International Handbook of White-Collar and Corporate Crime

International Handbook of White-Collar and Corporate Crime

Edited by

Henry N. Pontell
University of California, Irvine
Irvine, CA, USA

and

Gilbert Geis
University of California, Irvine
Irvine, CA, USA

Springer

Henry N. Pontell
Department of Criminology, Law and Society
School of Social Ecology
University of California, Irvine
Irvine, CA 92697-7080
USA
hnpontel@uci.edu

Gilbert Geis
Department of Criminology, Law and Society
School of Social Ecology
University of California, Irvine
Irvine, CA 92697-7080
USA
ggeis@uci.edu

Library of Congress Control Number: 2006925856

ISBN-10: 0-387-34110-2 e-ISBN-10: 0-387-34111-0
ISBN-13: 978-0-387-34110-1 e-ISBN-13: 978-0-387-34111-8

Printed on acid-free paper.

9 8 7 6 5 4 3 2 1

springer.com

For Miho and Dolores

And in memory of
Michelle Smith Pontell and
Robley Elizabeth Geis

Contents

Preface

By chance, we began writing the preface to this collection of 34 articles that consider various aspects of white-collar crime in different parts of the world on the day that the criminal trial of the two leading Enron executives opened in the federal courthouse in Houston, Texas. The Enron excesses both epitomized and adumbrated a deluge of exposed corporate wrongdoing, both in the United States and in other industrialized nations throughout the world. As this volume now goes to press some months later, the trial is now over, with both defendants—former Enron President, Kenneth L. Lay, and the onetime chief operating officer, Jeffrey K. Skilling having been found guilty. Lay reportedly died of a heart attack while vacationing in Colorado shortly after the verdicts.

As the trial began, there was considerable uncertainty regarding how the Enron case would turn out: i.e., what the jury would decide about either or both of the defendants. The news agency Reuter's quoted the lead editor of this volume as speculating that the defendants would claim that they were unaware of what was going on in Enron, and he pointed out that this was "the only thing the defense has to stand on." As it turned out the claim was insufficient in persuading the eight woman, four man jury, especially since several of the middle and high-level Enron managers already had entered guilty pleas and, in exchange for sentencing leniency, agreed to testify against their former bosses. But there were still indications at the time that the case was far from what Americans, adopting basketball terminology, call "a slam dunk," a sure thing for the prosecution. Skilling reportedly allocated $37 million to the legal team handling his defense. Daniel Petrocelli, one of the country's leading lawyers, headed that group although until then his practice had been confined to civil matters. Petrocelli was the attorney who picked up the pieces after the Los Angeles district attorney's office fared so poorly in its effort to convict O.J. Simpson of the (obvious) murder of his wife and a bystander who proved to be in the wrong place at the wrong time. He won sizeable civil judgments against Simpson for the victims' survivors, although they have never collected anything because Simpson's considerable income is arranged so that it is judgment proof. It was also notable that the lead federal prosecutor in the Enron case was appointed by President Bush to a judgeship only a few weeks before the trial began, and had to withdraw from the case. The president's move seemed odd, especially when viewed in light of the fact that he is known to have enjoyed close contacts with Enron executives—especially Kenneth Lay, who he reportedly referred to as "Kenny Boy."—when Bush was in the oil business and later as governor of Texas.

The Enron case and other white-collar crimes around the world for a time garnered great amounts of media attention until the invasion of Iraq by the United States, arguably another form of white-collar crime. That war preempted the major share of news reports that occupied the eyes and ears of readers and viewers. Nonetheless, the prominent fraud cases demonstrate the importance and the necessity, as the new Millennium moves along, of criminological attention to the crimes of persons in the upper echelons of society and the corporate entities that pay them so handsomely. There is a need for much greater transparency in business operations and for a regimen of corporate governance that stops members of boards of directors from bestowing what some persons regard as obscene amounts of money on the executives who appointed them to the boards. Absent adequate oversight both within the financial community and from scholarly sources, the estimated four trillion dollars in market losses suffered in 2002 around the world because of massive corporate and accounting meltdowns will continue apace.

Despite the enormity of the price paid for inadequate attention to white-collar and corporate crime, by and large criminologists and, more generally, social science scholars tend to bypass the subject and focus their research on traditional street crimes–murder, manslaughter, and assault, drug transactions, and since the feminist surge, rape, domestic violence, and child abuse. The chapters in this book stress the need for better information and understanding of white-collar and corporate crime. The facts and ideas that are presented by leading scholars from throughout the world provide a background for complementary and supplementary probes and theories.

Even including the corps of investigative journalists, the ranks of investigators and scholars who write about white-collar and corporate crime are relatively thin, undoubtedly in part because the pursuit of information about the subject is beset by a number of special complexities and structural barriers. For one, understanding of white-collar crime requires the command of knowledge located in a variety of disciplinary domains: business and finance, economics, law, criminology, sociology, psychology, and political science, among the more prominent sources. For another, governmental and private funding agencies are not hospitable to work that may question the legitimacy of their supporters, who donate large amounts to their campaigns and the corporate entities that supplied the moneys to establish the private foundations. For a third matter, access to relevant information can be a very difficult and wearing endeavor. It is a far more comfortable enterprise to do secondary analyses of data gathered in survey format and please journal editors and peer reviewers with elaborate tables and elegant statistical analyses, even if the results shed little to no light on matters of public understanding or policy.

Attempts to gain access to real or presumed white-collar offenders before the legal system has (or does not have) its way with them can be a dauntingly demanding task. If they are high enough on the business, political, or professional totem pole, they have receptionists, aides, secretaries, and other factotums who screen those to whom they will grant an audience. Crossing that barrier requires persuasive powers far beyond the reach of most of us. If you persist, typically you will be referred you to their attorney, who, if he or she is so gracious as to answer your telephone call or e-mail (or your fourth or fortieth such approach), will interdict any access to their client and offer, at best, platitudinous observations regarding the absurdity of the authorities' allegations and the blameless position of the suspect, not to mention his or her extraordinary contributions to the well-being of all of us.

On the other hand, if there is a public trial of a white-collar crime case, a researcher can find the court setting a particularly fruitful venue for gathering information. This is a resource that to date has been greatly underutilized; in the area of white-collar crime, we are aware only of Hazel Croall's courtroom observations of the trials of trading offenders in the United Kingdom. Court trials offer an opportunity to observe the emotions and hear the words of the leading players in a case, both during formal proceedings and in informal moments during court recesses and lunch breaks. There usually will be an opportunity to interview witnesses, kin of the accused, and sometimes the accused and the accusers. Court transcripts offer what can be extremely useful information and direct quotations.

In addition to the difficulty of doing fieldwork on white-collar crime, there is the dearth of governmental information. Since the 1930s in the United States, when the federal Department of Justice and the Federal Bureau of Investigation began tabulating data in the Uniform Crime Reports, information that tends to be similar to that available in other jurisdictions around the world, criminologists have had access to crime statistics as a basis for further analysis and theory building. The worldwide surge in surveys that tabulate reports by victims of their experiences with crime have added an important dimension to this statistical base. But neither criminal justice reports nor victim surveys attend to white-collar and corporate crime, so that it requires a sensational single case or a discovered panoply of illegal behavior in the upper echelons of the business, political, and professional world to at least momentarily place such behavior in the limelight. There are no systematic counts of white-collar crimes that occur in a given year, or the number of individuals who are arrested for such offenses. It is difficult enough to carry out satisfactory cross-national comparisons of criminal behavior, given the variations in definitions of crime, reporting distinctions (some countries count crimes known to the police, others only those offenses which eventuate in a court appearance, and still others only persons entering prison). It becomes significantly more complicated in regard to white-collar and corporate crime. Readers, for instance, will note the important differences that our contributors recite in regard to what their countries define as behavior that can be prosecuted as corporate crime, presuming their statutes have such a category at all.

Absent systematic information from public sources, scholars, as the ensuing chapters clearly demonstrate, often come to rely heavily on media sources, particularly newspapers. These can provide invaluable information and insights, yet it is worthwhile to keep in mind the caution from Diane Vaughan, a leading white-collar crime scholar who is represented by a contribution in the *Handbook*, about uncritical acceptance of media reports:

> We tend to see the media as our colleagues, for in keeping with our critical stance toward the power elite, journalists tantalize us with exposes that attack the powerful. In our enthusiasm for the bounty of information that the sensational case produces, we

must remind ourselves of what we know about the manufacture of news and the social construction of knowledge for public consumption.

John Kenneth Galbraith once remarked that he feared that economics was becoming an offshoot of applied mathematics. The same might be said of criminology, most particularly in regard to the forms that it is taking in the United States, which has been at the forefront of the criminological enterprise. It is informative to compare the contents of *Criminology*, the leading American disciplinary journal, with that of the *British Journal of Criminology* and the leading journals in Asia, Latin America, and on the European continent. One might suspect that they are dealing with two very disparate realms of knowledge, one heavily methodological, the other much more humanistic. The most prestigious criminological work in the United States appears to be a quest for "scientific respectability" and an enhanced status vis-a-vis more established areas of study. As a result, the tail of statistics and methods has been allowed to wag the dog of social and empirical relevance. Unfortunately, whatever the form of criminological work—heavily statistical or more qualitative—it typically fails to attend very diligently to white-collar and corporate crime. The intellectual imbalance reflected in the neglect of white-collar and corporate crime leads to the allegation that criminology essentially serves the state's interest in the social control of traditional kinds of law-breakers.

Indeed, part of the failure of academics to pay greater attention to white-collar crime lies in the original formulation of the concept itself. Edwin H. Sutherland, at the time a 56-year-old professor at Indiana University, introduced the term "white-collar crime" in his 1939 presidential address to the American Sociological Society. Ever since, its parameters have been a matter of considerable contention. Sutherland's was a muckraking enterprise, and he focused on the offenses of "respectable" persons in the upper reaches of society that were committed in the course of their work. This status emphasis contrasts with the contending and later position that white-collar crime can best be examined in regard to persons who violate specific laws, such as those against bribery and insider trading. The second definition allows for the study of a specified sample of violators, but it also comes to embrace a considerable array of persons who by no stretch of the imagination could be regarded as occupying positions of power that they abused. Many are unemployed, have been charged with fraud for writing insufficient fund checks, or have engaged in similar kinds of petty offenses. Some twenty years ago, the Australian scholar John Braithwaite concluded that using Sutherland's definition remained the best way to proceed with white-collar crime research, noting: "This at least excludes welfare cheats and credit card fraud from the domain." As a reader will discover, an overwhelming number of contributors to this volume who deal with specific white-collar offenses adhere to Sutherland's definition or else focus on corporate violations.

Nonetheless, it has been argued that while Sutherland's conception of white-collar crime was born from an effort to liberate traditional criminology from the "cognitive misbehavior" reflected in the spurious correlation between poverty and law-breaking, it has itself become an imprisoning framework that confuses the offender with the offense and inadequately attends to the structural aspects of white-collar crimes. Studies of the savings and loan debacle in the United States, for example, showed that high-status offenders were able to engage in acts resembling what is seen as "organized crime," acts that involved the same type of premeditated looting for personal gain that characterized the behavior of their underworld counterparts.

It has further been argued that both resource constraints and class bias affect the recognition and treatment of white-collar crime, laying a cloak over such acts by defining them as "non-issues." The result, we believe, represents a major shortcoming in law and society scholarship that traditionally has focused on the "law in action." A more critical approach views the "law in inaction" as equally if not more important, especially in regard to white-collar and corporate crime.

The chapters in this volume add greatly to our knowledge and interpretations of white-collar and corporate crime and, especially important, they involve scholars from around the world who approach the subject matter from different perspectives. Global understanding of white-collar and corporate crime is long overdue, considering that many large-scale organizations have for some time now expanded their domains beyond national borders and conduct business in multiple countries. Contributions from nine countries appear in the *Handbook:* Australia, Belgium, Canada, China, Italy, Japan, the Netherlands, the United Kingdom, and the United States. The great diversity of thought and approaches to the area of white-collar and corporate crime is well represented by case studies, historical analyses, theoretical treatments, development issues in the field, and legal interpretations. The topics addressed cover an even broader terrain, including corruption, fraud, financial crime, pollution, organizational decision-making and wrongdoing, criminal intent and motivation, computer crime, healthcare fraud, state-corporate crime, as well as prevention tactics, criminal justice responses, and punishment. There are a number of comparative studies and socio-political analyses as well as discussion of postmodern global issues, industrial manslaughter, corporate crime and criminal liability, stock market fraud, gender issues, the role of the media, white-collar crime in the professions, and theoretical issues regarding interpretative concerns.

The essays demonstrate the continuing need for an increased research focus on white-collar and corporate crime. Such work can have important scholarly and policy implications in regard to understanding organizational behavior, prevention strategies, crime theory, regulatory regimens, and legal change. Raising consciousness about the depth, dynamics, and disaster of white-collar crime hopefully will reshape notions regarding the social and economic significance of offenses such as insider trading and financial fraud, the tragedy of environmental pollution, the damaging consequences of corruption, and other major assaults on the quality of life in the global community.

Irvine, California, USA

Henry N. Pontell
Gilbert Geis

Acknowledgments

Our work in assembling this volume was greatly assisted by many persons on many levels, and we welcome the opportunity to thank them for the contributions they made on our behalf. First, we greatly appreciated the assistance we received from Welmoed Spahr of Kluwer Academic Publishers. She showed great excitement about getting the project underway and has been totally supportive from its birth to its delivery. She was responsive and invariably helpful in regard to every question that we posed about details of our work. She is an ideal editor, and we greatly appreciate her confidence and wisdom.

The volume also has benefited by having two outstanding editorial assistants—both at the time undergraduates at the University of California, Irvine. They kept in touch with contributors and assisted in numerous other essential chores. Crystal Tatco created the extensive initial files and took responsibility for seeing that some of the authors were located and enrolled in the endeavor. When Crystal graduated, she left the immaculately organized materials to another outstanding undergraduate student, Anny Lee. Not only did Anny redesign reference and endnote materials for a number of papers with meticulous care and intelligence—an arduous and demanding task—she also took charge of contacting authors about final details concerning their chapters. Without Anny's skillful involvement we would have been unable to meet our submission deadline. We were particularly fortunate to have been assisted by such talented young people.

We also want to thank Tokikazu Konishi, a doctoral student in law at Waseda University in Tokyo, for assisting in recruiting white-collar crime scholars both in Japan and China. We greatly appreciate his generous and skillful efforts toward broadening the geographical coverage that is one of the hallmarks of this volume.

We also owe a debt of gratitude to staff personnel at the University of California, Irvine, for their assistance during the different stages of the project. Dianne Christianson and Patty Edwards of the Department of Criminology, Law, and Society both kept track of manuscripts and reproduced numerous updated chapter versions, all with consummate amiability. Not least, we thank Judy Omiya, the department manager for the past 17 years, whose retirement at the beginning of 2006 marked the end of an era. Her loyalty to the department, and to us personally, was only surpassed by her trademark ability to get everything done that needed doing, quickly and in the right way. We wish her the best in the new phase of her life, and only regret that she will not be available to rescue us so competently when things seem to get a bit overwhelming.

Finally, we want to thank all the contributors to this volume for the energy and intelligence that went into their chapters. For those whose first language is not English, we owe a special debt for the effort and the skill that went into addressing the complex subject of white-collar crime in a vernacular other than their own. We believe that the cross-cultural insights afford a special quality to this volume that often is absent in more parochial scholarly endeavors.

Irvine, California, USA
February 2006

Henry N. Pontell
Gilbert Geis

Part I

Introduction: Theoretical Issues in Organizational and Corporate Lawbreaking

1

Beyond Macro- and Micro-Levels of Analysis, Organizations, and the Cultural Fix

Diane Vaughan

Since the mid 1980s, scholars theorizing about the causes of individual deviance and crime—street crime—have begun to consider the possibility of theoretical integration. Verifying the extensiveness of this activity and simultaneously reifying it, Travis Hirschi called it the "integrationist movement," identifying proponents as "integrationists."[1] Theoretical integration is an activity that involves the formulation of linkages among different theoretical arguments.[2] The fact that theoretical integration has been raised as a strategy worthy of consideration suggests an optimistic view about the status of causal theories of deviance and crime, particularly if we define theory consistent with the hypothetical-deductive model of the scientific process: a set of testable, interrelated propositions that explain some activity, event, or circumstance. From this perspective, the call for theoretical integration suggests that individual theories have attained sufficient rigor and explanatory power that refinement by integrating propositions from one with propositions from another is a logical next step. This is not the case.

While discussions of both the pros and cons and the possible methods of achieving integration have been extensive,[3] they have, for the most part, been at an abstract, theoretical level. Empirical practice indicates that the war-horses—traditional causal theories that have stood the test of time—are not ready for such a sophisticated step.[4] Indeed, the quantitative deductive positivistic approach that merges propositions for testing purposes is a road infrequently taken. Instead, most scholars seek to more adequately explain the causes of street crime by theory elaboration: inductive strategies for more fully developing existing theories that explain particular research findings by merging different theoretical perspectives in a more general way.[5] More specifically, the means to theory elaboration are theoretical tools in general (theory, models, and concepts) rather than a more restricted formal meaning (a set of interrelated propositions that are testable and explain some phenomenon). The data define which theory(theories) or concepts would apply. For example, Mertonian theory or Marxist theory could be joined with the Cloward and Ohlin version of opportunity theory and learning theory to explain drug use, sales, and drug-related crime.

Two theory elaborative strategies have appeared. One strives for theory elaboration by drawing together theories at the *same* level of analysis.[6] The other combines *different* levels of analysis to elaborate theory, so that a macro-level theory is supplemented by micro level component or vice-versa.[7] These macro–micro-theory elaborative efforts have arisen independently, but they reflect a shift in general sociological theory that emphasizes the importance of the macro–micro-connection as an accurate representation of how social life operates. The validity of synthesis between macro- and micro-levels of analysis has been so thoroughly discussed by social theorists[8] that it is safe to declare a consensus that social life is a consequence of both macro- and micro-level forces, working together in different ways. Ironically, this theoretical consensus stands without substantial empirical progress in this direction by researchers: making the macro–micro-connection is an unresolved empirical problem.

In this essay, I take the position that scholars of white-collar offending can take the lead in theory elaboration across macro- and micro-levels of analysis, which has, to date, remained a fledgling enterprise making slow but dubious progress, not only in explanations of individual crime and deviance,[9] but also in sociology as a whole. The crucial step in such a merger is the inclusion of the meso-level: formal and complex organizations. Historically, organizations and occupations have played important roles in white-collar offending. Moreover, organizational settings make visible the ways that macro-institutional forces outside of organizations and occupations are joined with micro-processes, thus affecting individual decisions and actions. Organizations provide a window into culture, showing how culture mediates between institutional forces, organizational goals and processes, and individual illegality so that deviance becomes normalized in organizational settings. At the same time scholars of white-collar offending are filling this research gap in sociological theory, important progress can be made in understanding how people in organizations make decisions to violate laws and rules.

I begin with an overview of the historic trajectory of competing theories of individual crime and deviance, showing that under the substantive differences is an unresolved and unarticulated debate about what level of analysis is appropriate for causal explanations. Then I show that the same pattern holds true in theorizing white-collar crime. Next, in order to establish the legitimacy of integrating macro-, meso-, and micro-levels of analysis in white-collar crime research and theory, I describe human behavior as *situated action* by drawing upon sociological theory about the relation between structure and agency. However, I draw from organization theory and economic sociology to add organizations and culture to the mix in order to develop the link between the meso-level component of situated action and the structure-agency relationship. Third, I argue that white-collar crime research can take the lead in studying the relationship between the three levels of analysis because scholars have already done the foundational theoretical and empirical work at the macro-, meso-, and micro-levels of analysis. White-collar crime research and theory can thus be an exemplar for general theory in sociology, but perhaps more important is what this strategy yields for our own project. A theory elaborative strategy that merges macro-, meso-, and micro-levels of analysis reveals how culture affects decisions to violate, with challenging implications for social control and future research and theorizing about white-collar offending.

Causes of Individual Crime and Deviance: The Covert Debate

Elaborating theories of individual crime and deviance by combining levels of analysis is a logical resolution to what has, to date, been an unacknowledged pattern in the historic chronology of theories of street crime. This historic chronology has been typified by shifts in dominant paradigms.[10] Hirschi observes that these shifts indicate an oppositional tradition of denying an established perspective and substituting a new one, therefore giving the impression of progress.[11] However, the impression of progress is a false one: these shifting paradigms are more accurately read as an ongoing and unresolved debate about the appropriate level of explanation. A quick and cursory overview, a vast oversimplification due to space limitations, nonetheless shows a contest between individualistic, social psychological, and structural theories of crime causation.

In 18th- and 19th-century Europe, the causes of crime and deviance were located in the individual by theorists as diverse as Beccaria, Lombroso, and Freud. "European Individualism" took a back seat when American sociologists shifted the causal debate to emphasize the importance of the social context in determining individual deviance. Structural explanations—the work of Merton, Cloward and Ohlin, Shaw and McKay—became the dominant paradigm from the 1930s to the 1950s. These structural theories persisted, but from the 60s through the early 1970s social psychological theories—learning theory, control theory, labeling theory—became the dominant paradigm. Interestingly, theory through the mid-80s was marked not by a single dominant paradigm, but two competing ones that located the explanation of individual crime and deviance at different levels of analysis: the structural, deterministic Marxist theory and in a return to the free-will, the rational choice model of Beccaria, reincarnated as deterrence theory. Since the mid-1980s, the theoretical terrain has not been dominated by any outstanding paradigm, but by multiple theories that, by virtue of the different positions they represent on the levels of analysis issue, draw attention to the lack of resolution to the historic covert debate about the appropriate level of analysis. Viewed against this history and the unarticulated levels of analysis question, current attempts to integrate and/or to elaborate theory by merging macro- and micro-levels of analysis take on significance as recognition that current modes of theoretical explanation aren't working.

The search for the causes of white-collar offending has followed this same evolutionary pattern, but in a more limited way. A chronological history shows fewer competing theories to explain this type of offending—Sutherland's learning theory, Marxist theory, Mertonian theory, and more recently, rational choice/deterrence theory—and, with the possible exception of learning theory, none of them can legitimately be called a dominant paradigm that has held sway over even a decade of white-collar crime research. This difference may be explained, at least in part, because as a specialized interest within the sociology of crime and deviance, white-collar crime has had less concentrated attention by fewer scholars over the years. Further, difficulty getting access to data on organizational offenders—corporations, government, small businesses—has been a problem unless the case was well-publicized, making data available. In addition, many of the extant theories that so readily applied to a variety of types of street crime (and thus could be applied successfully to a number of different kinds of offenses) did not apply to high-status offending: labeling theory, ecological theory, subcultural theory. These theories were neither directly importable nor could they be reconfigured to fit the problem. Whatever the relative importance of these reasons and others, the chronological trajectory of theories of white-collar offending shows the same lack of resolution about the appropriate level of analysis as do theories of street crime. Researchers locate cause in the individual, the social psychological, and/or the structural sources. Notably absent is consensus—or even debates—about elaborating theory that takes into account the macro–micro-connection. To ground my point that white-collar crime research should include efforts to elaborate theory that not only connects macro- and micro- but investigates organizations as meso-level structures, in the next section I draw upon social theory to show human behavior as situated action. I add the meso-level by drawing from organization theory and economic sociology to emphasize the central role that organizations and culture play in mediating between macro-level influences and micro-processes.

Situated Action: Institutions, Agency, and the Macro–Meso–Micro-Connection

Causal theories should correspond with empirical realities. It is a well-acknowledged sociological understanding that interaction takes place in socially organized settings. Rather than isolating action from its circumstances, the task of scholars is to uncover the relationship between the two. This argument appears in the history of sociological thought as a common thread running through the work of such otherwise diverse theorists as Herbert Blumer, Max Weber, George Herbert Mead, Harold Garfinkle, George Homans, and Talcott Parsons. More recent developments allow us to build upon these understandings about the situated character of social action, showing a more complex and complete picture.

Three theoretical developments are important. The first is the extensive theoretical literature that not only establishes that social life can best be understood as a consequence of macro–micro links, but also has raised extensive debates about how the relationship between structure and agency works.[12] At the same time that these debates ferret out the complexity of the structure/agency relationship, they lay the groundwork for research examining that relationship. The second development is that culture has entered the picture as a mediating link in the structure/agency relationship. Theorists are defining the link between an individual's position in a structure and interpretative practices, meaning, and action at the local level.[13] Although dramatically different perspectives, each draws attention to the tacit understandings, habits, assumptions, routines, and practices that constitute a repository of unarticulated source material from which more self-conscience thought emerges. Equally significant in this line of thought is the role of history: both the historic chronology of events at the macro-level and individual history and experience are critical to interpretation and meaning.

Two further developments, one in organization theory, one in economic sociology, reinforce the important role of both organizations and culture in situated action. One is the new institutionalism, which explains that organizational forms and behaviors take the form that they do because of prevailing values and beliefs that have become institutionalized to varying degrees.[14] New

Institutionalists argue that cultural rules constitute actors (state, organizations, professions, and individuals), thus defining legitimate goals for them to pursue, and therefore affecting action and meaning at the local level. The other is Mark Granovetter's work on the socially embedded character of economic action.[15] Granovetter points to the relative autonomy and/or relative dependence between the forms of economic action and social organization and the national frameworks of culture and institutional value within which they are constituted. In contrast to the new institutionalism, agency is at the heart of this analysis. Agents can be individual or organizational forms, but the embeddedness perspective prohibits reduction to a rational actor mode. Because agency is central, economic action can take a variety of forms, and thus in a common cultural frame there will be significant variations that cannot be explained only in cultural terms. Together, these perspectives draw attention to the need for research that examines larger institutional forces that influence individual cognition and action.

Both the new institutional theory and the embeddedness perpective make organizations central, thus laying the groundwork for going beyond macro- and micro-levels by bringing organizations in. Both acknowledge organizations as a force: the former showing the interplay of a number of organizations in an organization field as affecting the forms organizations take, the latter shows how relationships between an organization or organizations must be seen from the vantage point of their social context and relation to others. Further developments in organization theory show how organizations are recipients and carriers of as well as generators of culture and history.[16] Within the well-established theoretical importance of exploring the macro–micro- connection, these three theoretical developments demonstrate that organizations are meso-level actors that mediate between institutional forces and individual action and choice.[17] Culture is the mediating mechanism.

This complex conceptual and theoretical package goes beyond the sociological truism that all social life is organized. Based upon the above established theoretical principles, my argument is that a full theoretical explanation of any particular behavior needs to take into account, to the greatest extent possible, its situated character: individual activity, choices, and action that occur within a layered social context that affects cultural understandings, and thus interpretation and meaning at the local level. We can simplify and make a general theoretical argument as follows: a social actor's position in a structure affects that actor's understandings, choices, actions, and outcomes. The social actor could be an individual, organization (group, formal, or complex), or network; the structure refers to the actor's social location, which could be a family, neighborhood, community, organization, network, organization field, occupation, institutional environment, nation state, or global society. Reconceptualizing social life as situated action makes possible generating theory and research that explores macro-, meso-, and micro-connections in any and all of the possible combinations and permutations of these varieties of social life. What is true of all social life is true of white-collar offending. Because it tends to be enacted in organizations and occupations, it presents the perfect opportunity to pursue the links between these three levels of analysis. Historically, research confirms that institutional environments and organizational forms are significant causal factors and the question remaining is how they, in combination, affect individual offending.

Situated Action: The Empirical and Conceptual Foundation in White-Collar Crime

Specialists in white-collar crime can play a leading role in research that merges macro-, meso-, and micro-level factors because the foundational work has already been done. Sutherland's introduction of the concept of white-collar crime in his 1939 presidential address to the American Sociological Society was remarkable for its expansion of the concept of crime beyond street crime, but by emphasizing the high status of individual offenders, Sutherland's definition turned attention away from the organization as violator. However, in Sutherland's own research, the individual and the social psychological, and the structural levels of analysis were all acknowledged. The "white collar" concept focused attention on individuals; learning theory and differential social organization showed the role of groups and interaction at the social psychological level; large organizations and industries were the primary units of analysis. His data did not articulate the link between individuals, organizations, and industries, but the seeds for a theory elaborative strategy that merges levels of analysis were there. Ironically, the ambiguities about appropriate levels of analysis in his work and ambiguities about his definition spawned the foundational work for current theory and research that merges macro-, meso-, and micro-levels of analysis. The good news is that the lack of resolution to these controversies has had researchers working at all levels of analysis to explain white-collar offending since Sutherland's 1939 presidential address. Because white-collar offenses occurred in formal and complex organizations—corporations, small businesses, government, occupations, and industries—a substantial body of research exists that has explored institutions, organizations, and individual actions.

In the classic period of white-collar crime theory and research (1940–1960), scholars debated Sutherland's conceptual definition.[18] A main sticking point in the definitional disagreement was identifying the appropriate social location among the multi-layered and overlapping structures identifiable in his work: was it the social class of the individual offender, small groups and differential social organization, the organization, occupation, or the industry that was most important in theories of cause? While some scholars dedicated themselves to resolving the definitional issue, others didn't wait for it to be settled, instead initiating research that explord the separate pieces of the puzzle. Much of this work investigated the macro-level causes of corporate offending. For example, Vilhelm Aubert, examining the macro-institutional context of business,[19] argued that businessmen are confronted with contradictory structural pressures emanating from the legal and the competitive environments of firms: the normative obligation to obey the law and the equally compelling normative obligation to resist the law in certain situations, instead following business norms that justified violations. Although he did not write about institutionalized cultures, in retrospect his work set a precedent for research on industry norms. Richard Quinney's unit of analysis was the occupation. His pharmacy study examined the professional orientations of pharmacists, determining the relationship between that orientation (either business or professional) and violative behavior.[20] Because these were small pharmacies with pharmacist owners, this qualifies as one of the first studies of occupational and organization culture. Quinney's data did not allow him to trace the connection between the professional norms with the meanings and actions of individual violators. Subsequently, however, in the heavy electrical equipment conspiracy case, Gilbert Geis's data gave an unprecedented look at the macro–micro-connection: the relationship between industry norms and the meanings that individual violators gave their own actions.[21] The results were revealing: Geis found violators were conforming to industry norms, so in their view, their actions were not deviant, but conforming.

The mid-1960s marked a conceptual turning point: Albert Reiss called for a recognition of the role of social organization in explaining deviance, thus initiating the concept of "organizational deviance." [22] Focusing on organizations added the meso-level to the foundational work already done that examined normative environments outside corporations and government offenders, and the social psychology of learning theory. Not until the 1970s and 1980s, however, did organizations begin to receive substantial attention. New conceptual definitions of white-collar offending made organizations central to explanations.[23] A work of major impact was Christopher Stone's *Where the Law Ends: The Social Control of Corporate Behavior*.[24] A lawyer, Stone was first to take into account every facet of organization structure, including Boards of Directors. Edward Gross, an organization theorist who "crossed over" into the deviance specialization, added theoretical insight about the intersection of organization structure and organizational crime.[25] Also widely influential was David Ermann and Richard Lundman's theoretical framework by which acts of both government and corporations could be analyzed as organizational deviance.[26] Their framework allowed both the study of the crimes and deviant acts that were not specifically prohibited by the law. Further, this framework opened the possibility of studying organizational processes as well as structure, and in another advance, it emphasized contradictions between internal organization norms and norms in the institutional environment.

The competitive structure of industries and institutionalized norms, first explored by Aubert in 1952, was expanded by extensive research in the 1970s and 1980s. The shared reference point was "criminogenic" processes external to organizations: competitive pressures on industries and firms that were institutionalized at the societal level, a reflection of the American capitalism and the cultural emphasis on individual achievement. These competitive pressures affected both firms and industries by providing a structural inducement for illegality via a normative environment that supported it. The effects, research showed, materialized differently within and between industries, affecting some to a greater extent than others.[27] Pursuing these differences in the most extensive quantitative inquiries since Sutherland were two definitive works at the macro-level: Marshall Clinard and Peter Yeager's study of violations and industries and the longitudinal research of Sally Simpson, who explored antitrust offenses within industry context.[28] The recognition of capitalism as causal was made most explicit by Quinney, whose Marxist analysis showed the power of the state in constructing laws that protected the powerful, enabling crimes of domination by government, crimes of control by law enforcement, and corporate crime.

Definitional controversies about whether it was white-collar, organizational, occupational, or economic crime flourished into the 1990s, as did debates about what kinds of violative behavior should be included.[29] In June 1996, at a conference designed to investigate the definitional question, the same issues debated in the classic period of white-collar crime research still were being debated.[30]

The reason that the debate remains provocative, lively, and unresolved is because *all levels of analysis apply*. From the plethora of possible theoretical framings came four that began to explore the relation between macro-, meso-, and micro-levels of analysis. Ronald Kramer and Henry Finney and Lesieur imported ideas directly from organization theory to explain how organizational environments, goals, and structure were related to crimes and other illegalities of organizations.[31] Diane Vaughan and James W.Coleman worked out integrated models in the theory elaborative mode that recognized the interconnections between competitive environment, external norms, organization structures, goals, and processes, regulatory failure, and individual decisions to violate.[32] All four made organizations the central unit of analysis and drew heavily from organization theory, integrating it with theories of deviance and crime. A new direction in explanations of white-collar offending had begun: theory elaboration, built upon the foundational work of earlier periods, joined macro-, meso-, and micro-levels of analysis.

The Cultural Fix and The Normalization of Deviance

All the building blocks—theoretical and empirical—are there to continue these developments. The reason to elaborate theories of white-collar offending to include macro-, meso-, and micro-levels of analysis is that we know very little about decision-making and why people who are well educated, have opportunities, and are generally law abiding decide to engage in illegality in their occupational and organizational roles. Consensus about the importance of competitive pressures as a causal force has resulted in the assumption among scholars that this, of all crimes, is driven by utilitarianism and rational choice. However, testing this hypothesis is still in progress. Stanton Wheeler lamented our lack of knowledge about decisions to violate, calling it "the problem of white collar crime motivation."[33] Drawing upon principles of microeconomics and data from interviews with white-collar offenders, Wheeler concluded that it was not greed or striving for success that motivated offenders, but "fear of falling," a finding consistent with structural analysis showing that all organizations experience pressure to compete for scarce resources in order either to rise, remain the same, of keep from falling in rank in the organizational stratification system.[34] However, Wheeler's resolution also assumes a rational choice model of decision-making. Lack of access to good data has been a problem. Attempts to clarify the influences on decision-making by experimental designs rather than *in situ* have methodological limits and therefore have not produced clear results about how people would behave within the workplace. However, the work that has been done throws doubt upon the rational choice model, showing decision-making to be influenced by a variety of factors.[35]

Scholarship on organizations verifies that individual decisions are always rational, but that institutional and organizational forces narrow choice by shaping understandings about what is rational at a given moment. Alternative choices are limited: the range of choices is determined prior to and outside of the venues of decision-making themselves. Walter Powell and Paul DiMaggio point out that institutionalized cultural beliefs in environments external to organizations narrow choice.[36] By emphasizing the importance of normative environments and norms toward and/or against violations, many white-collar crime scholars have acknowledged culture as a causal factor without naming it as culture. This body of research, taken collectively, suggests that when white-collar offenders make decisions to violate, they are, in fact, conforming to cultural mandates. In their view, then, they may define their illegalities as conforming, rather than deviant. Thus, in some social settings deviance becomes normal and acceptable: it is not a calculated decision where the costs and benefits of doing wrong are weighed because the definitions of what is deviant and what is normative have been redefined within that setting. Building upon previous work indicating conformity to industry, occupation, organizational, and group norms, recent work affirms the role of culture and the normalization of deviance as an alternative perspective explaining why white-collar offenders violate.[37]

My analysis of the *Challenger* launch decision was a case study covering NASA decision-making over a number of years, culminating in the controversial decision to launch *Challenger* against the advice of NASA engineers.[38] The research project was based on data that allowed me to focus on the intersection of macro-, meso-, and micro-level factors. A main question was why NASA continued to launch for years with technical flaws recurring on the solid rocket boosters, flaws that ultimately were responsible for the demise of *Challenger*. Archival data, engineering documents, and interviews showed how a work group culture was created that normalized technical deviation in official risk assessments. In retrospect, each anomalous incident stood out as a clear indicator to outsiders that something was wrong; the public viewed NASA decisions to proceed as deviant. But as decisions were made, an engineering decision logic was created that determined flying again was normal and acceptable, not deviant. An important part of the decision context was influential: the space shuttle was an experimental technology, had problems on every launch, and having technical problems was normal at the agency. Change in what was acceptable behavior occurred gradually. The first incident of accepting risk of an anomaly and launching again became the basis for future decisions to do the same. At the micro-level, the understanding of the risk of the solid rocket boosters was normalized by a decision history based on engineering judgments that were proven correct by post-flight engineering assessments that showed that even more damage could be sustained without bringing the shuttle out of the sky. Flying with damage came to be routine practice, viewed as normal and acceptable. At the social psychological level, the history of decision-making about technical problems on the solid rocket boosters was one in which, incrementally, judgments were made about risk and safety that became the basis for moving forward and a constraint against stopping to fix the technical problem. The result was a cultural belief that it was safe to fly.

The normalization of deviance at NASA was explained by a combination of institutional, organizational, and social psychological factors, however. Like Geis's heavy equipment conspirators, NASA personnel saw their behavior as conforming to cultural imperatives, thus decisions that shocked outsiders in the aftermath of the accident were not deviant in the eyes of decision makers at the time these decisions were made. But the institutional and organizational levels of analysis were crucial. NASA personnel's decisions to continue launches conformed to cultural mandates institutionalized in the engineering profession and the aerospace industry. Cost efficiency, schedule, and safety were competing cultural imperatives. The industry was highly competitive, contractors were dependent upon the space agency for their funding, and the punishment for work not completed on time resulted in a monetary penalty. Further, engineering schools trained engineers that decisions must include considerations about cost, safety, and schedule. NASA decisions to move forward with a flaw that had in the past caused damage but was not perceived as a serious threat to safety conformed to mandates in both industry and the occupation about the importance of schedule and cost efficiency. The pattern continued due to another structural factor. The safety structure in place to give alternative interpretations of risk and challenge engineering practice and decisions was weak, so that no alternative interpretations of the situation penetrated and the cultural belief in risk acceptability persisted until the accident.

The normalization of deviance differs in important ways from Gresham Sykes and David Matza's "techniques of neutralization," a social psychological explanation of deviant acts whereby individuals employ a justification or excuse for a wrongful behavior before doing it, in order to alleviate guilt.[39] "Techniques of neutralization" is a form of the rational choice model because the motivation to find a justification or excuse *prior to a wrongful act* indicates the actor's awareness that the act is wrong. When deviance is normalized, the action is not seen as wrong by actors in that setting—thus making it important to study decision-making as situated action. It is not concealed from other members of the organization; it is, in fact, culturally approved and therefore rewarded. Deviant actions are viewed as normal because they fit with and conform to cultural mandates of the group to which the actor belongs. So powerful can these mandates become that not following them is deserving of reproach, negative sanctions, or ostracism by other members of the group. The example that comes to mind from street crime is from subculture of violence theory, in which the norm is for youthful males to use violence to resolve problems: when violence is deemed appropriate to a situation by the community but violence is not the response of the actor, that actor is viewed as cowardly and loses status in the group.

Other case studies offer support for the connection between institutions, organizations, culture and the normalization of deviance in white-collar offending. In their study of fraud in savings and loan institutions, Kitty Calavita, Henry Pontell, and Robert Tillman show that widespread criminal activity in the thrift industry was intentional and deliberate.[40] They pointed to changed macro-institutional conditions as presenting opportunities that affected the entire industry: the shift away from industrial capitalism to finance capitalism; a downturn in the economy; and a relaxation of regulation by government that allowed increased and unregulated business speculation with depositors' money. In response, certain patterns of fraud appeared that were repeated across the entire industry: misapplication of funds, nominee loans, check kiting, landflips, and kickbacks. Calavita et al. determined that many of these illegal activities were a form of "collective embezzlement" in which networks of top administrators and managers inside and outside of thrift institutions were co-conspirators embezzling from their own organizations. Their evidence suggests a parallel with the *Challenger* case: actions that the public saw as deviant after the fraudulent activities collapsed were not deviant to the top administrators and managers at the time they were engaged in them. In fact, in many cases these activities were company policy. Indeed, Calavita et al. determined that in some cases, the sole purpose of the organization was to provide a mechanism for its own top administrators and others to defraud it. How could these collective embezzlements occur in organizations engaged in the same business but geographically scattered, different sizes, different ownership? Although Calavita et al. do not invoke a cultural explanation, we might hypothesize that these similar outcomes resulted from industry and organizational cultures that normalized deviance in the industry.

Like the engineering profession, other occupations are based on common training, goals, and opportunities to pursue those goals. Thrifts operate within the structure and culture of competitive capitalism, in which the distinction between a clever business deal and illegality is blurred. The savings and loans operated within business norms that had an elastic quality, like the standards for risk that existed at NASA that were stretched to conform to external mandates during a time in the space agency's history when productivity became enormously important. Savings and loans were themselves engaged in risk and prediction, which were, for them, normal. Once engaged in risky decisions, altering the terrain of risk may have been simply an extension of existing practice, not a new and abnormal practice. And, like Donald Cressey's embezzlers, the skills they used to commit fraud were not deviant skills, but the same skills that they employed on the job every day, prior to the economic downturn and prior to the government relaxation of regulation. Industry-wide, top administrators and managers appear to have been conforming to institutional and organizational cultural imperatives for that industry. Significantly, Calavita et al. note the contribution of the state to collective embezzlement: not only did deregulation encourage it, but the interdependence of state interests with those of the thrifts undermined the effectiveness of regulatory actions taken as the crisis became public. As in the case of NASA, the interdependence of regulatory organizations with the regulated space agency appear to have perpetuated the normalization of deviance by failing to act to stop it.

The normalization of deviance demonstrated in the above two cases (proved in one, hypothetical in the other) suggests that culture can mediate between institutional and organizational forces to affect individual decisions to engage in white-collar offending. Individuals respond to the cultural imperatives of the social location in which they are situated, thus in their view their actions are conforming, not deviant. Three important books, written from other disciplinary perspectives, confirm the role of conformity in organizational deviance and misconduct: Hannah Arendt's *Eichmann in Jerusalem*; Herbert Kelman and D.Lee Hamilton's *Crimes of Obedience*, and most recently, Daniel Goldhagen's *Hitler's Willing Executioners*.[41] Each of these studies shows individual actors explaining horrific acts by referring to the norms of the organizations to which they belong—the military and others—with comments indicating they were not engaging in deviant acts; rather, they were following orders and cultural mandates. Because culture affects how individuals perceive what is rational at a given moment, research that further explores the macro–meso–micro-link can provide us with better understanding of the causes of white-collar offending.

The Connection Between Causes and Strategies for Control

The studies mentioned above that have successfully explored the connections between the institutional, organizational, and individual levels of analysis all are based on sensational cases, each of which had at its heart a form of organizational deviance that persisted for years. These cases produced enormous amounts of data that provided the kind of detail necessary to show macro-structure and micro-processes and how organizations and culture act as links between them. The researchers relied on historical records, archives, organization documents, official investigation testimony, and personal interviews and observations. The prospect of a project of such scope may seem daunting, precluding the initiation of such an investigation. It is easy to understand why the debates about macro–micro-connections in social theory have not spawned a flurry of empirical work aimed at bridging the gap. Instead, in white-collar offending as in other substantive areas of sociology, scholars investigate either the macro-, the meso-, or micro-level but not all three. They carve out a particular locus of inquiry, taking a slice of the whole, thus offering a measured but nonetheless partial view, a partial explanation, of situated action. Continuing to probe each level of analysis singly is a constant source of theoretical refinements and empirical insights and should continue. Then why should we pursue more complex inquiries that explore macro-, meso-, and micro-connections?

In the historic trajectory of theories of cause in the sociology of crime and deviance, which I described earlier, each theory of cause suggested a particular strategy of control that targeted the causal elements identified in that theory.[42] These social control strategies were invoked. For example, the free-will, rational choice model of Cesare Beccaria located cause in individual decision-making; the strategy for control was the attempt to alter decision-making by rationalizing the criminal justice system so that individuals' weighing of costs and benefits of particular acts would be manipulated by an appropriate system of punishments. The response to the social disorganization theory of crime causation was a crime control strategy to organize inner city life (e.g., the Chicago Area Project). The appropriate strategy for control implied by labeling theory was radical non-intervention (e.g., the deinstitutionalization movement) so that stigmatizing labels were not given to first and youthful offenders. The fact that deterrence theory and Marxist theory were competing paradigms during the 1970s takes on new significance when their contrasting implications for crime reduction are considered. The former directed strategies for control at individual offenders; the latter targeted the state, arguing for a redistribution of power. The level of analysis debate is not just a theoretical debate: it has both practical and political implications for social control.

Indeed, to be effective, strategies for control *should* target the causes of a problem. The better our understandings of the causes of deviance, the better the understandings on which social control can be based. Research and theoretical explanations that isolate one level of analysis for attention automatically and implicitly suggest strategies for control that do not take into account relevant factors at other levels. We need to bear in mind both the practical and political implications of our work. When we restrict our analysis to the individual, social psychological, or structural level of explanation, we have isolated one element from many that comprise situated action. A partial explanation, no matter how important the finding, leads to a partial, or incomplete, strategy for social control.

Consider the following. A rational actor model locates cause at the individual level of analysis, pointing to a preventive strategy that targets responsible individuals: ethics training, punishment, forced resignation, and so forth. While these are appropriate strategies, they are incomplete because they leave systemic social causal factors at the macro-, meso-, and micro-levels unaddressed. Industry norms, competitive pressures, professional cultures, organization culture and structure will exert similar pressures on a position, even if personnel changes are made. Focusing on individual offenders without attention to institutional factors and their effect upon organization goals, cultures, structures can reproduce the original situation for new personnel. In particular, organization culture is seductive: what is normal and acceptable within the culture may alter the costs and benefits of decisions, so that individuals do not view their actions as wrong. What happens when these social causes are not taken into account? When the social conditions precipitating an incident persist, the deviant actions may be reproduced. Revisit, for a moment, NASA's *Challenger* accident. In its 1986 Report, the Presidential Commission investigating that accident found that "flawed decision-making" was responsible for the technical failure.[43] Middle managers were blamed, as was a "silent safety system" that failed to intervene as risky launches proceeded. The main strategies for control that the commission recommended were tightening the procedures and processes to guide individual decision-making and a strengthened and independent safety system. Although the report acknowledged extensive schedule pressure, it attributed responsibility for that pressure to the NASA organization, mandating that in the future NASA bring goals and resources into alignment.

In response to the commission's identification of causes, managers responsible for the "flawed decisions" were transferred or retired; new reporting and documentation procedures and new decision rules were implemented to better control decision-making; the safety system was strengthened by adding new personnel. These strategies of control targeted individual decision-making, addressing the very causes identified in the report. However, many crucial social causes were omitted from the report, therefore not addressed by social control strategies. They persisted, as follows. After *Challenger*, at the institutional level, elite leaders in the White House and Congress were not called upon to take responsibility for political and economic decisions that thrust the agency into a business mode. NASA was not able to bring goals and resources into alignment because both goals and resources were determined outside the agency. These powerful leaders perpetuated the NASA organization culture of schedule pressure and cost-efficiency that undercut safety in the years leading up to *Challenger*. The emphasis on individual failings in decision-making rather than upon the cultural and structural conditions that led to the normalization of deviance left those cultural and structural conditions unchanged. Finally, the independent safety system with authority to override management decisions about technical anomalies never came about because the safety units were still dependent upon the agency for resources and authority. Resources continued to be scarce, and the pattern repeated: NASA again cut safety personnel.

In 2003, seventeen years after *Challenger*, the *Columbia* Accident Investigation Board (CAIB) declared that NASA's second accident occurred because once again NASA had normalized a technical anomaly.[44] For years preceding this accident, NASA had been flying with known flaws, this time not on the solid rocket boosters, but on the foam insulation on the external tank containing the fuel. The decision-making pattern was identical. The institutional, organizational, and cultural aspects of the NASA organization had remained the same, impinging on NASA decision-making in exactly the same ways as they had for *Challenger.* Indeed, the CAIB concluded that the macro-, meso-, and micro- causes of *Columbia* were the same as those for *Challenger*: the social causes of *Challenger* had not been fixed. The changes that had been made after *Challenger* did not target the institutional and organizational causes of NASA's problem; instead they focused on flawed decisions, risk-taking managers, and processes and procedures to guide decision-making, without understanding the role of larger social forces at the institutional and organizational level that impinged upon decision-making, normalizing deviance. This Report is worth reading by scholars of white-collar offending for the way it uses organizational analysis to demonstrate macro-, meso-, and micro connections as a causal constellation for both accidents.[45] The report gives equal weight to social causes and to technical causes, laying out a causal model that includes (1) historical and economic conditions in NASA's institutional environment; (2) organization structure, culture, and processes; and (3) the micro-level processes that combined to produce the normalization of deviance. The conclusion to be drawn from the two NASA cases is that replacing or punishing individuals who engage in organizational deviance without addressing the macro- and meso-level forces that shape decisions in the work place will only result in the new person or persons experiencing the same pressures and opportunities to engage in deviance as did the previous position occupants.

I have argued that we can benefit from a theory elaborative strategy that allows us to examine the links between macro-, meso-, and micro-levels of analysis to explain white-collar offending. In the new global economy, problems of organizational deviance and how to regulate it present new challenges, not only for research but for regulation. To meet this challenge calls for new thinking about our training, design of projects, and conceptual tools. A first step is recognizing that human behavior is situated action when designing research and doing analysis. This is not as simple and easy as it sounds. The structure of the profession, our professional training, and socialization train us to focus on either macro-, micro-, or meso-levels of analysis, but not macro- and micro- and especially we are not trained to think in terms of all three and the connections among them. Departmental specialization produces students with greater skills at research at either the macro-level or the micro-level, but not both. Or, their training may predispose them toward a particular theory or theoretical perspective because of the interest of their advisor.

From that graduate experience, individuals develop a research style that ties them to a particular style of research (quantitative, qualitative, survey, network analysis, ethnography, etc.) and the conceptual tools and theories that go with it. In other words, we grow up in departments that, to a great extent, create a professional world view that affects how we frame our research topics. Then, once published, the experience enhances our skills at that kind of work, while skills to work in other research modes atrophy. We associate more with colleagues working in the same way. Opportunities come that reinforce our initial interest and research style, perpetuating the path that our graduate experience began. We may diversify, but seldom do people who begin doing macro-level structural analysis switch to micro-level processes or vice versa. Because our training does not prepare us for research of multi-layered structures and processes, intentionally building it into a project at the design stage is an important first step.

We might revise the way that graduate training has traditionally progressed. Given that most white-collar offending occurs in organizations and occupations, a course or courses in formal and complex organizations, economic sociology, or on the professions could be made part of the requirement for a degree, or required as a minor, or (at least) included on a required reading list for the general exams. Case studies of organizations are most useful because they can expose macro-level influences, micro-processes, and cultural influences external and internal to the organization. These influences show up in what people say and do. Getting access to corporations to study deviance has always been a problem, which is why so often we are in the position of studying sensational cases after some misconduct has been revealed to the public. Although we must keep in mind what is unusual about sensational cases, they produce data—testimony and documents from government investigations, historical archives—making possible research that would not be possible otherwise. Our initial understanding of white-collar offending, based on Sutherland, was restricted to corporations. Then Ermann and Lundman expanded the scope of investigation to include governmental deviance. However, the reality of organizational offending is much more broad than these two possibilities. Small businesses, without complex structures and highly skilled lawyers, also offend and may be more accessible. Moreover, cases of organizational deviance and misconduct can be found in education institutions, the military, hospitals, churches, and prisons. Social control agents also can be organizational offenders and should be studied. These too, should be subject to investigation to advance our understanding of the causes of organizational offenses.[46]

Even when case studies of organizations do not provide data at three levels of analysis, or when case studies are neither desirable nor possible, research can take into account the macro– meso–micro-connection by incorporating relevant work by others. Other specializations in sociology offer resources in conceptual tools and research findings that fill in gaps in data about institutional conditions: network analysis, economic sociology, industrial relations, and the non-profit sector. To explain micro-processes affecting decision-making in white-collar offending, cultural anthropology, cognitive psychology, and organization theory offer numerous decision-making models that focus on social circumstances and can be tested against rational choice models. Another productive direction that research could take is cross-cultural comparison that targets differences in economic systems, institutional, organizational, and cultural context of offenses. Not only could this strategy be helpful in understanding differences in social causes, but also our discovery of these differences has important implications for global social control. In order to deal with the new problems of white-collar offending in the 21st century and provide data for improved strategies for regulation, we must have a better understanding of how macro-, meso, and micro-level forces combine to cause these socially harmful and costly incidents.

Endnotes

1. Travis Hirschi, "Exploring Alternatives to Integrated Theory," in Steven F. Messner, Marvin D. Krohn, and Allen E. Liska, eds., *Theoretical Integration in the Study of*

Deviance and Crime: Problems and Prospects. Albany: State University of New York Press, 1989, p. 39.
2. Allen E. Liska, Marvin D. Krohn, and Steven F. Messner, "Strategies and Requisites for Theoretical Integration in the Study of Crime and Deviance," in Messner et al., ibid., p. 2.
3. For a review, see Liska et al., ibid., pp. 5–17.
4. See Messner et al., op. cit.; Terance D. Miethe and Robert F. Meier, *Crime and its Social Context: Toward an Integrated Theory of Offenders, Victims, and Situations.* Albany: State University of New York Press, 1994; Ronald L. Akers and Christine S. Sellers, *Criminological Theories.* Boston: Roxbury, 2004.
5. Liska et al., op. cit., pp. 16–17; Terrance Thornberry, "Reflections on the Advantages and Disadvantages of Theoretical Integration," in Messner et al., op. cit., pp. 51–60; Diane Vaughan, "Theory Elaboration: The Heuristics of Case Analysis," in Charles C. Ragin and Howard S. Becker, eds., *What is a Case?* Cambridge: Cambridge University Press, 1992, pp. 173–203.
6. See, e.g., Ronald L. Akers, *Deviance: A Social Learning Approach.* Belmont CA: Wadsworth, 1985; Michael Gottfredson and Travis Hirschi, *A General Theory of Crime.* Stanford: Stanford University Press, 1990; Nikos Passas, "Anomie and Corporate Deviance," *Contemporary Crises* 14, pp. 157–78.
7. See, e.g., James F. Short, Jr., "Exploring Integration of Theoretical Levels of Explanation: Notes on Gang Delinquency," in Messner et al., op. cit., pp. 243–60; Robert Agnew, "Foundation for a General Strain Theory of Crime and Delinquency," *Criminology* 30: 1992, pp. 47–87, Robert J. Sampson, Stephen W. Raudenbush, and Felton Earls, "Assessing 'Neighborhood Effects': Social Processes and New Directions in Research," *Annual Review of Sociology* 28, 2002, pp. 443–478.
8. See, e.g., Anthony Giddens, *The Constitution of Society.* Berkeley: University of California Press, 1984; Jeffrey C. Alexander, Bernhard Giesen, Richard Munch, and Neil J. Smelser, eds., *The Micro-Macro Link.* Berkeley: University of California Press, 1987.
9. Akers and Sellers, op. cit., pp. 286.
10. See Stephen J. Pfohl, *Images of Deviance and Social Control: A Sociological History.* New York: McGraw Hill, 2nd ed., 1994
11. Hirschi, op. cit., 37–8.
12. Randall Collins, "On the Micro-Foundations of Macro-Sociology," *American Journal of Sociology* 86, 1981, pp. 984–1014; Gary Alan Fine, "Agency, Structure, and Comparative Contexts: Toward a Synthetic Interactionism," *Symbolic Interaction* 15, 1992, pp. 87–107; Karin Knorr-Cetina and and Aaron Cicourel, eds., *Advances in Social Theory and Methodology: Toward an Integration of Micro- and Macro-Sociology.* London: Routledge and Kegan Paul, 1981; David Maines, "Social Organization and Social Structure in Symbolic Interactionist Thought," *Annual Review of Sociology* 3, 1977, pp. 235–59; William H. Sewell, Jr., " A Theory of Structure: Duality, Agency, and Transformation," *American Journal of Sociology* 98, 1992, pp. 1–29.
13. See, for example, Pierre Bourdieu, *Outline of a Theory of Practice.* Cambridge: Cambridge University Press, 1977; Mustafa Emirbayer and Jeff Goodwin, "Network Analysis, Culture, and the Problem of Agency," *American Journal of Sociology* 99, 1994, pp. 1411–54; Peter M. Hall, "Interactionism and the Study of Social Organization," *Sociological Quarterly* 28, 1987, pp. 1–22; Sharon Hays, "Structure and Agency and the Sticky Problem of Culture," *Sociological Theory* 12, 1994, pp. 57–72.
14. Walter W. Powell and Paul J. DiMaggio, eds., *The New Institutionalism in Organizational Analysis.* Chicago: University of Chicago Press, 1991.
15. Mark Granovetter, "Economic Action and Social Structure: The Problem of Embeddedness," *American Journal of Sociology* 91, 1985, pp. 481–510; "Economic

Institutions as Social Constructions: A Framework for Analysis," *Acta Sociologica* 35, 1992, pp. 3–11.
16. Linda Smirchich, "Concepts of Culture and Organizational Analysis," *Administrative Science Quarterly* 28, 1983, pp. 339–358; Ann Swidler, "Culture in Action," *American Sociological Review* 5, 1986, pp. 273–86; Harrison M. Trice and Janice M. Beyer, *The Cultures of Work Organizations*. Englewood Cliffs: Prentice Hall, 1993.
17. William J. Sonnenstuhl and Harrison M. Trice, "Linking Organizational and Occupational Theory Through the Concept of Culture," *Research in Sociology of Organizations*, 9, 1991, pp. 295–318.
18. This section is an updated version of ideas I expressed earlier. For a more detailed chronological examination of the definitional question and the emergence of organizations as actors in white-collar crime research and theory from the 1940s to the 1980s, see Diane Vaughan, "Recent Developments in White-Collar Crime Theory and Research," C. Ronald Huff and Israel Barak, eds., *The Mad, the Bad, and the Different: Essays in Honor of Simon Dinitz*. Lexington MA: Lexington Books, 1981.
19. Vilhelm Aubert, "White-Collar Crime and Social Structure," *American Journal of Sociology* 58, 1952, pp. 263–71.
20. Earl R. Quinney, "Occupational Structure and Criminal Behavior: Prescription Violation by Retail Pharmacists," *Social Problems* 11, 1963, pp. 179–85.
21. Geilbert Geis, "The Heavy Electrical Equipment Antitrust Cases of 1961," in *Criminal Behavior Systems*, Marshall B. Clinard and Richard Quinney, eds., New York: Holt Rinehart and Winston, 1967, pp. 139–51.
22. Albert J. Reiss, Jr., "The Study of Deviant Behavior: Where the Action Is," *Ohio Valley Sociologist* 21, 1966, pp. 60–66.
23. Robert F. Meier, "Corporate Crime as Organizational Behavior," paper presented, American Society of Criminology Annual Meeting, Toronto, 30 October—2 November, 1975; Neal Shover, "Defining Organizational Crime," *in Corporate and Governmental Deviance: Problems of Organizational Behavior in Contemporary Society*, M. David Ermann and Richard J. Lundman, eds., New York: Oxford University Press, 1978, pp. 39–45; Laura Shill Shrager and James F. Short, Jr., "Toward a Sociology of Organizational Crime," *Social Problems* 25, 1978, pp. 407–19.
24. Christopher D. Stone, *Where the Law Ends: The Social Control of Corporate Behavior*. New York: Harper and Row, 1975.
25. Edward Gross, "Organizational Crime: A Theoretical Perspective," in Llewellyn Gross, ed., *Symposium on Sociological Theory*, New York: Harper and Row, 1978, pp. 5585; "Organization Structure and Organizational Crime," in Gilbert Geis and Ezra Stotland, eds., *White-Collar Crime: Theory and Research*, Beverly Hills: Sage, 1980, pp. 52–76.
26. M. David Ermann and Richard J. Lundman, eds., *Corporate and Governmental Deviance: Problems of Organizational Behavior in Contemporary Society*. New York: Oxford University Press, 1978.
27. Henry Farberman, "A Criminogenic Market Structure: The Automobile Industry," *Sociological Quarterly* 16, 1975, pp. 438–57; William N. Leonard and Marvin Weber, "Automakers and Dealers: A Study of Criminogenic Market Forces," *Law and Society Review* 4, 1970, pp. 407–24; Martin L. Needleman and Carolyn Needleman, "Organizational Crime: Two Models of Criminogenesis," *Sociological Quarterly* 20, 1979, pp. 517–28.
28. Marshall B. Clinard and Peter C. Yeager, *Corporate Crime*. New York: Free Press, 1980; Sally S. Simpson, "The Decomposition of Anti-Trust: Testing a Multi-level Longitudinal Model of Profit Squeeze," *American Sociological Review* 51, 1986, pp. 859–79.

29. Susan P. Shapiro, *Thinking about White-Collar Crime: Matters of Conceptualization and Research*. Washington DC: Department of Justice, National Institute of Justice, 1980; Susan P. Shapiro, "Collaring the Crime Not the Criminal: Liberating the Concept of White-Collar Crime," *American Sociological Review* 55, 1990, pp. 346–69; Gary S. Green, *Occupational Crime*. Chicago: Nelson Hall, 1997; Gilbert Geis, "White-Collar Crime: What Is It?" in Kip Schlegel and David Weisburd, eds., *White-Collar Crime Reconsidered*. Boston, Northeastern University Press, 1992, pp. 31–53.
30. James Helmkamp, Richard Ball, and Kitty Townsend, eds., *Definitional Dilemma: Can and Should There be a Universal Definition of White-Collar Crime?* Proceedings of the Academic Workshop. National White-Collar Crime Center Training and Research Institute. Morgantown, West Virginia.
31. Ronald C. Kramer, "Corporate Crime: An Organizational Perspective," in Peter Wickman and Timothy Dailey, eds., *White-Collar and Economic Crime*. Lexington, MA: Lexington Books, 1982, pp. 75–94; Henry C. Finney and H. R. Lesieur, "A Contingency Theory of Organizational Crime," in Samuel B. Bacharach, ed., *Research in the Sociology of Organizations*. Greenwich, CT: JAI Press, 1982, pp. 255–99.
32. Diane Vaughan, *Controlling Unlawful Organizational Behavior: Social Structure and Corporate Misconduct*. Chicago: University of Chicago Press, 1983; James W. Coleman, "Toward an Integrated Theory of White-Collar Crime," *American Journal of Sociology*, 93, 1987, pp. 406–39.
33. Stanton Wheeler, "The Problem of White-Collar Crime Motivation," in Schlegel and Weisburd, op. cit., pp. 108–123.
34. Vaughan, 1983, op. cit., pp. 54–66.
35. See, e.g., Sally S. Simpson, "Corporate Crime Deterrence and Corporate-Control Policies: Views from the Inside," in Schlegel and Weisburd, eds., op. cit., pp. 289–308; Sally S. Simpson, and Christopher S. Koper, "The Changing of the Guard: Top Management Team Characteristics, Organizational Strain, and Antitrust Offending, 1960–1980," *Journal of Quantitative Criminology* 13, 1997, 373–404; Sally S. Simpson and Nicole Leeper Piquero, "Low Self-Control, Organizational Theory, and Corporate Crime," *Law and Society Review* 2002, 36, pp. 509–48.
36. Powell and DiMaggio, op. cit.
37. I submit that the normalization of deviance also explains some kinds of street crime, but making that argument must await a future paper.
38. Diane Vaughan, *The Challenger Launch Decision: Technology, Culture, and Deviance at NASA*. Chicago: University of Chicago Press, 1996.
39. Gresham Sykes and David Matza, "Techniques of Neutralization: A Theory of Delinquency," *American Sociological Review* 22, 1957, pp. 664–670.
40. Kitty Calavita, Henry N. Pontell, and Robert Tillman, *Big Money Crime: Fraud and Politics in the Savings and Loan Crisis*. Berkeley: University of California Press, 1997.
41. Hannah Arendt, *Eichmann in Jerusalem: A Report on the Banality of Evil*. New York: Viking, 1964; Herbert C. Kelman and V. Lee Hamilton, *Crimes of Obedience*. New Haven, CT: Yale University Press, 1989; Daniel Goldhagen, *Hitler's Willing Executioners*. Cambridge: Harvard University Press, 1996.
42. Pfohl, op. cit.
43. Presidential Commission on the Space Shuttle *Challenger* Accident. *Report to the President by the Presidential Commission on the Space Shuttle Challenger Accident*. Vol. 1 of 5. Washington, DC: Government Printing Office, 1986.
44. *Columbia* Accident Investigation Board. *Report*. Washington, DC: Government Printing Office, 2003.
45. *Columbia* Accident Investigation Board, ibid., pp. 99–192. For a comparison of the social causes of the two accidents and the normalization of deviance, see pp. 195–202.

46. For the logic of developing general theory by comparing similar events in different organizational settings, see Vaughan, 1992.

References

Akers, Ronald L. (1985) *Deviance: A Social Learning Approach.* Belmont CA: Wadsworth.

Akers, Ronald L. (1989) "A Social Behaviorist's Perspective on Integration of Theories of Crime and Deviance." In *Theoretical Integration in the Study of Deviance and Crime: Problems and Prospects*, Editors Steven F. Messner, Marvin D. Krohn, and Allen E. Liska. Albany: State University of New York Press.

Akers, Ronald L., and Christine S. Sellers (2004) *Criminological Theories: Introduction, Evaluation, and Application.* Los Angeles: Roxbury.

Agnew, Robert (1992) "Foundation for a General Strain Theory of Crime and Delinquency." *Criminology* 30:47–87.

Editors, Alexander, Jeffrey C. Bernhard Giesen, Richard Munch, and Neil J. Smelser (1987) *The Micro–Macro Link.* Berkeley: University of California Press.

Arendt, Hannah (1964) *Eichmann in Jerusalem: A Report on the Banality of Evil.* New York: Viking.

Aubert, Vilhelm (1952) "White-Collar Crime and Social Structure." *American Journal of Sociology* 58:263–271.

Bourdieu, Pierre (1977) *An Outline of a Theory of Practice.* Cambridge: Cambridge University Press.

Calavita, Kitty, Henry N. Pontell, and Robert Tillman (1997) *Big Money Crime: Fraud and Politics in the Savings and Loan Crisis.* Berkeley: University of California Press.

Clinard, Marshall B. (1983) *Corporate Ethics and Crime.* Beverly Hills: Sage.

Clinard, Marshall B., and Peter C. Yeager (1980) *Corporate Crime.* New York: Free Press.

Coleman, James W. (1987) "Toward an Integrated Theory of White-Collar Crime." *American Sociological Review* 93:406–439.

Coleman, James W. (1996) "What is White Collar Crime? New Battles in the War of Definitions." In *Definitional Dilemma: Can and Should There be a Universal Definition of White-Collar Crime?* Editors James Helmkamp et al. Morgantown, WV: National White Collar Crime Center Training and Research Institute.

Collins, Randall (1981) "On the Micro-Foundations of Macro-Sociology." *American Journal of Sociology* 86:984–1014.

Columbia Accident Investigation Board (2003) *Report.* Washington D.C.: Government Printing Office.

Emirbayer, Mustafa, and Jeff Goodwin (1994) "Network Analysis, Culture, and the Problem of Agency." *American Journal of Sociology* 99:1411–1454.

Farberman, Henry (1975) "A Criminogenic Market Structure: The Automobile Industry" *Sociological Quarterly* 16:438–457.

Finney, Henry C., and Henry R. Lesieur (1982) "A Contingency Theory of Organizational Crime." In *Research in the Sociology of Organizations.* Editor Samuel B. Bacharach. Greenwich CT: JAI Press.

Fine, Gary Alan (1992) "Agency, Structure, and Comparative Contexts: Toward A Synthetic Interactionism." *Symbolic Interaction* 15:87–107.

Geis, Gilbert (1967) "The Heavy Electrical Equipment Antitrust Cases of 1961." In *Criminal Behavior Systems*, Editors Marshall B. Clinard and Richard Quinney. New York: Holt, Rinehart, and Winston.

Geis, Gilbert (1992) "White-Collar Crime: What is it?" In *White-Collar Crime Reconsidered*, Editors Kip Schlegel and David Weisburd. Boston: Northeastern University Press.

Geis, Gilbert (1996) "Definition in White-Collar Crime Scholarship: Sometimes It Can Matter." In *Definitional Dilemma: Can and Should There be a Universal Definition of White-Collar Crime?* Editors James Helmkamp et al. Morgantown,WV: National White-Collar Crime Center Training and Research Institute.

Giddens, Anthony (1984) *The Constitution of Society*. Berkeley: University of California Press.

Goldhagen, Daniel (1996) *Hitler's Willing Executioners*. Cambridge: Harvard University Press.

Gottfredson, Michael, and Travis Hirschi (1990) *A General Theory of Crime*. Stanford: Stanford University Press.

Granovetter, Mark (1985) "Economic Action and Social Structure: The Problem of Embeddedness." *American Journal of Sociology* 91:481–510.

Granovetter, Mark (1992) "Economic Institutions as Social Constructions: A Framework for Analysis." *Acta Sociologica* 35:3–11.

Green, Gary S. (1997) *Occupational Crime*. Chicago: Nelson Hall.

Gross, Edward (1978) "Organizational Crime: A Theoretical Perspective." In *Symposium on Sociological Theory*, Editor Llewellyn Gross. New York: Harper and Row 55–85.

Gross, Edward (1980) "Organizational Structure and Organizational Crime." In *White-Collar Crime: Theory and Research*, Editors Gilbert Geis and Ezra Stotland. Beverly Hills: Sage 52–76.

Hall, Peter M. (1987) "Interactionism and the Study of Social Organization." *Sociological Quarterly* 28:1–22.

Hall, Peter M. (1995) "The Consequences of Qualitative Analysis for Sociological Theory." *Sociological Quarterly* 36:397–423.

Hays, Sharon (1994) "Structure and Agency and the Sticky Problem of Culture." *Sociological Theory* 12:57–72.

Helmkamp, James, Richard Ball, and Kitty Townsend, eds. (1996) *Definitional Dilemma: Can and Should There be a Universal Definition of White-Collar Crime?* Morgentown, WV: National White-Collar Crime Center Training and Research Institute.

Hirschi, Travis (1989) "Exploring Alternatives to Integrated Theory." In *Theoretical Integration in the Study of Deviance and Crime: Problems and Prospects*, Editors Steven F. Messner, Marvin Krohn, and Allen E. Liska. Albany: State University of New York Press.

Jackall, Robert (1988) *Moral Mazes: The World of Corporate Managers*. New York: Oxford University Press.

Jamieson, Kate (1996) "The Role of the Collective in Defining White-Collar Crime." In *Definitional Dilemma: Can and Should There be a Universal Definition of White Collar Crime?* Editors Helmkamp et al. Morgantown, WV: National White Collar Crime Center Training and Research Institute.

Kelman, Herbert C., and V. Lee Hamilton (1989) *Crimes of Obedience*. New Haven, CT: Yale University Press.

Editors Knorr-Cetina, Karen, and Aaron Cicourel (1981) *Advances in Social Theory and Methodology: Toward and Integration of Micro- and Macro-Sociology.* London: Routledge and Kegan Paul.

Kramer, Ronald C. (1982) "Corporate Crime: An Organizational Perspective." Pp. 75–94 in *White-Collar and Economic Crime*, Editors Peter Wickman and Timothy Dailey. Lexington MA: Lexington Books.

Leonard, William N. and Marvin Weber (1970) "Automakers and Dealers: A Study of Criminogenic Market Forces." *Law & Society Review* 4:407–424.

Liska, Allen E., Marvin D. Krohn, and Steven F. Messner (1989) "Strategies and Requisites for Theoretical Integration in the Study of Crime and Deviance." In *Theoretical Integration in the Study of Deviance and Crime: Problems and Prospects*, Editors

Steven Messner, Marvin D. Krohn, and Allen E. Liska. Albany: State University of New York Press.

Maines, David R. (1977) "Social Organization and Social Structure in Symbolic Interactionist Thought." *Annual Review of Sociology* 3:235–259.

Meier, Robert F. (1975) "Corporate Crime as Organizational Behavior." Paper presented, American Society of Criminology Annual Meeting, Toronto 30 October–2 November.

Meier, Robert F. (1996) "Understanding the Context of White-Collar Crime: A Sutherland Approbation." In *Definitional Dilemma: Can and Should There be a Universal Definition of White-Collar Crime*, Editors James Helmkamp et al. Morgantown, WV: National White-Coller Crime Research and Training Institute.

Miethe, Terance D., and Robert F. Meier (1994) *Crime and its Social Context: Toward an Integrated Theory of Offenders, Victims, and Situations*. Albany: State University of New York Press.

Editors Messner, Steven F., Marvin D. Krohn, and Allen E. Liska (1989) *Theoretical Integration in the Study of Deviance and Crime: Problems and Prospects*. Albany: State University of New York Press.

Passas, Nikos (1990) "Anomie and Corporate Deviance." *Contemporary Crises* 14:157–178.

Pfohl, Stephen (1994) *Images of Deviance and Social Control: A Sociological History*, Second edition. New York: McGraw-Hill.

Editors Powell, Walter W. and Paul J. DiMaggio (1991) *The New Institutionalism in Organizational Analysis*. Chicago: University of Chicago Press.

Presidential Commission on the Space Shuttle *Challenger* Accident (1986) *Report to the President by the Presidential Commission on the Space Shuttle Challenger Accident*. 5 vols. Washington D.C.: Government Printing Office.

Quinney, Earl R. (1963) "Occupational Structure and Criminal Behavior: Prescription Violation by Retail Pharmacists." *Social Problems* 11:179–185.

Ragin, Charles C. (1994) *Constructing Social Research*. Beverly Hills: Pine Forge Press.

Reed, Gary E., and Peter Cleary Yeager (1996) "Organizational Offending and Neoclassical Criminology: Challenging the Reach of a General Theory of Crime." *Criminology* 34:357–382.

Reiss, Albert J. Jr. (1960) "The Study of Deviant Behavior: Where the Action is." *Ohio Valley Sociologist* 32:60–66.

Sampson, Robert J., Stephen W. Raudenbush, and Felton Earls (2002) "Assessing 'Neighborhood Effects': Social Processes and New Directions in Research." *Annual Review of Sociology* 28:443–478.

Schlegel, Kip (1996) "Recalling Status, Power, and Responsibility in the Study of White-Collar Crime." In *Definitional Dilemma: Can and Should There be a Universal Definition of White-Collar Crime?* Editors James Helmkamp et al. Morgantown, WV: National White-Collar Crime Research and Training Institute.

Sewell, William H., Jr. (1992) "A Theory of Structure: Duality, Agency, and Transformations." *American Journal of Sociology* 98:1–29.

Shapiro, Susan (1980) "Thinking About White-Collar Crime: Matters of Conceptualization and Research." Washington, D.C.: U.S. Department of Justice.

Shapiro, Susan (1990) "Collaring the Crime not the Criminal: Liberating the Concept of White-Collar Crime." *American Sociological Review* 55:346–369.

Short, James F. Jr. (1989) "Exploring Integration of Theoretical Levels of Explanation: Notes on Gang Delinquency." In *Theoretical Integration in the Study of Deviance and Crime: Problems and Prospects*, Editors Steven M. Messner, Marvin Krohn, and Allen E. Liska. Albany: State University of New York Press.

Shover, Neal (1978) "Defining Organizational Crime." Pp. 39–45 in *Corporate and Governmental Deviance: Problems of Organizational Behavior in Contemporary Society*, Editors M. David Ermann and Richard J. Lundman. New York: Oxford University Press.

Shrager, Laura Shil, and James F. Short, Jr. (1978) "Toward a Sociology of Organizational Crime." *Social Problems* 25:407–419.

Simpson, Sally S. (1986) "The Decomposition of Antitrust: Testing a Multi-level Longitudinal Model of Profit Squeeze." *American Sociological Review* 51:859–879.

Simpson, Sally S. (1992) "Corporate-Crime Deterrence and Corporate-Control Policies: Views from the Inside." Pp. 289–308 in *White-Collar Crime Reconsidered*, Editors Kip Schlegel and David Weisburd. Boston: Northeastern University Press.

Simpson, Sally S. (2002) *Corporate Crime, Law, and Social Control*. New York: Cambridge University Press.

Simpson, Sally S., and Christopher S. Koper (1997) "The Changing of the Guard: Top Management Team Characteristics, Organizational Strain, and Antitrust Offending, 1960–1986." *Journal of Quantitative Criminology* 13:373–404.

Simpson, Sally S., and Nicole Leeper Piquero (2002) "Low Self-Control, Organizational Theory, and Corporate Crime." *Law and Society Review* 36:509–548.

Smirchich, Linda (1983) "Concepts of Culture and Organizational Analysis." *Administrative Science Quarterly* 28:339–358.

Sonnenstuhl, William J., and Harrison M. Trice (1991) "Linking Organizational and Occupational Theory Through the Concept of Culture." *Research in Sociology of Organizations* 9:295–318.

Stone, Christopher D. (1975) *Where the Law Ends: The Social Control of Corporate Behavior*. New York: Harper and Row.

Sutherland, Edwin H. (1940) "White Collar Criminality." *American Sociological Review* 5:1–12.

Sutherland, Edwin H. (1949) *White-Collar Crime*. New York: Dryden Press.

Swidler, Ann (1986) "Culture in Action." *American Sociological Review* 51:273–286.

Sykes, Gresham, and David Matza (1957) "Techniques of Neutralization: A Theory of Delinquency." *American Sociological Review* 22:664–670.

Thornberry, Terence (1989) "Reflections on the Advantages and Disadvantages of Theoretical Integration." In *Theoretical Integration in the Study of Deviance and Crime: Problems and Prospects,* Editors Steven F. Messner, Marvin D. Krohn, and Allen E. Liska. Albany: State University of New York Press.

Trice, Harrison M., and Janice M. Beyer (1993) *The Cultures of Work Organizations*. Englewood Cliffs: NJ: Prentice-Hall.

Vaughan, Diane (1981) "Recent Developments in White-Collar Crime Theory and Research." In *The Mad, the Bad, and the Different: Essays in Honor of Simon Dinitz*. Editors C. Ronald Huff and Israel Barak. Lexington MA: Lexington Books.

Vaughan, Diane (1983) *Controlling Unlawful Organizational Behavior*. Chicago: University of Chicago Press.

Vaughan, Diane (1992) "Theory Elaboration: The Heuristics of Case Analysis." In *What is a Case? Exploring the Foundations of Social Inquiry*. Editors Charles C. Ragin and Howard S. Becker. New York: Cambridge University Press.

Vaughan, Diane (1996) *Challenger Launch Decision: Risky Technology, Culture, and Deviance at NASA*. Chicago: University of Chicago Press.

Vaughan, Diane (1999) "The Dark Side of Organizations: Mistake, Misconduct, and Disaster." *Annual Review of Sociology* 25:271–305.

Wheeler, Stanton (1997) "The Problem of White-Collar Crime Motivation." In *White-Collar Crime Reconsidered.* Editors Kip Schlegel and David Weisburd. Boston: Northeastern University Press 108–123.

2

Understanding Corporate Lawbreaking: From Profit Seeking to Law Finding

Peter Cleary Yeager

At least since Sutherland's pathbreaking publication in 1949,[1] American social science has had to conjure with the phenomena of "white-collar crime." If not quite reluctantly, it did so only haltingly in the quarter century following Sutherland's strong lead. Subsequent work was impeded by a combination of political disinterest in (even disdain for) the topic, the consequent lack of federal agency funds for research on it, and the focus of criminologists' work on rapidly rising rates of street crime in the United States.[2]

But following the social and political unrest associated especially with the Vietnam War in the 1960s and the Watergate scandal in the 1970s, research interest in white-collar crime took firmer root, and a variety of projects were launched. In contrast to the earlier years after Sutherland wrote—when a dominant cultural conservatism found itself married to the often visceral anti-Communism associated with the Cold War—the social disruptions and political mischief of this later period dislodged public trust in the nation's leading institutions of government and the economy, now seen as intertwined in deviant activities.[3] One result of this erosion of institutional legitimacy was the first-ever federal funding for large-scale studies of white-collar crime. The research arm of the U.S. Department of Justice financed three major research programs in the latter half of the 1970s, one each at the universities of Minnesota and Wisconsin, and at Yale University.

One of these, the Wisconsin project, explicitly followed Sutherland's lead in its effort to discover and explain patterns of lawbreaking by the largest American corporations.[4] While his study had focused on a sample of 70 of the largest companies of the period, the Wisconsin researchers compiled the records of violation of federal laws for the nation's 500 largest industrial corporations as listed in the annual Fortune 500 in the mid-1970s. This compilation remains the only such database of its size and breadth ever constructed.[5]

In the quarter century since the Wisconsin results were published, there has emerged a significant body of research on the wrongs done in and on behalf of American corporations. Despite a retreat in federal funding for such work, the last 25 years constitute history's longest sustained period of research on this topic. While still small in comparison to studies of conventional crimes, this body of research on deviancy in American companies far exceeds that done regarding any other nation's corporate businesses.

There is much to learn from the findings that have accumulated over this more recent 25 year period. My purpose in this essay is to highlight key findings and to sketch the explanatory portrait of corporate lawbreaking that they indicate. Where findings are more suggestive than definitive, I shall offer arguments more as hypotheses than as firmly rooted in evidence. As a related aim, the essay also will identify key gaps in knowledge and understanding, gaps that future research should one day fill.[6]

In what follows I shall first raise a few introductory analytic issues. Then I shall take up some key explanatory factors as suggested by the research literature on corporate offending, examining in turn the matter of profit seeking, the dynamics of corporate decision making and their institutional sources, and the role of law in lawbreaking.

Matters of Method

Before proceeding, several methodological points are in order. First is the matter of definition. The essay's focus on *corporate lawbreaking* distinguishes itself in a number of ways from Sutherland's fraught term of art "*white-collar crime*."[7] He had defined the concept as the crimes committed by "respectable persons" in the course of their legitimate occupations, by which he generally meant the offenses of middle- and upper-class professionals, whether committed only for personal gain or to meet organizational goals.[8] My interest is specifically in lawbreaking committed by corporate personnel for the purpose of meeting the goals of their private sector economic organizations. These personnel are often persons of the middle and upper classes, but they may also be blue-collar workers on the shop floor and pink-collar workers on corporate administrative staffs.

The other difference from Sutherland's usage lies in my preference for the term "*lawbreaking*" over "*crime*." Here the reason is practical rather than analytical. Sutherland had included in the category of "white-collar *crime*" almost all law violations, whether they were handled under the procedures of criminal, civil, or administrative law. He did so in part on the basis of the arguments that the government's choice of procedures registered the influence of elites rather than substantive legal differences and that the offenses could ultimately bring criminal penalties if violators persisted in their misconduct.[9] While these arguments were reasonable, his word choice created more heat than light. Rather than concentrating on the social dynamics that arguably underlie lawbreaking in and by corporations, many scholars have been distracted by the debate over the correctness of his categorization. Ironically, Sutherland's argument regarding political influence helped to politicize the analysis of corporate lawbreaking.[10]

In highlighting "lawbreaking" rather than "crime" I am seeking more neutral ground. My interest is in the explanation of any lawbreaking committed in the pursuit of corporate goals, no matter under which legal regimen the state seeks remedies. In this I agree completely with Sutherland's research focus. Indeed, research since he wrote suggests that there is no essential behavioral or legal difference between crimes as formally defined and other lawbreaking in pursuit of corporate purposes.[11] Regardless of what we call it, therefore, this category of lawbreaking should lend itself to focused social science theorizing, and this is best done without distracting disputes about language and ideology.[12]

The second methodological issue involves the matter of measurement. While crime statistics imperfectly tabulate crime of all types, estimates of the volume and rates of corporate lawbreaking are arguably among the least precise. A number of systemic factors contribute to this result, including the complexity of many corporate offenses that hides them from both regulators and victims and conceptual difficulties in determining how to calculate rates when violations occur over days and months and represent the work of many corporate hands.[13] Another major complication arises from the fact that the official data on corporations' lawbreaking register not only illegal behavior in firms, but also the priorities and capacities of regulatory officials, which are often politically shaped.[14] Explanations of offending based on such data therefore necessarily remain tentative at best. Confidence increases in such explanations when they are corroborated by research findings distributed over both time and investigative methods, both qualitative and quantitative.

Finally, just as crime has long frustrated the criminological pursuit of a grand theory of all lawbreaking,[15] it is not unlikely that different types of corporate offending will require varying explanations, or at least varying emphases on general causal factors. For example, it may be that the constellation of factors that contribute to antitrust violations by corporations may differ from that which influences discrimination against demographic categories of workers. In what follows below I will not attend closely to this potential variation. In part, this is because research has not yet taken us far enough to identify such variation with adequate confidence; in part it is because space limitations prevent adequate discussion of the possibilities, speculative as they are. Instead, I shall focus more on factors that are arguably generalizable, at least across many types of corporate lawbreaking. Future research will, one hopes, establish the accuracy of today's theoretical estimations.

Causes and Conditions of Corporate Lawbreaking

Given the mammoth size and multinational scope of operations of large U.S. corporations, it is likely that all of them violate federal or state laws from time to time. In principle, this could simply be due to the odds involved when a company's tens or hundreds of thousands of employees face dozens of major laws and thousands of associated regulations. The larger the company, the more difficult become internal communications and controls, which can increase both propensities and opportunities for lawbreaking. A large firm that is consistently compliant with all legal requirements is little more likely than a crime-free city.

Indeed, the Wisconsin research in the 1970s found that the largest of the sample of large industrial corporations were the most frequent violators of federal laws overall. The corporations' records of infractions correlated strongly with firm size.[16] Similar results have been found more recently in research on various types of corporate lawbreaking,[17] on antitrust offenses,[18] and on toxic emissions by chemical plants.[19]

However, the Wisconsin research also showed that the largest of its sample of big companies had no more violations of federal law per unit size of the firm than did the smaller companies; that is, relative to their sizes, the corporations violated laws at about the same rate, suggesting that perhaps larger companies offend more only because they do more business that is regulated, and hence more can go wrong.

But it is important to note as well that the relation between size of company and lawbreaking may vary according to other key factors, such as the relationship between specific industries or technologies and the specific regulatory laws in question. For example, with a sample of both large and small industrial corporations I found that company size was not related to firms' violations of pollution limits under the federal Clean Water Act but that larger firms violated government-imposed schedules for installing pollution control equipment less often than did smaller companies.[20] On the other hand, Grant and his colleagues[21] found that large chemical plants emitted toxic pollutants at higher rates than did smaller plants.

Like the Wisconsin research, these studies suggest therefore that tendencies to break laws vary systematically. Indeed, from Sutherland's foundational research in the 1940s onward it has been apparent that such offenses are not randomly distributed across the universe of companies. Instead, patterns of lawbreaking emerge consistently in research, patterns that distinguish seriously recidivist corporations from more law-abiding firms and patterns that distinguish offenses and violating firms by type and timing. It is these patterns that require both explanation and sustained policy responses.

Going into our research in the 1970s, Clinard and I made the assumption that large corporations differed in their propensities to violate federal laws; we did not assume that all firms broke whatever laws executives and managers figured they could evade without risk, and our findings bore this out. There was considerable variation between companies in the extent of their lawbreaking, with 40 percent not having been charged with any violations of federal law during the two year period we examined.[22]

On the basis of the few earlier, smaller-scale studies available, we had formulated a number of hypotheses about factors that might differentiate between corporations with higher and lower rates of offending. These hypotheses had to do with variation in firms' financial performances, in their organizational structures, and in their cultures. By the completion of our research in 1979, we had sharper focus on both causal patterns and unanswered questions.

Today, social science has a fuller view of the features of organizational life that promote lawbreaking in large companies. These include a more complex view of motivation than that simply entailed in profit seeking, and they involve an understanding of corporate life as comprising both structures and processes. They also include an appreciation of the role of law—of social control itself—as a potential enabler of corporate wrongdoing. Much has been accomplished over the past quarter century; much remains to be accomplished.[23]

Business Rationality and Legal Compliance

Research on corporate lawbreaking typically proceeds with the assumption that corporations are the preeminent rational form of human organization; that is, congruent with common sense it begins with the assumption that violations of federal law are motivated by the rational pursuit of profit. But because companies often comply with law, researchers have commonly hypothesized that corporate executives and managers are more likely to break laws when they are experiencing financial strain in their businesses and are less likely to do so when the corporate financial results are strong.

Unfortunately, measurement difficulties have limited efforts to detect connections between financial performance and lawbreaking by large corporations.[24] Nonetheless, although necessarily tentative, the empirical support for this argument has consistently proven to be modest, at best. The Wisconsin analyses discovered a tendency, but only a small one, for companies in financially strained industries to violate laws more often than those in better-performing industries. In other words, financial performance did not much distinguish between firms more or less likely to break laws.[25] Similarly, modest-to-null findings have since been reported by Simpson for corporate antitrust violations, by Gray and Shadbegian for air pollution violations in the pulp and paper mill industry, and by Keane in a reanalysis of the Wisconsin data using additional measures of financial performance and different statistical techniques.[26]

Further complicating the picture were some results that suggested the opposite conclusion. The Wisconsin study discovered evidence that companies experiencing improving profit trends were somewhat more likely to violate federal environmental laws than those with poorer results and that corporations experiencing greater rates of growth were more likely to violate product quality and safety laws.[27] Similarly, a later study found that while companies in industries experiencing financial strain were more likely to violate federal laws than were firms in industries doing moderately well economically, companies operating in the financially strongest industries were most likely to break the law.[28]

Some clues to this complex pattern of research findings may be found in Simpson's investigation antitrust offenses committed between 1927 and 1981 by a sample of 52 American corporations.[29] She discovered that firms were more likely to commit this type of violation when the economy was experiencing recession as well as when their industries were in financial difficulty, regardless of the firms' own levels of profitability.[30] She also found that economic strain was related only to firms' commission of *serious* antitrust offenses, such as predatory pricing or price-fixing conspiracies to eliminate competition. For relatively less serious offenses, such as false advertising or warranty violations, offenses that do not so directly and immediately assault competition in the marketplace, economic strain appears to play no part in the decision to break the law. Finally, her research also found that corporate antitrust violations occurred, or, at least, were detected, more frequently during Republican presidential administrations than during Democratic administrations.[31]

Collectively, these results suggest two important provisional conclusions and hypotheses for future research. First, broad economic and political conditions may be more relevant to rates of corporate lawbreaking than are firms' assessments of their own immediate financial circumstances. Regardless of past performance or current profitability, company personnel may make decisions about legal compliance based on their forecasts of future economic conditions in their industries and in the economy as a whole. They may also make these decisions with an eye toward their risks of prosecution for offenses, risks that are shaped by political forces. As Simpson points out, it appears that firms may consider Republican administrations less likely to enforce antitrust laws aggressively, a perception that raises the attraction of lawbreaking options that will improve the bottom line.[32]

Second, they suggest that companies' value or ethical systems—their corporate cultures—largely determine whether large corporations are inclined to break laws. These cultures may promote (or inhibit) lawbreaking regardless of whether companies are doing well financially and regardless of future prospects. Moreover, all corporate cultures, even those that are generally beneficent, may specify conditions under which laws may be broken as well as which laws may be broken under such conditions.

For example, there is evidence that—other things held equal—corporations are more inclined to break laws that govern the broader social consequences of business than they are to break laws designed to protect the competitive markets on which the companies' very existence depends. Clinard and Yeager found that large corporations much more often violated environmental protection, product quality and safety, and worker protection laws than they did antitrust and securities laws. This suggests that corporate executives and managers grant greater legitimacy to laws protecting markets than to those protecting values more remote from the core rules of competition that safeguard capitalist systems. This conclusion is also suggested by their findings that corporations with better profit results more often violated environmental laws and that those with greater growth rates more often violated product quality and safety rules.[33]

It is further suggested by Simpson's later finding that economic strain is associated with serious antitrust offenses, while such strain is unrelated to less serious breaches in this area of law,[34] and by Lane's much earlier finding that companies' economic decline was associated with unfair competitive practices but not with violations of labor relations law.[35] In sum, where legal requirements are considered less legitimate, less morally binding, no special motivation—such as financial troubles—may be required to justify lawbreaking in companies that are always looking to improve their bottom lines.[36]

This sense of law's legitimacy is reinforced when government punishes violations of market-protection rules much more aggressively than it does violations of other rules, as our research also demonstrated. The Wisconsin study found that while criminal sanctions were infrequently used for corporate offenses generally, they were applied to more than one-fifth of the trade (anticompetition) violations and to about 14 percent of violations of financial regulations but to less than 1 percent each of cases involving environmental, product quality, and safety and labor laws. In these latter three areas of offending, typically, lenient administrative sanctions accounted for from 78 percent to 96 percent of the legal responses.[37]

These possibilities therefore suggest the importance of separating law's potentially dual effects on corporate behavior: that of deterring noncompliance via fear of sanctions from that which brings compliance through shaping the normative views of corporate personnel. I shall return to this matter below.

Since the Wisconsin research in the late 1970s, there has been a series of costly corporate "crime waves" in the financial services sector of the U.S. economy, beginning with the savings and loan crisis in the 1980s and continuing in recent years with widespread lawbreaking in accounting practices, investment banking, mutual funds, and the insurance industry. With this sustained assault on investors' confidence, to say nothing of their personal savings, corporations have undermined the trust on which financial markets—and hence the economic system—depend.

But rather than contradicting earlier findings regarding the prevalence of different forms of corporate lawbreaking, these destructive crises tend to support them. In particular, they suggest that when law drops its regulatory guard,[38] a competitive business culture can promote even the eating of its own seed corn, the legitimacy of markets.[39] At the same time, although systematic studies are lacking, it is possible that broad patterns of deregulation in the areas of health, safety, and environmental controls since the 1980s have also spurred rates of offending, at least among some industries, types of firm, and difficult market conditions. This is further suggested in recent research on environmental law. On the basis of interviews with business officials in charge of compliance with U.S. environmental laws in two industries, Gunningham and his colleagues reported that "many acknowledged that in the absence of regulation, it is questionable whether many firms' current good intentions would continue indefinitely to maintain good environmental practice throughout the industry."[40] These possibilities establish a promising agenda for future research on trends in both corporate law violation and enforcement in the various regulatory arenas.

Corporations, Culture, and Choice

The research reviewed above suggests the limitations of the classical rational choice model of business behavior. In the aggregate the research shows little support for the hypothesis that profit strain produces significantly higher rates of offending by U.S. companies, as one would expect under the model. Limitations of this model are also suggested by research on the deterrent effects of legal sanctions on corporate misconduct. This body of deterrence research indicates generally either that the law has at best modest impacts on business compliance decisions or that law's effects operate more forcefully through its indirect influence on cultural and managerial norms than through its direct effect via fear of legal punishment.[41]

But corporations in markets are surely rational entities, and profit seeking is their *raison d'être.* One reasonable interpretation of the profit-strain findings is therefore that American companies' legal violations are generally motivated by their pursuit of profit, no matter how well they have done lately or even what their forecasts of future markets tell them.[42] On the other hand, no legitimate corporation regularly breaks the law, and many appear to do so infrequently, if at all.[43] The accumulated research has also documented systematic variation in violation records across types of firm, regulatory regimes, and types of offenses, size of companies, market structures, and so on.[44]

Explanations of corporate lawbreaking must therefore consider the potential causal action of such factors in combination with companies' fundamental economic purposes. The key observation to make here is as important as it should be obvious: These factors do not operate on their own. Instead, they work whatever effects they may have through the perceptions and behaviors of corporate personnel. Among other things, this suggests the importance of the analysis of *corporate cultures* to the understanding of lawbreaking in business. Happily, while there has been a substantial body of quantitative and macrosociological research aimed at discovering and conjecturing about such structural factors as markets, organizational size, and regulatory regimes, rather more recently, there has developed as well a body of qualitative and microsociological research aiming to understand the role of culture, social process, and choice in corporate lawbreaking.[45]

This research stream has highlighted a number of features that characterize much corporate lawbreaking. First, these offenses are not only reasonably common, but they are also mundane; that is, they typically occur as part of routine operations and reflect the customary patterns of thought in corporate work environments. They do not represent radical departures from standard operating procedures. Second, these offenses are typically the result of corporate executives' and managers' intentional decisions. Decisions that break laws, whether taken individually or collectively in work environments, are generally conscious and motivated behaviors that reflect persons' essentially moral assessments of their obligations and goals.[46] This means, for example, that executives and managers may break laws either because they judge the reaching of corporate goals as morally trumping legal requirements, at least in some situations, or because they simply regard legal requirements as morally insignificant.

Of course, executives' and managers' self-interests are key to these decisions as well. Considerations of self-interest here run a continuum from fear of failure and losing one's job through pursuing promotions and bonuses to the exercise of sheer greed. But—and this is the third point—cases of simple greed aside, persons' interests are *socially constructed* in their work environments. Through their experiences at work, executives and managers learn not only corporate purposes, strategies, and goals, they learn much else as well. In particular, their preferences—and moral evaluations—regarding both corporate means and ends are shaped by their socialization into corporate cultures. Here individual self-interest merges with corporate purposes, especially as the pursuit of these purposes is shaped by systems of incentives and rewards for individual and group performance.

Christopher Stone suggested 30 years ago how complex corporate organizations, with their hierarchies, fine divisions of labor, and blocked communication channels, segment and dim managers' senses of moral responsibility for wrongdoing.[47] The more recent qualitative research has demonstrated that in the process of learning to pursue the legitimate goals of companies—profits, growth, innovation—corporate personnel also absorb subtler messages, messages regarding the relative moral importance attached to competing goals (e.g., profitability and environmental safety) and to the often-perceived conflict between legitimate means and desirable business results. This research has established that these messages can form cognitive maps that govern managers' moral assessments of their choices such that they may not recognize anything wrong, even if their choices violate law.[48]

This is illustrated in the account of the former recall coordinator who failed to push adequately for the recall of the Ford Motor Company's Pinto automobile after its dangerous tendency to explode on rear-end impacts had been demonstrated. He argued that "cognitive scripts" to which corporate managers are socialized systematically orient decision makers to some sorts of information and interpretations, while screening out other sorts. He writes that

> the unexplored ethical issue for me is the arguably prevalent case where organizational representatives are not aware that they are dealing with a problem that might have ethical overtones. If the case involves a familiar class of problems or issues, it is likely to be handled via existing cognitive structures or scripts—*scripts that typically include no ethical component in their cognitive content.*[49]

As Diane Vaughan concludes from her close examination of the 1996 *Challenger* launch decision at NASA that cost the lives of all the astronauts aboard, "rather than acting illegally, then invoking techniques of neutralization to minimize their experience of guilt and culpability, many offenders may never define their behavior as wrong in the first place."[50]

Another, arguably more common dynamic finds corporate personnel experiencing dilemmas in which law violation is one recognized option in the choice about how to best meet corporate goals. Even here, the decision makers may learn to justify any legal and other ethical transgressions on what they find to be a moral basis. This was one of the conclusions from research based on extensive interviews that colleagues and I conducted in two large American companies, a high technology manufacturer and a financial services firm.[51]

For example, a middle manager reported that, under pressure from his superiors, he falsified the profits of the company by millions of dollars in a manner that violated standard accounting practices and U.S. law. A second manager in the same company reported a separate incident of a similar accounting maneuver to inflate profits. (Neither act came to the attention of legal authorities.) While the first manager struggled with the wrongfulness of this decision, ultimately, he came to justify it in terms of other legitimate aims and needs, including moral ones. Here he speaks of these, making reference to his boss, who had pressured him to inflate the profit statement:

> What he did was not unethical. It just . . . um . . . well, he knew exactly what he was doing. It's not that he did it out of ignorance or anything. What he did was not unethical. What he did was he made the best of a bad situation without having to sacrifice the company's progress. If we couldn't have gotten the [profits increased this way], I don't know how we would have gotten the money. We might have had to cut back on some things we didn't want to sacrifice, like our marketing budget, or on people. You know, I mean the alternatives to [the decision] were probably a lot uglier.[52]

The normalization of such behavior is indicated not only in its apparently routine appearance in this company—one, by the way, with a good corporate reputation—but also by its justification in essentially moral terms, including the financial health of a valuable business that serves important societal interests. Especially noteworthy is the reference to the unpleasant alternative of laying off employees to increase profits (by cutting costs), a move many American companies have made via either downsizing the firm or transferring work to overseas locations. Here the potential victimization of real people—colleagues and subordinates—by firing them stands in sharp psychological contrast to breaking faith with something as abstract as financial markets with their institutional investors. In a very real sense these managers perceived the choice to falsify the financial statements as involving no harm nearly so substantial as hurting loyal employees, if any at all. Where corporate violations involve "only" impersonal markets, therefore, the law may find less support in managers' own moral inhibitions, much as Geis's price fixers also demonstrated.[53] As I have indicated elsewhere, such "demoralization" of offenses may also characterize some types of pollution offense, with an assist from law (see below).[54]

These fundamentally moral characterizations of offenses appear to be conditioned by structural and cultural factors, both inside firms and in firms' social environments. In both companies we studied, for example, managers routinely reported that ethical dilemmas were *indiscussable* with their superiors. Instead of consultation that may have resolved dilemmas more ethically (and legally, where the law was involved), and despite formal norms of open communication (especially emphasized in the high technology company), the managers said that they were expected by their bosses to solve problems on their own. This was generally attributed to the view that what successful managers do—and what they are rewarded for doing—is solving problems. One consequence, of course, is that such tensions, as between profit making and legal and ethical requirements, may not be publicly addressed and resolved, hence reproducing them in the company's culture or subcultures.

It is noteworthy that "indiscussibility" appeared to be more salient in the high technology company with the flatter, decentralized managerial hierarchy than in the steeper, more traditional and centralized corporate hierarchy of the financial services firm. In addition to this finding's counterintuitive interest, it also suggests the interaction of cultural and structural features in firms as they condition the likelihood of lawbreaking.

Moreover, the characterization of the behavior as acceptable is furthered in this example by the *approval of outside institutional authorities:* The company's auditors, a large accounting firm, had endorsed the specific falsification, as it had also done with at least one other major corporate client. We see just this pattern of formal authorization in the roles played by investment banks, lawyers, and accounting firms in the large recent cases of illegal financial practices, as in the facilitation of Enron's crimes by its outside auditor, the now dissolved Arthur Andersen company.

Similar financial frauds have spanned the globe in recent years. For example, the Italian multinational corporation Parmalat has been embroiled in a major financial fraud scandal that involved numerous Italian and international banks and charges that the company's auditors—the major firm Deloitte & Touche—had helped to hide the firm's true financial picture from investors. The company was declared bankrupt in 2003, and thousands of small Italian investors were reported to have lost their savings when Parmalat's bonds proved worthless. Not surprisingly, given the similarities to the United States's paradigm case, the scandal came to be known as "Europe's Enron."[55]

From such evidence it is clear that the understanding of corporate misconduct requires consideration and integration of levels of analysis from the individual to the institutional.[56] Indeed, cumulatively, the research on corporate lawbreaking strongly suggests that the basic material from which managers' ethical views are constructed is found not only in deviant corporate or industry subcultures, although it is transformed there into fuel for chronic lawbreaking. Instead, much as Sykes and Matza long ago suggested regarding commonly used justifications for conventional crimes,[57] this material is located in our basic social institutions, especially in the economy and law and in the wider culture that reflects and sustains them.

The result is that corporate lawbreaking is endemic in our conventional social arrangements. What distinguishes infrequent from chronic corporate offenders is the absence—or presence—of a corporate culture that routinely privileges financial success over all else and discounts the moral weight of law. To a substantial degree, such a culture is likely to be conditioned by a combination of factors, from the personality of corporate leaders, to the characteristics of the markets in which firms compete, to the vigilance of law enforcers.

To see something of the interacting connections between such factors, consider the following proposed explanation for the financial scandals that have roiled American and world markets in recent years. The strong privileging of economic success over other social values uniquely characterizes American society as against other industrial capitalist nations.[58] This hierarchy of social values is visible in our institutional relations, in which the values and requirements of the economy supercede those of other institutions, such as education, the family, and communities. The animating values of these latter institutions are subordinated to those of the economy, and action within them is increasingly directed toward market requirements.[59]

This imbalance in American social values has been accompanied over the last several decades by the rise to prominence of finance capitalism in the direction of American industry.[60] Associated with key changes in markets and law, this development was, by the latter decades of the 20th century, increasingly focusing corporate management's attention on short-term financial gains, often at the expense of other considerations, including legal requirements. Finance capitalism emphasizes the pursuit of corporate growth and profitability through the acquisition of profitable assets—other firms—rather than through product innovation and other traditional modes of market competition.

This latter period also saw the growth of institutional investors as millions of American employees increasingly sought to build their retirement nest eggs through regular purchases of corporate stock, typically as sold and managed by mutual fund firms. The concerns of these investors and their mutual fund companies to see regular growth in stock values pressured the corporate orientation toward the achievement of short-term (quarterly) increases in stock prices. This orientation placed an even higher premium on the creative management by firms of their financial assets and accounting systems. The effective management of shareholder value became the touchstone of corporate success.

The consequence of these changes for corporate organization was the rise to prominence of chief executive officers (CEOs) with financial backgrounds—displacing those with backgrounds in sales, marketing, or manufacturing—along with the development of a new role in corporate leadership, the chief financial officer (CFO).[61] Recent decades have also seen the increased hiring of cadres of business school graduates professionally trained in the virtues of financial creativity and bottom-line achievement.[62]

This historic shift in the leadership structures and professional orientation of corporations is fateful for both rates and types of corporate lawbreaking. In his interview-based research with a sample of retired corporate middle managers, Clinard discovered an early indicator of such consequences.[63] These former managers reported that illegal and unethical acts in corporations were linked to the moral climate established by top management, and significantly, they viewed corporate leaders with engineering backgrounds as being more likely to establish positive ethical climates than were those with financial backgrounds, who they saw as focused on bottom-line results rather than on such factors as product quality.

In the increasingly turbulent world economy of the late 20th century, characterized by large-scale corporate restructuring (e.g., downsizing employees, outsourcing jobs to other nations, mergers, and acquisitions) to maintain competitiveness, the commitment to financial management deepened. In the ballooning stock market of the 1990s, many industries featured the recruitment of leadership from among a growing number of financially expert, highly mobile reorganization specialists with more compelling ties to stock markets and share prices than to firms' reputations for socially responsible behaviors, or to the communities they inhabited. This process was joined to the growing use of stock options in top management's pay and incentive packages, more firmly connecting management decisions to short-term financial results that boosted the price of their corporate stocks.[64] Together, these developments put a premium on creative accounting and financial management, and they did so in a laissez-faire regulatory climate, in which the federal government and major accounting firms had taken a hands-off approach to corporate governance. When the stock market bubble burst in 2001, it laid bare the great extent to which corporate management—especially in the telecommunications and energy industries—had engaged in massive financial frauds to prop up stock prices and the incomes of executives.

Finally, not only was the victimization from these large-scale frauds diffuse—spread over individuals and institutional investors the world over—it was also abstract in the sense that corporate officials, dealing over long distances with intangible investment vehicles and absentee consumers rather than with local customers purchasing tangible products, could not easily perceive real victims and moral harm. These characteristics of the market facilitated the crimes by reducing the role of conscience in them.

Prior to being pushed off the front pages and network television news by the American-led invasion of Iraq, these cases of fraud had commanded the attention of the nation, all the more as so many citizens were deeply victimized by them. But long before their public unmasking at the turn of the century, U.S. businesses had not only initiated such illegal practices, but they appear also to have normalized them—as indicated in the interviews discussed above—setting the stage for the ever greater frauds that later developed.[65]

Law and Lawbreaking

While the potential for lawbreaking is built into the structures and processes of all large corporations, we can expect to see differences in the rates and distribution of offenses over time, industries, and legal requirements. Importantly, the law does not stand only on the punishment side of the equation for explaining corporate wrongdoing; its role as a source of moral evaluation is central. This role is shaped by dynamic connections between legal action and corporate behavior.

As the discussion above suggests, corporate violations will increase when the enforcement of law retracts, other things held constant (such as strain and uncertainty in the economic climate of firms). As noted earlier, the law's deterrent effects on corporate conduct are generally modest at best. But the relative leniency or severity of enforcement is not the only legal characteristic that shapes compliance with law. Legal process and legal legitimacy also play important roles in conditioning the likelihood that corporate offenses will occur. The issue is the extent to which law either reinforces or undermines its own moral authority in the minds of corporate decision makers. When the moral force of law is reduced, managers and executives will find the prospect of legal violations less ethically troubling and hence more available as options.

Research on regulatory law finds that laws regulating corporate behavior generally lose some of their moral authority as they move from the typically well-publicized and often passionate moral arguments on the legislative stage to the mundane, technical, and obscure procedures of converting legal mandates into enforceable rules in the regulatory bureaucracies of government, and even onto enforcement in the field.[66] This is especially likely to occur in areas of law that are inherently technical and/or that seek to address aspects of corporations' *internal processes*, such as their production systems, research protocols, and management procedures. This is because the U.S. Government is reluctant to intrude into the prerogatives of management in private sector businesses. As a result, the government is unusually dependent on industry cooperation to provide information and ideas necessary for formulating and enforcing regulations.

Furthermore, to justify regulations, government agencies rely on cost-benefit analyses that favor business in two respects. First, the costs of regulations to businesses are typically more easily and precisely determined than are the proposed rules' wider social benefits, so the latter will be underassessed relative to the former. Second, the application of this formally neutral and highly technical analytic tool tends naturally to enhance a cultural perception, especially among businesspersons, that legally prohibited commercial conduct is *morally ambivalent* rather than clearly wrongful.

In research on the legal regulation of industrial water pollution I found these factors at play in the federal Environmental Protection Agency's (EPA) implementation of the Clean Water Act.[67] In the decades-long process of translating this ambitious statute into hundreds of specific regulations to control the industrial discharge of countless numbers of pollutants, the public interest voices for clean water were marginalized in the highly technical dialogue that was dominated by industry and government participants. Lacking both the financial and technical resources required for these deliberations, clean water advocates were typically unable to participate in the wide range of regulatory hearings and procedures that, in the end, produced environmental law. The results were regulations less stringent than had originally been anticipated, often less stringent yet for large companies that could most effectively participate in these deliberations. Moreover, countless water pollution violations went unpunished while industrial firms appealed the rules to the EPA and to the courts.

Lynxwiler and his colleagues discovered a related process in their study of enforcement discretion in the federal Office of Surface Mining Reclamation and Enforcement.[68] They found that, other things equal, larger mining companies' offenses were seen by inspectors as less serious, and were fined less, than were those of small firms. This was due, the investigators explained, to field inspectors finding larger firms to be more cooperative—and smaller firms less so—importantly because larger companies had the professional resources and expertise with which to engage the inspectors in discussions of their facilities' violations, discussions that characterized offenses more as technical rather than moral matters. Without such resources, smaller companies were more often seen by inspectors both as more recalcitrant and less technically able to comply with law.

It is reasonable to assume that such regulatory and enforcement processes both reflect and color corporate management's moral assessment of the rules and shape deterrent effects. Recent research on Occupational Safety and Health Organization penalties, for example, suggests that they do not prevent future injuries to workers in larger establishments.[69]

Propositions such as these regarding the "technological neutralization" of law are always *ceteris paribus* ones. But other things are never equal. Corporate perceptions of and compliance with law, however technical, are also likely to be shaped by economic factors and general cultural views of what constitutes appropriate commercial behavior, among other factors. For example, when environmental values become deeply rooted in a society, companies may comply more fully with environmental laws for reputational reasons and because of the general socialization of managers as citizens who share in these values. Law and law enforcement may serve largely to support such values and reputational concerns in the minds of corporate personnel, rather than primarily as classical deterrents to amoral calculators. Recent research by Gunningham and his colleagues on perceptions of corporate facility managers in two industries suggests this result, especially for larger, more sophisticated companies, while deterrence was more salient to smaller enterprises.[70]

A related consideration arises with respect to the *style of enforcement*. Here I have in mind specifically the contrast between adversarial and cooperative styles of enforcement. John Braithwaite has argued most forcefully for the virtues of the latter and the costs of the former.[71] Among other things, he asserts that cooperative enforcement—or restorative justice—would be more successful at shaping positive moral values toward greater compliance among regulated industries and argues that adversarial enforcement—which more often characterizes enforcement in the United States—produces more resistance to law and higher rates of noncompliance. In addition to some supportive evidence from his own research on coal mine safety in the United States and nursing home regulation in Australia, his general position has found support in comparative research on nations' successes in pollution control.[72]

Law also loses its efficacy when it acts capriciously or inconsistently. In these situations, regulated companies will withhold legitimacy from the law's commands, and the only legal force that will compel their compliance is the prospect of harsh punishment. As the government is reluctant to use such methods, especially against powerful multinational corporations that can readily move their business activities to more "friendly" states, the loss of legal legitimacy can promote lawbreaking.

This prospect is heightened when political winds blow government regulation back and forth between periods of aggressive enforcement and those of informal deregulation when legal controls are substantially reduced, as occurred from the 1980s through the early years of the 21st century in such areas of regulation as banking, securities, and environmental protection. Recent support for this process is found in interview-based research on compliance with U.S. environmental law, in which the "respondents indicated that they would be far less inclined to voluntary compliance if others were perceived to be 'getting away with it.'"[73]

Taken together, these ideas and findings suggest the value of future comparative research that examines corporate compliance with various regulatory regimes over time, taking into account such additional factors as economic climates (munificent or not), market characteristics (levels of competition, product characteristics, relations between producers and consumers), corporate structures and cultures, and political variables that reflect and reinforce societal values and the distribution of power.

Conclusion

Research on corporate lawbreaking conducted over the past 25 years has not only dwarfed that done in the quarter century after Sutherland's launching of the field; it has also "dwarfed" it in sophistication and variation in research methodologies and in contributions to our understanding of this important matter. In this essay I have sought to identify some of the most important findings from this recent period of work, and I have highlighted what I see as some of the more fruitful areas of future research.

Research in this area is not only analytically complicated, but it is also often challenging to mount. The reasons for this are well known to those who have taken it on. They include government databases on compliance and enforcement that make some research questions difficult to answer, insufficient government and foundation funding for research, proprietary data on some corporate characteristics that are unavailable to researchers, and understandable corporate resistance to having researchers on-site assessing their compliance behaviors. Given such challenges, the body of research that has been compiled since 1980 is all the more impressive. These challenges can render the rewards of such work even richer.

In these remaining lines I would like only to suggest a couple of particular areas of future research that should have high analytic payoffs. These areas are not the only ones of high potential value, as I trust the essay will have indicated, and certainly they are both complex and challenging types of studies to mount. But they should prove to be well worth the effort.

One area worth considerably more investment is the study of corporate cultures and decision-making processes from the viewpoints of those involved in them. We need more intensive, retrospective case studies that combine documentary analysis with interview data from participants, much like Diane Vaughan's excellent study of the disaster that befell the space shuttle *Challenger*.[74] We also need studies of corporate cultures and processes from inside the companies. Such fieldwork could combine interviews and observations regarding corporate values, cultures and subcultures, and communication and decision-making processes. As I've just noted, such studies face resistance from corporate leaders, who characteristically prefer to shield such matters from outsiders' view. But carefully planned and presented to potential research sites, such work is possible, and the potential payoff to knowledge—and ultimately, to policy—is high indeed.[75]

Another promising line of investigation is the historical analysis of the conditions under which industries were founded and in which they have evolved. From Sutherland onward, investigators have identified variation in industry cultures as a key to understanding differential rates of violation across industries. But we need more case studies, such as Norman Denzin on the liquor industry,[76] to better understand the nature and origins of cultures in specific industries. We need to know how cultural orientations favoring either compliance or breach may develop in industries. The relevant conditions include economic, legal, political, technological, and ideological factors. In a world increasingly dominated by multinational corporations from many countries, comparative cross-national work of this sort is increasingly indicated.

For example, the history of the oil industry in the United States suggests that the conditions of its early establishment are important to understanding its long record of violations of federal antitrust laws.[77] This industry was established and consolidated in a laissez-faire period prior to the passage of the Sherman Antitrust Act in 1890, which in large part was a response to the consolidated power of what came to be known as Big Oil. Thereafter, the record shows an industry that maintained a privileged relationship to antitrust enforcement, even in the face of suspect business dealings that appeared to clearly violate the statute. The history suggests that this preferential treatment was connected to the oil industry's control of a vital national resource which required development of foreign sources of crude oil and which therefore entailed key issues in international relations. It is likely that this control and role in national and international affairs has shaped the views of oil executives regarding the legal legitimacy of antitrust law.

It would be worthwhile from both social scientific and policy perspectives to generate comparative research on such histories. For example, one could then usefully compare industrial histories, such as those of the oil and computer hardware industries, to determine common and unique forces relating to compliance with such laws, such as those governing markets and those governing worker safety. Such work could be a hallmark of the next quarter century of research on corporate lawbreaking.

Endnotes

1. Sutherland (1949).
2. Among other difficulties (see, e.g., Clinard and Yeager, 1978).
3. As found, for example, in the evidence of illegal corporate contributions to the Nixon campaign for president in the 1972 election.
4. The results of the Wisconsin research were published in two monographs, *Illegal Corporate Behavior* (Clinard et al., 1979) and *Corporate Crime* (Clinard and Yeager, 1980). The research at the University of Minnesota examined the problem of employee theft (see, e.g., Hollinger and Clark, 1983), while the Yale series of studies were distributed across a number of specific types of white-collar offenses and their regulation at law (e.g., Rose-Ackerman, 1978; Wheeler et al., 1982; Shapiro, 1984).
5. The large data set has been archived since the early 1980s at the Inter-University Consortium for Political and Social Research (ICPSR) at the University of Michigan. With the accompanying codebook it is located in ICPSR's National Archive of Criminal Justice Data under the title "Illegal Corporate Behavior, 1975–1976" (http://www.icpsr.umich.edu/NACJD/archive.html).
6. I published a similar review of research progress a few years after the appearance of *Corporate Crime* (Clinard and Yeager, 1980); see Yeager (1986). Occasionally, in what follows, I will also footnote research done in other countries.
7. Criminologists and lawyers have wrangled over the definition of white-collar crime and its associated terms since Sutherland's work in the 1940s (see note 8 below). It is not my intention here to review these arguments and the range of definitions that have evolved over time. For some discussions of the debates and distinctions, see, for example, Clinard and Quinney (1973), Clinard and Yeager (1980: 17–19), Calavita and Pontell (1993), Shover and Wright (2001: section 1), and Kramer et al. (2002).
8. See, for example, Sutherland (1945, 1949).

9. Sutherland (1945).
10. The critiques of Sutherland's work had both analytic and political elements and continued decades later with the publication of my work with Clinard (Clinard et al., 1979; Clinard and Yeager, 1980). For examples, see Tappan (1947), Orland (1980), and Evans (1981).
11. This essay is not the place to defend closely this position. I pause here only to make two points. First, on the argument that the law of crimes requires proof of intent, it is noteworthy that the criminal law concepts of strict liability and negligence have been used to reach cases of corporate lawbreaking where clear intent may be absent (see, e.g., Wright and Huck, 2002; cf. Blum-West and Carter, 1983). Second, as the discussion below suggests, research on corporate lawbreaking indicates that most of it is done intentionally by personnel who know—or should know—the law.
12. It is also worth noting that my focus on illegalities differs from related concepts in this general field of research. Mine is narrower than that of critical or conflict criminologists, who are interested in explaining the broader category of harms done by corporations, whether proscribed by law or not (see, e.g., Young, 1981; Kramer et al., 2002). While for some such behaviors, there is likely to be strong agreement in the United States that firms are responsible for substantial and avoidable moral offenses (e.g., the aggressive marketing of "junk food" to children), about others there is less (e.g., outsourcing jobs to second- and third-world countries, to the detriment of local American communities and their workers). In contrast to the broader focus on what has been sometimes called "corporate deviance," I have chosen the less contentious legal definition to identify corporate harms. While legal prohibitions do not all register the same degree of society's moral condemnation, they commonly represent majority agreement that the behaviors should be prevented or at least minimized (cf. Stone, 1975).

    On the other hand, it may well be that corporate illegalities and forms of legal corporate deviance have etiological factors in common, as suggested by Diane Vaughan's (1999) important work on mistakes, misconduct, and disasters in organizations.

    My focus also excludes a type of organizational offending itself, one very usefully identified by Calavita and Pontell (1993) in their research on the savings and loan crisis of the 1980s. Much of this crime involved what they earlier called "collective embezzlement" (Calavita and Pontell, 1991), in which unscrupulous thrift owners used their control of banks to loot them *solely for personal gain*. The authors note that in both method and motive, these organizational crimes are more like conventional organized crime than they are like corporate lawbreaking as I define it here.

    Finally, I exclude important cases like those identified by Szasz (1986: 3, 23), in which corporations benefit in the way of cost savings from doing business with traditional organized crime. Szasz's study was of corporations' disposal of hazardous waste by contracting it out to organized crime–controlled businesses, knowingly or otherwise. Here legal responsibility rests typically on the final disposers of the waste rather than on the originating firm, given the structure of the law. While on such grounds I exclude these cases from my definition, Szasz has very importantly demonstrated the potential role of law in facilitating lawbreaking, a process to which I shall later return.
13. See, for example, Reed and Yeager (1996) and Yeager and Reed (1998).
14. See, for example, Yeager (1991); compare Geis and Salinger (1998).
15. Of course, this is not for lack of ambition and effort. Two of the most ambitious and prominent of such efforts—those of Sutherland, with his learning theory of differential association (e.g., Sutherland and Cressey, 1955), and of Gottfredson and Hirschi (1990), with their theory of low self control—explicitly and forcefully argued that these theories explained not only street crimes, but white-collar crimes as well. While Sutherland's theory has much merit in its focus on culture and learning

as key to understanding crime patterns, it neglects other factors in organizational and social processes that shape these patterns. Meanwhile, as Gary Reed and I have argued elsewhere, Gottfredson and Hirschi's argument that low self-control explains patterns of offenses of corporate personnel is clearly unconvincing (Reed and Yeager, 1996; Yeager and Reed, 1998; see also Steffensmeier, 1989; Benson and Moore, 1992; Simpson and Piquero, 2002).

16. Clinard et al. (1979); Clinard and Yeager (1980).
17. Baucus and Near (1991).
18. Simpson (1986); Jamieson (1994).
19. See Grant et al. (2002). The toxic emissions studied by Grant and his colleagues are generally unregulated by the U.S. Environmental Protection Agency. The agency instead requires only the reporting of such emissions, which states and localities may decide to regulate. The Grant et al. (2002) study also focuses on the size of the polluting plant, rather than on the size of the corporation as such. But the results showed not only that big chemical plants have higher rates of toxic emissions than do smaller plants, but that big plants' rates are especially high when they are part of a larger corporation.
20. Yeager (1991).
21. Grant et al. (2002).
22. See Clinard et al. (1979: chap. 6) and Clinard and Yeager (1980: chap. 5). Of course, the 40 percent figure may well include a number of companies who escaped legal scrutiny or charges for offenses they committed. Nonetheless, the variation between firms in lawbreaking is substantial enough to conclude that real differences exist in their rates of offending.
23. For contributions to our understanding of the roots of corporate lawbreaking and deviancy since we wrote *Corporate Crime*, see, for example, Vaughan (1982), Clinard (1983), Braithwaite (1984), Coleman (1987), Clinard (1990), Passas (1990), Ross (1992), Schlegel and Weisburd (1992), Tonry and Reiss (1993), Jenkins and Braithwaite (1993), Jamieson (1994), Geis et al. (1995), Pearce and Snider (1995), Punch (1996), Shover and Wright (2001), Simpson and Piquero (2002), and Simpson (2002). Helpful case compilations and texts include Mokhiber (1988), Coleman (2001), Ermann and Lundman (2001), Friedrichs (2003), and the other references in this essay.
24. Although financial data are available for all publicly held corporations in the United States those for the great majority of states have typically been available only for the entire firm. A better test of the financial strain hypothesis would use data for component parts of large, diversified corporations, such as for individual divisions or product lines, where financial pressures may build independently of the overall health of the corporation. It is at these lower levels that financial pressures act most forcefully on managers and executives eager to ensure their units' own successes in their competition for market share externally and for corporate resources and rewards internally. Unfortunately, such data have been difficult to come by (see Yeager, 1986: 99).
25. See Clinard et al. (1979: chap. 8); Clinard and Yeager (1980: chap. 5).
26. See Simpson (1986), Jamieson (1994), Gray and Shadbegian (2005), and Keane (1993). See also Jenkins and Braithwaite (1993), who found some evidence of the role of profit seeking in greater noncompliance among a sample of Australian nursing homes, and Barnett (1986), who found that poor profit indicators were not statistically significant predictors of tax noncompliance in Swedish industries. Barnett did find, however, that higher rates of bankruptcies distinguished higher rates of industry noncompliance.
27. The Wisconsin results were somewhat mixed, however, as other measures of financial performance (i.e., liquidity and efficiency) showed contradictory results. As profitability is the purpose of competitive enterprise and the focus of much research

on corporate behaviors, the results for this measure in respect of environmental offenses remains important. In a study with a subsample of the Wisconsin companies, but with a more complete measure of water pollution violations, Yeager (1981: 273) found no relationship between profitability and these offenses.

28. Baucus and Near (1991).
29. Simpson (1986).
30. Jamieson (1994: 52–63) made a contrary finding for antitrust offenses; her research indicated that guilty firms were more likely to come from industries with higher profitability than nonviolating firms. However, her findings are limited by the significantly shorter time frame studied as compared to Simpson's (1986) study and by a modified cross-sectional design as compared to Simpson's longitudinal design. As part of her design, Jamieson (1994) measured profitability at different time points for nonviolating firms (1981–1985) and for violating firms (the five year period before the illegal activity commenced), rendering comparisons fragile.
31. Simpson (1987).
32. See Simpson (1987). In his classic case study of the antitrust conspiracy in the heavy electrical equipment industry, prosecuted in 1961, Geis (1977) also suggested that perceived financial difficulties interact with corporate management's sense of legal risks in producing greater versus lesser likelihoods of such offenses: "When the market behaved in a manner the executives thought satisfactory or when enforcement agencies seemed particularly threatening, the conspiracy desisted. When market conditions deteriorated, while corporate pressures for achieving attractive profit-and-loss statements remained constant, and enforcement activity abated, the price-fixing agreements flourished" (130–131).
33. Clinard and Yeager (1980: chap. 5); Clinard et al. (1979: chap. 6).
34. Simpson (1986).
35. Lane (1953); compare Yeager (1986).
36. The Wisconsin study did not find that profit strain was more predictive of more serious offenses within offense types such as environmental and labor violations, but the study's measure of offense seriousness was exploratory rather than definitive (Clinard et al., 1979: chaps. 5–8, Appendix J, Tables 22, 24). The hypothesized relationships between seriousness of offenses as perceived by businesspersons and profit strain provide another area of investigation worthy of considerable further research.
37. See Clinard et al. (1979: 134–136).
38. As it—and the outside auditing firms—did regarding corporate financial reporting in the years leading up to the Enron/Andersen and other large corporate frauds and failures in the United States after the turn of the millennium (see, e.g., Yeager, 2004: 908–910).
39. Other structural and cultural features of business also shape such developments, as I discuss in the next section with respect to the recent pattern of offenses in finance and accounting in the United States.
40. Gunningham et al. (2005: 313).
41. See, for example, Simpson and Koper (1992), Simpson (2002), and Gunningham et al. (2005). For research showing some deterrent effects in air pollution regulation in the paper mill industry, see Gray and Shadbegian (2005). For research showing deterrent effects in antitrust enforcement, see Block et al. (1981). For research on the classical deterrence model in another country, with similar results, see Braithwaite and Makkai's (1991) study of the nursing home industry in Australia. For an excellent analysis of why the law's threats do not always reach corporate personnel, see Stone's (1975) classic and still definitive work on the topic.
42. A former staff economist for the Federal Trade Commission advised me during the Wisconsin research in the 1970s that this was precisely his view, based on his experience with that regulatory agency (personal communication).

43. As I said earlier, from both qualitative and quantitative evidence I believe it is unlikely that any large American corporations maintain perfect compliance records over time.
44. While for reasons of space limitations I shall not review all these various findings, see, generally, the references cited elsewhere in this paper. I have taken up the discussion of such factors in a number of other places, including Clinard et al. (1979: chap. 8), Clinard and Yeager (1980: chaps. 5 and 6), and Yeager (1986). Aspects of market structure have especially featured in research on antitrust violations as these offenses explicitly address and respond to market conditions (see, e.g., Geis and Salinger, 1998). For some recent case study research that examines the structures and processes of antitrust conspiracies, see Baker and Faulkner (1993) and Faulkner et al. (2003).
45. See, for example, Kram et al. (1989), Yeager (1995), and Vaughan (1996).
46. There are occasions of corporate lawbreaking that violate this assumption of intentionality, including offenses from inadvertence, error, and ignorance. Hopkins (1980) provided a useful example that demonstrates how the complex structure of an organization can bring about offenses without anyone necessarily intending to break the law. This was a case of false advertising, in which the company claimed that all its new car models had a particular type of brake, when two of the new models did not. The persons who reviewed the advertising copy in advance—the company's general manager and sales manager—were unaware of the difference between the models. Therefore this violation occurred because the firm failed to organize properly the information necessary for legal compliance. Of course, if this failure was intended, then the offense returns to the purposeful category.

    For a discussion of the sociology of mistakes in organizations, see Vaughan (1999).

    My assumption of intentionality is untested in rigorous research, but based on impressions from the existing research on corporate lawbreaking and regulation, it is likely that most *serious* offenses, and those committed by larger, better resourced corporations, are committed knowingly and not in ignorance of the law.
47. Stone (1975).
48. These studies include intensive case analyses (Vaughan, 1996, 1998; cf. Geis, 1977), depth interview studies inside firms (Kram et al., 1989; Yeager, 1995a; Yeager and Reed, 1998), and insider accounts of corporate deviancy (Gioia, 1996; cf. Vandivier, 1996).
49. Gioia (1996: 154) (italics in original).
50. Vaughan (1998: 52).
51. See Kram et al. (1989) and Yeager (1995a).
52. Yeager (1995a: 157–158).
53. Geis (1977).
54. See Yeager (1991, 1995b).
55. "Parmalat chief to face trial in Milan," *The Times of London*, June 27, 2005 (http://www.timesonline.co.uk). For another recent example of the internationalizations of financial fraud, see "Citigroup Fined $25 Million by U.K. Regulator for Bond Trades," *Bloomberg News*, June 28, 2005 (http://www.bloomberg.com/news/index.html).
56. In her research on the space shuttle *Challenger* launch decision, Vaughan (1996, 1998) has also very effectively demonstrated that full analysis of corporate decision making requires a linking of macro- and microsociological phenomena. On the integration of levels of analysis in the study of corporate deviancy and its social control, see also Yeager (1991, 1995a, 1998).
57. Sykes and Matza (1957).
58. This means that, other things equal, the United States should manifest higher rates of corporate lawbreaking than those found in other advanced capitalist societies.

59. Messner and Rosenfeld (2001). Thus, for example, education is valued principally for its job- and career-preparation functions rather than for such civic-minded aims as a well-informed, culturally sophisticated, and analytically minded citizenry. Compared to business in other industrial democracies, American industry (as well as law) displays a greater reluctance to foster family-friendly leave policies for employees with dependent children and parents and typically imposes the requirement that corporate human resource policies—including those relating to management ethics training and procedures—be justified as profitable activities. Meanwhile, U.S. global corporations routinely move jobs to cheaper sources of overseas labor, often leaving behind communities bereft of both jobs and a tax base adequate to support education and other civic needs.
60. See Fligstein (1990) and Zorn (2004).
61. Zorn (2004); Fligstein (1990).
62. Jackall (1988: 82–84).
63. Clinard (1983).
64. The use of such incentives was originally prompted by the concern that top corporate executives were being compensated with very high salaries, even when their companies were performing poorly in the marketplace. Tying their compensation to corporate financial performance as registered in stock prices was thought to be a positive solution that would both motivate high performance and reward it more fairly. That these incentives are linked to the recent wave of accounting fraud in major corporations is an ironic and unintended outcome of the original intentions.
65. See Calavita and Pontell (1991) for helpful additional discussion on the relationships between finance capital and fraud and some limitations on the legal control of such offenses.
66. On this theme, see, for example, Lynxwiler et al. (1983), Hawkins (1983, 1984), Shover et al. (1986), and Yeager (1991, 1993).
67. Yeager (1991, 1993).
68. Lynxwiler et al. (1983).
69. Gray and Mendeloff (2002), as cited in Mendeloff and Gray (2005).
70. Gunningham et al. (2005); see also Thornton et al. (2005).
71. See especially Braithwaite (2002). For a critical appreciation of his arguments, see Yeager (2004).
72. Verweij (2000).
73. Gunningham et al. (2005: 310). For another example in interview-based research, in this case involving the federal Bank Secrecy Act, see Yeager (1995a).
74. Vaughan (1996).
75. For a discussion of the challenges of mounting such research, and an example of surmounting them, see Yeager and Kram (1990). For some results of this research, see Kram et al. (1989) and Yeager (1995a).
76. Denzin (1977).
77. See, for example, Clinard and Yeager (1980: 145–147) and references therein; see also Coleman (1998: 47–53).

References

Baker, Wayne E., and Robert R. Faulkner (1993) "The Social Organization of Conspiracy: Illegal Networks in the Heavy Electrical Equipment Industry." *American Sociological Review* 58:837–860.

Barnett, Harold C. (1986) "Industry Culture and Industry Economy: Correlates of Tax Noncompliance in Sweden." *Criminology* 24:553–574.

Baucus, Melissa S., and Janet P. Near (1991) "Can Illegal Corporate Behavior Be Predicted? An Event History Analysis." *The Academy of Management Journal* 34:9–36.

Benson, Michael L., and Elizabeth Moore (1992) "Are White-Collar and Common Offenders the Same? An Empirical and Theoretical Critique of a Recently Proposed General Theory of Crime." *Journal of Research in Crime and Delinquency* 29:251–272.

Block, Michael K. et al. (1981) "The Deterrent Effect of Antitrust Enforcement." *Journal of Political Economy* 89:429–445.

Blum-West, Steve, and Timothy J. Carter (1983) "Bringing White-Collar Crime Back In: An Examination of Crimes and Torts." *Social Problems* 30:545–554.

Braithwaite, John (1984) *Corporate Crime in the Pharmaceutical Industry*. London: Routledge.

——— (2002) *Restorative Justice and Responsive Regulation*. New York: Oxford University Press.

Braithwaite, John, and Toni Makkai (1991) "Testing an Expected Utility Model of Corporate Deterrence." *Law & Society Review* 25:7–39.

Calavita, Kitty, and Henry N. Pontell (1991) "'Other People's Money' Revisited: Collective Embezzlement in the Savings and Loan and Insurance Industries." *Social Problems* 38:94–112.

Calavita, Kitty, and Henry N. Pontell (1993) "Savings and Loan Fraud as Organized Crime: Toward a Conceptual Typology of Corporate Illegality." *Criminology* 31:519–548.

Clinard, Marshall B. (1983) *Corporate Ethics and Crime: The Role of Middle Management*. Beverly Hills, CA: Sage.

Clinard, Marshall B. (1990) *Corporate Corruption: The Abuse of Power*. New York: Praeger.

Clinard, Marshall B., and Richard Quinney (1973) *Criminal Behavior Systems: A Typology*. Rev. ed. New York: Holt, Rinehart & Winston.

Clinard, Marshall B., and Peter C. Yeager (1978) "Corporate Crime: Issues in Research." *Criminology* 16:255–272.

Clinard, Marshall B., and Peter C. Yeager (1980) *Corporate Crime*. New York: The Free Press.

Clinard, Marshall B. et al. (1979) *Illegal Corporate Behavior*. Washington, DC: U.S. Government Printing Office.

Coleman, James William (1987) "Toward an Integrated Theory of White-Collar Crime." *American Journal of Sociology* 93:406–439.

Coleman, James William (1998) *The Criminal Elite: Understanding White Collar Crime*. 4th ed. New York: St. Martin's Press.

Coleman, James William (2001) *The Criminal Elite: Understanding White-Collar Crime*. 5th ed. New York: Worth.

Denzin, Norman K. (1977) "Notes on the Criminogenic Hypothesis: A Case Study of the American Liquor Industry." *American Sociological Review* 42:905–920.

Ermann, M. David, and Richard J. Lundman, eds. (2001) *Corporate and Governmental Deviance: Problems of Organizational Behavior in Contemporary Society*. 6th ed. New York: Oxford University Press.

Evans, Medford (1981) "Review of Marshall B. Clinard and Peter C. Yeager, Corporate Crime." *American Opinion* XX:73–76 (June).

Faulkner, Robert R. et al. (2003) "Crime by Committee: Conspirators and Company Men in the Illegal Electrical Industry Cartel, 1954–1959." *Criminology* 41:511–554.

Fligstein, Neil (1990) *The Transformation of Corporate Control*. Cambridge, MA: Harvard University Press.

Friedrichs, David O. (2003) *Trusted Criminals: White Collar Crime in Contemporary Society*. 2nd ed. Belmont, MA: Wadsworth.

Geis, Gilbert (1977) "The Heavy Electrical Equipment Antitrust Cases of 1961." In *White-Collar Crime: Offenses in Business, Politics, and the Professions*, rev. ed., Editors G. Geis and R. F. Meier. New York: The Free Press.

Geis, Gilbert, and Lawrence S. Salinger (1998) "Antitrust and Organizational Deviance." *Research in the Sociology of Organizations* 15:71–110.

Geis, Gilbert et al. (1995) *White-Collar Crime: Offenses in Business, Politics and the Professions*. 3rd ed. New York: Simon & Schuster.

Gioia, Dennis A. (1996) "Why I Didn't Recognize Pinto Fire Hazards: How Organizational Scripts Channel Managers' Thoughts and Actions." In *Corporate and Governmental Deviance: Problems of Organizational Behavior in Contemporary Society*, 5th ed., Editors M. David Ermann and Richard J. Lundman. New York: Oxford University Press.

Gottfredson, Michael R., and Travis Hirschi (1990) *A General Theory of Crime*. Stanford, CA: Stanford University Press.

Grant, Don Sherman, II et al. (2002) "Organizational Size and Pollution: The Case of the U.S. Chemical Industry." *American Sociological Review* 67:389–407.

Gray, Wayne B., and John Medeloff (2002) "The Declining Effects of OSHA Inspections in Manufacturing, 1979–1998." NBER Working Paper 9119. Cambridge, MA: National Bureau of Economic Research.

Gray, Wayne B., and Ronald J. Shadbegian (2005) "When and Why do Plants Comply? Paper Mills in the 1980s." *Law & Policy* 27:238–261.

Gunningham, Neil A. et al. (2005) "Motivating Management: Corporate Compliance in Environmental Protection." *Law & Policy* 27:289–316.

Hawkins, Keith (1983) "Bargain and Bluff: Compliance Strategy and Deterrence in the Enforcement of Regulation."*Law and Policy Quarterly* 5:35–73.

Hawkins, Keith (1984) *Environment and Enforcement: Regulation and the Social Definition of Pollution*. New York: Oxford University Press.

Hollinger, Richard C., and John P. Clark (1983) *Theft by Employees*. Lexington, MA: Lexington Books.

Hopkins, Andrew (1980) "Controlling Corporate Deviance." *Criminology* 18:198–214.

Jackall, Robert (1988) *Moral Mazes: The World of Corporate Managers*. New York: Oxford University Press.

Jamieson, Katherine M. (1994) *The Organization of Corporate Crime: Dynamics of Antitrust Violation*. Thousand Oaks, CA: Sage.

Jenkins, Anne, and John Braithwaite (1993) "Profits, Pressure, and Corporate Lawbreaking." *Crime, Law and Social Change* 20:221–232.

Keane, Carl (1993) "The Impact of Financial Performance on Frequency of Corporate Crime: A Latent Variable Test of Strain Theory." *Canadian Journal of Criminology* 35:293–308.

Kram, Kathy E. et al. (1989) "Decisions and Dilemmas: The Ethical Dimension in the Corporate Context." In *Research in Corporate Social Performance and Policy*, vol. 11, Editor J. E. Post. Greenwich, CT: JAI.

Kramer, Ronald C. et al. (2002) "The Origins and Development of the Concept and Theory of State-Corporate Crime." *Crime & Delinquency* 48:263–282.

Lane, Robert E. (1953) "Why Businessmen Violate the Law." *Journal of Criminal Law, Criminology, and Police Science* 44:151–165.

Lynxwiler, John et al. (1983) "The Organization and Impact of Inspector Discretion in a Regulatory Bureaucracy." *Social Problems* 30:425–436.

Mendeloff, John, and Wayne B. Gray (2005) "Inside the Black Box: How do OSHA Inspections Lead to Reductions in Workplace Injuries?" *Law & Policy* 27:219–237.

Messner, Steven F., and Richard Rosenfeld (2001) *Crime and the American Dream*. 3rd ed. Belmont, MA: Wadsworth.

Mokhiber, Russell (1988) *Corporate Crime and Violence: Big Business Power and the Abuse of the Public Trust*. San Francisco: Sierra Club Books.

Orland, Leonard (1980) "Reflections on Corporate Crime: Law in Search of Theory and Scholarship." *American Criminal Law Review* 17:501–520.

Passas, Nikos (1990) "Anomie and Corporate Deviance." *Contemporary Crises* 14:157–178.

Pearce, Frank, and Laureen Snider, eds. (1995) *Corporate Crime: Contemporary Debates*. Toronto: University of Toronto Press.

Punch, Maurice (1996) *Dirty Business: Exploring Corporate Misconduct*. London: Sage.

Reed, Gary E., and Peter Cleary Yeager (1996) "Organizational Offending and Neoclassical Criminology: Challenging the Reach of a General Theory of Crime." *Criminology* 34:357–382.

Rose-Ackerman, Susan (1978) *Corruption: A Study in Political Economy*. New York: Academic.

Ross, Irwin (1992) *Shady Business: Confronting Corporate Corruption*. New York: Twentieth Century Fund.

Schlegel, Kip, and David Weisburd, eds., (1992) *White-Collar Crime Reconsidered*. Boston: Northeastern University Press.

Shapiro, Susan (1984) *Wayward Capitalists*. New Haven, CT: Yale University Press.

Shover, Neal, and John Paul Wright, eds. (2001) *Crimes of Privilege: Readings in White-Collar Crime*. New York: Oxford University Press.

Shover, Neal et al. (1986) *Enforcement or Negotiation: Constructing a Regulatory Bureaucracy*. Albany: State University of New York Press.

Simpson, Sally S. (1986) "The Decomposition of Antitrust: Testing a Multi-Level, Longitudinal Model of Profit-Squeeze." *American Sociological Review* 51:859–875.

Simpson, Sally S. (1987) "Cycles of Illegality: Antitrust Violations in Corporate America." *Social Forces* 65:943–963.

Simpson, Sally S. (2002) *Corporate Crime, Law, and Social Control*. New York: Cambridge University Press.

Simpson, Sally S., and Christopher S. Koper (1992) "Deterring Corporate Crime." *Criminology* 30:347–375.

Simpson, Sally S., and Nicole Leeper Piquero (2002) "Low Self-Control, Organizational Theory, and Corporate Crime." *Law & Society Review* 36:509–548.

Steffensmeier, Darrell (1989) "On the Causes of 'White-Collar' Crime: An Assessment of Hirschi and Gottfredson's Claims." *Criminology* 27:345–358.

Stone, Christopher D. (1975) *Where the Law Ends: The Social Control of Corporate Behavior*. New York: Harper and Row.

Sutherland, Edwin H. (1945) "Is 'White Collar Crime' Crime?" *American Sociological Review* 10:132–139.

Sutherland, Edwin H. (1949) *White Collar Crime*. New York: Holt.

Sutherland, Edwin H., and Donald R. Cressey (1955) *Principles of Criminology*. New York: Lippincott.

Sykes, Gresham K., and David Matza (1957) "Techniques of Neutralization: A Theory of Delinquency." *American Sociological Review* 22:667–670.

Szasz, Andrew (1986) "Corporations, Organized Crime and the Disposal of Hazardous Waste: An Examination of the Making of a Criminogenic Regulatory Structure." *Criminology* 24:1–27.

Tappan, Paul W. (1947) "Who is the Criminal?" *American Sociological Review* 12:96–102.

Thornton, Dorothy et al. (2005) "General Deterrence and Corporate Environmental Behavior." *Law & Policy* 27:262–288.

Tonry, Michael, and Albert J. Reiss Jr., eds. (1993) *Beyond the Law: Crime in Complex Organizations*. Chicago: University of Chicago Press.

Vandivier, Kermit (1996) "Why Should My Conscience Bother Me? Hiding Aircraft Brake Hazards." In *Corporate and Governmental Deviance: Problems of Organizational Behavior in Contemporary Society*, 5th ed., Editors M. David Ermann and Richard J. Lundman. New York: Oxford University Press.

Vaughan, Diane (1982) "Toward Understanding Unlawful Organizational Behavior." *Michigan Law Review* 80:1377–1402.

Vaughan, Diane (1996) *The Challenger Launch Decision: Risky Technology, Culture, and Deviance at NASA*. Chicago: University of Chicago Press.

Vaughan, Diane (1998) "Rational Choice, Situated Action, and the Social Control of Organizations." *Law & Society Review* 32:23–61.

Vaughan, Diane (1999) "The Dark Side of Organizations: Mistake, Misconduct, and Disaster." *Annual Review of Sociology* 25:271–305.

Verweij, Marco (2000) "Why is the River Rhine Cleaner than the Great Lakes (Despite Looser Regulation)?" *Law & Society Review* 34:1007–1054.

Wheeler, Stanton et al. (1982) "Sentencing the White-Collar Offender: Rhetoric and Reality." *American Sociological Review* 47:641–659.

Wright, Ronald F., and Paul Huck (2002) "Counting Cases About Milk: Our 'Most Nearly Perfect' Food, 1860–1940." *Law & Society Review* 36:51–112.

Yeager, Peter C. (1981) "The Politics of Corporate Social Control: The Federal Response to Industrial Water Pollution." Ph.D. dissertation, Department of Sociology, University of Wisconsin, Madison.

Yeager, Peter C. (1986) "Analyzing Illegal Corporate Behavior: Progress and Prospects." In *Research in Corporate Social Performance and Policy*, vol. 8, Editor J. E. Post. Greenwich, CT: JAI.

Yeager, Peter C. (1991) *The Limits of Law: The Public Regulation of Private Pollution*. New York: Cambridge University Press.

Yeager, Peter C. (1993) "Industrial Water Pollution." In *Beyond the Law: Crime in Complex Organizations*, Editors Michael Tonry and Albert J. Reiss Jr. Chicago: University of Chicago Press.

Yeager, Peter C. (1995a) "Management, Morality and Law: Organizational Forms and Ethical Deliberations." In *Corporate Crime: Contemporary Debates*, Editors Frank Pearce and Lavren Snider. Toronto: University of Toronto Press.

Yeager, Peter C. (1995b) "Law, Crime and Inequality: The Regulatory State." In *Crime and Inequality*, Editors John Hagan and Ruth D. Peterson. Stanford, CA: Stanford University Press.

Yeager, Peter C. (1998) "Corporate Lawbreaking: A Conceptual Appraisal." Paper presented at the International Society for Criminology, Pre-Congress Symposium on Organized and Organizational Crimes: Research Frontiers. Kobe, Japan (Aug.).

Yeager, Peter C. (2004) "Law versus Justice: From Adversarialism to Communitarianism." *Law & Social Inquiry* 29:891–915.

Yeager, Peter C., and Kathy E. Kram (1990) "Fielding Hot Topics in Cool Settings: The Study of Corporate Ethics." *Qualitative Sociology* 13:127–148.

Yeager, Peter Cleary, and Gary E. Reed (1998) "Of Corporate Persons and Straw Men: A Reply to Herbert, Green and Larragoite." *Criminology* 36:885–897.

Young, T. R. (1981) "Corporate Crime: A Critique of the Clinard Report." *Contemporary Crises* 5:323–336.

Zorn, Dirk M. (2004) "Here a Chief, There a Chief: The Rise of the CFO." *American Sociological Review* 69:345–364.

3

Attributing Responsibility for Organizational Wrongdoing

Matthew T. Lee and Jeannine A. Gailey

The economic, social, and human consequences of organizational wrongdoing are enormous and well-documented.[1] The 21st century began with almost daily revelations about corporate and organizational misconduct, ranging from widespread economic abuses at Enron and other Fortune 500 corporations to human rights violations by the U.S. military at Abu Ghraib prison. Most observers agree that the costs of "crime in the suites" far outweigh those of "crime in the streets."[2] But who, or what, is responsible for these harms? Should we blame greedy or morally negligent individuals, referred to as "amoral calculators"?[3] Organizational cultures, structures, and processes?[4] Institutional logics and systemic environmental forces that transcend a "focal organization"?[5] Broader social norms and institutions, such as capitalism or "technical rationality"?[6] Or perhaps the very regulatory agencies charged with controlling organizational wrongdoing create criminogenic environments and deserve blame for placing organizations "beyond the law"?[7] Because the state plays the inherently contradictory dual role of both promoting and regulating business corporations, some scholars have come to see corporate wrongdoing as arising from functional interdependencies between corporations and the state, giving rise to the term "state-corporate crime."[8] To what extent do different audiences (e.g., prosecutors, scholars, laypersons) believe that such systemic causes absolve individuals of legal or moral responsibility and under what conditions? The big question—and judging by headlines in the daily news the one that contemporary society is desperate for an answer to—is how can human and organizational behavior be "both structurally caused and morally blameworthy."[9] And more importantly, what can we do about it?

These questions implicate a range of socio-political issues that can be explored at multiple levels of analysis and that are important to consider in any discussion of attribution of responsibility (AOR) for wrongdoing in organizations. But as we argue in this chapter, such attributions are first and foremost a function of how the facts and laws in a given case are socially contested and constructed, as well as the "bounded rationality"[10] of audiences who pass judgment on alleged wrongdoing. We first discuss the social construction of organizational wrongdoing, with special emphasis on the common scholarly and popular presumption of amoral calculation and willful violations of law. Then we develop a social contructionist, four-step, schematic model of attribution of responsibility for organizational wrongdoing that we hope will sensitize scholars to its multistage and multidimensional nature. We also encourage future researchers to draw on the insights of several disciplines in order to develop a better understanding of the attribution process.

Before moving on, we need to clarify what we mean by "attribution," "responsibility," and "organizational wrongdoing," concepts that have been the source of some confusion in the literature. An "attribution" concerns audience perceptions of why an act occurred. The issue is not what forces "objectively" generated a particular outcome, but rather what perceivers believe influenced relevant actors at the time of the occurrence. As for "responsibility," we view this concept not as a dichotomy, but rather as falling along a burden-of-proof continuum. Social responsibility is at the least restrictive end of the continuum, with public disapproval being weakly or not at all tied to legal standards. At the other end is criminal culpability, which requires guilt "beyond a reasonable doubt," as determined by legal procedures. Between these two extremes is the civil justice system's "preponderance of evidence" standard.[11] Furthermore, as discussed below, research indicates that responsibility is a multidimensional construct comprised of multiple dimensions. Finally, we prefer the term "organizational wrongdoing" instead of "crime" or "deviance" because organizations are frequently involved in acts that are not violations of extant criminal codes, and therefore not technically "crimes," but could still be considered by specific audiences as blameworthy or morally reprehensible.[12] "Deviance" is too broad because this may incorporate both positive and negative actions and outcomes.[13] Furthermore, our chapter is not about occupational crime (e.g., embezzlement for individual gain); instead, it addresses wrongdoing by individuals acting in a formal capacity on behalf of an organization to further organizational, not (exclusively) personal, interests.[14] In some cases, it may be inappropriate to reduce organizational actions to the "decisions" or behaviors of individuals, so we also pay attention to supra-individual levels of analysis.[15]

The Social Construction of Organizational Wrongdoing

Lessons from the Pinto and *Challenger* Cases

The importance of attending to social constructionist issues is illustrated by a consideration of a classic case of organizational wrongdoing: Ford Motor Company's production and marketing of the Pinto. Depicted by the media, and later academics, as a dangerous "firetrap"[16] and the product of greedy, amoral calculation, recent revisionist analysis has revealed that organizational and interorganizational actions with regard to the Pinto are more accurately understood using the conceptual language of institutional logics and organizational networks.[17] This raises a fundamental issue for responsibility attribution: the social construction of facts (and laws) plays a pivotal role in who or what will be blamed for untoward outcomes that occur in organizational contexts—a stance which echoes Yeager's[18] critique of the "standard approach" to studying "'pure' behavioral phenomena unconfounded by the form of law or the processes of its enforcement." If the Pinto case can be explained by the knowing and purposeful wrongdoing of powerful individual decision-makers, then the following moral condemnation may be appropriate: "One wonders how long Ford Motor Company would continue to market lethal cars were [top executives]

Henry Ford II and Lee Iacocca serving 20-year terms in Leavenworth for consumer homicide."[19] Another example: a reporter for *Fortune Magazine* writing an article on the "worst decisions of the last 75 years" asked the first author of this chapter, "Did anyone end up fired over this? Was there internal upheaval?" These questions were the product of the reporter's application of the rational choice model of organizational action, which views organizational outcomes as the result of strategic decisions, and grounded in a firm belief in the social construction of the Pinto as a deviant "firetrap." The reporter stated that she wanted to better understand "*decisions* at Ford that led to the Pinto fiasco" (emphasis added).

Similarly, following the conventional wisdom on the Pinto case (grounded in Dowie's explanation) has led social scientists to explicitly affirm the amoral calculation explanation:

> Documents surfaced in the Ford Pinto case showing, in writing, Ford executives' calculation of costs and benefits in a redesign decision that juxtaposed the cost of redesign against the quantified loss of human life in accidents if the redesign were not done. Lives had already been lost; nonetheless, production continued.[20]

But the conventional wisdom is not universally accepted. Writing shortly after the appearance of a revisionist account of the case,[21] this same author later argued that "no amoral calculators were found" at Ford and that "institutionally embedded unreflective action" was causally responsible for outcomes in the Pinto case.[22]

The changing discourse on the Pinto case suggests that beliefs about responsibility for wrongdoing derive from an interaction between how the facts of a case are publicly constructed and the ideological filters through which the facts are perceived. Although factual and legal ambiguity are ubiquitous features of real-world events, claim-makers draw on a variety of cultural resources in the unending activity to reduce complexity and construct unambiguous accounts that resonate with audiences.[23] If one subscribes to the "Nader paradigm of the American state and society"[24] (named after Ralph Nader, an influential consumer advocate and recent presidential candidate), one might limit the search for evidence of wrongdoing in the Pinto case to greedy and powerful individuals, who operate in an amoral cultural landscape shaped by the inequalities inherent in a capitalist economic system.[25] Conversely, if one is trained as an organizational sociologist, one might direct a disproportionate amount of attention to organizational influences on the behavior of Ford personnel.[26] Allison explains this unavoidable fact of life with a metaphor:

> Conceptual models both fix the mesh nets that the analyst drags through the material in order to explain a particular action or decision and direct him to cast his net in select ponds, at certain depths, in order to catch the fish he is after.[27]

Conceptual models can be challenged by anomalous facts, but only if the analyst has sufficient time and resources to attend to such facts and can afford to be open-minded about their implications.[28] This presents difficult obstacles for some analysts, such as newspaper reporters facing tight deadlines and prosecutors who feel pressure from voters to bring guilty parties to justice. For example, when the first author explained to a *Fortune* reporter that the decision-making framework was not the best analytical model for understanding the Pinto case and suggested an alternative, she responded that it was too late to alter the

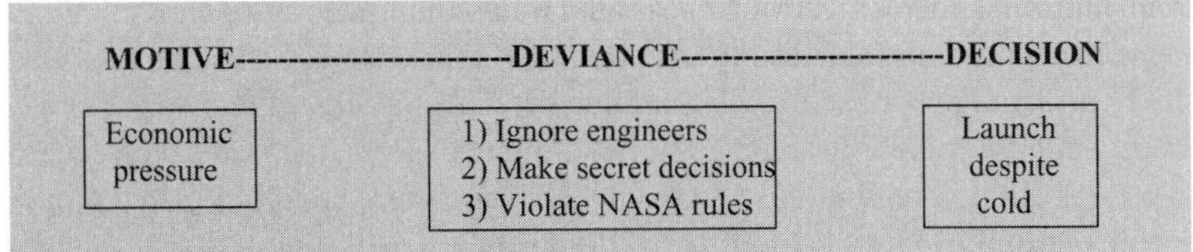

Figure 1. The Amoral Calculator Model of Organizational Deviance (*Challenger* Case).

emphasis on decision making. The article eventually expressed the conventional wisdom without mentioning the controversy.[29]

Scholars may have more flexibility in terms of time, but "publish or perish" pressures of the tenure system impose constraints. Vaughan spent nine years studying NASA's disastrous decision to launch the space shuttle *Challenger*, and her findings with regard to responsibility for the deaths of the *Challenger* astronauts differed sharply from the snap judgments of media and government investigators.[30] Before Vaughan, discussions of the case adopted what Allison[31] would call the "rational policy model" and focused on deviant rule breaking by NASA managers (amoral calculation). Vaughan describes the logic of the rational choice view as follows: "NASA managers, experiencing production pressure in a year when many important launches were planned that were essential to the future of the space program, ignored the advice of contractor engineers and went forward with the launch, violating rules about reporting problems up the hierarchy in the process."[32] This view, which provides the cognitive framework for conventional understandings of many cases of organizational wrongdoing, is summarized in Figure 1.

The contention that NASA managers and work groups explicitly or implicitly weighed the economic costs and benefits of the launch decision, but ignored or minimized moral/ethical issues, is based on faulty constructions of facts. As but one example, government investigators drew attention to NASA's alleged decision to abandon a single-piece design of the solid rocket booster (the part of the shuttle that failed, providing the technical cause of death) because it was cheaper to use the multi-part O-ring design. In fact, the single-piece design was scrapped because the engineers agreed that it would not work, not because of cost considerations. Despite such distortions of fact, in this case and in others (e.g., the Pinto), the amoral calculator explanation may be preferred over more systemic narratives because of political considerations. Rooting out amoral calculators requires only that organizations fire or otherwise punish individual decision-makers, often relatively powerless middle managers rather than elites, in order to provide a "quick fix" solution for a few "bad apples." But such scapegoating is a distraction from more important causal processes that, if unchanged, increase the likelihood that the wrongdoing will be repeated.[33]

Vaughan's revisionist account goes further than merely correcting distorted facts in the historical record to the social construction of wrongdoing itself.[34] Her analysis is firmly rooted in Allison's[35] organizational process and bureaucratic politics models, but also in the constructionist/labeling perspective on deviance that recognizes that organizational insiders may not share outsiders' definitions of wrongdoing. Organizational participants may perceive their actions to be normative, rather than deviant, according to organizational or institutional norms. The vagueness and moral ambiguity of legal rules, along with the negotiated nature of organizational offenses, may also encourage "outsider" government regulators to share insiders' definitions of reality.[36] For example, Yeager found "designated noncompliance" to be the norm with regard to water pollution regulations and that legal agents were complicit in redefining such violations as formal compliance with the law.[37] This orientation problematizes the idea of an objective violation of norms and instead views wrongdoing as a negotiated attribution with distinct meanings for internal and external audiences.

Working within this subjectivist tradition Vaughan found, contrary to her initial expectations of amoral calculation, that "the causes of the accident went beyond the actions of individuals to the environment, the NASA organization, and the developmental nature of the shuttle technology."[38] In terms of the environment, top NASA administrators, Congress, and Presidential Administrations politicized the space program while leaving it continuously under-funded. This created an organizational context where risks were taken or granted due to limited resources, while also merging three cultures: NASA's historical culture of technical excellence (rooted in "pure" quantitative science), with new cultures based on political (cost efficiency) and bureaucratic (ritualism regarding rules) accountability. Although the internal normative environment of NASA bears some of the blame for the fatal launch decision in Vaughan's account, it is important to keep in mind the aspects of this culture that were imposed from outside the organization.

Another contextual cause was a new organizational structure at NASA which included "external" contractor organizations as an adaptation to the new culture of political accountability. This structure exacerbated problems of bounded rationality because of "structural secrecy" that prevented the free flow of information across organizational subunits.[39] Writing about the eve-of-launch teleconference, Vaughan states, "Separated by distance and a mute button, no one at the other two locations knew that the contractor engineers still objected [to the launch]. Further, the contractor engineers were unaware that people in the other two locations were expecting the launch to be scrapped."[40]

In the *Challenger* case, the engineering data on the O-ring problem were not clear and convincing, as outsiders advancing attributions based on amoral calculation had argued—at least not to insiders working with risky technology under conditions of structural secrecy. The scapegoats, NASA managers, actually followed all rules for reporting on safety concerns to superiors; they did not hide the facts. But Vaughan's account required almost a decade of dispassionate scholarship, a rarity in the literature on organizational wrongdoing. In addition, it produced politically unpopular policy recommendations, such as the need to fundamentally reform organizational structures and cultures to minimize problems like structural secrecy, and it was highly critical of elites who had used the space program as a "political football." Vaughan's constructionist account has important implications for AOR for organizational wrongdoing, especially for explaining why individual "white collar criminals" are not held personally responsible for harmful organizational outcomes. In some cases, such as the Pinto and *Challenger*, blaming individuals may be inappropriate and counterproductive. In other cases, the social organization of the offenses raises difficulties for the formal attribution process, because often individual perpetrators must be given legal immunity in order for prosecutors or regulators to collect information that is central to understanding the extent and nature of wrongdoing.[41]

Of course, there is no reason to absolve individuals of moral or legal responsibility simply because systemic forces are at work. After all, systemic forces are present in all social situations. But the question arises, is it reasonable to blame Ford executives for wrongdoing in the Pinto case, or midlevel NASA managers in the *Challenger* case? Attributions in the Pinto case were based on faulty understandings of both the Pinto's alleged distinctiveness and Ford's alleged use of "cost/benefit" analysis in the Pinto "decision." while the conventional wisdom on the *Challenger* hinged on erroneous beliefs about rule violations and cover-ups by NASA managers. Does this mean that individuals in these two organizations are blameless? That depends fundamentally on the particular construction of facts that audiences perceive as authoritative and how they process those facts.

A brief reflexive discussion by one of the authors of the revisionist account of the Pinto case illustrates this point. I (Lee) was motivated to pursue graduate studies in sociology partly because of the moral outrage I felt after reading case studies of organizational deviance as an undergraduate. The Pinto episode epitomized my early understanding of such cases as fundamentally caused by amoral calculation and "captured" law enforcement. I began graduate studies as Professor David Ermann's research assistant and he suggested that I investigate "anomalies" in the Pinto narrative. Subscribing wholeheartedly to the "Nader paradigm,"[42] I saw no need to study such a broadly discussed case. Furthermore, I initially saw no anomalies. When I examined Ford's cost/benefit analysis (the Grush/Saunby Report), as reprinted in countless books,[43] I saw incontrovertible evidence that individual evildoers (i.e., decision-makers) at Ford had weighed the cost of lawsuits for Pinto occupants who died in fiery rear-end collisions against the cost of fixing the dangerous defect ($11 per car) and determined that it was cheaper to let people die. So strong was the Pinto mythology (and underlying worldview of corporate decision-making) in my mind that I did not notice that the document did not concern rear-end crashworthiness . . . or the Pinto. It related to a proposed "static rollover" test and covered all domestic cars and light trucks produced annually. Like many others, I believed that the $200,000 figure was an estimate produced by Ford's lawyers of the average cost of a lawsuit for a Pinto "victim's" fiery death, not a government estimate of an individual's value to society (measured by lifetime average earning potential, among other factors). It was not until I had spent the better part of a year examining countless original documents and talking with participants in the original Pinto drama (both defenders and supporters of Ford) that I began to see the anomalies—and the "obvious" misuse of the cost/benefit analysis that is at the heart of the Pinto's infamy.

Having disconfirmed my expectations and challenged my worldview, we crafted what we believe is a more accurate (and organizationally grounded) constructionist explanation of the case.[44] Does our explanation absolve individuals at Ford—executives, managers, engineers, among others—of personal responsibility for the safety profile of the Pinto? The fact that we understand the reasons for a person's behavior does not necessarily imply that we should absolve the person of responsibility for untoward outcomes. But perhaps a better question is who or what bears responsibility for cars produced by other manufacturers with comparable safety profiles in terms of rear-end crashworthiness? This is not a question with a simple answer, unless one relies on the faulty facts of the Pinto "landmark narrative" and a mindset consistent with the Nader paradigm.[45] There is no doubt that "boundary spanners" at Ford, such as the authors of the cost/benefit analysis, worked tirelessly to stall or defeat new regulatory standards with the full support of top executives like Henry Ford II and Lee Iacocca, who themselves were complaining to a sympathetic President Nixon about the adverse economic impacts of such standards. Will diverse audiences ever be able to agree on the legal or ethical responsibility of these individuals?

The political question of drawing the line between acceptable and unacceptable risk is the real issue here, what we refer to as the determination of "sensible bloodshed."[46] Laypersons who would find the fiery death of a loved one in a Pinto (or any other small car that meets the federal 30 mile-per-hour rear-end crashworthiness standard) to be an unacceptable risk may also vote for politicians who find such safety standard too onerous for the economy and work to freeze or repeal them. On what grounds, then, do outsiders attribute responsibility to engineers who produce cars that meet such government-legitimated standards? Because these engineers knew, or should have known, that consumers may perish in some small fraction of rear-end collisions involving not just Pintos, but all other cars? This is perhaps not the image of willfulness that outsiders have in mind when they contemplate organizational wrongdoing and certainly not the image conjured by the faulty Pinto landmark narrative. But the Pinto and *Challenger* cases, as described in revisionist accounts, may themselves be anomalous.[47] This begs the question of what we know about "willfulness" in cases of organizational wrongdoing.

Willfulness and Organizational Wrongdoing

As the previous discussion demonstrates, responsibility for organizational wrongdoing is a complicated and contested issue. Criminal intent, or *mens rea*, is especially difficult to determine in such cases. There may be differences by type of wrongdoing, such as economic transgressions or those that produce physical harm. One study found that middle managers generally expressed a strong conviction that they had a duty to report to regulators any legal violations with health and safety implications, but not ones with only financial consequences.[48] For the latter, norms of corporate loyalty and self-preservation outweighed the duty to report violations which to them involved much moral ambiguity. But even presumably "pure" cases of "willful" law violation, such as the infamous savings and loan crisis of the 1980s, have generated competing explanations.[49] Nevertheless, willfulness remains a core component of responsibility attribution in amoral calculator accounts and a foundation of the moral outrage that calls for stiffer penalties for white-collar crime.

The notion that the willful action of organizations routinely causes immense human suffering and death is quite prominent in a number of popular texts. For example, both Reiman's *The Rich Get Richer and the Poor Get Prison*, 6th edition,[50] and Kappeler, Blumberg, and Potter's *The Mythology of Crime and Criminal Justice*, 3rd edition,[51] discuss the "myth" that most corporate violence is unintentional. Reiman's book states—

> Since 1972, numerous studies have documented the astounding incidence of disease, injury, and death due to hazards in the workplace *and* the fact that much or most of this

> carnage is the consequence of the refusal of management to pay for safety measures and of government to enforce safety standards—and sometimes of willful defiance of the law.[52]

In the footnote supporting this statement, Reiman[53] provides a number of references and quotes Kappeler et al., who claim—

> James Messerschmidt, in a comprehensive review of research studies on job related accidents, determined that somewhere between 35 and 57 percent of those accidents occurred because of direct safety violations by the employer. Laura Shill Schrager and James Short, Jr. found 30 percent of industrial accidents resulted from safety violations and another 20 percent resulted from unsafe working conditions.[54]

The notion that "35 to 57 percent" of accidents are caused by "direct safety violations" is useful to scholars hoping to direct attention to organizational violence. However, we argue that the weak empirical foundation on which this particular estimate was based typifies the data scarcity problem that confronts corporate criminologists—and suggests that the willfulness argument itself requires much more empirical investigation before we can treat it as an article of faith. First, while Reiman cites Kappeler et al., who in turn cite Messerschmidt's[55] "comprehensive review." Messerschmidt himself cites an earlier edition of Reiman's book[56] to make his point that "the vast majority of all these [job related] injuries and deaths occur because employers either neglect or intentionally violate safety standards." Note also Messerschmidt's original sentence, subsequently misquoted by Kappeler et al. to include the phrase "somewhere between 35 and 57 percent," which was then cited verbatim by Reiman:

> ...in a New York study, 57 percent of the accidents investigated involved a code violation, and a Wisconsin study found that 35 of 90 lethal accidents occurred because of safety violations (Bacow, 1980:38–39).[57]

As it turns out, it was not Messerschmidt who "determined" after a "comprehensive review of research" that "somewhere *between* 35 to 57 percent" of job-related accidents occur "*because of* direct safety violations" [emphasis added], as Kappeler et al. claim[58]; rather, a single New York study found that 57 percent of *serious* accidents "involved a code violation" (which does not necessarily imply causality) and a different Wisconsin study found that almost 39 percent of "*lethal* accidents occurred because of safety violations" [emphasis added]. So, the estimate of the *range* of accidents caused by willful violations turns out to have derived from an erroneous reference to two isolated studies originally cited by Bacow in 1980,[59] and later by Messerschmidt in 1986, not from Messerschmidt's own determination after a "comprehensive review of research studies on job-related accidents." Tracing the estimate over two decades from Reiman (in 2001), through Kappeler et al., Messerschmidt, and Bacow (in 1980) still has not yielded the original source of the data.

Continuing the hunt, we learn that Bacow's two-page discussion relies on a U.S. Department of Labor contract evaluation from 1975 for the New York figures, and Ashford's 1976 report to the Ford Foundation, *Crisis in the Workplace: Occupational Disease and Injury*, for the Wisconsin data. Ashford himself cites "unpublished research" conducted by a group called the Wisconsin Safety Specialists, who utilized a sub-sample of 19 percent of "reported job deaths" investigated by the Wisconsin Safety and Buildings Division.[60] There is no indication whether this was a randomly selected sample and it is certainly possible that these were the most egregious cases reported to the Wisconsin agency. Nor is there any detailed description of the causal role, if any, played by the safety violation in the death, what the specific violations were, or even the year or years involved. At any rate, the numbers were provided to Ashford in the form of a "letter to the author" in 1974. Neither of the original studies of New York or Wisconsin job-related accidents is readily available to scholars.

Although the original figures contained in the letter to Ashford are not publicly available, it is interesting to note that he reports 93 total fatalities for the Wisconsin sub-sample, 37 of which were attributed to "Wisconsin Safety Code Violations."[61] The total number is listed as 90 in Bacow's[62] presentation, although he does reprint the correct percentage (39 percent). Messerschmidt uses Bacow's total (90) and reduces the "violation-related" deaths to 35.[63] Neither Bacow nor Messerschmidt point out that the Wisconsin data were drawn from a sub-sample of 19 percent of worker deaths. In 1976, Hagglund discovered that a Wisconsin state inspector initially claimed that all worker deaths in Wisconsin were investigated, possibly adding to the confusion, when in fact only 19 percent had been examined.[64] As stated above, Kappeler et al. (see also Reiman) convert Messerschmidt's *count* of 35 into a *percentage* in constructing their estimate ("somewhere *between* 35 and 57 percent" [emphasis added]).[65] Finally, Hagglund's hard-to-find report provides a more detailed discussion of the Wisconsin data—which appear to have been collected in 1973—and shows that the 19 percent sub-sample data revealed 39 percent of deaths were due to a "violation of Wisconsin Safety Codes." while another 19 percent were due to "other unsafe working conditions" that presumably were not treated as violations.[66] One conclusion from Hagglund's report, missing in all other discussions, is that—

> The results of this study should not be construed as supportive of a theory of unsafe acts or unsafe conditions—it is not intended to demonstrate that at all. It is more likely that accidents are caused by interaction of a variety of complex events and factors.... Accident causation research is not so simple that one needs only to look for an employee to "blame" or a hazardous working condition which can be held responsible in a particular accident. What is needed is more objective research into accident causes....[67]

Experts may speak as if they have a reasonable statistical picture of willfully caused worker deaths, but tracing the origin of the particular estimates cited in the literature raises doubts about even the little "hard data" that exists.[68]

The purpose of the preceding discussion was not to attack the scholarship cited. In fact, both authors of this chapter have made frequent use of the works cited above in teaching undergraduate students about the substantial costs of organizational wrongdoing. Furthermore, Reiman and others make an important point that a focus on *direct* causes obscures the fact that employers may *indirectly* cause job related accidents by setting high quotas, in turn providing incentives for employees to disobey safety regulations and take unreasonable risks. Our point is that it is difficult to locate even a basic fact like the range of worker deaths caused by direct safety violations, because of the lack of empirical data on the topic. Yet causal attributions for these deaths continue to dominate the literature, even in the absence of data.[69] Indeed, Schrager and

Short, also cited by Reiman, pointed out in their classic 1978 article that while OSHA collects data on both safety violations as well as worker deaths and injuries, it has "failed to document the crucial relationship between the two"—a judgment that continues to apply today.[70] Despite methodological advances in the intervening years, our current state of knowledge on such "basic"[71] matters remains extremely limited, as ideological and political barriers preventing research on the subject force contemporary scholars to cite studies that are decades old and described in detail only in obscure government documents or private correspondence. All too often, empirical data are irrelevant to the attribution process.

A Four-Step Model of Attributing Responsibility for Organizational Wrongdoing

The preceding discussion highlights some of the difficulties facing scholars who wish to study AOR for organizational wrongdoing. Most research to date has bracketed these potential problems and investigated AOR in quasi-experimental studies using short vignettes that abstract wrongdoing from its complicated and contested social contexts.[72] These studies have provided valuable insights into responsibility attributions in organizational settings, but more explicit attention to each step in the AOR process is required in order to better understand AOR outcomes. We cannot assume either "pure" or "willful" violations of "clear" or "objective" normative standards, as the vignette studies have done. In the following section, we provide a four-step schematic model of AOR for organizational wrongdoing that builds on the constructionist approach to the topic found in the previous section (see Figure 2). Our purpose in developing this model is not to provide a comprehensive list of factors that should be considered at each step. This is not possible. Rather, we hope to sensitize scholars to issues that their research might be omitting by arguing that each step in the AOR process be treated as a subject for empirical investigation, rather than as a "given" or "black box." AOR for organizational wrongdoing cannot be

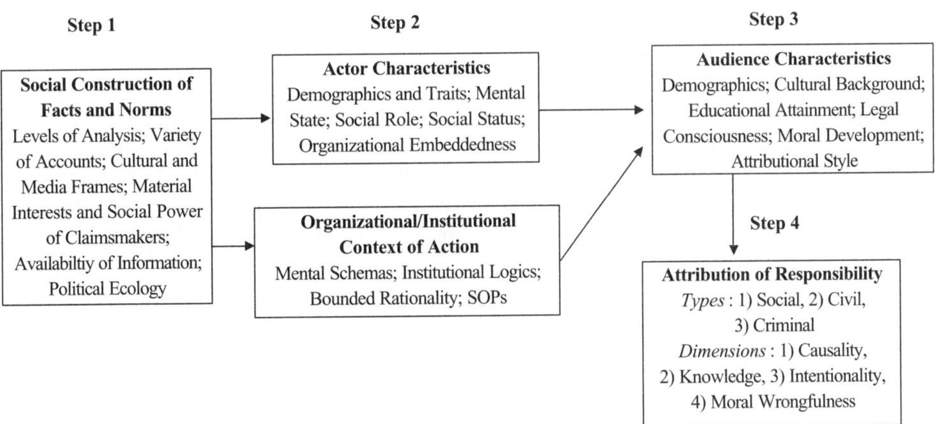

Figure 2. Steps in the process of attribution of responsibility for wrongdoing in organizations.

understood without attending to each of these four steps. We begin by pointing out that facts and norms are problematic social constructions and certainly never as clearcut as they are presented in vignettes, media representations of cases, or even scholarly discussions.

Step 1: The Social Construction of Facts and Norms

As mentioned throughout this chapter, responsibility attributions can be lodged at one or more levels of analysis, from the psychological traits of individuals construed to have the power to make decisions, a single organization's unique internal culture or structural arrangements, to broader institutional logics and ideologies that permeate societies. Facts, and norms that become linked to them, may be socially constructed by a variety of primary claims makers (e.g., advocates, politicians, religious leaders, moral entrepreneurs) and secondary groups that interpret, disseminate, and otherwise transform initial claims (e.g., media, social movements, commentators). The content of claims in terms of level of analysis impacts the rest of the attribution process, making some attributions plausible and others unthinkable. Because individualistic, and to a lesser extent organizational, levels of analysis dominate the extant literature, we focus our discussion on macrolevel factors that have often been obscured or minimized in attributional claims. We do this to illustrate the importance of attending to this often neglected level of analysis, while we also recognize that the other levels cannot be ignored.

At the broadest macro level are those institutionalized forces that transcend specific organizations, industries, or sectors. Capitalism is often the culprit at this level of analysis. However, most observers recognize that serious wrongdoing is a ubiquitous organizational reality, occurring in non-profit and government organizations, countries with non-capitalist economic systems, and ancient societies.[73] The primary issue at this level of analysis concerns how dominant social institutions select certain types of people for positions of power (e.g., those who are driven, amoral, and well-connected) and the attributes of human nature that are facilitated or suppressed by ideologies and cultures within a society.[74] One potential object of blame at this macrolevel is *technical rationality:* "a way of thinking that elevates the scientific-analytical mindset and the belief in technological progress over all other forms of rationality."[75] Related concepts include the cultural imperatives toward *objectification* and *routinization*—"to rob the world of its subjectivity . . . to turn everyone and everything into objects."[76] The outcomes of these imperatives are the dehumanization of out-groups and the institutionalization of blind obedience to authority.[77] Individual "decision-making" is constrained in these social contexts in ways that transcend a single organization or industry.

But such influences on behavior are often not fully perceived by organizational insiders or claims-making outsiders who seek to fix blame on internal organizational or individual causes. Abundant research has demonstrated that audiences are more likely to blame an individual when environmental forces are diffuse and difficult to discern. But when broad environmental factors are constructed in a discrete and obvious manner, the actor (whether individual or organizational) is more likely to be absolved of personal responsibility.[78] The construction and framing of facts and norms by the media and the ideological filters of the larger culture are particularly important in this regard.

For example, participants in a research study who viewed a video based on excerpts from television newsmagazine programs that highlighted institutional causes of the "Cold War human radiation experiments." as opposed to individual causes, were more likely to blame the government agency that sponsored the experiments than subjects who did not view the video. The latter were more likely to hold responsible the individual scientist who ran a given experiment.[79] This suggests that audiences are strongly influenced by the presentation of facts and that media representations may come to define the authoritative version of reality in the AOR process.

The literature on mitigators of responsibility (e.g., the norm of obedience to legitimate authority) are well known,[80] so we discuss lesser known scholarship on technical rationality in order to identify one emerging macro-level target of AOR for organizational wrongdoing. Components of technical rationality include the "shift from a belief in divine authority to a belief in the power of individual reason" and the "logical organization of tasks into smaller units . . . in the interest of efficiency."[81] Drawing on the classic works of Mannheim and Horkheimer, technical rationality is distinct from substantive rationality. The latter includes the "ability to understand the purposeful nature of the whole system of which a particular task is a part" and incorporates "ethical and normative concerns as well as the consideration of instrumental aims."[82] The result of the increasing technical rationalization of society has been an inordinate emphasis on instrumental objectives divorced from ethical considerations; a separation of means and ends, or a disregard of moral standards based on socially convergent understandings of universal ethics or fundamental human rights.[83] What are the implications of such research for AOR? We suggest that, depending on the extent to which facts are framed as products of institutional logics or cultural forces (such as technical rationality), individuals may be less likely to be held responsible for organizational wrongdoing.

As we pointed out, the media is one important player in the drama of fact construction, as illustrated by research on the "social ecology" of public accounts for wrongdoing.[84] Media frames can emphasize individual responsibility and motivation, or focus on systemic factors, or some combination of both. But the media are not the only players—scholars are important as well. A recent comprehensive review of cases of white collar crime, many of which involved organizational wrongdoing, concludes that greedy people are not the fundamental cause of such incidents, but rather that the "acts involve certain societal roles and transpire only under certain conditions."[85] This is a representative statement from the sociological perspective on organizational deviance and one that is consistent with the central arguments in our discussion of the Pinto and *Challenger* cases in this chapter. But portraying individuals as subject to forces beyond their control may unwittingly create a scholarly discourse of non-responsibility, at least at the individual level, and thereby contribute to a reluctance to hold individuals responsible for institutionalized offenses.

Some examples will clarify this point. Kelman and Hamilton's discussion of the My Lai massacre during the Vietnam War provides an example of the widespread public support for the American soldiers who murdered unarmed civilians—and in some cases raped and mutilated them—on the grounds that they were obeying lawful orders.[86] In other words, soldiers were not individually responsible for institutionally caused outcomes. The law as a legitimate social institution, combined with widely shared habits of obedience as a contextual social fact that resonated with audiences, mitigated personal responsibility. Although some soldiers argued that an order to kill an unarmed civilian was not a legal order at all, consistent with the civil disobedience tradition in law, the public and legal officials seemed to reject this particular construction of facts. Similarly, a recent report about forced, involuntary sterilization programs targeting poor and minority women that were implemented in the United States until the mid-1970s provided an account of one of the members of a state board that decided who would be sterilized. Although this person felt "uncomfortable" making such decisions, he argued, "We did it because the law obligated us to."[87] Ignoring the philosophical implications of such Sartrean "bad faith." it is instructive to note the rarity of prosecutions of individuals involved in such legally institutionalized organizational wrongdoing. Finally, despite the Nuremberg Code of 1947, no American has been prosecuted for violating a research subject's right to consent to participation in medical experiments, even when such experiments have caused death or serious injury.[88]

Why? A recent study of AOR for the "Cold War human radiation experiments" is suggestive. One focus group participant argued that nobody in an organizational setting is ever "autonomous." even if the "actor" in a vignette had been assigned to an autonomous condition (i.e., the actor "decided" to inject an unwitting subject with a potentially lethal dose of plutonium rather than being ordered to do so). According to this (atypical) respondent, an unusually thoughtful sociology major with work experience in organizational settings, all organization members are subject to similar socialization pressures and beholden to institutional norms and therefore never have "free will" to act on their own.[89] This research found that one element of institutional logic (e.g., standard operative procedures) was a statistically significant predictor of AOR.[90] Perhaps for perpetrators of organizational wrongdoing facts are routinely constructed at the institutional level, by the media or scholars, which mitigates personal responsibility, while discourse on street crime commonly emphasizes personality traits and individual decision/motivation, which suggest personal responsibility.[91]

We have devoted a significant proportion of this chapter to discussing the social construction and framing of facts because we believe that this is an under-appreciated content area in the AOR field generally and particularly in AOR studies of organizations. The level of analysis issue has been a dominant theme of this chapter. We have highlighted recent research on institutional forces that impinge on organizational wrongdoing because we believe that this work is especially important. AOR studies should not ignore empirical research that suggests that the line separating "safe" and "unsafe" working conditions or rule violations from normative behavior is a function of cognitive schemas shaped by interactions embedded in organizational routines and institutional logics, thus imposing limits on individual perceptions.[92] But our focus is also potentially problematic because such writings tend to minimize, although they certainly do not preclude, individual responsibility. We raise this problem as a point of debate rather than a settled issue and hope that others will reflect on it in their own studies. The implication for AOR work is, however, quite clear: audiences are strongly influenced by the institutionalized narratives that frame events as the product of forces as particular levels of analysis.[93]

Before we move on to other steps of the model, we offer a brief explanation of the additional items listed in the first box of Figure 2. Other influences on the construction of facts and norms include the diversity of viewpoints (*variety of accounts*) that are reflected in the prevailing discourse on a given case. For example, corporate press releases, statements by legal or other government officials, and claims by victims and victim advocates all have an impact in the construction of reality. Some voices are routinely silenced in social discourse, usually those of relatively powerless groups. In such a context, powerful organizations with highly trained and well-funded spokespersons are better able to present their claims, which highlights the importance of the *material interests and social power of claims makers*.[94] Furthermore, an organization's control of information and ability to keep damaging facts from becoming part of the public record (*availability of information*) is an important contingency in the AOR process.[95] Organizations may enlist powerful supporters to help redefine facts that are made public or redefine the laws that regulate the organizational behavior, thereby converting violations into normative behavior.[96] For example, organizational lobbyists convinced the United States Sentencing Commission to alter aggravating and mitigating circumstances in sentencing guidelines to the advantage of the business community.[97] These factors exert their influence in a particular *social and political ecology* where "ownership" of the definitions of public problems and the contours of responsibility determines which version of reality gains widespread acceptance as legitimate.[98]

Step 2: Actor Characteristics and Organizational/Institutional Context of Action

Actor Characteristics

AOR researchers commonly find that the characteristics of actors are important predictors of responsibility attributions in controlled studies involving vignettes. This makes sense, as social science research has a long tradition of finding that high status individuals (and by implication, organizations) are treated leniently for their crimes and deviance, while low status individuals are treated relatively harshly.[99] Organizational size might be an analog for status and studies have found that large organizations are treated more leniently than smaller ones.[100] In this section, we begin by discussing actor characteristics including individual actor *demographics and traits* (i.e., sex, gender, race, age, SES), positive/negative traits, mental state, and intentions, among others that we include in the actor characteristics box found in Figure 2.[101] Many of these factors have not been examined in organizational studies, but they have such broad support in the AOR literature that we argue that they should be incorporated in future research. They are also potentially relevant at the organizational level. For example, just as positively viewed actors are more likely to escape the criminal label, so might positively viewed organizations that engage in effective public relations campaigns be likely to avoid such unwanted labeling.

Considering first an actor's positive/negative traits, a large body of research has found that our interpretations of others' behavior is dependent on, for example, whether we are initially given favorable or unfavorable information about them.[102] If informed that a person is intelligent, we may interpret subsequent behavior as daring rather than reckless. Organization leaders may be absolved of personal responsibility for organizational deviance occurring on their watch if we have been previously presented with information that they are generally competent and ethical people. Similarly, other researchers have found that the actor's demographics, such as sex, socioeconomic status, and race all affect how perceivers attribute responsibility.[103] In a particularly striking example that involved a case of wrongdoing, Dion found that attractive children were less likely to be stigmatized by respondents for assaulting a dog with stones than unattractive children.[104] In this study, the assaultive behavior of an "angelic-looking" girl was explained by a respondent in terms of her having a "bad day"—a situational and unstable trait for an otherwise "well-mannered and basically unselfish" child—while the same act perpetrated by a "homely" girl elicited a response that points to an inherent and stable trait, "I think this child would be quite bratty and would be a problem to teachers . . . all in all, she would be a real problem."[105] This is possibly due to the fact that physically attractive people are perceived as having a number of valued attributes, including more socially desirable personalities.[106] Although the study did not involve organizations, it suggests that "attractive" organizations may be judged more favorably in the AOR process if they have built a favorable public reputation before wrongdoing was discovered, possibly by behaving as a "virtuous organization,"[107] by investing in public relations and advertising campaigns, or by having powerful allies promote a positive organizational image.[108] Research into corporate philanthropy patterns suggests that such considerations are not unwarranted.[109]

Another study varied the actor's *mental state* to determine how this consideration might mitigate responsibility.[110] Vignettes portrayed two actors and a sequence of events that led to damaged property. One manipulation was that one of the actors either did or did not display the symptoms of schizophrenia. Responsibility for the damaged property was judged to be greater when the actor showed symptoms of schizophrenia. Again, the link to organizational participants or organizations as actors was not made, but the result is nevertheless informative. It is plausible that organizational leaders may be judged differently depending on their mental state at the time of the wrongdoing.

In an especially relevant line of research, Hamilton promoted a "roles-and-deeds" model of AOR that has explicated the important influences of an actor's *social role* and *social status* on how observers (i.e., survey respondents) attribute responsibility for wrongdoing. In these studies, the deed involves behavior for which an actor may potentially be held responsible; different acts entail different judgments of responsibility (an obvious point that we do not discuss in the review that follows). Roles can best be conceptualized as the social location of actors and the level of authority they possess as well as the tasks they are expected to perform and the norms they are expected to follow in their performance (e.g., whether the actor is in an autonomous or obedient role). In passing judgment about responsibility, different roles seem to provide audiences with differing criteria of strictness in terms of level of intent necessary for "guilt." In other words, it is not what you did, but what you did given who you are and the social context, that determines which sanctioning rules apply. As we have discussed above, obedience to legitimate authority has often served as a mitigator of responsibility in cases of organizational wrongdoing.

One reason for the complexity of AOR in organizational cases is that responsibility may be attached to the organization itself as well as to the people who act as agents on behalf of the organization. Superiors can argue that an individual down the chain of command behaved contrary to instructions. At the same time the fact that one is acting as an agent for another may also be seen as an excuse for wrongdoing (e.g., a crime of obedience).[112] Thus, vocabularies of motive[113] that mitigate responsibility are an inherent feature of organizational life and an actor's perceived *organizational embeddedness* is especially likely to shape the impact of an actor's social role. An actor who audiences believe is both in an obedient role and also heavily embedded in an organization may be better positioned to draw on organizational vocabularies of motive than an actor who is in an obedient role but not heavily embedded (e.g., a "temp" worker or subcontractor).

Organizational/Institutional Context of Action

Although some variants of attribution theory have recently been applied to organizational contexts,[114] most involve self attributions and few have investigated AOR by outsiders for actors involved in organizational wrongdoing. This is unfortunate because attributional theories are especially well-suited to organizational settings.[115] Indeed, one of the most dominant features of bureaucratic life—the restriction of decision-making opportunities by processes that generate outcomes from unreflective action[116]—has yet to be modeled by AOR studies. Therefore, in addition to the actor characteristics discussed above, step 2 of our model includes a box that directs attention to features of an actor's organizational or institutional context that are relevant for responsibility judgments. As we have noted throughout this chapter, in some cases the organization or institution may be more appropriately labeled as the actor rather than an individual decision-maker.

Organizational scholars have produced an immense literature explicating the complex manner in which *mental schemas* and *institutional logics* contribute to unreflective actions.[117] The influence of these factors potentially cuts across social roles and even transcends the "focal organization" that has historically provided the social location for organizational responsibility claims.[118] Furthermore, institutional logic is an important source of causal schemas[119] that comprise a person's attributional style and on which observers rely to make sense of events such as organizational wrongdoing.[120] All of this hints at the value of a synthesis of the organizational and psychological literatures. The extent to which audiences perceive and understand the manner in which institutional logic transfoms "decisions" into unreflective actions and moral issues into routine procedures devoid of moral implications will likely determine the extent to which perceivers attribute responsibility to the other variables in Figure 2.[121] It is possible that a perceiver who has experienced this process first-hand by having worked in a large bureaucracy, or who is familiar with this literature (i.e., students or social scientists), may be more likely to perceive actions as stemming from institutional logic than individual choice.

It is because of the operation of an institutional logic that persons in organizational contexts rarely make decisions based on complete free will. Rather, they are subject to the constraints of a *"bounded rationality."*[122] In other words, actors may personally believe that they are making fully informed and unconstrained decisions, but in many cases the institution has provided behavioral scripts, also known as standard operating procedures (SOPs), and cognitive frameworks that limit the search for information and give meaning to actions (mental schemas) that guide behavior and shape what choices are preferred, required, or even unthinkable.[123] According to this perspective, decisions and decision-making are best understood in terms of social representations, not rational choices.[124] "Decisions" are constructed after-the-fact as narratives to help participants understand unreflective actions taken by the organization; they are not the cause of these actions. They subsequently influence processes, facilitate new actions, and give meanings to events that occur within the organization.

Recent research has incorporated such insights by empirically testing the effects of cognitive schemas and SOPs on AOR for organizational wrongdoing.[125] The findings indicate that both the organization studies literature and the AOR literature can mutually benefit by synthesizing the two fields when examining public perceptions of organizational wrongdoing, although the context of the wrongdoing will affect outcomes to some degree. Both qualitative and quantitative findings from this study show similar patterns for SOPs. If the wrongdoing was typical then respondents attributed more responsibility to the organization than where it was not typical. In other words, this research indicates that organizational features influence people, consciously or not, which affects how they make decisions in cases when an organization or a person within the organization is the defendant.

These patterns also support previous research which found statistically significant results for SOPs. Simpson and Piquero asked business executives and MBA students to read vignettes that involved a manager engaged in some type of wrongdoing (e.g., bribery, price-fixing, pollution, or sales fraud).[126] The respondents were then asked to indicate if they would have acted similarly based on the circumstances that were manipulated in the vignettes. One of those manipulations involved whether the act was common within the firm or common within the industry (SOPs). Results indicated that respondents were more willing to personally engage in misconduct because of organizational factors, such as the SOP that wrongdoing was common in the firm, but not because of SOPs in the industry, individual decisions, or low self-control.

We have much to learn from institutional approaches that move "beyond agency"[127] and incorporate ideas that are derived from, and promoted by, the dominant institutional logics of particular social systems at specific times.[128] We argue that scholarship on AOR for wrongdoing in organizations would benefit from increased attention to such issues.

Step 3: Audience Characteristics

In this section we discuss some of the more important audience characteristics that are likely to play a significant role in the AOR process. Although research findings are mixed with regard to differences in *demographics* across respondents in accounting for variations in AOR, and more research is needed before definitive answers can be provided, other studies have demonstrated that *cultural background* and *educational attainment* are particularly important.[129] One study of AOR for wrongdoing in organizations included the impact of the legal culture and economy of three countries (the United States, Japan, and Russia), while controlling for individual differences such as stratification, education, and social class.[130] With regard to culture, the opinions of American respondents about obedience to orders had implications for corporate accountability, but Japanese and Russian respondents' beliefs did not. This is not surprising, as a large body of literature has found that Eastern-origin group members have a very different social and intellectual history than Westerners, which affects processes of causal attribution and responses to social circumstances and situations.[131]

Perceptions of organizational and individual responsibility for wrongdoing are likely to vary because of cultural issues.

Another relevant factor is perceivers' "*legal consciousness*,"[132] which depends on their degree of familiarity with specific aspects of legal procedures and substantive rules. A person with a well-developed legal consciousness will tend to interpret actions according to legal criteria, often relying on legal frameworks and imagery as a cultural resource for making sense of events. Laypersons may develop a legal consciousness based on exposure to law through the media, their own personal experiences, or while jurors who are socialized into legal habits of reasoning through instructions from judges and witnessing the legal process in the courtroom. Entire communities may develop a collective legal consciousness that shapes how they perceive events and assign responsibility for wrongdoing.[133] Depending on how "legalistic" their cognitive orientations are, perceivers may differentially rely on legal criteria in attributing responsibility for wrongdoing in organizations. Sutherland's insight that much corporate criminality is not formally labeled as crime, but rather is treated as civil or administrative matters, may be seen as a limitation of collective legal consciousness.[134]

Similarly, the *moral development* of an audience may also shape the attribution of responsibility. Kohlberg's research is especially informative on this topic and we offer a condensed version of his stage model to illustrate the potential importance of this variable.[135] Kohlberg believed that there are several stages of moral development and that our behaviors, and by implication AOR, are influenced by the extent of our moral development. The preconventional stage is the lowest level of moral thinking. The individual in this stage shows no internalization of moral values and all moral thinking is based on punishments. The conventional stage finds individuals abiding by certain internal standards that derive from the standards of others, such as parents or the laws of society. The postconventional stage is Kohlberg's highest level of moral thinking; moral development is completely internalized and not based on the standards of others. The individual recognizes alternative moral courses of thought and action, explores a number of options, and then develops a personal moral code. Kohlberg believed these levels and stages occur in a sequence and are age-related. Some evidence for Kohlberg's theory has been found that indicates that few people reach the more advanced stages of development. Although AOR research has not yet incorporated his insights, it is reasonable to expect that a person in the preconventional stage will exhibit different AOR patterns than an individual in the postconventional stage. There may also be relationships between moral development and other demographic variables (e.g., education and gender).[136]

Finally, a perceiver's *attributional style* has been found to be a robust predictor of AOR.[137] For example, if audience members have an external locus of control,[138] they may be more likely to attribute responsibility to outside forces rather than to internal character or psychological traits of an actor. Similarly, the attributional effects of a relatively stable "causal schema"[139] or "underlying cognitive structure"[140] may persist even after controlling for situational and control variables. For example, one's score on the Attributional Style Questionnaire (a relatively stable personality trait scale) may explain more variance in how one attributes responsibility than one's score on the more situationally based Causal Dimension Scale.[141] Another study found that respondents who had a strong Protestant work ethic were more likely to point to internal factors to explain worker absenteeism while those who exhibited a positive explanatory style attributed absenteeism to external factors.[142] Despite strong findings in the attribution literature, the literature on AOR for organizational wrongdoing has not incorporated attributional style measures, which constitute a potential limitation of the existing research.

Step 4: Attribution of Responsibility

The context of attribution is important as jurors charged with applying either civil or criminal standards are likely to attribute responsibility differently than laypersons who are not subject (at least formally) to such demands.[143] Furthermore, jurors are also required to consider *mens rea* and *actus reus,* the intentions of the perpetrator and the nature of the act, while laypersons are formally free to consider or ignore information or base their attributions instead on the emotional impact of the nature of the wrongdoing. By giving explicit attention to the *types* of responsibility, our process model can be applied to laypersons as well as to civil or criminal jurors.

The measurement of responsibility in attribution research has been the subject of much debate within psychology, although the unidimensional concept of "responsibility" seems to be taken-for-granted within sociology. In one useful scheme, Shaver posits *five dimensions of responsibility* for an individual involved in wrongdoing.[144] The first of these is the *causal* dimension, a measure of the extent to which the actor was the direct cause of an occurrence for which the accusation is being made. The second dimension is *knowledge,* the degree to which the actor was aware of the consequences of the action taken. The third dimension is *intentionality,* a measure of the degree to which the action is thought of as intentional versus accidental. The fourth dimension is *coercion,* a measure of the degree to which responsibility for an intentional action can be mitigated by the presence of forces within the environment. Finally, the fifth dimension is *appreciation of moral wrongfulness* of the consequences that resulted from the actor's behavior. The judgment of this dimension should have less to do with the action per se than with the overall moral capacity of the actor or the moral views of the perceiver. Because perceivers may take into account all five of these dimensions, it is important to measure each when testing AOR.

Recent research has tested Shaver's theory using vignettes of the "Cold War human radiation experiments."[145] Using confirmatory factor analysis, the authors investigated a model that consisted of five latent constructs corresponding to the five dimensions of Shaver's AOR model. Findings supported only four of the five dimensions—coercion was not supported and therefore does not appear in Figure 2. However, the issue is far from settled and more research is needed to test Shaver's theory with different populations because the sample in this initial study was restricted to undergraduates and the results may not be generalizable.

Conclusion

In this chapter, we have argued that the attribution of responsibility for organizational wrongdoing is a rich and complicated area of study. At times, scholarship seems to oversimplify some issues while ignoring others. To some extent, this is a problem in most scholarly endeavors: we can subject only some aspects of social reality to our gaze at any given time. As a result, much of what we know about "willfulness" in organizational contexts, to mention just one example discussed in this chapter, may be problematic. To address the concerns that we have raised, we have offered a more holistic approach to AOR for organizational wrongdoing by proposing a four-step schematic model. We also conceive of responsibility as a multidimensional concept comprised of four dimensions (knowledge, intention, causality, and moral wrongfulness) and suggest that scholars would benefit from exploring each of these dimensions as they are impacted by the kinds of factors that we have included in our model. We believe that future research would benefit from empirically investigating the social construction of facts at multiple levels of analysis rather than assuming the existence of "pure behavioral phenomena," and that more attention to all four steps in our model is needed to advance our understanding of organizational wrongdoing.

Endnotes

1. Rosoff, Pontell, and Tillman, 1998; Simon, 1996.
2. Reiman, 2001; Kappeler, Blumberg, and Potter, 2000.
3. Kagan and Scholz, 1984; Vaughan, 1998.
4. Beamish, 2000; Haines, 1997; Shover and Hochstetler, 2002; Allison, 1969; Kriesberg, 1976.
5. Jackall,1988; Perrow, 1984; Lee and Ermann, 1999; Vaughan, 1996.
6. Friedland and Alford, 1991; Adams and Balfour, 2004.
7. Braithwaite,1993; Pontell and Calavita, 1993; Zimring and Hawkins, 1993; Yeager, 1991; 1993.
8. Kramer, Michalowski, and Kauzlarich, 2002.
9. Zimring and Hawkins, 1993:288.
10. Simon, 1957.
11. Gailey and Lee, 2005.
12. Hamilton and Sanders, 1995.
13. Spreitzer and Sonenshein, 2004.
14. Braithwaite, 1985.
15. Laroche, 1991; Kriesberg, 1976.
16. Dowie, 1977.
17. Lee and Ermann, 1999; Schwartz, 1991.
18. Yeager, 1993:117.
19. Dowie, 1977:32.
20. Vaughan, 1998:27.
21. Lee and Ermann, 1999.
22. Vaughan, 2001:60.
23. Llewellyn, 1951; Hayden, 1991; McEvoy, 1995.
24. Zimring and Hawkins, 1993:265.
25. cf. Simon, 1996.
26. cf. Ermann and Rabe, 1997.
27. Allison 1969:690.
28. Vaughan, 1996.
29. The Pinto case appears as number fourteen in *Fortune's* series of twenty "key decisions that made history" (see Bonamic, 2005). The subtitle of this story is "Ford decides to let the Pinto explode." The cost/benefit analysis is once again discussed incorrectly (including a statement that is was "cheaper... to pay off victims"), despite the fact that the first author of the current chapter spent a great deal of time explaining the revisionist account to Bonamic.

30. Vaughan, 1996.
31. Allison, 1969.
32. Vaughan, 1996:308–309.
33. Geis, 1967; Perrow, 1984; Lee and Ermann, 1999.
34. Vaughan, 1996.
35. Allison, 1969.
36. Reichman, 1993.
37. Yeager, 1993:117.
38. Vaughan, 1996:316–317.
39. Vaughan, 1998:41.
40. Vaughan, 1998:45.
41. Shapiro, 1990.
42. Zimring and Hawkins, 1993:265.
43. This analysis is also reprinted in Lee and Ermann, 1999:38.
44. Lee and Ermann, 1999.
45. Nichols, 1997.
46. Lee and Ermann, 1999:42.
47. Vaughan, 2001.
48. Clinard, 1983:162.
49. Zimring and Hawkins, 1993.
50. Reiman, 2001.
51. Kappeler, Blumberg, and Potter, 2000.
52. Reiman, 2001:79.
53. Reiman, 2001:102.
54. Kappeler, Blumberg, and Potter, 2000:124.
55. Messerschmidt, 1986:101.
56. Reiman, 1984.
57. Messerschmidt, 1986:101.
58. Kappeler, Blumberg, and Potter, 2000:124.
59. Bacow, 1980.
60. Ashford, 1976:113–114.
61. Ashford, 1976:114.
62. Bacow, 1980:39.
63. Messerschmidt, 1986:100.
64. Hagglund, 1976.
65. Kappeler et al., 2000:124; Reiman, 2001:102.
66. Hagglund, 1976:2.
67. Hagglund, 1976:3.
68. On the use of statistics more generally, see Best, 2001.
69. See also Zimring and Hawkins, 1993.
70. Schrager and Short, 1978:413.
71. Schrager and Short, 1978:413.
72. cf. Hamilton and Sanders, 1996; Gailey and Lee, in press.
73. Vardi and Weitz, 2004.
74. Mills, 1959.
75. Adams and Balfour, 2004:30.
76. Keeble, quoted in Jensen, 2002:38.
77. Milgram, 1974; Kelman and Hamilton, 1989.
78. Downs, 1996.
79. Gailey and Lee, 2004.
80. cf. Kelman and Hamilton, 1989.
81. Adams and Balfour, 2004:30.
82. Adams and Balfour, 2004:30.

83. Empirical studies of organizational life support contentions that technical rationality guides behavior in contemporary organizations to a large degree. Consider a classic study of "the most admired individuals in the best companies." in this case electronics multinationals widely recognized as corporate "models of excellence" and the "ideal future from a corporate point of view" (Maccoby, 1978:5–6). These companies were selected because they represented the best-case scenarios in terms of working conditions and management philosophies. Yet most of the highly admired managers employed by these pinnacles of the business world were preoccupied with technical rationality, to the detriment of the development of virtues such as "compassion, generosity, and idealism" (Maccoby, 1978:184). Furthermore, although 72 percent considered honesty "very important" to their work, only 12 percent believed that the structure of their work helped to develop this honesty. Similarly, while 80 percent indicated at least "moderate" interest in their work, less than half expressed a similar level of interest in *agape* (compassionate) love. Maccoby (1978:187) concludes that "The most loving were not the ones who moved up the ladder rapidly. Corporate work stimulates and rewards qualities of the head and not of the heart."

    Such findings are consistent with ethnographic research on organizational life. For example, Jackall (1988) found the patrimonial environment of the modern organization to be a far cry from the rational-legal order described in Weber's classic essay on bureaucracy. The core value prized by the "institutional logic" that pervades the contemporary corporate setting is "alertness to expediency." In other words, the ethics of managers must be situational, not absolute, and tied to the social norms of the corporation, not personal standards tied to one's religious background. This social setting transformed "all moral issues into immediately practical concerns." One manager summed up this situation by stating, "What is right in the corporation is what the guy above you wants from you." In this environment, insiders socially define "wrongdoing" as violations of localized variants of institutional logic, not external standards of conduct.
84. Cavender, Jurik, and Cohen, 1993.
85. Rosoff, Pontell, and Tillman, 1998:398.
86. Kelman and Hamilton, 1989.
87. Sinderbrand, 2005.
88. Rosoff, Pontell, and Tillman, 1998:398.
89. Gailey, 2005.
90. Gailey, 2005.
91. Zimring and Hawkins, 1993.
92. Lee and Ermann, 1999; Vaughan, 1996; 1998; Yeager, 1993; Gioia, 1992.
93. Gailey and Lee, 2004.
94. Best, 2001; Spector and Kitsuse, 1977.
95. Coleman, 1982.
96. Savelsberg, 1994; Yeager, 1991; 1993.
97. Etzioni, 1990.
98. Gusfield, 1981; Cavender et al., 1993.
99. Black, 1983; Chambliss, 1973.
100. cf. Yeager, 1993.
101. See also Gailey and Lee, 2005.
102. Asch, 1946.
103. Gleason and Harris, 1976; Hansen and O'Leary, 1985; Kleinke and Baldwin, 1993; Stewart, 1980.
104. Dion, 1972; see also Stewart, 1980.
105. Cited in Katz, 1999:330.
106. Dion, Berscheid, and Walster, 1972.

107. Haines, 1997.
108. Waegel, Ermann, and Horowitz, 1981.
109. Ermann, 1978.
110. Fincham and Roberts, 1985.
111. Hamilton, 1978; Hamilton and Sanders, 1999.
112. Sanders and Hamilton, 1997; see also Lofquist, 1997.
113. Mills, 1940.
114. cf. Martinko, 1995.
115. Weiner, 1995.
116. Laroche, 1995.
117. DiMaggio, 1997; Jackall, 1988; Powell and DiMaggio, 1991.
118. Lee and Ermann, 1999.
119. cf. Kelley, 1973.
120. cf. Gioia, 1991.
121. Laroche, 1995; Lee and Ermann, 1999; Gioia, 1991.
122. Simon, 1957; Jackall, 1988.
123. DiMaggio, 1997; Powell and DiMaggio, 1991; see also Perrow, 1986 on "premise controls."
124. Laroche, 1995; Fuchs, 2001.
125. Gailey, 2005.
126. Simpson and Piquero, 2002; see also Paternoster and Simpson, 1996.
127. Fuchs, 2001.
128. Friedland and Alford, 1991.
129. Sanders and Hamilton, 1987; 1997; Hamilton and Hagiwara, 1992; Hamilton and Sanders, 1983.
130. Hamilton and Sanders, 1996.
131. Nisbett, 2003.
132. Ewick and Silbey, 1998:45.
133. cf. Greene, 1991.
134. Sutherland, 1983.
135. Kohlberg, 1981.
136. See Gilligan, 1982.
137. Henry and Campbell, 1995.
138. Rotter, 1973.
139. Kelley, 1973.
140. Martinko, 1995:10.
141. Henry and Campbell, 1995.
142. Judge and Martocchio, 1995.
143. Weiten and Diamond, 1979.
144. Shaver, 1985.
145. Gailey, Falk, and Christie-Mizell, 2004.

References

Adams, Gary B., and Danny L. Balfour (2004) Unmasking Administrative Evil: Revised Edition. Armonk, NY: ME Sharpe.

Allison, Graham T. (1969) "Conceptual Models of the Cuban Missile Crisis." 63 American Political Science Rev. 689–718.

Asch, Solomon E. (1946) "Forming Impressions of Personality." 59 J. of Abnormal and Social Psychology 177–181.

Ashford, Nicholas Askounes (1976) Crisis in the Workplace: Occupational Disease and Injury. Cambridge, MA: MIT Press.

Bacow, Lawrence S. (1980) Bargaining for Job Safety and Health. Cambridge, MA: MIT Press.

Beamish, Thomas D. (2000) "Accumulating Trouble: Complex Organization, a Culture of Silence, and a Secret Spill" 47 Social Problems 473–498.

Best, Joel (2001) Damned Lies and Statistics: Untangling Numbers from the Media, Politicians, and Activists. Berkeley, CA: University of California Press.

Black, Donald (1983) "Crime as Social Control." 48 American Sociological Review 34–45.

Bonamic, Kate (2005) "1972: Ford Decides to Let the Pinto Explode." Fortune Magazine (June 27), www.fortune.com.

Braithwaite, John (1993) "The Nursing Home Industry." in Michael Tonry and Albert Reiss, eds., Beyond the Law: Crime in Complex Organizations. Chicago: University of Chicago Press.

Braithwaite, John (1985) "White Collar Crime." 11 Annual Review of Sociology 1–25.

Cavender, Gray, Nancy C. Jurik, and Albert K. Cohen (1993) "The Baffling Case of the Smoking Gun: The Social Ecology of Political Accounts in the Iran-Contra Affair." 40 Social Problems 152–166.

Chambliss, William (1973) "The Saints and the Roughnecks." 11 Society 341–355.

Clinard, Marshall B. (1983) Corporate Ethics and Crime: The Role of Middle Management. Beverly Hills: Sage Publications.

Coleman, James S. (1982) The Asymmetric Society. Syracuse, NY: Syracuse University Press.

Dimaggio Paul (1997) "Culture and Cognition." 23 Annual Review of Sociology 263–87.

Dion, Karen K. (1972) "Physical Attractiveness and Evaluation of Children's Transgressions." 24 J. of Personality and Social Psychology 207–213.

Dion, Karen K., Ellen Berscheid, and Elaine Walster (1972) "What is Beautiful is Good." 24 J. of Personality and Social Psychology 285–290.

Dowie, Mark (1977) "Pinto Madness." 2 Mother Jones 18–32.

Downs, Donald Alexander (1996) More than Victims: Battered Women, the Syndrome Society, and the Law. Chicago: University of Chicago Press.

Ermann, M. David (1978) "The Operative Goals of Corporate Philanthropy: Contributions to the Public Broadcasting Service, 1972–1976." 25 Social Problems 504–514.

Ermann, M. David, and Gary Rabe (1997) "Organizational Processes (Not Rational Choices) Produce Most Corporate Crimes." in William Lofquist, Mark Cohen, and Gary Rabe, eds., Debating Corporate Crime. Cincinnati, OH: Anderson Publishing.

Etzioni, Amitai (1990) "Going Soft on Corporate Crime." Washington Post, 1 April, sec. C, p. 3.

Ewick, Patricia, and Susan S. Silbey (1998) The Common Place of Law: Stories from Everyday Life. Chicago: University of Chicago Press.

Fincham, Frank D., and Caton Roberts (1985) "Intervening Causation and the Mitigation of Responsibility for Harm Doing." 21 J. of Experimental Social Psychology 178–194.

Friedland, Roger, and Robert R. Alford (1991) "Bringing Society Back In: Symbols, Practices, and Institutional Contradictions." in W. Powell and Paul DiMaggio, eds., The New Institutionalism in Organizational Analysis. Chicago, University of Chicago Press.

Fuchs, Stephan (2001) "Beyond Agency." 19 Sociological Theory 24–40.

Gailey, Jeannine (2005) "Factors Affecting How People Attribute Responsibility to Individuals and Organizations Involved in Wrongdoing: An Empirical Assessment of an Integrated Model of Responsibility Attribution." Ph.D. diss., Department of Sociology, University of Akron.

Gailey, Jeannine A., R. Frank Falk, and C. André Christie-Mizell (2004) "Is Responsibility a Multidimensional or Unidimensional Concept?" Presented at the American Sociological Association conference, San Francisco (14 August).

Gailey, Jeannine, and Matthew T. Lee (2005) "An Integrated Model of Attribution of Responsibility for Wrongdoing in Organizations." 6 Social Psychology Quarterly 338–358.

Gailey, Jeannine, and Matthew T. Lee (2005) "The Impact of Roles and Frames on Attributions of Responsibility: The Case of the Cold War Human Radiation Experiments." 37 J. Applied Social Psychology 1067–1088.

Gailey, Jeannine, and Matthew T. Lee (2004) "Does the Media Effect How Jurors Assign Guilt in Cases of Individual and Organizational Wrongdoing?" Presented at the American Society of Criminology conference, Nashville (17 November).

Geis, Gilbert (1967) "White-Collar Crime: The Heavy Electrical Equipment and Antitrust Cases of 1961." in Marshall Clinard and Richard Quinney, eds., Criminal Behavior Systems: A Typology, New York: Holt, Rinehart and Winston.

Gilligan, Carol (1982) In a Different Voice: Psychological Theory and Women's Development. Cambridge, MA: Harvard University Press.

Gioia, Dennis (1992) "Pinto Fires and Personal Ethics: A Script Analysis of Missed Opportunities." 11 J. of Business Ethics 379–389.

Gleason, James M., and Victor A. Harris (1976) "Group Discussion and Defendant's Socio-Economic Status as Determinants of Judgments by Simulated Jurors." 6 J. of Applied Social Psychology 6: 186–191.

Greene, Melissa Fay (1991) Praying for Sheetrock: A Work of Nonfiction. NY: Fawcett Columbine.

Gusfield, Joseph R. (1981) The Culture of Public Problems: Drinking-Driving and the Symbolic Order. Chicago: University of Chicago Press.

Hagglund, George (1976) "Causes of Injury in Industry—The 'Unsafe Act' Theory." OSHA School for Workers Safety and Health Publication, July. Washington, DC: GPO.

Hamilton, V. Lee (1978) "Who is Responsible? Toward a Social Psychology of Responsibility Attribution." 41 Social Psychology 316–328.

Hamilton, V. Lee, and Shigeru Hagiwara (1992) "Roles, Responsibility, and Accounts across Cultures." 27 International J. of Psychology 156–179.

Hamilton, V. Lee, and Joseph Sanders (1999) "The Second Face of Evil: Wrongdoing in and by the Corporation." 3 Personality and Social Psychology Rev. 222–233.

Hamilton, V. Lee, and Joseph Sanders (1996) "Corporate Crime Through Citizens' Eyes: Stratification and Responsibility in the United States, Russia, and Japan." 30 Law and Society Rev. 513–547.

Hamilton, V. Lee, and Joseph Sanders (1995) "Crimes of Obedience and Conformity in the Workplace: Surveys of Americans, Russians, and Japanese." 51 J. of Social Issues 67–89.

Hamilton, V. Lee, and Joseph Sanders (1983) "Universals in Judging Wrongdoing: Japanese and Americans Compared." 48 American Sociological Review 199–211.

Haines, Fiona (1997) Corporate Regulation: Beyond 'Punish or Persuade.' New York: Oxford University Press.

Hansen, Ranald D., and Virginia E. O'Leary. (1985) "Sex-Determined Attributions." in V. O'Leary, R. Unger, and B. Wallston, eds., Women, Gender and Social Psychology. Hillsdale, NJ: L. Erlbaum.

Hayden, Robert M. (1991) "The Cultural Logic of a Political Crisis: Common Sense, Hegemony, and the Great American Insurance Famine of 1986." 11 Studies in Law, Politics, and Society, 95–117.

Henry, John W., and Constance Campbell (1995) "A Comparison of the Validity, Predictiveness, and Consistency of Trait versus Situation Measure of Attributions." in M. Martinko, ed., Attribution Theory: An Organizational Perspective. Delray Beach, FL: St. Lucie Press.

Jackall, Robert (1988) Moral Mazes: The World of Corporate Managers. New York: Oxford University Press.

Jensen, Derrick (2002) The Culture of Make Believe. New York: Context Books.

Judge, Timothy A., and Joseph J. Martocchio (1995) "Attributions Concerning Absence from Work: A Dispositional Perspective." in M. Martinko, ed., Attribution Theory: An Organizational Perspective. Delray Beach, FL: St. Lucie Press.

Kagan, Robert A., and John T. Scholz (1984) "The 'Criminology of the Corporation' and Regulatory Enforcement Strategies." in Keir Hawkins and John Thomas, eds., Enforcing Regulation. Boston: Kluwer-Nijhoff.
Kappeler, Victor E., Mark Blumberg, and Gary W. Potter (2000) The Mythology of Crime and Criminal Justice. 3rd Edition. Prospect Heights, IL: Waveland.
Katz, Sidney (1999) "The Importance of Being Beautiful." in J. Henslin, ed., Down to Earth Sociology: Introductory Readings. NY: Free Press.
Kelley, Harold H. (1973) "The Process of Causal Attribution." 28 American Psychologist 107–128.
Kelman, Herbert C., and V. Lee Hamilton (1989) Crimes of Obedience: Toward a Social Psychology of Authority and Responsibility. New Haven: Yale University Press.
Kleinke, Chris L., and Michael R. Baldwin (1993) "Responsibility Attributions for Men and Women Giving Sane Versus Crazy Explanations for Good and Bad Deeds." 127 J. of Psychology 37–50.
Kohlberg, Lawrence (1981) The Philosophy of Moral Development: Moral Stages and the Idea of Justice. San Francisco: Harper and Row.
Kramer, Ronald C., Raymond Michalowski, and David Kauzlarich (2002) "The Origins and Development of the Concept and Theory of State-Corporate Crime." 48 Crime and Delinquency 263–282.
Kriesberg, Simeon M. (1976) "Decisionmaking Models and the Control of Corporate Crime." 85 Yale Law J. 1091–1129.
Laroche, Herve (1995) "From Decision to Action in Organizations: Decision-Making as a Social Representation." 6 Organization Science 62–75.
Lee, Matthew T. and M. David Ermann (1999) "Pinto 'Madness' as a Flawed Landmark Narrative: An Organization and Network Analysis." 46 Social Problems 30–50.
Llewellyn, Karl N. (1951) The Bramble Bush. New York: Oceana Press.
Lofquist, William S. (1997) "A Framework for Analysis of the Theories and Issues in Corporate Crime." in William Lofquist, Mark Cohen, and Gary Rabe, eds., Debating Corporate Crime. Cincinnati, OH: Anderson Publishing.
Maccoby, Michael (1978) The Gamesman: Winning and Losing the Career Game. New York: Bantam Books.
Martinko, Mark J. (1995) Attribution Theory: An Organizational Perspective. Delray Beach, FL: St. Lucie Press.
McEvoy, Arthur F. 1995) "The Triangle Shirtwaist Factory Fire of 1911: Social Change, Industrial Accidents, and the Evolution of Common-Sense Causality." 20 Law and Social Inquiry 621–651.
Messerschmidt, James W. (1986) Capitalism, Patriarchy, and Crime. Totowa, NJ: Rowman and Littlefield.
Milgram, Stanley (1974) Obedience to Authority: An Experimental View. New York: Harper and Row.
Mills, C. Wright (1959) The Sociological Imagination. New York: Oxford University Press.
Mills, C. Wright (1940) "Situated Actions and Vocabularies of Motive." 5 American Sociological Review 904–913.
Nichols, Lawrence T. (1997) "Social Problems as Landmark Narratives: Bank of Boston, Mass Media and 'Money Laundering,'" 44 Social Problems 324–341.
Nisbett, Richard E. (2003) The Geography of Thought: How Asians and Westerners Think Differently... and Why. New York: The Free Press.
Paternoster, Raymond, and Sally Simpson (1996) "Sanction Threats and Appeals to Morality: Testing a Rational Choice Model of Corporate Crime." 30 Law and Society Rev. 549–583.
Perrow, Charles (1986) Complex Organizations: A Critical Essay. New York: Random House.
Perrow, Charles (1984) Normal Accidents: Living With High-Risk Technologies. New York: Basic Books.

Pontell, Henry N., and Kitty Calavita (1993) "The Savings and Loan Industry." in Michael Tonry and Albert Reiss, eds., Beyond the Law: Crime in Complex Organizations. Chicago: University of Chicago Press.

Powell, Walter and Paul DiMaggio (1991) The New Institutionalism in Organizational Analysis. Chicago, University of Chicago Press.

Reichman, Nancy (1993) "Insider Trading." in Michael Tonry and Albert Reiss, eds., Beyond the Law: Crime in Complex Organizations. Chicago: University of Chicago Press.

Reiman, Jeffrey 2001 The Rich Get Richer and the Poor Get Prison: Ideology, Class, and Criminal Justice. 6th Edition. Boston: Allyn and Bacon.

Reiman, Jeffrey (1984) The Rich Get Richer and the Poor Get Prison: Ideology, Class, and Criminal Justice. 2nd Edition. New York: Wiley.

Rosoff, Stephen M., Henry N. Pontell, and Robert Tillman (1998) Profit Without Honor: White-Collar Crime and the Looting of America. Upper Saddle River, NJ: Prentice Hall.

Rotter, Julian B. (1973) "Internal-External Locus of Control Scale." in J. Robinson and P. Shaver, eds., Measures of Social Psychological Attitudes. Ann Arbor, MI: Institute for Social Research.

Sanders, Joseph, and V. Lee Hamilton (1997) "Distributing Responsibility for Wrongdoing Inside Corporate Hierarchies: Public Judgments in Three Societies." 21 Law and Social Inquiry 815–855.

Sanders, Joseph, and V. Lee Hamilton (1987) "Is There a 'Common Law' of Responsibility? The Effect of Demographic Variables on Judgments of Wrongdoing." 11 Law and Human Behavior 277–297.

Savelsberg, Joachim J. (1992) "Law that Does Not Fit Society: Sentencing Guidelines as a Neoclassical Reaction to the Dilemmas of Substantivized Law." 97 American J. of Sociology 1346–1381.

Schrager, Laura Shill, and James F. Short, Jr. (1978) "Toward a Sociology of Organizational Crime." 25 Social Problems 407–419.

Schwartz, Gary T. (1991) "The Myth of the Ford Pinto Case." 43 Rutgers Law Review 1013–1068.

Shapiro, Susan P. (1990) "Collaring the Crime, Not the Criminal: Reconsidering the Concept of White-Collar Crime." 55 American Sociological Review 346–365.

Shaver, Kelly G. (1985) The Attribution of Blame: Causality, Responsibility, and Blameworthiness. New York: Springer-Verlag.

Shover, Neal, and Andy Hochstetler (2002) "Cultural Explanation and Organizational Crime." 37 Crime, Law, and Social Change 1–18.

Simpson, Sally S., and Nicole Leeper Piquero (2002) "Low Self-Control, Organizational Theory, and Corporate Crime." 36 Law & Society Rev. 509–547.

Simon, David R. (1996) Elite Deviance. Boston: Allyn and Bacon.

Simon, Herbert A. (1957) Models of Man: Mathematical Essays on Rational Human Behavior in a Social Setting. New York: John Wiley and Sons.

Sinderbrand, Rebecca (2005) "A Shameful Little Secret: North Carolina Confronts its History of Forced Sterilization." Newsweek 33 (May 28).

Spector, Malcolm, and John I. Kitsuse (1977) Constructing Social Problems. Menlo Park, CA: Cummings.

Spreitzer, Gretchen M., and Scott Sonenshein (2004) "Toward the Construct Definition of Positive Deviance." 47 American Behavioral Scientist 828–847.

Stewart, John (1980) "Defendant Attractiveness as a Factor in the Outcome of Criminal Trials: An Observational Study." 10 J. of Applied Social Psychology 348–361.

Sutherland, Edwin H. (1983) White Collar Crime: The Uncut Version. New Haven: Yale University Press.

Vardi, Yoav, and Ely Weitz (2004) Misbehavior in Organizations: Theory, Research, and Management. Mahwah, NJ: Lawrence Erlbaum.

Vaughan, Diane (2001) "Sensational Cases, Flawed Theories." in Henry Pontell and David Shichor, eds., Contemporary Issues in Crime and Criminal Justice: Essays in Honor of Gilbert Geis. Upper Saddle River, NJ: Prentice Hall.

Vaughan, Diane (1998) "Rational Choice, Situated Action, and the Social Control of Organizations." 32 Law & Society Rev. 23–61.

Vaughan, Diane (1996) The Challenger Launch Decision: Risky Technology, Culture, and Deviance at NASA. Chicago: University of Chicago Press.

Waegel, William B., M. David Ermann, and Alan M. Horowitz (1981) "Organizational Responses to Imputations of Deviance." 22 Sociological Quarterly 43–55.

Weiner, Bernard (1995) "Attribution Theory in Organizational Behavior: A Relationship of Mutual Benefit." in M. Martinko, ed., Attribution Theory: An Organizational Perspective. Delray Beach, FL: St. Lucie Press.

Weiten, Wayne, and Shari Seidman Diamond (1979) "A Critical Review of the Jury Simulation Paradigm: The Case of Defendant Characteristics." 3 Law and Human Behavior 71–86.

Yeager, Peter C. 1993. "Industrial Water Pollution." in Michael Tonry and Albert Reiss, eds., Beyond the Law: Crime in Complex Organizations. Chicago: University of Chicago Press.

Yeager, Peter C. (1991) The Limits of Law: The Public Regulation of Private Pollution. NY: Cambridge University Press.

Zimring, Franklin E. and Gordon Hawkins (1993) "Crime, Justice, and the Savings and Loan Crisis." in Michael Tonry and Albert Reiss, eds., Beyond the Law: Crime in Complex Organizations. Chicago: University of Chicago Press.

Part II

White-Collar Criminogenesis: Structure, Motivation, and Rationalization

1

Generative Worlds of White-Collar Crime

Neal Shover

A complex of issues surrounding white-collar crime has flummoxed investigators for nearly seven decades. They originate in disagreement over how to distinguish and define the concept and whether there is significant analytic payoff from doing so. This paper begins by briefly noting this definitional controversy and lays out an approach that is employed in the remainder of the paper. Next the paper notes that regardless of how white-collar crime is defined research shows striking differences between white-collar and common offenders. The focus then shifts to class-based differences in lives and child-rearing that provide working-class citizens and citizens of privilege with significantly different cultural capital. A major focus is constructions of white-collar crime by the latter that distinguish them from what is characteristic of street offenders. The paper concludes with an interpretation of white-collar-crime that is committed by privileged citizens that situates it in context of social class and cultural capital.

Definitional Nets

There are few areas of criminological investigation plagued with the intractable controversies that envelop study of white-collar crime. From the introduction of the concept nearly 70 years ago, dispute has swirled around alternative definitional approaches. Sutherland's definition highlights the respectable status of its perpetrators as the most important characteristics of white-collar crime. This approach is adopted by all who believe that differentials of power and influence are key to identifying, framing satisfactorily, and unraveling fundamental questions about crime and crime control (Braithwaite, 1991). In contrast to those who prefer *criminal-based* definitions of white-collar crime, others contend that either there is no analytic advantage to be gained by highlighting offenders' privileged position or that the focus is misplaced. They counter with *crime-based* definitions, all of which look to formal characteristics of criminal offenses as the basis for distinguishing white-collar crime. As Edelhertz (1970:3) puts it, a white-collar crime is "an illegal act or series of illegal acts committed by nonphysical means and by concealment or guile, to obtain money or property, to avoid the payment or loss of money or property, or to obtain business or personal advantage." When using crime-based definitions of white-collar crime, the respectable status of those who commit it is reduced substantially or is rendered analytically insignificant. Thus, Edelhertz (1970:4) believes that "the character of white-collar crime must be found in its modus operandi and its objectives rather than in the nature of the offenders." His approach is matched by Shapiro (1990), who calls for "collaring the crime, not the criminal."

The democratic implications of doing so are clear. When it is defined on the basis of offense characteristics, white-collar crime can be "committed by a bank teller or the head of an institution. The offender can be a high government official with a conflict of interest [or] [h]e can be the destitute beneficiary of a poverty program" (Edelhertz, 1970:4). No longer is white-collar crime the province of the respectable, remote, and powerful; now the neighborhood automobile mechanic receives equal billing. Just how democratic the empirical implications of crime-based definitions can be is clear from studies that use the criminal code as template for identifying white-collar crimes. Investigators at Yale Law School, for example, began research on 1,094 individual offenders by drawing a sample from all persons who were convicted of or who pleaded guilty to any of eight statutorily defined crimes in seven U.S. District Courts in the years 1976–1978 (Weisburd et al., 1991). Securities fraud, antitrust violations, bribery, bank embezzlement, postal and wire fraud, making false claims and statements, credit and lending institution fraud, and tax fraud were designated white-collar crimes by investigators. By definition, individuals convicted of any of these offenses are white-collar criminals. In samples selected on this basis, a high proportion of offenders are anything but members of "elite groups, high status executives or large, multinational corporations, however loosely defined these terms may be" (Croall, 1992:56). Instead they are citizens of modest means and small business firms. Many individual offenders in fact are unemployed when they commit their "white-collar" crimes (Forst and Rhodes, 1980; Weisburd et al., 1991).

Regardless of how the behavior is defined, however, the demographic characteristics and backgrounds of white-collar offenders present a marked contrast to what is typical of street criminals. The contrast is reduced enormously when crime-based definitions are employed, but it is pronounced nonetheless. In one such study, 15 percent of white-collar criminals came from families that had trouble providing necessities, but the same was true of 25 percent of street offenders (Benson, 2002; Forst and Rhodes, 1980). Telemarketing offenders overwhelmingly are products of parental homes in which financial circumstances were secure if not comfortable (Doocy et al., 2001). Information on their educational attainment also shows a level of achievement beyond what is true of street criminals. Interviews with 47 convicted telemarketers revealed that eight dropped out of high school, but most graduated. Twenty-one attended college, and five held baccalaureate degrees (Shover, Coffey, and Sanders, 2004). Other research likewise shows that white-collar criminals are better educated than street offenders, significantly older and less often members of minority groups (Benson and Kerley, 2001; Benson and Moore, 1992; Shover and Hochstetler, 2005).

Class and Respectability

Controversy over alternative definitions of white-collar crime undoubtedly will continue, if only because the outcome is consequential for the kinds of persons who will bear the opprobrium of being labeled a *criminal*. The definition employed in this paper emphasizes the qualities of white-collar offenders rather than the crimes they commit. Approached in this way, a substantial proportion of white-collar criminals are distinguished by lives of material privilege and respectability. This means, most importantly, that they are free from the "daily struggle to keep themselves from falling over the cliff" into insolvency (Shipler, 2004:300). Preoccupation with meeting basic material needs, fiscal precariousness, and unceasing concern about it are largely alien to their worlds and lives. Dunk (1991:41) notes the obvious, that in stark contrast to their conditions of life, "the necessity of paid labor and the fear of losing it dominate the lives of working-class individuals." White-collar criminals generally do not live in families where injury to the breadwinner can plunge all into material desperation in a matter of days. Instead, their automobiles start on command; their refrigerators and wine racks are adequately, if not amply, stocked; their homes are commodious, comfortable and secure; and their children are well-clothed and well-fed. Material privilege is important because it shapes every aspect of life from options available at stages of the life course to the availability of leisure to evaluate them carefully.

Privilege and respectability are not dichotomous variables, however, and it would be foolish to pretend they are. The members of any population—this is true particularly of large and demographically heterogeneous nation states—can be arrayed on a continuum from those who have an adequate if precarious income and a modicum of respectability to citizens with multi-million dollar annual compensation packages and deference from elites. It includes those who cling to being counted among the middle-class as well as citizens who live in opulence. As it is used here, the privileged excludes those who are marginally above the floor of wealth and respectability in favor of citizens who are materially comfortable and routinely treated with respect by others. It excludes, therefore, clerks, bank tellers and similar low-paid and low-level organizational functionaries who generally are counted as white-collar criminals when crime-based definitions are employed.

Crime and other forms of rule breaking spring from a remarkably small number of base motives, but they are expressed in diverse meanings and rhetorical constructions. The worlds in which these are acquired vary structurally and culturally, but social class is an irreducible source of variation. Class, however,

> is largely missing as a category of identity offered by popular culture and political discourse in the early-twenty-first century United States. [It] is not a central category of thought..., and [it] is often conceptually displaced onto or read through other categories of difference like gender and race in such a way that [it] is rendered invisible (Bettie, 2003:195).

To speak of *class* is to highlight the material conditions of life and how they shape perspectives and understandings not only of crime and punishment but a host of matters. Class

> is script, map and guide. [It] tells us how to talk, how to dress, how to hold ourselves, how to eat, and how to socialize. It affects who we marry; where we live; the friends we choose; the jobs we have; the vacations we take; the books we read; the movies we see; the restaurants we pick; how we decide to buy houses, carpets, furniture, and cars; where our kids are educated; what we tell our children at the dinner table (conversations about the Middle East, for example, versus the continuing sagas of the broken vacuum cleaner or the half-wit neighbor) (Lubrano, 2004:5).

As class is used here, the analytic focus is on its cultural components, not its structural properties. This is class as lived experience.

In addition to their adequate if not substantial material resources, white-collar criminals are privileged also by respectability. Poverty and disrepute are inextricably linked, and, for many, "the worst thing about poverty is not the actual living of it, but the shame of it" (Parton, 1994:51). Reflecting on his materially impoverished Irish childhood, McCourt (1996:272) recalls,

> We go to school through lanes and back streets so we won't meet the respectable boys... We know they're the ones who will get jobs in the civil service and help the people who run the world.... We know they're the ones who will go to university, take over the family business, run the government, run the world. We'll be the messenger boys on bicycles who deliver their groceries or we'll go to England to work on the building sites. Our sisters will mind their children and scrub their floors ... We know that. We're ashamed of the way we look.

Referring to a typical male informant, investigators who interviewed 150 Boston-area working-class men and women said that "he sees himself as receiving the ultimate form of contempt from those who stand above him in society: he is a function, "Ricca the janitor," he is part of the woodwork" (Sennett and Cobb, 1972:50). Reflecting on her working-class background, Rubin (1976:13) notes that she was unable to examine it analytically for many years because "I was... eager to forget the pain and the shame of feeling deficient." Scholars and academics are not immune from the tendency to see working-class women and men as unworthy. Part of the intelligentsia, they characteristically see themselves as "people who hold the 'right' values [and] stand out from a mass whose understanding and sensitivity they believe inferior to their own" (Sennett and Cobb, 1972:69).

This is not to ignore substantial variation in the conditions and rewards of working-class lives (Bettie, 2003). They include men and women who earn high wages, who have adequate health insurance and who may own their home. Their work, perhaps in the highly skilled and unionized construction trades, is challenging, allows for exercise of some self-direction and results in visible and enduring products that they often point to with pride. Nevertheless, the changing labor market characteristic of contemporary Western nations has left an increasingly large fraction of the working class in economically marginal or desperate straits (Rubin, 1994; Johnson, 2002). Here, for example, are persons employed at the lowest levels of the nursing home industry; their work often requires cleaning the beds and bodies of incontinent residents. The nature of this work ensures that only those with few options choose to do it, particularly at the minimum wage it pays. Few working-class citizens do work that is exciting or newsworthy. This and their low status gives to many a sense of personal insignificance that is only strengthened by awareness that their views are not solicited and usually are not considered by people who count (Sennett and

Cobb, 1972). They are largely invisible to respectable people, and neither they nor their opinions matter much (Ehrenreich, 2002; Shipler, 2004).

Interpersonal and Cultural Correlates

The interpersonal and cultural correlates of materially precarious lives are as clear as they are different from what is commonplace in worlds of privilege and respectability. Observational studies of the daily lives of working-class families reveal distinctive patterns of child-rearing described as "natural growth" (Lareau, 2002:747). By this is meant that "parents [view] children's development as spontaneously unfolding, as long as they [are] provided with comfort, food, shelter and other basic support" (Lareau, 2002:773). Poor and working-class parents try to provide "the conditions under which children can grow but [leave] leisure activities to children themselves." Moreover, "these parents... use directives rather than reasoning." In blue-collar households, communication is implicit; much is understood but goes unsaid, and children do not engage in conversation with adults so much as receive opinions or edicts. This is one reason many do not develop self-assurance dealing with superiors and impersonal organizations. Parental discipline in poor and working-class families runs to the immediate, painful and quick. Corporal punishment is used more often by working-class parents than those at higher levels of the class structure (Strauss and Donnelly, 1994). Working-class children, however, develop a generalized conformism, and they generally see legal threats as legitimate and binding (Kohn, 1977).

In blue-collar employment worlds an easy, informal egalitarianism prevails in most circumstances. There is remarkably little competitiveness among workers. Most share a common status, and prospects for upward mobility are limited in any case. Those who work too rapidly or maintain distance from co-workers in hopes of being noticed by superiors are derided as "rate busters" or "company men." Dunk (1991:75) notes that in this world, a "[o]ne does not want to give the impression of being too eager or of trying too hard." Those with a background in the working-class who subsequently find themselves in middle-class work worlds often remark by contrast on the competitiveness they encounter:

> In the factories I've worked in, if you talk down to another worker you can expect to be "punched out." The basic operating procedure of academia and graduate school... are based on competitive game playing, which in working-class settings would make you an outcast.... In my previous work environments this type of behavior had specific names: "brown nosing," "kissing ass," and so on... The modus operandi among middle-class careerists is based on competition (Langston, 1993:66–7).

Fortune is not generous to most who must make their way in the working-class world, but they generally do not blame others for this. What has been said about chemical factory workers is true for most:

> [T]hese workers typically believe that their position in the class structure is of their own doing. They are factory workers because they want to be or, if they do not want to be, because "they missed the boat." They "had their chances." If they regret their position they tend to blame not their class origins but themselves (Halle, 1984:169).

Many realize as well that their lack of social connections or well-placed contacts limits their chances in life, but this is accepted as "the way the world works" and not something to lament for long.

Located near the bottom of the class structure, working-class citizens witness ample misfortune either personally or vicariously. They are cautioned from early life to expect and to take setbacks in stride. Their calloused dreams include a healthy dose of fatalism. "[Y]ou are always afraid that the good things in life are temporary, that someone can take them away" (Bragg, 1997:297). Lacking a sense of efficacy even, entitlement as a cultural or individual quality is the last thing encountered in their worlds (Croteau, 1995). Their lives have given them little reason to expect opportunities, and when they encounter them, wariness is a characteristic response. Many have come to understand that "the only thing worse than doing without is to be given something and then have it snatched away" (Bragg, 1997:309). Those with little if any material surplus do not rush headlong into schemes that could turn to dust and produce ruination.

When they run afoul of the law, men and women from these worlds are as likely as not to blame themselves. That economic or labor-market conditions may have shaped their actions and the actions of others like them is not considered at length. If they recognize that others influenced them, they are quick to add "I got myself into the situation" or "no one twisted my arm." Reflecting on his younger years, songwriter and singer Merle Haggard rejects the possibility that his upbringing was responsible for his later imprisonment. He concludes instead that "leaves only me to blame" (Haggard, 1968). There are millions like him.

They have available and employ a narrow range of acceptable explanations for their crimes. They likely did not belong to high-school forensic or debate clubs nor did they take classes that encourage search for arcane meanings and complex interpretations. The conditions of their work, moreover, do not facilitate or require development of these cultural skills. Their work days are filled with the need for physical action, immediate responses and outcomes that are readily apparent to others either as satisfactory or lacking. Their crimes share many of these qualities and seem not to permit or require from investigators a complex search for either the facts or their meaning. They discourage public exploration of motives and may interpret it as weakness, deception or whining. Street thieves, for example, typically refer to their activities as "stealing" or "doin' wrong," and the circumstances of their crimes leave little room for denial or creative explanations. Twenty-year old males arrested on the street carrying electronic equipment and a pry bar only blocks from where residents were burglarized readily invite the label "perp."

Backgrounds of material privilege provide those who later become white-collar criminals with experiences sharply different in many ways from what is commonplace in poor and working-class households. The amount of space available to family members and the accommodative patterns that produce a high rate of occupational density is an immediate example. "It is one of the distinguishing marks of . . . working-class family life that there's not enough room in the house either for the people who live in it or the things they collect as they pursue their lives" (Rubin, 1994:17). Family members as a result must accommodate to the wishes and schedules of others in matters as mundane as the nightly bathtub queue. Middle-class homes are spacious, families are small and space generally is close at hand for those who want to be alone. Children typically have private bedrooms. Throughout the homes of working-class families, empty space is public space, which makes for both a reduced sense of personal privacy and inability to get away easily to indulge the brain or emotions. In marked contrast to their living arrangements, middle-class homes "don't have a bed in the living room" (Bragg, 1997:98).

Other benefits of a materially secure and respectable upbringing are not nearly as apparent, but they are no less important. Lareau (2002:773) describes the child-rearing practices of middle-class parents as "concerted cultivation." In contrast to working-class parents, who see the lives of their children "unfolding," middle-class parents make a "deliberate and sustained effort to stimulate children's development and to cultivate their cognitive and social skills." They attempt to foster children's talents through organized recreational and activities. An assured and adequate family income has obvious implications for these efforts by making it possible for parents to pay financially for these pursuits. The leisure activities of working-class youth by comparsion are played out on geographically more restricted and less expensive terrain. Their parents have neither the fiscal nor cultural resources to provide the kind of support that is commonplace in middle-class households. This severely limits their children's participation both in school and extra-curricular activities (Lareau, 2003).

Middle-class children are encouraged verbally and included in conversations with their parents and other adults. Parents often defer to them, and middle-class children witness parental juggling of family schedules around them and their activities. Lareau suggests that this and other aspects of middle-class child-rearing produce a sense of entitlement in middle-class children, one that may find expression throughout life. In school, for example, they are singled out for special treatment by teachers who see in their class-based cultural skills and personal qualities evidence of leadership potential (Bettie, 2003). They have little knowledge of drudgery and subordinate status save perhaps for temporary employment .

In other ways as well, the contrast with working-class experience is striking. Children of privilege have little experience with crises of the kind that can send lives on a downward and irreversible spiral. They characteristically expect that things will go well for them. They expect opportunities to be available. Cultural skills and perspectives acquired gradually in the routine conversations and dynamics of family life shape characteristic responses to subsequent crises and opportunities. Crises are unexpected and generally are seen as unfair or undeserved, and, for this reason, extraordinary responses are thought to be justified. As for opportunities, they learn to recognize and exploit them when they appear.

The social and cultural conditions that prevail in their formative years generally are reproduced in the subsequent employment experiences of privileged citizens (Kohn, 1977). As adults, they generally do work that is morally and physically cleaner than work done by blue-collar employees; they generally do not return home at the end of the day with mud, grease, cotton dust or toxic chemicals on their clothing. For many their work is interesting and creative, and they are permitted considerable self-direction. They may occupy offices, access to which is restricted by secretaries or other subalterns. Personal assistants maintain their appointment calenders and smooth out problems in the workday, while the inconveniences and unpleasantries of life beyond the office are managed by paying others to take care of them. They and their superiors prefer not to know very much about those who do the world's dirty work. Nor do they want to know how things are going, just so long as they *are* going. This is one reason respectable citizens do not show up at local police stations unaccompanied by media representatives simply to talk with officers to let them know how much their work is appreciated.

Products of child-rearing in which communication is predominantly implicit, working-class citizens are attuned and pay attention to external qualities of behavior. In middle-class child-rearing communication is explicit, and much of it is devoted to unraveling the intentions behind puzzling or deviant actions. Children learn to look for and consider what is behind untoward conduct and to pay less attention to its formal status. Privileged citizens are more likely to view norms not as absolutes but as situationally applicable, and infraction, which is seen as a product of internal dynamics that explain if not justify it, is a matter for discussion and negotiation. It can be a protracted process. The reasons for punishment or correction must be explained defensibly, and middle-class children learn early that arguable lack of intent mitigates a wide array of misconduct. They gain experience evading moral and legal responsibility for their unpleasant actions. It is a lesson they learn well. Many convicted white-collar criminals have little experience as penitents.

Class, Culture and Criminogenesis

Interpretations of street crime and those who commit it invariably highlight the causal significance of childhood and family pathology. "[I]mpoverished families have long been stigmatized as dysfunctional. The father is a drunken or addicted ne'er-do-well, if he's around at all, and the mother an angry shrew or submissive incompetent. The parents don't read to their children, don't value education, don't teach or exhibit morality" (Shipler, 2004:161–62). Children of privilege by contrast have little material need, yet many appear as ready recruits to white-collar crime. Products of location in the class structure where material resources are adequate if not abundant and interpersonal respect is granted routinely, they commit acts of deceit and fraud and exploit positions of organizational power. Whether at home, at their places of employment or engaged in leisure activities, the culture and ethos of their worlds appear to generate ample if not increasing numbers of privileged citizens prepared to commit white-collar crime.

The ease with which they do so suggests there may be qualities and pathologies in their common backgrounds that are functional equivalents of family conflict and deprivation that figure prominently in the early lives of street criminals. The apparent flourishes and excesses of privilege are a starting point. Wright et al. (1999:178) have noted that social class "alters a variety of life contexts and chances" from differences in economic opportunities to culture, and these can increase delinquency by privileged youth." Hagan (1992) suggests as well that both the social power and risk taking characteristic of materially comfortable classes may contribute to crime and delinquency in their children. Three cultural conditions of their *generative worlds* may be significant for how they facilitate criminality: normatively unbridled competition, a pervasive sense of arrogance, and an ethic of entitlement. They are among the reasons why not only taverns and jails but also worlds of privilege and corporate offices can be breeding grounds for transgression.

Competition

Competitiveness is striving or vying with others for profit, prize, or position. It is a sense of rivalry. Lareau (2002, 2003) observed that middle-class children often develop and experience a sense of competitiveness with their siblings. As with their overall style of child-rearing, middle-class parents believe competition is a positive experience and one they try to provide for their children (Lareau, 2003:60–61). They monitor the progress of their children regularly and precisely so they will develop skills needed to thrive in the professional and managerial workforce. They push them to compete and excel. In countless ways, middle-class children are sent the message that their parents and others expect them to succeed. They expect life to offer rewarding opportunities. This is less common and salient in working-class homes.

In cultures of competition individuals are driven to strive for success, whether this be fortune, fame, or respect, and they worry ceaselessly about conditions that might stand in their way. Locales and time periods vary in how powerfully and pervasively an ethos of competitiveness dominates interpersonal relationships and individual actions. At Enron Corporation, management policies required each year that employees be evaluated on a forced curve so that fifteen percent would receive performance ratings of unacceptable (Cruver, 2002). The pervasive insecurity generated in competitive environments like this provides powerful motivational pushes toward misconduct. On the basis of interviews with convicted white-collar offenders, Spencer (1965) notes that they place an exaggerated emphasis on elevating their social position and prevailing in competition with others. It can become all-consuming and trump all obligations and commitments. In competitive worlds, progress is assessed by comparison with peers, and inevitably there are winners and losers. Desire to be the former is fueled in part by fear of becoming the latter. Enron's system of "rank and yank" bred intense fear:

> Suffice it to say any [annual] ranking that plummeted you lower than your previous assessment gave many people a reason to start a course of antidepressants or switch from beer to bourbon. A reduction in your ranking status would affect your salary, your self-esteem, your standing among your peers and, worst of all, your bonus. Once wounded with an "issues" ranking, like a stricken animal in a herd, other employees would begin to shun you as you might draw lions (Brewer, 2002:92).

A convicted telemarketer could be talking for most:

> You could be selling a $10 thousand ticket, you could be selling a $49.95 ticket, and it's the same principle. It's the same rules, it's the same game. I like to win. I like to win in all the games I play, you know. And the money is a reason to be there, and a reason to have that job. But winning is what I want to do. I want to beat everybody else in the office.

Nor is he alone in describing the power of culturally competitive worlds:

> [I] sold the first person I ever talked to on the phone. And it was just like that first shot of heroin, you know. I'm not a heroin addict.... I've only done heroin a couple of times. But it was amazing. It was like, "I can't believe I just did this!" It was incredible. It was never about the money after that.... Yeah, it was about the money initially, but when I realized that I could do this every day, it was no longer about the money. It was about the competition, you know. I wanted to be the best salesman, and I want to make the most money that day (Shover, Coffey, and Sanders, 2004:69).

In competitive cultures, people generally evaluate personal success in terms of wealth and material possessions. Competition need not be economic, however. Establishing or maintaining respect by peers for exceptional achievement is a priority for many, but humans compete for attention from superiors, plum assignments and career advancement. Charles Colson, once a White House staff member, remarks that

> Nixon and I understood one another—a young ambitious political kingmaker and an older pretender to the throne. We were both men of the same lower middle-class origins, men who'd known hard work all our lives, prideful men seeking that most elusive goal of all—acceptance and the respect of those who had spurned us in earlier years (Colson, 1976:31–2).

Desire to demonstrate through competitive struggle that respect is deserved plays no small part in some white-collar crimes.

Money, however, is unsurpassed as a medium for gauging competitive success. Its decimalized metric is far superior to the disputed and nuanced ones used to measure respect. The upwardly mobile son of an entrepreneur and small-business owner notes that

> [t]o those of us who raced along the Wall Street treadmill of the 80s, money assumed a mystical aura. Once you achieved a modest level of success, once you knew that you had your mortgage and your car payment covered, once you had a full belly, money simply became the way you gauged your level of success, compared to those about you.... [M]oney became the points on the scoreboard (Levine, 1991:390).

This suggests that not all who emerge as winners from competitive struggle find relief in victory; once achieved they know only insecurity over hanging on to what they have gained. For others, successful competition only kindles desire for more of the same:

> [A]t each new level of my career, I had pushed my goals higher. When I was an associate, I wanted to be a vice president. When I became a vice president, I wanted to be a senior vice president.... When I was earning $20,000 a year, I thought, *I can make $100,000....* When I was making $1 million, I thought *I can make $3 million.* There was always somebody one rung higher on the ladder, and I could never stop wondering: Is he really twice as good as I am? Ambition eclipsed rationality. I was unable to find fulfillment in realistic limits.... The hours grew longer, the numbers grew bigger, the stakes grew more critical, the fire grew ever hotter (Levine, 1991:391).

By elevating and rewarding success above all else, competitive environments provide both characteristic understandings and justifications for misconduct (Coleman, 1987). In these worlds normative restraints are transformed into challenges to be circumvented or used to advantage. The roots of workplace competitiveness reach well into the past for many who cannot elude its undertow. The morally corrosive effects of unbridled competition are seen in a range of settings, but they are evident most glaringly where competitors are young males. In places where their numbers and influence predominate, their perspectives define the collective ethos. Patriarchal notions of masculinity and competitors of privileged background predominate in worlds that breed tempted individuals and predisposed organizations.

Arrogance

Arrogance and an air of imperiousness occasionally are seen in the conduct of street criminals; the swaggering gun wielding figure is encountered in real life often enough to reacquaint us with this fact. But arrogance is a more likely springboard for crime in places and on the part of offenders who do not live so close to the material edge. The inhabitants of materially secure and respectable worlds are accustomed to being superordinates; they give orders, and others move to their dictates. Their views are solicited and taken seriously by people who count. They are waited on. Many of them have known success and emerged as winners from competitive struggle. All do not handle it well, however; the self-important, arrogant white-collar offender is a recurring figure in chronicles of white-collar crime. The face of arrogance is inescapable, for example, in decisions by powerful and wealthy public figures to award lucrative non-competitive contracts to friends and associates. In a large public meeting the chief executive officer of Enron Corporation reportedly referred to a pesky questioning accountant as an "asshole" (Cruver, 2001:54; Swartz and Watkins, 2003:265). Public lapses of respectability are uncommon for elite white-collar criminals; normally they do not display such inappropriate behavior. A securities fraudster recalls the sense of self-importance bordering on arrogance that he experienced before his scheme collapsed:

> [My wife] and I were becoming more and more in demand. I was successful enough that people were laughing at my stories. Even my brother-in-law invested with the kid brother who was taking the world by storm down there in Atlanta. . . .
>
> [M]y mother-in-law claimed I was a genius. I secretly admired her discernment. My office had to be enlarged to house a person of my intelligence, kindness, and shrinking humility. Class A personalities asked for my opinion about things (Lawson, 1992:67).

He and others like him may come to believe that "they [don't] have to follow the rules because they made them" (Swartz and Watkins, 2003:302).

Arrogance probably is less common among ordinary white-collar criminals, chiefly because many are employed in occupations that do not provide the requisite material, organizational and dramaturgical supports. It can find expression in disdain or indifference for legal restrictions and their creators, however. The idea that the state reserves the right to intervene in their work environments and restrain their decision-making is accepted only conditionally by many. Further, the presumption that they should exercise due diligence and responsible concern for details expected of ordinary citizens is rejected. Asked to explain his crimes, a former academic scientist, entrepreneur and corporate CEO who was convicted of insider trading replied,

> I think I was arrogant enough at the time to believe that I could cut corners. Not care about details that were going on and not think about consequences. [But] one of my great faults is—I refused to deal with everyday details that people have to deal with to make sure that mistakes aren't made. And I think, in that way, there may have been arrogance where I didn't have to deal with details—that these details were meant for other people, not for me (Waksal, 2003).

The arrogant are accustomed to a world they can manipulate, and their days are devoted to the search for shortcuts. When caught and convicted of crime, they deny everything or characterize it as a mistake and an aberration. Belief in their personal integrity is grounded in what they have accomplished and their success in other aspects of life. They distinguish themselves from "real criminals."

Entitlement

For children reared in families of privilege and respectability, "[p]arental ambition and high expectations, the pressure to succeed, the access to education, [and] the drive for professional achievement all add up to a sense of entitlement and opportunity" (Shipler, 2004:145). Cultures of entitlement cause actors in a range of circumstances to believe that benefits of some kind are due them and that questioning or disruption of delivery is illegitimate. Behn and Sperduto (1979:55) point out that this ethic is not a "conscious creed that prescribes personal or political conduct [but one that] . . . applies in specific situations, as a . . . constraint on . . . behavior." Lareau (2003) observed that middle-class children question and contest authority. They dispute and refute correction routinely. The children she observed were quick to offer advice to authority figures and to make special requests. They readily passed judgement and already had a sense that their efforts and accomplishments made them special. The investigators noted also that when privileges were denied, middle-class children badgered their parents until they were provided. These children acquired and operated with a sense of entitlement.

In a ground-breaking study of fraud among medical doctors, a team of investigators from the University of California interviewed 60 Medicare/Medicaid and American Medical Association officials, 42 physicians convicted of medical scams, and a control group of 32 physicians with no record of criminal conviction (Jesilow, Pontell, and Geis, 1993). The investigators found that among conditions that facilitate Medicaid fraud by physicians is their belief that insensitive external forces are interfering with their just desserts. In other words, felonious physicians believe they are *entitled* to pursue wealth without external restraint. What is instructive about this is confirmation that an ethos of entitlement can become so pervasive among occupational practitioners or organizational managers that it becomes taken for granted and erodes willingness to comply with law.

Professionals are hardly alone in this regard. The owners and managers of commercial establishments believe they contribute importantly to civic life and to community welfare generally by providing employment to citizens. They often point to the wealth returned to government by taxes of one kind or another paid by them and their workforce. Many donate time and money to civic organizations and causes. Professional persons, whether physicians, attorneys, or engineers, point to their work and its visible results as evidence of their importance. It is common for them and for high-level public-sector managers to believe that their contributions to community life and the sacrifices their families make because of their work entitles them to cut corners and claim perks not available to others.

Moral hierarchy is another source of entitlement. The privileged understand that fortune or luck has placed them in positions of power and control over organizations and others. They are not brick-layers, and they know it. They operate daily with understanding that their honor and respectability are a given, and they are entitled to be treated accordingly; privilege and deference is their due. Consequently, when austerity measures are called for the response may be something different. Throughout the corporate restructuring of recent decades, as employees made concessions in wages and benefits, management compensation skyrocketed. In 2000, before the collapse of Enron Corporation, the behavior of its CEO, the son of a minister,

> betrayed a powerful sense of personal entitlement. Long after his annual compensation... had climbed into the millions, Lay arranged to take out large personal loans from the company. He gave Enron jobs and contracts to his relatives. And Lay and his family used Enron's fleet of corporate jets as if they owned them. On one occasion, a secretary sought to arrange a flight for an executive on Enron business only to be told that members of the Lay family had reserved three of the company's planes (McLean and Elkind, 2004:3–4).

As their employer spiraled into bankruptcy and near-destruction, Enron employees,

> continued taking business-related trips, staying in the best hotels and eating in the best restaurants. These were the perks that the majority of Enron employees enjoyed—and it was a fair trade for being on the road, for being away from families, and for working fourteen-hour days. We considered it part of our compensation (Cruver, 2002:73.

Their sense of entitlement is only strengthened by the enormous amount of largesse that is made available to the privileged. This has been the case for so long and has become such an accepted part of life that it is no longer seen as discretionary.

Crime Constructions

Class origins and experiences account for how both crises and opportunities are experienced, and they also help to explain how easily transgression is resorted to and justified. When they violate the law the privileged have little difficulty fashioning and bringing to bear linguistic constructions that excuse or explain their actions. In part because they generally view their circumstances as exceptional, they generate, elaborate and employ complex interpretations of their motives. The great majority of individuals placed in positions of financial trust fulfill their fiduciary responsibilities honestly and faithfully. But not all. What has been learned about why some persons embezzle from their employers while others do not highlights the importance of self conversations in framing prospective acts. Ability to neutralize obeisance to law facilitates criminal decision-making; investigators have documented and catalogued the variety of ways criminal decision makers do so (Maruna and Copes, 2004). Men and women who embezzle are able to do so in part because they define the act of stealing in ways that enable them to maintain a favorable self-concept (Cressey, 1953; Zietz, 1981). Some define it as borrowing or as fair compensation due them for the long hours they put in without overtime pay. Others see it as something done to provide for their children or significant others that cannot be provided legitimately. Self-defined crises and attractive opportunities figure prominently in the explanations offered up by white-collar criminals, and apparently there is no shortage of either in their lives (Weisburd et al., 1991).

Class differences in cultural capital means that upper-class and middle-class children gain acuity with a larger and more diverse array of neutralizing justifications than less privileged citizens (Hazani, 1991). Computer hackers, who disproportionately are young middle-class males, engage in unending verbal and ideological disputes with state representatives over the harmfulness of their actions (Levi, 2001; Schell, Dodge, and Moutsatsos, 2002). They claim that they act not for personal enrichment but for the betterment of all by dispersing intellectual property and encouraging innovation. Hackers minimize their crimes also by claims that they could do much greater harm if they put their minds to it. By identifying points of system vulnerability, they contend what they do is no different from what security technicians are paid to do. That they might also be compared to trespassers, prowlers, or thieves is a possibility they are unprepared to appreciate.

The linguistic and conversational skills of privileged citizens give them an advantage at construing criminal decisions as legitimate and socially acceptable actions that is denied citizens of more humble circumstance. Where the latter must resort to drugs and the influence of others to overcome the bind of law, white-collar citizens accomplish this readily by using rhetorical devices. That they do so attests not to belief in the moral legitimacy of law but their crucial need to see and be seen as respectable. Perspectives and skills acquired in early generative worlds and reinforced in their occupational lives facilitate this process. They make it possible for respectable citizens to weigh and select criminal options without adopting a criminal identity. When weighing criminal opportunity, white-collar offenders employ rhetorical and linguistic constructions that make it seem acceptable and routine. They can draw from a rich repertoire of excuses and explanations.

White-collar offenders perhaps are more successful than street offenders at getting others to empathize when they explain their misfortune; accusers are portrayed as unjust and the government as obtrusive and inefficient. Some cite the necessity of cheating in order to compete with others who cut corners. Many white-collar offenders claim they committed crime to benefit their employer, which leaves them free to argue also that gains for employers benefit many people. Many draw on professional expertise to argue that overseers do not understand the requirements or realities of their work. In this way, "social controls that serve to check or inhibit deviant motivational patterns are rendered inoperative, and the individual is freed to engage in [crime] without serious damage to his self image" (Sykes and Matza, 1957:667).

Beyond Generative Worlds

The generative worlds of white-collar criminals do not exist in social vacuum. Nor are they immutable and unchanging. Instead, characteristics and dynamics of the larger worlds in which individuals are situated constrain their perceptions, assessments and the odds of resorting to crime. Three aspects may be critical for their effect on the readiness of privileged citizens either to move closer to or away from the breakwaters of the law: fluctuations of the business cycle, the culture of their work organizations and belief that credible oversight is lacking.

Fluctuation in the business cycle has been linked repeatedly to changes in the supply of those predisposed or tempted to commit white-collar crime, chiefly because economic downturns threaten both income and prospects for the future (Baucus, 1994; Clinard and Yeager, 1980; Simpson, 1987). The decades bounding arrival of the millennium witnessed increasing income inequality and "fear of falling" for a growing proportion of the population (Ehrenreich, 1989). The result has been heightened competition and willingness to cut corners ethically (Callahan, 2004). Economic upturns also may increase the number of individuals inclined to weigh criminal options because of widespread belief that "everyone is getting rich." At these times, many believe that it is foolish to hold back or to pass up opportunity. Many who commit white-collar crime do so in their occupational roles, which typically are situated in organizations, and the culture of these organizations repeatedly has been linked to the odds of crime (Baucus, 1994; Vaughan, 1996). Last, ensconced in their peculiar generative worlds, privileged citizens are aware of whether or not and how closely overseers are paying attention to them. Where their attention is hazy in focus and weak in application, the criminogenic consequences of competitiveness, arrogance, and a sense of entitlement increase. Where it is clear and strong, humility and self-restraint are ascendant. State actions alternatively can cause an optimistic or pessimistic assessment of the odds of criminal success and thereby stoke or dampen predispositions to crime.

Acknowledgments

I thank Stephen Cernkovich, Peter Grabosky, Andy Hochstetler, Annette Lareau, and Richard Wright for helpful comments on a draft of this paper.

References

Baucus, Melissa S. (1994) "Pressure, Opportunity and Predisposition: A Multivariate Model of Corporate Illegality." *Journal of Management* 20:699–721.

Behn, Robert D., and Kim Sperduto (1979) "Medical Schools and the 'Entitlement Ethic.'" *Public Interest* 57:48–68.

Benson, Michael L. (2002) *Crime and the Life Course: An Introduction*. Los Angeles: Roxbury.

Benson, Michael L., and Kent R. Kerley (2001) "Life-course theory and white-collar crime." Pp. 121–136 in *Contemporary Issues in Crime and Criminal Justice: Essays in Honor of Gilbert Geis*, Editors Henry N. Pontell and David Shichor. Upper Saddle River, NJ: Prentice Hall.

Benson, Michael L., and Elizabeth Moore (1992). "Are White-Collar and Common Criminals the Same?" *Journal of Research in Crime and Delinquency* 29:251–272.

Bettie, Julie (2003) *Women without Class: Girls, Race, and Identity*. Berkeley: University of California Press.

Bragg, Rick (1997) *All Over But the Shoutin'*. New York: Random House.

Braithwaite, John (1991) "Poverty, Power, and White-Collar Crime: Sutherland and the Paradoxes of Criminological Theory." *Australian and New Zealand Journal of Criminology* 24:40–58.

Brewer, Lynn (2002) *House of Cards: Confessions of an Enron Executive* (with Matthew Scott Hansen). College Station, TX: Virtualbookworm.com Publishing.

Callahan, David (2004) *The Cheating Culture: Why More Americans Are Doing Wrong to Get Ahead*. Orlando, FL: Harvest.

Clinard, Marshall B., and Peter C. Yeager (1980) *Corporate Crime*. New York: Free Press.

Coleman, James W. (1987) "Toward An Integrated Theory of White-Collar Crime." *American Journal of Sociology* 93:406–439.

Colson, Charles W. (1976) *Born Again*. Old Tappan, NJ: Chosen Books.

Cressey, Donald R. (1953) *Other People's Money*. Glencoe, IL: Free Press.

Croall, Hazel (1992) *White-Collar Crime*. Philadelphia: Open University Press.

Croteau, David (1995) *Politics and the Class Divide: Working People and the Middle-Class Left*. Philadelphia: Temple University Press.

Cruver, Brian (2002) *Anatomy of Greed: The Unshredded Truth from an Enron Insider*. New York: Carroll & Graf.

Doocy, Jeffrey H., David Shichor, Dale K. Sechrest, and Gilbert Geis (2001) "Telemarketing Fraud: Who are the Tricksters and What Makes Them Trick?" *Security Journal* 14:7–26.

Dunk, Thomas W. (1991) *It's a Working Man's Town: Male WorkingClass Culture in Northwestern Ontario*. Montreal: McGillQueen's University Press.

Edelhertz, Herbert (1970) *The Nature, Impact and Prosecution of White Collar Crime*. Washington, DC: U.S. Department of Justice, National Institute of Law Enforcement and Criminal Justice.

Ehrenreich, Barbara (1989) *Fear of Falling: The Inner Life of the Middle Class*. New York: Knopf.

Ehrenreich, Barbara (2002) *Nickel and Dimed: On (Not) Getting by in America*. New York: Henry Holt.

Forst, Brian, and William Rhodes (1980) *Sentencing in Eight United States District Courts, 1973*–1978. Ann Arbor, MI: Inter-University Consortium for Political and Social Research.

Hagan, John (1992) "The Poverty of a Classless Criminology." *Criminology* 30:1–20.

Haggard, Merle (1968) "Mama Tried." *Sony/ATV Songs*. Santa Monica, CA: Sony/ATV Tree Publishing.

Halle, David (1984) *America's Working Man*. Chicago: University of Chicago Press.

Hazani, Moshe (1991) "Aligning Vocabulary, Symbols Banks, and Sociocultural Structure." *Journal of Contemporary Ethnography* 20:179–203.

Jesilow, Paul, Henry N. Pontell, and Gilbert Geis (1992) *Prescriptions for Profit—How Doctors Defraud Medicaid*. Berkeley: University of California Press.

Johnson, Jennifer (2002) *Getting By on the Minimum: The Lives of Working-Class Women*. New York: Routledge.

Kohn, Melvin L. (1977) *Class and Conformity: A Study in Values,* Second edition. Chicago: University of Chicago Press.

Langston, Doris (1993) "Who Am I now? The Politics of Class Identity." Pp. 60–73 in *Working-Class Women in the Academy*, Editor Michelle M. Tokarczyk and Elizabeth A. Fay. Amherst: University of Massachusetts Press.

Lareau, Annette (2002) "Invisible Inequality: Social Class and Child Rearing in Black Families and White Families." *American Sociological Review* 67:747–776.

Lareau, Annette (2003) *Unequal Childhoods: Class, Race, and Family Life*. Berkeley: University of California Press.

Lawson, Stephen P. (1992) *Daddy, Why Are You Going to Prison*? Wheaton, IL: Shaw.

Levi, Michael (2001) "'Between the Risk and the Reality Falls the Shadow:' Evidence and Urban Legends in Computer Fraud (with apologies to T.S. Eliot)." Pp. 44–58 in *Crime and the Internet*, Editors David S. Wall. New York: Routledge.

Levine, Dennis B. (1991) *Inside Out: An Insider's Account of Wall Street* (with William Hoffer). New York: G.P. Putnam's Sons.

Lubrano, Alfred (2004) *Limbo: Blue-Collar Roots, White-Collar Dreams*. Hoboken, NJ: John Wiley & Sons.

Maruna, Shadd, and J. Heith Copes (2004) "Excuses, Excuses: What Have We Learned from Five Decades of Neutralization Research?" In *Crime and Justice: A Review of Research,* vol. 32, Editors Michael Tonry. Chicago: University of Chicago Press.

McCourt, Frank (1996) *Angela's Ashes: A Memoir of a Childhood.* London: Harper-Collins.

McLean, Bethany, and Peter Elkind (2004) *The Smartest Guys in the Room: The Amazing Rise and Scandalous Fall of Enron*. New York: Penguin.
Parton, Dolly (1994) *Dolly: My Life and Other Unfinished Business*. New York: HarperCollins.
Rubin, Lillian B. (1976) *Worlds of Pain: Life in the Working-Class Family*. New York: Basic Books.
Rubin, Lillian B. (1994) *Families on the Fault Line*. New York: HarperCollins.
Schell, Bernadette H., John L. Dodge, and Steve S. Moutsatos (2002) *The Hacking of America: Who's Doing It, Why, and How?* Westport, CT: Quorum Books.
Sennett, Richard, and Jonathan Cobb (1972) *The Hidden Injuries of Class*. New York: Alfred A. Knopf.
Shapiro, Susan (1990) "Collaring the Crime, not the Criminal: Reconsidering 'White-Collar Crime'." *American Sociological Review* 55:346–365.
Shipler, David K. (2004). *The Working Poor: Invisible in America*. New York: Alfred A. Knopf.
Shover, Neal, Glenn S. Coffey, and Clinton R. Sanders (2004) "Dialing for Dollars: Opportunities, Justifications and Telemarketing Fraud." *Qualitative Sociology* 27:59–75.
Shover, Neal, and Andy Hochstetler (2005) *Choosing White-Collar Crime*. New York: Cambridge University Press.
Simpson, Sally (1987) "Cycles of Illegality: Antitrust Violations in Corporate America." *Social Forces* 65:943–963.
Spencer, John C. (1965) "White-Collar Crime." Pp. 233–266 in *Criminology in Transition*, Editors Edward Glover, Hermann Mannheim and Emmanuel Miller. London: Tavistock.
Strauss, Murray, A. and Donnelly, Denise A. (1993) "Corporal Punishment of Adolescents by American Parents." *Youth and Society* 24:419–442.
Swartz, Mimi, and Sherron Watkins (2003) *Power Failure: The Inside Story of the Collapse of ENRON*. New York: Doubleday.
Sykes, Gresham M., and David Matza (1957) "Techniques of Neutralization: A Theory of Delinquency." *American Sociological Review* 22:664–670.
Vaughan, Diane (1996) *The Challenger Launch Decision: Risky Technology, Culture, and Deviance at NASA*. Chicago: University of Chicago Press.
Waksal, Sam (2003) "I Was Arrogant." *60 Minutes*. CBS Television. October 2.
Weisburd, David, Stanton Wheeler, Elin Waring, and Nancy Bode (1991) *Crimes of the Middle Classes*. New Haven, CT: Yale University Press.
Wright, Bradley R. Entner, Avshalom Caspi, Terrie E. Moffit, Richard A. Miech, and Phil A. Silva (1999) "Reconsidering the Relationship Between SES and Delinquency: Causation but Not Correlation." *Criminology* 37:175–194.
Zietz, Dorothy (1981) *Women Who Embezzle or Defraud: A Study of Convicted Felons*. New York: Greenwood.

2

Because They Can

Motivations and Intent of White-Collar Criminals

James Gobert and Maurice Punch

Why do high-status, eminently respected business executives and managers, earning handsome salaries and benefits, breach rules, violate the law, and engage in "deviant" behavior?[1] Seemingly this group of violators has no financial "need" to turn to law-breaking. What then is their motivation? How do they justify their actions and how "conscious" are they of offending?

Over a half century ago, Edwin Sutherland,[2] who is generally credited with being the first to identify the field of corporate and white-collar crime as worthy of serious study, asserted that senior executives in reputable companies routinely displayed what amounted to contempt for legal rules. Many of these law-breakers, he added, were "recidivists," who apparently believed that they could act with impunity either because their conduct was not criminal or, if it was, their chances of getting caught were miniscule. The absence of prosecutions no doubt reinforced this belief. Above all, even when their offenses were exposed, the white-collar criminals refused to think of themselves as criminals: "Their consciences do not ordinarily bother them."[3] From a criminal's perspective, white-collar crime approaches the perfect crime: it reaps substantial rewards, there is an excellent chance of getting away with it, and rarely does an offender have to confront the victim or a gruesome crime scene. As a result, the offender usually does not experience any guilt or remorse.

Our aim in this paper is to build on Sutherland's lapidary insights.[4] Recent scandals from the world of business suggest a close and complex relationship between the white-collar criminal and the company under whose guise he or she perpetrates the crime. The company often provides the context, the opportunity, the means, and the incentive for the misconduct.[5] While white-collar crimes are usually committed *for* the organization, the prototypical situation which Sutherland envisaged, they may also be committed *against* the organization. Or the organization may be the vehicle for achieving personal goals and exercising power.

A second point is that the corporate sector is constantly attempting to construct, influence, and control the legal and regulatory environment in which it conducts its business. It lobbies for deregulation and against legislation that would restrict its freedom to operate.[6] It provides financial support to parties, politicians, and candidates who share its philosophy and goals. It constantly contests laws and tries to manipulate regulators. In short, the corporate sector seeks to bring the law into conformity with its aims, rather than the other way around.

Keith Hawkins[7] described regulators as adopting a strategy of "bargain and bluff." One might say that white-collar criminals employ a strategy of "bluff and bargain." They probe the environment for market opportunities created by regulatory weaknesses, and continually and relentlessly attempt to expand the frontiers of the law to and beyond its proper limits. When confronted with resistance or controls, they resort to bluff; when threatened with exposure, they endeavor to bargain their way out of trouble.

Putting the above points together leads to a third point, which relates to the unique opportunities for deviance created by the business environment. Much ordinary crime is of an opportunistic nature, requiring few skills and little planning to carry out, and is indulged in by a substantial segment of the young male population.[8] The opportunities to commit a business crime, on the other hand, are typically confined to a few select persons who are mature, of high status, typically male, and who have risen sufficiently within the corporate hierarchy to be in a position to exploit the unique opportunities provided by their senior level management posts.[9] Only a relatively few "special" people ever are faced with the temptations engendered by the rarified atmosphere of high-level corporate management in a major company with its opportunities for deviance, pressures to perform, inducements, and substantial rewards for success, whether by legal or illegal means.

Our analysis leads us to the issue of motivation: Why do some but by no means all white-collar executives yield to "temptation," by which we refer to the rich opportunities for deviance on offer to those in a position of power and the ever-present seductions to abuse that power? An insight to the answer to this question may have been supplied by President Clinton when, in seeking to explain his affair with Monica Lewinsky, he reflected, "I did [it] for the worst possible reason . . . because I could."[10] While Clinton was obviously not engaged in white-collar criminality, his point about the near-irresistible opportunities that are presented by being in a position of almost absolute authority, combined with the perceived minimal risks of exposure, has resonance for the situation of white-collar criminals. They too may engage in illegal, immoral, deviant, or highly questionable behavior simply "because they can." Like Clinton, they too may have come to believe that they are somehow above the law.

It is never possible to know exactly what goes on inside an individual's mind. The statements which an executive makes after having been accused or convicted of a criminal offense, are after-the-fact rationalizations. Further, these rationalizations may be part of an overall defense strategy, a form of legal posturing designed either to lay the groundwork for a legal defense, or, in the event of a conviction, for a lenient sentence or early parole. On the other hand, post-event statements frequently can be fitted into a "vocabulary of motive,"[11] a set of formulaic responses that run the gamut from denial of responsibility and lack of injury or harm to the victim, to an impugning of the motives of one's accusers and an appeal to higher values and loyalties.[12] All self-serving explanations for personal and group actions have to be regarded with caution, however, and the analyst is inescapably forced into conjecture, assumptions, and interpretations.

The dearth of reliable data is a serious problem for researchers trying to unravel causation, motivation, and justification in the corporate context.

Comparable difficulties do not present themselves when the subject is "street" crime or violent crime. Jack Katz,[13] for instance, has vividly described the "seductions of crime"—a criminal may enjoy the excitement of face-to-face confrontations, actively cultivating a reputation for callousness and aggression, consciously adopting the self-image of an outsider, and deriving pleasure from the "sensuality" of the offense. In contrast, we have little insight into the personal world of the smartly dressed, well-spoken, and highly educated corporate executive who turns to crime. These individuals are not outsiders but rather quintessential insiders. They are seemingly "winners" at the other end of the social spectrum from the "losers" who commit street crimes. Yet one might ask whether, like the rogues in Katz's gallery, the executives who break the law experience the same excitement, and adrenalin "rush" that come from performing a deviant act. More likely, the white-collar criminal's satisfaction is derived from the creative manipulation of the legal system rather than imposing one's will on another through the exercise of brute force. The white-collar criminals pride comes from identifying and exploiting loopholes in the law, outwitting law enforcement personnel, and massaging regulatory systems to their and their company's financial advantage. In contrast to street criminals, who may boast of their triumphs, white-collar criminals are more likely to maintain a discreet silence regarding their exploits. Thus, not only is white-collar crime less likely to come to light,[14] but also white-collar criminals are less likely to reflect publicly on their offenses:

> [W]hite-collar criminals, perhaps from shame or because the ties to those whom they would have to incriminate are so intimate a part of their own identities that they can *never* be broken, rarely publicly confess; when they do confess, they virtually never confess with the sustained attention to detail that characterizes, for example, almost any mugging related by an ordinary, semi-literate hustler.[15]

Problems of access and funding, and the persistent and widespread neglect of this area by academics,[16] mean that one has to enter a blackhole of surmise, speculation, rationalization, doublespeak, obfuscation, and mendacious dramaturgy to discover the roots of white-collar crime.

Inevitably we are left to speculate about cause, motive, and intent. Yet such speculation is problematic because multiple variables at different levels can contribute to the decision to break the law or to engage in conduct that is subsequently held to be illegal. The critical point may occur at a strategic level (involving management boards or even segments of an entire industry), at a tactical level within a specific part of the organization, or as an opportunistic response to a set of highly specific circumstances. And in all this there is the further issue of intent and consciousness of wrongdoing. To explore this area we have decided to examine a select number of cases within three main categories:

- where the behavior is deliberate and fully conscious and there is an awareness of its being "wrong" and/or illegal;
- where the behavior is consciously planned but where the outcome is not intended and where some mechanism operates which "hides" the illegal dimensions of the behavior for those involved; and
- where the contextual ambiguities in the law encourage would-be offenders to believe (or be able to rationalize to themselves) that they are not engaged in unlawful behavior.

The categories, motives, and mental processes at work are not discrete and there is an inevitable overlap, but the illustrations have been chosen because they are broadly representative of the three typologies.

I. White-Collar Crime Committed with an Ostensible Awareness of the Criminal Implications

Deliberate and "Fully Conscious" Behavior

In this section we focus on decisions by white-collar criminals which are taken deliberately and consciously, with an awareness of their illegality. We examine four variations: (1) where the participants come to view deviant practices and polices as the normal way of doing business and begin to overlook the fact that what they are doing is illegal; (2) where there is antipathy to rules and regulators; (3) where executives, with criminal intent, have "looted" their own companies; and (4) where ostensibly the "best and brightest" managers have engaged in high-level manipulations leading to severe consequences not only for natural persons but also for the abstract entity commonly referred to as "the market."

League of Gentlemen: Business Crimes as "SOP" (Standard Operating Procedure)

An early and frequently cited study is that of the Heavy Electrical Equipment Antitrust cases.[17] This research, like that of Sutherland, revealed how complex, deliberate, and sophisticated white-collar crime can be. Antitrust violations typically involve strategic conspiracies within industries to evade legislation and to control the market. These conspiracies are carefully constructed and often elaborately concealed. Included within the scope of the conspiratorial activities may be cartel-forming, price-fixing, secret agreements on kick-backs, and covert deals on bid-rigging. Market conditions and the characteristics of the industry shape contexts in which companies such as in the pharmaceutical or construction industries, rig the bidding on contracts, bribe regulators, and arrange secret deals with professed competitors. Such offenses are deliberate and involve a conscious decision to break the law. However, to the participants they may be seen as "the most rational and cost-effective strategy for securing elusive resources."[18]

As Gilbert Geis[19] pointed out, those involved in the Heavy Electrical Equipment cases regarded price-fixing as an instrumental means of addressing a business problem. Ostensible competitors met and collectively reached agreements on prices. These clandestine meetings and agreements became routine to the extent that managers began to believe that they were standard industry practice: "[I]t had become so common and gone on for so many years that I think we lost sight of the fact that it was illegal."[20] When exposed, the participants were probably genuinely shocked to be treated as "criminals" and to receive custodial sentences. At a subconscious level, they probably were aware that what they were doing was "wrong" but they masked their deviance behind a battery of rationalizations and justifications—everyone was doing it, nobody was really "harmed," it was part of their job and, invoking higher loyalties, they were acting in the best interests of their company and not for personal gain.

These rationalizations served to divest their illegal practices of any "criminal" element.

Of course these excuses were disingenuous: there were duped consumers who did not receive the beneficial prices of a frcc and competitive market and disadvantaged companies which were not included in the conspiracy. And, while the participants in the Heavy Electrical Equipment and other cases may not have profited directly, they may well have been rewarded indirectly through bonuses and promotions for their company's success and/or for their "loyalty" to the company. The judge in this case described the defendants as "company men," conformists who go along with their superiors and "find balm for their consciences in the additional comforts and security of their place in the corporate organization."[21]

Although the white-collar conspirators in the antitrust cases were guilty of violating external rules, viewed from their perspective their actions were a rational and functional response to market conditions within their industry. Their personal motives were almost certainly mixed and their justifications essentially denied illegality and harm. When their activities were exposed, they forcefully rejected the criminal label "Illegal? Yes, but not criminal."[22]

Price-fixing had become a routine way of conducting business; in other words, *standard operating procedure*. Senior managers viewed establishing illegal arrangements as part of their job, performed ostensibly "on behalf of" their company, with no sense of engaging in criminal activity although they were clearly and deliberately breaking the law.

Condemning the Condemners: The Van der Valks Take on the Regulators

Conservative lawyers, economists, journalists, and politicians are ideologically opposed to the regulation of business and have a particular abhorrence for using the criminal law to control corporate practices which they believe are better regulated by the free market. There is also a category of business entrepreneurs who not only want minimum regulation with maximum freedom, as does most of the corporate sector, but who actively resent rules, hold regulators in contempt, and openly and brazenly flout the law. The Van der Valk case in the Netherlands illustrates the type of offender that we have in mind.

The Van der Valks operated a highly successful, family-run business in the hotel and restaurant sector.[23] The family's outlets were renowned for friendly service, low prices, and large helpings of food. They were popular and profitable, and the family was a household name. However, the Van der Valks also regularly violated employment laws, failed to register personnel (often illegal immigrants), and did not pay various taxes. They covered up their improprieties by maintaining poor, sloppy, or nonexistent records.

When challenged by the tax authorities, the Van der Valks adopted a confrontational and highly adversarial stance. As in many other countries, the tax authorities in the Netherlands favor compliance strategies aimed at recouping lost revenues through negotiated settlements. They are reluctant to go to court, except as a last resort or in the face of persistent recalcitrance. Unfortunately for them, the Van der Valks long record of rule-breaking, inadequate record-keeping, and general maladministration, coupled with their defiance and policy of vigorously contesting tax claims, made a courtroom confrontation virtually inevitable. By the time the cases reached the courts the amount involved was around $100 million.

Despite the seriousness of the charges, the Van der Valks' defiance of the tax authorities did not abate when they were faced with the prospect of a criminal trial. Their defense was that legal rules were little more than a nuisance that should not be applied to successful entrepreneurs like themselves, and that the regulators were pathetic bureaucrats who deserved to be treated with contempt.[24] Behind this cavalier attitude lay the family's power and their knowledge that any locality chosen for one of their hotels or restaurants would welcome the employment opportunities provided and the custom brought to the area. Weaving their way through a maze of rules, regulations, licenses, controls, and auditing requirements, the Van der Valks were able to find authorities willing, in implicit if not explicit agreement, to collude with them. Over a number of years the family was able continually and successfully to ignore rules designed to apply to all, with the result that law-breaking had become a profitable way of conducting their business.[25]

The goal of the Van der Valks was ostensibly power, status, and profit. No doubt they also aimed to maximize their profits by not fully declaring and paying taxes. But underlying their misconduct appeared to be a genuine and deep disdain for legal rules and an open contempt for those who tried to enforce them. When attacked, the Van der Valks counter-attacked. They compared the behavior of the tax authorities toward them to that of the Nazi occupiers during the Second World War, branding their accusers as "blackmailers and extortionists," who used arrest and interrogation methods associated with the Nazis in the war. This may well have touched a sensitive public nerve. After they were convicted and given custodial sentences, there was such a public outcry that an appeal court substituted suspended sentences and community service for the custodial sentences. This popular support for their stance and case served to enhance the Van der Valks reputation as folk-heroes. Ordinary people identified with their defiance of the tax authorities.

In "condemning the condemners" the implicit and not so subtle message of the Van der Valks was that "real" businessmen should be allowed to make money with as little hindrance from the state as possible: "Do people want to destroy a healthy company? Crime in the Netherlands is rising at a disturbing pace. Isn't it better that they [the government] spend their time on tackling that rather than on people who with hard work have built up a healthy business?"[26] Among the points made by the Van der Valks' in their counter-attack against the authorities was that they already paid considerable taxes, that they had created many jobs, and that their helping young people from abroad to earn a living, albeit illegally, was a form of "social work" ("you have to be really tough if you are going to drive someone away who is hungry"[27]). Their attack, however, was almost scattergun, with their emotive barbs being aimed at the government, the unions, the tax authorities, fiscal investigators, and the judiciary. Yet some authorities and regulators apparently covertly agreed with them to the extent of condoning their rule-bending and colluding in their law-breaking, while the public, for its part, regarded them as heroes rather than villains.

As we noted earlier, the corporate sector often vigorously contests the law, lobbies against legislation, and sponsors politicians and parties whom it regards as sympathetic and who it believes will support laws and regulatory regimes favorable to them. In short, corporations seek to shape the political, economic, and regulatory environment in which they operate. But all this goes on within a traditional and accepted political framework. The Van der Valks, by challenging and impugning all who stood in their way, took their campaign to a different level. They ignored the rules of "the game," libeled their accusers, and employed a wide-ranging repertoire of specious rationalizations for ways of doing business which were blatantly illegal, all the while strenuously rcjccting the criminal label. In essence they were saying that, because there were no victims, and because everyone from their employees to their customers to the community in which their businesses were located gained in some way, then their failure to pay taxes was not a "real" offense.

What set the Van der Valks apart from other white-collar criminals was the fact that, when their illegality came to light, they did not deny it, but rather seemed to take pride in it. Doubtless many executives and directors in large companies share their views but, for tactical reasons, tend to be more restrained in their public utterances. Self-made entrepreneurs like the Van der Valks, owners of small family firms, and independent professional groups may be more inclined to be vocally combative, exploiting the media, conveying contempt for regulators and officials, and showing little deference to the authorities. In response to being accused by the prosecution of being a member of a "criminal organization," one of the family was not afraid to retort "if running a business, managing to survive and working hard is criminal; then yes, we are criminals."[28]

Opportunistic and Predatory Deviance: The Savings and Loan Scandals

There are many cases where the opportunity to make money quickly and illicitly is created unwittingly by laws or government policies. The savings and loan (S&L) scandal in the United States, which wound up costing the American taxpayer billions of dollars, was a case in point. Originally allowed to take deposits and offer loans and low interest mortgages, the S&Ls, or "thrifts," were restricted in their financial practices by federal regulation. For a number of reasons, however, the thrifts found themselves in considerable difficulties by the 1970s. Following his election, President Reagan lifted existing controls, thereby allowing the thrifts to offer more services and compete with the commercial banks.

This exercise in deregulation sparked a virtual crime wave within the S&L industry. Calavita and Pontell[29] documented a wide range of conduct which they characterized as "looting" or "collective embezzlement". Many of the thrifts were brought down by "deliberately high-risk strategies, poor business judgments, foolish strategies, excessive optimism, and sloppy and careless underwriting."[30] Others were waylaid by actions which bordered more on the criminal: legally dubious real estate transactions, personal enrichment through exorbitant salaries and bonuses, excessive fees to "consultants," jobs for family members, trading on inside information, and setting up a shield of front companies through which to make loans to themselves. In essence, institutional funds were siphoned off for personal gain at the expense of the institution itself, typically with the implicit or explicit sanction of the company's management.

What distinguished the S&L cases from, for example, the improprieties of the Van der Valks and others was that the offenders were not committing crime *for* the benefit of their company, one of the major themes in the literature since Sutherland; these crimes were committed *against* the company. In other words, the **company was the victim**.

There was another significant feature that may have contributed to the white-collar offenses in question. Individual deposits in S&Ls were insured by the government against losses up to $100,000. This insurance may have allowed the S&L looters to rationalize their misconduct on the ground that ordinary savers were not being harmed. When the thrifts failed, the government as insurer had to pay the bill. Thus, the unintended consequence of an arguably enlightened government social policy was to create a criminogenic market that provided tempting, if not irresistible, opportunities. In the highly significant words of one consultant:

> "If you didn't do it, you weren't just stupid—you weren't behaving as a prudent businessman, which is the ground rule. You owed it to your partners, to your stockholders, to maximize profits. Everybody else was doing it."[31]

Unscrupulous individuals, some with criminal connections, flocked as a rat-pack to the S&Ls in order to fleece them through premeditated, organized, and systemic fraudulent conduct and falsification. The motivation was, of course, "greed," but greed here was stimulated by deregulation, protected deposits, weak controls, and changing market conditions. Illegality was justified by business rationality. Stripped bare, the white-collar criminals displayed the predatory rapaciousness usually associated with organized criminals: there was "easy money" to be made and, as suggested above, you were considered foolish, and even a poor business-person, if you did not avail yourself of the opportunities presented. As Calavita and Pontell[32] tellingly observed, "if you put temptation and the opportunity, and the need in the same place, you are asking for trouble."

Mega-Fraud at the Top

Sutherland had characterized white-collar and corporate crime as primarily "clean-hands" crime committed for the benefit of the company. His thinking was reflected in much of the early work conducted by criminologists who followed in his footsteps, including Geis, Marshell Clinard, and Clinard and Peter Yeager. In recent years, however, additional types of business-related misconduct have come to light which have served to alter both academic and public perceptions of the nature of corporate and white-collar crime. As discussed above, there was the identification by Calavita, Pontell, and their colleagues of a form of "looting," or collective embezzlement, where managers committed crimes not for the company but in a predatory fashion with the company as victim. Second, there has been an increased appreciation that deaths and serious injuries at work, often dismissed in the past as unfortunate "accidents," may in fact be attributable to reckless and grossly negligent decisions by those in a position of corporate power.[33] These cases of "*corporate violence*" will be discussed in a subsequent section of this chapter.

A new addition to the litany of corporate and white-collar offenses is required to take account of recent scandals where mega-frauds have shaken the very foundations of the capitalist system. As Alan Greenspan put it,

> An infectious greed seemed to grip much of our business community.... It is not that humans have become any more greedy than in generations past. It is that the avenues to express greed have grown so enormously."[34]

The high-level frauds perpetrated by top executives in various leading American-based firms in the "new economy"—Enron, WorldCom, and Tyco—created thousands of victims through unemployment and loss of life pensions.

On a broader and deeper level, the aftershocks included a serious diminution of confidence in the markets.

The frauds in question were perpetrated at the highest levels of management in companies previously regarded as exemplary.[35] Not only was there a failure of corporate governance but also of supposedly neutral audits and accountants' reports. These "objective" criteria, which are relied upon by investors in making decisions to purchase shares of companies, had been deliberately distorted by accountants and auditors who had colluded in covering up the deviance of the firms which had hired them to validate their books. Prospective investors were left to wonder whether other companies with far lesser reputations were engaged in comparable deception. The financial reports of the top accounting firms came under suspicion.

Most of the firms where this meltdown occurred appeared to have been flourishing at the time of their collapse. At Enron, for example, objective performance indicators soared, the company was the recipient of "company of the year" awards, and its executives were lauded in financial publications. Corporate directors were handsomely rewarded for the company's apparent success.

A key factor in judging corporate success must be that it is real, transparent, and verifiable. In typical cases of fraud, the fraudster tries to deceive others (usually regulators, government officials, and the firm's clients). At Enron outside analysts and the exchanges were deceived, but the deception also seems to have extended to the company's directors. Apart from a few persons at the highest level, and a smattering of suspicious employees whose warnings were ignored or disparaged, nobody seemed to appreciate in just how critical shape were Enron's finances.

Cases of mega-fraud are not confined to the United States. Since Enron, Worldcom, and Tyco, there have been comparable scandals uncovered in Europe. With respect to both AHOLD in the Netherlands and Parmalat in Italy, vast sums of money were suddenly found "missing" from the books.[36] In these cases, as in their American counterparts, management continued to function as if nothing was amiss. Were the CEO and other executives deceiving themselves as well? Or did they think that the shortfall was temporary and that they could right the ship whenever they wanted? The offenders appeared to believe that, no matter how many funds were diverted for their personal self-enrichment, a high level of corporate performance could be sustained. The possibility of exposure seems not to have been considered or, if it was, dismissed. The perpetrators displayed an apparently unshakeable confidence in their ability to continue to mislead the outside world and an undue faith in ostensibly objective figures which they believed were unlikely to be challenged, even by auditors. The consequences were a systemic failure on a grand scale where internal and external weaknesses in governance and control combined to threaten the very stability of the capitalist system.

Confidence and trust in business are underpinned by an effective system of checks and balances. The executives at Enron and elsewhere risked not only destroying themselves but also the very infrastructure upon which they and others were dependent to conduct their business affairs. Financial markets rely on accurate information. If the aim of most white-collar crimes is some form of financial gain, utilizing existing market structures, then it has to be recognized that the conduct of the mega-fraudsters threatened the structures and systems that they needed to make their offenses possible. There were many individual victims in these cases, but, at an institutional and systemic level, one has to include among the victims the "market," as well as public confidence in the ability of the capitalist system to regulate itself.[37]

II. White-Collar Crime Committed with an Ostensible Unawareness of the Criminal Implications: Filters, Blindness, and Pathology

In this section we focus on cases where the participants either did not intend or were not fully aware of the illegal dimensions and harmful consequences of their deviant conduct. One of the common characteristics of the descent into white-collar crime is that it conforms to the "slippery slope" metaphor. Relatively minor violations of rules escalate into serious law-breaking. At first, the deviance may cause significant moral hand-wringing, but over time it becomes progressively easier to rationalize and to neutralize, and the offense become that much easier to commit. Each step in the progression can be viewed as a stage in a deviant or criminal career (with "career" standing for a phased process into deviance over time[38]).

An excellent example of the slippery slope metaphor is provided by Nick Leeson of Barings Bank. We can get some inkling of his mindset during his deviant "career" as he has given a number of interviews, while a book and film also purport to present his story (*Rogue Trader*[39]). It would be incorrect, however, to view Leeson's case as simply that of an individual who has gone wrong. One needs also to appreciate the critical role played in his downfall by a broad range of environmental and situational factors, including glaring errors of judgment on the part of white-collar executives within Barings Bank.[40]

Cases involving deaths and serious injuries, either to employees or members of the public, present the consequences of white-collar crime in its most stark form. These cases often arise from a failure by management to consider the potential harmful consequences of ill-advised and sometimes criminally negligent policies. In this section we examine two cases of corporate violence. One involved a small transport company, where a fatal traffic "accident" was stimulated by poor management practices that encouraged dangerous, unlawful, and eventually fatal, risk-taking. The other case involved a major train company where the fatal decisions were made at a level far removed from the fatal "accident."

Lone Trader: Sliding Down the Slippery Slope at Barings

In the 1990s, Barings, a major merchant bank in London, sought to expand its operations into the booming Asian economy by establishing a strong presence in the futures and derivatives markets of Singapore and Japan. Nick Leeson, a young, inexperienced employee, who had been denied a trader's license in England, was dispatched by Barings to Singapore. The Singapore office was far removed from London not only geographically but also culturally. It was staffed by young, ambitious traders operating in an environment where large "positions" were regularly taken on volatile markets, where hospitality for clients was extravagant, where the life-style was opulent, and where the rewards for success seemed unlimited.[41] In this environment Leeson thrived, steadily assuming a leading role as a result of his daring on the exchange floor. Over time he came to enjoy an almost unchallengeable status, and brought in a large amount of business—which translated into huge bonuses not only for him and for his colleagues in Singapore but also, and equally important, for Barings executives in London. In short, Leeson had become a "major player" on the markets and an indispensable asset at Barings.

When an earthquake hit Kobe in Japan in 1995, Japanese stock prices fell. Previously, Leeson had Barings committed to the Japanese stock market's rising. Rather than taking offsetting positions on another exchange, as would a prudent trader, Leeson chose to gamble everything on the Japanese exchange rising. He assumed that the Japanese government would heavily invest in the rebuilding of Kobe. But for a number of reasons this rise did not materialize and Leeson found himself "overexposed." In a desperate attempt to force the market up on his own—a highly dubious strategy—he kept taking even more extreme "positions." In order to support these positions, he was forced to request large infusions of funds from Barings in London. The money was sent with few questions and little or no objection.[42]

The losses, which Leeson concealed in an "error account," continued to mount and he became increasingly desperate. Eventually, and in hindsight unbelievably, Leeson reached a point where he had committed more funds than were contained in the bank's reserves. At the point when his losses amounted to some $780 million and this became apparent in London, the Bank of England stepped in. Barings was forced to close and was declared bankrupt.

Seeing the impending crisis, Leeson left Singapore, attempting to return to Britain. On a stopover at Frankfurt, however, he was detained by the police and subsequently extradited to Singapore. In a German prison he gave an interview to David Frost in which he made illuminating comments about his motivations and the justifications for his actions.

- Leeson claimed that his first "deviant" step in Singapore involved a transaction of a mere £20,000, and was made to help a young, inexperienced employee (Leeson's description) who had made a minor error. In order to hide her mistake, Leeson had opened the "error account" (where mistakes could be temporarily "parked" until they could be later rectified). In the error account Leeson began to hide his own unsuccessful transactions.
- While Leeson maintained that his first entry on the error account had given him "sleepless nights," he also stated that, when the amount in the error account reached £40,000, it was easier for him to accept than the initial "error" of £20,000. Similarly, as the amount in the error account increased, it became progressively easier for Leeson to accept the nature of his actions—at least until the amount in the error account reached nearly £800 million and he was facing exposure.
- Leeson explained that, because he often dealt with huge amounts of money on a daily basis, the enormous sums involved ceased to be "real money" to him and were more akin to "monopoly money." It was as if he were playing a "game."
- Listening to Leeson, Frost commented that he sounded like a gambler. Leeson replied that was essentially the nature of his job—to gamble. Like a desperate gambler, Leeson had attempted to recoup his losses by taking increasingly large and questionable positions. Much as a gambler faced with debilitating

losses may double up his bets to recoup his losses in a single stroke, so too did Leeson dramatically increase the size of his positions in order to regain equilibrium. While conventional wisdom in dealing rooms cautions that one should never "take on" a market on one's own, that is precisely what Leeson tried to do.

- As Leeson slid down the slippery slope of his own making, it was apparent that he became less and less concerned not only with the amounts involved but also with the consequences for Barings. He seemed unable to face up to the immense risks he was taking and appeared immune to the fact that he was putting the entire enterprise and several thousand jobs in jeopardy.
- Throughout all of his interviews, Leeson insisted that he was not a "criminal."

The spectacular collapse of Barings is noteworthy for at least three reasons. First, it provides one of the most graphic examples of the *slippery slope* process at work in a business context. The metaphor assumes that once a person is on a slippery slope he or she will continue to "slide" down it until a psychological point of no return is reached. Obviously the metaphor does not hold true in all cases, and some individuals realize that they are "throwing good money after bad," and are able to quit. But for others hope seems to spring eternal. Leeson has been quite explicit about the manner by which he became more and more enmeshed in his web of deceit and deviance, and how he was able to rationalize his actions to himself. While one can never be totally sure what really went through Leeson's mind, he comes across as a person who lost all control of events, who engaged in self-deception, and who tried, ultimately unsuccessfully, to insulate himself from the consequences of his actions by fraud and bravado.

Second, it can be seen in retrospect that Barings management, whether deliberately or unwittingly, created the opportunity and provided the means and incentives for Leeson's transgressions. Not only did the bank send an inexperienced and unqualified trader to a difficult situation in Singapore, it also failed to supervise him adequately or audit his transactions. This lack of control allowed Leeson to assume a dominant position on the dealing room floor. Further, management's award of extravagant bonuses based on "results" encouraged high-risk business decisions in a field where fiscal responsibility is essential. Nor did it appear that the London management of Barings fully comprehended the nature of recent developments in investment banking (in particular, in the area of futures, derivatives, and arbitrage). Finally, and fatally, Barings management ignored or failed to see the warning signs, continuing to send additional funds to Leeson without seriously questioning why he might need the money.[43] It is indeed remarkable how top officials of a prestigious London bank could display so acute a lack of professionalism. In effect, the individual and the organizational were inextricably linked and Leeson and Barings slid down the slippery slope together, one to a Singapore prison and the other to bankruptcy.

Third, it is instructive to compare the Barings fiasco with the antitrust conspiracies that we examined previously. In the latter the participants had a conscious and covert strategy. They established alliances, negotiated agreements, employed secret codes, disguised the purpose of their meetings, camouflaged expenses, kept the conspiracy going for years, and adjusted their arrangements to changing market conditions. An antitrust conspiracy provides a pre-eminent example of a planned and deliberate white-collar crime where the people and processes are under control at all times. In contrast, Barings represents one of those cases where there seemed to be no overall strategy, where persons of questionable competence were making the key decisions, where one hand of the operation (Barings management) did not know what the other hand (Leeson in Singapore) was doing, where the principals reacted to events rather than thinking through the implications and consequences, and where nobody seemed to be in charge. Indeed, in the Barings fiasco, everything and everybody seemed out of control.

Eyes Wide Shut: The "Split Personality" Company

In the cases discussed so far there may well have been multiple victims and considerable financial harm done, but noone died as a direct result of the offenses, although perhaps there may have been some related suicides. When deaths and serious injuries to innocent victims occur, the risks created by managerial and corporate irresponsibility are exposed in their most stark form.

In the Roy Bowles case two deaths resulted from a road traffic accident on the M25 London ring-road.[44] A truck being driven erratically smashed into the rear of another truck, which then hit a car. Both the driver of the second truck and of the car were killed. The police investigation revealed that the original driver not only had been exceeding the speed limit at the time of the crash, but also was near to exhaustion. When the police looked more closely at the case, they discovered that the "odometer" (which records the driver's hours of driving) in the truck's cab had been tampered with to under-represent his time on the road. It further emerged that the employer, the Roy Bowles Transport Company, systematically encouraged and rewarded its drivers for productivity that could realistically be achieved only by exceeding speed limits and falsifying data on the odometers. Managers were in effect sending out trucks with drivers whom they knew were dangerously overtired.

The Roy Bowles Transport Company was relatively small and management was able to stay close to the primary activity. On the surface the company had an impressive record for complying with the law: it routinely passed regulatory inspections; and it possessed all the requisite quality certificates. Its principal officer had been awarded an OBE and was chairman of the local magistrates' court. Yet, at another level, "respectable" and compliant managers had engaged in systematic and deliberate rule-breaking that entailed an obvious risk of death for drivers, pedestrians, and other road users. What accounted for such unwarranted risk taking?

It appears that the decision-makers were able to dissociate their decisions from their possible consequences. It was as if the managers existed in a encapsulated world in which they were able to filter out the risks they were creating. This psychological defense mechanism allowed them to blind themselves to the dangers that they had generated. Effectively, the company had a "split personality" which enabled participants to function at two levels: one level involved dutiful compliance with legal requirements and the other was an "operational code"[45] which endangered life on a daily basis.

The theory of "cognitive dissonance"[46] posits that evidence that contradicts what one wants to believe is ignored, discounted, or rationalized to lessen the dissonance between what an actor wishes to do and the foreseeable consequences of his actions. This theory may help to explain the thinking of the Roy Bowles managers. A similar example of denial and cognitive dissonance occurred in respect to the thalidomide scandal.[47] Here, when an ostensibly harmless sedative taken by pregnant women led to reports of severely deformed children, the German manufacturer ignored the evidence of the serious side effects of the drug. Instead, it redoubled its marketing and production efforts and sought to discredit its critics.

It is not uncommon for "ordinary" criminal activity to be conducted with a measure of blindness to the consequences. The significance of the Roy Bowles case is that it is inconceivable that the managers were not aware of the risks they were taking. The dangers of driving when overtired are common knowledge within the transport industry and even among the general public. Yet the managers allowed themselves to remain "willfully blind" to the consequences of their decisions. They compartmentalized their thinking to the point where they became comfortable in sending overtired drivers on to the roadways. It seems perfectly clear that none of the company's officials or its drivers *intended* to kill, but in retrospect it seems equally clear that such a result was virtually inevitable.

The business pressures that gave rise to the Roy Bowles case are not unique to the transport industry, although they arise frequently in industries, like transport, which are highly competitive with low profit margins. In other industries too one can discern demands for enhanced profits by any means. Shortcuts involving non-compliance with the law are often abetted by the fact that the agencies responsible for regulating the industry are inadequately financed, under-staffed, and reluctant as a matter of policy to confront transgressors or to take them to court.[48] Those responsible for setting regulatory policies and the government departments which establish the agency's budget, although far removed from the crime scene, can thus be seen to be complicit in the commission of the offenses, a point that we will develop further in the next section.

When Corporate Strategy Kills: Great Western Railways and the Southall Train Crash

Some industries work routinely with risk and this is particularly true of transport—by road, air, sea, and rail. Safety is an ever-present concern, but safety is related to factors such as quality of management, the allocation of resources, government policies, and regulatory regimes. It is unimaginable that any manager of an airline, railroad, or ferry would intentionally take decisions that the manager knew would lead to fatal consequences or serious injury. On the other hand, as we saw in the Roy Bowles case, managers may deliberately engage in risk-taking behavior that can lead to death. This phenomenon can also be seen in a number of significant cases of "corporate violence" such as the dangerous placement of the gas tank of Ford Pintos, the capsize of the Herald of Free Enterprise, and the mass deaths at Bhopal.[49]

In contrast to a small trucking company such as Roy Bowles Transport, those who make the critical decisions relating to railroads may be far removed from operational levels and any fatal "accident" that might occur. Rarely is a director or senior officer present at the "scene of the crime" or likely to have to met the victims face-to-face, although families of victims are now becoming more assertive in confronting corporate executives believed to be responsible for the death of their loved ones. Yet the "accident" may be traceable to ill-advised and criminally negligent policy decisions taken at boardroom level. In some instances the relevant decisions are made by the industry as a whole. These decisions help shape the culture of the industry and of individual companies. In turn, this culture may encourage risk-taking that ultimately leads to deaths and disaster. The Southall crash illustrates the dangers.

At the time of the crash, the rail industry in Britain had been through a period of deregulation. What had previously been a state monopoly was fragmented and converted into a large number of private operating companies. Critics of deregulation maintained that this process both stimulated an emphasis on short-term profitability and a lack of investment in infrastructure and safety. The effects could be seen, they claimed, in the number of serious rail crashes with considerable casualties that occurred in Britain over the previous two decades.[50] One of those crashes took place at Southall, just outside of London.

The circumstances surrounding the crash were as follows. An express train at Swansea was preparing for its return journey to London. Standard on all trains in Britain is an Automatic Warning System (AWS) which alerts the driver if the train proceeds through a red warning light; the driver then has to intervene actively to respond to the situation. In contrast, in a number of continental European states trains are equipped with Automatic Train Protection (ATP), a system designed to stop a train automatically without driver intervention if it should pass a red light. Although the Southall train had been fitted with ATP on an experimental basis, the system had been disengaged, apparently because management had lost confidence in it. When the driver of the Southall train went to the original rear of the train for the return journey to London, he discovered that the AWS was at the wrong end of the train. He requested the station management to switch the locomotive at the rear to the front so that he could return with AWS. However, local management declined, apparently out of a concern that the time required to turn the train around would cause undue delay and lead to the company's incurring a possible penalty for a late arrival.

The driver on the London-bound train was alone in the cab and had never driven without AWS. On the return journey the train passed two warning lights and a red light. It then crashed into a freight train. Seven persons were killed and numerous others seriously injured. If the locomotive with AWS had been switched to the front, if ATP had been mandated in Britain, or if there had been a second driver assigned to the cab, then the accident would almost certainly not have happened.

Three elements arguably combined to produce the fatal crash. First was the decision of station management at Swansea not to turn the train around or to switch the locomotives. This decision reflected a not uncommon pattern in transport and other industries where a fixation on keeping to tight, self-established schedules is allowed to take priority over safety.[51] The government may have contributed to this prioritization by its practice of publishing "league tables" in which rail companies are ranked based on their "efficiency" in arriving on time and penalties are imposed for late arrivals.

A second, and crucial, factor in the crash was the decision taken by senior management to allow drivers to proceed in some instances without a functioning AWS and without a back-up driver. Not mandating that there be a second driver in the cab seems a misguided attempt to economize which ignored the existing research on human concentration levels and the possibility of human error. Allowing trains to proceed without a functioning AWS seems to be born of a willful blindness to the possibility of an accident similar to that which we encountered in the Roy Bowles case. Senior management can also be faulted for prematurely giving up on ATP, which was being tried out on an experimental basis. While directors blamed the technology, which appeared to work well on the Continent, critics noted that the company did not adequately train its drivers in the use of ATP and appeared reluctant to invest the time and money needed to iron out any problems with the system.

The third and final element contributing to the crash was the fact that the driver was almost certainly negligent. In reporting the accident—he survived the crash and alerted management by phone—he tearfully admitted that he had been "packing his bags" at the time of the crash. While it might seem that the most immediate cause of the crash was driver error—and, indeed, this was the conclusion reached by a subsequent public inquiry[52] —it must be recognized that human error is eminently foreseeable. As the Law Commission, the body charged by statute with making recommendations for law reform in England and Wales, stated in bringing forward its proposal for a law of corporate killing:

> If a company chooses to organize its operations as if all its employees were paragons of efficiency and prudence, and they are not, the company is at fault; if an employee then displays human fallibility, and death results, the company cannot be permitted to deny responsibility for the death on the ground that the employee was to blame. The company's fault lies in its failure to anticipate the foreseeable negligence of its employee, and any consequence of such negligence should therefore be treated as a consequence of the company's fault.[53]

The Southall crash led to a prosecution for manslaughter against both the driver of the Southall train and GWR. The Crown Prosecution Service's case against GWR failed in court because of the difficulty of linking the crash to decisions taken in the GWR boardroom. Under the law at the time, a company could only be convicted of an offense that had been committed by an officer or senior manager of a company—somebody who was part of its "directing mind and will."[54] Obviously neither the driver nor the middle-level managers at Swansea qualified. The strategic decisions taken in the boardroom were made by directors and officers who would qualify but these decisions were too far removed both in time and space from the crime scene to be identified as the cause of the crash. As a result, it could not be proved that any corporate executive in GWR had committed manslaughter. Consequently, neither the directors nor, derivatively, their company could be convicted of that crime. When the case against the company failed, it no doubt must have been thought to be too much like scapegoating to continue with the prosecution against the driver and this prosecution too was dropped.[55] As in the earlier trial stemming from the capsizing of the *Herald of Free Enterprise*, the upshot was that noone was convicted despite a major disaster where corporate fault had been identified in a public inquiry as a cause of the disaster.[56] Little wonder that families of the victims of a series of disasters were left with a deep sense that justice had not been done.

What can be learned from the Southall crash, apart from the obvious desirability of ATP? One lesson relates to the importance of corporate culture. Great Western Railway was not alone in declining to adopt ATP on its trains. The *entire*

British rail industry had rejected ATP on the grounds of its cost, even though it was presumably aware that this decision might cause unnecessary loss of life. The industry also persuaded the government not to make ATP mandatory. It was not that the industry was disregarding passenger safety completely; rather, safety simply no longer was given the same priority as it had received when the railroads were nationalized. Post-deregulation, the balance between safety and profitability shifted in favor of the latter. And, in a deregulated industry, the government was no longer in a good position to intervene. The resulting culture fostered an operational climate in which, at GWR, lower level functionaries felt pressured not to cause delays and to place adherence to schedules above passenger safety.

Yet another effect of deregulation was to lead to the recruitment of directors from other industries with little or no knowledge of the railways, no engineering background, and no appreciation of the operational dangers faced by train drivers on a daily basis. The primary focus of such directors tends to be on a return on investment, not surprising in light of the fact that they are appointed because of their reputed business acumen. While in their public utterances the directors may pay lip service to the paramount importance of safety, the record of the industry in practice suggests the disingenuousness of such pronouncements.[57] Although none of the relevant executives could have wished for a mass disaster, their collective view of appropriate business behavior produced just such an occurrence.

A second lesson relates to the criminal law as it is applies to companies. The strategic decisions made at the GWR boardroom level were deemed too far removed from the resulting fatalities to warrant the criminal prosecution of the company itself. This feature of the case highlights the pressing need for reform of the law of corporate criminal liability to take account of the connection between negligent (or worse) management decisions and deaths in practice.[58] While proposals for such reform had been advanced by the Law Commission in 1996 and had been repeatedly endorsed in election manifestos promulgated by the Labor Party, as of the beginning of 2006 they had yet to be enacted by Parliament, despite the fact that a Labor government had been in power for nine years.

In addition to deficiencies in the law and failings of individuals which contributed to the Southall tragedy, the role of the government merits examination. The lesson here relates to the well-known dangers of deregulation, privatization, and misconceived policies. The deregulatory climate that had swept Great Britain (and earlier the United States) had led to the downgrading of safety, and decreased funding of research and development departments formerly charged with improving safety. Management at GWR claimed to have lost confidence in ATP, but they probably were not prepared to invest the time, money, and resources needed to make ATP effective, and they were not required to do so. Beyond its philosophical preferences for deregulation and privatization, the government may be faulted for the priority it chose to give to efficiency over safety, its seeming obsession with "league tables" (in this instance relating to timely arrivals), penalty structures that encouraged risk-taking to avoid late arrivals, and an unwillingness to make ATP mandatory. Although no government minister was blamed for the Southall crash, let alone charged, it can be seen that government policies and priorities contributed significantly, even if only indirectly, to the crash.

III. Where the Contextual Ambiguities in the Law Encourage Would-be Offenders to Believe (or be Able to Rationalize to Themselves) That They are not Engaged in Illegal Activity

With respect to ordinary or common crime, the line between what is and is not criminal is generally self-evident to all, including the offender. There can be little dispute about the criminality of an assault, theft, or murder; and the perpetrator can be in no doubt that he or she is committing a criminal offense. The borderline between legal and illegal behavior becomes murkier in cases of white-collar crime.[59] There may be nothing to warn a would-be offender that he or she is about to cross the line and commit an offense. Unlike cases of homicide or theft, the conduct is not *per se* illegal in the absence of a successful defense. Unlike cases of fraud, the offender is not aware that he is skating on thin legal ice. The reason that the offender may not believe that the conduct in question is illegal may be because of advice and provided by a reputable lawyer, or because there have been known cases where comparable conduct has not led to a prosecution, or because there seem to be no criminal laws that clearly apply to the conduct in question. While none of these excuses is recognized as a defense in law, the actor's honest and reasonable belief that the conduct in question is not criminal distinguishes him or her from other criminals.

Pushing the Boundaries: The Guinness Affair

The Guinness affair arose against the backdrop of turbulent economic and political times in the City of London, the square mile containing the main financial institutions. Again, deregulation played a key role. Following the deregulation of the financial services industry, takeover practices that had become familiar in the United States were imported to the UK. Many may have assumed that the practices were not illegal, or else, in their enthusiasm to embrace the new opportunities presented, did not bother to consider the issue.

At the root of the Guinness affair lay a takeover battle between Guinness and Argyll to acquire a controlling interest in a third company, Distillers.[60] As part of its bid, Guinness offered shares in its own stock for shares in Distillers. This share swapping is a fairly common practice in mergers and acquisitions. Presuming that the Distillers' shareholders would accept the shares that were the most valuable, the chairman and CEO of Guinness persuaded wealthy associates to purchase shares in Guinness. The idea was to drive up the value of Guinness stock and thereby make its bid more attractive to the Distiller's shareholders. The associates who purchased the Guinness shares were promised that they would be indemnified for any losses that they might incur should the takeover bid fail, while they would be rewarded with "success fees" if the takeover bid was successful.

No doubt many in business would have regarded the plan as not only not illegal but positively ingenious. It was not clear who would be harmed by the stratagem. Guinness shareholders and creditors would benefit handsomely if the scheme succeeded, while Argyll shareholders would be no worse off than before the takeover battle had begun. Distillers' shareholders may have been deceived but they would have only themselves to blame, as prudent investors in this situation would have sought an independent financial analysis of the relative worth of Guinness and Argyll since stock prices can be inaccurate in the best of times. A possible and more intangible victim in the Guinness affair could be said to have been the London Stock Exchange. Potential investors may have been misled by the prices at which Guinness stock was trading, as it was artificially high as a consequence of the share support scheme. Again, one could assert that prudent investors would have based their buying decisions on financial reports and analyses. Nevertheless, if disgruntled investors, for whatever reason, were to lose confidence in the accuracy of prices quoted on the Exchange, they might cease to invest in the market, a phenomenon we noted previously in the mega-fraud cases.

The above analysis, presented in only summary form, is designed not to prove that the machinations of the Guinness CEO and its confederates were legal but only to show how they may have genuinely believed that their scheme was not illegal (even allowing for a measure of self-deception). Further support for this belief was provided by an American adviser who informed the group that "success fees" were commonplace in the United States and had not been held to be illegal. The fact that no prosecutions for comparable practices had ever been brought in Britain also may have reinforced the conviction that the price support scheme was lawful. Nonetheless, the Serious Fraud Office (SFO), which had recently been established (this was its first major case), decided to bring a criminal prosecution.

The CEO and his confederates were charged with a wide range of offenses, including the statutory crime of violating section 151 of the Companies Act 1985 (prohibiting financial assistance). The interpretation of this section turned on whether the success fees were given in "good faith" and were "in the interests of the company;" and also whether they were part of a "larger purpose" of the company.[61] Arguably the acquisition of Distillers satisfied the "larger purpose" requirement and showed that the price support scheme was "in the interests" of Guinness.

The SFO also argued that the unauthorized monies paid in success fees amounted to a theft from Guinness (not from the Distillers' shareholders). If this was theft, it was not the type of theft with which ordinary victims are familiar. Normally the victim of a theft is not aware at the time that her property is being taken or is deceived into parting with the property. The CEO, the legal embodiment of Guinness, voluntarily paid out money to his allies. The payments were consensual; and, at least among the participants in the scheme, there was no stealth or deception involved. Nor was there any intent to deprive Guinness shareholders permanently of any monies (except for the success fees, of course, but these could be looked at as part of the cost of doing business), as is generally required for theft. Indeed, if the scheme had succeeded, Guinness shareholders would have been financially better off.

Finally, the SFO included a virtually *pro forma* conspiracy charge. As conspiracy requires proof of an agreement to commit a criminal offense, this charge was dependent on the jury's decision that the other crimes charged had been proved. The alleged purpose of the conspiracy was to create a false market in Guinness shares, but the shares were in fact trading at their quoted value. Nevertheless, after a lengthy and contentious trial, the jury convicted the CEO and three co-defendants, although subsequently the European Court of Human Rights ruled that the trial had been unfair.[62] Three subsequent trials involving other of the alleged conspirators all failed.

The Guinness affair, if it indeed involved serious criminality, was a "crime" of its times. In order to make sense of the defendants' conduct, one has to take account of the context within which the Distillers takeover bid arose. Margaret Thatcher was Prime Minister in the UK and Ronald Reagan was President in the United States; both had championed entrepreneurialism, laissez faire capitalism, and business deregulation. Both subscribed to the view that governments should interfere as little as possible in business matters, and that the market was perfectly capable of regulating itself. Thus the Guinness group could be forgiven for believing that the government was not about to intercede in the takeover battle over Distillers.

With deregulation of the financial services industry there came a growing interest in mergers and acquisitions, and a change in the perception of those involved in takeover bids. So-called corporate "raiders" were no longer regarded as predators, let alone criminals, but as entrepreneurs who were performing a valuable public service by helping to weed out companies that were weak and inefficient. If a takeover target wished to resist, all it had to do was to reform its business practices and become more efficient. Another viable alternative would be for the target company to find a so-called "white knight," who would come to the company's rescue by taking it over on terms that it deemed to be more favorable. This medieval way of characterizing takeovers may have contributed to the Guinness CEO's belief that, for from doing anything improper, he was "rescuing" Distillers' from the "clutches" of Argyll. Even if this smacks of self-interest rather than disinterested chivalry, it is the case that the practices under consideration were widely exercised and accepted in the Unites States and were considered by some to be "overdue" in the United Kindom.

Not only did the British government of the day preach entrepreneurialism, it had also shown itself prepared to honor successful entrepreneurs (one of the alleged conspirators in the Guinness case had already been knighted). The Guinness CEO no doubt believed that he was more likely to receive a knighthood than be criminally prosecuted, and the criminal prosecution must have been seen by him and his co-defendants as akin to an ambush. Indeed, many years later, it emerged in the media that the SFO was aware of, but had not disclosed, at least six other share support operations. Had the defendants been informed of these other schemes, it would have supported their claim that they honestly believed that their plan was within the law and not unknown in the City of London.

The above analysis notwithstanding, the Guinness CEO may have been a victim of his own hubris. "Deadly Earnest," as he was known, was by all accounts an energetic and autocratic leader, who could be ruthless in business matters. Consumed by the takeover "game" which he was playing, he may have come to believe that he was bound only by the rules of that game and that these were being made up by the competitors themselves as the game unfolded. That Argyll may not have disagreed was evidenced by the fact that, at the same time that Guinness was trying to prop up its stock prices through the share support scheme, Argyll was apparently "selling short" Guinness shares in order to depress their price. Both company leaders appeared to have operated on the principle that all is fair in love, war, and mergers and acquisitions. This belief may well have been fuelled by political rhetoric, government policies, the laissez faire capitalist ethic of the times, and the frenzied takeover environment that had seized businessmen on both sides of the Atlantic.[63]

These factors also may have led to the belief that they were unlikely to be prosecuted. Under the circumstances, the prosecution must have come as a shock. Even the sentencing judge, addressing the Guinness CEO, stated, "I am satisfied you would not have been sucked into dishonesty but for the ethos of those days."[64]

The merger conduct was not unlike that of many enterprising and well-respected managers in dynamic times when there exists fluidity about rules, ambiguous laws, and new opportunities for massive profits.[65] In such circumstances the resourceful entrepreneur, according to business lore and management manuals, must be prepared to seize the initiative, pushing the boundaries of the uncertain law, inventing new rules of the game, exploiting weaknesses in the regulatory system and thinking "out of the box."[66] Following his early release from prison on "health grounds," the Guinness CEO continued to protest his innocence, to contest the fairness of his trial and conviction (on which point he eventually won in the European Court of Human Rights), and, now in robust health, to give self-justificatory lectures in business schools across Europe. Ruthless, ambitious, "no-holds-barred" entrepreneurs may be perhaps somewhat too eager to define their conduct as legal, or at least not yet illegal, but they are obviously walking a fine line between a brilliant coup or, in the words of John Galbraith, a stay in a "minimum security slammer."

Conclusion

There have been numerous attempts to explain white-collar and corporate crime and deviance.[67] Far less attention has been paid to the motivations, rationalizations, justifications, and mental processes of offenders. In this paper we have endeavored to place the white-collar criminal within an organizational framework where unique opportunities and sometimes near-irresistible temptations for misconduct exist. We have examined how the rarefied view from the upper echelons of a company can blind corporate executives to rules that apply to ordinary citizens and lead them to believe that they are somehow "above the law." We have also examined how corporate structures, market forces, and government policies can individually and collectively foster deviant and illegal conduct.

We have attempted to illustrate our theses with case studies that can be placed within a three-part typology: where business executives were fully conscious of committing an offense: where they may have "blinded" themselves to the illegal dimensions of their actions; and where they believed—or convinced themselves—that they were not breaking the law. These typologies in turn open up a plethora of possible organizational, social-psychological, and wider environmental explanations as to why white-collar criminals choose deviant options. Unfortunately, in the end our analyses inevitably run up against the fact that one can never know for certain what goes through another person's mind before he or she decides to break the law or engage in deviant behavior, and our understanding of the processes involved is not helped by the reticence of white-collar criminals, as least compared to that of "common" or "street" criminals, to explain themselves and their actions (except perhaps for the commercially oriented memoirs of ex-offenders[68]).

Those who write in this field are inevitably drawn to the insights of Sutherland, many of which remain as fresh and valid today as when they were first articulated. Sutherland, however, tended to focus on "clean-hands" crime that was fully conscious and deliberate and was committed "for" the benefit of the offender's company. Since then there have been at least two major developments that demand attention: one has to do with offenses "against" the organization and the other focuses on corporate "violence" causing death and severe injuries. Mega-frauds, where the primary victim may be the capitalist system itself, also need to be taken account of. In addition, the role of government policies, and, in particular, deregulation and privatization, must be considered for the extent to which they contribute to the commission of white-collar offenses. The picture is complex, and even limiting ourselves to individuals, we find that the motives of white-collar criminals are many and varied.

Clearly there are some offenses that are deliberate and highly articulated, but there are probably far more where no-one "intended" to cause harm, where executives blinded themselves to the consequences of their actions, where they believed they were not acting illegally, or where they were no longer in control of events. There is perhaps a tendency in the literature to overemphasize the rationality and orderliness of organizations. But, as the Barings case so graphically demonstrates, organizations can slide into deviance by ignorance, incompetence, neglect, lack of caution, and wilful blindness. In some cases, then, white-collar criminals commit crimes that noone wilfully intended and with consequences for which no-one would ever have wished.

Acknowledgments

We would like to thank Michael Clarke for his valuable comments on our paper.

Endnotes

1. We use the term "deviant" behavior to refer to proscribed, but not necessarily criminal, conduct. Often, however, the conduct in question escapes "criminal" categorization only because the business community has been able to effectively lobby the legislature (Gobert, 2005). There is a further technical question of whether conduct which does not lead to a prosecution or conviction is properly to be classified as "criminal" (Tappan, 1947). Also, much depends on who is characterizing the behavior in question. Take, for instance, the practice of giving gifts to valued clients (Reisman, 1979). Within the organization the gift giver is the conformist and not the deviant. An external oversight agency, on the other hand, may characterize such gift-giving as deviant or even constituting an illegal bribe. The point is that it is the defining audience that applies the deviant label (Downes and Rock, 1995). When we refer to "deviant" behavior in this article, we include violations of generally accepted norms and rules, as well as violations of the criminal law.
2. Sutherland (1949).
3. Sutherland (1983: 217).
4. See Slapper and Tombs (1999), Pearce and Snider (1995), Tonry and Reiss (1993), Ermann and Lundman (1996).
5. Gobert and Punch (2003); Punch (1996).
6. Gobert (2005).
7. Hawkins (1983).

8. Maguire (1997).
9. Clinard and Yeager (1980).
10. *The Associated Press* (2004).
11. Mills (1940).
12. See Sykes and Matza (1957).
13. Katz (1988).
14. Reed (1989).
15. Katz (1988: 321).
16. Tombs and Whyte (2003).
17. Geis (1978).
18. Jamieson (1994: 61).
19. Geis (1978).
20. Geis (1978: 68).
21. Geis (1978: 71).
22. Geis (1978: 67).
23. Gobert and Punch (2003).
24. Helmer (1997: 33).
25. Bogaarts and van Gelder (1996).
26. Helmer (1997: 44).
27. Helmer (1997: 43).
28. Helmer (1997: 46).
29. Calavita and Pontell (1990: 321).
30. White (1991: 117).
31. Texan S&L consultant in Calavita and Pontell (1990: 320).
32. Calavita and Pontell (1990: 319).
33. Gobert and Punch (2003); Slapper and Tombs (1999); Wells (2001).
34. Quoted in Partnoy (2003).
35. Fusaro and Miller (2002); Elliot and Schroth (2002).
36. Smit (2004).
37. Partnoy (2003).
38. Rock (1973).
39. Leeson (1996).
40. Punch (1966).
41. Rawnsley (1996).
42. Bank of England Report (1995).
43. Bank of England Report (1995).
44. Gobert and Punch (2003).
45. Reisman (1979).
46. Festinger (1957).
47. Sunday Times Insight Team (1979).
48. Hawkins (2002).
49. Mokhiber (1994); Punch (1966).
50. Jack (2002).
51. See also the Sheen Report (1987) relating to the capsize of the Herald of Free Enterprise.
52. Uff Report (2000).
53. Law Commission Report (1996).
54. See *Tesco Supermarkets Ltd. v. Nattrass* (1972) AC 153.
55. The company, however, did admit to breaches of health and safety regulations and was heavily fined.
56. Sheen Report; Uff Report (2002); and recently manslaughter charges were not brought against the rail company for a serious accident at Ladbroke Grove; Cullen Report (2002).
57. Jack (2002).

58. See Gobert and Punch (2003), Wells (2001).
59. Clarke (1990).
60. Kochan and Pym (1987).
61. See Companies Act (1985: Sec153).
62. *Case of Saunders v. The United Kingdom*, No. 43/1994/490/572 (European Court of Human Rights).
63. Punch (1996).
64. *The Times* (August 29, 1990).
65. Partnoy (2003).
66. Handy (1900).
67. Braithwaite (1985); Clarke (1990); Levi (1987); Clinard and Yeager (1980); Whyte and Tombs (2003).
68. Levine (1990: 390).

References

Bank of England Report (1995) Report of the Board of Banking Supervision Inquiry into the Circumstances of the Collapse of Barings. London: HMSO.

Bogaarts, René, and Harry van Gelder (1996) *Het Teken van de Toekan.* Amsterdam: Meulenhoff.

Braithwaite, John (1985) "White Collar Crime." *Annual Rev. of Sociology* 11: 1–25.

Calavita, Kitty and Henry N. Pontell (1990) "'Heads I Win, Tails You Lose': Deregulation, Crime and Crisis in the Savings & Loan Industry," *Crime & Delinquency* 36: 309–41.

Clarke, Michael (1990) *Business Crime.* Cambridge: Polity Press.

Clinard, Marshall B., and Yeager, Peter C. (1980) *Corporate Crime.* New York: Free Press.

Cullen Report (2002) *Ladbroke Grove Rail Inquiry*. London: Department of Transport.

Downes, David, and Paul Rock (2003) *Understanding Deviance, 4th ed.* Oxford: Oxford University Press.

Elliot, Larry A., and Richard J. Scroth (2002) *How Companies Lie: Why Enron is Just the Tip of the Iceberg.* London: Nicholas Brealey Publishing.

Ermann, M. David, and Richard J. Lundman, eds. (1996) *Corporate and Governmental Deviance*, 3rd ed. New York: Oxford University Press.

Festinger, Leon (1957) *The Theory of Cognitive Dissonance.* Stanford: Stanford University Press.

Fusaro, Peter C., and Ross M. Miller (2002) *What Went Wrong at Enron.* New York: Wiley.

Geis, Gilbert (1978) "White Collar Crime: The Heavy Electrical Equipment Antitrust Cases of 1961." In *Corporate and Governmental Deviance,* Editors M. Ermann and R. Lundman. New York: Oxford University Press.

Gobert, James (2005) "The Politics of Corporate Manslaughter—The British Experience," *Law Reform* 8(1): 138–152.

Gobert, James, and Maurice Punch (2003) *Rethinking Corporate Crime.* London: Butterworths.

Handy, Charles (1990) *The Age of Unreason.* London: Arrow.

Hawkins, Keith (1983) "Bargain and Bluff: Compliance Strategy and Deterrence in the Enforcement of Regulation." *Law and Policy Quarterly* 5: 35–73.

Hawkins, Keith (2002) *Law as Last Resort.* Oxford: Oxford University Press.

Helmer, Charlotte (1977) "De neutralisatie theorie togepast op witte boorden criminaliteit." Masters thesis, Faculty of Law, University of Utrecht.

Jack, Ian (2001) *The Crash that Stopped Britain.* Cambridge: Granta Books.

Jamieson, Katherine M. (1994) *The Organization of Corporate Crime*. Thousand Oaks CA: Sage.
Katz, Jack (1988) *The Seductions of Crime.* New York: Basic Books.
Kochan, Nick, and Hugh Pym (1987) *The Guinness Affair.* London: Helm.
Leeson, Nick (1996) *Rogue Trader*. London: Little, Brown.
Levi, Michael (1987) *Regulating Fraud: White-Collar Crime and the Criminal Process*. London: Tavistock.
Levine, Dennis B. (1991) *Inside Out: A True Story of Greed, Scandal and Redemption.* New York: Berkley Books.
Maguire, Mike (1997) "Crime Statistics, Patterns, and Trends: Changing Perceptions and their Implications." In *The Oxford Handbook of Criminology,* Editors M. Maguire et al. Oxford: Clarendon Press.
Mills, C. Wright (1940) "Situated Actions and Vocabularies of Motive." *American Sociological Rev.* 5: 904–13.
Mokhiber, Russell (1988) *Corporate Crime and Violence*. San Francisco: Sierra Club Books.
Partnoy, Frank (2003) *Infectious Greed.* New York: Holt.
Pearce, Frank, and Laureen Snider, eds. (1995) *Corporate Crime: Contemporary Debates*. Toronto: Toronto University Press.
Punch, Maurice (1996) *Dirty Business*. London: Sage.
Rawnsley, Judith (1995) *Going for Broke*. London: Harper Collins.
Reed, Michael (1989) *The Sociology of Management*. New York/London: Harvester/Wheatsheaf.
Reisman, Michael W. (1979) *Folded Lies*. New York: Free Press.
Rock, Paul (1973) *Deviant Behaviour*. London: Hutchinson University Library.
Sheen Report (1987) m.v. Herald of Free Enterprise: Report of Court No. 8074. London: Department of Transport.
Slapper, Gary, and Steve Tombs (1999) *Corporate Crime*. London: Longman.
Smit, Jeroen (2004) *Het drama Ahold.* Amsterdam: Balans.
The Sunday Times Insight Team (1980) *Suffer the Children: the Story of Thalidomide*. London: Futura.
Sutherland, Edwin H. (1949) *White-collar Crime*. New York: Drgden.
Sutherland, Edwin H. (1983) *White-collar Crime: The Uncut Version*. New Haven: Yale University Press.
Sykes, Gresham, and David Matza (1957) "Techniques of Neutralization: A Theory of Delinquency." *American Sociological Rev*. 22: 664–70.
Tappan, Paul W. (1947) "Who is the Criminal?" *American Sociological Rev.* 12: 96–102.
The Times (1990) "Judge's tough sentencing receives widespread support." *The Times*, 29 August, p. 3.
Tombs, Steve, and Dave Whyte, eds. (2003) *Unmasking the Crimes of the Powerful*. New York: Peter Lang.
Tonry, Michael T., and Albert J. Reiss Jr., eds. (1993) *Beyond the Law: Crime in Complex Organizations*. Chicago: Chicago University Press.
Uff Report (2001) *The Southall Rail Accident Report*. London: Department of Transport.
Wells, Celia (2001) *Corporations and Criminal Responsibility,* 2nd ed. Oxford: Oxford University Press.
White, Lawrence J. (1991) *The S & L Debacle: Public Policy Lessons for Bank and Thrift Regulation*. New York/Oxford: Oxford University Press.

Part III

Critical and Postmodern Approaches to Research

1

Researching Corporate and White-Collar Crime in an Era of Neo-Liberalism

Steve Tombs and Dave Whyte

Introduction: "Knowing" About Corporate and White-Collar Crimes

Research conducted within the discipline of criminology has been relatively blind to corporate and white-collar crime, a myopia that has remained even in the face of overwhelming evidence that in both Britain and in the United States of America the social and economic impact of corporate and white-collar crimes upon their victims massively exceeds the corresponding impact of conventional crimes.[1] This last fact is *acknowledged* in much contemporary criminology, though such acknowledgment tends to appear somewhat gesturally, as if mere recognition of the existence of corporate and white-collar crimes is enough to bolster the integrity of criminological research. The truth of the matter is that, despite such token recognition of the crimes of the powerful, criminological research rarely takes these types of offenses and offenders as an object of study.

Of course, there are complexities to be acknowledged within this overall generalization. For one thing, we cannot deny that we can find within (and, importantly, beyond) the disciplines of criminology and criminal justice bodies of work which do seek to document, understand, and theorize abuses of law and power by both relatively privileged individuals and organizations in Western democratic social orders.

Indeed, looking at the United States from the outside, there appears to be a great deal of corporate and white-collar crime research. However, despite this greater volume—measured, for example, by the number of books and journal articles—it is difficult to judge the extent to which this is simply a function of the far greater scale of publishing there in general or evidence of a greater academic interest in these areas. But even if the latter is the case, even if there is greater interest in corporate and white-collar crime in the American academy, then it is again incontestable that these types of crime remain peripheral to the issues which dominate academic criminology and criminal justice there.

Further, if the majority of academic work on corporate and white-collar crime hails from the United States, this is not problematic in the sense that some of this work raises empirical, conceptual, methodological, and theoretical issues of more general, international, relevance. But it can be problematic in that, given that much of this work is context specific, with its reference points being systems of law and enforcement which are specific to U.S. state and federal levels, then it may not be either generalizable across to, nor providing basic raw material for further research for those working in other jurisdictions. Indeed, some have remarked upon the insularity of U.S.-based corporate and white-collar crime research.[2]

What, then, are the prospects of an upsurge in academic interest in corporate and white-collar crimes—a central question of this chapter? Here, it is important to bear in mind the various milieus within which academic work proceeds, and which affect the questions it asks and thus the "answers" it can reach. As Cohen has noted,

> The development of social scientific theory and knowledge takes place not simply within the heads of individuals, but within particular institutional domains. These domains, in turn, are shaped by their surroundings: how academic institutions are organised, how disciplines are divided and subdivided, how disputes emerge, how research is funded and how the findings are published and used. In criminology, an understanding of these institutional domains is especially important for knowledge is situated not just, or not even primarily, in the 'pure' academic world, but in the applied domain of the state's crime control apparatus.[3]

Making a slightly broader point, Geis and colleagues, in their brief review of "scholarship on white-collar crime," noted how this history "shows rather clearly how close academic work can parallel political and social climates."[4] Thus it is unsurprising that there has hardly been an upsurge in corporate crime research either in Britain or the United States during the past 25–30 years, which have seen a reassertion of neo-liberal hegemony. Indeed, reviewing recent scholarship on *corporate* crime in the United States, Snider has documented how "interest and funding" for research "plummeted in the 1980s and the 1990s,"[5] and comments regarding much remaining research about "corporate and white-collar crime" that,

> The literature has become increasingly conservative in recent decades, the big empirical surveys and largest grants from major government and private agencies have gone to studies of occupational rather than organisational (corporate) crime.[6]

For Snider, the emergence to dominance of neo-liberalism has both effected and been a consequence of an increase in the structural power of capital and what she has called "the social credibility of capital."[7] The combined effect of these shifts has been a tendency to see the removal of (the control of) corporate crime from state agendas. As the legitimacy of business organizations has increased, so has the legitimacy of arguments for their control declined.[8] If one sets these processes in the context of the difficulties that have historically attached to labeling the illegal activities of corporations as criminal—not least, if most regrettably, due to the support of a succession of academics[9]—it is no surprise that this task has become much more difficult in the past two decades. Neo-liberalism has also raised the naked pursuit of profit to the status of almost moral exigency, which has the effect of legitimating virtually any activity because it is engaged in by business, and de-legitimating opposition and resistance—the bases of pro-regulatory forces—for its very "anti-business" rhetoric and practice. We should add that when external controls (both material and ideological) on profit maximization are weakened, then we can reasonably expect to see an increased incidence in illegal corporate activity.[10] Corporate and white-collar crimes become more pressing social problems at the same time as they are defined, literally, out of existence. It becomes "nonsensical" to speak of the increasing incidence of corporate and white-collar crime under conditions of rampant neo-liberalism—for one of the effects of the increasing structural power and social credibility of capital is that corporate crime as a phenomenon disappears:

> because its survival as an object of study is contingent on the passage and enforcement of "command and control" legislation, corporate crime can "disappear" through decriminalization (the repeal of criminal law), through deregulation (the repeal of all state law, criminal, civil and administrative), and through downsizing (the destruction of the state's enforcement capacity). All three have been used.[11]

In this chapter,[12] we attempt to highlight the dimensions of the increasing "problem" of subjecting corporations and high-status individuals to critical scrutiny from the university in a neo-liberal era. We begin, in the next section, by documenting some of the key aspects and consequences of the emergence to dominance of neo-liberalism for universities in general and in relation to criminology on particular. We then turn to consider how these new contexts for academic work frame the microprocesses of research around corporate and white-collar crime, arguing that long-standing difficulties in the research process have become exacerbated. Thus our concern is broadly with the march of the values and practices of neo-liberalism through the universities, and the particular effects of these processes for critical research around corporate and white-collar crime. In taking this focus, it is not our intention to play down the continuing importance of the prospect for carving out space to produce ideas that engage critically with and provide intellectual legitimacy for counter-hegemonic struggles. But it *is* our argument here that the enthusiastic promotion of universities as entrepreneurial in current government policy is an alarming prospect for those that wish to develop research which stands outside the agendas of states and corporations. The entrenchment of the utility value of research means that research agendas must be ever more tailored to what is useful to markets and to the state.

Neo-Liberalism and the Entrepreneurial University

Taking the University to Market

An underlying theme of this chapter concerns the marketization of universities and the commodification of academic knowledge. By the former, we mean the various means by which universities are increasingly required to perform as economic actors, both in external markets—as competitors for students, research funds, prestige, and so on—and through the development of internal markets, whereby courses, departments, and so on become individual cost centers which are required to generate a surplus or perish, where there is competition for students (as a resource) at all levels, and where academics are increasingly required to generate income to meet their wage or salary (and often employed upon fixed-term contracts to add the necessary discipline to this enterprise). This compulsion toward acting as economic units has also been furthered by universities turning to the business world for models, advice, prescriptions as to how to operate, and be organized. By the commodification of knowledge, we mean the variety of shifts toward the production of knowledge as something to be traded as a commodity, with a realizable exchange value within some internal or external market.[13] These trends toward marketization and commodification are not entirely new,[14] nor should their emergence be viewed in an unfolding, unilinear fashion; but over the past quarter of a century, such processes have become greatly intensified, as increasingly intimate links between university departments and corporate/state sponsors have been forged in the context of massive expansions of higher education sectors and, at the same time, steady cuts in state funding.

In the United States, this process of disinvestment has had a fundamental impact upon business–university relationships. As early as the mid-1970s it was estimated that about a third of the faculty in all United States universities had been involved in some form of corporate consultancy.[15] Yet the process of state disinvestment since the early 1970s has forced universities to attract ever greater corporate funds.[16] This trend has occurred partly as a result of military disinvestment as the restructuring of the military-industrial complex has gradually reduced state funding for research.[17] However, the story of the decline in state funding for research in the United States is not just the story of the changing imperatives of the military-industrial complex. In the 15 years between 1980 and 1995 there was a drop of 43% in non-military state funding in the United States.[18] Commenting upon higher education in Canada, Newson and Buchbinder have noted that a similar program of disinvestments, embarked upon in the late 1970s, following the liberal expansion of the universities in the 1960s, has prompted a severe funding crisis in recent years.[19] The result in both countries has been a creeping entrepreneurialization of the universities based on the expansion of research consultancies and joint ventures, ostensibly aimed at facilitating knowledge and technology transfer from the public sector to private corporations. Funding data analyzed by Slaughter and Leslie indicate that similar trends are unfolding in all Organisation for Economic Co-operation and Development (OECD) countries.[20] Recently, higher education systems in locations as diverse as Australia, Mexico, New Zealand, and South Africa have been forced to accept the conditions of essentially similar processes of marketization.[21]

What appears to be a growing assimilation of the universities into the neo-liberal project has also been encouraged via key international economic and political institutions associated with it. For example, the World Bank, in a 1994 report on higher education, urged an international shift within nation-state higher education regimes from state funding to "multiple sources" of income, noting that, "In short, higher education should resemble the United States model more closely."[22] Thus it continues to undermine the public provision of education in countries undergoing "structural redevelopment," challenging the principle of higher education provision as a public good, and increasingly forcing states to commodify their universities. Included in the World Bank's prescriptive measures are introducing tuition charges for students, limiting the number of scholarships available to the poor, forcing down costs in universities, and encouraging private schooling.[23] In South Africa, for example, foreign advisers have been drafted into institutions to teach the principles of the "market university,"[24] principles that have militated against the development of research around topics of social justice and poverty.[25] The World Bank's version of the market university in many countries has created the conditions whereby "[t]he fragile storehouse of indigenous knowledge is almost destroyed, along with the major source of independent critique. Local research by independent academics is minimal."[26]

In the United Kingdom, a similar regime of austerity has forced universities increasingly to look for alternative sponsors of academic work and thus to "embrace" marketization and commodification. Since 1979, the sector has been the subject of several waves of reductions in grants from central government.[27] Alongside these reductions in funding have occurred two equally significant developments: first, an opening up of universities to external market influences; second, attempts to introduce an era of mass higher education. Through the crudest mechanism of funding, universities are being repositioned as autonomous market actors, less and less able to rely upon an over-stretched state.

Moreover, in recent years, and particularly in relation to research, an intensified regime of austerity has swept through U.K. universities, entrenching the principle of utility, strengthening the reliance of academics upon external funding dominated by policy or industrial requirements. Indeed, we may be witnessing a trend akin to that identified in a recent review of state/corporate/university relationships in the United States during the Cold War era: "in the short-term, power typically *selects* ideas . . . while in the long term ideas tend to *conform* to the realities of power."[28]

While the current British government, compared with its Conservative predecessors, may be less hostile to social science research, there is very little difference in the degree to which it wishes to tie social science to government and industry's functional requirements. On the face of it, New Labour's 1997 election victory, preceded by Blair's insistence that the key issue facing the country was "education, education, education," did signify more than a simple rhetorical change for social science. Thus, for example, the Labour Government increased the Economic and Social Research Council (ESRC)[29] budget by 15% in real terms over three years. The current government support for the ESRC is linked closely to "evidence-based policy" rhetoric.[30] If researchers want to be involved in the right type of research and tie themselves into government or research council defined priorities, then being a social scientist at the moment can be a successful enterprise. Thus in a key speech by Lord (formerly prominent social scientist, David) Lipsey, he hammered home the need to view research as commodity: "Produce the right goods at the right time and promote them well, and they have every chance of success in the political marketplace."[31] While the ESRC's commitment has some welcome aspects, the signals it sends, coupled with other recent messages from the Council and Government, do not augur well for critical social research, least of all research that seeks to subject the powerful to critical scrutiny.

These commitments need to be seen in the broader context of the oft-stated aim of the New Labour governments that the United Kingdom should become the most business friendly environment in the world.[32] In almost all spheres of social and economic activity, and at every opportunity, the Blair governments have articulated, supported, and acted upon a dogmatic pro-business stance. When it comes to education, Labour's evangelical business-friendliness has been applied vigorously: for Blair, "in the knowledge economy, entrepreneurial universities will be as important as entrepreneurial businesses, one fostering the other."[33] At the forefront of this commitment is the Foresight program, which brings together representatives from industry, government, and the research base (largely the universities), ostensibly to maximize the role of the science in facilitating and maximizing future wealth creation and a better quality of life—though there are now many similar initiatives.[34] Foresight panels provide a forum for the incorporation of universities into the commercial strategies of the industrial sectors they represent, and, in so doing, they draw the universities into a general promotion (rather than scientific scrutiny) of the profitability of the sector. Many are dominated by corporate representatives, at least in numerical terms. In addition, civil servants and academics are selected on the basis of their support for the general aims of promoting the industry in which they are involved.[35] Indeed, the general direction of the work taken on by the panels is one that rarely deviates from promoting the commercial success of the sector.

The effects of such interactions have been deleteriously one-sided. Far from boosting the resources available to universities, evidence from the United States indicates that the growth of research parks and university/business consortia has, despite the hype, not been successful in producing profitable returns; indeed, such arrangements have often left universities in the red.[36] In the meantime, huge benefits are accrued by private corporations in terms of the training of managers and technical workers, from the transfer of technology to the private sector, and via the construction of ideologies and ways of interpreting the world consistent with the stability of capitalist social orders. Thus, the very idea that the marketization of research, and, more generally, the entrepreneurialization of the universities, is based upon a flow of resources from business to the universities is little more than an illusion. Corporations are now gaining vastly more resources from the universities for less money than ever before.[37] Yet this is the process that is used to justify programs of austerity in parts of the university that are deemed unprofitable or are resistant to commercialization.[38]

Criminology and "Power"

Now, there are good reasons to suggest that the general shifts identified above—the marketization and commodification of knowledge—have worked upon academic criminology as much as, if not more than, most other disciplines across and indeed beyond the social sciences. And within criminology and criminal justice research, such processes have, we argue below, particularly helped to construct a terrain of valid, acceptable research for academics, a terrain from which a focus upon corporate and white-collar crimes is more and more likely to be expunged.

Of course criminology—and, to an even greater extent, its more applied offspring, criminal justice—has had, since its very inception, an extremely intimate, indeed subservient, relationship to the state. In a famous passage, Foucault has claimed that "the *whole content* of criminology—with its "garrulous discourse" and "endless repetitions"—is to be explained with reference to its application by the powerful:

> Have you ever read any criminology text?... They are staggering. And I say this out of astonishment, not aggressiveness, because I fail to comprehend how the discourse of criminology has been able to go on at this level. One has the impression that it is of such utility, is needed so urgently and rendered so vital for the working of the system, that it does not even need to seek a theoretical justification for itself, or even a coherent framework. It is entirely utilitarian.[39]

For Garland, its relationship to power is a defining feature of criminology, which is "shaped only to a small extent by its own theoretical object and logic of inquiry. Its epistemological threshold is a low one, making it susceptible to pressures and interests generated elsewhere."[40]

This intimate relationship between criminology on the one hand, and the demands of the state and power on the other, has seriously infected the character of British criminology, a character which is long-standing and relatively resistant to change.[41] Even in the early 1980s it was suggested that British criminology was becoming even more pragmatic:

> [T]he Home Office Research Unit, the research branches of the prison department, the Metropolitan Police and allied state agencies have all expanded and become more professional and productive. This is particularly notable given the decline of government support for social science research. In line with what happened in the United States over this decade [the 1970s], the content of this type of criminology has switched (and is likely to switch even more) in the direction of "criminal justice": that is to say, an exclusive concern with the operation of the system. Research deals mainly with matters of decision-making, manpower, evaluation and classification.[42]

Examining the "Social Organisation of British Criminology," Paul Rock identifies the period of expansion of British higher education in the latter half of the 1980s as a crucial moment: it produced, among other things, a younger generation of criminologists, smaller in number, who "came to preoccupy itself with hunting grants for empirical research."[43] Thus,

> a growing proportion of criminologists were becoming increasingly dependent on soft money, obliged to work on short-term contracts to supply research to order for government departments, statutory agencies, and voluntary organizations.[44]

In a sense, the period described marks the beginning of a boom time for British criminology—one which continues as we write. Fuelled by the exponential expansion of the criminal justice system and the political priorities attached to crime and criminal justice, academic criminology in Britain currently finds itself in apparent good health—witness the proliferation of postgraduate and undergraduate courses, the ceaseless torrent of academic texts and journals, the seemingly increasing intrusion by criminologists in public and government-led debates around "crime, law, and order." This flourishing was given particular impetus by the New Labour administration's demand for what it calls "evidence-based policy." Thus, having introduced a significant piece of crime control legislation on entering office, the Crime and Disorder Act 1998, and having prioritized through this and related initiatives "crime reduction," New Labour increased Home Office external research spending by a massive 500% between 1998/99 and 2000/01. Most funding was for research to be done by university-based criminologists. On the face of it, this encouraged a more open exchange of ideas between the policy and academic communities, paving the way for a new knowledge base to tackle crime and promote justice. But this bonanza for academic criminology came with strings attached, strings pulled strategically by the Home Secretary. For example, according to an internal memo distributed to staff in the Home Office Research Development and Statistics unit at the behest of the Home Secretary Blunkett, no externally funded research is to be published unless it has Ministerial approval. One Home Office researcher told us, "You can't really publish anything without political acceptance, no matter how significant your findings are. The atmosphere is becoming so harsh that young high calibre researchers are leaving."

Thus, as criminologists were being forced to seek external research funding, a massive boom in such funding appeared—from the coffers of the Home Office. Certain types of research are therefore further marginalized from academic criminological agendas as academics compete for research grants provided by the state, generating reliance upon direct funding for specific, preordained research projects often with narrowly defined fields of inquiry and outputs. And so criminology does little to explore corporate and white-collar crimes, rather the discipline is tied to an even narrower state definition of the "crime problem"; it is increasingly committed to an endless reproduction and multivariate analyses of local and national surveys and statistics on youth offending, burglaries, car crime, shoplifting or graffiti and vandalism; and prioritises a self-fuelling cycle of evaluative research of a narrow "reform" measures.[45]

For us, such trends are the key context for understanding how the massed ranks of policy-driven academic criminology have swollen with such alacrity in recent years. These processes—the marketization and commodification of knowledge—have touched criminology as much as any other discipline in the social sciences, with significant effects for those who work within the discipline and, concomitantly, the work that they produce.

But more than this, the complementary programs of marketization and commodification within a mass higher education system have produced a series of highly disciplinary processes. That is, in a range of ways, the subordination of research workers to the imperatives of the market has played a crucial *disciplinary* role in the drive to fashion the academic, self-regulating subject, while simultaneously attempting to normalize those individuals and indeed institutions who might dissent from these imperatives, or at least harbor serious doubts about the moral and political discourses that underpin them. We can identify three associated trends[46]—all detrimental to the prospects for an upsurge in critical criminological scrutiny of the illegal activities of corporations and high-status business-people.

First, the rise in casualized and temporary posts may force researchers to seek funding wherever it is available. Since this is increasingly likely to be found in contract research, researchers may have little option but to conduct utility research. In 1998, 94.2% of research-only staff in universities were on casualized, fixed-term contracts.[47] By 2004, 45% of all university academics were on fixed-term contracts, and over one-third of all academic staff had their salaries funded from sources beyond their own institution.[48] Thus, the expansion of the university sector may well be ushering in a new generation of researchers entirely dependent upon policy and commercial research projects. This process is likely to be reinforced by the drive toward the evaluation studies discussed above: "the projects are short-term, the evaluations are time-restricted (usually 3–6 months) and survival (for practitioners and researchers) depends on positive outcomes."[49]

Second, those researchers are less likely to be in a position to carve out space for developing autonomous research agendas outside the agendas of large grant-holders. The further neutralization of critical criminological research may be one result of casualization. Thus van Swaaningen, in his recent analysis of critical criminology, has argued that the "heyday" of critical criminology has passed and that "criminology has shifted away from epistemological and socio-political questions and returned to its old empiricist orientation as an applied science . . . fuelled by the political issues of the day, and geared by the agenda of its financiers."[50] It is for us no coincidence that the heyday of critical criminology in the United Kingdom—the period marked by the emergence, formation, and immediate aftermath of the National Deviancy Conference—was a period of expansionism which was relatively generously funded, allowing far greater room for manoeuvre for academics whom Rock has referred to as the "fortunate generation."[51]

Third, casualization in universities is likely to produce increasing numbers of researchers that are relatively powerless, unorganised and atomised. The very conditions of security that allow workers in all industries to resist overbearing managerial regimes are therefore denied to the new generation of casualized researchers. To be blunt, "Say the wrong thing and you can be out of a job."[52] It is easy to see how the "wrong things" may include issues about the crimes committed by the relatively powerful in our society.

Researching Corporate and White-Collar Crime in an Era of Neo-Liberalism?

Let us, at this point, restate what the above arguments have to do specifically with researching corporate and white-collar crime. Researching such activities has always been at the margins of social science in general, and criminology in particular. However, in macro-level terms, the prospects for such research have been further diminished in the era of neo-liberalism as a series of changes have swept through universities. In particular, the social credibility of capital, and indeed the importance of the business world as models for and funders of university activity have been augmented. Universities have been subjected to processes of marketization and commodification, with the whip of external funding forcing researchers to turn to external sources of tightly controlled funding. Both within and beyond criminology, these new parameters of academic work have meant that certain types of research and research questions have been increasingly defined as useful, pressing, and legitimate, others as futile, irrelevant, or illegitimate. Within criminology, this trend has perhaps been particularly dramatic given the opening up of a massive pool of funds, funds tied to the Government's narrowing definition of what constitutes crime. Thus questions of corporate or white-collar illegality have clearly slipped further from constructions of acceptable research terrain.

These are, as we have indicated, macro-level considerations. In this section, we seek to link these to more micro-level considerations regarding various aspects of the process of researching corporations and high-status individuals. The problems to which we point here are mostly far from new—although for us many if not all of them have become *intensified* in the new wider "realities" set out above.

For the purposes of discussion, we consider separately three aspects of the research process—securing funding, gaining access, and disseminating results. These divisions are, however, to a large extent purely analytical devices rather than neatly reflecting separate elements of an overall process. And indeed what occurs within one "aspect" clearly often impacts upon others. Thus, for example securing high-level National Institute of Justice or Home Office research funding—through offering to ask "safe" questions—is itself one means of improving chances of both access and publication; at the same time, publication in the safest journals of highest prestige—the *British Journal of Criminology* or *Criminology*, for example—is itself viewed positively when it comes to securing prestigious research funding. These are, then, in many respects, mutually reinforcing stages or processes.

Regulating Funding: The Construction of Feasible Enquiry

Our starting point, then, following others,[53] is that sponsors—by which we mean those who demand, support, recognize as legitimate, fund, facilitate, and seek to disseminate—help to create research agendas. In this creation, some questions are organized *onto* agendas, others are by definition organized *off* these agendas. Now, while some of this organizing is highly conscious on the part of individuals and organizations who sponsor research activity, it would be wrong to cast this process as simply—or even largely—one involving direct or conscious manipulation. Certainly, concerted agency on the part of individuals and institutions frequently takes place. But the key issue about the creation and reproduction of research agendas is much more fundamental than simply the hands-on control that the powerful are able to wield; rather, it is their by-and-large taken for granted nature. Certain questions seem "naturally" to fall within the boundaries of the legitimate, feasible, and acceptable, and generally questions beyond those boundaries tend not to be raised, or if they are raised they are not taken seriously. This is, after all, one of the mechanisms by which the process of hegemony operates. In other words, while we do not dismiss the role of agency, we are talking about power operating in a structural fashion here.[54]

As we have argued in previous sections, under neo-liberal conditions, the tightening of government control over research agendas over the past two decades has had the effect of intensifying demand for utilizable and policy-relevant research findings in relation to the usual suspects of the criminal justice system. An intensifying demand for policy-relevant research findings has narrowed the scope for asking politically sensitive research questions, or for focusing upon more fundamental or long-term issues. One effect of this is that state-funded research projects increasingly tend to be empiricist and a-theoretical. This trend also has a constraining effect in terms of defining what is and what isn't possible to achieve, or even suggest, in terms of the reform or development of policy.[55]

Aside from these general points regarding funding, there are particular issues pertaining to possible funding of research into the illegal activities of the powerful. It is perhaps a truism to note that private capital is, all things being equal, not likely to be enthusiastic about sponsoring research into the activities of private corporations. Yet we also need to be clear that corporate and white-collar crime research does not necessarily look particularly attractive from the viewpoint of state funders either. For when we are speaking of academic attention to corporate and white-collar crime, it is also clear that we are speaking of attention directed to states and state agencies. This is much more than simply a reference to the effect of the state's regulatory functions. Rather, understanding corporate and white-collar crime raises methodological, empirical, and theoretical questions that lead us to enquire into state-capital relationships. Within capitalism, an economic order based upon private property with markets in capital and in labour, the limited liability corporation remains the main legal mechanism through which capital is brought together and interacts in various marketplaces. Thus, corporations are artificial entities created for the mobilization, utilization, and protection of capital within recent socio-historical state formations, entities whose very existence is provided for and maintained through the state via legal institutions and instruments, which in turn are based upon material and ideological supports. The corporate form and the state are thus inextricably linked. The nature, visibility, and treatment of corporate and white-collar crime can be approached only within a broader understanding of social constructions of crime and criminality, and in relation to the key role played in the development and maintenance of such constructions by states in general and key state institutions in particular.

Thus, critical attention to corporate and white-collar crime entails critical attention to states. If the research is itself funded by the state, then clear tensions are raised. Without descending into crude instrumentalism, it seems clear to us that certain implications do follow from state funding of academic research, implications which are of particular consequence for critical researchers. That the state does not relish the scrutiny by researchers who may present a particularly critical or even complex view of the role and activities of its institutions is no longer a controversial point. It has been well established through the experience of numerous researchers over the years, particularly in criminology.[56] But we should also be aware that, on one front, the neo-liberal project has made significant gains in assimilating social research into the "official" or business-friendly policy environment which rewards anyone who is "one of us."[57]

Once a group of researchers, or a university "department," to use a generic term, enters into a funding relationship with a state department, as a research council, or corporate grant holders, then it must accept that its research activities will, to some extent, be structured by those who hold the purse-strings.[58] Moreover, the pressure to accept such "direction" has increased—for many university departments that rely upon external funding, their future success may be gauged by their ability to secure and retain financial support from government and corporate sources. The increasing value being placed upon the securing of research grants means that loss of funding may have implications for the long-term sustainability of a university department's research output and the "success" of a department's research may be measured ultimately by the degree to which funders are satisfied with the output. With this measure as a primary performance indicator, it may become difficult to distinguish between the role of management consultancies and the role of some groups of researchers in universities.[59]

Regulating "Access": Power, Control, Exclusion

As all first year social science students of methodology know, gaining access to relevant data, organizations, people and so on is a common problem for social scientific research. And within criminology, access is problematic for researchers of conventional crime. Yet in comparison with offenders or potential offenders in the context of corporate and white-collar crime, conventional crime researchers are dealing with the relatively powerless, and this, whether we like it or not, renders such work immediately more feasible than dealing with, and seeking to focus upon, the relatively powerful. As Hughes has noted, studying relatively powerless groups is much more common than studying elite groups.[60] One reason for this is that, quite simply, "the inner sanctum of the company boardroom and the senior management enclaves within corporate hierarchies still remain a largely closed and secretive world."[61] And if we accept the accuracy of this observation by Reed, then it should be apparent that the inner sanctum is likely to be even more tightly sealed from outside scrutiny when the aim of the outside researcher is to investigate actual or possible illegality.

Of course, there is no obligation in the first instance for any corporation to agree to access or to provide information on request. If such requests are declined, there is very little by way of legal remedy: private corporations enjoy almost complete rights of ownership to information about their activities, save the requirement to submit the names and addresses of directors and basic annual financial returns to the public register at U.K. Companies House. In this sense, the very legal constitution of corporations is designed to avoid public disclosure of the details of their activities. Further, information *about* corporations gathered by the government, such as compliance information or tax returns, is in the main protected by that most mercurial of catch-all clauses, "commercial confidentiality."

Moreover, whether or not access is formally granted to social researchers, the opportunities afforded to corporations to obscure their structures, decision-making processes, lines of accountability, knowledge, and responsibility are socially and legally constructed in ways that limit, to say the least, opportunities for locating and understanding corporate illegality. And the increasing penetration of the private sector into state functions creates a further level of obstacles and complexity for the researcher. The incursion of private companies into spheres of activity such as prison management and policing means that previously accountable public authorities are supplanted by corporations who may deploy the privileges of the corporate veil (not least, again, on the basis of "commercial confidentiality"[62]). Thus, for example, details of contracts between the Prison Service and private companies that now run private jails may be hidden from the public—indeed, aspects of private prison management may even be withheld from state servants.[63]

Where access *is* successfully negotiated, this can quickly reveal itself as more apparent than real. As Jupp notes, often within organizations there are hierarchies of gatekeepers to be negotiated, with hierarchies of power and authority distributed among them.[64] Professor Hugh Pennington found precisely this after he was appointed by the government to lead an inquiry into a 1996 outbreak of *E. coli* in Lanarkshire (Scotland) which killed 18 people—a serial killing for which the offending shop owner was successfully prosecuted and fined £2,500. Formally, he was given access to all relevant government-held documents, but later found that key reports that detailed the filthy conditions of abattoirs were withheld by civil servants keen to avoid rigorous criticism of the industry and of poor regulatory standards.[65] Thus the problem of access does not end once you are "in"; it can be a continual process of negotiation and renegotiation. Formal access is often, then, only the beginning of securing real or adequate access.[66] We suggest that while these are common issues, they are more starkly raised when the objects of research are the powerful. Certainly, the possibility of deliberate obfuscation on the part of the researched is greater where one is dealing with individuals who are often well educated, possess highly developed social skills, are socialised into particular ideologies and cultures, and so on.

All in all, gaining access is highly problematic. The role of gatekeepers and the cooperation of the researched are common across social research,[67] the extent to which they may, or do, prove problematic varies according to the context. But these obstacles are particularly acute when researching the relatively powerful—corporations and high-status business-people. And they are, we have argued, even more acute where the social credibility of those potential research objects has been augmented, where their material power has increased (not least through performing functions previously carried out by state bodies), and where they increasingly are acting as funders, or potential funders, of research. Thus, in general, within the current neo-liberal conjuncture, there are good reasons to expect it to be more difficult to research the relatively powerful, where such research involves access to the powerful themselves.

Disseminating Research on the Crimes of the Powerful

We began this chapter by noting the relative dearth of work within criminology and criminal justice concerning the crimes of the powerful. Our arguments thus far—regarding the increasing commodification and marketization of universities and the commodification of "knowledge," and the trends toward funding research of immediate utility and our observations upon the nature of the research process—all help to explain this dearth of work. However, there is a final set of issues to be considered here. For where research on the crimes of the powerful *is* successfully conducted, then there remains the problem of disseminating that knowledge, which for university academics usually means having that work published in some form.

An obvious opening point is to note a reinforcing cycle of exclusion. If relatively few academic criminologists research corporate and white-collar crime, then this makes it less likely that book length studies of corporate and white-collar crime will appear. To the extent there are relatively few book length resources, particularly textbooks, there is likely to be relatively few undergraduate and postgraduate courses dedicated to these issues; this further undermines the market case for proposals for book length studies in these areas—and certainly not for textbooks, which, within the increasingly concentrated academic, and international, publishing industry,[68] not least due to rational calculations of potential markets and sales are increasingly the books of choice for publishers. In other words, there is simple market logic to the relative absence of books on corporate and white-collar crime when set against the mass of material concerned with "conventional" crimes.

Perhaps related are other, more subtle, "processes of exclusion." Thus, for example, Arrigo has referred, with echoes of the process of hegemony construction and maintenance, to "a suppressor effect"—and though his discussion was of critical criminology, it lends itself equally well to considering corporate and white-collar crime scholarship. Given that part of the struggle of critical criminology "is with dominant ideologies and how they are sustained through various means of communication," and that the marginalization of critical as compared with mainstream criminology is one function of a "journal-industrial complex," he claims that there exists a

> general "suppressor" effect operating within and throughout the Academy, particularly when critical scholarship is repeatedly denied recognition and thus legitimacy in the leading periodicals of our discipline. This is the presence of hegemony in the academy. What counts as "serious" scholarship and, hence, what is actively engaged in by critical criminologists is, all too often, circumscribed by the "chilling effect" found in the seemingly systematic exclusionary practices enacted and sustained by the more prestigious periodicals of our field.[69]

Of course, there are other, highly conscious processes whereby academic work on corporate and white-collar crimes is prevented from reaching a public audience. In the United Kingdom, researchers are commonly required by government agencies to sign the Official Secrets Act, and are bound to have any publication or dissemination cleared by the commissioning department.[70] An even more common tactic is the use of libel and other legal action on the part of the powerful designed to prevent publication of information which might expose their illegal activities. If recourse to law was part of a concerted effort by corporations to respond to the emergence of social activism and criticism in the late 1960s and the 1970s, more recently there has been an upsurge in the use of strategic lawsuits against public participation,[71] which have been developed partly as a means of preempting even the need to resort to libel laws. More generally, corporations have become rather adept at launching counter-offensive propaganda campaigns to discredit and persuade the withdrawal of research findings by deploying resources that invariably dwarf those available to scholars who conduct critical research.[72] This corporate counterattack has been facilitated by the general political shift to the right in both Britain and North America (which in itself has inhibited corporate and white-collar crime research). There is also reason to think that criminology will be the subject of legal control as much as—if not more than—any other field of social scientific study. For, as Carson has noted in relation to an attempt by the Australian attorney general to censor two papers presented at the 1996 Australian and New Zealand Society of Criminology Conference,

> Academic freedom in the field of criminology is perhaps even more problematic and more important than quite a few areas of academic endeavor because it's touching the State at a raw nerve. . . . Almost automatically, if we are studying crime, we are messing around with some of the most powerful constructs the State has at its disposal.[73]

Censorship of research findings remains a frequent state response to those who produce government-funded work that does not sit comfortably with government or departmental policy. Indeed, where the research is funded by government, censorship does not always require the threat of legal action. Several examples of "straight" censorship have been exposed in the U.K. media in recent years.[74]

Further, we should keep in our minds Edwin Sutherland's enforced self-censorship to protect the names of guilty corporations, a censorship demanded by his own university who were unprepared to defend Sutherland's academic freedom against the threat of libel action, and were also concerned about the impact of his book on corporate funding.[75] Preemptive action taken by universities in anticipation of either legal issues arising or simply to avoid upsetting corporate sponsors continues to plague corporate crime researchers. Following Tweedale's research into the major asbestos producer, T&N, he found his manuscript vetted by his university management—who then, supported by legal advice, demanded that, despite the successful conviction of T&N for health and safety crimes, this phenomenon should be described neither as murder or crime.[76] Maurice Punch has recorded that his book on corporate deviance[77] was held up for a year because of "legal issues," and that ultimately he was forced to make many incisions and deletions in order to avoid threats of libel.[78] Similarly, the publication of Braithwaite's (1984) classic study of *Corporate Crime in the Pharmaceutical Industry* was delayed for two years when managers whom he had interviewed used lawyers to haggle over "300 empirical claims that might be raised in court."[79]

In short, both conscious and unconscious efforts and assumptions may operate—often in combination—to exclude certain forms of work from prestigious publications and thereby challenge the legitimacy of this work. And these processes of exclusion combine with other, mutually reinforcing processes concerning funding and access to create a profound effect on our ability to subject the powerful to critical academic scrutiny.

Conclusion: Researching Corporate and White-Collar Crime in an Era of Neo-Liberalism

If there has ever existed some relative independence of academic work from the political imperatives of the powerful, an independence somehow turned toward the advancement of an "objective" knowledge, then this has been under sustained attack both within and beyond universities in the era in which neo-liberalism has reached national and international hegemony.

Yet we are not implying that the disciplinary effects of marketization and commodification have eradicated the space in which alternative research agendas can be developed. Certainly, there are good historical reasons for resisting such a pessimistic conclusion. As Nicolaus points out in his account of the Sociology Liberation Movement, the prolonged political struggle in American sociology during this period indicated that the relationship between the social sciences and the state is not always marked by passive servility and consensual acquiescence.[80] In the United States, notwithstanding the scale of academia, there appears to be both a vibrant critical criminology group within the ASC and a critical mass of corporate and white-collar crime scholarship. In the United Kingdom, criminology has in different periods and to varying degrees been the site of struggles between the criminological state technologues (described by Young as administrative criminology) and critical and radical critiques linked to social movements and counter-hegemonic groups outside the universities.[81] The protagonists of those struggles were thus differentiated not only by their opposing political perspectives, but also by the nature of their organic link to and engagement with the hegemonic bloc and with counter-hegemonic movements, respectively.

Nor is it the case that commodification and marketization have created the same conditions in all institutions. In fact, at least in the United Kingdom, these processes are at different stages of advancement across the sector[82] and there is still space within higher education to conduct relatively "independent" research, particularly in departments that continue to preserve the link between teaching and research. Furthermore, as Epstein has noted, although critical research may not be having much of an impact upon the culture of universities, even under difficult conditions "a surprising number of faculty manage to sustain some connection to progressive activism outside the university."[83]

From the outset, the neo-liberal assault upon the universities in Western democracies has unfolded with little or no opportunity for participation in political debate in the public arena or within internal university decision-making structures.[84] But this is not to say that the process of marketization of the universities has gone unchallenged. In an empirical sense, then, the march of neo-liberalism through the universities is not complete nor unstoppable. Moreover, in a theoretical sense, it is inconceivable that the marketization of the universities will proceed unobstructed. For one thing, the Gramscian concept of hegemony alerts us to the fact that dominance is never complete nor entirely secure, but always open to challenge and resistance. Given that corporations and the state continue to require a heavily subsidized publicly funded education system, it is likely the universities will continue to receive state subsidies for as long as they are required to perform a technological and educative role for capital. They will therefore be required, at one level, to account for the public subsidy that this entails. In this sense, the universities will remain an important site for struggle, and one where the contradictions inherent in the dominant representation of the function of universities as educative, independent, acting in the public interest and so on can be regularly and effectively exposed.

Indeed, the very processes of marketization render explicit the contradictory nature of the university within capitalist social orders—particularly between the ways in which universities' existence is represented and/or legitimated, and in terms of the rather schizophrenic ways in which they, and the academic staff within them, act. Certainly, there are several closely related reasons which indicate why universities cannot *simply* act as unfettered subjects of the market in the way that some other commercial operations might.

First, many universities have constructed for themselves long and proud histories, based upon reputations for the quality of their product, whether in terms of their teaching or their research. In this sense, there is reason to believe that the marketization of the universities has a limit; universities can never act as "pure" commercial concerns, responding to the demands of corporations without losing control over the quality of their product. A university which attempted to act purely commercially would at some point find itself losing market share in terms of both students and research grants—and would, in any case, be unattractive for private capital since one of the key commodities that such capital buys from universities is precisely the reputation for, or claims to, relative independence, objectivity, and so on.

Second, for all the drive toward utility in research activity and output, states themselves require universities to continue to meet ideological expectations of acting as "independent" voices, and thus require university research to air voices that are critical of existing social, economic, and political arrangements. Thus, liberal claims of state neutrality dictate that some funding be granted to critical voices, even where these are voices of resistance, since the liberal state must at least be seen to be supporting and acting on behalf of those who claim to take seriously its ideals of greater social equality, social justice, and democratic accountability.[85]

Third, universities, as publicly funded institutions, remain rather more vulnerable to public opinion than private corporations. This aspect of higher education institutions creates the space for critical debate. Relatedly, the fact of continuing public funding for universities renders them partially accountable, at least in principle. Even if we know that public bodies, including universities, regularly evade accountability, we also know that they can be reformed to improve standards of accountability: this is much more difficult in the case of the private sector, where companies have a fiduciary duty to their shareholders, are subject to the unrelenting imperatives of the stock market, and resist external scrutiny via the corporate veil and claims of commercial confidentiality.

Fourth, as (partially) publicly funded bodies, universities still retain some ideological commitment to democratic forms of management and functioning, and there remain some structural features which reflect these commitments. One such aspect is the existence of tenure or tenure-type arrangements in various countries' higher education systems. A second is the continued existence of academic trade unions. It remains the case that unions are recognized and nationally agreed conditions of service operate throughout many higher education systems. A third aspect is the persistence of some form of employee representation on boards and management committees and other quasi-democratic governance structures. Now, this is not to claim that such arrangements are operative or necessarily democratic, nor to deny that each has also been subject to considerable erosion; but it is to recognize that these structures persist, that they are worth defending (and, of course, seeking to extend), and that their existence is intimately related to the ideological cloth in which universities wrap themselves.

As the neo-liberal hegemonic project gains momentum, changed political, social, and academic climates pose fundamental challenges for critical social science in general and for critical criminologists in particular. But those who would shine a light on power, not least through researching the crimes of corporations and high-status business people, are feeling, and will feel, these challenges even more intensely. These are not challenges that we are all equally well placed to meet. Those academics who enjoy *relative* privilege—such as permanent contracts, institutional support, some traces of academic freedom and discretion—have a greater responsibility than others. In an atmosphere of creeping orthodoxy, criminologists must keep to the forefronts of their mind that being an academic means engaging in an inherently critical enterprise, one that requires us to ask awkward questions of power and the existent social order. It is time to face up to the realities of this task and resist the rising tide of corruption that looms before us both inside and outside the walls of educational institutions.

Endnotes

1. See Reiman, 1998, Slapper and Tombs, 1999.
2. Levi, 1987: xx.
3. Cohen, 1981: 220.
4. Geis et al, 1995: 13.
5. Snider, 2003: 63.
6. Snider, 1997: 6.
7. Snider, 2000: 171; and see Tombs, 2001.
8. Slapper and Tombs, 1999: 85–109, Snider, 2000.
9. Pearce and Tombs, 1990, Snider, 1990.
10. Pearce and Tombs, 1998, Tombs, 1990, 1996.

11. Snider, 2000: 172.
12. What we have to say here is much enhanced by collaboration with Paddy Hillyard and Joe Sim, whilst we have benefited greatly from working with a group of colleagues on an edited collection (Tombs and Whyte, 2003a) which explores in greater detail many of the themes set out in this chapter.
13. Barnett, 1994.
14. See Thompson, 1970, 1980, Miliband, 1973, Nicolaus, 1972, Shaw, 1972.
15. Marrer and Patton, 1976, cited in Stankiewicz, 1986: 44.
16. Soley, 1998: 230–31.
17. Geiger, 1992; Ovetz, 1996; and Rivers, 1998: 60.
18. Ovetz, 1996: 115.
19. Newson and Buchbinder, 1988: 11–19.
20. Slaughter and Leslie, 1997, Appendix.
21. See Slaughter, 1998, Ovetz, 1996, Kelsey, 1998, and Orr, 1997, respectively; and for an excellent overview of these trends at the international level, see the papers collected in Currie and Newson, 1998.
22. Currie, 1998: 6–7.
23. Kelsey, 1998: 53–54.
24. Orr, 1997; Kishun, 1998,
25. Orr, 1997: 63.
26. Kelsey, 1998: 54.
27. See, for example, Slaughter and Leslie, 1997: 41.
28. Simpson, 1998: xxix, emphases in the original.
29. The ESRC is the main social science research council, a QUANGO with an annual budget of over £100 million; http://www.esrcsocietytoday.ac.uk/ESRCInfoCentre/about/
30. ESRC, 1999: Chairman's Statement.
31. Lipsey, 2000: 1.
32. See, for example, Secretary of State for Trade and Industry Mandelson, cited in Monbiot, 2000: 7, Osler, passim, Hay, 1999, passim.
33. Blair, 1999.
34. Tombs and Whyte, 2003b.
35. For a case-study of the dominance of oil industry personnel on the relevant Foresight panels, see Muttitt and Lindblom, 2003: 42–43.
36. Ovetz, 1996: 120.
37. Tombs and Whyte, 2003b.
38. Ovetz, 1996: 126.
39. Foucault, quoted in Cohen, 1981: 220.
40. Garland, 1994: 28.
41. On which reading, the challenges to mainstream criminology of the labelling perspective, then of critical criminology in the late 60s and 1970, leading to the formation of the National Deviancy Conference, were somewhat fleeting and, in the medium term, largely unsuccessful; Cohen, 1981.
42. Cohen, 1981: 236.
43. Rock, 1994: 135.
44. Rock and Holdaway, 1998: 9–10.
45. Alvesalo and Tombs, forthcoming.
46. These are discussed much more fully in Hillyard et al., 2004.
47. *Times Higher Educational Supplement*, 20 November, 1998.
48. HESA, 2005.
49. Scraton, 2001: 3.
50. van Swaaningen 1997: 7, see also van Swaaningen, 1999.
51. Rock, 1994: 133.
52. Crace, 2001.

53. See, for example, Hughes, 1996, Jupp, 1989, Lee, 1993, 1997.
54. For all the problems associated with his own "third dimension" of power, not least for its failure to transcend completely the problematic of human agency, Lukes's (1974) critical discussion of agency-based theorizations of power is instructive on the distinction being made here.
55. Hillyard and Sim, 1997: 56–57.
56. For example, Baldwin and McConville, 1977; Cohen and Taylor, 1977; Scraton et al., 1991; see also Tombs and Whyte, 2003a.
57. Hillyard and Sim, 1997: 58.
58. Whyte, 2000.
59. See Whyte, 1999: 54–58
60. Hughes, 1996: 77.
61. Reed, 1989: 79, quoted in Punch, 1996: 4.
62. For example, Freiberg 1997.
63. See Sim et al., 1995. Indeed, in a rather more fundamental sense, and to turn full circle, the commodification of criminal justice provision itself has meant that academics who research prisons, policing, or other state justice agencies are increasingly working directly for private interest. This creation of sub-economies of research on demand creates myriad conflicts of interest and incentives to manipulate research findings in line with the requirements of paymaster (Geis et al., 1999).
64. Jupp, 1989.
65. *Daily Record*, 7 March 1997.
66. Jupp, 1989: 134.
67. Bryman, 1988.
68. Barnett and Low, 1996; Schiffrin, 2000.
69. Arrigo, 2000: 1.
70. And note the recent debate in the *Canadian Journal of Criminology* on the use of limited confidentiality clauses by government.
71. Beder, 1997, Monbiot, 1997, Rowell, 1996, Vick and Campbell, 2001.
72. Bosely, 2000: 1; Gelbspan, 1997: 3; Tweedale, 2000 and 2003.
73. Carson, quoted in Presdee and Walters, 1998: 158.
74. Travis 1994; Dyer 2000.
75. Geis and Goff 1983.
76. Tweedale, 2003.
77. Punch 1996.
78. Punch 2000: 247.
79. Punch 1996: 44.
80. Nicolaus, 1972.
81. Sim et al, 1987.
82. Edwards, 1998: 260.
83. Epstein, 2001: 201.
84. Newson and Buchbinder, 1988.
85. We are grateful to Laureen Snider for noting the need to make such points explicit.

References

Alvesalo, A., and S. Tombs (2004) *Evaluating Economic Crime Control?* Annual Meeting of the American Society of Criminology, November, Nashville.

Arrigo, B. (2000) "Critical Criminology's Discontent: The Perils of Punishing and a Call to Action." *The Critical Criminologist, http://sun.soci.niu.edu/~critcrim/critschool/barrigo.html.*

Baldwin, J., and M. McConville (1977) *Negotiated Justice*, Oxford: Martin Robertson.

Barnett, R. (1994) *The Limits of Competence: Knowledge, Higher Education and Society*. Buckingham, England: Society for Research into Higher Education and Open University Press.

Barnett, C., and M. Low (1996) *Lingua Franca: International Publishing and the Academy as Public Sphere*. British Sociological Association Annual Conference, University of Reading, 4 April.

Beder, S. (1997) *Global Spin. The Corporate Assault on Environmentalism*. Totnes, England: Green Books.

Blair, T. (1999) *Romanes Lecture*. Oxford, 2 December.

Bosely, S. (2000) "$2m Plot to Discredit Smoking Study Exposed." *The Guardian*, 7 April.

Bryman, A., ed. (1988) *Doing Research in Organisations*. London: Routledge.

Cohen, S. (1981) "Footprints on the Sand: A Further Report on Criminology and the Sociology of Deviance in Britain." Pp. 220–247 in *Crime and Society. Readings in History and Theory,* Editors M. Fitzgerald, G. McLennan, and J. Pawson. London: Routledge and Kegan Paul.

Cohen, S., and Taylor, L. (1977) "Talking About Prison Blues." In *Doing Sociological Research,* Editors C. Bell and H. Newby London: George Allen and Unwin.

Crace, J. (2001) "Free and Fair." *The Guardian. Education Supplement*, 29 May.

Currie, J. (1998) "Introduction." In *Universities and Globalisation,* Editors J. Currie and J. Newson. Thousand Oaks, CA: Sage.

Currie, J., and Newson, J., eds. (1998) *Universities and Globalisation. Critical perspectives*, Thousand Oaks, CA: Sage.

Dyer, C. (2000) "Home Office Censors Report from Anti-Torture Group." *The Guardian*, 13 January.

Edwards, M. (1998) "Commodification and Control in Mass Higher Education: A Double Edged Sword." In T*he New Higher Education: Issues and Directions for the Post-Dearing University*, Editors D. Jary and M. Parker. Stoke-on-Trent: Staffordshire University Press.

Epstein, B. (2001) "Corporate Culture and the Academic Left." In *Market Killing: What the Free Market Does and What Social Scientists Can Do About It,* Editors, G. Philo and D. Miller. London: Pearson Education.

ESRC (1999) *Annual Report 1998/99 www.esrc.ac.uk/esrccontent/publicationslist/arep9899/report9899.html*

Freiberg, A. (1997) "Commercial Confidentiality, Criminal Justice and the Public Interest." *Current Issues in Criminal Justice* 9:125–152.

Garland, D. (1994) "Of Crimes and Criminals: the development of criminology in Britain." in Maguire, M., Morgan, R. and Reiner, R., eds., *The Oxford Handbook of Criminology*, Oxford: Oxford University Press, 17–68.

Geiger, R. (1992) "The Dynamics of University Research in the United States: 1945–90." in Whiston, T. and Geiger, R., eds., *Research and Higher Education: the United Kingdom and the United States*, Buckingham, England: The Society for Research into Higher Education and Open University Press.

Geis, G., and Goff, C. (1983) "Introduction." in Sutherland, E, *White Collar Crime: the uncut version*, London: Yale University.

Geis, G., Meier, R. and Salinger, L. (1995) "Introduction." in Geis, G., Meier, R. and Salinger, L., eds., *White Collar Crime: Classic and Contemporary Views,* New York: Free Press.

Geis, G., Mobley, A., and Shichor, D. (1999) "Private Prisons, Criminological Research, and Conflict of Interest. A Case Study." *Crime and Delinquency* 45. 372–388.

Gelbspan, R. (1997) "Hot Air on Global Warming: science and academia in the service of the fossil fuel industry." *Multinational Monitor*, 18 (11), November.

Hay, C. (1999) *The Political Economy of New Labour*, London: Unwin Hyman.

HESA (2005) *Summary of Academic Staff in all UK Institutions 2003/04*, *www.hesa.ac.uk/holisdocs/pubinfo/staff/staff0304.htm*

Hillyard, P and Sim, J (1997) "The Political Economy of Socio-legal Research." in Thomas, P (ed.) *Socio-legal Studies*, Aldershot: Dartmouth.

Hillyard, P., Sim, J., Tombs, S., and Whyte, D, "Leaving a "Stain Upon the Silence": contemporary criminology and the politics of dissent." *British Journal of Criminology*, 44, (3), 369–90.

Hughes, G (1996) "The Politics of Criminological Research." in Sapsford, R (ed.) *Researching Crime and Criminal Justice*, Milton Keynes: Open University Press.

Jupp, V. (1989) *Methods of Criminological Research*, London: Unwin Hyman.

Kelsey, J (1998) "Privatizing the Universities," *Journal of Law and Society.* 25, (1), 51–70.

Kishun, R. (1998) "Internationalisation in South Africa." in Scott, P., ed., *The Meanings of Mass Higher Education*, Buckingham: Open University Press.

Lee, R. (1993) *Doing Research on Sensitive Topics*, London, Sage.

Lee, R. (1997) "Socio-Legal Research- what's the use?." in Thomas, P., ed., *Socio-Legal Studies*, Aldershot: Dartmouth.

Levi, M. (1987) *Regulating Fraud. White-Collar Crime and the Criminal Process*, London: Tavistock.

Lipsey, Lord (2000) "Ruling By Research." *Social Sciences—news from the ESRC, May 2000, www.esrc.ac.uk/news1.html.*

Lukes, S. (1974) *Power. A radical view*, London: Macmillan.

Miliband, R. (1973) *The State in Capitalist Society*, London: Quartet.

Monbiot, G. (2000) *Captive State: the corporate takeover of Britain*, London: MacMillan.

Monbiot, G. (1997) "Law and the Profits of PR." *The Guardian*, 21 August, Macmillan.

Muttitt, G., and Lindblom, H. (2003) *Degrees of Capture: an examination of the relationship between the upstream oil and gas industry and UK higher education institutions*, Oxford: Corporate Watch.

Newson, J., and Buchbinder, H. (1988) *The University Means Business*, Toronto: Garamond Press.

Nicolaus, M. (1972) "The Professional Organisation of Sociology: a view from below." in Blackburn, R. (ed.) *Ideology and Social Science: readings in critical social science*, London: Fontana.

Orr, L. (1997) "Globalisation and the Universities: toward the market university?." *Social Dynamics,* 23, (1): 42–67.

Osler, D. (2002) *Labour Party PLC. New labour as a party of business*, Edinburgh: Mainstream.

Ovetz, R. (1996) "Turning Resistance into Rebellion: student movements and the entrepreneurialisation of the universities." *Capital and Class*, 58, 113–152.

Pearce, F., and Tombs, S. (1990) "Ideology, Hegemony and Empiricism: compliance theories of regulation." *British Journal of Criminology*, 30 (4).

Pearce, F., and Tombs, S. (1991) "Policing Corporate 'Skid Rows.' A reply to Keith Hawkins." *British Journal of Criminology*, 31 (4).

Pearce, F., and Tombs, S. (1998) *Toxic Capitalism: corporate crime and the chemical industry*, Aldershot: Dartmouth.

Presdee, M., and Walters, R. (1998) "The Perils and Politics of Criminological Research and the treat to Academic Freedom." *Current Issues in Criminal Justice*, 10, (2), 156–167.

Punch, M. (1996) *Dirty Business: exploring corporate misconduct. Analysis and cases*, London: Sage.

Punch, M. (2000) "Suite Violence: why managers manage and corporations kill." *Crime Law and Social Change*, 33, 243–280.

Reiman, J. (1998) *The Rich Get Richer and the Poor Get Prison,* Boston: Allyn and Bacon.

Rivers, J. (1998) "Chomsky Warns of Corporate Secrecy Threat." *Times Higher Education Supplement*, November 20.

Rock, P. (1994) "The Social Organisation of British Criminology." in Maguire, M., Morgan, R., and Reiner, R., eds., *The Oxford Handbook of Criminology*, Oxford: Oxford University Press, 125–148.

Rock, P., and Holdaway, S. (1998) "Thinking about Criminology: 'facts are bits of biography'." in Holdaway, S. and Rock, P., eds., *Thinking About Criminology*, London: UCL Press, 1–13.

Rowell, A. (1996) *Green Backlash: Corporate subversion of the environment movement*, London: Routledge.

Schiffrin, A. (2000) *The Business of Books*, London: Verso.

Scraton, P. (2001) "A Response to Lynch and the Schwendingers." *The Critical Criminologist,* 1, 2, March, 1–3.

Scraton, P., Sim, J. and Skidmore, P. (1991) *Prisons Under Protest*, Milton Keynes: Open University Press.

Shaw, M. (1972) "The Coming Crisis of Radical Sociology." in Blackburn, R (ed.) *Ideology and Social Science: readings in critical social science*, London: Fontana.

Sim, J., Ruggiero, V, and Ryan, M (1995) "Punishment in Europe: perceptions and commonalities." in Ruggiero, V, Ryan, M and Sim, J (eds.) *Western European Prison Systems*, London: Sage.

Sim, J., Scraton, P., and Gordon, P. (1987) "Introduction: Crime, the State and Critical Analysis." in Scraton, P (ed.) *Law Order and the Authoritarian State*, Milton Keynes: Open University Press, 1–70.

Simpson, C. (1998) "Universities, Empire and the Production of Knowledge: an introduction." in Simpson, C., ed., *Universities and Empire. Money and politics in the social sciences during the cold war*, New York: the New Press, xi–xxxiv.

Slapper, G., and Tombs, S. (1999) Corporate Crime, Harlow Essex: Longman.

Slaughter, S., and Leslie, L. (1997) *Academic Capitalism: politics, policies and the entrepreneurial university,* Baltimore: Johns Hopkins University Press.

Slaughter, S. (1998) "National Higher Education Policies in a Global Economy." in Currie, J., and Newson, J., eds., *Universities and Globalisation*, Thousand Oaks, Calif.: Sage.

Snider, L. (1990) "Cooperative Models and Corporate Crime: panacea or cop-out?." *Crime and Delinquency*, 36 (3), 373–390.

Snider, L. (1997) *Downsizing, Deregulation and Corporate Crime*, Annual Meeting of the American Society of Criminology, 19–22 November, San Diego.

Snider, L. (2000) "The Sociology of Corporate Crime: an obituary (or: whose knowledge claims have legs?)." *Theoretical Criminology*, 4 (2), 166–206.

Snider, L. (2003) "No Funding, No Access, Then You Get Sued: methodological obstacles to studying corporate crime." in Tombs, S., and Whyte, D. (eds.), *Researching the Crimes of the Powerful*, Peter Lang: New York.

Soley, L. (1998) "The New Corporate Yen for Scholarship." in Simpson, C., ed., *Universities and Empire. Money and politics in the social sciences during the cold war*, New York: the New Press.

Stankiewicz, R (1986) *Academics and Entrepreneurs: developing university-industry relations*, London: Frances Pinter.

Sutherland, E (1983) *White Collar Crime: the uncut version*, London: Yale University Press.

Thompson, E.P. (1970) *Warwick University Ltd*, Harmondsworth, Middlesex: Penguin.

Thompson, E. P. (1980) *Writing by Candlelight*, London: Merlin.

Tombs, S. (1990) "Industrial Injuries in British Manufacturing." *Sociological Review*, 38, 2, May, 324–343.

Tombs, S. (1996) "Injury, Death and the Deregulation Fetish: the of occupational safety regulation in United Kingdom manufacturing industries." *International Journal of Health Services*, 26 (2), 327–347.

Tombs, S. (2001) "Thinking About 'White-Collar' Crime." in Lindgren, S-Å., ed., *White-Collar Crime Research. Old Views and Future Potentials. Lectures and Papers from a Scandinavian Seminar. (BRÅ-Rapport 2001:1),* Stockholm: Brottsförebyggande rådet/Fritzes, 13–34.

Tombs, S., and Whyte, D., eds. (2003a) *Unmasking the Crimes of the Powerful: Scrutinising States and Corporations?,* New York: Peter Lang.

Tombs, S., and Whyte, D. (2003b) "Scrutinising the Powerful: Crime, contemporary political economy and critical social research." in Tombs, S. and Whyte, D., eds., *Unmasking the Crimes of the Powerful: Scrutinising States and Corporations?,* New York: Peter Lang.

Travis, A. (1994) "Ministers Suppress Research." *The Guardian*, 4 July.

van Swaaningen, R. (1997) *Critical Criminology: Visions from Europe*, London: Sage.

Tweedale, G. (2000) *Magic Mineral to Killer Dust: Turner and Newall and the asbestos hazard*, Oxford: Oxford University Press.

Tweedale, G. (2003) "Researching Corporate Crime: a business historian"s perspective." in Tombs, S. and Whyte, D. (eds.), *Researching the Crimes of the Powerful*, New York: Peter Lang.

van Swaaningen, R. (1997) *Critical Criminology: Visions from Europe*, London: Sage.

van Swaaningen, R. (1999) "Reclaiming Critical Criminology: social justice and the European Tradition." *Theoretical Criminology*, 3, 1, 5–28.

Vick, D.W., and Campbell, K. (2001) "Public Protests, Private Lawsuits, and the Market: the investor response to the McLibel case." *Journal of Law and Society*, 28 (2), 204–241.

Whyte, D. (1999) *Power, Ideology and the Regulation of Safety in the post-Piper Alpha Offshore Oil Industry*, unpublished PhD thesis, Liverpool: John Moores University.

Whyte, D. (2000) "Researching the Powerful: toward a political economy of method?," in King, R. and Wincup, E., eds., *Doing Research on Crime and Justice*, Oxford: Oxford University Press.

2

An Age of Miracles?[1]

Frank Pearce

It is easy to believe that we live in an age of miracles and a time of spiritual revitalization. In Britain in the 1990s, Ernest Saunders was convicted and sentenced to prison for false accounting, two counts of theft, and conspiracy to contravene the Prevention of Fraud Act 1958, for his part in the illegalities involved in the Distillers/Guinness takeover bid. But before completing his sentence, he was released because of the onset of Alzheimer's disease. Yet, within months, his symptoms disappeared and he was communicating with the public on talk-shows, and back in business. Moreover, he and convicted co-conspirators were blessed with enough money, even 12 years later, to pursue an ultimately unsuccessful appeal against their convictions. Then, in the year 2000, General Pinochet was judged by the then British Home Secretary, Jack Straw, to be unfit for reasons of ill-health to stand trial in Spain for his role in the disappearance and death of people in Chile after his overthrow of the democratically elected government of socialist President Salvador Allende in the early 1970s, when as many as 30,000 people are believed to have died as a result of this U.S.-backed and CIA-aided coup. Yet, on his return to Chile, this frail old man, seemingly confined to a wheelchair, was able to get up, walk, and warmly greet his supporters.[2] Miraculous indeed!

If these seem isolated incidents, it is worth noting that in many nations and internationally there appears to be less evidence than before of white-collar and corporate crimes. In the United States, for example, there has been a recent and dramatic drop in the numbers of prosecutions and convictions for monopolistic practices, financial crimes, and environmental and occupational safety and health offenses compared to the 1970s and the 1980s. At the same time, there has been a growth in the belief that when these "illegalities" *do* occur, they are errors on the part of good corporate citizens, and any damaging effects are the inevitable costs of progress: after all, a risk-free world is as unlikely as one free of all sin. The Enron scandal shows that even the best human beings and human institutions are occasionally fallible, but, as U.S. Treasury Secretary Patrick O'Neill said, Enron's demise can also be read as part of the "genius of capitalism,"[3] no doubt a "market correction." So such events actually have as little relevance in understanding the fundamental dynamics of the modern world as did the savings and loan crisis of the 1980s.[4] President Bush has noted that widespread stock ownership creates a moral responsibility for the executives to run an honest company, and while, in fact, "the vast majority of businessmen and women are honest," a small minority have created problems and this means that there is as need for deepening of the ethic of corporate responsibility: "In the long run," Bush suggests, "there's no capitalism without conscience; there is no wealth without character."[5]

But moral Western societies are by no means free of "evil." Even with the development of the "compassionate conservatism" of Bush—which might in principle pay serious attention to discovering the factors that make criminal conduct more likely—there remains the focus on catching, punishing, and incapacitating those who are believed to commit a disproportionate number of what many criminologists call, or simply assume to be, "real crimes." This is not too surprising since, as Peter Singer has shown, there is a continuous tension between Bush's tax-cutting strategies and other promises he makes, such as ending "deep, persistent poverty."[6] There are also believed to be international problems linked with transnational organized crime.[7] While President Ronald Reagan had successfully destroyed the "Evil Empire" of the Soviets,[8] we are still living with aspects of its disordering aftermath. And there is a new and somewhat similar danger, namely, "terrorism." Amalgamating these concerns, Bush claims that "Al Qaeda is to terror what the mafia is to crime."[9]

Since 9/11, it has seemed clear that in all "civilized" countries the state must now deal with infiltration by new insidious external enemies, only too often financed and sheltered by terrorist states. This was seen to justify the armed assault on Afghanistan against Al Qaeda and the Taliban, while, incidentally, accepting as a major ally Pakistan, itself ruled by a leader of a military coup. Paving the ideological ground for attack was the identification of an "axis of evil"—Communist North Korea, fundamentalist Iran, and Saddam Hussein's Iraq.[10] (On occasion, Cuba, for years battered by a U.S.-led ideological, military, and economic offensive, has been linked with this axis.[11]) Of course, as is now clear, Iraq was illegally invaded, and with disastrous consequences.[12] U.S.-led action, it is claimed, is justifiable, since other institutions, such as the emergent International Criminal Court, are likely to be used cynically *against* the United States by its enemies.[13] Thus there are no non-American guarantors of international "justice." Quite the opposite, in fact.

Why is there so much opposition to the United States? Why were the Pentagon and the World Trade Center targeted, and why do American citizens and establishments around the world see themselves as potential "targets" of marginalized peoples? Two related reasons emanate from the U.S. administration. First, America was attacked because its opponents were simply "evil"—but God was with America, and America had "stood down enemies before" and would "do so this time."[14] In the light of this "struggle of good and evil" the Bush administration launched "Operation Infinite Justice." This seemed to be a new Christian "crusade" against Islam. The Bush administration soon changed its tone and claimed that its major target was a minority of Islamic fundamentalist terrorists and, indeed, it "acknowledged" the importance of reasonable Muslims by changing the name of its "Operation" to "Operation Enduring Freedom." After all, Saudi Arabia, home of Mecca, is one of America's staunchest allies; at the same time, it is a corrupt and thoroughly anti-democratic country, known for both religious and political repression.[15] Second, there is envy. As George Bush said in the immediate aftermath of 9/11, America was attacked because it was "the brightest beacon of freedom and opportunity in the world"[16] and, as he later elaborated, prior to caging "suspects" at Guantanamo Bay, "they hate our freedoms, our freedom of religion, our freedom of speech, our freedom to vote, and assemble, and disagree with each other."[17] America, on the other hand, supports, and is supported by, democratic, peace- and freedom-loving peoples, and their governments

Of course, the U.S. State—the corporate-guided engine of a globalizing neoliberalism and the self-appointed guardian of "freedom" and "democracy" and "freedom of faith"—has always been extremely selective in the applications of its publicly stated principles when deciding which political regimes to attack, tolerate, or actively support. When these are further elaborated their meaning shifts significantly, as was clear in some of Bush's remarks after the invasion of Afghanistan when he gave his only partially coded representation of the bases of human dignity: "Dignity requires the rule of law, *limits on the power of the state*, respect for women, *private property*, equal justice, religious tolerance."[18] Their meaning is rendered clearer by the actions of Lewis Paul Bremer III, installed on May 11, 2003, by the United States as head of the Coalition Provisional Authority. Soon after being appointed he fired 500,000 state workers, including not just soldiers, but doctors, nurses, teachers, publishers, and printers; he opened the boarders to unrestricted imports, planned to privatize 200 state-owned companies; he allowed foreign companies to own 100 percent of Iraqi assets (outside of the natural resource sector) and to repatriate all profits; but he left in place one of Saddam Hussein's policies—"laws restricting trade unions and collective bargaining."[19] In addition, the Bush administration was sympathetic to the attempted right-wing coup against democratically elected President Chavez of Venezuela until it manifestly failed[20] and is currently engaged in a propaganda war against Telesur, the television network co-founded by Venezuela, Argentina, Cuba, and Uruguay.[21]

Noam Chomsky has been documenting for many years the significant disjuncture between America's rhetoric and its effective guiding principles: his work provides a source of many of the examples used here.[22] The United States was born of European, and specifically English, Imperialism. Spanish, French, Dutch, and English settlers justified their presence and their expropriation of land in the Americas by the general Christian doctrine that God had given the world to mankind as a whole. The pre-conquest population of the Americas has been quite conservatively estimated by William Denevan to have been between 43 million and 65 million people, and Russell Thornton puts the figure at 57–112 million.[23] By the eighteenth century the population of aboriginal peoples was nearer 5% than 10% of that number.

The émigré English argued that since they and not aboriginal peoples cared for and improved land and (accurately enough on this one point) put in place regimes of private property, they had a right to this land. This was justified by the English Protestant interpretation of Genesis I: 28—"be fruitful and multiply."[24] The opposing savage native peoples, usually "heathens," could be vanquished by acts of war as indeed they were—to the point of genocide.[25] After the American War of Independence, it was not hard for the elite that ran a new country with a large number of slaves to feel free to assert an exclusive sphere of influence in the Americas nor to claim it had the "Manifest Destiny" to bring private property, Protestantism, and its version of democracy to other lands, whether they were nearby, like Mexico and Cuba, or distant but strategic states, such as the Philippines.[26] In 1839, John O'Sullivan provided a clear formulation of this doctrine:

> In its magnificent domain of space and time, the nation of many nations is destined to manifest to mankind the excellence of divine principles; to establish on earth the noblest temple dedicated to the worship of the most High—the Sacred and the True. Its floor shall be as hemisphere—its roof the firmament of the star-studded heavens, and its congregations an Union of many Republics, comprising hundreds of happy millions. . . .[27]

A similar rationale inspired U.S. involvement in World War I, which few would now see as much more than a struggle between rival Imperialist powers. Then, while World War II was undoubtedly primarily between the Allies—Britain and its empire, Russia and the United States—on the one side, and the Axis powers—Germany, Italy, and Japan—on the other, a key cause of the conflict in the Pacific theater was a pre-war rivalry between Britain, the United States, and Japan for the domination of China, and, in the background, the 1904/1905 war between Japan and Russia. The more general course of World War II was marked by rivalry between Britain and the United States and by a more fundamental struggle between Britain and the United States against Russia.[28] There is good evidence that strategic considerations about containing Russian power, rather than any calculation that their use would save American lives, played the key role in the decisions to drop the atomic bombs on Hiroshima and Nagasaki.[29] Yet, at the same time, retribution—indeed, seemingly divine retribution—was at work, for, immediately after the first bomb was dropped, President Truman warned that if the Japanese leaders did not accept the surrender terms, "they may expect a rain of ruin from the air, the like of which has never been seen on this earth"[30]; and in private, he thanked God that the bomb "has come to us instead of our enemies and we pray that he may guide us to use it in his ways and for his purposes."[31] Nine years later, under Eisenhower's Presidency, "In God We Trust" became America's national motto. During the cold war against the Soviet Union, when the United States led the "free world," the latter contained as many, if not more, dictatorships than democracies, and was marked more by poverty than affluence.

While each of these regimes may have imagined itself to be actuated by purely "political" or "religious" motives,[32] we do not need to share this illusion. Imperialist domination and expansionism seem to have been the major motivating factor and religious ideologies, while important, have been something of a gloss. After all, the strictly internal development of religions is only ever partial and of limited duration for, in the long run, the aspects of a specific religion that survive will be impersonally selected out for their compatibility with the development of other powerful social forces

The crucial point here is that it is naïve to take at face value the claims by states that they are essentially democratic, that they are responsive to the needs of an informed citizenry and that their societies are characterized by equality, either of opportunity or condition. Yet it is astonishing that so many people, after so much critical work has been written, leave generally unchallenged the claim that America is a democracy and one founded fundamentally on Judaeo-Christian moral ideals. The former makes sense only in terms of a very impoverished conception of democracy and the latter only through a very vulgarized, albeit widespread, version of the pastoral Calvinist ethic discussed by Max Weber[33]—worldly success being taken to indicate that one is of God's chosen. In fact, Bush's Protestantism and his "Compassionate Conservatism" as practical religious morality and as eschatological faiths are congruent with "Mammon" and the belief in the intrinsic good of the possession of money (above all, as capital.) There is one qualification to be made and that is that Bush allows for the value of non-Protestant, and, indeed, non-Christian faiths, provided they are monotheistic. Such a capitalist fundamentalism is well caught by Karl Marx's sardonic comment, "Money is the supreme good; therefore its possessor is good. Money, besides, saves me the trouble of being dishonest: I am therefore presumed honest."[34] The accumulation and expansion of capital, and the preservation and extension of its conditions of existence, remain the major determinants of domestic and international state activities in societies with capitalist economies. It is hardly surprising, then, that in a Confidential 1948 Policy Planning Study, George Kennan of the State Department argued that since "we have about 50% of the world's wealth but only 6.3% of its population . . . we cannot fail to be the object of envy and resentment" and that our "real task in the coming period is to devise a pattern of relationships which will permit us to maintain this position of disparity without positive detriment to our national security"; hence we "should cease to talk about vague—and for the Far East—unreal objectives such as human rights, the raising of the living standards and democratization."[35] Neither is it surprising that in 1999 Clinton's Secretary of Defense William Cohen declared the United States was committed to "unilateral uses of military power" to defend such vital interests as "ensuring uninhibited access to key markets, energy supplies, and strategic resources."[36]

It is this commitment that explains a long list of overt and covert support by the United States, in violation of international law, for attacking "unsound" democratic regimes and supporting and sustaining numerous repressive rulers. Examples abound: in 1954, by backing a coup in Guatemala that overthrew the democratically elected government of Jacob Arbenz, leading to four decades of military repression and more than 120,000 deaths; in 1965, by backing the coup that installed President Suharto, contributing to the death of more than 500,000 Indonesians and by defending his invasion of East Timor in 1975, leading to the death of at least 200,000 people there; in the 1980s backing paramilitary death squads in El Salvador, resulting in 80,000 deaths and by supporting the "contras," causing the death of 30,000 Nicaraguans. These judgments, moreover, are by no means subjective. Many of these actions have been judged by the World Court, and by U.N. resolutions to be in violation of international law and such treaty obligations as the Geneva Conventions and as undermining agreements for securing collective security through collectively sanctioned actions. But then, as President Clinton said to the U.N. in 1993, "the United States will act multilaterally when possible, but unilaterally when necessary."[37] Bush's withdrawal, only months before 9/11, of the United States (by far the world's major user of energy and also polluter) from the Kyoto protocol on measures to reduce emissions of "greenhouse" gases was a clear signal of U.S. unilateralism and the primacy of its own economic interests. Bush's willingness to apply to the pursuit of Bin laden the "Old West" maxim "Wanted: Dead or Alive"[38] and to dismiss the Taliban request for evidence of Bin Laden's guilt and to reject their offer to deport him from Afghanistan[39] has shown how little concern he has for the principle of national and international criminal law that a suspect is innocent until proven guilty and should be judged and tried by an independent and impartial legal system.

A commitment *not* to take the claims of the powerful at face value, to subject them to scrutiny, is now unusual among social scientific work in the academy. In the period from the late 1960s to the early 1980s, when critical scholarship was strong in the social sciences, and when Marxism played a significant role within this, critique meant engaging seriously with the positions held by one's opponents. In general, there was an expectation that positions with which one disagreed should be represented accurately and challenged conceptually, epistemologically, and empirically; it was also anticipated that an exchange might develop subject to the same rules. While this was not always achieved in practice, it nevertheless constituted a regulative ideal. By implication, social theory and social analysis were collaborative enterprises. However passionately a position was held, there existed a real possibility of its modification, its development, its abandonment, and, sometimes, the emergence of surprising, and non-eclectic, syntheses. A disturbing aspect of current academic practice is that differing but rigorous interpretations of the nature of the social world and of theories and theorists are often simply *ignored*, at times crudely parodied, or simply, and contemptuously, dismissed. This is to no one's benefit, and it seems important to find different ways of dealing with such disagreements.

Two experiences of Steve Tombs and myself in this respect are illuminating. In 1990 and 1991, through the pages of the *British Journal of Criminology*, we had a somewhat curious exchange with Keith Hawkins (as a key figure within a group of academics we termed "The Oxford School") regarding appropriate forms of regulatory enforcement.[40] There was also a curious aftermath for at least two reasons. First, because within the mass of work that has appeared subsequently, either within or broadly sympathetic to the views of the Oxford School, our own position, developed in those articles, is often ignored, at best footnoted and passed over. Second, because although the exchange is often referred to by other commentators on regulation, the position that we developed in those articles is often misrepresented, even by those who cite it approvingly. Thus our argument—that a corporation when acting as a sophisticated amoral calculator is aware of the distinction between long-term and short-term consequences, is sometimes caught within a disabling ideology, is sometimes less than competent and, as an organization, is often beset by conflicts—gets translated into the claim that corporations are coherent organizations with a consensus about goals and means and that as amoral calculators they focus only on immediate consequences, are omniscient and never make mistakes This is a clear illustration of how the deep incommensurability of positions becomes clear and is then negotiated or not negotiated. It is also an indication of the dominance of certain ways of looking at the world which do not see the need to engage with alternative knowledge claims. There is no need, it seems, for "The Oxford School" to engage in dialogue with its critics.

There seems to be little recognition that we were clearly drawing upon the work on hegemony of the Italian Marxist, Antonio Gramsci. This is particularly interesting because Gramsci explicitly refers to the issue of calculation albeit in his case in reference to national politics. He writes that "although politics is in fact at any given time the reflection of these tendencies of development of the structure... it is not necessarily the case that these tendencies must be realized" for any "particular political act may have been an error of calculation on the part of the leaders of the dominant classes"; the "principle of error" is a complex one: one may be dealing with an individual impulse based upon mistaken calculations, or equally it may be a manifestation of the attempts of specific groups or sects to take over hegemony within the directive grouping, attempts which may well be unsuccessful"; and "that many political acts are due to internal necessities of an organizational character, that is, they are tied to the need to give coherence to a party, a group, a society."[41] This lack of recognition suggests that there is a broader issue here, namely, the decline of familiarity with critical modes of thought in general and Marxist social science in particular. This aspect of the recent trajectory of social science will have the most destructive long-term consequences on the prospects for a vibrant tradition of critical social science. There is now a whole generation of academics, from undergraduates to post-doctoral teachers and researchers, many of whom lack any basic training in Marxist concepts or modes of analysis. This in turn significantly reduces the likelihood of Marxist social science being produced. This brings us to the second experience of Steve Tombs and myself. Somewhat more recently, we submitted an article to a leading socio-legal journal in Britain. The article was accepted, but only after we were required to write what amounted to five pages justifying a point made in one line in the original submission, to the effect that capitalist corporations, in the long run, had to maximize profits in order to survive as capitalist corporations. This is a central element of Marxist political economy; yet such political economy is rarely utilized within criminology now compared to, say, 20 years ago In other words, the return to dominance of mainstream criminology after the eruption of labeling and critical criminology in the late 1960s and early 1970s has left a generation of readers who need some basic "schooling" in the obviousness of some critical paradigms.

But, if "criminology" is a "discipline" that, as Foucault argued, experiences "no need to seek a theoretical justification for itself, or even a coherent framework,"[42] it is still a booming area and one on so much narrower ground than was the case in, say, the 1960s and 1970s. This is the case despite there being within social thought an abundance of sophisticated critiques, by Hirst, Cohen, O'Malley, Chambliss, Arrigo, and others[43] of its pretensions to a being a distinct discipline. In general, such pretensions demonstrate that it does not have its own social scientific "problematic" but rather one given to it by sundry state apparatuses. How is it possible that its main practitioners are able to choose not to engage with these critiques? It is perhaps worth mentioning here that there has also been a significant deradicalization of the work of Foucault—one to which he undoubtedly contributed himself—and this can be seen in the bulk of work—but by no means all of it—undertaken in the area of "governmentality.[44]"

Let me illustrate some of these issues with reference to a graduate/undergraduate course that I teach, "Towards a Sociology of Killing." Stunningly, the standard definition of murder taken up uncritically in most Criminology textbooks is simply "unlawful killing," and, like the law, there is a presumption that such acts (and not so many others also leading to death) are *mala in se*. The criminal statistics that are used follow state practice by excluding from their coverage all manslaughter except non-negligent manslaughter—which means not analyzing most motor-vehicle-related deaths, most "accidents" at work, and occupationally induced illnesses. There are some exceptions, but the work that exists on corporate crimes of violence is generally ignored. And even when these matters are addressed, commentators often remain within the parameters of the way in which the law actually has been implemented. For example, the Ford Pinto case is explored, but the grounds for treating the activities of the tobacco industry as engaging in reckless or negligent homicide or manslaughter during the 1970s—when they knew cigarette tobacco was highly carcinogenic, that nicotine was addictive, and when they often implicitly aimed advertising at very young people while publicly denying all three—are usually ignored. Four million or more premature deaths are the likely result of the addictions produced during this period, and there is every reason to define them as homicide or manslaughter. It is of no little consequence that current books on victimization and/or violence barely mention corporate crimes, if they mention them at all. With notable exceptions, criminology teaching and writing also excludes study of the failures by prison officers to fulfill their duties of care when such failures may lead to the injury or death of inmates; excessive force by the police is also treated as of marginal interest. True, there are books like Jack Katz's *Seductions of Crime*[45] that show that killing often involves quite a complex play of moralities, and hence it is not only police officers whose acts of life-risking violence are somewhat morally ambiguous, but even this interactionist text never frees itself from official definitions. State-sponsored violence in particular and state crimes in general are almost entirely absent from criminological discourses. The horrors of Nazism are generally also excluded from discussion, although most of their killing was "legal," and even if included the analysis is truncated, too often excluding the class dimensions of Nazi "success." How often are there discussions of the crucial role of the support of the military and of major capitalists in Hitler's rise to power or of how major German companies, such as I.G. Farben, took over the industries of those countries occupied by the Nazis?[46] How often are students led to understand the significance of, what is, according to his widow, the definitive version of Martin Niemoller's poem?

First they came for the Communists
but I was not a Communist so I did not speak out;
Then they came for the Socialists and the Trade Unionists
but I was not one of them, so I did not speak out;
Then they came for the Jews
but I was not Jewish so I did not speak out.
And when they came for me
There was no one left to speak out for me.

—Martin Niemoller, 1892–1984

Equally rare are discussions of the what, why, and wherefores of the genocides inflicted, in the name of Christianity, on the peoples of the Americas during Europeanization. The Spanish included as a justification for their appropriation of territory that Pope Alexander VI (Alejandro Borgia) had issued a "bull" giving to the kings of Castile and Leon and their heirs dominion over all lands which they discovered one hundred leagues to the west of the Azores, on condition that they were not already subject to the authority of a Christian King or Prince and that they converted to Christianity the pagans whom they found. This "present" was interpreted by the Spanish crown to mean that when contact was made with native peoples that they should be read the *Requerimiento*, which briefly outlined (in Spanish) the main tenets of the Catholic faith by which they claimed the land for the Spanish crown and called upon the natives to swear allegiance to the Pope and Spain. But, if the Indians refused to do this or delayed their acceptance of its terms, they were then told that—

> With the help of God we shall powerfully enter into your country and shall make war against you in all ways and manners that we can, and shall subject you to the yoke and obedience of the Church and of Their Highnesses. We shall take you and your wives and your children and make slaves of them, and as such sell and dispose of them as Their Highnesses may command. And we shall take your goods, and shall do you all the mischief and damage that we can, as to vassals who do not obey and refuse to receive their lord and resist and contradict him.[47]

The destruction of the Aztec city of Tenochtitlan/Tlatelolco by the Spanish and their native allies was at the cost over 200,000 Mexican lives.[48] Surely, these acts, and other such acts of Imperialism, then, and, above all, now, need to be an essential part of any course on murder.

In fact, in such courses, serial and spree killing are generally included, but war is generally excluded, as is the question of the rationales for dropping the atomic bombs and what that might tell us about state terrorism. Killing people is always morally problematic, but the moral and sociological questions are confused by accepting uncritically the definitions of murder by states or organized religions. As pointed out by Herman and Julia Schwendinger,[49] sociology and criminology cannot be morally neutral; as socially situated intellectual practices, they unavoidably have moral dimensions. Untheorized claims to neutrality implicitly endorse extant ideologies. Not surprisingly, this Sociology of Killing course finishes with an examination of the non-elitist implications of some of Nietzsche's perspectivalist interrogations, for example, implications of the human "will to power,"[50] that is of "eternal recurrence"[51] for the question of the foundations of morality and the nature of responsibility. With Nietzsche, one wonders how it is that so many people still do not acknowledge that the Gods of Religion and the Gods of the State are dead. And, it is important to add, the Gods of capitalism have rarely been given so much obeisance.

We should be concerned about all fundamentalisms, including those that provide false solutions to the real problems of inequality, racism, and dispossession that are found throughout the contemporary world. Any world view grounded in a "faith" which treats as taboo the continual rational reassessment of its premises is problematic and has a terrifying destructive potential—this is true of both Bush's capitalistic Christianity and of Islamic Wahhabist or warrior Salafiyya movements. No, this is not an age of miracles. And if there is a spiritual revitalization, it is to be seen in the ethics and courage of those who challenge the different forms of domination in the world currently subject to a capitalist "globalization." These challenges are taking place on the streets, across the globe; and there is some evidence that, while not equivalents, they are also still taking place through critical analyses and argument.

Endnotes

1. I am grateful to Steve Tombs, Tara Milbrandt, and Paul Datta for comments on earlier drafts.
2. See Levi (1995); Saunders appealed against his sentence of five years in prison, and on 16 May 1991, the sentence was reduced to two and a half years. Lord Justice

Neill was satisfied, "*on the balance of probabilities*," that Saunders was suffering from pre-senile dementia associated with *Alzheimer's disease*, which is incurable. Saunders was released from prison with full parole on *28 June 1991*. After release, he recovered from the symptoms which had led to the diagnosis and claimed the symptoms were a result of a "cocktail of tranquilizers and sleeping tablets" which he had been prescribed. Then in November 2002 the appeal by Saunders and three co-defendants against their original convictions was rejected, Clare Dyer "Still Guilty the Guinness Four Verdict: Law Lords Back Conviction and Legal Fight Ends," *The Guardian,* Friday, November 25, 2002.
The following letter in the *Guardian* discusses both cases.

> Your extracts from the medical report on General Pinochet (Mental barriers to Pinochet standing trial, February 17) inspire neither trust in justice nor confidence. The first, because the description of his condition recalls Josef Schwammberger, a doddery old man of 80, looking as though he was suffering from dementia, parkinsonism, or both, who, while not denying the charges against him, claimed he had no recollection of the second world war, but in May 1992 was sentenced to prison indefinitely for atrocities committed 50 years previously. Of course, the international lobby against Holocaust crimes may be more effective than that against abuse of civil rights of Chilean citizens, and he had no friends (even discredited ones) in high places to defend him.
>
> The second, because the medical conclusions are open to question. "Multi-infarct" dementia, always a speculative diagnosis, cannot, unlike Alzheimer's disease, even be verified at post-mortem. Nowhere in the history you publish is there hard evidence that General Pinochet has cerebrovascular disease. Linda Grant (I hate him, but send him home, February 17) appears to set great store by the fact that brain scans (not referred to in your reports) "demonstrate that [he] is not deliberately deceiving the doctors." No scans can do that.
>
> I am a consultant neuroradiologist. In 1980, I published with two colleagues one of the first papers on CT scanning in demented patients with cerebrovascular disease. There are general correlations, but these are statistical; many normally functioning people of General Pinochet's age have scans which show marked changes, and the reverse is also true.
>
> One cannot confidently diagnose "multi-infarct dementia (or Alzheimer's disease) by imaging. Your reports do not detail the abnormal findings and neither I nor my immediate radiological colleagues are aware of the scans having been reviewed by a neuroradiologist expert in dementia diagnosis.
>
> Thirdly, the grounds on which it is said General Pinochet would not be suitable for trial give cause for concern. Neither general debility (as in Schwammberger's case) nor deafness makes a trial impossible. One's cognitive abilities may influence the verdict or disposal, but are questionable as grounds that one should not undergo due legal process. The evidence for statements such as that "situational stress, as likely to be occasioned by trial... could accelerate the progression of vascular disease" would itself hardly stand up in court. Although there are concerns that the general could not follow a trial "his sense of humour remains intact."
>
> British neurology is still smarting from the disgrace of Ernest Saunders' unprecedented recovery from Alzheimer's disease (diagnosed by a senior, respected consultant) after being released from prison.
>
> One cannot imagine that the experts are supporters of General Pinochet, but one may suspect that they have bent over backwards to demonstrate that neither are they opponents. Should he recover in the clear air of the Andes, "multi-infarct dementia" may have to be added to the list of reversible diseases. Ivan Moseley London (Reader's Letters, *The Guardian,* Friday, February 18, 2000).

3. Cited in John Sweeney, "A Cancer in Our Economic System," *The Toronto Star* (Tuesday May 14, 2002: A-24).
4. Calavita (1997).
5. President Announces Tough New Enforcement Initiatives for Reform: Remarks by the President on Corporate Responsibility, Regent Wall Street Hotel, New York, New York, and White House Press Office July 9, 2002. The text of the speech is available through the White House Corporate Responsibility portal, *http://www.whitehouse.gov/infocus/corporateresponsibility/.*
6. Singer (2004).
7. For example, "Joint Statement by President George W. Bush and President Vladimir Putin on Combating Illegal Narcotics Trafficking" November 13, 2001; *http://moscow.usembassy.gov/bilateral/joint_statement.php?record_id=1* and President George W. Bush's Message to the Senate of the United States re.: United Nations Convention against Transnational Organized Crime, Office of the Press Secretary, February 23, 2004. *http://www.whitehouse.gov/news/releases/2004/02/20040223-7.html*
8. *http://www.whitehouse.gov/news/releases/20010206-4.html—34.1KB* (Knelman 1985: 177).
9. President Declares "Freedom at War with Fear." *http://www.whitehouse.gov/news/releases/2001/09/20010920-8.html#*).
10. Bush (2003: 108).
11. Speech by John Bolton "Beyond the Axis of Evil" (Monday, 6 May, 2002). *http://news.bbc.co.uk/1/hi/world/americas/852.stm*
12. Re.: Richard Perle, see Oliver Burkeman and Julian Borger, "War critics astonished as US hawk admits invasion was illegal." Thursday November 20, 2003 *The Guardian* 'Iraq war illegal, says Annan,' Thursday, 16 September, 2004, *http://news.bbc.co.uk/2/hi/middle_east/3661134.stm.*
13. Chomsky (2001); Chomsky(2002). "U.S. Punishes Foes in Fight Over World Criminal Court," *The Globe and Mail,* Wednesday (2 July, 2003).
14. Speech by President George W. Bush, Sept. 11, 2001.
15. Ali (2001).
16. Bush (2003: 2).
17. Bush (2003: 14).
18. Bush (2003: 145).
19. Klein (2005: 12).
20. Ed Vuillamy: "Venezuela coup linked to Bush team: Specialists in the 'dirty wars' of the Eighties encouraged the plotters who tried to topple President Chavez," *Observer,* Sunday, April 21, 2002); "Alfonso Daniels 'Chavez TV' beams into South America: Painful birth for new station in war of words with Washington," *The Guardian* Tuesday (26 July, 2005). *www.rethinkvenezuela.com/downloads/telesur.html*)
21. Chomsky (1969); Chomsky (1969).
22. Denevan ed. (1992); Thornton (1987).
23. Seed (1995).
24. Stannard (1992).
25. Merck (1963).
26. Sullivan (1839: 426–430).
27. Pearce (1976).
28. Alperovitz (1995).
29. President Harry S. Truman radio announcement (August 6, 1945).
30. Krieger (2004).
31. Marx and Engels (1975: 55).
32. Weber (2002: 79). This comment is not meant as an endorsement of Weber's idealist analysis—Calvinism tended to be interpreted from a framework which took for

granted the positive moral value of the way of life associated with different peoples' social positions and could generate critique as easily as accommodation; Tawney (1926); Maurice Merleau-Ponty (1974). It is worth noting two passages found close together in Calvin's Institutes:

a. In the second class of God's works, namely those which are above the ordinary course of nature, the evidence of his perfections are in every respect equally clear. For in conducting the affairs of men, he so arranges the course of his providence, as daily to declare, by the clearest manifestations, that though all are in innumerable ways the partakers of his bounty, the righteous are the special objects of his favour, the wicked and profane the special objects of his severity.
b. Conversely, when we see the righteous brought into affliction by the ungodly, assailed with injuries, overwhelmed with calumnies, and lacerated by insult and contumely, while, on the contrary, the wicked flourish, prosper, acquire ease and honour, and all these with impunity, we ought forthwith to infer, that there will be a future life in which iniquity shall receive its punishment, and righteousness its reward. Calvin (1962: Chapter 5).

33. Marx (1967: 128).
34. Kennan (1948: 509–529).
35. Cohen (1999: Chapter 1).
36. Chomsky (2001).
37. "Bush: Bin Laden Prime Suspect." *http://archives.cnn.com/2001/US/09/17/bush.powell.terrorism/*).
38. "Bush rejects Taliban offer to hand Bin Laden over," *The Guardian Sunday* (October 14, 2001).
39. Peace and Tombs (1990a); Hawkins (1990); Peace and Tombs (1990b); Hawkins (1991). The exchange was curious, because standard journal procedures were followed somewhat inconsistently. In 1989 we had submitted an article to the *British Journal of Criminology* and after the usual work of responding to comments, and simply improving the article and following guidelines for length etc. it was agreed that it would be published in 1990 in Volume 30:4. We had also been asked it we would agree to a response from Keith Hawkins, to which we agreed providing, of course, that we could write a reply. Hawkins' somewhat defensive article was "Compliance Strategy, Compliance Policy and Aunt Sally: A comment on Pearce and Tombs." There were three surprising features of this exchange: first, Hawkins' response was longer than our original article; second, the response was placed in the same issue as our original article but our response was placed in Volume 31:4, four issues later; and, third, and most surprising of all, Hawkins wrote a further response—a response to our response also published in Volume 31:4. Our understanding of normal journal policy is that an original article raises some questions, the analysis may well be challenged but as those who raised a set of questions the authors of the original article have the final word. We have never understood why this practice was not followed. Incidentally, for an attempt at a dialogical relation to theorizing and a non-syncretic synthesis, see Pearce (2001).
40. Forgacs ed. (1988: 190). For a further pertinent discussion of Gramsci, see Pearce and Tombs (1998b).
41. Foucault (1975/1980: 47).
42. Hirst (1973); Cohen (1998); O'Malley (1987); Arrigo ed. (1999); Williams and Arrigo (2004); Chambliss (1999).
43. Pearce and Tombs (1998a); Dupont and Pearce (2001); Pearce (2003).
44. Katz (1988).
45. Gluckstein (1999); Borkin (1978).
46. Keith and Parry (1984: 290).

47. The siege and destruction of the Aztec city of Tenochtitlan/Tlatelolco by the Spanish and their Tlaxcalan allies was at the cost of over 200,000 Mexican lives; Thomas (1994: 528).
48. Schwendingers and Schwendinger (1970).
49. Nietzsche (1968).
50. Nietzsche (1974).
51. Boal et al. (2005: Chapter 5).

References

Ali, Tariq (2001) "The Kingdom of Corruption: The Saudi Connection." *Znet* (23 Sept), *http://www.zmag.org/alisaudi.htm.*

Alperovitz, Gar (1995) *The Decision to Use the Atomic Bomb.* New York: Vintage Books.

Editor Arrigo, Bruce (1999) *Social Justice/Criminal Justice: The Maturation of Critical Theory in Law, Crime, and Deviance.* Belmont: West/Wadsworth.

Boal, Ian et al. (2005) *Afflicted Powers: Capital and Spectacle in a New Age of War.* London: Verso.

Borkin, Joseph (1978) *The Crime and Punishment of I.G. Farben.* New York: Free Press.

Bush, George (2003) *We Will Prevail: President George Bush on War, Terrorism and Freedom.* New York: Continuum International Publishing Group Inc.

Calavita, Kitty et al. (1997) *Big Money Crime: Fraud and Politics in the S&L Crisis.* Berkeley: University of California Press.

Calvin, John (1962) *The Institutes of the Christian Religion.* London: Hodder and Straughton.

Chambliss, William (1999) *Power, Politics, and Crime.* Boulder: Westview Press.

Chomsky, Noam (1969) *American Power and the New Mandarins.* New York: Pantheon Books.

Chomsky, Noam (2000) *Rogue States.* London: Pluto Press.

Chomsky, Noam (2001) *9/11.* New York: Seven Stores Press.

Chomsky, Noam (2002) "Questions On Israel: Chomsky responses in The ZNet Forum System." *ZNet Sustainer Program,* 30 June. *http://www.zmag.org/content/ showarticle.cfm?SectionID=22&ItemID=2053.*

Chomsky, Noam (2004) *Hegemony or Survival.* New York: Metropolitan Books.

Cohen, Stan (1998) "Intellectual Scepticism and Political Commitment: The Case of Radical Criminology." In *The New Criminology Revisited,* Editors Paul Walton and Jack Young. London: Macmillan.

Cohen, William S. (1999) *Secretary of Defense,* Annual Report to the President and Congress.

Editor Denevan, William (1992) *The Native Population of the Americas in 1492.* Second edition, Madison: University of Wisconsin Press.

Dupont, Danica, and Frank Pearce (2001) "Foucault contra Foucault: Rereading the 'Governmentality' Papers." *Theoretical Criminology* 5(May):2.

Editor Forgacs, David (1988) *An Antonio Gramsci Reader.* New York: Schocken Books.

Foucault, Michel (1975/1980) "Prison Talk." In *Power/Knowledge: Selected Interviews and Other Writings.* New York: Pantheon Books.

Gluckstein, Donny (1999) *The Nazis, Capitalism and the Working Class.* London: Bookmarks.

Hawkins, Keith (1990) "Compliance Strategy, Compliance Policy and Aunt Sally: A comment on Pearce and Tombs." *British Journal of Criminology* 30:4.

Hawkins, Keith (1991) "Enforcing Regulation: More of the Same from Pearce and Tombs." *British Journal of Criminology* 31(Autumn):4.

Hirst, Paul Q. (1973) "Marx and Engels on Law, Crime and the State." *Economy and Society* 1:1.

Katz, Jack (1988) *Seductions of Crime: Moral and Sensual Attractions in Doing Evil.* New York: Basic Books.

Keith, John H., and Robert G. Parry (1984) *New Iberian World: A Documentary History of the Discovery and Settlement of Latin America to the Early 17th Century*, vol. I. New York: Garland.

Kennan, George (1948) "PPS/23: Review of Current Trends in U.S. Foreign Policy." written for Secretary of State George Marshall, vol. I, Pp 509–529. Published in *Foreign Relations of the United States.*

Klein, Naomi (2005) *No War: America's Real Business in Iraq.* London: Gibson Square.

Krieger, David (2004) "US Policy and the Quest for Nuclear Disarmament." July, http://www.wagingpeace.org.

Levi, Michael (1995) "Serious Fraud in Britain: Criminal Justice versus Regulation." In *Corporate Crime: Contemporary Debates*, Editors Frank Pearce and Laureen Snider. Toronto: University of Toronto Press.

Marx, Karl (1967) *The Economic and Philosophical Manuscripts of 1844*, Translated by Martin Milligan. London: Lawrence and Wishart.

Marx, Karl, and Friedrich Engels (1975) *The German Ideology: Collected Works*, vol. 5. London: Lawrence and Wishart.

Merleau-Ponty, Maurice (1974) *Adventures of the Dialectic*, Translated by Joseph Bien. London: Heinemann.

Merk, Frederick (1963) *Manifest Destiny and Mission in American History: A Reinterpretation.* New York, Vintage Books.

Nietzsche, Friedrich (1968) *The Will to Power*, Translated by Walter Kaufmann and R.J. Hollingdale. New York: Random House.

Nietzsche, Friedrich (1974) *The Gay Science*, Translated by Walter Kaufmann. New York: Random House.

O'Malley, Pat (1987) "Marxist Theory and Marxist Criminology." *Crime and Social Justice* 29:70–87.

Pearce, Frank (1976) *Crimes of the Powerful: Marxism, Crime and Deviance.* London: Pluto Press.

Pearce, Frank (2001) *The Radical Durkheim*, Second edition. Toronto: Canadian Scholars Press.

Pearce, Frank (2003) "'Off with Their Heads': Caillois, Klossowski and Foucault on Public Executions." *Economy and Society* 32 (Feb.):21.

Pearce, Frank, and Steve Tombs (1990a) "Ideology, Hegemony and Empiricism: Compliance Theories of Regulation." *British Journal of Criminology* 30:4.

Pearce, Frank, and Steve Tombs (1990b) "Policing Corporate 'Skid Rows': A Reply to Keith Hawkins (1991)." *British Journal of Criminology* 31:4.

Pearce, Frank, and Steve Tombs (1998a) "Foucault, Governmentality." *Marx' Social and Legal Studies* 7:4.

Pearce, Frank, and Steve Tombs (1998b) *Toxic Capitalism: Corporate Crime and the Chemical Industry.* Aldershot: Dartmouth Publishing Company.

Schwendinger, Herman, and Julia Schwendinger (1970) "Defenders of Order or Guardians of Human Rights?" *Issues in Criminology* 5:123–157.

Seed, Patricia (1995) *Ceremonies of Possession in Europe's Conquest of the New World: 1492–1640.* Cambridge: Cambridge University Press.

Singer, Peter (2004) *The President of Good and Evil: The Ethics of George W. Bush.* New York: Dutton.

Stannard, David E. (1992) *American Holocaust. Columbus and the Conquest of the New World.* Oxford: Oxford University Press.

Sullivan, John L. (1839) "The Great Nation of Futurity." Pp 23 and 426–430 in *Afflicted Powers: Capital and Spectacle in a New Age of War*, Editors I. Boal et al, vol. 6. London: Verso.

Tawney, Richard H. (1926) *Religion and the Rise of Capitalism: A Historical Study.* New York: Harcourt Brace and Co.

Thomas, Hugh (1994) *The Conquest of Mexico*. London: Pimlico.

Thornton, Russell (1987) *American Indian Holocaust and Survival: A Population History Since 1492*. Norman: University of Oklahoma Press.

Weber, Max (2002) *The Protestant Ethic and the Spirit of Capitalism and Other Writings*, Edited, Translated and with an Introduction and Notes by Peter Baehr and Gordon C. Wells. NewYork: Penguin Books.

Williams, Christopher R., and Bruce Arrigo (2004) *Theory, Justice, and Social Change*. Norwell: Kluwer Academic/Plenum Publishers.

3

White-Collar Crime in a Postmodern, Globalized World[1]

David O. Friedrichs

We live in a world of boundaries. They include boundaries between academic disciplines and within disciplines, boundaries between areas of specialization. We live in a world of temporal boundaries, where it is common to differentiate between past, present, and future. We live in a world of geographical boundaries between communities, states, and nations. The erosion of boundaries in all of these realms, or the reconfiguration of such boundaries, is one of the guiding themes of this chapter. Developments pertaining to white-collar crime and its control bring this theme into especially sharp relief.

If the study of white-collar crime is a criminological topic, the complex nature of white-collar crime calls for attention to many different disciplines, including philosophy, history, economics, political science, psychology, sociology, jurisprudence, managerial sciences, and communications studies.[2] On a theoretical plane, we have witnessed some recent calls for the development of an integrated criminology, addressing multiple levels of explanation.[3] If the study of white-collar crime can be characterized as a specialization within criminology, this form of crime intersects in significant ways with other forms of crime, including organized crime, professional crime, and political crime.[4] If white-collar crime has been principally addressed in terms of the conditions of modernity, it increasingly manifests attributes of an emerging postmodern world. If white-collar crime was originally a largely local phenomenon, then a state or national phenomenon, it is increasingly a global phenomenon, with some of its most significant forms transcending national boundaries. A substantial literature has now developed on white-collar crime, on globalization, and on the postmodern, but to date there has been relatively little cross-fertilization between these realms of inquiry. As the various boundaries identified here increasingly disintegrate, such cross-fertilization will surely intensify.

E. H. Sutherland and the Discovery of White-Collar Crime: Traditional Roots and a Modern Context

Edwin Sutherland is universally recognized as the founding father of white-collar crime scholarship.[5] Although Sutherland's birth in 1883 occurred during a period of great expansion for an industrialized, modern America, he was personally a product of a small rural town, a traditional environment, born in Gibbon, Nebraska.[6] With maturity, Sutherland increasingly came into contact with a modern, urban society, especially during his pursuit of a doctorate at the University of Chicago and subsequent years as a professor there. Sutherland's interest in white-collar crime has been attributed, at least in part, to his revulsion at the practices of Wall Street manipulators who helped bring about the 1929 stock market crash (and subsequent Great Depression), as well as the increasingly conspicuous corporate empires of the first half of the 20th century. In one sense, Sutherland could be regarded as reacting against the corrupting elements of a modern society in relation to the traditional society familiar to him from his youth. The basic framework of Sutherland's work could be described as modernist, in its focus on modern industrialized (and bureaucratized) major corporations. Sutherland's *White-Collar Crime* can also be said to have a nationalist framework: he focused primarily on American corporations, operating principally within American borders.[7] Most white-collar crime scholarship—at least American white-collar crime scholarship—has adopted this modernist, nationalist framework. It has focused on professions operating within modern communities, or on small businesses, individual managers, employees, and entrepreneurs operating within such communities. It has also focused on national industries and major American corporations, and on federal and state bureaucracies regulating these corporations. One could cite many examples to support this claim.[8] Such a framework may continue to be adopted indefinitely within white-collar crime scholarship in the years ahead, but it misses or fails to encompass immensely significant (and in some cases emerging) forms of white-collar crime. Accordingly, white-collar crime scholarship must increasingly adopt a postmodern, globalized point of view.

Contemporary White-Collar Crime Criminologists and a Globalized Framework

While most criminologists—including students of white-collar crime—adopt a framework that is modernist and nationalistic, a relatively small number of them have sought to construct a broader, globalized framework.[9] An orientation toward globalization appears to be more pronounced among non-American than among American criminologists, although there are important exceptions to this proposition. Several key themes emerge from the literature linking crime with globalization. First, globalization itself is viewed as generating some significant criminogenic tendencies. Second, globalization has an impact on a wide range of different types of crime, including conventional forms of crime. Third, certain classes of people (for example, women) are especially vulnerable to victimization as a consequence of an ever-accelerating globalization. And fourth, transnational—or multinational—corporations have become immensely powerful in a globalized world, and are increasingly beyond the reach of existing agencies of social control and regulation. While nations have responded to some forms of globalized crime, they have done so quite selectively. New international norms and new global regulatory initiatives are now needed. The harmful human, environmental, and economic consequences of globalized crime are formidable.

On the Concept of White-Collar Crime and a Typology of White-Collar Crime

The concept of white-collar crime is invoked for different purposes (e.g., polemical, typological, and operational), and has no single meaning.[10] It is best treated as a heuristic term, to which various specific forms of illegal and harmful activity can be related. Some forms of illegal or harmful activity are best viewed as cognate, hybrid, or marginal forms of white-collar crime. The classic forms of white-collar crime—corporate crime and occupational crime—have been analyzed principally as local, state-wide, or national phenomena, although it is widely recognized that multinational or transnational corporations operate on a global level. Governmental crime is a cognate form of white-collar crime: crimes of the state have a significant domestic focus, but also often have transnational or global dimensions; political white-collar crime is treated as primarily a domestic phenomenon. Hybrid or marginal forms of white-collar crime—including enterprise crime, contrepreneurial crime, and avocational crime—are seen as mainly domestic phenomena, although enterprise crime (cooperative or interrelated activities of syndicated crime and legitimate businesses) has an increasingly transnational dimension to it.[11] Technocrime (crime carried out through high tech, especially computers) is also by its very nature, in the context of a world linked through the worldwide web, significantly global in nature. Finance crime (or crimes carried out by or through major financial institutions such as investment banks) has a significant global dimension as well, insofar as many such institutions today are transnational in character. State-corporate crimes—or cooperative and harmful ventures between the state and a corporation—also inevitably have a global dimension when the corporation is transnational. We have a classic example of such crime when a multinational corporation bribes the government of a developing country to enable it to engage in exploitative or environmentally harmful practices within that country.

The concept of "crimes of globalization" has been added to an evolving typology of white-collar crimes as an emerging hybrid form of such crime. Crimes of globalization largely have been neglected by criminologists. However, the anti-globalization movement contends that large-scale crimes are being carried out in the name of globalization. More specifically, international financial institutions such as the World Trade Organization, the International Monetary Fund, and the World Bank are alleged to be complicit in major crimes against large numbers of people in developing countries.[12] The alleged crimes have important elements of white-collar crime, although they do not correspond with its classic parameters. On the one hand, crimes of globalization are consequences of policy decisions by high-level officials of international financial institutions and government agencies who are attempting to realize positive outcomes (or avoid losses). Although typically it is not their specific intent to cause harm, their policy decisions can have devastating financial and human consequences for large numbers of especially vulnerable people. On the other hand, crimes of globalization do not necessarily involve either direct pursuit of profit or directly fraudulent activity, as would be true of much white-collar crime. The specific character of such crimes of globalization is considered in a subsequent section of this chapter.

White-Collar Crime in a Postmodern World

The term *postmodern* has been widely invoked in final two decades of the 20th century and into the early years of the 21st century, although it has a considerably earlier provenance. The term does not have a single, fixed meaning. The "post" in postmodernism reflects both the notion of "after" (or a time following the modern) and "against" (in opposition to modern sensibilities and assumptions). This term has some relevance for the contemporary understanding of white-collar crime and its control. In traditional, pre-modern societies various types of marketplace frauds were not unknown, but were predominantly a local phenomenon. In modern societies, the most significant forms of white-collar crime, especially corporate crime, increasingly have assumed a national character. Since the 1960s, in the view of some commentators, we have witnessed the emergence of a burgeoning postmodern world, at least in the West.[13] In this new era we have seen the collapse of the Euro-American colonial system around the globe, which has left the world without a dominating center and has produced widespread repudiation of the Euro-American value system.[14] In this postmodern era, globalization has also emerged, with various societies powerfully influencing each other and threatening the native culture and way of life in those societies.[15] The postmodern provides a new cultural logic for contemporary capitalism.[16] In one view, neither the capitalist nor the socialist models of modern societies are credible exemplars for an emerging postmodern society; hence, the search for a "third way."[17] But modernity itself is a complex phenomenon, and the developments of post-communist societies can also be viewed within the framework of modernity, not postmodernity.[18] The modern and the postmodern coexist.

Our postmodern society seems to be changing rapidly in many different ways. Our communities are fragmented, complex, and increasingly "virtual," for example, linking people via the Internet. We are in the heart of a global community, simultaneously transmitting and receiving materials and ideas to and from other societies. Conventional forms of bureaucracy are giving way to more flexible, adaptable "adhocracies," with constant changing of institutional arrangements and roles to fit specific situations. The computer has rapidly been replacing industrial machinery at the core of our technological existence. Mass communication is evolving with almost lightning speed into a form of interactive communication, as exemplified by cable television, the Internet, and home shopping. Growing "fluidity" is taking place in residence and career, with people moving back and forth between different residential locations and in and out of different careers. All these changes impact the character of white-collar crime and its control.

More specifically, we live in a world with coexisting premodern, modern, and postmodern dimensions. The basic theme here is that the postmodern dimensions are increasing—and perhaps will increase at an accelerating pace in the future—and it is therefore necessary for white-collar crime scholars to attend to how these different dimensions intersect, and specifically the impact of the emerging postmodern dimensions on the character and control of white-collar crime. In effect, the traditional, the modern, and the postmodern coexist in our world, as does the local, the national, and the global. The adoption of the notion of "a postmodern era" or "a globalized world" is probably only warranted when postmodern and globalized dimensions are adjudged to be dominant.

A sense of proportionality is necessary if we are to produce an appropriate contextual framework within which white-collar crime and its control is to be understood.

The term *postmodern thought* has been applied to a collection of ideas from a number of late-20th-century French philosophers. These ideas include the belief that there is no absolute truth nor stable, fixed meaning in the world, differences of ideas should be celebrated, any attempt to explain the whole of human social existence should be rejected, local action as opposed to collective or centralized action should be used to transform society and positivism, such as the scientific method, should be repudiated as a means of understanding the human condition.[19] Postmodernism challenges Western hegemony, then, as well as the massive development projects associated with globalization, and it favors locally controlled projects.[20] It also favors a methodology privileging an understanding of the effects of globalization "from the bottom up," or through the stories of ordinary people, as opposed to the "top down" interpretations of elite observers.

Two concepts that emerge out of this body of social philosophy can usefully be applied to an understanding of at least some forms of white-collar crime. The concept of "hyperreality"—introduced by Baudrillard[21]—can be applied to cases such as Enron. Hyperreality has been characterized as a circumstance wherein images breed incestuously with each other without reference to reality or meaning. When we increasingly experience our world in terms of simulations and can no longer clearly differentiate between conventional reality and simulations, then we have entered the realm of hyperreality. The related term hypermodernism has been applied to the hyper-intensification of modernism, and a circumstance where technology and economics merge. And hyperreal finance is a world of 24 hour hook-ups between worldwide financial markets, where transactions in cyberspace become dominant.

In the various accounts of the Enron case one is struck by a fundamental disconnect between the presumed "modernist" assumptions of most ordinary investors—that they are putting their money into something "real," into an appropriately assessed product or service with a good potential for growth—and the apparent postmodernist orientation of some of the central figures in this case, whose primary concern seemed to be the manipulation of assets and numbers in ways that maximized their own short-term gain, with almost complete indifference to the "real" demonstrable value of the "product" or service at the center of their business.[22] The question of whether the key figures in the Enron case were deliberately and consciously engaging in transactions that they knew to be outright fraud or that on some level they were no longer able to clearly discriminate between simulated transactions and transactions of substance is not entirely resolved. In more colloquial terms, did these key figures on some level confuse the "smoke and mirrors" they were generating with something of substance? Did they operate in an environment promoting a "dematerialization of the real" and a disconnect with the conventional reality of capitalist economy?

The concept of "intertextuality," as it has emerged from postmodernist discourse, may also have some relevance here. This key term refers to the idea that there is a complex and infinite set of interwoven relationships, "an endless conversation between the texts with no prospect of ever arriving at or being halted at an agreed point."[23] Absolute intertextuality assumes that everything is related to everything else. In the Enron case—as well as in some of the other corporate scandals—one is struck by the complexity of the many suspect deals, financial arrangements and instruments (e.g., derivatives), to the point that it seems possible that at a certain juncture none of the key players could any longer fully grasp the scope and character of the financial edifice they constructed. Second, and on a parallel plane, one is struck by the direct and indirect intertwined involvement of so many different parties in these transactions: i.e., corporate executives, corporate boards, auditors, investment bankers, stock analysts, lawyers, credit rating agencies, and the like. On the one hand, none of these different parties may have had a complete handle on all aspects of the complex financial transactions involved; on the other hand, these different parties may have mutually reinforced on at least some level the basic disconnect with conventional reality. None of the foregoing propositions should be interpreted as excusing the culpability of the different parties from their fiduciary responsibilities, denying the significant forms of conscious wrongdoing, or overlooking the role of greed and personal enrichment as motivating factors in individual and collective involvement in fraudulent transactions. But at the same time, a deeper understanding of Enron and other such corporate crimes, calls for attention to the potential role of an emerging postmodern environment in the corporate world.

In certain respects, the recognition of complex ties involved in law-breaking is hardly new.[24] But in a contemporary "network society" such ties and interdependencies are intensifying, facilitated by new forms of communication and information technology.[25] Traditionally, policing and prosecutorial entities have been organized to address individual actors and organizations. In a postmodern world such entities increasingly have to address webs and complex interrelationships.

White-Collar Crime in a Globalized World

White-collar crime and its control must today be increasingly understood in the context of globalization. Crime itself has become increasingly globalized.[26] Use of the term *globalization* has been ubiquitous, and the literature on globalization has expanded exponentially in the recent era. Although the term *globalization* has been in fairly wide use since the 1960s,[27] the meaning of the term is far from settled.[28] It is hardly a new phenomenon, if one means by it the emergence of international trade and a transnational economic order. But globalization has become one of the buzzwords of the transition into the new era due to the widely perceived intensification of certain developments.[29] It is not simply an economic phenomenon, although it is most readily thought of in such terms. Globalization also has important political and cultural dimensions.[30] The phenomenal growth in influence of transnational corporations, non-governmental organizations (NGOs), intergovernmental organizations (IGOs), international financial institutions (IFIs), and special interest groups, is a conspicuous dimension of contemporary globalization.[31] Governments are increasingly puppets of corporations and financial special interests.[32] Ordinary people lose control over their economic destiny.[33] World markets came to overshadow national markets, barriers to trade are reduced, and instant tele- and cyber-transactions are becoming the norm.[34] It is not interconnections per se but the speed of interconnections and technological developments that are the novel dimensions of globalization.[35] In the broadest possible terms, globalization today refers to the dramatic compression of time and space across the globe.

Globalization as a phenomenon is endlessly complex, is characterized by various contradictory tendencies and ambiguities, and is best seen in dialectical terms and as a dynamic process as opposed to a static state of affairs.[36] No one should dispute the claim that there are many "winners" in the move toward an increasingly globalized economy.[37] However, the winners are disproportionately wealthy multinational corporations, and the losers are disproportionately poor and disadvantaged peoples, especially indigenous peoples in developing countries.[38] But globalization is also alleged to be damaging to the health and well-being of its supposed beneficiaries, the people of the West or the global North.[39] In this view, the losers tend to outnumber the winners.

Globalization contributes to an overall increase in economic inequality, fostering impoverishment and unemployment for many.[40] Much evidence documents the increasing flow of wealth upwards, and growing inequality between the rich and the poor.[41] One-third of the world's population is estimated to live on incomes of less than $1 a day.[42] Accordingly, globalization has been characterized as a new form of the ancient practice of colonization.[43] Richard Falk argues that the logic of globalization is dictated by the well-being of capital rather than of people.[44] Amartya Sen regards the vastly unequal sharing of the benefits as the central issue relating to globalization today.[45] Some recent trends within a globalized world have cast doubt upon the more optimistic assessments of globalization, and these trends include a downward turn of the global economy, intensification of local and global political conflicts, increasing repression of human rights and civil liberties, and a general increase of fear and anxiety.[46] The global North is increasingly impacted by deteriorating economic conditions in the global South.[47] Some symptoms of this impact include growth in illegal trafficking of people, drugs, and weapons; the re-emergence of once-conquered diseases; and the further devastation of the ecosystem. In some interpretations, 9/11 and a general increase in fear of terrorism is linked with the intensification of poverty in the global South.[48]

Globalization policies are largely formulated by elite Western institutions that have set agendas and build coalitions to promote their interests.[49] Globalization has been disproportionately driven by the so-called "Washington consensus" of free market fundamentalism.[50] The rationale here holds that a free market, free trade environment "lifts all boats" and in the long run benefits people in both developed and developing countries. But the Washington consensus is often at odds with an agenda promoting human rights.[51] Faith in the Washington consensus has eroded in recent years, especially with many major setbacks in the context of this model (e.g., major failures of the economies of Thailand, and Argentina). Critics of the model now include not only progressives and leftist activists, but members of the economic establishment such as former World Bank Chief Economist (and Nobel laureate) Joseph Stiglitz and international financier and philanthropist George Soros.[52] One commentator challenges the morality and sanity of "free market fundamentalism"; another characterizes it as the capitalist equivalent of Wahhabism or Maoism.[53] But a global "free markets" hardly produces a level playing field. Traditional industries in poorer countries are overwhelmed by efficient multinational giants.[54] According to a World Bank report, "intellectual property rules will result in a transfer of $40 billion a year from poor countries to corporations in the developed world."[55] Furthermore, the policies promoted by this model reflect a monumentally hypocritical promotion of free trade rhetoric by developed countries such as the United States, which then embrace various protectionist policies. For example, a *New York Times* editorial addresses the rigged trade game of massive subsidies to American farmers (disproportionately, agribusiness interests) that have a devastating impact on farmers in developing countries.[56] These policies are "morally depraved" and "harvesting poverty" and will sow ever-greater resentment toward the United States, with a threat of a devastating backlash against American-backed globalization policies, or "atavistic rage" against the West.[57] The long-term costs of imposing "market fundamentalism" on the rest of the world are likely to be immense.

The demographic explosion and the evolving new world economy have been identified as primary shaping forces over the next twenty years.[58] The policies adopted in response to these forces over the decades ahead may chart historical developments for some time to come.[59] Tina Rosenberg has observed that "the largest story of our times" is this: "What globalization has done, or has failed to do."[60] Altogether, much is at stake.

The dimensions of globalization most pertinent within the realm of white-collar crime include the following: First, the growing global dominance and reach of neo-liberalism and a free-market, capitalist system that disproportionately benefits wealthy and powerful organizations and individuals. Second, the increasing vulnerability of indigenous people with a traditional way of life to the forces of globalized capitalism. Third, the growing influence and impact of international financial institutions (such as the World Bank), and the related, relative decline in the power of local or state-based institutions. And fourth, the nondemocratic operation of international financial institutions, taking the form of "globalization from above" instead of "globalization from below."

The Role of the World Bank in a Global Economy

The international financial institutions that play such a central role in contemporary globalization have become prime targets for criticism for their policies and practices in the global economy. These international financial institutions include the World Trade Organization, the International Monetary Fund, and the World Bank. They have also been characterized as the "unholy trinity of greed."[61] The World Bank and the International Monetary Fund have also been characterized as "the two most powerful financial institutions in the world."[62] Each has different key missions, with the World Trade Organization primarily focused on fostering trade, the International Monetary Fund primarily focused on maximizing financial stability, and the World Bank primarily focused on promoting development.[63] Of course, these institutions have many ties with each other and the lines of demarcation between their different activities can become quite blurred. Collectively, much evidence suggests that they have acted principally in response to the interests of developed countries and their privileged institutions rather than in the interests of the poor.[64] The international financial institutions may be taken to symbolize the new "colonial" powers in a globalized world.[65] The focus here is principally on the activities of one of these institutions, the World Bank.[66]

The World Bank (formally, the International Bank for Reconstruction and Development, or IBRD), was established at the Bretton Woods Conference in 1944 to help stabilize and rebuild economies ravaged by World War II. Eventually it shifted its focus to an emphasis on aiding developing nations.[67] The bank makes loans to governments of its member nations and to private development projects backed by the government. The projects are supposed to benefit the citizens of the country receiving Bank loans, which are made at a favorable rate of interest. The World Bank generally claims to contribute to the reduction of poverty and improved living standards in developing countries.[68] Today the bank is a large, international operation, with more than 10,000 employees, 180 member states, and annual loans of some 30 billion dollars.[69]

The World Bank was established (along with the International Monetary Fund) at the behest of the dominant Western nations, with little if any real input from the developing countries.[70] It is disproportionately influenced by or manipulated by elite economic institutions and has been characterized as an agent of global capital.[71] A critic claims that "corporate welfare," subsidized by American taxpayers, is one of the primary activities of the World Bank.[72] In the developing countries it deals primarily with the political and economic elites of those countries, with little direct attention to the perspectives and needs of indigenous peoples, a practice for which it has been criticized by U.S. Senators.[73] Historically, it has had a record of lending money to ruthless military dictatorships engaged in murder and torture, after it has denied loans to democratic governments overthrown by the military.[74] It favors strong dictatorships over struggling democracies because it believes that the former are more able to introduce and see through the unpopular reforms its loans require.[75] Borrowers of money from the World Bank typically are political elites of developing countries, and their cronies, although the repayment of the debt becomes the responsibility of people in these countries, most of whom do not benefit from the loans. In this reading, then, the privileged gain disproportionately from dealings with the World Bank, relative to the poor.

The World Bank and Crimes of Globalization

The World Bank has been characterized as paternalistic, secretive, and counterproductive in terms of any claimed goal of improving people's lives. More specifically, it has been charged with being complicit in policies with genocidal consequences, with exacerbating ethnic conflict, with increasing the gap between rich and poor, with fostering immense ecological and environmental damage, and with the callous displacement from their original homes and communities of vast numbers of indigenous people in developing countries.[76] Critics claim that many of the less developed countries which received World Bank loans are worse off today in terms of poverty, and that the severe austerity measures imposed on borrowing countries, deemed necessary to maximize the chances of bank loans being repaid, impact most heavily on the poorest and most vulnerable segments of the population.[77] The building of dams has been the single most favored World Bank project, but even its own experts concede that millions of people have been displaced as a result of these projects.[78] In many of them resettlement plans have either been non-existent—in violation of the bank's own guidelines—or have been inadequately implemented. In a notorious case in the 1970s anti-dam protesters in Guatemala were massacred by the military, with no direct reference to this atrocity in the World Bank's report on the project.[79] Such circumstances have led to claims of criminality directed at the World Bank. Indeed, at a World Bank meeting in Berlin in 1988 protesters called for the establishment of a Permanent People's Tribunal to try the World Bank (and the International Monetary Fund) for "crimes against humanity."[80] An American anthropologist has characterized the forced resettlement of people in dam-related projects as the worst crime possible, short of killing them.[81] An American biologist has characterized the World Bank's report on the environmental impact of one of its dam projects in a developing country as "fraudulent" and "criminal."[82].

The World Bank's complicity in the crimes outlined above is best understood in terms of its criminogenic structure and organization. Its Charter has called upon it to focus on economic developments and considerations, not on other kinds of consequences of its policies and practices.[83] Accordingly, throughout its history it has avoided addressing or taking a strong stand on human rights issues.[84] Furthermore, it has focused on a not very clearly defined mission of promoting "long-term sustainable growth" as a rationale for imposing much short-term suffering and economic losses.[85] This orientation has led the World Bank to apply somewhat one-dimensional economic models to its project-related analyses, with insufficient attention to many other considerations and potentially useful insights from other disciplines.[86] And once the projects are initiated they tend to develop a momentum of their own that often marginalizes or negates any real adjustments in response to reports indicating negative environmental or social effects.[87] The underlying incentive structure at the Bank encourages "success" with large, costly projects. Bank employees are pressured to make the environmental "as well as social" conditions fit. The World Bank has in common with other international financial institutions that it is structured in such a way that it rewards its personnel for technical proficiency rather than for concerning themselves with the needs of the ordinary people of developing countries.[88]

In terms of their own career interests World Bank officials are rewarded for making loans and moving large amounts of money, with no regard to any human consequences of these loans. Furthermore, World Bank personnel have not been held accountable for any of the tragic human consequences of their projects.[89] All of these institutional factors contribute to a criminogenic environment.

Since the World Bank has not been a signatory to international human rights treaties, it has manifested relatively little concern with human rights abuses.[90] The international financial institutions are, however, subject to the imperatives of international law and at a minimum are obliged to insure that they do not exacerbate conditions impinging on human rights. Most of the countries with which they have dealings have ratified the United Nations' Economic Covenants, and accordingly should be bound by its provisions.[91] Recently, some commentators have argued that the World Bank and other international financial institutions clearly have basic human rights obligations, and have to be held accountable for the social costs and fundamental harms to indigenous peoples that are products of some of the projects they fund.[92] This type of analysis is likely to be more widely disseminated in the years ahead.

It is not the specific intent and purpose of the policies of the World Bank to do harm. However, the World Bank's mode of operation is intrinsically criminogenic and it functions undemocratically. Its key deliberations are carried out behind a veil of secrecy, and it is insufficiently accountable to any truly independent entity. Furthermore, the World Bank is at a minimum criminally negligent when it: (1) Fails adequately to explore or take into account the impact of its loans for major projects on indigenous peoples; (2) adopts and implements policies specifically at odds with the protocols of the United Nations' Universal Declaration of Human Rights, and subsequent covenants; or (3) operates in a manner at least hypothetically at odds with both international law national law.

Crimes of Globalization, in Sum

Globalization, as defined here, is an increasingly important dimension of the context within which crime of all types occurs. The World Bank can be viewed as engaging in a noteworthy form of criminal activity; it is both necessary and useful to view some of its policies and practices this way, despite resistance to equating activities relating to global finance with global violence.[93] The project of raising consciousness about the criminal dimensions of the activities of international financial institutions ideally contributes both to the application of comparative criminological frameworks to this phenomenon and to direct activist responses to it on behalf of those most harmed by present trends.

The term *globalization* has been shown to be elusive and multifaceted. The premise here is that globalization as a fairly dramatic intensification of some existing international patterns is something real, although we need not accept the current direction in which globalization has been moving as inevitable. Critics of present global developments call for the development of popular accountability of both national and global institutions, more public control over these institutions, a true internationalism, and just alternatives to the present criminal activities of the international financial institutions.[94] Ideally, external pressures on international financial institutions such as the World Bank lead either to substantive internal reforms or to the demise of such institutions.

The Significance of the Global Justice Movement for White-Collar Crime

Although there has always been some significant level of public awareness of and anger toward certain forms of white-collar crime—e.g., the monopolistic and exploitative practices of the "robber barons" of the late 19th century—for most of our history white-collar crime has not been a major preoccupation of either citizens or of the criminal justice system. Jack Katz claimed that a "social movement" against white-collar crime emerged in the 1970s.[95] Public awareness increased from this period on in part as a function of an environmental movement and a consumer movement, and federal prosecutions increased as well. But the claim of a "social movement" against white-collar crime, analogous to the civil rights movement or the feminist movement, appears to be overstated. These movements had measurable effects on society and had a clear focus. A self-conscious social movement specifically targeting white-collar crime has not yet emerged. The corporate scandals of the 2001–2005 period did lead to white-collar crime's being one of the top news stories and to some significant legislation (for example, the Sarbanes-Oxley Act of 2002). This focus on corporate crime has not yet coalesced into a movement.

It may be that the global justice movement that emerged in full bloom in the late 1990s will provide the most substantial basis over time for an authentic and focused movement directed at white-collar crime. This movement achieved high visibility following its massive protests against the World Trade Organization meeting in Seattle in 1999 and subsequent meetings of international financial institutions in Washington, DC, Genoa, and elsewhere. The common term "anti-globalization movement" is a misnomer, insofar as this movement is opposed to neo-liberalism, corporate capitalism, and class divisions, not necessarily to globalization per se.[96] The global justice movement is made up of diverse constituents, with different agendas, and united principally in their opposition to globalization driven by corporate and other elite interests that produce a wide range of perceived harms to the global environment and to workers, people of color, women, indigenous peoples, and other non-elite segments of the population. A significant proportion of those involved recognize the inevitability of globalization, but want it to be "globalization from below" or globalization taking direction from those most affected, not from elite institutions and individuals, and not as "globalization from above."[97] This movement recognizes that the supranational entities now dominating globalization are not democratic, and accordingly it calls for democratizing the globalization process.[98] Since the pursuit of justice, broadly defined, is the basic mission of this movement, it is better named a global justice movement. As one commentator notes, evidence suggests that in many respects it is adherents of neo-liberalism who oppose authentic globalization; for example, U.S. border guards tripled following the implementation of NAFTA.[99] This commentator also notes that the movement does not manifest violence—there is no example, he claims, of anyone physically injured by a U.S. activist in the protests. The violence comes from the police; indeed, it is the absence of violence—which limits repression—that disturbs the powers that be.[100] The movement is focused mainly on exposing, delegitimizing, and dismantling the mechanisms of rule of the global powers rather than on seizing state power.

In a globalized world the global justice movement is able to mobilize especially rapidly and broadly through the Internet or world wide web in particular.[101] Jonathan Schell has suggested that this evolving movement represents the world's other superpower.[102] Such a claim may be premature and overstated, but the future potential of the development is still unsettled. Indeed, whether the global justice movement really merits the designation "movement" is also questionable, with an alternative characterization as a "protest field."[103] Accordingly, if this movement is a phenomenon of measurable significance, its specific character is still open to interpretation. It is quite widely conceded, however, that it has already had a measurable influence on the policies of the international financial institutions. It has the potential to influence the response to corporate forms of white-collar crime, especially the activities of transnational or multinational corporations.

Regulating White-Collar Crime in a Postmodern, Globalized World

If one accepts the argument that our world is increasingly postmodern and globalized, it follows that the regulation and control of white-collar crime will have increasingly to adapt to this evolving context. Insofar as the postmodern dimensions described earlier are concerned, new types of competencies have to be developed. A broad understanding of the character of postmodern institutions (such as adhocracies), the increasingly interactive character of mass communications, and the intensification of various forms of interconnections is quite essential. If complex—and often fundamentally artificial—financial transactions take place increasingly in the context of a hyperreal environment, the nature of this hyperreal environment has to be penetrated and understood.

Existing regulatory mechanisms are inadequate for an increasingly globalized world. The international financial institutions were in some respects established to "regulate" international finance and in the recent era have focused more on addressing elite crime and corruption.[104] But, as was suggested earlier, they have also been subjected to a sweeping critique of their own complicity in large-scale "crimes of globalization." There is a lack of agreement today among their critics on whether they should be reformed, or abolished entirely. If they are abolished, they should be replaced by international financial institutions with far more democratic input and oversight.

At the outset of the 21st century we have seen the establishment of a permanent international criminal court, directed at crimes of war. It remains to be seen whether this court will be successful in realizing its objectives. If the court is successful by some reasonable criteria, could it possibly serve as an inspiration and model for the establishment of a permanent international court that would have jurisdiction to address global white-collar crimes, broadly defined? John Eatwell and Lance Taylor have called for the establishment of a World Financial Authority (WFA) that would both regulate systemic risk in a global economy and coordinate national actions against market abuses and international financial crime.[105] They identify some of the tasks for such an entity as encompassing information, authorization, surveillance, guidance, enforcement, and policy.[106] The concentration of power in any such entity is unavoidable, and a major concern. The global justice movement can play a key role in influencing the development of global oversight entities that are fundamentally democratic and characterized by transparency. The challenges of developing global entities that are effective but also avoid complicity in crimes of globalization themselves are formidable.

Concluding Observations: New Challenges for White-Collar Crime Scholars

At the outset of the 21st century, white-collar crime scholars had to contend with some new challenges. Elements of the modern world will continue to be significant in understanding white-collar crime. For example, unsafe conditions of factories can be characterized as a modern condition with ongoing significance in terms of one form of corporate crime. But white-collar crime scholars will have to attend more fully to the emerging conditions of a postmodern world. Certainly white-collar crime will continue to have to be understood as a national, state-based, and local phenomenon. But white-collar crime scholars will increasingly have to understand it in terms of globalization. While traditional forms of white-collar crime—such as corporate crime and occupational crime—will remain important, the field of white-collar crime must also attend to emerging forms of "crimes of globalization." Accordingly, white-collar crime scholars must engage more fully with the literatures of the postmodern and globalization in the interest of achieving a richer and deeper understanding of both traditional and emerging forms of white-collar crime and in the interest of understanding the need for new types of regulatory and justice system entities to respond effectively to such crime in an increasingly postmodern, globalized world.

Endnotes

1. This chapter is based on a paper originally presented at the World Congress of Criminology in Rio de Janeiro, August, 2003. Versions of this chapter were presented as invited lectures at Western Michigan University and Eastern Kentucky University in Spring, 2004, and at Stonehill College in Spring, 2005. I wish to thank Dawn Rothe, Ronald Kramer, Carole Garrison, and Danielle McGurrin for their role in arranging these lectures, and for their encouragement and observations. My daughter Jessica Friedrichs provided basic inspiration for developing the concept of "crimes of globalization," as a consequence of her experiences while living in Thailand. I also wish to thank the Faculty Research Committee at the University of Scranton for ongoing support in connection with this project.
2. New forms of analysis, such as an emerging science of networks, have to be integrated into the study of white collar crime (See Duncan Watts, 2003). Networks are inherently complex, and difficult to understand, but play a central role in some of the most significant white-collar crime (See Alan Block and Sean Griffin, 2002). More generally, Gilbert Geis (2002) and John Braithwaite (2000), arguably the two most highly regarded white-collar crime scholars, have strongly advocated cross-disciplinary or multidisciplinary approaches in criminology.
3. See, for example, Gregg Barak (1998), Thomas Bernard and Jeffrey Snipes (1996), and Michael J. Lynch (1999).
4. Some recent attention to crimes of states considers connections with other realms of criminological inquiry (e.g., see David Friedrichs, 1998; Penny Green and Tony Ward, 2004; and David Kauzlarich and David Friedrichs, 2003).
5. For example, see Kip Schlegel and David Eitle (1999).
6. See Gilbert Geis and Colin Goff (1987).
7. E. H. Sutherland (1949).
8. For example, see James William Coleman (2002), David Friedrichs (2004a), and Stephen Rosoff, Henry Pontell and Robert Tillman (2004).
9. For example, see Gregg Barak (2001), John Braithwaite (2000), John Braithwaite and Peter Drahos (2000), Sergio Cuadra (2003), Richard Friman and Peter Andreas (1999), Fiona Haines (2000), Raymond Michalowski and Ronald Kramer (2003), Nikos Passas (1999, 2000), Frank Pearce and Steve Tombs (2002), Steve Russell and Michael Gilbert (1999, 2002), and Nancy Wonders and Mona Danner (2002).
10. See James Helmkamp, Richard Ball and Kitty Townsend (1996) for one extended discussion of the definitional disputes surrounding the term "white-collar crime." The term "economic crime" has been quite widely invoked in European and non-American contexts to refer to tem white-collar crime (e.g., see Anne Alvesalo,

2003). This term may too easily lend itself to the conflation of classic forms of white-collar crime with crimes having an economic dimension but no generic relationship to white-collar crime.

11. Contrepreneurial crime refers to businesses combining elements of legitimate enterprises with classic scams or cons; avocational crime is crime parallel in form to white-collar crime but carried out in a non-occupational context (e.g., personal income tax evasion, or making fraudulent claims to one's auto insurance company.)
12. See David Friedrichs and Jessica Friedrichs (2002) for one account.
13. See John Lukacs (2002) on this theme.
14. See Charles Lemert (1997) on this theme.
15. Seyla Benhabib (1999).
16. Douglas Kellner (2002: 285).
17. Otto Newman and Richard de Zoysa (2001).
18. Larry Ray (1997).
19. Pauline Rosenau (1992).
20. Barbara Stark (2000: 550, 551).
21. See Baudrillard (1994).
22. See Fox (2002) and Fusaro and Miller (2002). A more detailed discussion of the Enron case along the lines developed here can be found in Friedrichs (2004b).
23. Zygmunt Bauman (1990: 42).
24. For example, see William Chambliss (1988) on organized crime as a network.
25. Douglas Kellner (2002).
26. For example, see Alison Smale (2001).
27. Andreas Busch (2000: 22).
28. For example, see Christopher Chase-Dunn, Yukio Kawano and Benjamin D. Brewer (2000), Tim Dunne (1999), and Colin Hay and David Marsh (2000) for some discussion of the terminological discussion.
29. Andreas Busch (2000: 22).
30. See Douglas Kellner (2000), Bruce Mazlish (1999), Robert Schaeffer (2003), and Manfred Steger (2004).
31. Christopher Chase-Dunn et al. (2000); Bruce Mazlish (1999: 7).
32. See Bruce Mazlish (1999), Jan Nederveen Pieterse (2000), Ian Shapiro and Lea Brilmayer (1999), and Kimon Valaskakis (1999).
33. See William Greider (1997) and Douglas Kellner (2002).
34. See Christopher Chase-Dunn et al. (2000), John H. Jackson (2000), and William E. Scheuerman (1999).
35. Ray Kiely (2000) and Jan Nederveen Pieterse (2000).
36. See Douglas Kellner (2002: 286) and Robert McCorquodale with Richard Fairbrother (1999: 733).
37. Jagdish Bagwati (2004) and William Cline (2004) are two authors who emphasize the positive consequences of globalization. See also Michael Weinstein (2005).
38. See Adalberto Aguirre and Ellen Reese (2004) and Ellen Frank (2000).
39. See Teresa Brennan (2003).
40. See Surjit Bhalla (2004), Susan George (2000), and Joseph Kahn (2002).
41. See James K. Galbraith (2002).
42. Jan Nederveen Pieterse (2002: 1024).
43. See Tim Dunne (1999: 22).
44. Richard Falk (1993).
45. Amartya Sen (2000).
46. Douglas Kellner (2002: 290).
47. See Saski Sassen (2002).
48. See Joseph Kahn and Tim Weiner (2002).
49. Jan Nederveen Pieterse (2000: 3).
50. See Jan Nederveen Pieterse (2000) and Joseph Stiglitz (2002).

51. Jan Nederveen Pieterse (2000: 11).
52. Joseph Stiglitz (2002) and George Soros (2001).
53. Amy Chua (2003) and William Finnegan (2003: 43).
54. See David Leonhardt (2003).
55. Tina Rosenberg (2002: 33).
56. *New York Times* (2003).
57. Greg Grandin (2003).
58. See J. F. Rischard (2002).
59. See Anthony Scaperlanda (2002).
60. Tina Rosenberg (2002: 28).
61. Cary Nelson (2003: 4).
62. William Finnegan (2003: 44).
63. See Joseph Stiglitz (2002).
64. See Cary Nelson (2003), G. Sjoberg, Elizabeth A. Gill and Norma Williams (2001), Jackie Smith and Timothy P. Moran (2000), and Joseph Stiglitz (2002).
65. One commentator suggests that the policies of these institutions help explain support for the 9/11 terrorists, if not the motives of the terrorists themselves (See Bruce Robbins 2003).
66. A recently published collection of readings, *World Bank*, has as its premise that the World Bank can be viewed as an agent and a metaphor that helps us to comprehend the "wider context" of global capitalism (Amitava Kumar: 2003: xix. The term "World Bank literature" has been introduced as a new name for post-colonial studies (See Gautam Premnath 2003).
67. See Bryan T. Johnson (2000).
68. See World Bank (2000).
69. William Finnegan (2000: 44). Historically, the World Bank itself has been the principal source of information about its operations and programs, and inevitably such internally generated information can be strongly suspected of being self-serving (See Bruce Rich 1994).
70. See Ethan B. Kapstein (1998/1999: 28).
71. See William Greider (2000: 15).
72. See William Finnegan (2003).
73. Catherine Caufield (1996: 227) and Bruce Rich (1994: 145).
74. Shirin Ebadi and Amir Attaran (2004), and Bruce Rich (1994: 99).
75. Catherine Caufield (1996: 209).
76. See Sebastian Mallaby (2004) and Bruce Rich (1994: xii; 16; 30; 93; 151).
77. See Bryan T. Johnson (2000).
78. Catherine Caufield (1996: 12; 73); also, see David O. Friedrichs and Jessica Friedrichs (2002).
79. Catherine Caufield (1996: 207-208; 263.
80. Bruce Rich (1994; 9).
81. Catherine Caufield (1996: 262).
82. Bruce Rich (1994: 11-12.
83. Bruce Rich (1994: 199).
84. Rajagopal Balakrishnan (2003), Catherine Caufield (1996: 206) and Sigrun I. Skogly (2001).
85. Bruce Rich (1994: 189).
86. Bruce Rich (1994: 195).
87. Snigda Vallabhaneni (2000: 11).
88. Daniel D. Bradlow (1996: 75).
89. Bruce Rich (1994: 91; 307).
90. Daniel D. Bradlow (1996: 63; Barbara Stark (2000: 537).
91. Barbara Stark (2000: 536).
92. See Mac Darrow (2003) and Sigrun Skogly (2001).

93. See Bruce Robbins (2003).
94. See Barbara Crossette (2000), Ellen Frank (2000: 16,19), and Jesse Lemisch (2000: 10).
95. See Jack Katz (1980).
96. See Robin Broad (2002), Eddie Yuen, George Katsiiaticas and Daniel Rose (2001), David Graeber (2003) and Amory Starr (2000).
97. See Douglas Kellner (2002), Paul Kingsnorth (2004), and Amory Starr (2000).
98. See Rajagopal Balakrishnan (2003) and Michael Hardt and Antonio Negri (2003).
99. See David Graeber (2003).
100. David Graeber (2003: 329).
101. See Nick Crossley (2002) and Lauren Langman (2005).
102. See Jonathan Schell (2003).
103. See Nick Crossley (2002).
104. See John Brademas and Fritz Heimann (1998); Richard Pratt (2002).
105. See John Eatwell and Lance Taylor (2000).
106. John Eatwell and Lance Taylor (2000: 220).

References

Aguirre, Adalberto, Jr., and Ellen Reese (2004) "Introduction: The Challenges of Globalization for Workers: Transnational and Transborder Issue." *Social Justice* 31:1–20.

Alvesalo, Anne (2003) *The Dynamics of Economic Crime Control*. Helsinski, Finland: The Police College of Finland.

Aronowitz, Stanley, and Heather Gautney, eds. (2003) *Implicating Empire—Globalization and Resistance in the 21st Century World Order*. New York: Basic.

Barak, Gregg (1998) *Integrating Criminologies*. Boston: Allyn & Bacon.

Barak, Gregg (2001) "Crime and Crime Control in An Age of Globalization." *Critical Criminology* 10:57–72.

Baudrillard, Jean (1994) *Simulacra and Simulation*. Ann Arbor: University of Michigan Press.

Bauman, Zygmunt (1990) "Philosophical Affinities of Postmodern Sociology." *Sociological Review* 38:411–444.

Benhabib, Seyla (1999) "Sexual Difference and Collective Identities: The New Global Constellation." *Signs: Journal of Women in Culture and Society* 24:335–361.

Bernard, Thomas J., and Jeffrey B. Snipes (1996) "Theoretical Integration in Criminology." In *Crime and Justice: A Review of the Research,* Editor M. Michael Tonry. Chicago: University of Chicago Press.

Bhagwati, Jagdish (2004) In *Defense of Globalization*. New York: Oxford University Press.

Bhalla, Surjit (2002) *Imagine There's No Country: Poverty, Inequality and Growth in the Era of Globalization*. Washington, DC.: Institute for International Globalization.

Block, Alan A., and Sean Patrick Griffin (2002) "Transnational Financial Crime: Crooked Lawyers, Tax Evasion, and Securities Fraud." *Journal of Contemporary Criminal Justice* 381–393.

Brademas, John, and Fritz Heimann (1998) "Tackling International Corruption: No Longer Taboo." *Foreign Affairs* 77:17–22.

Bradlow, Daniel D. (1996) "The World Bank, the IMF, and Human Rights." *Transnational Law & Contemporary Problems* 6:47–90.

Braithwaite, John (2000) "The New Regulatory State and the Transformation of Criminology." In *Criminology and Social Theory,* Editors David Garland and Richard Sparks. Oxford, UK: Oxford University Press.

Braithwaite, John, and Peter Drahos (2000) *Global Business Regulation*. Cambridge, UK: Cambridge University Press.

Brennan, Teresa (2003) *Globalization and Its Terrors: Daily Life in the West*. New York: Routledge.

Broad, Robin, eds. (2002) *Global Backlash—Citizen Initiatives for a Just World Economy*. Lanham, MD: Rowman & Littleheld Publishers.

Busch, Andreas (2000) "Unpacking the Globalization Debate: Approaches, Evidence, and Data." In *Demystifying Globalization*, Editors C. Hay and D. Marsh. New York: St. Martin's Press.

Caufield, Catherine (1996) *Masters of Illusion: The World Bank and the Poverty of Nations*. New York: Henry Holt & Co.

Chambliss, William J. (1988) *On the Take*. (2nd Ed.), Bloomington: Indiana University Press.

Chase-Dunn, Christopher, Yukio Kawano, and Benjamin D. Brewer (2000) "Trade Globalization Since 1795: Waves of Integration in the World System." *American Sociological Review* 65:77–95.

Chua, Amy (2003) *World on Fire: How Exporting Free Market Democracy Breeds Ethnic Hatred and Global Instability*. New York: Doubleday.

Cline, William R. (2004) *Trade Policy and Global Poverty*. Washington, DC: Institute for International Globalization.

Coleman, James W. (2002) *The Criminal Elite*. Fifth edition, New York: Worth.

Crossette, Barbara (2000) "Making Room for the Poor in a Global Economy." *New York Times* 16 April, p. A4.

Crossley, Nick (2002) "Global and Anti-Corporate Struggles: A Preliminary Analysis." *British Journal of Sociology* 53:667–691.

Cuadra, Sergio (2003) "Globalization and the Capacity of Violence to Transform Social Spheres: Some Critical Points About the Latin American Debate." *Crime, Law & Social Change* 39:163–173.

Darrow, Mac (2003) *Between Light and Shadow—The World Bank, The International Monetary Fund, and International Human Rights Law*. Portland, OR: Hart Publishing.

Dunne, Tim (1999) "The Spectre of Globalization." *Indiana Journal of Global Legal Studies* 7:17–34.

Eatwell, John, and Lance Taylor (2000) *Global Finance at Risk: The Case for International Regulation*. New York: New Press.

Falk, Richard (1993) "The Making of Global Citizenship." In *Beyond the New World Order*, Editors J. Brecher, J. B. Childs, and J. Cutler. Boston: South End Press.

Finnegan, William (2000) "After Seattle." *The New Yorker* April 17:40–51.

Finnegan, William (2003) "The Economics of Empire—Notes on the Washington Consensus." *Harper's Magazine* May:41–54.

Fox, Loren (2002) *Enron—The Rise and Fall*. New York: John Wiley & Sons.

Frank, Ellen (2000) "Global Democratization: Spotlight on the United States." *New Politics* 8:14–19.

Friedrichs, David O. (ed.) (1998) *State Crime*, vols I & II. Aldershot, UK: Ashgate.

Friedrichs, David O. (2002) "State-Corporate Crime in a Globalized World: Myth or Major Challenge?" In *Controversies in White-Collar Crime*, Editor Gary. W. Potter. Cincinnati, OH: Anderson Publishing Co.

Friedrichs, David O. (2004a) *Trusted Criminals: White Collar Crime in Contemporary Society*. Belmont, CA: Thomson/Wadsworth.

Friedrichs, David O. (2004b) "Enron et al.: Paradigmatic White Collar Crime Cases for the New Century." *Critical Criminology* 12:113–132.

Friedrichs, David O., and Jessica Friedrichs (2002) "The World Bank and Crimes of Globalization: A Case Study." *Social Justice* 29:13–36.

Friman, H. Richard, and Peter Andreas (1999) *The Illicit Global Economy and State Power*. New York: Rowman and Littlefield.

Fusaro, Peter C. and Ross M. Miller (2002) *What Went Wrong at Enron*. New York: John Wiley & Sons.

Galbraith, James K. (2002) "A Perfect Crime: Inequality in the Age of Globalization." *Daedalus* Winter, 11–25.

Geis, Gilbert (2002) "On Cross-Disciplinary Qualitative Research: Some Homilies." *The Criminologist* 27:1 and 3–5.

Geis, Gilbert, and Colin Goff (1987) "Edwin H. Sutherland's White-Collar Crime in America: An Essay in Historical Criminology." In *Criminal Justice History*, Vol., 7 L. Knafla (ed.). Westport, CT: Meckler.

George, Susan (2000) "Carte Blanche, Bete Noire." *Dissent* Winter, 13–15.

Graeber, David (2003) "The Globalization Movement and the New New Left." In *Implication Empire—Globalization and Resistance in the 21st Century World Order*, Editors S. Aronowitz and H. Gautney. New York: Basic Books.

Grandin, Greg (2003) "What's a Neo-liberal to Do?" *The Nation* March 10, 25–29.

Green, Penny, and Tony Ward (2004) *State Crime: Government, Violence and Corruption*. London: Pluto Press.

Greider, William (1997) *One World, Ready or Not: The Manic Logic of Global Capitalism*. New York: Touchstrone.

Greider, William (2000) "Waking Up the Global Elite." *The Nation* October 2, 17–18.

Haines, Fiona (2000) "Towards Understanding Globalization and Control of Corporate Harm: A Preliminary Criminological Analysis." *Current Issues in Criminal Justice* 12:166–180.

Hardt, Michael, and Antonio Negri (2003) "Globalization and Democracy." In *Implicating Empire*, Editors S. Aronowitz and H. Gautney. New York: Basic Books.

Hay, Colin, and David Marsh, eds. (2000) *Demystifying Globalization*. New York: St. Martin's Press.

Helmkamp, James, Richard Ball, and Karen Townsend, eds. (1996) *Definitional Dilemma: Can and Should There Be a Universal Definition of White Collar Crime?* Morgantown, WV: National White Collar Crime Center.

Henderson, Hazel (2000) "Life Beyond Global Economic Warfare." In *Global Futures: Shaping Globalization*, Editor J. N. Pieterse. London: Zed Books.

Jackson, John H. (2000) *The Jurisprudence of GATT and the WTO*. Cambridge, UK: Cambridge University Press.

Johnson, Bryan T. (2000) "The World Bank Does Not Provide Effective Development Programs." In *The Third World—Opposing Viewpoints*, Editor L. K. Egendorf. San Diego, CA: Greenhaven Press.

Kahn, Joseph (2002) "Loving Faith: Globalization Proves Disappointing." *New York Times* 21 March, p. A8.

Kahn, Joseph, and Tim Weiner (2002) "World Leaders Rethinking Strategy on Aid to Poor." *New York Times* 18 March, p. A5.

Kapstein, Ethan B. (1998/1999) "A Global Third Way: Social Justice and the World Economy." *World Policy Journal* 15:23–35.

Katz, Jack (1980) "The Social Movement Against White Collar Crime." In *Criminology Review Yearbook*, Editors Egoh Bittner and Sheblon Messinger, vol. 2. Beverly Hills, CA: Sage.

Kauzlarich, David, and David O. Friedrichs (2003) "Crimes of the State." In *Controversies in Critical Criminology*, Editors Martin D. Schwartz and Suzanne Hatty. Cincinnati, OH: Anderson Publishing Co.

Kellner, Douglas (2002) "Theorizing Globalization." *Sociological Theory* 20:285–305.

Kiely, Ray (2000) "Globalization: From Domination to Resistance." *Third World Quarterly* 21:1059–1070.

Kingsnorth, Paul (2004) *One No, Many Yeses: A Journey to the Heart of the Global Resistance Movement*. New York: Free Press.

Editors Kumar, Amitava (2003) *World Bank Literature*. Minneapolis, MN: University of Minnesota Press.

Langman, Lauren (2005) "From Virtual Spheres to Global Justice: A Critical Theory of Internetworked Social Movements." *Sociological Theory* 23:42–74.

Lemert, Charles (1997) *Postmodernism is Not What You Think*. Oxford, UK: Blackwell.

Lemisch, Jesse (2000) "A Movement Begins: The Washington Protests Against IMF/World Bank." *New Politics* 8:5–11.

Leonhardt, David (2003) "Globalization Hits a Political Speed Bump." *New York Times* 1 June, sec. 3, p.1.

Lukacs, John (2002) "It's the End of the Modern Age." *Chronicle of Higher Education* 26 April, pp. B7–B11.

Lynch, Michael J. (1999) "Working Together: Towards an Integrative Critical Criminological Model for Social Justice." *Humanity & Society* 23:68–78.

Mallaby, Sebastian (2004) *The World's Banker: A Story of Failed States, Financial Crises, and the Wealth and Poverty of Nations*. New York: Penguin.

Mazlish, Bruce (1999) "A Tour of Globalization." *Indiana Journal of Global Legal Education* 7:5–16.

McCorquodale, Robert, and Richard Fairbrother (1999) "Globalization and Human Rights." *Human Rights Quarterly* 21:735–766.

Michalowski, Raymond, and Ronald Kramer (2003) "Beyond Enron: Toward Economic Democracy and a New Ethic of Inclusion." *Risk Management: An International* Journal 5:37–47.

Nelson, Cary (2003) "Consolations for Capitalists: Propositions in Flight from World Bank Literature." In *World Bank Literature*, Editor A. Kumar. Minneapolis, MN: University of Minnesota Press.

New York Times (2003) "The Rigged Trade Game." *The New York Times* 20 July, Week 10.

Newman, Otto and Richard de Zoysa (2001) *The Promise of the Third Way: Globalization and Social Justice*. Basingstoke, UK: Palgrave.

Passas, Nikos (1999) "Globalization, Criminogenic Asymmetries, and Economic Crime." *European Journal of Law Reform* 1:399–423.

Passas, Nikos (2000) "Global Anomie, Dysnomie, and Economic Crime: Hidden Consequences of Neoliberalism and Globalization in Russia and Around the World." *Social Justice* 27:16–44.

Pearce, Frank, and Steve Tombs (2002) "State, Corporations and the 'New World Order.'" In *Controversies in White-Collar Crime*, Editor Gary. W. Potter. Cincinnati, OH: Anderson.

Pieterse, Jan Nederveen (2000) "Shaping Globalization." In *Global Futures: Shaping Globalization*, Editor J. N. Pieterse. London: Zed Books.

Pieterse, Jan Nederveen (2002) "Global Inequality: Bringing Politics Back In." *Third World Quarterly* 23:1023–1046.

Pratt, Richard (2002) "Global Financial Business and the Implications for Effective Control of Money Laundering in Offshore Centers." *Journal of Financial Crime* 10:130–132.

Premnath, Gautam (2003) "The Weak Sovereignty of the Postcolonial Nation-State." In *World Bank Literature*, Editor A. Kumar. Minneapolis, MN: University of Minnesota Press.

Rajagopal, Balakrishnan (2003) *International Law from Below—Development, Social Movements, and Third World Resistance*. Cambridge, UK: Cambridge University Press.

Ray, Larry (1997) "Post-Communism: Postmodernity or Modernity Revisited?" *British Journal of Sociology* 48:543–560.

Rich, Bruce (1994) *Mortgaging the Earth: The World Bank, Environmental Impoverishment, and the Crisis of Development*. Boston: Beacon Press.

Rischard, J. F. (2002) *High Noon—Twenty Global Problems, Twenty Years to Solve Them*. New York: Basic Books.

Robbins, Bruce (2003) "Afterword." In *World Bank Literature*, Editor A. Kumar. Minneapolis, MN: University of Minnesota Press.

Rosenau, Pauline (1992) *Post-Modernism and the Social Sciences: Insights, Inroads, and Intrusions*. Princeton, NJ: Princeton University Press.

Rosenberg, Tina (2002) "The Free-Trade Fix." *New York Times Magazine* 18 August, pp. 28 and more.

Rosoff, Stephen M., Henry N. Pontell, and Robert Tillman (2002) *Profit Without Honor—White Collar Crime and the Looting of America*. Second edition, Upper Saddle River, NJ: Prentice Hall.

Russell, Steve, and Michael J. Gilbert (1999) "Truman's Revenge: Social Control and Corporate Crime." *Law and Social Change* 32:59–82.

Russell, Steve, and Michael J. Gilbert (2002) "Social Control of Transnational Corporations in the Age of Marketocracy." *International Journal of the Sociology of Law* 30:33–50.

Sassen, Saskia (2002) "Governance Hotspots: Challenges We Must Confront in the Post-September 11 World." In *Understanding September 11*, Editors C. Calhoun, P. Price, and A. Timmer. New York: The New Press.

Scaperlanda, Anthony (2002) "Global Society in 2052." *Review of Social Economy* 60:493–505.

Schaeffer, Robert K. (2003) *Understanding Globalization—The Social Consequences of Political, Economic and Environmental Change*. Second edition, Lanham, MD: Rowman & Littleheld Publishers, Inc.

Scheuerman, William E. (1999) "Economic Globalization and the Rule of Law." *Constellations* 6:3–25.

Schlegel, Kip, and David Eitle (1999) "Back to the Future: A Reminder of the Importance of Sutherland in Thinking About White Collar Crime." In *The Criminology of Criminal Law*, Editors Willinn S. Laufer and Freda Adler. New Brunswick, NJ: Transaction Press.

Sen, Amartya (2000) "How to Judge Globalism." *The American Prospect* Winter, A1–A6.

Shapiro, Ian, and Lea Brilmayer, eds. (1999) *Global Justice*. New York: New York University Press.

Sjoberg, Gideon, Elizabeth A. Gill, and Norma Williams (2001) "A Sociology of Human Rights." *Social Problems* 48:11–47.

Skogly, Sigrun I. (2001) The Human Rights Obligations of the World Bank and the International Monetary Fund. London: Cavendish Publishing Co.

Smale, Alison (2001) "The Dark Side of the Global Economy." *The New York Times* 26 August, Week 3.

Smith, Jackie, and Timothy Patrick Moran (2000) "WTO 101: Myths About the World Trade Organization." *Dissent* Sprint 66–69.

Soros, George (2002) *On Globalization*. New York: Public Affairs.

Stark, Barbara (2000) "Women and Globalization: The Failure and Postmodern Possibilities of International Law." *Vanderbilt Journal of Transnational Law* 33:503–571.

Starr, Amory (2000) *Naming the Enemy: Anti-corporate Movements Confront Globalization*. London: Zed Books.

Steger, Manfred B., ed. (2004) *Rethinking Globalism*. Lanham, MD: Rowman & Littlefield Publishers, Inc.

Stiglitz, Joseph E. (2002) *Globalization and Its Discontents*. New York: Norton.

Sutherland, Edwin H. (1949) *White Collar Crime*. New York: Holt, Rinehart & Winston.

Tombs, Steve, and Dave Whyte (2003) "Introduction: Corporations Beyond the Law? Regulation, Risk, and Corporate Crime in a Globalized Era." *Risk Management* 5:9–16.

Valaskakis, Kimon (1999) "Globalization as Theatre." *International Social Science Journal* 160:153–160.

Vallabhaneni, Snigdha (2000) *Inertia of Change in the World Bank: The Pak Mun Dam Project as a Case Study*. Honors Thesis. Providence, RI: Brown University.

Watts, Duncan J. (2003) "Unraveling the Mysteries of the Connected Age." *Chronicle of Higher Education* 14 February, pp.137–139.

Weinstein, Michael M., ed. (2005) *Globalization—What's New?* New York: Columbia University Press.

Wonders, Nancy, and Mona Danner (2002) "Globalization, State-Corporate Crime, and Women: The Strategic Role of Women's NGOs in the New World Order." In *Controversies in White-Collar Crime*, Editor Gary W. Potter. Cincinnati, OH: Anderson.

World Bank (2000) "The World Bank Provides Effective Development Programs." In *The Third World—Opposing Viewpoints*, Editor L. K. Egendorf. San Diego, CA: Greenhaven Press, Inc.

Yuen, Eddie, George Katsiaticas, and Daniel Burton Rose, eds. (2001) *The Battle of Seattle: The New Challenge to Capitalist Globalization*. New York: Soft Skull Press.

Part IV

Corporate Crime and State-Corporate Crime

1

Corporate Crime

Amitai Etzioni with Derek Mitchell

Can a Corporation be a Criminal?

The right to bring civil suits against corporations for the damage their activities have caused has long been established in American law. However, the notion that criminal charges can be brought against a corporation is less self-evident, for, as the saying goes, "One cannot jail a corporation." There is a tendency to confuse crimes committed by one corporate executive for his or her personal gain with corporate crime, or with crime committed by a corporation as a whole. Thus when Martha Stewart was charged and convicted of lying to investigators about insider trading, it was not Martha Stewart, Inc. (a corporation she founded and headed) that committed or facilitated a crime, or was otherwise involved in wrongdoing. Indeed Stewart's corporation (the shareholders, employees, clients) was considered one of the victims of her crime, albeit indirectly.

Corporations as a whole, however, can be charged with a crime because they are collective entities, made up of organizational networks and hierarchies, means of communication and transportation, office space, and other assets that can be put to criminal use. When agents of a corporation use the corporate infrastructure or assets to commit a crime meant to boost general profits and benefit shareholders, the corporation as a whole can legitimately be held as the culprit. Thus when the president and vice-president of Beech-Nut Nutrition Corp. systematically orchestrated the adulteration of purportedly pure apple juice for babies, and its shareholders reaped the benefits, that corporation was charged and convicted.[1]

Federal law recognizes corporations as subject to criminal laws by ascribing to them a legal status similar to that of an individual.[2] From the viewpoint of a communitarian sociologist, treating corporations as individuals means that they have the rights and responsibilities of individuals and therefore can legitimately be punished when they fail to discharge their legal and moral responsibilities properly.

As to the claim that shareholders remain innocent when corporate employees act illegally and thus should not be punished, it must be remembered that the shareholders are nevertheless the beneficiaries of the illegal behavior. The corporation as a whole is the transgressor when illicit profits are channeled into its coffers rather than pocketed by executives. Hence, it seems proper to hold the shareholders responsible. It is up to them, after all, as the ultimate source of corporate sovereignty, to see to it that the executives, acting as their agents, uphold the law. And if the executives do not, it is up to the shareholders to retain a law-abiding crew.

Legal scholars debating the costs and benefits of criminal versus civil prosecution for corporations focus on the distinction between deterrence through monetary fines available through civil sanctions and deterrence through the combination of monetary fines and moral condemnation available through criminal sanctions. Criminal sanctions typically assume the victim has a moral right to be free of the defendant's conduct, regardless of its profitability or its greater utility to the defendant or society.

Corporate nominalists such as V.S. Khanna, Alan Sykes, and Daniel Fischel view corporations as contractual associations of individuals, with a "personhood" limited to legal transactions. Corporations do not have an independent identity, cannot suffer moral stigma, and therefore only waste public resources when subject to criminal sanctions.[3] Communitarians will be quick to point out that the corporation is a social entity with a distinct personality in society. Those who manage and own them are far from unmindful of their reputation and know what is morally right corporate behavior. Thus and in fact many companies prominently advertise their efforts to practice corporate social responsibility.

Frequency

There are no definitive or reliable assessments of how common corporate crime is in the United States, either in this decade or previous ones. The F.B.I. does not compile comprehensive data on corporate crime in its Uniform Crime Reports. Indications exist, however, that many of the major corporations in any given industry have engaged in activities that are at least ethically wrong even if not outright illegal. The sociologist Edwin H. Sutherland published the first academic study of corporate crime in 1949, *White-Collar Crime*.[4] His study of 70 non-financial corporations found that in total they had been convicted of 980 criminal and civil charges, for an average of 14 convictions per corporation. In the 1970s, Marshall B. Clinard and Peter Yeager found that of 582 large U.S. companies they studied over a two-year period, 60 percent faced an average of four charges of violating the law.[5] In recent years, many of the major pharmaceutical companies have been investigated for withholding information about the negative side effects of drugs they have marketed.[6] The Corporate Crime Reporter found in June 2005 that 9 out of 30 Dow Jones Industrial Index Companies have been convicted of a crime, and this study did not include their subsidiary companies.[7] Finally, since its creation in July 2002, the President's Corporate Fraud Taskforce has helped federal prosecutors charge over 900 corporate wrongdoers and secure over 500 convictionsc, with many trials still pending.

Corporate crimes are often difficult to detect and prosecute, either because the wrongdoing can be passed off onto one or more individual employees or because the illegal behavior is buried in complex networks of transactions, hidden behind corporate fronts, or concealed in offshore accounts. However, one only has to open the *Wall Street Journal* on any day to learn about another allegation of corporate fraud, environmental destruction, antitrust violations, or some other form of corporate antisocial conduct.

A Short History of Corporate Crime in America

Corporate crime is hardly new. Throughout American history there have been major incidents that have caused great suffering and captured public attention.

In the early 1800s, banks within the United States began taking liberties and testing just how closely their internal operations were monitored. In 1832, President Andrew Jackson vetoed a motion to extend the charter of the Second Bank of the United States, attributing his decision to the bank's corrupt and tyrannical actions. In the same year, Pennsylvania revoked the charters of ten banks, citing operations contrary to the public interest.

One of the most infamous early examples of corporate corruption was the Crédit Mobilier scandal of 1872, during which Union Pacific Rail Road contracted with the Crédit Mobilier construction company to build a government-subsidized railroad. The company, owned by major Union Pacific shareholders, overcharged to the point of depleting all of Union Pacific's government grants. To avoid a congressional inquiry, the head of Crédit Mobilier sold stock to prominent members of Congress at sub-par prices; thus when Congressmen voted to increase government grants to Union Pacific, some of the money went directly into their own pockets.

In the early 20th century, Upton Sinclair and other muckraking journalists brought to light such scandals as the poor sanitation in food-processing plants, the large-scale adulteration of meat products, and the false claims of medicine advertisements, leading to massive public outrage. Journalist Ida Tarbell's revelations about the Standard Oil Trust stoked public fears about corporations that merged together into "trusts" and then dominated particular industries. In an early case of a corporation being caught defrauding the government, the Department of Commerce and Labor discovered in 1907 that the American Sugar Refining Company had failed to pay the government large sums in import duties.

War profiteering has been a part of American history since the Revolutionary War, and the period of the World Wars was no exception. Edwin Sutherland details widespread price inflation and tax evasion on the part of American corporations during World War I, as demonstrated by Federal Trade Commission investigations and the 1935 report of the Nye Committee.[8] Stuart Brandes has shown that during World War II, 14.4 percent of defense company profits were the result of price increases, despite government attempts to prevent war profiteering.[9] Moreover, the mean salary of presidents of corporations jumped 159 percent before taxes from 1939 to 1945. The 1980s saw a rash of defense procurement fraud, when upward of 50 U.S. contractors came under investigation for overcharging the Defense Department and other violations. Between 1983 and 1990, a quarter of the 100 largest Pentagon contractors were found guilty of procurement fraud. In the 1988 to 1990 period, there were 16 cases involvinged 14 of the largest weapons makers.

In the 1960s, the auto industry came under fire after revelations, largely by Ralph Nader, that it had systematically avoided incorporating safety features into automobiles in order to reduce costs. The case of the defective Ford Pinto, that was prone to exploding in rear-end collisions, was one of the most flagrant examples of an auto company's knowing of a car's safety problems but choosing not to fix them.

Environmental crime perpetrated by corporations became a serious cause of public concern during the 1960s and 1970s. Incidents such as the polluted Cuyahoga River's bursting into flames in 1969 and books such as Rachel Carson's *Silent Spring* alerted the public to the dangers that dumping chemicals into waterways and spewing pollutants into the air posed to human health.[10] Numerous cases have since come to light of companies exposing workers and communities to toxic substances with full knowledge of the dangers.

The 1980s are notorious for the savings and loan scandal, when the owners of savings and loan associations throughout the country fleeced their members of billions of dollars. These crimes, however, do not fit under the rubric "corporate crime" as defined here because the beneficiaries of the crime were not the shareholders of the company, in this case the depositors, but the individual owners.

The late 1980s and 1990s saw the first legal penalties imposed on the tobacco industry for misleading the public about the health risks of smoking. In 1988 the tobacco industry lost its first lawsuit holding it responsible for the death of a smoker, and this decision set off a flurry of suits brought by state attorneys general, culminating in a $206 billion dollar settlement with 46 states in 1998.

The beginning of the 21st century has seen a new wave of corporate scandal. Many of the most notorious cases—Enron, WorldCom, Tyco, Adelphia—have involved executives misleading investors about the financial health of the company and misappropriating company funds for personal use. While they do not qualify as corporate crimes as previously defined, the scandals have led to revelations that accounting firms have consistently failed to audit their clients' books properly. Their motivation for not questioning accounting irregularities appears to have been to hold on to their clients' business, especially the lucrative consulting services they provided on the side.

Historically, much of the focus on corporate crime has been on large corporations with many investors, but small corporations have also been charged with their share of corporate wrongdoing. Especially prominent in the media have been stories of nursing homes, doctors' offices, and pharmacies defrauding the government out of Medicaid and Medicare payments.

Waves of Disclosures, Reforms, and Backsliding

The history of counteracting corporate malfeasance in America has been one of public outcry, followed by spurts of reform, and then partial erosion of these reforms. For much of the 19th century, and especially during the Gilded Age (approximately 1876–1900), politicians often exhibited a laissez-faire attitude about corporate crime—when they were not complicit themselves. Tycoons of the period, often called "robber barons," were allowed by and large free rein in their business practices. However, as the power of the industrialists grew, and many corporations merged into even more powerful trusts, the public began clamoring for controls. In 1887 President Grover Cleveland signed one of the first significant pieces of federal legislation to regulate corporations, the Interstate Commerce Act. It was meant to prevent excessive charges, pools, rebates, and rate discrimination by railroad companies. However, the Supreme Court during the period struck down several key legal provisions needed to prosecute corporations. The federal government's first effort to break monopolies, the Sherman Antitrust Act of 1890, was similarly ineffective in the years following its passage.

It took Theodore Roosevelt and his "Square Deal" for America in 1901 to initiate a period of serious "trust busting." Empowered by the reform spirit of the Progressive movement, Roosevelt successfully broke up J.P. Morgan's Northern Securities railroad trust and John D. Rockefeller's Standard Oil. He signed legislation that gave the Interstate Commerce Act real authority, and created the Department of Commerce and Labor. When Upton Sinclair's *The Jungle* was released in 1906, Roosevelt called for immediate action against the meatpacking industry, resulting in the1906 Pure Food and Drug Act and the Meat Inspection Act. The regulation of industry continued through William H. Taft's administration and into Woodrow Wilson's term. Wilson created the Federal Trade Commission to investigate unfair and corrupt behavior by corporations, secured the passage of the Clayton Antitrust Act in 1914 to strengthen the government's ability to break up trusts, and in 1916 signed the Adamson Act to institute an eight-hour work day for railroad employees, the first initiative on the part of the federal government to regulate working hours in private companies. However, World War I brought an end to the wave of reform, and in the years between the war and the Great Depression, industry regained much of its autonomy. Large conglomerates once again dominated entire industries and antitrust laws were used mainly against labor unions.

This laissez-faire era came to a close with the election of Franklin D. Roosevelt. In his second Fireside Chat, May 1933, Roosevelt declared that "government ought to have the right and will have the right... to prevent... unfair practice [by industry] and to enforce this agreement by the authority of government." The Federal Securities Act of 1933 was intended to increase corporate transparency about the value of stocks and other securities, and thus better protect investors. In 1934 the Securities and Exchange Commission was established to monitor trading on the stock market and ensure that corporations properly disclosed their financial situation. To improve the conditions of working men and women engaged directly or indirectly in interstate commerce, Roosevelt signed the Fair Labor Standards Act in 1938. The Act established a maximum workweek, overtime standards, and a minimum wage and set up the Wage & Hour Division within the Department of Labor to ensure that employers complied. Roosevelt's ability to pass new regulatory laws began to fade after the 1937 recession, his failed attempt to pack the courts, and increased Congressional opposition. By the start of World War II, the wave of reform brought on by the Great Depression had effectively come to an end.

During the 1950s, corporations once again faced little in the way of new government regulation. Eisenhower staffed his cabinet primarily with business executives and believed in minimal government involvement in the economy. During the 1960s, however, government increasingly had to respond to public demands for corporate regulation, largely inspired by the rise of new consumer protection groups and the environmentalism movement. For example, Congress passed the Traffic and Motor Vehicle Safety Act of 1966, in part due to the efforts of Ralph Nader.

In 1963 the first major effort to counteract environmental pollution by corporations emerged with the passage of the Clean Air Act, which was further strengthened in 1970 and 1990. Rachel Carson's book *Silent Spring* is widely credited with spearheading the contemporary environmentalist movement and alerting Americans to the role of corporations in polluting the environment. Growing public demand for a cleaner environment led to the creation of the Environmental Protection Agency in 1970. The new agency was charged with setting environmental standards for industry and enforcing compliance. The Occupational Safety and Health Administration was also created in 1970 to protect workers and ensure that industries maintained healthy workplaces.

The 1980s under Ronald Reagan was a decade of rolling back much regulation of corporations. By the late 1980s, however, and then again at the beginning of the 21st century, government renewed its efforts to institute stiffer penalties for corporate crime and stricter oversight. The following account of these recent efforts provides a detailed sense of the tug of war between attempts to rein in corporations and their successes in getting out from under regulation.

The U.S. Sentencing Commission

The U.S. Sentencing Commission was formed in 1984 because judgments meted out for individuals in federal courts varied greatly, so that, for instance, a person caught with a "joint" of marijuana could get 20 years in one court and receive a suspended sentence in another. The commission formulated a set of guidelines that Congress enacted in 1987, and required judges to vary not more than 25 percent from these guidelines. (In January 2005 the Supreme Court ruled that sentencing guidelines could only be advisory and not mandatory).[11]

Heartened by its early success, in the late 1980s the commission decided to turn to studying the penalties for corporate rather individual crimes; it found that such penalties were often minimal. For example, in the 1980s, of the 60 some banks convicted of money-laundering, 25 received fines of $10,000 or less. Such small fines have a negligible effect; corporations can easily absorb them as part of the costs of doing business. Some economists argue that fines must take into account not only the potential for gain, but also the likelihood of being detected. Thus, Gary Becker of the University of Chicago said in a 1985 *Business Week* article, "[If the illegal] act does $1 million worth of harm with a 50-percent chance of going unpunished, then the fine would be $2 million."[12] This is indeed a valid observation except that the probability that a corporate crime will be detected, the responsible corporation will be tried and convicted, and the government will actually collect the fine is much lower—perhaps even closer to 0.5 percent, rather than 50 percent.

The U.S. Sentencing Commission published its first-draft guidelines in November 1989 and opened them to public hearing on February 14, 1990. While the commission asked for comments, it offered only two options: One option provided for fines ranging from two to three times the amount of damage caused (or illicit gains obtained) by a corporation; and the second established a 32-level sliding scale of fines that was dependent on the severity of the offense, nature of the crime, and mitigating circumstances.

The guidelines suggested the introduction of huge fines, up to one-third of $1 billion, for crimes that had previously resulted in fines of tens of thousands of dollars. For such serious crimes as drug companies neglecting to report data showing that drugs they sold caused multiple fatalities or for crimes causing major and repeated damage to the environment, fines could be as high as $364 million per single offense. In contrast, four-fifths of all corporate convictions between 1975 and 1976 resulted in fines of $5,000 or less. Between 1984 and 1987, the average corporate fine was $48,000, and 67 percent of the fines were $10,000 or less. Consider some specific cases: Eli Lilly & Company, the pharmaceutical manufacturer, was fined $25,000 for a guilty plea to a misdemeanor charge for failing to inform the government of four deaths and six illnesses related to its arthritis drug Oraflex. Though the company was charged with only a misdemeanor, the drug was linked to at least 26 deaths in the United States and even more from its sale overseas.[13]

The commission's proposed guidelines elicited a firestorm of opposition from major corporations, their lawyers, trade associations, and the columnists close to them. Liberal groups that might have fortified the commission's firm stance were barely aware of the hearings and initially played a rather minor role in the process. The result was predictable: the commission withdrew its recommendations and promised to reconsider them. It then swung full force in the opposite direction.

Its new set of recommendations, released March 6, 1990, drastically scaled back most of the penalties, in some cases by as much as 97 percent! For example, under the commission's original guidelines, a level 10 offense carried a penalty of up to $64,000; the new option reduced it to $17,500. Level 25 dropped from a hefty $136 million to $580,000. The maximum proposed penalty dropped from $364 million to about 3 percent of that, or $12.6 million.[14]

These much diluted and weakened guidelines were still not acceptable to the big corporations and their political allies. Liberal groups finally entered the arena, though rather weakly. Business groups by contrast, riding high on their recent victory over the commission's draft, went in for the kill. They called upon the commission either to withdraw its conclusions completely or adopt only *recommended* guidelines. They even successfully enlisted the White House to help restrain the commission.

The commission finally reached a formula acceptable to big business and, issued its final report on May 1, 1991, on all but environmental crimes. In a minor concession to the critical press and liberals, the commission somewhat enhanced the reduced penalties, but provided a list of extenuating circumstances that allowed offending corporations easily to reduce the remaining penalties to small amounts, if not to nothing.

One major avenue the commission allowed for mitigating penalties was the existence of internal policies deeling with criminal conduct. The guidelines contained detailed definitions of an effective compliance program, including designation of a specific high-level person to be responsible for the program, written policies and reporting procedures, and mandatory participation in training programs by employees.

In the end, the U.S. Sentencing Commission's mountain of deliberations and studies produced a molehill of enforcement. It zigzagged itself into a position that has some merit, but it made overwhelming concessions to the pro-business environment.

Sarbanes-Oxley Act of 2002 (SOX)

The corporate scandals revealed at the dawn of the 21st century led to Sarbanes-Oxley (or "SOX"), a Congressional act passed in 2002 in the aftermath of the Enron and WorldCom debacles to "protect investors by improving the accuracy and reliability of corporate disclosures."[15] It has tightened rules for corporate behavior, giving boards heightened responsibility (and liability) for eliminating illegal conduct. It was overwhelmingly approved by a vote of 423-3 in the House, and by 99-0 in the Senate, reflecting the public outcry to "do something." The act was signed into law on July 30, 2002, by President Bush, who explained that its intent was "to use the full authority of the government to expose corruption, punish wrongdoers, and defend the rights and interests of American workers and investors."[16] SOX was celebrated as the most sweeping legislation aimed at curtailing corporate scandal since the Glass-Steagall Act, which was instituted after the stock market crash of 1929.

The Sarbanes-Oxley Act applies to publicly traded companies and requires that their audit committees be composed of "independent" individuals, meaning those not belonging to the management team nor receiving compensation for other professional services. The act also defined a role for the Public Company Accounting Oversight Board, empowered to enforce new compliance standards.

The criminal provisions of the Act are found in Title VIII (the "Corporate and Criminal Fraud Accountability Act of 2002"), Title IX (the "White-Collar Crime Penalty Enhancement Act of 2002"), and Title XI (the "Corporate Fraud Accountability Act of 2002"). These fortify criminal sanctions by creating new federal criminal offenses, increasing penalties for existing federal criminal offenses, and mandating review of current federal sentencing guidelines to ensure they effectively deter criminal activity.

In the short time that has passed since the law was enacted, SOX has already faced the prospect of dilution, despite claims to the contrary from officials. For example, while SOX forbids accounting firms from providing many kinds of consulting services to the companies they are auditing, the SEC has made an exception for selling advice about matters such as tax shelters—even though part of what the firms audit are their clients' tax arrangements. The SEC has also backed down from requiring that every five years accounting firms rotate all the auditors working on a client's accounts, to prevent individual auditors from becoming too close with clients. In February 2005 *The New York Times* reported that "under heavy pressure from Bush administration officials, business groups, and Wall Street, Mr. Donaldson [former SEC chairman] denied that the agency was in a period of significant retrenchment, but said that it was part of his plan to reflect on the regulatory experience of the past two years and make some rules more 'cost-effective' without diluting their impact."[17] The SEC has already announced that it will allow small and foreign companies with shares traded in the United States more time to comply with provisions many contend are too expensive. It remains to be seen whether regulators will further give in to intense pressures from corporations to ease oversight and controls.

It follows that to deter corporate crime more effectively, fines may well have to be close to the stiff ones initially suggested by the U.S. Sentencing Commission, and monitoring will have to be at least as tough as that required by the 2002

Sarbanes-Oxley Act and other such measures. Given the public's mercurial interest in corporate crime, we are likely to see more cycles of scandals, public outrage, and reforms that are enacted and the in part rolled back, although some improvements will stick. The best course of all is to prevent corporate crimes, i.e., to lock the door of the barn rather than to try to go after the horse after it has bolted.

Preventing Corporate Crime

In addition to government regulation and stiff penalties, the literature on preventing corporate crime notes the importance of fostering a culture of respect for the law within corporations and creating internal controls to prevent misconduct. Several measures can be taken by corporations to encourage an atmosphere where management and employees abide by the law. General Dynamics represents one of the most notable examples of a corporation building such a culture after being found guilty of serious ethical and legal infractions. In the mid-1980s, General Dynamics became synonymous with defense procurement fraud and dubious overhead charges to the governments, such as country club memberships and kennel charges for an executive's dog. In May 1985, the Secretary of the Navy wrote a letter informing General Dynamics that the Navy would not do business with the company until it changed management and put a stop to misconduct. General Dynamics responded by creating a comprehensive ethics program and hiring Kent Druyvesteyn, a former head of the University of Chicago Business School, as staff vice-president of ethics.[18] Druyvesteyn set about ensuring that all employees and management were well aware of what was stipulated in the company's new code of ethics and knew how to communicate concerns. The company set up an ethics hotline that employees could call for information about the code or to report any wrongdoing. Thiry-three ethics program directors were hired to investigate cases of potential misconduct and serve as sources of information. To give teeth to the program, an enforcement system was put in place whereby those found guilty of a violation would be subject to various types of sanctions, including termination of employment and referrals for criminal prosecution. In 1988 there were 206 sanctions, with 35 of them resulting in discharge and four leading to criminal referrals.[19] Druyvesteyn contends that for an ethics program to work, it must be clear to employees that management is serious about creating a culture of respect for the law; if management does not respond to ethics concerns, and is apathetic about questions of legality, employees are unlikely to report misconduct. Numerous corporations have codes of ethics and other internal controls meant to ensure compliance with the law, but it is up to management at all levels to set the example of taking ethics seriously.

Education as a Preventive Measure

Business schools—the training grounds for corporate executives—have a role to play in preventing corporate crime by instilling respect for the law and more generally for moral values in their graduates. However, most business schools teach very little ethics or none at all. The Harvard Business School—which deserves particular scrutiny, as it is the school to which many others look when they design their own curriculums—had little in the way of formal ethics teaching until 1987. And that was typical. A 1988 survey of MBA schools found that only one-third had a required ethics class.[20] It was in 1987 that John S. R. Shad, then chairman of the Securities and Exchange Commission, made a personal donation of $20 million to the Harward Business School (HBS) to support the teaching of ethics. On April 21, 1989, after months of deliberations, an initial proposal for teaching ethics was put up for a faculty-wide vote. Reactions ranged from distrust to outright hostility. One economist argued, "We are here to teach science." Another faculty member wanted to know, "Whose ethics, what values, are we going to teach?" And a third pointed out that the students were adults who got their ethics education at home and at church. By meeting's end, the project had been sent back to the drawing board.

Debates continued regarding whether ethics should be a required course or a separate elective or, alternatively, whether the topic should be integrated into all classes. A member of the marketing department mused that if the latter policy were adopted, his department would have to close because much of what it was teaching constituted a form of dissembling: selling small items in large boxes, putting "hot" colors on packages because they encourage people to buy impulsively, and so forth.

A finance professor was also concerned about its effects on his teaching. Students later told me that they learned in his course how you could make a profit by breaking implicit contracts. Say, for instance, that you acquire controlling shares in a company such as Delta, where workers used to work harder and pose fewer demands than at other airlines because of an informal understanding that they had lifelong employment. The finance course would explain that once you take over, you could announce that you are not bound by any such informal arrangements. While such a change might be deemed a prudent move for the company, it could also bring personal gain to the new management: Your stock jumps (because your labor costs seem lower, absent commitments to carry workers during a downturn) and, bingo, you cash in your stock options and move on.

In the following years, an ethics course was taught at HBS, but it was only a minor requirement to be gotten out of the way as quickly as possible. These days, students take a required "mini" course on ethics upon arrival, and there is a required first-year course titled, "Leadership and Organizational Behavior." And that's it. The same situation can be found at other schools. One student at Stanford's business school, which until recently had a similar program, described his ethics class as "like going to church on Sunday." The George Washington University School of Business and Public Administration has an elective on moral reasoning (the art of clarifying what your values are, rather than educating you on how to develop higher moral standards). And the University of Michigan, which has an activist student group that pushed its business school to be mindful of social policy, requires only that students take one class in ethics or in law. Many other schools do less.

In recent years, many business schools have added courses that promote values other than the maximization of investors' and managers' incomes, and Harvard has been praised for being at the forefront of this trend with its "Social Enterprise Initiative." Such courses generally favor social values, and usually liberal ones, such as concern for the environment or the well-being of minorities and workers in the Third World rather than personal values, such as integrity, veracity, and loyalty.

An Aspen Institute study of about 2,000 graduates of the top 13 business schools found that business school education not only fails to improve the moral character of a student, it actually weakens it.[21] The study examined student attitudes three times while they were working toward their MBAs: on entering, at the end of the first year, and on graduating. Those who believed that maximizing shareholder values was the prime responsibility of a corporation increased from 68 percent upon entrance to 82 percent by the end of the first year. In another study, students were asked if, given a one percent chance of being caught and sent to prison for one year, they would attempt an illegal act that would net them (or their company) a profit of more than $ 100,000. More than one-third responded yes.

In light of continued corporate scandals, some business schools will attempt to strengthen ethics education. They should recruit more faculty members to teach ethics. And ethics courses should be approached not as a way to circumvent challenges by outsiders (such as the consumer protection movement or advocates of the poor) but as a moral obligation any decent person heeds. The ethics requirements set by the Association to Advance Collegiate Schools of Business, which is responsible for the accreditation of business schools, should be more straightforward: No MBA student should graduate without having taken at least one full-term course in a class aimed at heightening ethical standards. Even more important, all teaching material and class presentations should be examined to ensure that they do not promote unethical conduct. Although such changes will not end corporate crimes, they might make them less likely.

Endnotes

1. Leonard Buder, "Beech-Nut is Fined $2 million for Sale of Fake Apple Juice." *The New York Times*, November 14, 1987, p. 1.
2. 1 USCS §1 (2005): "The words 'person' and 'whoever' [in any Act of Congress] include corporations, companies, associations, firms, partnerships, societies, and joint stock companies, as well as individuals."
3. See V.S. Khanna, "Corporate Criminal Liability: What Purpose Does it Serve?" *Harvard Law Review* 109 (1996): p. 1487 and Daniel R. Fischel & Alan O. Sykes, *Corporate Crime*, Journal of Legal Studies 25, (1996): 323.
4. Edwin H. Sutherland, *White-Collar Crime*: *The Uncut Version* (New Haven, CT: Yale University Press, 1983), p. 15.
5. Marshall B. Clinard and Peter C Yeager, *Corporate Crime* (New York: The Free Press, 1980), p. 113.
6. See for example, Jonathan Mahler, "The Antidepressant Dilemma." *The New York Times Magazine*, November 21, 2004, p. 59; Brooke A. Masters, "Two Agencies Probe Merck's Handling of its Vioxx Drug." *The Washington Post,* November 9, 2004, p. A6.
7. Corporate Crime Reporter, June 20, 2005 (http://www.corporatecrimereporter.com/dowjones062005.htm).
8. Sutherland, p. 174–191.
9. Stuart D. Brandes, *Warhogs: A History of War Profits in America* (Lexington, KY: The University of Kentucky Press, 1997), pp. 264–265.

10. Rachel Carson, *Silent Spring* (Boston: Houghton Mifflin Company, 2002).
11. See The United States Sentencing Commission, www.ussc.gov.
12. Gary S. Becker, "Tailoring Punishment to White-Collar Crime." *Business Week*, October 28th, 1985, p. 20.
13. Philip Shenon, "Report Says Eli Lilly Failed to Tell of 28 Deaths." *The New York Times*, August 27, 1985, p. A16.
14. Amitai Etzioni, "Going Soft on Corporate Crime." *The Washington Post,* April 1, 1990, p. C3.
15. 107th Congress. H.R. 3763.
16. White House Press Release, July 30, 2002, http://www.whitehouse.gov/news/ releases/ 2002/07/20020730.html.
17. Stephen Labaton and Jenny Anderson, "SEC Chief, Under Cross-Pressure, Sees Some Modest Changes." *The New York Times*, February 10, 2005, p. C 9.
18. See Andrew Singer, "General Dynamics Corporation: An Ethical Turnaround." *Ethikos*, March/April 1990.
19. Adam Goodman, "Talking Business: Ethics Codes Help Raise Awareness." *St. Louis Post-Dispatch*, January 23rd, 1989, p. 1.
20. Christopher Stewart, "A Question of Ethics: How to Teach Them?" *The New York Times*, March 21, 2004, C 11.
21. Della Bradshaw, "Aspen Survey: Most Business School Programs Tend to Transform Concerned Consumers into Corporate Consultants." *The Financial Times*, April 8, 2002, p. 16.

References

Becker, Gary S. (1990) "Tailoring Punishment to White-Collar Crime." *Business Week*, 28 Oct., p. 20.

Buder, Leonard (1987) "Beech-Nut is Fined $2 million for Sale of Fake Apple Juice." *The New York Times,* 14 November, p. 1.

Bradshaw, Della (2002) "Aspen Survey: Most Business School Programs Tend to Transform Concerned Consumers into Corporate Consultants." *The Financial Times,* 8 April, p. 16.

Brandes, Stuart D. (1997) *Warhogs: A History of War Profits in America.* Lexington, KY: The University of Kentucky Press.

Carson, Rachel (2002) *Silent Spring.* Boston: Houghton Mifflin Company.

Clinard, Marshall B., and Peter C Yeager (1980) *Corporate Crime*. New York: The Free Press.

Etzioni, Amitai (1990) "Going Soft on Corporate Crime." *The Washington Post,* 1 April, sec. C, p. 3.

Fischel, Daniel R., and Alan O. Sykes (1996) "Corporate Crime." *Journal of Legal Studies* 25:323.

Goodman, Adam (1989) "Talking Business: Ethics Codes Help Raise Awareness." *St. Louis Post-Dispatch,* 23 January, p. 1.

Khanna, V.S. (1996) "Corporate Criminal Liability: What Purpose Does it Serve?" *Harvard Law Review* 109:1487.

Labaton, Stephen, and Jenny Anderson (2005) "SEC Chief, Under Cross-Pressure, Sees Some Modest Changes." *The New York Times,* 10 February, sec. C, p. 9.

Mahler, Jonathan (2004) "The Antidepressant Dilemma." *The New York Times Magazine,* 21 November, p. 59.

Masters, Brooke A. (2004) "Two Agencies Probe Merck's Handling of its Vioxx Drug." The *Washington Post,* 9 November, sec. A, p. 6.

Shenon, Philip (1985) "Report Says Eli Lilly Failed to Tell of 28 Deaths." *The New York Times,* 27 August, sec. A, p. 16.

Singer, Andrew (1990) "General Dynamics Corporation: An Ethical Turnaround." *Ethikos,* March/April.

Stewart, Christopher (2004) "A Question of Ethics: How to Teach Them?" *The New York Times,* 21 March, sec. C, p. 11.

Sutherland, Edwin H. (1983) *White Collar Crime: The Uncut Version.* New Haven, CT: Yale University Press.

2

State-Corporate Crime and Criminological Inquiry

Raymond J. Michalowski and Ronald C. Kramer

The term *state-corporate crime* refers to serious social harms that result from the interaction of political and economic organizations. The need for such a concept emerged from our examination of events such as the explosion of the space shuttle *Challenger* and the fire at the Imperial chicken processing plant in Hamlet, North Carolina.[1] This research made us aware of a class of organizational crimes that were the collective product of the joint actions between a state agency and a business corporation. This suggested that an additional conceptualization of deviant organizational relationships between government agencies and business corporations was needed. Since those original papers on the concept and theory of state-corporate crime, we, and a number of other researchers, have used the concept to analyze a wide variety of organizational harms.[2] This chapter will describe the origins and development of the concept of state-corporate crime, review some of the research that has been carried out under this rubric, present the theoretical framework that has been most often utilized, and assess where the study of state-corporate crime might go in the future. Before we will address these issues, however, we will sketch out the historical context for considering the relationship between power and crime and explore the relationship between state-corporate crime and criminological inquiry.

Power and Crime in Historical Context

Modern history is dense with crimes flowing from decisions taken by economic and political elites. From the physical and cultural destruction of Native people in North America, South America, Africa, and the South Pacific during the 18th and 19th centuries, to the World Wars, aerial bombings, genocides, and ethnic displacements of the 20th century, political leaders have authorized the ruination of uncountable millions of innocent human lives. In the 20th century alone, nearly 200 million civilians were killed in the great wars and politically orchestrated genocides.[3] Many times that number were maimed, lost loved ones, or had their material lives destroyed as a by-product of 20th-century power-games.

Political leaders of the 21st century show no inclination to break with the past habits of slaughter. In place of world wars, humanity now faces the threat of revolutionary terrorism in both rich and poor nations, imperial wars such as the U.S. invasions of Iraq and Afghanistan, continued ethnic cleansings, violent internal conflicts in so-called "failed states," and numerous "small wars" around the planet.[4] Instead of periods of the world *at* war, we may have entered an era of the world *in* war, characterized by constant conflicts through which leaders of both great and small nations maneuver for competitive advantage within a unitary capitalist world order. To the extent that this assessment is correct, the 21st century may rival its predecessor in terms of inflicted death and brutality, particularly as the tools of war designed and manufactured in developed nations become increasingly deadly and ever more available worldwide through legal and underground international arms trading.[5] It would be a mistake, however, to assign exclusive blame for history's great crimes of violence to political leaders alone. Political elites rarely act without the prompting or support of at least some economic elites. In the dominant social systems of modern history—fascism, communism, and liberal democracy—it is often difficult to determine where economic interests end and political ones begin. As C. Wright Mills noted, a "circulation of elites" ensures that major economic and political decision-makers are typically drawn from the same pool of powerful social actors pursuing a shared vision of a desired social order.[6] We may eventually find the same to be true of the 21st century's emerging social system of illiberal theocracy.[7]

Despite the close connections between wealth and power, the institutional arrangements and cognitive frameworks of liberal democratic societies, including the United States, create an image that economics and politics are, or should be, kept apart by a bright line that separates money from power. This is, of course, a social fiction. It is, however, an important one because the premise that the rich and poor are political equals is the very heart of democracy's claim to legitimacy.

Attractive and legitimizing though it may be, the idea that economic inequality does not intrude into the realm of political governance overlooks a fundamental social reality. What is economic is always political; what is political is always economic. Nevertheless, there is a tendency in liberal-democratic discourse to treat economics and politics as separate spheres. This is as true of academic discourse as it is of elite political narratives. Contemporary social scientists have largely forgotten what our 19th century counterparts knew so well. There is neither economics nor politics; there is only political-economy.

The indivisible linkage of economics and politics means that economic elites have been as guilty of letting the blood of innocents as their political counterparts. From the trade in selling Africans into New World slavery, to the multitudes whose bodies and spirits were broken by the unyielding machines and labor practices of early industrialization, to those who have died, are dying, and will die from the destruction of ecosystems in the pursuit of corporate profit, economic decisions have been the source of at least as much, if not more, human sorrow and suffering as decisions by political leaders.

Ever since Edwin Sutherland introduced of the concept of "white-collar crime,"[8] a small subset of criminologists have sought to understand the crimes and social harms generated by economic and political elites. Influenced, however, by hegemonic ways of thinking that imagine a fundamental distinction between economics and politics, early inquiries into crimes of the powerful soon divided into studies of white collar and corporate crime on the economic side[9] and studies of political criminality and state crime on the political side.[10] This division has remained largely unquestioned since these early inquiries into elite criminality. The concept of *state-corporate crime* that we have developed seeks to breach the conceptual wall between economic crimes and political crimes in order to create a new lens through which we can examine the ways crimes and social injuries often emerge from intersections of economic and political power.

Our approach to the problem of crime contradicts much of what has come to be taken for granted in criminology, sociology, and political science about elite crime. For this reason, before expanding further on the notion of state-corporate crime, we want to examine more fully the dominant consciousness that we hope to fracture.

Crime and Criminological Consciousness

Our approach to crimes of the powerful contradicts the ideological frame that dominates contemporary analyses of wrongdoing in two ways. First, as we already observed, contrary to the typical practice of separating economics and politics into distinct fields of inquiry, we begin with the premise that political and economic practices are mutually interrelated in ways that deserve serious investigation by criminologists and other analysts of elite wrongdoing.

Second, we question the utility of the dominant understanding of crime as it has been used by orthodox criminology and other social sciences—as well as by the wider society. Most of the cases of state-corporate crime that have been examined do not involve *crimes* in the juridical sense of the word. That is, most do not involve violations of *criminal law*. Some cases, such as the ValueJet crash,[11] Enron-era stock manipulations,[12] and the Firestone-Explorer rollover deaths,[13] involve one or more violations of *regulatory law*. From a legal standpoint, however, violations of regulatory law are not crimes. The distinction between crime and regulatory violations, however, is itself an expression of political power. The deployment of regulatory rather than criminal law systems to address harms that can *only* be caused by corporate and governmental elites was a juridical move prompted by the interests of the same economic and political elites it was designed to control.[14] By design, America's regulatory legal structure has ensured that elite offenses and offenders remain "administratively segregated" from the crimes of the poor.[15] This has important consequences. The creation of a regulatory legal system isolates elite wrongdoers from the harsh penal sanctions and social stigma that are routinely assigned to street criminals. Because they are categorized as "regulatory violations," most of the crimes typical of powerful actors are perceived as less serious than "real" crime," even though the measurable harm they cause vastly exceeds the physical and financial damage caused by street crime.[16]

Although violations of regulatory laws are not crimes in a juridical sense, criminologists who analyze white collar and corporate crimes have, for the most part, accepted the idea that regulatory violations should be examined as forms of legal wrongdoing.[17] The concept of state-corporate crime as used here, however, extends the scope of criminology even further, incorporating harmful social actions that violate neither criminal nor regulatory laws. Several recent situations, such as corporate collaboration with Germany's Nazi regime,[18] the U.S. invasion and occupation of Iraq,[19] and questionable linkages between military contractors and the U.S. government,[20] involve actions taken under the full authority of national laws. Thus, these social harms violated neither criminal nor regulatory law at the time of their commission. While these offenses may have been legal according to national laws, they and many other elite wrongs can be evaluated according to the laws and human rights standards established in the international arena, and therefore also fall within the legitimate purview of criminological inquiry.[21] By reaching beyond criminal and regulatory law, the study of state-corporate crime challenges the juridical and conceptual limitations that have kept criminology focused largely on private crimes among individuals. We contend that criminology's focus on interpersonal crimes is largely responsible for its general inattention to the ways that economic and political elites can bring death, disease, and loss to tens of thousands of persons through a single decision, and can impact entire human groups through the creation of systems of oppression and exploitation. It is these greater crimes we wish to examine.

When we speak about criminal systems of oppression and exploitation here we are referring to egregious structures such as slavery, genocide, ethnic cleansing, and political imprisonment that have been condemned by international law, rather than larger systems of exploitation such as capitalism, fascism, or communism. These latter systems, it might be argued, are also guilty of causing widespread and wrongful social harm by the ways in which they give some the ability to dominate others. Two of the three—communism and fascism—have been so condemned. The difference between fascism and communism on the one hand, and capitalism on the other, however, may be only that fascist and communist nation states have been defeated by capitalist ones and, in the aftermath of those defeats, their brutalities have been judged and condemned. The capitalist world has not yet faced any comparable defeat and judgment. There may be some validity to the idea that all accumulative social systems, whether fascist, communist, or capitalist, are guilty of great crimes. Such sweeping critiques are beyond the scope of our inquiry. Rather, we seek to understand specific moments when political and economic interests have intersected in ways that produced a specific set of demonstrable harms.

Elite Crime and Criminology

Despite the enormous costs of economic and political wrongdoing, those who study crime—i.e., *criminologists*—have devoted scant attention to the harms flowing from the misuse of political and economic power. One need do little more than examine the contents of major academic outlets for criminological writings to verify this claim. Between 2000 and 2005, the official journal of the American Society of Criminology, *Criminology*, the official journal of the Academy of Criminal Justice Sciences, *Justice Quarterly*, and the official journal of the British Society of Criminology, the *British Journal of Criminology*, published a total of 575 articles. Of these, 533 examined either patterns of street crime, the institutions of police, courts, and corrections designed to control street crime, or theory and research aimed at explaining the causes of street crime. Only 18 articles, a mere *3 percent* of the total, were in any way devoted to what could be considered crimes by those wielding some degree of concentrated economic or political power. [31]

This emphasis on street crime challenges the claim that criminology is an independent academic discipline shaped by internally generated intellectual guidelines. To the contrary, criminology is largely an extension of the political state, an academic enterprise whose subject matter is defined primarily by external political and ideological forces. There are a number of reasons for this.

First, criminology is typically defined narrowly as the study of *crime* rather than more broadly as a study of the ways humans can harm one another. This means that the subject matter of criminology, as Thorsten Sellin observed long ago, will always be shaped by what governments *choose* to criminalize, rather than by analytic criteria independent of these political processes. Political-economic arrangements and hegemonic consciousness dominate the definition of crime rather than any calculus of demonstrable social harm.

The use of illegal drugs, for instance, causes far fewer deaths and much less illness every year than cigarette smoking. Yet, the volume of research by criminologists studying patterns of illegal drug use, drug-related crimes, and drug law enforcement far exceeds that exploring the efforts of cigarette manufacturers to hide information about the hazards of cigarettes from the public, their efforts to market cigarettes to youth despite bans on such promotion, and their programs to purvey a known deadly substance in less-developed countries that do not have smoking bans or limitations on cigarette advertising.

It might be argued that such comparisons are not valid because cigarettes are legal, while marijuana, cocaine, and heroin are not. Moreover, hiding research findings and engaging in questionable marketing practices are regulatory violations, not crimes. But that is precisely our point. To the extent that criminologists take their lead from politically motivated decisions influenced by powerful economic interests, criminology will continue to buttress rather than analyze the dominant social order.

Second, criminological research is *ameliorative* in nature. Either explicitly or implicitly, most criminological research is aimed, not only at understanding crime as a category of human behavior, but toward reducing crime. For this reason, criminology is substantially influenced by contemporaneous social concerns. Like all social problems, crime problems are socially constructed interpretations of danger and risk.[25] Social harms become social problems only when moral entrepreneurs galvanize public sentiment around some area of private trouble, resulting in its redefinition as a public issue and the stimulation of popular demands for some form of public—usually governmental—relief.[26]

Since the rise of national mass media, beginning with newspapers and magazines in the 19th century, the successful construction of social problems has required that issues achieve relatively high-profile status within the channels of mass communication before they can become the focus of popular demands for change.[27] National mass media, however, are far more inclined to discuss public awareness about ordinary street crimes than about harms by economic and political elites.

The mass media have become adept at reporting interpersonal crimes committed anywhere in the country, imbuing them with a sense of immediate and *local* threat.[28] Elite criminality fits far less comfortably within existing channels of mass communication. In the last forty years, the United States has experienced a succession of media mobilizations of public sentiment—or "moral panics"—around issues of interpersonal victimization, such as crimes against the elderly, drive-by-shootings, missing children, crack babies, a supposed new generation of super-predators, and most recently the threats posed by "illegal" immigrants from Mexico and Central America.[29] Insofar as criminology is attentive to these social constructions, an ongoing parade of interpersonal threats take their turn as "the next big thing" in criminology, revealing the power of the social construction of social problems to shape what criminologists will find worthy of inquiry.

Third, criminology is *individualistic* in focus. Criminological inquiry tends to focus on the ways specific individuals cause willful harm to other identifiable individuals. Harms that deviate from this ideal-type of crime fit poorly with contemporary criminological consciousness. It is certainly understandable that people will fear the immediate and specific harm to their physical or material security posed by real or imagined threats (e.g., robbery, burglary, identity theft). What is important, however, is that this fear dominates: public consciousness of crime even though the likelihood of interpersonal victimization by street crime is lower than becoming the victim of less specific but far more widespread harms caused by corporate and governmental deviance. Each year in the United States, more people will suffer illness or early death due to environmental pollution than will suffer physical injury due to a violent street crime.[30] Similarly, relatively few people will be the victims of robbery or burglary, but nearly *everyone* in the United States will suffer financial loss due to malfeasance in high places.[31] Nevertheless, overall public sentiment remains far more focused on the threat of street crimes than potential victimization by corporate or governmental deviance.[32] Studies of perceived crime seriousness suggest that *when asked*, research subjects assign equal seriousness to both corporate and street crimes that cause injury or death.[33] Reported perceptions of seriousness are not the same as public action, however. Seriousness rankings are intellectual exercises. Fear of crime, however, is an emotional experience that is heightened by the idea of individuals who would deliberately harm others. For instance, the similarity in seriousness assigned to corporate and street crimes applied only to cases where the corporate offender *intentionally* pursued some action that caused death or injury.[34] This emphasis on *individual* guilt, deeply entrenched in American law, culture, and political ideology mutes potential public fear of elite wrongdoers because they do not cause harm directly, but through their control over institutions of power.

When it comes to public policy, the fear factor that surrounds street crime ensures that the acts committed by individual criminals against individual victims will receive more public and political attention than corporate or governmental crimes that harm larger numbers of people. This, in turn, directs criminology to focus its attention more toward explaining what causes *individuals* to become criminal than on understanding how organizational frameworks generate corporate and political crimes. These latter crimes rarely involve individual "bad guys" who intentionally plan to harm specific victims. As a result, they fit poorly within the individualistic consciousness of contemporary society and contemporary criminology.

Fourth, political and economic crimes involve *complex causal chains*. Crimes resulting from elite decisions are committed rarely, if ever, by the officials who authorize them. Consider the political crimes of the United States emanating from the Cold War. The U.S. *geo-policy* of containing the Soviet Union's influence within its Eastern European boundaries was transformed into *strategic goals* by leaders in a variety of governmental agencies such as the State Department, the Central Intelligence Agency, the Department of Defense, and the National Security Council. These strategic goals were then passed down the chain of command to military units, CIA operatives, and clandestine "assets" charged with designing and carrying out *tactical missions* in support of the strategic goals.[35]

The front-line cold warriors who helped agent provocateurs plant bombs in third-world countries, trained foreign police in the use of torture, helped plan and fund counterrevolutions in developing socialist nations, carried out assassinations of leaders who seemed to threaten U.S. Cold War interests, or fought in what came to be known as *low intensity warfare* against governments that did not support U.S. interests, were far removed from the leaders whose policies they were carrying out.[36] If anything questionable or illegal came to light, leaders could always claim "plausible deniability," saying they had not ordered the specific crimes in question. They may not have meant that some specific, heinous crime be committed in the name of freedom and democracy. Nevertheless, they created a political culture and organizational frameworks that ultimately led to heinous acts that would not have occurred without that culture and those frameworks.

We find a similar chain-of-command issue in the more recent scandals involving the torture of U.S. captives in the "war on terror." There is substantial evidence that in Afghanistan, in Camp X-Ray in Guantanamo Bay, Cuba, and in Iraq—most notably in the Abu Ghraib prison—members of the U.S. armed forces and privately contracted interrogators were enmeshed in a system where abuse of so-called "enemy combatants" had become routine.[37] The Bush Administration, however, was successful in using claims to plausible deniability to protect both its inner circle and military leaders by limiting prosecutions to the lowest levels of involvement.[38]

It is probably true that no high-level U.S. official specifically *ordered* torture. Yet, it is also true that the Bush Administration appointed an Attorney General who had previously drafted legal opinions justifying torture on narrow legal technicalities such as the fact that Al Qaeda is not a nation and has not signed the Geneva Convention.[39] Decisions of this sort at the top of the political pyramid go a long way toward creating an organizational climate in which the torture of suspected terrorists—regardless of how minimal the evidence—can easily be interpreted as heroic duty.

Similarly, when corporate managers mandate accelerated production, increased worker output, or reduced costs, they are not specifically ordering increases in injuries due to assembly-line speed-ups, intensification of repetitive-motion tasks, or reductions in expenditures for safety equipment or worker training, even though such outcomes are predictable.[40] Thus, like political leaders, plausible deniability means that those who issue such orders will normally not be seen as guilty for the causal chain leading to the harms those orders cause. When it comes to widely disbursed harms such as environmental damage or consumer injuries, the insulation between elites and the causal process leading to harm becomes even thicker. The ability of Union Carbide Corporation to isolate its managerial chain from responsibility for the deadly 1984 leak of methyl isocynante gas in Bhopal, India, that killed over 15,000 people is a particularly vivid case of plausible deniability in operation.[41] Contemporary narratives of harms resulting from decisions by economic and political elites lack clear villains. This is perhaps appropriate since many of these harms are the products of complex organizational arrangements, not the mendacity of specific individuals.[42] Without straightforward causal chains leading from criminal to victim, however, these crimes fit poorly within the dominant consciousness of criminology, and therefore receive less attention from criminology than the harms they cause would seem to warrant.

Fifth, criminology is an *academic discipline*. This means that criminologists are disciplined by the organizational demands of higher education. The ability to survive and advance in a university setting requires that criminologists not only teach, but also that they conduct research and publish research findings. As Tombs and Whyte have noted, governments provide little or no funding for research into wrongdoing by political leaders or their allies in business, industry, or the military.[43] When governments fund criminological research—and governments are the primary source of criminological research dollars—these monies are primarily designated for research into the causes and control of crimes and vices associated with poor and less powerful segments of society.[44]

The structure of research financing plays a significant role in determining what the majority of criminologists will investigate. Well-funded areas of study attract scholars anxious to advance their careers. Government-sponsored research also funds graduate students interested in criminology, thereby increasing the likelihood that many of these future scholars will develop research agendas along government-supported lines of inquiry. Meanwhile, as public financing of universities shrinks, university administrators become increasingly insistent that new faculty members bring in overhead-generating research dollars, further ensuring that most criminologists will have little choice but to dance to the tune played by the governmental pipers of research dollars. Finally, the most prestigious private and public universities are closely linked to governmental and business interests. Scholars who pose serious challenges to the hegemonic social system have long been seen as unattractive candidates for employment or promotion in these schools.[45]

State-Corporate Crime: Origins And Development

Knowing when an idea first appeared is far different than knowing how it began. Although the term *state-corporate crime* made its first public appearance in a series of papers presented in 1990,[46] unraveling its origins and evolution is a longer story that embraces more than two decades of collaborative effort to understand crimes of the powerful.

In the mid-1980s, as part of an early inquiry into globalization, we examined how the growing power of transnational corporations headquartered in cosmopolitan centers enabled them to shape laws of interest in the peripheral and semi-peripheral nations to which they were increasingly outsourcing components of production and distribution. This work was published in the journal *Social Problems* as "The Space Between Laws: Corporate Crime in the Transnational Context."[47] We came away from this initial inquiry with a heightened awareness of the importance of understanding the intersection of economics and politics in the production of corporate crimes and social harms.

About the time we were completing "The Space Between Laws," Ron began a project focused on unraveling the organizational origins of the *Challenger* explosion. As he examined the relevant documents, he became increasingly sensitized to how the controversial *Challenger* launch decision involved interactions between a political organization, The National Aeronautics and Space Administration (NASA), and Morton Thiokol, Inc., a private business corporation. Acting in concert, these two organizations produced a technological failure of far-reaching consequence.[48] This clearly suggested a need for criminology to develop clearer conceptualizations of deviant inter-organizational relationships between business and government.

In 1989, over dinner at the Society for the Study of Social Problems (SSSP) meeting in Berkeley, we discussed the issue, and Ray suggested labeling harms resulting from these interactions "state-corporate crime." Ron thought the term fit the problem, and began incorporating it into his work on the *Challenger*, including "State-Corporate Crime: A Case Study of the Space Shuttle *Challenger* Explosion," which he presented at the Edwin Sutherland Conference on White Collar Crime: 50 Years of Research and Beyond."[49] We continued working together to refine the concept of state-corporate crime, and to develop a more elaborated theoretical framework for it.

We presented our first joint efforts at the American Society of Criminology (ASC) meeting in 1990 in a paper titled "Toward an Integrated Theory of State-Corporate Crime." We noted that, despite their ubiquity, structural relations between corporate and governmental organizations had been largely left out of the study of corporate crime. Instead, two nearly independent bodies of research had developed. Theory and research in the area of corporate crime had concentrated primarily on organizational deviance within private business corporations. Paralleling that work, but seldom intersecting with it, others had examined crimes and malfeasance initiated by governments, what Chambliss had called "state-organized crime."[50] We suggested that, rather than seeing these as separate problems, it would be useful for criminologists to examine how organizational deviance frequently emerges at the interstices of corporations and government. We used the term state-corporate crime to denote these types of crimes and offered the following definition:

> State-corporate crimes are illegal or socially injurious actions that occur when one or more institutions of political governance pursue a goal in direct cooperation with one or more institutions of economic production and distribution.[51]

Less than a year later, in September 1991, a fire in the Imperial chicken processing plant in Hamlet, North Carolina, killed 25 workers and injured another 49. Based on reports about working conditions at the Imperial Processing Plant that Ray heard from his students at UNC-Charlotte, and from what he already knew about the North Carolina Occupational Safety and Hazards Administration (OSHA), he recognized the Imperial fire as another potential candidate for state-corporate crime inquiry. Ray began working with his colleague Judy Aulette to gather and analyze data on the distant and proximate causes of am increasingly apparent case of industrial murder. As part of this work, Ray analyzed the ways in which larger conditions created by the state, such as an anti-regulatory, pro-business climate and an under-funded North Carolina OSHA were important contributing precedents to the Imperial fire. This led him to revise the definition of state corporate crime as—

> illegal or socially injurious actions that result from a mutually reinforcing interaction between (1) policies and/or practices in pursuit of the goals of one or more institutions of political governance and (2) policies and/or practices in pursuit of the goals of one or more institutions of economic production and distribution.[52]

The deviant interorganizational relationships that serve as the basis for state-corporate crime can take several forms. Kramer's analysis of the space shuttle *Challenger* explosion,[53] and Kauzlarich and Kramer's study of the relationship between the U.S. government and weapons manufacturers in the nuclear weapons production process,[54] both emphasize the central and direct role of the state in initiating a cooperative activity involving government and business that led to a deviant outcome. Aulette and Michalowski's examination of the fire at the Imperial Food Products chicken processing plant in Hamlet, North Carolina,[55] and Matthews and Kauzlarich's analysis of the crash of ValuJet Flight 592,[56] suggest a different kind of relationship, one where government omissions permit corporations to pursue illegal and potentially harmful courses of action which, in a general way, facilitate the fulfillment of certain state policies

Corporate crime can take two distinct forms. One is *state-initiated corporate crime* and the other is *state-facilitated corporate crime*. State-initiated corporate crime occurs when corporations, employed by the government, engage in organizational deviance at the direction of or with the tacit approval of the government. State-facilitated corporate crime occurs when government regulatory institutions fail to restrain deviant business activities, either because of direct collusion between business and government or because they adhere to shared goals whose attainment would be hampered by aggressive regulation.

As a sensitizing concept the term "state-corporate crime" has three useful characteristics. First, it directs attention toward the way in which deviant organizational outcomes are not discreet acts but rather the product of the relationships between different social institutions. Second, by focusing on the relational character of the state,[57] the concept of state-corporate crime highlights the ways in which horizontal relationships between economic and political institutions contain powerful potentials for the production of socially injurious actions. This relational approach provides a more nuanced understanding of the processes leading to deviant organizational outcomes than approaches that treat either businesses or governments as closed systems. Third, the relational character of state-corporate crime also directs us to consider the vertical relationships between different levels of organizational action: the individual, the institutional, and the political-economic. These insights lead toward the development of a theory of state-corporate crime.

Toward a Theory of State-Corporate Crime

In addition to an important revision of the concept of state-corporate crime, our 1990 ASC paper also introduced an integrated theoretical framework to analyze organizational offenses such as state-corporate crimes. We noted that there were three major theoretical approaches to the study of corporate crime that and each corresponded to a different level of social action. The first was differential association theory as developed by Sutherland.[58] The second was based on organizational theory and it argued that organizations could be criminogenic either due to the performance emphasis on goals[59] or as a result of defective standard operating procedures.[60] This organizational approach would eventually be merged with an anomie perspective on corporate crime.[61] The third approach located the criminogenic forces in the wider political economic structure of capitalism.[62] Differential association addressed the individual level of action; organizational theory focused on specific institutional factors promoting or retarding corporate crime; and political-economic or radical approaches examined the way that broad, pre-existing societal characteristics interact with both the individual and organizational level of action.

Although the differential association, organizational, and political economic perspectives represented divergent approaches to explaining corporate and government crime, we believed that they could be brought together into an integrated theoretical framework. The structure, dynamics, and cultural meanings associated with the political economic arrangements of any particular society will shape the goals and means of economic and political organization, as well as the constraints they face. The organizational level of analysis links the internal structure of specific economic or political units with the external political-economic environment and with the way in which the work-related thoughts and actions of the individuals who occupy positions in those units are conditioned by the requirements of the positions they hold and by the procedures of the organization. Differential association, by focusing on the social relations that give meaning to individual experience, directs us to examine the symbolic reality derived from social interaction within bounded organizational niches.

Table 1 presents an analytic framework for this integrated theory of organizational deviance.[63] This framework links the three levels of analysis discussed above with three catalysts for action. These catalysts are (1) motivation or performance pressure, (2) opportunity structure, and (3) the operationality of control. This framework is designed to indicate the key factors that will contribute to or restrain organizational deviance at each intersection of a catalyst for action and a level of analysis.

This theoretical framework is based on the proposition that criminal or deviant behavior at the organizational level results from a coming together of pressure for goal attainment, availability, perceived attractiveness of illegitimate means, and an absence of effective social control. The first catalyst for action is the emphasis on goal attainment. Political and economic structures, organizations, and individuals may place greater or lesser emphasis on the attainment of rationalized goals as the engine for social action. A highly goal oriented individual, working in an organization that evaluates performance strictly on goal attainment by its workers, in a society whose cultural and institutional framework emphasizes goal attainment above all else, will be more susceptible to pursuing deviant organizational strategies than if one or more of these conditions are absent.

The second catalyst for action suggests that organizational deviance is more likely in a society where legitimate means are scarce relative to goals. The likelihood of deviance increases for those organizations or organizational subunits

Table 1. An integrated theoretical model of state-corporate crime

	Catalysts for Action		
Levels of Analysis	Motivation	Opportunity	Control
Institutional Environment	Culture of competition Economic pressure Organizational goals Performance emphasis	Availability of legal means Obstacles and constraints Blocked goals/strain Availability of illegal means Access to resources	International reactions Political pressure Legal sanctions Media scrutiny Public opinion Social movements
Organizational	Corporate culture Operative goals Subunit goals Managerial pressure	Instrumental rationality Internal constraints Defective SOPs Creation of illegal means Role specialization Task segregation Computer, telecommunication, And networking technologies Normalization of deviance	Culture of compliance Subcultures of resistance Codes of conduct Reward structure Safety & quality control Communication processes
Interactional	Socialization Social meaning Individual goals Competitive individualism Material success emphasis	Definitions of situations Perceptions of availability & attractiveness of illegal means	Personal morality Rationalizations & techniques of neutralization Separation from consequences Obedience to authority Group think Diffusion of responsibility

where the allocation of means by the internal structure is inadequate relative to the organization's goals, increasing the likelihood that individuals will perceive themselves to be blocked from access to legitimate means and will subsequently seek deviant alternative routes.

Finally, the operationality of social control at all three levels will serve as both an important constraint on organizational deviance and as a critical element in constructing symbolic frameworks that will operate at the societal, organizational, and personal levels as time passes. Thus societies with high operationality of social control are more likely to produce organizations with strong corporate cultures favoring compliance with laws and regulations. Individuals who function in these organizations in such a society will be more likely to develop forms of personal morality that would mitigate against engaging in organizational deviance.

By its very nature, state-corporate crime directs us to examine the linkages between levels of analysis and catalysts for action. When the topic is profit-oriented violations of law by some business, it is possible, although not necessarily sufficient, to treat the crime as organizationally self-contained. Injurious social actions that result from concerted actions by organizations operating in different social spheres (e.g., production vs. governance), however, require that we must expand the analysis, and that is what this theoretical framework attempts to do.

Conclusion

In the years following our initial inquiry into state-corporate crime, it appears that a number of criminologists have found the concept to be a useful way to think about the crimes of the powerful. State-corporate crime is discussed in several popular criminology textbooks[64] and in a number of textbooks on white-collar, corporate, and government crime.[65] Articles on the topic have also been published or reprinted in quite a few anthologies dealing with crimes of the powerful.[66] But most important, the development of the concept and theory of state-corporate crime has resulted in the production of a substantial body of criminological research.

Soon after the initial formulation appeared, other scholars began adapting the concept and its associated theoretical model to a number of other social harms. In addition to the case studies of the *Challenger* explosion, the fire at Hamlet, the contamination wrought by nuclear weapons production, and the crash of ValuJet 592, the concept of state-corporate crime has been used to analyze historical offenses such as corporate collaborations with the Nazi regime during World War II, and contemporary violations such as state-corporate corruption in the world of private military organizations. Some applications of the state-corporate crime model have examined offenses that begin with governments (e.g., the invasion and occupation of Iraq). Others have explored injurious collaborations that began in the realm of business but that could not develop without governmental acts of commission or omission (e.g., Firestone-Explorer rollover deaths). Much of this research has now been gathered together in an anthology titled, *State-Corporate Crime: Wrongdoing at the Intersection of Business and Government.*[67]

In the concluding chapter of *State-Corporate Crime,* David Kauzlarich and Rick Matthews take stock of theory and research regarding the subject.[68] They argue that much has been accomplished in this of study of elite deviance, considering that the concept of state-corporate crime is less than 20 years old. Much has been learned about the manner in which motivation, opportunity, and control impact the genesis and persistence of these organizational harms at the intersection of business and government. Penny Green and Tony Ward concur, and argue that "the approach developed by state-corporate crime scholars is a significant advance toward developing a powerful integrated theoretical model, and can easily be synthesized with our framework for analyzing state crime."[69]

As for the future, the study of state-corporate crime has enormous potential to contribute to criminology. Great power and great crimes are inseparable. It is only those with great power who, with the stroke of a pen, the giving of an order, or a knowing nod of the head can send thousands to their deaths or consign millions to lives to unrelenting want and misery. Those who occupy positions within the organizational structures of the state and transnational corporations have such power. As criminologists, we need to continue to engage in inquiries that identify, describe and explain the variety of social harms that emanate from the intersection of business and government. In particular, we need to examine harms that occur at the international level, such as crimes of globalization and crimes of empire.

In an era of economic globalization it is important to explore the impact of neo-liberal policies and practices. Transnational corporations (TNCs), national states, and international financial institutions act together to privatize the global economy and promote free market policies. New legal frameworks favorable to TNCs and investors are adopted, business regulations are gutted, taxes are cut, welfare services and other public interventions on behalf of social and economic equality are withdrawn. The consequences of these policies and practices are great crimes; that is, preventable social harms such as economic inequality, poverty, environmental destruction, hunger, disease, and premature death.[70] And, ironically, greater levels of what criminologists normally focus on: conventional forms of interpersonal violence and property crime.

Given the imperial designs of the current US government it is also imperative to analyze the crimes of empire. As the neo-conservatives who make up the George W. Bush administration have pursued their geo-political strategy to project American power, secure access to and control over oil supplies, reshape the political culture of the Middle East, and make that part of the world a laboratory for radical free market policies, massive state-corporate crimes have been committed. Under the cover of the global war on terrorism, the US has engaged in wars of aggression, violations of International Humanitarian Law (war crimes), torture, and other violations of human rights.[71]

In a significant number of criminologists began to analyze state-corporate crimes, such as the crimes of globalization and the crimes of empire, it would transform criminological inquiry and could have enormous political implications. As William Chambliss, one of the pioneers of the study of the crimes of the powerful, has observed, "If we begin our work today by researching and analyzing [these] crimes... we will be on the cutting edge of a revitalized science. If we fail to do so, we will have little relevance to the world of the 21st century."[72]

Endnotes

1. Kramer, 1990a; Kramer and Michalowski, 1990; Aulette and Michalowski, 1993.
2. See Michalowski and Kramer, 2006.
3. Rummel, 1994.
4. Coll, 2004; Berkeley, 2002; Pilger, 2001.
5. Greider, 1999; Keller, 1995.
6. Mills, 1956.
7. Clarkson, 1997.
8. Sutherland, 1940.
9. Sutherland, 1949; Hartung, 1950; Geis, 1967; Clinard and Yeager, 1980.
10. Turk, 1969; Schafer, 1974.
11. Matthews and Kauzlarich, 2000.
12. Michalowski and Kramer, 2003.
13. Mullins, 2006.
14. Pearce, 1976; Sklar, 1988.
15. Sutherland, 1949.
16. Hills, 1987; Reiman, 2003; Lynch and Michalowski, 2005.
17. Friedrichs, 2004.
18. Matthews, 2006.
19. Kramer and Michalowski, 2005.
20. Rothe, 2006.
21. Chambliss, 1989, 1995; Green and Ward, 2004; Kramer, Michalowski and Rothe, 2005.

22. It is interesting to note that while criminological inquiry into elite crime is relatively absent from criminology *journals*, since the publication of Sutherland's *White Collar Crime* criminologists have written or edited a number of influential books about crimes by political and/or economic elites. See, for instance, *Criminality and the Legal Order*, Austin Turk, 1969; *The Political Criminal*, Stephen Schafer, 1974; *Elite Deviance,* David Simon, 1982; *On The Take,* William Chambliss, 1988; *The Criminal Elite,* James Coleman, 1985; *Crimes by the Capitalist State,* Gregg Barak, 1991;*Beyond the Limits of the Law,* John McMullan, 1992;*Political Crime in Contemporary America,* Kenneth Tunnell, 1993; *Crimes of the American Nuclear State,* David Kauzlarich and Ronald Kramer, 1998; *Corporate and Governmental Deviance,* Erman and Lundman, 2001, *State Crime: Governments, Violence and Corruption,* Penny Green and David Tony Ward, Richard 2004.
23. Sellin, 1938.
24. Glantz et. al., 1996.
25. Spector and Kitsuse, 2000; Schehr, 2005.
26. Gusfield, 1984; Nelson, 1986.
27. Demers and Viswanath, 1999.
28. Altheide, 2002; Ferrell and Websdale, 1999.
29. Best, 1995; Cohen, 1972; Carpenter, 2005; Reinarman and Levine, 1997.
30. Burns and Lynch, 2004.
31. Shover, Fox and Mills, 2001.
32. Chiricos, Padgett, Gertz, 2000.
33. Rossi, et., al., 1974 ; Wolfgang et. al., 1985; Rebovich, 2002.
34. Rossi, et., al., 1974.
35. Kennan, 1967.
36. Blum, 2004; Herman, 1982; Klare and Kornbluh, 1989.
37. Danner, 2004; Hersh, 2004; Ratner and Ray, 2004; Lewis, 2005.
38. Schmitt, 2005.
39. Danner, 2004; Greenberg and Dratel, 2005.
40. Aulette and Michalowski, 1993.
41. Moro and Lapierre, 2002.
42. Kramer, 1984.
43. Tombs and Whyte 2003.
44. NIJ, 2005.
45. Schrecker, 1986.
46. Kramer 1990a; 1990b; Kramer and Michalowski, 1990.
47. Michalowski and Kramer, 1987.
48. For a more comprehensive analysis of the *Challenger* launch see Vaughan, 1997.
49. Kramer, 1990a, 1990b.
50. Chambliss, 1989.
51. Kramer and Michalowski, 1990.
52. Aulette and Michalowski 1993: 175.
53. Kramer, 1992.
54. Kauzlarich and Kramer, 1993.
55. Aulette and Michalowski, 1993.
56. Matthews and Kauzlarich, 2000.
57. Wonders and Solop, 1993.
58. Sutherland, 1940; 1949.
59. Gross, 1978; Finney and Lesieur, 1982; Kramer, 1982.
60. Hopkins, 1978.
61. Vaughan, 1982; 1983; 1997; Passas, 1990.
62. Quinney, 1977; Barnett, 1981; Young, 1981 Michalowski, 1985.
63. Created by Kramer and Michalowski, 1990 and revised by Kauzlarich and Kramer, 1998.

64. Barkan, 2006; Barlow and Kauzlarich, 2002; Siegel, 2001.
65. Friedrichs, 2004; Green and Ward, 2004; Ross, 2003; Simon, 2001; Slapper and Tombs, 1999.
66. Friedrichs, 1998; Geis, Meier and Salinger, 1995; Potter, 2002; Shover and Wright, 2001; Tunnell, 1993.
67. Michalowski and Kramer, 2006.
68. Kauzlarich and Matthews, 2006.
69. Green and Ward, 2004: 51.
70. Derber, 2002; Falk, 1999.
71. Kramer and Michalowski, 2005; Kramer, Michalowski and Rothe, 2005.
72. Chambliss, 1995:9.

References

Altheide, David (2002) *Creating Fear: News and the Construction of Crisis*. New York: Aldine.

Aulette, Judy, and Raymond Michalowski (1993) "A Fire in Hamlet: A Case Study of State-Corporate Crime." In *Political Crime in Contemporary America*, Editor Kenneth Tunnell. New York: Garland.

Barak, Gregg (1991) *Crimes by the Capitalist State: An Introduction to State Criminality*. Albany, NY: State University of New York Press.

Barkan, Steven E. (2006) *Criminology: A Sociological Understanding*. Third edition, Upper Saddle River, NJ: Pearson Prentice Hall.

Barlow, Hugh D., and David Kauzlarich (2002) *Introduction to Criminology. Eighth edition*, Upper Saddle River, NJ: Prentice Hall.

Barnett, Harold (1981) "Corporate Capitalism, Corporate Crime." *Crime and Delinquency* 27:4–23.

Berkeley, Bill (2002) *The Graves Are Not Yet Full: Race, Tribe, and Power in the Heart of Africa*. New York: Basic Books.

Best, Joel (1995) *Images of Issues: Typifying Contemporary Social Problems*. New York: Aldine.

Blum, William (2004) *Killing Hope: US Military and CIA Interventions Since World War II*. Updated edition, Monroe, ME: Common Courage Press.

Burns, Ronald, and Michael J. Lynch (2004) *Environmental Crime: A Source Book*. New York: LFB Scholarly Publishing.

Carpenter, Jan (2005) "Media Representation of Mexican Immigrants in Arizona: 1987–2004." Unpublished paper. Flagstaff, AZ: Department of Political Science.

Chambliss, William J. (1989) "State-Organized Crime." *Criminology* 27:183–208.

Chambliss, William J. (1995) "Commentary." *Society for the Study of Social Problems (SSSP) Newsletter* 26/1:9.

Chambliss, William J. (1988) *On the Take: From Petty Crooks to Presidents*. Second edition, Bloomington, IN: Indiana University Press.

Chiricos, Ted, Kathy Padgett, and Marc Gertz (2000) "Fear, TV News and the Reality of Crime." *Criminology* 38:755–785.

Clarkson, Frederick(1997) *Eternal Hostility: The Struggle Between Theocracy and Democracy*. Common Courage Press, Monroe, ME.

Clinard, Marshall, and Peter Yeager (1980) *Corporate Crime*. New York: Free Press.

Cohen, Stanley (1972) *Folk Devils and Moral Panics*. London: Routledge.

Coleman, James William (1985) *The Criminal Elite: The Sociology of White Collar Crime*. New York: St. Martin's Press.

Coll, Steve (2004) *Ghost Wars: The Secret History of The CIA, Afghanistan, and Bin Laden*. New York: Penguin.

Danner, Mark (2004) *Torture and Truth: America, Abu Ghraib, and the War on Terror*. New York: New York Review Books.

Derber, Charles (2002) *People Before Profit: The New Globalization in an Age of Terror, Big Money, and Economic Crisis*. New York: St. Martin's Press.

Demers, David P., and K. Viswanath, eds. (1999) *Mass Media, Social Control, and Social Change: A Macrosocial Perspective*. Ames: Iowa State University Press.

Ermann, M. David, and Richard J. Lundman (2001) *Corporate and Governmental Deviance: Problems of Organizational Behavior in Contemporary Society*. New York: Oxford University Press.

Falk, Richard (1999) *Predatory Globalization: A Critique*. Cambridge, U.K.: Polity Press.

Finney, Henry C., and Henry R. Lesieur (1978) "A Contingency Theory of Organizational Crime." In *Research in the Sociology of Organizations*, Editor Samuel B. Bacharach. New York: Random House.

Ferrell, Jeff, and Neil Websdale, eds. (1999) *Making Trouble: Cultural Constructions of Crime, Deviance and Control*. New York: Aldine.

Friedrichs, David O., ed. (1998) *State Crime. Volume I: Defining, Delineating and Explaining State Crime*. Aldershot, UK: Ashgate.

Friedrichs, David O. (2004) *Trusted Criminals: White Collar Crime In Contemporary Society*. Second edition, Belmont, CA: Wadsworth.

Geis, Gilbert (1967) "White-Collar Crime: The Heavy Electrical Equipment Antitrust Cases of 1961." In *Criminal Behavior Systems: A Typology*, Editors Marshall Clinard and Richard Quinney. New York: Holt, Rhinehart and Winston.

Geis, Gilbert, Robert F. Meier, and Lawrence Salinger, eds. (1995) *White-Collar Crime: Classic and Contemporary Views*. Third edition, New York: The Free Press.

Glantz, Stanton A., John Slade, Lisa A. Bero, Peter Hanauer, and Deborah E. Barnes, eds. (1996) *The Cigarette Papers*. Berkeley, CA: University of California Press.

Green, Penny, and Tony Ward (2004) *State Crime: Governments, Violence and Corruption*. London: Pluto Press.

Greenberg, Karen, and Joshua Dratel, eds. (2005) *The Torture Papers: The Road to Abu Ghraib*. New York: Cambridge University Press.

Greider, William (1999) *Fortress America: The American Military and the Consequences of Peace*. New York: PublicAffairs.

Gross, Edward (1978) "Organizational Crime: A Theoretical Perspective." In *Studies in Symbolic Interaction*, Editor Norman K. Denzin. Greenwich, CT: JAI Press.

Gusfield, Joseph (1984) *The Culture of Public Problems: Drinking-Driving and the Symbolic Order*. Chicago: University of Chicago Press.

Hartung, Frank E. (1950) "White-Collar Offenses in the Wholesale Meat Industry in Detroit." *American Journal of Sociology* 56:25–34.

Herman, Edward S. (1982) *The Real Terror Network: Terrorism in Fact and Propaganda*. Boston: South End Press.

Hersh, Seymour M. (2004) *Chain of Command: The Road from 9/11 to Abu Ghraib*. New York: Harper Collins.

Hills, Stuart (1987) *Corporate Violence: Injury and Death for Profit*. Totowa, NJ: Rowman & Littlefield.

Hopkins, Andrew (1978) "The Anatomy of Corporate Crime." In *Two Faces of Deviance: Crimes of the Powerless and Powerful*. Editors Paul R. Wilson and John. Braithwaite, Brisbane, Australia: University of Queensland Press.

Kauzlarich, David, and Ronald C. Kramer (1993) "State-Corporate Crime in the U.S. Nuclear Weapons Production Complex." *Journal of Human Justice* 5:4–28.

Kauzlarich, David, and Ronald C. Kramer (1998) *Crimes of the American Nuclear State: At Home and Abroad*. Boston: Northeastern University Press.

Kauzlarich, David, and Rick Matthews (2006) "Taking Stock of State-Corporate Crime Theory and Research." In *State-Corporate Crime: Wrongdoing at the Intersection of Business and Government*, Editors Raymond Michalowski and Ronald Kramer. Piscataway, NJ: Rutgers University Press.

Kennan, George F. (1967) *Memoirs: 1925–1960*. Boston: Atlantic Monthly Press.

Keller, William (1995) *Arm in Arm: The Political Economy of the Global Arms Trade*. New York: Basic Books.

Klare, Michael T., and Peter Kornbluh, eds. (1989) *Low Intensity Warfare: Counter Insurgency, Proinsurgency, and Antiterrorism in the Eighties*. New York: Pantheon.

Kramer, Ronald C. (1982) "Corporate Crime: An Organizational Perspective." In *White Collar and Economic Crime*, Editors Peter Wickman and Thomas Dailey. Lexington: Lexington Books.

Kramer, Ronald C. (1984) "Corporate Criminality: The Development of an Idea." In *Corporations, as Criminals*, Ellen Hochstedler (ed.) Beverly Hills, CA: Sage.

Kramer, Ronald C. (1990) "State-Corporate Crime: A Case Study of the Space Shuttle Challenger Explosion." Paper presented at the Edwin Sutherland Conference on White Collar Crime: 50 Years of Research and Beyond, Indiana University.

Kramer, Ronald C. (1990b) "The Concept of State-Corporate Crime." Paper presented at the Society for the Study of Social Problems, Washington, D.C.

Kramer, Ronald C. (1992) "The Space Shuttle Challenger Explosion: A Case Study in State-Corporate Crime." In *White Collar Crime Reconsidered.* Kip Schlegel and David Weisburd (eds.) Boston: Northeastern University Press.

Kramer, Ronald C., and Raymond Michalowski (1990) "Toward an Integrated Theory of State-Corporate Crime." Paper presented at the American Society of Criminology Meeting, Baltimore, MD, November, 1990.

Kramer, Ronald C., and Raymond Michalowski (2005) "War, Aggression, and State Crime: A Criminological Analysis of the Invasion and Occupation of Iraq." *British Journal of Criminology* 45: 1–24.

Kramer, Ronald, Raymond Michalowski, and Dawn Rothe (2005) "The Supreme International Crime: How the U.S. War in Iraq Threatens the Rule of Law." *Social Justice* 32 (No. 2, July).

Lewis, Neil A. (2005) "Documents Say Detainees Cited Abuse of Koran." *New York Times* (May 26): A1.

Lynch, Michael, and Raymond Michalowski (2005) *Crime, Power and Identity: The New Primer in Radical Criminology*. Fourth edition, Washington, DC: Criminal Justice Press.

Matthews, Rick (2006) "Ordinary Business: State-Corporate Crime in Nazi Germany." In *State-Corporate Crime: Wrongdoing at the Intersection of Business and Government*, Editors Raymond Michalowski and Ronald Kramer. Piscataway, NJ: Rutgers University Press.

Matthews, Rick A., and David Kauzlarich (2000) "The Crash of ValuJet flight 592: A Case Study in State-Corporate Crime." *Sociological Focus* 3:281–298.

McMullan, John (1992) *Beyond the Limits of the Law: Corporate Crime and Law and Order*. Halifax: Fernwood Press.

Michalowski, Raymond (1985) *Order, Law and Crime*. New York: Random House.

Michalowski, Raymond, and Ronald C. Kramer (1987) "The Space Between the Laws: The Problem of Corporate Crime in a Transnational Context." *Social Problems* 34:34–53.

Michalowski, Raymond, and Ronald C. Kramer (2003) "Beyond Enron: Toward Economic Democracy and a New Ethic of Inclusion." *Risk Management: An International Journal* 5:37–47.

Michalowski, Raymond J., and Ronald C. Kramer (2006) *State-Corporate Crime: Wrongdoing at the Intersection of Business and Government*. Piscataway, NJ: Rutgers University Press.

Mills, C. Wright (1956) *The Power Elite*. New York: Oxford University Press.

Moro, Javier, and Dominique Lapierre (2002) *Five Past Midnight in Bhopal: The Epic Story of the World's Deadliest Industrial Disaster*. New York: Warner Books.

Mullins, Christopher (2006) "Bridgestone-Firestone, Ford and the NHTSA: State-Corporate Crime in the Tire Separation Case." In *State-Corporate Crime: Wrongdoing at the Intersection of Business and Government*, Editors Raymond Michalowski and Ronald Kramer. Piscataway, NJ: Rutgers University Press.

National Institute of Justice. "Funding Opportunities, 2005." *www.ojp.usdoj.gov/nij/funding.htm*

Nelson, Barbara (1986) *Making an Issue of Child Abuse: Political Agenda Setting for Social Problems*. Chicago: University Of Chicago Press.

Passas, Nikos (1990) "Anomie and Corporate Deviance." *Contemporary Crises* 14:157–178.

Pearce, Frank (1976) *Crimes of the Powerful: Marxism, Crime, and Deviance*. London: Pluto Press.

Pilger, John (2001) "The Truths They Never Tell Us: Behind the Jargon about Failed States and Humanitarian Interventions Lie Thousands of Dead." *New Statesman* 130(November 26):14–16.

Potter, Gary W. (2002) *Controversies in White-Collar Crime*. Cincinnati, OH: Anderson Publishing.

Quinney, Richard (1977) *Class, State and Crime: On the Theory and Practice of Criminal Justice*. New York: David McKay.

Ratner, Michael, and Ellen Ray (2004) *Guantanamo: What the World Should Know*. White River Junction, VT: Chelsea Green.

Rebovich, Donald, and John L. Kane (2002) "An Eye for an Eye in the Electronic Age: Gauging Public Attitude Toward White Collar Crime and Punishment." *Journal of Economic Crime Management*. Volume 1, Issue 2 viewed at www.jecm.org/02_fall_art1.htm, 6-6-05.

Reinarman, Craig, and Harry Gene Levine (1997) *Crack in America: Demon Drugs and Social Justice*. Berkeley, CA: University of California Press.

Reiman, Jeffrey (2003) *The Rich Get Richer and the Poor Get Prison: Ideology, Class, and Criminal Justice*. Seventh edition, Boston: Allyn & Bacon.

Rothe, Dawn (2006) "War Profiteering and the Pernicious Beltway Bandits: Iraq and Halliburton." In *State-Corporate Crime: Wrongdoing at the Intersection of Business and Government*, Editors Raymond Michalowski and Ronald Kramer. Piscataway, NJ: Rutgers University Press.

Ross, Jeffrey Ian (2003) *The Dynamics of Political Crime*. Thousand Oaks, CA: Sage Publications.

Rossi, Peter H., Emily Waite, Christine E. Bose, and Richard E. Berk (1974) "The Seriousness of Crime: Normative Structure and Individual Differences." *American Sociological Review* 39:224–237.

Rummel, Rudolph (1994) *Death by Government*. New Brunswick, NJ: Transaction Press.

Schafer, Stephen (1974) *The Political Criminal: The Problems of Morality and Crime*. New York: Free Press.

Schehr, Robert (2005) "Conventional Risk Discourse and the Proliferation of Fear." *Criminal Justice Policy Review*. 16-1:38–58.

Schmitt, Eric (2005) "No Criminal Charges for Officer at Abu Ghraib Interrogations." *New York Times* (May 12):A1.

Schrecker, Ellen (1986) *No Ivory Tower: Mccarthyism and the Universities*. New York: Oxford University Press.

Siegel, Larry (2001) *Criminology: Theories, Patterns, and Typologies*. Seventh edition, Belmont, CA: Wadsworth.

Simon, David R. (1982) *Elite Deviance*. Boston: Allyn & Bacon.

Simon, David R. (2001) *Elite Deviance*. Seventh edition, Boston: Allyn & Bacon.

Sellin, Thorsten (1938) *Culture, Conflict and Crime*. New York: Social Science Research Council.

Shover, Neal, and John Paul Wright, eds. (2001) *Crimes of Privilege*. New York: Oxford University Press.

Shover, Neal, Greer Litton Fox, and Michael Mills (2001) "Consequences of Victimization by White-Collar Crime." In *Crimes of Privilege*, Editors Neal Shover and Jolin Paul Wright. New York: Oxford University Press.

Sklar, Martin J. (1988) *The Corporate Reconstruction Of American Capitalism, 1890–1916: The Market, The Law, And Politics*. New York: Cambridge University Press.

Slapper, Gary, and Steve Tombs (1999) *Corporate Crime*. Essex, UK: Longman.

Spector, Malcolm, and John I. Kitsuse (2000) *Constructing Social Problems*. New Brunswick, NJ: Transaction.

Sutherland, Edwin H. (1940) "White Collar Criminality." *American Sociological Review* 5:1–12.

Sutherland, Edwin H. (1949) *White Collar Crime*. New York: Dryden Press.

Tirman, John (1997) *Spoils of War: The Human Cost of America's Arms Trade*. Collingdale, PA: Diane Publishing Company.

Tombs, Steve, and Dave Whyte (2003) "Scrutinizing the Powerful." In *Unmasking the Crimes of the Powerful*, Editors S. Tombs and D. Whyte. New York: Peter Lang.

Tunnell, Kenneth (1993) *Political Crime in Contemporary America*. New York: Garland.

Turk, Austin T. (1969) *Criminality and the Legal Order*. Chicago: Rand McNally.

Vaughan, Diane (1982) "Toward Understanding Unlawful Organizational Behavior." *Michigan Law Review* 80:1377–1402.

Vaughan, Diane (1983) *Controlling Unlawful Organizational Behavior: Social Structure and Corporate Misconduct*. Chicago: University of Chicago Press.

Vaughan, Diane (1997) *The Challenger Launch Decision: Risky Technology, Culture, and Deviance at NASA*. Chicago: University of Chicago Press.

Wolfgang, Marvin E., Robert Figlio, Paul Tracey, and Simon Singer (1985) *The National Survey of Crime Severity*. Washington, DC: US Government Printing Office.

Wonders, Nancy, and Fred Solop (1993) "Understanding the Emergence of Law and Public Policy: Toward a Relational Model of the State." In *Making Law*, Editors William Chambliss and Marjorie Zatz. Bloomington, IN: Indiana University Press.

Young, T.R. (1981) "Corporate Crime: A Critique of the Clinard Report." *Contemporary Crises* 5:323–336.

Part V

Legal Perspectives: Theory, Irresponsibility, and Liability

1

A Normative Approach to White-Collar Crime

Stuart P. Green

The study of white-collar crime has been primarily the province of two fairly distinct academic disciplines. In the 1940s, sociologists and criminologists began to focus on the causes and effects of white-collar crime and the social status and circumstances of the offenders who commit such offenses.[1] A generation or so later, academic lawyers began directing their attention to the complexities of white-collar crime doctrine, the policies and procedures that underlie such offenses, and the sentencing of white-collar offenders.[2]

Curiously, however, the subject of white-collar crime has mostly escaped the notice of criminal law theorists. Such scholars have tended to focus their attention on "general part"[3] concepts such as act and omission, harm and culpability, and justification and excuse, as well as on a few specific core offenses such as murder and rape. To the extent such theorists have thought at all about what can fairly be described as white-collar crime, it has been almost exclusively in connection with the question of corporate criminality and with a handful of relatively exotic offenses such as blackmail and extortion.[4] My goal in this essay (which is excerpted from a book-length monograph on the moral theory of white-collar crime) is to begin to remedy this neglect.

So what is criminal law theory? The term is broad enough to encompass inquiry into matters such as what distinguishes the criminal from the civil law, the purposes of punishment, the proper scope and limits of the criminal law, the question of criminalization, and the manner in which the criminal law should address the citizenry. For present purposes, I shall be particularly interested in the task of describing the relationship between the criminal law and moral norms. Most criminal law theorists now agree that retribution is a necessary, if not sufficient, goal of criminal sanctions.[5] Although there are many versions of retributivism, the core notion is that punishment is justified when it is deserved, and that criminals deserve punishment when they are morally at fault.[6] Thus, much of my focus here will be on determining whether, and in what manner, the commission of white-collar crime entails moral fault.[7]

In undertaking such a project, we face an initial question about exactly what should count as a white-collar crime. While acknowledging the controversy surrounding this issue,[8] I shall for present purposes simply assume that the white-collar crime consists of those offenses typically dealt with in American law school white-collar crime courses and categorized as such by agencies, such as the Department of Justice's Bureau of Justice Statistics, which compile statistics concerning the incidence of crime. As such, my concern will be with offenses such as fraud, perjury, false statements, obstruction of justice, bribery, extortion and blackmail, insider trading, tax evasion, and certain regulatory crimes. Moreover, I shall regard an act as a white-collar offense only if it is actually treated by the law as a "crime" (rather than merely as a civil violation or mere "deviance") and regardless of the socio-economic or professional status of its alleged perpetrator or the particular social setting in which it was allegedly performed.

My approach here will consist of three basic steps. First, it will be necessary to say something about the moral content of criminal offenses generally. To that end, I offer a brief description of three different kinds of moral content that can be found in most criminal offenses, which I shall refer to as *mens rea* (or the mental element required to commit a crime), harmfulness, and moral wrongfulness. The second step is to show the distinctive forms of *mens rea*, harmfulness, and wrongfulness that are characteristic of this area of criminal law. In this context, we will observe certain patterns of moral "ambiguity" that seem to inhere in many white-collar crimes. The third step reflects the recognition that any adequate assessment of the moral content of white-collar crimes will ultimately require an offense-by-offense analysis. Although any such comprehensive assessment is beyond the scope of this chapter, I will offer, as an illustration of the approach I have developed in more detail elsewhere, a brief description of the moral content of the offenses of fraud and insider trading.

Finding Fault in Criminal Conduct

In determining whether and to what extent a given crime (whether or not a white-collar crime) entails moral fault, there are at least three basic kinds of moral element that need to be considered: *mens rea*, harmfulness, and moral wrongfulness.

Three Kinds of Moral Content

Mens rea is perhaps the most familiar element of moral content in criminal offenses. The term is used here in its narrow "elemental" sense to refer to the particular mental state required in the definition of an offense or with which a defendant actually commits a crime.[9] The Model Penal Code famously provides a concise list of *mens rea* terms—"purposely," "knowingly," "recklessly," and "negligently"[10]—though there are also many other such terms (including "intentionally" and "willfully") that are in regular use in non-MPC jurisdictions as well.

Assessments of *mens rea* are crucial to determining the extent to which an act entails fault and is therefore deserving of punishment. Other things (such as the amount of harm caused) being equal, we say that a criminal act committed purposefully or intentionally is more blameworthy (and therefore more deserving of punishment) than one committed recklessly, and that a criminal act committed recklessly is more culpable than one committed negligently.

The second basic kind of element in the moral content of criminal offenses is "harmfulness"—i.e., the degree to which a criminal act causes (or risks causing) harm. And what is harm? For present purposes, we can look to Joel Feinberg's definition of harm as some relatively lasting or significant setback to a person's interests.[11] An interest, in turn, is something in which a person has a stake.[12] For present purposes, we can also assume that the harm caused by criminal acts is "public" in a way that the criminal law considers relevant—i.e., that it is the sort of harm that somehow properly concerns the community as a whole rather than just individual citizens within such community.[13]

Once again, the more harm an act causes, the more deserving of blame it is likely to be. For example, murder involves one of the most serious harms a person can cause—namely, the death of a human being—and is therefore viewed as deserving of as serious a punishment as the system offers. Parking in a no-parking zone, by contrast, involves a fairly trivial harm and merits only a trivial punishment, if any.

The third element of moral content in criminal offenses—moral wrongfulness—refers to the violation of a moral norm that occurs when a criminal act is committed. The concept is primarily non-consequentialist, or deontological, in its orientation.[14] Under such an approach, what makes an act wrongful is some intrinsic violation of a free-standing moral rule or duty, rather than the act's consequences. Such wrongfulness is typically directed towards a particular person or group of persons who are "wronged"—as opposed to being, in Feinberg's term, a "free-floating" evil.[15]

The most familiar way of thinking of moral wrongfulness is, in the words of Jean Hampton, as "an affront to the victim's value or dignity."[16] In Feinberg's definition, "[o]ne person *wrongs* another when his indefensible (unjustifiable and inexcusable) conduct violates the other's right."[17] Thus, a murderer violates his victim's right to life, a rapist violates his victim's rights to sexual autonomy and bodily integrity, a larcenist or fraudster violates his victim's rights in property.

An alternative approach to thinking about the concept of moral wrongfulness is to examine the role that various everyday, but nevertheless powerful, moral norms play in the definition of white-collar crime. Such norms include, for example, the rules against cheating, deceiving, stealing, coercion, exploitation, disloyalty, promise-breaking, and disobedience.

Such an approach has several advantages over the generalized rights-based approach mentioned earlier. Unlike rights, which can be maddeningly abstract ("nonsense upon stilts," in Bentham's memorable phrase), such norms are fairly concrete. Although there will be significant disagreement over the precise content and application of such norms, almost every civilized person will have some rudimentary understanding that it is morally wrong, at least in certain core cases, to lie, cheat, steal, coerce, exploit, break promises, and the like. Moreover, such an approach is more suggestive of the richly nuanced way people actually think about the content of their moral lives. Even people who have never had occasion to read a single page of moral philosophy are capable of making remarkably fine-grained distinctions about, say, what properly constitutes cheating or stealing.

At the same time, it should be clear that the norms-based and rights-based approaches are not mutually inconsistent. I have no quarrel at all with the proposition that subjecting a fellow human being to coercion or deceit also constitutes a violation of such person's moral or legal rights. My point is that saying that *V*'s rights were violated is often less informative than saying that *V* was deceived or coerced or cheated.

Distinguishing *Mens Rea*, Harmfulness, and Wrongfulness

Although moral wrongfulness, harmfulness, and *mens rea* frequently overlap, the concepts are analytically distinct. First, an act can clearly be harmful without being wrongful. For example, if *X* and *Y* are boxing, there is a reasonable chance that *X* will cause *Y* serious harm. But, assuming that *Y* has "consented" to such conduct (and that *X* is playing by the rules), we would say that *X* had not *wronged Y*, and therefore that he should not be subject to prosecution for battery. Similarly, if *X* kills *Y* in justified defense of himself or others, we would once again say that *Y* has been harmed without being wronged, since one cannot be wronged by a justified act; and because *X*'s act was not wrongful, he would not be liable for criminal homicide.

It is also possible to do harm without intending to do so, or even being aware that such harm is likely to occur. For example, a person who, though driving in a cautious and lawful manner, hits a child who darts out from behind a parked car, thereby causing the child serious injury, has obviously done harm, but she has done so without *mens rea*. Ordinarily, a driver would not be criminally liable in such a case unless causing harm to a person while driving a car was a strict liability offense.

Acts can also be wrongful without being harmful. If I lie to you, but you do not believe me, I have certainly done you a wrong, but it is unlikely that I have caused you any significant harm. Similarly, a witness who lies on the stand about a matter that is not "material" to the proceeding has done an act that is wrongful, but is not harmful in the way that the law of perjury considers relevant.

Moreover, even when a single act entails both harmfulness and wrongfulness, the two concepts are conceptually distinct. For example, if *X* steals a car owned by *Y*, the *wrong X* has committed is done principally to *Y*, although *X* might also cause indirect harm to *Y*'s family (who are deprived of transportation) and to *Y*'s neighbors (who suffer a feeling of insecurity). Similarly, if *X* trades securities on the basis of inside information that is not available to *Y*, then it appears that *X* has wronged *Y*. But the *harm X* causes (at least in the aggregate) is more general: In theory, insider trading is detrimental to investor confidence and ultimately harmful to the market as a whole.

The concept of wrongfulness is also distinguishable from that of *mens rea*, though less clearly than it is from the concept of harmfulness. Whether an act is wrongful often depends on whether it is intentional. For example, *X* must intend for *Y* to believe something that is untrue in order for us to say that *X* has deceived *Y*. If *X* has been reckless or negligent in his attitude toward the truth, we might still say that *X* had done a wrongful act, but we would probably not say that he had deceived or cheated. On the other hand, one can certainly break a promise even if one does not intend to do so, such as when *X* fails to perform some promissory obligation because he has simply forgotten that he had it.

Some Generalizations About the Moral Content of White-Collar Crime

Having considered three different kinds of moral content in criminal offenses generally, we are now in a position to look at the distinctive forms of *mens rea*, harmfulness, and wrongfulness that occur, more narrowly, among the white-collar offenses. In this context, we will observe certain patterns of moral "ambiguity" that are characteristic of such crimes.[18]

The *Mens Rea* of White-Collar Crime

White-collar offenses are characterized by at least two distinct patterns of *mens rea*, which are in some sense direct opposites. The first pattern, which is particularly common in the regulatory area, requires a significantly lower level of *mens rea* than has traditionally been required by the criminal law. For example, Section 1319(c)(1)(B) of the Clean Water Act provides that "any person who negligently introduces into a sewer system . . . any pollutant or hazardous substance which such person knew or reasonably could have known could cause personal injury or property damage . . . shall be punished."[19] By requiring that the defendant act "negligently" rather than "intentionally" or even "knowingly," the level of moral fault required is reduced from what was commonly required at common law. Even more dramatic is the enactment of strict liability offenses, which do away with *mens rea* entirely as to one or more elements of the *actus reus* of the offenses. A good example here is the Federal Food, Drug & Cosmetic Act, which makes it a crime to introduce into interstate commerce any food, drug, device, or cosmetic that is adulterated or misbranded, regardless of whether the defendant had any knowledge of such adulteration or misbranding.[20]

There is also another distinctive pattern of *mens rea* that figures in white-collar criminal law which is in some sense the converse of the pattern of reduced culpability just described. Under this second pattern, proof of *mens rea* is so crucial to the definition of the white-collar offense that conduct performed without it either fails to expose the actor to criminal (as opposed to civil) liability, or is not even regarded as unlawful in the first place. For example, imagine that *X*, a private citizen, gives Congressman *Y* a check for $10,000. Assuming that *X* acts with the "intent to influence" an official act, he has committed a bribe.[21] Alternatively, if he has acted with the intent to "thank" *Y* for his services, then he has committed the offense of gratuities.[22] But if *X* acts with the intent neither to influence nor thank *Y* for his services, he has committed no offense; he has merely made a legal gift or campaign contribution. Thus, in such cases, the presence or absence of *mens rea* would provide an unusually decisive (though, in terms of proof, a frequently elusive) factor in determining whether *X* has committed a crime.

The Harms and Victims of White-Collar Crime

White-collar crime is also characterized by several distinctive patterns of harmfulness. First, it differs from conventional crime in the kind and quality of harm caused. Many conventional street crimes involve identifiable physical injury to the victim, such as death, serious injury, or physical violation; are committed through sudden violent force; and occur in an identifiable physical location in a brief, relatively discrete period of time. White-collar crime, by contrast, tends to: be committed through non-violent means; cause harm that is incorporeal, such as financial loss or injury to an institution; and occur at a nonspecific physical location over what can be a difficult-to-define period of time.

White-collar offenses also tend to involve harms that are more difficult to identify than in the case of conventional street crimes. For example, there is not likely to be much controversy about the proposition that the principal harm caused by homicide is the death of a human being. In the case of white-collar crimes such as tax evasion, bribery, and insider trading, however, the identification of harm presents real difficulties. Some direct harms seem relatively straightforward: Presumably, tax evasion leads to reduced revenues for the public treasury, bribery to biased governmental decision making, and insider trading to unfair transactions in the securities markets. But there are also significant indirect, diffuse, and aggregative harms caused by such conduct—e.g., loss of investor and consumer confidence, distrust of government, and bad decisions made by public officials—that are much harder to quantify.

The complexity of harms caused by white-collar crime is in part a function of the complexity of the underlying activity that white-collar crime statutes are meant to regulate. Such activities can occur over an extended period of time and in disparate locations. They frequently involve elaborate forms of behavior such as those associated with manufacturing and industrial processes, marketing, corporate finance, the stock market, document retention procedures, government contracts, financial auditing, trial and litigation procedures, and political fundraising. Such activity often occurs within large and complex organizations, involving numerous individuals occupying a wide range of different positions, and many series of complicated transactions. Understanding how such processes work can require a fairly sophisticated understanding of disciplines such as finance, economics, engineering, medicine, political science, organizational theory, management, accounting, environmental science, and information technology. It is often hard enough for the lay public to understand how these processes are supposed to work when they are conducted in a legal manner; it is all the more difficult to understand how they function when they involve criminal activity.

The harm caused by white-collar crime also differs from that caused by conventional crime in terms of the way in which it affects victims. In core, violent street crimes, such as murder or rape, the harm is focused and obvious: a human being is killed, a person's body is violated. We have no problem in saying that the principal victim of a homicide is the decedent and that the principal victim of the rape is the person whose body is violated. Even in the case of non-violent crimes such as larceny and forgery, a victim or discrete group of victims is easily identified. But white-collar crime presents much greater difficulties: How can we say exactly which citizens are victimized by environmental violations and government corruption; which taxpayers are the victims of false claims and tax evasion; which employees are wronged by labor law violations and accounting fraud; and which consumers are harmed by price fixing, violations of the food and drug and product safety laws, and fraudulent marketing practices? Many white-collar crimes involve small harms to a large number of victims, and are significant only in the aggregate.[23] And, of course, some victims of white-collar crime are never aware that they have been victimized. Indeed, the identity of the victims harmed may be unknown even to the white-collar offender herself.

White-collar crime also deals with inchoate (or incomplete) liability in a distinctive manner. The criminal law has traditionally distinguished between choate and inchoate forms of criminality. Inchoate offenses, such as attempt, conspiracy, and solicitation, are generally not punished as severely as completed offenses (although there is a lively scholarly debate about whether this should be so). White-collar crime statutes, by contrast, tend to conflate complete and incomplete conduct into a single offense, punishable by a single penalty.[24] And, often, they criminalize conduct that involves nothing more than the creation of a *risk* of harm.[25]

The Wrongs of White-Collar Crime

Another way in which white-collar crime differs from more traditional street crimes is in terms of moral wrongfulness. There are many harmful white-collar-type acts that become criminal only if they are also wrongful. For example, the kinds of harms caused by unlawful price fixing, insider trading, and fraud, on the one hand, and lawful (if ruinous) competition, on the other, are virtually indistinguishable from each other: all involve loss of money, a business, a job, or market share. But, assuming that the relevant players "played by the rules," and violated no one's rights, we would not consider the kinds of harms that result from lawful "fair" competition wrongful (unless, perhaps, we are looking at the situation from a Marxist perspective). And because such acts are not wrongful, they should not be subject to criminal sanctions.[26]

To some extent, of course, the same can be said of certain conventional offenses: For example, sexual intercourse without consent is rape; with consent, it is lovemaking. The taking of property without consent is theft; with consent, it is a gift or contract. Hitting someone in the face with one's fists without consent is battery; with consent, it is boxing. The difference is that the wrongfulness in white-collar crime seems more elusive than the wrongfulness in cases of conventional crime. While it should, at least in theory, be relatively easy to distinguish between rape and lovemaking and battery and boxing, it is potentially much more difficult to distinguish between extortion and mere "hard bargaining," fraud and "puffing," bribery and "campaign contributions," obstruction of justice and "routine document destruction," and the like.

The Moral Context of Fraud and Insider Trading

However exactly the concept of white-collar crime is defined, it clearly encompasses a wide range of related forms of conduct. Although it is possible to offer some helpful generalizations about what such offenses have in common (as I sought to do in the previous section), in the end, the only way to have a complete picture of the moral and legal (and, I would submit, sociological and psychological) content of the white-collar crimes is through an offense-by-offense analysis. To that end, this Part offers a discussion of two offenses that are widely acknowledged to be white-collar crimes: fraud and insider trading.

Fraud

The concept of fraud is ubiquitous in white-collar crime, reflecting a protean and proliferating range of meanings. Not only are the fraud offenses among the most frequently charged, but they are also among the most widely and variously codified.[27] In this section, I want to offer a brief survey of the range of moral concepts that have been associated with fraud.

The Concept of Fraud

Much of the difficulty in defining the concept of fraud lies in the often inconsistent ways in which the term has been used in the law. My focus here is on two points of contention: the means by which fraud must be carried out, and the object at which it must be aimed.

Traditionally, fraud has been thought to require the use of deceit.[28] But while deception, historically and conceptually, seems to be at its core, the means by which fraud must be carried out are, under modern statutes, frequently defined more broadly. As Brenda Nightingale has put it in her comprehensive treatise on the subject:

> Given the origin of the concept of fraud, in equity and at common law, as a concept tied, initially to misrepresentations in contractual relations and later to the tort of deceit, deceit was, for a time, the primary concept around which the law relating to the offense was developed. While deceit is no longer the defining characteristic of fraudulent conduct, it is still one of the most common means by which the offense is committed.[29]

So what might fraud mean in the absence of deceit? The term that is often used to describe non-deceptive fraudulent means is "dishonesty."[30] And what does "dishonesty" mean? The concept has been defined broadly enough to include, at various times, notions as diverse as breach of trust, conflicts of interest, non-disclosure of material facts, exploitation, taking unfair advantage, non-performance of contractual obligations, and misuse of corporate assets.[31] Indeed, the term *fraud* has been used to refer to a wrongful act of almost any sort—a violation of "moral uprightness, of fundamental honesty, fair play and right dealing in the general and business life of members of society,"[32] an act that is "discreditable as being at variance with straightforward or honorable dealings."[33]

There is also considerable variation in the way in which the authorities define fraud's object. The most common use of the term is to refer to criminal acts the purpose of which is to obtain, in the words of the federal mail fraud statute, "money or property,"[34] or at least something of economic value, such as an accommodation or service of some kind. A classic case of such alleged fraud is that involving Enron Vice President and Chief Financial Officer Andrew Fastow, who, in an effort to find investors for an Enron spin-off investment partnership known as LJM-2, allegedly gave such investors false information about the state of Enron's and LJM-2's finances, and thereby obtained from them nearly $349 million in equity.[35]

But the term *fraud* is also used more broadly to refer to schemes not just to obtain money or property, but also to achieve any "unjust advantage" or to "injure the rights or interests of another."[36] As the Supreme Court put it in *Hammerschmidt v. United States*, "[t]o conspire to defraud the United States means primarily to cheat the Government out of property or money, but it also means to interfere with or obstruct one of its lawful governmental functions."[37] Indeed, the term *fraud* has been used to refer to objects as broad and nebulous as the "evasion of statutory prohibitions."[38]

Under U.S. federal law, one of the most significant contexts in which fraud involves an object other obtaining property is that contained in the 1988 amendment to 18 U.S.C. § 1346, enacted in response to the Supreme Court's decision in *McNally v. United States*.[39] Under Section 1346, the term "scheme or artifice to defraud" is expressly defined to include a scheme or artifice to "deprive another of the intangible right of honest services."[40] When such fraud occurs in the public sector, the goal is to deny the public its rights to honest governmental services.[41] When it occurs in the private sector, the goal is to deny an employer his or her right to the honest services of an employee.[42]

The Moral Content of Fraud

The moral content of fraud follows directly from the way in which its statutory elements are defined. For example, according to its core, historically-based definition, fraud involves the use of (1) "false or fraudulent pretenses, representations, or promises" for the purpose of (2) "obtaining money or property."[43] Under such a definition, fraud seems to refer to two basic, and fairly discrete, forms of moral wrongfulness: stealing and deception.

But under alternative definitions of fraud, moral content varies significantly. Here we need to consider both means other than deceit and objects other than obtaining money or property. For example, if the object of a given fraud is some "unjust advantage" or "injury to the rights or interests of others" other than the obtaining of money or property, then such fraud would not violate the norm against stealing. And if such fraud is carried out by some "dishonest" but non-deceptive means of the sort mentioned above, then it would involve cheating, exploitation, disloyalty, or promise-breaking, rather than deceit. Indeed, if fraud really does refer to any "evasion of statutory prohibitions," then it would apply, as Arlidge and Parry point out in their treatise on fraud, even to such apparently non-fraud-like crimes as the smuggling of drugs and dissemination of pornography.[44]

Such diversity in the definition of fraud poses real impediments to the principles of fair labeling and of legality. If fraud really were to encompass not just stealing by deceit, but also deceptive and non-deceptive breaches of trust, conflicts of interest, non-disclosure of material facts, exploitation, taking unfair advantage, non-performance of contractual obligations, and misuse of corporate assets, it would be virtually impossible to distinguish between different offenses in terms of their nature and seriousness, and even to know whether and when one had committed a crime. Under such an approach, and subject to certain contingent jurisdictional limitations, there is no reason why the perjurer, the bribee, the tax cheat, and the extortionist could not all be convicted of fraud.[45]

Unfortunately, I have no immediate solution to this conceptual morass. Certainly, I would recommend that legislatures define, and courts interpret, the concept of fraud narrowly, to avoid such indeterminacy. But to the extent that my goal is to describe the moral content of white-collar crime as it currently exists, it will do no good to deny that such problems exist. Instead, I will in the discussion below focus on what seems to me the most characteristic feature of the traditional "core" notion of fraud—namely, the flexible way in which it defines the notion of deceit.

Fraud as a White-Collar Crime

Before we proceed further, there is one more preliminary matter that needs to be addressed. To the extent that I have defined the core concept of fraud as theft by deceit, it is reasonable to ask how such a concept differs from the traditional common law offense of false pretenses, which is defined as using false representations to wrongfully deprive another permanently of property.[46] More generally, it is worth asking in what sense fraud should be classified as a white-collar crime.

In terms of offense elements, there are three basic differences between fraud and false pretenses. First, whereas the offense of false pretenses always involves an attempt to obtain money or property, the object of fraud, as we have seen, is far more ambiguous. Second, whereas false pretenses requires a misrepresentation regarding a past or present fact, fraud can also involve a misrepresentation involving a promise or prediction of a future state of affairs.[47] Third, while false pretenses requires a completed theft, fraud frequently conflates the distinction between complete and inchoate criminality by requiring that the defendant either obtain, or attempt to obtain, property (or perhaps some other goal) through deceptive means.[48]

But fraud also differs from false pretenses in more than just its basic formal elements. The term *fraud* is typically used to describe a statutory offense that is committed by some specialized means or in some specialized context. Under American federal law, for example, there are now dozens of statutory provisions that criminalize offenses such as mail fraud, wire fraud, bank fraud, health care fraud, tax fraud, computer fraud, securities fraud, bankruptcy fraud, accounting fraud, and conspiracy to defraud the government.[49] Fraud is thus distinguishable from false pretenses most significantly in terms of its potential harms, victims, and perpetrators.

Fraudsters use means of mass communication and commerce—television and radio, the internet, and the mail—to perpetuate frauds that are capable of causing widespread, aggregative harms.[50] Such offenders are often privileged, highly compensated, ostensibly respectable citizens who are perceived as (and may in fact be) providing valuable goods and services, increasing stock value, and creating employment opportunities. They commit such frauds in the context of complex business contexts, such as securities offerings, health care financing, and bank transactions. Such activity can be hard to distinguish not only from civil frauds (in terms of their elements, the two offenses are virtually indistinguishable[51]), but also from lawful, if aggressive, business activity—"creative accounting," "puffing," "sharp dealing," and the like.

The victims of fraud can also be hard to identify. In addition to its immediate targets, fraud also causes more remote harms to less easily identifiable victims, including consumers and taxpayers. More generally, it can result in a loss of confidence in the system of free and fair enterprise. And even when a direct victim can be identified, such persons are sometimes themselves held to blame. As in the saying, "you can't cheat an honest man," the assumption is often made that only the greedy and dishonest are likely to be defrauded.[52] In light of such characteristics, fraud is appropriately classified as a white-collar offense.

The Deceit Element in Fraud

Although deceit is not always a required offense element under modern fraud statutes—"dishonesty," in all of its ambiguity, is a common alternative—it nevertheless plays a central role in fraud's history and modern understanding. In this section, I want to explore the particular form that deceit takes in the formulation of fraud and contrast it to the form of deceit required for perjury.

As defined earlier, deception consists of the communication of a message, or attempt to communicate a message, with which the communicator, in communicating, intends to cause a person to believe something that is untrue. Perhaps the clearest way to see the importance of deception in the concept of fraud is in connection with the law of theft. Indeed, it is precisely the element of deception that distinguishes fraud from other stealing offenses such as embezzlement (stealing by breach of trust), extortion (stealing by coercion), and robbery (stealing through force).[53]

The fact that property is taken *by deception* significantly affects the way in which fraud is experienced by the victim. One who has been defrauded of $50 by a confidence man is likely to feel very different from a person who has had $50 stolen by a larcener (or extortionist or robber). As Peter Alldridge has noted:

> [I]f a victim is going to suffer a particular harm, it is less painful for him or her and less culpable of the person causing it that the harm should be caused without whatever additional unpleasantness comes from the deception of the victim. In the case of frauds there is far more likely to be the loss of self-esteem consequent upon feeling responsible by reason of having been duped.[54]

Indeed, it is the recognition of the distinctive moral character of fraud that explains why, notwithstanding the widespread consolidation of theft law that has occurred in many jurisdictions, the fact that theft is committed by means of deception continues to play a role in various classificatory schemes. Good examples are provided by the Model Penal Code[55] and the English Theft Act of 1968.[56] Both statutes consolidate the traditional acquisitive offenses (larceny, embezzlement, false pretenses, extortion, blackmail, fraudulent conversion, and receiving stolen property) in a manner that obviously reflects the similarity in harms caused.[57] Yet, within the broad rubric of "theft offenses," each statute retains categories such as Theft by Deception (in the case of the Model Penal Code[58]) and Obtaining Property by Deception (in the case of the English Theft Act[59]). In both instances, the principal factor that distinguishes such offenses from other theft offenses is the presence of deceit.

Insider Trading

Having considered the broadly defined offense of fraud in the last section, I now want to focus on the more narrowly defined offense of insider trading, a crime that demonstrates with particular clarity the doctrinal relevance of the concept of moral wrongfulness.[60] As we shall see, the question of whether and how insider trading wrongs or harms its victims (if at all) bears directly on the scope of the doctrine. In the United States, the dominant, Supreme Court-formulated theory has been that insider trading is wrongful because it involves a breach of fiduciary duty—either to the shareholder from whom the stock was purchased or to the person from whom confidential information was misappropriated. Doctrinal results differ significantly based on which theory is adopted. In this Section, I will argue that, rather than thinking of insider trading as involving a breach of fiduciary duty, we would do better to think of it in terms of cheating. The stock market is viewed as a highly formalized, rule-governed game. Confidence in the market depends on investors feeling that the game is being played fairly. The fact that some investors have better *information* than others is not viewed as unfair. What is viewed as unfair is the possibility that some investors might have *access* to information to which other investors do not. Market participants who trade on undisclosed inside information in these circumstances are viewed as cheaters, and punishment is viewed as warranted.

Assessing the Moral Content of Insider Trading

In the United States, insider trading is a crime under both Section 10(b) of the Securities Exchange Act of 1934, which prohibits any "manipulative or deceptive device or contrivance,"[61] and Securities and Exchange Commission Rule 10b-5, which prohibits any "act, practice, or course of business which operates or would operate as a fraud or deceit upon any person, in connection with the purchase or sale of any security."[62] What exactly "insider trading" consists of, however, is not defined in either provision, so one must look elsewhere for enlightenment—to SEC rulings and federal case law.

In its 1961 decision, *Cady, Roberts & Co.*, the SEC enunciated the basic rule that a trader who possesses material non-public information that would affect his or her judgment about a given securities transaction must either "disclose" such information or "abstain" from trading.[63] In subsequent years, the courts and commentators have struggled to explain why violation of the "disclose or abstain" rule should be prohibited in some circumstances, but not others.[64]

Much of the scholarly literature on insider trading involves the question of whether and to what extent such conduct is harmful. A number of prominent law and economics scholars have argued that insider trading in fact makes the market more efficient by causing market prices to reflect more complete information about the value of the traded securities than would otherwise be possible, and that insider trading therefore ought not to be criminalized.[65] Suffice it to say that the question whether insider trading is harmful, and precisely how, is a controversial issue that cannot be resolved here.[66]

For our purposes, the most interesting thing to note about the law and economics literature on insider trading is the way in which it consistently ignores or trivializes the question of moral wrongfulness. For example, in his influential book on insider trading law, Henry Manne patronizingly reports the outraged reaction of "an anonymous lady law student who in a classroom discussion of the subject, stamped her foot and angrily declaimed, 'I don't care; it's just not right.'"[67] In relating this incident, Manne's purpose is to belittle the idea that insider trading might be understood as involving morally wrongful behavior. For Manne, the only relevant question is whether insider trading is harmful.

In response to critics such as Manne, a number of scholars argue that insider trading is, on one ground or another, morally wrongful. Making exactly the reverse of the error made by Manne, however, these scholars argue, or imply, that insider trading should be made illegal regardless of whether it is economically harmful. For example, Alan Strudler and Eric Orts have contended that "[e]ven if economic arguments conclusively favored unfettered insider trading, moral arguments would potentially give an independent reason for prohibiting insider trading. . . ."[68] As I understand them, Strudler and Orts are arguing that it would be permissible to criminalize insider trading even if it were shown to be harmless. This position seems to me wrong for the same reason I believe it is wrong to criminalize so-called "morals offenses" such as adultery, bigamy, and prostitution. In a liberal society of the sort described by Mill, Feinberg, and others, moral wrongfulness by itself is not sufficient to justify criminalization. Under the liberal view, we ought not to make something a crime unless it can also be shown to be harmful.

For our purposes, though, the interesting question is exactly why insider trading *is* morally wrongful. Indeed, there is a direct connection between the way in which the courts have conceptualized this issue and the precise circumstances under which the disclose-or-abstain rule should apply. Over the years, the courts and commentators have offered three basic theories as to whether, and when, trading on material non-public information is morally wrong and should be made illegal. I shall refer to these as the (1) "breach-of-duty-to-shareholder" theory, (2) "breach-of-duty-to-source-of-information" theory, and (3) "fraud" or "deception" theory. In my view, none of these theories adequately captures what is morally wrong with insider trading. After briefly reviewing each of the theories, I offer an alternative characterization of what's wrong with insider trading, based on the idea of cheating.

The breach of duty to shareholder theory (or "classical" or "traditional" theory, as it is usually known) is articulated most prominently by the majority opinions in *Chiarella v. United States*[69] and *Dirks v. SEC*.[70] Under this theory, the rule against insider trading is violated when a corporate insider breaches a fiduciary duty owed to shareholders of his company by using, for his own benefit, non-public information obtained in his role as an insider. A paradigm example is provided by the facts of *SEC v. Texas Gulf Sulphur Co.*, in which officers, directors, and employees of TGS learned of their company's rich ore strike in Canada and traded on this information before the news became public.[71] The defendants in *TGS* were liable for insider trading because, under the classical theory, they breached a duty of loyalty owed to the shareholders of their company. In contrast, the defendant in *Chiarella*—a markup man for a financial printing press who was able to determine the true identity of five companies that were takeover targets of a client bidder, and to use that information to purchase stock in the target companies—did not, according to the classical theory, commit insider trading. Unlike the defendants in *TGS*, defendant Chiarella owed no fiduciary duty to those with whom he had traded because "he was not a corporate insider and he received no confidential information from the target company."[72]

The "breach-of-duty-to-source-of-information" (or "misappropriation theory" as it is usually known) was adopted by a majority of the Court in *United States v. O'Hagan*.[73] Under *O'Hagan*, insider trading is viewed as morally wrongful because it involves a breach of fiduciary duty not to the shareholders of the insider's firm, but rather to the source of the information that is misappropriated.[74] For example, in *O'Hagan* itself, the defendant was a partner in a law firm that represented Grand Metropolitan, which planned to make a tender offer for Pillsbury. After learning of the prospective offer, defendant O'Hagan bought Pillsbury stock and call options. Because O'Hagan was not a corporate insider at Pillsbury, he had no fiduciary duty to Pillsbury shareholders to breach, and his purchase would not have constituted insider trading under the classical or traditional theory of *Dirks* and *Chiarella*. But under the misappropriation theory adopted by the Court in *O'Hagan*, the defendant was liable, since he had breached a duty of loyalty to the *source* of the information—namely, Grand Metropolitan. Likewise, had Chiarella's case been decided under the misappropriation theory, he would have been liable for insider trading, since he had breached his duty to his employer, the printer Pandick Press, by taking and using information to which he was not entitled.

The final approach, based on the concept of "fraud" or "deception," is one that can be found in Chief Justice Burger's theoretically eclectic dissent in *Chiarella*. Although a majority of the Court has never embraced it, the theory continues to find favor with various scholarly commentators.[75] According to this theory, insider trading involves a wrong of omission, rather than of commission. By failing to disclose certain material facts, the offending trader engages in a kind of misrepresentation; hence the term securities "fraud." And, like other forms of deceit, such failure to disclose interferes with the other party's deliberative process and thereby infringes on his autonomy.[76] Although its doctrinal implications are not completely spelled out, the theory would surely apply to a broad range of factual circumstances like those involved in *Texas Gulf Sulphur*, *Chiarella*, and *O'Hagan*, since in each case the defendant, whether insider or outsider, allegedly misled the market by failing to disclose material information.

In my view, none of the three theories adequately captures what's morally wrong with insider trading. The classical theory applies only when non-public information is used by a corporate insider. It does not apply when such information is used by an outsider. From the perspective of the person who buys or sells stock without access to such non-public information, however, it makes no difference whether the party on the other side of the transaction is an insider or an outsider. The wrong in both cases is identical. Therefore, the classical theory is too narrow: it fails to capture cases that should be subject to the insider trading laws.

Like the classical theory, the misappropriation theory also does a poor job of reflecting our moral intuitions about what's wrong with insider trading. The classical theory says that the wrong in insider trading comes from a breach of duty to the source of the information. Once again, however, to the victim of insider trading, it makes no difference how the offender has obtained the non-public information on which he relies. What does matter is that the offender enjoys an unfair advantage that is denied to the uninformed trader.

Finally, there is the deceit or fraud theory. Although this approach is preferable to the other two (for one thing, it has the virtue of tracking the "securities fraud" language of the statute under which insider trading is actually prosecuted), the fraud theory nevertheless fails to capture the real moral content of insider trading. As described above, "fraud" is best understood as theft by deception. Yet it is unclear that insider trading necessarily involves either theft or deception. Unlike the typical fraudster, who makes false representations regarding the quality, price, or quantity of goods or services,[77] the insider trader makes no affirmative representations at all. She simply acts on the basis of information that she knows or believes to be reliable. Indeed, if the insider trader does make any representations, she is signaling, quite accurately, that she regards the stock as either overvalued (which she does by selling) or undervalued (which she does by buying)—precisely the point that the critics of insider trading law make when they argue that insider trading provides an efficient means of telegraphing reliable information to the market.

Perhaps, then, buying stock in a company that one knows will soon be the target of a corporate takeover is like buying a dusty old canvas at a yard sale when one knows that the painting is a previously undiscovered Vermeer. Or perhaps selling stock in a company that one knows, on the basis of non-public information, to be headed for bankruptcy is like selling a used car without disclosing that the transmission is shot. Unfortunately for the fraud theory, the law does not generally regard nondisclosure of material information as deceptive,[78] and neither, it seems to me, does morality. If, as seems to be the case, nondisclosure of material information is not regarded as fraudulent in the context of ordinary commercial transactions (e.g., at a yard sale), it is hard to see why it should be regarded as fraudulent in the context of the securities markets. If we are to explain why nondisclosure should be illegal in the latter context, but not in the former, then we need some moral concept, other than deceit, that allows us to distinguish between the two.

Insider Trading as Cheating

A better characterization of what is morally wrongful with insider trading would take into account of the notion of cheating. The trader (1) violates the SEC rule that one must either disclose material non-public information or abstain from trading; and does so (2) with the intent to obtain an advantage over a second party with whom she is in a cooperative, rule-governed relationship. Under this characterization, the stock market is viewed as a highly formalized, rule-governed game, which is distinct from the game that is played at yard sales and on used-car lots.[79] The insider trader violates a rule that is ultimately intended to give investors confidence that the game is being played fairly, and thereby gains an advantage over the uninformed party with whom she is dealing.[80]

I am certainly not the first to characterize insider trading as a form of "cheating."[81] But I want to pursue this idea to see where it leads in considering two recurring questions in the law of insider trading: First, why does the law forbid trading securities on information that is not public, but nevertheless allow trading on the basis of vast inequalities in the quality and quantity of information that, theoretically, is publicly available? Second, should it be a crime to trade securities on the basis of material non-public information that is obtained by luck rather than through misappropriation?

In order to answer these questions, let us consider the following three hypotheticals:

- *X* is in a bicycle race with *A*. As a result of his exceptional talent, top-notch training, mental toughness, and superior equipment, *A* rides much faster than *X* and wins the race.
- *X* is in a bicycle race with *P*. While *X*'s back is turned, *P* violates the rules of bicycle racing by puncturing *X*'s tire and causing *X* to lose several minutes as a result of having to dismount and change his tire. *P* wins the race.
- *X* is in a bicycle race with *T*. During the course of the race, *X* has the bad luck to run over a nail. It takes *X* several minutes to change his tire. Rather than waiting for him (there is no requirement that he do so), *T* rides on ahead and wins the race.

The first hypothetical helps explain the answer to the first question—namely, why does the law forbid trading on non-public information but allow traders to exploit other kinds of informational advantages, such as those gained by superior research and knowledge of the market? Just as the average competitive bicyclist is unlikely to overcome the extraordinary talents of a Lance Armstrong, the average individual investor is unlikely to outwit the investment savvy of a Warren Buffett.[82] But we would not ordinarily say that it is "unfair" for such prodigies to exploit their natural talents, hard work, and superior resources. Cheating arises only when an advantage is obtained unfairly, through rule-breaking. The fact that Buffett is smarter, knows more about the stock market, and has access to more and better (at least theoretically) publicly available information than the average investor is not regarded as "unfair." What would be regarded as unfair is if he were to rely on information that was not even theoretically accessible to the public (for example, inside information obtained from his friend, Microsoft Chairman Bill Gates).

As for the second question—should it be a crime to trade on the basis of material non-public information that is obtained by luck rather than through misappropriation? Consider the case of the famous American football coach, Barry Switzer.[83] In June 1981, Switzer was in the stands at a high school track meet in Oklahoma when he overheard a man whom he knew to be a director of a publicly held corporation discussing with his wife the impending merger of one of the corporation's subsidiaries. Trading on the basis of this not-yet public information, Switzer turned a profit of more than $50,000.[84] Although the Supreme Court has not yet had occasion to consider this question straight on, it appears that, following the rule in O'Hagan, an outsider who obtains information fortuitously (say, by overhearing it on the train or at the beach), without breaching any fiduciary duty to the source of the information, would not be bound by the disclose-or-abstain rule, and would not have committed insider trading.

Would the result differ under my "cheating" approach to insider trading? At one level, the question whether Switzer cheated turns on nothing more than whether he violated a rule: If the disclose-or-abstain rule applies to information obtained fortuitously by outsiders, then he has cheated; if the rule does not apply in such cases, then he has not. The problem, of course, is that the precise question we are trying to answer is whether the disclose-or-abstain rule *should* apply in such circumstances.

Here a consideration of hypotheticals two and three might prove useful. There appears to be, at least at an intuitive level, a significant moral difference between creating a disadvantage for one's rival (e.g., by puncturing his tire), and exploiting a disadvantage that one's rival has come by naturally (e.g., by riding on while the rival changes a tire that was punctured as a result of his fortuitously running over a nail). The same distinction should apply in the context of insider trading. The trader who relies on non-public information obtained through his own efforts is analogous to the racer who punctures his rival's tire, while the trader who relies on non-public information that has been obtained fortuitously is analogous to the bicycle racer whose rival runs over a nail. The distinction is between creating an unfair informational disparity and exploiting an informational disparity that already exists. If this analogy is apposite, then the disclose-or-abstain rule should be construed so as not to apply to cases in which an investor comes across non-public information fortuitously (say, by overhearing it in an elevator or on the train), and trading on such information so obtained should not constitute insider trading.

Conclusion

The concept of white-collar crime is rich enough and diverse enough to sustain scholarly attention from a wide range of sources. To date, most of this attention has come from social scientists and from academic lawyers. In this essay, I have attempted to enlarge the boundaries, and, I hope, enrich the discourse, of white-collar crime studies by using some of the tools of criminal law theory to focus more explicitly and systematically on the moral content of such crime. What we have seen is that such moral content is complex, fine-grained, and at times quite ambiguous. Although generalizations are both possible and useful, any full understanding of the moral content of white-collar crime will ultimately require a careful offense-by-offense analysis.

Acknowledgments

The content of this chapter is derived from my book, *Lying, Cheating, and Stealing: A Moral Theory of White-Collar Crime* (Oxford University Press, 2006). I am grateful to Oxford University Press for its permission to reprint these materials here.

Endnotes

1. The seminal work is Edwin H. Sutherland, "White-Collar Criminality" (1940) 5 *American Sociological Review* 1, reprinted in Gilbert Geis and Robert F. Meier (eds.), *White-Collar Crime* (New York: Free Press, 1977).
2. A good example is Kathleen F. Brickey, *Corporate and White Collar Crime: Cases and Materials* (Boston: Little, Brown and Co., 1st ed. 1990. Of course, there are many works on white-collar crime that seek to bridge the gap between social science and law. See, e.g, David Weisburd et al., *Crimes of the Middle Classes: White-Collar Offenders in the Federal Court* (New Haven: Yale University Press, 1991); Herbert Edelhertz, *The Nature, Impact and Prosecution of White-Collar Crime* (Washington, D.C.: National Institute of Law Enforcement and Criminal Justice, 1970).
3. The general part is that part of the criminal law that contains supposedly general doctrines, rules, and definitions, as opposed to the special part, which contains the definitions of specific offenses. See R.A. Duff and Stuart P. Green, "Introduction: The Special Part and Its Problems," in R.A. Duff and Stuart P. Green (eds.), *Defining Crimes: Essays on the Special Part of the Criminal Law* (Oxford University Press, 2005) 1.
4. For theoretical literature on corporate criminality, see, e.g., Celia Wells, *Corporations and Criminal Responsibility* (Oxford: Oxford University Press, 2d ed. 2001). For theoretical literature on blackmail and insider trading, see, e.g., Leo Katz, *Ill-Gotten Gains: Evasion, Blackmail, Fraud, and Kindred Puzzles of the Law* (Chicago: University of Chicago Press, 1996).
5. Most criminal law scholars subscribe to a theory that mixes retributive and preventative (including both deterrent and incapacitative) goals. See, e.g., Andrew von Hirsch, *Doing Justice: The Choice of Punishments* (Boston: Northeastern University Press, 1986 reprint ed.); H.L.A. Hart, *Punishment and Responsibility* 158–85 (Oxford: Oxford University Press, 1968). Only "pure" retributivists believe that retribution should be the sole purpose of punishment. See, e.g., Michael S. Moore, *Placing Blame* (Oxford: Oxford University Press, 1997).
6. See generally Moore, above note 5; Jeffrie G. Murphy, "Retributivism, Moral Education, and the Liberal Estate" (Winter/Spring 1985) *Criminal Justice Ethics* 3; Joel Feinberg, "Justice and Personal Desert," in *Doing and Deserving: Essays in the Theory of Responsibility* (Princeton: Princeton University Press, 1970) 55, 67–73.
7. This is not to say that social scientists and academic lawyers are not also concerned with the moral content of white-collar crimes. Social scientists are concerned with the unfairness of treating white-collar offenses less harshly than apparently equally serious blue collar offenses, and with the corrosive effects that the immoral behaviors associated with white-collar crime have on society generally. For a useful treatment of some of the moral issues underlying white-collar criminality, written

by a social scientist, see Susan Shapiro, "Collaring the Crime, Not the Criminal: Reconsidering the Concept of White-Collar Crime" (1990) 55 *American Sociological Review* 346, 350 ("The violation and manipulation of the norms of trust—of disclosure, disinterestedness, and role competence—represent the modus operandi of white-collar crime."). Lawyers and legal academics, to the extent they want to distinguish white-collar crimes from other kinds of crimes, are inevitably forced to consider presumably moral questions concerning the way in which the harms associated with white-collar crime differ from those associated with more traditional offenses, and their mental elements. My point is simply that criminal law theory tends to be concerned with moral issues more explicitly and more systematically than these other disciplines.

8. See generally Proceedings of the Academic Workshop, "Definitional Dilemma: Can and Should There Be a Universal Definition of White Collar Crime?" (Richmond, VA: National White Collar Crime Center, 1996). The definitional issue is also dealt with in Stuart P. Green, "The Concept of White Collar Crime in Law and Legal Theory" (2004) 8 *Buffalo Criminal Law Review* 1.
9. See generally Stuart P. Green, "Six Senses of Strict Liability: A Plea for Formalism," in A.P. Simester (ed.), *Appraising Strict Liability* (Oxford: Oxford University Press, 2005) 1.
10. Model Penal Code § 2.02(2).
11. Joel Feinberg, *Harm to Others* (New York: Oxford University Press, 1984). See also Hyman Gross, *A Theory of Criminal Justice* (New York: Oxford University Press, 1979) 115 ("Harm is an untoward occurrence consisting in a violation of some interest of a person.").
12. Feinberg, *Harm to Others*, above note 11, at 33–34. The concept of harm was also helpfully characterized by Jean Hampton, who referred to it as "a disruption of or interference in a person's well-being, including damage to that person's body, psychological state, capacities to function, life plans, or resources over which we take this person to have an entitlement." Jean Hampton, "Correcting Harms Versus Righting Wrongs: The Goal of Retribution" (1992) 39 *UCLA Law Review* 1659, 1662; see also Gross, above note 11, at 115 ("Harm is an untoward occurrence consisting in a violation of some interest of a person.").
13. For a helpful discussion, see R.A. Duff, *Punishment, Communication and Community* (Oxford: Oxford University Press, 2001); Jonathan Schonsheck, *On Criminalization: An Essay in the Philosophy of Criminal Law* (Dordrecht: Kluwer Academic Publishers 1994).
14. For a helpful introduction to such concepts, see Samuel Scheffler, *Consequentialism and its Critics* (Oxford: Oxford University Press, 1988); Nancy (Ann) Davis, "Contemporary Deontology" in Peter Singer (ed.), *A Companion to Ethics* (Oxford: Blackwell Publishers, 1991) 205; Philip Pettit, "Consequentialism" in ibid., at 230.
15. See Joel Feinberg, *Harmless Wrongdoing* (New York: Oxford University Press, 1988) 18–20.
16. Hampton, above note 12, at 1666.
17. Feinberg, *Harm to Others*, above note 11, at 34.
18. The argument in this section was originally developed in Stuart P. Green, "Moral Ambiguity in White Collar Criminal Law," (2004) 18 *Notre Dame Journal of Law, Ethics and Public Policy* 501.
19. 33 U.S.C. § 1319(c)(1)(B).
20. 21 U.S.C. § 331(a).
21. 18 U.S.C. § 201(b)(1)(A).
22. 18 U.S.C. § 201(c)(1)(A).
23. See Feinberg, *Harm to Others*, above note 11, at 187–217 (assessing and comparing harms).

24. For example, fraud is fraud regardless of whether anyone's property is actually taken; bribery is bribery regardless of whether a bribe is actually accepted; perjury is perjury regardless of whether a lying witness is believed; and obstruction of justice is obstruction regardless of whether any proceedings are actually hindered. See, respectively, 18 U.S.C. § 1341; 18 U.S.C. § 201(b); 18 U.S.C. § 1621; 18 U.S.C. § 1503(a).
25. See generally R.A. Duff, "Criminalizing Endangerment," in R.A. Duff and Stuart P. Green (eds.), *Defining Crimes: Essays on the Special Part of the Criminal Law* (Oxford University Press, 2005) 43.
26. As Dan Kahan has put it, in explaining the difference between theft and legal, but nevertheless harmful, competition, only theft involves "disrespect for the injured party's moral worth." Dan M. Kahan, "The Secret Ambition of Deterrence" (1999) 113 *Harvard Law Review* 413, 420. See also A.P. Simester and Andrew von Hirsch, "Rethinking the Offense Principle" (2002) 8 *Legal Theory* 269, 270–72 (distinguishing between harms and wrongs).
27. For data on the number of fraud prosecutions, see Administrative Office of the U.S. Courts, *Federal Judicial Workload Statistics* (Washington, D.C., 1993) 52–57 (listing criminal cases commenced by major offenses); Bureau of Justice Statistics, *Sourcebook of Criminal Justice Statistics* (Washington, D.C.: U.S. Department of Justice, 1996). For estimates of fraud codifications, see Ellen S. Podgor, "Criminal Fraud," (1999) 48 *American University Law Review* 729, 740 (counting a total of 92 substantive fraud statutes in Title 18 of the U.S. Code alone).
28. The *OED*, for example, defines *fraud* as "criminal deception," requiring the use of "false representations." "Fraud" in *Oxford English Dictionary*. See also Podgor, above note 27, at 737 ("In United States federal criminal law the term is often synonymously used with the term 'deceit.'").
29. Brenda L. Nightingale, *The Law of Fraud and Related Offences* (Toronto: Carswell Pub., 1996) 2–4.
30. See, e.g., *Hammerschmidt v. United States*, 265 U.S. 182, 188 (1924) (although fraud has traditionally been committed by means of "deceit, craft or trickery," it can also be committed by other "means that are dishonest"); *R. v. Olan* [1978] 2 S.C.R. 1175, 1180 ("The words 'other fraudulent means' in [what is now s.338(1)] include means which are not in the nature of a falsehood or deceit; they encompass all other means which can properly be stigmatized as dishonest."). Criminal Code (Canada) 380(1), in turn, provides that "[e]veryone who, by deceit, falsehood, or other fraudulent means, whether or not it is a false pretence within the meaning of this Act, defrauds the public or any person, whether ascertained or not, of any property, money or valuable security or any service" is guilty of fraud.
31. Nightingale, above note 29, at 3–13 (cataloging meanings of "dishonest means").
32. *Gregory v. United States*, 253 F.2d 104, 109 (5th Cir. 1958).
33. *R. v. Doren* [1982] 66 C.C.C. (2d) 448, 450.
34. 18 U.S.C. §1341.
35. The solicitations are described in an October 15, 2001 Memorandum from Max Hendrick, III, outside counsel for Enron at Vinson and Elkins law firm, to James V. Derrick, Jr., Enron General Counsel, available on *Houston Chronicle* website, <http://www.chron.com/content/chronicle/special/01/enron/background/index.html>. See also David Ivanovich, "The Fall of Enron; Bankers Believed Deals Hinged on Investments," *Houston Chronicle* (Feb. 20, 2002), at A9; "Top Former Enron Executive 'to Plead Guilty,'" *The Guardian* (Jan. 8, 2004), <http://www.guardian.co.uk/enron/story/0,11337,1118744,00.html>.
36. "Fraud" in *Oxford English Dictionary*.
37. 265 U.S. 182, 188 (1924).
38. Anthony J. Arlidge and Jacques Parry, *Arlidge and Parry on Fraud* (London: Waterlow Publishers, 1985) 30 (criticizing this tendency).

39. 483 U.S. 350 (1987).
40. 18 U.S.C. § 1346.
41. For cases involving breach of duty to the public, see *United States v. Devegter*, 198 F.3d 1324, 1328 (11th Cir. 1999) ("Public officials inherently owe a fiduciary duty to the public to make governmental decisions in the public's best interest. 'If the official instead secretly makes his decision based on his own personal interests . . . the official has defrauded the public of his honest services.'") (quoting *United States v. Lopez-Lukis*, 102 F.3d 1164, 1169 (11th Cir. 1997)).
42. For cases involving breach of duty to private employers, see *United States v. Frost*, 125 F.3d 346 (6th Cir. 1997), *cert. denied*, 525 U.S. 810 (1998); *United States v. Vinyard*, 266 F.3d 320 (4th Cir. 2001); *United States v. Jain*, 93 F.3d 436 (8th Cir. 1996).
43. 18 U.S.C. § 1341; see also, e.g., the Canadian fraud statute, Criminal Code § 380(1) (making it a crime "by deceit [or] falsehood" to "defraud[] the public or any person, whether ascertained or not, of any property, money or valuable security").
44. Arlidge and Parry, above note 38, at 30.
45. Indeed, to cite just one example, acceptance of a bribe has been held to constitute a breach of honest services under the mail fraud statutes, provided that the requisite jurisdictional requirements are met. *United States v. Mandel*, 591 F.2d 1347 (4th Cir.), *aff'd per curiam by equally divided court*, 602 F.2d 653 (4th Cir. 1979), *coram nobis granted*, 862, F.2d 1067 (4th Cir. 1988). As the court explained:

    > [T]he fraud involved in the bribery of a public official lies in the fact that the public official is not exercising his independent judgment in passing on public matters. A fraud is perpetrated on the public to whom the official owes fiduciary duties, e.g., honest, faithful and disinterested service. When a public official has been bribed, he breaches his duty of honest, faithful and disinterested service. While outwardly purporting to be exercising independent judgment in passing on official matters, the official has been paid for his decisions, perhaps without even considering the merits of the matter. Thus, the public is not receiving what it expects and is entitled to, the public official's honest and faithful service.

46. See Wayne R. LaFave, *Criminal Law* (St. Paul, Minn.: Thomson/West, 4th ed. 2003), at § 19.7.
47. *Durland v. United States*, 161 U.S. 306, 313 (1896).
48. The mail fraud statute, for example, speaks in terms of devising or "intending to devise" any scheme or artifice to defraud. 18 U.S.C. § 1341.
49. U.S.C. § 1341 (mail fraud); 18 U.S.C. § 1343 (wire fraud); 15 U.S.C. §§ 77x, 78ff (securities fraud); 26 U.S.C. § 7201 (tax fraud); 18 U.S.C. § 1344 (bank fraud); 18 U.S.C. § 1030 (computer fraud);18 U.S.C. § 1347 (health care fraud); 18 U.S.C. § 371 (conspiracy to commit fraud against United States); 18 U.S.C. § 157 (bankruptcy fraud).

    The scholarly literature on mail fraud alone is enormous. For some leading examples, see Craig M. Bradley, "Foreword: Mail Fraud After *McNally* and *Carpenter*: The Essence of Fraud" (1988) 79 *Journal of Criminal Law & Criminology* 573; John C. Coffee, Jr., "Modern Mail Fraud: The Restoration of the Public/Private Distinction" (1998) 35 *American Criminal Law Review* 427; Peter J. Henning, "Maybe It Should Just Be Called Federal Fraud: The Changing Nature of the Mail Fraud Statute" (1995) 36 *Boston College Law Review* 435; Jed S. Rakoff, "The Federal Mail Fraud Statute (Part I)" (1980) 18 *Duquesne Law Review* 771; Geraldine Szott Moohr, "Mail Fraud Meets Criminal Theory" (1998) 67 *University of Cincinnati Law Review* 1.
50. For a discussion of the social costs of fraud, with particular reference to Canada, see Nightingale, above note 29, §1.3(a).

51. See, e.g., False Claims Act, 31 U.S.C. § 3730 (giving federal government and civil plaintiffs a cause of action against those who submit false claims to the government). Virtually the only differences between criminal and civil fraud concern burden of proof and remedies.
52. Nightingale, above note 29, at 1–29.
53. For example, in its decision in *Fasulo v. United States*, 272 U.S. 620, 628 (1926), the Supreme Court was explicit that, broad as the conception of fraud is, it does not include obtaining property through threats or coercion.
54. Peter Alldridge, "Sex, Lies and the Criminal Law" (1993) 44 *N. Ireland Legal Q.* 250, 251. See also Lloyd L. Weinreb, *Criminal Law: Cases, Comment, Questions* 395–96 (New York: Foundation Press, 6th ed. 1998) (making a somewhat similar point).
55. Model Penal Code § 223.1–.2.
56. Theft Act, 1968, ch. 60, §§ 1, 7 (Eng.).
57. See, e.g., Model Penal Code, Comments to § 223.1, at 131–32 ("[T]heft by a stranger and . . . theft by a fiduciary represent similar dangers requiring approximately the same treatment and characterization. . . . Prevailing moral standards do not differentiate sharply between the swindler and other 'thieves.' To that extent, at least, consolidation conforms to the common understanding of what is substantially the same kind of undesirable conduct.").
58. Model Penal Code § 223.3.
59. Theft Act, 1968, ch. 60, § 15 (Eng.).
60. The argument in this section was originally developed in Stuart P. Green, "Cheating," (2004) 23 *Law and Philosophy* 137, 175–84.
61. 15 U.S.C. § 78j(b).
62. 17 C.F.R. § 240.10b–5. Insider trading is also prohibited, though not necessarily criminalized, in numerous other countries. See Emerging Markets Committee, International Organization of Securities Commissions, "Insider Trading: How Jurisdictions Regulate It" (March 2003).
63. 40 S.E.C. 907, 912 (1961). *Cady, Roberts* assumed that the holder of non-public information would be a corporate insider, although subsequent cases have expanded the scope of "insider trading" to apply to outsiders as well.
64. Leading commentary includes Stephen Bainbridge, "The Insider Trading Prohibition: A Legal and Economic Enigma" (1986) 38 *Florida Law Review* 35; Allison Grey Anderson, "Fraud, Fiduciaries and Insider Trading" (1982) 10 *Hofstra Law Review* 341; Victor Brudney, "Insiders, Outsiders, and Informational Advantages Under the Federal Securities Laws" (1979) 93 *Harvard Law Review* 322.
65. The most influential such work is Henry G. Manne, *Insider Trading and the Stock Market* (New York: The Free Press, 1996).
66. For a useful overview of the issues, see Mark Klock, "Mainstream Economics and the Case for Prohibiting Inside Trading" (1994) 10 *Georgia State University Law Review* 297.
67. Manne, above note 65, at 233 n. 42.
68. Alan Strudler and Eric W. Orts, "Moral Principle in the Law of Insider Trading, (1999) 78 *Texas Law Review* 375, 383. Other moralized theories of insider trading can be found in Leo Katz, *Ill-Gotten Gains* (Chicago: University of Chicago Press, 1996); Kim Lane Scheppele, "It's Just Not Right: The Ethics of Insider Trading" (1993) 56 *Law & Contemporary Problems* 123; Ian B. Lee, "Fairness and Insider Trading" (2002) *Columbia Business Law Review* 119. I should note, however, that only Strudler and Orts are explicit in minimizing the importance of harm.
69. 445 U.S. 222 (1980).
70. 463 U.S. 646 (1983).
71. 401 F.2d 833 (2d Cir. 1968).
72. 445 U.S. at 43.
73. 521 U.S. 642 (1997).

74. Ibid. at 652.
75. See, e.g., Strudler and Orts, above note 68.
76. Ibid. at 380, 408–17.
77. See *United States v. Regent Office Supply*, 421 F.2d 1174, 1179 (2d Cir. 1970).
78. The leading case is *Laidlaw v. Oregon*, 15 U.S. (2 Wheat.) 178, 193–94 (1817) (buyers who learned that a peace treaty ending the War of 1812 had been signed, thereby ending the blockade of New Orleans, did not commit fraud when they failed to disclose such information to seller from whom they acquired large quantities of tobacco).
79. Cf. Boyd Kimball Dyer, "Economic Analysis, Insider Trading, and Game Markets," (1992) *Utah Law Review* 1 (characterizing stock market as a "game market").
80. The fact that the trader does not ordinarily know the actual identity of his trading partner does not seem to change the analysis.
81. See, e.g., William R. Lucas et al., "Common Sense, Flexibility, and Enforcement of the Federal Securities Laws" (1996) 51 *Business Law Review* 1221, 1233, 1237 ("Even though it is not specifically mentioned in the text of the statutes, insider trading, pure and simple, is cheating." "Insider trading is about cheating; cheating a shareholder, an employer, a client, or even a friend."); Strudler and Orts, above note 68, at 412 (characterizing insider trading as "cheating" in passing). Although she does not use term "cheating," my theory of the morality of insider trading is probably closest to Scheppele, above note 68 (focusing on fairness, level playing fields, equal access to information, and breach of contractarian obligations as key to understanding what is wrong with insider trading).
82. Warren Buffett, chairman of Berkshire Hathaway Co., is known as the world's most successful stock market investor.
83. *SEC v. Switzer*, 590 F. Supp. 756 (W.D. Okla. 1984).
84. The district court held, under then-current law, that Switzer had not committed insider trading. Ibid. at 760.

References

Administrative Office of the U.S. Courts (1993), *Federal Judicial Workload Statistics* (Washington, D.C.).

Anderson, Allison Grey (1982). "Fraud, Fiduciaries and Insider Trading," *Hofstra Law Rev.* 10:341.

Alldridge, Peter (1993). "Sex, Lies and the Criminal Law," *N. Ireland Legal Q.* 44:250.

Arlidge, Anthony J. & Jacques Parry (1985). *Arlidge & Parry on Fraud*. London: Waterlow Publishers.

Bainbridge, Stephen (1986). "The Insider Trading Prohibition: A Legal and Economic Enigma," *Florida Law Rev.* 38:35.

Bradley, Craig M (1988). "Foreword: Mail Fraud After *McNally* and *Carpenter*: The Essence of Fraud," *J. Criminal Law & Criminology* 79:573.

Brickey, Kathleen F. (1990). *Corporate and White Collar Crime: Cases and Materials*. Boston: Little, Brown and Co., 1st ed.

Brudney, Victor (1979). "Insiders, Outsiders, and Informational Advantages Under the Federal Securities Laws" *Harvard Law Review* 93:322.

Bureau of Justice Statistics (1996). *Sourcebook of Criminal Justice Statistics*. Washington, D.C.: U.S. Department of Justice.

Coffee, Jr., John C. (1998). "Modern Mail Fraud: The Restoration of the Public/Private Distinction," *American Criminal Law Rev.* 35:427.

Davis, Nancy (Ann) (1991). "Contemporary Deontology" in Peter Singer (ed.), *A Companion to Ethics*. Oxford: Blackwell Publishers.

Duff, R.A. (2001). *Punishment, Communication and Community*. Oxford: Oxford University Press.

Duff, R.A. (2005). "Criminalizing Endangerment," in R.A. Duff & S. P. Green, *Defining Crimes: Essays on the Special Part of the Criminal Law*. Oxford: Oxford University Press.

Duff, R.A., & Stuart P. Green (2005). "Introduction: The Special Part and Its Problems," in R.A. Duff & S.P Green, *Defining Crimes: Essays on the Special Part of the Criminal Law*. Oxford: Oxford University Press.

Dyer, Boyd Kimball (1992). "Economic Analysis, Insider Trading, and Game Markets," *Utah Law Review* 1992:1.

Edelhertz, Herbert (1970). *The Nature, Impact and Prosecution of White-Collar Crime* Washington, D.C.: National Institute of Law Enforcement and Criminal Justice.

Emerging Markets Committee, International Organization of Securities Commissions, "Insider Trading: How Jurisdictions Regulate It" (March 2003).

Feinberg, Joel (1984). *Harm to Others*. New York: Oxford University Press.

Feinberg, Joel (1988). *Harmless Wrongdoing*. New York: Oxford University Press.

Feinberg, Joel (1970) "Justice and Personal Desert," in Feinberg, *Doing and Deserving: Essays in the Theory of Responsibility.* Princeton: Princeton University Press.

Green, Stuart P (2004). "The Concept of White Collar Crime in Law and Legal Theory," *Buffalo Criminal Law Rev.* 8:1.

Green, Stuart P (2005). "Six Senses of Strict Liability: A Plea for Formalism," in A.P. Simester (ed.), *Appraising Strict Liability*. Oxford: Oxford University Press.

Green, Stuart P (2004). "Moral Ambiguity in White Collar Criminal Law," *Notre Dame Journal of Law, Ethics & Public Policy* 18:501.

Green, Stuart P (2004). "Cheating," *Law and Philosophy* 23:137.

Gross, Hyman (1979). *A Theory of Criminal Justice*. New York: Oxford University Press.

Henning, Peter J (1995). "Maybe It Should Just Be Called Federal Fraud: The Changing Nature of the Mail Fraud Statute," *Boston College Law Rev.* 36:435.

Ivanovich, David (2002). "The Fall of Enron; Bankers Believed Deals Hinged on Investments," *Houston Chronicle* (Feb. 20), at A9.

Hampton, Jean (1992). "Correcting Harms Versus Righting Wrongs: The Goal of Retribution," *UCLA Law Rev.* 39:1659

Hart, H.L.A. (1968). *Punishment and Responsibility*. Oxford: Oxford University Press.

Kahan, Dan M (1999). "The Secret Ambition of Deterrence," *Harvard Law Review* 113:413.

Katz, Leo (1996). *Ill-Gotten Gains: Evasion, Blackmail, Fraud, and Kindred Puzzles of the Law*. Chicago: University of Chicago Press.

Klock, Mark (1994). "Mainstream Economics and the Case for Prohibiting Inside Trading," *Georgia State University Law Rev.* 10:297

LaFave, Wayne R. (2003). *Criminal Law* (4th ed. 2003). St. Paul, Minn.: Thomson/West.

Lee, Ian B (2002). "Fairness and Insider Trading," *Columbia Business Law Rev.* 2002:119.

Lucas, William R. et al. (1996). "Common Sense, Flexibility, and Enforcement of the Federal Securities Laws" *Business Law Rev.* 51:1221.

Manne, Henry G. (1996). *Insider Trading and the Stock Market*. New York: The Free Press.

Memorandum from Max Hendrick, III (October 15, 2001) outside counsel for Enron at Vinson & Elkins law firm, to James V. Derrick, Jr., Enron General Counsel, available on *Houston Chronicle* website, <http://www.chron.com/content/ chronicle/special/01/enron/background/index.html>

Moohr, Geraldine Szott (1998). "Mail Fraud Meets Criminal Theory," *University of Cincinnati Law Rev.* 67:1.

Moore, Michael S. (1997). *Placing Blame*. Oxford: Oxford University Press.

Murphy, Jeffrie G. (1985). "Retributivism, Moral Education, and the Liberal Estate," *Criminal Justice Ethics* (Winter/Spring) 3.

Nightingale, Brenda L. (1996). *The Law of Fraud and Related Offences*. Toronto: Carswell Pub.

Pettit, Philip (1991). "Consequentialism," in Peter Singer (ed.), *A Companion to Ethics*. Oxford: Blackwell Publishers.

Podgor, Ellen S. (1999). "Criminal Fraud," *American University Law Rev.* 48:729.

Proceedings of the Academic Workshop (1996), "Definitional Dilemma: Can and Should There Be a Universal Definition of White Collar Crime?" Richmond, VA: National White Collar Crime Center.

Rakoff, Jed S. (1980). "The Federal Mail Fraud Statute (Part I)," *Duquesne Law Rev.* 18:771.

Scheffler, Samuel (ed.) (1988). *Consequentialism and its Critics*. Oxford: Oxford University Press.

Scheppele, Kim Lane (1993). "It's Just Not Right: The Ethics of Insider Trading" *Law & Contemporary Problems* 56:123.

Schonsheck, Jonathan (1994). *On Criminalization: An Essay in the Philosophy of Criminal Law*. Dordrecht: Kluwer Academic Publishers.

Shapiro, Susan (1990). "Collaring the Crime, Not the Criminal: Reconsidering the Concept of White-Collar Crime," *American Sociological Rev.* 55:346.

Simester, A.P. & Andrew von Hirsch (2002). "Rethinking the Offense Principle" *Legal Theory* 8:269.

Strudler, Alan & Eric W. Orts (1999). "Moral Principle in the Law of Insider Trading, *Texas Law Rev.* 78:375.

Sutherland, Edwin H (1940). "White-Collar Criminality," 5 *American Sociological Review* 5:1, reprinted in Gilbert Geis & Robert F. Meier (eds.) (1977), *White-Collar Crime*. New York: Free Press.

von Hirsch, Andrew (1986). *Doing Justice: The Choice of Punishments*. Boston: Northeastern University Press, reprint ed.

Weinreb, Lloyd L. (1998). *Criminal Law: Cases, Comment, Questions*. New York: Foundation Press, 6th ed.

Weisburd, David, et al. (1991). *Crimes of the Middle Classes: White-Collar Offenders in the Federal Court*. New Haven: Yale University Press.

Wells, Celia (2001). *Corporations and Criminal Responsibility*. Oxford: Oxford University Press, 2d ed.

Cases cited

Cady, Roberts & Co., 40 S.E.C. 907, 912 (1961)
Chiarella v. United States, 445 U.S. 222 (1980)
Devegter, United States v. 198 F.3d 1324 (11th Cir. 1999)
Dirks v. SEC, 463 U.S. 646 (1983)
Doren [1982] 66 C.C.C. (2d) 448 (Canada)
Durland v. United States, 161 U.S. 306 (1896)
Fasulo v. United States, 272 U.S. 620 (1926)
Frost, United States v. 125 F.3d 346 (6th Cir. 1997)
Gregory v. United States, 253 F.2d 104 (5th Cir. 1958)
Hammerschmidt v. United States, 265 U.S. 182 (1924)
Jain, United States v. 93 F.3d 436 (8th Cir. 1996)
Laidlaw v. Oregon, 15 U.S. (2 Wheat.) 178 (1817)
Mandel, United States v. 591 F.2d 1347 (4th Cir. 1979)
McNally v. United States, 483 U.S. 350 (1987)
O'Hagan, United States v. 521 U.S. 642 (1997)

Olan [1978] 2 S.C.R. 1175 (Canada)
Regent Office Supply, United States v. 421 F.2d 1174 (2d Cir. 1970)
SEC v. Switzer, 590 F. Supp. 756 (W.D. Okla. 1984)
SEC v. Texas Gulf Suphur Co., 401 F.2d 833 (2d Cir. 1968)
Vinyard, United States v. 266 F.3d 320 (4th Cir. 2001)

Legislation cited

15 U.S.C. §§ 77x, 78ff (securities fraud)
15 U.S.C. § 78j(b) (insider trading)
18 U.S.C. § 157 (bankruptcy fraud)
18 U.S.C. § 201(bribery)
18 U.S.C. § 371 (conspiracy to commit fraud)
18 U.S.C. § 1030 (computer fraud)
18 U.S.C. § 1341 (mail fraud)
18 U.S.C. § 1343 (wire fraud)
18 U.S.C. § 1344 (bank fraud)
18 U.S.C. § 1346 (mail fraud)
18 U.S.C. § 1347 (health care fraud)
18 U.S.C. § 1503 (obstruction of justice)
18 U.S.C. § 1621 (perjury)
21 U.S.C. § 331 (Food, Drug & Cosmetic Act)
26 U.S.C. § 7201 (tax fraud)
31 U.S.C. § 3730 (False Claims Act)
33 U.S.C. § 1319 (Clean Water Act)
17 C.F.R. § 240.10b-5 (insider trading)
Model Penal Code § 2.02(2)
Model Penal Code § 223 (theft)
Criminal Code (Canada) 380(1) (fraud)
Theft Act, 1968, ch. 60, §§ 1, 7, 15 (Eng.)

2

The Corporation as a Legally Created Site of Irresponsibility

Harry Glasbeek

The Argument

The recent Enron-type scandals were portrayed as assaults by venal corporate officials and their ethically challenged professional advisors on the legitimacy of the Anglo-American corporation and, therefore, as attacks on everything that is to be treasured. They were depicted as a form of terrorism by evil-doers who hate decency and achievement. The overblown analogy came easily to "spin doctors." The 9/11 assaults had destroyed the towers that symbolized the interconnection between the American way of life and the corporation. George W. Bush embraced this imagery when he signed the remedial Sarbanes-Oxley Act into law:

> During the past year the American economy has faced several sudden challenges and proven its great resiliency. Terrorists attacked the center and symbol of our prosperity.... And now corporate corruption has struck at investor confidence, offending the conscience of our nation. Yet, in the aftermath of September the 11th, we refuse to allow fear to undermine our economy. And we will not allow fraud to undermine it either.... [T]he law says to honest corporate leaders: your integrity will be recognized and rewarded, because the shadow of suspicion will be lifted from good companies that respect the rules."[1]

Despite the rhetoric, however, the steps taken did not amount to an attempt at regime change. Rather, the focus was to reassure the public that, as bad apples would be taken out of the barrel, it would be safer than ever to invest in private corporations and that this would help to provide ever-increasing economic welfare.

For the moment, it appears that this response has worked. The worst is over. The sharp edge of this, the latest of the recurrent legitimacy crises for Anglo-American corporations, has been blunted. Shareholders are still investing in the equity markets and there are no calls for a radical revamping, let alone an abandonment, of the corporate form. Indeed, at the time of writing, the corporate elites and their professional servants are calling for a dilution of the Sarbanes-Oxley Act. Its reforms, structurally unchallenging as they were, are portrayed as imposing too many costs on the corporate sectors which, once again, are posited as generally virtuous and benign.[2]

The resilience of the corporation is great. After all, the eye-catching Enron/Worldcom/Adelphia, etc. saga, has been followed by a daily parade of familiar-looking wrongdoings (at, for example, Fannie Mae, HealthSouth, Merck, AIG, Bristol-Myers, Nortel, General Re, Krispy Kreme, KPMG, New York Stock Exchange/Grasso). There is a long tradition of corporate excesses and abuses. Occasionally, they accumulate into a large cluster of ugliness and give rise to public outrage. Then policy-makers come in, adjust the sleeve of the emperor, and soon all goes on as before. This paper addresses questions and issues that arise from this sorry cycle of deviance–regulation–deviance.

The Anglo-American publicly traded corporation bestrides our political economy as a colossus. It is a center of economic and political power. Its exercise of that power needs to be seen as legitimate, lest overt coercion be used to enable it to attain its goals. The question that arises is, Why does the modern corporation, which has been mistrusted since its emergence as a dominant form of enterprise (Smith, Arnold, Hurst, Horowitz, Dahl), repeatedly engage in potentially self-destructive activities? The answer proffered is that it cannot help it. It is legally built that way. The argument is as follows:

1. The corporation is the principal legal device deployed to achieve capitalism's goals; the attainment of those objectives is the corporation's primary purpose.
2. The goals of contemporary capitalism may be summarized to be the private accumulation of socially produced wealth by means of competition. It envisages an unequal division of wealth in which a relatively few individuals control most of the wealth in the economy. In the competitive economic situations fostered, individual owners of wealth use their disproportionate economic clout to pit non-wealth-owners against each other and against their physical environment as they struggle to get the opportunity to produce and, thereby get a share of the pie that is primarily consumed by commanding owners of wealth. The nature of the exercise means that it is driven by avarice, fear, and luck and promotes the perpetuation of inequality in favor of those in the best position to take advantage. This is not an easy political "sell."
3. In mature capitalism, much of this philosophically and ethically troubling economic activity is engaged in by means of the corporation. The corporation is not only designed to facilitate the wealth-owners' agenda by making it mechanically easier to generate wealth and to accumulate it, but its legal trappings help hide the essential brutality and indifference to the plight of others that characterize these profit-maximizing activities. A good deal of intellectual and ideological massaging is needed to maintain the standing of the corporation, a pivotal economic actor, as an acceptable legal/political institution.
4. We do not proclaim ourselves to be a capitalist political economy but, rather, a liberal market capitalist democracy. The emphasis in conventional public discourse is on the concepts "liberal," "market", and "democracy" found in that phrase. Only since the fall of the Soviet Union has the word "capitalist" come to be used commonly in our political conversations. Its hard-to-sell characteristics now are less threatening to its hegemony. Law continues to describe itself as liberal law, dedicated to the maintenance of liberal values. These values posit the equal sovereignty of all individuals and eschew the notion of coercion of any kind. That our liberal legal regime purports to pursue these values is amply demonstrated by our repeated claims to adhere

to the rule of law, that is, to fair processes and neutral applications of the law by neutral adjudicators who treat all individuals as equals before, according to, and under the law. We continuously assert that to safeguard the autonomy of individuals the coercive powers necessarily bestowed on the State must be kept in check by watchful politicians, judges, and constitutional bills of rights.

5. But law is not just liberal law. Just as in a feudal political economy law rejected any notion that individuals were created equal, or just as, in a socialist polity, law would/should abide by basic socialist values—for example, that those who have abilities should provide for the needs of those that do not—in a capitalist political economy, our political economy, law strives to satisfy capitalism's needs. Its primary need is to allow individuals to accumulate socially produced wealth. This need may, indeed is likely to, demand the use of anti-liberal practices, of coercion and exploitation by the powerful of the powerless. It becomes important for law to mask that fact. This is important both to legal institutions that justify themselves on the basis that they advance liberalism and the equality of all and to the hegemony of capitalism. It becomes the task of law to hold out to the world that it pursues liberal democratic goals while it quietly promotes the private accumulation of socially produced wealth. In part, law does this by pretending that, when it creates a corporation, it is merely facilitating economic activities that dovetail with the ideological consensus, with liberal market principles. That is, law emphasizes its facilitative and ideological functions to hide the structural role it plays in the creation of the conditions necessary to capitalist relations of production. The maintenance of the structures that ensure the viability of capitalist relations of production is portrayed as a normal by-product of its facilitative/instrumental interventions, i.e., an unintended, not a legally engineered, result. This genie cannot be kept in the bottle. Corporate shenanigans cause it to pop out from time to time. This is so because the corporation is more than a piece of facilitative machinery established to support a liberal market economy. Primarily, it is meant to be a capitalist device. Given law's tightrope-walker's task of having to advance, simultaneously, the needs of both a mediated liberal market and of unvarnished capitalism, its chief vehicle, the corporation, has had the tension between the liberal market and raw capitalism built into its architecture.
6. In order to allow capitalists to pursue their goals, corporate law has given powers and incentives to wealth-owners that enable and invite them to avoid the restraints that liberal doctrines impose on citizens outside the corporate setting. This generates legitimacy difficulties in all sorts of circumstances, but they are most likely to get political attention when it is wealth-owners themselves who complain about other wealth-owners' use of the potential for coercion, exploitation, and abuse that inheres in the corporate form. These episodes are frequent because, while capitalist relations of production can be described as a system, its protagonists, capitalists, are anarchic. By definition, they look after their interests, not the system's. If an institution or process can be exploited to advantage, as the legally created Anglo-American corporation can be, it will be. This is tolerable to wealth-owners when it is not their class that is victimized, but not when—as in the Enron scandals—it is they who are plundered by those among them who have used the elasiticity of the corporate form in an unexpected manner.

The Legal Architecture of the Corporation I—Romance and Reality

For a long time, the notion that investors should have an unalloyed right to combine their wealth to garner more wealth by the registration of their business venture as a corporation was anathema to leading political thinkers. They believed that the ensuing concentration of perpetually accumulating wealth in private hands was a threat to the liberal democratic institutions they favored. It was seen as a potential source of abuse.[3] A much-cited passage from a judgment by Justice Brandeis, writing in dissent, captures the depth of this early angst:

> Although the value of this instrumentality in commerce and industry was fully recognized, incorporation for business was commonly denied long after it had been freely granted for religious, educational and charitable purposes. It was denied because of fear. Fear of encroachment upon the liberties and opportunities of the individual. Fear of the subjugation of labor to capital. Fear of monopoly. Fear that the absorption of capital by corporations, and their perpetual life, might bring evils.[4]

While the argument in this paper is that these fears were, and remain, well-founded, they are no longer permitted to stand in the way of corporate dominance. Today, incorporation by a simple act of registration is treated as a birthright in Anglo-American jurisdictions.

Any number of persons (indeed, a lone individual) may form a corporation by submitting the appropriate form and fee to a state-appointed bureaucrat. The firm should not have any overt criminal purposes, nor should its submitted name allow it to be confused with an existing business. There is no requirement to declare that the corporation will have a defined business goal, nor that it will have a certain amount of capital. Once the request for registration is accepted, a corporation comes into existence. It is to be a person with all the legal capacities of a human being. It is, therefore, a person distinct from all other persons in our polity, including its founders. They, in turn, because they may have invested some of their wealth in this creature in order to have it generate more wealth for them, are deemed to have a special relationship with it, one that is different from that which other suppliers of wealth, such as creditors or workers, have with the corporation. They are given a certificate that evidences their share of the contribution of capital made to the corporation. They are shareholders. Their certificate entitles them to the appropriate fraction of future income yielded by the corporation's profit-seeking uses of the contributed capitals. The contributed capitals became the property of the corporation upon the instant of its birth, upon registration. To ensure that the corporation engages in effective profit-maximizing activities, the shareholders are given the right to appoint an oversight board, a board of directors, whose legal duty it is to set appropriate policies. The directors are to appoint and monitor executives who are to implement these policies. Shareholders can dismiss directors who disappoint them and, in some defined circumstances, are entitled to submit policy proposals to their boards of directors.

Manifestly, this is legal machinery that has gone out of its way to facilitate the establishment of corporations. The instrumental convenience of the form has come to be seen as trumping the potential for abuse that so worried earlier policy-makers and commentators despite daily, often vivid, reminders—from the Enrons, the AIGs, WorldComs, to the asbestos producers, the Bhopals, Exxon-Valdezes, Love Canals, Dalkin Shields, Mercks—that the fears harbored by Justice Brandeis and his predecessors about the inherent dangers of the corporate form have relevance today. There are no serious suggestions that the utility of the corporation is to be questioned. In part, this is so because it is widely believed that the massive output of wealth achieved by means of the corporate business form cannot be matched by other forms of enterprise, certainly not by a return to greater reliance on sole ownership or small-scale enterprise. That is, the end results provide a reason for living with the publicly-traded corporation.[5] But, as this grounding of legitimacy is empirically contestable (Greenfield, 2005), the position of the corporation would be far less secure than it actually is if it were its only justification for existence: the ends might not be seen to justify the means, especially as some of the means employed to achieve these ends are notoriously odious. More, then, is needed to explain the corporation's apparent stranglehold on our faith in its virtue.

Political and economic support for the corporation's legitimacy is found in its legal design, the design that purports to facilitate the workings of a business form that dovetails with law's liberal market precepts. Let us return to the legal architecture of the corporation.

Romance

For legal purposes, the corporation is an individual, that is, it has the legal—if not the sentient—characteristics and attributes of any human being. The significance of this construction is that it has those characteristics and attributes that make it a political unit that is compatible with our notions of liberalism. Consequently, it is bestowed a political standing, one that enhances its legitimacy in our polity. This is reflected in the legal treatment it gets. It is not that which might be accorded a menacing institution, that is, the law does not start off by limiting the political rights of a corporation because its potential power is dangerous to our social relations. On the contrary, the corporation is, like you and I, put in a legal position to ask for protections and safeguards to ward off the potentially coercive power of the State. Like human beings, it may challenge the State's attempts to tell the corporation how to deploy its private property. Its arguments to have regulations invalidated or curbed have the resonance of all such arguments made by sovereign individuals in a liberal political system where the individual is king. The corporation has been allowed to claim due process, free speech rights, and the like, and it has done so to telling effect (Glasbeek, 2002).[6] While the corporation does not always succeed, it is the assumed legal justification for its claims that enhances its standing as a legitimate political unit in our liberal polity. Every time that a corporation plausibly exercises its claim to political rights accorded to human beings, it reinforces its political standing, it adds to the credibility of its proponents' contention that it is to be treated as a citizen, a valued member of civil society, not a danger to it.

In an analogous way, the legal characterization of this non-human person as a distinct property-owning individual gives it the appearance of being the equivalent of the individual self-seeking economic actor made famous by Adam Smith as the cornerstone of his idealized market model. The legal design of the corporation presents it as the equivalent of "the butcher, the brewer, or the baker," from whose egoistic, anarchic activities all of us can expect our dinner. The market was proffered by Adam Smith, and is advocated by his legion of contemporary followers, as a machine that leads to an efficient use of resources and talents if it is not fettered, corrupted by collusion, or spoiled by imperfect information and communication. Participants in the market are, therefore, unconscious, but effective, servants of the public weal. The legal design of the corporation presents it as just another market actor, another individual contributor to the public good. Obviously, this starting position does a lot to offset suggestions that the corporation is inimical to social welfare.

The ensuing enhancement of the corporation's legitimacy is given further impact by the fact that, in a liberal polity, the market machinery is not only seductive because of the economic benefits it promises, but also because of its political appeal. Liberal law's focus on the promotion of the sovereignty of the political individual dovetails with the tenets of the idealized market model. This model, like liberalism, emphasizes the centrality of the autonomy of all individuals to choose what to think, how to act, how to make the most of themselves. Not only is this economically efficient but, if all of us determine for ourselves what to do with our resources and talents in a competitive market setting, all of us, as individuals, will be making choices about what we want to do, make, purchase, exchange, etc. There will be little need for a planner, a coordinating authority, to tell us what to ask for, what to produce, how our resources and talents should be used, how the outcomes of our individual efforts should be allocated. In short, there will be little reason to have political decisions made on our behalf by others, by government. This makes *economic* market actors virtuous *political* actors in a liberal political regime.[7] A legal architecture that gives corporations an a priori standing as market actors gives corporations both economic and political legitimacy.

There is at least one other way in which the legal design of the corporation, in combination with the history of its economic development, supports the social and political legitimacy of this essentially capitalist device. It has been noted that, when investors determine to conduct their business by means of a corporation, they make a contribution of capital which, upon the registration of that business as a legal person, becomes the property of that new person, of the corporation. But, to call it a person does not actually make it one in the ordinary sense of that word; it is a legal description, not a biological one. It has no physical capacities, no intellect of its own: hence, the appointment of a board of directors and, in due course, a set of managers to execute this board's policies. In large, publicly traded corporations where many (hundreds, thousands, sometimes millions) of people come to be shareholders; this leads to the much-discussed separation between owners of capital and a management that controls that capital. This phenomenon is a source of anxiety for those who want to characterize the corporation as a market actor. After all, in Adam Smith's ideal world, the butcher, brewer, and baker both contributed the capital *and* decided how to deploy it. They could be counted on to be as efficient as their capacities permitted because they would reap all the rewards as owners/controllers of the invested resources and bear all the costs of the materialized risks their efforts produced. A separation of ownership of property from control over that property would lead to inefficiencies. This caused Adam Smith to be caustic about the utility of joint stock companies (whether incorporated or not), that is, of large businesses in which managers, not owners, made decisions about the uses of capital.[8]

This issue, the potential inefficiency of the large, widely held, corporation as a market actor, remains a central problematic preoccupying corporate scholarship. It was revived by the Berle and Means findings published in 1932. The issue will be revisited briefly in the next section. For the moment, however, the point is that, while the notion of ownership without control and control without ownership vexes many corporate cheerleaders, it also serves, in a rather unexpected manner, to boost the legitimacy of profit-maximization by means of the corporate vehicle.

As noted, capitalism involves the *private* accumulation of *socially* produced wealth. There is a taking; it is sought to make it acceptable by arguing that non-wealth-owners voluntarily agree to this taking, trying to make it appear to be the outcome of a fair exchange. This is not an easy position to maintain and the objective circumstance that there is a private accumulation of socially produced wealth obstinately continues to provide a basis for the argument that there is a basic conflict, a class conflict, between employers and workers, one that subjugates the rights and privileges of workers to those of employers, a subjugation that negates the tenets of a liberal political economy. When the owner of the invested capital also is the one who directly and daily controls its deployment, that is, when it is the butcher, brewer or baker who reaps the profits from what his workers produce, the subjugation, the class relations, tend to be readily visible. The existence of a pitched struggle between adversarial classes becomes less visible when the investors of capital in a specific firm are numerous and largely unknown to the workers directed by the investors' managerial cadres. The ownership of the property invested in the corporation becomes a legal fiction as shareholders are not effective owners, and the effective, deploying managers are not actual owners.[9] That is, the separation of ownership and control has an implicit meaning other than the one that worries market proponents so much. It provides fodder for an argument that the advent of the corporation has done away with the exploitation of non-property-owning workers by their property-owning employers. Indeed, this argument was—and still is—made by many corporate and labor relations theorists, who contend that the corporation is run by managers who are not extracting surplus value that is socially produced for the benefit of private accumulators but, rather, are professionals charged with the efficient deployment of socialized capital.[10] Hence, they may (and some would argue, should) eschew the maximization of profits on behalf of the capitalists who have invested equity capital in the corporation. They may (and, perhaps, should) take other investors and stakeholders' interests into account as they deploy the collectivized capitals entrusted to them.[11]

In short, there is suggestion that, once a large publicly traded corporation is an employer, the tension between private accumulation and socially generated wealth disappears. Any superior-inferior nexus of employment relations that remains is attributable to bureaucratic/managerial efficiency requirements rather than to antagonistic class relations reflecting the clash between owners of property, i.e., financial capital, on the one hand, and sellers of labor power, i.e., non-property owners, on the other. The legal design, then, when used to establish widely held corporations, allows for a different portrayal of giant corporations than the one proffered by Louis Brandeis and his fellow skeptics. Far from being a threat to our values and beliefs it may be presented as a progressive instrument in the advancement of liberalism.

In sum, the corporation is given great leeway because it produces the goods (in the sense of a lot of wealth) and, despite the recurrences of scandalizing behavior, the means that it uses to create wealth are adorned with legitimating features. In facilitating the formation of corporations, law has made the vehicle into one that, on its face, could, and should, act as sovereign individuals are expected to. But, the fly in the ointment is that this is not all that law does when it creates corporations.

Reality

Instrumentally, law creates an individual when it approves the registration of a corporation. It is this that permits the corporation to be cast as a potentially appropriate participant in an idealized market economy. But, the ideal market (contrast capitalism) is one in which no one individual is in a position to dictate prices or demands to any other individual. Individuals must rely on their own resources and talents and compete with all others who are doing the same. The market is to be free from coercion. By definition, collusion by individuals to gain competitive advantage is not to be tolerated. This is why, economically, we have antitrust legislation. This is why, politically, we hate collectives and combinations. It is these starting points that furnish law with the justification to restrict workers who want to form trade unions. Their purpose is to restrain competition,[12] a clear "no-no" in a market economy. This is why, after decades of struggle, trade unionism continually needs to fight for its political legitimacy.

Here is a difficulty. The corporation generates more wealth than individual discrete market investors might precisely because it has combined their wealth and brought them under a coordinating managerial team. *Legally* characterized as an individual, *functionally* the corporation is designed (by law) to be a collective of capitals and resources. This furthers the goal of capitalist accumulation of wealth but appears to undermine the approved means of wealth production in a liberal market society. Despite the technical appearance and popular portrayal of the corporation as a bunch of coordinating individuals, law has created an institution that, structurally, has potentially coercive powers. Theoretically, this is a threat to the supposed overall goals of liberal law and the idealized market model. But it is not just a theoretical problem. When the logic of promoting the collectivization of many capitals reaches its natural zenith, the legal corporate vehicle actually operates to distort the market as a whole.

The structured-in, but not necessarily activated, coercive power of the corporate aggregation of discrete capitals and human talents menace liberal market principles most when corporations have come to occupy a dominant position in a market because of their size. Their size then vastly exceeds that which isolated individuals could match because of their capacity to gather lots of discrete contributions and to have them *function* as one mass of collectivized capital. It is then that the fears harbored by Brandeis and his predecessors clearly show themselves as having been, and continuing to be, warranted.

Oligopolistic and monopolistic, that is, anticompetitive, practices dominate our economies despite public rhetoric about the benefits of fierce competition between a myriad of small firms.[13] Huge corporate enterprises dictate terms of trade to suppliers and workers. To take an admittedly extreme example—but one that illustrates the general situation—consider the case of Wal-Mart. Its success in capturing the lion's share of retail marketing means that smaller businesses compete fiercely to be allowed to supply it. In a sense, then, the large collectives enhance competition among the smaller fry. But, that competition is not easily described as autonomous activity. The suppliers are forced to deal with a particular person (Wal-Mart) and prices are set by Wal-Mart. In turn, the supplying corporations coerce whomsoever they can to meet Wal-Mart's demands, often workers in parlous circumstances in poorer countries. Their market activities are only notionally free. Fishman's study of Wal-Mart led him to conclude that "[t]he giant retailer's low prices often come with a high cost. Wal-Mart's relentless pressure can crush the companies it does business with and force them to send jobs overseas. Are we shopping our way straight to the unemployment line?"[14]

While large corporations may compete with each other for market share by waging advertising wars and the like, the clout of their critical mass of collectivized capital may lead to oppressions elsewhere. Or, to put it more politically: the legal architecture of the corporation promotes the functional collectivization of capitals. Not only is this collectivization abhorrent to market ideology in principle, but in large aggregations, private accumulators, instead of being islolated actors without power over the behavior of others, are put into a position, by law, to structure the markets in which these others must operate. They are empowered to do what liberal market proponents say elected governments should be inhibited from doing. From this perspective—one that underpins much publicly expressed unease with the so-called big business or the "corporate agenda"—the legally created corporation looms as a menace to liberal institutions (Deetz, Nadel).

This position is countered by very influential conservative scholars. Their technique is to argue that, whether an incorporated business is large or small, incorporation never creates an organization that transcends the rights and responsibilities of the individuals who set up the firm. The law and economics school is acknowledged to be the dominant provider of this kind of justificatory theoretical framework.[15] It contends that the corporate person is a mere convenience. The reality is that a number of individuals have decided to maximize their opportunities by collaborating with each other. They are contractually bound to each other; superficial judgments to the contrary notwithstanding, there is no collective, no combination, just a bunch of contracts between sovereign individuals using a legal facility. This line of argument furnishes a host of plausible ripostes to those who would cast doubt on the legitimacy of the corporation.

It posits that shareholders, despite the legal formal legal transformation of the corporation into a property owner, remain the real owners of the invested capital. This characterization of corporate ownership as a facilitating convenience rather than as a concrete change sideswipes those who would argue that claims for favored treatment of shareholders ought to be rejected. Similarly, this approach relieves the anxiety caused by the alleged separation between control and ownership. Under the law and economics umbrella, investors of capital are owners who have delegated control, not given it up. If there are glitches because the contract terms between the shareholders/owners and their managerial delegates are not detailed enough or because they are too difficult to police, judicial and statutory interventions imposing duties on the delegatees/agents to overcome these contractual imperfections may be warranted. From this vantage point, the troubling theoretical questions raised by the ownership without control and control without ownership phenomenon is transmuted into a series of technical problems, problems that are not sufficiently fundamental to undermine the legitimacy of the corporation as an efficient business form in a market economy. And, directly pertinent to the contention that the collectivization of capitals should not be an economic or political concern, the premise that a corporation is a convenient way to deal with a bunch of individual contracts between politically sovereign market actors means that the use of the corporation does not signal that there has been any erosion of the idealized liberal market model.

This is not the place to engage with this elegant line of justification of the corporation as an appropriate institution in a market economy, although there are many salient critiques of it.[16] But, even if it is granted some credibility, the contract-nexus theorization does not do away with some elemental facts. The large, widely held corporation does distort the operation of suppliers' and labor markets and does have an unwanted impact on the workings of liberal electoral democratic institutions. A wealthy business person or a large unincorporated business firm might well have great market leverage but nowhere near as much as the huge corporations that dot the contemporary scene. On the economic front, their size and power are unmatchable by other business forms for which the bringing together of so many investors has not been made as legally easy and, as we are about to see, so legally enticing. And, politically, while individual wealth-owners also can be very effective in having their goals cared for by elected politicians by funding their causes and campaigns and by their ultimate threat to withhold investment, none of those electorally disturbing strategies are as easily implemented by rich individuals as they are by large corporations. Once incorporated, the impact of the threat of de-investment is greater because the amounts that might be withheld are larger. More, it is politically easier to make the threat and to lobby. Individuals buried inside a corporation do not have to reveal their selfish and crass interests; corporate controllers of the capitals amassed in these corporations can be used to advertise ideas that serve the investors' avaricious interests, push for certain policies to frame politics so as to better suit their narrow needs, often via think-tanks and learned institutions that corporations fund for these purposes and that ostensibly speak for the public's welfare; and, via their corporations, the hidden investors can offer employment opportunities to policymakers, rendering them more receptive to entreaties to be kind to wealth-owners. All this can be done without the links between specific favor-seeking wealth-owners and particular politicians and policymakers becoming explicit. Equally important, as a matter of perception, it is more effective for wealth-owners inside corporations to cow elected officials by corporate threats of non-investment, as the decision-making can be presented to the world as a bureaucratic one impelled by market forces operating on an impersonal, apolitical institution. The wealth-owners, who hide behind this veil of technocracy, do not have to go public as they would have to do if they directly sought hand-outs for themselves; they do not have to reveal themselves as unpatriotic as they would have to do if they personally menaced the government with the threat of taking their capital to a foreign country.

In the words of Lewis Lapham (1996), there are now two governments, namely, a provisional government constituted by those institutions that formally govern us and that we subject to the rule of law, rather than the rule of men; and the permanent government, comprising the Fortune 500 corporations, their lobbyists, the media, the advertisers, and the financial and legal advisers they own or command. The provisional government is, says Lapham, expected to live "within the cage of high-minded principle," while many matters of substance, notionally subject to liberal democratic decision-making, are decided by the so-called permanent government because it generates the wealth on which the provisional government depends for its legitimacy. This permanent government is ruled by the rich, by "men," not by law.[17] Ironically, it is two other features of corporate law that make this rule by men peculiarly inimical to the legitimating liberal market model.

In return for agreeing to combine their personal capital with that of other investors in a corporation whose management is to coordinate the optimal deployment of the combined capitals, the shareholders are promised not only a right to a share of any future profits and the right to appoint directors and vote on significant issues, but they are also blessed with limited fiscal liability. That is, they cannot be asked for more money than they already have invested. They cannot be made to contribute to any debts or obligations owed by the corporation as a consequence of its pursuit of profits on behalf of these shareholders. All they ever have at risk is the amount they invested in the corporation when they bought the shares. That is, unlike the butcher, brewer, or baker, their other personal wealth cannot be subjected to these debts and obligations incurred when trying to maximize the return on their investment.

There are good arguments to justify this arresting departure from the market model. Like the arguments made in support of the corporation because of its capacity to generate economic welfare, they are based on the notion that the apparently aberrant grant of limited liability leads to efficiency in terms of wealth creation. Limited liability allows investors to spread their capital over a large number of risk-taking enterprises, rather than a few relatively less risky ones to which they would restrict themselves if their personal wealth was at risk in each enterprise. Further, in the absence of limited liability, the less well-off investors might invest in higher-risk firms than would investors with a great deal of personal wealth on which creditors might call. Wealthier investors would have a different sense of what a corporation's shares should be worth than would their less well-off cohorts. This would make for very unstable stock markets.[18] Such arguments to legitimate the departures from liberal and market tenets that limited liability entails are based on the notion that the ends justify the unacceptable means.

Limited liability for shareholders ought to be anathema to a political economy adhering to individual initiative and responsibility. The abdication from principle that limited liability represents is exacerbated when the benefiting investors have put their capital into either a very large, publicly traded corporation or a very small corporation whose shares are not to be bought and sold. In the first situation they can sell their shares, side-stepping any further impacts of risks created by the corporation in the past or future. This draws attention to what should be—to contract-based analysts—another problem generated by the legal design of the modern corporation: the relations between shareholders is based solely on their monetary ties. They have no personal relations.

Once again, the conservative scholars of the law and economics persuasion have to attempt a rescue, lest the legally devised corporation comes to be seen as a perverter of the market arrangements that they claim leads to an efficient economy and a free polity. They persist in their far-fetched claim that, despite the impersonality of relationships between the owners of investing capitals, they are contractually connected. More, they argue that limited liability for these sovereign contractors does not present a dilemma because it is only an illusory avoidance of market responsibility. After all, the *corporation* does not have the luxury of limited liability. *It* is fully responsible for the debts and obligations it incurs, just as any ideal market participant is meant to be.[19] Ireland has definitively and sharply noted the incoherence of this argument, coming as it does from those who insist that the corporate form is a mere convenience, that the real market actors are the investors and the other marketeers with whom they contract.

The strained nature of the law and economics justification of limited liability is further demonstrated by the difficulties this school has when the corporation is the vehicle for a small business with little capital. Then the argument that limited liability for shareholders is fine because the corporation bears the full risk is manifestly hollow. All too often, creditors and injured people will be left with a useless remedy against an impecunious corporate person. The combined operation of the separate personality and limited liability doctrines will let readily visible risk-creators off the hook for harms inflicted by their barely hidden selves.[20] This creates a cornucopia for lawyers and law teachers as they analyze the jurisprudence that has evolved as courts are asked to ignore the corporate person altogether in these situations. The result, of course, is incoherence and, worse, a questioning of the wisdom of the separate personality and limited liability doctrines. The operation of these doctrines in these small business settings not only brings the judiciary into disrepute, but also the claim that the corporate institution can be made consonant with a liberal market model.

To counter this questioning, the more thoughtful law and economics scholars have suggested that limited liability ought not to be available to investors in very small corporations or, more logically, in situations where the plaintiffs are involuntary creditors, such as workers in respect of a bankruptcy or victims of a tort committed by the corporation.[21] While such refinements would go some way to offset the delegitimizing aspects of limited liability for supposedly sovereign actors, they have not been given legal life, most likely because, once legislators embarked on this slippery slope, it would be harder and harder to maintain separate personality (with its property-owning and individualizing characteristics) and limited liability as the universal, founding principles of the corporation. In short, despite stout defenses in academic journals and books and despite some suggestions for amendments that would allow us to keep the corporate baby while purifying its bath water, limited liability remains available to investors in all types of corporations; it remains embedded as an anti-liberal, anti-market feature of the modern corporation. Its toxic effect is made more disagreeable by another feature of the legal design of the corporation.

As seen earlier, the law and economics scholars and their corporate allies insist that shareholders are the true owners of the corporate business and that they remain in control as principals who can discipline their agents. Yet, when a corporation, in its efforts to maximize profits on behalf of its shareholders, engages in violations of law, *it* will be held responsible, *it* may be punished. The investors will not be. There are a number of explanations for this, all of them discomfiting for the law and economics school. First, the legal irresponsibility of shareholders could be justified on the basis that, legally, their invested capital has become the property of the corporation, despite the right they have to share in the residue of the corporation's capital after it has been wound up and all of its debts paid. This reasoning fits with the law as written and with the concept of the corporation as a sovereign person distinct from its investors and every one else.[22] It does not dovetail with the reasoning of those who contend that the corporation does not distort the market schema because it is a mere convenience used by individual, responsible marketeers who have invested property they continue to own.

Another possible justification for the shareholders' immunity in respect of legal infractions committed as the corporation seeks profits on their behalf is that they are not in control of the corporation and its managers. Again, while, functionally, this is true of many of the shareholders, this line of argument is destructive of the one that maintains that the owners of the firm are in control, that they have—for efficiency reasons—assigned the task of implementing their wishes to agents whom they can control. The resulting erosion of legitimacy is palpable. To hold a corporation criminally responsible for, say, a wrongful killing in the workplace or for the injuries caused by products designed with a reckless indifference to the safety of consumers, while no flesh and blood human being who profited from these outrages is held to account, offends a public taught that serious departures from well-known standards of care should lead to personal sanctions.

Note here that the problem is aggaravated by the fact that corporations are rarely sanctioned criminally. It is hard to hold the bloodless corporation criminally responsible.[23] It is conceptually difficult: it has no mind to which the criminal intent can be attributed; it has no physical capacity to act on the intent. Its thoughts and conduct are those of human beings. It is necessary to find someone whose thoughts and acts can be said to be those of the corporation. Jurisprudence varies across jurisdictions but, for the most part, it is only those who can be said to occupy positions of significance in the corporation, its guiding mind and will, whose conduct will be held to be that of the corporation.[24] In those jurisdictions where such a person or persons must be found to have acted with the appropriate criminal state of mind before the corporation can be held criminally liable, another delegitimizing problem arises. When that person acts as the guiding mind and will, s/he will be acting as the corporation, rather than as a sovereign individual choosing conduct for her/his own reasons. That is, these corporate actors should, as shareholders are able to do, be able to claim personal legal immunity because the wrongful conduct was the corporation's, not theirs. This leaves no one but the corporation, a creature of law without any sentient attributes, to punish. Law and economic scholars argue that this is sufficient because the investing public and the potential managerial pool of labor will use their bargaining leverage to discipline corporations that attract liabilities of this kind. They will not want to invest in corporations that may face costly sanctions because of their management's conduct and/or that have had their reputation besmirched.[25] But, this reasoning does little to assuage the outrage of the public that witnesses the commission of many wrongs and harms with no one human being held responsible. In recent times, therefore, over the shrill objection of law and economic scholars, senior officials have had positive duties imposed on them and when their corporations breach those duties, machinery is set in motion that may lead to their punishment for these corporate infractions. The need for policy-makers to resort to this kind of stratagem is evidence of the legitimacy problems created by the twin attributes of limited liability and total legal immunity for shareholders.[26]

In sum, corporate law, infused by liberal market principles as it must be and as the first section showed it is, nonetheless reveals that the corporation is not just another way for individuals to participate in liberal market practices. It is manifest that the brute capitalist agenda, viz., the private accumulation of socially produced wealth, is central to the design of the corporation. Unsurprisingly, this inherent tension leads to deviance.

The Legal Architecture of the Corporation II—Incentives and Deviance

The law and economics scholars' contentions are logically problematic and historically threadbare. Yet, they rule the roost because their arguments to the effect that corporations are a legitimate convenience for competitive property-owning and controlling market actors are reflected in actual practices. The investing classes benefit from their arguments that justify their corporate law privileges and, in turn, the investors' success with legislators and policy-makers boosts the law and economics school's prestige. Whatever may have been the situation in the past, in the last twenty-five years or so, certainly in the United States, the United Kingdom, Australia, and Canada, it has been conventional wisdom that corporations should be, and are, run for their "real owners," for the shareholders. In the United States this is so clear that it was the unabashed rationale for the enactment of the Sarbanes-Oxley legislation. Elsewhere, a slew of government reports, recommendations, and studies has adopted this perspective (Hampel Committee, Cadbury Committee, Company Law Review Steering Committee, TSE, Committee on Corporate Governance), as have a plethora of academic assessments.[27] Echoing the observations about the end of class politics by Bell in the immediate aftermath of World War II and the end of history by Fukuyama after the fall of the Soviet, leading law and economic scholars have announced the end of history for corporate law: shareholder primacy can no longer be denied; stakeholder politics are not only passé, but have become irrelevant; moreover, the rest of the world will have no option but to follow the Anglo-American lead and promote the cause of corporate shareholders in order to create economic welfare.[28]

These to-be-privileged shareholders can make money in two ways. First, if they remain invested in a corporation that does well over the long haul, they will profit from its success as a productive entity. But the fact that the corporation is indifferent about who furnishes the capital, provided it is retainable by the corporation, means that relatively few shareholders are expected to remain invested for the long haul. After all, shareholders also can make money by buying and selling shares. The share has become property in its own right, tradeable like any other commodity.[29] To be sure, the value of shares is tied to the competitive success of the corporation, but only in the loosest way (Stout). Famously, and somewhat acerbically, John Maynard Keynes (1936) characterized the stock market (that he played so successfully) as no more scientific than a beauty contest. He suggested that the price of a share had only the vaguest relationship to its value calculated with respect to the flow of future corporate profits. At any one time, the price of a share is a guess as to the future, a guess heavily influenced by a barrage of scientific and quasi-scientific reports, neutral and not-so-neutral assessments, and gossip. The 1990s boom and subsequent bust in technology stocks presents a poster case for the dysfunctionality of these information flows. It was amusingly, but most aptly, described by Cassidy as "dot.con: The Greatest Story Ever Sold." In addition, sentiments fanned by nationalism, fear, sporting events, the latest electoral results or prospects, etc., all play a part in pricing shares. It is a circumstance that invites speculation and fabrication.[30]

As shareholders are to be the major beneficiaries of corporate activities, they will pressure corporate managers to give them what they want: more profits and/or improved share values. As the shareholders have limited liability for any of the fiscal risks incurred, risks further minimized by their ability to sell their shares, and as they bear no legal responsibility for any aggressive profit-chasing on their behalf that goes off the rails, they have no legal incentive whatsoever to ensure that the managers behave decently. Indeed, they have a negative incentive to disregard the well-being of others. Managers are rewarded in terms of enhanced reputation and remuneration if they make shareholders happy. They have positive incentives to push the legal and social envelopes as far as they possibly can be pushed. The scales are tipped in favor of deviance by the state of corporate law.

In terms of making the corporation a long-term success as a firm (something that, in theory, ought to militate to improved share values), efforts to maximize profits at any cost are easier to satisfy if the rules inhibiting aggressive market activities can be minimized. Here the impact of the political clout of major corporations comes into play. The ability to get government to regulate less, to diminish the burden of environmental, consumer, and worker protection schemes, allows more opportunities to make profits, even if it comes at the expense of our natural environment and physical well-being. As noted, the corporation's inherent political capacity to push governments in this direction springs from its creation as a functional collective. This potential has been given greater bite in recent years with the advent of new technologies, the tearing down of trade barriers, so-called globalized production and trade that make for more competitive pressures, all intensifying the salience of an ideology and politics that marginalizes government and privileges the unfettering of market forces. Governments are to privatize as many of their operations as possible, because, not being disciplined by the market, they are inefficient. This leaves more of what once were essential tasks to the mercies of private corporations.

These developments have led to increased vulnerabilities for the masses. Governments need to contain potential outbreaks of resistance and militance. Unsurprisingly, as they deregulate on behalf of corporate capital, they become more repressive in respect of the potential victims of corporate power. In her review of the relevant studies, Laureen Snider (2001) has noted that, throughout Western liberal democracies, "we have witnessed zero tolerance of the transgressions of the least privileged people and maximum tolerance of crimes of the powerful." And, inevitably, there are many harms inflicted (albeit not always criminally) by the powerful.

It is in this context that many progressive people are urging that corporate managers should be educated/pressured, in the first place, to abide by such laws as do restrain corporate behavior and, in the second, to try to make positive contributions to the general welfare, to be socially responsible. It is precisely because they are finding it harder and harder to get government to fetter market activities that they resort to private stick-and-carrot tactics, such as publicizing egregious corporate behavior, ethical investment, and economic boycotts. This is not the place to engage with the pros and cons of these strategies.[31] It is pertinent to note, however, that those who want to exercise control over the large publicly traded corporations must do so by suasion. There are no material/legal constructs to advance their perspective as to how corporations ought to be run. On the other side, the architecture of the corporation gives material and legal impetus to those who can benefit from antisocial corporate conduct. It is because they are virtually invisible, run little fiscal risk, and are legally immune that investors in corporations are content to have managers engage in dubious activities. They are happy to put their monies in enterprises that exploit people in other parts of the world or that use their economic and political leverage to destroy environments such as, say, the Amazon, to make U.S. shareholders wealthier; personally, they are not shamed when people are burned to death when a car is rear-ended because, to yield more profits for them, it was knowingly built to permit this to happen; they are not embarrassed by having been enriched by having a manufacturer peddle a formula that it knows will be harmful to babies when it is mixed with impure water, even though mother milk's would have fed those babies adequately. The list is long and growing every day. On March 6, 2005, *The New York Times* reported that, on Wall Street, tobacco remained a favored investment. In the previous five years, the Standard & Poor Index had fallen 2.2%, while its tobacco component grew by a staggering 26.4%. Despite the wide acceptance of the horrible consequences of tobacco peddling, there are large numbers of hidden and protected money chasers who do not see broken bodies and destroyed lives. All they see is gold in the killing that will result from their managers' deployment of their assets.

The legal design of the corporation gives a seductively green light to shareholders to have managers make money for them, only asking them to stay within clearly legal norms. They respond positively to those negative legal incentives, despite the brave attempts by social responsibility activists to have them think about where they should put their monies. The architecture of corporate law makes for an uneven contest between the greedy investing classes and the advocates for a more socially responsible corporate sector. The corporation is legally created as a site of irresponsibility. It is a crucible for deviant behavior. Shareholders will reward the managers who bring home the bacon, that is, increased profits and improved share prices, no matter how these are obtained.

Shareholders get angry, however, when they find that they have rewarded managers who led them astray. Then the managers' discretion to do as they see fit with the corporation's assets is fiercely questioned. Here the immediate legislative and administrative responses to the Enron-type scandals should be contrasted to the deafening silence emanating from the investing classes when a corporation has made huge profits for them by exploiting child labor or the pollution of a river. There have been no Presidential addresses telling the populace that asbestos producers, responsible for millions of premature deaths and pain-filled diseases, have assaulted the foundations of capitalism and the social bonds that tie. Such ire and hyperbole is reserved for the wrongs committed against quintessential capitalists—shareholders. At the core of the public anxiety aroused by the turn of the 21st-century stock market shenanigans is the fact that the same corporate law that makes it so tempting for shareholders to let managers do whatever it takes to maximize profits and share prices also makes shareholders vulnerable.

The managers are under pressure to raise share prices on behalf of all their shareholders. Recently, this pressure has intensified because large pools of capital are invested by fund managers who need very quick returns. These institutional investors compete for funds to invest. They need to be kept happy. Share prices are to be maintained and raised in the shortest possible time lest the investors sell their stake, putting a downward pressure on the share price. One way of meeting these demands, of course, is to improve the competitive position of the corporation. But, this is a long-term project. In the short term, different measures are needed. In recent years, managers of large publicly traded corporations have been given incentives to improve short-term share prices by having their compensation depend directly on the value of their corporation's shares. The option to buy shares at a set price was to be the incentive for managers to drive up the share's value above that guaranteed purchase price. This was an additional spur for corporate managers to be aggressive in their push for higher share prices.

The resulting excesses are well known. Corporations moved losses to related companies. Remember here how easy it is to set-up corporations, how the law treats them as distinct persons even if they are functionally integrated, that is, note how the basic legal design of the corporation militates toward deception and manipulation on behalf of financial capitalists. The accounts of the central corporation looked better after these manipulations, although objectively the losses had not been offset by real gains. The managers, their willing accountants, and lawyers also set up bookkeeping systems that manufactured earnings by characterizing increases in share values as actual earnings; they used limited partnerships and special purpose entities, i.e., notionally distinct legal enterprises, to hold out to investors that risks of the central corporation had been hedged although, because of the sleight of hand by managers and accountants and lawyers, they had not been shifted; they got banks and lenders to pretend that a transaction other than borrowing had occurred, avoiding to have to account for a debt, and they entered into "nod" and a "wink" sales with purchasers who knew very well that they would be able to return the goods "purchased" (with a "profit" that was actually the interest on the money they had lent) after the financial reporting statements had been finalized. Everyone made money: the executives, the brokers, analysts, bankers, lawyers, accountants, some of the shareholders who bought and sold as prices were churning—until it all collapsed. Then, all of a sudden, the investing classes discovered that neither they, nor anyone else, had exercised sufficient control over their agents.[32] There is a paradox here.

The major shareholders are quite happy to let those who contend that they are owners without control to have the best of the argument when this permits them to claim righteous ignorance and innocence when workers, consumers, and the environment are harmed by their executives' chase for profits and improved share values. But this gap becomes a bone of contention when it leads to adverse impacts for some of them and for the capital markets in general. Then the discretion given to managers is to be regulated because it was used to betray the interests of capital as opposed to those of the general public. When Enron, WorldCom et al., exploded, the otherwise content-to-be irresponsible major shareholders wanted *someone* to exercise control over these managers and their professional allies. The major shareholders' complaints had added resonance because some of the more hapless losers were small, often indirectly invested, shareholders who had been assured that someone, somewhere already was protecting their interests.

The Sarbanes-Oxley measures are nothing but a checklist for those designated to promote the shareholders' interests on how to abide by rules and principles that had been thought to have been well and truly internalized by them. As before, the legislation requires that there should be no lying about the true state of a corporation's operations and finances. As before, there is to be no abuse of corporate information by those charged with the welfare of the corporation. As before, there is to be strict compliance with professional codes of ethics and responsibilities by professional advisers, most particularly, they are not to put themselves in conflictual situations by giving supposedly independent advice when they are dependent for their profit on the goodwill of corporate management. What the legislation does is to spell out specifically what kind of conduct would breach these well-established norms of behavior.

In short, Sarbanes-Oxley is the kind of legitimating exercise that is engaged in after every episode of skullduggery that has threatened the further flourishing of capital markets. Each time, the latest specific misdeeds are addressed, but the raisons d'etre of the wrongdoings are left alone. This time, the pressure to be seen to do something vigorous was greater than it has been for some time. During the late 1990s an increasing number of small-time investors entered the markets as their social wages were eroded. Healthcare insurance had become more expensive as had education; unemployment benefits were harder to come by as job insecurity increased; workers' compensation regimes were paying less; public pension schemes were under attack at a time when collective private pensions were eroding with the fall in collective bargaining, a phenomenon that also had reduced the number of people covered by health insurance bought by unionized employers. Individuals had to find their own means to secure their futures. These incentives to play the stock markets were complemented by what Chairman Alan Greenspan had called "irrational exuberance," as share prices, pushed by the technology craze and boosters everywhere, as well as by the sense of triumph generated by the collapse of socialist economic regimes and the accompanying deepening of the ideology of individualism, self-reliance, and the perception of the inutility of democratically elected governments.

The capital markets depend on the players' staying in the game, something made easier if share prices are booming. Major players profit from having active share markets where they can make monies from commissions and the provision of services, such as preparing documents necessary for compliance, to buy and sell, to issue securities, to develop new kinds of instruments and securities in which people can invest, to write prospectuses, to furnish analyses for lenders and investors, to underwrite offers for takeovers, to set up defenses to takeovers, and so forth. Here, given one of the theses of this paper to the effect that the structural design of the corporation has the potential to distort liberal politics, it is pertinent to note that the large traded corporations and their allies had waged successful campaigns to get rid of many of the controls that had been imposed on them because of previous excesses.[33] Not only had the professional lobbyists and parasitic service-renderers successfully lobbied for not requiring corporations to treat the grant of expensive options to executives as a liability (Levitt), they had convinced government to release banks from the fetters imposed on them in the aftermath of the hyperspeculation that preceded the Great Depression. The Glass-Steagall Act had prevented them from using the enormous funds deposited with them in stock market investment activities. This ended,[34] letting loose a flood of money looking for somewhere to go during the technology boom days. Or, on another front, legislation was enacted making it much more difficult for investors to sue professionals for negligently misstated financial accounts. In short, conditions were created that rewarded advisers and their allies if they successfully encouraged speculative activities by those in charge of corporations. They, in turn, were operating in a context where they had been given material incentives to drive up the prices of their corporations' shares in any way possible. All of this fuelled already overheated markets as money flowed around the world in unprecedented amounts.[35] The temptation to push the letter of what was allowed under law by way of devising new investment instruments and corporate organization to make a corporation look attractive to would-be investors was intense and, inevitably, led to practices that became risible examples of wrongdoing by the captains of the financial world.[36] The potential for deviance inherent in the architecture of the corporation materialized—in spades.

Of course, the legislative reforms that explicitly name and prohibit some of the practices that led to the problems may have an ameliorative impact. For instance, if options are to be calculated as a capital expense by the corporations granting them, they are less likely to be bestowed as easily or as carelessly as they had been. And, similarly, the economic conditions that underlay the mad dash for stock speculation may turn out to have been extraordinary. But, it is to be noted that, every time that these kinds of reforms are wrought, a novel means of taking advantage has been spawned. Take the option payment scheme. It was largely a result of the restraints imposed by government when high executive salaries had led to public protests. A tax was placed on corporations when they paid an executive more than $1 million in cash. Executives expected more and this led to the option device, a way to pay those executives a lot without incurring the cost of the punitive payroll tax. Note that it was shareholders, the very ones who today complain so loudly about their underperforming/cheating fat cat executives paid by options, who provided the rationale for the option-payment regime. They wanted executives to have discretion to run the corporation without having to bother about the daily decisions, but not so much discretion that executives might feel free to pay some attention to interests other than those of shareholders (Coffee Jr.).[33] In addition to the legal rules that require the executives to act in the best interests of the corporation—that judicially was mostly perceived to be the same as the best interests of the shareholders—they wanted to make sure that the executives should be completely preoccupied with optimizing share values. They were happy to give executives a monetary incentive that they believed would align their interests with those of their principals—the shareholders.

In the absence of changes to the basic legal design of the corporation, we should expect further outbreaks of harmful deviance. The reforms set out to promote shareholder interests. The ruling wisdom is that individuals should continue to be encouraged to participate in stock market activities. Indeed, there is a continuation of the movement to drive more and more people to rely on this kind of investment to provide for their individual and family security. The debates initiated by the Bush Administration about the changes it would like to see in the social security scheme illustrates this political trend. Somehow it must be believed that the English Board of Trade's 1696 caution about the dangers to ignorant men drawn in by false information artfully spread has no resonance in modern Anglo-American settings, despite the mountains of evidence to the contrary. By endorsing the notion that shareholder values should retain, indeed be given greater, privileges, all that the changes are ensuring is that everything will remain the same: the potential for deviance remains embedded; it will manifest itself, again and again.

Summary and a Question

1. The large, publicly traded corporation aggregates a great number of capitals that can be used as a collectivized force. It has coercive economic and political powers. These powers make it an ideal vehicle for wealth-owners to exercise disproportionate market and political influence. The wealth-owners remain hidden. This gives them the inclination to act with reckless indifference toward others.
2. The inclination of the investors to serve their own interests, regardless of the impact and/or the legality of the means used, is sharpened by the privileges bestowed on them by corporate law. In capitalism, a political economy based on the satisfaction of greed and the pursuit of self-interest, the grant to (virtually invisible) people of limited fiscal liability and total legal immunity for the way in which their greed and self-interest are to be satisfied, generates pressures for wrongdoing.
3. The managers are charged with satisfying the shareholders' interests. They are driven by market capitalism's competitive pressures and by the punishment/reward system scheme that disciplines them on behalf of the shareholders. In their role as the corporation's instrument they fight for freedom from government's mediating restrictions and the enforcement thereof and to exploit any means available within this contested (and, recently, increasingly ramshackle) framework of protections to maximize profits. Their productive and marketing practices are a drive to the bottom of the ethical barrel. Pressured by shareholders who are not made to care by dint of law, managers who still are relatively safe from personal prosecution for wrongs committed by their corporations cause corporations not only to behave in a socially amoral way, but also to commit a huge number of illegal acts. Indeed, there is a good deal of recidivism (Glasbeek, 2002).[6] The economic and personal costs of harms inflicted are great, even as a large amount of private wealth is accumulated within corporations. Shareholders, hidden and protected, are content to collect the profits made from conduct that is anti-social and/or illegal, even

if it causes dreadful pain and harm. They show this by continuing to invest their capital in harm-causing firms, safe in their knowledge that corporate law will keep them out of sight and irresponsible for the harms done. Gross cultural, environmental, and personal physical harms will continue to be inflicted and the legitimacy of the corporation will come into question, again and again.

4. The managers are expected to drive up the value of shares in the short term. If they succeed, the rewards they receive are extremely generous. A great number of middle-persons benefit from these pushes, as do a number of professional advisers who are there to furnish legitimacy to the corporation in the first place. This leads to the letter of any law being pushed way beyond the spirit that imbued its passage. This generates pressures to exaggerate performance and to falsify the prospects and financial status of their corporations. Shareholders are content to profit from these exaggerations and falsifications until the bubble bursts. Governments then step in to reassure the shareholding classes that they will be safeguarded in the future from betrayal by managers and their hired professionals and bankers, although all these people are to continue to promote share values as energetically as ever. Shareholders are told, in other words, that their greed and selfishness are prime concerns in our polity and that the corporation that allows them to satisfy their goals at the expense of others is a sacrosanct institution. Charitably, it is to be assumed that the harms (deaths, diseases, horrible working conditions, poisoned environments, a world filled with untruths, etc.) and erosion of democratic institutions (as the $1,000/1 vote replaces the 1 person/1 vote polity) to which this wealth-generation vehicle's modus operandi are perceived to be (in some crude way) offset by the abundance created. But, this remains a contestable claim. The legitimacy of the corporation will come into question, again and again.

The Question

Is it too simplistic to argue that the corporation, despite its portrayal, is a vehicle that hides capitalists so as to enable them to escape the economic and political restrictions a well-functioning market economy in a liberal polity might impose on them? After all, in widely held, large, publicly traded, corporations, there is a multitude of shareholders/investors. Most of them exercise no control over the management of the corporate assets and/or are passively invested via institutions over which they have no control. Should they be considered a driving force of any kind, let alone a malevolent one? How can they exercise pressures to which corporate managers must respond? These thousands of marginal investors have conflicting agendas. A corporation's maximization of profits by shifting operations overseas may suit them as shareholders but not as workers, as consumers; the encouragement of shoddy product manufacturing to improve their fortuitously held shares' value may harm their overall well-being; takeovers may suit them as shareholders in the target corporation, but not as investors or workers elsewhere. Their investment in any one corporation does not mean that their self-interest is the single-minded pursuit of profit by that corporation of the capitalist goal of private accumulation of socially produced wealth at any cost. In part, these arguments buttress those who would have the corporation be more socially responsible and altruistic, who claim that stakeholders other than shareholders must have their non-monetary interests safeguarded by corporate management.[37]

This paper cannot examine these important questions fully in the way they deserve to be treated. An elaborated discussion must be attempted in the future. In the meanwhile, an initial response intended to support the central points made in this paper is sketched-out.

The proliferation and the resultant diffusion of shareholding may be characterized as evidence supporting the socialization of capital that gave rise to the managerialist schools discussed earlier. But, there is another way of looking at this phenomenon. It is that, precisely because in many large, publicly traded corporations, the shares are so diffusely held, a few people can actually control these huge corporations with relatively small holdings. This is another way to come to terms with the conundrum of the separation between ownership and control, somewhat like that favored by the law and economics scholars in that it posits that *some* investors are akin to owners, but different in that it does not pretend that all investors possess the same power although their legal contractual rights are the same. That is, while legal ownership, vested in the multitude of shareholders, may be divorced from control, real economic control, in the sense of being able to dictate the terms of assignment and disposition of the assets, is vested in a few shareholders. The diffusion in shareholding may lead to greater control for the few in many firms as control requires less investment.[38] These shareholders' desires and goals will exert real influence over the managers' behavior.[39] The de facto invisibility of these shareholders, added to their limited fiscal liability and legal immunity, will lead to the behavioral problems identified in this paper. In part, this is acknowledged in the practices of corporate laws and reflected in the actual shareholding patterns that exist.

Whenever a takeover or acquisition is to occur, it is clear to managers and shareholders alike that the group bidding for dominance will be in position to dictate new terms to the management, to make different business decisions, affect strategies, sizes of workforce, and the like. The directors, executives, brokers, and share markets will react to such news; securities regulators will demand disclosures to enable people to get equal access to deal with the new opportunities and dangers. Moreover, there are regulations that require that, when some significant shareholders do things, e.g., sell or purchase shares, sell or purchase goods or services to or from the corporation, they must tell the capital markets about their doings. The idea is to give other, less economically well-placed and control-possessing shareholders an opportunity to protect themselves against the acknowledged leverage that some shareholders have over the corporation and its managers. This understanding that some relatively few shareholders are not just technical legal owners like all other shareholders, but rather may be economic owners—with the inherent and material power that ownership of a firm's assets implies—is given life by the pattern of shareholding in large, publicly traded corporations. Despite the steady growth in equity market investors, the bulk of the wealth, that is, the bulk of legal voting, appointing and controlling power, remains in the hands of a small group of capitalists. In the United States, in 1998, while about 48% of households owned shares, directly and indirectly, the richest 10% of them accounted for 78% of the wealth the value of those shares represented.[40] Their demands for maximization of profits at any cost, for the improvement of share value, no matter how artificially contrived, carry weight. Their demands are unprincipled because—like all shareholders, small, active or passive—they do not have to worry about being held to account.

The question needs further exploration, but, on the face of it, the diffuse nature of shareholding does not affect the argument that the legal architecture of the corporation has created a vehicle that, in liberal market terms, is a site of irresponsibility, a site where hard-to-see fundamentalists can practice capitalism while purporting to have accepted this political economy's harsher aspects mediated by liberal democratic and market institutions.

Endnotes

1. *Transcript of Bush Remarks At Signing of Sarbanes-Oxley Act*, 30 July, 2002, U.S. Newswire; http://www.usnewswire.com.topnews/prime/0730–115.html
2. Jonathan D. Glater (2005) "Here It Comes: The Sarbanes-Oxley Backlash," New York Times, 17 April, BU 5; Jacquie McNish (2005), "Corporate America's Reign of Terror Waning," Globe & Mail, Report on Business, 14 July, B1 (reporting that U.S. Congressman Michael Oxley has noted that the legislation "was not a perfect document," perhaps "excessive" in some ways).
3. Cronald Chen and Jon Hansen (2004) "The Illusion of Law: The Legitimating Schemas of Modern Policy and Corporate Law" 103 *Mich. L.R.* 1, at pp. 135 et seq., cite such notables as Maddison, Jefferson, Lincoln, Presidents Cleveland and Van Buren, to this effect.
4. *Louis K. Liggett Co.* v. *Lee* 288 U.S 517 at pp. 548–9 (1933).
5. In the passage from *Liggett* quoted in the text above, Brandeis also wrote that the evils visited upon society by corporations had come to be perceived as "the inescapable price of civilized life and, hence, to be borne with resignation."
6. See Mandel, Bakan, Tollefson, Grossman and Adams, Friedman, Nader, Green and Seligman, Miller from the reference section.
7. This argument to the effect that the market is not only an economically beneficial institution but also an ideologically appealing one has been made most famously by Milton Friedman in his *Capitalism and Freedom*. There Friedman argued that, while economic efficiency was more likely to be achieved via the market than by reliance on government planning, it was not inconceivable that a planning system could be efficient. But, he contended, a planned economy would still liberty by constraining individuals' right to choose. The influence of this argument is well known. It provides the philosophical underpinnings for the many political parties that run on platforms of non-intervention with the private sector and on promises to open up more spheres for private market activities. It also has made it appear natural to equate a turn toward private market economics, as in the former planned economies of the Soviet Bloc or in China, as freedom-enhancing reforms and with the advance of political democracy. For my own critical comments on these issues, see *Wealth by Stealth*.
8. *An Inquiry.... Wealth of Nations,* Book III, chap. 1: "The only trades which it seems possible for a joint stock to carry on successfully are those, of which all the operations are capable of being reduced to what is called routine, or to such an uniformity of method as admits of little or no variation." Given the respect accorded them today, it is amusing to note that the father of market ideology thought that routinized businesses that required virtually no management included banking, insurance, digging holes for canals and the delivery of water.
9. This notion of a legal fiction to describe the disappearance of private ownership when the firm used was a widely held corporation of the socialization of capital was put forward by Daniel Bell, "The Corporation and Society in the 1970's," *The*

Public Interest, 24, Summer, 1971, p. 21. It echoed his famous arguments that, post-Second World war, the class divide had disappeared as had all ideological conflict; (1965) *The End of Ideology: On the Exhaustion of Political Ideas in the Fifties,* New York: Free Press. In a more populist way, a similar argument underpinned the thesis that, since shareholding was becoming ever more pervasive, especially as private pension schemes spread, we had all become owners and the distinction between the owning class and the working class had become otiose; Drucker, P. (1976) *The Unseen Revolution: How Pension Fund Socialism Came to America.* New York: Harper & Row.

10. As early as 1926, John Maynard Keynes had noted that the rise of managerial control and power was evidence of the tendency for enterprise carried on through the widely held corporation to socialize itself and that, therefore, shareholders should be given adequate, rather than maximum returns, so that managers could avert criticism of the abuse of corporate power. This kind of argument, based on the concept of managerial theory, inheres in many of the contemporary social responsibility/stakeholder proponents' arguments. The managerial theorists (Burnham, Galbraith, Dahrendorf) who followed Keynes, after his observations were given weight by the empirical work of Berle and Means, argued that the separation of control from ownership had led to a qualitative change in capitalism, one that made contentions that the owning class had antagonistic/unequal relations with non-owners old hat. In labor relations scholarship, this line of argument, buttressed by increased collective bargaining powers of workers, lent support to those who saw employer–employee relations as essentially arising out of struggles between a team of producers who had reached a consensus on the need to produce for profit and who shared political goals and values, even as they differed about the share of the pie produced. Their struggles were about the web of rules that should govern their relations, not over the nature of those relations (Dunlop, Cox, Task Force on Labor Relations). The oppression and exploitation of workers was no longer seen as a factor of division and the socialization of capital that had given rise to a technocratic revolution and played a pivotal role in this development.
11. Recently, this line of argument has been given a different and more persuasive slant by Blair and Stout. These scholars argue that the efficiency of the corporation is enhanced by the separation of ownership and control, that, indeed, the history of the American corporation demonstrates that this separation was one of the prime impulses for the increased use of the corporate vehicle. These progressive scholars then argue that, as the entrustment of invested capital leads to certainty for investors in that the capital will be retained by the firm and not be subjected to the whims of fellow individual investors, the goal of the investors can be said to be that it is the firm as a whole that should prosper. To them, this means that the controlling managers are there to coordinate a team of producers and that they should pay heed to the needs and desires of all members of the team, not just those of shareholders. This is not the place to discuss this intriguing and very sophisticated line of reasoning, but it is suggested that, even if Blair and Stout are right about the original impulse for entrusting property to relatively autonomous managers, this does not mean that the same goals are being pursued by contemporary investors. Below, an argument will be made to show that to-day's equity investors have no serious interest in the well-being of the other producers in the corporate firm and little interest in the eventual well-being of the corporation.
12. The earliest English statutes giving some legal standing to trade unions defined them as 'combinations in restraint of trade'; *1871 Trade Union Act*, 39 & 40 Vic. c.22 (U.K.) .
13. This is reflected in our daily discourses. We speak of Big Business, Big Pharma, Big Oil, etc., pay homage and respect, tinged with fear, to business leaders. We listen to their political and economic pronouncements (often made through think-tanks

they fund) and entice them to be good to us. We know that some market actors are far more important than others, economically, socially and politically. If more formal evidence is needed, either for the tendency toward the development of anti-competitive conditions or the existence thereof, see Galbraith, John Kenneth, 1956, *American Capitalism: The Concept of Countervailing Power,* Boston: Houghton Mifflin; Hovenkamp, Herbert (1991) *Enterprise and American Law, 1836–1937,* Camb. Mass.: Harvard University Press; Baran, Paul A., and Sweezy, Paul M. (1966) *Monopoly Capital: An Essay on the American Economic and Social Order,* New York: Monthly Review Press; Campbell, David (1996) *The Failure of Marxism: The Concept of Inversion in Marx's Critique of Capitalism,* Brookfield, VT.: Dartmouth. For my own documentation of the relative unimportance of the multitude of small businesses in Canada, see *Wealth by Stealth.*

14. Fishman, Charles, 2003, "The Wal-Mart You Don't Know," *FastCompany*, Issue 77, p. 68. Another powerful retailer, keen to match Wal-Mart on low prices is Costco. It proudly told reporters that it seeks to match Wal-Mart by simply carrying less items of the same kind, increasing the sales volume of each, permitting "Costco to squeeze deeper and deeper bulk discounts from suppliers"; Greenhouse, Steven, 2005, "How Costco Became the Anti-Wal-Mart," New York Times, 17 July, BU1. It is possible to argue that competition has not been stilled as Wal-Mart and Costco struggle for market share. But, it is a struggle that oppresses, directly and indirectly, a whole host of other would-be market actors. As Fishman points out, Costco's (and K-Mart's and a few other smaller giants') strategies vis-a-vis suppliers of goods and labour are dictated by Wal-Mart because, amongst the dominant firms, it is by far and away the largest.
15. Greenfield, Kent (2005) "New principles for Corporate Law" 1:1, *Hastings Business L.J.*, at p. 87, writes that the "group... includes most of the legal scholars who teach and write in the area". Fine examplars of this scholarly strain include, Posner, Richard A. (2003) 6 ed., *Economic Analysis of Law*, New York: Aspen Publishers; Posner, Richard A. and Scott, Kenneth E., eds. (1980) *Economics of Corporate Law and Securities Regulation*, Boston: Little, Brown; Richard Hansmann, Henry and Kraakman, Reinier (2001) " The End of History for Corporate Law" 89 *Georgetown L.J.* 439; Clark, Robert (1986) *Corporate Law*, Boston: Little, Brown ; Easterbrook and Fischel (1991) *The Economic Structure of Corporate Law* , Camb., Mass.: Harvard University Press; Bebchuk, Lucian A., ed. (1990) *Corporate Law and Economic Analysis*, Camb, Eng./ New York: Cambridge University Press; Cheffins, Brian R., (1992) *Company Law: Theory, Structure and Operation*, Oxford: Clarendon Press; Harris, Doug, Daniels. Ron, Iacobucci, Ed MacIntosh, Jeff, Pooman, Puri, and Ziegel, Jacob S. (2004) *Cases, Materials and Notes on Partnerships and Canadian Business Corporations*. 4th ed., Toronto: Carswell.
16. The literature is voluminous. Some of the most important works and ideas are discussed and refined in the many sharply critical writings of the legal historian and theoretician, Paddy Ireland; see for instance, Ireland, P., Grigg-Spall, I., and Kelly, D. (1987) "The Conceptual Foundations of Modern Company Law," 14 *J. of Law and Society* 149; Ireland, P., 1983, "The Triumph of the Company Law Form 1856–1914" in Adams, John, ed., *Essays for Clive Schmithoff*, Abingdon, Eng.:Professional Books; 1996, " Capitalism Without the Capitalist: The Joint Stock CompanyShare and the Emergence of the Modern Doctrine of Separate Corporate Personality" 17 *J. of Legal History* 40; 1999, "Company Law and the Myth of Shareholder Ownership" 62 *Modern L.R.* 32;2002, "History, Critical and Legal Studies and the Mysterious Disappearance of Capitalism" 65 *Modern L. R.* 128. For my own attempts at criticism, see (1995) "Preliminary Observations on Strains of, and Strains in, Corporate Law Scholarship" in Pearce, Frank and Snider, Laureen, eds., *Corporate Crime: Contemporary Debates*, Toronto: University of Toronto Press; also in *Wealth by Stealth*.

17. Many serious theoreticians offer arguments in support of this proposition. Amongst them, see Polanyi, Karl (2001) *The Great Transformation: The Political and Economic Origins of Our Time*, Boston: Beacon Press (Foreword by Joseph E. Stiglitz, Intro. by Fred Block), who argues that a market economy cannot produce anything but a market polity, that is, one in which decision-making is determined by market power and ideology; Samin, Amir (2004) *The Liberal Virus: Permanent War and the Americanization of World*, New York: Monthly Review Press (Trans. by James H. Membrez), who contends that market capitalism leads to "low-intensity democracy".
18. For a good summation of these arguments made by leading law and economics scholars, see Gabaldon, T. (1992) " The Lemonade Stand: Feminist and Other Reflections on the Limited Liability of Corporate Shareholders," 45 *Vanderbilt L.R.* 1387.
19. See Easterbrook and Fischel, 1991 from the reference section.
20. For an overview of the many struggles, academic and practical, arising out of the uses and abuses of limited liability, see Ziegel, Jacob (1991) "Is Incorporation (with Limited Liability) Too Easily Available?" 31 *Cahiers de Droit* 1075.
21. Hansmann, H., and Kraakman, R., 1991, "Toward Unlimited Shareholder Liability for Corporate Torts," 100 *Yale L.J.* 1878; Halpern, P., Trebilcock, M., and Turnbull, S. (1980) "An Economic Analysis of Limited Liability in Corporation Law" 30 *Uni. Toronto L.J.* 117.
22. Not only does it fit with the fact that the corporation is an individual property owner, capable of investing its assets as it determines best—the essence of the argument that, legally, an individual market participant has been created—it also resonates with the historical analysis of Ireland, op. cit., who emphasises the evolution of the fictitious anture of shareholder ownership and that of Blair and Stout, op. cit., who claim that the evolution of the U.S. corporation denotes that shareholders willingly gave up their property to the corporation so that the firm's business endeavors would not be subject to the whims of property claims by former individual contributors of capital.
23. To this end, there is pressure on governments to make it easier to do so, as a way to offset the argument that no one, not even a corporation is held responsible for serious wrongdoing. For an overview of these efforts in England, Australia and Canada see the Special Edition: Industrial Manslaughter, 2005, vol. 8, issue 1, *The Flinders Journal of Law Reform*.
24. A great deal depends, then, on judicial interpretation. Crudely it can be said that English and Australian courts look for very senior officers to have been involved in the decision-making and that Canadian courts are more willing to look at the functional realities of decision-making inside corporations; in the U.S. both these tendencies are reflected in different jurisdictions and, in some, there is willingness to attribute corporate responsibility when even the lowest level of corporate employee has violated the standards in the course of his/her duties. For an overview of the many lines taken by different courts, see *Canadian Dredge and Dock Co. Ltd.* v. *The Queen* (1985), 19 *Can Crim. Cases(3d)* 1, (Sup. Ct. Canada).
25. See Kraakman, Posner, Elzing and Breit, Daniels from the reference section.
26. I have discussed some of the U.S literature and the Canadian situation in 1995b, "More Direct Responsibility: Much Ado About... What?" 25 *Canadian Bus. L.J.* 416.
27. See Armour, Deakin and Konzelmann, Tomasic, Wheeler, Ireland, Hopt, Roe, Greenfield from the reference section.
28. See Hansmann and Kraakman, 2001; OECD, 2004 from the reference section.
29. See Serra, Pettet, Penner, Ireland, 1996 from the reference section.
30. This was understood as soon as it became the fashion to trade corporate stock. Hadden reports that, in 1696, the English Board of Trade lamented that the company form was being abused by ther sale of shares "to ignorant men, drawn in by

the reputation, falsely raised and artfully spread, concerning the thriving of the stock"; Hadden, T. (1972) *Company Law and Capitalism*, London: Weidenfeld and Nicolson, p. 14.

31. I have made an attempt in *Wealth by Stealth*.
32. See Bryce, Fusaro and Miller, Swartz, with Watkins, Blasi, Kruse and Bernstein, Toffler and Reingold, Levitt, with Dwyer, Partnoy, McLean and Elkind from the reference section.
33. See Coffee Jr. from the reference section.
34. With the passage of the *Competitive Equality Banking Act of 1987*, 12 USC § 1903.
35. See Brenner, 2002, 2003, Kotz from the reference section.
36. One result of rewarding executives by means of options was to stimulate these worthies into ever more clever means to push up the price of shares—something that the shareholders wanted them to do. Inevitably, some of those means were more questionable than others; see Coffee, Jr. (2003), Graybow, Martha (2005) "Stock Option Plans Linked to Figure Juggling: Study," *Financial Post,* 8 August, 2005, FP2; Nocera, Joseph (2005) "Stock Options: So Who's Counting?" *The New York Times*, 6 April, 2005, B1. Linked to the loosening of liability for carelessly prepared financial statements by the *Private Securities Litigation Reform Act*, 15 USC § 78a (1995) was an amazing instance of increased restatements by corporations. Coffee, Jr., notes that, between 1997 and 2002, there were restatements in 10% of initial corporate financial statements, causing these corporations' stocks to drop by 10% upon this news, indicating the extent to which investors felt they had been fooled.
37. See Greenwood, Stout, Greenfield, 2005 from the reference section.
38. See Hilferding, Bettelheim, De Vroey from the reference section.
39. To take just on example that popped-up at the time of writing: the investor Icahn, with only 2.6% of shares in Time Warner has been invited to meet with its CEO to discuss Icahn's demand that Time Warner use its money to buy back shares for the explicit purpose to drive up the price of the shares outstanding. That is, with few shares, this investor has enough power to sway corporate policy; Suel, Seth, "Investors lean on Time Warner," *Toronto Star*, 16 August, 2005, D1.
40. See Wolff, Gates from the reference section.

References

Amin, Samir (2004) *The Liberal Virus: Permanent War and the Americanization of the World*. Trans. by James H. Membrez. New York: Monthly Review Press.

Armour, John, Simon, Deakin, and Suzanne, J. Konzelmann (2003) "Shareholder Primacy and the Trajectory of UK Corporate Governance." *British J. Ind. Rel.* P. 531.

Arnold, Thurman W. (1937) *The Folklore of Capitalism*. New Haven: Yale University Press.

Bakan, Joel (2004) *The Corporation: The Pathological Pursuit of Profit and Power.* Toronto: Viking Canada.

Baran, Paul A., and Paul M. Sweezey (1966) *Monopoly Capital: An Essay on the American Economic and Social Order.* New York: Monthly Review Press.

Bebchuk, Lucian A., Editor (1990) *Corporate Law and Economic Analysis*. Cambridge, England/New York: Cambridge University Press.

Bell, Daniel (1965) *The End of Ideology: On the Exhaustion of Political Ideologies in the Fifties*. New York: Free Press.

"The Corporation and Society in the 1970's." (1971) *The Public Interest* (24)12 (Summer).

Berle, A.A., and C.G. Means (1932) *The Modern Corporation and Private Property*. New York: Commerce Clearing House.

Bettelheim, Charles (1970) *Calcul Économique et Formes de Proprieté.* Paris: Maspero.

Blair, Margaret M. (2003) "Locking in Capital: What Corporate law Achieved for Business Organizers of the 19th Century." *UCLA L.R.* 51:2.

Blair, Margaret M., and Lynn A. Stout (1999) "A Team Production Theory of Corporate Law." *Virginia L.R.* 85:247.

Blasi, Joseph, Douglas Kruse, and Aaron Bernstein (2002) *In the Company of Owners: The Truth about Stock Options (and Why Everyone Should Have Them).* New York: Basic Books.

Brandeis, Louis D. (1967) *Other People's Money and How the Bankers Use It.* Editor Richard M. Abrams. New York: Harper Torchbooks.

Brenner, Robert (2002) *The Boom and the Bubble: Crisis of Global Capitalism.* London:Verso.

"Toward the Precipice." (2003) *London Review of Books,* p. 18 (Feb. 6).

Bryce, Robert (2002) *Pipe Dreams: Greed, Ego and the Death of Enron.* New York: Public Affairs.

Burnham, James (1972) *The Managerial Revolution—What is Happening in the World?* Westport, CT: Greenwood Press.

Cadbury Committee (1992) *Report of the Committee on Financial Aspects of Corporate Governance.* London: Gee.

Campbell, David (1996) *The Failure of Marxism: The Concept of Inversion in Marx's Critique of Capitalism.* Brookfield, VT: Dartmouth.

Cassidy, John (2002) *dot.con: The Greatest Story Ever Sold.* New York: HarperCollins.

Cheffins, Brian R. (1992) *Company Law: Theory, Structure and Operation.* Oxford: Clarendon Press.

Chen, Ronald, and Jon Hanson (2004) "The Illusion of Law: The Legitimating Schemas of Modern Policy and Corporate Law." *Michigan L.R.* 103:1.

Clark, Robert (1986) *Corporate Law.* Boston: Little, Brown.

Coffee Jr., John C. (2003) "Limited Options." *legalaffairs* p. 52 (Nov./Dec.).

Company Law Steering Committee (2001) *Modern Company Law for a Competitive Economy: Final Report—vol. I.* London: DTI.

Cox, Archibald (1957–58) "The Duty to Bargain in Good Faith." *Harvard L.R.* 71: 1401.

Dahl, Robert A. (1985) *A Preface to Economic Democracy.* Berkeley: University of California Press.

Dahrendorf, Ralf (1959) *Class and Class Conflict in Modern Society.* London: Routledge and Kegan.

Daniels, Ron (1994) "Must Boards Go Overboard? An Economic Analysis of the Effects of Burgeoning Statutory Liability on the Role of Directors." In *Conference on Canadian Corporate Governance.* C.D. Howe Institute Toronto. (Feb.).

Deetz, Stanley (1992) *Democracy in an Age of Corporate Colonization.* Albany: SUNY Press.

Drucker, Peter (1976) *The Unseen Revolution: How Pension Fund Socialism Came to America.* New York: Harper & Row.

Dunlop, John T. (1958) *Industrial Relations Systems.* New York: Holt.

Easterbrook, Frank H., and David R. Fischel (1991) *The Economic Structure of Corporate Law.* Cambridge, MA: Harvard University Press.

Elzinge, Kenneth G., and William Breit (1976) *The Anti-Trust Penalties: A Study in Law and Economics.* New Haven, CT: Yale University Press.

Everest, Larry, and Leonard Innes (2002) *Z Magazine*, p. 24–28 (Mar.).

Fishman, Charles (2003) "The Wal-Mart You Don't Know." *Fast Company* 77:68.

Friedman, Lawrence M. (1973) *A History of American Law.* New York: Simon and Schuster.

Friedman, Milton (1962) *Capitalism and Freedom.* Chicago: Chicago University Press.

Fusaro, Peter C., and Ross Miller (2002) *What Went Wrong at Enron: Everyone's Guide to the Largest Bankruptcy in U.S. History.* New York: Wiley and Sons.

Gabaldon, Theresa (1992) "The Lemonade Stand: Feminist and Other Reflections on the Limited Liability of Corporate Shareholders." *Vanderbilt L.R.* 45:1387.

Galbraith, John K. (1956) *American Capitalism: The Concept of Countervailing Power.* Boston: Houghton Mifflin.

Galbraith, John Kenneth (1975) *Economics and the Public Purpose.* New York: New American Library.

Gates, J. (with Foreword by Schmidheiny, S.), (1999) *The Ownership Solution: Toward a Shared Capitalism for the Twenty-first Century.* Reading, MA: Perseus Books.

Glasbeek, Harry (2002) *Wealth by Stealth: Corporate Crime, Corporate Law and the Perversion of Democracy.* Toronto: Between the Lines.

Glasbeek, Harry (1995a) "Preliminary Observations on Strains of, and Strains in, Corporate Law Scholarship." In *Corporate Crime: Contemporary Debates,* Editors Pearce, Frank and Laureen Snider. Toronto: University of Toronto Press.

Glasbeek, Harry (1995b) "More Direct Director Responsibility: Much Ado About... What?" *Canadian Bus. L. J.* 25:416.

Glater, Jonathan D. (2005) "Here It Comes: The Sarbanes-Oxley Backlash." The *New York Times*, 17 Apr. BU p. 5.

Graybow, Martha (2005) "Stock Option Plans Linked to Figure Juggling: Study." *Financial Post*, 8 August, FP p. 2.

Greenfield, Kent (2002) "September 11th and the End of History for Corporate Law." *Tulane L. Rev.* 76:1409.

Greenfield, Kent "New Principles for Corporate Law." (2005) *Hastings Business L.J.* 1:87.

Greenhouse, Steven (2005) "How Costco Became the Anti-Wal-Mart." *The New York Times*, 17 July, BU p. 1.

Greenwood, Daniel (1996) "Fictional Shareholders: For Whom Are Corporate Managers Trustees?" *So. Cal. L.R.* 69.

Grossman, Richard L., and Frank T. Adams (1993) *Taking Care of Business: Citizenship and the Charter of Incorporation.* Cambridge, MA: Charter, Ink.

Halpern, Paul J., Stuart M. Trebilcock, and S. Turnbull (1980) "An Economic Analysis of Limited Liability in Corporation Law." *Uni. Toronto L.J.* 30:117.

Hansmann, Henry, and Reiner H. Kraakman (1991) "Toward Unlimited Shareholder Liability for Corporate Torts." *Yale L.J.* 100:1878.

Hansmann, Henry, and Reiner H. Kraakman "The End of History for Corporate Law." (2001) *Georgetown L.J.* 89:439.

Hampel Committee (1997) *Final Report of the Committee on Corporate Governance.* London: Gee.

Hilderfing, Rudolf (1970) *Le Capital Financier.* Paris: Editions de Minuit.

Hopt, Klaus J. (2002) "Common Principles of Corporate Governance in Europe." In *Corporate Governance Regimes,* Editors J. McCahery, P. Moerland, T. Raaijmakers, and L. Rennneboog. Oxford: OUP.

Horwitz, Morton (1992) *The Transformation of American Law 1870–1960: The Crisis of Legal Orthodoxy.* Cambridge, MA: Harvard University Press.

Hovenkamp, Herbert (1991) *Enterprise and American Law, 1836–1937.* Cambridge, MA: Harvard University Press.

Hurst, J. Willard. (1970) *The Legitimacy of the Business Corporation in the Law of the United States, 1780–1970.* Charlottesville: University of Virginia.

Industrial Manslaughter (2005) *Special Edition: Flinders Journal of Law Reform* 8(1).

Ireland, Paddy, Ian Grigg-Spall, and Dave Kelly (1987) "The Conceptual Foundations of Modern Company Law." *J. of Law & Society* 14:149.

Ireland, P. (1983) "The Triumph of the Company Legal Form 1856–1914." In *Essays for Clive Schmithoff,* Editor John Adams. Abingdon, England: Professional Books.

Ireland, P. 1983 "Capitalism Without the Capitalist: The Joint Stock Company Share and the Emergence of the Modern Doctrine of Separate Corporate Personality." (1996) *J.. of Law & Society* 17:40.

Ireland, P. 1983 "Company Law and the Myth of Shareholder Ownership." (1999) *Modern L.R.* 62:32.

Ireland, P. 1983 "History, Critical Legal Studies and the Mysterious Disappearance of Capitalism." (2002) *Modern L.R.* 65:128.

Keynes, John Maynard (1926) *The End of Laissez-Faire.* London: Hogarth Press.

Keynes (1936) *The General Theory of Employment, Interest and Money.* London: Macmillan.

Kotz, David M. (2003) "Neoliberalism and the U.S. Economic Expansion of the '90 s." *Monthly Review*, 54 (Apr.). 15–33.

Kraakman, Reiner H. (1984) "Corporation Liability Strategies and the Costs of Legal Controls." *Yale L.J.* 93:857.

Lapham, Lewis (1996) "Lights, Camera, Democracy!" *Harper's Magazine* (Aug.).

Levitt, Arthur, and Paula Dwyer (2002) *Take on the Street: What Wall Street and Corporate America Don't Want You To Know*. New York: Pantheon Books.

Mandel, Michael (1994) *The Charter of Rights and the Legalization of Politics*. rev. ed. Toronto: Thompson Education Publishing Inc.

McLean, Bethany, and Peter Elkind (2003) *The Smartest Guys in the Room: The Amazing Rise and Scandalous Fall of Enron.* New York: Portfolio.

McNish, Jacquie (2005) "Corporate America's Reign of Terror Waning." *Globe & Mail, Report on Business,* 14 July, B p. 1.

Miller, Arthur Selwyn (1968) *The Supreme Court and American Capitalism*. New York: The Free Press.

Nadel, Mark V. (1975) "The Hidden Dimensions of Public Policy: Private Governments and the Policy-making Process." *Journal of Politics* 37: 2–34.

Nader, Ralph, Mark, Green, and Joel, Seligman (1976) *Corporate Power in America.* New York: Norton.

Nocera, Joseph (2005) "Stock Options: So Who's Counting?" *New York Times*, 6 August, B p. 1.

OECD (2004) *Principles of Corporate Governance—Annotations.* (Jan.).

Partnoy, Frank (2003) *Infectious Greed: How Deceit and Risk Corrupted the Financial Markets*. New York: Times Books/Holt & Co.

Penner, J.F. (1996) "The Bundles of Rights Picture of Property." *UCLA L.R.* 43:711–820.

Pettet, Ben. (2001) *Company Law.* Harlow, England: Longmans.

Polanyi, Karl (2001) *The Great Transformation: The Political and Economic Origins of Our Time.* Foreword Joseph E. Stiglitz. Introduction Fred Block. Boston: Beacon Press.

Posner, Richard A., and Kenneth E. Scott, Editors (1980) *Economics of Corporate Law and Securities Regulation.* Boston: Little, Brown.

Posner, Richard A. (2003) *Economic Analysis of Law.* 6th edition. New York: Aspen Publishers.

Posner Richard A. (1985) "An Economic Theory of the Criminal Law." *Col. L.R.* 85:1193.

Sarra, Janis (2003) "Rose-Coloured Glasses, Opaque Financial Reporting and Investor Blues: Enron as Con and the Vulnerability of Canadian Corporate Law." *St. John's L.R.* 73.

Smith, Adam (1994) *An Inquiry into the Nature and Causes of the Wealth of Nations.* Editor Edwin Cannon. New York: Modern Library.

Snider, Laureen (2001) "Abusing Corporate Power: The Death of a Concept." In *[Ab]using Power: The Canadian Experience,* Editors Susan C. Boyd, Dorothy E. Chunn, and Robert Menzies. Halifax, Nova Scotia: Fernwood Publishing.

Stout, Lynn A. (2005) "Share Price as a Poor Criterion for Good Corporate Law." Research Paper No. 05–7. *http://ssrn.com/abstract=660622.*

Suel, Seth (2005) "Investors Lean on Time Warner." *Toronto Star,* 16 August, D p. 1.

Swartz, Mimi, and Sharron Watkins (2003) *Power Failure.* New York: Doubleday.

Task Force on Labour Relations (1968) *Final Report.* Ottawa: Privy Council. (H.D.Woods, Chair).

Toffler, Barbara L., and Jennifer Reingold (2003) *Final Accounting: Ambition, Greed, and the Fall of Arthur Andersen.* New York: Broadway Books.

Tollefson, Christopher (1993) "Corporate Constitutional Rights and the Supreme Court of Canada." *Queen's L.J.* 19:309.

Tomasic, Roman (2001) "Good Corporate Governance: The International Challenge." *Aust. J. Corp. L* 12:142.

Toronto Stock Exchange (TSE) Committee on Corporate Governance (1994) *Where Were the Directors?—Draft Report.* (Chairman P. Dey). Toronto.

U.S. Newswire (2002) "Transcript of Bush Remarks at Signing of Sarbanes-Oxley Act of 2002." 30 July. *http:// www.usnewswire.com/topnews/prime/0730–115.html.*

de Vroey, Michel (1975) "The Separation of Ownership and Control in Large Corporations." *Rev. of Radical Pol. Eco.* 7(2):1.

Wheeler, Sally (2002) *Corporations and the Third Way.* Oxford/Portland, OR: Hart Publishing.

Wolff, Edward N. (2000) "Recent Trends in Wealth Ownership from 1983 to 1998." In *Assets for the Poor: The Benefit of Spending Asset Ownership*, Editors Thomas M. Shapiro and Edward N. Wolff. New York: Russell Sage Press. pp. 74–83.

Cases

Canadian Dredge & Dock Co. Ltd. v. The Queen, (1985), 19 Can. Crim. Cases (3d), 1 (Sup. Ct. Canada)

Louis K. Liggett Co. v. Lee 288 U.S. 517 (1933).

Statutes

Competitive Equality Banking Act of 1987, 12 USC 1903.

Private Securities Litigation Reform Act, 15 USC 78a (1995).

3

Preventive Fault and Corporate Criminal Liability: Transforming Corporate Organizations into Private Policing Entities

Richard S. Gruner

Since 1990, federal officials in the United States have used increasingly sophisticated preventive fault standards for assessing corporate criminal liability. Under these standards, the scope of corporate efforts to prevent offenses, usually as reflected in the presence of substantial corporate law compliance programs, is considered in determining whether corporations should be charged with offenses undertaken by employees for corporate gain and, if they are so charged and convicted, in determining what sorts of penalties and compelled reforms the corporations should bear.

The use of these preventive fault standards has injected a new element of organizational justice into the allocation of corporate criminal liability. These standards promote justice at an organizational level by treating firms which have taken responsible steps to promote law compliance more favorably than firms which have ignored efforts to prevent offenses in the course of activities they initiate. By attaching concrete corporate advantages of a large magnitude to the pursuit of crime prevention and detection activities, these corporate criminal liability standards have strongly encouraged corporations to undertake a private policing function in support of law enforcement efforts by public officials. In short, the shift in incentives reflected in corporate criminal standards has transformed many corporations from willing beneficiaries of criminal conduct by corporate employees (or at least relatively unconcerned observers) into strongly interested parties seeking to prevent such misconduct in a "practical partnership" with prosecutors and other law enforcement officials.

This chapter will trace the development of preventive fault standards in federal criminal laws, the policies supporting such standards, some of the changes in criminal law enforcement dynamics resulting from these standards, and the desirability of extending these standards into foreign contexts.

Injecting Organizational Culpability into Federal Criminal Law: A Brief History

Beginning in the 1990s, two trends have successfully injected organizational culpability standards into federal criminal laws, thereby focusing courts, prosecutors, and potential corporate defendants on the quality of corporate efforts to prevent offenses by employees and other corporate agents. First, corporate fines and other penalties threatened for illegal corporate activities have escalated markedly, leading to new concern over such penalties on the part of corporate executives and a new willingness of prosecutors to expend extensive resources on corporate prosecutions aimed at imposing these large penalties. Second, crime prevention efforts on the part of corporate organizations have increasingly been viewed as legitimate criteria for withholding or reducing corporate criminal liability that would otherwise impact corporations whose employees or agents have undertaken misconduct for corporate benefit. These trends have developed in tandem with the heightened threat of corporate penalties inspiring increased willingness on the part of corporations to undertake extensive crime prevention efforts and to cooperate diligently with prosecutors and law enforcement officials in exchange for the avoidance of corporate criminal charges and liability.

Increasing Corporate Penalties

For many years, corporate criminal sentences for federal offenses were few in number and generally insignificant in size. Between 1984 and 1989, only 41 publicly traded firms were prosecuted for federal crimes.[1] The mean fine imposed on the 288 corporations sentenced by federal courts during this period was only $48,164.[2] In part, the paucity of corporate prosecutions stemmed from the small fines available for corporate offenses and a corresponding lack of prosecutorial interest in corporate prosecutions.[3] Given that corporations cannot be incarcerated, the maximum corporate penalties threatened for most offenses are the maximum fines. Before 1984, the maximum corporate fines for most federal offenses were quite small. For example, federal wire fraud was formerly punishable by up to five years in prison, but a maximum fine of only $1,000 per offense.[4]

The unavailability of large corporate fines led to anomalous sentencing proceedings in which federal courts imposed modest penalties on firms convicted of serious crimes. In some cases, maximum corporate fines were far less than the illegal profits or cost savings which firms gained through illegal conduct given that such conduct was only occasionally detected and punished. With such an imbalance of gains and penalties, the implicit sentencing message was that corporate crime paid.

Amidst this backdrop of limited corporate sentencing options, the Sentencing Reform Act of 1984 (the Act) implemented "the most broad reaching reform of federal sentencing in this century."[5] This legislation made two key changes in corporate sentencing standards for federal crimes. First, the Act raised maximum fines for corporate offenders. Second, the Act created the United States Sentencing Commission and authorized the Commission to enact guidelines governing the sentencing of organizational offenders including corporations.

The Act raised maximum fines for corporate felonies and serious misdemeanors to $500,000 per offense.[6] Separate legislation established potentially higher fine limits of twice the gross loss or gain resulting from a corporate crime.[7]

Congress instructed the Sentencing Commission to draft guidelines to aid sentencing courts in furthering the goals and purposes of federal sentencing. The sentencing goals and purposes contemplated by Congress included—

1. the need to reflect the seriousness of offenses, to promote respect for the law, and to provide just punishment;
2. the need to afford adequate deterrence to criminal conduct;
3. the need to protect the public from further crimes of the defendant; and
4. the need to provide the defendant with educational or vocational training, medical care, or other correctional treatment in the most effective manner.[8]

Under organizational sentencing guidelines issued by the Sentencing Commission in 1991 and significantly revised in 2004, corporations convicted of federal offenses face several potentially burdensome types of sentences: (1) large fines, reduced where corporations have implemented systematic crime prevention efforts in law compliance programs adopted before offenses, (2) restitution orders establishing victim compensation for most federal offenses, (3) remedial orders mandating cleanups and other restorative measures beyond restitution payments, (4) notices to crime victims to spur individual recoveries, (5) restrictive probation sentences to prevent repeat offenses, and (6) adverse publicity to modify public attitudes toward corporate offenders.[9]

The corporate penalty provisions of the Sentencing Reform Act and the organizational sentencing guidelines have significantly increased the size and number of corporate fines for federal offenses committed by corporate employees and agents. In 2003, an advisory panel working at the behest of the Sentencing Commission to evaluate the impact of the organizational sentencing guidelines summarized the impact of the guidelines on corporate penalties as follows:[10]

> Sentencing Commission data reflects that 1,642 organizations have been sentenced under [the organizational sentencing guidelines] since the Commission began receiving this information.[11] ... [A] recent study concluded that criminal fines and total sanctions are significantly higher in cases constrained by the Guidelines than they were prior to the Guidelines. Controlling for other factors, criminal fines in cases constrained by the Guidelines are almost five times their previous levels. Total sanctions are also significantly higher, with the percentage increase about half that for criminal fines.[12]

According to commission data, the average organizational fine in fiscal year 1995 was $242,892, and the median fine was $30,000. In fiscal year 2001, the average fine was $2,154,929, and the median fine was $60,000.[13]

The Impact of Organizational Culpability on Corporate Fines

Fines recommended under the federal sentencing guidelines for convicted corporations are increased or decreased based on the organizational culpability of the corporations concerning the offenses committed by their employees and agents. The guidelines use culpability assessments for convicted corporations to determine how much recommended fine ranges should be shifted upward or downward. For two firms convicted of similar offenses, differences in culpability assessments can produce large differences in recommended fines. If one firm obtains the maximum culpability assessment under the guidelines and the other receives the minimum, the mid-point of the recommended fine range for the first firm is approximately twenty-four times higher than that for the second corporation.[14] Should courts choose to make further culpability distinctions when setting fines within recommended ranges, sentencing disparities based on corporate culpability can be even greater. The harshest recommended fine for a corporate defendant with a maximum culpability assessment is eighty times the minimum recommended fine for a defendant with a minimum culpability score.

Several different types of offender characteristics affect corporate culpability assessments. In general, corporate practices that promote offenses increase corporate culpability assessments, while practices that prevent or deter crimes lower corporate culpability assessments. Corporate fines are varied based on these criteria to ensure that, for identical criminal conduct by their agents, firms promoting or tolerating offenses receive harsher fines than corporations that diligently attempt to prevent and stop offenses.

While the organizational sentencing guidelines use organizational culpability indicators to adjust corporate fines, they do not specify a general definition of organizational culpability. However, the culpability standards adopted in the guidelines seem to reflect a "crime promotion" test for organizational culpability. Organizational culpability is present for purposes of the guidelines when organizational policies or practices are likely to increase the probability of criminal behavior by corporate employees and agents over the probability that would have prevailed in the absence of corporate action or surroundings. That is, a corporate organization is culpable to the extent that actions of its managers and employees promoted, tolerated, or otherwise made offenses more likely than would have been the case outside a corporate setting.[15] Some practices, like corporate managers' toleration of illegal conduct, increase corporate culpability by encouraging additional offenses. Conversely, corporate compliance programs or other corporate actions that reduce the probability of criminal conduct or increase the probability such conduct will be detected and stopped lower corporate culpability in connection with offenses.

Framed this way, heightened corporate culpability turns on diverse actions that make offenses by corporate employees more likely than equivalent offenses by individual offenders who are unaffiliated with corporate organizations. However, not every corporate activity that enhances the risk of incidental crimes is an indicator of corporate culpability. Only those activities that increase the likelihood of crimes in a foreseeable manner suggest culpability. In short, corporate culpability depends on characteristics of corporate organizations that intentionally or foreseeably promote illegal conduct.[16]

Actions that promote corporate offenses include managerial policies or practices that are themselves illegal because they authorize or compel criminal behavior by subordinates.[17] Corporate managers may also promote illegal conduct through policies or practices which, although lawful in themselves, encourage illegal conduct in foreseeable ways. Defective managerial responses to detected offenses may signify managerial support for similar conduct in the future. Hence, managerial conduct acquiescing in offenses and implying that a firm accepts and supports such illegal actions is another indicator of corporate culpability. Such acquiescence can be reflected in standard operating procedures tolerating observable criminal behavior, thereby institutionalizing a form of systematic blindness toward illegal conduct. Alternatively, acquiescence in corporate crimes can be shown from failures to address known criminal departures from lawful operating procedures.[18]

Corporate culpability of a different sort is present where firms fail to institute internal monitoring systems and other control mechanisms to detect and prevent offenses. The absence of such measures indicates corporate culpability because it reflects a failure to couple management-initiated corporate actions with appropriate law compliance safeguards. The corporate sentencing guidelines imply that corporate managers have a responsibility to police the business-related activities of corporate employees and balance performance demands with checks and limitations which ensure that performance demanded of employees is achieved lawfully. The guidelines provide firms with substantial sentencing rewards if managers undertake this sort of private policing.[19] Some industry observers have objected that this places corporate managers in the undesirable position of serving as surrogate law enforcement officers in policing internal business conduct.[20]

The assumption by the Sentencing Commission that every corporation has law enforcement duties concerning its employees' actions is consistent with corporate criminal liability standards under federal law. Firms are held criminally liable for offenses by their employees in part to encourage corporate managers to take actions to prevent such offenses.[21] It seems sensible to determine corporate culpability and fines based on how well those functions are undertaken and the extent to which corporations aid in the detection and punishment of individual offenders as means to increase future deterrents.

Yet another type of corporate culpability is present where corporate managers fail to monitor the impact of their incentive systems to determine if those systems are encouraging illegal behavior by corporate employees. Once corporate managers create strong incentives encouraging their employees to increase profits and minimize law compliance costs, firms have a corresponding duty to monitor whether the incentives have gone too far and created substantial crime risks. Corporate culpability in this respect is particularly clear where employee compensation is based primarily on performance measures (e.g., sales commissions or production volume bonuses), and corporate monitoring systems carefully evaluate the features of employee performance affecting corporate profits, but give less attention to law compliance by the same employees. When an employee, operating under this combination of incentives and partial monitoring, commits an offense to increase corporate profits and his own compensation, his firm bears some culpability due to its failure to balance its incentives with law compliance checks.

Some culpability of this sort underlies many offenses committed by corporate employees for corporate benefit. While not explicitly encouraging unlawful conduct, corporate managers indirectly promote offenses aimed at corporate gains or cost savings by adopting corporate compensation schemes that reward profit-making and cost-saving performance. These systems can strongly encourage employees to pursue conduct that achieves greater corporate revenues. This will, in turn, make employees more willing to consider illegal conduct for corporate gain than otherwise would be the case. Furthermore, to the extent that employees perceive profit or performance goals as being manifestly unattainable through lawful behavior, they may see the imposition of such goals as a sign that senior managers understand and approve of achieving those goals through illegal means. This shifting of employee preferences toward a greater willingness to engage in gain-producing crimes is inherent to some degree in all performance-based corporate compensation systems. Hence, a corresponding degree of corporate culpability is present in most or all employee offenses committed for corporate gain under such compensation schemes.

Indeed, offenses for corporate gain should generally be taken as circumstantial evidence of imbalances in corporate incentives and crime deterrence threats. This type of offense implies that the employee committing the offense felt he had more to gain in corporate compensation and rewards than he had to lose in potential discipline or criminal penalties. In short, the offense probably reflects a weakness in corporate monitoring and discipline in that there were no perceived net penalties for illegal conduct in the eyes of the individual offender.

The linkage between corporate profit-making incentives and corporate crimes—and the difficulty of assessing individual culpability and liability for those crimes instead of corporate criminal liability—is captured in the following description of typical corporate crimes in large firms:

> [D]ecision making tends to be diffused in a group context. Time and again the same pattern recurs. At the highest levels of the corporation generalized directions are given for corporate conduct. The board or CEO will exhort all managers to increase revenue. Managers further down the chain interpret these directions based on a variety of inputs. Somewhere near the bottom of the chain, managers make specific decisions that may run afoul of the law, but believe that more senior managers have supported this conduct. Attempting to impose penalties at any one point along the chain yields a very unsatisfying result. While one may chastise the senior managers for not being specific or thoughtful enough in their direction, it is usually very difficult to find specific intent to violate the law. At the lower levels one can identify individuals who clearly broke the law, but in most cases these individuals received little or no direct benefit from the violation. Enforcement officials sense that these small fish should not be the real targets, but they cannot find big fish with specific intent.[22]

Extending the Impact of Organizational Culpability to Prosecutorial Discretion

The federal sentencing guidelines implement an organizational culpability scheme as a basis for scaling corporate penalties at the sentencing phase of criminal proceedings. Standards governing federal prosecutors have injected similar culpability assessments into decisions at earlier stages about whether to charge corporations where their employees or agents have committed offenses for corporate gain. These offenses are ones for which federal law indicates that corporations can be held criminally liable. However, prosecutors can choose to withhold such liability by simply failing to institute corporate prosecutions.

The decision by a prosecutor whether to withhold criminal charges against a corporation—as well as the similar decision about what charges to bring where an array of charges are potentially applicable to conduct undertaken on a corporation's behalf—is critically important in determining the scope of corporate penalties that will result from an offense by corporate employees and agents. Where corporate charges are not filed, a corporation can not only avoid corporate criminal fines entirely, it can also avoid collateral consequences of a conviction such as debarment from government procurement programs and impairment of a convicted company's reputation in the eyes of corporate employees, customers, and community members. Hence, federal prosecutorial discretion standards relying on corporate culpability considerations are a second important means whereby corporate culpability has shaped the size of threatened criminal penalties and consequences associated with corporate offenses.

Under prosecutorial guidelines issued by the United States Department of Justice (DOJ) in 2003, federal prosecutors are instructed to consider a corporation's systematic efforts to detect and stop offenses by corporate employees and agents in determining whether to charge the corporation for a crime committed by an employee or other agent.[23]

These prosecutorial guidelines focus on several features of corporate law compliance programs related to the detection, prevention, and reporting of offenses. Specifically, where a corporate employee or agent has committed a crime, federal prosecutors deciding whether to bring criminal charges against the corporation involved are instructed to consider the following factors, among others:

1. the corporation's timely and voluntary disclosure of wrongdoing and its willingness to cooperate in the investigation of its agents, including, if necessary, the waiver of corporate attorney-client and work product protection;
2. the existence and adequacy of the corporation's compliance program; and
3. the corporation's remedial actions, including any efforts to implement an effective corporate compliance program or to improve an existing one, to replace responsible management, to discipline or terminate wrongdoers, to pay restitution, and to cooperate with the relevant government agencies.[24]

Shaping Criminal Investigations Through Prosecution Referral Standards

Personnel in federal regulatory agencies may detect and review corporate misconduct to determine whether it is serious enough to refer to prosecutors for possible criminal changes. In making these referral decisions, several federal agencies have indicated that they will consider corporate culpability as indicated by corporate crime prevention and self-reporting efforts.

For example, the federal Environmental Protection Agency (EPA) has promulgated standards that call for agency officials not to refer offenses by corporate employees to federal prosecutors where the offenses were detected and reported by a corporation through an environmental auditing process meeting the EPA's standards.[25] The EPA will withhold a criminal referral where a violation of federal environmental laws meets the following criteria:

1. The violation must have been discovered through either (a) an environmental audit, or (b) a compliance management system that reflects due diligence in preventing, detecting and correcting violations.
2. The violation must have been identified voluntarily, and not through a monitoring, sampling, or auditing procedure that is required by statute, regulation, permit, judicial or administrative order, or consent agreement.
3. The corporation must disclose the violation in writing to the EPA within 21 calendar days after discovery.

4. The corporation must discover the violation independently before the EPA or another government agency identified or was likely to have identified the problem either through its own investigative work or from information received through a third party.
5. The corporation must remedy any harm caused by the violation and expeditiously certify in writing to appropriate Federal, State, and local authorities that it has corrected the violation.
6. The corporation must agree to take steps to prevent a recurrence of the violation after it has been disclosed.
7. The corporation must not have experienced the same type of violation or a closelyrelated type of violation at the same facility within the past 3 years.
8. The violation involved must not have resulted in serious actual harm to the environment or have presented an imminent and substantial endangerment to public health or the environment.
9. The corporation must cooperate as required by EPA and provide the Agency with the information it needs to determine the applicability of the EPA's penalty reduction policy.

If a corporation establishes that it satisfies all of the conditions of the audit policy or all of the conditions of the audit policy except for systematic discovery, the EPA will not recommend to the United States Department of Justice or other prosecuting authority that criminal charges be brought against the disclosing entity, as long as the EPA determines that the violation is not part of a pattern or practice that demonstrates or involves:

1. a prevalent management philosophy or practice that conceals or condones environmental violations; or
2. high-level corporate officials' or managers' conscious involvement in, or willful blindness to, violations of federal environmental law.

Whether or not the EPA recommends a company for criminal prosecution, the EPA may recommend individual managers or employees for prosecution in connection with violations that are disclosed in accordance with the audit policy.

Implementing Corporate Culpability Assessments Through Deferred Prosecution Agreements

The culmination of trends toward greater corporate penalties and increased consideration of corporate culpability is also reflected in the increased use of deferred prosecution agreements to resolve corporate criminal charges.[26] Under these agreements, corporate criminal charges are filed against a firm based on misconduct in the firm's activities, but prosecutors agree not to pursue a trial on the charges and to eventually drop the charges so long as the corporation involved aids public officials in investigations of the individuals responsible for the offenses charged and the corporation institutes reforms to ensure that similar offenses are not committed in the future. These sorts of deferred prosecution agreements make corporations' post-offense culpability—as measured from corporate assistance with law enforcement efforts and the implementation of corporate reforms during the life of a deferred prosecution agreement—a key influence on corporate criminal penalties and consequences.

Deferred prosecution agreements have proven popular with prosecutors and corporations alike. For prosecutors, these agreements offer a chance to obtain timely corporate cooperation in the pursuit of evidence against individual offenders and to strongly encourage corporations to provide the types of investigative assistance and reforms that prosecutors feel are significant. For corporations, advantages of deferred prosecution agreements include (1) opportunities to avoid potentially devastating corporate fines and restrictive probation sentences, (2) the absence of corporate convictions triggering further adverse consequences like automatic debarment from government contracting or exclusion from government benefit programs, (3) avoidance of the stigma of corporate convictions, and (4) guidance regarding adequate future corporate conduct in terms of the obligations specified in the deferred prosecution agreements.

The attractive features of deferred prosecution agreements to both prosecutors and corporations seem likely to make these agreements increasingly common in the resolution of cases in which corporate criminal charges are meaningful threats. Indeed, by increasing the options for encouraging substantial corporate cooperation with prosecutors and internal corporate reforms, the availability of deferred prosecution agreements ensures that prosecutors will consider the scope of corporate liability and penalties under the sentencing guidelines in more and more cases as preliminary steps toward discussions of deferred prosecution arrangements with potential corporate defendants.

As of mid-2005, deferred prosecution agreements had been used to resolve corporate criminal charges against a number of large firms, including[27]—

American Electric Power (2005)
Monsanto (2005)

American International Group (AIG) (2004)
AmSouth Bancorp (2004)
AOL (2004)
Computer Associates (2004)
Invision (2004)
MCI (Worldcom) (2004)
Symbol Technologies (2004)

Banco Popular de P.R. (2003)
Canadian Imperial Bank (2003)
Merrill Lynch (2003)
PNC Financial Services (2003)

Arthur Anderson (proposed and rejected) (2002)

Prudential Securities (1994)

Criteria for Recognizing Low Organizational Culpability: Features of a Reasonable Compliance Program

By focusing on crime prevention efforts as indicators of low organizational culpability and the basis for reduced corporate criminal penalties, the federal sentencing guidelines and related standards used by prosecutors and regulators have increased the legal significance of systematic crime prevention measures carried out through corporate law compliance programs. While effective crime prevention measures in organizations can take many forms, there is now a substantial consensus that organizational law compliance programs should have certain minimum features in order to have a reasonable chance of success. These minimum features encompass the basic features that any effective organizational management system should have, whether that system is aimed at managing marketing, manufacturing, safety, or other aspects of corporate performance. A reasonable law compliance program is one in which a corporation has applied standard management tools to the particular problem of ensuring corporate law compliance.

In some settings, legal standards have identified the minimum compliance program features needed to obtain special legal treatment for a corporation. For example, federal sentencing guidelines for organizational offenders describe the minimum features of a generally effective "compliance and ethics program" warranting consideration in sentencing analyses.[28] The operation of such a program in advance of an offense committed by a corporate employee will qualify the corporation involved for a reduced sentence.[29] The sentencing guidelines' standards provide a useful blueprint for constructing compliance and ethics programs. A firm that operates a compliance and ethics program with the features specified in the guidelines stands to realize two sorts of criminal liability reductions. To the extent that a firm prevents illegal conduct through such a program, the company will avoid criminal prosecutions and penalties altogether. However, if a firm is not successful in preventing all offenses, its criminal penalties for offenses that do occur will still be reduced in recognition of its law compliance efforts.

Beyond their significance in corporate sentencing, the provisions of the sentencing guidelines are likely to be consulted by prosecutors and other government officials as they evaluate the quality of corporate compliance programs. Given their specificity and completeness in comparison with other available legal measures, the compliance program standards of the sentencing guidelines will generally serve as valuable, if not authoritative, tests for evaluating compliance programs in a variety of legal contexts. This section summarizes the guidelines' standards governing the adequacy of corporate law compliance programs.

General Criteria for an Effective Program

A compliance and ethics program must satisfy five types of tests under the sentencing guidelines.[30] These tests require the following:

1. *Due Diligence:* An effective compliance and ethics program for purposes of the guidelines must reflect an organization's "due diligence to prevent and detect criminal conduct" and efforts to "otherwise promote an organizational culture that encourages ethical conduct and a commitment to compliance with the law." Such a program must "be reasonably designed, implemented, and enforced so that the program is generally effective in preventing and detecting criminal conduct."
2. *Targeting Principles:* The design and implementation of a compliance and ethics program must take into account such factors as a firm's organizational

size, the nature of a firm's business, the types of offenses likely to be undertaken by corporate employees, and the prior offense history of a firm.

3. *Disqualifying Characteristics:* Certain compliance and ethics program characteristics will cause a program to fail to meet the guidelines' standards. These disqualifying characteristics include a program's lack of compliance with industry standards or with the requirements of an applicable government regulation. A compliance and ethics program may also be found to be inadequate under the guidelines' standards due to the recurrence of misconduct in a firm, the involvement of top executives or law compliance officials in an offense, or the failure of corporate managers to report an offense to public officials within a reasonable time after ascertaining that the offense occurred.
4. *Required Features:* A compliance and ethics program must incorporate seven key components in order to meet the guidelines' standards. These required features include (1) compliance standards and procedures, (2) high-level management leadership of the compliance and ethics program, (3) responsible authority delegation, (4) steps to communicate standards and procedures, (5) monitoring, auditing, and evaluation practices to achieve compliance and ensure program sufficiency, (6) discipline, incentives, and enforcement actions applied so as to promote compliance, and (7) active organizational responses to misconduct that are aimed at preventing future misconduct and correcting program deficiencies.
5. *Ongoing Risk Assessments:* A compliance and ethics program must include ongoing efforts by an organization to periodically assess the risks of criminal misconduct in the course of the organization's activities and to adjust its compliance and ethics program practices to reduce those risks. Compliance risk assessments must include evaluations of both the nature and seriousness of potential corporate offenses.

The Nature of Due Diligence in Organizational Law Compliance Efforts

The guidelines' treatment of the due diligence expected of a corporate organization in pursuing law compliance offers particular insights into the nature of responsible crime prevention actions rewarded under the guidelines. According to the sentencing guidelines, the hallmarks of an effective compliance and ethics program are "due diligence" to prevent offenses, targeting of the program to match the offense risks identified in a company's compliance risk assessments, and program results indicating that the program is "reasonably effective" in eliminating offenses. Efforts to prevent offenses should not be limited to the implementation by a company of law compliance standards and internal controls, but should also include measures to create a corporate culture which promotes law compliance by making such compliance the expected norm among corporate employees.

These criteria for measuring adequate crime prevention steps constituting "due diligence" in the pursuit of corporate law compliance suggest four key tests for the adequacy of compliance and ethics programs.

First, an effective compliance and ethics program must be aimed at preventing those types of offenses that are likely to be present in an organization. Offenses that can be anticipated through reasonable projections of future misconduct should be given attention in a compliance and ethics program. Conversely, offenses outside this range need not be addressed in preventive measures until the occurrence of one of those apparently rare offenses suggests a need for retargeting the program.

Second, the degree of program efforts that will constitute "due diligence" to prevent offenses depends on the seriousness to the public of the potential offenses arising out of a corporation's activities and the probable costs and other negative business impacts of corporate measures to reduce the public impacts of such offenses. Corporations must consider the likely impacts of offenses by their employees and agents if the corporations are to properly target and scale their offense prevention efforts in compliance and ethics programs.

Third, an effective compliance and ethics program should include both compliance standards governing conduct by corporate employees and agents, monitoring procedures that limit opportunities for illegal conduct, and measures to create an ethical culture and establish a commitment to law compliance throughout a corporation. The creation of this type of culture and commitment will depend on actions by corporate leaders which convincingly convey management's expectations that law compliance should be the norm in corporate actions and that all corporate employees must work to further this end.

Fourth, with respect to foreseeable types of offenses, a compliance program must only be reasonably successful in preventing offenses. Corporate law compliance programs should include reasonable steps to prevent predictable offenses, but need not prevent every such offense. Programs must be generally successful, not perfect. The failure to prevent or detect an offense that was in some way significantly unpredictable or unusual should not preclude a compliance program from being seen as substantial and a basis for favorable corporate treatment.

Policy Underpinnings of Corporate Culpability Standards and Increased Corporate Self-Policing of Internal Activities

Corporations as Public Trustees Regarding the Prevention and Detection of Internal Crimes

The organizational sentencing guidelines—and related prosecutorial and regulatory standards derived from the sentencing guidelines' criteria for an effective compliance and ethics program—implement a new model of criminal law enforcement in corporate organizations.[31] Rather than viewing all crimes by corporate agents as offenses subtly initiated or promoted by corporate principals, the guidelines recognize that many corporate crimes involve misconduct by low-level corporate employees in which corporate managers have little or no role. Federal criminal laws and the sentencing guidelines impose criminal penalties on corporations for crimes like these not because corporate managers caused or promoted the crimes, but rather to encourage managerial attention to preventing and detecting them.

Conceived this way, corporate criminal liability encourages a corporation (acting primarily through its managers) to serve as a public trustee, with responsibilities to actively promote law compliance and the administration of justice in connection with business activities initiated by the corporation.[32] This quasi-official role involves obligations that are coextensive with a firm's business reach. It entails both duties to assist public authorities in preventing crimes and to aid in law enforcement investigations once crimes are committed by corporate employees or agents.

While service by corporations as law enforcement trustees is not explicitly recognized in federal statutes as a factor affecting corporate criminal liability, federal *respondeat superior* standards for attributing criminal liability to firms have been interpreted in a manner consistent with such a trustee model. Corporate criminal liability is imposed under federal case law for most employee crimes, even where employees are acting contrary to instructions from their superiors in committing offenses.[33] Such cases suggest that corporate criminal liability is imposed not because an employee committing an offense has been authorized to engage in illegal conduct, but rather because an offense by an employee carrying out corporate affairs reflects a failure of corporate managers to fulfill their law enforcement obligations. That is, criminal liability is imposed on a firm due to its failure to adequately serve as a public trustee for law enforcement within the firm.

An Agency Analysis of Criminal Law Enforcement Through Corporate Trustees

The imposition of corporate criminal liability on this basis and the creation of corresponding law enforcement incentives for corporate managers have sound underpinnings in agency principles. Corporations are expected to serve as agents of the public in carrying out crime prevention functions. The use of corporate managers and employees as law enforcement agents is aimed in part at overcoming barriers to effective law enforcement within corporations through traditional means. To the extent that large corporate organizations operate in substantial isolation from public scrutiny, the information gathering costs for detection of corporate crimes by traditional means are often large. However, equivalent information is often available to corporate managers during normal management activities. Furthermore, corporate managers can use their accumulated insight into a firm's operating methods to identify sources of useful information and to interpret data gathered on possible misconduct. Finally, corporate managers will typically be more effective in gathering information from employees than outside investigators since managers can threaten termination or other discipline against employees who are hesitant to disclose information needed in investigations.

However, if corporate managers are to serve as a sort of private police force regarding corporate misconduct, some very substantial corporate rewards for effective law enforcement efforts are probably necessary to encourage diligent action. Viewing corporate managers as agents of the public for law enforcement purposes, the challenge in agency terms is to provide positive incentives for successful law enforcement efforts or negative consequences for failures in these efforts. These positive or negative incentives must be sufficiently large and apparent to motivate corporate managers to act as public agents and to undertake desired law enforcement efforts.

The sentencing guidelines establish these types of incentives in several ways. Two important types of rewards for the pursuit of law compliance are created by provisions for fine reductions based on corporate compliance programs and post-offense responses aiding law enforcement. In providing for reduced fines based on these types of desirable conduct, the federal sentencing guidelines encourage corporations and their managers to perform in a socially desirable fashion as public agents or trustees for corporate law enforcement purposes.

This attempt under the guidelines to shift responsibilities from public to private law enforcers has not gone unnoticed. Some corporate counsel view the operation of compliance programs as "doing the government's job" and have argued for more substantial corporate rewards to compensate for this private allocation of law enforcement responsibilities.[34] Beyond the fine reductions provided for in the organizational sentencing guidelines, additional corporate rewards for sound compliance programs might include complete corporate immunity from liability for offenses committed by employees, qualification for special government opportunities (such as granting a company with a substantial compliance program a preferred status as a government supplier), or public recognition by government officials of superior compliance efforts to improve the reputations of the firms involved.

While these more substantial rewards might motivate greater voluntary efforts, for the moment corporations and their managers are expected to undertake criminal law enforcement efforts as conscripts, not volunteers.[35] Internal law enforcement duties are demands placed on business managers in exchange for the privilege of operating their businesses through the corporate form. To the extent that operating a business through a complex and often socially isolated corporate organization tends to shield internal misconduct from detection, this mode of business operation may foster more criminal activities than would be undertaken by independent individuals engaged in similar business activities without the cloak of a corporate organization. It is fair to expect parties operating businesses through corporate organizations and receiving the business and legal benefits of this mode of operation to take extra law enforcement steps to counteract the relative isolation of many corporate activities from scrutiny by traditional law enforcement personnel.

Demands for Private Policing in Corporate Organizations

The sentencing guideline's emphasis on private policing in corporate organizations and reliance on corporate managers as law enforcement monitors akin to private police forces within corporate organizations[36] is consistent with society's increasing demands for police activities in general. Societal demands for policing by state agents tends to increase where three circumstances are present (1) inequality in social conditions is large; (2) crime victims and persons who are in positions to monitor and reveal illegal conduct by offenders have few if any social relationships such that the persons capable of revealing criminal conduct are unlikely to act on behalf of crime victims; and (3) there are few institutions other than police forces to discourage illegal conduct.[37] In connection with traditional types of crime, if public resources do not meet demands for police activity under these circumstances, various forms of nonstate policing such as private guard services or citizen anti-crime organizations may be called on to fill the gap.[38]

Demands for policing stem from two characteristics of social fragmentation. First, persons who are not in daily contact with parties they perceive as potential criminals lack the information sources about incipient criminal activities that would exist in a small, close-knit community. Persons expect police personnel to obtain this information. Second, potential victims in a fragmented society may expect that persons sharing community backgrounds with criminals will identify with offenders more readily than with remote crime victims and, therefore, will not come forth to aid in law enforcement efforts. Hence, demands for police activities of various sorts grow with increases in the diversity of populations and with the isolation of particular community segments from others.

The growing complexity and isolation of large corporate organizations from other portions of society at least partially explain increasing public demands for regulatory oversight and criminal investigations of corporate activities. Many persons with little or no access to corporate operations have no basis to evaluate the social responsibility of corporate actors. However, they fear—correctly in some cases—that strong pressures for corporate profits may result in the sacrifice of public interests to corporate gains. Coupled with this fear is a sense that when misconduct occurs inside a firm, the tendency of corporations toward secrecy and a desire to protect co-workers will encourage concealment of the misconduct rather than revelations to public authorities. In light of such suspicion about corporate motives and the forthrightness of corporate disclosures concerning internal misconduct, the public increasingly looks to regulators, law enforcement personnel, and prosecutors to provide checks on illegal corporate conduct that individual citizens cannot adequately monitor themselves. Many individuals no doubt perceive themselves as potential victims of misconduct by large corporations, yet feel helpless to prevent and avoid injuries absent the deterrent efforts of public officials. Hence, they expect regulators and law enforcement personnel to undertake corporate crime prevention efforts on their behalf.

The emphasis in the organizational sentencing guidelines on encouraging law enforcement steps by corporate managers is an outgrowth of these expectations. If present resources of traditional law enforcement personnel do not permit sufficient enforcement efforts to achieve a high level of corporate crime prevention, it may be possible to produce equivalent results through the efforts of corporate managers. From this instrumental perspective, reliance on internal corporate law enforcement efforts is a way to accommodate increased public suspicion of isolated corporate bureaucracies in a period when decreasing public resources make public officials less and less able to provide an independent law enforcement check on those bureaucracies.

Altered Managerial Relationships Following Internalization of Corporate Law Enforcement

While the expanded involvement of corporate managers in crime detection and prevention may improve law enforcement and compliance in corporate organizations, these activities are also likely to alter relationships between corporate managers and traditional law enforcement personnel and between managers and their employees. On the one hand, law enforcement officials and corporate managers may move toward greater cooperation instead of the adversarial confrontations that have generally characterized their relationships to this point. On the other hand, firms and their employees (particularly those engaged in misconduct or with information about internal misconduct but not wishing to divulge it) may move toward more adversarial relationships.

The nature of the relationship between corporate managers and law enforcement personnel that is encouraged under the organizational sentencing guidelines is a matter of continuing debate. According to some law enforcement personnel, the guidelines recognize that federal prosecutors, investigators, and corporate managers share a "practical partnership" in combating corporate crime. However, unlike a business partnership, corporate membership in this arrangement is compulsory, not voluntary. As one United States Attorney has observed—

> Managements of publicly held corporations are left with few alternatives to attempting to prevent wrongdoing in the corporation, detecting it when it occurs and reporting it to the authorities.[39]

If a true law enforcement partnership is to develop between law enforcement officials and corporate managers, their relationships will need to be premised on a much higher degree of trust than presently prevails between these parties. Changes in both managerial and prosecutorial behavior are needed.

For corporate managers, the trust of prosecutors can only be gained through a track record of reliable assistance to law enforcement officials. If managers wish to be seen as promoting law enforcement in a responsible manner, the managers cannot pick and choose when to aid law enforcement officials and when to resist. Rather, they must consistently engage in active crime detection and disclosure, erring, when in doubt, toward over-inclusive rather than under-inclusive revelations. With such a pattern of cooperation and public service, prosecutors will have good reasons to believe they are receiving complete corporate cooperation in particular cases.

For their part, prosecutors need to provide greater assurances of desirable corporate treatment following law enforcement assistance if they are to build managerial trust in the desirability of such assistance. Two types of prosecutorial actions would be beneficial. First, prosecutors need to establish concrete standards for withholding corporate prosecutions or filing lesser corporate charges when corporations detect, disclose, and seek to prevent internal crimes. Binding standards governing prosecutorial discretion will help to ensure consistency among prosecutors. Such standards would also provide corporate managers with compliance practice targets to aim for without fear that criteria for beneficial corporate treatment will be constantly changed so as to be kept just out of reach. Second, if formal standards for beneficial treatment are not met, but firms nonetheless provide significant assistance in disclosing illegal conduct and bringing responsible individuals to justice, prosecutors should recognize this desirable corporate conduct with favorable charging decisions. A consistent practice of withholding prosecutions on these grounds will help to reassure corporate managers that, regardless of the formal status of corporate compliance programs, their cooperation and efforts to reveal incriminating information to public prosecutors will work to their company's advantage by reducing corporate liability. It will also indicate that prosecutors have due regard for the legitimate interests of innocent shareholders, managers, and employees and will not impose fines and related hardships on companies in which these persons are stakeholders so long as corporate managers and employees have served the public by contributing meaningfully to law enforcement.

The notion that firms cooperating with prosecutors should never be treated more harshly than they would probably have been treated absent such cooperation suggests a strategy for government decisions about prosecuting corporate defendants. Where firms (1) cooperate by revealing information about corporate offenses that prosecutors would probably not have detected from other sources and that was not otherwise required to be revealed and (2) undertake significant self-studies and reforms to reduce the chances of a repeat offense, favorable prosecutorial treatment should follow. In most cases, this treatment should include the withholding of corporate charges. Where one or more of these steps is lacking, but some desirable corporate actions are taken which promote law enforcement, then less favorable treatment should follow, such as withholding the most serious charges available against the firm and filing only lesser charges.

This strategy for targeting corporate prosecutions is desirable because, absent positive prosecutorial treatment of corporations in a predictable pattern, corporate managers will have no reason to cooperate with prosecutors concerning offenses that are detected within firms but unlikely to be detected or fully investigated by outside authorities. Given that managerial cooperation with investigations concerning such offenses may result in increased corporate costs if this cooperation is followed by corporate charges and liability, managers will tend to refuse to cooperate unless they are confident that prosecutors will reciprocate in kind. Put into economic terms, corporate managers possessing information about a corporate offense and considering cooperation with prosecutors are placed in a form of prisoner's dilemma. Their optimal result would be achieved by cooperating with prosecutors and having prosecutors cooperate with them through favorable prosecutorial treatment producing no corporate penalty. However, if corporate managers perceive that disclosures to prosecutors may hurt their firm by triggering new corporate charges and liability, they may conclude that their optimal strategy is to withhold cooperation with prosecutors. That is—in the absence of certainty about prosecutors' responses—corporate managers may believe, perhaps correctly, that the interests of their firm are best served by avoiding disclosures. They will tend to adopt this view in the hope that, absent the information the managers hold, prosecutors will not detect the crime involved (or will feel that they are unable to prove the facts necessary to establish corporate liability for the crime) and no prosecution will follow. The only way out of this dilemma is to increase managerial confidence in the linkage between corporate cooperation and beneficial corporate treatment by prosecutors.

Changes in corporate criminal liability standards that increase managerial incentives to monitor and disclose offenses by corporate employees will also change relationships between corporations and their employees.[40] If firms adopt the sorts of internal policing activities encouraged by the guidelines, corporate managers conducting internal audits and investigations and regularly disclosing detected misconduct will pose obvious threats to internal wrongdoers and those who wish to shield such wrongdoers from punishment. These changes are likely to create new tensions between corporate managers and employees. In settings where employees are unsure about the bounds of lawful activities, the adoption of a significant internal "policing" apparatus may also hamper legitimate employee creativity and lower employee morale.[41]

To avoid these problems, firms must prepare employees for law compliance monitoring and the investigative aftermath of an internal offense. Corporate employees engaging in offenses in their jobs must be characterized as acting as much against corporate interests as employees stealing corporate property.

Employee attitudes toward corporate offenders should be shaped accordingly. A firm must also convince employees that resisting an audit or investigation or altering evidence with the aim of protecting an individual offender is not in their company's interest. To the extent that employees are convinced of this by internal discipline imposed on employees who engage in such abuses, law compliance audits, investigations and disclosures will proceed more smoothly. Perhaps more important, potential offenders will be more strongly deterred because they will not count on internal corporate shelters to protect them from prosecutions and criminal punishments.

Expanding Corporate Culpability Tests into International Criminal Law Systems

As described here, the notion that corporations which make substantial efforts to prevent and detect illegal misconduct by corporate employees should avoid some or all liability for that misconduct is a central feature of United States criminal laws and has substantial policy underpinnings. The policy advantages already discussed would suggest that similar corporate culpability standards and criminal liability gradients would also be valuable components of foreign legal systems. This section considers some of the features of foreign criminal law systems that may create barriers to the type of corporate criminal liability standards turning on preventive fault that have emerged in United States criminal laws and prosecutorial standards.

Limits on Corporate Criminal Liability

A fundamental limitation on the use of corporate criminal liability as a means to encourage responsible crime prevention efforts by corporate organizations is the complete failure of some foreign legal systems to recognize organizational criminal liability under any circumstances. These foreign systems refuse to accept this type of liability because they maintain a strict requirement that criminal liability be based on personal scienter or bad intent and do not accept the notion that an organization can have that intent. Given that corporations cannot possess the characteristic which is the lynchpin of criminal liability, corporations are exempt from criminal liability under these systems, although their culpable employees remain criminally liable as individuals.

Professor John C. Coffee, Jr., has summarized the limited recognition of corporate criminal liability in some foreign legal systems as follows:[42]

> [C]ivil law regimes uniformly dismissed the idea of corporate criminal law liability, largely because the concept of *mens rea* seemed inconsistent with that of a fictional person.[43] British law went only a modest half step further. As late as 1971, the House of Lords showed itself still wedded to a narrow "alter ego" theory of corporate criminal liability under which only officers at very senior executive levels within the corporation could "be identified with it, as being or having its directing mind and will, its centre or ego, and its brains...."[44] Under this simplistic—and indeed anthropomorphic—model of corporate decision-making, if an individual does not qualify as a "corporate organ," his acts and intent cannot be imputed to the corporation, even though he may be responding to pressures or incentives created by higher ranking personnel within the corporation. Underinclusive as this theory seems, it nonetheless remains the dominant paradigm in those legal systems that follow British precedent.[45]

Systems which maintain a strict requirement of individual scienter and culpability in order to impose criminal liability do possess several advantages. They focus serious criminal penalties on personal decisions to act in a culpable manner and thereby clarify the deterrent message of criminal liability. These systems also reassure corporate managers that their organizational treasuries or resources will not be unexpectedly impaired by criminal penalties, although individual corporate employees or agents may be subjected to such penalties where they engage in culpable conduct either for their own gain or that of their corporation. Criminal law systems lacking corporate criminal liability may also streamline certain criminal proceedings by avoiding complex disputes about the scope of corporate misconduct and related crime prevention efforts by corporations to the extent that such efforts bear on sentencing decisions.

Despite these advantages, criminal law systems having no corporate criminal liability are probably undesirable on balance. Since corporations have no stake in the criminal penalties at issue, these legal systems lose the opportunity to strongly interest corporate managers in the prevention and detection of misconduct in the course of corporate affairs. They also fail to offer differential incentives and rewards to corporations undertaking extensive crime prevention efforts relative to firms undertaking no such efforts. In short, while there are advantages and superficial simplicities in criminal law systems limiting criminal liability to individuals with personal culpability, these systems seem unnecessarily inflexible and ill tailored to the realities of modern corporate crime characteristics and settings in which corporations and their managers may often be the only effective law enforcement actors. Criminal law systems lacking corporate criminal liability fail to capitalize on the crime prevention capabilities of corporate organizations and the ability of differential criminal penalties, varied in accordance with the quality of corporate compliance and ethics programs, to motivate company executives to use these crime prevention capabilities. Criminal law systems having this type of complete blindness to corporate criminal liability would probably be improved by enhanced threats of such liability, mediated by corporate culpability criteria.

Cultural Impediments to Compliance Program Features

Values present in some cultures may impair the operation of certain compliance program features regarded as essential in compliance programs operated in the United States and force foreign legal systems to adopt different criteria for assessing the reasonableness of a compliance program.

For example, in some foreign settings, systems for receiving anonymous whistleblower reports are viewed in a much less positive light than they are by most managers of United States companies.[46] In these foreign settings, anonymous reports on asserted misconduct by fellow employees are seen by some persons as undesirable counterparts to false reports made on fellow citizens in such repressive regimes as Nazi Germany. Likewise, a system calling for employees to monitor misconduct by their fellow workers and to report detected instances of misconduct to corporate managers may call up images of the oppressive surveillance of earlier repressive regimes in particular countries, leading to a unusual hostility to law compliance monitoring and reporting systems in corporate organizations.

In terms of managerial effectiveness, these concerns over whistleblower and compliance monitoring features of compliance programs are probably misguided. Such program features are needed to overcome the peculiar isolation from public scrutiny that corporate internal misconduct would otherwise enjoy given the separation of many corporate activities from outside observers and the tendency of coworkers sharing corporate activities to maintain secrecy about corporate activities. Hence, corporate whistleblower processes and compliance monitoring efforts probably do not implement an oppressive environment in most cases, but rather establish a balanced level of compliance scrutiny and information flow as corporate-initiated activities go forward.

However, even if corporate whistleblower programs and compliance monitoring and auditing efforts are perceived as having positive net consequences such that they should be encouraged under legal standards developed in foreign legal systems, the types of compliance-promoting practices that are needed in a reasonable compliance program will depend on the degree of countervailing resistance and hostility encountered in employee populations. This suggests that standards for reasonable compliance efforts may vary considerably as employee and societal values regarding surveillance and misconduct reporting differ.

Developing Compliance Program Standards Through Fragmented Common Law Processes

In common law systems where many legal standards are developed in case analyses, generally applicable standards for assessing the quality of compliance programs may not emerge clearly due to the narrow factual focus of particular cases and the fragmentary quality of compliance program assessments related to the facts of particular cases. Court assessments of compliance practices in any particular case may focus on specific compliance program elements that are at issue without consideration of the broader features of a corporate defendant's compliance program or the overall effectiveness of the program.

Following an extensive review of corporate criminal cases, the Law Reform Commission for New South Wales (NSW), Australia, noted the often fragmentary and incomplete assessments of corporate compliance programs by criminal courts:

Corporate Compliance Systems

> 4.32 The absence or inadequacy of procedures in the corporation to prevent the contravention of the law may aggravate the penalty. On the other hand, the existence of such a system may result in a more lenient penalty. For example, steps taken by the company to educate employees prior to the breach or the existence of a company policy against breaches of the law have been held to be relevant. Steps taken by the corporation after the occurrence of the offense, such as the adoption or improvement of policies and procedures to prevent further contravention may be taken into account to mitigate the penalty.
>
> 4.33 Most of the New South Wales cases where the presence or absence of corporate compliance systems have been held relevant have been in the areas of occupational health and safety, environmental protection and contempt by publication. There is, however, a lack of clarity in the cases as to what is required for a compliance system to help mitigate the severity of corporate penalties. There is some confusion over whether the mere existence of a compliance system is sufficient or if the corporation

must prove that the system has the capacity to prevent and detect violations of the law. The standards by which the effectiveness of such programs could be gauged are not apparent.[47]

In general, the lack of experience and specialized knowledge of criminal courts regarding corporate crime prevention systems, coupled with the often narrow concern of such courts with the types of compliance program features that have failed in a particular criminal case, will tend to produce analyses by courts in common law systems that do not assess the full range of compliance program elements which are relevant in determining if a company operated a generally effective law compliance program. Absent such complete assessments, common law courts may tend to allocate reduced corporate criminal penalties to firms that do not possess generally effective systems or fail to grant penalty reductions to firms that have such systems. In addition, the narrowly focused analyses of these courts may provide little guidance to company executives regarding the overall characteristics of compliance programs that will qualify their firms for reduced penalties in the future.

Developing Compliance Program Criteria Based on General Management Tools

In contrast to the problems raised by fragmentary analyses of compliance programs by criminal courts, efforts by law reform commissions or equivalent bodies in foreign legal systems offer means to develop comprehensive criteria for evaluating compliance program features and to link those criteria to tests for good corporate management tools.

In the United States, the Sentencing Commission adopted a similar approach to assessing and revising federal sentencing standards for evaluating compliance programs. Upon the tenth anniversary of the effective date of the Sentencing Commission's organizational sentencing guidelines implementing reduced sentences for corporations with responsible compliance programs, the Commission appointed an Advisory Group on the Organizational Sentencing Guidelines to assess the impact of the guidelines and to evaluate the need for changes in the guidelines' standards for identifying effective compliance programs. The Advisory Group reflected a broad range of experience with organizational sentencing and compliance programs, being comprised of present and former prosecutors (including a former Deputy Attorney General, the former head of the Justice Department's Antitrust Division, and several present and former U.S. Attorneys), criminal defense attorneys, compliance program experts, organizational ethics specialists, and legal and business school academics.[48]

After conducting an 18-month study of organizational sentencing practices and evolving knowledge in the business community regarding effective compliance practices, the Advisory Group recommended several modifications in the sentencing guidelines' criteria for an effective compliance program.[49] These recommendations building on expanded experience with compliance methods and improved understanding of the linkage between those methods and corporate management generally were largely accepted by the Sentencing Commission, resulting in new sentencing guidelines effective on November 1, 2004.[50]

Foreign legal systems with law reform commissions have recognized the advantages of using such commissions to develop complete compliance program standards for inclusion in criminal laws. Studies by such commissions have produced recommendations that compliance program standards require corporations to implement effective management tools for preventing offenses in order to qualify for favorable legal treatment. The conclusions of the NSW Law Reform Commission, reached after an extensive study of organizational sentencing practices worldwide, are typical of the emphasis on effective management tools in newly developed criminal law standards:

> 4:35 The Commission is of the view that it should not be sufficient for a compliance program to exist or for a corporation merely to exhort its officers and employees to obey the law. Case law supports the view that a compliance program must also be a successful management tool with the demonstrated capacity to prevent, detect and remedy breaches that may occur in the daily conduct of the company's business.[51]

Studies such as the evaluations of the NSW Law Reform Commission, while difficult to complete, offer the promise of saving governmental resources over time by assisting sentencing courts in numerous organizational sentencing analyses, ensuring that these analyses are complete and well constructed, and sending clear signals to corporate executives about the characteristics of generally effective compliance and ethics programs and the types of corporate actions that are necessary to qualify for favorable legal treatment under corporate criminal laws.

Conclusion

Beginning with the federal sentencing guidelines for organizational offenders promulgated by the United States Sentencing Commission in 1991, substantial criminal liability reductions have been available for corporate concerns that take reasonable efforts to self-police their operations, to instruct their employees how to obey the law, to detect violations of law in company activities, and to report detected offenses to public authorities. This basis for varying corporate liability has proven attractive to lawmakers in both criminal and regulatory contexts and is now a primary consideration in corporate criminal liability standards, prosecutorial discretion criteria, and regulatory liability measures in such diverse fields as health care fraud, money laundering, environmental offenses, and securities law violations.[52]

Liability reduction incentives for companies that engage in reasonable crime prevention have proven to be effective means to focus management attention on crime control and to marshal the power of organizational management tools and resources to prevent and detect criminal offenses in corporate contexts. The reaffirmation of these rewards by the Sentencing Commission in amendments to the sentencing guidelines enacted in 2004 confirms the Commission's belief in the success of this sentencing approach over its first decade of operation.[53] As threats of criminal liability rise in size and number, the criminal sentencing rewards available for substantial compliance efforts should cause more and more corporations to follow the lead of the sentencing guidelines and to adopt effective compliance and ethics programs. In addition, the reliance of numerous regulatory agencies on the reward logic and the compliance program definitions of the sentencing guidelines will ensure that governmental encouragement of corporate self-policing proceeds in regulatory as well as criminal contexts.

As both guidelines for corporate action and bases for harsh treatment of convicted corporations lacking reasonable crime prevention practices, standards for identifying generally effective corporate compliance and ethics programs are at the heart of the most important shift in corporate criminal law in many decades—the transformation of business corporations from passive beneficiaries of many corporate offenses into self-policing entities that are intensely interested in preventing corporate crimes and other internal misconduct.

Endnotes

1. Cohen, "Corporate Crime and Punishment: An Update on Sentencing Practice in the Federal Courts, 1988–1990," 71 B.U. L. Rev. 247, 252 (1991).
2. Id. at 254.
3. Rakoff, "The Corporation as Policeman: At What Price?" New York Law Journal, p. 3 (Jan. 9, 1992).
4. See 18 U.S.C. § 1343 (1984).
5. Nagel, "Structuring Sentencing Discretion: The New Federal Sentencing Guidelines," 80 J. Crim. L. & Criminology 883, 883 (1990).
6. 18 U.S.C. § 3571(c). The $500,000 maximum fine applies to all corporate felonies and those corporate misdemeanors that result in the loss of human life. Id. For Class A misdemeanors that do not result in the loss of human life, the maximum corporate fine is $200,000. Id. For non-Class A misdemeanors that do not result in death and for all infractions, the maximum corporate fine is $10,000. Id.
7. 18 U.S.C. § 3571(d).
8. 18 U.S.C. § 3553(a).
9. U.S. Sentencing Commission, Sentencing Guidelines Manual ch.8 (2004).
10. Advisory Group on the Organizational Sentencing Guidelines, U.S. Sentencing Commission, Final Report 25 (2003) (available at http://www.ussc.gov/corp/advgrprpt/advgrprpt.htm).
11. [FN98] 28 U.S.C. §§ 995(14) & (15) empower the Commission to "publish data concerning the sentencing process" and "collect systematically and disseminate information concerning sentences actually imposed. . . . " The PROTECT ACT recently amended the Sentencing Reform Act at 28 U.S.C. § 994(w) to require that the Chief Judge of each district ensure certain sentencing documents be submitted to the Commission: the judgment and commitment order; the statement of reasons for the sentence imposed (including the written reason for any departure); any plea agreement; the indictment or other charging document; and the presentence report). See Section 401(h) of Pub. L. No. 108–21 (April 30, 2003).
12. [FN99] Cindy R. Alexander, Jennifer H. Arlen & Mark Cohen, The Effect of Federal Sentencing Guidelines on Penalties for Public Corporations, 12 Fed. Sentencing REP. 20, 20 (July/Aug.1999); see also Cindy R. Alexander, Jennifer H. Arlen & Mark A. Cohen, Regulating Corporate Criminal Sanctions: Federal Guidelines and the Sentencing of Public Firms, 41 J. Law & Econ. 393 (1999).
13. [FN100] See the Sentencing Commission's Annual Reports, collected at http://www.ussc.gov/corp/organizsp.htm.
14. See U.S. Sentencing Commission, Sentencing Guidelines Manual, § 8C2.6 (2004).
15. This definition of corporate culpability is very similar to that developed by Jennifer Moore. Based on a lengthy study of corporate culpability and its relationship to corporate criminal laws, Moore concluded that the following features characterize corporate fault and culpability:

> By substituting an organizational decision-making process for its agents' individual autonomy, the corporation shapes and controls their behavior. When this process is likely to result in violations on behalf of the corporation on the part of its agents, the corporate entity may be said to be at fault.

Moore, "Corporate Culpability Under the Federal Sentencing Guidelines," 34 Ariz. L. Rev. 743, 796 (1992). See generally, Laufer, "Corporate Bodies and Guilty Minds," 43 Emory L.J. 647, 664–674 (1994) (reviewing several standards for evaluating corporate culpability).

16. Cf. French, Collective and Corporate Responsibility, 134 (1984) (a corporate person, acting through its managers, is accountable for actions of others that were intended by the managers or which the managers were willing to have occur as the result of actions they initiated).
17. See Foerschler, "Corporate Criminal Intent: Toward a Better Understanding of Corporate Misconduct," 18 Cal. L. Rev. 1287, 1288, 1307–10 (1990).
18. See French, Collective and Corporate Responsibility, 155–160 (1984) (the failure to follow up on detected misconduct conveys a message to corporate employees that managers acquiesce in such conduct, thereby encouraging further misconduct).
19. Richard S. Gruner, Corporate Criminal Liability and Prevention § 10.03[2] (2004).
20. See Zornow & Klubes, "The New Organizational Sentencing Guidelines," American Lawyer at 8 (March 1992) (objecting to the recasting of corporate management as gestapo-like law enforcers, ever monitoring employee behavior). But see, Obermeier, "A Practical Partnership," National Law Journal, p. 13 (Nov. 11, 1991) (recognizing a new partnership between corporate executives and U.S. Attorneys in carrying out the law enforcement processes envisioned in the guidelines, but reassuring managers of the productive potential of this partnership).
21. See, e.g., New York Central & Hudson River Railroad Co. v. United States, 212 U.S. 481, 29 S.Ct. 304, 53 L.Ed. 613 (1909).
22. Sigler & Murphy, "Corporate Conduct in the 1990s," in Corporate Lawbreaking and Interactive Compliance, 153, 161 (1991).
23. U.S. Department of Justice, Principles of Federal Prosecution of Business Organizations (Jan. 20, 2003), http://www.usdoj.gov/dag/cftf/corporate_guidelines.htm (memorandum from Larry D. Thompson, Deputy Attorney General, to Heads of Department Components and United States Attorneys).
24. Other factors which federal prosecutors are instructed to consider in deciding whether to prosecute a corporation include the following:

    - the nature and seriousness of the offense, including the risk of harm to the public, and applicable policies and priorities, if any, governing the prosecution of corporations for particular categories of crime;
    - the pervasiveness of wrongdoing within the corporation, including the complicity in, or condemnation of, the wrongdoing by corporate management;
    - the corporation's history of similar conduct, including prior criminal, civil, and regulatory enforcement actions against it;
    - collateral consequences, including disproportionate harm to shareholders, pension holders and employees not proven personally culpable and impact on the public arising from the prosecution;
    - the adequacy of the prosecution of individuals responsible for the corporation's malfeasance; and
    - the adequacy of remedies such as civil or regulatory enforcement actions.

    See id.

25. United States Environmental Protection Agency (1995) "Incentives for Self-Policing: Discovery, Disclosure, Correction and Prevention of Violations," 60 Fed. Reg. 66706 (Dec. 22, 1995).
26. See generally Vanessa Blum, "Justice Deferred: The Feds' New Weapon of Choice Makes Companies Turn Snitch to Save Themselves," Legal Times, March 21, 2005, p. 1 (describing six deferred prosecution agreements entered into with major corporations during the prior six months); Steven R. Peikin, "Deferred Prosecution Agreements: Standard for Corporate Probes," New York Law Journal, p. 4 (Jan. 31, 2005)(describing 12 deferred prosecution agreements entered into since 2003).
27. The deferred prosecution agreements concerning these companies are profiled in Steven R. Peikin, "Deferred Prosecution Agreements: Standard for Corporate Probes," New York Law Journal, p. 4 (Jan. 31, 2005).
28. United States Sentencing Commission, Sentencing Guidelines Manual § 8B2.1 (2004).
29. See id at §§ 8C2.5(f), 8C2.6.
30. See id. at § 8B2.1.
31. See Weintraub & Chaset, "Federal Sentencing Guidelines for Organizations," Champion, pp. 4, 7 (May 1992).
32. See Obermaier, "Drafting Companies to Fight Crime," New York Times, p. C13 (May 24, 1992) (observation by the U.S. Attorney for the Southern District of New York that, under the guidelines, "[g]ood corporate citizenship is now defined by expanded obligations: the traditional prevention and detection of crime, and now the reporting of crime when detected"); Rakoff, "The Corporation as Policeman: At What Price?" New York Law Journal, p. 3 (Jan. 9, 1992) (the guidelines treat a corporation like "an arm of the law").
33. See, e.g., United States v. Hilton Hotels Corp., 467 F.2d 1000 (9th Cir. 1972), cert. denied 409 U.S. 1125 (1973).
34. See Sigler & Murphy, "The Corporate Lawyer As Unsung Hero," Pennsylvania Lawyer, pp. 12, 13 (June 1989).
35. See, e.g., Obermaier, "Drafting Companies to Fight Crime," New York Times, p. C13 (May 24, 1992) (describing the sentencing guidelines as having "conscripted" corporations into the fight against crimes).
36. See Rakoff, "The Corporation as Policeman: At What Price?" New York Law Journal, p. 3 (Jan. 9, 1992) (observing that sentence reductions under the corporate sentencing guidelines are aimed at "having private corporate managers act as policemen").
37. See Black, The Manners and Customs of the Police (1980).
38. See generally, Ziegenhagen & Brosnan, "Citizen Orientations Toward State and Non-State Policing," 13 Law & Pol'y 245 (1991).
39. Obermaier, "A Practical Partnership," National Law Journal, p. 13 (Nov. 11, 1991).
40. See id.
41. See Zornow and Klubes, "The New Organizational Sentencing Guidelines," American Lawyer, p. 8 (March 1992).
42. John C. Coffee, Jr., "Emerging Issues in Corporate Criminal Policy" in Richard S. Gruner, Corporate Criminal Liability and Prevention v (2004).
43. Gerhard Mueller, "Mens Rea and the Corporation," 19 U. Pitt. L. Rev. 21 (1957).
44. See Tesco Supermarkets Ltd. v. Nattrass, [1971] 2 W.L.R. 1166, 1196. This organic theory dates back to several English decisions in the 1940s. See Kent and Sussex Contractors, Ltd., [1944] K.B. 146, 155–156; ICR Haulage Ltd., [1944] 30 Cr. App. Rep. 31; Moore v. Bresler, [1944] 2 A11 ER 515.
45. See Lederman, "Criminal Law, Perpetrator and Corporation: Rethinking a Complex Triangle," 76 J. Crim. Law 285, 292–293 (1985).

46. Advisory Group on the Organizational Sentencing Guidelines, United States Sentencing Commission, Hearings, Breakout Group 2, at 84–85 (November 14, 2002) (available at http://www.ussc.gov/corp/ph11_02/BRKOUT2.pdf).
47. New South Wales Law Reform Commission, Report 102: Sentencing: corporate offenders 65–66 (2003).
48. The author served as a member of the Advisory Group. For a complete list of the members of the Advisory Group and the text of its Final Report discussing the proper impacts of compliance programs on corporate criminal liability, see Advisory Group on the Organizational Sentencing Guidelines, United States Sentencing Commission, Final Report (2003) (available at http://www.ussc.gov/corp/advgrprpt/advgrprpt.htm).
49. See id.
50. See United States Sentencing Commission, Sentencing Guidelines Manual § 8B2.1 (2004).
51. New South Wales Law Reform Commission, Report 102: Sentencing: corporate offenders 67 (2003).
52. See Richard S. Gruner, Corporate Criminal Liability and Prevention (2004).
53. See United States Sentencing Commission, Sentencing Guidelines Manual § 8B2.1 (2004).

References

Advisory Group on the Organizational Sentencing Guidelines, United States Sentencing Commission (2003) Final Report. Washington: Sentencing Commission (available at http://www.ussc.gov/corp/advgrprpt/advgrprpt.htm).

Alexander, Cindy R., Jennifer H. Arlen, and Mark Cohen (1999a) "The Effect of Federal Sentencing Guidelines on Penalties for Public Corporations." *Federal Sentencing Reporter* 12 :20.

Alexander, Cindy R., Jennifer H. Arlen, and Mark A. Cohen (1999b) "Regulating Corporate Criminal Sanctions: Federal Guidelines and the Sentencing of Public Firms." *J. of Law & Economics* 42:393.

Alschuler, Alan (1992) "Ancient Law and the Punishment of Corporations: Of Frankpledge and Deodand." *B.U. L. Rev.* 71:307, 312.

Arkin, Stanley S. (1991) "Corporate Sentencing Guidelines." *New York Law Journal,* June 13, p. 3.

Black, Donald (1980) *The Manners and Customs of the Police*. Orlando: Academic Press.

Braithwaite, John (1984) *Corporate Crime in the Pharmaceutical Industry.* London: Routledge and Kegan Paul.

Braithwaite, John (1982) "Enforced Self-Regulation: A New Strategy for Corporate Crime Control." *Michigan Law Rev.* 80:1466.

Braithwaite, John, and Gilbert Geis (1982) "On Theory and Action for Corporate Crime Control." *Crime and Delinquency* 28:292.

Brown, H. Lowell (1995) "Vicarious Criminal Liability of Corporations for the Acts of Their Employees and Agents." *Loyola Law Rev.* 41:279.

Bucy, Pamela H. (1991) "Corporate Ethos: A Standard for Imposing Corporate Criminal Liability." *Minnesota Law Rev.* 75:1095.

Cohen, Mark A. (1996) "Theories of Punishment and Empirical Trends in Corporate Criminal Sanctions." *Managerial and Decision Economics* 17:399.

Cohen, Mark A. (1991) "Corporate Crime and Punishment: An Update on Sentencing Practice in the Federal Courts, 1988–90." *Boston University Law Rev.* 71:247.

Coffee, John C. (1981) "'No Soul to Damn: No Body to Kick': An Unscandalized inquiry into the Problem of Corporate Punishment." *Michigan Law Rev.* 79:356.

DiMento, Joseph F.C., Gilbert Geis, and Julia M. Gelfand (2001) "Corporate Criminal Liability: A Bibliography." *Western State University Law Rev.* 28:1.

Fisse, Brent (1983) "Reconstructing Corporate Criminal Law: Deterrence, Retribution, Fault and Sanctions." *Southern California Law Rev.* 56:1141.

Fiorelli, Paul E. (1992) "Fine Reductions Through Effective Ethics Programs." *Alabama Law Rev.* 56:403.

Foerschler, Ann (1990) "Corporate Criminal Intent: Toward a Better Understanding of Corporate Misconduct." *California Law Rev.* 18:1287.

French, Peter (1984) *Collective and Corporate Responsibility*. New York: Columbia University Press.

Goldsmith, Michael and Chad W. King (1997) "Policing Corporate Crime: The Dilemma of Internal Compliance Programs." *Vanderbilt Law Rev.* 50:1.

Gruner, Richard (2004) *Corporate Criminal Liability and Prevention*. New York: Law Journal Press.

Gruner, Richard S. (2000) "How Compliance Program's Fail: Lessons from the Con Edison Probation Sentence." *PLI/CORP* 1177:495.

Gruner, Richard S. (1994) "Towards an Organizational Jurisprudence: Transforming Corporate Criminal Law Through Federal Sentencing Reform." *Arizona Law Rev.* 36:407.

Gruner, Richard S. (1992) "Just Punishment and Adequate Deterrence for Organizational Misconduct: Scaling Economic Penalties Under the New Corporate Sentencing Guidelines." *Southern California Law Rev.* 66:225.

Gruner, Richard S., and Louis M. Brown (1996) "Organizational Justice: Recognizing and Rewarding the Good Citizen Corporation." *J. of Corporate Law* 21:731.

ICR Haulage Ltd. (1944) 30 Cr. App. Rep. 31.

Jordan, Kirk S., and Joseph E. Murphy (2000) "Compliance Programs: What the Government Really Wants." *PLI/CORP* 1177:529.

Kaplan, Jeffrey M., Joseph E. Murphy and Winthrop M. Swenson, eds. (1998) *Compliance Programs and the Corporate Sentencing Guidelines: Preventing Criminal and Civil Liability.* St. Paul: West Group.

Kent and Sussex Contractors, Ltd. (1944) K.B. 146, 155–156.

Laufer, William (1999) "Corporate Liability, Risk Shifting, and the Paradox of Compliance." *Vanderbilt Law Rev*. 52:1343.

Laufer, William (1994) "Corporate Bodies and Guilty Minds." *Emory Law J.* 43:647.

Lederman, Eliezer (1985) "Criminal Law, Perpetrator and Corporation: Rethinking a Complex Triangle." *J. Crim. Law* 76:285.

Moore, Jennifer (1992) "Corporate Culpability Under the Federal Sentencing Guidelines." *Ariz. L. Rev.* 34:743.

Moore v. Bresler (1944) 2 A11 ER 515.

Mueller, Gerhard (1957) "Mens Rea and the Corporation." *U. Pitt. L. Rev.* 19:21.

Murphy, Diana E. (2002) "The Federal Sentencing Guidelines for Organizations: A Decade of Promoting Compliance and Ethics." *Iowa Law Rev.* 87:697.

Nagel, Ilene H., and Winthrop M. Swenson (1993) "The Federal Sentencing Guidelines for Corporations: Their Development, Theoretical Underpinnings, and Some Thoughts About Their Future." *Washington University Law Quarterly* 71:205.

New South Wales (NSW) Law Reform Commission (2003) Report 102: Sentencing: Corporate Offenders. New South Wales: Law Reform Commission.

New York Central & Hudson River Railroad Co. v. United States, 212 U.S. 481, 29 S.Ct. 304, 53 L.Ed. 613 (1909).

Obermaier, Otto (1992) "Drafting Companies to Fight Crime" *New York Times,* May 24, p. C11.

Obermaier, Otto (1991) "A Practical Partnership." *National Law Journal,* November 11, p. 13.

Office of the Inspector General, United States Department of Health and Human Services (2005) "Compliance Program Guidance," www.oig.hhs.gov/fraud/ complianceguidance.html.

Parker, Jeffrey S. (1993) "Rules Without...: Some Critical Reflections on the Federal Corporate Sentencing Guidelines." *Washington University Law Quarterly* 71:397.

Peikin, Steven R. (2005) "Deferred Prosecution Agreements: Standard for Corporate Probes." *New York Law Journal*, Jan. 31, p. 4.

Rakoff, Jed S. (1992) "The Corporation as Policeman: At What Price?" *New York Law Journal,* Jan 9, p. 3.

Sentencing Reform Act of 1984, 18 U.S.C. §§ 3551–3742 and 28 U.S.C. §§ 991–998.

Sigler, Jay, and Joseph E. Murphy (1991) "Corporate Conduct in the 1990s." In *Corporate Lawbreaking and Interactive Compliance,* Editors Jay A. Sigler and Joseph E. Murphy. New York: Quorum Books.

Tesco Supermarkets Ltd. v. Nattrass (1971) 2 W.L.R. 1166, 1196.

United States Department of Justice (2003) Principles of Federal Prosecution of Business Organizations (Jan. 20, 2003), http://www.usdoj.gov/dag/cftf/corporate_ guidelines.htm (memorandum from Larry D. Thompson, Deputy Attorney General, to Heads of Department Components and United States Attorneys).

United States Environmental Protection Agency (1995) "Incentives for Self-Policing: Discovery, Disclosure, Correction and Prevention of Violations." *Fed. Reg*. 60:66706 (Dec. 22, 1995).

United States Sentencing Commission (1995) Corporate Crime in America: Strengthening the "Good Citizen" Corporation: Proceedings of the Second Symposium on Crime and Punishment in the United States. Washington: United States Sentencing Commission (available at www.ussc.gov/sympo/wcsympo.pdf).

United States Sentencing Commission (2004) *Sentencing Guidelines Manual.* Washington: Sentencing Commission.

United States v. Hilton Hotels Corp., 467 F.2d 1000 (9th Cir. 1972), cert. denied 409 U.S. 1125 (1973).

Webb, Dan K., and Steven F. Molo, "Some Practical Considerations in Developing Effective Compliance Programs: A Framework for Meeting the Requirements of The Sentencing Guidelines." *Washington University Law Quarterly* 375:71.

Wells, Celia (2001) *Corporations and Criminal Responsibility*. Oxford: Oxford University Press.

Wells, Celia (2001) "Corporate Criminal Developments in Europe." *Law Society J.* 39(7):62.

Weintraub, Benson B., and Alan J. Chaset (1992) "Federal Sentencing Guidelines for Organizations." *The Champion,* May, p. 4.

Ziegenhagen, Eduard A., and Dolores Brosnan (1991) "Citizen Orientations Toward State and Non-State Policing." *Law & Policy* 13:245.

Zornow, David M., and Benjamin B. Klubes (1992) "The New Organizational Sentencing Guidelines." *American Lawyer,* March, p. 8.

Part VI

Forms of White-Collar Crime

1

Gold-Collar Crime

The Peculiar Complexities and Ambiguities of War Crimes, Crimes Against Humanity, and Genocide

Chrisje Brants

'The peculiarity of the role of perpetrator [. . .] consists in this: that he acts not only himself but also with the help of a complex executive machinery. [. . .] These are not some Tom, Dick, or Harry of unknown lineage, without hearth or home. These are titled personages, upper classes [. . .]'[1] *'A multitude of enthusiastic collaborators, at all levels of the [. . .] hierarchy had cooperated in organizing and executing [the crimes].'*[2]

Such statements now seem commonplace to the student of white-collar and corporate crime, yet these were penned not long after Edwin Sutherland defined white-collar crime as "a crime committed by a person of respectability and high social status in the course of his occupation,"[3] and long before the term "corporate crime" became normal usage in criminology. Written in 1944 and 1947, respectively, they refer to the difficulties of understanding and judging the international crimes committed by the Nazis during World War II—acts we now know as war crimes, crimes against humanity, and genocide, although then the terminology was slightly different. For the purpose of this article, I shall use the term "international crimes" as synonymous with the three categories in current use.

A great deal has been written about the trials at Nuremberg and Tokyo, and the individual and collective responsibility of the perpetrators. And there exists today a large body of scholarship concerned with the doctrine and practice of bringing to justice the perpetrators of international crimes under the statutes of the International Criminal Tribunals for the Former Yugoslavia (ICTY) and Rwanda (ICTR), which are situated at The Hague in the Netherlands and Arusha in Tanzania; More recently, and at present engaged in getting its first cases underway, there is the International Criminal Court (ICC), also at The Hague. The approach in such writings, however, is most commonly from a legal perspective and the criminological significance of criminalizing those ultimately responsible for war crimes, crimes against humanity, and acts of genocide, and of the sentences passed on them, is largely ignored. It is perhaps in the nature of criminal law, which reduces behavior to the (provable) guilt of culpable individuals, to remove crime from its wider context. While that may serve to ensure that principles of due process are met and that only the actually guilty individual is convicted for his or her own part in a crime, it does not contribute much to our understanding of the phenomenon of collective criminality that so often accompanies armed conflict.

Criminologists have paid little attention as a distinct form of criminality to the grave breaches of human rights that international crimes entail. Following the pioneering work of Stanley Cohen in this field, a certain body of literature has arisen, more especially after the advent of the different international tribunals, though it can by no means compete with the libraries full that legal scholars have produced and often still seems to be searching for a sound theoretical basis. Certainly, those who have attempted to include the problem of human rights in criminological texts have rarely drawn on the theory of white-collar and corporate crime to enhance our understanding of crimes against humanity. The only really notable exception is Cohen, who has argued consistently for state criminal liability,[4] while Nelken and Cottino mention genocide in passing in their overview of white-collar crime.[5] Neither have criminologists examined the peculiar legal difficulties experienced in the practice of dealing with the criminal liability of high-ranking military personnel and other officials who are involved in such atrocities. In this contribution I want to try to close that gap a little by taking a closer look at whether it is helpful or even feasible to consider these international crimes as forms of white-collar and corporate crime; or, given that this might further complicate and fudge already existing definitional disagreements, whether we could at least use the analogy to promote insight into what is becoming an increasingly important topic in the field of criminal law. It is a wide and complicated subject, both from a legal and criminological perspective, and I can do little more than attempt to outline an approach that could be fruitful in bringing these crimes within the purlieu of criminology.

A Catalog of Necessary Questions

The first question of course must be, What are the similarities and what the differences between international crimes and white-collar and corporate crime? Given that the latter are in themselves contested concepts, the most helpful approach may well be the very fact of that contestation. Can it be that such generally abhorred crimes as the killing and mistreatment of prisoners of war, the mass rape of civilians by the military, the subjugation of populations through the destruction of their livelihoods, or the extermination of people because they belong to a certain group, are somehow shot through with the sort of ambivalence that characterizes white-collar crime? Or that the official reaction to crimes against humanity, which is now embodied in international criminal law, itself puts obstacles in the path of bringing the perpetrators to justice? Identifying possible ambiguities is a first step toward unraveling the context in which these international crimes occur, without which our understanding of them will be fragmentary at best.[6]

Following from this, we must then try to distinguish between the different types of perpetrators that commit war crimes, crimes against humanity, and genocide. There are, of course, the men—and they *are* almost always men—who actually do the killing, the maiming, the burning, and the torturing. They are the blue-collar workers of the forces engaged in armed conflict, and, as in white-collar and corporate crime, they complicate the issue of who is to be held criminally responsible and whether such responsibility can be laid at the door of those who do not get their hands dirty and take no active physical part in the commission of the crimes. For the significance of Sutherland's definition of white-collar crime, however vague and debatable it may be,[7] lies first and foremost in the combination of "high social status and respectability" and "occupation." In not only highlighting one of the reasons for the ambivalent reaction to such crime, but also in paving the way for the work later done on corporate crime, it guides us toward the complexities of (criminal) responsibility within an organizational context; eventually it points to the shortcomings of the criminal law, with its emphasis on individual guilt, and to the selectivity of the prosecution process. The difference between white and blue collars, indeed the definition of respectability and status as Sutherland understood it, may be redundant in late-modern society, but hierarchical order in organizations is not: some still (are paid to) do the thinking and the planning and derive their responsibility and authority from that status, while others do the (dirty) manual work and are not encouraged to question policy or strategy.

The difficulties of translating occupational (and moral) responsibility into criminal liability[8] also apply in the case of international crimes.[9] While we cannot ignore the contribution of the "foot soldier," especially in the light of the question of ambivalent attitudes to such crimes, equally pressing concerns are the responsibility of military commanders (for which all of the international statutes provide), and the problems of apportioning criminally relevant blame to those who never fired a rifle, set fire to a house, left women and children to starve, turned a blind eye to the actions of their subordinates, or were perhaps even ignorant of them, were one or sometimes many steps removed from what actually happened in the field.

However, the actions and omissions of military commanders—"gold-collar crime"—form only one part of the problem. The context of crimes committed by military actors must take us further, away from the majors and generals and behind the scenes of military action to the political backrooms where wars are planned and the resulting atrocities either intentionally incorporated into military strategy or wittingly or unwittingly taken for granted. The military do not operate in a vacuum, so we must also examine the responsibility of influential political and civilian officials: those who are in a position to direct the conduct of military action, who devise policies of war and sometimes of genocide, who use the mass media to stir up conflict and hatred. This type of superior responsibility too is catered to in the international criminal statutes.

Simply examining the ambitions, intentions, or state of mind of individual civilian superiors still does not put the crimes they incite or facilitate completely in context. So we must go further still and look at the contribution of the organizations for which such people work (in the final event the state), which bear all the hallmarks of corporate crime but for which there is no equivalent under international criminal law. And finally there are the legitimate business enterprises and their executives, who provide the means of committing crimes against humanity or who help prolong conflicts in which such crimes are committed. They may, for example, deliver the components for poison gas or contravene arms embargoes, or provide finance for a state and therefore for its security forces, which then go on to commit grave infringements of human rights. Corporations and their executives sometimes risk prosecution (for economic crimes) under national laws, but they are seldom if ever held responsible for the international crimes they have helped commit. In both theory and practice, this is probably by far the most intransigent legal problem of the context in which international crimes are committed.

In the coming pages, I will highlight a number of aspects from this catalog of questions. To keep matters of law as simple as possible, I will refer to the Statute of the International Criminal Court only as the relevant international statutory law. The statutes of the ICTY and ICTR, which differ somewhat from that of the ICC in wording and scope, are of course still in force and will remain so as long as the tribunals continue to operate. However, the ICC is the only court to have geographically unlimited, if secondary, jurisdiction, and its statute is not only the most recent but also incorporates the case law based on its predecessors. This whole body of international law regards as its sources customary international law, legal doctrine from national criminal justice systems, international human rights instruments, and case law from all international tribunals, including Nuremberg and Tokyo. I will, of course, cite such sources where appropriate.

International Crimes and the Analogy with White-Collar and Corporate Crime

The ambiguities of both white-collar crime and the reaction to it have often been remarked upon, although equally often simply taken as a starting point to examine one or another aspect of the phenomenon. Some, however, have seen ambiguity and ambivalence as its outstanding characteristics. The first of these was the Norwegian sociologist Vilhelm Aubert.[10] Nelken, following in his footsteps, argues that while there is still much disagreement over how to define and explain white-collar crime, the "ambiguity about [its] nature and the best way of responding to it, forms an essential key to the topic."[11] Such ambiguity exists at a number of levels. There is uncertainty as to what range of crimes is being referred to, and as to whether they actually are crimes, given that not all, or even a few, infractions are prosecuted under criminal law and that society at large does not regard all or even much of such behavior as criminal. Then there is the question of whether the organizational context of white-collar crime means that the perpetrators are simply engaging in conventional behavior within their own group and are therefore not "really" deviant.

In any event, that context may provide sufficient justification to engage widely in neutralizing techniques that allow perpetrators not to think of their actions as crime and themselves as criminals—a self-indulgence to which the lack of identifiable victims almost certainly contributes. The official response is equally ambivalent, often shaped by a lack of political will and with forms of control other than prosecution frequently preferred, or blind eyes turned as the collateral costs of effective control (loss of production, possible bankruptcy, unemployment) are weighed against the acceptance of the "reasonable" consequences of doing nothing at all; all of which reinforces the notion that the behavior in question is not really criminal and its consequences not really serious. At the same time, ideologically loaded communication as to the state's intentions of cracking down on such crime conceals these ambiguities.[12]

At first sight, none of these ambiguities attach to war crimes, crimes against humanity and genocide. Not only does it appear perfectly clear what these crimes are—the behavior that constitutes being set out in detail in Articles 6, 7, and 8 of the ICC Statute and continually interpreted and clarified in the case law of the international tribunals—there is no question about whether they are "really" crimes. Involving murder, inflicting grievous bodily harm, rape, arson, wanton destruction of property, and in general the negation of what are held to be universal civilized values, they are crimes under most if not all national systems of criminal justice, and in the specific context of international criminal law universally held to be the most heinous of all. Those who commit such crimes are often perfectly aware of this and are at pains to cover their tracks. Neither can there be said to be no readily identifiable victims; rather, the opposite.

The preamble to the statute also makes it quite clear that prosecution of perpetrators, and especially those in a position to give orders and to control events, must be the first goal of international criminal justice: the ICC is not concerned with the "little guys," nor with finding alternative, less "expensive" ways of expressing the sternest moral disapproval:

> . . . Mindful that during this century millions of children, women and men have been victims of unimaginable atrocities that deeply shock the conscience of humanity,
>
> Recognizing that such grave crimes threaten the peace, security and well-being of the world,
>
> Affirming that the most serious crimes of concern to the international community as a whole must not go unpunished and that their effective prosecution must be ensured by taking measures at the national level and by enhancing international cooperation,
>
> Determined to put an end to impunity for the perpetrators of these crimes and thus to contribute to the prevention of such crimes . . . [13]

Nevertheless, ambivalence and ambiguities exist on a par with those that characterize corporate and white-collar crime. To start with, and notwithstanding the declarations of ideological good intent that accompany the whole venture of international justice, there is the ambivalence of the community of states that have joined together in creating a sphere of international criminal justice. The statute of the ICC has a long and troubled history,[14] and was finally threshed out during negotiations in Rome in 1998 and amended and reamended in the following years until it entered into force on July 1, 2002. Leaving aside the eventual withdrawal of the United States, which somewhat undermined the ideological clout of this joint enterprise, the ICC, or Rome, Statute is, inevitably, the result of political and legal compromise. Parties, envisaging situations in which they themselves might wish to engage in international armed conflict, or could become embroiled in wars outside of the authority of the United Nations, were, for example, unable to agree on the crime of aggression that ranked so prominently at Nuremberg; much to the chagrin of Germany and Japan, it was tabled, to be reconsidered when the statute comes up for review after seven years (Articles 5, 121, and 123).

There were also disagreements on which system of law (common or civil) should prevail and on a number of doctrinal issues, among other things whether the court would have jurisdiction over corporate actors.[15] More importantly, perhaps, the problem of the sovereignty of states has been solved through the principle of subsidiarity or complementarity: the ICC has secondary jurisdiction only—namely, if states are unwilling or unable to prosecute the relevant crimes themselves in a fair and impartial manner (Article 17). This in its turn produces selectivity in prosecution and affects the ideological message produced by international criminal justice about who the international criminals are—and more especially, who they are not. And finally, where the politicians have dragged their feet, this has sometimes resulted in lack of financial and other support.[16] The ICTY and ICTR, for example, were and sometimes still are notoriously short of money and staff.

If the international context has affected the ambit of the law and the jurisdiction of the court, then the national context in which international crimes are committed and the organizational context in which the actual acts are perpetrated and the decisions leading up to them have wide implications for the social and psychological significance of behavior in the social setting of conflict in which it takes place. War crimes are distinguished from crimes against humanity and genocide, in that they are defined as taking place in the context of armed conflict, while both crimes against humanity and genocide may also be committed in "peacetime." Since the first case to come before the ICTY,[17] "armed conflict" is interpreted as being both international and internal. All are crimes that occur on a mass-scale, in the context of systematic violence.[18] Although war crimes may be committed by individual soldiers on an entirely individual basis, the ICC is mainly concerned when they occur on a large scale or as part of a plan or policy. Such crimes represent collective wrongdoing as do crimes against humanity and genocide that by definition imply systematic organization—what has been called system-criminality.[19] It is in this sense that the analogy with corporate crime is strongest, and it is to this characteristic that we must look to uncover ambiguities as to the nature of behavior that would, in any other context, be considered criminal by the perpetrators.

It is obvious that such large-scale criminality requires preparation and organization and that this in its turn almost always involves the machinery of the state (or in the case of a disintegrating state with competing or rebel factions, of the local geographical entity to which they belong): the cooperation of armed forces and the connivance and backup of (local) politicians, bureaucrats, and society at large. This complex network of organizational relationships forms the environment in which both fighters in the field and commanders and other superiors work toward a common goal—prevailing over the enemy. As Punch has said of organizational crime in which normal people do deviant things,[20] this is a "messy, dirty environment" (and war is the dirtiest business of all), in which deviance becomes a means of survival. But only if it can be rationalized and justified, for "ordinary men" do not "normally" deviate from compelling social and moral norms. Techniques of neutralization abound in situations of armed conflict, ranging from "only obeying orders" to the negation of the very humanity of the enemy, the "other." International crimes take place in a group culture of fear and violence that through such techniques becomes a culture of normality.[21] But, as Nelken exhorts us with regard to corporate and white-collar crime,[22] we must appreciate the perspective of those who engage in international crimes in order to understand them, however difficult or morally repugnant that may be.

Two aspects of this "culture of normality" deserve special attention, for they form the organizational context within which ordinary men do extraordinary things, and they have been well documented in the criminology of corporate crime. The first is the bureaucratic nature of organizations, be they commercial or political (or indeed the army), in which it is the job of middle management to control and monitor organizational progress towards organizational goals. In its humdrum banality, however, bureaucracy and the strain of conforming to organizational goals which are politically and culturally determined and "normalized" can serve to disguise the criminal nature of that progress and of the means by which it is achieved. Balance sheets showing figures of profit and loss, time schedules to be met, and the everyday costs and logistics of organizational business are simply so many piles of paper and normal bureaucratic pressures. But precisely because of that they hide the horrors of a concentration camp just as easily as they hide a price-fixing scam or the damage done to the environment and people by illegal emissions of polluting agents.[23]

The second is "the consensus-producing machinery in society" that allows situations to be redefined and individuals to perceive their behavior as legitimate. Science, law, and religion all play a role in providing notions that can be used by collective or individual actors to negate their own or other people's responsibility.[24] Studies of German soldiers who committed atrocities on the Eastern front and were involved in the mass-murder of Jews and partisans have shown that not only could most give no explanation for their behavior afterward, they also could not conceive of themselves as ever having behaved in such a way, although some were still able to recall the rationalizations that appear to have guided them.[25] Indeed, an important part of the consensus about what constitutes legitimate action is achieved by the development of a rationalizing vocabulary that either neutralizes or justifies the deviance. Already in 1953, Cressey had identified as a contributing factor to white-collar crime "verbalizations which could permit the commission of a crime while the idea of honesty was maintained,"[26] rendering reality "opaque" and, in the case of international crimes, depriving acts of violence of their criminal nature and victims of their actual status.[27]

The development of a rationalizing vocabulary that allows perpetrators of international crimes to justify their individual behavior and at the same time promotes acceptance of their actions by society at large—for which the connivance of the mass media is indispensable—may take two forms. On the one hand we find, in the systematic portrayal of the victims as an inhuman plague of vermin to be sought out and eradicated, the creation of a legitimate identity for the perpetrators as saviors of their own group in the face of overwhelming danger. In films and cartoons, the Nazis regularly portrayed Jews as rats. More recently *Radio Télévision Libre des Milles Collines* in Rwanda consistently referred to Tutsis as "cockroaches."[28] On the other hand, subtler but no less effective in paving the way for ordinary men to commit acts of which they would otherwise not be capable, there is the vocabulary of moral neutrality or even moral justification. The bombing of civilians becomes "collateral damage," bulldozing villages and destroying crops is "punishment" and "deterrence" for harboring insurgents, deportation of groups of the population—often a prelude to or part of a program of genocide—goes by the benevolent name of "ethnic cleansing."

So, if the international community defines, albeit in practice somewhat selectively, these acts as heinous crimes, the national community in which they take place, or a proportion of it, need not and indeed in many cases does not. Given the social construction of legitimacy that is characteristic of the systemic nature of international crimes, bringing the perpetrators to justice presents particular problems, one of which is that segments of the population may continue to regard them as heroes rather than villains and protect them against the efforts of an international prosecutor to secure their arrest. International courts have no police force and are dependent on co-operation on the territory of the state concerned, although under certain circumstances the Prosecutor may call on United Nations forces to assist. It is indicative of the aura of legitimacy that still surrounds them on their home territory that the Bosnian Serb commander and president, respectively, Mladić and Karadić, have still not been caught after ten years and are thought to be hiding with the aid of the local population.

The Criminal Liability of Figures of Authority

Understanding the legitimizing context in which individual members of armed forces or groups of civilians actually commit atrocities does not absolve them from their individual guilt or responsibility, any more than the corporate context absolves middle management or factory workers for acts which, in any other setting, they would know to be criminal. In recognition of the fact that international crimes could not be committed if ordinary men were not prepared to kill and maim or to submit to the evil banality of the bureaucratic procedures that accompany systemic and officially condoned violence, from Nuremberg onwards the defense of "superior orders" as such (*Befehl ist Befehl*) has never been admitted:[29] the test is whether moral choice was in fact possible[30]—in legal terms whether the absence of that choice constitutes duress.[31] Very rarely is that found to be the case, although it may be a factor in mitigation, while the lower the rank of the perpetrator, the more likely it is that some form of duress will be recognized.[40]

Superior Responsibility

Although concerned with individual culpability, as is all criminal law, the statutes and case law of international justice recognize the context in which individuals have acted and the systemic nature of the crimes that come under international jurisdiction. They are concerned with crimes against humanity that involve "widespread and systematic attacks" on a civilian population (Article 7, Rome Statute), with war crimes as "part of a plan or policy" (Article 8), while the nature of the acts that constitute genocide implies, through the requirement of special intent "to destroy, in whole or in part, a national, ethnical, racial, or religious group as such" (Article 6), the existence of some sort of program, plan, or policy that has been communicated to the actual perpetrators. In limiting jurisdiction to "the most serious crimes of concern to the international community," international criminal justice also concentrates on those with whom the most serious responsibility rests. These are the figures of authority who give the orders, who plan and control policy and strategy, who in general create or manipulate the social conditions in which the atrocities occur, or who are in a position to prevent them.

It is not their physical actions that constitute their crimes, but their functional behavior, their (mal)functioning in positions of authority, be they military or civilian. Their criminalization represents that particular form of *noblesse oblige* that requires superiors to have, and demonstrate, higher moral standards than their subordinates. There is a word for this in German legal doctrine: *Garantenstellung*, a concept that allows the criminal prosecution of superiors for acts that others, their subordinates, have committed. This goes further than accomplice liability with its difficult proof of intent, but stops short of strict liability deriving simply from "the accused's position and duty of care" as applies in the United States with regard to public welfare offenses.[33] Rather it interprets the required degree of *mens rea* as extending from intent to culpable negligence and closely resembles the way in which Dutch law deals with corporate executives.[34]

Article 28 a. and b. sets out the conditions under which commanders and other superiors can be held responsible for crimes committed by their subordinates, because their own actions—or rather omissions—are culpable (other than giving the actual orders, which incurs direct individual liability).[35] The requirements for criminal liability are identical in so far as they attach only if the superior, military or otherwise, had effective command, authority, or control over those subordinates, and failed to so exercise it as to repress or prevent the crimes, or failed to refer the matter to the competent authorities. Clearly, culpable failure to exercise authority and control requires some form of knowledge of the (foreseeable) event and its probable or possible consequences. There is, however, a subtle difference in the degree of *mens rea* required here. According to Article 28 a. 1, military commanders or others acting effectively as a military commander are criminally responsible if they "either knew or, owing to the circumstances at the time, *should have known* [my italics] that the forces were committing or about to commit such crimes." For superior–subordinate relationships outside of military situations, proof is needed that "the superior either knew, or *consciously disregarded* [my italics] information which clearly indicated that the subordinates were committing or about to commit such crimes" (Article 28b. 1).

On the one hand, there is something to be said for this distinction: in a military setting, superiors are perhaps more likely to be in a position to be able to know what happens in the field, and in any event, where they have special responsibility for preventing war crimes by individual combatants or groups of combatants under their command, their very position requires them to do just that. On the other hand, requiring a conscious disregard of information in non-military situations presupposes that the information actually reaches the superior and points toward intent rather than negligence. That is a more stringent form of *mens rea* that requires more stringent proof. This not only means that those higher in the civilian hierarchy are less likely to be called to account, it also ignores the organizational context of events and relationships. As in corporate crime, what happens on the "shop floor" need not necessarily come to the attention of executives, and information is more likely to get stuck at management level. Indeed, while the "managers" of international crimes are held responsible for not reporting information to the "competent authority," Article 28 b.1 opens the way for their civilian superiors to make sure that nothing gets reported that they should but would rather not know about. There is not a little of the "officer responsible for going to jail" in all of this.

Joint Criminal Enterprise

In many cases the connivance or even explicit intentions of the political figures that control the state apparatus, including the mass media, is a constituent element of international crimes. Whatever their status and official capacity, they may still come under the jurisdiction of the ICC, as Article 27 makes abundantly clear:

> [...] This Statute shall apply equally to all persons without any distinction based on official capacity. In particular, official capacity as a Head of State or Government, a member of a Government or parliament, an elected representative or a government official shall in no case exempt a person from criminal responsibility under this Statute [...]

The criminal responsibility to which this provision primarily refers is individual and direct, and may be very difficult to prove, especially in the case of politicians. Although directly and publicly inciting to genocide is a separate offense of a specific type of complicity and has been used to successfully prosecute politicians and senior media figures for broadcasting the messages that were instrumental in sparking the genocide in Rwanda, other charges of complicity (and crimes other than inciting to genocide) may be less easy to sustain, let alone the conscious disregard of information that is needed to prove superior responsibility. One way of avoiding such problems, and indeed any problems that may arise in proving that superiors are individually responsible as perpetrators, is to regard the state or other corporate entity as being a joint criminal enterprise in which its officials have participated. To this end, Article 25d of the Rome Statute extends accomplice liability to an individual who in any way contributes to the commission or attempted commission of a crime by a group acting with common criminal purpose, while they either intended to further the criminal aim of the group or at least knew that it intended the crime. This provision was used to prosecute the Bosnian Serb general Krstic, who commanded the transport of Muslim women and children and was therefore directly involved in the unfolding humanitarian crisis at Srebenica in 1995, but against whom there were insufficient indications that he could be held responsible for the ensuing massacre of the men.[36]

While at first sight this has the attraction of covering both the collective nature of the crime and the relationship between the perpetrator and the man behind the scenes, the usefulness of the concept of joint criminal enterprise has severe limitations. It neither fully expresses the implications of the corporate or other organizational network that often governs that relationship,[37] nor does it always meet the due process principle of *nullem crimen sine lege praevia* in that it may require more than a little creative interpretation on the part of prosecutors and judges to make the law fit the facts.[38] The main characteristic of the joint criminal enterprise is that there is a certain degree of cohesion and mutual understanding between the participants that speaks of knowledge of each other's individual intentions and of conscious agreement as to the plan or actual activities. However, the greater the physical and structural distance between the actual perpetrators and others indirectly involved, the less appropriate the concept becomes.[39] This is a complication that could undo the prosecutor in the case now underway against Slobodan Milosevic, where the charges rely heavily on the joint criminal enterprise doctrine.[40] Moreover, the larger the corporate entity and the more complicated the network of responsibilities and lines of communication, the more difficult it becomes to prove individual involvement sufficient to warrant individual criminal responsibility. In international criminal law, however, there is no concept of corporate crime, let alone of corporate criminal liability.

Corporations, the State, and Commercial Enterprises

The nature of international crimes such as genocide and the moral stigma that they carry goes some way to explaining why international criminal law lays such emphasis on individual immorality as the basis of criminal liability. It is this moral element, of which corporations are judged incapable, that leads many lawyers to cling to the idea that corporations are fictions and therefore cannot commit criminal offenses;[41] and moreover to fear that, were it to be otherwise, evil and responsible individuals would be able to hide behind the very corporate façade they themselves have created. These are familiar arguments in many national legal systems into which I do not want to go in any detail here. Suffice it so say that, in so far as the criminological understanding of the context of international crimes is concerned, the fact of the corporate entity in which specific individuals even at a very high level are dispensable and can be replaced with others, and recognition of its propensity to facilitate criminality, is of the greatest importance. Whether this then translates into corporate criminal liability is a secondary consideration from that perspective, although the discursive power of the criminal law in the social construction of crime should certainly not be overlooked. Moreover, from a point of view of ambivalence and ambiguity, the fact that the ICC is concerned with individuals only is important for two reasons. The first is that the lack of corporate criminal responsibility precludes the criminal liability of the state, the second that the involvement of legitimate (often foreign) business corporations in international crimes will all too easily fall outside the scope of the ICC's jurisdiction.

In its refusal to recognize that corporations are capable of criminal acts, even if they rely on human actors, and that they can be liable for those acts, international criminal law lags behind many national jurisdictions. Van der Wilt believes that the greatest barrier to accepting state criminality lies in the sovereignty of states that is the leading principle in international law[42]: the international legal order functions through agreement between equal, sovereign states and would collapse if states could sit in judgment of each other. He also believes that it may be a matter of time. The immunity of heads of state no longer applies and many scholars of international law favor the introduction of the criminal responsibility of the state.[43] On the other hand, the International Law Commission has dropped its suggestion in its Draft Articles on State Responsibility that "a serious breach on a widespread scale of an international obligation of essential importance for safeguarding the human being, such as those prohibiting slavery, genocide, and apartheid" should be regarded as an international *crime*, which, given the wording, could mean a crime committed by the state.

While the legal construction is not always easy, from a criminological point of view, there are very good reasons to regard the state, and state institutions such as the army as criminal actors in their own right.[44] Many international crimes of the gravest nature are simply unthinkable outside of the institutional state context and are sometimes the result of intentional state policy. This need not let state leaders off the hook any more than it makes corporate executives immune from prosecution in national jurisdictions that recognize corporations as criminally liable perpetrators but also prosecute the decision-makers. Even more important criminological considerations from the corporate crime perspective, however, concern the ambivalence of powerful states when it comes to relinquishing the idea of state sovereignty, which to all intents and purposes amounts to state impunity.

Finally, on the subject of corporations, there is the problem of legitimate and often foreign commercial enterprises that cooperate with criminal regimes or factions for the simple reason that it is profitable to do so. Without their contribution, many international crimes would be impossible, so that they must be regarded as an—often essential—element of the political and economic context in which those crimes take place. While this was already recognized at Nuremberg,[45] such corporate actors themselves cannot be held criminally liable. The current Prosecutor, Ocampo, has announced that he intends to include possible crimes by the executives of corporations involved in atrocities, in order to "deter business executives from assisting or empowering those who plan and carry out crimes within the jurisdiction of the Court."[46]

However, under the current statute an ICC prosecutor would have difficulty in proving the criminal involvement of corporate executives, who would have to be prosecuted under the same provisions as any other "superior." That is to say, they could be accomplices in a joint criminal enterprise, in which case their complicity must be intentional and either have the aim of furthering the criminal act or they must have knowledge that the criminal group itself intends the crime. Prosecution could possibly succeed in the examples given by AMICC, where corporations provide Somali war lords with weapons, buy diamonds from breakaway criminal factions in the Congo or Sierra Leone or from companies who use torture, deportation, and murder to control the civilian population around their mines, or where banks launder stolen money from dictators, although proving knowledge and intent would be far from easy. Such executives could also be prosecuted on the basis of superior responsibility, in which case prosecution could well founder on the requirements that the executive consciously disregarded information and was in a position of effective authority and control with regard to the perpetrator.

There is a great deal of legal work on the accountability of multinational corporations in international law, with most writers advocating criminal liability and effective means of prosecution. There could certainly be legal solutions to the problem of the current impunity of legitimate corporations that are simply pursuing their legitimate aims of profit and growth. But, as in a national context, the criminologist should look first and foremost to the ambiguities of the response to corporate crime: to the question of political will when the stakes are as high as the international criminalization and prosecution of the economic pillars of society who control multinational oil companies, banks, construction firms and arms manufacturers, with all of the economic interests and power they command in the (probably Western) states where they are based—states that themselves profit from the gains of such international trade and finance.

Conclusion

The final category of potential international criminals, legitimate business, well illustrates both the difficulties and ambiguities involved in the official international response to international crimes. It also demonstrates that it makes criminological sense to look at war crimes, crimes against humanity, and genocide from the perspective of white-collar and corporate crime. This is not to advocate including them in the definition as it now stands, even if all could agree on that. This would simply lead to further confusion. At the same time, while recognizing that international crimes form a category of criminality in their own right, the many different approaches to, and the immense body of work on, white-collar and corporate crime provide insights that can applied to international crimes by analogy—the more so because, while there are great differences between the actual acts that constitute white-collar and international crimes, there are also significant similarities. More than anything else, the identification of the ambiguities that surround the social construction of white-collar and corporate crime as "not really criminal" could be helpful in coming to understand the criminological significance of war crimes, crimes against humanity, and genocide.

Deconstructing these international crimes is a difficult enterprise, fraught with the dangers of confusing legal and social definitions, and all the more complicated because the law and legal institutions that constitute international justice are new and ever developing. Nevertheless, criminological work in this field must take into account the implications of the legal response to international crimes in so far as the law itself contributes to the ambiguities that surround them. In some ways international criminal law is better equipped than many national jurisdictions in how it deals with the translation of the moral responsibility of leaders into the criminal liability of commanders and other superiors. The criteria for superior responsibility show some understanding of the way in which organizational aspects may contribute to international crimes, but at the same time demonstrate the legal difficulties of holding individuals responsible for crimes committed by others. In any event, international criminal law lags sorely behind many national jurisdictions in refusing to countenance organizations themselves—including the state, state institutions such as the armed forces and business corporations—as both criminally responsible and criminally liable for international crimes. This legal preoccupation with individual culpability, however understandable from the point of view of individual justice, should not blind criminologists to the organizational context in which human actors operate (and it is here that most is to be gained from the analogy with corporate crime), nor to the discursive value of law in the social construction of criminality.

There is another analogy that we would do well to keep within our sights. Many criminologists who study white-collar and corporate crime, and discover the impunities that all too often result from the ambiguous social and legal response to it, are at pains to argue that this is serious crime that causes immense damage and harm and must be prosecuted as such. Such moral indignation and normative exhortations are sometimes inclined to confound the issue when it comes to research. The same is true, but to a very much greater degree, in the case of international crimes and the massive and very serious breaches of fundamental human rights that they involve. No one can regard what happened in Rwanda and the former Yugoslavia, indeed what is happening right now in so many different parts of the world, dispassionately, or feel morally neutral about whether those responsible are brought to justice. In international criminal justice, all issues are magnified: that applies to the crimes themselves, but also to the difficulties of realizing the goals of international criminal law and to the very expectations that we have of it. More than of any other body of criminal law and in the light of the crimes with which it is concerned, we expect too much of its deterrent and instrumental properties. And yet, precisely because of the nature of those crimes and their perpetrators, international criminal justice has as many, if not more shortcomings than, and is as ambiguous and selective as, any national system.

We must question how instrumental it can be in deterring genocide, for example, in the light of the political and social circumstances that form both the precursor and the backdrop to actual mass killing. The political will of the international community to intervene at an early stage—through diplomacy, with economic sanctions, and in the final event with force—seems a much more feasible means of prevention. We must also question whether the claims made for international criminal law that it can provide satisfactory retribution and redress for victims as a first step toward social reconciliation, can hold true. Like all criminal trials, an international trial reduces the narrative of crime to a few provable soundbites, and in many ways devalues the victim's experience by taking individual culpability out of the context that was the reality of that experience. No trial of an individual murderer can ever do justice to the collective reality of genocide. In that respect, truth commissions are probably more effective in helping a society deal with its violent past.

An important and related issue, often overlooked in criminology especially when moral issues block out other considerations, is that ensuring the instrumental success of a criminal trial by securing a conviction often has its costs in detracting from that other function of criminal procedure: guaranteeing due process. Justice done and seen to be done is only legitimate if it is fair and seen to be fair. In the prosecution of influential figures from a society that has recently undergone the severe trauma of collective violence and is usually still very much divided, often with other responsible persons still in positions of influence, it is, for example, no easy matter to get victims into court to testify. Although the trials are adversarial in nature, the prosecutor is in a much more powerful position than the defense and many convictions at the tribunals have already relied on (sometimes anonymous) testimony that could not be challenged in court. And as to the presumption of innocence, the guilt of the defendant is often a foregone conclusion and trial by media an inevitability: who could honestly start on the assumption that Milosevic is innocent? But in an international trial the fairness of the procedure is paramount, for its very legitimacy lies in the demonstration that civilized values must prevail over barbarity.

To be sure, the advent of the International Criminal Court is a small but important step toward ending the impunity of those responsible for genocide, crimes against humanity, and war crimes, one of many that began at Nuremberg. But consider this: Not without some justification, the Allies were accused of exercising victor's justice at Nuremberg. That charge cannot be leveled at the international community now, but the political compromises that underlie the international tribunals and the drafting of Rome Statute send out a selective ideological message about the nature of international crimes and their perpetrators, and it also does the legitimacy and deterrent value of international criminal justice a disservice. There have been tribunals for Yugoslavia, Rwanda, East Timor, and Pol Pot's Cambodia, but not for Algeria or Vietnam. Disintegrating states, failed states, and rogue states form the context of the crimes that the ICC will judge, for they are the ones unable and unwilling to prosecute the perpetrators; neither do they have the power to remove themselves *per se* from its jurisdiction. Good states, nice democratic members of the international community, will not see their citizens and soldiers before the international court. In any event, some of the things that nice states do in war are not always crimes under the statute: just as the Nazi bombing of Rotterdam and Conventry counted as crimes of war and the allied destruction of Dresden did not, the use of poison gas and dum-dum bullets is a war crime under article 8 of the Rome Statute, and deploying anti-personnel mines and atomic weapons is legitimate. The real-politik of international criminal justice is highly significant to its capability to deliver the goods. It is one more factor, but not an unimportant one, to be taken into consideration in pursuing the analogy with white-collar and corporate crime.

Endnotes

1. Trainin (1944), Hitlerite Responsibility under International Law: 79.
2. Leventhal et al. (1947), The Nuerenberg Verdict: 877.
3. Sutherland (1949), *White Collar Crime:* 9.
4. Cohen (2001), *States of Denial: Knowing About Atrocities and Suffering.*
5. Nelken (2002), *White-Collar Crime*; Cottino (2003) *White-Collar Crime.*
6. Clarke (1990) Business *Crime: Its Nature and Control*; Van der Wilt (2005) *Het kwaad in functie.*
7. Nelken, note 5 *supra.*
8. Hart (1968) *Punishment and Responsibility. Essays in the Philosophy of Law:* 225
9. Van Sliedregt (2003) *The Criminal Responsibility of Individuals for Violations of International Humanitarian Law:* 347–349.
10. Aubert (1952) *White-Collar Crime and Social Structures.*
11. Nelken, note 5 *supra.*
12. Nelken, idem; see also Brants and Brants (1991) *De sociale constructie van fraude.*
13. The full text of the ICC or Rome Statute is available on the ICC website: *http://www.icc-cpi.int.* From there links may also be accessed to the statutes and case law of the ICTY and ICTR
14. Cassese (1999) *The Statute of the International Criminal Court: Some Preliminary reflections.*
15. Schabas (2004) *Introduction to the International Criminal Court:* 13–20.
16. Cf. on corporate crime: Calavita and Pontell (1992) *The Savings and Loan Crisis.*
17. Prosecutor v. Tadić (1997).
18. Van Sliedregt (2003) *The Criminal Responsibility of Individuals for Violations of International Humanitarian Law:* 5.
19. Jokić (2001) *War Crimes and Collective Wrongdoing. A Reader.*
20. Punch (1996) *Dirty Business. Exploring Corporate Misconduct: Analysis and Cases.*
21. Cf. Box (1983) *Power, Crime and Mystification,* and Coleman (1987) *Toward an Integrated Theory of White-Collar Crime.*
22. Nelken (1997) *White-Collar Crime.*

23. On the holocaust: Arendt (1963) *Eichmann in Jerusalem. A Report on the Banality of Evil;* Bauman (1989) *Modernity and the Holocaust.* Cf. on corporate crime: Vaughan (1996) *The Challenger Launch Decision;* Slapper and Tombs (1999) *Corporate Crime.*
24. Cottino, note 5 *supra*: 353.
25. Browning (1992) *Ordinary Men. Reserve Police Batallion 101 and the Final Solution in Poland.*
26. Cressey (1953/1973) *Other People's Money. A Study in the Social Psychology of Embezzlement.*
27. Galtung (1990) *Cultural Violence:* 292.
28. Prosecutor v. Akayesu (1998): §148–149.
29. Dinstein (1965) *The Defence of Obedience to Superior Orders.*
30. Friedman (1972) *The Law of War. A Documentary History,* vol. II: 940.
31. Van Sliedregt note 18 *supra:* ch. 6.
32. Prosecutor v. Erdemović (1998); see especially dissenting opinion Judge Cassese: §51
33. *U.S. v. Dotterweich* (1943); *U.S. v. Parks* (1975).
34. Stessens (1984) *Corporate Criminal Liability: A Comparative Perspective*; Brants and De Lange (1996) *Strafbare vervolging van overheden*; key decisions are Supreme Court of the Netherlands (1982 and 1987) Kabeljauw and Slavenburg II, respectively.
35. See *Prosecutor v. Blaskic* (2004).
36. *Prosecutor v. Kristić* (2001): §616.
37. Van der Wilt, note 6 *supra*: 12–13.
38. Powles (2004) *Joint Criminal Enterprise; Criminal Liability by Prosecutorial Ingenuity and Judicial Creativity.*
39. *Prosecutor v. Brđanin* (2001).
40. *Prosecutor v. Milosević* (1999 ff.).
41. Dugard (1999) *Criminal Responsibility of States.*
42. Van der Wilt, note 6 *supra*: 16–20.
43. Pellet (1999) Can a State Commit a Crime? Definitely, Yes!.
44. Cohen, note 4 *supra*.
45. *Vide* the I.G. Farben and Krupp cases.
46. AMICC (2005) *Information Regarding the Potential Liability of Businesspersons for Atrocity Crimes under the Rome Statute.*

References

AMICC, American Non-Governmental Organizations Coalition for the International Criminal Court, *Information Regarding the Potential Liability of Businesspersons for Atrocity Crimes under the Rome Statute*, *www.amicc.org*, 2005 (accessed 12 July 2005).

Arendt, Hannah (1963) *Eichmann in Jerusalem. A Report on the Banality of Evil.* New York: The Viking Press.

Aubert, Vilhelm. (1952) "White-Collar Crime and Social Structures," *American Sociological Rev* 58: 263–271.

Bauman, Zigmunt (1989) *Modernity and the Holocaust.* Cambridge: Polity Press.

Box, Steven (1983) *Power, Crime and Mystification.* London: Tavistock.

Brants, C.H., and and K.L.K. Brants (1991) *De sociale constructie van fraude.* Arnhem: Gouda Quint bv.

Brants, C.H., and and R. De Lange (1996) *Strafbare vervolging van overheden.* Deventer: Gouda Quint bv.

Browning, Christopher R. (1992) *Ordinary Men. Reserve Police Batallion 101 and the Final Solution in Poland.* New York: Harper Collins.

Calavita, Kitty and Henry Pontell (1992) "The Savings and Loan Crisis," In: *Corporate and Government Deviance,* Editors M. David Erdmann, and Richard J. Lundman (eds.), *Corporate and Government Deviance*. Oxford: Oxford University Press.

Cassese Antonio (1997) *Dissenting Opinion to Prosecutor v. Erdemović*, Case No. IT-96-22-A, A.Ch.

Cassese, Antonio (1999) "The Statute of the International Criminal Court: Some Preliminary reflections," *European J of International Law* 10: 144–171.

Clarke, M. (1990) *Business Crime: It's Nature and Control*. Oxford: Polity Press.

Cohen, Stanley (2001) *States of Denial: Knowing About Atrocities and Suffering*. Malden, MA: Polity Press.

Coleman, J.W. (1987) "Toward an Integrated Theory of White-collar Crime.", *American Journal of Sociology*, 93(/2): 406–439.

Cottino, Amedeo (2003) "White-Collar Crime," In: *The Blackwell Companion to Criminology,* Editor Colin Sumnerr (ed.), Oxford: Blackwell.

Cressey, Donald R. (1953) *Other People's Money. A Study in the Social Psychology of Embezzlement*. Glencoe, III: Free Press.

Dinstein, Y. (1965) *The Defence of 'Obedience to Superior Orders*.' Leiden: Sijthoff.

Dugard, John (1999) "Criminal Responsibility of States" In: *International Criminal Law*. 3rd ed., Editor M. Cherif Bassiouni, *International Criminal Law*. 3rd ed., New York: Transnational Publishers.

Friedman, Lawrence (1972) *The Law of War. A Documentary History*. Vol. II., New York: Random House.

Galtung, Johan (1990) "Cultural Violence," *Journal of Peace Research*, 3: 291–305.

Hart, H.L.A. (1968) *Punishment and Responsibility. Essays in the Philosophy of Law*. Oxford: Clarendon Press.

Jokić, A. (ed.) (2001) *War Crimes and Collective Wrongdoing. A Reader*. Oxford: Blackwell Publishers.

Leventhal, H. et al. (1947) "The Nuerenberg Verdict" *Harvard Law Rev* 60: 857–907.

Nelken, David (1997) "White-Collar Crime," In: *Oxford Handbook of Criminology*. 2nd ed., Editors M. Maguire et al. (eds), Oxford: Oxford University Press.

Nelken, David (2002) "White-Collar Crime," In: *Oxford Handbook of Criminology*. 3rd ed.: M. Maguire et al. (eds), Oxford: Oxford University Press.

Pellet, A. (1999), "Can a State Commit a Crime? Definitely, Yes!", *European J of International Law*, 10: 425–434.

Powels, S. (2004) "Joint Criminal Enterprise; Criminal Liability by Prosecutorial Ingenuity and Judicial Creativity," *J of International Criminal Justice*, 2: 606–619.

Punch, Maurice (1996) *Dirty Business. Exploring Corporate Misconduct: Analysis and Cases*. London: Sage.

Schabas, William A. (2004) *Introduction to the International Criminal Court*. 2nd ed., Cambridge: Cambridge University Press.

Slapper, Gary, and Steve Tombs (1999) *Corporate Crime*. Harlow: Longman.

Sliedregt, E. van (2003) *The Criminal Responsibility of Individuals for Violations of International Humanitarian Law*. The Hague: T.M.C. Asser Press.

Statute of the International Criminal Court, *http://www.icc-cpi.int*.

Stessens, G. (1994) "Corporate Criminal Liability: A Comparative Perspective," *International and Comparative Law Quarterly* 43: 493–520.

Sutherland, Edwin (1949) *White Collar Crime*. New York: Dryden.

Trainin, A.N. (1944) *Hitlerite Responsibility under International Law*. London: Hutchison and Co.

Vaughan, Dianne E. (1996) *The Challenger Launch Decision*. Chicago: University of Chicago Press.

Wilt, van der, H. (2005), *Het kwaad in functie*. Amsterdam: Vossiuspers, UvA.

Cases

Decision on Motion for Judgement of Acquittal, *Prosecutor v. Milosević*, Case No. IT-02-54-T, Tr. Ch. 16 June 2004.
I.G. Farben case (Krauch et al.), *Trials of War Criminals (TWC)*, vol. VIII, 1081–1210.
Krupp case (Krupp et al.), *Trials of War Criminals (TWC)*, vol. IX, 1327–1484.
Judgment *Prosecutor v. Akayesu*, Case No. ITCR-96-4-T, T. Ch. I, 2 September 1998.
Judgment *Prosecutor v. Erdemović*, Case No. IT-96-22-T*bis*, T. Ch., 5 March 1998.
Judgment *Prosecutor v. Krstić*, Case No. IT-98-33-T, 2 August 2001.
Judgment *Prosecutor v. Brđanin*, Case No. IT-99-36-T, Tr. Ch., 2 November 2001.
Judgment on Appeal *Prosecutor v. Blaskić*, Case No. IT-95-14-A, A. 19 July 2004.
Supreme Court of the Netherlands, *Kabeljauw-decision*, HR 1-7-1981, NJ 1982, 80.
Supreme Court of the Netherlands, *Slavenburg II-decision*, HR 16-12-1986, NJ 1987, 321.
United States v. Dotterweich, 320 U.S. 277 (1943).
United States v. Park, 421 U.S. 658 (1975).

2

Environmental Pollution by Corporations in Japan

Minoru Yokoyama

1. Prosecuting Private Corporations as Social Entities

Corporations pursue as much profit as possible in the free market. One of the ways private corporations do this is to become larger by adopting a joint-stock form. The joint-stock corporation has a large number of stockholders and employees[1] and supplies products or services to many people. If it pursues profits egoistically, great damage to society can occur.[2] Therefore, some believe that a private corporation, especially a large one, comes to be regarded more as a social entity rather than simply as a private one.

After recovering from the damage left by World War II, Japan became a welfare state.[3] Under this model the state and the municipal governments guide, supervise, and regulate activities of corporations through a system of bureaus and committees. Through this system it gives warnings to corporations at risk of violating the law. In serious cases it imposes administrative sanctions. In addition, a corporation that commits a serious offense may receive criminal punishment.[4] As Japan has taken a more serious stance against organizational crimes, formal sanctions for corporations have increased.

A corporation as a private entity may be inclined to commit antisocial or illegal activities in the overzealous pursuit of profits. If such an antisocial or illegal activity causes intolerable damage, or is reported to authorities by an insider, corporate wrongdoing becomes a social reality and the company may be formally charged and prosecuted. In the most serious cases, both the corporation and its executives may be convicted of crimes.

Japan has witnessed serious tragedies in which many people suffered bodily injury or death because of corporate crimes. Such acts were severely criticized during the upsurge of social movements in the late 1960s. At that time a corporation that did not admit responsibility for its egotistic operation was sued for damages. In addition, the corporation was forced to take measures to prevent such damage in the future. Criminalization occurred in all fields of private corporate activities that might endanger life and health. In this paper I will focus on how environmental crimes that have caused death and bodily injury in Japan have been punished more seriously over time and criminalized by the legislature and law enforcement agencies.

In the United States, violence perpetrated on the environment which affects both humans and the natural habitat is widely considered to be a form of white-collar crime. For example, according to Frank Schmalleger,[5] environmental crime entails the violation of environmental laws, including the discharge of toxic substances into the air, water, or soil, especially when those substances pose a significant threat of harm to people, property, or the environment. Reactions to such crimes have gathered strength over time. In the most serious cases, corporations violating environmental laws receive criminal punishments.

In the United States environmental crimes are considered to be a relatively new area of corporate crime.[6] Japan has been experiencing many serious tragedies due to environmental pollution for some time. An analysis of two major historical cases of environmental pollution in Ashio and in Minamata highlight the differences in how these white-collar crimes are reacted to in both countries.

2. Copper Mining in Ashio

2.1. Environmental Pollution in Ashio

The most famous case of environmental pollution in Japan occurred at a copper mine in Ashio. In 1877, Ichibei Furukawa, a founder of Furukawa Kogyo Co. Ltd., began to operate this mine.[7] It was the largest copper-mining operation in Japan at a time when the government had adopted policies to enrich the country through the development of modern industry and to strengthen its military forces. Furukawa Kogyo's efforts were thus strongly supported by the state.

Furukawa Kogyo operated the mine at Ashio to yield as much profit as possible without considering the effects of environmental pollution. As a result, many villagers living near the refinery suffered great harm. For example, slag dumped near the refinery was washed into the Watarase River. Toxic substances contained in the run-off caused massive harm to many farmers and fishermen. In addition, the refinery discharged sulfuric acid from which villagers participating in the forest industry suffered great damage. Ashio was the first recorded case of complex environmental pollution caused by a modern factory in Japanese history.[8]

2.2 Reactions to the Incident

2.2.1 The Social Movement Against Pollution at the Ashio Copper Mine

In 1890, when the pollution became too serious for villagers to ignore, the Azuma Village Assembly adopted a resolution to demand that Furukawa Kogyo stop the operation of the refinery. Kogyo ignored it.

Angered by the company's recalcitrance, villagers organized against the company. The famous leader of this movement was Shozo Tanaka. He was elected to the House of Representatives in the first national election in 1890,[9] which occurred immediately after the enactment of the Constitution in 1889. Tanaka demanded the suspension of operations at the refinery in Ashio at a session of the House of Representatives. However, it was ignored due to the state's interest in the rapid development of modern industry. Securing native industry and protecting the life and health of the citizens from environmental pollution was not a concern. Even now this same prioritization of policy can be seen in many developing countries in the world.

In response to the social movement, research on environmental pollution began on Ashio. In 1892 the Tochigi Prefectural Government published its first report on the situation. It pointed out that the soil pollution in farmlands was caused by flooding from the Watarase River. The report provided the first evidence showing a causal relation between the pollution and harm.

As a consequence, Furukawa Kogyo had to negotiate with victimized villagers. In 1895 a president of the company succeeded in concluding a private settlement. Without admitting responsibility for the pollution, he promised to pay compensation with the condition that the villagers could not demand any further recompense. This obviously favored the company, as additional damage could occur in the future.

Shozo Tanaka severely criticized the settlement in the House of Representatives in March in 1896. That autumn villagers suffered more damage from flooding from the Watarase River. The state issued an order to Furukawa Kogyo to take measures to prevent further copper poisoning. In response, the company purchased special equipment to dispose of the slag; however, this proved to be insufficient.

2.2.2. Rise and Fall of the Movement

In March 1897 many victimized villagers walked to Tokyo to bring their plight to the attention of people throughout the country. Other large-scale demonstrations were carried out four times over the next three years. At the last one, police arrested many of the demonstrators. Of the arrested persons, 51 were prosecuted at the Maebashi District Court; five months later, 29 persons were convicted and 22 were acquitted of charges. This incident involved severe suppression of the social movement by the police, who, in this case, served to maintain order for the emperor (Yokoyama, 2001: 189).

In 1901 Shozo Tanaka resigned his position as a member of the House of Representatives. He then attempted in vain to appeal directly to a Meiji Emperor who had been given sovereignty by the Constitution of 1889.[10] After Tanaka's death in 1913, the movement against Ashio Copper Mining waned, although both Furukawa Kogyo and the government had not taken adequate measures to prevent pollution.

2.2.3 The Movement During World War II

In 1917, despite a report by the Committee on Supervision of Pollution presented to Gunma Prefecture that there was no pollution from the copper mine in Ashio, villagers living in the seriously polluted area had to leave their homes. Many victims felt great dissatisfaction and demanded compensation from Furukawa Kogyo. However, if they had sued the company for damages, they could not have won. At that time plaintiffs had to prove that the company had damaged them intentionally or negligently. It was almost impossible for victimized villagers to prove this without detailed information from the company or the assistance of specialists in the area. Thus, they refrained from suing for compensation in civil court.

Instead, in 1925 thousands of victims signed a petition to the Diet, the Minister of Agriculture, and the Minister for Home Affairs. They asked to be compensated for damages from the pollution caused by Furukawa Kogyo and succeeded in receiving some compensation in 1938.[11] In addition, villagers petitioned the

Minister for Home Affairs to clean up the Watarase River to prevent further damage. The petition was promulgated 22times up to 1940, just before World War II. However, at that time the country had no budget for adequately improving the river, and the restoration was only completed after the war.

2.2.4 Reactions Toward Furukawa Kogyo Co., Ltd., after World War II

With an upsurge in the environmental movement in the late 1960s, victims living in Ashio demanded greater compensation from Furukawa Kogyo. In 1974, using mediation procedures under the Law to Dispose Conflicts on Environmental Pollution of 1970, the plaintiffs reached a settlement with the company totaling 1,550 million yen (US $5,200,000). In 1973 mining in Ashio was closed due to exhaustion of the copper vein, although the refining of copper continued until 1989. With the closing of the refinery, Furukawa Kogyo was renamed "Furukawa Machine Metal Co., Ltd." This renaming was an attempt to remove public stigma from the company by burying the past.

2.2.5 Learning from the Ashio Case

For 100 years Furukawa Kogyo engaged in copper mining in Ashio, pursuing as much profit as possible. The company continued neglecting people harmed by environmental pollution without taking adequate measures to prevent it. Initially, the company agreed to only a small amount of compensation without admitting any responsibility for the harms suffered by victims. This same pattern exists today in many capitalist societies.

After the withdrawal of Furukawa Kogyo from Ashio in 1989, the state and Gunma Prefecture continued cleaning up forests and rivers. When the natural environment is seriously damaged by the operation of an egoistic company, it takes a long time and a lot of money to restore it.[12]

With globalization, Furukawa Machine Metal has invested overseas. For example, it bought a copper refinery in Australia in 1996. Regulations are less strict in Australia than in Japan, and it remains to be seen whether the company will engage in similar polluting activities.

3. Reactions to Damage Caused by Corporate Activities in the 1960s

During the period of high economic growth in the 1960s, heavy industry developed with the help of state subsidies. Companies operated their factories using highly toxic substances developed by new technologies. Again, they did so for the purpose of pursuing profit without considering the resulting damage to the environment. As a result, in the 1960s many people suffered bodily harm from pollution of the air, soil, water, from noise, and from the sinking of land. In some cases people died or became seriously ill. As in the Ashio case, both companies and the government neglected victims for long periods of time. In the late 1960s, a victims' movement arose to force action by corporations and the government.

As part of this movement, victims began to sue private corporations for the damage caused by environmental pollution. Suits were brought by victims suffering from the Minamata disease in Minamata and Niigata, Itai-itai disease in Toyama,[13] and asthma in Yokkaichi.[14] These suits drew worldwide attention through reports in the mass media. With the support of the public, many of the plaintiffs were successful.

As mentioned earlier, in previous civil suit judges had demanded that plaintiffs prove a direct causal sequence between environmental pollution and claimed damages. However, with the new social movement against environmental pollution, judges also had to think about relief for victims. The judges hearing the above-mentioned four cases sentenced defendants to pay compensation to plaintiffs and to admit an "indirect" causal sequence from an ecological viewpoint. Thus, here we see a more severe reaction against corporations causing environmental pollution.

In the late 1960s many new laws were enacted to regulate environmental pollution. Under these laws, guidance, supervision, and regulation by the government became more severe. This was largely due to the events that transpired during the outbreak of Minamata disease, which is discussed below.

4. Reactions to Corporations Causing Minamata Disease

4.1. Reactions Before World War II

Minamata disease became the most serious social problem caused by environmental pollution after World War II.[15] In 1908, Chisso Manure Co., Ltd., was founded in Minamata. The company's chemical factory discharged dirty water into Shiranui Bay, poisoning fish and other marine life. In 1925, the fishermen's association demanded that the company pay compensation for damage to their industry. The following year, the company agreed to do so with a condition that the association would not demand further compensation in the future. This result was similar to the settlement of claims against Furukawa Kogyo Co., Ltd., in 1895.

In 1932, the factory in Minamata began to discharge water containing mercury into Shiranui Bay. In 1941, Chisso produced vinyl chloride for the first time in Japan. Water containing methyl mercury was drained from the factory into the bay, poisoning residents who ate fish from the site. Although the company did not admit responsibility, it bought the fisherman's association's fishing rights in 1943 to calm future criticism. During World War II, Minamata's residents could not complain to Chisso, because the the factory was regarded as an important munitions facility for the country. By 1945, the factory had ceased operations due to serious damage caused by allied bombings.

4.2. Reactions Immediately After World War II

After the war, the factory opened again, causing further pollution in Shiranui Bay. By 1952 cats in the area first went beserk and then died from eating contaminated fish. In order to continue draining wastewater into Shiranui Bay, Chisso reached an agreement with the fishermen's association in 1954 which had the company pay 500,000 yen (US $1,390) a year as compensation for their loss of fishing rights. The association agreed to make no future demands.

4.3. Finding the Cause of Minamata Disease

In May 1956, Hajime Hosokawa, director of the hospital attached to Chisso, reported the first case of Minamata disease, although the cause of the illness was not known at that time. Medical personnel began to conduct research on the disease. By December 1956, a total of 54 cases had been found and 17 persons had died. In July 1957, based on research about the disease conducted up to that time, the director of the Public Health Bureau of the Ministry of Health and Welfare announced that Minamata disease was caused by eating fish poisoned by some chemical substances which the factory of Chisso drained into Shiranui Bay. Chisso immediately disputed this claim.

In July 1959, a research team at the Medical Faculty of Kumamoto University published a report stating that Minamata disease was caused by methyl mercury drained from the Chisso factory. Again, the company denied it. Without providing any evidence to the contrary.

Without the help of specialists, it would have been impossible for victims to prove a causal sequence between the pollution and their disease. In the case of Minamata disease, such specialists as Hajime Hosokawa and medical doctors from Kumamoto University played an important role in clarifying this causal sequence. However, Chisso denied their findings, hoping to continue to pursue profits while avoiding penalties. Other chemical companies engaged in polluting activities of their own supported the denial. In September 1959, the director of the Japanese Association of Chemical Industry announced that fish in Shiranui Bay were tainted not by wastewater from the Chisso factory, but by an explosive compound found in the water. In addition, medical doctors at Kumamoto University who were not affiliated with the above-mentioned research team announced that Minamata disease would end by about 1960. This announcement supported Chisso's initial response to victims.

4.4. The Fishermen's Movement Against Chisso

Fishermen living along Shiranui Bay continued to sustain damage to their livelihoods because of the contaminated fish. Knowing the results of research on Minamata disease and the denial of these results by Chisso eventually pushed the group into action. In 1959 they resumed demands for compensation from Chisso. After a meeting on October 17, fishermen marched to the factory. When Chisso refused to negotiate with representatives of the association, demonstrators threw stones at the factory. On November 2, another meeting was held, after which demonstrators rushed past police and into the factory. Many persons were injured in this clash. However, the police did not arrest any demonstrators because they knew that the public supported them. If such an incident had occurred before World War II, many demonstrators would have been arrested, as we saw in the Furukawa Kogyo case of 1900.

4.5. The Victims' Movement against Chisso

The Chisso factory was the largest industry in Minamata. As most citizens enjoyed prosperity because of its presence, those afflicted with Minamata disease were neglected. However, in August 1957, patients organized an association to help each other. Two years later members of the Association to Aid Families of Patients with Minamata disease began to take collective action against Chisso. On November 28, 1959, they conducted a "sit-in" in front of the factory to demand compensation. A month later, Chisso promised the group that it would compensate victims and their families, but they did not admit responsibility for the disease.

4.6. Regulation of Environmental Pollution by New Laws

As the Minamata disease case drew public attention to water pollution, in 1958 the Law to Preserve the Quality of Water in Public Water Areas and the Law to Regulate Factory Wastewater were enacted, which criminalized water pollution by private corporations. However, the state did not provide sufficient guidelines for Chisso to prevent future pollution.

In October 1959, the Ministry of International Trade and Industry (MITI), which had promoted the development of industry without considering the prevention of environmental pollution, directed Chisso to install equipment by the end of that year for the purification of water. Using this equipment, Chisso continued producing acetaldehyde through May 1968.

In September 1968, the state admitted that the disease in both Minamata and Niigata was caused by wastewater containing methyl mercury, which drained from the factory. In February 1969, the government began to regulate the discharge of wastewater into Shiranui Bay through the Law to Regulate Factory Wastewater. The delay in this regulation caused an increase in the number of patients with Minamata disease.

4.7. Minamata Disease in Niigata

In May 1965, Tadao Tsubaki, a professor at Niigata University, published a finding that patients along the Aganogawa River in Niigata were suffering from Minamata disease. These patients had eaten fish containing methyl mercury discharged from the factory of Showa Electric Co., Ltd. On June 12, 1967, these patients sued the company for damages.

On January 12, 1968, patients in Minamata had a meeting with those in Niigata. Following this, 112 patients in Minamata sued Chisso. Both Showa Electric and Chisso denied a casual sequence between their discharging wastewater and Minamata disease. However, in 1971 and in 1973, respectively, judges ruled that an indirect causal sequence in fact existed.

4.8. Corporate Criminal Responsibility

In Japan the corporation itself is not regarded as a wrongdoer upon which criminal punishment can be imposed under the Criminal Code, although both an offender and the corporation employing him/her can receive a criminal fine under other statutes, especially administrative laws.[16] In the past it was rare for a president or a manager of a company to be prosecuted for causing public harm. However, this action was brought in the Minamata case.

In response to severe criticism against Chisso, law enforcement began to investigate officers of the company. In May 1976, the public prosecutor in Kumamoto charged a former president of Chisso and a former superintendent of the factory in Minamata with professional negligence causing death and bodily injury. In March 1979, they were sentenced to two years' imprisonment without compulsory labor with the penalty suspended for three years. Although they appealed, the High Court and the Supreme Court upheld the convictions.[17]

4.9. Relief of Patients Under the Law

In addition to the strengthening of regulations to prevent environmental pollution, the state established a policy to aid persons who were harmed. In December 1969, the Special Law to Relieve Victims from Health Damage Caused by Environmental Pollution was enacted, followed by the Law of Compensation for Health Damage From Environmental Pollution of 1973. Almost 300 victims of Minamata disease received compensation under this law.

In 1995 the Murayama Cabinet decided to take additional measures to help patients suffering with Minamata disease by proclaiming that the state should also accept responsibility for the delay in confirming the cause of the disease. After this announcement, about 1,300 persons requested that the government recognize them as patients under the law. Chisso paid a large amount of the compensation awarded to these victims, although it was able to avoid bankruptcy only through government subsidies. By 1998 it had incurred so much debt that it was essentially operating for the sole purpose of providing victim compensation.

4.10. Severe Sentence by Supreme Court

The state and the Kumamoto Prefectural Government wanted to spend as little as possible on Minamata patients and insisted that they were not responsible for their illness. Thus, the government did not recognize victims suffering minor health damage under the Law of Compensation for Health Damage by Environmental Pollution. Victims whose applications were rejected sued for damages. The suit continued until the autumn of 2004, at which time the Supreme Court found Chisso, the State, and the Kumamoto Prefectural Government responsible for damages and ordered them to compensate plaintiffs.

Usually, the court only finds responsibility for corporation damages that are caused by intent or negligence. However, in this case the court ruled that the state and the Kumamoto Prefectural Government were responsible for compensating 36 plaintiffs. The decision was based on the following facts:

First, the court pointed out three incidents that took place in January 1960: (1) the state and Kumamoto Prefectural Government had evidence that many citizens had died or had been injured by Minamata disease; (2) they could have recognized that the cause of this disease was methyl mercury drained from the Chisso factory; and (3) they could have analyzed the wastewater containing mercury. In other words, the state should have exercised power to regulate wastewater from the factory under the Law to Preserve the Quality of Water in Public Water Areas and the Law to Regulate Wastewater from Factories. Nevertheless, it did not exercise this power, so there was increased damage caused by the wastewater. This non-use of power was found to be illegal, and thus the state was responsible for compensating plaintiffs.

In Kumamoto Prefecture there was a Rule to Regulate the Fishing Industry. Since the local government admitted to the above-mentioned situations, it also had an obligation to regulate wastewater from the Chisso factory. However, this did not occur. Thus, it was also ordered to compensate plaintiffs.

The Supreme Court found that the state and local government had a major responsibility to prevent environmental pollution caused by corporations. If they failed to prevent it because of insufficient guidance and supervision, or if they did not exercise their power to regulate it, they were responsible for damages and obliged to relieve the suffering incurred by victims.

4.11 Changes in the Relief System for Patients

At the end of February 2005, the number of recognized Minamata patients was 2,955.[18] Chisso paid between 16,000,000 yen (US $145,500) and 18,000,000 yen as one-time compensation to each patient. In addition, it continues paying all medical expenses for recognized victims.

For unrecognized patients, the government established two kinds of relief systems. A medical note is given to unrecognized patients with major medical needs, while a health note is provided to those with less health damage.[19] In February 2005 there were 8,396 patients with a medical note and 729 with a health note. After the sentencing by the Supreme Court, the state foresaw the heavier financial burden by estimating that the total number of unrecognized patients to be given health notes would increase to about 3,000.[20] To cope with this projected liability, the proportion of payment between the state and the Kumamoto government was changed in April 2005 from 50 percent for each to 80 percent and 20 percent, respectively. As this case demonstrates, the restoration of the environment and the relief of victims can be quite costly. It is a heavy burden that should be borne not only by the corporation causing the pollution but also by the government, which was at the time legally responsible for stopping it.

5. Regulation of Environmental Pollution under Laws Enacted Since the Late 1960s

With an increase in public awareness of the dangers of environmental pollution in the 1960s, the state drafted new laws to regulate the activities of corporations.

In the first stages of this process there was conflict within the government. The Ministry of Health and Welfare took the initiative of drafting laws to prevent environmental pollution, while the Ministry of International Trade and Industry (MITI) opposed such regulation, as it would make Japanese corporations less competitive in the international market. Through subsequent compromise by both ministries, the Law to Regulate Dirty Smoke was enacted in 1962. However, the law that was agreed upon was largely ineffective and was severely criticized. In an attempt to rectify this, the Fundamental Law to Cope with Environmental Pollution was enacted in 1967. In the following year, the Law to Prevent Air Pollution was enacted to strengthen regulation under the former Law to Regulate Dirty Smoke. At the same time, the Law to Regulate Noise was proclaimed.

In December 1970 a special session was held at the Diet to discuss new laws that addressed environmental problems. In this session the Fundamental Law to Cope with Environmental Pollution and the Law to Prevent Air Pollution were revised in order to strengthen regulation, and an additional 14 laws were enacted, including the Law to Prevent Water Pollution. As these laws contained articles prescribing criminal punishment, there was now an official recognition of environmental crime in Japan.

In 1971 the Ministry of Environment was established. The agency took the initiative to aid people because of the harms caused by environmental pollution. For example, a month after the agency was established, its vice minister announced that the link between Minamata disease and methyl mercury pollution could not be denied. In addition, the agency strengthened regulations against environmental pollution. Corporations were compelled to take measures to prevent environment pollution, and in certain cases were also subsidized by the government when they installed expensive preventive equipment.

Japan's private corporations were now regarded as social entities responsible for maintaining the environment and as such they could be placed under the guidance and supervision of the government. If they broke the law, they could be subject to criminal punishment.[21]

6. Present Sanctions for Environmental Crimes

In 1973 oil prices rose dramatically, causing serious inflation. After the short economic recession that ensued, Japan enjoyed prosperity in the 1980s, including rapid development in the high-tech industry.[22] At the same time, heavy industry gradually waned. With the aid of government subsidies, companies introduced equipment to prevent pollution. These subsidies contributed to the improvement of the natural environment[23] and, at the same time, facilitated the development of high-tech methods to prevent pollution.[24]

In the early 1980s, many companies began to move their factories from Japan to neighboring Asian countries that provided cheaper labor. These new factories usually had little economic incentive to take measures to prevent environmental pollution.[25] Thus Japan was blamed for exporting environmental pollution to developing countries, where there were few existing laws to regulate pollution.[26]

The maintenance of a clean environment became an international issue with the development of more industries that caused pollution.[27] In 1992 many Japanese officials participated in the Earth Summit—the UN Conference on Environment and Development—held in Rio de Janeiro. Five years later, the United Nations Framework Convention on Climate Change was held in Kyoto, Japan, resulting in the "Kyoto Protocol," which set limits on gas emissions in order to minimize what most scientists agree is a "greenhouse effect," or the warming of the Earth's atmosphere, which could dramatically change weather patterns throughout the world. If these emissions are not reduced, the earth will cease to exist as we now know it. The United States continues to deny this officially and has yet to agree to reduce its emissions, unlike the vast majority of developed countries throughout the world who have signed the Kyoto Protocol.[28]

As the reaction to environmental pollution has become more severe, fewer corporations directly pollute the environment. However, pollution scandals still occur, such as the case of fraud by Mitsui & Co., Ltd., a large commercial company operating in the international market.[29] In addition, there are still accidents that cause damage to the environment, brought about by the overzealous pursuit of profits, such as the explosion at the nuclear power plant of the Kanasi Electric Power Co., Ltd.[30] The next section analyzes this accident and more recent reactions to corporate crime in Japan.

7. The Mihama Nuclear Power Plant Incident

7.1. The Regulation of Nuclear Power

Nuclear power has many purposes. Used properly, it can provide clean energy to large populations. As a weapon of war, it can cause massive destruction and widespread death and injury, as the Japanese experienced from the atomic bombs dropped on Hiroshima and Nagasaki in 1945.

In 1955 Japan enacted the Fundamental Law on Nuclear Power, by which the country is obliged to use nuclear power only for peaceful purposes. Under this law there are many provisions to control the use of nuclear power. Moreover, the law prescribes administrative and criminal punishments to make these controls effective.

With major economic development following World War II, electric power was in short supply. The state encouraged the construction of a nuclear power plant at Tokai Village, although many local residents living at the scenic seaside area where it was to be built participated in a movement against its construction.[31] In 1966 Japan Nuclear Power Electric Co., Ltd. operated its first nuclear power plant at Tokai Village.

Following the oil shock, many nuclear power plants were built; the law strictly regulating their construction and operation. However, regulations were sometimes neglected by the electric power company. The accident at Mihama Nuclear Power Plant of the Kansai Electric Power Company provides one major example.

7.2. Rescue and Research Immediately After an Accident

At 3:28 P.M. on August 9, 2004, a water-cooling pipe of the Unit No. 3 Reactor at the Mihama plant exploded, killing five workers and injuring six others. The steam emitted did not contain any radioactivity. The emergency control system operated properly and shut down the reactor after the pipe had burst. If this system had not functioned, a major disaster including wide-spread environmental consequences would have occurred.[32]

Immediately after the accident the fire station dispatched firefighters to save victims.[33] However, they failed to rescue four workers who were trapped in a room filled with hot steam. The police also came to the site. After completing rescue operation, they began an investigation into whether professional negligence had caused the accident.[34]

Under current law, investigation teams other than the police may be dispatched by the government.[35] In the Mihama accident the Nuclear and Industrial Safety Agency in the Ministry of Economy, Trade, and Industry (METI) and the Fukui Prefectural Government established headquarters to deal with the accident. On August 11th, the Nuclear and Industrial Safety Agency dispatched five specialists to look into the accident. As Kansai Electric Power cooperated with their research, the cause of the accident was easily found.[36] The investigators concluded that the explosion had occurred at a thinner part of the pipe. At Unit No.3, the pipe thickness was reduced from 12.7 mm to 0.6 mm at its thinnest part, and, moreover, it had not been inspected since the unit began operating in December 1976.

Immediately after this finding the companies concerned began to incriminate each other. Mitsubishi Heavy Industries Co., Ltd. was responsible for inspections at the Mihama plant until 1996. It made an inspection checklist in 1991 on which the pipe broken in this accident was not listed. In 1996 this list was delivered to Nihon Arm Co., Ltd., a company affiliated with Kansai Electric Power.[37] In April 2003 the company found some thinned parts of the broken pipe and reported this to Kansai in November 2003. Kansai blamed Nihon for leaving this situation unresolved for seven months before the accident. On the other hand, Nihon insisted that it could not fix a thinned pipe on its own because the contract with Kansai gave the latter the right to decide on the improvements regarding the main checkpoints on the inspection list. These charges and counter-charges elicited severe criticism from the public. The research found that the broken pipe was used for over nine years beyond its intended lifespan.

7.3. Apology by Kansai Electric Power

In Japan victims request that an offender express a sincere apology for an accident or a crime.[38] In the Mihama accident, "Y.F.," president of Kansai Electric Power, apologized at a press conference five hours after the accident. The next day he visited both the hospital treating the injured workers and the homes of bereaved families. At the funeral of one of the victims he expressed his sincerest apology by striking the ground with his forehead.[39]

The public, especially residents living near the Mihama plant, were angered by the accident and wanted to know its cause. On August 17th, Kansai held a meeting to explain the accident to residents, at which Y.F. again expressed his apologies.

On August 27th, in a formal apology, Kansai announced the imposition of disciplinary actions against seven of its officials: Y.F., three executives, and three managers responsible for the operation of Unit No.3. As president, Y.F. received the harshest punishment—a 50 percent salary reduction for three months.

The Mihama case drew attention throughout Japan. Y.F. was summoned to meetings of the Diet on three separate occasions.[40] At a meeting of the Committee on the Economy and Industry on August 31st, he expressed his apology and explained the accident. At this meeting, the Minister of Economy, Trade, and Industry stated that his agency would thoroughly investigate the cause of the accident and endeavor to prevent such incidents in the future.

7.4. Government Direction of Power Companies

The state has facilitated the utilization of nuclear power for peaceful purposes. Since nuclear power has the potential to produce a serious disaster if used carelessly, the state must strictly supervise and regulate it.

The government was truly shocked by the Mihama accident. Immediately after the accident the Nuclear and Industrial Safety Agency directed electric power companies to check all pipes at the nation's 52 nuclear reactors. As a result, many pipes of substandard thickness were reported to the agency, which indicated that many large electric power companies were operating nuclear power plants unsafely.

7.5. Government Reaction to Kansai Electric Power

The Minister of Economy, Trade, and Industry has responsibility for policy regarding the use of nuclear power in Japan. Two days after the Kansai incident he visited Mihama to inspect the accident site. After the inspection he publicly criticized the company for its defective safety system.

In Japan there are many laws designed to give government the power to investigate corporate crime. On August 13th the Nuclear and Industrial Safety Agency carried out a formal inspection at the Mihama plant under the Electricity Enterprises Law. The same day, Kansai Electric Power decided to stop operating eight nuclear reactors in order to check the thickness of all pipes.

The Fukui Labor Bureau and the Tsuruga Labor Standards Inspection Office found that Kansai had exposed its workers to danger because it failed to check the pipe that had ruptured. On August 23rd they indicted Kansai Electric Power for this offense, which was a violation of the Law for Labor Safety and Health.

Since the government can demand that suspected offenders present a report, it required that Kansai Electric Power submit a review of the accident. In addition, on August 30th, using the Electricity Enterprises Law, the Nuclear and Industrial Safety Agency directed Mitsubishi Heavy Industries and Nihon Arm to present a report on their failure to check the pipe involved in the accident. In early September, both companies presented their reports to the agency. The Nuclear and Industrial Safety Agency continued its research and published an interim report on September 27, 2004, and a final report on March 30, 2005.

7.6. Establishment of Preventive Measures by Kansai Electric Power

In response to the interim report, the Minister of Economy, Trade, and Industry directed Y.F. to take measures to prevent future accidents. The same day, Kansai Electric Power published new concrete safety measures.

The Fukui Prefectural Governor had not given permission to restart operation of the Mihama plant because of the continued concerns of residents. On November 26th he permitted Units 1 and 2 to resume operations, as their pipes were thoroughly checked and repaired where needed.

On March 1, 2005, Kansai presented its final report on the cause of the accident and the preventive measures taken since the accident to the Ministry of Economy, Trade, and Industry. The report was criticized and resubmitted again later that month. It stated that the company would give the highest priority to safety in all aspects of its operation. The same day it announced that Y.F. would resign as president at the general meeting of the stockholders in June 2005.[41] The delay in his resignation was severely criticized.

On March 30, 2005, the Nuclear and Industrial Safety Agency published its final report on the accident, in which it pointed out the culpability of Kansai Electric Power, Mitsubishi Heavy Industries, and Nihon Arm. Kansai received the harshest criticism. In addition, the agency criticized the state for trusting electric power companies to check the thickness of pipes without outside scrutiny or verification.

8. Conclusion

Serious cases of a corporate crime related to environmental pollution have occurred in Japan. Like many other corporate crimes, they were largely committed through the overzealous pursuit of profits, with little actual oversight by the government.

During periods of rapid economic growth, people naturally desire a better standard of living. In such situations they may also be more tolerant and neglectful of corporate crimes. In the late 1960s environmental pollution caused by corporations became a serious issue in Japan. Social movements led to the enactment of laws designed to regulate industry better. The same impetus led to the beginning of criminalization of such acts in an effort to prevent their reoccurrence in the future.

Japan has experienced serious corporate crimes in which not only executives of large corporations have been involved, but politicians as well.[42] In the most serious cases, leaders of the underground such as *Sokaiya* (dissidents at general meetings of stockholders) have played an important role mediating between corrupt executives and politicians.[43] As more cases of corporate crime were reported in the mass media, societal reactions became more severe in terms of both public opinion and the law.

Over time, Japan has become more sensitive to accidents and corporate crimes causing death or injury. Even if someone is killed or injured by an accident in the legal operation of a business, people tend to blame the company concerned. Thus, in Japan the public may regard such accidents as "corporate crime." This is especially the case when a corporation causes death or injury without appearing to take sufficient preventive measures.

As companies compete in the marketplace, the reputational costs of corporate crime can cause great damage to offending entities.[44] For example, bankruptcy can result from consumer boycotts.[45] Such actions can cause dramatic drops in sales and revenues, as was seen in the cases of Snow Brand Milk Products, Co., Ltd., after an incident of food poisoning,[46]and Mitsubishi Motors, Co., Ltd., and Mitsubishi Fuso Truck and Bus, Co., Ltd. after improper recall procedures.[47] Severe reactions to such cases involve not only such informal sanctions but formal ones as well.

Through laws the government is obliged to guide, supervise, and regulate corporations so as not to allow such accidents to occur. Therefore, every time an incident happens, the government directs the company under question to take further measures (or adhere to the original ones that were not followed in the first place) to provide for adequate safety and prevention. As the introduction of such measures can be expensive, this functions as a sanction to the corporation as well. If a corporation causes an accident involving heavy casualties by not incurring the costs to take preventive measures, it suffers a great loss through the subsequent payment of compensation to victims. In addition to providing direction, government can also impose administrative sanctions on corporations violating the law. In serious cases it can bring criminal charges against the company.

Recently, we have seen increased prosecution by law enforcement agencies. For example, if an employee of a corporation kills or injures someone, not only is the employee causing the harm charged, but so too are the manager in charge of supervising him/her and the executive in charge of overseeing required preventive measures. Every time an accident occurs, the police begin an investigation to determine whether an offense has occurred.

Criminalization may contribute to a decrease in corporate wrongdoing. However, it is also just as important that corporations be made aware of their social responsibility to avoid causing damage and harm to society by taking necessary measures to maintain safety. As shown here, curtailing such costs in the pursuit of profit may lead not only to injury and death of victims and harm to the environment, but the demise of the offending companies themselves.

Endnotes

1. In Japan corporations were regarded as a kind of a family, which respected employees more than stockholders. However, with the recent decline of such a model, corporations are more frequently required by stockholders to increase dividends.
2. (Yokoyama, 1984).
3. Previously, an insider reporting about corruption to an outsider was blamed and discriminated against as a betrayer in his/her affiliated corporation. The Law to Protect Insider Reporting for Public Interests was enacted in June in 2004. However, the protection is not sufficient, because this law was drafted after a compromise with corporations who opposed it.
4. Scholars in criminal law regard criminal punishment as a last resort. However, many articles in the law prescribed criminal punishment especially to make administrative regulation effective. For example, the Law to Cope with Polluted Soil was enacted in May in 2002. Under this law companies are obliged to test for polluted soil at the ruins of their factory when they plan to redevelop the site. In addition, a prefectural governor can order an owner of polluted ruins to remove toxic substances from the soil to prevent future endangerment. The maximum punishment imposed on the owner neglecting this order is imprisonment with compulsory labor for one year, or a fine of 1,000,000 yen (US $9,090).
5. (2004: 372).
6. (Schmalleger, 2004: 378).
7. (Shoji and Sugai, 1992: 18).
8. (Sugai, 1999: 5).
9. At this election only those persons who paid a certain amount of tax were given suffrage. Although many poor villagers victimized by the pollution could not vote for Shozo Tanaka, he won the election.
10. In the Edo Period farmers could appeal to their village manager for some help. If their appeal was not heard, they could appeal directly to a feudal lord as a last resort.
11. However, sufficient compensation was not realized until 1974.
12. In the economic depression starting in 1990 many factories in large cities were closed. With the recovery from this depression the ruins of these factories were sold for redevelopment. During this redevelopment we saw scandals such as the one involving soil pollution in Osaka. In December 1989 a refining factory of Mitsubishi Metal Co., Ltd. renamed Mitsubishi Material, was closed. Investigators found that soil at the ruins of this factory contained toxic substances. Nevertheless, Mitsubishi Estate Co., Ltd. bought the ruins from Mitsubishi Material. It constructed buildings for a luxury hotel, offices, and apartments. In January 1997 it began to sell apartments without notifying buyers of the polluted soil. On March 29, 2005, the police indicted Mitsubishi Estate, Mitsubishi Material, and ten officials and executives including the presidents of both companies for an offense against the Housing and Construction Enterprises Law, because they continued selling these apartments until September 2002 while knowing about the polluted soil (Nihon Keizai, March 30, 2005). To prevent future scandals the Law to Cope with Polluted Soil was enacted in May 2002 (see note 3).
13. A refinery at Kamioka Mining of Mitsui Metal Co., Ltd. discharged water containing cadmium into th Jintu River over a long time period. Farmers used the river water to grow rice. As a result, residents living along this river suffered from cadmium poisoning from eating the contaminated rice. As patients cried "Itai-itai (Ouch! Ouch!)" their condition became known as Itai-itai disease. Although it was reported

for the first time in 1912, research on its cause was not conducted until decades later. In 1961 two scholars pointed out that Itai-itai disease was caused by cadmium. However, Mitsui Metal ignored this finding. Later, victims of Itai-itai disease sued the company for damages in the Toyama District Court in 1968. They won their suit in 1971.

14. In 1950 a large-sized petrochemical complex was developed in Yokkaichi. In this complex a thermoelectric power plan was constructed in 1959. In the early 1960s many citizens living in Yokkaichi suffered by asthma. Nine patients sued six large companies for damages in 1967 by insisting that the sooty smoke discharged from these companies was the main cause of their illness. They won this suit in 1972.
15. (Ui, 1992: 103).
16. Article 9 of our Criminal Code prescribes seven kinds of criminal punishment: death penalty; imprisonment for life, one with compulsory labor, one without labor; fine; short-term confinement; minor fine, and forfeiture. The main criminal punishment imposed on a corporation for its illegal activity is a fine.
17. One of the main issues was whether a fetus could be an object of a homicide, because a person who had been poisoned by methyl mercury in the womb died 11 years later. On February 29, 1988, the Supreme Court ruled that two defendants were guilty for causing the death of this person by the discharge of methyl mercury. In this sentence we see the judges' admission of an indirect causal sequence and subsequent imposition of severe punishment on defendants whose activities in the company caused serious harm to individuals.
18. (*Asahi News,* April 7, 2005).
19. To the former the government paid a total of 2,600,000 yen as a one-time allowance, and continues paying money to cover all medical costs. The latter are not paid any one-time allowance, while receiving money to cover medical costs. Previously, the money for covering medical costs was limited. But under a new system started in April 2005, this limit was abolished.
20. Many victims who are not relieved under the law did not fall under this new policy. Instead of applying for the health note, they may file suit for relief as a recognized patient (Nihon Keizai, May 2, 2005).
21. (Yokoyama, 1989).
22. (Yokoyama, 1983).
23. For example, around 1970 there was dirty, oil-slicked water in Tokyo Bay. Nowadays we enjoy fishing and boating in the bay, as the water was subsequently cleaned up.
24. For example, Japanese automobile companies have competed to improve engines to conserve gasoline and to invent equipment to purify the emitted gas. They have succeeded in mass sales of their products all over the world, while American automobile companies have declined because of their failure to deal with environmental conservation and pollution issues.
25. In this decade modern industry has developed rapidly in East Asian countries such as Korea, China, and Thailand. China especially has become a base for heavy industry for the world. However, many factories in China do not have the equipment to purify toxic substances. Thus, the Chinese suffer serious environmental pollution. Recently, individuals sued a company for damages caused by pollution. Chinese lawyers representing them want to learn from experiences in Japan (*Asahi News,* April 19, 2005).
26. (Yokoyama, 1993: 70).
27. For example, a strong wind in the spring brings acid rain and toxic dust from the industrial area in Northeast China to Korea and Japan.
28. One-hundred fifty countries ratified the Kyoto Protocol in April 2005. In this protocol, the European Union, the United States, and Japan were to reduce gas emissions

by 8%, 7%, and 6% respectively, between 2008 and 2012 from their levels in 1990. However, in March in 2001 the Bush Administration broke away from the protocol, because it feared it would stifle economic growth. In Japan the state has enacted many policies to reduce gas emissions through initiatives introduced by the Ministry of Environment. However, the Ministry of Economy, Trade, and Industry has resisted these policies from the viewpoint of economic development. For example, this ministry wants to change the reduction target of 6% from a requirement to a goal (Nihon Keizai, May 5 in 2005).

29. In October 2003 four prefectures—Tokyo, Kanagawa, Chiba, and Saitama—decided to regulate gas emitted from diesel engine cars. Under an ordinance in Tokyo enacted in April 2006, a diesel car emitting gas over a specified amount will be prohibited from operating in the city, and violators will be fined up to 500,000 yen (US $4,550). To cope with this situation, Pures Co., Ltd., an affiliate of Mitsui & Co., Ltd., designed equipment to purify gas emitting diesel engines, which Mitsui & Co. then sold. The company, subsidized by four prefectural governments, presented false data on the effectiveness of the equipment. The scandal was exposed through a confession of an officer dispatched from Mitsui & Co. to Pures on November 22, 2004. On November 29th an executive of Mitsui & Co. announced that the company would return a total of 8,000 million yen (US $73 million) to the four prefectures. On December 4th the Tokyo Metropolitan Government decided to prohibit Mitsui & Co. from participating in bidding for government contracts. On December 25th Mitsui & Co. announced that two officers of the company and a vice-president and another officer of Pures participated in the fraud. On December 27, 2004, the police conducted an investigation at the main office of Mitsui & Co. and indicted four suspects on fraud charges. In January 2004 the Tokyo Metropolitan Government demanded that the company pay a total of 2,000 million yen (US $18 million) including an administrative fine of 200 million yen (Nihon Keizai, February 24, 2005). Through these sanctions Mitsui & Co. suffered not only monetary losses, but the loss of public confidence.
30. Kansai Electric Power is one of the most important companies in the Kansai area, including Osaka and Kobe, because it supplies electric power monopolistically in the region.
31. (Sugai, 2003: 4).
32. Japan experienced emission of radioactivity for the first time in September 1999, which was caused by an accident at a factory of JCO, an affiliated company of Sumitomo Metal Mining Co., The way to process uranium had been changed to reduce costs without the permission of the state. Two workers were killed and one was seriously injured by radioactivity. About 250 persons, including 59 workers of JCO and 3 members of a rescue team dispatched from a fire station, were also exposed to radioactivity. Farmers suffered great damage because their products could not sell at market. In October 2000, six officials of JCO, including an executive in charge of production and another executive in charge of managing the factory, were arrested for professional negligence causing death. In addition both JCO and Sumitomo Metal Mining had to pay compensation to victims. In March 2000 Sumitomo Metal Mining appropriated 13,900 million yen (US $116 million) to settlethe case.
33. Almost all Japanese know two telephone numbers for an emergency: 119 for the fire station, and 110 for the police. The fire station and the police dispatch the rescue team and the investigation team to the site of an accident, disaster, or crime immediately after receiving an emergency call. Using this system, Japan has a high probability of rescuing an injured or ill person and of arresting a suspect. In addition, the fire station and the police ask companies to establish a system to deal with the emergency. The law requires the establishment of such a system.

Thus, if companies cause an accident without establishing this system or if the system is not functioning properly, they usually receive administrative or criminal punishment.

34. Since the late 1990s we have seen an increase in victims' rights movements. As they insist on the imposition of severe sanctions for offenders, the police always are on the lookout for professional negligence causing death and/or injury if an accident, even one causing minor injury, occurs. If a serious accident occurs through the negligence of a company, officers of the company can also be criminally charged. For example, on March 26, 2004, a six-year-old boy died after being caught in an automatic revolving door. After careful investigation, the public prosecutor judged that this accident would not have occurred if the companies concerned had taken proper preventive measures. An executive and a chief in charge of managing this building for Mori Building Co., Ltd. and an executive in charge of production of the automatic revolving door of Sanwa Tajima Co., Ltd. were prosecuted for professional negligence causing death (Nihon Kaizai, March 17, 2005). Through this prosecution both companies were severely criticized for overzealous pursuit of profits without providing adequate safety measure.
35. Typical is the Aircraft and Railway Accidents Investigation Commission in the Ministry of Land Infrastructure and Transport. Officers affiliated with this commission began to investigate a major railway accident on April 25, 2005, in which 107 persons were killed and 460 injured. It was found that West Japan Railway Co., Ltd., urged drivers to operate trains punctually without taking measures for safe driving. This accident was regarded as a crime committed by the company rather than by the driver who operated the train above speed limits in order to make up a delay of only a minute and a half.
36. Usually a company is inclined to hide information about the cause of an accident. For example, West Japan Railway did not disclose the confession of a conductor that the train was speeding just before it overturned. Instead, at the press conference the company suggested that the accident could have been caused by a stone on the tracks that someone intentionally placed there (*Nihon Kaizai,* May 2, 2005).
37. This change to Nihon Arm might be carried out to curtail costs for maintenance. With the change, Kansai Electric Power reduced the number of days for regularly checking its nuclear plants. The days were shortened from over 100 in 1996 to about 60 after 1997 (*Nihon Keizai,* March 26, 2005).
38. Previously, we had a custom to express apology immediately after a wrongdoing. However, recently many wrongdoers hesitate to express an apology mainly because they are afraid of financial liability. Victims often get angry about this hesitation. The negotiation regarding compensation then becomes more complicated.
39. This was the way to express the sincerest apology in the feudal era, which we rarely see today.
40. He was summoned to a meeting of the Committee on Economy and Industry of the House of Representatives on August 31st and on September 29th, and to a meeting of the same committee of the House of Councilors on October 6th.
41. Companies in Japan do not want to admit responsibility by the resignation of their top executive. Therefore, Kansai Electric Power announced that Y.F. would resign at the general meeting of stockholders as a "normal retirement."
42. (Yokoyama, 2005).
43. (Yokoyama, 2003a).
44. (Yokoyama, 1985: 511).
45. (Yokoyama, 2003b: 31).
46. Snow Brand Mild Products Co., Ltd., supplied milk of bad quality in June and July, poisoning over 10,000 persons. As the company did not account properly for the cause of the poisoning, it was severely criticized. In addition, in January 2002

the mass media reported that Snow Brand Food Products, Co., Ltd., an affiliated company, Snow Brand Milk Products, had received a subsidy through fraud. As a consequence of this, and the negative publicity it brought, not only was the company closed, but the entire Snow Brand Conglomerate was disbanded because of the resulting drastic decrease in sales.

47. On January 11, 2001, a tire coming off a trailer produced by Mitsubishi Motors killed a mother and injured her two sons. Investigation of this accident found that the trailer had a serious defect. It was later revealed that Mitsubishi Motors and Mitsubishi Fuso Truck and Bus had repaired many defective automobiles secretly for the purpose of curtailing the costs of a major vehicle recall. After this accident, both companies continued hiding defective automobiles, which delayed a general recall for repairs. As they lost public confidence, the company declined dramatically. The total number of new cars sold by Mitsubishi Motors and Mitsubishi Fuso Truck and Bus in 2004, in 2003 decreased by 43.6% and by 35.8%, respectively, while the rate of sale of all automobiles in Japan fell by only 2.2% during the same time periods (*Nihon Keizai,* April 2, 2005).

References

Kumamoto Daily News. "Chronological Table of Minamata Disease." http://kumanichi.com/feature/minamata/nenpyou/m-nenpyou.html (accessed 2 May 2005).

Nuclear and Industrial Safety Agency. "Automatic Shut-Down of Unit 3, Mihama Power Plant (Kansai Electric Power Co. Inc.)." http://www.nisa.meti.go.jp/english/index.htm (accessed 3 May 2005).

Schmalleger, Frank (2004) *Criminology Today* (Third Edition). Upper Saddle River, NJ: Pearson Education, Inc.

Shoji, Kichiro, and Masuro Sugai (1992) "The Ashio Copper Mine Pollution Case: The Origin of Environmental Destruction." In *Industrial Pollution in Japan.* Editor Jun Ui. Tokyo, Japan: The United Nations University Press.

Sugai, Masuro (1999) "The Development of the Copper Industry and Environmental Destruction, 1980s." *The Kokugakuin University Economic Review* (47)1: 1–20.

Sugai, Masuro (2003) "Present Stage of Local People's Movements in Japan: Focus on Anti-Nuclear Power Movements." *Bulletin of Center for Transnational Labor Studies,* 8 Nov.:2–19.

Ui, Jun (1992) "Minamata Disease." In *Industrial Pollution in Japan,* Editor Jun Ui. Tokyo, Japan: The United Nations University Press.

Yokoyama, Minoru (1983) "Change in Industrial Structure and Social Pathology." In *Sociology of Present Pathology*, Editor S. Nasu. Tokyo, Japan: Gakubun-sha.

Yokoyama, Minoru (1984) "Crimes of Private Corporation in Japan." Presented at the Conference on Crime and Development, United Nations Latin American Institute for Crime Prevention and Treatment of Offenders in San Jose, Costa Rica (December 17–19).

Yokoyama, Minoru (1985) "Corporate Crime." In *Criminal Policy,* Editors T. Sawanobori, K. Tokoro, K. Hoshino, and I. Maeno. Kyoto, Japan: Sorin-sha.

Yokoyama, Minoru (1989) "Sanctionalization." In *Przymus w Spoleczenstwie,* Editor Andrzei Kojder. Warsaw, Poland: Warsaw University.

Yokoyama, Minoru (1993) "Social Pathology with Internationalization." In *Pathology in Mature Society*, Editors S. Yonekawa and M. Yajima. Tokyo, Japan: Gakubun-sha.

Yokoyama, Minoru (2001) "Analysis of Japanese Police from the Viewpoint of Democracy." In *Policing, Security and Democracy: Theory and Practice*, Editors M. Amir and S. Einstein. Huntsville, TX: The Office of International Criminal Justice.

Yokoyama, Minoru (2003a) "Analysis of Corruption by *Sokaiya* (Hoodlums at General Meeting of Stockholders) in Japan." *Kokugakuin Journal of Law and Politics* 40(4):59–86.
Yokoyama, Minoru (2003b) "Political and Economic Power" (in Japanese). In *Society with Desire,* Editors M. Inoue, K. Sasaki, H. Tajima, S. Tokii, and T. Yamamoto. Tokyo, Japan: Gakubun-sha.
Yokoyama, Minoru (2005) "Analysis of Political Corruption in Japan." *Kokugakuin Journal of Law and Politics* 42 (4):1–49.

3

Crime in the World of Art

Christine Alder and Kenneth Polk

In these pages we shall address an under-researched aspect of white-collar crime—namely, illegal activity in the art world, specifically problems arising with art theft, fraud in the art market, and the illicit traffic in cultural heritage material. The art world is, of course, exceptionally diverse, consisting of paintings, sculptures, works in glass, works on paper, photography, works in fabric, and many other art forms. It is, as well, widespread in a geographical sense with material for collectors and collections coming from all parts of the globe. There are, further, many layers to the art market in terms of cost, with some objects at the low end being little more than trinkets, ranging upward to the rarefied heights of the art auction rooms where some items are sold for millions of pounds or dollars. It should come as no surprise that it is this expensive end of the market that attracts the interest of those willing to seek illicit avenues to wealth, although as we shall see the pathways such illegal activity can take are multiple and diverse.

Art Theft

The first form of illegal activity in the art world to be addressed here consists of the theft of artworks. At regular intervals newspaper readers will encounter a story about the theft of a major work of art somewhere in the world. The list of such artworks stolen in recent months alone includes artists such as Pieter Brueghel the Younger, Jan Brughel, Salvador Dali, Leonardo Da Vinci, Georgia O'Keefe, Edvard Munch (including his iconic "The Scream"), and Pablo Picasso, among others, and in addition such important objects as a golden salt cellar by Cellini and a cello by Stradivarius. This is, of course, but a partial list of works of art that have been stolen, since objects produced by less well-known artists may not be so widely reported. As we widen the time span we encounter such notable events as the theft in 1990 of an estimated $200 million worth of art (including works by Vermeer and Rembrandt) from the Isabella Stewart Gardner Museum in Boston, the theft of major Impressionist works from the Marmottan Museum in 1985, the loss of major works from the National Museum of Anthropology in Mexico City in 1985, and from the Montreal Museum of Fine Arts in Canada in 1972, or more recently from the

National Museum in Stockholm in 2000 (including a Rembrandt self-portrait), and the theft of an entire exhibition of the works of Grace Cossington Smith from a private gallery in Sydney in 1977. In short, the problem is worldwide, and includes thefts from some of the best-known museums in major capital cities.[1]

At this point we are not yet into a discussion of white-collar crime, since most of the thefts result from burglaries, which would usually be treated as a form of street crime. What makes art theft relevant to a discussion of white-collar crime is what happens after the item is stolen, and concerns the ways that the wider art market can be bent to serve illicit purposes. The situation facing a criminal who has stolen a major work of art is quite different than that faced by the common burglar. The ordinary burglar, research tells us, disposes of his loot in a very short space of time (often within hours of the theft), and will seek out disposal sources such as a drug dealer, someone in the informal social network (friend, acquaintance, family), perhaps a professional fence, or even market resources such as bent dealers or stores which specialize in the rapid turnover of second hand merchandise.

Put simply, this is no way to sell a stolen Picasso or Munch. For art to realize even a fraction of its true value, it is likely that it will have to pass overtly or covertly onto the legitimate art market. There are two main levels to this art market: a primary market that deals in sale of original works for the first time by living artists; and a secondary market that provides a venue for the sale of works which are re-entering the market after some previous sale. While there are occasional exceptions, one of which will be discussed below, in general living artists do not command prices significant enough to attract the attention of knowledgeable art thieves, so there is little movement of stolen art at this primary level. By definition, if a potential thief is planning to realize a significant profit from stolen art, a buyer must be found either in the open secondary market, or perhaps through a covert sale (to a source, for example, that some in the trade refer to as "gloaters").

There are barriers in the contemporary secondary art market that make the sale of stolen work problematic. There are international registers of stolen artworks that operate both in the private sector (for example, the Art Loss Register) and in public policing (for example, both Interpol and the FBI maintain files of stolen art). There are market forces that compound the problem, since in fact there are only a relatively few dealers and auction houses that operate at the top end of the secondary market; and in general those involved tend to be extremely careful in purchasing works, especially works with suspicious provenance. Many dealers assert that they will not buy "off the street" from vendors unknown to them. The auction houses, further, routinely compare their prospective sale catalogues with the available lists of stolen art, and this step accounts for a significant trickle of stolen works back to their original owners.

Despite all the protections, there are examples of unscrupulous dealers who provide a portal for stolen work into the open market. A recent example can be found in Australia where, as the well-known artist Albert Tucker was nearing the end of his life, he was befriended by an art dealer who took advantage of the open access he was given to Tucker's remaining personal collection, stealing a small flow of works and putting them onto the market through his own art gallery. In this rare case we see a configuration of conditions that contributed to the success (for a time, at least) of these thefts: the thief had considerable *knowledge about the working of the art market*, he had an established *reputation* that meant that other dealers and collectors would trust him so that they could purchase art from him, his own gallery gave him a clear *portal* into the art market, and his personal connection with the artist gave him the *access* he needed to steal the valuable art.

The configuration of factors in this case, successful for at least a brief period of time, suggests why it is that theft is not a major issue for students of white-collar crime in the art world. It will be rare that an individual, or group for that matter, has the combination of knowledge of what art is valuable and where it can be stolen from, the position within the art market that makes any sale potentially credible, and direct access to a portal for sale of material onward onto the market. It seems clear, in fact, that many thieves have little understanding of the difficulties they will face in negotiating art objects. It is not uncommon for stolen work simply to be returned by some surreptitious route, or more tragically, to drop out of sight altogether as has happened with the recent theft of Munch's "Scream," and the many invaluable works stolen from the Gardner Museum in 1990. As thieves become aware of the difficulties in arranging a sale or ransom of a highly valuable work, there is the worry that they might destroy the works altogether, which occurred in a recent case in Europe where a mother threw several valuable paintings into a canal when she feared that police were closing in on her art thief son.

Fraud in the Art Market

A more vexing problem, and one more central to concerns about white-collar crime, is that related to fraud, especially what would commonly be understood as faking. It is virtually axiomatic that if there is a vigorous and prosperous market for legitimate art, then individuals will emerge who will attempt to take advantage of the opportunities for deception and fraud in that market. Recent decades have seen waves of fakers whose names are now notorious, including van Meegeren in the 1930s,[2] deHory[3] and Keating in the 1950s and 1960s,[4] Hebborn in the 1970s and 1980s,[5] and Myatt/Drew in the 1980s and 1990s.[6] But such activities are not unique to art in the European tradition, as Clunas[7] has observed that faking and deceptive practices emerged in China as early as the 15th and 16th centuries as a consequence of the rapid expansion of the art market that occurred in the Ming period.

However evocative the terms *fake* or *faker* may be, in fact there are a number of both logical and legal issues that emerge that urge caution in the use of these terms. These arise especially in regard to the intent element necessary for a criminal charge of fraud, such as the commonly used charge in Australia of "obtaining financial advantage through deception." A successful prosecution will have to address the following material elements: (1) it must be shown that the defendant obtained some financial advantage; (2) in the case of art fraud, that advantage must be a result of the negotiation that can be demonstrated to be deceptive—for example, it might be a painting with a signature of a well-known artist where that artist was not responsible for its creation; and (3) it must be proven that the defendant intended to deceive the victim.

While these may seem to be relatively clear elements in a legal sense, matters can become cloudy very quickly when the realities of the art market are addressed. One common problem results from the fact that there is a long tradition of legitimate copying of existing works, at times for purposes of training art students, and at other times for the purposes of obtaining a copy of a popular work. Indeed, in many major metropolitan centers, and on the Internet, there is a thriving trade in producing quite legitimate copies of famous artworks (some advertised, in fact, as "genuine fakes").

Considerable confusion and mischief can occur when these works, especially if they are decades or centuries old, enter the art market with their correct attribution lost, and their provenance murky. The popular word *fake* presumes knowledge and intent of the person passing the work into the market. In the case of the famous fakers in history, as when van Meegeren magically produced his "new" Vermeers, the issue of intent is clear, and a charge of fraud could be sustained. But if a victim purchases such a painting in good faith, paying a reasonable market price, then later sells that work on the secondary market, still believing the object to be genuine, then the critical intent element necessary to sustain a charge of fraud is not present.

It is not uncommon for works to recirculate in the secondary market. If a work is not authentic (for example, if the attribution, such as the artist's signature, is not correct), each time that it enters the market the question of fraud will hinge on what the seller can be demonstrated to know about the origins of the work. It might be, for example, that for some reason a previously naïve victim has obtained expert advice that the attribution is not correct. If the owner attempts to sell the painting with its original attribution after having such advice, and if it can be proven that the owner thought that advice correct (not necessarily easy to prove, of course), then a charge of fraud might be sustained.

Other matters may arise to cloud the issue even further. For example, in recent years there have been allegations of fraud and deception in the market for Aboriginal art in Australia, and, in fact, there has been one case where an art dealer of European descent was convicted of fraud involving the production of art that was not authentic (in that it was established that the dealer himself had created works, and then had these signed with the name of a noted Aboriginal artist). Difficulties can arise in these works because of the distinctive approach to ownership taken within the Aboriginal community.[8] Within traditional communities, there is a keen sense of "ownership" and custodial responsibility regarding who "owns" the specific Dreaming story that might be featured in a painting. Given this, the indigenous view will be that the work is "owned" not necessarily by the person who actually produced it, but by the person who owns the story itself. Consistent with such an interpretation, the person who signs the work may be the person who owns the story, not the actual artist. Needless to say, this can cause at a minimum confusion in the art market, and certainly in any potential courtroom.

It is because of such complications that many in the art market are wary of the term *fake*. Those who are in the business of authenticating art tend to focus on the probabilities that the work is what it seems to be—that it is *authentic*. However popular and dramatic the word *fakery* may be, it presumes a particular cluster of intent elements that actually may not be accurate in describing a work that is not authentic.

It also underscores the growing importance of the availability of provenance information regarding works that come onto the market. If the purchaser is in the rare position of knowing the ownership history of a work that stretches back to the original artist, then there is the possibility of some safety in the assumption of authenticity of the work. It must immediately be said, of course, that if works can be faked, then so can provenances. Indeed, one of the more ingenious schemes for selling fraudulent art, thought up by John Drewe in England, involved precisely the development of false provenances and the successful insertion of these into the records of venerable art institution libraries.

There are, of course, many other avenues for fraudulent activity in the art market. It involves, after all, commercial activity with the participation of many different kinds of players. Conklin[9] in his extensive analysis of art fraud discusses such forms as insurance and tax fraud by collectors; fraud against artists, collectors, museums and auction houses by dealers; and especially fraud by auction houses. The art world was scandalized at the onset of 2000 by an announcement of a major antritrust suit against the two largest and most prestigious art auction houses, Sotheby's and Christie's, which ultimately resulted in 2003 in both a negotiated settlement of a class action suit involving over $500 million dollars, and criminal convictions of leading players, including a jail term of one year and a day for the 76-year-old head of Sotheby's, A. Alfred Taubman, and a fine of $7.5 million assessed against him.

The Illicit Traffic in Plundered Antiquities

A third component of the art market significant to a discussion of white-collar crime is that concerned with the international traffic in illicit cultural heritage material. This antiquities market is exceptionally diverse, and consists of stone sculptures stolen from such places as Khmer temples in Cambodia or ancient Hindu sites in India, Pakistan or Indonesia, brass material taken from Tibet or Thailand; ancient paintings ripped off of walls of churches in Italy; mosaics pulled out of the ground in diverse locations controlled in earlier centuries by the Romans; material from Greek temples and graves; various items from Egyptian tombs; and diverse objects (ceramic, stone, precious metals, weaving) from Pre-Columbian sites in various parts of Latin America, among others.

In the early days in the study of white-collar crime there was concern regarding whether the term *crime* was strictly appropriate, but when it comes to antiquities there is no question that the traffic is illegal. There is now a complex web of criminal laws and treaties that define the trade as unlawful. Virtually all countries that are the source of stolen material have laws prohibiting the export of cultural artifacts, but most now take the further step of defining the taking of such objects as theft. There are as well complex international treaties and conventions that strengthen the hands of nations desiring to limit this trade.

Having said that, it also must be pointed out that these laws are imposed upon cultures with a long tradition of appropriation of the cultural heritage of other peoples. From the 19th century onward, one of the devices used by the politically powerful and economically dominant nations was to gather up diverse material to be housed in such central institutions as the Louvre in Paris, the British Museum in London, or the Metropolitan Museum in New York. "Collecting" has been defined as a desirable activity, especially for social elites. In places such as New York one way of establishing a visible symbol of elite status is to endow a particular section of a major museum, often by making available choice items from one's own private collection.

The issue of the destruction of cultural heritage sites to feed the collecting market has become especially visible with recent events in Iraq (and just before that, in Afghanistan). With the United States and its allies unable to protect the very lives of its service personnel, it should come as no surprise that there has been a dismal record in terms of the protection of some of the most valued cultural sites in the world. Atwood[10] describes how within hours of the downfall of the Iraqi government, looters had overrun archaeological museums in both Bagdad and Mosul. Thus, added to massive looting in the countryside, released a flood of material onto the antiquities markets of both Europe and North America. By the middle of 2004, U.S. customs agents had seized some 600 objects stolen from the Bagdad museum alone.[11]

In many respects this traffic in cultural heritage material shares features with other criminal markets.[12] Such markets function within a dynamic of demand, exerting pressure upon potential criminals to provide a supply of material to satisfy that demand. Some criminal markets are highly localized, as is the case with most household burglaries where the thief will most often rapidly dispose of the stolen objects. One of the defining characteristics of the antiquities trade, in sharp contrast, is that the market is international in character (a characteristic shared with such other complex criminal markets such as that dealing with drugs, or the traffic in women).

Much follows from this important element. For one thing, the attempt to counter the illegal traffic results in a network of complex laws at the state and national level, supported by a cluster of international treaties that give supporting guidance and direction. By definition this creates a number of awkward problems for criminal justice enforcement resulting from issues of compatibility of laws, problems of coordination of intelligence and enforcement actions, language difficulties, differences that arise from different political systems and approaches, and a host of related problems. Put simply, it is difficult to create an efficient and effective enforcement strategy that appropriately mirrors and meshes with the international workings of such international criminal markets as antiquities or drugs.

With antiquities as with drugs, the international trade is countered by a web of not necessarily coherent criminal laws at the national or even state level, with the laws of the individual states not necessarily sharing common interests, objectives or legal principles. Given the presence of such laws, however, those engaged in the trafficking of the illicit material must arrange for the successful smuggling of material out of one country and into another. Where considerable money is involved (true in both antiquities and drug markets), for the smuggling to be consistent enough to satisfy market demand, forms of corruption emerge directed at customs officials, police, and politicians. Often in both markets, the source countries are relatively poor, and the destination nations rich, further aggravating the situation by increasing the motivation at source for the local residents to play their role in the production of illicit material (in the case of antiquities by engaging in illegal digs), and making possible greater opportunities to corrupt local officials. Further, both the drug and antiquities markets are internally diverse, with different distribution and sales pathways for different kinds of objects. (For antiquities, there are quite different origins, smuggling routes, and ultimate market destinations for small jade objects from China, ornamental chests from Tibet, woven objects from Peru, or small ornamental bronze objects from Roman Britain).

There are, however, some unique features in the market for illicit cultural heritage material that give it a different shape than that encountered in some other illegal markets. One of the distinctive features of the antiquities market is that, by and large, the sale of material, illegally removed from often remote original sites, is perfectly legal in the major market states. While there have been a handful of arrests, and some seizures of cultural heritage material by customs authorities, it is still true today that one can walk into shops in London, New York, and Paris, as well as, of course, Brussels, Amsterdam, Berlin, Stockholm and elsewhere, and openly and legally purchase a wide variety of cultural objects from places such as Cambodia, China, Thailand, Tibet, and Latin American, among others.

Put another way, the international market in illicit antiquities is quite different from some other illicit markets, such as that involving drugs. The markets for drugs, and many other illicit items, are in general illegal both in source and destination environments. To be sure, those in the trade have to negotiate carefully, since it technically is possible in countries such as Australia, the United Kingdom, and the United States that if theft in the source state can be proven beyond reasonable doubt, and if there are clear criminal laws prohibiting such theft in the country of origin, then a prosecution in the destination country becomes technically a possibility, as one of the major figures in the trade in New York found when he was convicted and sentenced to over two years in jail in a courtroom in New York for handling goods that were established to have been stolen in Egypt.

This open and legal sale of material occurs for a number of reasons. For one, there is an accepted, but odd, convention in this arena of the art trade that in virtually all sales, and even in exhibitions of material by museums or collectors, no provenance information is provided for the potential purchaser or viewer. It should be noted that archaeologists when they speak of ownership history ask for considerably more information than is usually implied by the term *provenance*. A more specific term is sometimes used, *provenience,* which asks for information not simply of ownership history, but of the origins of the object, where it originally came from—and if it was produced through an archaeological dig, where the material was found, who found it, when it was extracted, and information about any publications that have resulted. Such information is almost never provided by vendors in the antiquities market.

This is somewhat odd because the art trade generally has learned from experience with works stolen by the Germans in World War II that unprovenanced material might be seized and turned over to its rightful owners. This has alerted the general art community to the issue of provenance, and one can now find at least some provision of provenance information for some objects in major art sales and auctions, although this trend has yet to carry over into the antiquities market.

Perhaps an even better reason for questioning the absence of information on provenance in the sale of antiquities is the strong possibility that the material is not authentic: that is, it has been faked. Antiquities dealers in locations such as Bangkok and Hong Kong often will provide elaborate stories of how the material had been dug up from a tomb, and then smuggled out of the country of origin (for example, China or Cambodia), as a way of countering questions about possible fakery. In one shop in Asia the authors observed some unique Thai ceramic material on sale, with a huge photograph pasted over the display showing what was presumed to be the illegal dig in process. One thus comes away with the conclusion that the material is either faked or smuggled.

The continuation of the trade is made possible, however, by the fact that prospective purchasers of antiquities do not demand information on provenance, much less provenience, and because dealers do not feel an obligation to provide such information. Put simply, if there were no purchase of objects that lack proper provenience, there would be no demand for illegal material, and without demand the trade would dry up.

A second factor that allows the trade to continue is the elaborate process by which objects are laundered through key trade "portals" and emerge onto the market as legitimate exported goods. Because of the gradual passage of various international treaties and conventions over recent years, and the workings of the criminal law at an international level, those in the illicit antiquities trade have learned that it is dangerous, if not illegal, simply to ship material directly to the market state from the country of origin. The United States, for example, has signed treaties that prohibit the illegal export of cultural heritage material from countries such as Cambodia, China, and Italy. If it can be proven that the material has been illegally removed, then the objects can be seized and returned to the country of origin. While this has happened to a few objects, often with considerable publicity, the legal requirements are exceptionally strict, requiring, for example, specific proof that the object was known, even inventoried, in its original location. While this is possible in the case of material illegally removed from the archaeological museum in Bagdad (both because the items still possessed their inventory numbers and at least some had been photographed) it should be obvious that this is hardly a likely possibility when the material is produced by an illegal dig in a remote area where there is little or no effective surveillance.

Such material, however, still must enter the destination country as legal export goods. The major avenue historically is for such material to pass through a "free port" portal, such as Switzerland, Hong Kong, Macao, or Singapore, or perhaps through a portal where it is possible to evade customs examinations, such as Bangkok. Typically what will happen is that dealers from destination centers such as New York or London will negotiate with what are essentially middlemen or brokers who work as dealers in the transition portal location. The goods are then sent onward to the destination country with what now becomes legitimate export documentation. This process might have elaborations, as when the transition broker arranges for a real or fictitious sale of the material to a resident in the transition country, whence the material is moved on, bearing such provenance—as one can see commonly in the catalogs of major auction houses— as "from the collection of a Swiss gentleman."

A third issue which both differentiates this market and also serves to inhibit control on the illicit antiquities traffic is the fact that both historically and at present, the purchase of ancient art involves many who are part of the economic and social elite. In the past, certainly, one of the ways of establishing elite status was to acquire fine objects from ancient cultures, for example, the material brought back by young English gentlemen returning from their "Grand Tour" in the 18th and 19th centuries (some of which, of course, over time have found their way into the British Museum holdings). The Chinese have long appreciated antique art, and in an odd twist one of the common sets of objects that turn up in illegal digs in China are even older material which in turn had previously been looted in antiquity from an even older tomb. There is even a wonderful painting of two elite gentlemen from the Ming Period, dated to the late 15th century, which bears the title that translates into English as "Enjoying Antiquities." This theme of social elites wanting to possess antique materials continues to this day, and one factor which works against the development of more effective laws and strategies to counter the illicit traffic is the opposition exerted by leading societal figures who, of course, often have direct links to leading political figures.

One of the important roles that a market analysis can play is to help focus debates regarding effective strategies to control this illicit traffic. Criminologists are likely to take a somewhat different position on approaches to this task than the lawyers and archaeologists who currently dominate the movement to bring this illegal market under control. Currently such strategies tend to be tilted strongly in the direction of the use of legal prohibitions on the trade, most often having their greatest strength in source environments. The criminologist, on the other hand, is likely to look at the dismal record of such legal approaches, as seen in the failure of Prohibition in the United States in the early 20th century and the current and continued unsuccessful outcomes of the various wars on drugs that have gone on since the middle of the 20th century, and urge caution about the potential success of legal prohibition, especially when demand remains high in the wealthy market countries.

There is, of course, some role for clear legal prohibition, especially if more effective regulations could be developed in the rich market environments. In addition to the important moral symbolism involved in the statements made in the criminal law, the very nature of the acts involved in the purchase of antiquities make it somewhat more vulnerable to deterrence-based strategies that rely on potential criminal penalties. The decision to purchase an object, especially an expensive one, is more likely to meet the conditions of "rational choice" presumed in deterrence; and further, the fact that social elites might suffer public humiliation as a consequence of an arrest and prosecution adds further weight to consideration of deterrence-based measures.

Nonetheless, there are inherent limits to the control of illicit activity based on deterrence. Such approaches work only if effective law enforcement is possible (a condition emphatically not met in many of the poorer countries that provide the source of much of the illicit material); and even where it might be achieved, it could result simply in some form of displacement. As an example, in current research conducted by the authors, it has been observed that while in recent years there has been an apparent decline in the sale of Cambodian material in leading Bangkok antiquities venues (because, it has been suggested, of agreements between the Thai and Cambodian governments, as well as actions by the United States), the result has been that now the shops sell more material from Burma and Laos. An alternative, one familiar to those studying white-collar crime, is to aim for a "culture of compliance" that is based in strategies that attempt, in the words of one prominent criminologist, to persuade rather than punish.[13] The target of such strategies must be clear: that is, to protect the important cultural heritage sites that are being irrevocably destroyed by the looters. The theoretical task is to reduce demand, by a combination of criminal justice strategies (based in the use of appropriately severe punishments) supported by wider educational projects designed to convince buyers in the market place that they should not purchase antiquities that lack clear and legitimate provenience.

Conclusion

From the foregoing we see that the art market consists of commercial activity involving demand and supply, or selling and buying. As a form of commercial activity it is vulnerable to a range of illegal activities that are core issues to the student of white-collar crime. To be sure, one element that tends to differentiate at least some parts of art crime is that it involves social or political elites. It is notable that in recent years, it has been crime involving an artwork that has been responsible for the downfall of such noted entrepreneurs as Alan Bond in Australia and L. Dennis Kozlowski in the United States. The involvement of social elites, including the likes of Bond and Kozlowski, in the art market assures that more accounts of art crime will find their way into the media. There will be more art thefts involving prominent collections, and new waves of faking and other forms of art fraud will inevitably emerge. Even as this chapter is being written, the prestigious Getty Museum is being rocked by allegations of impropriety, including criminal charges being brought in Italy against its curator of antiquities as a result of allegations of improper purchase of material stolen from Italy. Our analysis has argued that a key to understanding art crime rests in a careful analysis of the dynamics of market behavior with regard to the movement of art. It is the theoretical grasp of these dynamics that creates some possibility for focusing effective measures of prevention and control on various form of art crime.

Endnotes

1. Conklin (1996).
2. Hoving (1996).
3. Irving (1969).
4. Keating et al. (1977).
5. Hebborn (1997).
6. Landesman (1999).
7. Clunas (1997).
8. Alder and Polk (2004).
9. Conklin (1996).
10. Atwood (2004).
11. Atwood (2004:11).
12. Alder and Polk (2005).
13. Braithwaite (2002).

References

Alder, Christine, and Kenneth Polk (2004) "Examining Claims of Fraud and Deception in Australian Aboriginal Art." *Art, Antiquity and Law* 9:117–142.

Alder, Christine, and Kenneth Polk (2005) "The Illicit Traffic in Plundered Antiquities." In *Handbook of Transnational Crime & Justice*, Editor P. Reichel. Thousand Oaks, CA: Sage Publications.

Atwood, Roger (2004) *Stealing History: Tomb Raiders, Smugglers and Looting of the Ancient World.* New York: St. Martin's Press.

Braithwaite, John (2002) *Restorative Justice and Responsive Regulation.* Oxford: Oxford University Press.

Clunas, Craig (1997) *Art in China.* Oxford: Oxford University Press.

Conklin, John E. (1996) *Art Crime*. London: Praeger.
Hebborn, Eric (1997) *The Art Forger's Handbook*. London: Cassell.
Hoving, Thomas (1996) *False Impressions: The Hunt for Big-Time Art Fakes*. New York: Simon & Schuster.
Irving, Clifford (1969) *Fake! The Story of Elmyr de Hory, the Greatest Art Forger of Our Time.* New York: McGraw-Hill.
Keating, Tom et al. (1977) *The Fake's Progress: Tom Keating's Story*. London: Hutchinson.
Landesman, Peter (1999) "The Art Con Of The Century." *The New York Times Magazine* 31–38 (18 July).

4

Computer Crime and White-Collar Crime

Peter Grabosky and Sascha Walkley

The concepts white-collar crime and computer crime share one feature—an unfortunate degree of ambiguity. Depending on how one defines each term, there is a matter of overlap. There is also much that is unique to each. This essay will attempt a delineation of the two concepts and will seek to demonstrate how they intersect. It will conclude by testing the fit of routine activity theory and the importance of trust to both types of crime.

Computer Crime Defined

Crimes involving digital technology have been given a number of labels, including computer crime, computer-related crime, cyber crime, digital crime, high-tech crime, Internet crime, e-crime, electronic crime, and netcrime. Although one could spend a great amount of time trying to articulate and differentiate these, the following discussion will address three basic forms:

- Offenses where digital technology is the *tool* or the *instrument* of the crime in question
- Offenses where digital technology is the *target* of criminal activity
- Offenses where digital technology is *incidental* to the crime

Digital Technology as the *Instrument* of Crime

Many conventional offenses can be committed with digital technology. The significance is the speed and efficiency that this technology contributes to execution of the crime in question. The production, reproduction, storage, and dissemination of child pornography are all much easier today than they were in the days of ordinary photography and magazine or film production. Fraudulent solicitations in many varieties, from Nigerian advance fee requests to false rumors about share prices in furtherance of stock market manipulation, can now be disseminated to millions of people instantaneously, and at negligible cost. Millions of items are offered for sale on the Internet, either privately or through organized auctions. Online auctions have become an increasing source of consumer complaints, where the vendor delivers inferior products or none at all, or when the purchaser fails to pay for the product. Digital technology permits perfect reproduction of text, images, sound, vision, and multimedia combinations, greatly facilitating piracy of software and entertainment products. Sophisticated scanning devices and graphics software are commercially available and reasonably priced. Even designer labels can be easily and perfectly forged. Official documents such as birth certificates and other documents that can be used in fabricating a false identity can also be produced. Credit card details can be stolen by persons obtaining unauthorized access to computer systems.

The Internet can also be used for harassing, threatening, or intrusive communications. The traditional obscene telephone call has given way to its contemporary manifestation in "cyber-stalking," in which persistent messages are sent to an unwilling recipient.

Offenses Where Digital Technology Is the *Target* of Criminal Activity

Advanced industrial societies are dependent on digital technology as never before. Interference with or damage to information systems can have catastrophic consequences. The earliest form of such interference was given the colloquial name *hacking*. Originally, it entailed obtaining unauthorized access to information systems out of curiosity or with benign intent. The term *cracking* was used to designate activity of a malicious nature such as the destruction of data. Eventually, *hacking* took on both meanings. Hacking has evolved to entail the dissemination of malicious codes, such as viruses and worms, which can spread through computer networks and slow them down or even destroy data. Another form of targeting is the distributed denial of service attack, where the hacker obtains unauthorized access to a number of computers and then directs them against a target, effectively shutting it down.

Defacing of websites is a popular pastime in some hacker circles. This can entail mere self-expression and exhibition of artistic prowess (as is the case with much ordinary graffiti), or it can involve explicit political statements. On one occasion the CIA home page was altered to read, "Central Stupidity Agency."

The term *cyber-terrorism* has received considerable attention in the post-9/11 age. A precise, if narrow definition is that of Denning (2000, p. 10), who defines cyberterrorism as "unlawful attacks against computers, networks and the information stored therein when done to intimidate or coerce a government or its people in furtherance of political or social objectives." Of course, digital technology can be incidental to "terrestrial" terrorism, as will be noted below.

The two categories discussed above are not mutually exclusive. Although it is possible to attack and damage information systems physically (i.e., with an actual or proverbial sledgehammer), criminal attacks on systems usually employ digital technology. For example, the illegal electronic transfer of funds from a legitimate bank account will entail obtaining unauthorized electronic access to that account. Electronic attacks against critical infrastructure will usually be preceded by unauthorized access to the information systems supporting that infrastructure.

Digital Technology as Incidental to the Crime

Digital technology may play an indirect role in many kinds of ordinary criminal activity. Financial records of conventional criminal enterprises are no longer kept manually in ledger books. The convenience of spreadsheets is no less apparent to drug dealers than it is to directors of legitimate enterprises.

Communications in furtherance of criminal conspiracies is greatly facilitated by digital technology. Just as researchers on opposite sides of the planet can communicate in real time for practically no cost, so too can terrorists, drug dealers, and people-smugglers. Technologies of encryption and anonymity may place these communications beyond the reach of law enforcement.

As digital technology becomes increasingly pervasive, it will be present at nearly every crime scene. Global tracking technologies are becoming routine features of motor vehicles. Electronic toll collection systems permit the reconstruction of vehicular movements on toll roads. Hand-held computers, not to mention mobile telephones, all contain data that may be retrieved in furtherance of an ordinary "terrestrial" criminal investigation. Some may even permit identification of the bearer's physical location. Once the subject of jokes, the idea of networked toasters and refrigerators is now becoming a reality. The day is fast approaching when some evidence of most crimes will exist in digital form.

White-Collar Crime Defined

The classic definition of white-collar crime was, of course, the gift of Sutherland: "a crime committed by a person of respectability and high social status in the course of his occupation." The lack of precision in Sutherland's definition has been nicely dissected by Geis (1992). Although Sutherland's work focused largely on offenses committed in furtherance of professional activities, usually by executives or senior employees of large organizations, his definition was somewhat elastic. He did allude in passing to overcharging by mechanics.

For some time now, commentators have pondered whether the term "white-collar crime" refers to the social status or occupational role of the offender, the nature of the offense, or some combination of the three. In today's labor market, lower-level clerical staff who work in large organizations are not generally regarded as people of high social status; they may, however, be in a position to commit forgery, embezzlement or fraud.

There are some white-collar crimes that are unambiguously central to Sutherland's ambiguous conceptualization. Conspiracies in restraint of trade such as those documented by Geis (1967) are a classic example.

By contrast, if a doctor were to commit a sexual assault against a patient during the course of an examination, the act might technically fall within the parameters of Sutherland's definition, but it is not quite what he had in mind. Indeed, he excluded "most cases" of murder, adultery, and intoxication, because they were not customarily part of the offenders' "occupational procedures."

Sutherland's ambiguity is perhaps a blessing. By failing to exclude all cases of murder and intoxication, he created conceptual space for the offense of corporate homicide, as well as for civil or criminal liability for the negligent management of intoxicated employees, such as that alleged in the Exxon Valdez disaster. We will leave the intersection of adultery and white-collar crime to those of more prurient inclination, except to note that extramarital affairs involving senior executives have been deemed to be deleterious to the ethical climate in some organizations (Wayne, 2005).

The elasticity of Sutherland's definition notwithstanding, one usually associates the term "white-collar crime" with a variety of financial transgressions, including fraud (in its various forms), forgery, embezzlement, money laundering, and tax evasion. An expansion of the concept to include offenses committed *by or on behalf of organizations* will include offenses against the environment, violations of occupational health and safety regulations, discrimination against employees, unfair labor practices, etc.

Fraud (obtaining something of value by deception) may strike some as the quintessential white-collar crime. Although a large number of high-status individuals exploit their positions in furtherance of fraud, it is by no means the monopoly of elites. In Australia, many prosecutions for fraud are brought against welfare recipients who make false declarations in order to obtain government benefits. These are hardly the persons of high social status that Sutherland had in mind. He would, presumably, be happy to apply the label to an affluent tax evader, but perhaps not to a domestic cleaner who is paid in cash and chooses not to declare his or her income. Classic studies of white-collar offenders by Shapiro (1987) and by Weisburd at al. (1991) reveal them to be drawn not from the Social Register, but rather from the ranks of ordinary middle-class people.

Computer Crime That Is Not White-Collar Crime

What of the relationship between computer crime and white-collar crime? A look at the types of computer crime discussed above will suggest that there is nothing inherently "Sutherlandian" about any of them. The acceptance of digital technology, at least in advanced industrial societies, is such that computers are accessible to the masses as well as to the elites. While one day not long ago the use of digital scanning equipment and specialized software to produce counterfeit currency may have been regarded as the work of the technological elite, today it requires no particular sophistication (*United States v. Godman* (223 F.3d 320, 323 (6th Cir. 2000)). The earliest computer criminals tended to be individuals who were technologically skilled, but hardly of relatively high social status (Sterling, 1991).

A great deal of computer crime might be excluded from the domain of white-collar crime because it is not committed by persons of relatively high social status or because their employment status is irrelevant. An unemployed laborer is as capable of accessing online child pornography as is a corporate executive. Operation Candyman was an international child pornography ring that involved more than 7,200 members and included a range of people of different social status: a bus driver, a member of the armed forces, a janitor, a security guard, and an office manager (Heimbach, 2002). The role and status of the offender has little significance for at least some types of crime perpetrated in cyberspace.

Moreover, young people who have come of age in the digital era often have acquired a proficiency in computing that rivals that of IT professionals. Not all of these skills are devoted to socially responsible ends. Digital technology provides young people with capacities that they did not possess a few years ago.

They can be, and indeed have been, engaged in a great deal of serious criminal activity from the privacy of their bedrooms. The distributed denial of service attacks against a number of e-commerce sites in February 2000 was the work of a 15-year-old. A great deal of computer hacking is the work of young adventurers (DeMarco, 2001). A 16-year-old hacker was the first juvenile to have received a custodial sentence in the United States for intercepting communications on military computer networks and for illegally obtaining information from NASA computer networks. (*http://www.cybercrime.gov/comrade.htm*, visited 31 January 2005). Another 15-year-old was charged with manipulating shares on the NASDAQ (Lewis 2001).

The key to classic white-collar crime was opportunity. Access to an employer's or client's assets is a precondition of embezzlement. It was impossible to participate in a price-fixing cartel without being a company executive. Stock-market manipulation usually required at least the complicity of financial publishers and stockbrokers. Historically, the key to opportunity was a modicum of occupational status. The rapid democratization of digital technology, and its availability across class and occupational boundaries, have provided criminal opportunities to those who were previously excluded.

Computer Crime That Is White-Collar Crime

The pervasiveness of digital technology in the modern workplace has created a range of new opportunities to commit crime. These opportunities are available to ordinary workers, not just those of high social status. They may be directly related to one's employment, or merely incidental. The digital technology provided to ordinary workers brings with it abundant criminal opportunities.

Organizations may use information systems as instruments of crime. One of the earliest examples of this was the Revco case, where a large drugstore chain initiated a computer-generated double-billing scheme that cost federal and state governments in the United States hundreds of thousands of dollars (Vaughan, 1985). The increasing prevalence of online billing and payment systems would suggest that computers will soon become the primary instruments of fraud if they are not already. One type of white-collar crime to which information technology is ideally suited is "high volume-low value" theft, otherwise known as the "salami" technique, in which a tiny amount is sliced from each of a very large number of transactions. One penny diverted from each of ten million transactions would deliver a criminal profit of $100,000. In January 1993, four executives were charged with defrauding at least 47,000 car rental customers using a salami technique. It was alleged that the defendants modified a computer-billing program to overstate the actual gas tank capacity of their rental cars. Over a three-year period, every customer who returned a car with less than a full tank was charged for a falsely inflated total of gasoline (Kabay, 2002).

Organizations may also be implicated in incidents involving illicit material stored on their computers. In many jurisdictions, internet service providers are not criminally liable for content where they are not aware of its nature. Moreover, they are usually not required to monitor, keep records, or make inquiries about Internet content which they host or carry. They may, however, be required by law to remove prohibited content or take reasonable steps to prevent users from gaining access to the content.

In February 2001, a New York ISP pleaded guilty to the misdemeanor charge of knowingly providing access to child pornography. The prosecution was launched when the company, having been notified by the state attorney-general's office that child pornography was being distributed over one of the company's newsgroups, failed to take action.

(http://www.weil.com/wgm/CWGMPubs.nsf/683629e9ec75ae8f8525691a006d6af3/4fbee5a85d0473f3852569fa007587df?OpenDocument; visited 12 May 2005)

The managing director of CompuServe Germany was charged under criminal law for child pornography located on a news server of CompuServe USA (Eberwine, 2004). It was alleged that Felix Somm aided in the distribution of child pornography after 282 newsgroups (located on CompuServe's server) contained child pornography and images of violence involving children and animals. CompuServe was informed by a Munich District Attorney that criminal sanctions might apply if members could still gain access to the illegal content (Determann, 1999). Prosecutors argued that online servers should block images that are deemed illegal. As such, CompuServe blocked the newsgroups to avoid sanctions; however, this was short lived. CompuServe reinstated the newsgroups two months later, giving limited access to Germans. CompuServe's approach to preventing young children from gaining access to images included providing members with access to "Cyber Patrol," an Internet filtering program (Determann, 1999). However, this approach did not change the fact that child pornography is a criminal offense in Germany and the United States. In 1998, Somm was sentenced to two years' probation although in late 1999 the ruling was overturned and he was acquitted by the Munich Court of Appeals.

Yahoo! was charged in France with making Nazi memorabilia available for sale on its website. Accompanying civil actions moved Yahoo! to seek assurances in U.S. courts that French judgments would not be enforceable there. *La Ligue Contre le Racisme et l'Antisemitisme* (LICRA) and *L'Union Des Etudiants Juifs De France* (UESF) filed a complaint against Yahoo! Inc. objecting to the exhibition and sale of Nazi memorabilia and propaganda on its website (Yahoo! Inc v. LICRA, 169 F. Supp. 2d 1181 (N.D. Cal. 2001). The Superior Court of Paris ordered Yahoo! Inc. to prevent users from gaining access to Nazi memorabilia through its website.[1] In 2000 Yahoo! Inc. was ordered by a French Judge to install filters to eliminate access to French users to Nazi memorabilia. Subsequently, Yahoo! Inc. banned the sale of hate-related merchandise on their sites, although some months later Nazi memorabilia was still available. In August 2004, the U.S. Court of Appeals reversed the District Court's judgment (379 F. 3d 1120 (9th Cir. 2004)).

Organizations may also target other information systems. The practice of industrial espionage may entail unauthorized access, interception of telecommunications content, or other means of obtaining competitors' sensitive information (Nasheri, 2005). Disgruntled or greedy insiders may also engage in industrial espionage. One example is a recent case that involved a contract employee at Gillette Company who was caught using email to sell stolen plans for the company's new Mach-3 razor. http://www.taborcommunications.com/dsstar/02/1217/105217.html (Visited 11 July 2005).

Organizational Complicity in Employee Crime

An interesting question at the intersection of computer crime and white-collar crime is where responsibility for the misuse of a company's computers should lie. The range of misconduct that employees can engage in using their employer's information technology is surprisingly diverse. Much of it may entail significant civil and/or criminal implications for both employer and employee.

Perhaps the most common form of electronic transgression by employees is the excessive use of the employer's digital technology for matters unrelated to employment. Activities that occur *in the course of* one's employment need not be *related to* one's employment. Employees can waste considerable time at work surfing the web, or sending and receiving personal emails. The web or email content may be perfectly innocent, but the time spent perusing or producing it is time not spent on one's work. The employee who regularly raids the office stationery cupboard is costing her employer money. So too is the employee who spends two hours per day on Internet or web activities unrelated to work. Their own work time, and their employer's storage space, is wasted (Snider 2001). In the words of one IT specialist, "Beware of the employee who comes to work with an MP3 player... They can store up to 40 GB of music, movies and programs and kill your network performance" (Exinda Networks, 2004).

Of course, not all employee misuse of an employer's information resources can be rationalized as innocent. Some of it may entail accessing patently illegal content. The music and movies just referred to may have been pirated. Some computer misuse may entail the display of content that other employees may find offensive or harassing. Some may involve the unauthorized downloading and reproduction of copyrighted or otherwise illicit material.

Even innocent use of an employer's information systems can have more sinister implications. An employee who ventures into some corners of cyberspace may unwittingly render her organization's information systems vulnerable to intrusion, or susceptible to worms and viruses. As recent experience has shown, this can have major consequences. Major virus epidemics of the past ten years have led to significant system degradation around the world, entailing millions of hours of lost productivity and billions of dollars of lost revenue and system maintenance costs. Organizations in both public and private sectors can be unwitting accessories to crime. So it is that the distributed denial of service attacks launched by "Mafia Boy" in 2000 were routed through computers at the University of California at Santa Barbara, among other sites. Another skilled hacker, Kevin Mitnick, routed one attack through a computer at Loyola University of Chicago. A server at the Arkansas Highway and Transportation Department was allegedly used by Al-Qaeda to transfer digital files (United Press International, 2004).

In the unfortunate event that an organization's computers are seized in furtherance of a criminal investigation, the financial implications can be serious indeed. (Steve Jackson Games, Inc., v. U.S. Secret Service., 36 F.3d 457, 458-59 (5th Cir. 1994))

Depending upon the legal system, the liability of employers for crimes committed by employees may be a significant consideration. Under the doctrine of *respondeat superior*, if the employer knew or should have known that the employee was engaged in criminal activity, and failed to inquire or failed to act, then the employer might be liable.

Under the negligent retention theory, even when an employee's acts are not within the scope of employment, an employer may be liable if the employer's management or retention of the employee is negligent (Papa and Bass, 2004; Davis, 2002; Ishman, 2000). Of course, employers may incur civil liability for damages resulting from negligent management of their information systems.

Almost all business records exist today in electronic form; Thus, it would appear that most if not all corporate crime has a digital component. The role of information systems as incidental to the offense thus represents the most significant overlap between white-collar crime and computer crime.

The Restatement of Agency provides that—

> [the] conduct of an employee is within the scope of employment if, but only if, (a) it is of the kind he is employed to perform; (b) it occurs substantially within the authorized time and space limits; (c) it is actuated, at least in part, by a purpose to serve the [employer], and (d) if force is intentionally used by the [employee] against another, the use of force is not [unforeseeable to the employer]. Restatement (Second) of Agency 228 (1958).

An employer's civil or criminal liability for the crimes of employees will depend on a number of factors. The first of these is forseeability. If the potential for the acts in question was known or should have been known to the employer, the employer may be liable or if the employer was willfully blind to the criminal conduct of the employee. Obviously if the employer condoned or encouraged the criminal conduct, the employer is likely to be found culpable.

Employees may commit securities fraud using their employer's IT systems. For example, in April 1999, a fabricated page resembling a product of the financial news service Bloomberg posted a report that a particular company, PairGain Technologies, was about to become the subject of a takeover. The report included apparently credible quotations, purportedly from officials of the company. Within minutes, the stock was being touted in chatrooms, and the price rose by more than thirty per cent before the hoax was discovered. The perpetrator was a 25-year-old employee of the company. PairGain cooperated in the investigation, and there was never any suggestion that they encouraged or condoned the behavior. One could, however, imagine a situation wherein demonstrated negligence on the part of a company might lead to liability for losses arising from an overzealous employee.

Another important factor is the nature of the employer's business. When the motives of the employee are not related to the employer's business, or when the employee's actions are so outrageous that they do not serve a rational business purpose, the employer may not be liable. By contrast, if the criminal act did further the employer's interest, liability may be an issue.

If the job provided by the employer creates an opportunity for the employee to commit the illegal act, the employer may be liable, depending upon the degree of control the employer has over the employee. When does control over the employee cause an employee's act to be imputed to the employer? There are a number of cases where employers have been pursued civilly as a result of the electronic indiscretions of their employees. In one unsuccessful case, an unfortunate woman sought damages from an Internet service provider after contracting the HIV virus from an employee with whom she engaged in consensual, unprotected sex after she met him over the Internet in one of the ISP's chat rooms (Haybeck v. Prodigy Services Company, 116 F.3d 465, 1997 (2d Cir 1997)).

The distinction is not trivial, because employers may be criminally or civilly liable for misconduct committed by employees within the scope of employment. Debates over surveillance of employees' computer use often overlook such considerations.

Employers may at the very least be civilly liable for employees' infringements of copyright. In Playboy Enterprises, Inc., v.Webbworld 991 F. Supp. 1361 (N.D.Tex 1997), an Internet services provider was held vicariously liable for infringements of Playboy's copyright. In the United States, the Digital Millennium Copyright Act holds ISPs (along with the primary offender) liable for copyright infringement if ISP had been informed by copyright holder of the infringement and does not inform subscriber of complaint or does not remove offending content. An Arizona business agreed to a $1 million out-of-court settlement with Recording Industry Association of America arising from employee use of a corporate file server to distribute MP3 files over the Internet (RIAA, 2002).

Explaining White-Collar Crime and Computer Crime

Routine activity theory, one of the more elegant and robust theories in criminology, would appear to provide a very good explanation for both white-collar crime and computer crime, both when they intersect, and where they are distinct.

According to Cohen and Felson (1979), all crime can be explained by the conjunction of three factors:

1. a supply of motivated offenders;
2. the availability of suitable targets or victims; and
3. the absence of capable guardians (someone to "mind the store" so to speak).

Conventional White-Collar Crime

Motivation

Traditional observers of white-collar crime tend to attribute motives for offending to one of the most universal and enduring human characteristics—greed. To be sure, individual crimes of acquisition are usually driven by the desire for greater wealth. In addition, corporate offenses, whether explicitly financial in nature or related to such issues as occupational health and safety or environmental harm, are often inspired by "bottom-line" considerations.

But there is more to white-collar crime than just greed. Theories of white-collar crime tend to overlook what might be described as the sensual element of offending (Katz, 1988). White-collar crimes are rarely crimes of passion, but they nevertheless contain elements that may be described as seductive.

Maurer (1940) in his classic study of con men, describes the intense satisfaction arising from the successful manipulation of a victim. Shover, Coffee, and Hobbs (2003) describe the pleasure derived by telemarketing fraudsters when they snare a victim. The satisfaction transcends any financial element. Revenge can also be a significant motivator for fraud. Disgruntled employees (or former employees) are among the most common examples. But the desire to get back at an old enemy, or a perceived wrongdoer (Black, 1984) may also be apparent. So too can the feeling of satisfaction at having "outsmarted" a target. These latter motives were apparent in the classic film, *The Sting*, in which Paul Newman (Gondorff) and Robert Redford (Hooker) flawlessly execute a sophisticated and complex con against an adversary whose henchmen had brutally killed a close friend of theirs. At the end of the film, the despised adversary, fearing that his involvement in an illegal betting room will attract police attention, flees the scene, leaving a large amount of his own money with the two successful con men. The film ends with an exchange between Gondorff and Hooker which vividly illustrates that Hooker's motives were not financial (Ward, 1973):

> Gondorff: You beat him, kid.
> Hooker: Your're right, it's not enough. But it's close!
> Gondorff: You not gonna stick around for your share?
> Hooker: Nah. I'd only blow it.

Duffield and Grabosky (2001) identify a number of non-financial motives for fraud. One of these might be described as "the thrill of the deal." Offenders may simply enjoy sailing close to the wind, to see what they can get away with. Success in executing a complex fraud may be exhilarating. The sensation of power over another individual or individuals seems to be a powerful motivating force for some fraud offenders to the point that it becomes an end in itself. As one confidence man put it, "For myself, I love to make people do what I want them to, I love command. I love to rule people. That's why I'm a con artist" (quoted in Blum, 1972, p. 46).

To quote another, "Half of being a con man is the challenge. When I score, I get more kick out of that than anything; to score is the biggest kick of my whole life" (quoted in Blum, 1972, p. 44).

Opportunity

White-collar crime can also be explained by the availability of targets or prospective victims. In years past, one would comment upon the under-representation of women in the ranks of white-collar offenders by suggesting that women were not necessarily less criminally disposed, but rather lacked the opportunity to offend.

Correlatively one would notice the more equal representation of women charged with social security fraud and attribute this not to a lack of virtue, but rather to the fact that social security frauds were among the few criminal opportunities available to them.

Guardians

A classic bulwark against the commission of white-collar crime is what Kraakman referred to as "gatekeepers"—professionals in a position to prevent, detect, or disclose client illegality. Gatekeepers are by no means guarantors of virtue, as the many failures of Arthur Andersen to flag client illegality will attest. Black (2005) relates how most of the failed S&L's of the 1980s had received clean audits shortly before their demise. In addition to accountants, lawyers are in a position to play the gatekeeper's role too. Indeed, this may even be required by law. Under Australia's Financial Transaction Reports Act (1988), lawyers are required to report transactions involving $10,000 or more of their clients' funds to Australia's anti-money-laundering regulator and financial intelligence unit.

Nevertheless, Grabosky (1990) suggests that corporate lawyers may identify too closely with their clients, or may become financially dependent upon them to the extent that they are incapable of making an independent professional judgment. In his study of white-collar defense attorneys, Mann (1985, p. 110) notes the widespread view among practitioners that it is *not* the attorney's responsibility to enforce his or her client's compliance with the law.

But in the grander scheme of things, every little bit helps. Accountants, lawyers, and financial journalists, when they are not part of the problem, can be part of the solution.

Explaining Computer Crime

Motivation

A great deal of computer crime simply entails the commission of "old" crime using new methods. As such, the motivations will remain the same. The rapid uptake of digital technology has made it nearly ubiquitous in Western industrial societies and the exponential growth of people on line has meant that there are more prospective offenders with access to digital technology than ever before. At the same time, basic human motivations have not changed significantly. Crimes of acquisition are often driven by greed; offenses relating to sexual activity such as child pornography are grounded in lust. Expressive as well as instrumental computer crime also arises from the desire for power. In contemporary society, this can include the desire to achieve mastery over complex systems. Computer crimes of varying kinds can also arise from revenge and ideology. Aside, perhaps, from the intellectual challenge of mastering complex systems, none of the above motivations is new.

Dreyfus (1998, pp. 5–6) interviewed a number of computer hackers, whose remarks revealed the very significant influence of excitement and challenge:

- "The kick of getting into a system. It's the ego boost from doing something well where other people try and fail. Once you are in, you very often get bored and may never call back. Because once you've gotten in, it's a challenge over."
- "Once you get into the first system, it's like, you get into the next one, and the next one, and the next one . . . like forbidden fruit."
- "[At first it was] possibly the sheer lust for power or [the desire] to explore an intricate piece of technology. [Now] my first and foremost motivation is to learn."
- "It ain't a malicious thing. It's a challenge—the thrill of the chase. Sometimes I think I hack just to be able to say that I do something, like it's a fad or something."

One of the more significant aspects of the digital age is what might be called *disintermediation*. People can send investment solicitations directly to millions of people, without so much as advertising in a newspaper. They can buy and sell shares directly, without going through a stockbroker. They can disseminate information (truthful or otherwise) about publicly traded shares without using the services of Forbes, Bloomberg, or Dow Jones. They can withdraw funds from a bank without encountering a teller.

Another characteristic of the digital age is what might be termed disinhibition. To many people, the Internet and world wide web contain an air of unreality.

One deals, it seems, with ones and zeroes, not with people. Most computer crime occurs in the absence of a face-to-face relationship between offender and victim.

The disembodied nature of electronic interactions may well lower inhibitions on the part of prospective offenders. It takes a particular type of person to engage in face-to-face fraud. It is a great deal easier to relieve the proverbial little old lady of her life savings by remote control than by a con.

The element of challenge, the thrill of the illicit, ego and revenge—all are evident in some cases of Internet piracy, especially those in which the offender does not profit from his or her deeds. Anthony LaMacchia, a Massachusetts Institute of Technology (MIT) student (*United States* v. *LaMacchia*) (871 F. Supp. 535 (D. Mass. 1994)), set up a bulletin board in 1994 for people to access and exchange copies of software applications and computer games free of charge on the Internet. LaMacchia operated the bulletin board on an MIT computer for approximately six weeks before it was shut down. Despite the estimated value of the software at $1 million, LaMacchia operated alone and did not profit from his activity.

Given the widespread penetration of digital technology and its wide accessibility or "democratization," one might predict that women might be equally represented among the ranks of computer criminals. This appears not to be the case. Most cyber-criminals are male. This appears particularly true in cases that involve hackers. Hacking has attracted a largely male audience. Kevin Mitnick, one of America's most recognized cyber-criminals, caused in excess of $290 million dollars damage by hacking into a wide range of high-tech companies. Mitnick's history of computer crime began in the 1980s, when he was caught stealing a number of computer manuals from a telephone company (Power, 2000, p. 57). Mitnick has committed a broad range of computer crimes, such as breaking into several different computer systems, monitoring e-mails, stealing software, committing computer and wire fraud, and damaging computers (Power, 2000, p. 58). Mitnick has served time in prison for multiple computer-related offenses.

In 1988, Robert Tappan Morris, a 23-year-old graduate student at Cornell University released the Internet's first worm that infected a large proportion of UNIX computer systems connected to the Internet (Hafner and Markoff, 1991). In 1995, under the pseudonym of the "Black Baron," Christopher Pile, the author of a virus toolkit Smeg and viruses Queeg and Pathogen, was the first person to be prosecuted in the United Kingdom for writing and distributing computer viruses. These programs were publicly and freely available on the Internet and through bulletin boards (Jackson, 1995). Pile was sentenced to 18 months in prison, an indication of how seriously the crime was regarded.

In 1999, two Chinese citizens, Hao Jing-Long and Hao Jing-Wen, were prosecuted for hacking. It was alleged that Hao Jing-Long conspired with his brother, Hao Jing-Wen, to break into the computer network of the Zhejiang branch of the China Industrial and Commercial Bank in furtherance of stealing funds. It was further alleged that Hao Jing-Long, an employee of the bank, entered the bank and secretly connected a modem to the bank's computer, which allowed his brother access to the network. This access led to Hao Jing-Wen transferring a total of 720,000 yuan into 16 different accounts set-up by the two brothers (Hong Kong Voice of Democracy, 1998, p. 1). The two brothers were found guilty of hacking and sentenced to death. This case represents one of the harshest punishments against a computer hacker (Hong Kong Voice of Democracy, 1998 p. 1)

Opportunities

Just as the proliferation of digital technology and its exponential dissemination have increased the number of motivated offenders, so too have they increased the number of prospective victims. The emergence of online commerce has been accompanied by a proliferation of e-commerce sites, from online auctions, to online share trading, to online banking. Each of these, and many other types of e-commerce sites, has attracted criminals.

Information technologies such as the Internet provide unprecedented capacity to accomplish things that have traditionally been difficult to achieve on a global scale and maintain in the physical world. For example, the Nigerian fee scheme that emerged over a decade ago relied on postal messages to reach millions of potential victims or targets. The cost to set up, print and distribute letters would amount to hundreds if not thousands of dollars and in addition, the speed of response would be much slower than the Internet. Today, these letters can be produced through digital technology at very little cost and reach millions of users instantaneously.

The number of prospective victims of online securities fraud has expanded with the advent of online share traders, and with numerous ways people communicate and exchange information on the Internet through chat rooms, news group and bulletin boards. Trading on the Internet, which can be carried out privately, thus bypassing intermediaries such as brokerage houses, allows investors to buy direct and create information previously monopolised by intermediaries. This open means of trading has created new opportunities for criminals to provide false and misleading information to other investors. This can make it difficult for users to identify with the individual or organization that is the provider of information. In fact, offenders may intentionally disguise their identity through the use of remailing facilities in order to defraud individuals later and avoid detection (Grabosky et al., 2001, p. 89). These methods have meant that the fraudster can operate at a level that in the terrestrial world was limited by intermediary institutions.

The storage of valuable information by individuals, companies and government on the Internet increases the accessibility of the information to prospective offenders, and depending on the type of information available contributes to the attractiveness of the item as a target. The challenge to e-commerce in the digital age has been to foster the proliferation of commercial activity while reducing criminal opportunities. The architecture of computer systems, especially relating to access control, contributes to this end (Lessig, 1999).

Guardianship

The absence of capable guardianship characterizes computer crime no less than conventional white-collar crime. Just as many terrestrial crimes occur because of the lack of internal control systems or the lack of external oversight mechanisms, so too does much cybercrime. Part of the attraction to prospective criminals in the digital world is its global reach and absence of capable guardianship. The lack of guardianship on the Internet can also be attributed to limited law enforcement, low security consciousness, lack of self-defense, lack of willingness to report cyber crime, and vulnerable systems, to name a few.

Lax cyber-security at the individual and organizational level has opened the door to countless examples of unauthorized access, many of which have been the predicate to a variety of serious offenses. Philip Cummings was employed as a helpdesk operator at a U.S. communications company and had access to passwords and codes, which enabled him to download credit reports. Cummings illegally accessed this information and stole more than 30,000 reports from the company's database, then sold them at $30 per report. The estimated loss to the company equated to between $50 million and $100 million. Cummings was sentenced to 14 years in jail (KRT, 2005, p. 35).

At the same time, guardians in the form of law enforcement agencies have not always had the capacity to respond. Just as no city can afford to place a police officer on every street corner, no state can afford to position a police officer next to every computer terminal or even in every cyber-café. Given the various ways people invest on the Internet, challenges have arisen for law enforcement agencies to keep apace with criminal techniques. In the United States, the Securities and Exchange Commission (SEC) investigates criminal activity relating to securities fraud with the cooperation of the National Association of Securities Dealers (NASD), the Commodities and Futures Trading Commission (CFTC), the FBI, and related state agencies. Clandestine and overt investigative techniques by law enforcement agencies have been used to investigate a range of securities scams. The cooperation between these agencies is instrumental in information gathering, which has resulted in a number of successful prosecutions against fraudsters.

Guardianship in the digital age also entails the watchful eye of human beings, such as systems administrators, or technological surveillance provided by electronic security systems. These can entail such things as intrusion detection and alarms and technological tools such as firewalls and anti-virus software to increase the security of computer systems and networks. Guardianship can also be enhanced by market forces. By 2003 Microsoft began responding to consumer demand for products less vulnerable to security breaches (Charney, 2005). Other forms of guardianship include less formal methods of social control, such as private monitoring, parental supervision, auction escrow services, online watch groups such as cyber-angels, and methods of surveillance (Grabosky, 2000).

Cyber Trust

Just as motivations, opportunity, and an absence of guardianship explain criminal behavior in the terrestrial and digital worlds, cyber-trust also forms an important aspect of understanding criminal behavior most commonly through lying, misrepresentation, and role conflict. Following on from Sutherland's pathbreaking work, Shapiro (1990) applied a range of strategies to demonstrate how individuals establish and exploit trust relationships in furtherance of criminal opportunities: misrepresentation of the use of charitable funds to underdeveloped countries; fabrication of data for experiments; declaring a fictional account of a heroin addict to be a work of nonfiction (it was awarded a Pulitzer Prize); and falsification of test results by pharmaceutical companies.

These strategies are equally applicable in the digital world. Internet users lie in various ways to commit different forms of crime: Internet predators who lie about their age in order to meet children off-line in furtherance of illegal activity; a Nigerian fraud scam which deceives people into parting with money or providing account details by falsely offering a fee for assistance in transferring funds; auction fraud, which can involve money sent by the successful bidder to the seller while the goods are never received; misrepresenting true intentions when communicating in chat rooms as a prelude to harassment and cyber-stalking, and deceiving investors by falsely declaring that a company is about to announce a new discovery, resulting in causing a company's share price to rise.

However, one may see that differences of trust are evident between the terrestrial and digital worlds. In the terrestrial world, trust is based on personal relationships, while online trust is based on confidence in processes (Grabosky, 2001). In one case, a buyer bidding for a laptop via an online auction was persuaded to trade privately after being convinced by the seller's knowledge of the product (Adams, 2003). Thus, the buyer of the laptop relied on confidence in processes of communication. The confidence proved to be misplaced when the vendor took the money and ran.

Many factors have shaped the reliance on confidence in processes on the Internet. These can be identified through the absence of face-to-face interaction (which is also evident in many forms of transactions in the physical world), absence of physical proximity of Internet users, and anonymity.

"Phishers" have targeted customers with access to Internet banking facilities. Trusted brands such as financial institutions have been one of the key vectors for phishers who violate trust for financial gain. An email message may indicate to the customer that their bank's website is experiencing technical difficulties and instructs the customer to click on a link to a "temporary" website and provide their account details or password. This method manipulates the customer into accessing a counterfeit website that exposes their personal and financial information, giving perpetrators access to account details in furtherance of criminal activity.

Trust relationships on the Internet are also formed through email, chat rooms, bulletin boards, and newsgroups. A number of techniques are used to identify and pursue victims: direct contact via email, harassment abuses through live chat rooms, providing false information about the victim and posting it on newsgroups for wider distribution, establishing a webpage on the victim with personal and spurious information, and assuming the victim's identity online in chat rooms. Many examples exist where individuals have fallen victim to this type of crime. According to Cyberangels (2000), approximately 63,000 Internet stalkers monitor the Internet, stalking more than 470,000 targets (cited in USDOJ, 2000, p. 1).

A recurrent pattern of breaches of trust is evident in the digital world. Deception through exploiting an architecture of anonymity is the largest overarching pattern. Deception may then take the form of lying, phishing, bid-rigging, market-rigging, and, more widely, self-dealing, role conflict, espionage, stalking, hacking, seducing and tricking children, and acquiring false identities. Not all breaches of trust are best conceived as fundamentally about deception. There are forms of theft that are not particularly deceptive, such as pirating music, and forms of exploitation that are not very deceptive, such as exchange of child pornography between consenting adults. Yet abuse of trust norms to deceive is one of the dominant patterns. Some forms of trust create opportunities for would-be cyber-offenders; and as a result, more victims are available and trusting individuals may not mobilize available safeguards, such as firewalls, which imply less guardianship.

Conclusions

The coming of the digital age has further blurred the concept of white-collar crime. The intentional dissemination through online chat rooms of false rumors about a company's likely share price movements is certainly a white-collar crime when committed by a senior executive of the company, or even a low level employee. When the same act is committed by an ordinary high-school student, the "Sutherland connection" is harder to make.

Nowadays, most organizations are dependent on digital technology for practically everything, from heating and lighting to physical security, to communications (both internally and externally) to record-keeping. Now that "almost everything depends on software," almost any offense by or against an organization, or with the organization's resources, will leave some digital evidence. The distinction between computer crime and white-collar crime becomes largely obscured.

Endnote

1. Although Yahoo! France does not host auctions for Nazi memorabilia, users can access the United States website Yahoo.com which offers large amounts of Nazi-related memorabilia for sale.

References

Adams, D. (2003) "Foiling the Online Conmen." *The Sydney Morning Herald,* 17 June 2003.

Black, Donald (1984) "Crime as Social Control." Ch. 1 in *Toward a General Theory of Social Control*, Vol. 2, Editor D. Black. Orlando, FL: Academic Press.

Black, William (2005) *The Best Way to Rob a Bank is to Own One*. Austin: University of Texas Press.

Blum, Richard H. (1972) *Deceivers and Deceived: Observations on Confidence Men and their Victims, Informants and their Quarry, Political and Industrial Spies and Ordinary Citizens.* Springfield, IL: Charles C Thomas.

Charney, Scott (2005) "Combating Cybercrime: A Public-Private Strategy in the Digital Environment" Presented to the Workshop on Measures to Combat Computer Related Crime." 11th United Nations Congress on Crime Prevention and Criminal Justice, Bangkok, 18–25 April 2005.

Cohen, Lawrence, and Marcus Felson (1979) "Social Change and Crime Rate Trends: A Routine Activity Approach." *American Sociological Review* 44:588–608.

Cyberangels (2000) United States Department of Justice NVAA. Text 2000: Chapter 22 Supplement Special Topics, Section 2: Stalking.

Http://www.ojp.usdoj.gov/ovc/assist/nvaa2000/academy/V-22-2ST.htm

Davis, Erin (2002) "The Doctrine of Respondeat Superior: An Application to Employers' Liability for the Computer or Internet Crimes Committed by their Employees." *Albany Law Journal of Science and Technology* 12:684–713.

DeMarco, Joseph V (2001) " 'It's Not Just Fun and 'War Games'—Juveniles and Computer Crime.' " *United States Attorneys' Bulletin* 49(3):48–55. http://www.usdoj.gov/criminal/cybercrime/usamay2001_7.htm (Visited 31 January 2005)

Denning, Dorothy E. (2000) "Cyberterrorism." *Global Dialogue* 2 (Autumn): 10–16.

Determann, L. (1999) "Case Update: German CompuServe Director Acquitted on Appeal." *Hastings Int'l & Comp. L. Review* 23:109–123.

Duffield, Grace, and Peter Grabosky (2001) "The Psychology of Fraud." *Trends and Issues in Crime and Criminal Justice #200*. Canberra: Australian Institute of Criminology. *http://www.aic.gov.au/publications/tandi/ti199.pdf* (visited 12 May 2005).

Eberwine, Eric T. (2004) "Sound and Fury Signifying Nothing: Jurgen Bussow's Battle Against Hate Speech on the Internet." *New York Law School Law Review* 49:353.

Exinda Networks (2004) "P2P downloads cost Australian businesses $60m pa Businesses could cut $225 million a year from Internet bills." *http://www.exinda.com/public/news/news_20041021.htm* (Visited 18 April 2005)

Geis, Gilbert (1967) "The Heavy Electrical Equipment Antitrust Cases of 1961." Pp. 139–150 in *Criminal Behavior Systems,* Editors Clinard and Quinney. New York: Holt Rinehart and Winston.

Geis, Gilbert (1992) "White Collar Crime: What is It?" Pp. 31–52 in *White Collar Crime Reconsidered,* Editors K. Schlegel and D. Weisburd .Boston: Northeastern University Press.

Grabosky, P. (1990) "Professional Advisers and White Collar Illegality. Towards Explaining and Excusing Professional Failure." *University of New South Wales Law Journal* 13(2):1–24. *http://www.aic.gov.au/publications/proceedings/10/grabosky.pdf* (visited 11 July 2005).

Grabosky, P. (2001) "The Nature of Trust Online." *The Age*, 23 April 2001, I.T.1, pp. 1,12 *http://www.aic.gov.au/publications/other/online_trust.html* (visited 11 July 2005).

Grabosky, P., R.G Smith, and G. Dempsey (2001) "Electronic Theft, Unlawful Acquisition in Cyberspace." Cambridge: Cambridge University Press.

Hafner, K., and J. Markoff (1991) *Cyberpunk, Outlaws and Hackers on the Computer Frontier*. New York: Touchstone, Simon & Schuster.

Heimbach, M.J. (2002) Criminal Investigative Division—Crimes Against Children Unit. Federal Bureau of Investigation on Internet Child Pornography before the Subcommittee on Crime, Terrorism, and Homeland Security Committee on the Judiciary United States House of Representatives. http://www.fbi.gov/congress/congress02/heimbach050102.htm

Hong Kong Voice of Democracy (1998) "Two Chinese Hackers Given Death Sentences." http://www.democracy.org.hk/pastweek/dec27_jan2/hackers.htm

Ishman, Mark (2000) "Computer Crimes and the Respondeat Superior Doctrine: Employers Beware." *Boston University Journal of Science and Technology Law* 6:6.

Jackson, D. (1995) Virus Writer Christopher Pile (Black Barron) Sent to Jail. http://www.cryonet.org/cgi-bin/dsp.cgi?msg=5184

Katz, Jack (1988) *Seductions of Crime: The Moral and Sensual Attractions in Doing Evil*. New York: Basic Books.

Kabay, M. (2002) "Salami Fraud" Network World Security Newsletter, 07/24/02. *http://www.networkworld.com/newsletters/sec/2002/01467137.html* (visited 10 May 2005).

Kraakman, R.H. (1986) "Gatekeepers: The Anatomy of a Third-Party Enforcement Strategy." *Journal of Law, Economics and Organization* 2:53–104.

KRT (2005) "US Agents Play Catch-Up." *The Australian,* 5 July 2005.

Lessig, L. (1999) *Code and Other Laws of Cyberspace*. New York: Basic Books.

Lewis, Michael (2001) "Jonathan Lebed: Stock Manipulator, SEC Nemesis—and 15." *The New York Times Magazine,* February 25. *http://www.kentlaw.edu/classes/chill/strona/Jonathan%20Lebed%20Stock%20 Manipulator, %20S_E_C_%20 Nemesis% 20–%20and%2015.htm* (visited 24 January 2004).

Maurer, David (1999) [1940] *The Big Con: The Story of the Confidence Man*. New York: Anchor Books.

Nasheri, Hedieh (2005) *Economic Espionage and Industrial Spying*. Cambridge: Cambridge University Press.

Papa, Louis, and Stuart Bass (2004) "How Employers Can Protect Themselves from Liability for Employees' Misuse of Computer, Internet, and E-Mail Stystems in the Workplace." *Boston University Journal of Science and Technology Law* 10:110–123.

Power, R. (2000) *Tangled Web, Tales of Digital Crime from the Shadows of Cyberspace.* Indianapolis, IN: Que Corporation.

RIAA (2002) "RIAA Collects $1 Million From Company Running Internal Server Offering Thousands Of Songs." http://www.riaa.com/news/newsletter/040902.asp (visited 12 May 2004)

Shapiro, Susan (1987) *Wayward Capitalists: Target of the Securities and Exchange Commission.* New Haven: Yale University Press.

Shapiro, Susan (1990) "Collaring the Crime, Not the Criminal: Liberating the Concept of White Collar Crime." *American Sociological Review* 55:346.

Shover, Neal, Glenn S. Coffey, and Dick Hobbs (2003) "Crime ON THE Line: Telemarketing and the Changing Nature of Professional Crime." *British Journal of Criminology* 43:489–505.

Snider, L. (2001) "Crimes Against Capital: Discovering Theft of Time." *Social Justice* 28:3.

Sterling, Bruce (1992) *The Hacker Crackdown: Law and Disorder on the Electronic Frontier*. New York: Bantam Books.

Totten, J.A. (2004) "The Misuse of Employer Technology by Employees to Commit Criminal Acts." Presented to the ABA Section of Labor and Employment Law Technology Committee Midyear Meeting, Miami, 2123 April. *http://www.bna.com/bnabooks/ababna/tech/2004/totten.pdf* (visited 10 May 2005).

United Press International (2004) "Al-Qaida Hacker Hits Arkansas System." *http://www.washtimes.com/upi-breaking/20040714-090047-9427r.htm* (visited 31 January 2005).

Vaughan, Diane (1985) *Controlling Unlawful Organizational Behavior: Social Structure and Corporate Misconduct.* Chicago: University of Chicago Press.

Ward, David S. (1973) *The Sting*. Los Angeles: Universal Pictures.

Wayne, Leslie (2005) "Boeing Chief Is Ousted After Admitting Affair." in document *The New York Times*, 8 March, page 1.

Weisburd, David, Stanton Wheeler, Elin Waring, and Nancy Bode (1991) *Crimes of the Middle Classes: White Collar Offenders in the Federal Courts*. New Haven: Yale University Press.

Part VII

Professional and Occupational White-Collar Crime

1

From Pink to White with Various Shades of Embezzlement: Women Who Commit White-Collar Crimes

Mary Dodge

In 2001, Martha Stewart's image was scorched by allegations of an insider-trading scandal that suggested she had cooked up a scheme to sell 3,928 shares of ImClone stock based on privileged information that the company would fail to receive FDA approval of a lucrative cancer drug. Overall, the core aspects of the case and seriousness of the crime were relatively insignificant during a time of major corporate wrongdoing, including the collapse of Enron and WorldCom. Stewart's powerful home-making image, corporate status, and gender, however, stood out as unique attributes compared to previous and contemporary white-collar offenders. Much of the controversy surrounding her indictment, trial, and sentence was brought about by the intense media maelstrom it created, and gender-related characteristics clearly emerged as variables that contributed to the hoopla. The Stewart case, along with those of other prominent female offenders such as Leona Helmsley, Diane Brooks, and Lea Fastow, offer insight into the historical and current debates surrounding gendered varieties of white-collar crimes.

Traditionally, and not surprisingly, white-collar crimes almost exclusively have been concocted and conducted by men. The primary obstacle to female involvement in elite crime is linked to limited opportunities and less participation in the upper echelons of the corporate milieu. In the United States, the number of women involved in the public sphere continues to increase, despite a developing trend toward "opting out" that shows female executives are choosing to leave corporate positions for less demanding employment that is more conducive to personal freedom and family life.[1] In 2004, about 59 percent of the women in the United States were involved in the work force, though they continue to play relatively minor roles in corporate, political, and medical realms. In 2005, the U.S. Bureau of Labor Statistics reported that women represented 29 percent of the physicians and surgeons nationwide.[2] Worldwide, political leadership remains in the hands of men with a count (as of the 1990s) of 42 women who have served as presidents or prime ministers.[3] Upper-level positions in corporations and financial institutions also continue to be male dominated. Over the past three years, only eight women have or are holding CEO positions in Fortune 500 companies and, in 2002, just 9 of the 1,000 largest companies in the United States were headed by women.[4] Women compose about 14 percent of board members in Fortune 500 companies and represent only 5.2 percent of the top-earning corporate officers.[5] Additionally, Wall Street remains primarily a male domain with men accounting for 82 percent of the salespeople, while women continue to hold low-level jobs as sales assistants.[6]

Gaining acceptance into male-dominated enterprises continues to be problematic for women who face sexual and gender discrimination, and other structural barriers that prevent them from moving up the ranks even after breaking through the glass-ceiling—a term coined by *Wall Street Journal* reporters in 1986.[7] The limited opportunities in corporate America for women also have been referred to in more graphic terms as the "sticky floor," "concrete ceiling," and "pink collar ghetto."[8] Even women who rise to the higher ranks in male-dominated cultures continue to face obstacles based on gendered stereotypes and exclusionary practices. Journalist Michael Lewis notes that "[the] curious problem of women on Wall Street is that even the ones making a million and a half dollars a year too often feel like outsiders, or oddballs or people whom their firms might be about to burn. And they are!"[9]

Critiques of the achievements and failures of women executives often are cast in gender-related terms instead of professionalism and competence. Linda Wachner, the former Chief Executive Officer (CEO) of Warnaco who successfully transformed the clothing company into a $2.2 billion-a-year business, was hailed as the darling of Wall Street until the business filed for bankruptcy protection in 2001. Her aggressive manner and lavish lifestyle that garnered so much respect during her reign as CEO became liabilities when she was labeled the "iron maiden of lingerie" and colleagues denigrated her aggressive leadership style and called her tough behavior inappropriate.[10] Generally, women in the corporate world tend to view their experiences as similar to male peers and, ultimately, they take the same risks and use similar tactics, but scrutiny of their actions is intrinsically linked to gender. Obtaining gender equity in the public sphere relies on developing a framework that teaches women "the rules of the game," removes structural barriers, and shifts the focus from eliminating differences to embracing differences.[11] Women, when given the opportunity to participate in corporate or political positions, may develop a different way of "doing business," though the established patterns of practice often demand that women "do gender" in the workplace by mimicking traditional masculine behavior.

Some commentators and scholars have argued that women bring a more ethical perspective to the workplace. A Canadian study, for example, found that 94 percent of the corporate boards with three or more women had established conflict-of-interest guidelines compared to 68 percent of the companies with all male boards and that 91 percent of the boards with women members verified audit information compared to 74 percent of all male boards.[12] The study results are suggestive, though preexisting policies for each company were not included in the analysis. Another survey of 515 women and 608 men from companies with more than 1,000 employees found that women placed a higher value on family/home, fairness/equity, teams/collaboration, friends/relationships and recognition/rewards; whereas men tended to value pay/money/benefits, and power/status/authority.[13] An unpublished study by Judith Collins, a professor at Michigan State University, that examined the characteristics of 71 female executives incarcerated in federal prisons for white-collar crimes compared to 172 non-criminal female executives in managerial positions found that personal and situational factors related to friends and family had an enormous impact on the actions of women.[14] According to Collins, females score more positively compared to men on measures of socialization, self-control, empathy, responsibility, and social involvement. Overall, women in her study tended to act in ways that were "other-directed" and often viewed their crimes as benefiting friends and family.[15]

The "different voice" of women in business may carry a sense of community and connectedness and perhaps a more ethical way of doing business. The concept of a different voice is associated with notions of variations in moral reasoning between males and females. Carol Gilligan's work on moral reasoning and women debunked the traditional six stage model put forth by Lawrence Kohlberg in the 1970s that suggested men were more likely to achieve higher levels on his measurements. Kohlberg, who placed women at an intermediate, more simplistic level of development, noted that stage three "is a functional morality for housewives and mothers; it is not for businessmen and professionals" who rise to more advanced and complex levels.[16] Gilligan's research found that women tended to view moral issues as a network of inter-connecting responsibilities, whereas men focused more on individual rights based on formal rules.[17] More recent research, however, suggests that moral reasoning and ethical behavior are deeply embedded in situational contexts and that these factors offer better explanatory power than gender. Care-based approaches are more likely to emerge when interacting with a friend than a stranger and when others are seen as in-group members.[18] The connectedness to others typically attributed to women may fail to predict ethical decision making as the social distance between self and others increases, particularly in corporate environments.

Speculations among journalists, business executives, and scholars that women are engaging in more white-collar crime have triggered intense scrutiny. Anthony Paonita, in his journalist account of "women behaving badly," notes that females are "involved in high-profile misdeeds in numbers that would have been unthinkable a few years ago."[19] The controversy over how and why women engage in white-collar crime, however, is far from settled. The assumption that women will behave like men in similar situations was disputed by Eileen Leonard who noted that historical, social, and economic experience may forecast less white-collar crime among female even when given the opportunity.[20] In 1989, feminist scholar Kathleen Daly first called attention to lower-level clerical and administrative wrongdoing among women and noted that female embezzlers and fraudsters are more appropriately considered pink-collar criminals committing "petty" acts.[21] The focus of who commits white-collar crime, along with feminist theories of why women commit crime, is rapidly changing from victims to perpetrators as the 21st century progresses.[22]

Challenging Masculine Theory and Practice

Edwin Sutherland's ground-breaking work on white-collar crime, which began in the late in 1930s, understandably focused on male offenders. The emergence of feminist theory and criminality shifted attention from men as an increasing number of scholars sought explanation for the rising involvement of women in crime. In 1975, in a controversial look at women and crime, Freda Adler challenged the status quo when she predicted the emergence of a new breed of women criminals who would, like men, use their power, status, and position to commit crimes for economic gain. In her widely acclaimed and often critiqued book, *Sisters in Crime*, Adler noted:

> In the future a greater proportion of this wealth and power will pass through feminine hands, and almost all of it will be wielded responsibly. But it would be an unrealistic reversion to quixotic chivalry to believe that, for better or worse, women will be any more honest than men.[23]

That same year, Rita Simon also predicted increases in female participation in white-collar crime as opportunities became available, particularly for embezzlement and fraud.[24] Not all scholars agree on the accuracy of these forecasts and the actual involvement of women in upper-echelon crimes. Darrell Steffensmeier has quibbled over women's involvement; specifically, he notes that larceny, fraud, forgery, and embezzlement on a small scale involving low sums of money fail to fit within the of traditional white-collar crime definitions. Trends that indicate a rise in shoplifting, check kiting, welfare fraud, and credit card fraud more aptly come within the notion of traditional female criminal activities based on available, limited opportunities. Steffensmeier argues that women rarely are arrested for occupation-related frauds or "real white-collar crimes." He notes that female crimes of insider trading, price-fixing, restraint of trade, toxic waste dumping, and official corruption, for example, are practically nonexistent.[25]

In 1993, Jay Albanese examined data from the United States and Canada and found a "dramatic" increase in the number of women who were employed in white-collar jobs and a similar pattern in arrests for fraud, forgery and counterfeiting, and embezzlement during the 1970s and 1980s.[26] Sandy Haantz, a research assistant at the National White-Collar Crime Center, reported a pronounced upward progression of women who engage in elite deviance and noted that of the 1,016 federal prisoners incarcerated for white-collar crime in 2000, nearly one in four were women.[27] The Bureau of Justice Statistics reported a 55 percent increase in the number of women convicted of fraud felonies in state courts from 1990 to 1996.[28] The increase in arrests for embezzlement skyrocketed over the last 20 years and rates for forgery/counterfeiting have steadily increased for women.[29] Simon and Ahn-Redding's recent analysis of women and crime data notes that "[t]he increase in arrests for serious offenses can be attributed largely to women's greater participation in property offenses, especially larceny, embezzlement, fraud, and forgery."[30]

Adler and Simon's early forecast of greater female involvement in white-collar crimes is yet to be put to the test, although the ideas appear to represent a legitimate aspect of criminological inquiry, despite the backlash regarding the validity of their claims. Currently, in fact, there is neither reason nor evidence to support the belief that women when presented with the opportunity will be any less likely than men to commit crimes from positions of power and through occupational opportunities. The difficulty of testing any thesis about women and white-collar crime, however, is limited by real-world circumstances and inadequate data. As noted by Simon and Ahn-Redding, "we have no systematic evidence regarding the qualitative nature of contemporary women's white-collar offending relative to that of contemporary men."[31] Consequently, like much of the early work in white-collar crime, case studies offer valuable insight into understanding the participation of women in white-collar crime.[32] Women who have committed white-collar crimes may stand out as the exception to the rule, though the following cases suggest that gender plays an important role in the conceptualization and treatment of female white-collar offenders. From the well-publicized incidents beginning with the prosecution of Leona Helmsley in 1992 to the sentencing of Martha Stewart in 2004, the behavior of women who are involved in white-collar crime is becoming remarkably similar to that of their male counterparts. The case study method, though limited in explanatory power, provides insight and understanding into what occurs when women cross the line into elite law-breaking.

Case Studies

The Queen of Mean

In 1992, Leona Helmsley became one of the first high-profile female entrepreneurs to be convicted of a white-collar crime. Her tough and sometimes nasty persona defied the stereotypes associated with femininity. The labeling of Helmsley as unladylike was widespread: New York Mayor Edward Koch called her the "Wicked Witch of the West" and *Newsweek* headlined a description of Helmsley as "Rhymes with Rich."[33] Even her defense attorney Gerald A. Feffer commented that his client was one "tough bitch."[34] The personification of Helmsley based on gender was not unlike the traits attributed to Martha Stewart eight years later and demonstrates that participation in the corporate world, legal or illegal, may require women to redefine their role to fit in a "man's world," but they are still be held to societal expectations of traditional femininity. Men who commit white-collar crime rarely are heralded in media headlines as ruthless, tough bastards—characteristics that are associated with success in the corporate world.

Helmsley, who was 69 years old at the time of the federal indictment and her 80-year-old husband Harry were charged with conspiracy, fraud, and tax evasion. The charges stemmed partly from a billing scheme that involved extensive renovations to the couple's 28-room Greenwich, Connecticut, mansion that were paid for by charging the expenses to legitimate Helmsley business enterprises using phony invoices. The renovations to the Hemsley home included a $1 million swimming pool enclosure and dance floor; and $500,000 worth of artwork, furniture, interior decorating, and gardening.[35] Leona also allegedly charged personal items such as clothing and gifts for her husband to the company.

The federal grand jury indictment issued on April 14, 1988, by prosecutor Rudolph Giuliani included 41 charges that carried a total maximum sentence of 182 years (see Table 1). Michael Moss, author of *Palace Coup*, noted that the grand juries, state and federal, initially included as many as 188 counts of tax fraud.[36] The federal indictment on conspiring to commit extortion accused Leona and her personal aide of demanding and receiving free goods and services from contractors and vendors and of instructing employees to prepare fraudulent travel vouchers.[37] The Helmsleys also allegedly underpaid their

Table 1. Helmsley's federal indictment.

Number of counts	Charge	Maximum sentence
1	Conspiracy to defraud the government and the IRS	5 years
3	Tax evasion	15 years
3	Making and submitting false income tax returns	9 years
16	Aiding and assisting the filing of false tax returns	48 years
17	Mail fraud	85 years
1	Extortion conspiracy	20 years

personal income tax by as much as $1.2 million over a three-year period—an amount noted by some as petty compared to the $140 million in taxes that were paid.[38]

Helmsley's 1992 trial, along with those of her two co-defendants, former company officials Joseph Licari and Frank Turco, contained all the elements of a high-profile "bitch hunt" that centered on the charges of tax evasion. Harry Helmsley was found to be mentally incompetent and did not stand trial. In his opening statement Assistant U.S. Attorney James R. DeVita, known for his prosecution of the Reverend Sun Myung Moon, noted, "This defendant, Leona Helmsley, and her husband Harry Helmsley, used their position in society of privilege, and power and wealth to evade one of the most important... responsibilities of citizenship... to pay their fair and accurate share of income taxes."[39] In a surprising move, Helmsley's defense attorney claimed that the couple actually had overpaid their income taxes by almost $600,000. Also, hoping to downplay the reputation of his client, he acknowledged her status and toughness to the jury: "I don't believe Ms. Helmsley is charged in the indictment with being a tough bitch. In this country, we do not put people in jail because they're unpopular, or because they think differently, or because they are wealthy."[40]

The jury found Helmsley guilty of 33 felonies, including conspiracy, tax evasion, filing false tax returns, and mail fraud.[41] Whether her husband would have been treated differently by the courts raised some speculation about his role in the fraudulent activities and rumors that he kowtowed to his wife's bullying. Certainly, Harry's introverted mild personality and his reputation for integrity and honesty in the business community would have offered a much more sympathetic image to the jury.

Expectations regarding Helmsley's sentencing created a great deal of speculation based on her age and gender. One defense attorney commented, "Look, she's 69 years old. That's clearly a consideration. She's no spring chicken and her husband's sick."[42] Many people involved in the case expected a long sentence. Research data showed that from July 1, 1984, to June 30, 1986, of the 188 people convicted of extortion conspiracy in the United States 65 percent were sentenced to an average of 8 years in prison and the average sentence for income tax evasion was 2.8 years.[43] Any leniency in the sentencing of Helmsley seemed unlikely, and, in fact, her haughty and acerbic personality probably had a negative impact on the judge's decision.

Gender bias in sentencing has been extensively explored by scholars but remains controversial. Overall, empirical research has shown that women defendants receive preferential treatment.[44] Kathleen Daly, however, argues that any statistical analysis of disparity in sentencing based solely on gender is faulty because it ignores other important variables. She notes that decisions regarding sentencing based on equal or gender-neutral treatment neglect variables such as family and fail to recognize "the variations in women's lives and the circumstances of their lawbreaking."[45] The controversy over judicial paternalism in sentencing remains unsettled, particularly when crimes are designated as white-collar, though Helmsley's sentence appeared somewhat lenient, perhaps because of her age and gender, which were employed in later court maneuvers seeking to reduce her prison time.

Helmsley's sentence included a four-year prison term, a $7.1 million fine, and a payment of $1.7 million in back taxes. In June 1993, a district court judge reduced her sentence to 30 months after the parole commission denied her release during the discretionary period for time-served of 16 to 32 months. The judge noted, in his opinion, that Helmsley is "a 72-year-old woman" with a husband who "is a person of advanced age and in seriously ill health" and concluded that "32 months of prison is unduly harsh."[46] Helmsley served a total of 18 months in Danbury prison and 3 months under house arrest in her Manhattan residence at the luxurious Park Lane Hotel.

Helmsley, who turned 85 on July 4, 2005, continues to run her hotel empire, though she is reported to suffer from memory and health problems.[47] She denies any ailments and manages the $4 billion enterprise that she inherited after the passing of her husband in her traditional tough and abrasive manner. In an interview just prior to her 84th birthday she described herself as very much in charge and living up to her self-described reputation as a mean bitch, though she acknowledged the inherently negative role that greed and wealth had played in her life: "It's all about money . . . Money is the root of all evil."[48]

Ironically, Helmsley offered survival advice to Martha Stewart based on her own prison experiences. Helmsley, who continues to claim, "I did nothing wrong," expressed her regrets that Stewart was being sent to prison, because from her perspective Martha had engaged in no misdeeds. Helmsley simply stated, "I'll give you my advice—don't go! There are no nice jails."[49] Helmsley, when asked by a female journalist to reflect on the difficulties of prison life, commented that she was a "good girl" and explained, "If people are going to be contrary, there's really nothing that's going to help them. Darling, they're not there to torture you. They're there to reform you. I think [prison] does that. I think it helps people to go there."[50] Helmsley also continues to display an acute sense of toughness in her business dealings. In 2004, she lost a breach of contract lawsuit that was filed by a former employee who claimed that she backed out of a landscaping deal and she was ordered to pay $100,000.[51] That same year, Leona topped the list in a *Forbes* poll that inquired, "Which billionaire would you least like to work for?"[52]

The behavior of Leona Helmsley is analogous to that seen in male white-collar criminals, though the negative labeling of her persona as a woman surely contributed to the final outcome. Obviously, Helmsley's position allowed her opportunity and greed played a central role in motivation, but the acquisition of power is fundamental in explaining her actions. Michael Moss argues that her thirst for power trumped all other motives, though amusement also explained much of her behavior:

> Leona's motivation is clear to those closest to her. If she cooked the company books as her aides say she did, she did not cook them for money. If she screwed contractors out of their payments as they say she did, she did not screw them for money. And if she fired hotel employees willy-nilly without regard to justice or feelings as they say she did, she did not do it for her guests. Rather, she did all that for fun.[53]

Prisoner of Park Avenue

Diana "Dede" Brooks was a well-known and high-profile CEO for Sotheby's auction house in New York. Her innovative efforts to modernize Sotheby's by establishing an online network and partnering with Amazon.com were heralded as moves that helped overcome a serious financial crisis in the company. Brooks, raised on the North Shore of Long Island, was the oldest of six children in an upper-class family. From her childhood she remembers her father's encouragement that she could accomplish the same goals as her brothers and recalled: "I believed him. When I was eight, I announced I wanted to go to Yale."[54] After completing her studies at Miss Porter's high-society finishing school, she attended Yale University and graduated in 1972. Her initial employment at Sotheby's as director of financial planning required that she eliminate 90 staff positions through buyouts and firings, and in 1987, she was promoted to president of Sotheby's America and regarded as the most powerful woman in the art world.

Brooks, an imposing figure at six feet tall, is well known among associates for her competitive nature; she is an avid golfer, who often beats male employees on company outings. She was described by colleagues as smart and aggressive, and she had a reputation for toughness, almost to the point of being tyrannical. Author Christopher Mason notes that "lesser mortals found it hard to cope with Brooks' enormous energy, her demands and verbal abuse."[55] She also was no stranger to corporate scandal. Brooks had left the board of the family-owned company JWP Incorporated just before the computer reseller collapsed in bankruptcy after allegations of bookkeeping fraud emerged.[56]

After a three-year criminal probe, Brooks and former chairman of Sotheby's A. Alfred Taubman were charged in an antitrust conspiracy that rocked the international art world. The price-fixing scheme also involved Christie's, the most prominent auction house in England. The two companies controlled almost 95 percent of a $4 billion worldwide auction market. The Sotheby's and Christie's antitrust scheme included exchanging confidential lists of top customers who were not charged a commission and coordinating auction dates to avoid competition. Overall, their actions were said to have defrauded art sellers out of more than $400 million during the 1990s.

Brooks, who was granted conditional amnesty from prosecution for her testimony, pled guilty in October 2000 to price-fixing. At the trial, she testified that Taubman, who was in his mid-seventies at the time, directed her to meet with Christie's chief executive Christopher Davidge to discuss details of the schemes. She recalled a meeting with Taubman after the story of the scandal first appeared in print in which he told her, "You know, just don't act like a girl," a comment that she interpreted as meaning she should remain tough.[57] Brooks also told the jury about Taubman's offhanded remark that she would "look good in stripes" when her picture appeared on the front-page of the *Financial Times*, suggesting that the blame and punishment for the illegal actions would fall on her. Her testimony helped to convict Taubman for his part in the price-fixing conspiracy, and he was sentenced to a year and a day in prison and fined $7.5 million.

Brooks was sentenced to six months of home arrest, three years' probation, and 1,000 hours of community service, and was fined $350,000 fine. At the sentencing hearing Brooks, who was deathly afraid of receiving time in jail, apologized for the hurt she caused and accepted responsibility for her actions. U.S. District Judge George Daniels scoffed at her attempt to act contrite: "Your words are the all-too-familiar refrain of the white-collar criminal; the rationalization that somehow their theft is less serious because theirs is not a crime of violence and is committed while wearing a business suit."[58] Brooks was dubbed the "Prisoner of Park Avenue" by the *New York Daily News* while she served time in her $5 million apartment on 79th Street.

Brooks, like other high-profile women offenders, suffered a great deal of public humiliation. A professional who during the heyday of her career had been hailed as a tough executive regardless of gender, was now a woman who had dared to enter and participate in the male-dominated culture, and challenge the male patriarchy, that dominated Sotheby's. Journalists focused on her appearance and apparel during the trial, describing her "mane of blond hair [that] had turned almost entirely gray" and her "black, fur-trimmed coat." The *Times of London* referred to her as "the reincarnation of Cruella De Vil."[59] A columnist for the *New York Post* described Brooks a "dragon lady" and wrote that Taubman was the "victim of a conniving woman."[60]

> Dede Brooks is an admitted third-rate crook who hid behind a skirt . . . The fact that the old fella [Taubman] had to be put through this, rich or not, by a Wagnerian tank commander called Dede Brooks is just bloody outrageous . . . He is a bit of a darling old fella—and she would eat a barracuda without taking out the bones.[61]

The characterization of Brooks is reminiscent of the more primitive description of female criminality offered by Otto Pollak that assumes a sense of deception is endowed socially and physiologically in women.[62] The idea that Brooks failed to act like a woman by undermining the male patriarchy and was solely responsible for the price-fixing scheme is nonsensical. While the decision-making processes in the illegal acts are vague, it seems likely that Brooks readily agreed to play the game under the rules established by her colleagues. The ill-gotten gains surely boosted her career, income, and ego, which at the time outweighed the cost of getting caught.

The Domestic Diva

In 1991, Martha Stewart Living Omnimedia, Inc. had an estimated worth of more than a billion dollars. Stewart had risen through the corporate world by combining domesticity with her acumen for high finance after starting a small catering company that was run from her home. By the time the ImClone stock scandal emerged Stewart was heralded as one of the most powerful business executives in the county. On the day that the charges became public she was slated to take her position as a member of the New York Stock Exchange board of directors.[63]

Martha Kostyra was born the second of six children on August 3, 1941, in the working class neighborhood of Nutley, New Jersey. Her parents, Eddie Kostyra, a pharmaceutical salesman who never achieved his dream of being a doctor, and her mother, a schoolteacher—lived a modest, working-class life-style. The Kostyras set strict rules and high expectations for their children; Stewart credits her drive and ambition to her father.[64] She began her career in media as a model for television and print advertisements at the age of 13. Always an overachiever with straight A's in school, she received a partial scholarship to study European and architectural history at Barnard College, where she met Yale law student Andy Stewart, whom she married in 1961. Martha Stewart joined the Wall Street firm of Monness, Williams, and Sidel six years later as a stockbroker and worked there until 1972, when the family moved to Westport, Connecticut. She stayed at home to care for the couple's infant daughter and worked on restoring "Turkey Hill" their 1805 farmhouse.

In the late 1970s, Stewart started a small catering company that offered gourmet menus and high-quality services. The company in time developed into a $1 million-dollar business that served a host of corporate and celebrity clients. Her first book, *Entertaining*, released in 1982, became a best seller and Martha Stewart soon was an icon of the American Dream, embodying the unique combination of prosperous homemaker and business entrepreneur.[65] Her life was not without conflict, however, and in 1987 after 27 years of marriage her husband left her to pursue a relationship with her former assistant.

Martha Stewart experienced enormous growth in her professional life as she focused her energy on business. Martha Stewart Living Omnimedia, Inc. (MSLO) publishes magazines and books, produces cable television and radio shows, runs a syndicated newspaper column, and supplies an exclusive product line for Kmart with an estimated $730 million in annual retail sales. MSLO stock went public in 1999 and the first day of trading generated almost $130 million for the company.

On December 27, 2001, Stewart was enroute to San Jose del Cabo in Mexico, when she made a phone call to her broker to sell her shares of ImClone stock that changed the course of her life. Also on the plane was Mariana Pasternak, the ex-wife of a doctor, who sold 10,000 ImClone shares the next day. News was spreading among the inner circles that the Food and Drug Administration (FDA) was planning to reject approval of Erbitux, a cancer drug developed by ImClone. Peter Bacanovic had placed a call to Stewart, leaving a message that ImClone had started "trade downward." Stewart's phone conversation with Bacanovic's assistant resulted in an order to sell her 3,928 shares of the stock. It had fallen to $58 per share, and Stewart allegedly had established a preexisting arrangement to sell if the value dropped below $60. She claimed that the verbal "stop-loss" order was in place in late November, though Bacanovic disputes this version and says that he placed the agreement in December (by that time some ImClone executives knew that the drug would not receive FDA approval). Stewart's stock sale reaped less than $230,000. Ultimately, the trip would cost Stewart far more than the value of the stock and the $17,000 vacation at the exclusive Las Ventanas resort that included a $1,500 per night suite, $1,500 in massages, and a $1,060 "sea grill dinner" all claimed as business expenses, although the request for reimbursement was rejected by the company's chief financial officer.[66]

Stewart's phone call to Bacanovic's assistant Douglas Faneuil included a discussion of the price of the stock and the trading volume, that had reached almost 8 million shares compared to about 1 1/2 million the day before.[67] Faneuil, who eventually pled guilty to a misdemeanor charge of misleading investigators, claimed that Stewart knew that Samuel Waksal CEO and founder of Imclone had unloaded his stock.

Waksal had tried unsuccessfully to dump substantial shares of stock—almost 80,000 which were worth nearly $5 million—and four family members had sold more than $10 million worth of the stock. Waksal was a close personal friend of Stewart's and had briefly dated her daughter Alexis. On the same day that Stewart dumped her shares, Waksal had allegedly tipped an unidentified seller in Florida, who sold 50,000 shares and another person who sold 40,000 shares. Waksal was arrested on June 12, 2002, and charged with insider trading; conspiracy to commit securities fraud by tipping people to sell stock in the biotech company the day before the cancer drug was rejected; and lying to the Securities and Exchange Commission.

Stewart claimed to have received no inside information on ImClone and released the following statement:

> I did not speak to Dr. Samuel Waksal regarding my sale, and did not have any nonpublic information regarding ImClone when I sold my ImClone shares. After directing my broker to sell, I placed a call to Dr. Waksal's officer to inquire about ImClone. I did not reach Dr. Waksal and he did not return my call.[68]

According to the notes from the phone recording taken by Waksal's secretary, the call was related to the stock: "Martha Stewart something is going on with ImClone and she wants to know what."

Waksal's wrongdoing, however, was soon forgotten as the media focused unmercifully on Stewart.[69] In June 2002 on the CBS *Early Show* Stewart chopped cabbage and expressed a desire to "focus on my salad," though she commented, "I will be exonerated of any ridiculousness." This incident became fodder for jokes and snide comments. A satirical cover of *Martha Stewart Living Behind Bars* that showed a decorated prison cell was distributed over the Internet and late-night hosts were relentless in their one-liners.

On June 4, 2003, after a year-long investigation by the U.S. Attorney's Office and the Securities and Exchange Commission (SEC), Stewart and Bacanovic faced a nine-count indictment. The difficulties of proving that Stewart engaged in insider-trading prevented officials from pursuing what appeared to be the most serious allegation. In order to win an insider-trading case against Stewart, the government needed to show that she received information from a person with a legal duty to keep it confidential, that she knew it was an improper disclosure, and that she traded based on that information.[70]

The indictment was based on her alleged actions surrounding the sale of the stock and her behavior during the investigation. Stewart was charged with conspiracy to obstruct justice, making false statements, and committing perjury, because she allegedly lied about the stop-loss order and knew that Waksal was selling his stock. Stewart was charged with making false statements to the government, because when questioned she denied that the conversation with Bacanovic included any non-public information. Bacanovic was charged with making and using false documents based on allegations that he had added in a different ink color the stop-loss notation "@60" as a cover-up. Both parties were charged with obstruction of justice for giving false information to the SEC. The charge of securities fraud was based on Stewart's public announcement that she had a prearranged stop-loss order. Prosecutors argued that the public statement was designed to defraud investors.[71]

Many experts found the absence of insider-trading charges perplexing and some commentators believed that the indictment of Stewart was an attempt to undermine her status in the corporate world. U.S. Attorney James Comey noted that Stewart was not being prosecuted for who she is, but for what she did: "This is a criminal case about lying—lying to the FBI, lying to the SEC and investors."[72] Others disagreed and maintained that gender was central to Stewart's treatment by prosecutors. An editorial titled, "White-Lace-Collar Crime" noted that, "Stewart is being made an example because she's a high-profile woman."[73] Fans visited her website to read her statement of innocence—in a strong show of support, the site received 1.7 million hits in 17 hours.[74]

Stewart maintained her plea of innocence, but stepped down as chair and CEO of her company. She commented, "It's sort of the American way to go up and down the ladder, maybe several times in a lifetime. And I've had a real long up—along the way my heels being bitten at for various reasons, maybe perfectionism, or maybe exactitude, or something. And now I've had a long way down."[75] Stewart placed the blame on a "small personal matter" that was criminalized unfairly and worsened by overzealous prosecutors and the intense scrutiny by the media.[76] Her defense attorneys argued that the government was determined to make an example of her: "She is a woman who has successfully competed in a man's business world."[77] For Stewart her reputation as being bossy and demanding bolstered arguments that she was singled out for prosecution because of her gender, not her crime. Carol Stabile notes that "[p]owerful women who do not conform to subservient and heteronormative models of female behavior . . . are simply not tolerated for long (if at all) within the highest levels of private or public institutions."[78] Stabile's analysis of the media coverage compared Stewart with Kenneth Lay, the former CEO of Enron, showed that from June 1, 2002, until June 30, 2003, a total of 1,279 articles in major New York area newspapers appeared on Stewart, while only 23 were published on Lay.[79] Analyses of Stewart's behavior based on gender are hard to ignore given her dedicated, almost compulsive need for perfection in domestic and business affairs. The "noxious, misogynistic language" in the media, according to Stabile, portrayed Stewart as a rich, mean, lying woman who got what was coming to her. Newspaper reporters seemed to revel in describing Stewart's attire, commenting on her recent 15- to 25-pound weight gain, and discussing how she tucked her 38-year-old daughter Alexis into bed and slept with her after the verdict.

At the trial, the securities fraud charge, which carried a maximum 10 years in prison and a $250,000 fine, was dismissed. Federal Judge Mariam Goldman Cedarbaum ruled that "no reasonable juror can find beyond a reasonable doubt that the defendant lied" to change market perceptions of her company.[80] On the other charges, some of the most damaging testimony was given by Stewart's assistant Ann Armstrong, who claimed that the call she had taken from Bacanovic on December 27th, did not match what he had told investigators, and that Martha had tried to delete the message "Peter Bacanovic thinks ImClone is going to start trading downward." Martha changed the message to read, "Peter Bacanovic. Re: imclone." Faneuil, who had cut a deal with prosecutors, provided powerful testimony that he had informed Stewart that Waksal and his family had dumped stock. The defense attorneys worked to undermine his testimony by characterizing Faneuil as a "liar, drug user, and weirdly fixated on Stewart."[81]

On March 2004, a jury of eight women and four men found Stewart guilty of making false statements to the FBI, engaging in a conspiracy, and obstructing justice. A public statement by juror Chappell Hartride, a 47-year-old computer technician at an insurance company, called the verdict a victory for "the average guy" and commented that he was unimpressed by celebrity appearances and not swayed by testimony that Stewart was "above everyone."[82] Lawyers quickly filed a motion for a new trial after information emerged that Hartride had lied about a previous arrest for assault and had allegedly embezzled money as treasurer of a little league team.[83] The judge refused the request. Stewart's second attempt to get a new trial argued that charges of perjury against a Secret Service laboratory director had sullied the verdict. This motion also was dismissed by the judge.[84]

Many legal experts believed that the judge needed to avoid an appearance of showing favoritism. Cedarbaum sentenced Stewart to five months in federal prison and five months of house detention. Stewart reported to Danbury federal prison camp in October 2004 to serve her sentence—obviously, not heeding the advice of Helmsley. At Danbury, about 2 percent of the inmates are considered white-collar—the majority are incarcerated for drug-related offenses. According to the U.S. Bureau of Prisons, approximately 1,100 women of the total 11,800 female inmates are in the Federal Prison System.[85] Stewart was released from prison in March 2005 to finish her sentence under house arrest.

Political, Professional, and Corporate Crime

The rooster of professional women who have perpetrated fraud continues to grow, despite the relatively small number of women in high-profile positions. The following examples show that some women when given the opportunity will engage in white-collar crimes that are clearly occupationally related and involve high dollar amounts. "Petty theft" now appears to be inaccurate terminology for many elite women offenders. In 2003, Sara Bost made headlines when the city of Irvington, New Jersey, discovered a serious deficit in its budget. Bost, who previously had worked as a bank auditor, was elected the first African American mayor in Irvington. She was charged with taking bribes from developers and with witness tampering—she allegedly received a $1,500 kickback and $7,000 in bribes from contractors and developers.[86] Boost pled guilty to attempted witness tampering and was sentenced to one year, 150 hours of community service, and fined $2,000. Frances Cox in her position as treasurer for Fairfax, Virginia, embezzled $48,000. Betty Loren-Maltese, former town president of Cicero, Illinois, bilked $12 million from the city in an elaborate insurance fraud. Mary Hudson, board chair of Hudson Oil Company, pled no contest to charges of price-fixing gas pumps to shortchange customers. Nancy Young, an attorney in New York, stole $300,000 from clients over a nine-year period.

Lea Fastow was one of the few women executives who became entangled in the corporate misdeeds surrounding the collapse of Enron. The 2003 indictment of Fastow, former Assistant Treasurer of Enron, included charges of wire fraud, money laundering conspiracy, tax fraud, and aiding and abetting. Her husband, chief financial officer Andrew Fastow, faced nearly 100 charges for his part in the scandal.

Lea Fastow was a socialite heiress to a grocery and real estate fortune. She was born to Mariam Hader, a former beauty queen who was crowned Miss Israel and was a semifinalist in the 1958 Miss University pageant, and Jack Weingarten, a member of one of Houston's wealthiest families. Lea, had a difficult childhood because of the divorce of her parents in 1970 and insecurities over her weight.[87] She graduated in 1984 from Tufts University, where she first met Andrew during his freshman orientation and they married a year after finishing college. Lea eventually received her masters in Business Administration at Northwestern University's night program while working at the Continental Bank in Chicago.

The couple lived in a 4,666-square-foot home in Southhampton and owned vacation homes in Galveston, Texas, and Norwich, Vermont. They were in the process of building a $4 million home at the time of their arrest. Lea had left her position at Enron in 1997 after the birth of the couple's first child. In 2001 and 2002, she became a member of the Enron art committee with a $20 million budget to assemble a contemporary art collection.[88]

The Enron schemes included numerous off-the-book partnerships and secret deals. The Fastows were accused of laundering money from the transactions by bestowing phony gifts on family members and falsifying tax returns. Lea, said by colleagues to be the smarter half of the couple, reportedly created an elaborate tax shelter while still at Enron in 1994, subsequently the Treasury Department sought to ban such practices.[89] The couple's success was readily apparent from their tax returns. The Fastows showed an incredible growth in income, primarily from the underhanded partnership deals and the sale of Enron stock, despite the underreporting that was claimed by the Internal Revenue Service. Their joint tax return in 1997 reported an income of just over $1 million, 2000 their income had risen to $48½ million.[90]

Lea's plea bargain negotiations included one count of filing a false tax return by failing to report $47,800 on her 2000 personal taxes and an estimated $204,000 undeclared income over four years. Skirmishes between Fastow and U.S. Federal Judge David Hittner began when he rejected the plea bargain that limited his sentencing options. Ultimately, she pled guilty to signing tax forms that hid income obtained illegally from the Enron schemes. Her lawyer argued for leniency in sentencing because of her position as a mother and her prospects for a new career as a nurse.[91] The change of career for Fastow appeared to be a blatant attempt to sway the judge with notions that she would make amends for her misdeeds by engaging in a more nurturing career in the future—an idea likely met with skepticism. In July 2004, Fastow was sentenced to one year at the Federal Detention Center in Houston for a misdemeanor conviction of signing a fraudulent tax return not related to her tenure at Enron. Her husband was sentenced to 10 years and agreed to cooperate with further investigative efforts. The couple ultimately forfeited control of assets worth more than $29 million. Lea and Andrew also negotiated serving consecutive sentences so that at least one parent would be home with their two children, ages eight and four.

Women of the Saving and Loans Scandal

The savings and loan scandal in the 1980s represents perhaps the most widespread and insidious example of fiduciary fraud by persons in positions of trust. The debacle has been called the worst financial disaster of the 20th century and experts estimate the cost of the S&L incident to American taxpayers as high as $500 billion.[92] By October 1990, a total of 331 convictions had resulted in an average sentence of 3½ years and included the involvement of at least 49 women.[93] While only a small percentage of the crimes were committed by women their behavior and seriousness mirrored that of their male counterparts (see Table 2). Women involved in the S&L scandal, based on 15 cases, embezzled or stole over $3 million (mean = $204,080). In one instance, Luann Price, a loan officer, worked with her husband to kite $2 million in checks.[94] Many of the women held high-level positions, and, undoubtedly, were playing the game of fraud according to the same rules and for the same reasons as their male colleagues.

Pink and White Embezzlers

The definitional issues of what offenses and offenders fit within the framework of white-collar crime continue to plague the field and, in many respects, have limited much of the discourse on the participation of women. Embezzlement ignores the conceptual tenets of white-collar crime established by Sutherland and is regarded by many experts as not really counting as white-collar crime. Scholars disagree as to whether or not embezzlement is more aptly described as an occupational crime, though this categorization is rarely considered as separate and distinct from traditional typologies of elite deviance.[95] The term "pink-collar crime" was coined by Kathleen Daly during the 1980s to describe embezzlement type crimes that typically are committed by females. Women are more likely to commit low-level crimes such as check-kiting and bookkeeping fraud from positions of less power compared to men who engage in acts of white-collar crime.

Embezzlement represents an equal opportunity crime and overall rates for women tend to be slightly higher than men. In 2002, a reported 5,917 embezzlement crimes were attributed to women compared to 5,898 to men. According to the Association of Certified Fraud Examiners, that same year men were responsible for stealing larger amounts of money (median =$185,000) compared to women (median = $48,000). A handful of embezzlement studies, though dated, have focused on female offenders and have confirmed trends that women tend to commit embezzlement at a higher rate, steal less money, and invoke different rationalizations for their actions compared to men.

Donald Cressey's 1953 study of male embezzlers noted that frequently offenders were attempting to solve "non-shareable problems" and neutralized their behavior as "borrowing."[96] In contrast, an study by Dorothy Zietz of women embezzlers discovered that they tended to be motivated by family needs and rarely rationalized their behavior as "borrowing." Similarly, the embezzlers in Daly's study were twice as likely as man to use the rationalization of needs of the family. Men appeared to be motivated by self-interest or greed.[97] Overall,

Table 2. Women of the savings & loan scandal.

Name	Position	Offense	Sentence
Byrn, Peggy	Unknown	Charged 18 vehicles to the company	1 year
Crooks, Frances	Sales Officer	Siphoned $103,000	6 months
Crawford, Judy P.	VP of Operations	False loan worth $263,350	15 months
Davis, Pamela	Account Manager	Embezzlement from escrow accounts, losses estimated at $102,000	2½ years $98,000 restitution
Feezel, Mary	Assistant Treasurer	Embezzled $597,657	3 years
Grimm, Carol Lee	Purchasing Agent	Kickbacks $15,000	2 years' probation
Hulon, Susan	Real Estate Co. Owner	Undervaluing possessions in a bankruptcy	4 years
Killen, Rebecca	Assistant Manager	Kited $80,000 in checks	9 months
Lawler, Janet	Branch Manager	Stole $510,000	Unknown
Lee, Janis	Clerk	Skimmed $100,000 from dormant accounts	Unknown
Lickiss, Mary Jo	Secretary/ Treasurer	Altered minutes of the board of directors on loan approvals	80 days
Loren, Gina	Investment Manager	Misused clients money for personal luxuries	6 years
Luker, Rebecca L.	Real Estate Agent	Falsified collateral to borrow $10,000	4 years' probation
Mallet, Mildred	Vice President	Embezzled $600,000	6 months in jail 5 years' probation
Martin, Kipi Elaine	Unknown	Stole $48,729 in loans using fake identities & documents	6 years and restitution
McKinzie, Janet	Executive Assistant	Set up a fake escrow account and submitted phony invoices	20 years
Newbill, Sharon	Vice President	Embezzlement	3 years' probation
Payne, Sandra L.	Vault Teller	Embezzled $100,000	5 months
Peters, Darlene	Vice President	Created a fictitious loan & spent the money	1 year
Powers, Linda	Unknown	Transferred $300,000 into her personal account	1 year 2 years' probation
Price, Luann	Loan Officer	Kited $2 million in checks	4 years
Sears, Sherilane	Branch Manager	$27,000 withdrawn from dormant customer accounts	5 years' probation
Schaefer, Lori	Loan Officer	Made secret loans to herself ($128,000)	15 months
Skidmore, Alice	Assistant Branch Manager	Made 50 bogus loans to herself	1 year
Smith, Mary	Head of Title Company	False policies for real estate backing $3.7 million in loans	5 years $10,000 fine
Stawinski, Laura	Accounting Supervisor	Embezzled $91,471	3 years' probation
Wilson, Mary Jane	Officer Manager	Submitted fictitious invoices	5 years' probation

Source: Farnham, Alan (1990) *Fortune*.

according to Daly, crimes by men were more serious and were committed with a work group using organizational resources. The data also showed that women bank embezzlers were younger, less educated, reported lower incomes, and acted alone.

More recent cases, however, show that embezzlement schemes by women given the opportunity can be and are comparable to the those of men. Carol Braun, the former controller of Goodwill Industries of North Central Wisconsin and a trusted employee for 26 years, embezzled more than half a million dollars to cover her gambling debts. In 2003 she pled no contest and was sentenced to serve five years.[98] Sharon Wertz stole more than $700,000 in a case that appeared to be motivated by greed. Authorities found that she had bought new vehicles and gambled away a fortune—some speculate as much as $420,000—at a local casino. Wertz stated that she committed the fraud to "better my own life, I guess," and her defense attorney noted that "greed" and "the thrill of getting away with it" served as powerful motivators.[99]

Conclusions

The corporate environment and ethos, along with opportunity, may play an important role in the decision-making processes connected to conducting illegal or unethical business practices. A woman, for example, allowed in the inner circle of men, may find saying no difficult.[100] Betty Vinson was a mid-level accountant for WorldCom when company executives requested that she enter fraudulent numbers into the accounts. Initially, she refused to take part in the scheme, but because she feared losing her job, which she needed to support her family, she acquiesced.

How and why women engage in white-collar crime appear to be somewhat mediated by the strength of the existing patriarchy and perceptions of who's in charge. Generally, males are seen by others as having more influence than women. This perception may develop out of notions that women are less competent and thus not as influential.[101] Women may be more likely to commit white-collar crimes when given the chance to enhance career opportunities because of the pressures to perform and higher standards that demand they work harder than men to achieve the same goals. Women may also wish to avoid being ostracized and become "one of the boys" by participating in illegal schemes. In addition to career limitations, opportunities for women to engage in white-collar criminal activities are hindered by closer supervision and exclusion from social networks.[102]

The motivational differences between male and female white-collar offenders, as noted by scholar James Coleman, remain unresolved. Some insight into motivation can be gained from Jody Miller's exploration of gender and street robbery.[103] She found that women who participate in a male-dominated environment are likely to have similar motivations. Likewise, the female police officers in a study conducted by Deborah Parsons and Paul Jesilow were attracted to the job for the excitement rather than "helping others."[104] The women tended to hide their femininity while on the job in order to fit within the male culture and conform to public images of law enforcement. Crime, according to some scholars, may represent "a resource for accomplishing gender—for demonstrating masculinity within a given context or situation."[105] Greed, fame, and power, however, are likely to impact both genders in a similar fashion, despite sociological and biological differences in how "gender is done."

The idea that women are taking on masculine qualities in order to compete, according to Adler, who stands by her assessment 30 years later, ignores the real issue about a human nature of which is not about gendered socialization, though the "masculinity thesis" continues to spark debate. Simon and Ahn-Redding note a lack of evidence for increases in aggressive criminality among women and that research that documents the competitive nature of aggressive women looking for their "piece of the action" is scant.[106] Adler argues that opportunity is central to understanding the involvement of women in white-collar crime:

> There is no "masculinization." Women have made it because the doors have been opened. They use the same tactics as men. These are human characteristics not male or female—they are not gender issues in science. Women are making a lot of money now and it will only increase as their opportunity increases. They too will take advantage of the opportunity to go further—cut corners, make more money as it presents itself—legal and illegal. They are driven by the same factors and motivations as men.[107]

Perceptions of women by male counterparts create a catch 22 for females striving for standing as a competent professionals. Achieving success in male-dominated spheres means being tough, aggressive, competitive, and, sometimes, ruthless, though women must also maintain some modicum of femininity or suffer the denigration seen in the Helmsley, Stewart, and Brooks cases. "When women are perceived to be as competent as men, they are often seen as violating prescriptive gender role norms that require women to be communal."[108] Deborah C. Hopkins, chief financial officer for Lucent and next in line to serve as CEO, for example, lost her job allegedly because she was seen as being too "pushy."[109] Stabile notes,

> Thus, behavior that is socially sanctioned among male executives (perfectionism, self-absorption, coolness, self-confidence) is an indication of full-blown malevolence in women. Expected to be more caring and giving than men, women who do not conform to these still dominant stereotypes about maternal warmth and proper womanly behavior always risk vilification. They are just not normal.[110]

Ironically, the trend today toward greater involvement of women in white-collar crimes seems no more certain than predictions made by scholars some 25 years ago. National data that distinguish types of fraud by gender, amount stolen, and circumstances of the crime are difficult to obtain. The increase of women in the workplace may correlate with higher levels of elite deviance, though the difficulties of determining the accuracy of this statement represent a challenge for future research.

Endnotes

1. Carol Kleiman, "Many Women Opting to Quit Corporations," *Denver Post*, Aug. 16, 2004, p. 2C.; Career Women, "Are Women Opting Out of Corporate Careers?" 2004, *http://www.careerwomen.com/resources/resources_optingout.jsp* (accessed April 5, 2005).
2. U.S. Bureau of Labor Statistics, "Women in the Labor Force: A Databook," 2005, *http://www.bls.gov/cps/wlf-intro-2005.pdf.* (accessed May 26 2005).
3. Nancy J. Adler, "Global Leaders: Women of Influence." In Gary N. Powell, ed., *Handbook of Gender and Work*, Thousand Oaks, CA: Sage, 1999, pp. 239–261; Linda L. Carli & Alice H. Eagly, "Gender, Heirarchy, and Leadership: An Introduction," *Journal of Social Issues*, 57(2001):629–636.
4. Catalyst "Women in the Fortune 500," 2004, *www.catalystwomen.org* (accessed May 26, 2005); Alessandra Stanley, "For Women, to Soar is Rare, to Fall is Human." *New York Times*, January 13, 2002, sec. 3, p. 1.

5. Stacy A. Teicher, "Do Female Execs Have Cleaner Hands?" *Christian Science Monitor*, March 15, 2004, p. 14; Carol Hymowitz, "Through the Glass Ceiling," *Wall Street Journal*, Nov. 8, 2004, p. 1R.
6. Patrick McGeehan, "Discrimination on Wall St.? The Numbers Tell the Story," *New York Times*, July 14, 2004, p. 1C.
7. Carol Hymowitz & Timothy Schellhardt, "The Glass Ceiling: Why Women Can't Seem to Break the Invisible Barrier that Blocks Them from Top Jobs," *Wall Street Journal*, March 24, 1986, p. 1R.
8. Katherine Giscombe & Mary Mattis, "Women in Corporate Management at the New Millenium: Taking Stock of Where We Are," *Women in the Workplace: A Status Report*, 11(2003), pp. 5–10.
9. Michael Lewis, "Still a Man's World: Morgan Stanley Case Illustrates Wall Street's Persistent Gender Gap," *Rocky Mountain News*, July 24, 2004, p. 2C.
10. Marci McDonald, "Lingerie's Iron Maiden is Undone," *U.S. News & World Report*, 130(2001), p. 37.
11. Deborah Kolb, Joyce K. Fletcher, Debra. Meyerson, Deborah Merrill-Sands, & Robin Ely, "Making Change: A Framework for Promoting Gender Equity in Organizations." In Robin J. Ely, Erica G. Foldy, & Maureen A. Scully, eds., *Reader in Gender, Work, and Organization*, Oxford, UK: Blackwell Publishing, 2003:10–15.
12. Teicher, op. cit.
13. Mark Koebrich & Quynuh Nguyen,"Gender Role Found in Workers' Health," *Denver Post*, July 21, 2004, p. 1, 5C.
14. Judith Collins, Personal Communication, Feb. 28, 2005.
15. Deb Pozega Osburn, "Women's Integrity a Plus for Corporate Suite Jobs," *Michigan State University News Bulletin*, Dec. 3, 2003 *http://newsbulletin.msu.edu/nov11/integritywomen.html*, (accessed June 24, 2005); Associated Press "Corporate Crime Low for Women," *The Record*, July 27, 1987, p. 2C.
16. Lawrence Kohlberg, *Stages in the Development of Moral Thought and Action*. New York: Holt, Rinehart, & Winston, 1969, p. 372 cited in Michelle Ryan, Barbara David & Katherine J. Reynolds, "Who Cares? The Effect of Gender and Context on the Self and Moral Reasoning," *Psychology of Women Quarterly*, 28(2004):246–255.
17. Gilligan, Carol, *In a Different Voice: Psychological Theory and Women's Development*. Cambridge: Harvard University Press, 1982.
18. Ryan et. al., op. cit.
19. Anthony Paonita, "Crime Wave" *More*, January 2004, pp. 110–113, 114.
20. Eileen Leonard, *Women, Crime and Society: A Critique of Theoretical Criminology*. New York: Longman, 1982.
21. Kathleen Daly, "Gender and Varieties of White-Collar Crime," *Criminology*, 27(1989):769–794.
22. For a discussion of women as victims of white-collar crime see Elizabeth Szockyj & James G. Fox, *Corporate Victimization of Women*. Boston: Northeastern University Press, 1996.
23. Freda Adler, *Sisters in Crime: The Rise of the New Female Criminal*. New York: McGraw-Hill, 1975.
24. Rita Simon, *Women and Crime*. Lexington, MA: Lexington Books, 1975.
25. Darrell Steffensmeier, "Gender and Crime: Toward a Gendered Theory of Female Offending," *Annual Rev. Sociology*, 22(1996):459–487.
26. Jay Albanese, "Women and the Newest Profession: Females as White-Collar Criminals." In Concetta C. Culliver, ed., *Female Criminality: The State of the Art*, New York: Garland, 1993, pp. 119–131.
27. Sandy Haantz, "Women and White Collar Crime," National White Collar Crime Center, 2002 *http://www.nw3c.org/downloads/women_wcc1.pdf* (accessed June 24, 2005).

28. Ibid.
29. Ibid.
30. Simon, Rita J. & Heather Ahn-Redding, *The Crimes Women Commit, The Punishments They Receive* 3rd ed. New York: Lexington, 2005, p. 68.
31. Ibid, pp. 13–140.
32. Gilbert Geis, "The Case Study Method in Sociolgical Criminology." In Joe R. Feagin, Anthony M. Orum, & Gideon Sjoberg, eds., *A Case for the Case Study*, Chapel Hill, NC: University of North Carolina Press, 1991, pp. 200–223.
33. Andrew Blum, "A 'Queen's Defense: Countering Bad Press," *National Law Journal*, Aug. 28, 1989, p. 8.
34. See also Ransdell Pierson, *The Queen of Mean: The Unauthorized Biography of Leona Helmsley*, New York: Bantam Books, 1989.
35. *United States v. B. Helmsley*, 864 F.2d 266 (U.S. App. 1988).
36. Michael Moss, *Palace Coup: The Inside Story of Harry and Leona Helmsley*. New York: Doubleday, 1988.
37. Ibid.
38. Ibid.
39. Blum, op. cit.
40. Ibid.
41. Ronald H. Jensen, "Reflections on United States v. Leona Helmsley: Should 'Impossibility' be a Defense to Attempted Income Tax Evasion," *Virginia Tax Review*, 12(1993):335–396.
42. Gregg Krupa, "Helmsley's Trials May Continue: Tough Judge is Expected to Order Time in Prison," *Manhattan Lawyer*, August 29, 1989, p. 3.
43. Blum, op. cit.
44. Ilene Nagel & Johnson, Barry L. "The Role of Gender in a Structured Sentencing System: Equal Treatment, Policy Choices, and the Sentencing of Female Offenders under the United States Sentencing Guidelines," *Journal of Criminal Law & Criminology*, 85(1994):181–221. See also David B. Mustard, "Racial, Ethnic and Gender Disparities in Sentencing: Evidence from the U.S. Federal Courts," *Journal of Law & Economics* 44(2001):285–314.
45. Kathleen Daly, "Gender and Sentencing: What We Know and Don't Know From Empirical Research," 8 Fed. Sent. R. 163,1995 Vera Institute of Justice, Inc. Federal Sentencing Reporter; Kathleen Daly & Rebecca L. Bordt, "Sex Effects and Sentencing: An Analysis of the Statistical Literature, *Justice Quarterly*, 12(1995):141–175.
46. *United States v. Leona M. Helmsley*, 88 Crim. (U.S. Dist. 1993).
47. Joanna Molloy, "Friends Fear Leona Failing," *New York Daily News*, June 15, 2004, p. 3.
48. Andrea Peyser, "Leona: I'm One 'Mean Bitch,' But a Sane One," *New York Post*, June 16, 2004, p. 25.
49. Andrea Peyser, "Take it from Leona—Martha, Listen to your Fellow Billionaire Con and You'll Get Along in Jail," *New York Post*, March 14, 2004, p. 9.
50. Ibid.
51. Joe McGurk, & Cynthia R. Fagen, "Gardener Prunes 117G from Leona," *New York Post*, May 6, 2004, p. 17.
52. Anonymous, *Rocky Mountain News*, March, 13, 2004, p. 1C.
53. Moss, op. cit., p. 335.
54. Carol Vogel & Ralph Blumenthal, "An Auction Season Dominated by an Absence," *New York Times*, May 8, 2000.
55. Christopher Mason, The *Art of the Steal: Inside the Sotheby's-Christie's Auction House Scandal*. New York: Berkley Books, 2004, p. 202.
56. Vogel & Blumenthal, op. cit.
57. Mason, op. cit.

58. Dan Ackman, "Sotheby's Brooks Sent to Her Room, But No Jail," April 29, 2002, *http://www.forbesimg.com/2002/04/29/0429brooks_print.html* (accessed June 27, 2005).
59. Cruella De Vil is a villainous Walt Disney character who stole puppies to use their fur for a coat in the movie 101 Dalmatians.
60. Mason, op. cit.
61. Steve Duleavy, *New York Post*, April 19, 2002 cited in Mason, op. cit., p. 334.
62. Otto Pollak, *The Criminality of Women.* New York: Barnes, 1961.
63. Carol A. Stabile, "Getting What She Deserved: The News Media, Martha Stewart, and Masculine Domination," *Feminist Media Studies*, 4(2004):315–332, p. 317; Stephen M. Rosoff, Henry N. Pontell, & Robert H. Tillman (2004), *Profit Without Honor: White-Collar Crime and the Looting of America* 3rd edition. Upper Saddle River, New Jersey: Prentice Hall, 2004.
64. Christopher Byron, *Martha Inc.: The Incredible Story of Martha Stewart Omnimedia.* New York: John Wiley & Sons, 2002; Jerry Oppenheimer, *Just Desserts: Martha Stewart Unauthorized Biography*. New York: Avon, 1998.
65. Mary Dodge, "Stewart Martha (1941-)" In Lawrence M. Salinger, ed., *Encyclopedia of White-Collar and Corporate Crime* Volume 2, Thousand Oaks, CA: Sage, 2005, pp. 766–767.
66. Keith Naughton, Barney Gimbel, Daniel McGinn et al "Martha's Fall" *Newsweek*, March, 15, 2004, p. 28, 9p., 18c, 4bw.
67. Toobin, Jeffrey, "Lunch at Martha's: Problems with the Perfect Life," *New Yorker*, Feb.3, 2003, p. 38.
68. CBSNEWS.com "Securities Fraud Charges for CEO," June 12, 2002.
69. Rosoff, Pontell, & Tillman, op. cit.
70. Toobin, op. cit.
71. *New York Law Journal* "Federal Charges Against Martha Stewart and Peter Bacanovic," June 5, 2003, 229(2003), p. 1.
72. Mark Hamblett, "Prosecutors say Martha Stewart's Lying was her Downfall," *The Recorder*, 6 (2003).
73. Columbus Dispatch, "White-Lace-Collar Crime: Martha Stewart Joins Host of Corporate Honchos Hit with Federal Indictments," June 16, 2003, p. 8A.
74. Bruce Horovitz, "Stewart Uploads her Cause to Web Site." *USA Today*, June 6, 2003, p. 3B; Rosoff, Pontell, & Tillman, op. cit.
75. Toobin, op cit.
76. Bill Hewitt, Sharon Cotliar, & Jennifer Longley , "I'll Be Back," *People*, Aug. 2, 2004, pp. 54–59.
77. Hamblett, op. cit.
78. Stabile, op. cit.
79. Ibid.
80. Erin McClam, "Stewart Judge Tosses Most Serious Charge," *Rocky Mountain News*, Feb. 28, 2004, p. 1, 6C.
81. News Wire Reports, "Martha Goes 0–4," *Rocky Mountain News*, March 6, 2004, p. 1, 6C.
82. Larry Neumeister, "Juror Says 'Average Guy' Won," *Denver Post*, March 6, 2004, p. 6C.
83. Constance L. Hays, "Martha Stewart Seeks New Trial, Saying a Juror Lied," *New York Times*, April 1, 2004, p. 3C.
84. Erin McClam, "Stewart Cites 'Lies' in Bid for New Trial," *Denver Post*, June 11, 2004, p. 2C.
85. Edward Iwata, "Prison Wouldn't Look Like 'Club Fed," *USA Today*, March 8, 2004, p. 3B.
86. Kevin C. Dilworth, "Bost Admits Witness Tampering, Ends Trial," *Star-Ledger*, April 24, 2003.

87. Fox, Loren, *Enron The Rise and Fall*. Hoboken, New Jersey: John Wiley & Sons, 2003; Bethany McLean & Peter Elkind, *The Smartest Guys in the Room*. New York: Penguin Group, 2004.
88. Bill Murphy, "Some Attribute Greed to Couple's Ultimate Downfall," *Houston Chronicle*, January,15, 2004.
89. Paul Krugman, "Enron and the System," *New York Times*, January, 9, 2004; McLean & Elkind, op. cit.
90. McLean & Elkind, op. cit.
91. Carrie Johnson, "Lea Fastow Withdraws Plea Agreement," *Washington Post*, April 7, 2004.
92. Kitty C. Calavita & Henry N. Pontell, "Heads I Win," Tails You Lose: Deregulation, Crime and Crisis in the Savings and Loan Industry *Crime & Delinquency*, 36(1990):309–341; Kitty C. Calavita, Robert Tillman, & Henry N. Pontell, "The Savings and Loan Debacle, Financial Crime, and the State," *Annual Review of Sociology*, 23(1997):19–38.
93. Alan Farnham, "The S&L Felons," *Fortune*, Nov. 5, 1990, p. 90 (15).
94. Franham, op. cit.
95. Gary S. Green, "White-Collar Crime and the Study of Embezzlement," *Annals of the American Academy of Political and Social Science*, 525 (January 1993):95–106.
96. Donald Cressey, *Other People's Money: The Social Psychology of Embezzlement*. Glencoe, Il: Free Press, 1953.
97. Kathleen Daly, "Gender and Varieties of White-Collar Crime," *Criminology*, 27(1989):769–794.
98. Associated Press "Former Goodwill Official Waives Right to Preliminary Hearing," August 8, 2003; Associated Press "Former Goodwill Exec Pleads No Contest to Theft," Sept. 15, 2003.
99. David Doege, "Former Bookkeeper Accused of Spending Money on Gambling," *Milwaukee Journal Sentinel*, Oct. 10, 2003, p. 1B; David Doege, "Embezzler Gets 4-Year Sentence," Milwaukee Journal Sentinel, April 13, 2004, p. 1B.
100. Anthon Paonita, "Crime Wave," *More,* December/January 2003/2004, pp. 110–113, 114.
101. Carli & Eagly, op. cit.
102. Coleman, James William, *The Criminal Elite* 2nd ed. New York: St.Martin's, 1989; see also Steven Box, *Power, Crime and Mystification*. New York: Tavistock, 1983; Rosabeth Kanter, *Men and Women of the Corporation*. New York: Basic Books, 1977.
103. Jody Miller, "Feminist Theories of Women's Crime: Robbery as a Case Study." In Sally S. Simpson ed., *Of Crime & Criminality*, 2000, pp. 25–46. Thousand Oaks, CA: Pine Forge.
104. Deborah Parsons & Paul Jesilow, *In the Same Voice: Women and Men in Law Enforcement*. Santa Ana, CA: Seven Locks, 2001.
105. Miller, op. cit., Sally S. Simpson & Lori Elis, "Doing Gender: Sorting Out the Caste and Crime Conundrum," *Criminology*, 33(1995):47–81, p. 50; James Messerschmidt, *Masculinities and Crime*. Lanham, MD: Rowman & Littlefield, 1993.
106. Simon & Ahn-Redding, op. cit.; Ngaire Naffine, *Female Crime: The Construction of Women in Criminology*. Boston, MA: Allen and Unwin, 1987.
107. Freda Adler, Personal Interview by Emily Unkefer November 20, 2003, Denver, CO; Emily Unkefer, "Predictions of More to Come," Unpublished Manuscript, 2003.
108. Carli & Eagly, op. cit., p. 633.
109. Stanley, op. cit.
110. Stabile, op. cit.

References

Ackman, Dan (2002) "Sotheby's Brooks Sent to Her Room, But No Jail." 29 April, *http://www.forbesimg.com/2002/04/29/0429brooks_print.html* (accessed 27 June 2005).

Adler, Freda (1975) *Sisters in Crime: The Rise of the New Female Criminal*. New York: McGraw-Hill.

Adler, Nancy J. (1999) "Global Leaders: Women of Influence." In G. Powell, ed., *Handbook of Gender and Work*, pp. 239–261. Thousand Oaks, CA: Sage.

Albanese, Jay (1993) "Women and the Newest Profession: Females as White-Collar Criminals." Pp. 119–131 in *Female Criminality: The State of the Art,* Editor Concetta C. Culliver. New York: Garland.

Blum, Andrew (1989) "A 'Queen's Defense: Countering Bad Press." *National Law Journal* 28 Aug., p. 8.

Box, Steven (1983) *Power, Crime and Mystification*. New York: Tavistock.

Byron, Christopher (2002) *Martha Inc.: The Incredible Story of Martha Stewart Omnimedia*. New York: John Wiley & Sons.

Calavita, Kitty C., and Henry N. Pontell (1990) "Heads I Win, Tails You Lose: Deregulation, Crime and Crisis in the Savings and Loan Industry." *Crime & Delinquency* 36:309–341.

Calavita, Kitty C. et al. (1997) "The Savings and Loan Debacle, Financial Crime, and the State." *Annual Review of Sociology* 23:19–38.

Carli, Linda L., and Alice H. Eagly (2001) "Gender, Heirarchy, and Leadership: An Introduction." *Journal of Social Issues* 57(4):629–636.

Coleman, James William (1989) *The Criminal Elite.* Second edition. New York: St. Martin's.

Cressey, Donald (1953) *Other People's Money: A Study in the Social Psychology of Embezzlement*. Glencoe, IL: Free Press.

Daly, Kathleen (1989) "Gender and Varieties of White-Collar Crime." *Criminology* 27:769–794.

Daly, Kathleen (1995) "Gender and Sentencing: What We Know and Don't Know From Empirical Research." *8 Fed. Sent. R. 163*, Vera Institute of Justice.

Daly, Kathleen, and Rebecca L. Bordt (1995) "Sex Effects and Sentencing: An Analysis of the Statistical Literature." *Justice Quarterly* 12:141–175.

Dilwork, Kevin C. (2003) "Bost Admits Witness Tampering, Ends Trial." *Star-Ledger* April 24.

Dodge, Mary (2005) "Stewart Martha (1941–)." Pp. 766–767 in *Encyclopedia of White-Collar and Corporate Crime Volume 2*, Editor Lawrence M. Salinger. Thousand Oaks, CA: Sage.

Doege, David (2003) "Former Bookkeeper Accused of Spending Money on Gambling." *Milwaukee Journal Sentinel* 10 Oct. (sec. B), p. 1.

Doege, David (2004) "Embezzler Gets 4-Year Sentence." *Milwaukee Journal Sentinel* 13 April (sec. B), p. 1.

Farnham, Alan (1990) "The S&L Felons." *Fortune* 5 Nov., p. 90.

Fox, Loren (2003) *Enron: The Rise and Fall.* Hoboken, NJ: John Wiley & Sons.

Geis, Gilbert (1991) "The Case Study Method in Sociological Criminology." Pp. 200–223 in *A Case for the Case Study,* Editors Joe R. Feagin, Anthony M. Orum, and Gideon Sjoberg. Chapel Hill, NC: University of North Carolina.

Gilligan, Carol (1982) *In a Different Voice: Psychological Theory and Women's Development*. Cambridge: Harvard University.

Giscombe, Katherine and Mary Mattis (2003) "Women in Corporate Management at the New Millenium: Taking Stock of Where We Are." *Women in the Workplace: A Status Report* 11(1):5–10.

Green, Gary S. (1993) "White-Collar Crime and the Study of Embezzlement." *Annals of the American Academy of Political and Social Science* 525:95–106.

Haantz, Sandy (2002) "Women and White Collar Crime." National White Collar Crime Center *http://www.nw3c.org/downloads/women_wcc1.pdf* (accessed 24 June 2005).

Hamblett, Mark (2003) "Prosecutors Say Martha Stewart's Lying Was Her Downfall." *The Recorder* 6(5).

Hays, Constance L. (2004) "Martha Stewart Seeks New Trial, Saying a Juror Lied." *New York Times* 1 April (sec. C), p. 3.

Hewitt, Bill, et al. (2004) "I'll Be Back." *People* 2 Aug., pp. 54–59.

Horovitz, Bruce (2003) "Stewart Uploads Her Cause to Web Site." *USA Today* 6 June (sec. B), p. 3.

Hymowitz, Carol, and Timothy Schellhardt (1986) "The Glass Ceiling: Why Women Can't Seem to Break the Invisible Barrier that Blocks Them from Top Jobs." *Wall Street Journal* 24 March (sec. R), p. 1.

Iwata, Edward (2004) "Prison Wouldn't Look Like 'Club Fed'." *USA Today* 8 March (sec. B), p. 3.

Jensen, Ronald H. (1993) "Reflections on United States v. Leona Helmsley: Should 'Impossiblity' be a Defense to Attempted Income Tax Evasion." *Virginia Tax Review* 12:335–396.

Johnson, Carrie (2004) "Lea Fastow Withdraws Plea Agreement." *Washington Post* 7 April.

Kanter, Rosabeth (1977) *Men and Women of the Corporation*. New York: Basic Books.

Kleiman, Carol (2004) "Many Women Opting to Quit Corporations." *Denver Post* 16 Aug. (sec. C), p. 2.

Koebrich, Mark and Quynuh Nguyen (2004) "Gender Role Found in Workers' Health." *Denver Post* 21 July (sec. C), p. 1 and 5.

Kohlberg, Lawrence (1969) *Stages in the Development of Moral Thought and Action*. New York: Holt, Rinehart, & Winston.

Kolb, Deborah, et al. (2003) "Making Change: A Framework for Promoting Gender Equity in Organizations." Pp. 10–15 *Gender, Work, and Organization* in Robin J. Ely, Erica G. Foldy, and Maureen A. Scully. Oxford, UK: Blackwell Publishing.

Krugman, Paul (2004) "Enron and the System." *New York Times* 9 January.

Krupa, Gregg (1989) "Helmsley's Trials May Continue: Tough Judge is Expected to Order Time in Prison." *Manhattan Lawyer* 29 August, p. 3.

Leonard, Eileen (1982) *Women, Crime and Society: A Critique of Theoretical Criminology*. New York: Longman.

Lewis, Michael (2004) "Still a Man's World: Morgan Stanley Case Illustrates Wall Street's Persistent Gender Gap." *Rocky Mountain News* 24 July (sec. C), p. 2.

Mason, Christopher (2004) *The Art of the Steal: Inside the Sotheby's–Christie's Auction House Scandal*. New York: Berkley Books.

McClam, Erin (2004) "Stewart Judge Tosses Most Serious Charge." *Rocky Mountain News* 28 Feb. (sec. C), p. 1 and 6.

McClam, Erin (2004) "Stewart Cites 'Lies' in Bid for New Trial." *Denver Post* 11 June (sec. C), p. 2.

McDonald, Marci (2001) "Lingerie's Iron Maiden is Undone." *U.S. News & World Report* 130(25):37.

McLean, Bethany and Peter Elkind (2004) *The Smartest Guys in the Room*. New York: Penguin Group.

McGeehan, Patrick (2004) "Discrimination on Wall St.? The Numbers Tell the Story." *New York Times* 14 July (sec. C), p. 1.

McGurk, Joe, and Cynthia R. Fagen (2004) "Gardener Prunes 117G from Leona." *New York Post* 6 May, p. 17.

Messerschmidt, James (1993) *Masculinities and Crime*. Lanham, MD: Rowman & Littlefield.

Miller, Jody (2000) "Feminist Theories of Women's Crime: Robbery as a Case Study." Pp. 25–46 in *Of Crime & Criminality*, Editor Sally S. Simpson. Thousand Oaks, CA: Pine Forge.

Molloy, Joanna (2004) "Friends Fear Leona Failing." *New York Daily News* 15 June, p. 3.

Moss, Michael (1988) *Palace Coup: The Inside Story of Harry and Leona Helmsley*. New York: Doubleday.

Murphy, Bill (2004) "Some Attribute Greed to Couple's Ultimate Downfall." *Houston Chronicle* 15 January.

Mustard, David B. (2001) "Racial, Ethnic and Gender Disparities in Sentencing: Evidence from the U.S. Federal Courts." *Journal of Law & Economics* 44:285–314.

Naffine, Ngaire (1987) *Female Crime: The Construction of Women in Criminology*. Boston, MA: Allen and Unwin.

Nagel, Ilene and Johnson, Barry L. (1994) "The Role of Gender in a Structured Sentencing System: Equal Treatment, Policy Choices, and the Sentencing of Female Offenders Under the United States Sentencing Guidelines." *Journal of Criminal Law & Criminology* 85:181–221.

Naughton, Keith, et al. (2004) "Martha's Fall." *Newsweek* 15 March, p. 28.

Neumeister, Larry (2004) "Juror Says 'Average Guy' Won." *Denver Post* 6 March (sec. C), p. 6.

Oppenheimer, Jerry (1998) *Just Desserts: Martha Stewart Unauthorized Biography*. New York: Avon.

Osburn, Deb Pozega (2003) "Women's Integrity a Plus for Corporate Suite Jobs." *Michigan State University News Bulletin* 3 Dec. *http://newbulletin.msu.edu/nov11/ integritywomen.html* (accessed 24 June 2005).

Paonita, Anthony (2004) "Crime Wave." *More* January, pp. 110–113 and 114.

Parsons, Deborah and Paul Jesilow (2001) *In the Same Voice: Women and Men in Law Enforcement*. Santa Ana, CA: Seven Locks Press.

Peyser, Andrea (2004) "Take It From Leona—Martha, Listen to Your Fellow Billionaire Con and You'll Get Along in Jail." *New York Post* 14 March, p. 9.

Peyser, Andrea (2004) "Leona: I'm One 'Mean Bitch,' But a Sane One." *New York Post* 16 June, p. 25.

Pierson, Ransdell (1989) *The Queen of Mean: The Unauthorized Biography of Leona Helmsley*. New York: Bantam Books.

Pollak, Otto (1961) *The Criminality of Women*. New York: Barnes.

Ryan, Michelle, et al. (2004) "Who Cares? The Effect of Gender and Context on the Self and Moral Reasoning." *Psychology of Women Quarterly* 28:246–255.

Rosoff, Stephen, et al. (2004) *Profit Without Honor: White-Collar Crime and the Looting of America*. Upper Saddle River, NJ: Prentice Hall.

Simon, Rita (1975) *Women and Crime*. Lexington, MA: Lexington Books.

Simon, Rita J. and Heather Ahn-Redding (2005) *The Crimes Women Commit, The Punishments They Receive*. Lanham, Maryland: Lexingon Books.

Simpson, Sally and Lori Elis (1995) "Doing Gender: Sorting Out the Caste and Crime Conundrum." *Criminology* 33:47–81.

Stabile, Carol A. (2004) "Getting What She Deserved: The News Media, Martha Stewart, and Masculine Domination." *Feminist Media Studies* 4(3):315–332.

Stanley, Alessandra (2002) "For Women to Soar is Rare to Fall is Human." *New York Times* 13 Jan. (sec. 3), p. 1.

Steffensmeier, Darrell (1996) "Gender and Crime: Toward a Gendered Theory of Female Offending." *Annual Review of Sociology* 22:459–487.

Szockyj, Elizabeth and James G. Fox eds. (1996) *Corporate Victimization of Women*. Boston: Northeastern University.

Teicher, Stacy A. (2004) "Do Female Execs Have Cleaner Hands?" *Christian Science Monitor* 15 March, p. 14.
Toobin, Jeffrey (2003) "Lunch at Martha's: Problems with the Perfect Life." *New Yorker* 3 Feb., p. 38.
Unkefer, Emily (2003) "Predictions of More to Come." Unpublished Manuscript.
Vogel, Carol, and Ralph Blumenthal (2000) "An Auction Season Dominated By An Absence." *New York Times* 8 May.

Cases Cited

United States v. Harry B. Helmsley, Leona M. Helmsley, Joseph V. Licari, and Frank J. Turco, 864 F.2d 266 (U.S. App. 1988).
United States v. Leona M. Helmsley, 88 Crim. (U.S. Dist. 1993).

2

The Itching Palm: The Crimes of Bribery and Extortion

David Shichor and Gilbert Geis

"Let me tell you, Cassius, you yourself are much condemn'd to have an itching palm."
William Shakespeare, *The Tragedy of Julius Caesar*

Two days before Christmas in 1939, while the United States was deeply immersed in a wrenching decade-long depression, the city of Philadelphia hosted a joint meeting of the American Sociological Society and the American Economic Association. The presidential address to the Society was delivered by Edwin H. Sutherland, a 56-year-old professor from Indiana University. His topic, "White Collar Criminality," would in time significantly affect the way in which the study of crime would be conducted throughout the world. Sutherland began his talk by noting that economists, while well acquainted with the methods of business, rarely looked at these methods in terms of crime, while sociologists, though sometimes students of crime, rarely considered it as an ingredient of business. Sutherland disingenuously, in keeping with the scientific ethos of the time, maintained that his only interest was to shore up theoretical understanding, but his clearly was a muckraking attack on the law-breaking activities of persons in the business world and in politics. "White-collar criminality is found in every occupation," he proclaimed, "as can be discovered readily in casual conversation with a representative of an occupation by asking him, 'What crooked practices are found in your occupation?'"[1]

Sutherland offered examples of bribery as indications of white-collar crime, and maintained that business was a more tainted enterprise than politics, however rotten politics might be. For this judgment, he relied on writers who presumably were in a position to know, including John T. Flynn, a highly respected investigative reporter, who had written: "[T]he average politician is the merest amateur in the gentle art of graft, as opposed to his brother in business."[2] Flynn's position was supported by a quotation from Walter Lippmann, a nationally syndicated political commentator: "Poor as they are," Lippmann had written, "the standards of public life are so much more social than those of business that financiers who enter politics regard themselves as philanthropists."[3] Three decades earlier, a mayor of New York City had observed that the truly corrupt were the "so-called 'leading citizens' who get millions of dollars out of the city dishonestly while 'the Boss' gets a thousand."[4]

Sutherland offered the following report in regard to these assertions:

> Political graft almost always involves collusion between politicians and businessmen. Judge [Martin T.] Manton was found guilty of accepting $664,000 in bribes but the six or eight important commercial concerns that paid the bribes have not been prosecuted. [Tom] Prendergast, the late boss of Kansas City, was convicted for failure to report as part of his income $315,000 received in bribes from insurance companies, but the insurance companies which paid the bribes have not been prosecuted.[5]

A decade later, Sutherland updated this report by noting that the Missouri insurance companies finally had been prosecuted. He emphasized that Prendergast had been tried rapidly and sentenced, but that it took another decade before the justice system got around to the corporate bribe-givers and that the penalty for them was only a fine. No company officer was charged.[6]

During the two-thirds of a century that have elapsed since Sutherland's presidential address, economists have come to take at least a glancing interest in crime, a move pioneered by Nobel–prize-winner Gary Becker's foray into the subject.[7] Business and finance scholars also occasionally have focused on crime, usually euphemistically looking at it in terms of ethical violations rather than legal offenses. For their part, criminologists have followed Sutherland's call and built an impressive, though often inconclusive, body of knowledge regarding white-collar crime.[8] Criminologists are likely to take issue with what they see as a largely sterile mind play of econometric scholarship,[9] while legal scholars are wont to scrutinize legislative acts and judicial decisions to the neglect of a close look at the participants in bribery and the social dynamics of bribery and extortions acts.

After a brief historical tour, it is this latter task that will be addressed in this chapter, though we must grant at the outset that the absence of reliable comprehensive information on bribery and extortion offenses will limit the reach of our effort. On the question raised at the outset, for instance, concerning the suggested disequilibrium between the response of the criminal justice system to business bribers and political bribe-takers there is no accurate information either for the time when this was claimed or at present. As one of the leading authorities on bribery and a colleague of his have pointed out, what comes to our attention is far from the product of systematic inquiry into the full realm of bribery. "Historically," they observe, "prosecutors have depended on chance to bring cases to their attention."[10] It is extremely likely that chance turns up violations only of a certain nature rather than an acceptable sample of all instances of bribery.

An alternate approach to addressing matters of bribery lies in an examination of case histories. Case histories cannot prove a general point, but they are useful for generating hypotheses and for providing fleshed-out information about law-breaking behavior, and they can be especially valuable to disprove ad hoc positions unsupported by empirical data. Quantitative studies of matters such as bribery, though valuable, will tend to overlook details and nuances in order to construct numerical portraits that can be manipulated statistically.[11]

The Background

Bribery and its juridical mate, extortion, have a long legal history. The Code of Hammurabi, promulgated in Babylonia about 1770 B.C.E., specified penalties for accepting bribes, and in ancient Egypt death was decreed for officials or priests who took bribes related to the performance of their duties. Both Greek and Roman law also contained stiff penalties for acts of bribery.[12]

The *Old Testament* makes mention of bribery several times. *Exodus* 23:8 commands, "Do not take bribes, for bribes blind the clear-sighted and upset the pleas of the just," a dictate that is repeated in *Leviticus* 16:19, where it is addressed specifically to officers and judges. In *Chronicles* 19:7, King Jehoshaphat is reported to have told the judges he appointed to each fortified town in Judea, "Keep the Law, apply it, for Yawheh our God has no part or partiality in the taking of bribes." English common law also condemned bribery as a penal offense,[13] and there have been cases in which judges solicited bribes from both parties, and ruled in favor of the one who offered the largest sum. Judicial bribery in the seventeenth-century was difficult to determine because it was the custom for the victorious party in a lawsuit to present the judge with something valuable as a token of appreciation.[14] It is an axiom of historical legal analyses that a pattern of persistent lawmaking on a subject is a strong indicator of a pattern of law-breaking; otherwise, why bother? Judges most certainly often had itching palms, but it is necessary to note that in earlier times the relatively low level of economic diversification meant that there were rather few persons who had sufficient power and authority to make it worthwhile to bribe them.

The first major English bribery cases arose more than a hundred years ago and illustrated the rise of commercial enterprises that invited efforts at bribery to make sure that their financial rewards were assured. The South Sea Company was chartered in England in 1711, one of the very first enterprises offering shares to the public to foster its advertised desire to establish trade with South America. Adam Smith, the renowned economist, later would hurl a collection of epithets at the effort: "folly," "malversation," "extravagance," and "knavery."[15] A fierce speculative fever fueled by bribes and artfully planted misinformation sent the price of South Sea stock on a wild upward ride that lasted almost a decade. Later, after the stock collapsed, a Parliamentary inquiry found that 12 members of the House of Lords and 462 members of the House of Commons had invested in the stock and between 40 and 50 had been bribed to support its aims. A major surprise was that there was no statute that would allow criminal proceedings to be launched against the malefactors. Robert Molesworth, a parliamentarian who had lost a considerable sum of money, plunged into the juridical gap, unsuccessfully as it turned out, by arguing that the company directors should be charged with parricide since they had in effect strangled their country, the father of all English citizens. If found guilty, he declared, they should receive the penalty decreed in ancient Rome for that offense by being sewn into sacks with a monkey and a snake and cast into the river.[16]

The ranks of persons today who can usefully be bribed have, of course, increased dramatically along with the explosion of populations. Stuart Green points out that under current American law the term "public official" is now broadly defined to include members of Congress, virtually all officers and employees of the three branches of government, jurors, and persons who act for or on behalf of the federal government, such as private employees who receive federally administered grants.[17]

An analytical problem then and now in regard to bribery is that it is characterized by reciprocity and most always is a consensual act. It is criminalized today in the United States despite the fact that reciprocity is an accepted norm in

American society. The ambiguity between the norm and the law is reflected in the fact that giving money to a headwaiter to secure a good table is regarded as a legitimate act, but giving money to a legislator to ensure a favorable vote is not. In his magisterial study of bribery, John Noonan challenges readers by asking whether "prayer and sacrifice to God are different from bribes."[18] There is a significant body of philosophical literature that seeks to establish why bribery should be outlawed. Some maintain that it is morally repugnant because it provides "unfair benefit or advantage,"[19] a principle that the eminent thinker John Rawls declares to be the cornerstone of justice.[20] Others, most notably some economists, see nothing untoward about bribery under certain circumstances: to them, it speeds up creaky bureaucratic processes and permits poorly-paid civil servants to achieve a more acceptable standard of living.[21]

For our purposes we will adhere to the legal definition of bribery since, however tainted by special interests, it permits some agreement on what the act does and does not embrace. In legal terms, bribery involves payments for (1) a positively unlawful act (malfeasance, such as rendering a judgment in a trial because of the payment; (2) the imperfect performance of a duty (misfeasance) such as not properly supervising a building construction; and (3) failure to perform a required duty (nonfeasance) such as not investigating a known toxic emission. Bribery involves the violation of a trust, explicit or implicit, bestowed upon the public official, but it need not require a situation of trust between the briber and bribe taker; both are said to be committing a criminal act.[22] Max Weber, in his classic analysis of bureaucracy, denoted the "ideal type" as a rational person "bound by rules" and embedded in a rigid hierarchical structure which closely supervises his or her behavior.[23] The ideal, it hardly needs be said, may not mirror the real: accepting bribes is common enough, and it does not represent playing by the rules.

Bribery and treason are the only crimes identified by name in the United States Constitution. In federal law (18 U.S. 201), bribery is codified as "corruptly attempting to influence a public official in the performance of official acts through the giving of valuable considerations. It is barter for an official act or omission to be taken other than on its merits." Generally, both the briber and the recipient of the bribe are culpable. Whether one party might be regarded as "more guilty" than the other is dependent on the circumstances.

Susan Rose-Ackerman recently noted different aspects of the criminal law of bribery. Her first point was that bribery should be decriminalized, that it should no longer remain the law's business. She analogized the situation to the legalization of gambling which both in the United States and elsewhere in the world eliminated many unsavory practices that had sprung up when gambling was outlawed. She notes that if bribery is to remain illegal more efficient procedures need to be developed to discover its occurrence. Since most bribery is uncovered as a result of insider reports she suggests that there be a policy of leniency toward those who disclose such practices. She also mentions approvingly the example of Taiwan, where bribing is not forbidden, but accepting bribes is a criminal act. Rose-Ackerman also advocates that the allocation of law enforcement resources in regard to bribery should be driven by the extent of the harm involved. In addition, she suggests that the penalties for corporate criminal liability should be enhanced. In many instances, it is the lower level or middle management employees who actually carry out the bribery transaction, while the chief executive officer hides behind a veil of "plausible deniability," professing that he or she was totally unaware of what was going on.[24] By holding the corporate entity criminally responsible there is a much stronger possibility of satisfactory financial recovery and, hopefully, the prospect that adverse publicity will lead to internal investigations that will locate and remedy the corrupt situation.[25]

Extortion is a considerably more complex concept than bribery to get a grip on. In his definitive tracing of the historical development of the law of extortion and its meaning today, James Lindgren concludes that "[u]nlike bribery, extortion has no generally recognized definition." He notes that the existing literature offers "lots of help" in pinpointing extortion, but that "most of it [is] poor,"[26] and he seeks to pin it down in the following terms: "Broadly speaking, coercive extortion [the form almost invariably charged] can refer to any illegal use of threat or fear to obtain property or advantages from another, short of violence that would be robbery." The kinds of threats or fear noted by Lindrgen are such matters as the threat to commit a crime, injure a person or property, expose a crime, or expose contemptible information.[27]

In American law, the doctrine of strict entity liability for an act of extortion by a corporate employee is set out in the leading case of *United States v. Hilton Hotel Corp.* The president of the corporation as well as the manager of the chain's Portland, Oregon, hotel testified that on two occasions they informed the hotel's purchasing agent that he was to take no part in a boycott of suppliers who declined to pay into a fund that was alleged to be used to promote tourism. Ignoring these instructions, the agent refused to deal with the non-compliant suppliers. The appellate court ruled that "liability may be imposed on a corporation without proof that the conduct was within the agent's actual authority, and even though it may have been contrary to actual instructions."[28] The outcome of the case was that the purchasing agent was acquitted and the Hilton corporation convicted.

Bribery is often considered to be synonymous with corruption, but, as Robert Brooks observes, it is "narrower, more direct, less subtle." He elaborates on the distinction: "There can be no bribe-taker without a bribe-giver, but corruption can and frequently does exist when there are no personal tempters or guilty confederates."[29] A case in point might be a legislator who buys up vacant land in a friend's name at a cheap price and then successfully sponsors a bill for the state to purchase that land for a much higher price in order to build a public hospital.

Arnold Heidenheim delineated three categories of corruption, including bribery, based on social perceptions in diverse countries: (1) "white" bribery—where such acts are viewed tolerantly. This is prevalent in societies based on family ties and patron-client relationships; (2) "gray" bribery—where a less tolerant view prevails. While such acts are considered morally reprehensible the individuals involved do not introject a sense that they are doing anything really wrong; and (3) "black" bribery—where the acts are outlawed and, if discovered, tend to be punished, a position generally taken in modern industrial societies.[30]

Receiving bribes clearly is related to the opportunities a person possesses to substantially influence decisions. Richard Cloward and Lloyd Ohlin, in their classic study of gang delinquency, pointed out the importance of the availability of illegal opportunities for committing criminal acts,. They found that access to opportunities were controlled by the mob members who recruited neophytes based on an evaluation of their suitability for the enterprise, be it drug-dealing, strrong-arm "persuasion," or other efforts that required particular traits and skills.[31] No intermediaries are necessary to carry out bribery, beyond those involved in helping the incumbent achieve a position where important favors may be granted for a price.

Not only are there differences in the opportunity to acquire bribes, the monetary level of such bribes will be determined by personal and marketplace factors. Generally, one's standing in the hierarchical order will be related to the size of the bribe that a public official can negotiate. On the other hand, the literature on the police has documented the way payoffs, often from merchants, are distributed. The cop on the beat typically takes the largest share, since he or she runs the greatest risk. The higher- ranking officers generally receive less from each of those paying off, but in aggregate are likely to realize a good deal more than street or squad car officers because of the latters' geographically limited operations.[32] Another pattern also finds the donor discriminating on the basis of officer rank. Liz Smith, a celebrity gossip columnist, tells how she handled police bribes when she was a young gofer working for a television producer:

> I hated our show and begged to be given the job nobody wanted, going out on the street "shaking hands" with the cops. ("Shaking hands" is a euphemism for paying off the police for looking the other way . . . to not move our trucks, not to harass our crews and cameramen). I'd step up to each policeman, shake hands and give him $20. When the big brass with gold braid on their hats and shoulders showed up, I shook hands holding $50 bills. I would be out on the streets with thousands in cash.[33]

Similarly, and at about the same time, the police in Chicago routinely were bribed by the mobsters controlling gambling to protect themselves and to make certain that no competition was tolerated in the area. As St. Claair Drake and Horace Cayton observed, "The police were paid off regularly, at a 'union wage,' with a sliding scale for patrolmen, plainclothesmen, and headquarters officers. Honest law enforcement officers often found themselves transferred to the cemetery beat. 'It's lonely out there,' one resident noted wryly. 'Nothing ever happens out there.' "[34]

The relationship between hierarchical status and bribery was demonstrated in two cases, one in Europe, the second in Japan. In the Netherlands, Prince Bernhard, the husband of Queen Juliana, received $1 million in the early 1960s for his assistance to Lockheed in its sale of fighter planes to the Dutch Air Force. In 1978, Lockheed paid several high-level officials in Japan, including Prime Minister Kakuei Tanaka, to arrange that Japanese government purchase 21 Tri-Star fighter aircraft. Both incidents contradicted Sutherland's hypothesis, which was noted at the outset of this chapter, that the bribe-taker, if caught, will suffer more than the person who gave the bribe. Prince Bernhard, after declaring, "I am above such things," received a mere slap on the wrist, despite further information that he had bribed Juan Peron, the Argentinian dictator, to buy railroad equipment from the Netherlands. Bernhard was made to apologize, to resign his directorships in a score of Dutch companies, and to give up his military positions.[35] Tanaka was arrested and sentenced to four years imprisonment and a fine of 500 million yen ($4.4 million), but by delaying maneuvers he managed to avoid serving time. More impressive, he later was reelected by the largest majority of any of the 834 persons running for a seat in the Japanese Diet that year. A sizeable segment of the country's electorate must have agreed with the statement by Japan's Minister of Justice at the time of Tanaka's trial: "Tanaka is being lynched," the cabinet member declared. "Looking for honesty in a politician is like shopping for fish in a green-grocer."[36] Obviously, at least in overseas venues or perhaps in regard to especially highly placed persons, there is a notable insulation from the heavier penalties that Sutherland maintained were the lot of American bribe-takers. For its part, Lockheed was fined heavily.

There has been no recent American scandal of the magnitude of the Bernhard and Tanaka scams. The two most notorious recent United States case involved Congressman. James A. Trafficant, Jr., of Ohio accepted money, equipment for his farm, and other expressions of gratitude for doing favors for corporate executives. He became only the second member of the Congress since the Civil War to be expelled by a vote of his colleagues.[37] Randy Cunningham, representing a district in San Diego, California, pleaded guilty to tax evasion, conspiracy to commit bribery, and mail and wire fraud for having accepted several million dollars in bribes for in a variety of forms. Cunningham resigned from the Congress at the end of November 2005.

Lobbying

Political lobbying and campaign fund contributions represent particularly interesting elements of the operation of self-interested suasion that falls short of the legal characterization of, bribery, but nonetheless displays many of its ingredients. Efforts to control lobbying in the United States have taken the form of having lobbyists register and indicate on whose behalf they are working. The ubiquitous nature of lobbying at the national level in the United States is reflected in the fact that 27 of the former staff members of Representative Tom DeLay (R-Texas), onetime majority leader of the House of Representatives, who was indicted for accepting illegal campaign contributions and for money laundering, had left DeLay's employ and taken up work as registered lobbyists. Reform of the campaign contribution regulations is persistently pressed by those who say they are working to level the playing field, but it may be too much to expect incumbent legislative bodies to control more effectively an approach that very often got them where they are. When some reforms are enacted it is not long afterwards that skilled attorneys find ways to evade their restrictions. Today, some corporations circumvent the law's limits by funneling money to their executives, workers, and friends and family members, who then donate it to the political party of the company's choice. While many contributors agree with the agenda of those they finance, most also presume that they are purchasing access. Those who resist efforts to limit campaign contributions often rely on the constitutional right to free speech to defend what they are about. After all, they also say, money always exerts power, and to try to restrict that power is to corrupt an essential ingredient of the capitalistic system.

Lobbyists say that they merely "inform" law-makers about their clients' problems and plans, hoping that this information will be sufficiently persuasive to influence the introduction of a desired bill or to sway a vote on a pending measure. But their activities often assume a more ominous form. Take the case of a health insurance company that fought against legislation that would have made insurance more accessible to the public by prohibiting various forms of "cherry picking"—that is, the enrolment in their program of only the heathiest applicants. The company hired lobbyists to press its cause and, according to a Congressional report, in Indiana the company lobbyist left envelopes containing checks for $100 to $250 on the desks of state House members.[38] Special interest groups, representing all segments of the political and social spectrum, often invite influential politicians, judges, or other officials to speak at events they organize, and pay them hefty honoraria. The proximity of lobbying and political contributions to outright bribery is reflected in the extensive coverage given to these subjects in the leading monographs on bribery.[39]

Transnational Bribery

Criminological interest in the topic of transnational bribery was aroused by the spate of scandals involving the operations in foreign countries of several major American oil companies (e.g., Gulf and Mobil) and defense contractors (e.g., Lockheed, Norton, Boeing, McDonnell Douglas). Marshall Clinard and Peter Yeager, studying corporate criminal behavior, had this to say about these events:

> The investigation of foreign payments of bribes, perhaps more than anything else, reveals the ingenuity and deviousness of large corporations in violating business ethics and laws. In nearly all cases examined, the efforts to conceal payments were so elaborate and cunning that even a casual examination would clearly indicate that the corporation involved had regarded such behavior as potentially illegal and unethical and, at least, highly embarrassing.[40]

The scandal led the Congress and the Securities and Exchange Commission (SEC) to engage in a comprehensive investigation of overseas bribery transactions. The Commission survey found that about 350 companies were involved to the tune of $750 million in bribing foreign officials and contributing to foreign political campaigns for the purpose of securing government contracts. In the wake of the scandals, Congress enacted the Foreign Corrupt Practices Act in 1977, making the bribery of foreign officials by American companies or their subsidiaries a criminal offense.[41] The Act was criticized by corporate interests because, they claimed, it made it more difficult for them to compete with enterprises from other nations that do not so constrain them. They sought successfully to exclude from the Act relatively small payments to lower level officials in order to expedite the issuance of licenses and other documents required to complete purchases. They maintained that such "greasing"[42] was essential in several countries in order to do business. Two major loopholes remain in the Act. One allows payments for promotional expenses such as travel and lodging for foreign officials visiting American companies to view products they are considering buying. The second, a gaping exception, allows payments to foreign officials if such payments are regarded as lawful in their native countries.

By mid-2004, fewer than one hundred cases had been prosecuted during the more than a quarter century since the Foreign Corrupt Practices Act had become law. Critics observe that penalties tend to lack a deterrent force. They cite a $300,000 fine that International Business Machines paid in 2000 to settle charges that its Argentine subsidiary had paid bribes totaling $4.5 million to facilitate a trade deal. It is also claimed that about two-thirds of the big multinationals have found legal ways around antibribery statutes, like bartering goods and services.[43]

An international survey of corruption constructed an index of such behavior that included episodes of bribery, and focused on conditions that ordinary citizens confront when dealing with public officials. The results showed a negative correlation between corruption and the level of national income and development. This may indicate that corruption—at least of the kind that the inquirers focused on—is a recourse deemed necessary to achieve a decent income. It could also mean that in first world countries corruption is not concerned with penny-ante matters but involves much higher financial stakes.

The survey also learned that tax and customs were the most corruption-tainted government enterprises, and that this was particularly pronounced in less developed nations. There also was a positive correlation between public sentiments that a tax system was inequitable and the amount of cheating in the form of bribery of tax code enforcers. A powerful conclusion was that "independence and fairness of the judiciary emerged as the single most important determinant of both street-level and high-level corruption in the public sector."[44]

Bribery also has been prominent in the arena of government procurement where large sums of money are awarded to private companies, sometimes on the basis of presumably competitive bidding and at other times on a sole source arrangement. The amount of discretion accorded an official to award contracts is believed to be a strong correlate of the level of bribery likely to exist. In this regard, countries have begun to put in place laws that forbid government employees from accepting jobs for stipulated periods of time with businesses with which they have had financial dealings, but like so many attempts to attack a problem, those intent upon evading the rule have little difficulty in doing so: in this situation, for instance, a company that a public official had favored financially might arrange an executive position for him or her in another organization which, for its part, will seek reciprocation in regard to government employees stepping down who have aided them.

The degree of supervision exercised over customs agents is believed to influence the level of bribery to avoid levies. Tina Rosenberg, an investigative reporter for *The New York Times,* noted the widespread presence of corruption in the Mexican customs offices until the inauguration of the NAFTA agreement in 1989 and the appointment of an energetic and scrupulously honest chief to head the service. Before that, a mafia-like organization had controlled the Mexico City international airport, where most merchandise from abroad arrived. For the first time after the reorganization, a registry of goods coming into the airport was maintained. Besides, the sixteen steps necessary to get goods past customs had provided sixteen opportunities for bribery; otherwise, the process was likely to drag on for at least a month. Reforms reduced the sixteen steps to only three and the time involved to about ten minutes. Bribery was significantly reduced.[45]

When discovered, bribery cases involving politicians often support the essence of the remark by the Japanese Minister of Justice that the term "honest politician" is an oxymoron. In Costa Rica, for example, three former presidents of the country were implicated in receiving bribes from foreign companies. By then, two of them had gone on to prominent positions in international organizations. One had to resign as chief executive of the World Economic Forum after admitting that he obtained almost $1 million from Alcatel, a French communications organization. The second had been bribed by the same company; he had to give up his position as head of the Organization of American States. The most recent past president of Costa Rica, the third of that trio, was under investigation for taking bribes on a contract with a Finnish company. That case is especially notable because a recent survey by Transparency Internatonal rated Finland as the least corrupt nation in the world.[46]

The Victimology of Bribery

It has been said that white-collar offenders such as those who engage in bribery transactions are much like juvenile delinquents in regard to how they maintain a self-image of decency, employing "techniques of neutralization"[47] to justify their wrongdoing.[48] Prominent among such techniques is a "denial of victim" which rests on the defensive belief that nobody really was hurt by the episode, a claim that commonly can be supported by the fact that "material injury that bribers and bribees inflict is often undemonstrable."[49] But it can be said regarding bribery of public officials that the government is victimized because its authority is compromised. The public itself may also be enumerated among the victims of bribery because of the violation of the "common good" that officials are supposed to protect.[50] Such injuries, however, are rarely tangible, and unless gross or very well publicized may prove to be of little public concern. On a more concrete level, bribes add to the cost of products in order to compensate the person giving the bribe for his or her financial outlay.

Competitors of the briber also suffer because they are denied the preferential treatment given to the person who had paid the price for that advantage. And they may try to do something in their defense, as in the case of *W.S. Kirkpatrick & Co. v. Environmental Tectonic Corp.* which in 1990 ended up before the United States Supreme Court. The chairman and chief executive of Kirkpatrick had bid about $7 million to build an aeromedical facility at the air force base in Karduna, Nigeria. He was referred to a middleman who said that he could secure the contract but would require a 20 percent "commission" to do so. The bribe money could be added to the bid, and on payment would be deposited to accounts of the intermediary in two Panama banks, and thereafter distributed to a number of Nigerian government officials and agencies. All told, Kirkpatrick received $10 million for its work and deposited $3 million in the Panama accounts.

Environmental Tectonics had submitted a significantly lower bid than Kirkpatrick for the work and when it did not receive the contract it complained of fraud to Nigerian officials and to the American Embassy in Nigeria, which referred the case to the FBI. Ultimately, there were grand jury indictments for violations of the Foreign Corrupt Practices Act, followed by guilty pleas on the part of the (former) Kirkpatrick chief executive and the company itself. The judge fined the company's onetime leader $10 million and ordered that he perform 200 hours of community service. The company itself suffered a $750,000 fine to be paid over five years.[51] By all accounts, the Nigerian government took no action against any participant in the scheme, though the country since 1975 has had a law against giving or accepting bribes. For a time before that, and at times now, Nigeria has been regarded as the most corrupt nation in the world, run by people dubbed "kleptocrats."

The *Kirkpatrick* case involved complicated jurisprudential issues. The defendant company argued that a legal doctrine known as the Act of State, which has roots going back to common law and early American law, precluded such a legal action because it might jeopardize relations between the United States and a sovereign country.[52] Kirkpatrick had prevailed in the trial court, but lost in the federal appeals court before it won in the Supreme Court.

One basis for the Environmental Tectonic action, besides it having been unfairly left out in the cold, is that when some of the leading companies in the United States show dazzling earnings from cooking their books or other illegal tactics, executives in businesses in the same corporate sector who have been operating honestly came under fire for their failure to match the reported profits of the law-breakers. Smaller companies also are likely to find themselves at a disadvantage because they do not have the financial wherewithal to compete in the bribery market with the giants.

Finally, victimization from bribery can produce very ominous consequences that involve national security. There have been a number of cases of consular officers who received bribes from terrorist-intent foreigners that led them to issue visas to them.

Some tentative evidence appears to support the view expressed by Sutherland that we noted at the outset of this chapter, at least for run-of-the-mill bribery cases. Businesspersons, it seems, typically escape with a figurative slap on the wrist, while those who pocket the bribe are dealt with more harshly. One likely consideration is the public and criminal justice appraisal of the different levels of evil shown by the participants in the business of bribery. In a recent study, respondents were asked which they regarded as more serious: a public official accepting a bribe or a private citizen giving a bribe to such an official. Seventy-four percent said that they saw the first as more serious; only 12 percent regarded the giving of the bribe as worse, with 14 percent maintaining that they were equally serious.[53]

Corporate officials can claim, with at least some semblance of truth, that they were primarily seeing to the interests of their employer. They can also claim that their action was impelled by equivalent actions by their competitors. What they did, they can argue, was done out of a sense of loyalty to their company: jurors value loyalty. It may be somewhat obvious that finalizing a lucrative deal will produce dividends for the individual as well as the company in terms of salary, a bonus, and promotion, but that is not likely to be demonstrable in a court trial.

It is also important to appreciate that business executives are not sitting ducks for federal prosecutors and district attorneys. Their employer typically will foot the considerable legal bill accused executives incur, and probably will indemnify them if they're found guilty and fined, a situation that one writer believes "encourages criminal conduct by employees.[54] The defense attorneys hired will likely be former staff members in the U.S. Attorney's office. They are almost invariably very competent and can be ruthless.[55]

Different conditions prevail in regard to the government officials and politicians as takers of bribes. For one thing, there probably is some agreement that it is more malevolent to solicit, demand, or accept a bribe than to offer one. In one of the few research forays into this subject, a student-based questionnaire found that a hypothetical United States Senator was held by respondents to be more "responsible" for work-related bribery—in this case taking a $1,000 payment from a lobbyist to withhold information during a committee hearing—than for accepting the same sum from a neighbor who was being sought by the police and had asked that his whereabouts not be divulged. The study's authors were well aware of the failure of their probe to convey more than a barebones vignette and note that the conclusion should be taken with caution—as well it should.[56]

Other considerations also come into play in cases involving businesspersons and public officials caught in a bribery situation. For one thing, enforcement agents and prosecutors are themselves part of the government apparatus: they understand it better than they understand the structure and ethos of business and therefore are better able to deal with offenders who operate in the same realm that they inhabit. The paper trail, so crucial in bribery prosecutions, is very likely to be more accessible in the political arena than in the business world. In addition, there generally is greater publicity to be obtained by going after a government official, particularly a prominent one, than in proceedings against a less publicly known corporate figure. Prosecutors (and their agencies) depend on public notice, though they may run the risk if they become too aggressive of alienating members of the legislature or others who control their purse strings. Finally, more than any other persons in public life in the United States, it is prosecutors who typically aim for higher office, for judgeships, attorney general posts, or Congressional seats. Name recognition is an important asset in such a quest.

Empirical Inquiries

Criminological research regarding bribery is entangled in the revisionist debate that currently characterizes the field of white-collar crime scholarship in general. Sutherland's definition, focusing on the status of the offender, held sway for decades until a group of scholars housed at the Yale Law School decided that the best research approach lay in a definition based on legal categories. They designated eight offenses, including bribery, as the realm of white-collar crime. This approach resulted in a sample in which less than thirty percent matched Sutherland's definition. Many of the offenders they studied were unemployed, including almost a third of the women,[57] and a considerable portion had committed what reasonably could be regarded as petty offenses, such as passing small-amount checks with insufficient funds to back them up.

Eighty-four of the 1,094 persons in the Yale sample had been charged with bribery. In most instances, the person arrested had offered the bribe and in four of ten instances it was not taken. Most cases involved attempts to have rules waived or ignored. In ten of the cases, bribes were offered to a certified public accountant or to an IRS agent. The study concluded that there was a greater diversity—that is, a lack of homogeneous scenarios—in bribe offenses than in any of the other white-collar categories. Among the jobs held by those taking of offering bribes were health administrator, bill collector, hairdresser, truck driver, and professional athlete.[58]

A much earlier survey sponsored by the President's Commission on Law Enforcement and Administration of Justice provides some teasing information on bribery that was derived from the country's pioneering victimization study. Persons were asked to respond to the following question: "Within the past 12 months, have you or anyone in your household had to pay money to a public officer, such as a policeman or inspector, or some official like that, so that he would not make trouble for you, even though you had not done anything wrong?" The affirmative response rate was 9.1 per 100,000 persons and it was supposed that the results represented considerable underreporting because "there is an aura of victim involvement in these situations and this will tend to diminish forthrightness in the interview."[59] Multiplied out this response indicates that bribery has a considerable place in American culture.

Public Integrity Section Data

To flesh out our examination of bribery and extortion we can offer information regarding such activity in the United States that appears in the five volumes of annual reports (covering 1999 to 2003) to the Congress by the Public Integrity Section (PIS) of the U.S. Department of Justice. The Public Integrity Section was established pursuant to the Ethics in Government Act of 1978. It focuses on offenses involving abuses of the public trust by government officers, including acts of bribery and extortion. The Section possesses a considerable degree of discretion in regard to those events to which it will attend. It is noted, "Decisions to undertake particular matters are made on a case-by-case basis, based on Section resources, the type and seriousness of the allegation, the sufficiency of factual predication reflecting criminal conduct and the availability of federal prosecutive theories to reach the conduct."[60] Its caseload primarily represents four categories:

1. Recusals by U.S. Attorneys' Offices. Typically, these cases involve a substantial conflict of interest between the local U.S. prosecutor's office and the accused. In particular, cases involving the judiciary commonly are referred to the Public Integrity Section.
2. Sensitive cases that arrive at the PIS often involve classified information requiring coordination with intelligence agencies or they may concern issues that could be explosive if aired at a local level.
3. Multi-district cases involve allegations of wrongdoing by public officials that fall under the jurisdiction of more than one U.S. Attorneys' office.
4. Federal agencies may refer cases to the PIS that involve their own personnel.
5. The section also becomes involved in cases that are shared with other governmental agencies or a U.S. Attorney's office. This may occur when the cooperating office lacks the resources to take the case on alone.

The caseload at PIS can be categorized generally as involving the federal judicial, legislative, and executive branches, state and local governments, and election crimes. Obviously, the discretion that marks the section's involvement in particular cases does not result in a sample of bribery cases that represents more than those that come to someone's attention and which the PIS decides to pursue, either on the basis of its regulations and, perhaps, whim, and on the ingredients of the cases. That these criteria may shift from year to year is, of course, self-evident. What we have then is a nonrandom sample of bribery episodes that seem to be somewhat serious occurrences and that offer us an opportunity to examine their characteristics.

All told, 61 of the 93 cases included in the PIS reports involved clear instances of bribery or extortion involving public officials., though the episodes were variously described as payoffs, kickbacks, solicitations, cash payments, and even as gratuities. U.S. Attorney's offices in different locations obviously use variant terminology to label bribery and extortion cases. We can look at the

2003 PIS report to Congress, the most recent one available, to obtain a sense of what the Section handles. Very few of the cases involved the federal judiciary branch of government. One involved allegations of the theft of $1.4 million of government funds from the AIDs Institute in San Juan, Puerto Rico to bribe public officials in connection with a grand jury investigation. Most involved federal employees holding positions that allow them to make contracting or purchasing decisions. Mostly, the offenders received bribes from vendors but on occasion they themselves initiated contacts by soliciting payments to induce purchasing decisions. The items involved office supplies, promotional materials, and included stationery for the 2000 census. A typical case that appears in the 2003 report is that of James W. Brown, Jr., who had pled guilty to one count of bribery:

> Brown, who worked as a general supply specialist at the United States Department of Energy (DOE), was responsible for awarding contracts for cleaning carpets at various DOE facilities. For contracts worth less that $25,000, Brown was authorized to select the most qualified bidder and to issue payments on a government-issued purchase card. Between late 1996 and early 1998, a carpet cleaning contractor paid Brown cash in exchange for being awarded various carpet cleaning contracts. On at least one occasion, Brown provided the carpet cleaning contractor a copy of the price list of a competitor, so that the contractor could place the lowest bid.
>
> On June 5, 2003, Brown was sentenced to one year of incarceration, split between six months in jail and six months of home detention with electronic monitoring, and a $5,000 fine. In sentencing defendant Brown, the Court found that the defendant accepted bribes on multiple occasions, and that the amount of the bribe was between $5,000 and $10,000.[61]

This case, and many of similar ilk, convey, perhaps a bit subtly, that the courts may not be overly exercised regarding such petty bribery incidents. Brown suffered time in jail and constraint at home, and presumably lost at least a year's salary and very likely reduced job opportunities in the future. There also was the shame that goes with a criminal conviction. But from a financial viewpoint, how many were the "multiple occasions" on which Brown collected between $5,000 and $10,000? If there were 50 such transactions (although we do not learn this from the report), Brown's take would have been $375,000, at least arguably demonstrating a satisfactory cost–benefit ratio for the illegal behavior.

A number of the 2003 PIS cases were concerned with attempts to obtain visas to enter the United States. In one such scheme, an employee of the Department of Agriculture whose duties included the invitation of Chinese agricultural experts for meetings with USDA officials conspired to obtain visas for non-eligible individuals who offered to pay about $10,000 each to be invited, perhaps with the intention of defecting. The American official and his wife took in $82,000 from these deals.

In another instance, the Deputy Consul General in Prague processed visas for a fee that he personally appropriated. In two years, he arranged for at least 85 visas and received bribes totaling at least $50,000. He was sentenced to a two-year prison term.

A noteworthy case involving the bribing of four Mississippi judges, one of them sitting on the state Supreme Court, who were paid off by a personal injury lawyer. In return, the attorney won cases tried before these judges, including one that had a multi-million-dollar award.

Besides, there were 11 cases based on vote-buying in the May 1998 primary election for the County Judge Executive position in Knox County, Kentucky. Ten cases involved buying votes for the eventual winner; one for purchasing votes for the loser. What is not stated in these cases is the implication that the money expended will, if the briber is successful, provide an opportunity to recoup the amounts of the bribes, and probably to do so in an illegal manner.

Conclusion

Enforcement of the laws against bribery is almost exclusively a reactive enterprise. Typically, a lead is brought to the attention of government officials; they investigate it and if the results and other considerations appear to warrant it they go forward toward a prosecution or settlement. It is a process that is rather haphazard, neither especially efficient nor effective. It forces researchers to try to generate independent data that will be responsive to sophisticated research questions. The record shows that such an effort is rarely productive and, as the present chapter has, reliance ultimately has to be placed on case studies, anecdotal evidence, and consideration of the scattered aggregate evidence that might be available.

Discussions of bribery therefore almost invariably stick rather closely to details of a case or a panoply of cases. They identify the cast of characters, the scenes and the acts, and spell out the denouement. Little is said about the "dark figure"—the bribery cases that do not come to light. We do not know whether the participants or the modi operandi in those undiscovered plots differ in a significant manner from those that come to light. This is, of course, characteristic of almost all crimes. There are formidable difficulties involved in relying on data supplied by enforcement agencies.[62] Among other things, agency enforcement priorities can vary from year-to-year and often more dramatically from administration to administration. Enforcement agencies always have to decide whether to accumulate a large number of convictions against small-time easier targets or whether to expend a large amount of limited resources to go after a major malefactor.

These are among the tasks necessary to enhance our understanding of bribery and extortion:

1. It is necessary to construct a taxonomy of the offenses that identifies distinctive forms and subgroups of the behaviors.
2. There is a pressing need for comprehensive case studies that will provide information to flesh out our understanding of the nature and the dynamics of various forms of bribery and extortion and the persons who engage in them. These almost invariably must be post hoc: Vaughan's investigation of the elements of the *Challenger* disaster, which was blessed with comprehensive source material that the author doggedly examined and evaluated, provides an outstanding exemplar of how such work might be done and the insights it can yield.[63]
3. Interviews with persons who have been involved in bribery arrangements need to be conducted, and information gathered about their understanding of what went on. Absent such access, it could be profitable to talk with

present or retired businesspersons and to ask them not about what they had done but about what others of their colleagues might have done in the line of bribery and extortion.

4. Once a useful core of information has been gathered it becomes essential to try to make theoretical sense out of what has been learned. Existing theoretical constructs need to be brought to bear on bribery and extortion and new postulates formulated where current theories prove inadequate. It is likely that no overarching theory will adequately explain bribery and extortion but that crime-specific formulations will be necessary to account for their ingredients and perpetrators.

Endnotes

1. Sutherland, 1940, p. 2.
2. Flynn, 1931, p. 55.
3. Lippmann, 1961, p. 30.
4. Gaynor, 1910, p. 666; Weinstein, 1968; see also McCormick, 1981.
5. Sutherland, 1940, p. 7.
6. Sutherland, 1949, p. 239.
7. Becker, 1968.
8. For an extensive bibliography see Friedrichs, 2004.
9. See, e,g., Braithwaite, 1981–1982; Makkai and Braithwate, 1993.
10. Noonan, Jr., and Kahan, 2002, p. 110a.
11. Geis, 1991.
12. Coleman, 1998.
13. de Bracton, 1968.
14. Geis and Bunn, 1997.
15. Smith, 1937, pp. 703–704.
16. Carswell, 1960l Erleigh, 1933; Mackay, 1869.
17. Green, 2003, p. 5.
18. Noonan, 1984, p. 57.
19. Phillips, 1984, p. 629.
20. Rawls, 1971.
21. See, e.g., Annechiarico and Jacobs, 1006/
22. Von Alemann, 2004.
23. Weber, 1996, pp. 330–331.
24. Rose-Ackerman, 2002.
25. Geis and DiMento, 2002.
26. Lindgren, 1988, p. 816.
27. Lindgren, 1986, p. 825.
28. *United States v. Hilton Hotel Cort.*, 467 F.2d 1000, 1004 (9th Cir., 1972), cert. denied, 409 U.S. 1125 (1973).
29. Brooks, 1910, p. 45.
30. Heidenheimer, 1970.
31. Cloward and Ohlin, 1960.
32. Rubinstein, 1973.
33. Smith, 2000, p. 150.
34. Drake and Cayton, 1945, p. 474.
35. Boulton, 1978; Hunt, 1983.
36. Hunziker and Kamimura, 1994, p. 117.
37. United States Congress, House of Representatives, 2002.
38. Tillman, 1998.

39. Noonan, 1984; Rose-Ackerman, 1999.
40. Clinard and Yeager, 1980, p. 171.
41. Roebuck and Weeber, 1978; Shichor, 2004.
42. Boulton, 1978
43. Finney, 2005.
44. Buscaglia and van Dijk, 2003, p. 15.
45. Rosenberg, 2002.
46. Transparency International, 2004.
47. Sykes and Matza, 1957
48. Benson, 1985.
49. Noonan, 1984, p. xxiii.
50. Shichor, 1989,
51. *W. S. Kirkpatrick v. Environmental Tectonics Corp.*, 499 U.S. 400 (1990).
52. Bazyler, 1986.
53. Rebovich, et al., 2000.
54. Bucy. 1991, p. 1140.
55. Mann, 1985.
56. Riordan, Marley, and Kellogg, 1983.
57. Daly, 1989
58. Weisburd, et al., 1991, p. 57.
59. Enis, 1967, p. 10.
60. U.S. Department of Justice, 2000, p. 1.
61. Ibid., 2003, p. 15.
62. Biderman and Reiss, 1980.
63. Vaughan, 1996.

References

Anechiarico, Frank, and James B. Jacobs (1996) *The Pursuit of Absolute Integrity: How Corruption Control Makes Government Ineffective.* Chicago: University of Chicago Press.

Bazyler, Michael J. (1986) "Abolishing the Act of State Doctrine." *University of Pennsylvania Law Review,* 134:325–398.

Becker, Gary (1968) "Crime and Punishment: An Economic Approach." *Journal of Political Economy* 76:169–217.

Benson, Michael L. (1985) "Denying the Guilty Mind: Accounting for Involvement in White-Collar Crime." *Criminology* 21:583–608.

Boulton, David (1978) *Lockheed Papers.* London: Jonathan Cape.

Biderman, Albert, and Albert J. Reiss, Jr. (1989) *Data Sources on White-Collar Law-Breaking.* Washington, D.C.: U.S. Government Printing Office.

Bracton, Henry de (1968) *On the Laws and Customs of England.* Cambridge, MA: Harvard University Press.

Braithwaite, John (1981–1982) "The Limits of Economism in Controlling Harmful Corporate Conduct." *International Journal of Sociology of Law* 7:125–142.

Brooks, Robert C. (1910) *Corruption in American Politics and Life.* New York: Dodd, Mead.

Bucy, Pamela H. (1991) "Corporate Ethos: A Standard for Imposing Corporate Criminal Liability." *Minnesota Law Review* 75:1095–1184.

Buscaglia, Edgardo, and Jan Van Dijk. (2003) "Controlling Organized Crime and Corruption in the Public Sector." *Forum on Crime and Society* 3 (1,2):3–34.

Carswell, John (1960) *The South Sea Bubble.* Stanford, CA: Stanford University Press.

Clinard, Marshall B., and Peter C. Yeager (1980) *Corporate Crime.* New York: Free Press.

Cloward, Richard, and Lloyd Ohlin (1960) *Delinquency and Opportunity.* New York: Free Press.

Coleman, James W. (1998). *The Criminal Elite: Understanding White-Collar Crime* (4th ed.). New York: St. Martin's Press.

Daly, Kathleen (1989) "Gender and Varieties of White-Collar Crime." *Criminology* 27:769–793.

Drake, St. Clair, and Horace Cayton. (1945) *Black Metropolis: A Study of Negro Life in a Northern City.* New York: Harcourt, Bace.

Ennis, Philip H. (1967) *Criminal Victimization in the United States: A Report of a National Survey.* Washington, D.C.: U.S. Government Printing Office.

Erleigh, Gerard R. (1933) *The South Sea Bubble.* New York: Putnam's.

Finney, Paul Burnham (2005) "Shaking Hands, Greasing Palms." *The New York Times*, May 17:C8.

Flynn, John T. (1931) *Graft in Business.* New York: Vantage Press.

Friedrichs, David O. (2004) *Trusted Criminals: White Collar Crime in Contemporary Society* (2nd ed.). Belmont, CA: Thomson/Wadsworth.

Gaynor, William J. (1910) "The Problem of Efficient City Government." *Century* 80:663–670.

Geis, Gilbert (1991) "The Case Study Method in Sociological Criminology." Pp. 200–223 in *A Case for the Case Study, Editors* Joe R. Feagin, Anthony M. Orum, and Gideon Sjoberg. Chapel Hill: University of North Carolina Press.

Geis, Gilbert, and Ivan Bunn (1997) *A Trial of Witches: A Seventeenth-Century Witchcraft Prosecution.* London: Routledge.

Geis, Gilbert, and Joseph F. C. DiMento (2002) "Empirical Evidence and the Legal Doctrine of Corporate Criminal Liability." *American Journal of Criminal Law* 29:341–375.

Green, Stuart (2003) "What is Wrong with Bribery?" In *Defining Crimes: Essays on the Special Part of the Criminal Law, Editors* R. A. Duff and Stuart P. Green Oxford: Oxford University Press.

Heidenheimer, Arnold J. (ed.). (1970) *Political Corruption: Readings in Comparative Analysis.* New York; Holt, Rinehart, Winston.

Hunt, G. Cameron (1983) *The Tanaka Decision: Tanaka Kakuei and the Lockheed Scandal.* Hanover, NH: Universities Field Staff International.

Hunziker, Steven, and Ikuro Kammura (1994) *Kakuei Tanaka: A Political Biography.* Los Gatos, CA: Daruma International.

Lindgren, James (1988) "The Elusive Distinction between Bribery and Extortion." *UCLA Law Review* 35:815–909.

Lippman, Walter (1961) *Drift and Mystery: An Attempt to Diagnose the Current Unrest.* Englewood Cliffs, NJ: Prentice Hall.

Mackay, Charles (1869) "The South Sea Bubble." In *Memoirs of Extraordinary Popular Delusions and Madness of Crowds.* 45–84. London: George Routledge.

Makkai, Toni, and John Braithwaite (1993) "The Limits of Economic Analysis of Legislation." *Law and Policy* 15:271–291.

McCormick, Richard L. (1981) "The Discovery that Business Corrupts Politics: A Reappraisal of the Origins of Progressivism." *American Historical Review 86*" 247–274.

Mann, Kenneth (1985) *Defending White-Collar Crime: A Portrait of Attorneys at Work.* New Haven, CT: Yale University Press.

Noonan, John T., Jr. (1984) *Bribes.* Berkeley: University of California Press.

Noonan, John T., Jr., and Dan M. Kahan (2002) "Bribery." Pp. 105–111 in *Encyclopedia of Crime & Justice* (2nd ed.), Editor Joshua Dressler. New York: Macmillan Reference.

Phillips, Michael J. (1984) "Bribery." *Ethics* 94:621–636.

Rawls, John (1971) *A Theory of Justice.* Cambridge, MA: Harvard University Press.

Rebovich, Donald J., Jenny Layne, Jason Jiandani, and Scott Hage (2000) *The National Public Survey of White Collar Crime.* Morgantown, WV: National White Collar Crime Center.

Riordan, Catherine A., Nancy A. Marlin, and Ronald T. Kellogg (1983) "The Effectiveness of Accounts Following Transgression." *Social Psychology Quarterly* 46:213–219.

Roebuck, Julian, and Stanley C. Weeber (1978) *Political Crime in the United States: Analyzing Crime by and Against Government.* New York: Praeger.

Rose-Aclerman, Susan (1999) *Corruption and Government: Causes, Consequences, and Reforms.* New York: Cambridge University Press.

Rose-Ackerman, Susan (2002) ("Corruption and the Criminal Law." *Forum on Crime and Society* 2:3–22.

Rosenberg, Tina (2003) "The Taint of the Greased Palm." *The New York Times* (August 10):section 6:28.

Rubinstein, Jonathan (1973) *City Police.* New York: Farrar, Straus, Giroux.

Shichor, David (1989) "Corporate Deviance and Corporate Victimization: A Review and Some Elaborations." *International Review of Victimology* 1:67–88.

Shichor, David (2004) "The Foreign Corrupt Practices Act." Pp. 329–330 in *The Encyclopedia of White Collar Crime, Editor* Lawrence M. Salinger. Thousand Oaks, CA: Sage.

Smith, Adam (1937) *An Inquiry into the Nature and Causes of the Wealth of Nations.* New York: Modern Library.

Smith, Liz (2000) *Natural Blonde: A Memoir.* New York: Hyperion.

Sutherland, Edwin H. (1940) "White Collar Criminality." *American Sociological Review* 5:1–12.

Sutherland, Edwin H. (1949) *White Collar Crime.* New York: Dryden.

Sykes, Gresham M., and David Matza (1957) "Techniques of Neutralization: A Theory of Delinquency." *American Sociological Review* 22:644–670.

Temporary International Corruption Perception Index. 2004. http://www.transparency.org/cpi/2003.en.html.

Tillman, Robert (1998) *Broken Promises: Fraud by Small Business Health Insurers.* Boston: Northeastern University Press.

United States Congress, House of Representatives, Committee on Standards of Official Conduct. *In the Matter of Representative James A. Trafficant, Jr.* 107th Con., 2nd Sess.

United States Department of Justice, Public Integrity Section. (2000) *Report to Congress.*

United States Department of Justice, Public Integrity Section. (2003) *Report to Congress.*

Von Alemann, Ulrich (2004) "The Unknown Depths of Political Theory: The Case for a Multidimensional Concept of Corruption." *Crime, Law and Social Change* 42:25–34.

Vaughan, Diane (1996) *The Challenger Launch Decision: Risky Technology, Culture, and Deviance at NASA.* Chicago: University of Chicago Press.

Weber, Max (1966) *The Theory of Social and Economic Organization.* A. Henderson and Talcott Parsons, trans. New York: Free Press.

Weinstein, James (1968) *The Corporate Ideal in the Liberal State, 1900–1918.* Boston: Beacon Press.

Weisburd, Daivd, Stanton Wheeler, Elin Waring, and Nancy Bode (1991) *Crimes of the Middle Class: White Collar Offenders in the Federal Courts.* New Haven, CT: Yale University Press.

3

Crimes by Lawyers in Japan and the Responsibilities of Professionals

Shin Matsuzawa and Tokikazu Konishi

In Japan, as well as in other countries, professional occupational crimes, including crimes by lawyers, occur frequently and draw keen social attention. By the term *professional occupational crime*, we mean crime that is committed through the use of professional status—especially a status which is certified by the government or a public authority. Such offenses include those committed by a certified public accountant, a chartered patent agent, a certified tax accountant, a lawyer, a doctor, or a professor. These acts can have serious effects on society and the economy as a whole. Among other things, crimes by lawyers may cause significant economic damage and produce not only a dislike of the legal profession but also distrust of the entire justice system.

Crimes by lawyers in Japan have not been researched criminologically, nor has the responsibility of professionals been analyzed jurisprudentially. It is necessary to study them from a scientific standpoint, since such occupational crimes have a significant effect on Japanese society.

First, from the perspective of criminal policy and criminology, we'll discuss the nature and characteristics of crimes by lawyers in Japan and the penal and autonomous sanctions against such offenses. In the course of this discussion, we'll present several recent cases of crimes by attorneys and will discuss the current disciplinary system for such misconduct by lawyers. Second, we'll analyze the responsibility of professionals from the perspective of criminal law.

Crimes by Lawyers and Formal Sanctions

Characteristics of Legal Services in Japan

Before discussing the characteristics of crimes by lawyers, we'll briefly point out the characteristics of the services of lawyers.

In Japan, the three elements of the judicial community—the judge, the prosecutor, and the lawyer (in this paper, we use the term *lawyer* to mean a private-practice attorney)—are separated almost entirely professionally. That is, they don't form a single unified legal profession. Although all successful applicants from the bar exam enter the national legal training center where the legal profession is nurtured, after graduating, they can take up any of the legal professions, as a judge, prosecutor, or lawyer. Each of the three elements of the judicial community has a very different occupational culture. They have been known to be antagonistic in regard to policy-making. However, after resigning as a judge or a prosecutor, legal practitioners often register at bar associations as lawyers.

The services of a lawyer are comprehensive. They include the services of a chartered patent agent and a certified tax accountant. Moreover, a lawyer can act as a judicial and administrative scrivener. Thus far, lawyers have exclusively practiced in broad "general legal affairs."[1] The unauthorized practice of law is strictly prohibited.[2]

Also, as a characteristic of the services of lawyers in Japan, a lawyer is always required to "strive for the maintenance of a high degree of sophistication and the cultivation of a sterling character."[3] Thus, even if a lawyer engages in misconduct unrelated to his or her professional practice, he/she can be disciplined by a bar association.

Crimes by Lawyers

In this paper, we define *crime by a lawyer* as an offense which is committed through the use of the professional status of being a lawyer. Crime by a lawyer would not include, for example, groping, illegal gambling, or drunk driving. Lawyers who commit these crimes may be reprehensible in terms of legal ethics, and can be disciplined. But since these aren't committed as part of their occupational role, we don't consider these acts to be *crimes by lawyers.*

So what acts can we classify as *crime by a lawyer?* Three major categories of such offenses include *fraud against clients*, *cooperating and collaborating with a client's offenses,* and *crimes based on Lawyers Law*.

Fraud against clients typically entails embezzlement in the course of business dealings. Generally, lawyers often know a client's financial condition inside and out and may administer a client's property. Such duties give lawyers the opportunity to commit crimes of this type.[4] One recent case involved a former president of the bar association who was sentenced to ten years of imprisonment with forced labor. Though sentencing of white-collar criminals is generally regarded to be lenient in Japan; it seems that in this case the defendant was punished relatively harshly. He had been accused of embezzlement in the course of business. About ten years ago, the court had appointed him as an administrator in the bankruptcy of several companies, and, as such, he had control of the property of the bankrupt companies. During this time, he siphoned off money from these companies. Without the court's permission, he had withdrawn the companies' deposits and used the money for gambling in South Korea, erecting a new home, and taking up with a Korean girlfriend, among other activities. He managed to spend more than 150 million yen on entertainment and the payment of his debts. Compared with similar cases in the past, this was unprecedented in terms of the amount of money involved.

Second, we can cite cooperating and collaborating with a client's offenses as another category of *crime by a lawyer*. It is exemplified in the crimes of documentary forgery and the instigation of perjury. Since lawyers act on the client's behalf, and endeavor to tip the scales in favor of their client, they can easily cross legal boundaries in the interest of their client, and aid and abet their offenses.[5]

In Japan, it is no secret that criminal organizations (criminal syndicates and cults that engage in unlawful activities) and companies that pursue fraudulent business, such as Ponzi schemes, have had their own lawyers. Attorneys have counseled such organizations and advanced their activities. Even if these lawyers haven't been charged with any crimes, they often have been disciplined by the bar.

Third, crime based on "Lawyers Law" forms the last category of *crime by lawyers*. Lawyers Law prescribes several acts relating to a lawyer's practice as crimes. Lawyer's "bribery,"[6] lawyer's "practicing together with persons who are non-lawyers,"[7] and lawyer's "obtaining any right in dispute"[8] are included here.

Lawyer's "acting together with persons who are non-lawyers" has drawn attention as a serious social problem in Japan. Some lawyers collude with *syoukai-ya,* who charge heavily indebted people high referral fees in exchange for obtaining a consumer loan for them, and *seiri-ya,* who charge heavily indebted people high fees in exchange for adjusting multiple debts, and reap a considerable reward. This form of crime typically constitutes two types of acts: *procurement* and *name lending*. In some cases, for example, the *syoukai-ya* or *seiri-ya* introduces the colluding lawyer to heavy debtors to adjust their loans. This falls under procurement. In name lending, there are three known patterns.[9] In some cases, the *seiri-ya* adjusts multiple debts in the law office of the colluding lawyer. In other cases, colluding lawyers work at the *seiri-ya's* office, or the new office that *seiri-ya* sets up. It is not uncommon for lawyers who have received some disciplinary action, or who can't fully practice because of advanced age or illness, to be invited by *syoukai-ya* or *seiri-ya* to collude with them in financial crimes.[10]

To date, few researchers in Japan have empirically studied which factors generate crimes by lawyers. In recent years, the Japanese judicial system has been dramatically reformed. For the first time in history, law schools have been established as the institutions where legal professionals are trained. Additionally, the lay judge system has been created and will be inaugurated in May 2009. Moreover, it is expected that, as a sequel to the establishment of law schools and an increase in persons passing the bar exam, the number of lawyers will increase considerably. On the other hand, in 2002, as part of the reform of the judicial system, as well as deregulation, judicial scriveners were authorized to act as counsel at summary courts. These changes regarding the profession will affect opportunities to commit crime in the course of legal practice. It is necessary to conduct more empirical research to determine exactly how these transformations are related to criminal activities engaged in by lawyers.

Formal Sanctions for Crime and Misconduct by Lawyers

Punishment and disciplinary actions constitute the two formal sanctions in Japan for crime and misconduct by lawyers. If a lawyer commits any of the above-mentioned crimes, a punitive sanction can be imposed on him/her. Moreover, in examining cases of crimes by lawyers, there appears to be more severe culpability in criminal trials involving lawyers than in proceedings entailing similar offenses by non-lawyers. This is difficult to prove, however, since there are no readily available official or unofficial statistical data on the subject.

Besides criminal punishment as a formal sanction, there is disciplinary action by the bar association. This constitutes an administrative disposition. Through such actions, bar associations and the Japan Federation of Bar Associations foster the discipline of lawyers autonomously without State intervention.[11] Since a lawyer is obliged to join a bar association, action by these organizations has major significance for lawyers. Such disciplinary action is expected to have a deterrent effect.

The disciplinary system is designed to function in the following manner. When a lawyer (1) infringes upon Lawyers Law; (2) violates rules of the bar association that he/she belongs to, or those of the Japan Federation of Bar Associations; (3) negatively impacts the order or confidence of the bar association; or (4) commits other misconduct with or without reference to the profession, he/she can be disciplined by the bar association or, in some instances, the Japan Federation of Bar Associations.[12] These causes for disciplinary action don't necessarily mean that criminal punishment will follow.

The disciplinary procedure begins with a claim for action against a certain lawyer. After acceptance of the claim, the bar association's discipline maintenance committee investigates to determine whether it is appropriate that its disciplinary actions committee inquire further into the claim. If the former committee considers it appropriate that the latter does so, the bar association then requires a formal investigation to take place. The findings of the investigation determine whether disciplinary action should be imposed. When those who make claims for disciplinary actions are dissatisfied with the judgment of the bar association, they can file an appeal with the Japan Federation of Bar Associations.

Lawyers Law provides that the disciplinary action can be composed of four types of actions: reprimand, suspension from the practice of law for not more than two years, an order to withdraw from the bar association that the lawyer belongs to, and disbarment[13]. However, since the lawyer who withdraws from a bar association due to the disciplinary action usually will not be taken in by other bar associations, the order to withdraw from the bar association and disbarment perform similar, if not identical functions.

It is useful to compare this disciplinary system with the one employed in the United States. Unlike the role of the American Bar Association, the bar association in Japan plays a vital role in internal control. In practice, though, most of the cases involving the violation of rules of the bar association that the lawyer belongs to regard payment defaults of bar association dues. And, as is stated in Lawyers Law, it is provided that misconduct not related to professional practice can lead to disciplinary action. So, unlike the American disciplinary system, the causes for disciplinary action aren't limited to the transgression of professional ethics.[14] The American disciplinary system, however, has more types of disciplinary sanctions, including admonition and probation.

Finally, available statistical data show how the Japanese disciplinary system has actually operated. Examining the number of claims for disciplinary action in all bar associations from 1988 to 2004, it is clear that there has been a significant increase over time (Figure 1). Similarly, the number of disciplinary actions, as a whole, has been increasing since about 1980 (Figure 2). In particular, the number has increased sharply in recent years. Calculating the ratio of the number of disciplinary actions to the number of demands for disciplinary action from 1988 on, it turns out that it hovers around 6 percent (Figure 3).

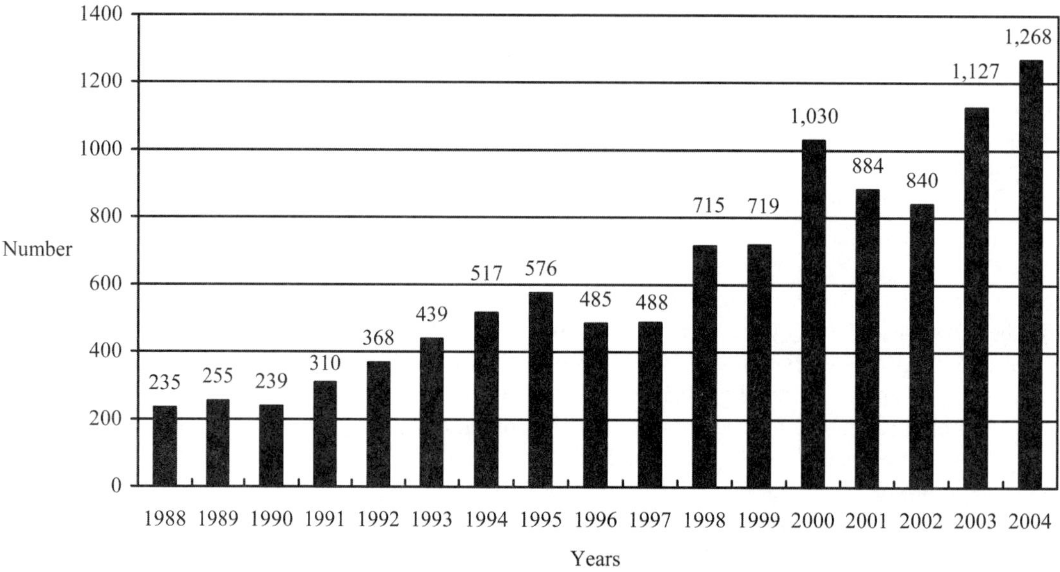

Figure 1. Number of Claims for Disciplinary Action, 1988–2004

When a lawyer is convicted, the public prosecutors office informs the bar association. However, there are no data on how many convicted lawyers are further disciplined by the bar association, nor how many disciplined lawyers are subjected to further criminal sanctions. Thus, we cannot currently explain the relationship between the application of disciplinary action and criminal punishment. Considering the latent contradiction between the guarantee of relative freedom in legal practice, and the social obligation to protect individuals from crime and misconduct by lawyers, it is necessary to refine both the disciplinary and criminal justice systems in order to affect better control of these offenses.

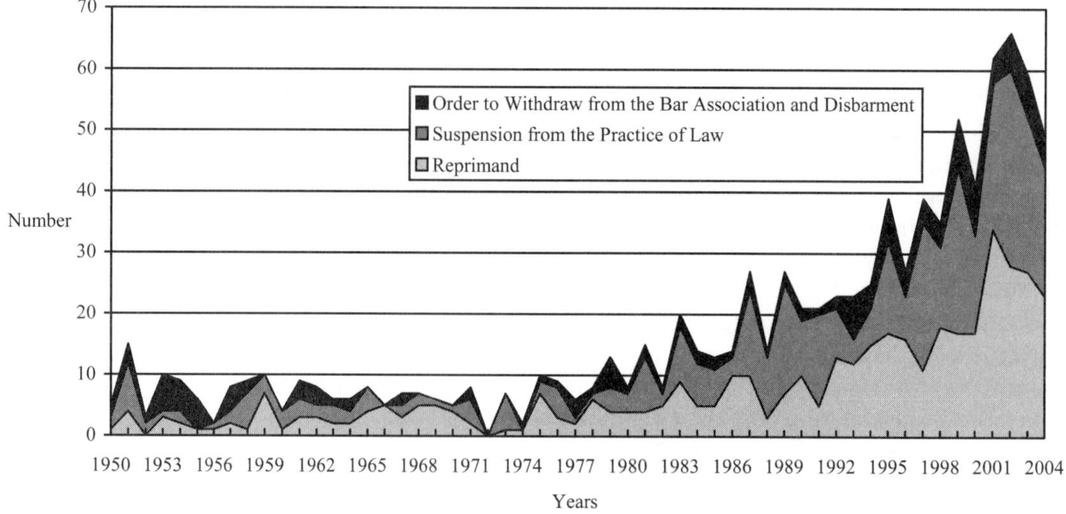

Figure 2. Number of Disciplinary Actions, 1950–2004

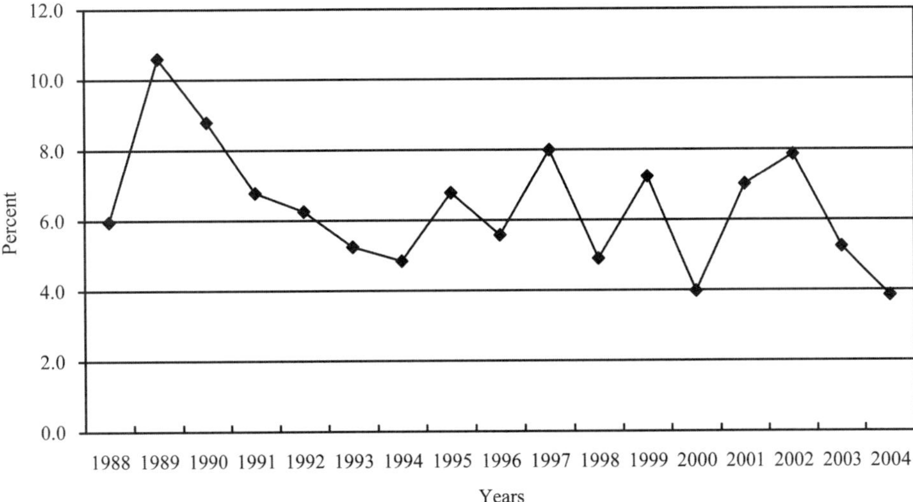

Figure 3. Variations in the Ratio of the Number of Disciplinary Actions to the Number of Claims for Disciplinary Action, 1988–2004
Source: Data from the Japan Federation of Bar Associations.

The Responsibility of Professionals

Jurisprudential Aspects

Professional responsibility has numerous jurisprudential dimensions. What is considered the responsibility of professionals is jurisprudentially divided into two major categories: civil and criminal responsibilities.

The following discussion focuses largely on the criminal aspects of professional responsibility. However, in order to define it, we need to recognize the reach of the civil responsibility of professionals. Because criminal responsibility is a matter of criminal law and control, there should be recognition of the different legal controls that come into play up to that point as well as the division of roles among these controls.

In Japan, the civil responsibility of professionals is usually treated as tort liability. Article 709 of the Japanese Civil Code provides for tort. According to this article, the occurrence of intentional or negligent damage and its causation are the contents of tort, and, the tort-feasor is liable for damages. This article is used to determine the civil responsibilities of professionals. But, usually, in the case of negligence by professionals, the duty of care is defined quite strictly.

In Japanese law, the fair apportionment of loss is emphasized in civil responsibility. Though some researchers argue over so-called punitive damages, generally, its examination remains at the starting point of formal legal controls. Even if damages have in fact a social function very similar to a criminal penalty, they are perceived differently. Although the vindicatory function of damages cannot be ignored, at the same time we should consider in principle that criminal responsibility takes on a very different function. Thus, since we can state that the role of the civil responsibility in the sanctioning of professional remains limited, it is necessary to consider the aspect of criminal responsibility.

Regarding the responsibility of lawyers specifically, there are dual sanctions that may be applied; a criminal penalty and/or a disciplinary action. It is necessary to examine the functions and segregation of these different social sanctions in Japanese law from a theoretical standpoint.

The Basis of the Criminal Responsibility of Professionals: The Case of Japanese Law

According to Japanese legal theory, crimes are defined as illegal and culpable acts in correspondence to constituent elements. When someone's act meets these prerequisites, criminal responsibility will be assigned.

The notion of "constituent elements of crime" (*Tatbestand*) is derived from German penal law theory, and it has given rise to a great deal of discussion among jurists in Japan. Here, it will be translated into crime types. Since these types of crime typify illegal and culpable acts, we can say that the substance of crime is, eventually, "an illegal and culpable act." "Illegality" (*Rechtswidrigkeit*) is *actus reus* in Anglo-American law, and "culpability" (*Schuld*) corresponds roughly to *mens rea*. However, in recent arguments, quite different contents have been included in these notions.

Illegality is, formally, the transgression of law. Though illegality in principle represents an objective side of crime, we can see that there are theoretical conflicts over its meaning. Among others, the conflict between the "negative value inherent in acts" (*Handlungsunwert*) theory and the "negative value inherent in results" (*Erfolgsunwert*) theory is well known.[15] The former places emphasis not on illegal results, but on illegal acts. The breach of socio-ethical norms is considered to be central to illegality. In the latter, which was established as an antithesis of the former, illegal results are believed to be essential to the existence of a crime. And, the violation of legal interest or the high probability of the violation is thought to be central to illegality.

Culpability means blameworthiness. There are few theoretical conflicts over this point. Formerly, in Japan scholars of criminal law debated the philosophical question of whether it is necessary for perpetrators of crime to have free will so that they can be blamed for their crimes. However, recently, this metaphysical question has not been considered very much.

In discussing the criminal responsibility of professionals in terms of these premises, it needs to be kept in mind that according to Japanese legal theory criminal responsibility does not depend on the "individual characteristics of perpetrators." According to criminal theory derived from the so-called "modern school" (*moderne Schule* in Germany), "the perpetrator, not the act, should be punished" (*Nicht die Tat, sondern der Täter ist zu bestrafen*). This school tended to attach the consideration of criminal policy to the jurisprudential understanding of crime. If one takes the position of this school, the introduction of "individual characteristics of perpetrators" into criminal law theory might be permitted theoretically. But, under contemporary Japanese criminal legal theory (which is an extension of the so-called "classic school"—*klassische Schule* in Germany), that is based upon retributive notions. The degree of blame according to the attributes of the perpetrator is only determined in the finding of culpability. Moreover, theoretically, it's difficult to incorporate the attributes of perpetrators into criminal law theory. For example, we can imagine the idea that in the case of crime by lawyers heavy culpability could be involved, and that the extent of the illegality of the crime would be high. However, it is difficult to generalize this into criminal law theory.

But, even if it is impossible to generalize about individual characteristics of perpetrators, it is not impossible to incorporate them into the general part of criminal law theory, if they are used as a "lodestar of interpretation." It may be useful to do so, especially considering the segregation of duties of the two types of sanctions—the sanctions of criminal responsibility and those of the disciplinary system. It seems that this problem should be looked at theoretically since the current disciplinary system for lawyers lacks a broad theoretical framework for understanding its limitations, and, since the criminal law acts as *ultima ratio*, the limits of criminal responsibility should be strictly considered as well.

Two theoretical points can be considered regarding the individual characteristics of perpetrators in Japanese criminal law theory. The first is the relationship between these characteristics and the ethical standards of an act. This is based on the traditional "negative value inherent in acts" theory described above. When "negative value inherent in acts," or unethicalness, is considered theoretically, there is resolution of the degree of the "breach of ethics" into an "extent of illegality." Second, we can note the relationship of the individual characteristics of perpetrators to both sentencing and culpability. As noted above, we can see that when lawyers are convicted, their sentencing is inclined to be heavier than when non-lawyers are found guilty. If sentencing is proportional to the amount of culpability, there is reason to relate the weight of responsibility of lawyers (who should know better, given their profession) to blameworthiness.

Besides, one can note crimes of "death caused by negligence in the course of business,"[16] crimes related to personal status, and so forth, as acts where, in substantive law, "professionalism" tied to illegality or culpability could be considered. But, such "professionalism" can become meaningful theoretically only when included in provisions of the Penal Code. However, if "professionalism" were included within the Penal Code, it would be possible to incorporate it into the theories regarding interpretation of the criminal law.

Illegal Activity

In Japan, the dispute over whether the ethical side of crime should be considered in the finding of illegality appeared as the above-mentioned conflict between the "negative value inherent in acts" theory and the "negative value inherent in results" theory. If we seek conflicts similar to it in the context of Anglo-American law, we could cite the controversy between John Stuart Mill and James Fitzjames Stephen as well as that between H. L. A. Hart and Patrick Devlin.

In the 1950s, Hart debated with Devlin about the Wolfenden Report regarding private prostitution and male homosexual acts. In this controversy, Hart insisted, from a utilitarian point of view, that morality should not be enforced through law, whereas Devlin argued the affinity between law and morality. This controversy had concrete practical significance, particularly regarding the problem of the decriminalization of victimless crime. From the perspective of Japanese criminal law theory, Hart's view paralleled the "negative value inherent in results" theory, which regards the violation of legal interest or the high probability of the violation as the core of illegality, and that Devlin's view corresponded to the "negative value inherent in acts" theory, which regards the breach of socio-ethical norms as the core of illegality.

In Japan, after World War II, under the newly established constitution, the emphasis was on the individualistic sense of values. The view that saw a close relationship between law and morality was liable to be seen as nationalistic. Most scholars in the academic circles of criminal law after the war firmly backed the "negative value inherent in results" theory, which is highly critical of the enforcement of morality through law.

As time has gone by, the "negative value inherent in acts" theory has gradually lost its power of persuasion. At present, Japanese jurists wouldn't deny that it is impossible to make mere breaches of ethics (morality) crimes. In terms of the context of Anglo-American law, this can be understood as the guarantee of substantive due process. The due process of law has to be guaranteed, not only formally in criminal procedures, but also as an appropriate notion of what crime is, in material criminal law.

But, even if mere breaches of morality are excluded from illegality, it cannot be denied that illegality differs from person to person. In other words, one can consider the personal illegality of an act that is related to the violation of legal interest. For example, Hans Welzel, a German scholar of criminal law, who created the "negative value inherent in acts" theory, maintained that the estimation of illegality turns on personal factors peculiar to the actor.

So, although the assertion that mere breaches of ethics should not be punished seems to be valid in principle, we can also observe the violation of legal interest that status as professionals makes possible. This makes it clear that in discussing the criminal responsibility of lawyers, we should not consider, in principle, the lawyer's breaches of ethics, and that the personal illegality of an act that the status as lawyer brings should be regarded in enacting new legislation that provides for criminal responsibility.

In Japan, the responsibility of lawyers can be enforced through two formal sanctions—criminal penalty and disciplinary action. As we mentioned above, the use of the criminal penalty needs to be restricted to cases where a lawyer violates a legal interest or there is a high probability of violation. Theoretically, we can conclude that the bar association should discipline the lawyer's breach of ethics because it represents autonomous control over the members.

But, at the same time, we should take into account the actual function of disciplinary action. Among the disciplinary actions, the heaviest is disbarment. In Japan, the entry into the legal profession is based on the successful completion of the bar examination. So, even if a lawyer is disbarred, theoretically he/she could work as a judge or a prosecutor. However, in fact, there would be no chance of this happening because of the person's infamy. Seen in this light, disbarment is such a potent sanction that it threatens the existence of the legal professional in society. Therefore, particularly careful consideration would be required for the utilization of disbarment.

Given the high status of lawyers in Japanese society and the image of lawyers in the minds of Japanese people, it may not be so easy to separate breaches of ethics completely from the other reasons for taking disciplinary action. In Japanese, the Chinese character ("*shi*") that means samurai is contained in the word *lawyer* (*bengo-shi*). So, we can suppose that in Japanese society lawyers are required to have nobility that parallels the spirit of the samurai, or Japanese chivalry. Given such consciousness, culture, and tradition in Japan, this would seem to require that ethical aspects be contained within the roster of disciplinary action.

Culpability

In many cases of crimes committed by lawyers, they receive longer sentences than in cases of crimes committed by non-lawyers. Does this have to do with the culpability that is derived from the lawyer's status? Japanese criminal law theory has a tendency (or tradition) to consider it to be the role of the jurisprudential understanding of a crime to explain why a perpetrator can be punished, taking the notions of illegality and culpability into consideration. That is to say, it tries to explain why a criminal is punished and why the punishment is heavy, or light, by analyzing the content and extent of illegality and culpability. If sentences for lawyers are stricter than there for non-lawyers, the culpability of lawyers is greater, and it may be necessary to incorporate a rational explanation of that into the theory of culpability.

Regarding the question of whether sentencing can be theoretically related to culpability, those who would approve have made various attempts to theorize about it. For example, they have asserted that culpability fixes the maximum of sentencing, and postulated "the theory of width" (the theory that culpability has a width, and that this forms the boundaries of sentencing) and "the theory of point" (the theory that punishment based on culpability is fixed at a point) in sentencing.

But, sentencing, in reality, is determined within the range of "sentencing quotation" (*ryoukei-souba*), and, if the sentencing is within that range, the demands of the culpability principle are met. Legal practitioners have a tendency to hardly take the theoretical examinations by scholars into account.

Actually, in Japanese legal practice, when sentencing is determined, the affairs that cannot be related to the notion of culpability in the existing criminal law theories are then taken into consideration. As is stated above, the notion of culpability stands for blameworthiness. And, in Japan where the "classic school" based on the individual acts of perpetrators has been dominant after the war, scholars have disputed whether some acts are blameworthy or not. As examples of matters playing into the sentencing decision, we can cite the personality of the defendant, personal matters, previous conviction and previous life, degree of regret, presence or absence of restitution, society's emotional request for a harsh penalty, victim matters, and so on.

As for the sentencing conditions relating to lawyers, the personal matters of the defendant are the most significant. In this regard, the following comments by judges serve as a useful reference.[17] "The high status of the defendant doesn't always affect the sentencing." "When the defendant betrayed the societal high obligation not to commit any crime, or when the defendant committed the crime by using his/her social status, more blame can be laid on him/her." "Even if the defendant contributed a good deal to the society before, his/her culpability isn't mitigated. However, it may be taken into account, from the point of view of special prevention, as an expression of good personality, etc." For example, in a recent case, it was pointed out that the high degree of blame leveled by the society becomes a factor in toughening the sentencing and that the social contributions of the lawyer become a factor in extenuating the sentencing.[18]

There are at least two ways to explain these conditions theoretically. One is through separating sentencing and culpability. If we adopt this method, the function of explaining why a perpetrator of a crime can be punished, which the jurisprudential understanding of a crime has, couldn't be fulfilled.

The other way is that of reconstructing the theory of culpability so as to be able to contain these conditions. Among criminal law theories in Japan, the theory of "culpability of personality formation" may be of some help.[19] Using it, we could build a bridge between sentencing in practice and culpability in criminal law theory.

More specifically, by breaking down culpability into types on the basis of this theory, we could introduce the notion of "individual characteristics of perpetrators" into criminal law theory.

Conclusion

In Japan, few researchers have attempted to tackle the area of study examined here. However, it is and will be increasingly important to explore crimes by lawyers and the responsibility of professionals. As a result of legal system reforms and the deregulation of professions, the social status of lawyers has gradually changed. And, in the course of this change, crimes and misconduct by lawyers have become a major social problem. Hence, from the perspective of criminal policies and criminology, it is necessary to empirically research crimes committed by lawyers, which clearly fall within the category of white-collar crime. And, from the perspective of criminal law, it is important to establish a legal theory regarding the responsibility of professionals, on the basis of which lawyers and other professionals who commit crimes would be punished. The issues related to criminal policy, criminology, and criminal law discussed here provide initial pathways to developing larger frameworks for accomplishing these necessary tasks.

Endnotes

1. Lawyers Law art. 3 (1).
2. Lawyers Law arts. 72, 77 (iii).
3. Lawyers Law art. 2.
4. Friedrichs, David O. *Trusted Criminals: White Collar Crime in Contemporary Society* (2nd Edition). Belmont, CA: Wadsworth, 2004: 97; Green, Gary S. *Occupational Crime* (2nd Edition). Chicago, IL: Nelson-Hall Publishers, 1997: 206–210.
5. Friedrichs, op. cit., pp. 97–98.
6. Lawyers Law arts. 26, 30–19, 76.
7. Lawyers Law arts. 27, 77 (i).
8. Lawyers Law arts. 28, 77 (ii).
9. Japan Federation of Bar Associations, Task Force on the Issues of Lawyer's "Acting Together with Persons Who Are Non-Lawyers." *Tajyuu-Saimu-Syori-Jiken no Hiben-Teikei-Jian-Cyoukai-Jirei-Syuu: 2003-Nen no Jirei* (The Casebook on Disciplinary Actions against the Lawyer's "Acting Together with Persons Who Are Non-Lawyers" in Relation to the Adjustment of Multiple Debts: The Cases in 2003). Tokyo, Japan: Japan Federation of Bar Associations, 2005: 6–8.
10. Nomura, Minoru. *Keizai-Keihou no Ronten* (The Issues in Economic Criminal Law). Tokyo, Japan: Gendai-Houritsu-Shuppan, 2002: 217.
11. In Japan, there is no nationwide bar association. Bar associations are set up in district court jurisdictions. The Japan Federation of Bar Associations consists of these separate bar associations.

12. Lawyers Law art. 56 (1).
13. Lawyers Law art. 57 (1).
14. Sumiyoshi, Hiroshi, "Genkou-Bengoshi-Cyoukai-Shisutemu no Hihanteki-Kentou (The Critical Examinations of Current Disciplinary System for Lawyer)." *Hanrei-Jihou* 1778, 2002:3–17.
15. Matsuzawa, Shin. "Danish Criminal Law and the Pragmatic Science of Criminal Law from a Japanese Perspective." In *Kriminalistisk Årbog 1998*, edited by Peter Kruize and Lene Ravn. Copenhagen, Det retsvidenskabelige Institut D, Københavns Universitet, 1999: 138.
16. Penal Code of 1907 art. 211 (1).
17. Harada, Kunio. *Ryoukei-Handan no Jissai* (The Actualities of the Decision of Sentencing). Tokyo, Japan: Gendai-Houritsu-Shuppan, 2003. (Authors' translation).
18. 52 Keishuu 343 (Sup. Ct., July 14, 1998).
19. Dando, Shigemitsu. *The Criminal Law of Japan: General Part*. Littleton, CO: Fred B. Rothman & Co., 1997:133–140.

References

Dando, Shigemitsu (1997) *The Criminal Law of Japan: General Part*. Littleton, CO: Fred B. Rothman & Co.

Friedrichs, David O. (2004) *Trusted Criminals: White Collar Crime in Contemporary Society*, 2nd ed. Belmont, CA: Wadsworth.

Green, Gary S. (1997) *Occupational Crime*, 2nd ed. Chicago, IL: Nelson-Hall.

Harada, Kunio (2003) *Ryoukei-Handan no Jissai* (The Actualities of the Decision of Sentencing). Tokyo, Gendai-Houritsu-Shuppan.

Japan Federation of Bar Associations, Task Force on the Issues of Lawyer's "Acting Together with Persons Who Are Non-Lawyers" (2005) *Tajyuu-Saimu-Syori-Jiken no Hiben-Teikei-Jian-Cyoukai-Jirei-Syuu: 2003-Nen no Jirei* (The Casebook on Disciplinary Actions against Lawyer's "Acting Together with Persons Who Are Non-Lawyers" in Relation to the Adjustment of Multiple Debts: The Cases in 2003). Tokyo, Japan: Japan Federation of Bar Associations.

Matsuzawa, Shin (1999) "Danish Criminal Law and the Pragmatic Science of Criminal Law from a Japanese Perspective," in *KriminalistiskÅrbog* 1998, Editors P. Kruize and L. Ravn. Copenhagen: Det retsvidenskabelige Institut D, Københavns Universitet.

Nomura, Minoru (2002) *Keizai-Keihou no Ronten* (The Issues in Economic Criminal Law). Tokyo: Gendai-Houritsu-Shuppan.

Sumiyoshi, Hiroshi (2002) "Genkou-Bengoshi-Cyoukai-Shisutemu no Hihanteki-Kentou (The Critical Examinations of Current Disciplinary System for Lawyer)." *Hanrei-Jihou* 1778 :3–17.

Cases Cited

52 Keishuu 343 (Sup. Ct., July 14, 1998) (Japan).

Statutes Cited

Civil Code art. 709 (Japan).

Lawyers Law arts. 2, 3 (1), 26, 27, 28, 30-19, 56 (1), 57 (1), 72, 76, 77 (@) (A) (B) (Japan).

Penal Code of 1907 (as amended) art. 211 (1) (Japan).

Part VIII

Corruption: Narratives, Definitions, and Applications

1

Corruption Kills

William K. Black

Narrative is a powerful force. The stories we use to explain and support our theories— and the stories we exclude from our narrative—are often decisive. There is such overwhelming evidence that corruption is a severe problem that can lock nations in poverty that this article will not undertake to prove that point. Nevertheless, many conservative scholars continue to argue that corruption is benign, even desirable. The defense of corruption relies almost entirely on rhetoric—even when it initially appears to be objective and empirical. The defenses of corruption are internally inconsistent. The defense of corruption springs from a (typically unstated) conservative, or libertarian, view that government is inherently evil and a burden on honest businessmen and women and the citizenry.

Defenses of corruption rely on three primary rhetorical techniques. They exclude morality from the narrative and substitute euphemisms for bribery. They argue that excluding moral considerations makes them more objective and maintain that euphemisms for bribery such as "side payments" represent "neutral" phraseology.

Defenders of corruption minimize its negative aspects and emphasize its advantages by using stories of baseless bureaucratic denials of routine applications. The predominance of such stories may even cause scholars opposed to corruption to term such behavior "petty corruption." Petty, of course, is a word used to describe the inconsequential.

Corruption's defenders demonize government officials and praise the private bribers as the entrepreneurs who produce economic development. Corruption's defenders see the government as the problem, never the solution. In their view, bribery enhances freedom by removing government restrictions. The stories the defenders of corruption tell show private bribers seeking relief only from foolish governmental restrictions—not ones crucial to public safety.

The persistence of these defenses in the face of overwhelming empirical evidence that corruption makes nations less efficient demonstrates the power of narrative. That persistence is all the more remarkable because the scholars who hold these beliefs all purport to be devotees of empiricism.

The stories that defenders of corruption employ are highly selective. This chapter is also selective. It uses stories that show bribery in some of its worst applications. It shows that the term "petty" bribery is a dangerously inaccurate rhetorical device. This article focuses on four exemplars of how corruption kills and maims. It does not discuss the most common causes of death due to corruption. Corruption causes millions of unnecessary deaths by keeping nations poor and incompetently managed. Millions die and are maimed unnecessarily from drinking bad water, from being infected as a result of inadequate sewage disposal, and from wars that corrupt regimes engage in as an opportunity for profit. While these things are true, the narrative is less compelling for many because it is indirect.

For narrative purposes, this chapter presents illustrative examples of situations in which corruption leads directly to death and serious injury. The common theme is that the government does many things that are essential to maintaining public safety. Private actors have a strong incentive in situations where corruption is common to bribe government officials in order to avoid safety restrictions. The incentive is typically financial—a bribe is profit-maximizing. However, sometimes the incentive is that the governmental restriction prevents murder and the individual pays the bribe in order to commit individual or mass murder.

The four illustrative examples are Chinese coal mines, Turkish construction, Russian security, and Illinois truck licenses.

In China, operators of illegal mines bribe government officials to keep the mines open. The illegal mines do not follow essential safety procedures, and so thousands of Chinese die unnecessarily each year in these mines.

Turkey responded to its severe seismic risk by adopting advanced building codes based on California's approach, mandating that construction be designed to withstand severe earthquakes. Building in compliance with the Turkish codes is far more expensive than bribing the building inspectors, so construction firms frequently bribe the inspectors and construct buildings that collapse in earthquakes and kill or maim their occupants.

Chechen terrorists have killed hundreds of Russian civilians. They bribe Russian police and other security officials in order to send heavily armed groups through Russian security points and individual bombers onto airplanes.

The State of Illinois recently experienced a scandal in which hundreds of individuals bribed officials to secure commercial truck licenses. Many of these individuals were not competent to drive trucks and they caused accidents that killed at least eight people.

Note that each of these examples involves the kind of very small bribes to relatively low- level government officials that are typically considered "petty" corruption. Yet these examples are virtually never addressed by defenders of corruption and are rarely mentioned by those who employ the classification of "petty" corruption in their research. We should abandon the use of the term "petty" corruption. The next section explains why defenders of corruption employ such misleading rhetoric when they discuss corruption.

Narrative Defenses of Corruption: Euphemisms and Minimization

Conservative economists and political scientists have long employed a narrative that minimizes corruption's harms. James Q. Wilson states:

> I am rather tolerant of some forms of civic corruption (if a good mayor can stay in office and govern effectively only by making a few deals with highway contractors and insurance agents, I do not get overly alarmed).[1]

Samuel Huntington famously opined that "In terms of economic growth the only thing worse than a society with a rigid, overcentralized, dishonest bureaucracy is one with a rigid, overcentralized, honest bureaucracy."[2]

Conservative economists have been even more dismissive of the purported ills of corruption. Some have attempted to produce models that would support Huntington's dictum.[3]

Others have employed experiments designed to show that corruption can be beneficial. Gonzalez, Guth, and Levati[4] designed a three-party ultimatum game to test the "efficient grease" hypothesis, which posits that corruption speeds regulatory approvals and enhances efficiency. They acknowledged that econometric studies of the effect of corruption supported the opposite conclusion—corruption increases inefficiency—but expressed skepticism about those results and suggested that laboratory experiments were a superior test of the "efficient grease" hypothesis.

> As we do not want to discuss corruption from an ethical viewpoint or to take moralistic positions, we use a neutral experimental frame and refer to the transfers of money as "greasing."[5]

Economists frequently employ euphemisms for corruption (e.g., "transfers of money" or "making a few deals" or "side payments" or "grease") and commonly exclude morality from their narrative—even when morality may be the key factor discouraging individuals from engaging in corrupt behavior. They also fail to investigate whether acting in an immoral fashion could cause harm in other, unrelated transactions or spheres of life. This is puzzling because Gonzalez, Guth, and Levati acknowledge that "people are motivated by 'social' concerns and, in particular, ... by 'fairness,' especially in bargaining games."[6] Their game design, however, excludes morality. The (student) participants that the authors claim are accurate surrogates for government officials were not told that they were playing that role. There is no government in the experiment. There is no substantive decision, e.g., whether to approve a license, in the experiment. There is simply a division of "tokens" among three student subjects. The subjects were not told that the division of tokens was to model bribery (or "grease"), and there was no way to infer from the experimental design that the division of funds was a bribe. Indeed, the game design *mandated* that the student (unknowingly) playing the role of the putative businessman pay both of the students (unknowingly) playing the role of the putative regulators. It is difficult to understand why the authors felt the study could be a realistic test of bribery when they designed it to remove any moral concerns.

The third rhetorical device is implicit. Gonzalez et al. refer to government officials as "bureaucrats." The title of their article is "Speeding Up Bureaucrats by Greasing Them: An Experimental Study." The authors explicitly assume that "bureaucrats" engage in "opportunistic" behavior in which they seek to maximize their self-interest. At no time does the article suggest that government officials ever do anything useful or anything in the public interest (unless they are bribed!). The authors appear to view the perfidy of public officials as so universally understood that it does not require discussion or proof.

The fourth rhetorical tactic is also implicit. The authors state that the benefit of grease is reducing "excessive red tape."[7] The authors do not understand the substantive importance of these critical third and fourth narrative devices. Implicitly, they have assumed that bribery is beneficial, for they have created an experiment in which it is certain that paying a bribe will increase the likelihood and speed of approval. Only "excessive red tape" prevents such immediate approval. They implicitly assume that "bureaucrats" do not deny, or delay processing, applications for meritorious reasons. In their view, as a matter of course, the government should approve—immediately—any request made by a businessman.

The assumption that government officials should approve any proposal a businesswoman makes is a bizarre assumption. "Public choice" theory suggests that business will be "rent seeking" and attempt to loot the nation. The authors allude to this danger in a preliminary section of their paper.[8]

One of the two illustrative examples they give of the kind of real-world conduct their experiment might model is that of a lobbyist seeking "tariff protection."[9] The vast majority of economists view lobbying for "protective" tariffs as a classic example of rent-seeking behavior that produces reduced competition, higher domestic costs, inefficiency, and supranormal profits for those with political power. The authors appear to assume that "grease" is "efficient" if it produces "a positive monetary surplus."[10] A "positive monetary surplus" exists, when, after bearing the cost of bribing the "bureaucrats," the businessman still makes a net profit from the prompt approval of the protective tariff. That "surplus" is created, however, because the tariff decreased competition and allowed the businessman to charge higher prices to consumers. Noncorrupt legislators would improve efficiency were they to *reject* lobbyists' requests for "tariff protection." The authors do not recognize that their example undercuts their "efficient grease" hypothesis.

Their game design is a "one-time" transaction. As soon as one allows for repeated transactions, their logic (which assumes that the actors will act in an "opportunistic" fashion) requires that rational (immoral) "bureaucrats" would *increase* red tape in order to extort larger bribes. Thus, grease would appear efficient in any *individual* regulatory filing but would produce *systemic* inefficiency. Again, the authors' preliminary discussion shows that they were aware of this dynamic, but they still chose an experimental design that excluded the dynamic.[11] Similarly, economics predicts that it is the most inefficient firms and industries—ones that should close—that will have the greatest incentive to bribe officials to secure "protective" tariffs. The authors ignore this *selective* nature of corruption.

These analytical and game-design defects lead to the authors' inevitable finding that bribes are efficient and to badly flawed policy advice.

> [O]ur data show that the likelihood of immediate acceptance is positively correlated with greasing. [T]his implies that grease money may help public administrations and private firms to reduce the effective burden and delay they face. On the other hand, it suggests that greasing (above all in its illegal form of bribery) can be reduced or even prevented by reducing discretion in internal organization.[12]

The authors do not see any costs to "reducing discretion" because they implicitly assume that government officials use discretion only to cause harm (in order to extort larger bribes). But "judgment" is impossible without discretion, and a system of government that forbids the exercise of judgment will impose enormous costs on society.

Even some economists who generally see corruption as harmful show clear evidence of how powerful a hold the narrative of corruption's virtue has had on the profession. For example, Kimberly Ann Elliott wrote:

> Corruption may also be a second-best response when a bureaucrat is bribed to ignore official duties that entail enforcement of regulations that are inefficient, duplicative, or simply unnecessary. In this case there may also be a welfare gain. Edward Banfield (1975, 595, 23n) offers the example of the New York City construction industry, which at the time was governed by an 843-page building code that required as many as 130 permits from a variety of city departments for large projects. Banfield cites a city commission study that found that most builders typically applied for only the most important permits, often bribed officials to get those permits quickly, and then paid off the police or inspectors to avoid harassment for not having the others. The commission concluded that none of the bribes they investigated "... resulted from the builder's effort to get around the requirements of the building code. What was being bought and sold, an official said, was time.[13]

The builders in this narrative are ideal. They provide a public service by taking the risk of being prosecuted for bribery (a felony). Their willingness to bribe allows them to avoid stupid permit requirements that would cost consumers without adding to safety. Though they have an economic incentive to cut costs and increase profits even further by bribing the inspectors to allow them to compromise safety, they universally refuse to do so. The New York City builders meet the Goldilocks standard of morality—they are just corrupt enough to produce the optimal response to (stupid) regulation.

But notice the rhetoric within the narrative. An inspector or police officer that would cite the builders' failure to secure a permit as a violation is described as engaging in "harassment." This is obviously the most negative phrase possible for the act of upholding the law and doing one's duty as an inspector. How many bribes had the commission "investigated"? What facts were available to the commission that could support a claim that none of the builders wished to avoid any requirement of an 843-page building code? How did they discern the subjective intent of the builders? Who was the "official" that provided the punchy one-liner that the only thing being sold was "time"? Did he have an incentive to minimize the harm? Isn't this story too good to be true? Is it really conceivable, in a situation in which corruption was endemic, that no builder sought to avoid a single building code requirement? In other nations with grotesque permit requirements noncompliance through bribery or evasion is the norm.[14] Why is New York City's corruption so different than Peru's corruption?

But the story becomes magical when one takes into account the fact that organized crime was a major force in the industry at the time of commission that Banfield cites. Even today:

> Extortion, bid rigging, bribery and other illegal practices are pervasive in the construction industry and add to the cost of new construction. These illegal practices often take place because organized crime has infiltrated labor unions and construction

> companies. Efforts by federal, state and local law enforcement agencies to investigate and prosecute corruption in the industry have made progress, but much more needs to be done to ameliorate the problem and safeguard the gains that have been made.[15]

Banfield's portrait of mob builders and mob unions as ideal citizens is idiosyncratic, to say the least. New York City's building code has the most stringent construction worker protection rules of any jurisdiction. Not surprisingly, these rules have generated corrupt efforts to evade the safety rules. Salama, Schill, and Springer updated the 1989 study of the City's construction industry and concluded that while prosecutors had made some progress against mob influence, corruption remained endemic. They also found that it was very difficult to get members of the industry to speak candidly and that bribery was used not simply to expedite approvals but to cause inspectors to "overlook problems at job sites."[16] Both of these findings suggest that the unknown official that Banfield relied on to assert that corruption raised no safety concerns had no basis for his claim.

The New York City building code remains awful. It remains awful largely because its provisions provide incentives to bribe public officials and benefit some labor unions. These officials and unions have prevented efforts to reform the code for decades. Labor opposition is delaying the ongoing serious effort to adopt the model building code.

The examples I have discussed illustrate how defenders of corruption rely on narrative to support their claims because the empirical evidence and case studies have falsified their predictions that corruption increases efficiency. Their narrative, in turn, relies on the following three rhetorical techniques: (1) The defenders exclude morality from consideration and typically employ euphemisms for corruption. (2) They minimize the importance of corruption by studying only examples of (purportedly) foolish requirements being avoided or expedited. (3) They portray the government as inept (creating foolish rules) and rapacious (honest New York City inspectors that enforce rules are engaged in "harassment"); and they portray the private-sector actors as entrepreneurs forced to use bribes to prevent financial ruin. In their view, the government does not act properly, it does not reject applications for good reasons, and it does not have any useful role in protecting safety.

Once the rhetoric is considered it becomes clear that the defense of corruption continues, despite the overwhelming evidence that corruption is harmful, for ideological reasons. The greatest intellectual threat to deeply conservative and libertarian scholars is idea that the government could be largely a force for good. The ultimate insult to government is the claim that a corrupt government is superior to an honest government. If a corrupt government were less bad than an honest government, then government would in truth always be the problem and never the solution. Conservative and libertarian economists conceive of bribery as a means of expediting government approval of routine licenses that should always be approved—because the licensure requirement never should have been imposed. If they were to admit that government approval should be required for some activities and that the "bureaucrats" might improve public safety by denying unmerited applications, they would be admitting that government could be the solution to some problems.

The claim that corrupt governments are superior rests on a logical contradiction. The claim rests on the assumption that "bureaucrats" act opportunistically for self-benefit—not in the public interest. If that assumption is true, however, then private-sector actors must do the same. The rational strategy, if one ignores morality, then becomes "crony capitalism" in which bribery is used to convince bureaucrats to award private parties lucrative opportunities through grants of state monopolies, e.g., the exclusive right to import a product. Conservative economists assert that such "rent-seeking" behavior causes severe inefficiency.

Worse, there is no reason to assume that corruption will cause only financial injury. Businessmen and criminals willing to harm others have a strong incentive to bribe "bureaucrats" to prevent them from protecting public safety. There is no basis in economic theory, or human experience, for assuming that they would not bribe these bureaucrats when public safety was at risk. The next section shows that businessmen and terrorists have been willing to employ bribery (and public officials have been willing to accept those bribes) even where it is predictable that private action and governmental inaction will combine to cause the death of large numbers of people.

Corruption Kills: Half Forgotten American History

Private rapacity and the bribery of public officials have combined to cause some of America's worst tragedies. On June 15, 1904, over 1,000 people died in a fire on the ferry *General Slocum* in the waters off New York City. Few Americans could swim in this era. The crew made only feeble efforts to put out the fire. They had no training in fire suppression and the fire hoses burst because they had been allowed to rot. The lifeboats could not be lowered because they were improperly rigged. The cork in the life vests had turned to dust. The deficiencies were so widespread and obvious that the company must have bribed the inspector who inspected the boat only a month before the fire.[17] However, only the captain was found guilty.

The other case caused far fewer deaths but is far more famous and proved an impetus for many progressive movements. The March 25, 1911, fire at the Triangle Shirtwaist building killed 146 people. Triangle's factory was overcrowded and vulnerable to fire. It had previously made insurance claims for six fires. Instead of increasing safety precautions, however, management responded to trivial theft of cloth by some workers by illegally locking all but one door. Workers had to line up single file when they left so that they could be searched for pilferage. The fire escapes did not reach the ground and, in any event, collapsed during the fire when the workers tried to use them. Again, the public believed that the violations were so recurrent and obvious that the inspectors must have been bribed to ignore them. The fire trapped large numbers of workers on the ninth floor. Many of them jumped to their deaths.[18]

Fortunately, as corruption declined in America these direct, mass losses of life due to corruption ended. The next section, however, demonstrates that corruption continues to kill people by the thousands in other nations, that it continues to kill some Americans, and that it is one of the greatest threats to the lives of citizens of many lands in an era when terrorists may employ weapons of mass destruction.

Corruption Kills Thousands in China's Mines

China's rapid economic growth has caused a surge in the demand for energy. China has experienced electrical shortages when some of its generators could not get enough coal to burn to produce steam. China has abundant coal supplies, but many of them are deep underground.

Even a well-run coal mine is an inherently dangerous work site. Coal mines are vulnerable to explosion (from methane and coal dust), collapse, and flooding. Each of these events can occur quickly and kill hundreds. Mines are often deep and rescuing trapped miners is difficult, dangerous, and often takes days. Miners also risk asphyxiation and confront the danger of developing "black lung" and work daily in an environment in which explosives, high speed drills, picks, shuttle trains, and falling rocks pose recurrent dangers. There are proven techniques and precautions that can prevent the vast majority of deaths and serious injuries. However, mines operators have to make an intense commitment to safety to avoid killing workers.

For example, in the United States, improved safety research, enhanced safety regulation, and reduced corruption have led to precipitous reductions in coal-mining deaths. A Chinese professor of mining made this point in an October 23, 2004, interview with the *People's Daily:*

> *Wang Deming:* The main work-safety indexes are accident and fatality rates per million tons. China has a poor safety record among coal-producing countries: in fact, we can say it has the poorest safety record. Last year, China produced 1.7 billion tons of coal. With 6,434 miners dead in accidents, the fatality rate per million tons was nearly 4. Look at the US, a big coal producer. Its output is 1 billion tons per year, but its death toll is only 50 miners, putting the rate per million tons at 0.04. The death rates per million tons in Russia and South Africa were 0.34 and 0.13. The fatality rate in developed countries averages 0.4. Although mine safety has improved since 2002, we have still a long way to go.[19]

China's safety record is actually worse than these statistics show because, as the same article admits, many deaths are not reported to the government because most of the deaths occur at illegal mines. While the fact that China is a developing nation means that more miners are likely to die, even absent corruption, the bulk of the disparity is due to the corruption that allows these illegal mines to remain open and operate in a wholly unsafe manner. Moreover, the key issue is not cost—safer mines are cheaper and more profitable. Killing and maiming workers is a poor way to run a mine. Honest government regulation and mine operations would be more efficient as well as more humane. As Professor Wang explained:

> *Wang:* This is a longstanding problem resulting from operators' mistaken thinking. Safety equipment requires a very large lump-sum investment. Many operators of small mines trust to luck and are loathe to spend money on safety equipment. In a highly dangerous industry like coal mining, the ratio of safety equipment investment to benefit should be 1:7. When an accident happens, the cost of dealing with the resultant problems is usually 1.5 times that of investment in safety, and that calculation does not include losses caused by the halt in production.[20]

He went on to explain that the best mines in China had fatality rates comparable to those in the United States. Those mines are state-owned and relatively high technology operations with a serious safety culture. Safer mines are also less polluting, and pollution released by illegal mines also kills non-miners.

The most acute problem is that there are thousands of illegal Chinese coal mine operators "trust[ing] to luck." But trusting to luck in deep coal mining as a long-term strategy is equivalent to trying to draw to an inside straight. The strength and the perversity of the corruption in China is so great that the problems continue even though (1) the grotesquely unsafe manner in which illegal mines typically operate reduces efficiency, (2) the unnecessary deaths of thousands of Chinese miners is deeply embarrassing to the Party, (3) the illegal mines produce recurrent scandals by compounding the deaths through cover-ups and hiding or refusing to recover corpses—often with the active connivance of corrupt Party members,—a that have produced anti-Party demonstrations, and (4) the Party has made repeated promises to stamp out the corruption and illegal mines. The Chinese web site that reported the interview with Professor Wang about the October 2005 mine disasters has a link to an earlier article reassuring readers that earlier mine explosions in China that caused hundreds of deaths were not falling on deaf ears and promising that all small mines would be closed by June 2005.

Corruption also adds to the death toll in Chinese mines because the owners of illegal mines recognize that they are likely to get in trouble when a disaster occurs. In some cases they have fled from the site—leaving no one to guide rescue operations.[21] In addition to fearing arrest after a disaster, the owners of illegal mines are liable for death benefits. Both of these concerns may have prompted an illegal mine in Xinhua secretly to ship corpses to other areas, including Inner Mongolia, and report that 19 miners had died. The actual death toll was 36.[22] Firms that are able to operate unlawfully through bribery have perverse incentives prior to disaster, but disasters greatly intensify those incentives.

Corruption Kills Thousands of Turks: The Building as Weapon

The mantra of those that who study earthquakes is that earthquakes don't kill people, buildings do. Much of Turkey is subject to severe seismic risk. A series of major quakes have occurred in recent decades—and they are moving along a major fault line toward Istanbul, Turkey's largest city. Turkey's government has long recognized the problem and adopted building codes, patterned on California's codes, to reduce the risk of building collapse. Buildings that comply with Turkey's codes should not have collapsed in its recent earthquakes. Indeed, compliant buildings near the epicenter of the 1999 earthquake often suffered minimal damage.[23] Unfortunately, far too many newly constructed buildings collapsed, killing more than 10,000 Turks.

After the 1999 quake, it became apparent that bribery and blatant noncompliance with the existing building codes proved to be the norm in Turkey. The residents of one resort city sought to lynch the builder after 7 of the 16 buildings he constructed collapsed. The builder had boasted before the disaster that he saved money by substituting cheap building materials. Interior Minister Sadetin Tantan declared, "The contractors who built those buildings and those who issued permits committed murder" (ibid.). However, the Turkish government had long been put on notice by engineers and seismologists—and by experience—that corruption was endemic and led to widespread noncompliance with the building codes. It also knew that earthquakes were likely to occur and that the many illegally constructed buildings would not survive even a moderate earthquake. The failure of the government to launch a major initiative against corruption prior to 1989 suggests that higher-level corruption of senior officials may also have occurred.

Even if the government had been unwilling to uproot corruption in the construction industry and among government inspectors it could have made a major effort to alert Turks to the danger of noncompliant buildings and could have informed buyers which construction firms were honest. Turkey has a number of superb construction firms.[24] Instead, with the exception of adopting (but not enforcing) good seismic codes, the general response of Turkish leaders to the repeated, unnecessary loss of thousands of lives has been fatalism. Earthquakes are natural disasters—but buildings are not. They are planned and constructed by people, and if this is done well they will protect rather than kill residents even in severe earthquakes.[25]

This problem is not limited to Turkey. Investigations into building construction practices after Mexico City's 1985 earthquake showed that many buildings that collapsed did not comply with the building codes. The contractors bribed the inspectors to obtain permits despite cost-saving construction practices that made it likely that the buildings would collapse in a moderately severe earthquake. Mexico City is known to face serious seismic risk because it is near fault lines likely to produce powerful quakes and because it is built on a dried lakebed. The government owned many of the buildings that collapsed. (Many seismologists, while acknowledging the corruption, believed that the severity and length of the earthquake were so great that even had the government buildings complied with building codes many might have collapsed.[26])

Most Mexicans, however, took a far harsher view of the corruption and the pathetic government response to the disaster. Many political scientists view 1985 as the year in which the PRI, which had completely dominated Mexican government for decades, lost its legitimacy. One aspect of the disaster harkened back to the Triangle fire. Among the buildings that were badly damaged were sweatshops employing female seamstresses. The owners are believed to have promptly bribed the police to bring in heavy equipment—to save their *machinery*—while ignoring the injured employees trapped in the building. A union activist's column describes the event from labor's perspective:

> In Mexico's capital, many of the buildings that crumbled were found to be substandard constructions where money saved on cheap materials and feeble foundations had gone straight into the pockets of corrupt politicians.
>
> Survivors told horror stories of being locked in overcrowded rooms with no escape routes, no direction, and no hope as the buildings fell. Their indignation turned to rage when, left jobless, their bosses refused to pay wages due and severance pay. Then their rage turned into a union.[27]

Construction/corruption problems were documented by in the report of a team of international seismic experts investigating the 2001 Gujarat earthquake.[28] India was a poorer nation than Turkey in 2001 and its building codes' seismic provisions, though modern and professional in content, were advisory. Properly engineered buildings did not collapse even when they were close to the epicenter, while poorly engineered, recently constructed buildings located far from the epicenter (230 km) often collapsed.[29] Evidence of poor design and construction was pervasive in collapsed buildings of recent construction. Engineers did not serve as an effective barrier because there were no professional engineer societies in India. Bribery was less of a factor in Gujarat than in Turkey because the seismic code provisions were voluntary and because *builders* conducted most "inspections" in India! Of course, those factors may simply mean that the corruption is more fundamental, pervasive, and high-level in India than in Turkey. The builders have influenced elected Indian officials to avoid meaningful building regulation. In India, such inducements frequently involve bribery. Again, the result is widespread death and maiming and economic inefficiency. The international study team investigating the Gujarat quake summarized its findings in harsh terms:

> The current state of the engineering profession and construction industry in India is appalling. Major reforms must be implemented if another catastrophe is to be avoided.[30]

The team also found a more complex contribution of corruption to the loss of life.

> While adequate drawings were made for legal sanction from the municipality, the actual construction was left to the contractor who may or may not follow these drawings. After execution, the municipality was only responsible for checking certain building byelaws regarding ground coverage, floor area ratio and height regulations. They were not responsible for ensuring the technical details have been followed as per the drawings. This has led to poor structural design and in some cases the use of poor building material due to corruption, black marketeering and simple economic considerations on the part of the client/builder. In addition, there appeared to be considerable ignorance of earthquake risk in the area.[31]

It appears that fraud was the norm for large numbers of builders. They filed phony building plans rather than bribe the officials.

The tragic aspect of these deaths is that earthquake safety is a field in which the professionals have often done an exceptional job. Civil engineers and seismologists have sought to warn us of the danger of collapsing buildings, designed cost-effective means to keep us safe, and created effective codes and initiatives to implement those designs. They have organized and lobbied and educated and been proactive. Their efforts have saved many lives—but corruption has turned what should have been a brilliant success into a marginal gain. Engineers, scientists, the United Nations, Transparency International, and others have cooperated to create over a half dozen groups devoted to stopping buildings from killing and maiming people. The architect James Lewis summarized the situation:

> In the past 15 years, there have been more than 400 recorded earthquakes in 75 countries, rendering almost 9 million people homeless, injuring 584,000, and causing 156,000 deaths. These deaths were the result of buildings that folded in on themselves because concrete was diluted, steel bars were excised, or otherwise substandard building practices were employed. It is difficult to evaluate the extent to which corruption might have played a role. However, the accompanying examples from Italy and Turkey illustrate that the marriage of corrupt contractors and corrupt building inspectors and other public officials resulted in ignored building codes, lax enforcement and the

absence of on-site inspection, which is deadly when it occurs in earthquake-prone areas.[32]

As this section was being completed a new scandal broke in Japan, a first-world nation. The architect Hidetsugu Aneha, who specialized in calculating safety requirements to prevent seismic risk, admitted that he had deliberately grossly underestimated the amount of reinforcing elements required in order to save construction firms costs. He claimed that the construction companies pressured him to do so (they deny the claim). Preliminary estimates are that the buildings were designed in a manner that makes them susceptible to collapse in a moderate earthquake. The buildings are being abandoned and may have to be destroyed. Aneha did work for a number of Japanese construction firms, including two of its most prestigious. There is no evidence at this point that any public officials were bribed to approve Aneha's designs or to approve construction of inadequate support elements. Aneha's confession and charges have caused a large scandal in Japan.[33]

The key fact known at this point is that a professional employed as a seismic specialist was willing to engage in fraud while designing dozens of unsafe buildings in one of the seismically most active areas of the world. He did so for financial gain, knowing that he was putting thousands of Japanese lives at risk. The Japanese assumed that such behavior was unthinkable. As with conservative U.S. scholars, they assumed that no one wearing a white-collar would be willing to put public safety at risk for purposes of self-gain.

This refusal to see the non-financial risks to the public caused by white-collar crime is particularly strange in the context of the Japanese construction industry. Corruption is endemic in that industry. The primary example is the *dango*—the Japanese bid rigging conspiracies that determine the winner of public construction contracts. Corruption is essential to these cartels because the government officials must leak the secret maximum acceptable bid ("reserve price") to the *dango* so that the winning bid can come in at the maximum price. This aspect of the *dango* is made possible by the legal, but corrupt, practice of *amakudari* ("descent from heaven") and kickbacks to the LDP "construction tribes."[34] Senior government officials are given lucrative sinecures in private or quasi-private non-governmental organizations (QUANGOs) when they retire (at a relatively young age). An official who did not cooperate with the *dango* by leaking the reserve price would not be given a sinecure and would find his career stunted.

Chechen Terrorists Exploit Russian Corruption

Chechens have found that Russian corruption is endemic and that small bribes permit terrorists to penetrate even supposedly secure areas far outside Chechnya. On August 24, 2004, two Chechen women carried bombs on board separate Russian planes at a Moscow airport. They had no reservations and at least one was late for the flight she wished to board. Russia's pervasive corruption has spawned expert agents who can be hired cheaply to bribe officials. The women used such an agent to purchase tickets and entrée to the airplanes they wished to destroy. The agent, in turn, bribed an airport official for 1,000 rubles (about $35) to hold the flight and allow his client onto the plane.[35] The bombers destroyed both planes in midair—killing 90 people.

Corruption is widespread in Russia[36]: The police forces are notoriously corrupt,[37] and the military is particularly susceptible to bribes because most of its members serve involuntarily and are poorly paid, poorly housed, poorly led, and badly abused by their officers. The *Economist* reports that

> The defence minister was recently obliged to issue a special order designed to stop officers hiring troops out as day labourers, and using them to build dachas.[38]

Chechen terrorists employed bribes to allow them to travel hundreds of kilometers outside of Chechnya to commit attacks. The *Economist* article went on to explain:

> But Russian corruption doesn't just make life inconvenient, or hold back the economy: it kills people.... After the Beslan attack [in September 2004], reporters in Moscow proved it was possible to obtain official documents while using a photograph of Aslan Maskhadov, the Chechen leader who was later killed. The Beslan hostage-takers are thought to have bribed their way across internal borders. And how did over a hundred militants gather and arm themselves before launching the city-wide battle that struck Nalchick, not far from Beslan, last week?[39]

The Beslan atrocity killed hundreds of civilians, primarily schoolchildren and teachers. The first Chechen act of mass terrorism outside Chechnya occurred in 1996.

> Shamil Basayev, the Chechen guerilla leader, led an assault force that took over a hospital with more than 1,000 people in the southern city of Budennovsk. The attack ended with more than 100 civilian deaths. Basayev later told an interviewer that he had gotten past police road stops with $10,000 in bribes and had intended to go all the way to Moscow but stopped in Budennovsk because he ran out of money.[40]

Another spectacular terror attack outside Chechnya occurred when—

> gunmen paid off police in 2002 as they transported a virtual armory of assault rifles, hand grenades and explosives all the way from the south to Moscow, where they seized a theater filled with patrons. The subsequent standoff left 129 hostages dead.[41]

Corruption is essential to the Chechen terrorists' strategy of killing large numbers of non-Chechen civilians. The widespread and recurrent willingness of large elements of the many different Russian security agencies to be bribed—even when the bribes lead to enormous loss of civilian life—is the ultimate proof of the stranglehold that corruption has taken on Russia's soul. Russian soldiers, who once gave their lives by the millions to protect the *Rodina,* now sell it out to enemies they despise. And they sell themselves cheaply.

This is obviously disastrous for Russia, but it may also be disastrous for the world. Chechen terrorists train non-Chechen terrorists who then export their skills. Russia had more weapons of mass destruction than any other nation. Russia's endemic corruption threatens to make it the supplier of choice to terrorists who may either bribe officials to purchase the weapons or exploit weak security by stealing them. Corruption is likely to be key also to the transport of such weapons to countries like the United States. A small bribe in many nations can lead to a crate's being added to a container bound for a U.S. port.

The final section demonstrates that U.S. corruption continues to kill American citizens. The particular form of corruption it addresses—providing drivers licenses to unqualified drivers—is one that poses a realistic risk of facilitating the entry of terrorists into the United States, their movement within the nation, and their ability to perpetrate either a large conventional truck bomb attack or an attack with weapons of mass destruction.

Illinois: Safe Truck Drivers Don't Need To Bribe To Get a License

Illinois is one of several states that have recently suffered corruption scandals in which would-be truckers bribe state officials in order to receive commercial truck licenses. These bribes kill people because the primary reason to bribe an official in order to receive a trucker's license is that one is not a safe truck driver.

The Illinois scandal became known because the official in charge of the driver's license system during the period when thousands of truckers secured licenses through bribery, Illinois secretary of state George Ryan, was elected Governor. Ryan has been indicted and charged with creating the corrupt system that led to the widespread bribery. The indictment charged that the proceeds of bribery and other forms of corruption were used to help fund his election.

Further, some of the truck drivers who obtained their licenses through bribery were at fault in fatal accidents. One accident in Wisconsin killed six Illinois children. The truck driver had been involved in four accidents in the two years prior to the fatal episode.[42] To compound the scandal, the inspector general for the secretary of state's office—the individual who is supposed to root out corruption— pleaded guilty to obstructing the internal investigation into the allegations of bribery and lying to the FBI.[43] Of 510 truckers retested because they were suspected of having bribed the examiners, only 171 passed their retests.[44] The *Chicago Sun-Times* captioned its story on the scandal with the phrase U.S. Attorney Patrick Fitzgerald had used: "The State of Illinois was for sale."[45]

A broad criminal scheme also existed in New Jersey in which "brokers" competed with each other to provide drivers licenses for fees (of over $1,000).[46] The brokers had corrupt state officials on their payroll and created a recognition code, which changed on a daily basis, to enable the employees to identify the individual who had hired the brokers. The documents were sold primarily to individuals who could not legally obtain such a license. This primarily meant illegal immigrants, who wished to work peacefully in the United States, but it could also include terrorists. Georgia, Florida, Ohio, and Pennsylvania all had major bribery scandals contemporaneous with the Illinois and New Jersey scandals regarding the improper issuance of hundreds of commercial truck driver's licenses.[47]

I will close by returning to the power of narrative. Many Illinois state officials have now plead guilty to corruption charges arising from the bribery scandal. It is indisputable that there was pervasive corruption that led to hundreds of unsafe truck drivers' being granted licenses. It was morally certain that this corrupt scheme would kill people. But former Governor Ryan, like other former senior officials indicted for their roles in the corruption scandal, are not being charged with homicide. Indeed, his attorneys are fighting to prevent the introduction of evidence about the fiery deaths of the six children described earlier. That is, of course, consistent with their ethical obligation to provide zealous advocacy on behalf of their client. What is incomprehensible is the pre-sentencing report for one of Ryan's aides convicted of corruption. The report urged, under the then controlling U.S. sentencing guidelines, that the sentence not be enhanced because the link between the defendant's conduct and the risk of serious bodily injury was "too tenuous."[48]

Results like this can only occur because we as a society are so loath to believe that white-collar criminals would be willing to take a bribe in exchange for an act that places the public at risk of death. We need to reinforce the notion that there is nothing "tenuous" about the link between corruption and death. It is predictable that one will lead to the other wherever a government official is performing a health, safety, or security function. Millions of government employees perform these functions. Corruption kills.

Endnotes

1. Wilson (1975: xix).
2. Huntington (1968: 498–499).
3. Lui (1985).
4. Gonzalez et al. (2004).
5. Gonzalez et al. (2004: 4).
6. Gonzalez et al. (2004: 11).
7. Gonzalez et al. (2004: 6–7).
8. Gonzalez et al. (2004: 2).
9. Gonzalez et al. (2004: 6).
10. Gonzalez et al. (2004: 6).
11. Gonzalez et al. (2004: 3).
12. Gonzalez et al. (2004: 13).
13. Elliott (1997: 187).
14. de Soto (2000).
15. Salama et al. (1989: 9).
16. Salama et al. (2005: 124).
17. O'Donnell (2003).
18. Stein (2001); Drehle (2003).
19. *People's Daily* (2004).
20. *People's Daily* (2004).
21. BBC News (December 6, 2005).
22. BBC News (July 14, 2005).
23. *The New York Times* (August 20, 1999).
24. *The New York Times* (August 29, 1999).
25. Penny Green emphasizes and develops this point in greater detail in her recent article "Disaster by Design" (2005).
26. *Washington Post* (September 20, 1986).
27. Carlsen (2005).
28. Mistry et al. (2001).
29. Mistry et al. (2001: Sec. 2.2.1.2).
30. Mistry et al. (2001: Sec 2.3.6).
31. Mistry et al. (2001: Sec 4.2.2).
32. Lewis (2005: 23).
33. BBC News (November 29, 2005); *Time Asia* (December 5, 2005).
34. Black (2004).
35. *Washington Post* (September 18, 2004).
36. Wedel (1998).

37. *Los Angeles Times* (November 8, 2004); *Washington Post* (September 18, 2004).
38. *Economist* (October 20, 2005).
39. *Economist* (October 20, 2005).
40. *Washington Post* (September 18, 2004).
41. *Washington Post* (September 18, 2004).
42. *Kansas City Star* (December 16, 2001).
43. CNN.com NewsNet (March 16, 2000).
44. CNN.com NewsNet (March 16, 2000).
45. *Chicago Sun-Times* (December 18, 2003).
46. *Criminal Justice News* (June 24, 2002).
47. *Kansas City Star* (December 16, 2001).
48. *The Leader*—Chicago Bureau (June 27, 2003).

References

BBC News (2005) "Chinese Mine Owner 'Disappears'." *BBC News* 6 Dec. *http://news.bbc.co.uk/1/hi/world/asia-pacific/4502022.stm.* (accessed 6 December 2005).

BBC News (2005) "Japanese Scandal Prompts Quake Fears." *BBC News* 29 Nov. *http://news.bbc.co.uk/2/hi/asia-pacific/4527294.stm.* (accessed 16 December 2005).

BBC News (2005) "China Mine Concealed 'Death Toll'." *BBC News* 17 July. *http://news.bbc.co.uk/1/hi/world/asia-pacific/4683137.stm.* (accessed 6 December 2005).

Black, William K. (2004) "The Dango Tango: Why Corruption Blocks Real Reform in Japan." *Business Ethics Quarterly* 14(4):602–623 (Oct.).

Carlsen, Laura (2005) "Two Decades of Aftershocks from 1985 Quake." *Counterpunch* 22/23 Oct. *http://www.counterpunch.org/carlsen10222005.html.* (accessed 16 December 2005).

Chicago Sun-Times (2003) "The State of Illinois Was for Sale." *Chicago Sun-Times*, 18 Dec. *http://www.ilcampaign.org/press/news/ scandal/articles/2003-12-18The State.html.* (accessed 9 December 2005).

CNN.com NewsNet (2000) "Illinois Alerts States to Bogus Truck Driver's Licenses." *CNN.com NewsNet* 16 Mar. *http:// archives.cnn.com/2000/US/03/16/truck.licenses/.* (accessed 9 December 2005).

Criminal Justice News (2002) "Criminal Indictments Charge 36 persons With Trafficking in Fraudulent New Jersey Driver's Licenses and Identification Documents." *Office of the Attorney General* 24 June. *http://www.state.nj.us/lps/dcj/releases/2002/dmv0624.html.* (accessed 9 December 2005).

von Drehle, David (2003) *Triangle: The Fire that Changed America*. New York: The Atlantic Monthly Press.

Economist. (2005) "Blood Money." *Economist,* 20 Oct. *http://www.economist.com/PrinterFriendly.cfm?story_id=5061669.* (accessed 9 December 2005).

Elliot, Kimberly A. (1997) "Corruption as an International Policy Problem: Overview and Recommendations." In *Corruption and the Global Economy*, Editor K.A. Elliot. Washington: Institute for International Economics.

González, Luis, et al. (2004) "Speeding up Bureaucrats by Greasing them—An Experimental Study." *Working Paper* MPI Jena.

Green, Penny (2005) "Disaster by Design." *British Journal of Criminology* 45:(4)528–546.

Huntington, Samuel P. (1968) *Political Order in Changing Societies*. New Haven: Yale University Press.

Kansas City Star (2001) "Commercial Driver's License Program Flawed." *Kansas City Star*, 16 Dec. *http://www.knightridder.com/papers/greatstories/kansas/truckers11.html.* (accessed 9 December 2005).

Leader-Chicago Bureau (2003) "Feds link Fawell's actions to deaths of Willis Children." *Leader-Chicago Bureau*, 27 June. *http://www.illinoisleader.com/news/newsview.asp?c=6588*. (accessed 9 December 2005).

Lewis, James (2005) "Earthquake Destruction: Corruption on the Fault Line." *Transparency International* 23–30.

Los Angeles Times (2004) "Russia May Pay for Bribes in Lives." *Los Angeles Times*, 8 Nov. *http://www.globalpolicy.org/nations/launder/regions/2004/1108bribeslives.html*. (accessed 9 December 2005).

Lui, Francis (1985) "An Equilibrium Queuing Model of Bribery." *Journal of Political Economy* 93(4): 760–781 (Aug.).

Mistry, Ravi et al. (2001) "Interdisciplinary Observations on the January 2001, Bhuj, Gujarat Earthquake." *http://www.rms.com/Publications/Bhuj_EQ_Report.pdf*. (accessed 16 December 2005).

New York Times (1999) "The Turkish Quake's Secret Accomplice: Corruption." *The New York Times*, 29 Aug. *http://www.library.cornell.edu/colldev/mideast/tquak.htm*. (accessed 9 December 2005).

New York Times (1999) "Turkish Earthquake Survivors Blame Corruption." *The New York Times*, 20 Aug. *http://wakingbear.com/Political/Gems/turkey1.htm*. (accessed 9 December 2005).

O'Donnell, Edward T. (2003) *Ship Ablaze: The Tragedy of the Steamship General Slocum*. New York: Broadway Books.

People's Daily (2004) "Interview with Wang Deming." *People's Daily*, 23 Oct. *http://www.beijingportal.com.cn/7838/2004/11/06/207@2359924.htm*. (accessed 16 December 2005).

Salama, Jerry J. et al. (2005) *Reducing the Cost of New Housing Construction in New York City 2005 Update*. New York: Furman Center for Real Estate and Urban Policy, New York University School of Law and Robert F. Wagner Graduate School of Public Service.

Salama, Jerry J. et al. (1999) *Reducing the Cost of New Housing Construction in New York City*. New York: The New York University School of Law Center for Real Estate and Urban Policy.

de Soto, Hernando (2000) *The Mystery of Capital: Why Capitalism Triumphs in the West and Fails Everywhere Else*. New York: Basic Books.

Stein, Leon (2001) "The Triangle Fire." *Paper*. New York: Cornell University Press.

Time Asia (2005) "All Shook Up." *Time Asia* 12 Dec. *http://www.time.com/time/asia/magazine/article/0,13673,501051212-1137711,00.html*. (accessed 16 December 2005).

Washington Post (2004) "Russian Plane Bombers Exploited Corrupt System." *Washington Post*, 18 Sept. *http://www.washingtonpost.com/wp-dyn/articles/A30042-2004Sep17.html*. (accessed 9 December 2005).

Washington Post (1986) "Thousands Still Homeless 1 Year after Mexico Quake." *Washington Post*, 20 Sept. *http://www.washingtonpost.com/wp-srv/inatl/longterm/mexico/stories/860920.htm*. (accessed 16 December 2005).

Wedel, Janine R. (1998) *Collision and Collusion: The Strange Case of Western Age to Eastern Europe, 1990–1997*. New York: St. Martin's Press.

Wilson, James Q. (1975) *Thinking about Crime*. New York: Vintage Books.

2

On the Comparative Study of Corruption*

Franklin E. Zimring and David T. Johnson

This essay has two ambitions. The first is to show that a transnational comparative perspective can be of value in identifying topics worth studying in criminology and criminal law as well as an important method of conducting such studies. The second aim is to use the comparative perspective and method to explore the topic of corruption, a pervasively important and distinctive behavioral phenomenon that is of critical importance in both developing and developed nations. A comparative perspective on corruption provides insight about the role of this peculiar form of crime in various cultures and stages of development (p. 809). Moreover, we also believe that a focus on corruption as a special category of crime helps to explain the passions and politics that have been involved in discourse on white-collar crime.

We begin our tour with a plea for the increasing value of comparative study as a tool for criminological agenda setting and research. A brief second section defines corruption as a special subcategory of criminal behavior defined as the unlawful use of power. A third section then speculates on the relationship between corruption and features of social and governmental organization. A final section applies this comparative perspective to some long-standing issues in criminological discourse. We show that the same mix of condemnation and imprecision that has frustrated efforts to define white-collar crime produces ambiguity in the definition of corruption. We also suggest that the core focus of our criminology of corruption—the use of power as an instrument of crime—also helps to explain why white-collar crime has evoked concern, particularly among criminologists on the left. The unifying substantive theme in this analysis is the view of corruption as the criminal misuse of power.

Comparative Criminology: Necessity and Promise

In the early years of the 21st century, there are two important respects in which citizens of most regions are living on a smaller planet than a generation ago. In the first place, the impact of problems in one place on conditions in other places is more pronounced and faster in the current era than ever before. Whether the particular event is a bond default in Moscow, avian flu virus in China, political repression in Burma, or unemployment and low birthrates in France, the swift impact of many events far from their origins has become a commonplace observation of those who study globalization in culture, politics, public health, and economics.

The second important aspect of globalization is the more rapid dispersal of promising innovations in both the private and public sectors of institutional activity. With frequent travel and multinational business entities, both the lapsed time before innovations get transferred and the chances of transfer have increased to an extraordinary degree. So if the first impact of globalization is the larger susceptibility to problems, the second impact may be the faster transmission of solutions to problems. There is no indication in the current shrinkage of the globe that the homogenization of commerce and the speed of communication will soon end major differences in society and government, but a pervasive environment of mutual influence is a broad and important part of current events in most fields.

Criminology is no exception. International exchanges and organizations are proliferating in the developed world, including a new European association and international collaborations of scholars and organizations. Multinational research projects have included written surveys with common questions and estimation techniques that were published in the mid-1990s for a variety of developed nations,[1] followed by an attempt to measure victimization by survey in less developed nations. These findings have already been integrated into some discussions of transnational risks of crime and violence.[2] There have also been more limited international comparisons of criminal case processing and case outcomes.[3] Such efforts are in their pre-history, with much more work and greater sophistication to be anticipated in a relatively short time.

Two comments on the promise of comparative criminology here deserve emphasis. First, the value of comparative work is not simply to document differences and similarities among counties and systems for the comparative perspective is also a valuable tool for analyzing the distinctive character of one's own domestic practice and policy. The special nature of life-threatening violence in the United States, for example, is nowhere more apparent than when cross-national comparisons demonstrate that broadly similar rates of non-violent and even non-lethal violent crime contrast starkly with rates of lethal violence that differ markedly between nations.[4] So the value of comparison is much greater than its utility for describing observed variations between states and societies. It is an essential device for understanding what is distinctive (and problematic) about domestic arrangements.[5]

The second point about the promise of a comparative perspective is that the incentives to conduct comparisons are not evenly distributed throughout developed nations. Those who live in small countries are more easily convinced of the necessity of comparative work than those who live in big countries, if only because national variation is a much more visible element in Switzerland or Australia than in the United States.[6] Yet the value of comparisons in illuminating domestic problems is just as important for big countries as for small ones. If this is right, then it may be a special necessity to promote and illustrate the domestic values of comparative methods in the United States. The less natural a comparative perspective seems in the study of social behavior, the greater the chances that errors are made and opportunities for understanding are missed because of its absence. Similarly, the more students of a system assume its own uniqueness, the easier it will be to avoid evidence of non-uniqueness and the harder it will be to identify differences that are dysfunctional and problematic. The assumption of uniqueness thus frequently defeats opportunities to study how American behavior and institutions are exceptional.[7]

This essay explores the value of a comparative perspective in thinking about corruption as a distinct and widely present type of behavior that is criminal in a wide variety of complex societies. We first define that term and illustrate the distinctiveness of the category of behavior and the importance of the phenomenon as an impediment to economic development and social justice. We then apply the perspective obtained from a comparative approach to an analysis of white-collar crime as the criminal misuse of social or economic power.

Defining Corruption

Rather than constructing a definition of the crime of corruption in isolation, we wish to seek a definition of this particular offense in the context of the other types of methods of obtaining property that are usually considered criminal. By situating a definition of corruption in this larger tapestry, we hope to keep the distinctions between types of crime clear and to maintain consistent criteria for what makes violations of the interests of persons or institutions criminal.

There are, in criminal law, at least four methods of wrongfully obtaining control over the property or personal interests of others. One recurrent threat is the thief or burglar who takes by stealth, removing property when owners and custodians are not looking. A second method of victimization is to obtain property or compliance by use or threat of unauthorized personal force. "Your money or your life" is the choice the robber seeks to impose on his victim without any legal authority to use force. A third class of criminal method involves the use of fraud or falsity to induce victims to part with things of value because they believe facts the offender has misrepresented. Frauds and confidence games are as old as recorded history but as up-to-date as the hundreds of millions of e-mails sent out by persons purporting to have access to Nigerian bank millions but who require the assistance of "honest citizens" to secure mutual riches.

The fourth method of obtaining control over the property or person of another is the use of social or institutional power. When power granted to persons for restricted purposes is used instead for unauthorized personal aims, unlawful and socially wasteful exchanges take place: The government official charged with selecting the most qualified firm to provide trash collection to the city instead chooses the firm that offers him the most money in a personal bribe or as a "contribution" to a non-governmental organization; the schoolteacher with the power to assign grades on a merit basis to student work instead trades high grades for cash or personal favors from students or their families; the company official with the power to sell property for the benefit of the firm gives a major price concession to a buyer in exchange for a personal payment; the president of a nation grants public licenses that are not supposed to be given away to his friends and family rather than auctioning them off and making the proceeds available for the common good. In all these cases the offender has power for limited purposes and uses the power in prohibited ways.

While acts of corruption, which we define as *the illegal use of power for personal gain*, are no less or more dishonest than crimes involving force or stealth, the social structure of corruption and its distribution in society are different than crimes of personal force, fraud, or stealth. Anonymous acts of force or secret taking are typically acts of persons who lack social or government power. In contrast, corruption is, by definition, an act of a person who has either the economic power to bribe another or the power to provide a favor for a bribe. So corruption is a crime of the powerful, even though the power that triggers corrupt acts may often be minor and of special purpose. Traffic cops, sixth-grade teachers, and those who audit the tax records of small businesses are by no means potentates, but they do hold special purpose authority that can be of great importance.

Bribery and Corruption

What makes a bribe into a crime rather than a legitimate exchange of money for value or a gift? The answer has been another source of uncertainty and complexity in penal theory.[8] We define a bribe as the payment for a corrupt act, making the wrongfulness of the payment depend on the forbidden nature of the consideration for the payment. As long as the favor provided should not be exchanged for money, the act is corrupt, and the payment for it should be considered a bribe. There may be in local law specific prohibitions against selling discretionary power where the only unlawful use of the power is the acceptance of money itself. This type of "per se" corruption rule might seem to challenge the derivative nature of our definition, but we do not think the fact that it is the offering of money that makes the use of power wrongful undermines the utility of our definitional approach. Even here, it is the power holder's deviation from legal regulations constraining his acts which makes the transfer of money or other favors in exchange for benefits into a forbidden act.

Two Definitional Issues

Once the distinguishing feature of corruption is seen as the abuse of power, the next important question concerns the breadth of abuses of power to be regarded as corrupt. One definition would restrict the concept's scope to the unlawful use of power *for personal gain or other personal objectives*, thus limiting corruption to the venal and self-serving acts which are the archetypical illustrations of graft and bribery. In settings such as the break-in of Daniel Ellsberg's psychiatrist's office during the Nixon years, when national security powers were misused for a conception of governmental interest, or in the Iran-Contra case, where illegal exchanges were made to advance the government's political interests without personal gain, a definition of corruption that requires personal benefit would exclude such acts from being considered corrupt, while a definition of corruption that spanned the unlawful use of power *for all purposes* would clearly include such acts. The question—on the scope of the abuses of power that should be called corrupt—is a difficult one. Our position is that the element of personal gain should probably be required but would include more in regard to the concept of personal gain than money or tangible property.

A second question is easier to resolve: Should *unintended* abuses of power be considered corrupt? A totally objective standard of when power is unauthorized seems an unjust and therefore unnecessary element of the definition of criminal corruption. Where honest mistakes can be made about the scope of authorized power, such errors should not be regarded as criminal and therefore should not be considered corrupt. Mistakes of this sort might well produce civil liability, but they are not properly blameworthy in the criminal law and therefore should not be regarded as crimes. In our view the proper *mens rea* for corrupt abuse of power should be the Model Penal Code's notion of recklessness, and the criminological category of corrupt behavior should also be restricted to purposely unlawful uses of power.

The usefulness of our definition of corruption can best be explored by comparing it with its competitors. Although the last decade of the 20th century witnessed more publications on corruption than any previous period, key conceptual and definitional questions remain "largely ignored."[9] On the one hand, corruption is such a deeply contested concept that a coherent theory of it "has never been fully articulated."[10] On the other hand, "there is considerable overlap between various components of proposed definitions."[11] All analysts agree that corruption involves a deviation from certain *standards* of behavior. The key question, therefore, and the pivot around which conflict revolves, is what criteria to use to establish those standards. There seem to be three main candidates: law, public interest, and public opinion.[12]

The *legal approach* defines corruption in terms of the criteria established by official statutes and judicial interpretation. Thus an act is corrupt if it is prohibited by laws, and if it is not prohibited, it is not corrupt, even if it is unethical or abusive.

The *public interest approach* focuses on the effects of an act rather than on its legal status. In this view, if an act is harmful to the public interest, it is corrupt, even if it is legal. Conversely, if an act benefits the public, it is not corrupt, even if it violates the law.

Public opinion is the third source of criteria that has been used to define standards of integrity. This approach posits that an act is corrupt if some public defines it as such. Since public opinion may vary, analysts in this school must attend to the differences between "black," "gray," and "white" corruption.[13] Black corruption exists when a majority of both elite and mass opinion condemn it and want to see it punished. In contrast, gray corruption indicates that some observers, usually elites, want to see the action punished, while others do not—and the majority may be ambivalent. White corruption is corruption that is tolerated by the majority of both elite and mass opinion; neither wants to see the conduct punished.

Entering the contest to define corruption requires assessing the usefulness of these competing definitions. Because variations in definition affect research and law enforcement (not to mention democracy and development), we believe that definitional questions should be decided based on criteria of utility. In our view, law provides the most useful standard in terms of which corruption should be defined.

The Need for a Legal Standard

Only a legal standard can provide a definition of corruption that qualifies both analytically and morally as a crime and thus allows us to compare offenses of corruption with those of stealth, fraud, or force. Reserving the label of corruption only for acts which appear to the observer to have resulted in substantial social harm is both too broad and too restrictive. If any failed economic policy is harmful to the public, are all those policies that produce more harm than good to be judged, after the fact, as corrupt? Calling lawful acts corrupt when there is no intent to do harm is senseless. Conversely, a harm-centered definition is also too narrow because why should graft and self-dealing, which don't produce any obvious victims, be exempted from blameworthiness?

Necessary Versus Sufficient Conditions

Similarly, while a standard based on public opinion rather than legality provides some notice of wrongfulness if public opinion is stable, it provides no social protection in precisely those environments when illegal self-dealing is most rampant because it is tolerated by local mores—even though the behavior is unlawful.

There turns out to be no principled argument against making the unlawful use of power into a *necessary* element of the concept of corruption. Thus no use of power may be simultaneously authorized by law and called corrupt. In adhering to this as an ironclad requirement, there is the loss only of "corrupt" as an adjective of derision for condemning some forms of undesirable behavior. Given the many other negative terms available in modern languages for denouncing bad practices, this appears to us to be no great loss.

Still, should all unlawful uses of power be regarded as corruption? We have already excluded accidental illegality from the scope of our concern. Should there also be some *de minimus* exemption for acts that are not obviously harmful? We think not because of the consequences that one faces if the *sine qua non* requirement of corruption is either a violation of "public interest" or the presence of critical "public opinion." If the behavior was unlawful, why need we prove that this led to bad results any more with bribery than with larceny by stealth or deception?

Rather than making ill repute or bad outcome a requirement of the *actus reas* of corruption, the law can provide two affirmative defense-style exclusions to the solely legal definition of corruption in addition to the defense described earlier: the lack of intent to violate the law. The first would exclude from corruption acts where the actor's deviation from legal standard was objectively trivial. The second would provide an exclusion when the illegal use of power was justified by the greater harm avoided or the greater good achieved in a particular case. This second exception would be narrow and rarely successful—as in the exclusion from the category of corruption of illegal conduct by immigration officials to avoid Nazi internment policies. It would not become a standing invitation for political figures to justify broad programs of law violation.[14]

Because the opportunity to be involved in corruption is positively associated with increased power, corruption is one category of crime where the strong will prey on the weak and where the net effect of many acts of corruption may be regressive rather than redistributive of income. In many, if not most, settings where corruption flourishes, the offense pattern produces greater, rather than lesser, concentrations of wealth among advantaged populations.

Victimless Crime?

Because corruption frequently involves an exchange where the immediate parties to a transaction all gain from the unauthorized use of power, many corrupt acts lack a self-defined victim willing to report the conduct to law enforcement authorities. This fact distinguishes corruption from crimes such as larceny, burglary, or robbery, in which there often are angry victims. Further, since it is only the unauthorized use of power or its benefits that are regarded as wrongful, the criminal law of corruption is highly sensitive to legal and cultural factors that distinguish authorized from unauthorized motives and effects of discretionary choices by persons in authority. Though a particular state may have a few cultural or legal rules which vary the normal boundaries between illegal and lawful force or claim of right to property, questions of local law and custom will far more frequently be important in dividing permitted from prohibited uses of power in cases of alleged corruption. In short, local variations in law and culture will often be important in deciding whether conduct is corrupt.

Local customs and mores may also fail to condemn some acts of corruption because an obviously harmed individual victim is not present. Thus even when local law makes the criminality of conduct clear, local morals may all but excuse it.

Although the settings and practitioners of corruption will vary widely—from petty officials to presidents and from trivial material advantage to treason—there are also systematic differences between corruption and other forms of crime. Practitioners of corruption have power or money, or both, and are thus more likely to be of high or middle status than most of the burglars or robbers identified in modern states. The combination of higher-status offenders and the frequent lack of a direct victim to complain makes acts of corruption much harder to detect and prosecute than crimes with complainants.

Varieties of Corruption

As we define it, the essential element of corruption is the abuse of power, yet there are a wide variety of forms of corrupt behavior that ought to be distinguished. One distinction relates to the types of power abused—public or governmental power versus private power. The violation of public standards usually threatens the government or the collective benefit of its public as the interest diminished by corrupt acts. In contrast, private corruption involves the abuse of power by those given power over private interests who advance their own interests at the expense of the owner's interests. Accepting a bribe to avoid collecting a tax is an uncomplicated case of public corruption. An agent who sells private property to a friend for less than the market price he could get is corruption with a private victim.

A second important distinction is between predatory and cooperative offenders, with the predatory offenders seeking to keep rather than share with those they solicit all of the gains from an unauthorized transaction, either money or favors, rather than trying to create a natural alliance with those who need the benefits of the power they possess by creating a better outcome for them as well as for the primary offender. The cooperative pattern produces a more stable relationship that is harder to discover and stop. It is associated with social popularity and not infrequently with political power. The predatory pattern does not produce stable long-term relationships, unless its victims and customers fear the power holders. Moreover, the predatory pattern of corruption may often be mixed with uses of force as well. Where there is such a mixture, the charges exacted by the unauthorized users of power may exceed the costs of services in non-corrupt settings.

One final distinction in modes of corruption is between instrumental and affective motivations for participation in corrupt uses of power. In instrumental settings, one type of power is exchanged for other types, typically an exchange of favors for money. What the power holder wants with the money is not obvious in the exchange. By contrast, in an affective misuse of power, the primary motive of the authority is often that the benefit be conferred on a family member, loved one, or some other person whose gain is the primary motive of the power holder. On some occasions, power may be misused simply to assert the offender's ability to do so. While the misuse of power for affective purposes may be a violation of social norms, loyalty to family or friends may itself be a socially approved value, so a decision that must sacrifice either standards of probity in using power or loyalty to friends or family can generate value conflicts.[15]

Some Comparative Perspectives

A Tale of Two Potentates

Joseph Mobuto, the late and unlamented president of a nation he chose to call Zaire, and King Fahd Bin Abdul Aziz of Saudi Arabia were two of the richest and most free spending figures in the last decades of the 20th century. Both were notorious for throwing money at projects with no apparent social purpose in a world full of hunger and poverty. King Fahd built a replica of the American President's White House in the hills outside Marbella on the Costa del Sol in Spain. President Mobuto spread billions of dollars over European capitals and Swiss banks, with personal zoos and palaces as prominent landmarks in a country where starvation was not uncommon.[16] From a modern Western perspective the behavior of both these fin-de-siècle potentates was silly and immoral. But only one of the two was corrupt in the technical sense that we use the word.

King Fahd was wasteful and stupid with regard to the several billions of petro-dollars that came under the control of the royal family of Saudi Arabia. But evidently, the money he wasted was, under Saudi law, wholly under the control and personal dominance of the king. President-for-life Mobuto came to be known as "the man who stole a country" because of his conversion of public funds to private purposes: The extortion of bribes and the sale of publicly owned assets for private advantage were violations of the law of the nation he plundered. Mobuto was a criminal, while Fahd was merely a fool. In this sense the definition of corruption that we favor depends on local substantive law.

In one sense the dependence on local principles might make the presence or absence of a corruption label morally trivial. Would Mobuto have been any less monstrous if a duly elected parliament had passed legislation declaring all income from mineral rights to be his personal property? When it is a violation of legal standards that transforms the use of power into a category of criminal behavior, many varieties of despotic behavior are properly regarded as non-criminal, because those who fully dominate the institutions of government may be in the position to manipulate legal principles to avoid the label of corruption. In the vast majority of potential corruption situations, however, no such power to avoid legal conclusions will be present. Even in most cases where the central government's leadership is involved in plunder, the legal standards by which the behavior can be classified as illegal have been left intact.

To require that the use of power be unlawful as a matter of the law of the place where the behavior occurs is to provide a neutral standard that can be used to separate corrupt behavior from permissible discretionary acts. Relying instead on non-local norms for judging the appropriateness of particular discretionary acts is difficult to justify on a principled basis. Indeed, the best comparative history of bribery defines the core concept as "an inducement improperly influencing the administration of a duty meant to be gratuitously exercised."[17] Although the author of this definition displays some generalizing impulses (as when he asserts that bribery is everywhere shameful), as a conceptual matter, the meanings of the key terms in the definition—*inducement*, *improperly*, *duty*, and so on—cannot be discerned independently of the law and norms of a particular place. Thus even if bribery is everywhere shameful and secretive, what counts as bribery is locally defined.

Complexity and Corruption

What are the conditions of social structure and social value which influence the rate and the varieties of corrupt behavior in a particular place? The comparative perspective might be a useful tool for addressing this kind of question, but care must be taken to specify the salient sub-questions. There is, for example, an important distinction between the conditions which increase the opportunities for corrupt acts and social features which actually increase the rate of corrupt behavior. A major influence on the number and variety of potential cases of corruption is social and political complexity, with the number of opportunities for corrupt uses of power increasing as a function of the amount of power distributed throughout a social and political system and the complexity of restraints placed on the exercise of power in that system. The more complex an economic system, the greater the number of occasions when people will make important decisions which affect the property and interests of others. There are not only more different types of power in complex arrangements, there is a much greater tendency for the exercise of power to be constrained by the specialized roles of the people with access to it. When people put their savings under their mattresses, the primary custodians of the property are also its owners. In a society with banks, there are bank tellers and vice presidents with power over the money of others which is constrained by legal conditions. The opportunity to abuse power arises with the combination of physical control and legally limited power. The greater the complexity in a system, the larger the number of relationships of authorities with constrained power: toll takers, bank tellers, customs inspectors, tax auditors, mayors, and head waiters. In this sense, complexity in social and material relations is the mother of corruption.

The King Fahd example reminds us, however, that it is not merely the amount of property or power that determines the potential for corruption, it is also the constraints on its use. An absolute monarch cannot, by our definition, be a corrupt actor because there are no normative limits on his exercise of power. In the sense in which we use the term, it is not true that "absolute power corrupts absolutely." Rather, "absolute power" removes the constraints on power that make corruption possible when those constraints are not respected.

If opportunities for corruption expand with increases in complexity, do the rates of corruption also expand with an increase in the number of opportunities for exercising unlawful power? We suspect that a survey of developed and non-developed nations in the world at the turn of the 21st century would reveal little evidence of a positive correlation between complexity and corruption. If anything, poor and simple societies tend to be more corrupt than rich and complex ones.[18] In fact, when viewed from an external perspective, comparative judgments about corruption that business rating groups publish suggest that visible corruption is more often associated with more primitive levels of economic and political development. Conversely, complexity is associated with lower levels of corruption.[19] Of course, there are many less open societies in which a limited capacity for investigation and communication makes even rampant corruption unmentioned in public media, but that is not why complexity does not breed corruption because most closed societies are not economically advanced.

There are at least three reasons why the rate of corruption does not grow as a function of thc number of the opportunities for it to occur. First, many of the same technical processes which encourage the growth of complexity can be used to monitor the exercise of discretionary power and thus to control corruption through direct observation and deterrence. Hence accountability can also grow with complexity.

Second, increased complexity does not inevitably increase corruption because people learn social roles that impose an obligation of constraint. A culture of conformity with social roles of limited power is one important aspect of socialization in many complex modern societies. Being a responsible bank teller is learned behavior, and those who are socialized into roles with limitations on power will learn to respect and internalize the relevant rules of restraint. The material rewards for observing rules or restraint can be substantial; so can punishments for dereliction of duty. The incentives to conform are therefore great. In some less developed societies, by contrast, less effort may have been expended trying to socialize people to internalize a commitment to restraint in the performance of their public roles, and fewer rewards are given those actors who do try to act with integrity.

There is a third reason why visible corruption might decrease in more complex societies: the evolution of forms of corruption into less visible behaviors to avoid the deterrents and preventive measures that grow with complexity. More complicated societies not only generate lower rates of corruption, but a smaller proportion of the corruption that is present in such systems will be visible and easily measured. Crude and visible forms of corruption disappear more quickly than subtle and hidden abuses. This is a form of natural selection that accompanies increased complexity. There is thus good reason to suppose that the "dark figure" of corruption will encompass a larger proportion of corrupt acts in complex and developed societies than in less developed nations. As a result, the lower visibility of corruption in more complex societies is not just evidence of less crime, it also reflects the adaptive tendency to hide higher-status offending in developed nations.

While cross-sectional comparisons of the variations between nations in the amount and variety of corrupt behavior are ambiguous evidence of causation, longitudinal analysis of the development in particular countries might better reveal patterns that would help to answer the following questions. Is there a recurrent pattern of change in the levels and types of corruption associated with various stages of economic or political development—a single "natural history," in which particular stages of development are associated with particular patterns of corruption? Or are there different evolutionary patterns associated with different cultural values that interact with stages of economic and political development? Are there some cultural conditions that retard the growth or accelerate the decline in levels of corruption, while other value patterns provoke it? If there are, what are these values, and what are the magnitudes of their effects? And are there circumstances in which levels and types of corruption tend to be stable over long periods of time, despite changes in other aspects of government and economy?

Similarly, how important is corruption to total economic activity and to the functions and responsiveness of the political system at different times and stages of development? If levels of corruption are much greater in some systems than in others of comparable economic development, how important are patterns of corruption in explaining the different prospects for economic growth and for the distribution of income? In particular, is corruption on the whole a regressive influence on income distribution, and are other types of crime more likely to reduce income inequality, and if so, at what cost to economic growth?

Some features of social and economic development provide increased opportunities for many types of crime. Larger cities with efficient transportation systems encourage offenses of both stealth and force by creating the opportunity to come and go without fear of identification and detection. The same features of development facilitate fraud by enabling false identities to be assumed and dropped as people come and go.

If there are generalizations to be made about the criminological impact of increased complexity on corruption, we suspect that both trickery and corruption will be more prominent types of offending in wealthier and more complex social settings. This does not mean that *rates* of criminality of these types will actually increase as a number per thousand citizens or as a percentage of total economic activity, but rather that the proportion of all crime that is committed by fraud and corruption will go up with levels of social complexity and material wealth.

Complexity and Types of Corruption

Analysts of corruption in Western history argue that one corollary of the illegal nature of bribes is a universal penchant for secrecy.[20] However, many patterns of governmental and political corruption are best classified as "open secrets." Indeed, strong circumstantial evidence of political favor trading and dynastic favoritism to the family members of those in political power were all but acknowledged in regimes such as the Suharto government in Indonesia and the Marcos government in the Philippines[21] as well as among the government officials engaged in narcotics trafficking in places such as Mexico and Panama. The lack of a frightening deterrent should not motivate openness as long as visibility increases to some extent the risk of apprehension. To explain open corruption, we need, instead, to search for positive utilities—benefits of openness—that reveal why even small risks may be thought worth taking.

Perhaps the phenomenon of the "open secret" is simply evidence of inefficient or inept criminality so that the notoriety of corrupt behavior is a manifestation of the parties to the corruption failing to keep their shameful secrets hidden. But there are at least two other explanations of notorious corruption. The first is the "learning curve" notion mentioned previously. To the extent that there is real novelty in the restrictions on power that get imposed with governmental and economic complexity, relatively open patterns of corruption may take place because those who hold power use it without regard to relatively novel restrictions. President Mobuto, at some level, may have thought himself just as unconstrained in his personal use of his nation's treasure as did King Fahd with his obscene royal allowance. Under these circumstances the open abuse of power might be a developmental stage that is quickly replaced by more cautious and prudent behavior as examples of the punishment and disgrace of the improprieties accumulated.

The problem with this "learning curve" explanation in the age of the jet set is that so many intelligent and sophisticated people still seem prone to let favoritism, the conversion of vast sums of governmental resources, and the use of public power for personal gain, become public knowledge. It is almost as if there were some benefit to corrupt behaviors being well known.

And there might be. Just as corruption is, at its core, a use of power, the visibility of corruption can be an advertisement of the corrupt actor's power. Favoring one's relatives and spending vast sums that can only have come only from a public treasury are evidence of the powers possessed by the actor, so public knowledge of the wrongful act may be a risk worth taking where it demonstrates the magnitude of the offender's power. This instrumental and expressive value of "showing off" may be particularly pronounced when the corrupt act serves other favored social values, such as helping the poor,[22] being good to one's family (*chaebol* conglomerates in South Korea), or serving the national honor.

One final motive for open corruption is that it can be a way of asserting that the actor's power is not limited after all. The publicly corrupt act becomes a way of asserting its own legality. The openly corrupt activities may serve the offender as evidence that his behavior is not really wrong. Certainly, this is the dictator's usual defense when well-known abuses of power are the basis for later charges. Where this applies, it is a complete explanation for the utility of openness in the unlawful use of power for the offender for it is only in the open defiance of a legal standard that the claim of rightfulness, and therefore the validation of unconstrained power, can be asserted.

Corruption and Other Crimes

It might also be useful in conducting comparative analyses over time or cross-sectionally to inquire about the relationship between rates of corruption and rates of other types of criminal offenses. The relationship between rates of various types of offenses over time and across different types of societies has not been a major topic in theoretical or empirical criminology. The general assumption has been that environments with high rates of some types of criminal offenses would also have high rates of other varieties, but such analyses usually have been confined to various classes of crimes of stealth and force.[23] The assumption is that many of the environmental features that provoke or repress one kind of offense will have the same kind of effect on other kinds. There is also, of course, the notion that periods and places with large numbers of persons willing to commit crimes will have high rates of all sorts of offenses. If the proximate cause of high crime rates is a large number of potential offenders, then the general level of all types of crime should reflect the level of potential offenders.

Once the relation between types of crime considers both corruption and crimes of stealth and force, assumptions about rates are complicated by the different distribution of criminal opportunities that exist for crimes of corruption. Corruption is an offense that requires power—either political or economic—for the meaningful opportunity to gain from its criminal use. So not all of those who can employ force, stealth, or fraud for criminal purposes can resort to corruption. To the extent that crimes of force and stealth are concentrated in the least powerful elements of a society, there may be very little overlap between the most likely common criminals and those persons with the best opportunities to profit from corruption. Does this mean that there should be no significant relationship between rates of common offenses and rates of corruption? Probably not.

Even if particular offenders cannot or do not commit both types of offenses, the environmental conditions that foster or discourage common and corruption offenses might still generate systematic relationships between corrupt and common crimes. If the populations of potential offenders are distinct, there should be no substitution between common and corrupt offenses. But if there are environmental conditions, such as high or low tolerance of dishonesty or levels of effort or efficiency in detection and prosecution of offenses, that have a common influence on different types of crime, then one would expect rates of non-corruption and corruption offenses to rise and fall together.

There also may be social conditions which favor some forms of criminality and disfavor others. In Asia, for instance, Japan exhibits middling levels of many types of corruption offenses but has extremely low rates of crimes of force and stealth,[24] whereas Thailand has higher levels of both lethal violence and corruption,[25] while Singapore has more lethal violence but substantially less corruption.[26] In Europe, Italy has high levels of corruption and high homicide rates (at least by European standards), while the United Kingdom has lower rates of both corruption and homicide. And in the United States, Louisiana has high levels of corruption and lethal violence, while Hawaii has high levels of corruption but low levels of violence.[27] As these examples illustrate, different types of crime often move independently of one another. The comparative study of crime and corruption may help to identify patterns within that variation.

Corruption and the Problematics of White-Collar Crime

The extraordinary history of the study of "white-collar crime" can inform the analysis of corruption in two respects. First, it provides a cautionary tale of how problems of definition and classification can promote confusion and inhibit research. Second, some of the important themes that characterize writing about white-collar crime turn out to be at the core of corruption as a crime type as well. Students of corruption can learn from the definitional problems of the white-collar category at the same time that the focus on the abuse of power in corruption can teach important lessons about one sub-type of white-collar crime with distinctive characteristics.

Stanton Wheeler[28] began his analysis of definitional issues in white-collar crime by quoting E. A. Ross's[29] comment about the perfidy of "the man who picks pockets with a railway rebate, murders with an adulterant instead of a bludgeon, burglarizes with a 'rake off' instead of a jimmy, cheats with a company prospectus instead of a deck of cards."[30] The problem with this rhetorical assemblage of the sins of the powerful is the lack of analytic precision in identifying the agency of criminal harm. How, for example, does one "pick pockets with a railway rebate"? Such metaphors are both a wonderful tool for condemning conduct and a step away from rigor in defining the wrongfulness and the criminal agency that characterize the offending.

The first formal attempt to define white-collar crime was provided by Edwin H. Sutherland, the author of the concept. According to Sutherland,[31] "White collar crime may be defined approximately as a crime committed by a person of respectability and high social status in the course of his occupation." But why is the social status of the offender important? If it was to demonstrate that crime is not solely the product of poverty, then why was the job-related aspect also deemed important? And if there were supposed to be any distinctive elements attached to the job-related aspect of this definition of white-collar crime, what were they?

Moreover, Stanton Wheeler[32] says that Sutherland's definition and his empirical focus diverged from the start: "His book was devoted . . . to the crimes of organizations not of persons . . . thus a firm basis for ambiguity had been laid. Those following Sutherland sometimes focused on persons of high status, sometime on occupation, and sometimes on corporate bodies." The "crimes" that Sutherland counted included both violations of regulatory standards and civil contract cases. Though organizational offenses are an important criminological category,[33] they are only one part of the white-collar crime category in all of the usual definitions. For this and other reasons Wheeler claimed that "the concept of white collar crime is in a state of disarray."[34] Nothing in subsequent analyses has clarified the core conception.

There are important parallels in the definitional problems found in the white-collar and corruption categories. First, the symbolic or adjectival character of some definitions of both terms has generated conceptual confusion. Just as the need to stigmatize the corrupt official or influence peddler has blurred definitional boundaries in corruption, so does the metaphor of "picking pockets with a railway rebate" owe none of its rhetorical power to precision. Denunciations of white-collar crime "reflect a concern for the weakening of the social fabric created when people in privileged positions destroy trust by committing crimes."[35] Although the same language can be used to describe popular disgust with corruption, the cost of such broad rhetorical sweeps has been substantial. Most importantly, the loose and denunciatory usage of both these terms hampers the search for conceptual clarity and analytical utility.

We go even further to suggest that one reason for special public concern with white-collar crime can be found in the technical conception of corruption that we urge: the abuse of power. Whether combined with fraud or merely concealed, the essence of corruption is the misuse of power (and this is also what Wheeler would regard as the misuse of privilege). In some settings the misuse of power is manifest as classic organizational offenses, while in other settings, organizations are the primary victims of corrupt offenses by individuals or groups. In either case it is not merely a crime by a powerful person that invites special condemnation; it is the criminal misuse of power.

The parallels between white-collar crime and corruption provide another context in which to reconsider the question of whether personal gain should be a definitional requirement of criminal corruption. In the annals of white-collar crime, when combinations to restrain prices, for example, are discovered, there is no reason to worry about whether those who fix prices were only operating for the benefit of the corporations they represented or whether they personally would gain from the artificially high prices. Certainly, the General Electric heavy equipment conspiracies would have been just as socially injurious if their only beneficiaries had been the corporation. So why require personal gain as an element of the definition?

It is no answer to this that personal advantage can always be found through creative contortions in cases where organizations will benefit from restraint of trade. The essence of the anti-social nature of price fixing depends in no obvious way on whether the corporate conspirators obtained raises or stock options. If the corrupt bank teller or government official passed all her material gains to favored friends, how would that diminish the corruption?

Our focus on the misuse of power in both corruption and white-collar crime may help to distinguish degrees of wrong in notorious behavior by public officials. The mayor of Washington, D.C., Marion Barry, was caught red-handed ingesting crack cocaine. Barry's drug dependency certainly compromised his ability to serve as a public official, but the degree of public blame in this case was sufficiently tempered so that even after his drug treatment, Barry was deemed a credible candidate in the next election. When he was president, William Clinton had a sexual relationship with an intern and lied about it. What may separate these offenses from the Watergate scandal and the Daniel Ellsberg burglary case is the distinction between crimes involving powerful people and the criminal misuse of power. It is not merely the misbehavior of those with power that generates special condemnation; it is when power becomes the instrument of criminality that deeds are deemed most blameworthy. This, more than class resentment, may explain the angry response to the symbolism of some forms of white-collar crime and corruption. What is distinctively modern and threatening in the criminal use of power are the modern innovations and mechanisms that are utilized to achieve criminal ends. Whether this is a part of crimes against organizations or of crimes on behalf of organizations, it turns the tools of modernity against the public welfare and therefore elicits especially intense disapprobation.

Conclusion

The central principle of this article is that corruption is the criminal misuse of power. This feature of corruption as a crime suggests that it is an offense that will be committed more often than others by persons of higher social and economic status who hold the power that generates the potential for corruption. Because the criminal misuse of social or political power can be viewed as an abuse of trust, there is a reason to predict that corrupt offenders will be viewed as more blameworthy than those who take by deception or stealth. This same tendency to condemn the misuse of power may explain some of the passion in the criminological discourse about white-collar crime.

Endnotes

* We thank the following for helpful commentary: Susan Rose-Ackerman, Richard Leo, Henry Pontell, Michael Tonry, Andrew Von Hirsch, José Luis Díez Ripollés, and the participants in the eighth annual Nigel Walker Lecture at Cambridge in May 2004. An earlier version of this paper was published in the British Journal of Criminology 45:793 (2005).

1. Van Dijk and Mayhew (1992).
2. Zimring and Hawkins (1997).
3. See, for example, Farrington and Langan (1998).
4. Zimring and Hawkins (1997: chap. 3).
5. Langbein (1995); Lipset (1996).
6. American criminology is provincial. In *Criminology*, the flagship journal for the American Society of Criminology, just 7.4 percent of articles published between 1990 and 1999 had "any kind of international/comparative focus" (Barbaret 2001). For the same period the *Australia and New Zealand Journal of Criminology* published 190 articles, of which 11 percent were international or comparative, by our standards still a low figure, even if it is 50 percent higher than the parallel American figure. American law and society scholarship is also provincial. Between 1966 and 2000, for example, *Law & Society Review* published 352 "original research" articles, of which only 23 (6.5 percent) can be called "comparative analysis" (Silbey 2000: 864). The analogous figure for 1990–2000 was 6.6 percent.
7. Assumptions of singularity that have been tested—such as the views that America is a "high-crime society" or that American criminal justice is uniquely characterized by "leaky pipe" caseload attrition—often prove to be false.
8. See Noonan (1984).
9. Heidenheimer and Johnston (2002: xiii).
10. Ibid., p. 5.
11. Ibid., p. 13.
12. Scott (1972); Gardiner (2002).
13. Heidenheimer (1989).
14. See, on this theme, the defense of necessity in American Law Institute (1963: sec. 3.02).
15. A fourth distinction, between bribery and extortion, has an extensive academic pedigree, but it seems less conceptually and practically important than the distinctions we make here (Noonan, 1984; McChesney, 1997; Kang, 2002). Our distinction between predatory and cooperative corruption is not parallel to the boundary between extortion and bribery because often, those who extort may leave their victims with material advantages from the transaction. This certainly happens in corrupt labor relations.
16. Transparency International (2004).
17. Noonan (1984).
18. Rosenberg (2003).
19. See, for example, the cross-national Corruption Perceptions Indices that have been published by Transparency International every year since 1995 (Hodess et al., 2001).
20. Noonan (1984).
21. Transparency International (2004) ranks these leaders numbers 1 and 2 in total corruption loss.
22. As in the case of Eva Peron.
23. Zimring and Hawkins (1997: chap. 2).
24. Schlessinger (1997).
25. Phongpaichit and Piriyarangsan (1994).
26. For violence, see Johnson (forthcoming).

27. Compare Bridges (1999) with Cooper and Daws (1990), and see Federal Bureau of Investigation (2003) for violence.
28. Wheeler (1983).
29. Ross (1907).
30. Ibid., p. 7.
31. Sutherland (1949: 9).
32. Wheeler (1983: 1653).
33. Tonry and Reiss (1993).
34. Wheeler (1983: 1655).
35. Ibid., p. 1656.

References

American Law Institute (2003) *Model Penal Code*. Philadelphia: American Law Institute.

Barbaret, Rosemary (2001) "Global Competence and American Criminology—An Expatriate's View." *Criminologist* 26(2):3–5.

Bridges, Tyler (1999) *Bad Bet on the Bayou: The Rise of Gambling in Louisiana and the Fall of Governor Edwin Edwards*. New York: Farrar, Straus and Giroux.

Cooper, George, and Gavan Daws (1990) *Land and Power in Hawaii: The Democratic Years*. Honolulu: University of Hawaii Press.

Federal Bureau of Investigation (2003) "Uniform Crime Reports: Crime in the United States," http://www.fbi.gov/ucr/03cius.htm.

Gardiner, John A. (2002) "Defining Corruption." Pp. 25–40 in *Political Corruption: Concepts and Contexts*, 3rd ed., Editors A. Heidenheimer and M. Johnston. Piscataway, NJ: Transaction Publishers.

Heidenheimer, Arnold (1989) "Perspectives on the Perception of Corruption." Pp. 149–163 in *Political Corruption: A Handbook*, Editors A. Heidenheimer and M. Johnston. Piscataway, NJ: Transaction Publishers.

Heidenheimer, Arnold, and Michael Johnston, eds. (2002) *Political Corruption: Concepts and Contexts*. Piscataway, NJ: Transaction Publishers.

Hodess, Robin, ed. (2003) *Global Corruption Report 2003*. Berlin: Transparency International.

Hodess, Robin et al., eds. (2001) *Global Corruption Report 2001*. Berlin: Transparency International.

Johnson, David T. (forthcoming) "The Vanishing Killer: Postwar Japan's Homicide Decline." *Social Science Japan Journal*.

Kang, David C. (2002) *Crony Capitalism: Corruption and Development in South Korea and the Philippines*. Cambridge: Cambridge University Press.

Klitgaard, Robert et al. (2000) *Corrupt Cities: A Practical Guide to Cure and Prevention*. Oakland, CA: Institute for Contemporary Studies.

Langan, Patrick A., and David P. Farrington (1998) *Crime and Justice in the United States and England and Wales, 1981–96*. NCJ 169284, United States Department of Justice. Washington, DC: U.S. Bureau of Justice Statistics.

Langbein, John H. (1995) "The Influence of Comparative Procedure in the United States." *American Journal of Comparative Law* 43(4):545–554.

Lipset, Seymour M. (1996) *American Exceptionalism: A Double-Edged Sword*. New York: W. W. Norton.

McChesney, Fred S. (1997) *Money for Nothing: Politicians, Rent Extraction, and Political Extortion*. Cambridge, MA: Harvard University Press.

Noonan, John T., Jr. (1984) *Bribes*. New York: Macmillan.

Phongpaichit, Pasuk, and Sungsidh Piriyarangsan (1994) *Corruption and Democracy in Thailand*. Bangkok: Silkworm Books.

Rose-Ackerman, Susan (1999) *Corruption and Government: Causes, Consequences, and Reform*. Oxford: Cambridge University Press.

Rosenberg, Tina (2003) "The Taint of the Greased Palm." *New York Times Magazine*, 10 August, 28:30–33.

Ross, Edward A. (1907) *Sin and Society: An Analysis of Latter-Day Iniquity*. Boston: Houghton, Mifflin. Reprint, Glouster, MA: Peter Smith, 1965.

Schlessinger, Jacob M. (1997) *Shadow Shoguns: The Rise and Fall of Japan's Postwar Political Machines*. New York: Simon and Schuster.

Scott, James (1972) *Comparative Political Corruption*. Upper Saddle River, NJ: Prentice Hall.

Shapiro, Susan (1980) *Thinking About White Collar Crime: Matters of Conceptualization and Research*. Washington, DC: National Institute of Justice.

Silbey, Susan (2000) "From the Editor." *Law & Society Review* 34(4):859–871.

Sutherland, Edwin (1949) *White Collar Crime*. New York: Dryden Press.

Tonry, Michael, and Albert Reiss Jr., eds. (1993) "Beyond the Law: Crime in Complex Organizations." In *Crime and Justice: A Review of Research*. Chicago: University of Chicago Press.

Transparency International (2004) *Global Corruption Report 2004*. London: Pluto Books.

Van Dijk, Jan, and Pat Mayhew (1992) *Criminal Victimization in the Industrialized World*. The Hague: Ministry of Justice.

Wheeler, Stanton (1983) "White Collar Crime: History of an Idea." In *Encyclopedia of Crime and Justice*. New York: Macmillan.

Wrong, Michela (2001) *In the Footsteps of Mr. Kurtz: Living on the Brink of Disaster in Mobutu's Congo*. New York: Harper Collins.

Zimring, Franklin, and Gordon Hawkins (1997) *Crime Is Not the Problem: Lethal Violence in America*. New York: Oxford University Press.

3

Corporate Corruption in the New Economy

Robert Tillman and Michael Indergaard

In popular usage the "New Economy" refers to developments in the late 1990s such as the rise of the Internet, a boom in tech stocks, an explosion of dot-com start-ups, and the appearance of new business doctrines and cultures. Countless revelations that surfaced after the boom came to an illegal end, suggesting that epic fraud was as much a part of the New Economy as the dot-coms had been. The epidemic of crime among the ranks of prestigious corporations and professionals puzzled observers across the intellectual spectrum. Federal Reserve Chairman Allan Greenspan, formerly an exuberant fan of the New Economy, rued its "infectious greed." Law professor Frank Partnoy asked whether, in the wake of regulatory and cultural shifts, it was possible to convict business actors of financial crimes.[1] Sociologist Paul Hirsch remarked that the participants in the frauds had occupied central positions but apparently "rejected" the "legal culture" of the mainstream.[2] Robert Tillman and Michael Indergaard asked, "How was it that such a broad spectrum of Corporate America ended up a *field of schemes*?"[3]

The puzzling scandals of the New Economy add weight to earlier calls—made in the wake of the savings and loan and junk bond scandals of the 1980s—that new frameworks be developed for analyzing white-collar crime.[4] Indeed, analysts of white-collar crime have struggled for a quarter century to keep up with a terrain roiled by corporate restructuring, organizational innovation, deregulation, new technologies, globalization, and financialization. For many scholars this long-term transformation constitutes the real "New Economy." Relevant for our purposes is that these changes set the scene for the New Economy scandals circa 1999. Most basic was a shift in corporate organization from self-contained hierarchies to network forms. Economic sociologist Paul DiMaggio notes that this "network economy," with its permeable firm boundaries and new forms of coordination, poses "dilemmas" for corporate governance. The "valuation of companies increasingly must take into account the worth of assets held outside the firm," while "the acute flexibility that facilitates adaptiveness and innovation" may make accountability problematic.[5] At the same time, the governance system was altered by institutional changes linked with neoliberalism—namely, deregulation as well as new doctrines. New Economy doctrine—as espoused by business schools, the financial media, and business professionals—advocated insurrection against the "old rules" for investing and business development.

Brandishing a narrative about the rise of a new kind of firm, they advised would-be New Economy firms to become "first movers" that command new market niches. To this end, they should:

> . . . line up a chain of high status business intermediaries to help the firm gain credibility—and have a high profile IPO; and boost the share price so that the stock could be used as a currency, allowing one to acquire talent, capital, and other firms at less cost, fueling a spiral of growth that, in turn, would reinforce the stock's standing.[6]

However, in the wake of deregulation the same business intermediaries (e.g., lawyers, accountants, financial analysts) increasingly were being relied on as "reputational intermediaries" in the system of corporate governance. It is in the workings of this altered governance system for an economy increasingly organized around networks that one should look to understand the New Economy scandals. On the surface the most striking feature of this system was that so many prominent firms and professionals acted as if the only rule that truly mattered was that deception is normal.

One confounding aspect of the corrupt corporate practices in the late 1990s is that while many clearly violated civil and regulatory law, they may not have violated any criminal statutes and thus, technically, did not commit crimes. In key respects the situation was analogous to swindles and corruption surrounding the development of the railroads in the 19th century. Charles Perrow has shown that elite business interests of the era both helped alter the institutional environment and engaged in novel forms of misdeeds whose legal statuses were murky.[7] He argues that these deceptions were unethical abuses of power that entailed corruption in an institutional sense, if not always in a legal sense. For much the same reason we use the terms "corporate corruption" and "corporate crime" interchangeably. Following the line of reasoning first proposed by Sutherland and more recently advocated by Clinard and Yeager, Michalowski and Kramer, Mann, and Reed and Yeager, we assume that for many forms of corporate misconduct the legal distinction between criminal and civil wrongs may be arbitrary and misleading, and therefore we consider a broad array of practices that have in common the goal of misleading and defrauding investors.[8]

The next section begins with an empirical sketch of the New Economy crimes; it presents evidence on their scope, considers assessments of their economic consequences, and delineates the forms they have taken. The theoretical section that follows revises the criminogenic markets approach to deal with the shift to network forms of organization as well as the particular institutional framework that contributed to corporate corruption.

Crimes of the New Economy

There is ample evidence that fraud and other financial deceptions were widespread during the New Economy boom and bust. Moreover, the misdeeds in question had a distinctive empirical profile: (1) they were generally tailored to exploit gaps left by regulatory changes; (2) they often entailed collaboration across the boundaries of individual firms, with high-status business professionals playing prominent roles; and (3) they focused on boosting revenue numbers rather than profit figures, the common goal in financial frauds of earlier periods.

Scope and Consequences

While statistical data on white-collar crime, particularly corporate crime, are scant, clues to the magnitude of what a number of observers referred to as a "corporate crime wave" can be found in two sources: data on financial restatements and class action lawsuits involving allegations of securities fraud. Financial statements submitted to the SEC by publicly traded companies that include basic information about companies' assets, liabilities, revenues, and earnings may be restated if those facts later change. One of the primary reasons, in recent years, for these restatements has been "material errors and fraud." Thus financial restatements can be seen as an indirect measure of corporate misconduct, specifically intentional efforts to mislead investors.

A study by the General Accounting Office found that between 1997 and 2002, restatements increased from 92 in 1997 to an estimated 250 in 2002—an increase of 170 percent. The study found that during the period, restatements had been filed by a total of 845 companies, representing 10 percent of all those listed on the three major stock exchanges: the New York Stock Exchange, the American Stock Exchange, and Nasdaq. GAO researchers examined changes in stock values following restatement announcements for a subset of 689 companies and calculated that investor losses resulting from those restatements totaled more than $100 billion.[9]

A second indicator, one that more directly measures corporate fraud, is the number of class action lawsuits filed annually that allege securities fraud. These suits typically are brought by shareholders who claim that they suffered monetary damages, usually resulting from a decline in the value of their shares, because of the fraudulent actions of executives, managers, or other corporate insiders. Data collected by researchers at Stanford University show that the number of class action securities fraud lawsuits increased from 108 in 1996 to a peak of 483 in 2001. Significantly, a large number (312) of the 2001 suits involved initial public offering (IPO) allocations, in which shareholders typically alleged that company insiders, investment banks, and analysts conspired to drive up stock prices in IPOs in order to profit from pre-market allocations to insiders of the stock at below-market prices—leaving non-insiders to pay inflated prices for their shares.[10]

Two studies provide a basis for determining the broader impact of corporate corruption on the economy and on ordinary individuals. The Brookings Institution estimated that corporate scandals occurring in the period beginning with Enron's bankruptcy in December 2001 and ending with WorldCom's bankruptcy announcement in July 2002 caused a loss of $35 billion in the gross domestic product in the year following the WorldCom announcement.[11] Using the Brookings Institution methodology, the New York State Office of the Comptroller estimated that the scandals cost that state's economy $2.9 billion in fiscal year 2002–2003 and cost the state retirement fund for state and municipal employees $9 billion. And it estimated that in the period from mid-March 2002 through mid-July 2002, corporate scandals caused the average 401(k) plan participant who was in his sixties to lose $10,450 from his account.[12]

While these studies are open to criticism, they begin to provide a sense of the macro- and micro-level costs of the corporate scandals in the late 1990s. Among other things, they confirm the fact—often noted by criminologists but rarely by politicians—that the monetary costs of white-collar crimes, including corporate crimes, dwarf those of street crimes. The costs of many corporate crimes are often diffused over large numbers of victims, for example, shareholders. It is only when the brunt of these costs are felt by individuals that the public fully grasps the harm that these crimes inflict.

Basic Forms

While the corporate scandals of the late 1990s tainted a wide variety of companies, they seemed to occur in disproportionate numbers in three industries: the energy trading industry, in which companies like Enron transformed gas and electricity into commodities to be traded on financial markets; the dot-com industry, where start-up Internet companies could raise millions in cash, despite having no history of earnings or even reasonable business models; and the telecom industry, in which companies like WorldCom saw their stock prices multiply in a matter of months on the promise of the potential of fiber optics. All three industries had been identified as centers for the emerging New Economy. As the stock market boomed in the late 1990s, corporate insiders in these industries, along with their professional accomplices in the fields of accounting, banking, and law, contributed to the organized "exuberance." They also began to develop and pass along common strategies for defrauding investors and consumers. Here we describe several of these strategies.

Swapping/Round-Tripping

One of the much-touted features of the New Economy was the development of new types of transactions that relied less on cash exchanges and more on the bartering of goods and services. "Swaps" of various kinds between businesses became normalized parts of what Tillman and Indergaard refer to as the "New Economy Barter Circuit."[13] Swapping reflected the fact that the energy-trading, telecom, and dot-com sectors each relied on a network system. In each system, there were some commodities that just about any member firm could make use of or exchange (e.g., electrical power, telecom capacity, online advertising). More important, the ambiguous economic values of these commodities abetted swapping economies, as was the case with the stock of New Economy firms (especially start-ups). The nebulous value provided a great deal of flexibility for firms that wished to manipulate financial statements. In such cases the real utility of these commodities was that they facilitated collective efforts to engage in financial manipulations.

The origin of many swapping tactics may have been the energy trading industry, where federal legislation of the 1990s encouraged companies to exchange gas and electricity and to share transmission lines in an effort to increase efficiency. These tactics evolved into more deceptive and fraudulent practices that came to be known as "round-tripping," in which energy companies falsely boosted their revenues by buying and selling electricity to each other in mirror transactions whose only purpose was to inflate their reported sales. The *Wall Street Journal* described one such transaction that took place between two of the largest energy-trading companies, Dynegy and CMS, on November 15, 2001:

> At 10:08 A.M. CST, Dynegy bought a month's worth of electric capacity at $25.50 per megawatt hour. At exactly the same time, Dynegy sold CMS the same amount at the

> same price. Twenty minutes later, at 10:28 A.M. CST, Dynegy conducted another trade to simultaneously buy and sell a year's worth of electric capacity from CMS, at a price of $34 per megawatt hour.[14]

The Securities and Exchange Commission would later charge that in the first quarter of 2002 Dynegy reported $236 million in revenues from round-trip trades.[15] A number of the country's largest energy companies would eventually admit that they, too, had engaged in round-trip transactions.

The idea of inflating revenues through the use of round-trip transactions, thereby increasing the value of a company's stock, also caught on quickly in the telecommunications industry. In the mid-1990s the telecom industry was one of the high flyers of the New Economy, dazzling investors with promises of a brave new world, where everything from phone conversations to movies would flow through a global network of fiber optic cables. As the 1990s came to a close, however, the promises turned out to be hollow as it became apparent that capacity far outstripped demand and that there was a glut of fiber optic capacity on the market. In desperation, many telecom executives turned to "swaps" with other telecoms to keep their numbers high. Telecom giants like Global Crossing, Qwest, and WorldCom would sell access to their fiber optic networks to one another in deals that ended in no actual income but allowed each of the firms to report the revenue on their balance sheets. In the first three quarters of 2000, for example, Qwest sold $870 million in capacity, while buying $868 million in capacity from the same parties, suggesting that the transactions were "round-trips" that cancelled each other out.[16]

In a similar fashion, firms in the dot-com industry used swapping to boost their revenue numbers "on the way up" (especially leading up to IPOs) and, more desperately, to maintain revenue totals after the stock market crashed and the Internet economy began its downward slide. A number of them found it easier to create phony rather than real income by engaging in "round-trip" transactions. The classic example of these elaborate swaps may well be Homestore.com. An Internet start-up that became the largest online provider of real estate listings, Homestore allegedly was the nexus for a series of complex swaps that involved more than a dozen dot-coms as well as major firms such as Cendant and AOL. Homestore was, in essence, buying its own revenue in deals that took place in three "legs." In the first leg Homestore paid other dot-coms cash "purportedly for services, technology, advertising and/or content." This first leg "was a sham transaction because Homestore received nothing of value in return"; the real purpose was "to supply money to these companies so that they could fund the third leg."

> In the second leg, AOL paid cash to Homestore for advertising. The third hidden leg was the bridge between these two transactions and was the "round trip" which was the quid pro quo for the deal. This is where the third party company used the money received from Homestore to buy advertising from AOL .... AOL recycled the money back to Homestore which recognized the same as revenue.[17]

Such machinations generated large profits for company insiders, who sold their stock options at artificially inflated prices before the scheme collapsed. AOL itself proved to be a leader in the use of swaps and other illicit tactics to pump up its reported revenue.

Creative Accounting

At the heart of many New Economy schemes to defraud investors were accounting tricks that caused corporate debt to either disappear or to be magically transformed into assets. The magicians who performed these illusions worked for the Big Four accounting firms, which had shed their roles as independent auditors and had taken on the role of consultants to their clients. In many cases, accountants devised ways for firms to be in technical compliance with accounting rules using financial arrangements that made a mockery of the substance of the rules. For example, WorldCom's accounting of its huge merger deals made it appear as if its revenues were continually rising, while its costs were dropping—a ruse which set an unobtainable standard for other telecoms, many of which, in turn, engaged in fraud so as to keep up with the leader. Enron was arguably the most aggressive player when it came to gaming the rules; many of the deceptive accounting practices came to light after the fall of Enron, when investigators began looking at how accounting firms had colluded with company insiders to, in essence, "cook the books."

Soon after the Enron debacle began, investigators learned that the energy company had for years grossly inflated its revenues by utilizing an accounting method known as "mark-to-market," under which a firm can record all future revenues and profit from an energy contract in the quarter in which the contract was signed. Under more traditional accounting rules, revenues and profits (as well as any losses on the deal) would be recorded as they came in. Using mark-to-market rules, however, energy companies could record as revenue on their financial statements the entire amount of an energy contract so that if the company signed a contract to sell $1 million worth of natural gas, but they also had to buy the same amount of gas for $900,000 in order to resell it, they could still record the $1 million as revenue. If a securities brokerage firm had done a similar deal, they would have recorded the difference of $100,000 as net revenue. Had the latter method been used, the $101 billion in revenues that Enron reported in 2001 would have turned into $6.3 billion, and the company that claimed to be the seventh largest corporation in America would have dropped to 287th in the rankings.[18]

At the same time that revenues were being inflated, debt was being hidden in "special purpose entities" and removed from the company's balance sheet. In one year alone, 2000, Enron (aided by accountants, bankers, and lawyers) used these tactics to erase $10 billion of debt from its balance sheet. The deals worked like this: Enron insiders would create a partnership as part of a "special purpose entity" and then transfer ("sell") an asset, typically one that was performing poorly and incurring debt, to the partnership, thereby removing the debt from the balance sheets. According to accounting standards, in order for the partnership's finances not to be included on Enron's statements, at least 3 percent of the entity had to be owned by independent outsiders. The remaining 97 percent of the capital used to fund the partnership typically came from banks, usually large Wall Street investment banks such as J. P. Morgan, Citigroup, and Merrill Lynch, in the form of loans or lines of credit. The Enron insiders would include large commissions and fees to be paid to themselves by the partnerships.[19]

Enron was not the only energy company to engage in these practices. In 2002, Dynegy, one of Enron's competitors, agreed to pay a $3 million civil penalty to settle charges filed by the Securities and Exchange Commission that it misled investors in 2001 by artificially boosting its cash flow by 37 percent ($300 million) with money it received from special purpose entities that was, in fact, a loan.[20]

Biased Analysis

Stock values of many New Economy companies were kept artificially high through the efforts of what Tillman and Indergaard refer to as "professional pumpsters." In addition to the accountants who helped firms manipulate their financial statements, these included members of the financial media and, significantly, stock analysts at major investment banks. In the late 1990s a number of these analysts had achieved celebrity status, appearing frequently in the media, where they were often treated as financial gurus, and having spectacular salaries lavished on them by their employers. Because the reports they issued on the prospects of specific companies were often used by institutional investors, like pension fund managers, to make investment decisions, their professional opinions had a significant impact on the value of the stock of the companies they covered and thus on the value of the stock options awarded to those companies' executives. When large companies like Enron, Global Crossing, and WorldCom began to collapse amid allegations of fraud, many observers began to ask why these analysts were unable to foresee these events, and indeed, why many of them continued to give the companies strong ratings until just before they imploded. The answer lies in the fundamental conflict faced by the analysts. They were supposed to provide objective, independent assessments of corporations, despite the fact those same corporations were banking clients of the analysts' own employers who were eager to keep the CEOs of those companies happy.

These conflicts were exemplified in an incident involving Citigroup's CEO, Sanford Weill, telecom giant AT&T, and Jack Grubman, a star telecom analyst at a subsidiary of Citigroup. AT&T was a major banking client of Citigroup, and in the summer of 1998, AT&T management began complaining to Weill about the less than enthusiastic ratings that Grubman had been giving the company. Weill asked Grubman to "take a fresh look" at AT&T. Grubman responded with a memo to Weill with the title "AT&T and 92nd Street Y," in which he outlined the steps he would take in re-evaluating AT&T and asked Weill for help in getting his children admitted to an exclusive New York City preschool (the 92nd Street Y). Eventually, Weill made a phone call to a board member of the school, the Citigroup Foundation pledged to donate a million dollars to the school, and Grubman's children were admitted.[21]

This small example illustrates a much larger pattern of conflicts of interest among stock analysts that sparked an investigation by New York Attorney General Eliot Spitzer, who would later comment on how he and his staff came to see the problem as pervasive: "There was a tipping point, where we went from viewing this as a problem that was isolated and could be carved out, probably one analyst or two analysts and no more, to the recognition that we had suddenly arrived at that the entire structure was fraud."[22]

IPO Allocation Schemes

Wall Street investment banks also had a prominent role in another series of New Economy corporate scandals involving initial public offerings by private firms that had decided to "go public" by selling stock in their companies. Typically, the firm going public employs an investment bank to underwrite the offering: to set the initial price of the stock and to oversee its sale. Underwriters have the option of allocating a certain proportion of the shares to be sold at the initial offering price to specific individuals and organizations. Other investors purchase the stocks in the open market (or "aftermarket") at a price that fluctuates as demand rises or falls. A watershed event in the stock market boom of the 1990s occurred in 1995, when Netscape's stock price soared 108 percent on the first day it was offered to the public. Suddenly, everyone wanted to get in on the Internet gold rush; there was a flood of dot-com IPOs, surrounded by a frenzy of investors desperate to participate in what appeared to be a sure thing. Between January 1998 and December 2000 more than 460 high-tech and Internet firms went public, and many saw the value of their stock increase over 100 percent on the first day of the offering.[23] This meant that many who had been allocated shares at the initial offering price more than doubled their money in a single day.

The considerable power that the situation gave to underwriters opened the door for various kinds of abuses of the IPO process. One of the most common was a "tie-in arrangement," in which IPO allotments were made on the condition that the recipient purchase shares in the same stock in the aftermarket, thereby driving up demand and the price of the stock. This practice was extremely common during the boom years for dot-com IPOs. A massive class action suit filed in the wake of the dot-com bust charged that over 300 firms that filed for IPOs, their top officers, and 55 investment banks participated in a scheme to defraud the investing public. The suit alleged that investment banks underwriting the IPOs granted allotments of initial offerings of "hot" stocks—typically under-priced—to institutional investors or business notables who were important customers in exchange for their implicit agreement to participate in follow-up offerings of the stock—a hidden *tie-in* that provided *undisclosed compensation* to the banks and also resulted in the *manipulation of market prices.* In June 2003, the 309 companies that issued the stock in the IPOs offered to settle the suit with a payment of $1 billion.[24]

A related practice, known as "spinning," involved banks handing out IPO allotments to their favored customers in exchange for their future business. Given the near-certainty of the stock price rising dramatically higher than the initial price, these allocations are hard to describe as anything other than bribes. One of the most egregious examples of this corrupt practice involved investment bankers at Salomon Smith Barney and WorldCom CEO Bernie Ebbers. WorldCom was a major banking client of Salomon Smith Barney (later a subsidiary of Citigroup), and Salomon kept a steady stream of extraordinary allotments flowing to Ebbers, who made the decisions that kept a steady stream of fees flowing to the investment bank. Between June 1996 and November 1997, Ebbers received a total of nearly 750,000 IPO shares (and 90,000 secondary offering shares), which returned him a total profit of $11 million; Salomon received a total of $65 million in fees from WorldCom.[25]

All these schemes, whether they meet the legal definition of crime or not, represent efforts by corporate insiders and their accomplices to enrich themselves by defrauding investors, both individual and institutional. Many of these corrupt practices have been around for a long time. What distinguished them in the late 1990s was their frequency and the manner in which they were carried out by coordinated networks of high-level corporate officers and their professional advisors from the fields of banking, accounting, and law. It is this level of coordination across industries and across different sectors of the financial services industries that suggests the emergence of new forms of corporate crime and corruption that may force social scientists to rethink their approach to these phenomena.

Theoretical Interpretation

The *criminogenic markets* approach is a promising theoretical foundation for analyzing the New Economy scandals, given the prominent role of changing economic structures. However, just as important have been constant efforts by business interests and their political allies to remake institutional rules—ranging from laws and regulations to informal business norms and doctrines. Thus we propose to revise the notion of *criminogenic markets* to distinguish between *market structures* and *institutional frameworks. Criminogenic market structures* refers to the realm in which inter-firm networks are supplementing, if not supplanting, self-sufficient hierarchies; *criminogenic institutional frameworks* refers to the realm of culture and politics involved in the making and enforcement of various kinds of rules. We will see that a heightened focus on rules and rationalities is most appropriate.

Criminogenic Market Structures

In the 1970s and 1980s, theorists of white-collar crime demonstrated that certain markets were "criminogenic" in that they provided more opportunities and motivations for white-collar crime.[26] One key example concerned oligopolistic sectors where corporations could exercise greater control over their markets, such as the auto industry.[27] Maverick economists made complementary observations about the prevalence of fraud in markets where the structure of information favored some actors over others.[28] Sociologists noted related situations where market actors had to rely on "agents" to represent their interests; access to information was a key advantage agents possessed that could be used to abuse the trust given them. Moreover, the complex structure of the organizations in which agents operated often helped them to secrete their acts from law enforcement.[29] Sociologists have shown the criminogenic traits that networks can possess in frauds involving inter-firm collaborations. For example, price-fixing conspiracies that involve complex information processing require executives to engage in a considerable amount of face-to-face interaction.[30]

Analyses of financial frauds in the 1980s and 1990s have found new conjunctions of factors suggesting novel criminogenic conditions.[31] This has led some researchers to issue a call for new analytic frameworks. They have proposed, for instance, that deregulation and financialization were changing the nature of white-collar crime: Schemes now often were for personal gain, and the organization itself might be treated as if it was "disposable."[32] More fundamentally, the structural terrain that had given rise to the *criminogenic markets* thesis was giving way as large corporations reduced the range of activities they exercised direct control over, oftentimes through the use of networks. In some sectors the combination of corporate restructuring and deregulation was leaving gaps, or "structural holes,"[33] that deceitful "brokers" could exploit. Now it was the complexity of networks that helped agents hide their actions; moreover, their network positioning provided them with knowledge and social skills that aided their construction of deceptions.[34]

In various respects, networks were integral to the criminogenic conditions that spawned the New Economy scandals of the 1990s. Networks became ubiquitous in the New Economy, and, as is often the case, business arrangements that were established for legitimate reasons later came to abet fraud once an enterprise slid into illegitimate activities.[35] One of the most common new uses of networks was to link individual business units with the financial sector. Related to this, New Economy scandals frequently involved a complex web of financial arrangements among multiple parties. Moreover, the governance system increasingly made use of network as, in the aftermath of deregulation, it relied more on monitoring by business professionals (accountants, banks, financial analysts, lawyers, ratings agencies) or "reputational intermediaries."[36] These business professionals often became accomplices in the roundabout financial webs. Some of the most prominent orchestrators of New Economy schemes were bankers or financial analysts, who derived leverage from their positioning as brokers who controlled access to lucrative deals. Examples include Jack Grubman, a financial analyst who helped reorganize the telecom sector, and Frank Quattrone, a banker who brokered ties between Wall Street investment banks and Silicon Valley tech firms. Some power brokers also possessed considerable power because of their positions within a corporate hierarchy, which they also used to insert themselves as intermediaries in networks. Quattrone is one example, as are Bernie Ebbers (WorldCom CEO) and Andy Fastow (Enron CFO), both of whom positioned themselves as brokers between their own firms and a web of banks. The inner circles that coordinated frauds were composed of executives and teams of business professionals who assisted in promoting a stock or in manipulating its value. Brokering access to these inner circles was a key form of power used in the scandals.

Networks were also implicated in the workings of *criminogenic institutional frameworks*. Various researchers have reported that networks are involved in the branching out or diffusion of fraudulent schemes[37] and New Economy business models.[38] Furthermore, many of the same persons that orchestrated frauds also worked with political allies to orchestrate deregulatory policies that figured a great deal in the rise of criminogenic conditions.

The idea that corporate corruption can best be understood by analyzing the relationships among networks of market actors has also found its way into the business and finance literature. Several studies of the IPO process, for example, have focused on the relationships between the issuing firm and the bank that underwrites the IPO.[39] One frequently cited study of the underpricing of IPOs (in which insiders receive pre-market allocations of IPO shares at greatly reduced prices) concluded that a "corruption hypothesis," which "argues that venture capitalists and the executives of issuing firms have been co-opted through the setting up of personal brokerage accounts to which hot IPO shares are allocated," could explain much of the phenomenon.[40]

Criminogenic Institutional Frameworks

The aspect of the New Economy scandals that is most perplexing concerns the apparent failure of "the rules" on the one hand and of "rationality" of participants on the other. A flood of revelations about frauds left many asking, What had happened to "the rules," and what could "they" (high-status perpetrators with a lot to lose) have been thinking?

The institutional dimension of criminogenic markets—as domains where meaning is constructed, enacted, and manipulated—has received much less attention than their structural dimensions. One exception is Shapiro's model of "wayward" agents, which argues that they often take advantage of the trust that is generated by well-institutionalized settings (i.e., corporate organizations).[41] A second and more extensive treatment of institutional processes is the theory of "normalized corruption," which delineates the social dynamics set in motion when corruption is collective in nature. Blake Ashforth and Vikas Anand, for instance, discuss the role of socialization, task division, and routinization and the development of group cultures that rationalize deviance. They also stress the culpability of top executives who possess superior knowledge of the whole as well as control of "institutional levers" that can make corrupt practices seem normal.[42] Despite their virtues, neither model is equipped to deal with key New Economy traits: the shift to network forms of organization and efforts to alter institutions at various levels.

Tillman and Indergaard have offered a comprehensive treatment of the New Economy scandals by showing how the rationality of participants was "instituted"—framed by multiple kinds of rules. This assumption allows them to synthesize different levels of analysis concerning the remaking of the regulatory environment, the formulation of New Economy business doctrine, and the operation of the inner circles of fraud that were also epicenters for its normalization. They assert that the New Economy scandals,

> . . . resulted from the intersection of rules nested at three levels of corporate governance: (1) Congress under the influence of corporate contributors and free market ideologies set the general tone by promoting "market" rules while gutting protections for ordinary investors; (2) business professionals who were supposed to monitor corporations cashed in on their positions of institutionalized trust by joining executives in propagating New Economy Business rules in particular sectors; and (3) small circles that controlled access to the "deal flow" in effect made their own rules as they developed norms and routines that helped organize (and normalize) collective corruption.[43]

This conception stresses the role of active agents in "instituting" rationality at various levels of the governance system. Regarding lobbying for deregulation by corporate interests and free market ideologues, Tillman and Indergaard contend that "it was a political mobilization—not models or new technologies—that changed the rules in a manner that opened the door for a wave of fraud."[44] More often than not, networks were implicated. Enron executives, for example, "systematically changed the economic rules" by building "an elaborate network of interlocking connections to politicians, regulators, bankers, accountants, public relations experts, and media heads."[45]

Free market ideologies and deregulation at the federal level shaped, in turn, corporate governance activities at the next level. A reduction in government monitoring, in combination with court decisions and laws that reduced the liability of "corporate advisors," caused many business professionals to orient themselves to commercial roles at the cost of their professional duties as neutral monitors. They used their strategic network positions as reputational intermediaries to become carriers of New Economy doctrines and specific models. For example, accounting firms provided "swapping" models to telecom firms that abetted their financial manipulations. And in the inner circles of fraud, strategically positioned ringleaders used a mix of bullying and bribes to institute their own particular versions of "relationships" and "reciprocity"—by brokering access to hot IPO allocations or lucrative banking accounts.

Future Issues

It will take more time and research to fully assess the significance of the New Economy crimes, given that fewer than five years have elapsed since revelations surfaced about the epic flood of corruption. More scholarly investigations are needed to determine the extent of fraud that germinated in the late 1990s. A prime candidate for scrutiny is the financial sector, whose various branches were set free to engage in new kinds of deal making by the 1999 repeal of the Glass Stegall Act—the Depression Era law that forced a separation among banks, securities firms, and insurance companies.[46] Indeed, investigators continue to uncover frauds in one financial industry after another—earlier exposés of biased financial analysis, disguised loans, and shady IPO allotments have been followed by revelations of misdeeds in mutual funds and insurance as well as bank involvement in abusive tax shelters. Moreover, researchers should continue to search for dubious connections between the financial sector and other sectors such as those that tainted energy trading, telecommunications, and dot-coms in the 1990s.

Looking at the long-term picture, researchers need to systematically assess the criminogenic propensities of the network economy. There is little reason to think that its "valuation" and "accountability" dilemmas[47] have been solved or that much has changed in the institutional framework that allowed corporate governance to deteriorate so dramatically in the 1990s. The reforms implemented by the Sarbanes-Oxley Act and a series of successful prosecutions and financial settlements might be taken to mean that Congress and regulators have made significant progress in re-establishing boundaries for corporate conduct.[48] However, we need continued scrutiny to determine how effective these responses will be in changing the orientations of executives and the reputational intermediaries who are relied on to supplement or replace government regulators. It is hardly encouraging that Sarbanes-Oxley and modest attempts by regulators to increase corporate accountability have brought howls of protest from lobbyists and sparked efforts by their Congressional allies to stop or roll back reforms. As yet, there has been little challenge mounted against the neoliberal ideologies and policies which anchored the institutional framework that made pervasive corruption possible. In sum, future work should consider whether the response to the New Economy crimes has significantly reformed the corporate governance system or was merely "damage control"—as was the case following the savings and loan scandals in the 1980s.[49]

Finally, analysts should look for ways in which corruption has been a constitutive force in economic restructuring. Charles Perrow makes such a claim about the rise of the corporate economy in the 19th century which produced a separation between ownership and control that still problematizes corporate governance.[50] The prosecution of Frank Quattrone—who brokered a marriage between Wall Street finance and Silicon Valley technology—led some commentators to question Silicon Valley's distinctive brand of insider capitalism, but by that time it had spread across a great deal of the U.S. corporate economy.

Conclusion

Our review of the literature shows that researchers increasingly are seeking to link new forms of corporate crime with transformations in economic structures and institutional frameworks. In particular, the New Economy scandals of the late 1990s were associated with the rise of a network economy and institutional alterations (e.g., deregulation) that left corporate governance relying much more on reputational intermediaries. Indeed, the combination of novel organizational arrangements, new regulatory environments, and political obstruction of regulators had, in many cases, left the lines blurred between an "aggressive" bending of the rules and blatant fraud. Thus we have proposed that the New Economy scandals be characterized as a wave of *corruption* rather than of crime per se, although a series of recent felony convictions indicates that aggressive law enforcement can produce compelling criminal cases in especially egregious instances of fraud.

Our review also produced evidence on the scope and nature of the New Economy frauds, suggesting that they reflect a systemic problem in corporate governance rather than the deeds of a small number of "bad apples." A distinctive empirical profile emerged: The frauds typically were organized by inter-firm networks wherein executives and business professionals collaborated in devising deceptions that exploited regulatory gaps so as to pump up revenue numbers in financial statements. The New Economy frauds were striking in terms of the prominence of the lead culprits, the institutional mechanisms they commanded, and the extent to which they "normalized" corruption. The participants,

> ... included entrepreneurs who were celebrated as New Economy heroes, reputable professionals, prestigious financial institutions, and business notables with the highest of political connections.... Their modus operandi was to exploit normal institutional mechanisms for gaining expert approval and public notices. And, to an extraordinary extent, they came to see even the most egregious organized deceptions to be "normal" practice in their line of business.[51]

In contrast to moralistic approaches that would scrutinize the character of individual participants in the New Economy frauds, sociological treatments have illuminated the social settings in which individuals found meaning, motivation, opportunities, resources, and collaborators. This allows us to understand the New Economy scandals as an enterprise that was collective, and even conformist, in nature. Focusing on institutional frameworks as well as social structures that set the scene for the crimes also allows one to capture the socially situated agency of lead participants, who used their strategic positioning in organizations and/or networks to actively exercise power in constructing and manipulating relationships and meanings.

Endnotes

1. Partnoy (2003).
2. Hirsch (2003: 5).
3. Tillman and Indergaard (forthcoming).
4. Calavita et al. (1997); Tillman and Pontell (1995); Calavita and Pontell (1990); Zey (1993).
5. DiMaggio (2001: 226, 228).
6. Tillman and Indergaard (forthcoming).
7. Perrow (2000).
8. Sutherland (1945); Clinard and Yeager (1980); Michalowski and Kramer (1987); Mann (1992); Reed and Yeager (1996).
9. General Accounting Office (2002).
10. Securities Class Action Clearinghouse (2001).
11. Graham et al. (2002).
12. New York State Office of the Comptroller (2003).
13. Tillman and Indergaard (forthcoming).
14. Beckett and Sapsford (2002).
15. *Securities and Exchange Commission v. Dynegy, Inc.*, XXXX (S.D. Tex. 2002).
16. Berman and Solomon (2002).
17. *In re Homestore.com*, Master File No. 01-Cv-11115 MJP (E.D. Cal. 7 2001) ("First Amended Consolidated Complaint"), 27.
18. Morgensen (2002).
19. Tillman and Indergaard (forthcoming).
20. Securities and Exchange Commission (2002).
21. Tillman and Indergaard (forthcoming).
22. Ibid.
23. *In re Initial Public Offering Securities Litigation,* XXXX (S.D. N.Y. 2003).
24. Tillman and Indergaard (forthcoming).
25. *In re WorldCom, Inc. et al.,* XXXX (Bankr. S.D. N.Y. 2002), 140.
26. Farberman (1975); Denzin (1977); Needleman and Needleman (1979); Clinard and Yeager (1980).
27. Leonard and Weber (1970).
28. Akerlof (1970).
29. Shapiro (1990).
30. Baker and Faulkner (1993).
31. Calavita et al. (1997); Berenson (2003); Partnoy (2003); Stiglitz (2003).
32. Pontell and Calavita (1993); Tillman and Pontell (1995); Calavita et al. (1997).
33. Burt (1992).
34. Tillman and Indergaard (1999); Tillman (1998); Tillman and Indergaard (forthcoming).
35. Baker and Faulkner (2003).
36. Gourevitch (2002); Berenson (2003); Partnoy (2003); Stiglitz (2003); Tillman and Indergaard (forthcoming).
37. Tillman and Indergaard (1999); Tillman (1998); Baker and Faulkner (2003).
38. Davis (2003).
39. Schenone (2004); Ljungqvist and Willhelm (2003).
40. Loughran and Ritter (2003: 31).
41. Shapiro (1990).
42. Ashforth and Anand (2003).
43. Tillman and Indergaard (forthcoming).
44. Ibid., p. 272.
45. Ibid., p. 76.
46. *Gramm-Leach-Bliley Act of 1999*, S 900, 106th Cong., 1st sess.

47. DiMaggio (2001).
48. The *Sarbanes-Oxley Act of 2002* (HR 3763, 107th Cong., 2nd sess.) contained a number of provisions designed to curb widespread corporate abuses of the 1990s, including creating a semi-independent accounting oversight board, requiring CEOs and CFOs to certify their firms' financial reports, and increasing criminal penalties for a variety of corporate offenses.
49. Calavita et al. (1997).
50. Perrow (2000).
51. Tillman and Indergaard (forthcoming).

References

Akerlof, George (1970) "The Market for Lemons." *Quarterly Journal of Economics* 84:488–500.

Ashforth, Blake, and Vikas Anand (2003) "The Normalization of Corruption in Organizations." *Research in Organizational Behavior* 25:1–52.

Baker, Wayne, and Robert Faulkner (1993) "The Social Organization of Conspiracy." *American Sociological Review* 58:837–860.

Baker, Wayne, and Robert Faulkner (2003) "Diffusion of Fraud: Intermediate Economic Crime and Investor Dynamics." *Criminology* 41:1601–1634.

Beckett, Paul, and Jathon Sapsford (2002) "Size and Timing of Dynegy Trades Draw Scrutiny." *The Wall Street Journal*, 9 May, sec. A, p. 1.

Berenson, Alex (2003) *The Number*. New York: Random House.

Berman, Dennis, and Deborah Solomon (2002) "Optical Illusion?: Accounting Questions Swirl Around Pioneers in the Telecom World." *The Wall Street Journal*, 13 February, sec. A, p. 12.

Burt, Ronald (1992) *Structural Holes*. Cambridge, MA: Harvard University Press.

Calavita, Kitty, and Henry Pontell (1990) "Heads I Win, Tails You Lose: Deregulation, Crime, and Crisis in the Savings and Loan Industry." *Crime and Delinquency* 36:309–349.

Calavita, Kitty, Henry Pontell, and Robert Tillman (1997) *Big Money Crime: Fraud and Politics in the Savings and Loan Crisis*. Berkeley: University of California Press.

Clinard, Marshall, and Peter Yeager (1980) *Corporate Crime*. Glencoe, IL: Free Press.

Davis, Gerald (2003) "American Cronyism: How Executive Networks Inflated the Corporate Bubble." *Contexts* 2(3):34–40.

Denzin, Norman (1977) "Notes on the Criminogenic Hypothesis." *American Sociological Review* 42:905–920.

DiMaggio, Paul (2001) "Conclusion: The Futures of Business Organization and Paradoxes of Change." Pp. 210–243 in *The Twentieth Century Firm*, Editor Paul DiMaggio. Princeton, NJ: Princeton University Press.

Farberman, Harvey (1975) "A Criminogenic Market Structure." *Sociological Quarterly* 16:438–457.

General Accounting Office (2002) *Financial Statement Restatements*. Washington, DC.

Gourevitch, Peter (2002) "Collective Action Problems in Monitoring Managers." *Economic Sociology–European Electronic Newsletter* 3:3–16, http://econsoc.mpifg.de/archive/esjune02.pdf (accessed September 24, 2005).

Graham, Carol, Robert Litan, and Sandip Sukhtankar (2002) "The Bigger They Are, the Harder They Fall: An Estimate of the Costs of the Crisis in Corporate Governance." Report. Washington, DC: Brookings Institution.

Hirsch, Paul (2003) "The Cultures of Economic Sociology." *Accounts: A Newsletter of Economic Sociology* 3(2):5–7.

Leonard, William, and Marvin Weber (1970) "Automakers and Dealers: A Study of Criminogenic Market Forces." *Law and Society Review* 4:407–410.

Ljungqvist, Alexander, and William Wilhelm (2003) "IPO Pricing in the Dot-com Bubble." *Journal of Finance* 57:723–752.

Loughran, Tim, and Jay Ritter (2003) "Why Has IPO Pricing Changed Over Time?" Unpublished paper, University of Florida, Gainesville, http://www.nber.org/~confer/2002/bfs02/ritter.pdf (accessed September 24, 2005).

Mann, Kenneth (1992) "Punitive Civil Sanctions: The Middle Ground Between Criminal and Civil Law." *Yale Law Journal* 101:1795–1873.

Michalowski, Raymond, and Ronald Kramer (1987) "The Space Between Laws: The Problem of Corporate Crime in a Transnational Context." *Social Problems* 34:34–51.

Morgensen, Gretchen (2002) "How 287 Turned into 7: Lessons in Fuzzy Math." *The New York Times*, 20 January, sec. 3, p. 1.

Needleman, Martin, and Carolyn Needleman (1979) "Organizational Crime: Two Models of Criminogensis." *Sociological Quarterly* 20:517–539.

New York State Office of the Comptroller (2003) "Impact of the Corporate Scandals on New York State." Report. Albany, NY.

Partnoy, Frank (2003) *Infectious Greed*. New York: Times Books.

Pontell, Henry, and Kitty Calavita (1993) "The Savings and Loan Industry." In *Beyond the Law*, Editors M. Tonry and A. Reiss. Chicago: University of Chicago Press.

Reed, Gary, and Peter Yeager (1996) "Organizational Offending and Neoclassical Criminology: Challenging the Reach of a General Theory of Crime." *Criminology* 34:357–382.

Schenone, Carola (2004) "The Effect of Banking Relationships on the Firm's IPO Underpricing." *Journal of Finance* 59:2903–2958.

Securities and Exchange Commission (2002) "Dynegy Settles Securities Fraud Charges Involving SPE's, Round-Trip Energy Trades." Press release. Washington, DC.

Securities Class Action Clearinghouse (2001) Homepage, http://securities.stanford.edu (accessed August 10, 2004).

Shapiro, Susan (1990) "Collaring the Crime, Not the Criminal: Reconsidering the Concept of White-Collar Crime." *American Sociological Review* 55:346–365.

Stiglitz, Joseph (2003) *The Roaring Nineties*. New York: W.W. Norton.

Sutherland, Edwin (1945) "Is 'White-Collar Crime' Crime?" *American Sociological Review* 10:132–139.

Tillman, Robert (1998) *Broken Promises: Fraud by Small Business Health Insurers*. Boston: Northeastern University Press.

Tillman, Robert, and Michael Indergaard (1999) "Field of Schemes: Health Insurance Fraud in the Small Business Sector." *Social Problems* 46:572–590.

Tillman, Robert, and Michael Indergaard (forthcoming) *Pump and Dump: The Rancid Rules of the New Economy*. New Brunswick, NJ: Rutgers University Press.

Tillman, Robert, and Henry Pontell (1995) "Organizations and Fraud in the Savings and Loan Industry." *Social Forces* 73:1439–1463.

Zey, Mary (1993) *Banking on Fraud: Drexel, Junk Bonds, and Buyouts*. New York: Aldine de Gruyter.

4

Cesare Beccaria and White-Collar Crimes' Public Harm

A Study in Italian Systemic Corruption

Gabrio Forti and Arianna Visconti

As the great Italian Enlightenment thinker Cesare Beccaria put it, "The true measure of crimes is . . . *the harm done to society*."[1] For Beccaria, a humanitarian legal reformer and the forerunner of the classical school of criminological thought, law should be employed only to control behavior that is harmful to society, and to punish only insofar as the punishment is proportionate to the harm done. Beccaria observed that "they were in error who believed that the true measure of crimes is to be found in the intention of the person who commits them."[2]

The word *harm* is both vague and ambiguous, as Joel Feinberg has observed, but "it is a more convenient abbreviation for a complicated statement that includes, among other things, moral judgments and value weightings of a variety of kinds."[3] However abstruse, especially from a legal point of view, "harm" has played a significant role in criminology, figuring in crime seriousness ratings[4] and in criteria used to define "crime" independent of legal dictates.[5]

We will advance the idea that Beccaria clearly understood how "harm" cannot be conceived apart from the social status of the offender (better still, that such status is an essential yardstick to measure the amount and level of harm inflicted and especially to characterize the harm as "public" rather than "private"). He believed that persons who have achieved prominence and power commit crimes inflicting the most harmful effects because of their elusiveness and their potential for replicating themselves and threatening the whole legal and moral fabric of society.

We will focus on the crime of corruption to illustrate this point, discussing in some detail the Italian experience of *tangentopoli*, in the nineties, when there was a crackdown ("*mani pulite* operation") on massive kickbacks that threw some light on a pattern of systemic corruption. First, however, we will address some general definitional issues related to white-collar crime and to corruption.

I. Beccaria and Public Harm

Beccaria's discussion of harm is related to the principle *nullum crimen sine lege* (no crime without law), a principle he "vehemently advocated." Also, anticipating the great psychological and psychoanalytical achievements of the

19th and 20th centuries, Beccaria displayed remarkable insight into the human mind, pointing out how the disregard of legal principles by states or the ruling class could impact people's feelings, attitudes, and behavior. As emphasized by late-modern discussions on uncertainty arising from the inability of governments to check savage free-market struggles,[7] he anticipated how a perception of widespread anomie among citizens is bound to generate fear and, consequently, to undermine a clear understanding of social reality that is essential if people are to make correct public choices. "Fear" is deemed to have a significant bearing on human behavior so that "the fear of being injured is greater than the desire to injure."[8]

Beccaria emphasized that enlightened minds must be free of fear:

> The view that each citizen should have within his power to do all that is not contrary to the law, without having to fear any other inconvenience than that which may result from the action itself—that is, the political dogma that should be believed by the people and inculcated by the supreme magistrates, with the incorruptible guardianship of the laws. [It is] a sacred dogma without which there can be no lawful society; a just recompense to men for their sacrifice of the universal liberty of action over all things, which is the property of every sensible being limited only by its own powers. This shapes free and vigorous souls and enlightened minds; this makes men virtuous with that virtue which can resist fear, and not that of pliant prudence, worthy only of those who can endure a precarious and uncertain existence.[9]

It is also to protect society against public harm arising from the sway of "the right of the strongest" that especially "the great and rich" should be kept in check by law:

> Within this class [of the greater crimes] are included not only the assassinations and thefts committed by men of the lower classes but also those committed by noblemen and magistrates, the example of which *acts with greater force and is more far-reaching*, destroying the ideas of justice and duty among subjects and substituting that of *the right of the strongest*, equally dangerous, in the end, to those who exercise it and to those who suffer it [...]. The great and rich should not have it in their power to set a price upon attempts made against the weak and the poor; otherwise riches which are, under the laws, the reward of industry, become the nourishment of tyranny. There is no liberty whenever the laws permit that, in some circumstances, a man can cease to be a *person* and become a *thing:* then you will see all the industry of the powerful person applied to extract from the mass of social interrelations whatever the law allows in his favor. This discovery is the magic secret that changes citizens into beasts of burden; in the hands of the strong, it is the chain with which they fetter the activities of the incautious and weak.[10]

Moreover, in the chapter on the "punishments of nobles," Beccaria sees the true "measure" of such punishments not in "the sensibility of the criminal," but in "the public injury, which is all the more grave when committed by a person of rank."[11]

Beccaria details other features of crimes by the "great" and the "rich." Foremost, he notes the potential for affecting a large number of people and, relatedly, breeding new crime. In his words: "[*W*]*rongs breed new wrongs*; hate is a more lasting sentiment than love—so much more lasting as the former acquires strength from continuation of the acts that weaken the latter."[12]

Beccaria develops the idea that no overt state capture by a tyrant is needed to have a tyranny established, but only a situation where "the right of the strongest" is affirmed, and people cease to be *persons* and become *things*, seeing destroyed *in their minds* the ideas of justice and duty. Beccaria employs a kind of pre-Kafkeske metaphor of the insect: "Men generally set up the most solid embankments against open tyranny, but do not see the imperceptive insect that gnaws at them and opens to the flooding stream a way that is more secure because more hidden."[13] Beccaria shows here deep awareness of another feature of economic crime and corruption, namely, their elusive nature, which usually frustrates most attempts to prosecute them effectively.

If one considers another chapter of Beccaria's work, on "the spirit of the family" (which, by the way, would suffice to attest its modernity, and even its late-modernity), it is possible to understand better the way through which any break of the legality principle, especially by "the greats," can lead to further crimes, how wrongs can breed new wrongs.

> Family spirit is a spirit of details, limited to trifling facts. The spirit that rules republics, sustained by general principles, observes the facts and classifies them in the order of their importance for the good of the majority. [. . .] Such contradictions between the laws of a family and the fundamental principles of a commonwealth are a fertile source of other contradictions between domestic and public morality; they occasion, therefore, a perpetual conflict in every mind. Domestic morality inspires submission and fear; the other, courage and liberty: the first teaches the limitation of beneficence to a small number of persons, involving no spontaneous choice; the second calls for the extension of it to all classes of men. One commands a continual sacrifice of self to a vain idol, called "the good of the family" (which is often the good of no one of its components); the other teaches the pursuit of personal advantage without violation of the laws.[14]

Equalling the focus of many contemporary criminal policy discussions, Beccaria was able to outline causes and effects of crime and thus the sensitive area on which any legislator should crack down to cope with it, namely, reducing the citizens' fear by which most crimes (including white-collar crime and corruption) are fed, ensuring that laws are clear, simple, and based on the idea "which is the foundation of human justice," namely, "common utility" and therefore "relations of equality" among human beings ("see to it that the laws favor not so much classes of men as men themselves"),[15] as well as fostering and spreading knowledge, "which breeds evils in inverse ratio to its diffusion, and benefits in direct ratio."[16]

These same recipes may be deemed suitable to dissolve what Beccaria calls the harmful "spirit of the family," a spirit precisely incompatible with an effective legality principle.

II. White-Collar Crimes' Harm

Edwin H. Sutherland

Edwin H. Sutherland, almost two centuries later, echoed Beccaria's stress on the harmful consequences of crimes by the great and rich. Sutherland's definition of what he labeled white-collar crime is crucial for our consideration of social harmfulness. "White-collar crime," Sutherland wrote, "may be defined approximately as a crime committed by a person of respectability and high social status in the course of his occupation."[17] Equally relevant for our purposes is the definition that Sutherland put forward in his 1939 presidential address to the American Sociological Society: "White-collar crimes in business and the professions consist principally of violations of delegated or implied trust."[18] The crucial aspects of these definitions is their focus on the criminal's status and the emphasis on the harmful consequences of abuses of trust:

> [The] financial loss from white-collar crime, great as it is, is less important than the damage to social relations. White-collar crimes violate trust and therefore create distrust, and this lowers social morale and produces social disorganization on a large scale.[19] [...] How can we expect boys of the inner city to have standards of honesty, decency and morality higher than the standards they observe in their own public officials.[20]

On a yet more general level, it is Sutherland's peculiar and well-known definition of "crime" that emphasizes the relevance of the social harmfulness of a conduct in order both to define it a "crime" and to qualify, on a more substantial basis, as "criminal" even all those white-collar offenses that, in spite of their harmfulness, are not punished on first instance by criminal law because of a heavy-rooted "benefit of business."[21]

Recent Research

The study of the harm inflicted by white-collar crime has expanded far beyond the computation of financial losses, and now encompasses physical, psychological, moral, and social harms. Attempts to document these harms have been hampered by inherent characteristics of white-collar crime, such as low visibility, secretive perpetrators, diffusive victimizations, and variations in what might be an acceptable definition of white-collar crime.[22] Should law be the measuring stick of the offenses to be considered or should harmful consequences be the criterion for consideration?

The latter route has been taken by David Simon and Stanley Eitzen, who include in their review of "elite deviance" not only criminal and unethical acts of government and corporations, but also violations of fundamental human rights committed by people whose position within organizations (i.e., large corporations, government, and the military) have provided them the greatest amount of wealth, power, and often prestige. Simon and Eitzen examine work-related diseases and injuries, harms inflicted on consumers and the entire economic system by monopolies, as well as dangers to health and survival from environmental pollution. They also consider political and economic scandals that undermine citizens' trust and society's moral standards. They maintain that corporations' influence on criminal policies favor race- and class-based discrimination and that elite deviance's frequent and strong links with organized crime largely contribute to the expansion and strengthening of the latter. On a more general level, this great imbalance of power and wealth to elites' advantage—obtained through illicit means—increases social strain and thus leads to an escalation of street crimes.[23] Along these lines, it's also worth mentioning Grant Stitt's and Davil Giacopassi's suggestion[24] to substitute "corporate harm" for "corporate crime."

As to physical damages, the terms "white-collar violence," "corporate violence," and "corporate homicide" made their appearance following the trial of the Ford company for the burning deaths of passengers after a rear-end gas tank explosion of their Pinto model. It extended to conduct involving matters such as violations of safe working conditions and product safety, toxic waste violations, pollution, and the activities of the tobacco industry.

There remains, however, a scarcity of empirical research on the psychological harms of white-collar crime. The impact on individuals is mediated by the characteristics of the particular offense, the diffusion of the injuries, and the fact that the perpetrator often is not readily identifiable as a human being, but rather is an organization. One study examined the psychiatric consequences for victims of violent crimes and white-collar frauds and concluded that anxiety and depression followed on the heels of both.[25] Then there is the further psychological trauma that white-collar crime victims sometimes suffer when they deal with control agents who tend to regard their complaints as less serious than those of victims of street offenses,[26] which can in turn strengthen and enlarge a dangerous feeling of insecurity and of distrust towards institutions.

This latter feeling is one of the aspects of the moral and social harm[27] inflicted by white-collar crime. Social harms caused by economic crime and, more specifically, by corruption are quite numerous and serious[28]: in an economic system which is largely based on collection and investment of savings through institutional agents, a breakdown of the public's trust in institutions which run and survey this system can lead to recessions. Widespread illicit electoral contributions to political parties and vote bargaining, as well as corruption, finally produce a diffuse mistrust of government and business, which can also undermine democratic principles and respect for law in general. Public perception of a state "strong with the weaker ones and weak with the stronger ones," whose penal system, both in legislation and in law enforcement, is marked by a disparity of punishment for offenses of lower classes and higher ones—the latter often sheltered by complex organizations—leads almost inevitably to a general cynicism toward law and institutions, to a large perception of the whole system as fundamentally unjust, and to a diffuse feeling of social strain and rebellion. Finally, the public's wide and frightening perception of victimization risks, everyday more frequent, huge, and pervasive,[29] caused by uncontrollable acts by individuals or powerful, impersonal entities that are not checked at all by those institutions which should defend citizens but instead are seen as corrupt or incapable, largely feeds and strengthens that feeling of uncertainty which, as the great sociologist Zygmunt Bauman put it,[30] is nowadays a common characteristic of late-modern societies. This seriously undermines the individual's faith in a rational world, in which long-term projects and engagements are possible and sensible.

Definitions of White-Collar Crime and Implications of Harm

There are many criminologists today who believe that social status and reputation of the criminal are too amorphous and confining as white-collar-crime criteria to provide adequate theoretical value. Consequently, some suggest that the label "white-collar crime" should be tied to special formal features, with little or no regard to the personal characteristics of offenders—that the aim should be to "collar the crime, not the criminal."[31] But when legal categories are employed they tend to be conducive to a selection of samples that includes a considerable array of representatives of the lower sectors of economic life.[32]

Definitions that better capture the concept of harm related to economic crime (and, more specifically, to corruption) are those that focus on personal attributes of the offender. Not so much because it is the status that provides people opportunities, means, knowledge, and rationalizations that are needed to commit these notably harmful offenses, but rather because the positions that the persons occupy can heavily aggravate the extent of the harm that they inflict.

Elusiveness and Double Standards

First of all, white-collar criminals, as we denoted them, can employ their professional skills and the complex organizational structures into which they are embedded[33] to conceal their misdeeds. They have the advantage that as businesspersons they are legitimately present at the site of their illegal activity.[34] Victims fail to understand that they have been exploited in what they perceive to be normal business routines. Besides, even if they suspect or know that they were harmed, they often do not possess information about the procedures they need to undertake for redress.[35] The low visibility of white-collar crimes ensures that only egregious cases in which the offenders often manifest a lack of strategic skills are uncovered. The absence of social awareness and alarm undoubtedly influences criminal policy and tilts control agencies to focus on more obvious street offenses,[36] which are less harmful for society.[37]

The "discovery" of white-collar crime by criminologists occurred rather late and there are still relatively few specialists in the field. Street crimes (and, today, terrorism) hog public resources devoted to crime prevention. Besides, white-collar crime research suffers from technical difficulties inherent in unreliable statistics and problems with recourse to self-report and victimization surveys,[38] and even from the fact that a large number of socially harmful offenses aren't punishable by criminal law but are, instead, regulated by civil or administrative law.

The influence of business and industry on legislation, though pervasive, cannot simply be reduced to class or conspiracy theories, given the dynamic interactions of varying interest groups.[39] The web of interactions and balances of power among different lobbies and government forces are complex and easy to change, so that mechanisms like lobbying and political fundraising,[40] or agency capture, or the larger economic means (so much larger than public ones) corporations can use in scientific research and image promotion campaigns in order to sustain their plants' and products' safety,[41] generally lead to a web-like kind of influence on legislation, a so-called model of coherence without conspiracy.[42] Where there are clear instances of collusion between the world of business and legislatures, we most often will find that they occur in places with high levels of systemic corruption, traditions of buying and delivering of votes, and the diffusive presence of conflicts of interests.

This model attests to the so-called double standard of justice for white-collar crime and street crime,[43] which can be observed not only in legislators' regulatory and sanctioning choices, but even in the different terminologies adopted while coping with these two kinds of deviance.

Political debates in regard to white-collar crime typically use the word *regulation* and refer to street offenses in terms of "crime control" and declare "wars" against offenses such as drug trafficking and terrorism. The "fight" against common crimes is often based on ethical claims, while white-collar crimes are subject to a colder, cost-benefit approach by legislators, generally not interested in a moral evaluation of corporations' and businessmen's harmful actions[44] and more inclined to neo-liberal claims adverse to public interference in market dynamics. They may even place a positive "spin" on white-collar crimes, claiming, for instance, that corruption is "functional" because kickbacks "grease the wheels of the economy."

Laureen Snider has pointed out that corporate crime has tended to be characterized as obsolescent though recourse to specialized knowledge claims by powerful elites. This did not occur because superior knowledge was obtained but because new truth claims were developed which were more compatible with the core concerns of dominant interest groups and hence were more likely to be used in developing criminal policies.[45]

There also is a kind of blackmail that corporations can use against communities where they occupy a key position in economic life by providing jobs and paying taxes. They can threaten to close down or transfer their operations elsewhere, threats that can exert great pressure on authorities to grant concessions to the companies.[46]

Media and White-Collar Crime

Corporate violence such as environmental disasters, workplace deaths, and toxic torts as well as monstrous financial scandals stand as exceptions to the usual absence of attention in the media regarding white-collar crime.[47] Media attention is particularly likely when well-known corporations or business celebrities are involved in a scandal.[48] But the media are prone to sensationalism and only rarely do they provide sophisticated scrutiny of the facts of the situation and its causes: they may emphasize the large and palpable harms, especially when there is a butcher's list of such consequences. Media coverage of white-collar crime, however, even in the most striking instances, is largely reactive. Original inquiries by journalists are rare; the choice between an active investigative approach and a passive one is strongly influenced by media resources, by considerations of possible implications for advertising revenue, by the risk of becoming involved in legal actions, and by an evaluation of reader interest. Most media coverage of business is complimentary, supportive, and consonant with the media's role in reproducing the dominant ideology.[49]

III. Corruption and Its Tangles

Corruption generally is classified as a white-collar crime; however, it may possess a wide variety of differing characteristics both in terms of the offense and the offenders. Two different kinds of corruption coexist and interact. The first operates on a high, elite level, and consists of violations by business executives as well as politicians and public officials. The second involves low-level, blue-collar citizens and low-level public employees, and is usually concerned with matters such as avoiding red tape, securing a phony medical certificate, having a traffic citation canceled, or avoiding military service.

Corruption is strictly entangled with other crimes, primarily other forms of economic crime: first, it is instrumental in allowing others to commit white-collar crimes (frauds, antitrust violations, product safety violations, abusive toxic waste disposal, money laundering, etc.); in its turn, corruption itself is made possible or facilitated by other economic crimes, especially false corporate financial reports, tax evasion, money laundering, etc. In modern democracies the costs of politics—especially for electoral campaigns—follow a kind of inflationary trend that is a fertile field for corruption to take root in, fed as it is both by economic lobbies and organized crime.[50] And especially notable in the Italian socio-political environment, where traditionally the presence of organized crime is very prominent, is what Simon and Eitzen label "organized white-collar crime,"[51] which embraces all economic enterprises of criminal entities. Here corruption serves as a fundamental link and lubricant for relationships between organized crime groups and the world of business and politics.

First, there is the instrumental use of corruption by criminal organizations, even in the more subtle shape of vote bargaining, which allows the progressive abandonment of violence for more subtle white-collar tactics which are used in the service of cementing relationships with politicians. At the same time, these strategies grant to organized crime a stronger hold on the legitimate economic life of the country;[52] there follows a retreat of honest businesspersons from participation in the economic life of the country, that in turn increases market domination by criminal enterprises. Second, citizens are forced to confront the growing and inescapable corruption of the public administration, demonstrated daily by its ineffectiveness. This tends to push them toward illicit solutions to their problems and needs. It also encourages liaisons with underworld forces who wield power (the protection of the "family," as Beccaria would have put it) and appear to represent the only forces capable of guaranteeing attainment of their goals. It is quite clear, then, that the moral harm stemming from such diffusive and systemic corruption—which, besides its connecting with organized crime's expansion—is certainly larger and more serious than all economic damage already caused by the irrational allocation of scarce public resources and by organized crime's illicit activities—these being of a traditional kind or not—that corruption caused or helped. Moreover, these harms are already very difficult to classify because of their diffusive character, their ramifications, their low visibility, and their tendency to show up only over time.

In summary, economic crime and corruption overlap and reinforce each other practically and culturally as well. Both often have common roots, and their joint operations add to their harmful nature and their hold on society. Interactions between organized crime and corrupt practices demonstrate an inextricable network. Both take advantage and benefit from each other in a kind of an embrace. Also, the respective subcultures undermine the roots of civil and democratic communities.

IV. Italian "Systemic" Corruption

We will focus on recent Italian episodes of corruption in order to exemplify our previous general statements regarding harm and the dynamics of white-collar crime.

February 17, 1997, was the date of the disclosure by the Italian judiciary of a massive network of systemic corruption. That date saw the arrest of the president of the Pio Albergo Trivulzio (PAT), a public body responsible for the care of elderly people in Milan. He soon began to inform investigators about massive amounts of bribery in the public sector, pinpointing a myriad number of cases that would be studied by scholars seeking to document episodes of corruption.[53] It was learned that "corruption had become the norm" and that public life rewarded people prone to illegal acts and punished those who held to standards of good conduct.[54] There was a great spurt in the number of corruption cases uncovered at this time, but subsequently the figure declined as (illegal) business returned to its usual pattern.

It was found in the wake of the PAT scandal that corruption was more than a limited and occasional pathology—that it had attained a "systemic" shape, with a network of tangles in business and organized crime, a vast extension and, partly, an organization on an international basis with the strength to enforce a network of informal, illegal rules. To describe adequately some of the main features of corruption in Italy we need to put aside terminological subtleties, such as those regarding the difference between "corruption" and "bribery." We will treat both as if they had virtually the same meaning, though we are well aware that corruption is the more generic term, whose most obvious reference is to the receipt of a bribe by a public official. At its core, Italian corruption, apart from its pervasive hold on the political and administrative apparatus, has not differed greatly from corruption in other countries: an exchange of money or other goods for privileged treatment from public officials.[55] The underlying dynamic of corruption is the power of officials to influence at their discretion the assignment of property rights to scarce resources.

A more detailed analysis reveals the following features of corruption in Italy: (1) it is the result of highly rational choices by the persons involved; (2) it has grown *from* but not *into* a framework of stable and *continuous* relationships between public officials and private businesspersons; (3) it has been "circular" in its effects and nature as it has expanded; (4) it has been extremely difficult to attack with the traditional tools of criminal justice since the obvious aim of the bribers and bribees is to carry out a secret transaction that is profitable for both.[56]

We will deal with these features of Italian corruption in sequence. Such an overview will involve some simplification as we describe the features that play a predominant role in the behavior.[57] After this assessment we will seek to conceptualize the relationship that links the main features of systemic corruption, showing how they support and exemplify Beccaria's ideas regarding the inner structure of "public harm."

1. Rationality

Corruption is a crime of calculation, not of passion.[58] However complex the network of Italian corruption may seem as it relates to stylized models of a political economy approach,[59] we need to recognize that most partners to a bribery in Italy act on the basis of a rational assessment of the costs and benefits of their behavior. Benefits, besides the obvious economic gain, encompass other advantages accruing from the transaction, including the acquisition of prestige as a "great briber" or "leading bribee." This may establish opportunities to garner additional future bribes, or to enlarge and strengthen one's political influence. We believe that economic gain plays a more significant role for the private briber than for the public bribee. The former, generally a businessperson, generally an executive or tycoon, is accustomed to balancing advantages and disadvantages before acting or restraining from action. The public official operates in a less flexible environment, shackled by a bundle of regulations that involve status and income. Basically, he or she will likely be attracted to engage in an illicit transaction when the difference between his or her fixed wages and the bribe amount, which is relatively stable according to the Italian experience, becomes enticing.[60] Of course, both the likelihood of discovery and the "moral cost" figure into the calculation of whether to participate in a bribery scheme.

We think that this moral cost is likely to lie more heavily on the mind of the public official, as the private businessperson can readily mobilize a more impressive apparatus of neutralizations and rationalizations, self-justifying excuses that usually focus on company survival or the preservation of employees' jobs. Court trials demonstrate a generally tolerant judicial response to the offenses of businessmen who resort to these kind of explanations for their actions. The businessperson-briber develops a dual attitude: he complies with the legal order as a whole, but deftly and without embarrassment ignores rules that hinder achievement of personal and professional goals. The vulnerability to crime derives from the opportunities for profit that are seen as being obstructed by unreasonable political and bureaucratic tangles, so that the law comes to be viewed as a façade.

2. Stable Illicit Relationships

The stablility-continuity element of corruption has achieved such a significance in the Italian experience that it requires separate and close attention. The dynamics of corruption have been deeply affected by an intense search for guarantees of smooth and favorable conditions for illicit transactions. Such guarantees are often achieved through the protection of a politician who is able to inflict, or at least threaten to inflict, sanctions in the event that the illicit agreement is broken by one of the parties.

A main goal pursued during the initial phase of the corrupt transaction is the establishment of rules that allow an ordered operation of the illegal plan. In some instances, the payment of bribes becomes a kind of admission fee to the distribution of public resources, which also serves to check, regulate, or prevent new entries.[61] The crucial role played by such stability explains the presence of intermediaries (the *faccendieri*) who are endowed with special talents for illicit practices and who handle problems related to the reliability of the parties. Using the terminology of game theory, we could say that bribers and bribees try to establish a "cooperation."[62] The expectation of a marked continuity offers good guarantees that agreements will be respected, allowing long-term transactions between reliable partners. Such confidence shared by the group, a terrific lubricant for the machinery of systemic corruption, also enables the infliction of strong and convincing sanctions, which may involve the exclusion of the violator from future lucrative relations with the administration.[63]

3. Feedback

Another feature which the analysis of corruption must take into account is what we call "circularity," which also explains and contributes to its highly harmful effects. This feature is the key to the genetic code of corruption. It refers to the fact that what is touched by corruption—be it a person, an act, or a value—is bound to be transformed into a salable item. A main effect of corruption is that it stimulates the supply and demand for kickbacks, gradually pushing honest people to the margins. Moreover, the increase in the number of corrupt people enlarges the opportunities for corruption and makes them more enticing as it reduces the risk of being identified.

"The loss of confidence in the impartiality of the administration undermines the ethical basis of the community and encourages people to breach the social contract"; "the existence in itself of an illegal market where benefits may be purchased from public officials, diminishes the incentives to develop a reputation of honesty in the industry"; as illegality comes into common use, public reproach of wrongdoings is weakened.[64] At the same time, with the spread of bribery, the "moral costs" of corruption, together with any guilty consciences and fear of falling into disrepute, sink, while the likelihood of finding a "trustworthy" partner in illicit transactions is markedly increased.[65]

Whenever citizens are no longer able to get the protection of their rights to services and resources, lack of confidence in the soundness and efficacy of public procedures usually gives rise to a demand for private protection, even in relationships between ordinary citizens and public bodies. This result has deep roots and need not depend upon a particular corrupt official who actually makes demands or threats. It inheres rather in a degenerative situation, characteristic of Italy, that is dubbed *corruzione ambientale* (environmental corruption).

Corruptions replicate themselves in a horizontal as well as a vertical manner. Horizontal extension take the form of a general increase in the same or related offenses. Some instances of this dynamic is the support organized crime gets from corruption and vice versa, as well as the expansion of bribery beyond national boundaries. Corruption also proliferates vertically, from top to bottom and, though less often, from bottom to top, weaving a tight and wide network of complicities at various levels of the political, administrative, and economic life and disrupting any social hierarchy based on real consensus, merit, and ability to sustain competition.[66]

An intrinsic effect of corrupt transactions is that they weaken the objectivity that is needed for satisfactory public decisions, giving place to an invasive market dominance, which disrupts most rules governing administrative action. As a consequence, a tear is progressively opened in the fabric of the state apparatus, which should pursue the public interest and should clearly remain detached from business logic.[67] Corruption is apt to make interchangeable everything of value with which it comes into contact, transforming due services into arbitrary favors. Then, as it worms its way into the delicate texture of public sector, it erodes the foremost values on which public action should be based.[68] Such an invasive commercial perspective shows an intrinsic tendency to spread and consolidate, gradually overrunning every sanctuary for impartiality and selflessness still extant in the administration.[69]

This evolution is further fostered when findings about corruption in public administration discredit politicians and high-ranking bureaucrats. Public blame tends to extend fatally from single politicians to politics as a whole, and from single officials to the entire administrative apparatus, reducing public life to a heap of rubble.

Meaningful, though not entirely conclusive, are Italian statistical data on reported crimes which show a marked reduction in the number of extortions (*concussioni*) in comparison with the number of bribes (*corruzioni*). Since the beginning of the "clean hands" campaign led by the public prosecutors—the latter have been reported twice more often than the former.[70] Such a trend could be construed as a progressive strengthening of the role played by private businessmen in the illicit transactions with public officials, since bribery, in contrast to extortion, being something like an illicit contract, is usually preceded by negotiations where the businessman freely, actively, and somewhat aggressively enters into agreement, in order to achieve a profitable outcome, not simply to avoid bad treatment.

Elusiveness

An analysis of Italian corruption must examine the element of secrecy that characterizes it, its elusive nature, which generally frustrates attempts to detect and prosecute it. Corruption, it has been written, "thrives in the dark."[71] Sutherland and Donald Cressey pointed out that bribery is an "extremely prevalent crime for which arrests are seldom made" and that its private sector elusiveness lies in the fact that "the cost of the gifts is added to the price of the merchandise being sold, so that the employer and, eventually, the consumer are forced to subsidize the employee." They noted further that "persons who have experience in both business and politics claim that standards of honesty among politicians are higher than they are among businessmen."[72]

Italian networks of corruption are complex; in part this is traceable to the customs of the country and the communications code among those who participate in the illegal dealings.[73] With its enormous presence in the ranks of government administrators, it is bound to generate special skills in the art of illegality. Such sophistication is evident in the multiplication of individuals involved nowadays in such activities—intermediaries, business personnel, politicians, administrators, and others. The roster goes far beyond the traditional dyadic structure of bribery, when only a private briber and a public bribee were involved.

The Italian media coverage of corruption follows the path of white-collar crime in general, with one peculiarity: it is characterized by bouts of sensationalism devoid of satisfactory analytical and critical interpretation and background. The initial media reports are generally followed by a well-orchestrated response aimed at counteracting public indignation. It is alleged by the culprits that the prosecutors are acting as agents of the dominant political party and scapegoating the suspects. To date, the maneuver seems to have enjoyed considerable success in Italy.

V. The Harm of Corruption

Corruption has a devastating impact on society as a whole, an outcome that has been amply demonstrated in research by Italian economists.[74] A prominent German criminologist noted the toll that corruption can take: "It not only drains valuable human resources," he pointed out, "it undermines the self-image, credibility and legitimacy of the governing elites in the minds of the public".[75] For its part the English Law Commission took the position that "short of high treason it is almost impossible to imagine an offense more grave than to corrupt one of the public servants and cause neglect of his duties."[76] Similarly, in a conference held several years ago in Cambridge, corruption was depicted as a cancer which eats into the social fabric, undermining trust and destabilizing state institutions. Corruption aptly was named "the enemy within."[77]

Neither Italy's public nor the "new" politicians ruling the country have proven to be sensitive to the pressing need of a concrete solution to the problem of corruption. Though plagued by massive corruption, and despite the thorough purges of the recent years, Italy remains unable to devise new legislative solutions to combat corruption, despite an enormous growth of concern about the situation in other countries, a concern exemplified in numerous congresses, reform measures, and an upsurge in scientific publications devoted to diagnoses of corruption. A similar interest has been manifest by international organizations, including the United Nations, O.E.C.D., G.A.T.T., the European Union, and the Council of Europe.

There are several explanations for the weakness of current Italian anti-corruption policies. After the original dramatic reaction to a major scandal, public opinion concerned with the issue appears to wane, perhaps because the high level of disgust with politics turns people away from desiring to have anything to do with a possible political solution. At the same time, politicians unmasked for engaging in corrupt activities nonetheless retain their followers, while the activities of anti-corruption forces draw very little media attention. There also tend to be responses that represent symbolic gestures against corruption rather than enforcement policies with "teeth."

The authoritative *Transparency International Corruption Perception Index 2005 CPI* (Corruptions Perception Index) reports the degree of corruption presumed by business people and analysts to be present in a nation: scores range between 10 (very clean) to 0 (highly corrupt). A total of 117 out of 159 countries considered scored less than 5; and 72 countries, less than 3. Corruption is perceived to be most acute in Bangladesh, Turkmenistan, Nigeria, Chad, Myanmar, Haiti, Nigeria, Equatorial Guinea, and the Ivory Coast, all of which have a score of less than 2. In 2005, Italy ranked 40th with a CPI total of 5.0 compared to 9.7 for Iceland, the country ranking first: Italy was 29th in 2001, 31st in 2002, 35th in 2003, and 42nd in 2004. Despite the slight improvement of the latest year, data indicate an overall deterioration of the corruption level in Italy since 2001.

An adequate response to corruption should entail effective punishment for the criminals. There also is a need for people who have acted as whistleblowers to be spared the fearsome sanctions usually imposed for behaviors, i.e., the banishment from future public work—a sanction politicians and bureaucrats will be able to inflict whenever the judiciary is impaired (as it has been almost regularly in the past) in its ability effectively to punish and remove from office all criminals, or the administration lacks the means or the will to get rid of most wrongdoers.

Systemic corruption is particularly elusive because any attempt to crack down on it is bound to antagonize large sectors of the entrenched establishment. The situation is not confined to Italy. In spite of the growing awareness of the dangers of corruption in countries belonging to the European Union, very few trials in which corruption is charged have taken place in member states.

The decline in general institutional trust may reverberate to produce a diminution in the prestige of and confidence in the judiciary, leading to further complications in the prosecution of corruption. It is undeniable that many cases of bribery in Italy have been set aside because of corrupt justice officials. Certainly, this appears evident when information surfaces about briberies known to officials that had long evaded prosecution. Such situations arouse suspicion of collusion that involves judicial participants. Prosecutors cannot help being selective in terms of the cases that they pursue, a matter that allows those who are charged to emphasize how arbitrary their choice has been and to question the objectivity of the judicial process. This is particularly prominent when those who are prosecuted are known to be members or supporters of the opposition political party.[78]

A particularly devastating aspect of corruption stems from its often being perpetrated by offenders, to use Sutherland's words, "of respectability and high social status." The two major features highlighted in our analysis of systemic corruption in Italy—elusiveness and circularity—are the core elements of the harm that the behavior inflicts. Systemic corruption is actually the final stage of a longer process. It differs from endemic, sporadic, routine, and petty corruption, which, notwithstanding the dark figure associated with them do not create the pervasive sense of social malaise associated with systemic corruption. It undercuts civic culture and undermines the faith of citizens who "have developed strong community-regarding norms" and "do not feel they need to work through an influential intermediary in order to get the benefit of the laws and administrative programs."[79] They do not require protection for exercising their rights because they have obtained a stable objectivity in their social setting that allows individuals and social groups to have their identity and status recognized by the state without recourse to friendly and sometimes venal politicians. Giulio Sapelli regards the main feature of the control by the governing class in Italy to be a resistance to constructing institutional rules which would interfere with its personal interest. He points to a fragmented and scattered collection of responses to social needs.[80]

Any anti-corruption policy should first and foremost seek to develop and cherish a civic culture. This entails making the public, in accord with the criminal justice agencies, aware of the elusive nature and systemic extent of corruption. It needs to focus on the abuse of power by those Beccaria designated as the "noblemen," since their misbehavior has effects that are notably farreaching, destroying ideals of equitable justice and substituting for them the unfettered rule of the strongest.

To build a civil culture by fighting corruption involves at least two main elements, which today may sound bold and especially difficult, especially in Italy. First, any anti-corruption strategy should fry the big fish. When a culture of impunity exists, the only way to destroy it is for a number of major corrupt individuals to be caught, convicted, and punished. This would work most effectively if those so treated were from the party in power. Second, successful campaigns need to involve ordinary citizens, who can serve as fertile sources of information by way of hot lines, oversight bodies, call-in shows, educational programs, and village and borough councils.[81]

To this recipe we would add a third ingredient, particularly for Italy. There needs to be a reform of the deplorable "moral" condition of public administration that will enhance the status and self-esteem of civil servants, reducing the demoralization that has played so prominent a role in undermining their resistance to bribery. Such upgrading should include an increase in salaries that is related to merit and professionalism,[82] however anachronistic such a proposal might sound when there are shrinking government budgets, and public opinion reflects a general dislike for bureaucrats. But such measures are essential at a time when self-worth is measured in terms of income and when there is a crying need to rebuild the shattered image of administrators and significantly raise their resistance against corrupt infections. Today, we must also overcome the general lack of loyalty to the state in the Italian bureaucracy, which is a result of the overriding importance of political patronage and protection upon which successful careers largely depend.[83] Pride in one's position should be improved. It is so essential to internalize objective rules[84] and thus to counterbalance—at least in a symbolic way—what is perceived to be the overwhelming social status and power enjoyed by white-collars belonging to the higher echelons of the world of business.

A reader might readily relate these recommended strategies conductive to the establishment of a civic culture and to a real (not phony) equality before the law to the "sacred dogma" praised by Beccaria, "without which there can be no lawful society," namely, the view that "each citizen should have it within his power to do all that is not contrary to the law, without having to fear any inconvenience than that which may result from the action itself, which shapes free and vigorous souls and enlightened minds and prevents citizens from being changed into "beasts of burden" struggling in the service of the strong.

Endnotes

1. Beccaria, 1764/1994, pp. 23–24. From the following footnotes on our Beccaria references will be to the English translation by Henry Paolucci, quoted as Beccaria-Paolucci.
2. Beccaria-Paolucci, p. 65.
3. Feinberg, p. 31.
4. See Brown et al., pp. 3–10 for references.
5. See Hagan, 2000, pp. 48–51; Forti, pp. 346–375.
6. Brown et al., p. 182.
7. Bauman, 2003, pp. 216–220.
8. Beccaria-Paolucci, p. 77.
9. Beccaria-Paolucci, p. 67.
10. Beccaria-Paolucci, p. 69. Italics added.
11. Beccaria-Paolucci, p. 70.
12. Ibid., pp. 88–89.
13. Ibid., p. 69.
14. Ibid., pp. 89–91.
15. Ibid., pp. 94–95.
16. Ibid., pp. 94–95.
17. Sutherland, 1983, p. 7.
18. Sutherland, 1940, p. 3.
19. Sutherland, 1983, pp. 9–10.
20. Sutherland and Cressey, 1970, p. 234.
21. Sutherland, 1983, p. 57.
22. Stitt and Giacopassi, pp. 58–63.
23. Simon and Eitzen, pp. 12–41, 91–93, 121ff.
24. Stitt and Giacopassi, pp. 63–67.
25. Ganzini, et al., pp. 93–94.
26. Shover, 1995, pp. 141–144; Shichor, pp. 93–94.
27. Stitt and Giacopassi, pp. 69–79; Conklin, pp. 102–103; De Maglie, pp. 266–267; Simon and Eitzen, pp. 1–12, 40–42; Shover, 2001, pp. 81–85; Moore and Mills, pp. 51–54.
28. Levi, 1992, p. 342 ff.
29. Beck, pp. 130–132; Stella, p. 398 ff.
30. Bauman, 1999, pp. 7–24; 2003, p. 61 ff.

31. Shapiro, pp. 346–365; Poveda, pp. 69–70.
32. Croall, 1992, pp. 157–174.
33. Shapiro, p. 346.
34. Clarke, p. 21.
35. Shover, 1998, pp. 142–143; Jesilow et al., pp. 165–168.
36. Paradiso, pp. 147ff.
37. Poveda, p. 10 ff.
38. Shover, 1998, p. 139; Brown et al., 91 ff.
39. Simon and Eitzen, pp. 20ff.
40. Rosoff et al., 1998, pp. 277–279; Simon and Eitzen, pp. 24–29, 220 ff.
41. See, among others, Snider, 1993, pp. 177–188; Croall, 1994, pp. 140–141.
42. Croall, 1994, pp. 142–144; Nelken, 2002, p. 869.
43. Poveda, p. 45ff.; Croall, 1994, p. 130ff.; Bauman, 2000, p. 218ff.
44. Snider, 1993, p. 193.
45. Snider, 1993, pp. 169–189; 2001, 419ff.
46. Benson, 2001, pp. 388–390.
47. See, among others, Goff, pp. 191–196; Evans et al., pp. 88–92; Lynch et al., pp. 112–113; 121–124.
48. Forti and Bertolino, pp. xi–xxviii.
49. Rosoff, pp. 497–498; Tumber, p. 418.
50. Simon and Eitzen, pp. 25ff.; Della Porta and Vannucci, 1999, pp. 162ff.; Della Porta, 1995, pp. 49–66.
51. Simon and Eitzen, pp. 25ff.
52. See Fantò, pp. 15ff., 81ff.
53. For details of the cases see Barbacetto.
54. Della Porta, 1992; Della Porta and Vanucci, 1994, 1999, 2000.
55. Gardner and Lyman, p. 5.
56. Kaiser, 1995, p. 160.
57. See further, Forti, 1987, p. 414.
58. Klitgaard, p. 367.
59. Rose-Ackerman, 1978.
60. On the widespread "percentage rule" in Italian public works, see Sapelli, p. 134.
61. Sapelli, p. 141.
62. Della Porta-Vannucci, 1994, p. 376, fn. 19.
63. Vannucci, 1995, p. 36.
64. Vannucci, 1993, pp. 23, 40.
65. Della Porta-Vannucci, 1994, pp. 45, 462.
66. Ruggiero, p. 16.
67. See Della Porta and Vannucci, 1994, p. 253.
68. See Ruggiero, p. 17.
69. See also Ruggiero, p. 16.
70. See ISTAT (1993, 1994, 1995): public extortions ("concussioni") have steadily increased from 462 reported crimes in 1992 (when "clean hands" operation started) to 690 in 1994 (+49%), while in the same periods briberies have passed from 447 to 858 (+91%).
71. The World Bank, p. 44.
72. Sutherland and Cressey, 1978, pp. 44–45.
73. Della Porta-Vannucci, 1994, p. 227f.
74. Arnone and Iliopulos; Cabiddu. For further references see Forti, 1992.
75. Kaiser, p. 143.
76. Great Britain, Law Commission, p. 1.
77. "Corruption—The Enemy Within," 14th International Symposium on Economic Crime." Jesus College, Cambridge University, Sept. 13, 1996.
78. Cazzola, p. 14.

79. Heidenheimer, p. 27.
80. Sapelli, p. 148.
81. Klitgaard, pp. 368–369.
82. Della Porta-Vannucci, 1994, p. 472.
83. Cazzola, p. 150.
84. See Della Porta-Vannucci, 1994, p. 48.

References

Arnone, Marco, and Eleni Iliopulos (2005) *La corruzione costa*. Milano: Vita e Pensiero.

Barbacetto, Gianni et al. (2002) *Mani pulite. La vera storia*. Roma: Editori Riuniti.

Bateson, Gregory (1972) *Steps to an Ecology of Mind*. New York: Ballantine Books.

Bauman, Zygmunt (2000) "Social Issues of Law and Order." *British Journal of Criminology*, 40(2):205–221.

Bauman, Zygmunt (2003) *La società sotto assedio*. Bari: Editori Laterza. (Engl. ed. *Society Under Siege* (2002)) Cambridge: Polity Press.

Bauman, Zygmunt (1999) *La società dell' incertezza*. Bologna: II Mulino

Beccaria, Cesare (1764–1994) *Dei delitti e delle pene*, Editor F. Venturi. Torino: Einaudi.

Beck, Ulrich (1992) *Risk Society*. London: Sage Publications.

Becker, Paul J. et al. (2000) "The Pinto Legacy: The Community as an Indirect Victim of Corporate Deviance." *Justice Professional* 12: 305–326.

Benson, Michael J. (2001) "Prosecuting Corporate Crime: Problems and Constraints." In *Crimes of Privilege*, Editors N. Shover and J. P. Wright. New York: Oxford University Press.

Benson, Michael J. et al. (1992) "Community Context and the Prosecution of Corporate Crime." In *White-Collar Crime Reconsidered*, Editors K. Schlegel and D. Weisburd. Boston: Northeastern University Press.

Blankenship, Michael B. ed. (1993) *Understanding Corporate Criminality*. New York: Garland.

Braithwaite, John, and Gilbert Geis (1982) "On Theory and Action for Corporate Crime Control." In *On White-Collar Crime*, G. Geis. Lexington: Lexington Books.

Braithwaite, John (1992) "Poverty, Power and White-Collar Crime. Sutherland and the Paradoxes of Criminological Theory." In *White-Collar Crime Reconsidered*, Editors K. Schlegel and D. Weisburd. Boston: Northeastern University Press.

Brown, Stephen E. et al. (2004) *Criminology, Explaining Crime and its Context*, 5th edition. Cincinnati, OH: Anderson Publishing Co.

Cabiddu, Maria Agostina, ed. (2005) *Appalti e responsabilità. Da Tangentopoli agli attuali scenari*. Milano: Franco Angeli.

Caiden, Gerald E. and Naomi J. Caiden (1977) "Administrative Corruption." *Public Administration Review* 37:301–308.

Calavita, Kitty and Henry N. Pontell (1994) "Heads I Win, Tails You Lose": Deregulation, Crime and Crisis in the Savings and Loan Industry." In *White-Collar Crime* Editor D. Nelken, Aldershot: Dartmouth.

Cassese, Sabino (1991) *La Repubblica*. December 28, 1 and 12.

Cazzola, Franco (1992) *L'Italia del pizzo*. Torino: Einaudi.

Cazzullo, Aldo (2005) "Di Pietro: ora il porto delle nebbie è diventato il tribunale di Milano." *Corriere della Sera*, June 6, 14.

Chambliss, William, and Robert B. Seidman (1971) *Law, Order, and Power*. Reading, MA: Addison Wesley.

Clarke, Michael (1990) *Business Crime*. Cambridge: Polity Press.

Clinard, Marshall B. (1990) *Corporate Corruption*. New York: Praeger.

Conklin, John E. (1989) *Criminology*. New York: Macmilla.

Council of Europe—GMC (The Multidisciplinary Group on Corruption) (1996) First Conference for Law-Enforcement Officers Specialised in the Fight against

Corruption, Document GMC (96) 53, Strasbourg, 26 April 1996, Conclusions and recommendations of the *General Rapporteur (Mr Lorenzo Salazar, Italy), Strasbourg, 24–25 April 1996*.

Croall, Hazel (1989) "Who is the White-Collar Criminal?" *British Journal of Criminology* 29:157–174.

Croall, Hazel (1994) *White-Collar Crime*. Philadelphia: Open University Press.

Davigo, Piercamillo (1998) *La giubba del re*. Bari: Editori Laterza.

De Maglie, Cristina (2002) *L'etica e il mercato*. Milano: Giuffrè.

Della Porta, Donatella (1995) "I circoli viziosi della corruzione in Italia." In *Corruzione e democrazia. Sette paesi a confronto*, Editor D. Della Porta and Y. Meny. Napoli: Liguori Editore.

Della Porta, Donatella, and Alberto Vannucci (1994) *Corruzione politica e amministrazione pubblica. Risorse, meccanismi, attori*. Bologna: II Mulino.

Della Porta, Donatella, and Alberto Vannucci (1999) *Un paese anormale*. Bari: Editori Laterza.

Della Porta, Donatella, and Alberto Vannucci (2000) Corruption and Public Contracts: Some Lessons from the Italian Case. Paper prepared for the Conference on "Corrupt Exchanges: Empirical Themes in the Politics and Political Economy of Corruption." Bielefeld (May 18–19).

Della Porta, Donatella (1992) *Lo scambio occulto. Casi di corruzione politica in Italia*. Bologna: II Mulino.

Della Seta, Piero, and Edoardo Salzano (1993) *L'Italia a sacco*. Roma: Editori Riuniti.

Dezalay, Yves (1997) *I mercanti del diritto. Le multinazionali del diritto e la ristrutturazione dell'ordine giuridico internazionale*. Milano: Giuffrè.

Enciclopedia Einaudi (1978) Torino: Einaudi.

Evans, David et al. (1993) "Public Perceptions of Corporate Crime." In *Understanding Corporate Criminality*, Editor M. B. Blankenship. New York: Garland.

Fantò, Enzo (1999) *L'impresa a partecipazione mafiosa*. Bari: Dedalo.

Fattah, Ezzat A. (1997) *Criminology: Past, Present and Future*. Basingstoke: St. Martin's Press.

Feinberg, Joel (1984) *The Moral Limits of the Criminal Law, I, Harm to Others*. New York-Oxford: Oxford University Press.

Fisse, Brent, and John Braithwaite (1983) *The Impact of Publicity on Corporate Offenders*. Albany: State University of New York Press.

Forti, Gabrio (1992) *La corruzione del pubblico amministratore*. Milano: Giuffrè.

Forti, Gabrio (2000) *L'immane concretezza*. Milano: Raffaello Cortina editore.

Forti, Gabrio, ed. (2003) *Il prezzo della tangente*. Milano: Vita e Pensiero.

Forti, Gabrio and Marta Bertolino, eds. (2005) *La televisione del crimine*. Milano: Vita e Pensiero.

Ganzini, Linda, et al. (2001) "Victims of Fraud: Comparing Victims of White-Collar and Violent Crime." In *Crimes of Privilege*, Editors N. Shover and J. P. Wright, New York: Oxford University Press.

Garland, David, and Richard Sparks (2000) "Criminology, Social Theory and the Challenge of our Times." *British Journal of Criminology* 40(2):189–204.

Garland, David (2000) "The Culture of High Crime Societies: Some Preconditions of Recent "Law and Order" Policies." *British Journal of Criminology* 40(3):347–374.

Geis, Gilbert (1992) "White-Collar Crime: What Is It?" In *White-Collar Crime Reconsidered*, Editors K. Schlegel and D. Weisburd. Boston: Northeastern University Press.

Geis, Gilbert (1993) "The Evolution of the Study of Corporate Crime." In *Understanding Corporate Criminality*, Editor M. B. Blankenship. New York: Garland.

Goff, Colin (2001) "The Westray Mine Disaster: Media Coverage of a Corporate Crime in Canada." In *Contemporary Issues in Crime and Criminal Justice*, Editors H. N. Pontell and D. Shichor. Upper Saddle River NJ: Prentice Hall.

Grabosky, Peter N. et al. (1987) "The Myth of Community Tolerance Toward White-Collar Crime." *Australian and New Zealand Journal of Criminology* 20:33–43.

Hagan, John (1987) *Modern Criminology. Crime, Criminal Behavior, and its Control.* New York: McGraw-Hill.

Heidenheimer, Arnold, ed. (1978) *Political Corruption. Readings in Comparative Analysis.* New Brunswick, NJ: Transaction Books.

Instituto Nazionale di Statistica—I.S.T.A.T. (1993, 1994, 1995) *Annuario di Statistiche Giudiziarie. Roma*: Poligrafico dello Stato.

Jesilow, Paul et al. (1992) "Reporting Consumer and Major Fraud." In *White-collar Crime Reconsidered*, Editors K. Schlegel and D. Weisburd. Boston: Northeastern University Press.

Kaiser, Günther (1995) "Kriminalität der Mächtigen"—Theorie und Wirklichkeit. In *Festschrift für K. Miyazawa*. Baden-Baden: Nomos Verlag, 159–175.

Kaiser, Günther (1984) *Criminologia*. Milano: Giuffrè.

Katz, Jack (1995) "What Makes Crime "News"?" In *Crime and the Media*, Editor R. W. Ericson. Aldershot: Darthmouth.

Klitgaard, Robert (2000) "Roles for International Organisations in the Fight against Corruption." In *Responding to Corruption. Social Defence, Corruption, and the Protection of Public Administration and the Independence of Justice*, Editor Paolo Bernasconi. Napoli: La Città del Sole.

Kramer, Ronald C. et al. (2002) "The Origins and Development of the Concept and Theory of State-Corporate Crime." *Crime and Delinquency* 48(2): 263–282.

Levi, Michael (1992) "White-Collar Crime Victimization." In *White-Collar Crime Reconsidered.* Editors K. Schlegel and D. Weisburd. Boston: Northeastern University Press.

Levi, Michael (2001) "Transnational White-Collar Crime: Some Explorations of Victimization Impact", In *Contemporary Issues in Crime and Criminal Justice*, Editors H. N. Pontell and D. Schichor. Upper Saddle River NJ: Prentice Hall.

Levi, Michael (2005) "I Colletti bianchi e crimine organizzato nei notiziari britannici: alcune riflessioni sociologiche." In *La televisione del crimine*, Editors G. Forti and M. Bertolino. Milano: Vita e Pensiero.

Loos, Fritz (1974) Zum "Rechtsgut" der Bestechungsdelikte. In *Festschrift für Hans Welzel*, Editors G. Stratenwerth et al. Berlin-New York: De Gruyter.

Lynch, Michael J. et al. (2000) "Media Coverage of Chemical Crimes. Hillsborough County, Florida, 1987–97." British Journal of Criminology, 40(1):112–126.

Mannheim, Hermann (1975) *Trattato di criminologia comparata*. Torino: Einaudi.

Mannheim, Hermann (1972) *Pioneers in Criminology*, 2nd ed. Montclair, NJ: Patterson Smith.

Moore, Elizabeth and Michael Mills (2001) "The Neglected Victims and Unexamined Costs of White-Collar Crime." In *Crimes of Privilege*, Editors N. Shover and J. P. Wright. New York: Oxford University Press.

Nelken, David (2002) "White-Collar Crime." In *The Oxford Handbook of Criminology*, Editor M. Maguire et al. New York-Oxford: Oxford University Press.

Ostendorf, Heribert (1996) Korruption. Eine Herausforderung für Staat und Gesellschaft. *Neue Kriminalpolitik* 17.

Paolucci, Henry (1963) English translation of Beccaria, Cesare (1764) *On Crimes and Punishments*. New York: Macmillan Publishing Company.

Paradiso, Pietro (1983) *La criminalità negli affari. Un approccio criminologico*. Padova: Cedam.

Poveda, Tony G. (1994) *Rethinking White-Collar Crime*. Westport; CT: Praeger Publishers.

Punch, Maurice (2000) "Suite Violence: Why Managers Murder and Corporations Kill." *Crime, Law and Social Change* 33:243–245.

Reiner, Robert (2002) "Media Made Criminality: The Representation of Crime in the Mass Media." *The Oxford Handbook of Criminology*, Editors M. Maguire et al., New York: Oxford University Press.

Rose-Ackerman, Susan (1978) *Corruption. A Study in Political Economy*. New York: Academic Press.

Rosoff, Stephen M., et al. (1998) *Profit Without Honor: White-Collar Crime and the Looting of America*. Upper Saddle River, NJ: Prentice Hall.

Rosoff, Stephen M. (2005) "I mass media e il crimine dei colletti bianchi." In *La televisione del crimine*, Editors G. Forti and M. Bertolino. Milano: Vita e Pensiero.

Ruff, Charles F.C. (1977) Federal Prosecution of Local Corruption: A Case Study in the Making of Law Enforcement Policy. Geo. L.J. 65:1171–1228.

Ruggiero, Vincenzo (1994) "Scambio corrotto e vittimizzazione in Italia." *Dei delitti e delle pene*, 19 ss.

Sapelli, Giulio (1994) *Cleptocrazia. Il "meccanismo unico" della corruzione tra economia e politica*. Milano: Feltrinelli.

Schmalleger, Frank (1996) *Criminology Today*, Englewood Cliffs, NJ: Prentice Hall.

Shapiro, Susan P. (1990) "Collaring the Crime, Not the Criminal: Reconsidering the Concept of White-Collar Crime." *American Sociological Review*, 55:346–365.

Shichor, David, et al. (2001) "Victims of Investment Fraud." In *Contemporary Issues in Crime and Criminal Justice*, Editors H. N. Pontell and D. Shichor. Upper Saddle River NJ: Prentice Hall.

Shover, Neal (1998) "White-Collar Crime." In *The Handbook of Crime and Punishment*, Editor M. Tonry, New York-Oxford: Oxford University Press.

Shover, Neal, et al. (2001) "Consequences of Victimization by White-Collar Crime." In *Crimes of Privilage*, Editors N. Shover and J. P. Wright. New York-Oxford: Oxford University Press.

Simon, David R, and Frank E. Hagan (1999) *White-Collar Deviance*. Needham Heights, MA: Allyn and Bacon.

Simon, David R, and D. Stanley Eitzen (1992) *Elite Deviance*, Needham Heights, MA: Allyn and Bacon.

Snider, Laureen (1993) "Regulating Corporate Behavior." In *Understanding Corporate Criminality*, Editor M. B. Blankenship. New York: Garland.

Snider, Laureen (2000) "The Sociology of Corporate Crime: An Obituary." *Theoretical Criminology* 4(2):169–206.

Snider, Laureen (2001) "Cooperative Models and Corporate Crime: Panacea or Cop-Out?" In *Crimes of Privilege*, Editors N. Shover and J. P. Wright. New York: Oxford University Press.

Stella, Federico (2001) *Giustizia e modernità*. Milano: Giuffrè.

Stitt, B. Grant, and David J. Giacopassi (1993) "Assessing Victimization From Corporate Harms." In *Understanding Corporate Criminality*, Editor M. B. Blankenship. New York-London: Garland.

Sutherland, Edwin H. (1940) "White-Collar Criminality." *American Sociological Review*. 5:1–12 (February).

Sutherland, Edwin H. (1983) *White-Collar Crime. The Uncut Version*. New Haven: Yale University Press.

Sutherland, Edwin H. (1987) *Il crimine dei colletti bianchi. La versione integrale*, Editor G. Forti. Milano: Giuffrè.

Sutherland, Edwin H., and Donald R. Cressey (1970) *Criminology* (8th edition). Philadelphia: J. B. Lippincott Company.

Tanzi, Vito (1994) *Corruption, Governmental Activities, and Markets*. IMF Working Paper, August 1994.

The World Bank (1997) *Helping Countries Combat Corruption. The Role of the World Bank, Poverty Reduction and Economic Management*. The World Bank, September 1997.

The Law Commission (1997) Legislating the Criminal Code: Corruption. Consultation paper n. 145.

Titus, Richard M. (2001) "Personal Fraud and Its Victims." In *Crimes of Privilege*, Editors N. Shover and J. P. Wright. New York: Oxford University Press.

Tumber, Howard (1995) "Selling Scandal": Business and the Media." In *Crime and the Media*, Editor R. W. Ericson. Aldershot: Darthmouth.

Turk, Austin (1969) *Criminality and Legal Order*. Chicago, IL: Rand McNally.

Wright, John P. et al. (1996) "Chained Factory Fire Exists. Media Coverage of a Corporate Crime That Killed 25 Workers." In *Corporate and Governmental Deviance*, Editors M. D. Ermann and R. J. Lundman. New York: Oxford University Press.

Part IX

Case Studies

1

The Role of the Mass Media in the Enron Fraud

Cause or Cure?

Stephen M. Rosoff

The relationship between crime and the mass media often has been described by researchers as paradoxical. Perhaps the most striking of the proposed paradoxes are the dual contentions that the media can serve as both a *cause* of crime and a *cure* for crime. This paper posits that the recent financial scandals in the United States—which began in 2001, when Enron tipped over the first domino in a stunning fission of corporate failures—are a reflection of these contradictory notions of cause and cure.

Cause

When scholars like Surette[1] and others have written about mass media as a cause of crime, their focus generally has been on violent crime. They cite an abundance of evidence from laboratory studies in which media depictions of violence stimulate aggression in subjects.[2] They report classic empirical studies of modeled aggression[3] and copious anecdotal evidence of copycat crimes.[4] Although white-collar crime can in fact be very violent, especially in the areas of environmental contamination and unsafe consumer products, this is not the case with the corporate Ponzi schemes and "pump and dump" scams that opened the New Millennium. If modeling of illegal conduct has occurred—and it clearly has—the models typically have been deviant leaders, supervisors, or associates, whose crimes have been rewarded. It seems very unlikely that the media could have stimulated an explosion of fraudulent financial reports. It is tautological that there can be no copycat crime unless there is a crime being reported that someone could copy. This did not happen. The media failed to recognize—or chose not to report—that crimes of unprecedented magnitude were even being committed. They published and broadcast the fraudulent hyperbole but not the fraud.

So one must look elsewhere for a causal link between the mass media and the corporate scandals. If the media did not abet the fraud through imitation or social learning, how did they? In the best case, they did it through negligence or naiveté; in the worst case, through co-optation and complicity.

When one considers the role of the media in the Enron debacle, the primary referent is a journalistic segment largely ignored by criminologists—the financial press, both print and electronic. Excavating back issues of magazines like

Forbes, *Fortune*, *Business Week*, as well as the *Wall Street Journal* and the business sections of other major daily newspapers, for Enron stories is like taking a journey through a fantastic looking glass and entering a parallel universe of cheerleading and obsequiousness, a universe where applause drowns out skepticism, where down is up and nothing succeeds like failure. Like the treacly poetry in cheap greeting cards, it can be painful to read.

Naiveté

The naiveté was manifest in the extravagant praise heaped on Enron from the late 1990s through much of 2001. Enron was held up as the epitome of a new post-deregulation corporate model. As far back as 1998, the highly regarded *Kiplinger's Personal Finance Magazine*, for example, was touting Enron as "good value," adding that "Enron's estimated rate of long-term growth—15 percent per year—is roughly twice that of the market's."[5]

A reporter for the Dow Jones News Service beat the drum even louder in 1999: "In contrast to the 'boringly predictable' regulated utilities of old, which were safe havens for widows and orphans, the newcomers hold the promise of skyrocketing returns." His article listed the most interesting energy companies. Enron topped the list.[6]

Also in 1999, a *Los Angeles Times* business columnist rejoiced that the energy market was no longer a "staid business of regulated monopolies," but a "beehive of financially savvy companies like Enron."[7]

In 2000, *Business Week* was celebrating Jeff Skilling's vision of Enron as a cutting-edge company that could securitize anything and trade it anywhere.[8]

A headline in one *Dallas Morning News* branded Enron a "global e-commerce leader," and the article gushed over how Enron is a "global go-getter that has created a corporate culture that rewards risk-taking."[9] The *Houston Business Journal* used the adjective "sizzling" twice in three paragraphs, noting, "Enron has shown a widely recognized knack for innovation that consistently generates additional sources of revenue."[10] Both of these Texas publications were basically (and uncritically) rewriting Enron press releases.

On August 13, 2001, *Business 2.0* hit the streets, declaring, "The Revolution LIVES," with a photo of Enron president Jeff Skilling on the cover.[11] The following day Skilling resigned.

In September 2001, only a month before the implosion, *Red Herring*, one of the bibles of the New Economy, proclaimed, "Forget about Microsoft. America's most successful, revered, feared—even hated—company is no longer a band of millionaire geeks from Redmond, Washington, but a cabal of cowboy/traders from Houston: Enron."[12]

Even *The New York Times* called Enron a "model for the new American workplace."[13] It labeled CEO Ken Lay "an idea machine."[14] *Fortune Magazine* named Enron "America's Most Innovative Company" *six years in a row*.[15]

Negligence

Enron was, of course, a Houston-based company. As such, one would have expected the *Houston Chronicle*, the only daily newspaper in America's fourth largest city, to be on top of the story. When a major scandal breaks in a newspaper's hometown, it often gives local reporters and editors a chance to shine in the national spotlight. But this was not at all the case. On the *Chronicle's* website a link was offered to what it called "full coverage" of the Enron collapse. Interestingly, the stories went back only as far as October 23, 2001. Not available for examination was the *Chronicle's* shameless trail of cheerleading. An especially memorable piece appeared in the business section on August 28, 2001. The headline read, "Taking a Long View: Enron Works to Shore Up Confidence." The lead sentence was, "Even though *nothing major appears to be wrong at Enron* Corp., investor confidence in the world's largest energy trader remains shaky [emphasis added]."[16] Perhaps that shakiness stemmed from investors reading other publications, which, by that time, had been aggressively reporting Enron's troubles.

Another memorable *Chronicle* column that same month was titled, "Enron Making Way to Weather Storm." The column insisted, "It's still a company with innovative people who have shown they can turn ideas into profitable businesses. That's why the *current problems will blow over* [emphasis added]."[17]

Perhaps the *Chronicle's* most ignominious moment came on November 11 in a story covering Enron's public announcement that it had overstated its income by about $600 million over the previous four years. The *Chronicle's* lead on this story was astonishingly flippant: "Ever have to fix an error in your checkbook when you get your monthly bank statement in the mail? Imagine the headache Enron Corp. is facing."[18]

The *Chronicle* at times seemed to operate as Ken Lay's public relations arm. One story about his "humble beginning" said, "He is often described as a folksy man of the people who never lost sight of his origins—or his drive to succeed."[19] By that time, no one except the *Chronicle* was describing Lay in such sympathetic terms. Another story bemoaned, "Like the vast majority of the company's employees and shareholders, he [Lay] could now lose nearly everything." The newspaper wept for a hometown boy who was secretly dumping his own shares for hundreds of millions of dollars while still encouraging employees to invest all their retirement savings in Enron stock. The *Chronicle* somehow found a way to equate Ken Lay's mounting legal problems with the devastating financial losses suffered by Enron's faithful rank-and-file workers.

Ironically, since the collapse no newspaper has been more aggressive in its Enron coverage than the *Chronicle*. But its sad record of negligence in its own backyard may never be fully erased. In January 2002 the *Chronicle* ran a story headlined "The Myth of Enron." It said, "Years before its spectacular fall there were signs that Enron was never what it seemed. A close look at its history shows that the company relied on a steady stream of hype and distractions to gloss over its failures."[20] The story identified those taken in by the Enron propaganda machine: Wall Street analysts, investors, and "others." One might well wonder if it included itself in the "others" category, given its egregious record of fawning over the company—something never alluded to in the article. The *Chronicle's* belated outrage seems somewhat akin to marching onto the field *after* the battle and shooting the wounded.

Co-optation and Complicity

The press, needless to say, depends on public trust. It now appears clear that some prominent columnists and commentators placed that trust at risk by accepting substantial fees from Enron. Though purportedly meant as compensation for services rendered, the actual work involved seems so patently small that many critics have characterized the exchanges as ill-disguised bribery.

New York Times economics columnist Paul Krugman received $50,000 from an Enron advisory group shortly before joining the *Times*. The liberal Krugman later blamed the criticism on a conservative attempt to link Enron to the left—and thus help obscure the company's questionable ties to the Bush administration. It seemed a weak and self-serving argument, given that most of the journalists benefiting from Enron largesse were from the free-market right. Krugman denied he had done anything inappropriate, insisting that the Enron advisory board "had no function that I was aware of."[21] Krugman's curious neutralization was reminiscent of former Congressman Ozzie Meyers, who went to prison in the wake of the notorious ABSCAM sting operation of the 1970s. Meyers admitted taking a $50,000 bribe from a bogus Arab sheik but denied any culpability because he claimed he had no actual intention of using his position to help "Abdul"[22]—as if that makes a $50,000 payoff to Meyers or, in this case, to Krugman, ethically acceptable.

Weekly Standard editor William Kristol, one of the leading conservative voices in the America media, received $100,000 from the Enron advisory board.[23]

Lawrence Kudlow, contributing editor of *National Review* and host of a daily financial program on CNBC, was paid $50,000 for what was termed "consulting and research."[24]

Financial columnist Irwin Seltzer of the *Times* of London received about $50,000 from Enron. Perhaps coincidentally, perhaps not, Seltzer became one of Ken Lay's fiercest defenders.[25]

Wall Street Journal columnist Peggy Noonan (a former presidential speech writer) earned a fee of $25,000 to $50,000 (she claims not to remember the amount) from Enron for doing something—although no one is quite sure what that something was.[26]

It should be noted that all of the afore-mentioned beneficiaries—except Seltzer—later acknowledged in print their financial arrangements with Enron. And some of them, such as Krugman and Kudlow, became strong critics of the company. But the cooptation of the media by a criminogenic corporation is so fraught with danger that even journalistic *mea culpas* and after-the-fact piling on raise disturbing questions. When Enron set out to buy favorable press coverage by turning *muckrakers* into *buckrakers*, it placed its targets in a no-win situation. If their so-called consultants later recused themselves from Enron coverage—as some critics demanded—the company would have in effect bought their silence. If, on the other hand, their purchased pundits later turned on them, as most did, they risked the appearance of biting the hand that fed them just to flaunt their independence and courage.

Journalists are ever quick to rage when politicians appear to be doing the bidding of those who fill their campaign coffers. For those in the mass media, feeding at the same corporate trough is an engraved invitation for trouble.

Apologists for the financial press argue that the media were hoodwinked like everyone else. After all, the doctored financial reports of companies like Enron—as well as WorldCom, Qwest, Global Crossing, Adelphia, and others—had been certified by external auditors, most notably the once-giant corporate accounting firm of Arthur Andersen and Company, now deservedly a rotting corpse. There may be some measure of truth to this contention. There is no question that the Enron books were cooked by master chefs. But Enron's use of layer upon layer of interlocking limited partnerships should have raised a red flag to an attentive press. Consider just one example: Enron made a $12.5 million loan to Kafus Industries, a Canadian company that makes recycled fiberboard. In 1999 Enron increased the loan to $20 million and received a note convertible into Kafus shares. It then sold the Kafus stake to another partnership, SE Thunderbird. SE Thunderbird was controlled by Blue Heron, which in turn was controlled by Whitewing Associates, a partnership whose sole member was Whitewing Management, which was controlled by Egret I, another Enron affiliate.[27] If these Byzantine machinations seem incomprehensible, that's the whole idea. And the media should have understood that—even if they couldn't understand the precise details. Beyond a certain point, complexity *is* fraud.

Perhaps most importantly, the media fell asleep at the switch while a dangerous revolution in the corporate culture was occurring under their noses. The American economy had been largely built on what has been termed *patient wealth*. Earlier generations of executives were the products of a time when almost nobody got rich quickly. Going public and making a billion dollars a few months later was not in their mentality or imagination.

Today's business leaders grew up in a very different America—a more materialistic America that showcased enormous amounts of wealth. It now appears clear that many of them brought into the arena a profound sense of entitlement. They expected things sooner rather than later. "In your face" extravagance that once would have been embarrassing had become the norm. Not only do today's corporate elite believe they should make fortunes quickly, but there are also far fewer restrictions on conspicuous consumption. One need only think of now-imprisoned former Tyco CEO Dennis Kozlowski's infamous $15,000 umbrella stand and $6,000 shower curtains—paid for by victimized shareholders.

This dramatic transition was fueled by a greed so out of control that a generation of entrepreneurs who *make* things was replaced by a generation who *take* things. The wealth they possess or aspire to possess is not a patient wealth. But to merely call it "impatient" wealth is to understate what has happened in corporate America. It may be more apt to borrow a term from the psychiatric lexicon, a term used to describe persons intensely selfish, conspicuously lacking in human empathy, and dispositionally unable to delay gratification. We entered an age of *psychopathic wealth*—and the press hardly seemed to notice.

And even if most of the mass media are still not yet ready to admit it, they helped create Enron. The media had become participants in the New Economy. Today's news media are themselves frequently a part of large, often global, corporations, depending on advertising revenues that increasingly come from other large corporations. As public companies, the news media are under the same kind of pressure to create shareholder value and increase earnings as other public companies. Consequently, there are always potential conflicts of interest—perhaps more now than ever. The so-called "Chinese Wall" in journalism, between doing business and reporting business, rests on shifting sand.

White-collar crime, like most crime, is photosensitive. It does best in darkened rooms behind closed doors. The media, of course, have had centuries of experience in shining a spotlight on crime, but have probably been least successful in revealing the malfeasance of large corporations—particularly before the damage was done. The impact of large corporations on our environment, our political system, the distribution of wealth around the world, the security of our investments, even our health, continues to grow. The recent corporate failures and frauds served as a warning to the press that it needs to be dedicated to finding the next Enron. Finding the first Enron, thousands of days late and billions of dollars short, was surely not the media's finest hour. From 1995 to 2001, reporters gave a remarkably free ride to some amazingly unsupportable businesses. Perhaps writing about all those 20-something dot.com millionaires spawned some combination of envy and admiration that turned into a perverse Stockholm Syndrome.

But that was then, and this is now. Just as the political media were changed irrevocably by Watergate, the financial press seems far different in the post-Enron era.

Cure

Media scholars long have debated the notion of agenda setting—that is, the manner in which the mass media can influence public opinion. It is generally accepted that people tend to judge the significance of a social concern by the extent to which it is emphasized in the media. But whether that proposed nexus between media and public opinion effects changes in public policy is less clear. Some have proposed a simple linear model: a story appears; the issue increases in importance to the public; and policy makers respond.[28] Some critics contend that a linear model is *too* simple. Doppelt and Manikas suggest an ecological model, in which the relationship among media, public opinion, and policymaking is multidirectional.[29] Molotch and colleagues argue that the linear model may be truncated at any point, noting, for example, that the American media have reported decades of dramatic and tragic stories involving gun deaths, which have bent public opinion strongly in favor of tighter gun laws; but that (for a variety of reasons) this has resulted in very little in the way of major policy changes.[30]

Nevertheless, if the media are to play a role in "curing" grand-scale corporate corruption, they are most likely to do so by elevating the position of such crimes on the public agenda. In the past, this has proved to be difficult. Street crime has always dominated the public's attention. White-collar crime usually has been dismissed as the "other" crime problem. Even the massive savings and loan and insider trading scandals of the 1980s had surprisingly little traction, beyond the public's fascination with a few high-profile "star" offenders like Charles Keating, Michael Milken, and Ivan Boesky. To the average citizen, Wall Street often seems a million miles from Main Street. And while the cost of the S&L collapse to taxpayers was enormous (The cost of bailing out Keating's corrupt Lincoln Savings exceeded the total cost of all the bank robberies in American history[31]), these scandals failed to resonate in any lasting, visceral way.

But the Enron story *did* resonate. In journalistic parlance, it had "legs." The tragic tales of hard-earned retirement funds being wiped out almost overnight, while top executives continued to live like maharajahs, struck a collective nerve. And the more Enron horror stories the media told, the angrier the public became. Here, at last, was traction.

In its belated "Myth of Enron" story, *the Houston Chronicle* complained angrily about how the company had avoided answering tough questions. As usual, the *Chronicle* got it wrong. The fall of the House of Enron occurred because someone finally asked the *simplest* of questions: How do you make money?[32] It is a question not likely to be overlooked again by the financial press.

So, have the media reasserted their traditional public watchdog role? Have increased scrutiny and skepticism led to increased public outrage and a louder demand for corporate accountability? Have politicians and agency decision makers been listening? Perhaps it's too early to say for certain, but the signs are encouraging. Congress surely was listening when it passed the Sarbanes-Oxley Act of 2002—the toughest piece of corporate governance legislation ever enacted. The law imposes new duties on public corporations and their executives, directors, auditors, and attorneys, as well as securities analysts. The act requires significant rulemaking by the Securities and Exchange Commission and the creation of the Public Company Accounting Oversight Board.[33] Among the act's 11 major provisions is the requirement that corporate CEOs assume personal responsibility for the integrity of their company's financial statements. Misrepresentation could mean prison time.[34] At least two repercussions are worth noting. First, in the year following the passage of Sarbanes-Oxley, more than 300 publicly traded corporations revised and restated their earnings reports.[35] Second, there have been no major corporate scandals even approaching Enron proportions since Sarbanes-Oxley was enacted.

Another indication that the post-Enron media have sensitized their consumers to the seriousness of white-collar crime and the arrogance of control fraud is the spectacle of disgraced captains of industry voluntarily entering into plea bargains involving lengthy prison terms. Defendants such as Samuel Waksal[36] (former CEO of ImClone), Martin Grass[37] (former CEO of Rite-Aid), and Andrew Fastow[38] (former CFO of Enron) agreed to accept tough sentences of seven, eight, and ten years, respectively, rather than go to trial. These men presumably were represented by skilled, highly paid attorneys and surely would not have pled guilty without a compelling reason. Simply put, they were afraid to face an angry, punitive jury.

Moreover, the media finally have discovered psychopathic wealth and its newsworthiness. Consider one illuminating example: In April 2003, a story broke that CEO Donald J. Carty of American Airlines, in an effort to avert bankruptcy, had successfully negotiated a $1.8 billion savings package with the company's three labor unions. He had convinced his pilots, mechanics, flight attendants, and baggage handlers that they must accept major pay cuts of between 15 and 25 percent or AMR would collapse, taking their jobs and pensions down with it.[39]

What Carty failed to make clear at the time was that his plea for shared sacrifice did not include himself. On April 15, AMR filed a required report with the Securities and Exchange Commission. Only then was it revealed that—at the same time Carty was negotiating the labor pay cuts—he secretly was crafting hefty retention bonuses for himself and a handful of top executives that would reward them for staying at their posts until 2005. Carty's bonus would total $1.6 million, twice his annual salary.[40] The press wanted to know how this could have happened. And why a CEO whose company had lost over $5 billion dollars in the previous two years deserved a seven-figure bonus just for showing up.

This was the type of story that once easily could have gone unnoticed—especially at a time when the drums of war were drowning out competing noises. But an incensed public noticed it. As a result, the bonuses were rescinded, and Carty was forced to resign. Perhaps the media indeed had re-asserted its watchdog role. Even *Fortune*, long a bastion of the corporate status quo, the magazine that once had voted Enron America's best company six years in a row, did a cover story in 2003 on exorbitant CEO compensation. The cover featured pigs in designer suits.[41]

A chastened U.S. media have vowed "never again," and now promise to replace cheerleading with hardnosed, skeptical reporting. Will this pledge endure? No one can predict that with any real confidence. Forever is a long time. But the renascent financial press seems likely to last for a while—at least until the next giddy boom.

Endnotes

1. Surette (1992).
2. Garofalo (1983); Phillips (1982); Comstock (1983).
3. Rosekrans (1967).
4. Cook et al. (1983).
5. Stover (1998).
6. Sherman (2002).
7. Flanigan (1999).
8. Rebello (2000).
9. Thompson (2002).
10. Greer (2000).
11. *Business 2.0* (2001).
12. Locke (2001).
13. Salpukis (1999).
14. Ibid.
15. Enron Press Release (2001).
16. Goldberg (2001).
17. Barlow (2001).
18. Fowler (2001).
19. Fergus (2002).
20. Goldberg (2002).
21. Kurtz (2002).
22. Rosoff et al. (2004).
23. Kurtz (2002), op. cit.
24. Ibid.
25. Ibid.
26. Ibid.
27. Rosoff et al. (2004), op. cit.
28. Surette (1992), op. cit.
29. Doppelt and Manikas (1990).
30. Molotch et al. (1987).
31. Rosoff et al. (2004), op. cit.
32. McLean (2001).
33. Rosoff et al. (2004), op. cit.
34. Ibid.
35. *Boston Business Journal* (2003).
36. Usborne (2003).

37. WCVB-TV Boston (2003).
38. TalkLeft (2004).
39. Guardian Newspapers (2003).
40. Ibid.
41. Useem (2003).

References

Barlow, Jim (2001) "Enron Making Way to Weather Storm." *Houston Chronicle,* 19 August, sec. C, p. 1.

Boston Business Journal (2003) "Study: More Companies Restating Earnings." *bizjournals.com* (accessed 29 July 2003).

Business 2.0 (2001) "The Revolution LIVES!." *business2.com* (accessed 1 September 2001).

Comstock, George (1983) "Media Influences on Aggression." In *Prevention and Control of Aggression,* Editors A. Goldstein and L. Krasner. Elmsford, NY: Pergamon.

Cook, Thomas D. et al. (1983) "The Implicit Assumption of Television Research: An Analysis of the 1982 NIMH Report on Television and Behavior." *Public Opinion Quarterly* 47:161–201.

Doppelt, Jack C. and Peter Manikas (1990) "Mass Media and Criminal Justice Decision Making." in R. Surette, ed., The Media and Criminal Justice Policy. Springfield, IL: Charles L. Thomas.

Enron Press Release (2001) "Enron Named Most Innovative for Sixth Year." Propaganda Critic, *propagandacritic.com* (accessed 6 February 2001).

Fergus, Mary Ann (2002) "The Fall of Enron: Ken Lay Known as a Man of Humble Beginnings." *Houston Chronicle,* 25 January, sec. A, p. 19.

Flanigan, James (1999) "Energy Deregulation Helps Power U.S. Productivity Gains." *Los Angeles Times,* 14 March, sec. C, p. 1.

Fowler, Tom (2001) "Enron Adds Up 4 Years of Errors." *Houston Chronicle,* 11 November, sec. A, p. 1.

Garofalo, James (1983) "Crime and the Mass Media: A Selective Review of the Research." *J. of Research on Crime and Delinquency* 18:319–350.

Goldberg, Laura (2001) "Taking a Long View: Enron Works to Shore Up Confidence." *Houston Chronicle,* 28 August, sec. C, p. 1.

Goldberg, Laura (2002) "The Myth of Enron." *Houston Chronicle,* 27 January, sec. A, p. 1.

Greer, Jim (2000) "Enron Stock Hits New Heights As Market Applauds Diversification Plan." *Houston Business Journal, houston.bizjournals.com* (accessed 21 January 2000).

Guardian Newspapers (2003) "American Airlines Chief Quits in Business Row." *buzzle.com* (accessed 25 April 2003).

Kurtz, Howard (2002) "The Enron Pundits." *Washington Post, washingtonpost.com* (accessed 30 January 2002).

Locke, Christopher (2001) "Enron Experiences Exchange Overload." *Red Herring, redherring.com* (accessed 1 September 2001).

Molotch, Harvey L. et al. (1987) "The Media-Policy Connections: Ecologies of News." In *Political Communication Research,* Editor D. Paletz. Norwood, NJ: Ablex.

McLean, Bethany (2001) "Why Enron Went Bust." *Fortune, Fortune.com* (accessed 24 December 2001).

Phillips, David (1982) "The Behavioral Impact of Violence in the Mass Media: A Review of the Evidence From Laboratory and Non-Laboratory Investigations." *Sociology and Social* Research 66:387–398.

Rebello, Kathy (2000) "New Faces at the Party." *Business Week E.Biz, businessweek.com* (accessed 15 May 2000).

Rosekrans, Mary A. (1967) "Imitation in Children as a Function of Perceived Similarities to a Social Model of Vicarious Reinforcement." *J. of Personality and Social Psychology* 7:307–315.

Rosoff, Stephen M. et al. (2004) *Profit Without Honor: White-Collar Crime and the Looting of America* (Third Edition). Upper Saddle River, NJ: Pearson/Prentice Hall.

Salpukis, Agis (1999) "Firing Up an Idea Machine: Enron Is Encouraging the Entrepreneurs Within." *The New York Times,* 27 June, sec. 3, p. 1.

Sherman, Scott (2002) "Enron: Uncovering the Uncovered Story." *Columbia Journalism Review, cjr.org* (accessed April 1, 2003).

Stover, Stacy (1998) "Experts' Pick: Enron." *Kiplinger's Personal Finance Magazine, kiplinger.com* (accessed 30 September 1999).

Surette, Ray (1992) *Media, Crime & Criminal Justice: Images and Realities.* Pacific Grove, CA: Brooks/Cole.

TalkLeft (2004) "Andrew Fastow Pleads Guilty, Cooperates." *talkleft.com* (accessed 11 January 2004).

Thompson, Clive (2002) "Bad Energy." *Media Bistro, mediabistro.com* (accessed 24 January 2002).

Usborne, David (2003) "ImClone's Waksal Jailed for Seven Years." *The Independent, news.independent.co.uk* (accessed 17 June 2003).

Useem, Jerry (2003) "Oink! CEO Pay is Still Out of Control." Fortune 147:56–64 (April).

WCVB-TV Boston (2003) "Former Rite-Aid CEO Pleads Guilty to Conspiracy." *thebostonchannel.com* (accessed 17 June 2003).

2

Crime? What Crime? Tales of the Collapse of HIH[1]

Fiona Haines

The collapse of HIH Insurance Limited on March 15, 2001, was arguably the largest corporate collapse in Australia's history. While the losses, estimated at between 3.6 and 5.3 billion Australian dollars, were dwarfed by examples such as the savings and loan collapse in the United States[2] as well as, more recently, Enron[3] and WorldCom,[4] the HIH collapse has had a great impact within Australia. Many people lost disability pensions and superannuation savings. Further, due to the collapse of the second largest insurer in the country, the Australian insurance market was seriously affected. In an attempt to restore the industry to health, the Australian government announced a review[5] and followed through on its recommendations for drastic reductions to company exposure to public liability claims. Public access to compensation through civil action against negligence by companies has decreased and in some cases, it has been completely eliminated.

This chapter reviews HIH and the factors that led to its collapse. In doing so, it is clear that the demise of the HIH Group of companies has many hallmarks that criminologists view as indicative of corporate crime. The size of the financial losses, the key actors involved in the disaster, the complexity of the web of companies that made up the HIH Group, the use of various accounting methods to place profit in the best possible light, and the multiple conflicts of interest between company and auditor all are familiar to students of white-collar and corporate crime.

However, this chapter argues that simply enumerating the elements of the HIH collapse that resonate with other examples of white-collar and corporate crime can be problematic. Compiling lists and typologies that define and classify "criminal" businesses too easily can create the impression that there is some enduring distinction between "criminal" and "virtuous" businesses. Further, the condemnation of companies and the pillorying of executives (often only after their fall from grace) detracts attention from both the essentially contested nature of such crime as well as broader factors that lead to such events occurring. Neat distinctions between criminal and normal business behavior, however, are not so easy to make. Indeed, the ever-changing legal and regulatory framework that follows collapses such as HIH suggests an ongoing and progressive definition of what is "normal" and what is "criminal." With this in mind the analysis of HIH in this chapter suggests that a more fruitful approach is to examine the context of the collapse, where similar behavior can lead to praise of the company as "entrepreneurial" and "dynamic" while it succeeds and to the labeling of its key players as "criminal" when the company fails. Following Aubert,[6] the analysis below is directed at unpacking the essential ambiguity of white-collar crime, where heroic and criminal behaviors are closely aligned. To understand why this is the case, the chapter looks to the essential nature of advanced capitalist societies as well as to the particular features of the insurance industry and the Australian market that led to the demise of HIH.

HIH: Two Tales of a Corporate Collapse

At first glance the collapse of HIH appears simply as yet another example of corporate greed and corporate crime. Its charismatic founder and CEO, Ray Williams, was known as a generous man who donated large amounts to charity, in particular, to medical foundations. Much of this money, however, was donated at the expense of creditors and policyholders of HIH. Further, while Williams was known as a philanthropist, he also exhibited behavior common among those schooled in the art of corporate excess. In response to a journalist's question about the cost of his second Rolls Royce, for example, he quipped, "If you needed to know what it cost, you shouldn't be buying a Rolls Royce."[7]

The misplaced nature of his generosity was brought into sharp relief when HIH collapsed. Investigations revealed that the company had been insolvent for some time, propped up by suspect reinsurance schemes and a massive dependency on new business as a way of paying old debts.[8] This revelation led to some comparing HIH to a massive "Ponzi scheme",[9] a classic form of white-collar crime where company directors and senior managers build up personal and company wealth by bringing new customers into the business. However, the benefits of the services sold never materialize. There are only hollow promises and empty pockets. The comparison between such a scheme and the situation at HIH seemed particularly apt given the essential nature of insurance contracts. As a result of the collapse, many lost their insurance coverages, essentially promises that should financial need arise through some mishap, money would be forthcoming. In the case of HIH, it was not.

The harm to the Australian public was tangible and widespread. The Royal Commission set up to investigate the failure[10] found that as a result of the collapse, about 200 permanently disabled people no longer received their regular payments. Further, those who had invested their superannuations or life savings with HIH were left with nothing. Thousands lost insurance coverage, from community groups to builders, creating both immediate hardship and long-term uncertainty.[11] While some received compensation under the government-funded HIH Claims Support scheme recommended by the Commission,[12] many were left considerably worse off.[13] In short, the story of HIH's demise appears as a classic "crime in the suites," whereby those at the top benefit at the expense of ordinary citizens "foolish" enough to trust a large, apparently respectable Australian insurance giant.

What exactly, though, was criminal about the HIH collapse? Several elements appear in popular accounts of the case. First is the size of the financial loss. A failure of such dimensions would seem to demand the epithet of a massive crime.[14] Further, there was a veritable cast of characters that appeared to view other people's money as an extension of their own bank accounts. Ray Williams was a dominant presence[15] whose largesse both to charity and himself is noted above.[16] He was not alone: prominent also was Larry Adler, a post–World War II Hungarian immigrant with big ideas and the founder of FAI, a large insurer acquired by HIH. The insurance industry (about which Adler admitted very little knowledge) seemed the perfect vehicle to fund high-yield investments. There would be regular premium money generated, ripe for canny investment. Adler's son Rodney, who became a director of HIH after the takeover of FAI by HIH, followed in his footsteps on a high-risk, high-yield strategy of corporate growth.[17] There were also the "hangers on": Rodney Adler fancied himself as a "Guardian Angel,"[18] a business mentor providing expertise and capital to budding entrepreneurs, and his support of Brad Cooper, a "Young Turk" of the 1990s business scene, eventually cost FAI and HIH combined over $80 million.[19]

Deception about the profitability that surrounded HIH also is worthy of attention. Financial accounts were carefully crafted to give the best possible appearance of profitability and success.[20] HIH used its accounts to create a façade with which it could manipulate the share price. Such misinformation meant that the purchase of insurance and pension policies as well as investment in the HIH Group of companies (which included FAI) continued well after the group was insolvent. Common with other cases of corporate crime, too, was the nature of record and bookkeeping at HIH. Both were less than transparent, marking the company as secretive and unwilling to divulge information to outsiders.[21] This lack of transparency was compounded by the complex business and company structures of both HIH and FAI, which arguably were enough to indicate criminality.[22] At the height of the activities of the company it was estimated that there were over 280 individual companies in the group.[23] An investigation into the collapse by John Palmer, a Canadian accountant and expert on the insurance industry,[24] noted that despite the number of companies in each group (FAI and HIH), both ran their operations with the line of business at the fore, taking scant regard for the solvency of individual entities that were created under the HIH umbrella.[25] Finally, there were the multiple conflicts of interest between auditor, actuary, and company. HIH's accountant, Arthur Andersen, met its demise following the Enron debacle. Andersen had a close relationship with HIH, with several of their auditors leaving the firm and immediately joining the HIH board.[26] In conclusion, HIH would appear as yet another classic example of corporate crime. The size of the loss, the characteristics of key individuals, the deception of investors, poor record keeping, the complexity of the HIH Group, and the multiple conflicts of interest would certainly attract the attention of many scholars in the area.

However, this depiction of HIH does little to explain why such behavior persists, despite solutions that appear self-evident: Simply bring corporate criminals and their organizational practices to account, through a process of identification and excision employing criminal and other forms of law. A different approach, though, sensitive to the place of HIH within the insurance industry and Australia, might be able to shed more light both on the persistence of corporate harm and the difficulties of promoting greater use of criminal law as the best solution to financial harm of this scale. In this account the inter-relationship between the company and the business environment moves to center stage. It is not the "criminal" aspects of the demise of HIH per se that are under scrutiny, but the connection between collapse and context. Such an analysis suggests that epithets of criminality are somewhat capricious labels applied to certain companies in some circumstances, rather than beacons of distinct problematic and harmful acts.

This requires some greater understanding of the case itself, one that shows the difficulty of viewing the collapse of HIH as merely a "giant Ponzi scheme". The history of HIH, as outlined by the Commission, reveals the standard business practices that comprised much of the company's activity.[27] HIH came to life when the two founders, Ray Williams and Michael Payne, saw a profitable opening in the insurance industry through the Lloyds of London franchise.[28] They began in 1968 as M.W. Payne, working as agents in Australia for two Lloyds of London syndicates, mainly in workers' compensation insurance, first in Victoria, then in Tasmania, and other states. Three years later, the success of the business attracted CE Heath, a major U.K. insurance company, and in 1971 Payne was acquired by Heath, becoming known as CE Heath (Underwriting).[29] The company continued successfully until, in the mid-1980s, legislative changes in, namely, the nationalization of workers' compensation insurance in key Australian states saw CE Heath (Underwriting) diversify into different insurance classes (property, commercial, and professional liability) and also internationally, with business expanding into Hong Kong and California. The company also acquired additional businesses, notably CIC, a large general insurer, that could complement CE Heath's other products. CIC was controlled by Winterthur, a large Swiss insurer, and as a result of the deal, Winterthur became a significant shareholder in the group.[30] Over time, though, differences of business strategy saw Winterthur sell its shares in 1998[31] by way of a fully subscribed float that demonstrated confidence by the Australian public in the (now named) HIH.[32]

It is clear, however, that HIH was encountering progressive problems. Overseas operations, both in the United Kingdom and California, were not going well.[33] The business strategy adopted by HIH of aggressive sales of budget-priced insurance combined with optimistic costing of long-tailed liabilities saw debt looming. This was not fatal, however, since many insurers at the time made their profits on investments, not on core underwriting business. But the failed realization of a profit on key investments coupled with the business strategy was critical. The acquisition of FAI insurance in 1999, with its own problems of significant debt, compounded HIH's difficulties.[34] Despite various attempts to save the company, provisional liquidators were appointed on March 15, 2001, and on August 27 of that year the HIH Group was placed into official liquidation.[35]

The narrative above and that detailed by the Commission suggest a more complex problem than one representing the collapse as merely one giant fraud scheme. Rather, the picture formed is one of an aggressive, rapidly diversifying company chasing premiums and acquiring new businesses with a confident, ultimately over-confident, senior management. Indeed, even the elements that would perhaps suggest mismanagement and potential criminality—over-confident management, poor record keeping, and acquisition of debt-laden companies, for example—can be found in other cases where companies continue to trade and indeed to attract significant investment and praise from the business community.[36]

The Criminological Problem of HIH

The two accounts of HIH presented above, one delineating the criminality of the collapse and the other emphasizing business context and the strategic nature of company decisions that bring with them the potential for either success or failure, point to different methods of studying corporate crime. The first exudes condemnation and draws distinct lines between criminal and non-criminal behavior. Criminal behavior is further classified into a variety of forms with the aim of allowing the removal of undesirable companies and their executives from the business community. To this end, criminal prosecution appears a useful option. The second method emphasizes ambiguity, where the harm of business activity is intertwined with the benefits to both company and society. Here the potential for law and law enforcement alone to reduce harm is restricted since strategy and risk taking lie at the heart of both desirable and undesirable business practices.

The first form of analysis is prominent within the field. Condemnation and denunciation have had an enduring role in criminology[37] and in the analyses of white-collar crime in particular, with the rebuke of the powerful that is central to Sutherland's[38] seminal study. The aim was to radicalize, to demonstrate the inequity of treatment between powerful individuals and groups who escape criminal sanction in contrast to those convicted of more mundane (and less harmful) street offending. This initial censure by Sutherland, however, was quickly followed by demands from others for clarification of what actually constituted "white-collar" crime. Commentators pushed Sutherland and like-minded criminologists to define specifically what it was about such cases that comprised such crimes. Was the status of the offender, for example, the key variable?[39] Or perhaps the victim? Or the use of criminal law as distinct from civil law?[40]

This demand for greater precision led to the various typologies of "crimes of the powerful" found throughout the white-collar crime literature[41] that purport to "fix" the attention of the criminologist onto discrete variants of the phenomenon to aid both understanding and amelioration. Such classifications attempt to isolate the different forms of offending into distinct groups: White-collar crime is behavior perpetrated by high-status individuals (often against a corporation), while corporate crime is defined as a crime by a corporation against the public. Added to this is a variety of other types of crime, such as occupational crime (a crime by high-status individuals using the opportunities provided by their occupations);[42] crimes by professionals, such as doctors or lawyers, abusing their professional knowledge or the trust placed in them by the public; the multiple definitions of computer-related crime (cybercrime, computer crime, digital crime, and e-crime)[43]; and so on.

Such typologies, however, gloss over multiple ambiguities. First, a clear distinction is drawn between "crime" and "non-crime," although the line is both difficult to draw and constantly changing. Further, the multiple distinctions made among different forms of white-collar crime in practice may be very hard to make.[44] This can be well illustrated by the HIH example. A case so large can easily fit into several categories. Certainly, it would appear as a corporate crime as the harms were perpetrated by the corporation for the benefit of the corporate entity. These include the dubious reinsurance[45] schemes set up to save the bottom line for annual reports in 1999 and 2000[46] that had a central purpose of keeping the company alive. Yet, individuals within the company might also be viewed as white-collar criminals in their own right. Several, including Ray Williams and Rodney Adler, have been convicted of criminal offences, Adler of personally benefiting from his actions while ostensibly acting on behalf of the company.[47] Other examples from the collapse appear more as "crimes of the professions," exemplified by the actuaries and accountants concerned with HIH whose behavior fell well short of what might be expected from their professional mandates.[48] Finally, a large proportion of the losses FAI accumulated were hidden because of a disastrous computer data system, which was supposed to calculate reserve case estimates but which chronically and systematically under-reported FAI long-term liabilities. When the Aegis database was tallied with the "bordereaux" (grouped files coming in from the various subsidiaries), it was found that Aegis had under-estimated liabilities[49] by as much as 200 percent. In light of this, perhaps FAI at least could be classified as a major example of "computer crime."

A typologist might observe that separating out each element of the overall case assists in determining both the multiple causes and useful crime prevention measures for such incidents. In contrast, what is argued here is that this dissection and isolation process can be part of the problem. The disaggregation of discrete instances of "white-collar crime" contained within the case detracts from understanding the dynamic nature of the event as a whole and the critical role context played in the harms that eventuated. In doing so, the inter-relationships between context and case and between the various actors and roles within HIH would be underplayed.

White-Collar Crime and Context: Common Elements

Analysis of the case itself and comparisons with other examples, however, remain important. Common elements can point to common weaknesses in the underlying economic and political system within contemporary industrialized societies that give rise to such events. It may then be possible to suggest ways that to reduce the instance of financial harm. Following on from this, identification of elements particular to place (in this case, Australia) or industry (here insurance) might be used to identify the particular challenges for harm reduction that pertain to particular places and particular industries.

What elements, then, of the collapse of HIH resonate with other high-profile examples of corporate harm? A number have already been mentioned, such as the manipulation of accounts so that the best light could be shed on the profits of the company, a feature common both to the HIH collapse and other examples.[50] In the case of HIH the manipulation of accounts took the following forms. The first was the use of reinsurance contracts that could be booked as profit rather than as disguised loans.[51] A second method was to increase the amount of "goodwill" that could be booked on the "assets" side of the ledger, while the debts mounted and other sources of income plummeted. In one case a shortfall in the FAI accounts of $163 million was transformed into "goodwill" gained from the acquisition of FAI and hence into profit.[52] The autocratic nature of the senior executives at both HIH and FAI is found in other cases of this kind. Both Williams and Adler ran their respective public companies as if they were the sole owners, leaving investors in the dark about the true state of affairs. These characteristics are reminiscent of others in Australia, such as Alan Bond, Christopher Scase, and John Avram.[53] To these similarities might be added the final days of indiscretion and looting, when those within the higher echelons of the company know their creation is past redemption and so rush to protect their own assets. At HIH these "rescue packages" involved various dubious schemes, through which executives "found" willing buyers of their own increasingly worthless shares. In the case of HIH, as in other examples, the shares were paid for by the ailing company itself through various shell companies; companies end up buying their own worthless shares, a classic example of an entity cannibalizing itself, aided by senior management.[54]

A key difference from common conclusions drawn from such features lies in their interpretation. Rather than seeing them as obvious indicators of crime and so amenable to excision through law and law enforcement, the focus turns to the endemic and enduring nature of corporate harm that survives *despite* reforms that have occurred. Further, common features such as these challenge the myth that corporate and white-collar crime is somehow peripheral and marginal to the economic system. Surely, a prominent feature of white-collar harm is its continuing presence in the economic landscape. In Australia the experience of HIH in 2001 echoes that of Bond Corporation and Quintex in the 1980s, Minsec and Cambridge Credit in the 1970s, and Reid Murray and Stanhill in the 1960s.[55] The label of the "excessive eighties" gives way to the "greedy nineties," where each decade seems to label the previous 10 years as somehow lesser, more reprehensible, with the understanding that "we know better now."[56] This suggests, rather, that corporate harm is endemic and well embedded within the economic system.

To endure for so long further implies that the risk taking involved is both desirable and damaging. Strategic but risky business behavior is rewarded when successful. The same behavior can be judged differently, depending on outcome. Rodney Adler, for example, was given the Order of Australia in 1999 for his services to philanthropy and the insurance industry. What was attractive about him in 1999 was his aggressive and creative investment strategy that seemed to personify the "new Australia," one that was ready to compete in an increasingly competitive region.

Further, the rewards gained by both investors and entrepreneurs from such risk taking are central to capitalist societies. The superannuation system in Australia, for example, is dependent on significant returns on investment, returns that depend, in part, at least, on high-risk, high-return strategies that focus on short-term gains.[57] Our economic system as it is currently structured is then dependent on investment that demonstrates short-term profitability. Yet, it could be argued that only those with supreme confidence (perhaps over-confidence) would be able to live up to the market's expectations of such high levels of profitability. When their creations thrive, these actors and their companies are heroes; when they fail, they are criminalized. If this argument is valid, then the label "criminal" is more contingent than many analyses of corporate and white-collar crime suggest.[58] Separating "good" from "bad" business obscures this contingency.

Investigations in the aftermath of HIH indicated that the investment community's demands for shorter and shorter terms of profitability generated creative accounting, high-risk investment strategies, and the like. John Palmer, in his report on the HIH collapse, noted that:

> it is important to recognize that financial institutions today face many pressures, of which pressure from the regulator is but one. Most important by far are pressures from shareholders and financial markets for performance, including historically (and some, including the writer, believe unsustainably) high returns on equity and growth in those returns.[59]

For Palmer, this pressure lies behind the increasing complexity of corporate arrangements. Complexity is not then an indicator of criminality per se, but rather an indication of economic stress on financial institutions. Incentives within financial institutions exacerbate demands to "perform," with finance managers creating increasing numbers of technical instruments and complex arrangements to extract greater and greater levels of profit and provide increased dividends to shareholders. Palmer continued:

> These pressures are overwhelmingly strong, and, in many cases are augmented by the compensation systems of financial institutions, which are increasingly performance based, and tied to earnings and share price performance. These pressures have led to highly complex financial engineering to boost income, reduce capital levels, enhance tax efficiency of capital and reduce the risk-weighting of the balance sheet for regulatory capital purposes. Financial engineering techniques include asset and liability securitization, increasingly complex derivative products, ever more creative forms of financial reinsurance and innovative capital instruments.[60]

This suggests that corporate harm (and benefit) is embedded in the financial system; it is central and intrinsic, not peripheral and marginal. Any serious analysis of white-collar harm, then, must understand the way harm is intertwined with the system of economic reward.

Clearly, there are malevolent actors who exploit economic systems, corporate forms, and financial instruments for personal gain. However, their capacity to do so, to act as parasites on the system, if you will, exists because the current economic system has to encourage and protect risk taking. Enacting tough laws that prohibit certain forms of behavior threatens the wealth creation of both legitimate and illegitimate businesses alike.

The blurring between labels of "embezzlement" and "support of fledgling businesses" that occurred toward the end of HIH's life can also be understood in this light. Had those businesses turned out to be dazzling successes it is probable that the history books would view Brad Cooper and his associates in a very different light. Corporate collapses such as HIH's, replete with their post-disaster investigations, degradation ceremonies, and vilification of key players, perform a reassuring function that provides a way to deflect criticism from the inequities within the existing economic structure of a society and so to maintain the status quo. As much as Levi Strauss[61] might view the ritual of a rain dance and its function relative to the structure of a society and the maintenance of key relationships, the process of defining a corporate collapse as "preventable" and the behavior of certain key players as "reprehensible," "unethical," or "criminal" allows for the maintenance of existing economic relationships and key institutions.

The association of white-collar criminality with larger than life figures, with immigrants failing, or with supreme confidence coming before a fall, might be but one side of the Janus that is the contemporary capitalist system and its ambivalence toward greed. Condemnation reassures us of our morality, our essential abhorrence of avarice, yet the fundamental premise of the market is that self-interest is ultimately what allows the system as a whole to succeed. For those ambitious individuals who succeed, there is the myth of individual achievement: the belief that with enough effort and confidence, anyone, even a penniless migrant, can achieve great wealth. Courageous entrepreneurs who "bend of the rules" can be forgiven, even admired, if the outcome is success. Better to forge ahead with strong conviction and be a dynamic presence in the financial community than a pedant, adhering to the rules but missing opportunities for economic success and continuing high returns on investment.

Certainly, recognition of this ambiguity and ambivalence which characterizes white-collar crime has been an important, if less visible, element of research and writing in the field. Writers from this perspective argue that it is the process of definition of behavior as criminal or acceptable that should hold criminological attention.[62] Since the distinction between acceptable, even praiseworthy, behavior and criminally reprehensible acts is blurred and malleable, exploration of the process of criminalization can shed light on the nature of power in a particular context. Further, this attribute of white-collar crime also can reveal how both social benefit and harm are embedded in the same economic and political systems within a given society.[63]

Unique Aspects of HIH: Insurance and Australia

Finally, there are lessons to be learned from the collapse of HIH that provide insight into the unique challenges posed by harms associated with the insurance industry and insurance in Australia in particular. Insurance plays a critical role in the market as a "spreader of risk," and the reassurance it provides underpins a market economy.[64] This sharing of risk allows services to be performed and goods to be produced. If risks remaining uninsured, consumers could not claim adequate compensation should a building suffer due to poor workmanship, for example, nor could builders ply their trade lest someone sue them and reduce them to penury. Trade is inhibited by the inability to gain insurance. Indeed, legislation specifically prohibits some business activity without satisfactory insurance coverage. Insurance, in very tangible ways, then, affects what economic activity is undertaken and by whom.[65] Within advanced capitalist economies a crisis in insurance is a serious problem for the market in general.

Partly for this reason, insurance has often been protected from the full impact of competition, through nationalization, cartels,[66] and mutual company structures. Under mutual arrangements, policyholders and owners are one and the same group so that the conflict between demands for profit by shareholders and investors and the needs of policyholders for significant company reserves is circumvented.[67] A further benefit from some of these arrangements, such as mutuals, is that they can also reduce the likelihood of certain forms of risk being realized. Barriers to entry into a particular insurance "club" can ensure that only those with a proper attitude toward risk reduction are covered by insurance. Insurers thus reduce their overall liability by acting as secondary regulators to reduce overall risk.[68] Care is taken by members to be safe, reduce fire risk, and so on in order to retain the all-important insurance coverage.

Despite these advantages, there has been a progressive move toward greater levels of competition and "for profit" or stockholder arrangements.[69] In part, this has been championed by the General Agreement on Trade in Services (GATS) initiative of the World Trade Organization.[70] The concurrent impetus behind demutualization has arisen ostensibly to increase access to capital markets, augment accountability of management to the market, enhance flexibility of the insurer,[71] and, in certain cases, undercut anti-competitive tendencies.[72] Despite the advantages, increasing competition, including the move to stock holding forms of insurance, brings built-in weakness: critically, by providing opportunities for stockholders and senior management to profit at the expense of policyholders. The long-term relationship of some policyholders (such as those with pension schemes, medical indemnities, and other holders of "long-tailed" forms of insurance) with their providers makes this weakness particularly onerous for them to bear. The consequence of the collapse of HIH on these forms of insurance in particular brought this into sharp relief.

The actual price of premiums may not assist in assessing the worth of any particular shifts toward a more competitive set of arrangements since low premiums may indicate either the health or ill-health of the industry. Mutuals, for example, historically have been understood to provide low-cost insurance by virtue of their control over membership.[73] However, HIH, a public corporation, aggressively competed in the market by providing both low premiums and coverage to a wide range of marginally profitable clients. It did so because of its focus on generating profit from investment, not underwriting. There was some (short-term) benefit from this. Community groups, small businesses, and ordinary citizens reaped the advantage of competitive pressure on premiums, with HIH a leading-edge discounter, and hence HIH policyholders reaped the greatest benefits of low-cost premiums. Harm and benefit, then, may be intertwined with low premiums.

One further element of insurance deserves mention, namely, the recourse to reinsurance as a way of spreading risk, particularly long-tailed and catastrophic risk. Reinsurance illustrates well the ambiguity of labels and financial methods within the insurance industry. Reinsurance has developed ostensibly to create actuarial instruments by which risk, particularly catastrophic risk, can be atomized and shared so that in the case of realization, the industry can remain solvent.[74] However, the HIH Commission argued that the reinsurance arrangements put in place by HIH were actually no more than a cover for declining profits.[75] Reinsurance contracts were a means to create rosier accounts. Reinsurance, then, can be used either to insulate insurers from calamity that results from a catastrophe, such as a hurricane or earthquake or from the "calamity" of declining profits at the time of the annual report.

In the case of HIH the strategy it pursued within a highly competitive market, of low-cost insurance combined with an aggressive investment strategy covered by a comforting patina of reinsurance contracts, led ultimately to its demise. Because of its large size relative to the Australian market, it necessarily created two crises: one in the perceived viability of the insurance market within Australia and the second in the capacity of insurers to be both profitable and to act as responsible "secondary regulators."

The reforms that followed the collapse of HIH illustrate well the primary concern of the Australian government to support the viability of the industry as a whole, by which it meant the remaining Australian insurers.[76] The role of insurance either to provide financial support for consumers in the case of adverse events or as a secondary regulator to reduce risk were downplayed. Post-HIH reforms included tightened restrictions on the right of consumers to sue business. A good example is provided by the recreational service provider sector. Those who horseback ride, bungee jump, or canoe with a recreational business on their vacations now are fully responsible for the risks they take as a result of the Trade Practices Amendment (Liability for Recreational Services) Act of 2002. Should a horse bolt, a bungee cord break, or a canoe sink, even if the provider is at fault, the consumer has no right to sue. The emphasis returns to "buyer beware." As a result, the roles of insurance either as assuring consumer well-being or as secondary regulator are entirely lost. There is no incentive provided by the insurer for the business to reduce these risks to its consumers since it faces no liability. In other cases, such as community events, there was a "nationalization" process whereby the state, or in some cases, local councils, underwrote the liability of certain local activities to ensure they continued. The public purse stepped in where the private sector saw no profit.

These reforms indicate the political nature of white-collar harm. In the current neo-liberal climate, government could no longer legislate to reduce premium costs—this would be a direct intrusion into the mechanisms of the market through price controls, which, in a post-GATS market, are frowned on.[77] Rather, liability for risk was transferred from business to consumer and government. The small size of the Australian market and its consequent dependence on a few key providers of insurance meant that the demands of these insurers and the government legislation to reduce their liabilities met with a sympathetic response.

Conclusion

This chapter has described two tales of the demise of HIH. In the first account the qualities the HIH collapse shared with other "criminal" collapses were outlined, with an emphasis on the considerable size of the financial loss, the amoral character of key players, the deception of investors, the complexity of the HIH Group, and the multiple conflicts of interest. Its purpose was to highlight the criminality of the behavior of those involved in the collapse. By contrast, the second account suggested that HIH had a genuine role to play in the insurance business. It acted to exploit economic opportunity much as any other business might. When governments closed one avenue for business in the market (by nationalizing insurance, for example), the company expanded both internationally and into other insurance markets. Failure resulted more from poor judgment and over-confidence than from criminality.

These two accounts prefigure two different criminological trajectories. In the first, moral condemnation is followed by categorization, where neat lines are drawn between criminal and normal behavior and between one type of white-collar offending and another. The collapse of HIH, however, makes both these distinctions problematic. The second account illustrated the blurred boundaries between "criminal" and "normal" business behavior as well as between the various "types" of white-collar harm. Separation and isolation can detract from sufficient attention to context.

The latter part of the chapter revisited the initial narrative and explored the similarities between the HIH collapse and other "criminalized" collapses. Here, though, the aim was to shed light on how harm is embedded within the economic and political context of contemporary capitalist societies so that such harm persists over time. Identical behavior is both lauded and condemned since it is both creative (generating wealth for superannuation funds, for example) as well as destructive and harmful.[78] Criminalization, then, is a contingent process that depends on the context: failure precedes criminalization, as praise follows success. Condemnation and criminalization, however, allow the legitimacy of the economic system to remain intact. Evidence for this is provided by the reforms that followed HIH, legal change aimed at shoring up the insurance industry, an industry essential to the Australian economy. Reforms meant that financial and physical risk were pushed back to the consumer and to the public purse.

This chapter has highlighted the value of exploring both case and context in analyzing the collapse of HIH. Its striking similarities with other examples, however, should not simply be read as yet another example of greed and abuse of power. Rather, they demonstrate through their persistence that harm is embedded in contemporary capitalist societies that depend on particular economic structures to provide wealth. Further, understanding the role insurance plays in economies such as Australia's can show why reforms were targeted toward enhancing the health of the insurance business, rather than that of its own citizens.

Endnotes

1. I would like to extend grateful thanks to Adam Sutton for his helpful ideas and comments on earlier drafts of this chapter.
2. Losses estimated at around $153 billion U.S.
3. Losses estimated at around $60 billion U.S.
4. Losses estimated at around $30 billion U.S.
5. Andrew Ipp, Peter Cane, Don Sheldon, and Ian Macintosh, "Final Report of the Review of the Law of Negligence," Commonwealth of Australia, September, 2002.
6. Vilhelm Aubert, "White Collar Crime and Social Structure," *American Journal of Sociology* 58 (1952): 263–271.
7. Andrew Main, *Other People's Money: The Complete Story of the Extraordinary Collapse of HIH* (Sydney: Harper Colllins, 2003), p. 34.
8. Ibid.
9. Ibid., p. 57.
10. HIH Royal Commission, *The Failure of HIH Insurance,* vols. 1–3, ed. Royal Commissioner, the Hon. Justice Neville Owen (Canberrra, Australia, 2003). Hereinafter referred to as "the Commission" and referenced as "Owen" followed by the volume number.
11. Ibid., vol. 1, pp. xiv–xvi.
12. Ibid., vol. 1, chap. 11.
13. Parliament of Australia, "HIH Insurance Collapse and Government Assistance Packages: Who's Covered and Who's Not," in "HIH Insurance Group Collapse," E-brief, Parliamentary Library, 2001, *http://www.aph.gov.au/LIBRARY1 intguide/econ/hih_insurance.htm* (accessed May 23, 2005).
14. See, e.g., Editorial, "Doing Time for the HIH Crime," *Sydney Morning Herald,* February 18, 2005.
15. Owen, vol. 1, p. xxvi.
16. Main, *Other People's Money*, chap. 3; see also Owen, vol. 3, pp. 310–311.
17. Main, *Other People's Money*, chap. 4.

18. And continues to do so while in prison; see Alex Mitchell, "Adler: Inside Trader," *The Sunday Age,* June 19, 2005, p. 1.
19. Main, *Other People's Money*, chap. 15.
20. Owen, vol. 1, p. xlvii.
21. Owen, vol 1., p. xvi–xvii.
22. Robert Tillman and Henry Pontell, "Organizations and Fraud in the Savings and Loan Industry," *Social Forces* (1995): 1439–1463.
23. John Palmer, "Review of the Role Played by the Australian Prudential Regulation Authority and the Insurance and Superannuation Commission in the Collapse of the HIH Group of Companies," report to Messrs Corrs, Chambers Westgarth from John Palmer FCA, 2002, *http://www.apra.gov.au/Media-Releases/loader.cfm?url=/commonspot/security/getfile.cfm&PageID=5206* (accessed May 23, 2005); Commission Transcripts, transcripts from December 19, 2001, *http://www.hihroyalcom.gov.au/Documents/Transcript/Transcript_2001_12_19.pdf* (accessed May 23, 2005).
24. John Palmer's specific brief was to investigate the role of one of the regulators involved in the collapse, the Australian Prudential Regulatory Authority (APRA).
25. Op. cit. Palmer, "Review," pp. 95–99.
26. Op. cit. Main, *Other People's Money*, pp. 264–265; Owen, vol. 2, pp. 86–88, 166–169.
27. Op. cit. Owen, vol. 1, chap. 3.
28. Ibid., pp. 51–52.
29. Ibid., p. 51.
30. Ibid., pp. 52–55.
31. Ibid., p. 55.
32. Ibid.
33. Ibid., pp. 56–59.
34. Ibid., p. 56.
35. Ibid., p. 61.
36. Australian Securities and Investments Commission, "ASIC Urges Companies to Act Early to Avoid Insolvent Trading," media release, September 28, 2004, *http://www.asic.gov.au/asic/ASIC_PUB.NSF/byid/5E1DA4E9EE4A230CCA256F1D00249B24?opendocument* (accessed May 23, 2005); Stephen Mayne, "Trevor Sykes and Tumbling Share Prices," 2005, *http://www.crikey.com.au/articles/2005/04/05-1632-4409.html* (accessed May 23, 2005).
37. Fiona Haines and Adam Sutton, "Criminology as Religion: Profane Thoughts about Sacred Values," *British Journal of Criminology* 40 (2000): 146–162.
38. Edwin Sutherland, *White-Collar Crime: The Uncut Version* (New Haven, CT: Yale University Press, 1983). First published in 1949.
39. Marshall Clinard and Richard Quinney, "Corporate Criminal Behavior," in *Criminal Behaviour Systems: A Typology,* rev. ed., ed. Marshall B. Clinard and Richard Quinney (New York: Holt, Reinhart and Winston, 1973), pp. XX–XX; Marshall Clinard and Peter Yeager, *Corporate Crime* (New York: Free Press, 1980); M. David Ermann and Richard J. Lundman, *Corporate and Governmental Deviance: Problems of Organizational Behaviour in Contemporary Society* (New York: Oxford University Press, 1987).
40. Compare the arguments of Roman Tomasic, "Corporate Crime," in *The Australian Criminal Justice System: The Mid 1990s*, ed. Duncan Chappell and Paul Wilson (Sydney: Butterworths, 1994), chap. 12, with Clinard and Yeager, *Corporate Crime*.
41. See, e.g., Mary Langan, "Hidden and Respectable. Crime and the Market," in *The Problem of Crime,* ed. John Muncie and Eugene McLaughlin (London: Sage, 1996), chap. 6; David Friedrichs, *Trusted Criminals: White Collar Crime in Contemporary Society* (Belmont, CA: Wadsworth, 1996).

42. Op cit Clinard, "Corporate Criminal Behavior"; Clinard, *Corporate Crime*.
43. Russell Smith, Peter Grabosky, and Gregor Urbas, *Cyber Criminals on Trial* (Cambridge: Cambridge University Press, 2004).
44. Aubert, "White Collar Crime"; Stuart P. Green, "Moral Ambiguity in White Collar Criminal Law," *Notre Dame Journal of Law, Ethics and Public Policy* 18 (2004): 501–519.
45. Reinsurance is a central part of insurance and involves diversifying the risk taken on by the underwriter. The underwriter, in this case, HIH, on-sells part of the risk it has acquired through writing premiums. These reinsurance contracts can then be booked as profit. However, in the final years of HIH, reinsurance schemes took more the form of a loan. The reinsurer paid HIH money, which was booked as profit for the year, with HIH paying back the loan in subsequent years. The "risk" taken on by the reinsurer was minimal or non-existent, such as the risk of earthquake losses in Australia of over $10 billion: Australia is a stable continent. The most damaging earthquake in recent history, in Newcastle, New South Wales, cost insurers less than $2 billion. Further, the executives of HIH wrote side letters, kept secret, which stated that HIH would never claim on the reinsurance "contracts" set up. The existence of these side letters became a key concern of the Royal Commission.
46. Owen, vol. 2, chap. 16, pp. 467–529.
47. Editorial, "Doing Time."
48. Owen, vol. 3, p. 76.
49. Main, *Other People's Money*, p. 91.
50. Trevor Sykes, *Two Centuries of Panic: A History of Corporate Collapses in Australia* (Sydney: Allen and Unwin, 1988).
51. Owen, vol. 2, pp. 467–512.
52. Palmer, "Review," p. 101.
53. Trevor Sykes, "Wasters of the Universe," *The Bulletin with Newsweek,* August 3, 1993, pp. 65–71.
54. Main, *Other People's Money*, pp. 237–248; Trevor Sykes, *The Bold Riders: Behind Australia's Corporate Collapses*, 2nd ed. (Sydney: Allen and Unwin, 1996), pp. 174–185.
55. Frank Clarke, Graeme Dean, and Kyle Oliver, *Corporate Collapse: Accounting, Regulatory and Ethical Failure,* 2nd ed. (Cambridge: Cambridge University Press, 2003).
56. Sykes, "Wasters"; op cit Sykes, *Bold Riders*, 1996.
57. Stephen Bell, *Ungoverning the Economy: The Political Economy of Australian Economic Policy* (Melbourne: Oxford University Press, 1997).
58. Aubert, "White-Collar Crime"; W. G. (Kit) Carson, "The Challenge of White-Collar Crime," Inaugural Lecture as Professor of Legal Studies, La Trobe University, Melbourne, 1983; Adam Sutton and Fiona Haines, "Corporate and White Collar Crime," in *Criminology: An Australian Textbook*, 2nd ed., ed. Andrew Goldsmith, Mark Israel, and Kathleen Daly (Sydney: LBC Publishing, 2003), chap. 8, pp. 148–158.
59. Palmer, "Review," p. 140.
60. Ibid.
61. Claude Levi Strauss, *Structural Anthropology* (New York: Basic Books, 1963).
62. Aubert, "White Collar Crime."
63. Sutton, "Corporate and White Collar Crime."
64. Susan Strange, *The Retreat of the State: The Diffusion of Power in the World Economy* (Cambridge: Cambridge University Press, 1996).
65. This complex relationship goes beyond this paper. Nonetheless, it is clear that the marketplace is intrinsically bound up with available insurance arrangements; see Brian Glenn, "Risk, Insurance and the Changing Nature of Mutual Obligation," *Law and Social Inquiry* 28 (2003): 295–314.
66. Strange, *Retreat*.
67. Swiss Re, "Are Mutual Insurers an Endangered Species?" *Sigma* 4 (1999): XX–XX.

68. Glenn, "Risk, Insurance"; Paul Bennett, "Environmental Governance and Private Actors: Enrolling Insurers in International Maritime Regulation," *Political Geography* 10 (2000): 875–899. Note that this secondary regulation aspect can be socially beneficial but can also promote private or anti-social interest.
69. Swiss Re, "Mutual Insurers."
70. World Trade Organization, General Agreement on Trade in Services (GATS), *http://www.wto.org/english/news_e/news01_e/guide_gats_e.htm* (accessed June 27, 2005). Insurance forms part of the agreement on financial services aimed to increase competition in this area.
71. Op cit Swiss Re, "Mutual Insurers."
72. Paul Bennett, "Anti-Trust? European Competition Law and Mutual Environmental Insurance," *Economic Geography* 76 (2000): 50–67.
73. Swiss Re, "Mutual Insurers"; Glenn, "Risk, Insurance."
74. Strange, *Retreat.*
75. Owen, vol. 2, p. 467–468.
76. Commonwealth of Australia, "Reform of Liability Insurance Law in Australia," February 2004, *http://www.treasury.gov.au/documents/799/PDF/complete.pdf* (accessed June 23, 2005).
77. Op cit World Trade Organization, GATS.
78. See Joseph Schumpeter, *Capitalism, Socialism and Democracy* (New York: Harper and Row, 1950).

References

Aubert, Vilhelm. 1952. "White-Collar Crime and Social Structure." *American Journal of Sociology* 58:263–71.

Australian Securities and Investments Commission. 2004. "ASIC Urges Companies to Act Early to Avoid Insolvent Trading." Media release, September 28, *http://www.asic.gov.au/asic/ASIC_PUB.NSF/byid/5E1DA4E9EE4A230CCA256F1D00249B24?opendocument* (accessed May 23, 2005).

Bell, Stephen. 1997. *Ungoverning the Economy: The Political Economy of Australian Economic Policy*. Melbourne: Oxford University Press.

Bennett, Paul. 2000. "Anti-trust? European Competition Law and Mutual Environmental Insurance." *Economic Geography* 76:50–67.

Bennett, Paul. 2000. "Environmental Governance and Private Actors: Enrolling Insurers in International Maritime Regulation." *Political Geography* 19:875–99.

Carson, W. G. (Kit). 1983. "The Challenge of White-Collar Crime." Inaugural Lecture as Professor of Legal Studies. La Trobe University, Melbourne.

Clarke, Frank, Graeme Dean, and Kyle Oliver. 2003. *Corporate Collapse: Accounting, Regulatory and Ethical Failure*. 2nd ed. Cambridge: Cambridge University Press.

Clinard, Marshall B., and Richard Quinney. 1973. "Corporate Criminal Behaviour." Pp. XX–XX in *Criminal Behaviour Systems: A Typology*, rev. ed., Editors M. B. Clinard and R. Quinney. New York: Holt, Reinhart and Winston.

Clinard, Marshall B., and Peter C. Yeager. 1980. *Corporate Crime*. New York: The Free Press.

Commission Transcripts. 2001. "Transcripts of the HIH Royal Commission from December 19 2001," *http://www.hihroyalcom.gov.au/Documents/Transcript/ Transcript_2001_12_19.pdf* (accessed May 23, 2005).

Commonwealth of Australia. 2004. "Reform of Liability Insurance Law in Australia," *http://www.treasury.gov.au/documents/799/PDF/complete.pdf* (accessed June 23, 2005).

Editorial. 2005. "Doing Time for the HIH Crime." *Sydney Morning Herald,* February 18, *http://www.smh.com.au/news/Editorial/Doing-time-for-the-HIH-crime/2005/02/17/1108609343363.html* (accessed June 27, 2005).

Ermann, M. David, and Richard J. Lundman. 1987. *Corporate and Governmental Deviance: Problems of Organizational Behavior in Contemporary Society*. New York: Oxford University Press.

Friedrichs, David. 1996. *Trusted Criminals: White-Collar Crime in Contemporary Society*. Belmont, CA: Wadsworth.

Glenn, Brian. 2003. "Risk, Insurance and the Changing Nature of Mutual Obligation." *Law and Social Inquiry* 28:295–314.

Green, Stuart P. 2004. "Moral Ambiguity in White Collar Criminal Law." *Notre Dame Journal of Law, Ethics and Public Policy* 18:501–19.

Haines, Fiona, and Adam Sutton. 2000. "Criminology as Religion: Profane Thoughts about Sacred Values." *British Journal of Criminology* 40:146–62.

HIH Royal Commission. 2003. *A Corporate Collapse and Its Lessons*. Vol. 1. *The Failure of HIH Insurance*, Editor Royal Commissioner, the Hon. Justice Neville Owen. Canberra, Australia.

HIH Royal Commission. 2003. *Reasons, Circumstances, Responsibilities*. Vol. 2. *The Failure of HIH Insurance*, Editor Royal Commissioner, the Hon. Justice Neville Owen. Canberra, Australia.

HIH Royal Commission. 2003. *Reasons, Circumstances, Responsibilities (Cont)*. Vol. 3. *The Failure of HIH Insurance*, Editor Royal Commissioner, the Hon. Justice Neville Owen. Canberra, Australia.

Ipp, Andrew, Peter Cane, Don Sheldon, and Ian Macintosh. 2002. "Final Report of the Review of the Law of Negligence." Commonwealth of Australia, September, *http://revofneg.treasury.gov.au/content/Report2/PDF/Law_Neg_Final.pdf* (accessed June 27, 2005).

Langan, Mary. 1996. "Hidden and Respectable: Crime and the Market." Pp. 283–319 in *The Problem of Crime*, Editors J. Muncie and E. McLaughlin. London: Sage.

Levi Strauss, Claude. 1963. *Structural Anthropology*. New York: Basic Books.

Main, Andrew. 2003. *Other People's Money: The Complete Story of the Extraordinary Collapse of HIH*. Sydney: Harper Collins.

Matthews, Race. 2000. "Looting the Mutuals: The Ethics and Economics of Demutualisation." Background paper for "Success and Continuance of Mutuals," address to the Continuing and Emerging Examples Conference, Brisbane, June 16, *http://www.australia.coop/rm_lm_2000.htm* (accessed June 27, 2005).

Mayne, Stephen. 2005. "Trevor Sykes and Tumbling Share Prices," *http://www.crikey.com.au/articles/2005/04/05-1632-4409.html* (accessed May 23, 2005).

Mitchell, Alex. 2005. "Adler: Inside Trader." *The Sunday Age*, June 19, p. 1.

Palmer, John. 2002. "Review of the Role Played by the Australian Prudential Regulation Authority and the Insurance and Superannuation Commission in the Collapse of the HIH Group of Companies." Report to Messrs Corrs, Chambers Westgarth from John Palmer FCA, *http://www.apra.gov.au/Media-Releases/loader.cfm?url=/commonspot/security/getfile.cfm&PageID=5206* (accessed May 23, 2005).

Parliament of Australia. 2001. "HIH Insurance Collapse and Government Assistance Packages: Who's Covered and Who's Not." In "HIH Insurance Group Collapse," E-brief, Parliamentary Library, *http://www.aph.gov.au/LIBRARY/intguide/econ/hih_insurance.htm* (accessed May 23, 2005).

Schumpeter, Joseph. 1950. *Capitalism, Socialism and Democracy*. New York: Harper and Row.

Smith, Russell G., Peter N. Grabosky, and Gregor Urbas. 2004. *Cyber Criminals on Trial*. Cambridge: Cambridge University Press.

Strange, Susan. 1996. *The Retreat of the State: The Diffusion of Power in the World Economy*. Cambridge: Cambridge University Press.

Sutherland, Edwin. 1983. *White-Collar Crime: The Uncut Version*. New Haven, CT: Yale University Press. First published in 1949.

Sutton, Adam, and Fiona Haines. 2003. "Corporate and White-Collar Crime." Pp. 148–158 in *Criminology: An Australian Textbook*, 2nd ed., Editors A. Goldsmith, M. Israel, and Kathleen Daly. Sydney: LBC Publishing.

Swiss Re. 1999. "Are Mutual Insurers an Endangered Species?" *Sigma* 4: 1–36, *http://www.swissre.com/INTERNET/pwswpspr.nsf/fmBookMarkFrameSet?ReadForm&BM=../vwAllbyIDKeyLu/mbar-4vhqdv?OpenDocument* (accessed June 27, 2005).

Sykes, Trevor. 1988. *Two Centuries of Panic: A History of Corporate Collapses in Australia*. Sydney: Allen and Unwin.

Sykes, Trevor. 1993. "Wasters of the Universe." *The Bulletin with Newsweek*, August 3, pp. 65–71.

Sykes, Trevor. 1996. *The Bold Riders: Behind Australia's Corporate Collapses*. 2nd ed. Sydney: Allen and Unwin.

Tillman, Robert H., and Henry N. Pontell. 1995. "Organizations and Fraud in the Savings and Loan Industry." *Social Forces* 73:1439–63.

Tomasic, Roman. 1994. "Corporate Crime." Chap. 12 in *The Australian Criminal Justice System: The Mid 1990s*, Editors Duncan Chappell and Paul Wilson. Sydney: Butterworths.

World Trade Organization. 1994. "General Agreement on Trade in Services," *http://www.wto.org/english/news_e/news01_e/guide_gats_e.htm* (accessed June 27, 2005).

3

Enron, Lernout & Hauspie, and Parmalat

Comparative Case Studies

Georges Kellens, Michäel Dantinne, and Bertrand Demonceau

Enron, Lernout & Hauspie (L&H) and Parmalat were three very different companies, yet they shared what became very similar destinies. Due to criminal activities, the companies were caught up in the eye of a media cyclone. We propose to use case studies of their behavior and fate to highlight regularities and distinctive qualities of the situations in which the three companies, located in three different jurisdictions, found themselves.

First, we will examine the types of victimization inflicted by the fraudulent acts of the entities, noting the general and unfortunate failure of the authorities and the general public to regard the consequences of white-collar offenses as seriously as harm from violent crimes. Then we will consider the procedures employed by the companies as part of our criminological analysis. Finally, we will examine the facts that might explain why the scandals arose. Our aim is to employ the case studies in order to suggest preventive measures that might be taken to forestall such events.

To avoid undue repetition, we will consider each of the three major issues noted above in detail for one case and refer to the remaining two only to draw attention to similar occurrences or meaningful distinctions.

Information: The Common Denominator

The legal charges filed in the three cases by themselves fail to convey their essential nature. Such allegations as "conspiracy to commit wire fraud," "insider trading," "money laundering," and "filing false income tax returns" do not provide a satisfactory analytical foundation. Besides, a domestic legal model comes up against the transnational nature of the events involved.

The three companies share in common having been or still being (in the case of Parmalat) listed on regulated markets (the New York Stock Exchange for Enron, NASDAQ for L&H, and the Borsa Milano for Parmalat). Investor confidence is an essential element if these markets are to succeed: in each case, revelations of company misbehavior, as we shall see, undercut such confidence. In general, accurate and comprehensive information is necessary to guarantee trust of those trading in company shares. Listed companies are required to provide very precise information about their activities, starting with the initial public offering (IPO). There are also required quarterly and annual financial reports, such as the SEC's 8K, 10K, 10Q forms. Insider trades by executives are expected to be publicly announced too. People use this information to assess the likely performance prospects of a business; in this regard, specialists in decoding and analyzing available information emerge. For listed companies the management of business information has become a central issue.

It is in this realm, the realm of information fraud, that we believe the fundamental common denominator linking the three cases lies. In each case, the corporate swindlers provided a distorted image of the well-being of the organizations they represented.

Enron

On December 2, 2001, Enron, headquartered in Houston, Texas, sought the protection of Chapter 11 of the bankruptcy laws, whose main goal is to allow a company to continue to operate despite the wishes of its creditors whose demands it alleges it is presently unable to meet. The American and the world's financial systems were shaken by this cataclysmic development. In ten years, Enron, originally a regional gas supplier, had become a huge multinational trading player in the natural gas and electricity industries. It had particularly made the most of the deregulation in the United States of the energy business.[1] The earlier collapse of the technology sector exposed the precarious financial condition of Enron and, in time, led to the discovery of innumerable accounting frauds that misrepresented the company's true and desperate condition. The downfall of Enron was the first installment of what came to be called "a scandalous situation," subsequently involving companies such as Tyco, Ahold, Worldcom, and others.[2]

Lernout & Hauspie

The case of Lernout & Hauspie, at one time the world leader in voice recognition technology, never reached the level of notoriety that marked the Enron debacle. That was so for at least three reasons: the smaller size of the company, the lesser media coverage, and the location of the company in Belgium, off the main track. The company was named after the founders and directors, and its rapid early rise was fueled by successive issues of financial instruments and the buying out of competitors.

In August 2000, an article in the *Wall Street Journal* questioned the truth of the financial statements of L&H and showed it to be a paper tiger. The directors denied the report, but rot had set in and soon it became obvious that there was a wide abyss between the real situation and what had been reported by the company. The burst in the L&H bubble led to the bankruptcy and dismantling of the company and its installation in the hall of fame of Belgian financial scandals.

Parmalat

Unlike L&H, Parmalat was an old and well-established company. It became the European leader in the food sector, featuring a diverse roster of products and in particular long-life milk (UHT) in Tetra-Pak cartons. The Parmalat scandal erupted in 2003. Early in the year, the company sought to float a bank issue of

300 to 500 million euros. Analysts were puzzled by the apparent need for additional funding when accounting ledgers indicated no such necessity. Parmalat's inadequate response to inquiries fueled a sharp drop in its share price and led the Italian Stock Exchange Authority to call the company's directors to account. They had to admit that 496 million euros had been placed in a Cayman Island investment fund that specialized in high-risk leisure sector operations. The Cayman investment was a violation of official management regulations, and it had fared very poorly. A further investigation showed an 800-million euro hole in Parmalat's declared assets. It was learned that the company had used chain liquidity transfers from one affiliate to another by means of off-shore entities based in tax havens. By the end of the year Parmalat had to declare bankruptcy and its chief executives had been arrested.

Victimization, with a Focus on Parmalat

Positioning

Our approach borrows from Sellin and Wolfgang's distinction between primary, secondary, and tertiary victimization.[3] Primary victimization concerns personal victims, that is, a victim in the usual sense of the term. Secondary victimization has to do with impersonal victims, though the harm is not sufficiently disseminated to concern the wider community, while tertiary victimization injures a whole community and undermines public order.

In the Parmalat case the shock waves were much like the result of throwing a stone into water, that is, a series of concentric eddies of victimization.

Primary Victimization

The number of primary victims of the Parmalat disaster (mainly shareholders and bondholders) has never been adequately tabulated. By October 2004, a total of 8,000 small savers had filed civil suits against the company.[4]

Shareholders

There were an estimated 40,000 members of the "general public" owning shares of Parmalat. Their holdings went into a dramatic tailspin. The shares had been sold at a high of 2.48 euros in January 2003 and fell to 0.11 euros by the end of the year when the Italian stock exchange suspended trading and announced its investigation of the company. Because of Parmalat's deep indebtedness and the fact that shareholders are placed at the end of the roster of creditors, it is presumed that none of them will recover any part of their investment unless the company is allowed to continue in business under a new arrangement that would integrate all previous holdings that remain viable.

Creditors

Standard & Poor, the corporate rating organization, awarded an excellent rating to Parmalat until December 2003, although the company "was crumbling under a EUR 14.3 billion debt... where bonds accounted for 9.5 billion and bank loans for 4.2 billion.[5] The relief offered creditors today by the special administrator involves transforming the group's bond debt into capital which will be used to create a new company out of the ruins. The Parmalat Spa bond creditors would be allocated 73 shares for each EUR 1,000 invested. The Parmalat Finanziari bonds would be accorded a slightly higher rate. The reorganization plan also envisages providing each bondholder with free warrants that would allow them to purchase other securities at a nominal price between 2005 and 2015. Moreover, the Italian government has ruled that the reorganized Parmalat should pay its shareholders at least fifty percent of is distributable profits over the next fifteen years.

In addition, a large number of injured creditors have filed legal suits, and the Securities and Exchange Commission in the United States has opened an inquiry. Also, a major American law firm has filed a class action suit on behalf of the South Alaska carpenters' pension fund, which names as defendants groups such as Citicorp and the accounting firm of Deloitte and Touche.[6]

Banks

The total exposure of the banks that had advanced money to Parmalat amounted to EUR 4,200,000,000. It is unclear as yet how much of the total involved Italian banks and how much those outside the country: the list of creditors ran to 63 pages. Some banks took a particularly large hit, including Wells Fargo, Unicredit Banca d'Impresa, Deutsche Bank, and Credit Suisse First Boston.

The case of the Bank of America is particularly interesting. In December 2003 it had brought matters to a head by notifying the Italian Stock Exchange Authority that the statement issued in its name and showing the presence of \$3.9 billion in the account of a Parmalat subsidiary in the Cayman Islands was untrue. The Parmalat administrator is seeking \$10 billion in damages from the Bank of America. For its part, it is attempting to initiate civil proceedings against Parmalat, claiming that it was the victim of a fraud that was covered up by the company's employees on behalf of its directors.

Suppliers

The Parmalat catastrophe affected thousands of suppliers, mostly located in the dairy industry. Many faced bankruptcy. Toward the end of January 2004, the Italian government promised 5,000 Italian milk producers that they would be paid in cash for a period of 45 days for their product, and the Parmalat receiver negotiated loans to continue to pay milk suppliers, whose situation was of special concern to the government.

The Work Force

In 2003, Parmalat employed 36,356 persons throughout the world. The receivership envisages selling off affiliates, which employ about half that total, cutting back on the domestic staff, and establishing early retirement plans. There are plans as well to eliminate a wide range of products and focus primarily on dairy products and fruit juices. Parmalat had about 9,000 employees in Brazil during the 1970s, but financial difficulties forced it to sell off affiliates and cut the work force to 6,000 persons. The Argentine affiliate, wth 1,200 employees, had severed its relationship with Parmalat before the collapse, but affiliates in Uruguay (300 employees) and Paraguay (140) were threatened with their demise when the Brazilian group declared bankruptcy.

Secondary Victimization

The fate of the Parma football club offers an example of secondary victimization. The head of Parmalat had purchased the club and then installed his son to head it. After Parmalat's collapse, the receiver chose to sell the club, which by then had accumulated liabilities of 182 million euros. Given Italians' passion for football, we can justly claim that this stands as an instance of victimization, noting as well the uncertain fate of the club's employees, players, and others whose life was linked to the team.

Tertiary Victimization

Tertiary victimization concerns what most often are intangible victims. For all three of our case studies the main tertiary victim in each instance was the market and, more specifically, the fundamental ingredient of public trust and confidence in the manner in which it operates. That trust was abused by the promulgation of deceptive information. In the Parmalat case, confidence was shattered in the following spheres:

- confidence in the bankers who recommended the bonds of companies whose solvency state they were presumed to know;
- confidence in the credibility of the guarantees given to these companies by the rating organizations;
- confidence in the figures certified by external auditors who are expected to play a critical role in determing the accuracy of the ledgers of the companies they inspect;
- confidence, finally, in the operations of the financial markets, which cannot be viewed as games of chance where the investors bet their money on the future of companies without satisfactory information with which to evaluate that future.

However subtle and far-reaching the diminution of confidence may have been, it should be noted that the Parmalat frauds, in measurable terms, did not appear to have strong reverberations on the well-being of the market. From the beginning of November, when the scandal broke, to the end of the following January, the MSCI Consumer Staples Index, which includes Parmalat, suffered only slight downward pressure, and this trend did not persist beyond February. This would tend to demonstrate that investors considered Parmalat as an isolated episode and did not extrapolate its situation to the relevant market as a whole.

Schemes, with a Focus on Enron

In general, the deceptive techniques employed in the Enron case were similar to those that occurred with Parmalat. However, beyond these commonalities there were distinctions, most notably involving the use of sophisticated techniques by Enron (and L&H) compared to the cruder violations of the Parmalat group. The main tactics used in the Enron case can be divided into seven categories:

1. Illegally structuring financial transactions to create the illusion that earnings were booming, and hiding debts primarily by recourse to fraudulent third-party entities that were falsely said to be independent so that the accounts did not have to be consolidated.
2. Creating fictitious income and thereby improving Enron's profit-and-loss statements.
3. Not respecting accepted accounting principles regarding the sale of financial credits in order to hide the extent of the company's debt and to make profits appear more hefty than they actually were.
4. Hiding large losses in two Enron divisions, EBS and EES, linked to the "new technologies" sector.
5. Manipulating the true financial state of the company by using reserve accounts in order to camouflage Enron's financial condition.
6. Failing to respect accepted accounting principles relating to the disclosure of reductions in goodwill.
7. Making false declarations and omitting significant facts that would have made Enron reports more faithfully reflect the company's true condition.

We will select three illustrations of the first point above to provide a sense of the manipulations and maneuvers to which Enron personnel resorted.

The Cuiaba Project, Nigerian Barges, and the Grayhawk Projects

The Cuiaba Project

Toward the end of 1999, Enron participated in a project to build an electrical power station in Cuiaba, Brazil. The arrangements were notably complex, with the involvement of an array of company affiliates and divisions. Enron held a 65.6 percent share in the endeavor through Holding Enron du Brazil and a smaller percentage through a Brazilian company whose Texas parent controlled 25 percent. The other shareholder was a Shell Oil affiliate. Enron appointed three of the four directors of the company and Shell the fourth.

Enron was looking for a solution offering two advantages: to deconsolidate a poor investment and also to be able to record the income from a contract to supply energy worth $65 million through a company that it controlled.

This was when a partnership came into play, known as LJM Cayman, which had been created under the aegis of Jeffrey K. Sklling, Richard A. Causey, and Andrew Fastow, respectively COO, CAO, and CFO of Enron. It was a fraudulent set-up aimed at hiding the capital supplied by Enron. Through LJM Brazil Co., which was controlled by LJM Cayman, Enron negotiated the purchase of 13 percent of the shares held by Enron do Brazil Holding Ltd. A result of this change in the shareholding stakes, the distribution of the rights to appoint directors was changed so that Enron no longer held the de facto control of EPE, which meant that it could deconsolidate the accounts of this structure and consolidate the income from the aforementioned contract ($65,000,000). As was always the case with Enron manipulations, the individuals and companies involved received compensation—for this transaction, it amounted to nearly $3,500,000.

The Nigerian Barges Transactions[7]

At the end of 1999, after the breakdown of negotiations with a potential purchaser, the Enron directors began looking to unload a project that involved construction and operation of barges located along the coast of Nigeria in order to improve its financial statement for the previous quarter and half year. The project was already far behind schedule. Jeffrey McMahon, Enron's treasurer and executive vice president, contacted Merrill Lynch, an investment bank, which at the time was involved in numerous Enron commercial enterprises. Enron wanted Merrill Lynch to purchase its stake in the Nigeria project so that Enron could include $12 million in income in its 1999 profit-and-loss statement, though in fact $7 million was the actual asking price. In return, Enron guaranteed that it would find a partner that would repurchase the stake within six months and add 22.5 percent interest.

Merrill Lynch was sorely tempted, despite a meeting of its Debt Markets Commitment Committee during which a series of questions, fears, and criticisms were raised. These included concerns about control of the barges and reservations about Enron's ability to fulfill the repayment guarantee. But a simple contract and verbal assurances from Fastow overrode the objections in short order.

Just six months after the completion of the contract, the stake held by Merrill Lynch was purchased by a partnership known as LJM for $7,500,000, plus inflated consultancy fees of $250,000. LJM posed as an independent entity but in actuality was totally tied to Enron. The complete absence of due diligence by Merrill Lynch before becoming involved in the deal is notable. Its representatives never sought to negotiate the purchase price, and paid little or no heed to the fact that the business in question was radically outside the usual field of Merill Lynch's work. The company had no experience in Nigeria or, for that matter, in any of Africa. Nor did Merill Lynch apparently attend to the fact that the barges were not operative when the deal was cut.

The Grayhawk Project

January 20, 2000, was a key date in the history of the fall of Enron. During a press conference, Jeffrey Skilling declared that Enron Broadband Services (EBS), the group's Internet division, had in hand its broadband network and the software to make it operational. Skilling also claimed that a "conservative" estimate would establish the net worth of EBS at $30 billion. All the while he knew perfectly well that the broadband network still was not in place and that EBS did not have the software. Since EBS in many respects represented what was regarded as the future of Enron, every ruse was employed to camouflage its true condition.

Enron resorted to a variety of other schemes as well. The JEDI partnership was mainly employed by Enron, with remarkable ingenuity, to use profits from various speculations with its own securities and to credit this income to represent the result of industrial activities. JEDI had several hedging contacts with Enron. Furthermore, the shares contributed by Enron when establishing JEDI, where the link was both official and unofficial and involved consolidated accounts, contained a clause that determined JEDI's value beforehand. Therefore, the value of the investment that JEDI represented was not sensitive to the changes in the price of Enron shares.

As the important conference of January 20, 2000, approached, it was essential to present favorable figures. The Enron managers then imagined the following scenario. Enron was going to post figures including income of $85,000,000, which would then be posted as the result of Enron's ordinary energy activities, and which in reality was only the early result of the security increase that would be caused by this conference (during which false information would be given about EBS). More specifically, the Enron directors predated an amendment to the contract with JEDI, which allowed that partnership, whose results were consolidated to incur capital gains if the price went up. The securities leaped from $47 to $67 after the conference. That was how a cocktail based on financial products, partnerships, accounting consolidations, false accounts, and good communications can artificially create $85,000,000![8]

Comparing the Cases

The similarities between the Enron and the L&H cases are numerous, much more so than between either of them and Parmalat. For Enron and L&H, the role played by various financial institutions and the consequences for victims were nearly identical, despite the fact that much of the L&H story was shrouded in the secrecy that is part of Belgian law.[9]

The tactics used in the two cases were much the same. A large portion of the reputed sales were made to related companies. These small companies benefited from payment schemes (which blatantly contradicted the company's policy). Yet, more significantly, they benefited from loans guaranteed by L&H with their customary bankers in order to pay for the licenses, which the former leading company in voice recognition technology considered to be synonymous with income. What is worse, it was sometimes just the employees on the L&H payroll who were in charge of developing this software. And when the previous options were not chosen, L&H resorted to factoring, a method of pre-financing debts by supposedly abandoning certain rights in order to improve the image of its financial position. The factoring agreements were posted as non-recourse arrangements, when in reality they allowed the lender to demand that L&H remit the whole sum should it fail to pay up at the maturity date.

The similarity of methods suggests the hypothesis that while the two companies were very different in terms of history, culture, core business, and other matters, there are intrinsic considerations that influenced the modus operandi of the crimes, which appear to contain a strong opportunistic element. Just like the executives at L&H, Enron's managers took advantage of loopholes present in accepted accounting regulations and interpreted every principle so that it worked to their advantage.

Revisiting the L&H Case

The L&H scandal is first and foremost the story of a market dealing with a new-technology company that engaged in a whirlwind of transactions. It was basically a market situation where the company's future appeared much more promising than the present worth of its securities indicated. The state of mind that prevailed at the time is captured by Paul A. Gompers of the Harvard Business School: "Before the warning shot [in spring 2000], most of the companies were not assessed according to their business, but highly subjectively," Gompers noted. "If the investors believed the concept of the start-up was good, they did not hesitate to back it financially, as they hoped to make a profit from the fact of the dynamics of the Internet economy."[10] Put another way, investors would back what essentially an idea, a concept whose appeal was almost exclusively based on its presumed and sometimes highly imaginative prospects. And these prospects were heightened by both bluff and deception.

L&H's founders perfectly assimilated this ethos. Yet their company was more than a product of its time. Its activity touched on a area, voice recognition, which resonated with people's dreams of a better future produced by innovative technology. In popular culture, there was the film *2001: A Space Odyssey*, which showed a man talking to a computer on a space vessel, calling it by its first name. L&H sought to duplicate in actuality this fantasy, focusing both on speech-to-text applications that would allow machines to react to vocal commands and text-to-speech programs which would allow machines to talk. L&H arranged an agreement with Microsoft to integrate its technology into Office applications. Machines, it was envisaged, would be able to read e-mails. So L&H sold a humanistic dream, that of removing language barriers. Everyone would be able to speak with everyone else in their own languages with the machines providing instant and accurate translations.

However, the pitfalls were as numerous as the principles were seductive. They included the need to reduce extraneous noise, the necessity to deal with diverse accents, the problem of slang and ungrammatical usage, and issues of tonal expression, not to mention the need to be able to sell the product at an affordable price.

The nature of the market partly explains some of the tribulations of L&H, their investors, and their creditors. There seemed to exist what criminologists have called a "criminogenic industry" or "criminogenic market."[11] Nonetheless, we would stress that such influences do not inevitably lead to criminal acts, that when all is said and done the directors still have an element of free will.

An Idol and Groupies

The L&H "dream" seduced the Flemish world of politics and finance. The company's beginning was difficult, with the founders laying out virtually their last cent on the venture. But it soon became the standard bearer for Ieper, its home site, and for the West Flanders region. The beatification of the company was part of the industrial recovery of the area, which until then primarily had been known for the fierce battles fought on its territory during the first World War. L&H transformed a relatively moribund area into a jewel of the Flemish technology industry. Its aim was to operate successfully in a global marketplace.

Many people now wonder if the Flemish authorities did not exceed the limits of normal public support because they were intoxicated by the prospect of seeing the glory from L&H's possible success reflect on them. The unconditional support of the Flemish authorities and the alleged fraudulent use of public funds testify to this outpouring of unexamined aid to L&H. In addition, the Flanders Language Valley, where L&H was located, was declared a tax-free zone. As a risk capitalist stated in the Belgian press: "The combination of ambitious entrepreneurs and a government that desperately wanted a local technological champion was a volatile mix. It was dangerous."[12] The explosive mixture suggests three key questions: Did the Flemish authorities scrupulously respect the law? Did L&H benefit from a discriminatory system? What was the exact role of the Flemish authorities in blowing up the speculative bubble?

The minister in the Flemish government in charge of loan guarantees admitted that he had not tried to learn the identity of Dictation shareholders when the authorities underwrote 75 percent of a $15 million loan to the company (Dictation was a subsidiary of L&H). Was this carelessness or had the proximity of the relationship between the government and the company brought this situation about? Certain prominent politicians were known to have a direct interest in the company. Nor are we as yet aware of who exactly held stock in L&H, which makes adjudication of the concessions granted the company an uncertain enterprise. In Belgium friendship and reciprocity play a significant role in the founding and funding of a new enterprise. Companies aid one another by exchanging capital and administrators. While the "Belgium network" should not be demonized by comparing it, say, to the Mafia, its influence in the L&H scandal needs to be explained. Its transparency certainly leaves a great deal to be desired.

A set of players in the L&H case have attracted the attention of the justice system. The company's founders are suspected of a string of offenses ranging from fraud to falsification of accounts as well as money laundering and insider trading. Also implicated are a former CEO and onetime CFO of the company and the external auditor, KPMG. It will take some time and effort to unwind this tangle of responsibility and guilt. It remains unclear whether the problems were created by fraud or were the result of poor management. For its part, KPMG defines itself as a victim of organized fraudulent maneuvers by company officials. They point out that L&H's main Korean client was pressured to hide from KPMG the actual content of the contracts that had been negotiated. The crisis report requested from PriceWaterhouseCooper further documented that other L&H clients were offered compensation (bribes) to conceal evidence from auditors. All told, the elements of the L&H case provide an example of a "corporate crime" carried out for the benefit of the company rather than a "white-collar crime" motivated by the quest for personal gain.

We cannot conclude this review without considering the failure of the system of checks and balances aimed at preventing such fraudulent behavior. The L&H decline has rekindled the debate regarding the competence and actual power of the boards of directors of corporate entities. How could L&H's directors have allowed the situation to deteriorate to such a point? Are directors appointed because of their presumed passivity and obligations to management? Are they kept in the dark by the ability of corporate executives to feed them only sanitized information? Should impartial representatives of the public be accorded a seat on the board of directors to play a more confrontational role in its deliberations?

The External Auditor

A central player in the L&H case was the Anglo-Dutch auditor Klynveld Peak Marwick Goerdeler (KPMG), which came in for sustained criticism, mainly from small shareholders. They were upset that the auditor who certified the accounts had not discovered that the books were cooked. They criticized KPMG for its Panagruelian fees and ineffective oversight, though others maintain that the auditors were audaciously duped and that if a company uses sufficiently sophisticated methods it is almost always beyond the capabilities of any outside auditors to detect the fraud. To unravel the mess, the courts have charged the KMPG CEO in order to obtain the release of information otherwise held in secret under the strict rules of professional secrecy laid down by Belgian legislators.

More fundamentally, the L&H case reopened the controversy surrounding the role of external auditors. KPMG had a far-reaching relationship with L&H, acting as its tax and legal advisor, a setup that was rife with conflicts of interest. Dependent on the goodwill (not to mention the high fees) of an entity whose wrongdoing it also is charged with detecting, auditors tread carefully. The worldwide spate of legislation that is barring auditors from providing auxiliary services to their clients is now being carefully examined in Belgium.

Banks and Market Authorities

The banks were the creditors of L&H and the greatest victims in terms of losses, but were they not reckless in granting so much credit—in the literal and figurative meaning of the word—to the company from Ypres? The so-called Chinese wall that in theory separates the loan and financial analysis bank departments is now being questioned. Would it not be more effective if the groups shared information that permitted a more realistic and comprehensive determination of the company's condition?

Finally, the Stock Exchange Authority also turned out to be ineffective. The investigation by the Securities and Exchange Commission in the United States was begun only after an exposé by the *Wall Street Journal*, even though rumors of wrongdoing had been circulating much earlier.

Conclusion

Similarities between the three cases we have highlighted stand out in bold relief. The patterns of victimization are probably the least surprising of these. Nonetheless, thay are a reminder of the diverse nature of damage that such frauds, which we have grouped under the label "information fraud," can inflict. The equivalence between the methods employed also is striking. The companies were not predestined to go along parallel paths. They were vastly different organizations on a multitude of levels. This circumstance leads us, without denying the influence of endogenous factors, to turns our attention to exogenous issues.

At this stage, considerations of form join with those of content. The case study method, a direct descendant of LaPlay's contributions though it was supplanted to some extent by the arrival of quantitative methods in the social sciences, remains an important means of obtaining scientific truth.[13] This approach fits well with inductive analysis that avoids becoming locked into predefined models. Yin has emphasized the benefits of a research program that places the subject into his, her, or its context, using a variety of sources and centering on questions of how and why rather than who and how much.[14] This method is especially useful in the examination of frauds such as those we have addressed in this chapter. It is also particularly suitable for the study of crimes linked to finance, where access to hard data is a particularly delicate issue and the quantitative tools of mainstream criminology often are not appropriate or useful.

Endnotes

1. Berenson (2002).
2. Lascoumes (1997).
3. Sellin & Wolfgang (1964).
4. "Rome tire les leçons du Krach Parmalat," *L'expansion*, 3 Feb. 2004.
5. "Parmalat espère un retour au bénéfice en 2005," *La Tribune*, 16 July 2004.
6. "Parmalat, les diverses enquêtes se poursuivent au pas de course," *L'Echo*, 7 Jan. 2004.
7. United States v. Bayly, Cr. No. H-031-363 (S.D. Tex.); United States v. Fastow, Cr. No.H-02-0665 (S.D. Tex.).
8. Securities and Exchange Commission, First Amended Complaint, H-04-0284 (S.D. Tex.).
9. "L&H: Plaintes contre Dexia?" *La Libre Belgique*, 20 Jan. 2005.
10. "C'est la (le) Temps du Grand Nettoyage," *Libération*, 21–22 Oct 2000.
11. Slapper and Tombs (1999).
12. "Splendeurs et misères d'une rêve high-tech flamand," *Le Soir*, 11 Dec. 2000.
13. Le Play (1989).
14. Yin (1994).

References

Berenson, Alex (2002). "Mystery of Enron and California's Power Crisis," *New York Times*, 9 May.

Lascoumes, Pierre (1997). *Elites Irrégulières: Essais sur la Délinquance D'Affaires*, Paris: Gallimard.

Le Play, Frédéric (1989). *La Méthode Sociale: Abrégé des Ouvriers Européens, Ouvrage Destiné aux Classes Dirigeantes*. Paris: Méridiens Klincksieck.

Sellin, Thorsten and Marvin Wolfgang (1966). *The Measurement of Delinquency*. New York: John Wiley.

Slapper, Gary and Steve Tombs (1999). *Corporate Crime*. Harlow, England: Longman.

Yin, Robert K. (1994). *Case Study Research: Design and Methods*. London: Sage.

4

White-Collar Crime and Reactions of the Criminal Justice System in the United States and Japan

Tomomi Kawasaki

Since the 1990s, Japan has faced increasing numbers and types of white-collar crime. Some of them are similar to major cases in the United States. For example, both the savings and loan crisis in the United States and the "Jusen" Housing Loan Company debacle in Japan relate to financial fraud involving thrift institutions. Similarly, both the U.S. Department of Defense scandal and the Japanese Defense Agency scandal concern contract fraud. The Ford Pinto case and allegations against Mitsubishi Motors Co. raise issues of purported "corporate homicide."

Although the cases may be similar, the reaction of each country's criminal justice system has been different. Reviewing these differences is important because it can provide an indication of what the Japanese legal system may be lacking in fighting white-collar crime.

It is often said that the Japanese criminal justice system is more permissive toward white-collar criminals than that of the United States. Is that really so? This article first compares white-collar crime cases and the legal reaction to them in the two countries. Then, based on these comparisons, it addresses measures to be taken to deal with white-collar crime in the Japanese criminal justice system.

The Savings and Loan Crisis and the "Jusen" Housing Loan Company Debacle

Savings and Loan Crisis

Many investors and depositors in the United States were swindled out of billions of dollars by savings and loans (S&Ls) in the 1980s. The national scandal ultimately resulted in the conviction of thrift insiders and outside conspirators. The S&L crisis has been called "one of the worst financial disasters of the twentieth century"[1] and "the biggest white-collar crime in U.S. history."[2]

Brief History of S&Ls

S&Ls are a type of financial institution conceived in the early 1930s to promote the construction of new homes. The Federal Home Loan Bank Act of 1932 created the Federal Home Loan Bank Board (FHLBB) to provide additional reserve funds and oversight to the savings and loan programs. The National Housing Act of 1934 provided for the development of the Federal Savings and Loan Insurance Corporation to insure S&L deposits. At the beginning, savings and loan programs provided by those acts were restricted geographically and in terms of the kind of loans they could make. But in the 1960s these restraints were slowly eased.

Though the business of S&Ls expanded gradually, the thrifts were unable to offer adjustable rate mortgages in the 1970, because inflation had reached 13.3 percent by 1979. In 1980, the Depository Institutions Deregulation and Monetary Control Act phased out restrictions on interest rates paid by S&Ls. The federal government and Congress allowed the formerly restricted S&Ls to expand their business beyond residential housing loans under the Garn-St. Germain Depository Institutions Act. S&Ls were able to engage in high-risk commercial real-estate lending and offer corporate or business loans. The U.S. entered "an era of a massive deregulation of the S&L industry,"[3] giving it broad financial opportunities.

The sharp increase in interest rates in the 1980s created serious business problems for S&Ls as their inventories of low-interest, fixed-rate loans became increasingly unprofitable. The total cost to taxpayers of S&L difficulties has conservatively been estimated at $500 billion.[4] A total of 1,700 thrifts, about one-half of the industry, eventually collapsed. Government reports indicated that fraudulent activities had been a central factor in 70 to 80 percent of these cases.[5]

Looting

The unlawful activities fell into a number of categories.[6] The first was "looting," a kind of "collective embezzlement." In essence, thrift insiders robbed funds from the thrift itself.

In the case of Centennial S&L of California, the owner who had taken over in 1980 threw a Christmas party that cost $148,000. He and his companion, who was a senior officer at Centennial, traveled extensively around the world in private airplanes, purchased antique furniture at the S&L's expense, renovated their house at a cost of more than $1 million, and equipped it with a gourmet chef at an annual cost of $48,000. A fleet of luxury cars was put at the disposal of Centennial personnel and the thrift's offices were adorned with art from around the world.[7] The owner died before formal charges could be filed. However, his companion was eventually convicted of having embezzled $2.8 million. The FHLBB estimated the cost of Centennial's eventual insolvency at $160 million. In 1987, the commissioner of the California Department of S&Ls stated, "The best way to rob a bank is to own one."[8]

Unlawful Risk-Taking

A second tactic was "unlawful risk-taking," including making risky loans to commercial real estate developers. Kickbacks were often made to encourage loans. This type of S&L fraud is distinct from the same type of traditional white-collar crime. Traditional white-collar crime has an aim to steadily increase profits, but the unlawful risk-taking in S&L frauds was more like a gamble and often resulted in the bankruptcy of the institution.[9]

The owner of Lincoln S&L duped Lincoln's customers into buying worthless junk bonds of the American Continental Corporation. Lincoln's owner received a 12-year prison sentence after being convicted in a court of fraud, racketeering, and conspiracy. His federal conviction was thrown out because the jury in Tucson, Arizona improperly dealt with knowledge of his earlier state conviction.[10]

Cover-Up

A third category was "cover-ups." Thrift insiders manipulated accounting books and records and hid the fact from regulators that the thrift lacked the capital required by statute and regulation. This was "the most common form of insider abuse in the S&L crisis."[11]

The above-mentioned owner of Lincoln S&L, called "the king of cover-up,"[12] forged numerous documents in an attempt to deceive regulators. When examiners studied Lincoln's records after it was taken over, they discovered thousands of forged documents. At the owner's direction, Lincoln's employees were apparently involved in creating some of these phony documents, which included more than a thousand pages of board meeting minutes extending over a two-year period.

In addition, the head of the FHLBB intervened on behalf of Lincoln's owner to ward off FHLBB regulators in San Francisco who were investigating the thrift. He attempted to move the investigation from San Francisco to Washington, D.C., and to delay closure of the insolvent thrift for two years. The delay is estimated to have cost the Federal Savings and Loan Insurance Corporation fund $2 billion.[13]

Negative Legacy of S&Ls

From October 1, 1988, to March 18, 1992, more than 1,000 defendants had been charged by U.S. attorneys, 580 had been convicted and sentenced, and 451 sent to prison in major S&L cases.[14] Furthermore, the S&L crisis brought forth a new political scandal, the "Whitewater affair." President Bill Clinton was suspected of, but never prosecuted for, involvement in fraud and conspiracy for dipping into funds at an Arkansas-based S&L that was bankrolling risky business schemes. The scars left by the overall S&L crisis are still visible in the United States It has been conservatively estimated that over the next 40 years, the total cost of rectifying these problems could cost taxpayers $500 billion.[15]

"Jusen" Housing Loan Companies Debacle

Japan's "Jusen" housing loan company debacle was brought to light in 1995. It is often regarded as similar to the S&L crisis in several ways.[16] At the time it occurred, however, few people knew how deep and serious the scandal was.

Outline of "Jusen" Housing Loan Company

The "Jusen" housing loan companies were non-bank financial institutions established by groups of major financial institutions (city banks, regional banks, life insurance companies, trust bank, securities companies and agricultural financial institutions) in the early 1970's, principally for the purpose of providing housing loans to individuals.[17] They made loans but didn't take deposits. The funds lent by the "Jusen" housing loan companies were obtained by borrowing from the founders and other financial institutions. At the beginning, their earnings were firm. The demand for housing grew rapidly at that time, but Japanese commercial banks had placed a priority on corporate finance in the postwar period and the public housing loan corporation was increasingly unable to meet the demand.

"Jusen" in the Bubble Economy

Financial liberalization in the 1980s seriously eroded the "Jusen" housing loan companies' market niche because their sponsoring institutions actively increased mortgage lending to individuals and the government expanded the public housing loan corporation. The "Jusen" housing loan companies then turned aggressively to corporate borrowers. They were real estate developers with insufficient credit in the eyes of the banks. At the same time, the "Jusen" housing loan companies began borrowing huge sums from agricultural cooperatives that had sought a vehicle in which to invest their ballooning deposits. The "Jusen" housing loan companies increasingly loaned their funds to corporate borrowers. Just at that time, an ultra-easy monetary policy touched off a bubble economy in Japan. Land prices in cities skyrocketed. "Jusen" housing loan companies had been able to keep achieving good results through lending big money to corporations of real estate brokers. It was said a modern "alchemist" had appeared in Japan.

In the early 1990s, the Japanese "bubble" economy burst. It is said that the causes of the development and the collapse of bubble economy were compound,[18] but there is no doubt that nonperforming loans played a big part. Unrecoverable loans amounted to as much as ¥13 trillion (about $120.4 billion), "Jusen" housing loan companies were in serious trouble. Avoiding management responsibility, officers and agents of those companies tried to conceal the facts in illegal ways.

Japan Housing Loan Co. Case

For example, in the Japan Housing Loan Co. case, the former president, the former managing director, and the director of loan development section were indicted on a charge of aggravated breach of trust causing huge losses to their company.[19] They were involved in extending ¥1.595 billion (about $14.8 million) in loans to a golf course developer and ¥1.87 billion (about $17.3 million) to a real estate company, in spite of knowing the two firms didn't have the financial strength to repay the money. Furthermore, the former managing director and the director of loan development section acted as guarantors for ¥300 million (about $2.8 million) in loans to the golf course developer. Through such acts, they were said to have inflicted financial damage to their company.

On November 30, 2001, the Tokyo District Court sentenced the former president to a 38-month prison term, the former managing director to 30 months, and the director of the loan development section to 28 months, suspended for three years.

The End of Alchemy

In 1996, the Japanese government decided to inject a great deal of money directly or indirectly into "Jusen" housing loan companies to save the financial market, similar to the U.S. government's action in the S&L cases. The "Jusen" housing loan companies fell into dissolution. Public opinion was in a ferment over this policy.

The causes of the "Jusen" scandal were complex.[20] There was quite an outcry to clarify who was responsible. However, the only case brought to court was the Japan Housing Loan Co. case discussed above. The "Jusen" company scandal is a symbol of not only of the collapse of the bubble economy but also a later series of financial crimes in the 1990s.

Department of Defense Scandal and Japan Defense Agency Scandal

Department of Defense Scandal

The U.S. Department of Defense (DOD) purchases equipment and supplies for the military every year. In 1982, the General Accounting Office concluded there was a 91 percent chance of a major cost overrun on the average military contract, and that fraud and waste cost the DOD at least $15 billion a year. The media widely publicized the DOD's gross overpayments for spare parts and tools. For example, DOD paid $110 for a diode available elsewhere for 4 cents, $1,118.26 for a plastic cap for the leg of a navigator's stool, for which the usual price was $10, $2,043 for a nut worth 13 cents, and $9,606 for an Allen wrench available for 12 cents at hardware stores.[21] People became angry as it became clear the DOD was drowning in a vortex of contract fraud.

General Dynamics Scandal

In May 1985, the Secretary of the Navy announced a crackdown on General Dynamics (GD), the nation's second largest defense contractor at that time. As a result of "Operation DEFCON," the 1984–85 Department of Justice's criminal investigation, it became clear that GD had fraudulently overcharged for its work on nuclear submarine contracts. The Navy canceled some $22.5 million in contracts, imposed $676,283 in fines, and mandated a series of remedial measures. After that, six people retired—including the chairman, vice president, financial officer, and division general manager. In the same year, GD was charged with fraud stemming from earlier development work for an Army air-defense gun system, known as the Division Air Defense weapon.

But GD did not feel any severe pain. "Although some management changes were made, the value of the canceled contracts amounted to only 0.1 percent of the firm's billings the previous year. The partnership with the Pentagon was soon resumed, and the culpable executives received no prison sentences, merely a comfortable retirement."[22]

Packard Commission and DII

Successive defense contractor scandals reinforced pressures on suppliers to develop effective regulatory procedures. In 1985, President Ronald Reagan appointed David Packard, chair of the Hewlett-Packard Corporation and a former deputy secretary, to an independent commission on defense management. The

Packard Commission concluded that procurement problems were "symptoms of the same fundamental problem: the lack of an effective management structure in the [defense] department"[23] and recommended a system of self-regulation rather than governmental control.

The Packard Commission encouraged the reform and development of ethical codes.[24] First, in its interim report, the Commission encouraged major contractors to endorse a set of principles known as the "Defense Industry Initiatives on Business Ethics and Conduct" (DII). The 46 contractor signatories agreed to adopt and enforce codes of conduct. Second, the Commission urged the DOD to stipulate that contractors should develop internal control systems "to promote [high standards of business conduct], to facilitate the timely discovery and disclosure or improper conduct in connection with Government contracts, and to assure that corrective measures are promptly instituted and carried out." In 1988, a Memorandum from the Fraud Division Chief to United States Attorneys mentioned that where a defense contractor voluntarily discloses an illegal activity and could be prosecuted for it, the existence prior to commencement of the illegal activity of an effective compliance program is a factor to be considered in the decision to prosecute.[25]

Sequel to Scandal

The DII Defense Contractors' self-regulation was a positive step. However, defense fraud has not stopped. For example, an investigation from 1988 to 1990 into defense fraud code-named "Operation Ill Wind" resulted in almost thirty-six guilty pleas. Eleven Unisys officials pleaded guilty to tax evasion and bribery, three United Technologies officials were convicted of fraud, and nine other contractors pleaded guilty to defense contracting fraud. They were fined $1 million to $5.8 million. Furthermore, according to a 1996 General Accounting Office report, eighty percent of the Navy's purchase orders were inaccurate, and an Air Force purchase order of $888,000 worth of ammunition was listed as $333 million; a 37,500 percent overprice.[26]

Japan Defense Agency Scandal

The U.S. Department of Defense scandal resembles a problem involving the Japan Defense Agency. It too involved contractors' fraud for defense institutions in the 1990s.

Outline of Japan Defense Agency

After World War II, the General Headquarters (GHQ) set about dismantling the Japanese armed forces. However, the GHQ and U.S. government changed their policy as Cold War tension mounted. The Japan Defense Agency (JDA) was established in 1954 to control and operate three military services and manage their affairs for the purpose of defending the peace and independence of Japan.[27] The JDA consists of the military services, the Joint Staff Council, organizations such as the National Defense Academy, the Technical Research and Development Institute, the Central Procurement Office, and the internal bureaus including procurement sections.

The JDA procurement section had broad discretion over all equipment, from uniforms to missiles for the Self-Defense Forces. Its purchases totaled about ¥1.24 trillion (about $11.5 billion) covering about 9,800 items. That was one-third of the agency's budget in 1998.

Detection of JDA Scandal

In the middle 1990s, it became clear that contractors had overcharged the JDA by billions of yen for equipment. The former chief and deputy chief of JDA's procurement section feared they would be blamed for neglect. On the other hand, directors and officers of contractors feared being taken to task at stockholders' meetings for management irresponsibilities. They conspired to reduce the reimbursement payments to hush up the affair. However, the Mainichi newspaper reported this development in September 1997, revealing the back-scratching alliance of JDA's procurement section and contractors.

Toyo Communication Equipment Co. Route

Toyo Communication Equipment Co., an affiliate of NEC Corp., had received overpayments of ¥2.99 billion (about $27.7 million) for equipment for JDA over several years. In March 1994, the former Toyo chairman visited the JDA deputy chief of the procurement office and asked him to reduce the refund amount illegally, attempting to make the problem appear slight. After the meeting, the amount was reduced to ¥874 million (about $8.1 million), costing the state ¥2.12 billion yen (about $19.6 million).

A deputy chief of JDA's procurement section who had taken the initiative in the conspiracy had received ¥3 million yen (about $27,700) in cash from Toyo Communication Equipment Co. as a reward in September 1994.

Nico Electronics Co. Route

Nico Electronics Co. is another subsidiary of NEC Corp. It overcharged JDA about ¥1.72 billion (about $15.9 million) from fiscal 1990 to 1995 for the purchase of cryptographic and other items such as decoders, parachutes, and shells. In June 1995, four directors, including a chief director of Nico Electronics Co., two directors and three officers of NEC Corp., and a former chief and deputy chief of JDA's procurement section conspired to repay ¥296 million (about $2.7 million), causing losses of more than 1.42 billion yen (about $13.1 million) to the state.

Furthermore, a deputy chief of JDA's procurement section received ¥5.38 million (about $49,800) from Nippon Koki Co., also a subsidiary of NEC Corp., under the pretext of an advisor's fee after his retirement.

Sentencing

Of the 14 people indicted in this scandal, only the deputy chief of JDA's procurement section pleaded not guilty. On October 13, 1999, the former chief of JDA's procurement section was sentenced to three years in prison, suspended for five years, for conspiring in the breach-of-trust. Twelve other defendants—including six directors or officers of NEC Corp., four directors of Toyo Communication Equipment Co., and two directors of Nico Electrics Co.—also received from two- to three-year sentences for their role.

On May 8, 2003, the deputy chief of JDA's procurement section was sentenced to four years in prison and a ¥8.38 million fine for conspiring in the breach-of-trust and acceptance of bribes. According to the decision, he played a central role, his actions were malicious and tarnished public trust in defense administration, and his motive was self-protection. Only the deputy chief filed an appeal with the Tokyo High Court. That case is pending.

Impact of JDA Scandal

The scandal had great influence in Japan. The long-time chairman of NEC Corp. resigned. The JDA procurement office was split into two sections (cost accounting and contracts) in January 2001.

Japanese people took an increasing interest in the back-scratching alliance of government officials and big business. In particular, the "amakudari" system, by which former government officials are appointed to high positions in companies, received a great deal of criticism. But that system has not been abolished.[28] On the contrary, a new scandal has arisen involving suspicion that other contractors overcharged the JDA by billions of yen for various equipment purchases.

The Ford Pinto Case and Mitsubishi Motors Co. Case

Ford Pinto Case

In 1971, the Ford Motor Co. (FMC) introduced a new style of car, the Pinto, as its entry into the subcompact market. Although FMC was the fourth biggest company in the world at that time, it feared that foreign competitors, mostly from Japan, were going to capture the entire U.S. subcompact market. Against strong competitors and with the small car market growing more lucrative, FMC rushed the Pinto into production in much less than the usual time. It shortened the product-development process from 43 months to 25 months.[29] Engineers were told to make the car weigh less than 2,000 pounds and cost less than $2,000.[30] Because these organizational goals were made paramount, safety was not a priority for the Pinto.

The Defect and Legal Reaction

Because of lesser attention to safety, the 1971–1976 model Pintos had significant troubles. According to an article published in May 1978 in *The New York Times:* "Low to moderate speed rear-end collisions of Pintos produce massive fuel tank leaks due to puncture or tearing of the fuel tank and separation of the filler pipe from the tank."[31] Internal documents showed the company knew about these safety defects. Although the gas tank design defect could have been modified for $11 per car, Ford decided not to take action. It conducted a cost–benefit analysis of these safety defects:[32] "The $11 repairs for all Pintos would cost $137 million but 180 burn deaths and 180 serious burn injuries and $21,000 burned vehicles would cost only $49.5 million (each death was figured at $200,000 and each injury at $67,000). Therefore, the company could anticipate a savings of $87.5 million by continuing to make and sell the cars that were expected to kill or injure several hundred people."[33] Furthermore, to reach this conclusion, Ford asked the National Highway Traffic and Safety Administration about the average wrongful death claim in a vehicle accident in order to estimate the monetary worth of a human life. It got a reply of about $200,000.[34] Between 500 and 900 persons died in rear-end collisions of Pintos that resulted in fuel tank explosions.[35]

In April 1974, the Center for Auto Safety petitioned the National Highway Traffic Safety Administration to recall the Pinto, based on reports from attorneys of three deaths and four serious injury cases. This report remained in the NHTSA offices until 1977. Finally, however, FMC was forced to recall 1.5 million Pintos as a result of investigations of the NHTSA Office of Defect Investigations in

June 1978. Moreover, an Orange County, California, jury awarded a plaintiff $125 million in punitive damages for injuries he suffered as a passenger in 1971 when a Pinto was struck by another car at 28 mph.

Elkhart County Case

FMC was indicted for three cases of negligence arising from the deaths of three young women burned in a Pinto. On August 10, 1978, the women were driving in a 1973 Ford Pinto going to church. Their car was struck from the rear by a van on U.S. Highway 33 in northern Indiana. Within seconds, the car was engulfed in flames.

In the grand jury, three points were discussed.[36] First, whether the word "person" in the Illinois Criminal Code could be applied to corporate entities. Second, whether the county prosecutor could indict corporations, despite the fact that the federal government had established an apparatus to supervise the automobile industry under the National Traffic and Motor Vehicle Safety Act. Third, whether Pinto case prosecution was a breach of the ex post facto provision of both the Indiana and U.S. Constitutions: though the Pinto was produced in 1973, the new reckless homicide crime category in the Illinois Criminal Code became effective on Jury 1, 1978, and the Elkhart County crash happened on August 10, 1978.

On February 2, 1979, the Illinois Circuit Court judge denied FMC's motion to dismiss and rendered the following decision. First, a corporation could be responsible for homicide under the Illinois Criminal Code. Second, the federal regulatory scheme couldn't prevent the state from seeking retributive and deterrent goals unique to the criminal sanction. Third, because of the ex post facto restriction, Ford could not be charged with recklessly designing and manufacturing the Pinto, but it could be charged for failure to fulfill its obligation to repair at 41 days before the Elkhart County crash.[37]

In the trial, the company attempted to limit evidence for the prosecution and insisted it had announced a recall of Pintos on June 9, 1978, two months before the Elkhart County fatal crash. Ford's defense of FMC was successful. After eight weeks of testimony and four days of exhausting deliberations, a jury returned a not guilty verdict. It is said that the trial's outcome hinged on a legal technicality.[38]

The Significance and Impact of the Ford Pinto Case

The Ford Pinto case has been called "one of the most significant criminal court trials in American corporate history."[39] The U.S. criminal justice system had accepted the idea that a corporation might be responsible for homicide since the late 19th century.[40] However, defendants had been almost exclusively small corporations. The Pinto case was the first in which one of the world's biggest corporations was indicted on a charge of manslaughter. Despite the verdict, the case "demonstrate[d] that many people in our society are coming to recognize the serious physical costs associated with corporate crime, and that they feel something needs to be done to control the behavior of corporations."[41]

Mitsubishi Motors Co. Case

The Mitsubishi Motors Co. (MMC) case is often compared with the FMC Pinto case.[42] MMC, which belongs to Mitsubishi group, is the fourth-largest motor vehicle manufacturer in Japan, particularly prominent in the production of trucks and buses. Mitsubishi Motors Co. had spun off the large-vehicle manufacturer Mitsubishi Fuso in January 2003.

Yokohama Case

On January 2002, a 140-kilogram wheel came off a Mitsubishi trailer truck in Yokohama and hit a mother and her two young children. The mother was killed and the children injured. Mitsubishi Motors reported to the Land, Infrastructure, and Transport Ministry that the accident was caused by a failure to maintain the vehicle. But at that time, MMC had information about defects in the wheel hubs of some of its large vehicles.

Yamaguchi Prefecture Case

On October 19, 2002, another a fatal truck crash occurred in Yamaguchi prefecture. The driver was unable to stop the truck as it was passing through an expressway tollgate. It hit a building, killing the driver. Police suspected that one of the truck's propeller shafts separated from the chassis because of a defective clutch system and broke the braking mechanism. MMC had been aware of the possibility of defects in the clutch system. It had received complaints from a company that owned 11 Mitsubishi trucks, indicating that clutch system trouble had contributed to accidents and that the clutch systems of those trucks had been repaired ten times.

Violation of Road Truck Vehicle Law Case in 2000

In June 2000, before these accidents, the Transport Ministry got a call from a whistleblower, saying that MMC had covered up consumer complaints about defective cars to avoid recalls. The Ministry inspected the head office of MMC. After that, the company admitted its managers had knowingly and systematically concealed 64,000 consumer complaints about defective cars since 1977. On August 2 and September 3, 2000, the Tokyo Metropolitan Police raided MMC's office in search of evidence for a prosecution. On September 8, officials of Transport Ministry filed a criminal complaint with the police, alleging false declarations in violation of the Road Trucking Vehicle Law of 1951. MMC was ordered to pay ¥4 million (about $37 thousand) as an administrative penalty by Transport Ministry. MMC and four former executives (including a former vice-president) were sent to summary criminal proceedings and received fines of ¥400,000 (about $3,703) and ¥200,000 (about $1,852).

Japanese people were shocked by MMC's dishonest acts. The then-president resigned, taking responsibility. MMC's current-account deficit hit an all-time high of ¥756 billion (about $7 billion) in that year. Recall expenses amounted to about ¥215 billion (about $1.99 billion). In spite of such facts, MMC continued to engage in manufacturing misconduct, resulting in accidents involving injury and death.

Reaction of Criminal Justice System

In the Yokohama case, Kanagawa Prefectural Police arrested MMC and five former executives (including the former chairman) on suspicion of making false declarations to the competent authority in violation of the Road Trucking Vehicle Law of 1951. Furthermore, two former officers in charge of quality control were arrested on charges of negligent homicide. All of them were indicted by the Yokohama District Public Prosecutor's Office and have pleaded not guilty. The trials are currently in progress.

In the Yamaguchi Prefecture Case, the former chairman, former president, and two former directors were arrested and indicted on a charge of negligent homicide. In this case, the former chairman and former president pleaded not guilty. However, the two former directors pleaded guilty.

Studies

From the preceding survey, we can find similarities between white-collar crime cases in the United States and Japan. Damages were serious, with diverse and complex causes. Blame could be placed not only on faulty acts of the participants but also on business conditions and omissions by regulators. Viewed from the standpoint of the legal reaction, however, there are many differences in what happened.

Criminal Justice Structure: Japanese Precise Justice

As mentioned, it is often said that Japanese criminal justice system is more permissive toward white-collar criminals than the United States' courts. It is certain that there are as many indictments of white-collar criminals in Japan. For example, the Japanese criminal justice system's approach to the "Jusen" Housing Loan Company debacle was more passive than that of U.S. courts dealing with the S&L crisis.

One of the significant features of Japan's criminal justice system is a high conviction rate. For example, in 2003, the conviction rate of the first trial at all district courts in all parts of the country was 99.9 percent.[43] Prosecutors have made use of the wide power of indictment. Foreseeing the likely outcome at trial, they can drop prosecutions or change charges in cases that risk acquittal. This has been called "precise justice."[44] Japanese precise justice has developed over about 60 years, as prosecutors reflected on abuse of power and trampling of human rights under the pretext of maintaining public order during World War II. Moreover, the Japanese criminal justice system doesn't have "leniency programs" and plea-bargaining which the American criminal Justice system uses effectively to fight white-collar crime. In white-collar crime cases, Japanese prosecutors are necessarily required to demonstrate a careful handling of indictments, because the mechanism of such crimes is often very complex and the investigation difficult.

But this neither directly connects a permissiveness of the Japanese criminal justice system with white-collar crime nor indicates that the Japanese criminal justice system is ignorant of the seriousness of such crimes. In the JDA scandal, the Japanese criminal system was more aggressive than that of the United States in the Department of Defense scandal. The U.S. government attempted to tighten self-regulation of the contractors through the introduction of compliance programs.[45] On the other hand, in the JDA scandal, 14 people were indicted and found guilty at the district court. Therefore, it is a mistake to believe that the Japanese criminal system is always permissive in white-collar crime cases.

Corporate Criminal Liability

There are essential and systematic limits in the Japanese criminal law in regard to white-collar crime. One of them concerns corporate criminal liability. In the

United States, a corporation is liable for the actions of its agent, regardless of the agent's position within the corporation. Federal courts have used a three-pronged inquiry to determine whether a corporation will be held vicariously liable for the acts of its employee. First, the agent must be acting within the scope and nature of his or her employment. Second, the agent must be acting, at least in part, to benefit the corporation. Third, the act and intent must be imputed to the corporation. As a general rule, a corporation can be liable for all kinds of crime including manslaughter.

On the other hand, a corporation in Japan is criminally liable only under specific circumstances, such as when the officer, employee, or agent of the corporation violates the law for the corporation in relation to its business. Today, this provision, called "ryobatsu-kitei"—meaning the punishing of both an individual violator and a corporation—is specified in more than 500 acts, such as the Antitrust law, Securities Exchange law, and Environmental Protection law. However, many kinds of crimes are not specifically included, such as murder, manslaughter, negligent homicide, bribery, libel, arson, and theft. As a result, as the MMC case shows, companies are immune from prosecution for actions that—if done by individuals—would be criminally prosecuted.[46] In addition, more than 60 percent of the "ryobatsu-kitei" call for corporate fines of less than ¥1 million yen (about $ 9,259). Present fine rates are insufficient to deter big corporations from committing crimes. As pressure on corporations to introduce compliance programs becomes more important, the Japanese criminal justice system will have an incentive to take note of the American approach.[47]

Grand Design of Strategy for Fighting White-Collar Crime

It is often said that corporations are afraid of punitive damages more than criminal sanctions. The U.S. Ford Pinto case provides an example. Ford executives realized that a criminal conviction would be powerful evidence of culpability in any subsequent civil suits. With the potential costs of a prosecution running high, they strenuously tried to avoid conviction.[48] Civil penalties play an important role too. The regulatory agencies imposed severe civil penalties on S&Ls and defense contractors. Though U.S. criminal sanctions are stricter than those of Japan they are merely one type of measure to fight white-collar crime.

Japan does not allow punitive or treble damages. Generally speaking, damages for corporate defendants in civil suit are low. Corporations have been able to consider these as necessary expenses. As a result, we can't expect too much of civil penalties. Fighting white-collar crime will require a grand design of strategy to reinforce not only criminal sanctions but also civil penalties and damages.

However, there have been recent arguments to the contrary. The Japan Business Federation of "Nippon Keidanren," whose membership (as of May 27, 2004), of 1,623 included 1,306 companies, including 91 of foreign ownership, 129 industrial associations, and 47 regional employers' associations, claims that violations of corporate control laws such as the Antitrust Law or Security Exchange Law should not be criminal matters. Rather, in their view, sanctions for these violations should be restricted to civil penalties. This would mean that Japanese people would lose an important approach to fighting corporate misconduct. Laying down our arms of criminal sanctions to fight white-collar crimes would be an irreparable error.

Conclusion

In this article, we have surveyed three white-collar crime cases in Japan and compared them with those in the United States These cases indicate that white-collar crime is serious in Japan and that the Japanese criminal justice system is not sufficiently prepared to deal with it. While the United States has updated its approach to fighting corporate crime, especially since the 1980s, Japan has remained stuck in the past. White-collar crime has brought about great financial burdens and social costs. To fight white-collar crime, Japan's criminal justice system should be reformed as soon as possible.

Endnotes

1. Calavita et al. (1997: 1).
2. Hagan (2002: 339).
3. Pontell et al. (2001: 322).
4. Pontell and Calavita (1992: 195).
5. Siegel (2000: 396).
6. Calavita et al. (1997: 46–85); McGregor (2005: 712–716).
7. Calavita et al. (1997: 23–24); Siegel (2000: 397); McGregor (2005: 713).
8. Calavita et al. (1997: 58).
9. Pontell and Calavita (1992: 202).
10. Calavita et al. (1997: 27); Purdy (2005: 476).
11. Pontell et al. (2001: 328).
12. Calavita et al. (1997: 66).
13. Calavita et al. (1997: 108–109).
14. Calavita et al. (1997: 156–157).
15. Johnston (1990: A1); Pontell and Calavita (1992: 195).
16. See e.g., Sapsford (1995: A10), Bremmer et al. (1997: 119); Chandler (1997: A1), Zitner (1997: A1); Felson (1997: 568); Pontell et al. (2001: 322).
17. Milhaupt and Miller (1997: 25).
18. Miyazaki (1992: 103–247).
19. Japanese Commercial Code (Sec. 486.I).
20. Felson (1997: 573–77).
21. Clinard (1990: 69–90); Friedrichs (2004: 74).
22. Sims and Spencer (1995: 14–15).
23. Morganthau et al. (1986: 22).
24. Groskaufmanis (1997: 5.02[1]).
25. Perry and Dankin (1994: 18–6).
26. Simon (2002: 164–167).
27. The Establishment of Japan Defense Agency Law of 1954 (1954: sec. 4–1).
28. Handa (1998: 107–108); Saizen (1998: 26–28); Maeda and Handa (1999a: 175–178); Maeda and Handa (1999b: 204–206).
29. Dowie (1977: 20–21).
30. Kramer (1982: 83).
31. Stuart (1978: 22).
32. Malloy (1990: 148–154).
33. Thio (1998: 425).
34. Simon and Hagan (1999: 40).
35. Simon (2005: 327).
36. Cullen et al. (1984: 117).
37. Strobel (1980: 55–56); Cullen et al. (1984: 117–118).

38. Friendly et al. (1980: 74); Cullen et al. (1984: 123); Frank and Lynch (1992: 41).
39. Friendly et al. (1980: 74).
40. Kawasaki (2004: 324–345).
41. Kramer (1982: 77).
42. Kobayashi (2005: 84–86).
43. Research & Training Institute, Ministry of Justice (2004: 123).
44. Matsuo (1994: 1271–1276); Segawa (1998: 9); Mitsui (2003: 22); Johnson (2002: 264–275).
45. Kawasaki (2004: 233).
46. Kawasaki (2004: 322).
47. Kawasaki (2005: 2426–2427).
48. Cullen et al. (1984: 115–116).

References

Baker, John S. Jr. (2004) "Reforming Corporations through Threats of Federal Prosecution." *Cornel L. Rev.* 89:310–355.

Bremner, Brian et al. (1997) "Rescuing Asia." *Business Week* 116–119 (17 Nov).

Calavita, Kitty et al. (1997) *Big Money Crime: Fraud and Politics in the Savings and Loan Crisis.* Berkeley: University of California Press.

Chandler, Clay (1997) "Japanese Feel Markets' Tremors." *Washington Post* A1 (24 Dec).

Clinard, Marshall B. (1990) *Corporate Corruption: The Abuse of Power.* New York: Praeger.

Coleman, James William (1998) *The Criminal Elite: Understanding White-Collar Crime,* 4th ed. New York: St. Martin's Press.

Cullen, Francis et al. (1984) "The Ford Pinto Case and Beyond: Corporations as Criminals: Crime, Moral Boundaries, and the Criminal Sanction." In *Corporations as Criminals*, Editor Eilen Hochstedler. Beverly Hills, CA. Sage.

Cullen, Francis T. et al. (1987) *Corporate Crime under Attack: Ford Pinto Case and Beyond.* Cincinnati: Anderson.

Dowie, Mark (1977) "Pinto Madness." *Mother Johns* 18–32 (Sept–Oct).

Felson, Howard M. (1997) "Closing the Book on Jusen: An Account of the Bad Loan Crisis and a New Chapter for Securitization in Japan." *Duke L. J.* 47:567–612.

Frank, Nancy K., and Michael J. Lynch (1992) *Corporate Crime, Corporate Violence: A Primer.* Albany: Harrow and Heston.

Friendly, David T. et al. (1980) "Ford's Pinto Not Guilty." *Newsweek* 74 (24 March).

Friedrichs, David O. (2004) *Trusted Criminals: White Collar Crime in Contemporary Society,* 2d ed. Belmont: Wadsworth.

Fujita, Yasuhiro (1997) "Mass Exposure of S&L Crime in the U.S. and Jusen Problem in Japan." *J. of the Japanese Institute of International Business Law* 25:339–346 [Japanese].

Geis, Gilbert (1992) "White Collar Crime: What Is It?" In *White Collar Crime Reconsidered,* Editors Kip Schlegel and David Weisburd. Boston, MA: Northeastern University Press.

Geis, Gilbert (2002) "White-Collar Crime." In *Controversies in White-Collar Crime,* Editor Gory W. Potter. Cincinnati, OH: Anderson.

Groskaufmanis, Karl A. (1997) "Corporate Compliance Programs as a Mitigating Factor." In *Corporate Sentencing Guidelines: Compliance and Mitigation,* Editors J. Rakoff et al. New York: Law Journal Seminars-Press.

Hagan, Frank E. (2002) *Introduction to Criminology: Theories, Methods, and Criminal Behavior,* 5th ed. Belmont : Wadsworth.

Handa, Shigeru (1998) "Darkness of Japan Defense Agency's Procurement Section." Foresight 9:106–109 [Japanese].

Johnson, David T. (2002) *The Japanese Way of Justice: Prosecuting Crime in Japan.* New York: Oxford Universal Press.

Johnston, Oswald (1990) "GAO Says S&L Cost Could Rise to $500 Billion." *Los Angeles Times* A1 (7 April).

Kawasaki, Tomomi (2004) *Corporate Criminal Liability*. Tokyo, Japan: Seibundo.

Kawasaki, Tomomi (2005) "New Stage of Compliance Program in the U.S." *Doshisha L. Rev.* 56:2395–2440.

Kinugawa, Megumu (2002) *Japanese Bubble.* Tokyo, Japan: Nihon Keizai Hyoron Inc. [Japanese].

Kobayashi, Hideyuki (2005) *Mitsubishi Motors Company Sat in Judgment On*. Tokyo, Japan: Nippon-Hyoron-sya [Japanese].

Kramer, Ronald C. (1982) "Corporate Crime: An Organizational Perspective." *In White-Collar and Economic Crime: Multidisciplinary and Cross-National Perspectives,* Editors Peter Wickman and Thomas Dailey. Lexington, MA: D.C. Heath.

Lee, Matthew T., and M. David Ermann (1999) "Pinto Madness: Flaws in the Generally Accepted Landmark Narrative." *Social Problems* 46:30–47.

Lofquist, William S. (1997) "A Framework for Analysis of the Theories and Issues in Corporate Crime." In *Debating Corporate Crime,* Editors W. Lofquist et al. Cincinnati, OH: Anderson.

Maeda, Tetsuo, and Handa Shigeru (1999a) "Japan Defense Agency's Procurement Section and Structural Corrupt(1)" 660 SEKAI 170–182.

Maeda, Tetsuo and Handa Shigeru (1999b) "Japan Defense Agency's Procurement Section and Structural Corrupt (2)" 660 SEKAI 661 SEKAI 196–206.

Malloy, Robin Paul (1990) *Law and Economics: A Comparative Approach to Theory and Practice*. St. Paul: West Publishing.

Matsuo, Koya (1994) "Criminal Procedure in Japan: Its History, Features and Reform." *Lawyers Association* J. 46:1–33 [Japanese].

McGregor, Michael (2005) "Savings & Loan Fraud." In *Encyclopedia of White-Collar & Corporate Crime,* Editor Lawrence M. Salinger. Thousand Oaks, CA: Sage.

Milhaupt, Curtis, and Geoffrey P. Miller (1997) "Cooperation, Conflict, and Convergence in Japanese Finance: Evidence from the "Jusen" Problem." *Law & Policy in International Business* 29:1–78.

Milhaupt, Curtis (1999) "Japan's Experience with Deposit Insurance and Failing Banks: Implications for Financial Regulatory Design." *Washington University Law Quarterly* 77:399–286.

Mitsui, Makoto (2003) *The Law of Criminal Procedure II.* Tokyo, Japan: Yuhikaku.

Miyazaki, Yoshikazu (1992) *Complicated Recession.* Tokyo, Japan: Chuo-Koron [Japanese].

Morganthau, Tom et al. (1986) "Pentagon Manifesto." *Newsweek* 22–23 (10 March).

Neumann, Caryn E. (2005) "General Dynamics." *Encyclopedia of White-Collar & Corporate Crime,* Editor Lawrence M. Salinger. Thousand Oaks, CA: Sage.

Nicholson, Tom, with William D. Marbach (1980) "A Dead Stop in the Ford Pinto Trial?" *Newsweek* 65 (25 Feb).

Nihon Keizai Shinbun Inc., ed. (2000) *The Decade of Financial Stray*. Tokyo, Japan: Nihon Keizai Shinbun Inc [Japanese].

Nikkeizai Bussiness, ed. (2000) *The Real Story of Bubble.* Tokyo, Japan: Nikkei BP Co. [Japanese].

Okumura, Hiroshi (2005) *What is Mitsubishi?* Tokyo, Japan: Ohta Books [Japanese].

Perry, William K., and Linda S. Dankin (1994) "Compliance Programs and Criminal Law." In *Compliance Programs and the Corporate Sentencing Guidelines: Preventing Criminal and Civil Liability,* Editors J. Kaplan et al. Eagan, MN: West Group.

Pontell, Henry N., and Kitty Calavita (1992) "Bilking Bankers and Bad Debts: White-Collar Crime in the Savings and Loan Crisis." In *White-Collar Crime Reconsidered,* Editors Kip Schlegel and David Weisburd. Boston, MA: Northeastern University Press.

Pontell, Henry N., and Kitty Calavita (1993) "White-Collar Crime in the Savings and Loan Scandal." *ANNALS, AAPSS* 525:31–45.

Pontell, Henry N. et al. (2001) "The Role of Fraud in the Japanese Financial Crisis: A Comparative Study." In *Contemporary Issues in Crime and Criminal Justice: Essays in Honor of Gilbert Geis,* Editors Henry Pontell and David Shichor. Upper Saddle River, NJ: Prentice Hall.

Poveda, Tony G. (1994) *Rethinking White-Collar Crime*. Westport: Praeger.

Research & Training Institute Ministry of Justice (2004) *The White Paper on Crime 2003*. Tokyo, Japan: The National Printing Bureau [Japanese].

Purdy, Elizabeth (2005) "Keating, Charles (1924–)." *Encyclopedia of White-Collar & Corporate Crime,* Editor Lawrence M. Salinger. Thousand Oaks, CA: Sage.

Rosoff, Stephen M. et al. (2004) *Profit without Honor: White-Collar Crime and the Looting of America.* Upper Saddle River: NJ, Pearson Prentice Hall.

Saizen, Teruo (1998) "The Way of Exterminating Amakudari-System." *AERA* 11.9:26–28 [Japanese].

Sankei Newspaper Reporter's Team (2001) *Why Did the Brands Fall Down?* Tokyo, Japan: Kadokawa Publications [Japanese].

Sapsford, Jathon (1995) "Japanese Banks' Bad Loans Constitute Bigger Burden Than U.S. S&L Debacle." *Wall Street J.* A10 (7 June).

Segawa, Akira (1997) "50 Years of Criminal Policy after Establishing the Constitution of Japan." *Crime & Punishment* 35:5–13 [Japanese].

Siegel, Larry J. (2000) *Criminology,* 7th ed. Belmont: Wadworth/Thomson Learning.

Simon, David R. (2002) *Elite Deviance,* 7th ed. Boston: Allyn & Bacon.

Simon, David R. (2005) "Ford Pinto." In *Encyclopedia of White-Collar & Corporate Crime,* Editor Lawrence M. Salinger. Thousand Oaks, CA: Sage.

Simon, David R., and Frank E. Hagan (1999) *White Collar Deviance*. Needham Heights: MA, Allyn & Bacon.

Sims, Ronald R., and Margaret P. Spencer (1995) "Understanding Corporate Misconduct: An Overview and Discussion." In *Corporate Misconduct: The Legal, Societal, and Management Issues,* Editors M. Spencer and R. Sims. Westport, CT: Quorum Books.

Strobel, Lee Patrick (1980) *Reckless Homicide?* South Bend: IW, And Brooks.

Stuart, Reginald (1978) "U.S. Agency Suggests Ford Pintos Have a Fuel System Defect." *The New York Times* 22 (9 May).

Thio, Alex (1998) *Deviant Behavior,* 3d ed. New York: Harper & Row.

Zitner, Aaron (1997) "S&L Crisis in Japan May Take Wide Toll." *Boston Globe* A1 (24 Dec).

Cases Cited

United States

Grimshaw v. Ford Motor Co., 119 Cal. App. 3d 757, 174 Cal. Rptr. 348.

State v. Ford Motor Co., No. 5324 (Indiana Super. Ct., filed Sept. 13, 1978).

Japan

Tokyo District Court, Hanrei Jiho No. 1770, 3 (Oct. 22, 2001) [Japanese].

Tokyo District Court, LEX.DB No.28085708 (May 8, 2003) [Japanese].

Tokyo District Court, Hanrei Joho No. 1698, 53; Hanrei Times No. 1021, 292 (Oct. 12, 1999) [Japanese].

Part X

Policing White-Collar Crime

1

Policing Healthcare at the Dawn of the New Millennium

Paul Jesilow

The present problem of policing healthcare was delineated three-quarters of the way through the 20th century. On the one hand, were the billions of dollars of healthcare needs of a burgeoning population that was supplied by an extensive array of providers. On the other hand, were a small group of individuals mandated to insure that monies were spent on legitimate healthcare expenses. A form of "tightrope enforcement" was practiced by the control agents in response to this situation; they had to show wrongdoing without offending the healthcare industry as a whole, or at least too many of its members.[1] At the time, the problem manifested itself as a conflict between government agents and physicians. Henry Pontell and his colleagues commented on the matter with respect to California's Medicaid program for the indigent:

> Government control units need the cooperation of medical societies to inform physicians about program policies and guidelines and to help insure that regulations are taken seriously. Officials believe that if they "go too far" in regulating physicians in the program, they are likely to forfeit the support of medical societies, and that this would result in a lowered rate of participation by physicians in the Medi-Cal program. This in turn would further restrict the sources of healthcare for the population served by Medi-Cal. It could also raise costs, since patients would likely go for care to more expensive facilities, such as the emergency department of hospitals, if a Medi-Cal physician was not available.

Control agents, as a response to the dilemma, only pursued cases that involved blatant wrongdoing, and where evidence was unequivocal.[2]

Tightrope enforcement continues to be practiced by control agents in the new millennium. The visible conflict, however, has gone beyond physicians and control agents and now involves growing segments of the population and a panoply of actors. In this chapter, I highlight some of the areas of healthcare policing, discuss some of the interested actors and their conflicts, and demonstrate how these matters create the targets of healthcare investigations. Specific areas covered include legal torts and medical licensing, government regulation of Medicare and Medicaid, and the efforts of criminal enforcement agents.

Torts and Medical Licensing

The new millennium was greeted by many states passing tort reforms in response to rising liability insurance costs for physicians and other healthcare providers.[3] Proponents of tort reform claim that plaintiffs' attorneys bring too many inappropriate cases and charge excessive fees in liability cases, thereby contributing to the increase in healthcare costs. Most state legislatures have enacted changes in tort law that limit healthcare providers' liability and make it more difficult for potential plaintiffs to bring suits. The legal modifications are favored by physicians, hospitals, and other healthcare organizations, who have had their incomes reduced by rising malpractice costs. Insurance companies have been a less visible but active participant in the tort reform debate. Legal limits on malpractice cases benefit insurance companies by limiting their liabilities.

Plaintiffs' lawyers and some consumer groups find fault with tort reforms. The problem, they posit, is with those individuals and groups who are proposing the legal modifications. They contend that there is too much malpractice by healthcare providers and that is the reason for malpractice suits. They point to numerous public health studies to support their position. For example, a well-publicized report by a component of the National Academy of Sciences concluded that each year somewhere between 44,000 and 98,000 Americans die due to preventable medical errors.[4] They note that only a small portion of malpractice cases actually result in civil suits. The evidence, they contend, contradicts the tale of increasing medical liability suits and resultant jury awards.[5] Bernard Black and his colleagues, for example, studied data for Texas and concluded that—

> Controlling for population growth, the number of large paid claims . . . was roughly constant from 1991–2002 . . . [and] the number of small paid claims declined sharply. Payout per claim on large claims was constant over 1988–2002, while jury awards were constant or even declined.[6]

Opponents of tort reforms posit that the legal modifications are unlikely to much alter malpractice premiums, which research has shown to be more tied to insurance practices and economic cycles,[7] although caps on physician liability probably have played some role in holding down malpractice premiums in some states.[8]

Lost, for the most part, in the current debate about malpractice tort reform is the original intent of the legal doctrine. Awards in malpractice cases were meant to compensate victims and to deter healthcare providers from negligent behavior.[9] Historically, torts were established as a means to compensate plaintiffs adequately as a matter of fairness, but also so that they did not become burdens on others or the state. Compensation of successful plaintiffs allocated "the costs of an activity to those who benefit from it."[10] Malpractice insurance, in this regard, can be viewed as serving the interests of torts, in that it spreads the cost of liability among specific groups of physicians. Obstetricians and hospitals that have maternity wards, for example, have high malpractice insurance.

The other pillar of malpractice litigation is the prevention of negligent care by providers.[11] Oliver Wendell Holmes is usually credited with isolating negligence as a tort doctrine late in the 19th century.[12] Holmes' theory of tort liability fingered defendants as culpable if they failed to take the same precautions that a reasonable individual in their position should take to avoid foreseeable harms.[13] Important for the applicability of Holmes' ideas to healthcare providers is his "free will" perspective that individuals choose to perform procedures that can result in legal liability. They can also choose to eschew such actions.[14] The threat of liability, the theory goes, acts as a general deterrent in that physicians will avoid risky procedures in order to prevent future financial obligations. In addition, physicians may be encouraged to take precautions during procedures to avoid potentially costly accidents.[15]

Malpractice suits are necessary to establish proper parameters of care. Findings of culpability warn practitioners what is expected of them—that is, the steps a reasonable physician should take to avoid harm. Without a system of malpractice jury awards, the government would need to create a bureaucracy to establish proper parameters of care. Sweden, for example, relies on a system that "provides compensation without proof of provider fault."[16] A National Board of Health and Welfare (*Socialstyrelsen*) is entrusted with the task of establishing and propagating guidelines. The Board relies on reports from hospitals to indicate where problems exist. Some of the hospitals, however, never report errors, although Swedish healthcare policy experts believe they must have some.[17]

Insurance may undermine the deterrent, or preventive, effects of tort litigation. Adventurous physicians, who have malpractice insurance, may engage in risky procedures because they know that their liability for errors will likely be covered by their insurance companies. They gain a financial advantage by performing expensive procedures that others will not. But they pay no more for their insurance than their more wary colleagues. There is also the concern that other physicians, who might not perform hazardous procedures, may take less caution in their everyday practices or ignore literature that suggests better ways of doing things because they do not fear extensive liability. These beliefs are somewhat balanced by the fact that insurance does not always cover the entire amount of an award for negligence. Cognizant physicians may avoid procedures that might result in extraordinary awards that exceed the limits of their coverage. Physicians may also exercise some caution in order to avoid increased insurance premiums that would likely result from successful malpractice suits financial.

Tort reforms, the purpose of which are to protect medical doctors from punishment, may make matters worse by leaving the door open for more abusers. Findings of malpractice, as well as actions taken against practitioners by insurers, hospitals, professional societies, and state medical and dental boards, must be passed along to the National Practitioner Data Bank (NPDB), which then makes the information available to licensing boards, hospital appointment committees, and other professional groups.[18] State boards and medical societies often take adverse malpractice findings as triggering events for sanction hearings Researchers have concluded that claims history is a reasonable screening tool for this purpose.[19]

Efforts aimed at decreasing the number of civil suits might well be expected to impact physician sanctioning. Claudia Lavenant and her colleagues, for example, examined the relationship between changes in tort rules and the sanctioning of physicians by state medical boards between 1985 and 1994. They compared sanctioning rates for doctors in states that had passed specific tort reforms with the rates in states that had not made the same legislative changes. The results suggest that the addition of pre-trial screening panels and the regulation of attorney fees may have undermined improvements in healthcare by decreasing the likelihood that errant physicians would be detected by their states' licensing boards. Both tort reforms were associated with lower levels of licensing boards actions. Alternatively, their findings suggest that alterations to the joint liability rule may have enhanced the state's goal of improved healthcare. The tort reform was associated with higher rates of negligent physicians being placed on probation or having their licenses revoked or suspended. Alterations to the legal principle change the potential for monetary remuneration. Individuals and organizations, under the joint liability rule, could be held responsible for the entire extent of damages. The reform of this tort results in defendants being responsible only for the portion of damages they caused. As a result, attorneys may press cases against physicians that, prior to reform, would have resulted in settlements with hospitals. The ensuing findings of malpractice are passed along to medical boards and the National Practitioner Data Bank, which then make the information available to all licensing boards. Increased physician sanctioning is an expected outcome.[20]

The tort reforms that are being passed at the beginning of the 21st century are likely to further reduce the sanctioning of healthcare providers by state licensing boards. There is the suggestion from the corporate world that legal reforms may increase unsafe behavior by unscrupulous physicians, and, in the long run, increase the number of malpractice suits. A 1995 federal law that restricted class-action lawsuits against corporations, the argument goes, may have led to less concern among corporate executives and widespread defrauding of investors. The resulting crash at Enron, Worldcom, and HealthSouth led to increased numbers of civil suits by defrauded investors.[21] In the world of healthcare, the suggestion is that providers will move into riskier procedures where the potential profits are greater. An expected outcome might be a greater number of suits involving serious injury or death. Indeed, recent research has indicated that outcome. Neil Vidmar and his colleagues found a statistically significant rise in the percentage of Florida malpractice awards that involved serious injury or death. They hypothesized that one explanation for the increase was that it reflected actual hikes in the number of serious injuries and deaths resulting from medical malpractice.[22] Researchers might compare, by state, the percentage of malpractice awards each year that involved serious injury or death to determine if previous tort reforms might be associated with these changes. The irony is that the tort reforms, meant to limit awards and lower malpractice fees, may actually increase them as the result of higher awards for more serious injuries.

Government Regulation of Medicare and Medicaid

In this section, I identify crucial issues related to government regulation of Medicaid and Medicare. Medicaid is a predominantly state-funded program administered largely for the benefit of the needy. Medicare, in contrast, is federally funded and designed for the elderly. The inauguration of these programs in 1966 created new kinds of medical malefactors. There would be no gain, for instance, in performing extensive diagnostic tests on a poor person unable to pay for them; but if an insurer will meet the charges, there is a great deal to be garnered by doing such work, needed or not, and by doing it as cheaply as possible.

The stature of the medical profession and the trust the nation had in its doctors led to few safeguards that relied upon the existing insurance structure to accomplish many tasks. There was little warning from the private insurance companies that fraud would be a significant matter and sponsors of the legislation were wary of provoking new waves of antagonism from the medical establishment. Congress feared a wholesale unwillingness by disgruntled physicians to participate in the voluntary programs. In addition, the government ignored fraud issues at the inception of the benefit programs because it needed to establish public confidence in the new efforts.[23]

The present healthcare system and its enforcement apparatus grew in a haphazard manner, expanding as the extent and cost of the fraudulent behavior became known.[24] Debate among the healthcare industry, government enforcement agents, congressional leaders, and others helped defined the extent of the problem and acceptable cures. In the early days of the programs, the problem had been perceived as the result of a few rotten apples in an otherwise pristine barrel. The view suggested minimal losses due to fraud, that could be controlled by a limited response.[25]

At first, some providers stumbled upon the possibility of stealing from the programs. One physician, for example, tired of waiting for Medicaid payment, worried that the government might have lost his bills. He sent in duplicates and, in time, was paid twice. When such stories spread in the medical community, some doctors were convinced that "nobody was minding the store." For other physicians, the opportunity to provide medical care without concern about the cost proved attractive bait for illegal behaviors. Under lax scrutiny, these physicians had only to convince themselves that certain services would benefit their patients, a conclusion made more appealing when the services also benefited the physicians' pocketbooks.

Within a decade of the inauguration of the programs, the government was paying for patients who were never seen, X-rays done without film, blood and urine specimens that were never analyzed, and treatments much different—and more expensive—from those actually carried out. Oftentimes the behaviors seem outlandish. Ambulance services, for example, requested payments for round-trip transportation for patients who died en route to hospitals.[26] One doctor pled guilty to cheating Medicaid of $2.6 million; he was buying huge quantities of human blood drawn from drug addicts and other ill or poor people and then running unordered and unnecessary tests on the blood. He had purchased the blood for about $10 a vial and each pint yielded as much as $2,000 in billing for tests.[27] In a 1980s fraud, mobile laboratories attracted individuals for free tests and then billed the patients' insurers for costly procedures. A General Accounting Office (GAO) report estimated that one billion dollars was fraudulently obtained in this single case.[28] These experiences of enforcement agents suggested a much larger and costlier problem, which required substantial remedies.

Early patterns of fraud and abuse in healthcare that surfaced were strongly connected to the fee-for-service nature of most third-party payment programs. Physicians and other providers under this payment mechanism are compensated for each service or product they supply, which gives them a fiscal incentive to bill for as much as possible. The fee-for-service payment system was blamed for the rapid rise in costs for healthcare. Fraud was still considered to be only a small portion of the total bill. Abuse, from most people's perspective, was much more common. Expensive, and perhaps unnecessary, procedures were being performed because there was money to be made from doing so. Illustrative was the experience of former President Jimmy Carter, who had served on the Sumter County Hospital Authority in Georgia before he went into electoral politics. At the beginning of his term as president, he regretted the local policies he had once supported:

> I have seen in retrospect, from a little different perspective, that we were naturally inclined to buy a new machine whenever it became available and then to mandate, to require that every patient who came into the hospital had to submit to a blood sample or some other aspect of their body to the machine for analysis, whether they needed it or not, in order to rapidly defray the cost of the purchase of the machine. I did not realize that I was ripping off people, never thought about it too much. It was a fact.[29]

In 1983 Congress passed legislation that introduced a prospective payment system (PPS) for hospital billings for Medicare patients in an effort to control costs. The system established more than 400 diagnostically related groups (DRGs), which were to be used to establish payment. At admission, the patient would be diagnosed and that diagnosis would be the basis for a somewhat flat payment. That is, the government reimbursed the hospital based on the diagnosis and not on the actual services delivered. The belief was that under PPS hospitals and other providers would have no incentive to provide unnecessary services and that fraud, which was commonly defined by government agents at the time as billing for services never rendered, would disappear.[30]

At first, the new payment system seemed to work well and initial research on the matter suggested a decline in hospital costs.[31] The reduction in costs fueled the belief that organizational change is the cure for fraud and abuse in government health programs. Government officials insisted that newly evolving managed-care systems, such as health maintenance organizations (HMOs), would decrease the extent of dishonesty. An important part of the belief structure that clouded their thinking about crime in healthcare was the idea that under managed care the primary mechanism for illegal behaviors, which was considered at the time to be fee-for-service, would disappear.[32] A different payment mechanism, they reasoned, would have different results. Health maintenance organizations care for an individual's healthcare needs at a fixed rate and hire salaried physicians. Under such a system, the logic held, there is little, if any, financial incentive for conducting unnecessary services.

It should not be surprising that both private and government sectors have turned to the new models to control costs. Blue Cross/Blue Shield, for example, bought into HMOs in order to lower costs. California's Medicaid system instituted a health maintenance arrangement in which contracts are negotiated with HMOs to care for all the indigents in an area. Controlling fraud is not the primary concern associated with the organizational changes. Officials are much more concerned with controlling costs. The new model supposedly guaranteed stable, if not lowered, costs since the fiscal incentive for increased treatment was no longer present.[33]

The new delivery systems have been implemented at a rapid pace, but only superficial attention is afforded to the vulnerability of the programs to widespread illegalities. Despite wishful thinking, fraud and abuse appear to be a larger and more significant problem under the newer approaches than they were in the older Medicaid and Medicare medical programs. They merely changed form.[34] This time the offenders represent corporations as medicine increasingly is being pushed from the single-practitioner model to a form more like that of the industrial and big business firm.[35] The sole practitioner is unable to provide all-inclusive healthcare for thousands of individuals. Corporations in the United States (or the government in most industrialized countries) are the only entities believed to posses that capability. Corporate wrongdoing is much more difficult to uncover. The cases usually are highly complex, particularly when compared to the earlier forms of healthcare fraud. Individuals within the industry, lawyers, and accountants who are supposed to notify the public of wrongdoing have failed at the task. Government efforts to identify illegal behavior have also missed the mark (I discuss this issue in the next section). The cases that have come to light have primarily been the result of whistleblowing, prompted by the False Claims Act.

First enacted in 1863 during the Civil War, the False Claims Act originally was used to prosecute profiteers who provided the Union Army with shoddy equipment. In its updated 1986 version, the law has been employed to reward whistleblowers in industries that do business with the government. In the past, employees who reported company violations could expect only corporate retaliation. Under the new law, however, whistleblowers can collect up to 30 percent of any court award. The whistleblower brings the original suit, but the government, if it chooses, may take over the action.[36] Whistleblower cases, referred to as *qui tam* actions, are easier for investigators and prosecutors because the company employee often knows exactly where to look for evidence of the wrongdoing. There were 17 *qui tam* actions in 1992; there were about 2000 in 1999.[37]

The whistleblowers' actions, combined with federal investigations, have revealed widespread corporate illegalities that in some ways reflect earlier frauds, but on a much larger scale. "Upcoding" is illustrative. Upcoding is billing by a provider for a more expensive procedure or product than the one actually provided. A patient, as a simple illustration, receives a generic drug, but is charged for a name brand. A similar practice by physicians has been called "upgrading."[38] Upcoding, however, is much more a corporate behavior. It is believed that the introduction of the Prospective Payment System in 1983 for the reimbursement of hospitals for treating Medicare patients galvanized substantial upcoding. Naomi Soderstrom explains how hospitals can increase profits under the system:

> Reimbursement is an increasing function of the DRG weight, so the higher the weight, the greater the revenue for the hospital. Holding the treatment for the patient fixed, if the hospital can claim a higher-weighted DRG, profit will increase. To provide an incorrect report, the hospital can misclassify patients or code a second (higher weighted) diagnosis as the principal diagnosis. (Reimbursement is for the principal diagnosis only.)[39]

There is substantial evidence that upcoding in hospitals (also known as "code creep" or "DRG creep") is common.[40]

Bruce Psaty and his colleagues calculated that U.S. hospitals may annually be reimbursed more than $900 million in excess of what they should receive for patients with a Medicare discharge diagnosis of heart failure. The researchers found that in more than one-third of the cases they reviewed there was no evidence to support the hospitals' billing claims that the cases were worthy of a higher fee.

Other well-documented situations involve "game playing" by hospitals, in which patients are moved from inpatient care to alternative settings in order to maximize Medicare payments. Medicare utilizes PPS for inpatient services, but outpatient payments are cost-based.[41] The payment a hospital receives from the government for a hip replacement, for example, includes some monies for rehabilitation. Offending corporations discharge patients as soon as they can safely leave the hospital and move rehabilitative care to more profitable outpatient settings that are also owned by the corporate behemoth. Recent investigations have also revealed widespread violations of the 72-hour rule. The mandate is often associated with pre-surgery activities, such as drawing blood and X-rays, that occur within three calendar days of admission."[42] Payment for such services are included in PPS. Violators of the rule are usually the outpatient arms of healthcare corporations. They individually bill for services that are also covered in the DRG payment the hospital receives. In both instances the corporation is effectively paid twice for the services.

Despite widespread cheating, the federal government has been hesitant to ban offending corporations from participation in Medicare. Their reluctance is the outcome of a dilemma that has faced the programs since fraud and abuse first appeared. Crooks steal from the programs, but if they are not allowed to participate, who will there be to provide the services? Originally the problem was associated with sole practitioners, who provided healthcare to underserved populations and padded their billings to make their practices lucrative. Today, the dilemma is associated with corporations. A hospital, which is owned by a corporation that has engaged in dishonest practices, for example, may be the only healthcare provider in an area. Not allowing government payments to the offending corporation might result in the community's losing the hospital. At least the corporation's attorneys will present that possibility to the government officials. The federal solution is to allow the corporation to pay a hefty fine, establish a compliance plan, and continue to provide, and be paid, for healthcare services.

In 1996, Congress enacted The Health Insurance Portability and Accountability Act (HIPAA). The law expanded the range of weapons available to enforcement agents. Foremost, it promised continued funding to fight healthcare fraud, which allowed for the establishment of programs that coordinate federal, state, and local efforts. The law also expanded the applicability of the anti-kickback statute to extend to every federal healthcare program and allowed the extension of the power of the federal government into the regulation of private healthcare. The law set up a national database of sanctioned providers in an effort to prevent violators from moving from state-to-state to resume operations. Concomitantly, it enlisted private citizens into fraud detection by creating the Beneficiary Incentive Program. Similar in some aspects to *qui tam* actions, the law provides a share of recovered monies to beneficiaries who provide information which leads to criminal or civil sanctions.

Enforcement Efforts

Law enforcement agents who fight healthcare fraud seem to have almost no limit on the number of their potential targets. No one has been able to determine the exact extent of fraud and abuse associated with Medicare and Medicaid and other third-party payment programs, but it is extensive. A representative of the Blue Cross and Blue Shield Association estimated the 2003 loss to health insurance fraud at $85 billion or 5 percent of the total healthcare expenditures.[43] The General Accounting Office, a decade ago, estimated the total tab at 3 percent to 10 percent.[44] The same year the Office of the Inspector General (OIG), for the U.S. Department of Health and Human Services (HHS), estimated Medicare overpayments for the fiscal year at $23.2 billion, or 14% of the Medicare total.[45] These numbers probably underestimate the true extent of healthcare fraud.

Fraud cases that become known are the result of a selective funneling process common to many offenses, but most pronounced with white-collar crimes.[46] Initially, the hidden nature of many white-collar misdeeds prevents victims from uncovering the offenses and entering the complaint process. The third party nature of most healthcare fraud exacerbates the situation. Patients may be the victims of unnecessary surgery, but the direct victims of the thefts are government benefit programs and insurance companies. These entities were not physically present when providers supposedly supplied services. They must rely on others to determine whether a demand for payment is accurate or fallacious. Patients, on occasion, receive notification of payments that were made to providers on their behalf. The mailed announcements, however, rarely produce reports of fraud. Beneficiaries often ignore such mailings. The money is not theirs. Moreover, they are often unable to understand the medical terminology reported in the statements. As Edwin Sutherland, a pioneer in the study of white-collar crime, noted, "These crimes are not as obvious as assault and battery, and can be appreciated readily only by persons who are expert in the occupations in which they occur."[47]

Patients, who suspect the honesty and integrity of their healthcare providers, may be unaware as to where to report their suspicions. A call to the police is sufficient for most street crimes, but an array of agencies exist to handle the offenses of healthcare providers. The majority of individuals probably are not cognizant of such bodies, and if they are they possess at best only sketchy knowledge of the agencies' duties. Finally, suspicious patients may assume that if they report their misgivings, the authorities may not, or cannot, respond to their complaints. Only half of the respondents to a survey conducted by the American Association of Retired Persons believed that the government or insurance company would do anything if they registered a complaint about suspicious behavior.[48]

Under the current system, law enforcement agents rely on referrals from the intermediaries. Their detection work, therefore, becomes vital for identifying enforcement targets. Intermediaries hold federal and state contracts to pay healthcare providers for services rendered to benefit program participants. The intermediaries are expected to review the bills, but the compensation they receive covers the costs of processing and paying the bills. No money is specifically earmarked or reimbursed for uncovering fraud or abuse. Lacking any budget or fiscal incentive to scrutinize the requests for payment, the intermediaries limit their efforts to determining that the proper forms have been completed correctly. The result is that the computer screens primarily identify errors, and almost never point to frauds. Malcolm Sparrow, a health fraud expert, commented that such screens would not catch:

> The bulk of "false claims," nor claims involving falsified diagnoses, nor fabricated medical episodes, nor claims involving illegal kickbacks, nor computer generated fictitious billings.... In fact, it would not have caught most of the major types of fraud schemes that we see proliferating within the industry.[49]

The hidden nature of healthcare fraud affects who becomes the target of enforcement efforts. Enforcement agencies' limited budgets play a significant role in restricting the detection and sanctioning of frauds. In the words of a high-ranking Medicare enforcement official: "To go after these guys we need an army and all we've got is a battalion, if that." Investigators almost universally feel that if they had more time and resources to devote to seeking out medical crime, it would readily be found, and in huge amounts. Recently, an agent compared the situation to a cesspool. "Have you ever had the memorable experience of opening a cesspool? You know that a lot of bad stuff rises to the top and is easy to find. The rest of the water is polluted but the stuff is not obvious."[50]

Long Life Healthcare is illustrative of the type of cases that easily catch enforcement agents' attention. Law enforcement became interested in the activities of the owner of Long Life Healthcare after her former lover, a physician, was murdered and robbed of the laptop computer he was carrying at the time. Left untouched on the body, however, was more than $1,500 in cash. The murder investigation revealed that the doctor had been involved in Medicaid fraud with the owner, but the romance had soured. He had threatened to go to the authorities with evidence of the widespread criminal activity. Long Life Healthcare was supposedly a nonprofit home health-care agency, but the murdered doctor and the owner had been able to steal large sums of money from Medicaid by diverting into their own pockets some of the more than $35 million a year the company received from the government. The doctor, who was also a lawyer, had established shell corporations, which were used to hide the illegal payments. The company had also received Medicaid payments for numerous illegal activities, including payments to phantom employees.[51] The owner of the business and her son were convicted of the doctor's murder and Medicaid fraud.[52] But it was the threat of the doctor going to the authorities and his resultant murder that led to the Medicaid fraud conviction. Otherwise, the government might have indefinitely continued the illegal payments.

The Long Life Healthcare case illustrates that illegal billings can be hidden in a high-volume organization. Large-scale businesses not only provide dishonest individuals with camouflage for larceny but also allow them to place barriers between themselves and proof of their criminal culpability. Proving guilt beyond a reasonable doubt under such circumstances is, at best, difficult. Recently, for example, the founder and former chief executive officer of HealthSouth was found innocent of wrongdoing by a jury, this after15 former high-ranking corporate executives–including some of the CEO's closest and longest-serving aides–had already pled guilty.[53] The acquittal illustrates that the long-held advantages of white-collar defendants still are in place. A century ago, Edward Alsworth Ross noted the difficulties of convicting leading citizens of communities.[54] Community affiliations and activism, then and now, serve to defray criminal intent.[55]

Matters are unlikely to get easier for enforcement agents. The move toward electronic records, desired by policymakers to ease record-keeping problems, is increasingly removing the paper trail so necessary for enforcement agents.

At the same time, enforcement units have had their budgets reduced, while other investigators have been moved to other projects. The FBI, for example, following the September 11 attacks, improperly moved resources, earmarked by Congress for investigating health-care fraud, to anti-terrorism activities.[56] It is difficult to get criminal investigators and prosecutors interested in healthcare fraud when there are much more exciting and easier targets to be had. The words of the head of a Medicaid enforcement unit are as true today as they were in the past:

> To do a white-collar crime takes a lot of teamwork. Your grand juries have to be available, your subpoenas have to be timely. . . . These things are very, very important. They can't be piecemeal. You cannot go out and conduct a good white-collar crime investigation by just utilizing the services of the so-called "good investigator and auditor." It won't work because someplace along the line, you're going to be stiffed. Then you have to go to a district attorney or a federal prosecutor who really is not trained, nor does he have the patience to do a white-collar crime investigation. White-collar crime calls for a lot of patience, and most of the young attorneys want to go into the court with John Dillinger by the nape of the neck, and it just doesn't work that way.[57]

The multimillion dollar fraud cases that have been successfully handled by enforcement agents are primarily the result of whistleblower suits. State investigators are in no better shape today to handle such cases than they were a decade ago. As a result, the targets of their actions remain the weak and unsophisticated. Rather than uncovering and prosecuting the misdeeds of criminal corporations, they go after individual providers, such as home attendants, who foolishly bill for more hours than they could have been at work. Such individuals prove easy convictions for otherwise outgunned control units.

Conclusion and Discussion

Tightrope enforcement continues to shape enforcement responses to healthcare fraud. The actors involved in the debate, however, have expanded beyond physicians and government agents. Conflict between medical personnel, insurance companies, and lawyers, for example, has resulted in tort reforms that have lessened the likelihood that private citizens, by bringing civil suits, will be able to assist state medical licensing boards to spot errant doctors. Faced with less oversight, some doctors may be emboldened to practice medicine more for profit than for the health of their patients.

Medicine has become dominated by corporations, who are more formidable legal opponents than sole practitioners and have affected tightrope enforcement. Private citizens, through whistleblower suits, have assumed a major role in the uncovering of corporate fraud. Corporations, however, cannot be jailed, and the corporate death sentence—banning them from Medicare and Medicaid participation—would undermine the healthcare of the patients they serve. The federal solution is to allow corporations to pay substantial fines and establish compliance plans. Still, for corporations, legal fees and fines are often merely the cost of doing business. There is no reasonable way to assure that corporations will not once again venture into what corporate officials may define as "gray areas" in order to increase profits.

Enforcement agents continue to have difficulty identifying the human perpetrators of complex illegal schemes. Obtaining criminal convictions against white-collar individuals involved in healthcare fraud remains a formidable challenge for prosecutors, despite changes in the law. Enforcement units seek criminal convictions against relatively weak opponents as the solution to their dilemma.

Despite numerous efforts to control fraud, the impact of illegal behavior in healthcare is likely growing and becoming more expensive. For one thing, the cost of healthcare continues to rise as the market for healthcare products expands. The Medicare Modernization Act of 2003, for example, guaranteed that additional billions of dollars will be spent on pharmaceuticals. The law created a discount drug card that will operate until 2006. That year a voluntary outpatient prescription drug benefit will be available to Medicare beneficiaries. In addition, employers who provide retirees with drug coverage will be eligible for a federal subsidy and Medicare beneficiaries whose incomes fall below 150% of the federal poverty level will also be eligible for federal subsidies.[58]

The Centers for Medicare and Medicaid Services (formerly Healthcare Financing Administration) predicts that healthcare costs will account for 17 percent of the gross national product in the year 2011.[59] The additional funds will be increasingly attractive to unscrupulous individuals and the size of the industry will allow them to expand and hide illicit activities. There is already plenty of evidence that this is occurring.[60]

Direct losses due to healthcare fraud are only part of the problem and underestimate the true cost of fraud. For one, fraud has undermined the validity of studies on healthcare practices, financing, and organization. In the past, such frauds were often associated with corporate efforts to obtain government approval for a new healthcare device, drug, or procedure. Physicians, for example, have submitted fraudulent data as part of clinical trials, at times with the tacit approval of corporate personnel. Corporations have withheld damaging information that come to light during drug and device testing, or lied to the government about the procedures that were being used or the results that were obtained. Pharmaceutical corporations have also withheld from the FDA damaging data about products that have already been released, and they have used misleading data in the marketing of their products.[61]

The problem of poor policy decisions caused by fraudulent data is likely to get worse.[62] Healthcare studies, for example, increasingly rely on Medicare and other expanded data sets. These studies are of critical importance for public policy and for the development of strategies to contain escalating healthcare costs, but they often use data that have been corrupted by fraud and abuse. Mistaken conclusions as to the effectiveness of policy and procedures are likely being reached in studies that have used such data. Early studies of the effects of the introduction of PPS, for example, signaled that the change in billing had lowered Medicare costs.[63] But later studies indicated that there were no savings, once the costs of the illegal billings were considered.[64] Failure to consider the effects of illegal activities on expanded data sets will likely result in other erroneous policy decisions.

Fraud in healthcare is also increasing the cost of healthcare by increasing the number of uninsured. States are dramatically diminishing their Medicaid coverage as the result of skyrocketing costs, which have been fueled by fraud. Without the government funded insurance, many individuals postpone seeking services until minor problems become major, and much more expensive. And when they finally do seek medical help, they go to emergency rooms, which only furthers the unnecessary expense of their illnesses.

At some point, it seems likely that taxpayers will put a halt to continuing to foot the bill. Radical changes in healthcare delivery are very probable. The most likely, given the pattern of the rest of the industrialized world, is a shift to some form of universal healthcare. Hopefully the next time around policymakers will build fraud prevention into the program.

Endnotes

1. Jesilow et al. (1993).
2. Pontell et al. (1982).
3. AMA News Release (October 6, 2003).
4. Institute of Medicine (2000).
5. Black et al. (2005); Cohen (2001); Vidmar et al. (2005).
6. Black et al. (2005: 2).
7. Black et al. (2005); Thorpe (2004); Treaster and Brinkley (2005); Zuckerman et al. (1990).
8. Thorpe (2004); Zuckerman et al. (1990).
9. Cane (1982); Holmes (c2005/1881); Kinney (1996); Schwartz and Komesar (1978); Thorpe (2004).
10. Cane (1982: 49).
11. Schwartz and Komesar (1978).
12. Rosenberg (1995); White (1977).
13. Holmes (1873).
14. Holmes (c2005/1881).
15. Cane (1982).
16. Danzon (1994).
17. Personal interviews with members of Sweden's National Board.
18. Harmon (1990).
19. Bovbjerg and Petronis (1994).
20. Lavenant et al. (2002).
21. Granelli (June 3, 2005).
22. Vidmar et al. (2005).
23. Jesilow et al. (1993).
24. Gardiner and Lyman (1984).
25. Jesilow et al. (1985).
26. Jesilow et al. (1993).
27. Jesilow et al. (1995).
28. General Accounting Office (1992).
29. McCormack (April 25, 1979).
30. Jesilow (2005).
31. Guterman and Dobson (1986); Prospective Payment Assessment Commission (1992).
32. Richardson (1994).
33. Jesilow et al. (1995).
34. Jesilow et al. (1995).
35. Starr (1982).
36. Moses (2003).
37. Cone et al. (2003).
38. Jesilow et al. (1993).

39. Soderstrom (1990).
40. Brown (1994); Brown (1999); Report to Congressional Committees (March 2001); Harrington (2003); Psaty et al. (1999); Traska (1990); U.S. Department of Health and Human Services and U.S. Department of Justice (2002); United States Files Suit Against Tenet Healthcare Alleging False Claims Billing to Medicare (January 9, 2003).
41. Eldenburg and Kallapur (1997); Eldenburg and Kallapur (2000).
42. Mitchell et al. (2003).
43. Maltin (July 14, 2004: D1).
44. General Accounting Office (May, 1966: GAO/GGD-96-101).
45. Department of Justice (August 5, 1999).
46. Geis (1975); Sutherland (1945).
47. Sutherland (1945: 138).
48. Sparrow (2000).
49. Sparrow (2000: xiv).
50. Personal interview.
51. Jet Magazine (November 17, 1997); Discovery Health Channel (9 am June 26, 2005).
52. "Two Family Members Convicted." http://ny.yahoo.com/external/rnn/storyid/19980731011.html.
53. The Washington Post (July 3, 2005: F2); *The Deseret News* (July 4, 2005).
54. Ross (January, 1907).
55. Beck (July 3, 2005: 6D).
56. Pear (May 16, 2005).
57. Personal interview.
58. Active Project Report (2004).
59. Cone et al. (2003:713).
60. Sparrow (2000).
61. Broad and Wade (1982); Klein (1991); Pollock and Evans (1985).
62. Jesilow (2005).
63. Guterman and Dobson (1986); Prospective Payment Assessment Commission (1992).
64. Eldenburg and Kallapur (1997); Eldenburg and Kallapur (2000).

References

Active Project Report (2004) "Facts About the Centers for Medicare and Medicaid Services." Centers for Medicare and Medicaid Services. http://www.cms.hhs.gov/researchers/projects/APR/2004/facts.pdf

American Medical Association (2003) "States in Crisis: 19 States Now in Full-blown Medical Liability Crisis." *AMA News Release* (6 Oct).

Beck, Rachel (2005) "Ignorance Still a Viable Defense." *Charlotte Observer* 6D (July 3).

Black, Bernard et al. (2005) Stability, Not Crisis: Medical Malpractice Claim Outcomes in Texas, 1988–2002. (draft March) Columbia Law School, Law and Economics Working Paper No. 270, University of Illinois, Law and Economics Research Paper No. LE05-002, University of Texas Law School, Law and Economics Working Paper No. 30. Social Science Research Network electronic library at http://papers.ssrn.com/abstract=678601.

Bovbjerg Randall R., and Kenneth Petronis (1994) "The Relationship Between Physicians' Malpractice Claims History and Later Claims. Does the Past Predict the Future?" *Journal of the American Medical Association* 272(18):1421–6 (9 Nov).

Broad, William, and Nicholas Wade (1982) *Betrayers of the Truth*. New York: Simon and Schuster.

Brown, June G. (1994) A Compendium of Reports and Literature on Coding of Physician Services (OEI-03-91-00921). Washington, DC: Inspector General, Department of Health and Human Services.

Brown, June G. (1999) Interoffice Memorandum, to: Nancy-Ann Min DeParle, Administrator, Health Care Financing Administration. SUBJECT: monitoring the accuracy of hospital coding (OEI-01-98-00420) (January 21). http://oig.hhs.gov/oei/reports/oei019800420.pdf#search='NancyAnn%20Min%20DeParle%20%20January%2021%2C%201999%2C%20%20SUBJECT%3A%20monitoring%20the%20accuracy%20of%20hospital%20coding%20%28OEI019800420%29'

Cane, Peter (1982) "Justice and Justifications for Tort Liability." *Oxford Journal of Legal Studies* 2(1):30–62 (Spring).

Cohen, Thomas H. (2005) "Civil Justice Survey of State Courts, 2001. Punitive Damage Awards in Large Counties, 2001." U.S. Department of Justice/Office of Justice Programs. Bureau of Justice Statistics, NCJ 208445 (March).

Cone, Jonathan et al. (2003) "Health Care Fraud." *American Criminal Law Review* 40:713.

Danzon, Patricia M. (1994) "The Swedish Patient Compensation System: Myths and Realities." *International Review of Law and Economics* 14:453–466.

Department of Justice (1999) "Health Care Fraud Report: Fiscal Year 1998." Washington, DC (5 Aug). http://www.usdoj.gov/dag/pubdoc/health98.htm.

Eldenburg, Leslie, and Sanjay Kallapur (1997) "Changes in Hospital Service Mix and Cost Allocations in Response to Changes in Medicare Reimbursement Schemes." 23 Journal of Accounting and Economics 31–51.

Eldenburg, Leslie, and Sanjay Kallapur (2000) "The Effects of Changes in Cost Allocations on the Assessment of Cost Containment Regulation in Hospitals." 19 Journal of Accounting and Public Policy 97–112.

Gardiner, John A., and Theodore R. Lyman (1984) The Fraud Control Game: State Responses to Fraud and Abuse in AFDC and Medicaid Programs. Bloomington: Indiana University Press.

Geis, Gilbert (1975) "Victimization Patterns in White-Collar Crime." in I. Drapkin and E.Viano, eds., Victimology: A New Focus. Exploiter and Exploited, vol 5. Lexington, Mass.: DC Heath.

General Accounting Office (1966) Health Care Fraud. Information-Sharing Proposals to Improve Enforcement Efforts. GAO/GGD-96-101 (May).

General Accounting Office (1992) "Health Insurance: Vulnerable Payers Lose Billions to Fraud and Abuse." in U.S. House of Representatives, Committee on Government Operations, Subcommittee on Human Resources and Intergovernmental Relations (May). Washington, DC: Government Printing Office.

Granelli, James S. (2005) "Laws to Curb Suits May Have Missed the Mark." *Los Angeles Times*. (3 June). http://www.latimes.com/news/printedition/asection/lafitort3jun03,1,7612887.story?page=1&coll=la news a_section.

Guterman, Stuart, and Allen Dobson (1986) "Impact of the Medicare Prospective Payment System for Hospitals." *Health Care Financing Review* 7:97–115.

Harmon, Robert G. (1990) "The National Practitioners Data Bank." *Journal of the American Medical Association* 264 :945.

Harrington, Kirsten B. (2003) Clamping down on Upcoding: Government Efforts to Curb a Medicare Billing Fraud and Abuse. Unpublished paper, The University of Nebraska, Lincoln.

Holmes Jr., Oliver W. (c2005/1881) The Common Law. New Brunswick: Transaction Publishers.

Holmes, Jr., Oliver W. (1873) "The Theory of Torts." *A. L. Rev. v. 652* 7:660.

Institute of Medicine (2000) To Err Is Human: Building a Safer Health System.

Jesilow, Paul et al. (1985) "Medical Criminals: Physicians and White-Collar Offenses." *Justice Quarterly* 2:149–166 (June).

Jesilow, Paul et al. (1993) *Prescription for Profit: How Doctors Defraud Medicaid.* Berkeley: University of California Press.
Jesilow, Paul et al. (1995) "Doomed To Repeat Our Errors: Fraud in Emerging Health Care Systems." *Social Justice* 22(2)125–138.
Jesilow, Paul (2005) "The Effects of Fraud on the Evaluation of Health Care." *Health Care Analysis: An International Journal of Health Care Philosophy and Policy* 13:239–245.
Kinney, Eleanor D. (1996) "Malpractice Reform in the 1990s: Past Disappointments, Future Success?" *Journal of Health Politics, Policy and Law* 21:1 (Spring).
Klein Donald F. (1991) "Scientific Fraud and Misconduct." Journal of Clinical Psychopharmacology 11(6):337–9.
Lavenant, Claudia E. et al. (2002) "Tort Reform and Physician Sanctioning." 24 Law and Policy 1–16.
Maltin, Vanessa (2004) "Fraud Plagues U.S. Health Care." The Atlanta Journal-Constitution D1 (14 July).
Jet Magazine (1997) "Manhattan, NY, Doctor Slain." http://www.findarticles.com/p/articles/mi_m1355/is_n26_v93/ai_20028174. (17 Nov).
McCormack, Patricia (1979) "Once Hospital Board Insider: Carter Reveals Taking Part in Medical 'Ripping Off.'" *Los Angeles Times* (25 Apr.).
Mitchell, Colby L. et al. (2003) "Billing for Inpatient Hospital Care." *American Journal of Health-System Pharmacists* 60:S8–S11.
Moses, Jennifer (2003) "False Claims." *American Criminal Law Review* 40:495.
Pear, Robert (2005) "F.B.I. Said to Misuse Funds for Health Fraud Cases." *New York Times* (16 May) http://www.nytimes.com/2005/05/16/politics/16fraud.html?
Pollock Alan V., and Michael Evans (1985) "Bias and Fraud in Medical Research: A Review." *Journal of the Royal Society of Medicine* 78:937–940.
Pontell, Henry N. et al. (1982) "Policing Physicians: Practitioner Fraud and Abuse in a Government Medical Program." *Social Problems* 117-125 (30 Oct).
The Deseret News: Salt Lake City (2005) "Prosecutors Aren't Finished with Health-South." (4 July) p. 1.
Prospective Payment Assessment Commission (1992) Medicare and the American Health Care System: Report to Congress. Chicago, IL: Commerce Clearing House.
Psaty, Bruce M. et al. (1999) "The Potential Costs of Upcoding for Heart Failure in the United States." *The American Journal of Cardiology* 84:108–109.
Richardson, Sally K. (1994) "Health Care Reform in the United States." Paper presented at Annual Conference of the National Association of Surveillance and Utilization Review Officials. Seattle, Washington.
Rosenberg, David (1995) *The Hidden Holmes: His Theory of Torts in History.* Cambridge: Harvard University Press.
Ross, Edward A. (1907) The Criminaloid. *Atlantic Monthly* 99:44–50 (January).
Schwartz, William B., and Neil Komesar (1978) "Doctors, Damages and Deterrence. An Economic View of Medical Malpractice." *New England Journal of Medicine* 298(23):1282–9.
"Setback in Birmingham After . . . " *The Washington Post* F2. (3 July).
Soderstrom, Naomi S. (1990) "Are Reporting Errors under PPS Random or Systematic?" *Inquiry Blue Cross and Blue Shield Association* 27:234–241.
Sparrow, Malcolm K. (2000) *License to Steal: How Fraud Bleeds America's Health Care System.* Boulder: Westview Press.
Starr, Paul (1982) *The Social Transformation of Medicine.* New York: Basic Books.
Sutherland, Edwin H. (1945) "Is 'White Collar Crime' Crime?" *American Sociological Review* 10:260–271.
Thorpe, Kenneth E. (2004) "The Medical Malpractice 'Crisis': Recent Trends And The Impact Of State Tort Reforms." *Health Affairs* W20-W30 (January).

Traska, Maria (1990) "Unbundling Could Be Costing You a Bundle." *Business and Health* 20–27 (March).

U.S. Department of Health and Human Services and U.S. Department of Justice (2002) Health Care Fraud and Abuse Control Program Annual Report for FY 2001. http://oig.hhs.gov/reading/hcfac/HCFAC%20Annual%20Report%20FY%202001.htm

United States Files Suit Against Tenet Healthcare Alleging False Claims Billing to Medicare (2003) (9 Jan) http://www.usdoj.gov./opa/pr/2003/January/03_civ_007.htm.

United States General Accounting Office (2001) "DOJ Has Improved Oversight of False Claims Act Guidance." Report to Congressional Committees (March).

Vidmar, Neil et al. (2005) Uncovering the "Invisible" Profile of Medical Malpractice Litigation: Insights from Florida. 54 *DePaul Law Review* 315–354.

White, Edward G. (1977) "White: The Intellectual Origins of Torts in America." *The Yale Law Journal* 86:671–693.

Zuckerman, Stephen et al. (1990) "Effects of Tort Reforms and Other Factors on Medical Malpractice Insurance Premiums." *Inquiry* 27:167, 182.

2

Policing Financial Crimes

Michael Levi

All crime control involves—consciously or not—the management of risk. The policing of crimes of deception presents special—though not unique—problems because of (a) the social status of *some* suspects and (b) the relative inaccessibility of *most* offenses to routine observation and to normal police informant development strategies. This varies over time and place. To the extent that people conventionally defined as "organized criminals" become involved in frauds of various types and in laundering the proceeds of these and other crimes, routine police styles of dealing with racketeering are more likely to pick up frauds earlier. Likewise, the same need of the internet telemarketer to communicate with unknown potential victims also renders them vulnerable to police and regulator surveillance and—perhaps when law-enforcement is motivated, resourced, and provided with a legal mandate to do so—intervention. However, policing frauds and other financial crimes creates particular financial and institutional difficulties because of the regularity with which such investigations cross jurisdictions, even at a fairly modest level of victimization. As the comments above imply, the policing of financial crimes overlaps organized crime and white-collar crime (as defined, however vaguely, in police practices). It may be helpful to outline a typology of such crimes, as it would be a mistake to think that all have similar policing styles: for a more developed analysis, see Levi and Pithouse.[1]

Box 1 Types of Economic Crime

1. Harm government/taxpayer interests
2. Harm *all* corporate as well as social interests
   - i.e., systemic risk frauds that undermine public confidence in the system as a whole; domestic and motor insurance frauds; maritime insurance frauds; payment card and other credit frauds; pyramid schemes; high-yield investment frauds
3. Harm social and some corporate interests but benefit other "mainly legitimate" ones
   - some cartels, transnational corruption (by companies with business interests in the country paying the bribe)

4. Harm corporate interests but benefit mostly illegitimate ones
   - several forms of intellectual property theft—sometimes called "piracy"—especially those using higher-quality digital media

We can see that the ideological and practical pressures to deal with different sorts of business offenses come from different directions, even if one excludes health and safety and environmental violations.

Let us briefly review the behavioral context in which such offenses take place. Influenced as we are by cultural images of the Sicilian Mafia and the Italian-American Mafia that have brought *The Godfather* and *The Sopranos* to our screens, it is difficult not to be seduced by the assumption that this hierarchical, deeply embedded cultural and family mode of organization is the natural evolution of serious crime: the general public, criminals, and the police are all subjected to (and sometimes entranced by) these images of power and "threat to society."[2] However, let's take for a moment the paradigmatic case of Italy: before his assassination, Investigating Judge Falcone appreciated that this threat was much more complex than a subculture or alien conspiracy model, and that the organized crime phenomenon could not be controlled without tackling political and business alliances, as well as police, prosecutorial, and judicial corruption. This is equally true of contemporary countries in the Balkans and elsewhere. However, where it is harder to develop corrupt alliances between criminal justice officials, politicians, and suppliers of illicit commodities or predatory criminals, organized crime is unlikely to flourish. This is important because to the extent that organized criminals represent a set of people who are "really dangerous" to the essential integrity of the state, and who trigger (especially in continental European legal systems) special investigative powers because of this threat, it would be helpful to know how special are their threats and what they constitute. Some academics[3] consider that—at least in Britain—all crime is essentially local in character (though connected somehow to the global economy); others[4]—though understanding that value-added tax and European Community frauds require transnational networks (or, with the aid of corruption or counterfeiters, paperwork that *simulates* the transnational movement of goods)—regard the issue of transnational organized crime as overblown and under-analyzed by the "threat assessment industry," and others still regard the skeptics as naïve theorists who fail to appreciate the creeping threat posed by cross-border criminal cooperation.[5] The nature of what Hobbs[6] termed "criminal collaboration" varies in different countries but affects the kind of control strategies (policing and administrative) that it makes sense to adopt; history, culture, and personal/institutional interests shape actual responses, despite the rhetoric of "asymmetric warfare."

"Organized crime" used to be a phenomenon that was central only to American and Italian crime discourses about "the Mafia," but—stimulated by the growth of the international drug and people migration trades[7] and by the freeing up of borders since the collapse of the Soviet Union—the debate about it and specific national and transnational powers to deal with "it" has extended to Britain and other parts of Europe and beyond in the course of the 1990s. However unclear it may be about how "we" can assess whether crime is "organized" or not, the term is a unifying framework around which international police and judicial cooperation can be structured. Definitional ambiguities do not seem to inhibit confident statements about the "scale of the problem" of transnational organized crime, which is always asserted to be "growing" and often said to be using hi-tech methods, as if crossing borders by plane, motor vehicle, digital phone, or computer were not also done by businesspeople, professionals, and the general population, probably in greater proportions than criminals at work do. Some crimes such as "identity theft," associated with fraud, organized crime, and terrorism, are also plausibly said to be growing.[8]

By contrast, "white-collar crime" is a term used more by criminologists[9] than by police and politicians, especially in Britain where it has only rarely been a major crime issue (and then only in relation to identity fraud and deposit and investment "widows and orphans" frauds), and where prosecutors almost never go into politics in the way they do in the United States. Despite the more invasive and aggressive nature of capitalism in the United States compared to the more mixed social democratic economies of the European Union, in keeping with the more general moral entrepreneurship of U.S. "law and order" politics, U.S. media, politicians, and law enforcement officials are paradoxically *more* likely to discuss white-collar crimes, both (a) for crimes *against* business (like credit card fraud) and (b) for crimes against investors *by* prestigious and by racketeer-run business alike, as investigated by New York Attorney-General Eliot Spitzer since the late 1990s and by New York DA Robert Morgenthau over some decades. I will deal primarily here with the policing of one subset of white-collar crime—fraud—which itself encompasses a range of victim-offender activities and social statuses. "The problem of fraud" and official responses to it lack the "Evil Empire" rhetoric of the construction of the "organized crime problem," even though *some* large aggregate frauds against the Treasury—evasion of excise duty on alcohol and tobacco—are included in the category of the most serious organized crime threats facing Canada, the United States and the United Kingdom (e.g., in the assessment of the U.K National Criminal Intelligence Service and its Canadian counterpart[10]) and, peculiarly, tend to be seen as "organized crime" rather than "fraud." Nevertheless, if we look at frauds not so much by the number of each type reported but by the amount of money lost, we can better appreciate why they occupy the attention of so many FBI agents and why institutions such as the U.S. Securities and Exchange Commission (SEC) and the U.K Serious Fraud Office (SFO) were created and still exist. They exist because the "new classes" of victim—for example, shareholders in privatized utilities and collectors of early retirement and redundancy pay—are a *political risk* that calls for a response. The SFO exists also because Britain was concerned about its reputation in the global marketplace and, given that (despite large redundancies in 2002 and 2003) as many as one in five Londoners employed works in financial services, they are strategically important in an economy of seriously declining manufacturing and agricultural industries.

The standard method of dealing with the wide range of *non*-police "fraud" cases is advice and prodding of the uncooperative, with slowly escalating sanctions for persistent violation: Corporations are seen as amenable to restorative justice methods.[11] These differences may be justifiable on a risk-based model of policing, but we tend to take for granted the assumptions on which they are based. As one long-firm (bankruptcy) fraudster told me, "I only wanted to make enough money to afford to be honest."[12] This may be equally true of *some* drugs traffickers and other organized crime targets, but a policy decision has been taken not to allow them to integrate into the legitimate enterprise world, both on moral grounds and on the assumption of future dangerousness.

The Organization of Policing Deception

To help us analyze the threat and the problems that policing confronts, we should consider the tasks that need to be performed to commit serious crimes over a long period:

1. Obtain financing for crime.
2. Find people willing to commit crimes (though this may not always be necessary if one has an inside position and/or specialist skills that enables one to commit major crimes alone, in which case one does not fall within the legal category of "organized crime," but one might still be a fraudster and/or a threat[13]).
3. Obtain equipment and transportation necessary to commit the crimes.
4. Convert products of crime into money or other usable assets (unless they are already cash).
5. Find people and places willing to store crime proceeds (and perhaps transmit and conceal their origin).
6. Neutralize law enforcement by technical skill, by corruption, and/or by legal arbitrage, i.e., using legal obstacles to enforcement operations, admissibility of evidence, and prosecutions that vary between states.

Unlike racketeers, who must advertise illegal goods and services, fraudsters do not need to make themselves vulnerable to inspection. At the international level, policy responses have been to pressure states into passing legislation and setting up mutual legal assistance mechanisms to facilitate international exchanges of intelligence and to process cases.[14] This is part of the world anti-money laundering movement.[15]

Policing Fraud: The Contexts of Police Undercover Work

Most policing of any type of fraud happens *reactively*, i.e., after a scandal or a less sensational report, and the object in big cases is to ascertain and prove who was most responsible (responsibility often being shared): as in the Enron case, plea bargaining can be a powerful tool to induce incrimination of superiors. However, there are occasions in which covert policing is used, such as when the police already have a conspirator—usually associated with "organized crime"—under surveillance,[16] or when in the course of an ongoing scam, an insider comes to them voluntarily or under pressure and agrees to cooperate.[17] Gary Marx[18] observes that there are a number of types of police undercover work which, adapted to white-collar policing, are as follows:

1. Intelligence operations, in which agents are relatively passive, though they may need to participate in crime in order to gain credibility. Such operations can be *after* or *before* a particular crime. The Internal Revenue Service (IRS) gained access to a taxpayer's books by having an agent pose as a potential buyer of his business. When asked to justify this, he said, "We are not inducing anybody to break the law. The tax returns have already been filed, and the crime has already been committed long before we've come around." But such *ex post facto* investigations are relatively rare: *anticipatory* undercover operations are much more common. This can involve the creation of false fronts, in the classic "sting" operation mode, in which U.S. investigators adapted to white-collar crime the method first used on policing the poor.
2. Such operations can also be used to *prevent* crimes from taking place, or for educational purposes: via an alias, the U.S. Postal Inspection Service[19] placed enticing advertisements offering an easy way to earn money or to lose weight. People who responded received politely worded letters advising them that they ought to be more careful about offers that sound too good to be true, and containing stamps for the postage expended and a booklet on mail fraud schemes. My interviews suggest that there has been a reluctance to use this kind of tactic in the United Kingdom because of fear of complaints from the public.
3. Facilitative operations, in which the agent is either victim or co-conspirator. In the white-collar arena, the classic examples of this are in U.S. money-laundering investigations or cases such as those in which a professional confidence trickster allegedly involved former General Motors executive John De Lorean—who was suspected of defrauding the Northern Ireland Development Agency of many millions of dollars—in a purchase in the United States of large amounts of cocaine to pay off his debts. De Lorean was acquitted. Several U.K. investigations of excise tax evaders on alcohol and tobacco used this method, though to the chagrin of HM Customs & Excise, many of the trials later collapsed or convictions were overturned due to the failure to disclose to the defense or prosecution that the insider was a participating informant rather than simply an unprosecuted intermediary and witness.[20]

Covert Investigations of White-Collar Crime in America

Before Watergate, the American approach to investigating white-collar crime was not unlike that of the United Kingdom. It had a very low priority in police circles. Undercover investigations—except against "political subversives"—were greatly deprecated by J. Edgar Hoover, though Nixon allegedly used the Internal Revenue Service to investigate his political opponents and protect his political and financial friends.[21] However, post-Watergate, the FBI started to take white-collar crime very seriously, and though most investigations remained reactive, it decided in 1978 to tackle political corruption by planting an undercover agent as an Arab head of Abdul Enterprises, and spread the word that the "sheikh" needed help in an immigration matter. A professional confidence trickster of some notoriety was employed on the government payroll as an undercover agent, to look for legislators who would help the sheikh with work permits. This led to successful prosecutions of six congressmen and one senator, and a lot of publicity. In 1973, the FBI mounted 53 undercover investigations; in 1980, there were 300, mainly in "kickback" cases involving the underworld, but some "up-market" white-collar cases too. More recent examples are unknown, but often involve cases prosecuted as money-laundering. As always, there were problems: In Operation Corkscrew, an undercover con man gave $100,000 of FBI money in bribes to someone posing as a "judge," who was actually a friend of his, and who ran off with the money.

Technological improvements in audio- and video-recording were used in Operation Greylord to try to crack the corrupt state level judiciary and public officials in Cook County, Illinois. By 1983, this operation had netted only nine people—three judges, three lawyers, and three "bagmen"—but the FBI and prosecutors hailed it as a major breakthrough nonetheless. However, as a result of the same process employed in later insider-dealing cases, those charged in the first round plea bargained with their colleagues' liberty in the next round; and altogether, 9 judges, 37 lawyers, and 19 police and clerks were convicted in Greylord. (There were more convictions subsequently.)

In 1984, a major commodities producer with a grievance against the Chicago Board of Trade was referred by the Chicago Futures Trade Commission to the FBI. The moral entrepreneurial ambience for criminal investigation was right. As one investigator expressed it: "We were being told that if you were an honest man in the pits, you couldn't make it because nobody would deal with you.... Nobody believed me, until this guy showed up."[22]

The FBI then set up a meeting with the U.S. Attorney for approval to organize an undercover operation in the commodities exchange. (By the time the case came to trial in 1989, the same U.S. Attorney was a defense lawyer for the first person to plead guilty in the prosecution, and advised the Chicago Board of Trade on its defense to racketeering charges.) The operation required a major financial investment by the FBI: a $300,000 seat on the Exchange, a Mercedes, a subscription to a fashionable exercise club, and even a Rolex! The project went through a local undercover review board, the agent in charge, a national undercover panel, and finally was signed off by the FBI director. Unlike the usual white-collar sting operations, this did not have the problem of disreputable prosecution witnesses that bedeviled a number of trials.[23] It was only a slight complicating factor that the commodities producer, ADM, was fined $50,000 (reduced on appeal to $25,000) for refusing to give evidence in a disciplinary hearing for manipulating the soybean-oil market. (The charges that gave rise to the refusal were dismissed later for lack of evidence: for a brilliant exploration of the dynamics of this case, see Eichenwald.[24])

The agents were chosen from a pool of 8,000 who volunteered for undercover assignments. But the FBI decided that to avoid charges of favoritism on behalf of the Chicago Mercantile Exchange, which also had a poor reputation, it would have to mount a parallel sting there also. They found a sponsor for their FBI agents in a disillusioned older broker there. The agents had a six-week general undercover training course, but for the specific area of work, they had just three afternoons of classroom instruction on the futures business. The 1987 stock market crash led one agent to lose $30,000 in trading, plus the general costs of dealing.

One trader frisked the FBI people for hidden recorders but found nothing, since the whole room was bugged. After a lengthy enquiry, which was terminated when information began to leak, the FBI issued 500 subpoenas, conducted well over 500 interviews, and reviewed more than a million documents. A total of 1,275 pages of charges and 608 counts were issued against 46 defendants. However, no major exchange personnel were indicted, and the amounts of money involved in the alleged frauds—some of which were as low as $12.50—were not aggregated, assisting the defense claims that the prosecutors were scraping the bottom of the barrel in order to justify themselves. Those unlucky enough to have traded with the agents found themselves indicted, some with as many as 96 counts.

When the indictments were issued, some of the accused went for plea bargains and cooperated with the government; others fought. In the trials, however, which started nine months after the indictments, things became less clear-cut. Audiotapes turned out to be far more ambiguous and inaudible than the FBI believed—there were sometimes significant disparities in defense and prosecution versions—and agents' discretion about when to turn them on was used by the defense to allege selective bias, which argument found favor with some jurors. (Similar issues arose in other unsuccessful prosecutions using professional confidence tricksters as undercover informants.)

Covert tape-recording by participating informants was also employed in a series of insider trading investigations,[25] and the interview transcripts make it clear that the questions asked by people such as Ivan Boesky were aimed to get their business colleagues to implicate themselves. These occurred in the context of criminal conspiracies already known (in general terms) to the Department of Justice, where the informants were seeking to obtain credit for use in sentencing proceedings.

In cases such as Enron (and earlier savings & loans frauds), the corporate collapse preceded the police investigations, so the main method there was careful analysis of the documentation—paper, e-mails, and audio records (when not destroyed)—followed by pressure on defendants to incriminate those further up the corporate ladder. Likewise, with the "bubble" cases such as ImClone/Martha Stewart, WorldCom, in 2004–2005. Lengthy sentencing guideline norms and steep discounts for those who plead guilty and give "substantial assistance to the prosecutor" are the standard pressure tools. Other telemarketing and boiler room operations may first be investigated by the Securities and Exchange Commission and then passed on to the Department of Justice, or—as mentioned earlier—proactively handled by federal, state and/or local Organized Crime Task Forces if committed by associates of the New York Crime Families. What is critical here is the time to fraud discovery and/or fraud reporting by victims or professionals.

Covert Policing of White-Collar Crime in Britain

In many countries the amount of police attention to white-collar crimes, whether *by*, or *against* corporations is very low.[26] In spite of their surprisingly high seriousness ratings, crimes involving organizations rank near the bottom in the priorities of populist law and order. Under these conditions, an uneasy friendship develops between public and private sector organizations, since the private police come in to fill the regulatory gap and are also more responsive to the wishes of corporate chiefs. On the one hand, the police see the private sector as a future employer for their services and as a method of reducing the police input into a "cleared up" case; on the other, they are resentful of them for reasons that are obscure, but relate probably to some regulatory megalomania. Corporations would prefer to see much more public police attention than they get,[27] largely because they do not wish to pay for their policing except where they want control over investigations (e.g., over investigations against their own staff[28]).

Additionally, in the United Kingdom, there are semi-public investigation agencies, such as the Royal Mail Investigation Department, which unlike the U.S. postal service, is licensed by the government but is expected to make a profit on its operations. Very large social security investigation departments exist within the Department of Work and Pensions, the National Health Service Counter-Fraud Service, and Local Authority Housing Benefit departments, that are much larger than the number of police officers devoted to fraud investigations. In addition to the normal range of *reactive* investigations, the Royal Mail infiltrate postal sorting offices to observe activities of postal workers, who often steal check and credit cards—which is also common in the United States.

In the cases above, the existence of specific crimes is known. In other cases, however, investigations can be aimed at getting "dirt" on target people who are giving the government trouble on political or commercial grounds. In the United Kingdom, there have been several complaints of political interference in white-collar investigations, but these have not included allegations of *covert* police activity, unless by "covert" one wishes to include deceptions about the purposes for which information is being obtained. In the case of Manchester businessman Kevin Taylor, the police had a strong interest in finding out about his business dealings during the 1980s because he was a friend of Deputy Chief Constable John Stalker, whom they allegedly wished to see removed from his over-zealous investigation of the unofficial "shoot-to-kill" policy in Northern Ireland.[29] To get access to Taylor's bank accounts without arresting him, the Crown Prosecution Service applied for an order to search for evidence, telling the judge that they had grounds for suspecting Taylor's involvement in drug trafficking. (In fact, the police probably had no need to show the prosecutors their information and could have applied for the warrant themselves.) When, at the subsequent trial of Taylor on fraud charges, the judge found that there was no drug connection, he was furious and dismissed all the charges against Taylor, who successfully sued the police for millions of pounds over lost business and collateral damages.

Covert white-collar crime operations have mainly been in the private sector, such as the notorious Dixons/Woolworths takeover battle, and the Guinness/Bells one, during the 1980s, where private detectives allegedly searched target people's dustbins, tapped their telephones, and interviewed all persons having prior contact, in the hope of generating some personal "dirt" on company directors. One might describe this as a form of private sector integrity vetting. There are a number of private detectives who carry out surveillance operations, sometimes long-term ones, on business rivals. British Airways illicitly interrogated the Virgin upper class flight-booking database to try to "poach" customers with special offers to fly BA. Finally, there are random tests in the attempt to find out whether violations are occurring: "mystery shopping" test purchasing with marked notes, for example. (In addition, there is surveillance of private sector activity, such as the—generally non-secret—recording of all financial services telephone conversations by the firms themselves, principally to provide an objective test of disputes about the nature of oral contracts to buy and sell products, but consequentially to provide an audit trail for those dishonest practices which are conducted from the business premises.) During 1993, former SAS officers and a director of National Car Parks were acquitted of all criminal charges, though they admitted an operation in which they planted an undercover agent in their rivals Europarks, whom they suspected of having inside information about National Car Parks. They also admitted searching waste material from Europarks for clues.

To place this in context, in most white-collar crimes, covert activity is restricted mainly to the informal obtaining of financial information or, again depending on the definition of "covert," the official obtaining of information about suspected bank accounts without the knowledge of the account-holder. For example, without judicial oversight and without prior notice to the suspect unless s/he is the holder of the information wanted, the Director of the Serious Fraud Office may issue a notice under s.2 of the Criminal Justice Act 1987 to a banker or anyone else to disclose information relevant to a serious fraud investigation: this is done on many hundreds of occasions annually for documentary evidence. (Bankers risk prosecution for "tipping off" if they inform customers either before or after the court order, as well as where money laundering suspicions exist.) However, there are some *proactive* police fraud investigations, particularly in London, where informants—some of whom are regulars—tip off the police that a "scam" is being mounted and they are given permission (on strict guidelines) to act as Covert Human Intelligence Sources. (As noted earlier, in recent years to 2005, undisclosed use of such participating informants has led to the quashing of convictions and collapse of many multi-million-pound excise fraud prosecutions by HM Customs and Excise.[30]) There, unless customs/police officers are used as undercover "plants" (which is extremely rare), the problem arises that the police cannot readily know the extent to which their informant actually acted as an *agent provocateur* or more serious co-conspirator, let alone disprove such allegations when made by the defense lawyers.[31] The financial rewards (from the police, banks, or insurers) can be lucrative and could induce high levels of activism on the part of informants. Given the disclosure rulings discussed earlier, the police would then have the dilemma of whether to inform prosecutors (and risk them disclosing to the defense or dropping the case), or whether to keep the information to themselves and risk embarrassing questions in court about how they came to suspect that a fraud was in operation, given that they broke it up in the course of its commission. The police generally adopt the line that unless their informant is willing to give evidence in court, they would rather let the case collapse than reveal their identity.

One of the areas examined by Marx relates to whether the undercover work takes place in natural or artificial environments. Agents may work in a setting that is already there: in the United Kingdom, Automobile Association, Consumer's Association, and (municipal) trading standards officials regularly test for fraud by garages in "identifying" nonexistent motor ailments. As in the United States, a considerable amount of computerized market surveillance is carried out on securities transactions to attempt to detect insider trading. These monitor patterns of unusual transactions, particularly price changes in advance of the release of company results or takeovers, and serve as a heuristic to guide the detailed audit of who acted as principals and nominees in the deals. (Whether anything further happens depends on the competence and number of investigators, and on the opacity of the nominees and/or their bankers under the law of the country in which they were incorporated. In some jurisdictions such as England, shares can be frozen until the beneficial owners are revealed. However, sustaining a loss may be better than being prosecuted.) Similar heuristics based on developed mathematical risk analysis are used by tax authorities, particularly in America and Australia as well as the United Kingdom, to test the integrity of tax returns.

However, unlike the United States, there are no examples in the United Kingdom of strategic testing of nursing home fraud by undercover work, though with rising healthcare costs this may happen in the future. Then there are operations started by the police to function in a "normal" criminal environment, for example, classic stings involving fencing and money laundering. Here, too, the United Kingdom lags behind the United States in refusing normally to contemplate many such stings apart from drug busts.[32] Cyber-infiltration by the National Hi-Tech Crime Unit in the United Kingdom and its American equivalents is quite common, but especially in pedophile "grooming" and (supplemented by the intelligence agencies) in national security cases rather than to deal with fraud.

Finally, there are more problematical areas in which police come into a *milieu* which is *not* known to be criminal. This can emerge from an obsession with uncovering "hidden areas of criminality," but it can easily degenerate into a Dr. Strangelove-like psychosis, neatly combined with self-interest in sustaining operations. (However, this is so only in a fairly cost-uncontrolled environment such as some U.S. Federal bodies and the NYPD, in which resources are not a major problem: i.e., not the United Kingdom, where overtime payments are tightly limited and have to be justified very specifically). It may be that covert operations lead to a greater chance of guilty pleas, thus saving enormous court costs: lawyers are paid more than police. However, the police and legal budgets are separate, and the problem of cost in policing operations is a very real one: surveillance operations in white-collar crime—which are only sometimes tied in with "undercover" ones—are greatly discouraged because of budgetary problems in the financial environment of the 1990s and early 21st century. Even in a short-term operation at least ten people are needed for surveillance, and the cars and personnel are not normally available for continuous coverage over a long period of time. They can be available where reliable informants are involved—who, partly for economy reasons, are viewed as preferable to "police undercover" plants or to longer-term, untargeted surveillance—and the main trend is toward this sort of covert operation. There, sometimes in collaboration with overseas agencies, operations may be mounted to discover counterfeiting, narcotics trafficking, or money-laundering organizations. Sometimes, as in the case of actions against collusive traders who pass transactions through their books using credit card numbers obtained from insiders in hotels or on the phone (telemarketing), whether by simply typing in the numbers or making up crude counterfeit embossed cards ("white-carding"), the police may cooperate with private sector organizations such as credit card companies. Indeed, there is some potential for sting operations by setting up traders who will be approached by credit card fraudsters to cooperate in this way. (In Italy and other "organized crime" environments, many traders are made "an offer they cannot refuse" to accept stolen cards.) But except where they are suspected of involvement in terrorism or drugs trafficking (both of which can involve the use of businesses as "fronts"), covert operations have never to my knowledge been used by the U.K police against members of "the elite" (however problematic that is to define). Surveillance operations by HM Revenue and Customs in relation to value-added tax fraud are probably the closest analogy to what happens in United States, but apart from some participating informant excise fraud cases, even they are for the most part passively covert (e.g., simple surveillance of, say, meetings between already suspected conspirators) or are involved with test purchases or sales: they seldom use long-term dummy companies.

There are two sorts of shift in approach to the control of financial organized crime. The first shift relates to traditional criminal justice approaches, and the second—which is not incompatible—relates to prevention. Criminal justice approaches include—

1. substantive legislation, relating especially to money-laundering and proceeds of crime legislation;
2. procedural laws involving mutual legal assistance (including the establishment of Eurojust, whose detached national prosecutors and investigative judges are expected to facilitate urgent cases, and the European arrest warrant and asset freezing orders); and
3. investigative resources, including the formation of specialist organizations and police units. In the United Kingdom, this includes the National Hi-Tech Crime Unit and even some privately funded units such as the Dedicated Cheque and Plastic Crime Unit (established April 2002 for an initial two-year experiment and then continued wholly funded by the banking sector, though with no operational control by them over individual cases).

There has been ongoing reform of anti-laundering and crime-profits legislation around the world,[33] making bankers and lawyers accountable (under threat of imprisonment and being banned from doing business) by requiring them to keep records, actively look for "suspicious" transactions, and report their suspicions to Financial Intelligence Units (FinCEN in the United States, NCIS in the United Kingdom). There has been greater policing (including customs and excise) involvement in financial investigation, still mainly in the drug field, but increasingly in excise tax fraud and, post– September 11, 2001, terrorism.[34] Laundering is the cleansing of funds so that they can be used in a way indistinguishable from legitimate money; and in essence, bankers and (in Europe) lawyers have been forced to keep tight records and report their suspicions of their clients to central bodies. If and when those official surveillance capabilities increase—as they did steadily during the 1990s, accelerating after the millennium and especially after the spectacular attacks on New York and Washington on September 11, 2001—funds that were just hidden become vulnerable to enforcement intervention and perhaps confiscation.[35]

The Egmont Group of Financial Investigation Units (FIUs) worldwide, whose aim (not always realized in practice) is to facilitate inter-FIU enquiries across borders, has transformed the *potential* for intelligence-led policing (and disruption) of financial and other organized crime activity across borders.

The "cross-border" concept may be understood differently by those who have national police forces and/or are concerned with crimes across national boundaries. In the United States, geographic and other territorial conflicts are commonplace at federal, state, and local levels. However, in the United Kingdom, the concept has to be seen within the traditional constabulary divisions and the typical orientation of the geographic sector policing toward the local, which was originally a specific reaction to the French Revolution and the risks that this sort of centralized policing was held to pose for freedom of the bourgeoisie and landowning classes.[36] Militating against the policing of fraud is management reluctance to commit resources to out-of-force investigations, especially into frauds that are not highlighted as performance targets; knowledge about who to contact in another force; incompatible equipment; and a lack of relevant intelligence. There has been a growing bifurcation between (a) the growing decentralization of efforts at a neighborhood level and (b) the growing internationalization of links with other countries by national police agencies, as well as in the policing and prosecution of fraud.

The explanation for the neglect of fraud by the police is far from clear, but it appears to relate in part to some Victorian conception of prudence whereby everyone who does not take sufficient care of their own property deserves little sympathy. There are also a number of pragmatic factors, three of which are key:

1. there has been little central or local political pressure on forces to do more about fraud (e.g., via key performance indicators or local ones in policing plans);
2. the low productivity of fraud squad staff in relation to standard police performance indicators, fraud being more labor-intensive to investigate; and
3. chief officers' own relatively unsophisticated appreciation of the business world and the possible impact of fraud losses on the local and national economy.

Observation by this author over the past three decades indicates little evidence in the United Kingdom to support the notion advanced by Richard Ericson and Kevin Haggerty[37] that the police act as handmaidens and risk managers for the commercial sector. The main pressure for fraud policing comes from (a) the impact of globalization on the demand for investigation in key financial services countries (e.g., to investigate bribes paid to foreign leaders), and (b) broadened share ownership, both direct and via stock market investments by pension funds, creates demand for regulation of abuses and investigations of "failed" entrepreneurs.[38]

A number of changes—broadly summarized under the rubric of "new public management"—have affected public services, including frauds and police responses to them, in the past 25 years. Under the Conservative government during 1979–1997, Next Steps agencies were expected to create the organizational context for cultural change from public to private sector high-energy service values. These included the Benefits Agency (now JobCentre Plus), which deals with social security fraud investigation as well as service delivery, and the Revenue departments, which deal with tax fraud.

Outsourcing of public sector contracts generated more corruption and public sector fraud enquiries for the police, but the stripping-out of middle ranks, the devolution of most policing responsibilities to divisions, the downsizing of headquarters staff, and pressure on staffing complements of central squads was commonplace. Within this context of organizational change, several relevant reports and developments had implications for the policing of fraud, of which the most important were the shift (now reversed, but with irreversible loss of expertise) to short-term postings, and the shift from specialized squads to generic "major crime" units, which tends to neglect frauds that have to be policed reactively rather than on an "intelligence led" basis (informants, surveillance of the "usual suspects").

Fraud policing may be usefully bifurcated into (i) high policing, represented by the work of the Serious Fraud Office (SFO) and (ii) (relatively) low policing, represented by the regulation of plastic fraud with only a modest input from the police. At the "low policing" end of the fraud spectrum, the pressure on diminishing fraud squad resources was increased by the rise in high-volume, low-cost fraud in the private sector during the 1980s in those industries who had traditionally seen fraud squads as responsible for dealing with the threats from "white collar" criminals, leading to a further loss of interest in the high-volume credit card crimes (and reduction of service to businesses relocating from London). This was understandable because reactive investigation was inhibited by poor forensics—customers could take away the signed receipt with their fingerprints on, it or bank handling of checks made data recovery difficult—while plastic fraudsters were not "dangerous enough" either in terms of their nodal salience to organized crime groups/networks nor committing high enough priority offenses to interest force or national squads dealing with "serious crime."

Not only the private sector, but also internal corruption excepted, the public sector has largely taken fraud inquiries out of police hands. There are some 9,000 non-police fraud investigators in the public sector, from the Department of Work and Pensions Fraud Investigation Service and Jobcentre Plus (with some 7,000–7,500), HM Revenue and Customs, to the Charity Commissioners and local authorities (where up to 1,000 investigators deal primarily with housing benefit fraud). Further, a number of these agencies have both discrete legislation and their own prosecution capability that substantially mitigates the need to rely on the police, the Crown Prosecution Service, or more generic legislation.

There is also much "partnership fraud policing," especially in the United Kingdom. Again, however, there is enormous variation in quality of joint work and differences in objectives—especially in civil recovery or taking people off benefit versus criminal prosecution. The principal aims of the tax authorities and, in a different way because they are an expenditure body, social security agencies, are to maximize revenue: fraud reduction (and, *a fortiori*, prosecution) are very much subsidiary to this core purpose, by contrast with the police which is primarily a court-oriented body. Additionally, there are issues of investigative timing, since the tax investigators have longer time frames than the police and social security investigators.

Prosecution and Relationship to Policing Fraud

As noted earlier, the United Kingdom Serious Fraud Office was set up by the Criminal Justice Act 1987 to pursue more effectively and quickly "serious or complex fraud" in the aftermath of the Fraud Trials Committee chaired by Lord Roskill.[39] The size of the SFO was determined by the Treasury, and Lord Roskill's intention (personal interviews, 1986 and 1992) to include Customs, Department of Trade and Industry, and Inland Revenue investigations and prosecutions within it failed due to bureaucratic maneuvering. The Serious Fraud Office is a government department, responsible to the Attorney General, staffed by lawyers, financial investigators, forensic accountants, and administrative support personnel. It is not part of the police service, but police officers are provided "on loan" to the SFO at the discretion of their Chief Constables or Commissioners, in theory according to a Memorandum of Understanding agreed between the SFO Director and the Association of Chief Police Officers. Police officers are needed to execute search warrants in order to enter premises to seize evidence, to make arrests and to charge suspects, and to monitor compliance with bail conditions. The police also conduct interviews (other than those under s.2 of the CJA 1987 in which there is no right to silence but which are inadmissible in evidence in criminal courts). Policing priorities mean that the SFO is not always able to count on as many policing resources as it would like to have, and resource conflicts sometimes mean that officers prefer to work from their own offices rather than from those of the SFO.

Notwithstanding bodies such as the SFO, an unintended effect of policing policy and the practice of requiring firm proof of fraud before accepting cases was to shift the economic burden of crime investigation onto victims, in particular corporate victims, thus transferring public law back into the sphere of private law. At the high end of the fraud policing spectrum, there has been tension between some fraud squads and the SFO over what some police see as the "cost (in)effective" deployment of resources and whether the SFO in-house lawyers who act as Case Controllers are the best judges of how to manage cases,[40] while police "Authorized Investigator" schemes in the late 1990s to license private investigators (at the victims' own expense) to conduct fraud enquiries "in collaboration" with the police had very limited success.[41] The configuration of relationships in the United States takes a different form, since prosecutor management is more routine and investigative resources less constrained (at least until the post-"9/11" diversion towards terrorism and homeland security). Nevertheless, cases involving less than $1 million are unlikely to be investigated by the FBI.

All the components of the criminal justice system are "loose-coupled" in the sense that they have an interactive relationship in which one part's expectations of what the others will do inform their own behavior (though this can sometimes lead to deviance to achieve crime control goals). The United States tries to achieve this by separating prosecution decisions from actual investigative help or control by lawyers within organizations; likewise, with the U.K prosecutors, except in SFO cases, police investigations have limited lawyer input. In Continental Europe, investigative judges normally conduct the investigations and then hand over to prosecutors who, like the police, have a much more restricted role in fraud and in other investigations.

The Future of Fraud Investigation

Policing fraud is shaped by scandal: the United States has had more severe financial scandals than Europe, from the savings & loans debacle onward,[42] due in part to the U.S. fashion for deregulation; but in New York, there has been a push towards proactive as well as reactive (e.g., post-Enron, WorldCom) corporate crime investigation that has been unmatched in Europe except for the very particular case of the Milan *mani pulite* ("clean hands") investigations into the corrupt nexus between business, politics, and organized crime.

Additionally, the involvement of New York organized crime gangs in securities fraud brought them into the net of surveillance and infiltration policing by the NYPD.[43] However, everywhere in the Western world, since "9/11" as well as the Madrid and London bombings, policing resources have been redeployed to dealing with terrorism. Some of these have come from fraud investigation. In theory, the anti-terrorist focus on financial intelligence should yield more evidence of fraud, but in practice those bodies looking for terrorists are unlikely to pass on cases that indicate fraud because that it not their personal or institutional focus. Moreover, between the high-value, high-level focus of the national bodies (such as the FBI) and the very local focus of other forces, cases of fairly high value but considerable effort are unlikely to be followed up. A substantial gap is left in the service offered to fraud victims, which is hardly unique in contemporary policing but is seldom the result of explicit policy analysis or reviews of either harms or clear-up possibilities. There are many things victims with resources can and will do through the civil sphere, including asset-freezing injunctions and search-orders to freeze assets and require entry (though usually accompanied by a police officer), but though there may be some regional consolidation, there seems little chance of any substantial rise in police resources. The London Dedicated Cheque and Plastic Crime Unit is an intriguing example of public/private partnership policing, but there is limited private sector willingness to pay for public policing. In the United States, the police are better resourced and, to the extent that asset forfeiture generates income and fraudsters have assets to forfeit, this provides an incentive for investigation that is also creeping into the United Kingdom.

Finally, we have a different mode of controlling financial abuses, namely, the regulation of financial services and, less rigorously, elsewhere through the power to request a court to have a company wound up "in the public interest." Within the financial sector and in professional organizations, regulators have extensive powers to vet the moral suitability and competence of potential employees ("fit and proper person" tests)—which criteria may vary depending on the level of employment—and to discipline both individuals and firms, including financial penalties. Whether the policing Panopticon will ever extend to encompass all types of fraud, however, is extremely unlikely, for despite the growth in public concern about their direct and indirect (via pension funds, etcetera) investments in the stock markets and identity theft and other crime risks associated with the cyber-world, the iconography of fear of crime is more difficult to develop and sustain for "white-collar" than for "organized" crime.

Endnotes

1. Levi, Michael, and Andrew Pithouse (2006) *Victims of White Collar Crime: The Social and Media Construction of Business Fraud.* Oxford: Clarendon.
2. See Levi, Michael (2002) "The Organization Of Serious Crimes," in M. Maguire et al., eds. *The Oxford Handbook of Criminology*, 3rd edition, Oxford: Oxford University Press; Levi, n.1
3. Hobbs, Dick (1997) "Criminal Collaboration," in M. Maguire et al. eds., The *Oxford Handbook of Criminology,* Second edition, Oxford: Oxford University Press; Hobbs, Dick (1998) "Going Down the Glocal: The Local Context Of Organized Crime," 37 *The Howard Journal of Criminal Justice* 407–422.

4. van Duyne, Petrus (1996) "The Phantom and Threat of Organized Crime." 24 *Crime, Law and Social Change* 341–377.
5. Berdal, Michel, and Monica Serrano. eds. (2002) *Transnational Organized Crime: New Challenges to International Security*. Boulder: Lynne Rienner; Fijnaut, Cyrille and Letizia Paoli, eds. (2005) *Organized Crime and its Control in Europe*. Dordrecht: Springer.
6. Hobbs, Dick (1997) "Criminal Collaboration," in M. Maguire et al., eds. *The Oxford Handbook of Criminology,* Second edition, Oxford: Oxford University Press.
7. Analytically, both of these trades are artifacts of criminalization in the sense that if no artificial constraints were placed on demand, there would be no need for illegal businesses. However, though true, a similar argument could be made about property rights generally so it is not as profound a point as is often claimed.
8. Croall, Hazel (2001) *White-Collar Crime.* Buckingham: Open University Press; Nelken, David (2002) "White-Collar Crime," in Maguire et al., eds. *The Oxford Handbook of Criminology,* 3rd edition, Oxford: Oxford University Press; Levi, Michael, and Andrew Pithouse (2006) *Victims of White Collar Crime: The Social and Media Construction of Business Fraud.* Oxford: Clarendon.
9. Though there is a statistical inflation from treating all deceptions as to who we are as 'identity theft': see www.cifas.org.uk for some data on increased identity fraud.
10. NCIS (2005) UK Threat Assessment, 2005. London: National Criminal Intelligence Service; CISC (2005) Annual Report on Organized Crime in Canada. Ottawa: Criminal Intelligence Service Canada Braithwaite, John (2002) *Restorative Justice and Responsive Regulation.* New York: Oxford University Press.
11. Braithwaite, John (2002) *Restorative Justice and Responsive Regulation.* New York: Oxford University Press.
12. Levi, Michael (2005) *The Phantom Capitalists: the Organization and Control of Long-Firm Fraud.* Aldershot: Ashgate, 2nd edition; Levi, Michael (1999) "Regulating Fraud Revisited," in P. Davies et al., eds. *Invisible Crimes.* Basingstoke: Macmillan.
13. Some cybercriminals and hackers fall within this set of 'lone actors' though they are often treated as major social threats by cyberpolice.
14. Andreas, Peter, and Ethan Nadelmann (2006) *Policing the Globe.* New York: Oxford University Press.
15. Gilmore, William (2004) *Dirty Money: The Evolution of Money Laundering Counter-Measures.* 3rd edition, Strasbourg: Council of Europe Publishing; Reuter, Peter, and Edwin Truman (2004) Chasing Dirty Money. Washington, DC: Institute for International Economics; Stessens, Guy (2000) *Money Laundering: an International Enforcement Model.* Cambridge: Cambridge University Press.
16. Diih, Sorle S. (2005) *The Infiltration of the New York's Financial Market by Organised Crime: Pressures and Controls,* unpublished Ph.D.thesis, Cardiff University.
17. Eichenwald, Kurt (2001) *The Informant.* New York: Random House.
18. Marx, Gary (1988) *Undercover.* Berkeley: University of California Press, p.62.
19. Id. P.65.
20. Butterfield, Lord Justice (2004) *Review of Criminal Investigations and Prosecutions Conducted by HM Customs and Excise.* London: The Stationery Office.
21. Block, Alan (1990) *Masters of Paradise: Organized Crime and the Internal Revenue Service in the Bahamas.* London: Transaction Books.
22. Greising, David, and Laurie Morse (1991) *Brokers, Bagmen, and Moles.* New York: John Wiley, p.183.
23. Marx, op. cit.
24. Op. cit.
25. Levine, Dennis (1992) *Inside Out.* London: Century Books; Stewart, James (1991) *Den of Thieves.* New York: Simon and Schuster.

26. Levi, Michael (1987) *Regulating Fraud*. London: Routledge; Levi and Pithouse, op. cit.
27. Levi and Pithouse, op. cit.
28. Williams, James (2005) "Reflections on the private versus public policing of economic crime," 45 *B J Criminol*. 316–339.
29. Taylor, Kevin (1990) *The Poisoned Tree*. London: Sidgwick and Jackson.
30. See Butterfield, op. cit.
31. See Eichenwald, op. cit.
32. Dorn, Nicholas et al. (1991) *Traffickers*. London: Routledge.
33. See n.15
34. Cuellar, Mario-Fiorentino (2003) "The Tenuous Relationship Between the Fight Against Money Laundering And the Disruption of Terrorist Finances," 73 *J. of Criminal Law and Criminology* (2–3) 311–466; Levi, Michael, and William Gilmore (2002) "Terrorist Finance, Money Laundering and the Rise of Mutual Evaluation: A New Paradigm for Crime Control?" 4 *European Journal of Law Reform* 337–364.
35. Levi, Michael (2002) "Money Laundering and its Regulation," 582 *The Annals of the American Academy of Social and Political Science* 181–194.
36. Emsley, Clive (2002) "The Birth and Development of the Police," in Tim Newburn, ed. *Handbook of Policing*. Cullompton: Willan.
37. Ericson, Richard, and Kevin Haggerty (1997) *Policing the Risk Society*. Oxford: Clarendon Press.
38. Levi and Pithouse, op. cit.
39. Roskill, Lord (1986) Report of the Fraud Trials Committee. London: HMSO.
40. Levi, Michael (1993) The Investigation, Prosecution, and Trial of Serious Fraud. Royal Commission on Criminal Justice Research Study No.14, London: HMSO.
41. Levi and Pithouse, 2006.
42. Calavita, Kitty et al. (1999) *Big Money Crime: Fraud and Politics in the Savings and Loan Crisis*. Berkeley: University of California Press.
43. Diih, op. cit., n.16.

References

Andreas, Peter, & Ethan Nadelmann (2006) *Policing the Globe*. New York: Oxford University Press.

Berdal, Mats and Monica Serrano, Editors (2002) *Transnational Organized Crime: New Challenges to International Security*. Boulder: Lynne Rienner.

Block, Alan (1990) *Masters of Paradise: Organized Crime and the Internal Revenue Service in the Bahamas*. London: Transaction Books.

Braithwaite, John (2002) "Rewards and Regulation," *J. Law and Society* 29:12–26.

Butterfield, Lord Justice (2004) *Review of Criminal Investigations and Prosecutions Conducted by HM Customs and Excise*. London: The Stationery Office.

Calavita, Kitty, et al. (1999) *Big Money Crime: Fraud and Politics in the Savings and Loan Crisis*. Berkeley: University of California Press.

CISC (2005) *Annual Report on Organized Crime in Canada*. Ottawa: Criminal Intelligence Service Canada.

Croall, Hazel (2001) *White-Collar Crime*. Buckingham: Open University Press.

Cuellar, Mario-Fiorentino (2003) "The Tenuous Relationship between the Fight against Money Laundering and the Disruption of Terrorist Finances." *J. of Criminal Law and Criminology* 73(2-3): 311–466.

Diih, Sorle S. (2005) *The Infiltration of the New York's Financial Market by Organised Crime: Pressures and Controls*. unpublished Ph.D. thesis. Cardiff University.

Doig, Alan, & Michael Levi (2001) "New Public Management, Old Populism and the Policing of Fraud." *Public Policy and Administration* 16:91–113.
Dorn, Nicholas, et al. (1991) Traffickers. London: Routledge.
van Duyne, Petrus (1996) "The *Phantom and Threat of Organized Crime*." *Crime, Law and Social Change* 24:341–377.
Eichenwald, Kurt (2001) *The Informant*. New York: Random House.
Emsley, Clive (2002) "The Birth and Development of the Police." In *Handbook of Policing*, Editor T. Newburn. Cullompton: Willan.
Ericson, Richard, and Kevin Haggerty (1997) *Policing the Risk Society*. Oxford: Clarendon Press.
Fijnaut, Cyrille and Letizia Paoli, Editors (2005) *Organized Crime and its Control in Europe*. Dordrecht: Springer.
Gilmore, William (2004) *Dirty Money: The Evolution of Money Laundering Counter-Measures*. 3rd Edition, Strasbourg: Council of Europe Publishing.
Greising, David and Laurie Morse (1991) *Brokers, Bagmen, and Moles*. New York: John Wiley.
Hobbs, Dick (1997) "Criminal Collaboration." In *The Oxford Handbook of Criminology*. Second Edition. Editors Mike Maguire, et al. Oxford: Oxford University Press.
Hobbs, Dick (1998) "Going Down the Glocal: the Local Context of Organized Crime." *The Howard Journal of Criminal Justice* 37:407–422.
Levi, Michael (1993) *The Investigation, Prosecution, and Trial of Serious Fraud*. Royal Commission on Criminal Justice Research Study No. 14. London: HMSO.
Levi, Michael (1998) "Organising Plastic Fraud: Enterprise Criminals and the Side-Stepping of Fraud Prevention." *The Howard Journal of Criminal Justice* 37:423–38.
Levi, Michael (1999) "Regulating Fraud Revisited." In *Invisible Crimes*. Editors P. Davies, et al. Basingstoke: Macmillan.
Levi, Michael (2002a) "The Organization of Serious Crimes." In *The Oxford Handbook of Criminology*. Third Edition. Editors Mike Maguire, et al. Oxford: Oxford University Press.
Levi, Michael (2002b) "Money Laundering and its Regulation." *Annals of the American Academy of Social and Political Science* 582 :181–194.
Levi, Michael (2005) *The Phantom Capitalists: the Organization and Control of Long-Firm Fraud*. Second Edition. Aldershot: Ashgate.
Levi, Michael (forthcoming) "The Organization of Serious Transnational Crimes and Terrorism," In *The Oxford Handbook of Criminology* Fourth Edition. Editors Mike Maguire, et al. Oxford: Oxford University Press.
Levi, Michael and William Gilmore (2002) "Terrorist Finance, Money Laundering and the Rise and Rise of Mutual Evaluation: A New Paradigm for Crime Control?" *European Journal of Law Reform* 4:337–364.
Levi, Michael and Jim Handley (1998) *The Prevention of Plastic and Cheque Fraud Revisited*. Home Office Research Study 184. London: Home Office.
Levi, Michael and Jim Handley (2002) *Criminal Justice and the Future of Payment Card Fraud*. London: Institute for Public Policy Research.
Levi, Michael and Andrew Pithouse (2006) *Victims of White Collar Crime: The Social and Media Construction of Business Fraud*. Oxford: Clarendon.
Levine, Dennis (1992) *Inside Out*. London: Century Books.
Marx, Gary (1988) *Undercover*. Berkeley: University of California Press.
Naylor, R. Tom (2002) *Wages of Crime*. Ithaca: Cornell University Press.
NCIS (2005) *UK Threat Assessment, 2005*. London: National Criminal Intelligence Service.
Nelken, David (2002) "White-Collar Crime" In *The Oxford Handbook of Criminology*. Third Edition. Editors Mike Maguire, et al. Oxford: Oxford University Press.
Reuter, Peter and Edwin Truman (2004) *Chasing Dirty Money*. Washington, DC: Institute for International Economics.

Roskill, Lord (1986) *Report of the Fraud Trials Committee*. London: HMSO.

Stessens, Guy (2000) *Money Laundering: an International Enforcement Model*. Cambridge: Cambridge University Press.

Stewart, James (1991) *Den of Thieves*. New York: Simon and Schuster.

Taylor, Kevin (1990) *The Poisoned Tree*. London: Sidgwick and Jackson.

Williams, James W. (2005) "Reflections on the Private versus Public Policing of Economic Crime." *Br J Criminology* 45:316–339.

Part XI

Regulation, Prevention, and Control

1

Situational Crime Prevention and White-Collar Crime

Michael L. Benson and Tamara D. Madensen

Abstract

It is common knowledge that many white-collar crimes arise out of the special opportunities that accompany the offender's access to a particular occupational or organizational position. However, there have been few attempts to think systematically about how organizationally based opportunity structures facilitate the commission of different forms of white-collar crime. In this paper, we explore the applicability of ideas drawn from situational crime prevention theory to white-collar crime. The theory of situational crime prevention is based on the premise that crime can be reduced, if not altogether prevented, by altering various dimensions of the opportunity structures that are available to potential offenders. We argue that this theory offers a new and potentially effective approach to white-collar crime control.

Criminal opportunities are now recognized as an important cause of all crime.[1] Crime results when a potential offender perceives a situation as a criminal opportunity and decides to take advantage of it. The situational and ecological factors that create or facilitate opportunities for crime have accordingly become important objects of study for criminologists.[2] This development has had both theoretical and practical benefits. Theoretically, it has led to a greater understanding of how and why crime rates vary over time and over geographical areas. These variations often appear to be driven more by differences in criminal opportunities rather than by differences in the supply of potential offenders or their motivations. In addition, the focus on criminal opportunities has helped us to better understand why particular crimes recur repeatedly in particular places at particular times. On the practical side, research on criminal opportunities has led to a new approach situational crime prevention to the control of street crime. In this paper, we explore how situational crime prevention might be applied to white-collar crime.

We begin by describing the origins, assumptions, and basic tenets of the situational crime prevention approach. Then, we identify some distinctive characteristics of white-collar type crimes that may require us to modify standard situational prevention strategies. Next, we attempt to illustrate how the situational approach can be applied to white-collar-type crimes. We conclude with a general discussion of current methods used to control white-collar crime and the benefit of using the situational approach as a framework for choosing among crime control techniques.

Situational Crime Prevention

The situational crime prevention perspective differs from traditional criminological theories in several ways. The most notable is that situational crime prevention focuses on the criminal event, whereas traditional theories are directed toward the criminal offender and the sources of criminal motivation. By traditional theories, we refer to the theories of criminal motivation that are typically covered in standard textbooks, such as strain, control, and learning. Traditional theories provide much insight into the origins of criminal and delinquent behaviors. With respect to their crime prevention implications, these theories focus on somehow changing the factors that produce motivated offenders. The situational approach, however, is less concerned with why people are motivated to commit crimes. Instead, it asks how crimes occur and what situational factors can be manipulated to prevent them from recurring in the future. In other words, following Gottfredson and Hirschi,[3] situational crime prevention theorists make a distinction between *crime* and *criminality*, and they focus on the former rather than the latter.

The Origins of Situational Crime Prevention

The situational crime prevention approach developed at about the same time in Great Britain and the United States. In Britain, the birth of the perspective can be traced to the early work of Ronald V. Clarke. Clarke began to develop the ideas that would later form the basis of the situational approach while working in the Home Office Research Unit, the British government's criminological research department, during the 1960s and 1970s.[4] During this time, Clarke and colleagues were investigating why some juvenile correctional facilities had higher rates of absconding or re-offending than other facilities. The researchers found that the situational and environmental characteristics of the correctional institutions were stronger predictors of misbehavior than the background or personality factors of the juveniles.[5] They also found that by manipulating these characteristics, they could reduce rates of absconding and re-offending. This discovery led the researchers to speculate that the same ideas might work outside of institutions as well. Just as misconduct in institutions apparently could be reduced by manipulating the situational and environmental characteristics of facilities, everyday crimes in society might also be reduced or prevented by altering existing opportunity structures.[6]

In the United States, the relationship between situational variables and crime was also receiving attention from a variety of different disciplines. The concepts of "crime prevention through environmental design" or CPTED[7] and "defensible space"[8] both draw attention to the role that physical environments play in helping to encourage or inhibit criminal activity. Additionally, "problem-oriented policing"[9] developed as a way to approach specific crime problems, construct practical responses, and gauge the effectiveness of police efforts. These perspectives informed Clarke's later work in the area of situational prevention and have helped to guide the development of the major principles of the present-day situational crime prevention perspective.

According to Clarke, "situational prevention comprises opportunity-reducing measures that (1) are directed at highly specific forms of crime, (2) involve the management, design or manipulation of the immediate environment in as systematic and permanent way as possible, [and] (3) make crime more difficult and risky, or less rewarding and excusable as judged by a wide range of offenders."[10] Recent work has also incorporated the notion of controlling situational precipitators of crime, or removing situational factors that tend to incite criminal responses.[11]

The situational perspective offers five general crime prevention principles. These principles represent different ways of reducing the attractiveness of crime to potential offenders. In Table 1, the five principles are listed in brief form in the column headings. Here we spell them out in greater detail: (1) increase the degree of effort necessary to carry out the offense; (2) increase the risk of detection prior to, during, or after the completion of the criminal act; (3) reduce the rewards that can be obtained by engaging in the offense; (4) reduce situational conditions that may provoke an unplanned criminal action; and (5) remove the offender's ability to make excuses that justify criminal actions or that absolve the offender from responsibility. It is important to recognize that the five principles are meant to operate from the perspective of a person who is contemplating committing an offense. That is, they depend on the offender's perceptions of the effort, risks, rewards, provocations, and justifications that a particular situation offers.

There are 25 specific tactics or techniques that have been used to implement these crime reduction principles. This matrix of 25 opportunity-reducing techniques can be used as an analytical tool to assist construction of potential strategies to prevent or reduce specific crime problems. It provides a framework that encourages the strategist to think systematically about how existing opportunity structures can be altered to make an offense seem less attractive to potential offenders.

Although situational crime prevention has gained popularity among criminal justice academics and practitioners over the last two decades, the opportunity-reducing techniques of the perspective have been applied primarily to direct-contact, predatory crimes,[12] that is, to ordinary street crimes. Very little attention has been paid to white-collar type crimes.[13] Our goal here is to explore how this approach can be applied to white-collar crime. Before we do that, however, we must discuss some important features of white-collar crime.

Features of White-Collar Crime

For the purposes of this paper, we define white-collar crime in the manner proposed by Edelhertz[14] as a property crime committed by non-physical means through the use of deception or concealment. We are aware that this definition is not universally accepted by white-collar scholars, many of whom prefer to define white-collar crime along the lines proposed by Sutherland.[15] Those who follow Sutherland's "offender-based" approach to defining white-collar crime define it in terms of some combination of the social and occupational characteristics of the offender.[16] The offender characteristics typically referenced in offender-based definitions include such attributes as high social status, respectability, and occupancy of a prestigious or powerful occupational[17] position.

Table 1. Twenty-five techniques of situational preventions[17]

Increase the Effort	Increase the Risks	Reduce the Rewards	Reduce Provocations	Remove Excuses
1. Target harden • Steering column locks • Anti-robbery screens • Tamper-proof packaging	**6. Extend guardianship** • Take routine precautions: go out in group at night, leave signs of occupancy, carry phone • "Cocoon" neighborhood watch	**11. Conceal targets** • Off-street parking • Gender-neutral phone directories • Unmarked bullion trucks	**16. Reduce frustrations and stress** • Efficient queues and polite service • Expanded seating • Soothing music/muted lights	**21. Set rules** • Rental agreements • Harassment codes • Hotel registration
2. Control access to facilities • Entry phones • Electronic card access • Baggage • screening	**7. Assist natural surveillance** • Improved street lighting • Defensible space design • Support whistleblowers	**12. Remove targets** • Removable car radio • Women's refuges • Pre-paid cards for pay phones	**17. Avoid disputes** • Separate enclosures for rival soccer fans • Reduce crowding in pubs • Fixed cab fares	**22. Post instructions** • "No Parking" • "Private Property" • "Extinguish camp fires"
3. Screen exits • Ticket needed for exit • Export documents • Electronic merchandise tags	**8. Reduce anonymity** • Taxi driver IDs • "How's my driving?" decals • School uniforms	**13. Identify property** • Property marking • Vehicle licensing and parts marking • Cattle branding	**18. Reduce emotional arousal** • Controls on violent pornography • Enforce good behavior on soccer field • Prohibit racial slurs	**23. Alert conscience** • Roadside speed display boards • Signature for customs declarations • "Shoplifting is stealing"
4. Deflect offenders • Street closures • Separate bathrooms for women • Disperse pubs	**9. Utilize place managers** • CCTV for double-deck buses • Two clerks for convenience stores • Reward vigilance	**14. Disrupt markets** • Monitor pawn shops • Controls on classified ads • License street vendors	**19. Neutralize peer pressure** • "Idiots drink and drive" • "It's OK to say NO" • Disperse troublemakers at school	**24. Assist compliance** • Easy library checkout • Public lavatories • Litter bins
5. Control tools/weapons • "Smart" guns • Disable stolen cell phones • Restrict spray paint sales to juveniles	**10. Strengthen formal surveillance** • Red light cameras • Burglar alarms • Security guards	**15. Deny benefits** • Ink merchandise tags • Graffiti cleaning • Speed humps	**20. Discourage imitation** • Rapid repair of vandalism • V-chips in TVs • Censor details of modus operandi	**25. Control drugs and alcohol** • Breathalyzers in pubs • Server intervention • Alcohol-free events

These characteristics do play an important role in complicating white-collar crime control. However, it is an indirect role. The social and occupational characteristics of the offenders are important because they influence access to opportunities. However, in regards to white-collar crime control they are, in our opinion, less important than the characteristics of white-collar crimes that we review below.

Decades of case studies and empirical research has documented that white-collar crimes and white-collar criminals differ in many ways from common street crimes and criminals. Suffice it to say that white-collar crimes are typically more complex, better organized, longer lasting, and more profitable than conventional street crimes.[18] White-collar criminals tend to be older, better educated, more socially integrated, and wealthier than conventional street offenders.[19] For our purposes, these well-known facts are less important than four other characteristics of white-collar type crimes. The characteristics that we highlight are those that have special relevance for situational crime prevention. They are typical features of many white-collar crimes that require us to modify or rethink the situational prevention approach to controlling white-collar crime. We can illustrate these four features via the offense of healthcare fraud committed by a physician.

First, the offender has *specialized access to the victim or target* by virtue of an occupational position.[20] All would-be offenders must solve the general problems of identifying a target and then gaining access to it. Many white-collar offenders hold an occupational position which provides them with the necessary access to the victim or the target. For example, physicians who wish to commit healthcare fraud against the government have legitimate access to patients, their medical records, and the Medicare or Medicaid reimbursement systems as a result of their occupational positions.

Second, the offender uses *deception or concealment* to hide the offense and its effects from the victim and from law enforcers. A key feature of white-collar crime is that the offender engages in a fraudulent transaction in which the victim is unaware of the offender's true intent or objective. For example, physicians submit claims to Medicare that look like normal, legitimate forms. However, the forms do not reflect either what actually was done or what was medically necessary to do in regard to the treatment of particular patients.

Third, the offender has an *ambiguous state of mind* at the time of the offense. By ambiguous state of mind, we mean that the offender's state of mind cannot be easily determined from his or her actions. State of mind is used in the legal sense to refer to criminal intent. In most street crimes, the physical actions that the offender goes through while committing the offense clearly indicate criminal intent. With many white-collar crimes, the offender's physical actions are not out of the ordinary and thus cannot be used to infer criminal intent. Physicians submit claims to Medicare all the time. The fact that any one claim is not entirely accurate does not necessarily mean that a physician intended to commit fraud. He or she may just have made a mistake.

Fourth, the offender may be *physically distant or separate* from the victims of the offense. White-collar crimes may arise out of transactions that occur electronically, over the telephone, or through the mail. There is often no need for offenders to come into physical contact with victims or their property. Physicians who commit healthcare fraud do not steal directly from the government's coffers. Instead, they steal at a distance. From the confines of their offices they submit fraudulent claims to a government office located perhaps hundreds of miles away.

Separately and in combination, these features require us to modify several of the specific crime control tactics of the situational approach if we wish to apply them to white-collar crime. Before we discuss these modifications, we must also explore in greater detail a few assumptions of the situational approach and their implications for white-collar crime control.

Assumptions of Situational Prevention

To apply the situational approach to the prevention of white-collar offenses requires a reexamination of three elements of the situational perspective: (1) the approach must focus on highly specific forms of crimes, (2) manipulation of situational factors must occur in the immediate environment, and (3) the applied interventions must affect the judgment of a wide range of offenders. The following sections consider these elements and their applicability to white-collar crime.

Focus on Highly Specific Forms of Crime

Situational prevention is only applicable to "highly specific forms of crime." This is an essential limitation, especially when attempting to apply the situational perspective to a broad category of offenses such as "white-collar" crimes. The term "white-collar crime" is typically used to describe a wide array of heterogeneous offenses. To use the situational approach effectively, much more specific offense types must be targeted. For example, healthcare fraud is widely recognized as an important and extremely costly white-collar offense.[21] However, fraud in the healthcare system comes in a variety of different forms.[22] These different forms have different opportunity structures. Hence, applying the techniques of situational crime prevention requires a more detailed definition of the problem to be addressed. A more appropriate definition of a crime problem involving healthcare fraud would be "*physicians billing Medicare for services that were not actually provided to patients.*"

The more specific the definition of the offense, the greater the likelihood that the interventions derived using the situational approach will be effective in reducing or eliminating the problem. This is because a well-defined crime problem has a distinctive opportunity-structure that may overlap but is never fully replicated by other crime types. Every criminal opportunity structure is defined by characteristics of the offender, target/victim, mechanics, site, and situation that are unique to the particular offense.[23]

The challenge of appropriately defining a crime problem raises an additional consideration that requires us to modify how the situational approach is used. From the perspective of situational crime prevention, rare or isolated crimes are not *problems*.[24] Criminal activity becomes problematic when it recurs, that is, when it becomes patterned. Patterning is important for two reasons. It permits the crime analyst to identify the essential features of the crime's opportunity structure. It also makes devoting resources to crime prevention efforts worthwhile. If recurrence is not anticipated, then implementing an intervention would be an unproductive and inefficient use of resources.

Many high-profile white-collar crimes, such as the recent scandals at Enron and WorldCom, may be isolated events. Because these types of crimes often are not detected, it is difficult to know how many of them there are. If they truly are one-time events, then it makes little sense to apply situational preventive techniques. On the other hand, if we assume that these seemingly rare events are rather common, then it is appropriate to use the situational approach. However, when dealing with seemingly uncommon white-collar offenses, we use the approach in a different way. Rather than analyzing a large number of known criminal events to identify the important features of the opportunity structure of a particular type of crime, we must analyze in detail the few cases that have been discovered. We assume that the cases that are detected are not isolated events but rather representative of a class of similar crimes that have not yet been detected. If, as Sutherland argued long ago, the techniques of white-collar crime diffuse throughout industries by a process of differential association, then this assumption is more likely to be right than wrong most of the time.[25]

Even if some white-collar crimes really are one-time events, many other white-collar crimes happen over and over again. For example, Calavita and Pontell provide many examples of crimes that were repeatedly committed during the savings and loan crisis of the 1980s.[26] For these crimes, patterns can be investigated and the underlying opportunity structures identified. It is for these repeated events that situational prevention may hold the greatest promise for reducing levels of white-collar crime.

Immediate Environment

The situational crime prevention perspective maintains that the most effective way to change a crime opportunity structure involves altering the immediate environment. This assertion is rooted in the theoretical assumptions of routine activity theory. The most current version of routine activity theory states that a crime will occur if a target and offender intersect in a place that lacks an effective guardian, handler, or manager.[27] In other words, routine activity theory assumes that crimes happen in particular physical locations and at particular times. In the case of white-collar crime, we must rethink the concept of "place."

Many white-collar crimes are not like direct-contact predatory crimes in which the offender has some sort of direct physical contact with the victim or target. The white-collar offender may be physically separated from the victim. White-collar crimes can be committed by multiple offenders, in multiple locations. White-collar offenders may never come into contact with, or in some cases even know, the identity of their victims. Therefore, the concept of place or the immediate environment needs to be re-conceptualized before situational crime prevention can be effectively applied.

Rather than thinking in terms of the characteristics of physical locations, we must focus on the transactional network that links the offender and the target.[28] Interaction between the offender(s) and target may be facilitated at a distance through networks. The concept of transactional networks provides a way of analyzing, from a crime prevention perspective, offenses that do not occur in a concrete, physical environment. Provided that the target and the offender(s) are part of the same network, the network provides the offender(s) with the "place" to commit the offense. For example, computers that are linked to organizational resources provide opportunities in which theft of records, secret information, or funds can be accomplished without breaking and entering.[29] Transactional networks provide access to the target and may also offer an offender a form of concealment that is not granted to offenders of direct-contact predatory crimes. Therefore, the application of the situational approach to white-collar crimes will often require interventions that limit access to victims or targets by altering the characteristics of networks, rather than places.

Offender Judgment

The last element that defines the situational perspective concerns the offender and his or her perceptions. Situational interventions are constructed to alter offenders' perceptions of the costs and benefits associated with a particular crime in ways that discourage the offender from committing the offense. This approach assumes that offenders make more or less rational assessments of their situations when choosing whether or not to commit offenses. It is understood, of course, that offenders do not always make the best possible choices when seeking to benefit themselves. Like everyone else, criminal offenders are not perfectly rational calculators. They have only bounded or limited rationality. Nevertheless, the situational approach is based on the assumption that offenders are rational to some degree and are sensitive to changes in the immediate situation that influence the perceived costs and benefits of crime. Even seemingly "bad" choices are the product of the offender's evaluation of the risks and uncertainties associated with any criminal undertaking.[30] If the risks and uncertainties can be made great enough, then presumably even the most motivated of potential offenders will be less likely to make "bad" choices.

With respect to white-collar offenders, the assumption of rationality seems even more defensible than it is for ordinary street offenders. White-collar offenders are typically better educated and less likely to suffer from the sort of alcohol or drug abuse that undermines rational thinking.[31] In regard to the effectiveness of the situational crime prevention approach against white-collar crime, the greater rationality of white-collar offenders may be a double-edged sword. On the one hand, because of their greater rationality white-collar offenders may be more attuned to changes in opportunity structures that promote crime prevention. Situational interventions that raise the risk of detection only slightly, for example nevertheless, may have large effects on white-collar offender decision-making. On the other hand, the greater rationality of white-collar offenders may enable them to adapt to situational interventions in ways that permit them to continue to offend undetected.

White Collar Crime and Situational Prevention: A Summary of General Considerations

The features of white-collar crimes and the assumptions of the situational perspective considered above suggest that some modification to the situational approach may be necessary. In particular, we must remember that for most white-collar offenses: (1) offenders often have specialized access to victims and targets; (2) deception or concealment is used by offenders to hide evidence that an offense was committed; (3) it is often difficult to prove intent or malice since the actions taken by the offender are not obviously different from legitimate activities; and (4) the offender is often physically distant or separate from the victim when the offense takes place. Additionally, the basic assumptions of the situational crime prevention perspective requires us to (1) focus on the opportunity structures of highly specific crime types and move away from general descriptions of offenses (e.g., fraud), (2) re-conceptualize the concept of place and examine the structure of *networks* that link offenders and victims, and (3) recognize that some white-collar criminals may have a greater degree of rationality than street offenders and that this may make them more sensitive to changes in opportunity structures.

We now attempt to demonstrate the applicability of the situational approach to white-collar crime control. Little effort is needed to envision the application and effectiveness of many of the 25 techniques. However, some techniques appear more difficult if not impossible to implement based on the issues previously outlined. Below, we give greater consideration to the general principles, the specific techniques they encompass, and their potential for controlling white-collar crimes.

Using Situational Crime Prevention to Control White-Collar Crime

As shown in Table 1, the five general principles of situational crime prevention have been implemented using a variety of specific techniques. Numerous evaluation studies have shown that when these techniques are used separately or in combination they reduce rates of particular types of offenses in particular types of situations. In other words, these techniques appear to influence the decisions made by potential offenders so that they become less likely to commit specific offenses.

Can these principles and techniques be applied to white-collar crime? We believe that they can, but to do so will require modifications at times to the standard approaches. In the following sections, we provide examples of how the principles can be applied and the modifications that are needed. We do not wish to claim any originality in our examples or analyses. Many are drawn from the work of others and from our analysis of current law and regulations. Indeed, in many cases, current law and regulations are written in such a way that they illustrate or manifest one or more of the five principles of crime prevention. We hope, however, that by drawing attention to how regulations work in terms of the principles of situational crime prevention, it will become easier to identify ways to extend and improve current efforts at white-collar crime control.

Increasing the Effort

For most ordinary street crimes, a basic crime prevention strategy is to block or restrict potential offenders' access to the target or victim. As indicated in Table 1, this can be accomplished in several ways, such as by hardening the target itself, controlling access to where the target is located, deflecting offenders away from the target, or controlling access to the tools necessary to carry out the offense. Unfortunately, for white-collar crimes that involve specialized access via occupational roles, physically blocking access is not feasible in most cases. Consider, for example, the physician who orders unnecessary tests for patients or who bills Medicaid for work that was not performed. Obviously, to block the physician's access to the target (either the patient or the Medicaid reimbursement system) would have the undesirable side effect of preventing legitimate occupational activities, that is, preventing physicians from practicing medicine. In general, physically blocking access to the target is not a feasible crime prevention technique for any white-collar crime in which the offender misuses a legitimate occupational role, especially occupational roles in which a product or service is supplied to a customer or client.

However, there are ways to control access without blocking legitimate activities. For example, the Centers for Medicare and Medicaid Services have successfully controlled access to their reimbursement system by visiting new home healthcare providers and medical equipment companies before these agencies are assigned a provider number. This allows officials to identify illegitimate providers and deny access to the Medicare/Medicaid system before claims are submitted. Also, the Balanced Budget Act of 1997 has denied access to repeat offenders. The act requires permanent exclusion from government reimbursement systems for those who are convicted of three healthcare related crimes. The general idea here is to restrict access to the occupational role that provides access to the target. Restricting access to the occupational role makes it more difficult for potential offenders to access the target.

Since white-collar crimes often involve specialized access that arises out of the offender's occupational role, any policy or requirement that restricts who may assume particular occupational roles has the effect of blocking access to the tools of white-collar crime. Thus, regulations requiring licenses or certifications can be viewed as ways of blocking access to particular types of white-collar crime. They increase the effort that would-be offenders have to extend in order to get access to the target or victim. The process of occupational licensing and certification also provides opportunities to screen applicants for good moral character, that is, to reduce the number of motivated offenders who have access to the tools of white-collar crime. Granted once an individual obtains a license or certification, he or she has access to the tools of white-collar crime. Possession of the license facilitates rather than blocks opportunities for white-collar crime. As Malcolm Sparrow put it, a physician's license can be a license to steal.[32] So, restricting access to occupations does not stop the "Trojan Horse" scenario, where the offender takes the time and effort necessary to obtain the occupational role legitimately knowing that it will provide access to criminal opportunities. Nevertheless, requiring a license or certification to practice a particular occupation or profession imposes constraints on the number and type of people who are able to practice that line of work. It increases the effort for would be offenders.

Although physically blocking access to the target or victim is not feasible for all white-collar crimes, there are analogous ways to increase the effort needed to commit certain types of white-collar offenses. For example, consider all forms of consumer fraud. All of these frauds have a similar opportunity structure. It involves three components.

1. The offender must somehow contact the victim and make him or her aware of some service or product that the offender has to offer.
2. The offender must convince the victim via fraudulent statements or documents that he or she is legitimate and that the product or service is a good deal.

3. The offender must convince the victim to voluntarily give money or some other type of consideration to the offender for the product or service.

The second step in this chain of events presents opportunities for intervention. If it can be made harder for the offender to convince the victim of his or her legitimacy, then the likelihood that a successful fraud will occur is reduced. We can make it harder for offenders to fool victims by educating victims. This is in effect a form of target hardening. As the general level of education regarding particular forms of fraud increases, it becomes harder for fraudsters to find gullible victims or to convince potential victims of the fraudsters' legitimacy.

Increasing the Risk of Detection

Although there are many ways of increasing the risks of ordinary street crime, most of them involve some sort of increase in surveillance. That is, they all attempt to raise the chance that the offender will be observed while committing the offense. Neighborhood watches, improved street lighting, place managers, burglar alarms, closed-circuit video monitors, security guards—all of these crime prevention strategies supposedly work by making potential offenders more likely to feel that they are under surveillance and likely to be detected if they do something illegal. With ordinary street crime, surveillance is designed to spot the offender. Against white-collar crime, surveillance is used in a different way. White-collar crimes are committed by deception or concealment. The offender does not try to hide his or her identity. Rather, the offender tries to hide the true nature of his or her activities. Thus, for white-collar crime, surveillance must be designed to spot the offense. That is, surveillance must show that what appears to be legitimate on the surface is really fraudulent or illegitimate underneath. Finding the offender is not the problem. Finding the offense is.[33]

Attempts to prevent white-collar crime often rely on increasing the penalties associated with committing such acts. For example, the Health Insurance Portability and Accountability Act of 1996 (HIPAA) reclassified healthcare fraud as a federal criminal offense that carries significant financial penalties as well as a prison term of 10 years to life, depending on the specifics of the offense. However, research indicates that increasing the risks of being detected is more likely to deter would be offenders than is increasing the severity of the sanctions. The risk of detection can be increased by extending guardianship, utilizing place managers, assisting natural surveillance, strengthening formal surveillance, or reducing anonymity.

With respect to heathcare fraud, a simple way to extend guardianship and increase the risks associated with filing fraudulent claims is to hire more investigators to review claims submitted. The more claims reviewed, the greater the likelihood that an illegitimate claim will be detected. However, hiring more personnel is costly and given that most submitted claims are legitimate, this tactic might not yield the desired cost-ratio benefit. Improving fraud detection training for existing auditors and others who process submitted claims might be a more fiscally conservative approach to increasing the likelihood of detection. These individuals can be thought of as place managers who are responsible for the supervision of the network that links patients, physicians, and the organizations that provide monetary reimbursement. Enhancing the ability of these place managers to detect illegitimate activity will necessarily increase the risks associated with engaging in healthcare fraud.

The government has also increased the likelihood of detection by providing reporting incentives for individuals who are aware of others who engage in healthcare fraud. Medicare's Incentive Reward Program provides a monetary reward for information that leads to the recovery of inappropriately obtained funds. This practice encourages "natural surveillance" by individuals who are not employed by the government (e.g., patients, physicians' office assistants) but can provide information to assist fraud investigators. Alternatively, technology now offers a means to strengthen formal surveillance. Some private insurance companies are using software programs designed to detect claims anomalies that suggest fraudulent practices such as unbundling, or billing services separately when they should be included in a single service fee.

Operation Restore Trust, also known as the Senior Medicare Patrol Project, has worked with the Centers for Medicare and Medicaid Services to require providers and suppliers to use a unique billing identification number. This procedure effectively reduces the anonymity of those who submit claims. Unique identification numbers make it easier to track repeat offenders and to detect suspicious activities, including multiple claims submissions for a single procedure.

In general, to increase the risk of detection for white-collar criminals, it is important to make it difficult for them to maintain an ambiguous state of mind or to practice what Katz has called concerted ignorance.[34] For example, laws and regulations that require emails and other documents to be maintained can be effective means of increasing the risks for certain white-collar crimes because potential offenders now have to worry that if their crimes come to light they will not be able to claim that it was just a mistake or that they did not know what was going on.

Reducing the Rewards

Another way to alter the opportunity structure of white-collar crimes is to reduce the rewards associated with engaging in illegitimate activities. The situational crime prevention perspective argues that this could be accomplished by concealing targets, removing targets, identifying property, disrupting markets, or denying the benefits that result from crime. Reducing rewards may prove to be a more difficult task when dealing with white-collar crimes. The techniques of concealing or removing targets and identifying property are often not possible or are generally ineffective in reducing white-collar criminal opportunity unless the cash or property can be physically taken.

Street crimes can often be prevented by concealing or removing targets. For example, police often advise people to keep valuables in vehicles out of sight by locking them in the trunk whenever possible. Also, jewelry stores often remove their merchandise from shop windows after closing. However, it is not possible to conceal or remove reimbursement funds from healthcare professionals or patients. While bank employees keep cash behind counters or in locked drawers to deter robbers, reimbursement transactions do not take place in a physical location. Since reimbursement funds are not taken by force, "hiding" this money from perpetrators is not possible.

The task of identifying property, or in the case of healthcare fraud, government money, is accomplished by the very nature of these transactions. A paper trail is generated whenever funds are issued based on a claim submission. Receipts of electronic or paper bank transactions can be used to prove that an individual received government funds. For cases of healthcare fraud, it is rarely the receipt of money that is in question, but rather the legitimacy of the claim submission based on the actual services provided.

The rewards associated with healthcare fraud can most effectively be reduced by focusing on disrupting illegitimate markets and by denying the benefits associated with fraudulent claims. The Federal Bureau of Investigation's Healthcare Fraud Unit was established in 1992. This unit has been able to successfully use proactive techniques including undercover operation to identify and prosecute individuals and organizations involved in defrauding Medicare and Medicaid. This activity has led to the disruption of numerous illegitimate markets and the recovery of millions of dollars of government funds.

It is difficult to deny the benefits associated with fraudulent billing practices unless the activity is detected. However, once detected, quick denial or lengthy delays for suspicious claims could possibly deter less experienced offenders. Unfortunately, the Centers for Medicare and Medicaid Services evaluates contractors based on the timeliness and efficiency of their claims processing and payments. Since contractors are penalized for any claims not paid within 30 days, this makes it difficult to thoroughly review suspicious activity and makes the denial of payment less likely.

Reducing Provocations

The situational crime prevention perspective has recently recognized that situational factors can provoke people to commit crimes, and that it is helpful to reduce situational provocations that can encourage criminal activity. For example, relieving crowded conditions in bars can make physical confrontations less likely. Situational provocations can be reduced by helping individuals to avoid disputes, reducing emotional arousal, limiting frustration and stress, neutralizing peer pressure, and discouraging imitation.

Unlike some street crimes, white-collar crimes are not crimes of passion. The complex nature of the majority of these offenses often requires planning on the part of the perpetrator. Consequently, these crimes generally do not result from impulsive decision-making. This means that helping individuals to avoid disputes and reducing emotional arousal may prevent physical or violent crimes from occurring, but these techniques may hold less potential for controlling healthcare fraud. However, it should be noted that the banking industry has reduced the emotional arousal associated with dealing with large sums of cash by requiring dual custody of funds that exceed a specified limit. The other three techniques of reducing provocations have been used and are theoretically more applicable when attempting to prevent healthcare fraud.

First, the existing system for filing claims for Medicare and Medicaid payments has been designed to make the process as simple and easy as possible. By making it easy to file legitimate claims, the government reduces the frustrations and stress that would result from a confusing and complicated system. Second, the American Medical Association offers continuing medical education credits for attending seminars on professionalism. The ethical guidelines used to encourage professionalism may serve to neutralize peer pressure by dispelling the myth that "all physicians do it." Third, imitation has been discouraged or reduced by the refusal to publicize the methods used by those who have engaged in fraudulent schemes. While many examples of successfully perpetrated fraud cases can be found on the web or in government documents, the specific methods used by these individuals or organizations to fraudulently obtain funds are usually kept confidential.

Removing Excuses

The fifth and final category of situational techniques focuses on the rationalizations offenders use to commit offenses. Removing possible excuses prevents offenders from being able to neutralize feelings of guilt or shame. It also makes it difficult for offenders to justify their actions in hindsight. Excuses can be removed by setting rules, posting instructions, assisting compliance, alerting conscience, and by controlling drugs and alcohol.

Setting rules and posting instructions are important in the effort to reduce healthcare fraud. Those who submit claims should be aware of what services are and are not covered by the program. Government agencies have been explicit in defining submissions that constitute a fraudulent claim (e.g., billing for services never rendered, billing for a more expensive procedure than the one performed, or misrepresenting services). Additionally, instructions for submitting claims must be available and easy to understand. This allows authorities to challenge claimants who dispute charges by maintaining that they were unaware of the illegality of their actions. Training, signed affidavits stating that they have read and understand the rules of submission, and information readily available on the Internet can assist with this goal.

In addition to setting rules and posting instructions, insurance agencies can reduce the likelihood of frauds, especially those committed out of negligence, by assisting compliance. Those who are submitting claims must have access to resources that can help them answer questions about the submission process. When assistance is readily available, justifications for improper reporting become less tolerable. Also, paper or electronic forms that are clear and easy to file are likely to reduce the number of honest mistakes made by claimants.

Multiple agencies and organizations have compiled statistics and produced reports that describe the costs associated with healthcare fraud. Publications like these that address the negative effects of fraud for patients and society as a whole can be used to alert the conscience of those who might abuse insurance systems. For physicians who have taken an oath to protect their patients, knowledge of the consequences of healthcare fraud may increase the guilt associated with perpetrating these offenses and deter future misconduct.

Again, because white-collar offenses are not crimes of passion, efforts to control drugs or alcohol so that the judgment of a white-collar offenders is not impaired at the time they consider the offense are not likely to have a substantial impact on the prevalence of white-collar crime overall. While it is likely that some healthcare fraud occurs due to personal drug or alcohol habits, the interventions necessary to address this issue is a subject beyond the scope of the situational perspective.

Final Thoughts

The problem of how best to control white-collar crime, especially white-collar crime committed in organizational settings, is notoriously complex. There are any number of competing schools of thought, ranging from economism through self-regulation, legal regulation, and criminalization. A discussion of the strengths and weaknesses of these different approaches is far beyond the scope of this article. Rather, we would like to suggest that the approach presented here—crime prevention via the alteration of opportunity structures—represents a more fundamental way of thinking about the problem of white-collar crime control. It is more fundamental in the sense that it implicitly underlies the other approaches.

Depending on how they are used, economism, self-regulation, regulation, and criminalization can be thought of as ways of implementing one or more of the five general principles of crime prevention, and we should evaluate their effectiveness in terms of how well they match these principles. For example, advocates of greater criminalization often call for harsher sanctions for white-collar crime. While harsher sanctions may increase the risks for potential offenders, they are simply one way of increasing the costs associated with engaging in white-collar crime. The important question is whether harsher sanctions represent the best or most cost effective method for deterring potential offenders. From the perspective of situational crime prevention, harsher sanctions represent a very inefficient and ineffective way of increasing risks. They are too far removed from the immediate decision making context that confronts potential offenders. The situational approach maintains that increasing the risk of detection during or immediately after the offense is likely to be more effective. The evidence gathered over the last few decades through deterrence research suggests that this claim is correct.[35]

From the perspective of situational crime prevention theory, the key questions to ask are how do potential offenders assess the costs and benefits associated with a particular criminal opportunity structure, and what steps can be taken to alter these various dimensions of risk and reward. Whether this is accomplished via harsher sanctions or some sort of regulatory innovation is less important than the fundamental idea of considering how effective these proposed interventions will be in altering one or more the five dimensions (i.e., effort, risk, reward, provocation, excuse) of a particular opportunity structure.

As is the case with all forms of crime, the problem of white-collar crime will never be solved, but it can be made more tolerable. We think that the situational prevention approach provides a very effective way of accomplishing that end. We urge white-collar crime scholars and practitioners interested in reducing the harms imposed by white-collar crime to apply the principles and strategies of the situational prevention approach. The first step is to develop a detailed understanding of the opportunity structures of particular forms of white-collar crime, and the second step is to figure out the simplest and most cost-effective way of altering opportunity structures.

Endnotes

1. (Felson, 2002).
2. (Cohen and Felson, 1979; Felson, 2002; Clarke, 1997).
3. (Gottfredson and Hirschi, 1990).
4. (Clarke and Cornish, 1983).
5. (Tizzard, Sinclair, and Clarke, 1975).
6. (Clarke, 1995).
7. (Jeffery, 1971).
8. (Newman, 1972).
9. (Goldstein, 1979).
10. (Clarke, 1997).
11. (Wortley, 2001) (Cornish and Clarke 2003).
12. (Clarke, 1997).
13. But see Felson (2002) for an interesting start in this direction.
14. (Edelhertz, 1970).
15. (Sutherland, 1940).
16. (Reiss and Biderman, 1980; Albanese, 1995).
17. (Cornish and Clarke, 2003).
18. (Weisburd, Wheeler, Waring, and Bode, 1991).
19. (Weisburd et al., 1991; Benson and Kerley, 2000).
20. (Felson, 2002).
21. (Sparrow, 1996).
22. (Sparrow, 1996) Leiderbach; (Geis, Jesilow, Pontell, and O'Brien, 1985).
23. (Brantingham and Brantingham, 2001).
24. (Clarke and Eck, 2003).
25. (Sutherland, 1983).
26. (Calavita and Pontell, 1990).
27. (Felson, 2002).
28. (Eck and Clarke, 2003) (Vaughan, 1982).
29. (Vaughan, 1982).
30. (Clarke and Cornish, 2000).
31. (Benson and Moore, 1992; Benson and Kerley, 2000) .
32. (Sparrow, 1996).
33. (Braithwaite and Fisse, 1990).
34. (Katz, 1979).
35. (Pratt et al., 2005).

References

Albanese, Jay (1995) *White-Collar Crime in America.* Englewood Cliffs, NJ: Prentice Hall.

Benson, Michael, and Elizabeth Moore (1992) "Are White-Collar and Common Offenders the Same? An Empirical and Theoretical Critique of a Recently Proposed General Theory of Crime." *Journal of Research in Crime and Delinquency* 29(3):251–72.

Benson, Michael L., and Kent R. Kerley (2000) "Life Course Theory and White-Collar Crime." Pp. 121–36 in *Contemporary Issues in Crime and Criminal Justice: Essays in Honor of Gilber Geis*, Editors Henry N. Pontell and David Shichor. Saddle River, NJ: Prentice Hall.

Braithwaite, John, and Brent Fisse (1990) "On the Plausibility of Corporate Crime Control." *Advances in Criminological Theory* 2:15–37.

Brantingham, Paul J., and Patricia Brantingham (2001) "The Implications of the Criminal Event Model for Crime Prevention." Pp. 277–303 in *Process and Structure of Crime:*

Criminal Events and Crime Analysis, Editors Robert F. Meier, Leslie W. Kennedy, and Vincent F. Sacco. Somerset, NJ: Transaction Publishers.

Calavita, Kitty, and Henry N. Pontell (1990) "'Heads I Win, Tails You Lose': Deregulation, Crime, and Crisis in the Savings and Loan Industry." *Crime & Delinquency* 36:309–41.

Clarke, Ronald V. (1995) "Situational Crime Prevention." Pp. 94–150 in *Building a Safer Society: Strategic Approaches to Crime Prevention*, vol. 19, Editors Michael Tonry and David Farrington. Chicago: University of Chicago Press.

Clarke, Ronald V. (1997) *Situational Crime Prevention: Successful Case Studies.* New York: Harrow and Heston.

Clarke, Ronald V., and Derek B. Cornish (1983) *Crime and Control in Britain: A Review of Policy Research.* Albany, NY: State University of New York Press.

Clarke, Ronald V. (2000) "Rational Choice." Pp. 23–42 in *Explaining Crime and Criminals: Essays in Contemporary Criminological Theory*, Editors Raymond Paternoster and Ronet Bachman. Los Angeles: Roxbury.

Clarke, Ronald V., and John E. Eck. (2003) *Become a Problem-Solving Analyst.* London: Jill Dando Institute of Crime Science.

Cohen, Lawrence E., and Marcus Felson. (1979) "Social Change and Crime Rate Trends: A Routine Activity Approach." *American Sociological Review* 44:588–608.

Cornish, Derek B., and Ronald V. Clarke (2003) "Opportunities, Precipitators, and Criminal Decisions: A Reply to Wortley's Critique of Situational Crime Prevention." *Crime Prevention Studies* 16:41–96.

Eck, John E., and Ronald V. Clarke (2003) "Classifying Common Police Problems: A Routine Activity Approach." *Crime Prevention Studies* 16:7–39.

Edelhertz, Herbert (1970) *The Nature, Impact and Prosecution of White-Collar Crime.* Washington, D. C.: U. S. Department of Justice.

Felson, Marcus (2002) *Crime and Everyday Life.* Thousand Oaks, CA: Pine Forge Press.

Geis, Gilbert, Paul Jesilow, Henry Pontell, and Mary J. O'Brien (1985) "Fraud and Abuse of Government Medical Benefit Programs by Psychiatrists." *American Journal of Psychiatry* 142:231–34.

Goldstein, Herman (1979) "Improving Policing: A Problem-Oriented Approach." *Crime and Delinquency* 25:236–58.

Gottfredson, Michael R., and Travis Hirschi (1990) *A General Theory of Crime.* Palo Alto, CA: Stanford University Press.

Jeffery, C. Ray (1971) *Crime Prevention Through Environmental Design.* Beverly Hills, CA: Sage Publications.

Katz, Jack. (1979) "Concerted Ignorance: The Social Construction of Cover-Up." *Urban Life* 8:295–316.

Newman, Oscar (1972) *Defensible Space: Crime Prevention Through Urban Design.* New York: Macmillan.

Pratt, Travis C., Francis T. Cullen, Kristie R. Blevins, Leah E. Daigle, and Tamara D. Madensen (2006) "The Empirical Status of Deterrence Theory: A Meta-Analysis." pp. 367–395 In *Taking Stock: The Empirical Status of Criminological Theory—Advances in Criminological Theory, Volume 15*, Editors Francis T. Cullen, John Paul Wright, and Kristie R. Blevins. New Brunswick, NJ: Transaction Publishers.

Reiss, Albert J., and Albert D. Biderman (1980) *Data Sources on White-Collar Lawbreaking.* Washington, D.C.: National Institute of Justice.

Sparrow, Malcolm K. (1996) *License to Steal: Why Fraud Plagues America's Health Care System.* Boulder, CO.: Westview Press.

Sutherland, Edwin H. (1940) "White-Collar Criminality." *American Sociological Review* 5:1–12.

Sutherland, Edwin H. (1983) *White Collar Crime—The Uncut Version.* New Haven, CT: Yale University Press.

Tizzard, Jack, Ian Sinclair, and Ronald V. Clarke (1975) *Varieties of Residential Experience*. London: Routledge & Kegan Paul.

Vaughan, Diane (1982) "Transaction Systems and Unlawful Behavior." *Social Problems* 29:373–79.

Weisburd, David, Stanton Wheeler, Elin Waring, and Nancy Bode (1991) *Crimes of the Middle Classes: White-Collar Offenders in the Federal Courts*. New Haven: Yale University Press.

Wortley, Richard (2001) "A Classification of Techniques for Controlling Situational Precipitators of Crime." *Security Journal* 14:63–82.

2

"This Time We Really Mean It!"

Cracking Down on Stock Market Fraud

Laureen Snider

Canada's First Mining Scandal?
Between 1576–78, Martin Frobisher made 3 extended trips to Canada, convinced that he had found gold on Baffin Island. However, recent analyses reveal that the gold-containing assays were fraudulently "salted" by crooked chemists in London.
(Globe & Mail, July 6, 2004: A1)

"For more than 20 years, the [American] federal government has given companies fairly free rein, allowing them to operate with less and less regulation. . . . Suddenly, . . . the race to regulate is on."
(The New York Times, February 10, 2002, Section 3, Page 1)

On February 12, 2004, the federal government in Canada passed Bill C-13, amending the *Criminal Code* to increase penalties for insider trading, augment the investigative resources of the Crown, and strengthen whistleblower protection.[1] In December, 2003, a high-level report told the federal government it must create a new national regulatory body and a single regulatory code, thereby ending 100 years of decentralized provincially-based stock market regulation.[2] Both initiatives were responses to high-profile corporate scandals, particularly Worldcom and Enron in the United States, which followed the 1999 collapse of the technology stock market bubble. The new measures exemplify what media and officialdom trumpet as the state's crackdown on corporate crime. Two decades of government-sponsored deregulation and downsizing, of denying the ubiquity and severity of corporate crime, and forgetting the lessons of the past have now ended. Laissez-faire "see-no-evil, speak-no-evil" attitudes to business, and the deregulatory policies they inspired, are no more. Governments today are expanding corporate criminal liability, extending it to CEOs and Boards of Directors.[3] In the Unites States voices bemoaning "overregulation" are strong: Chambers of Commerce suggest governments are on "witch hunts that imperil the American dream"; conservative politicians decry draconian new regulations that will destroy the New York Stock Exchange (*The New York Times,* February 10, 2002: 3–1, *Globe & Mail,* June 1, 2002: F8).

The history of business regulation should make us cautious of such claims. More than 200 years of struggle, with many more defeats than victories, were necessary to force capitalist states, first, to recognize that corporations must be held responsible for corporate acts that cause death, injury, and financial damage to millions of people; second, to pass laws with teeth; and third to actually resource and enforce these laws.[4] State reluctance to hold capital to account in the past has produced a series of regulatory cycles, each beginning with a high-profile event—a major bridge collapse or ferry accident, a series of frauds, massive corporate bankruptcies. Such an event typically is followed by volumes of lofty rhetoric from politicians and officials, and eventually by draft legislation. After a series of revisions, new laws are passed. They usually are much weaker than originally promised, and in some cases totally unenforceable, as was the case with Canada's first anti-combine laws.[5] If the laws are useable, and the issue is still politically salient, a flurry of well-publicized charges will follow, then plea bargains, convictions, fines, and appeals. Once the media spotlight has moved away, the regulatory body reverts to status quo ante and normal regulatory patterns, characterized as "benign neglect" or "capture," reappear. In the 1980s a new wrinkle in this pattern surfaced, first in the United States and Britain, now globally. Under the sway of neoliberal doctrines, the economic and political power of business dramatically increased. Instead of reverting to status quo ante, governments began aggressive campaigns against regulation (euphemistically called regulatory reform). In the United Kingdom, this took the form of wholesale privatization of publicly owned enterprises.[6] In the United States and eventually Canada, public relations campaigns attacked regulators as inefficient, empire-building bureaucrats, regulatory agency budgets were slashed, and self-regulation replaced public bodies.[7]

Stock market fraud is a type of financial crime which is itself a category of corporate crime. Corporate crime refers to "illegal acts committed by legitimate formal organizations aimed at furthering the interests of the organization and the individuals involved."[8] Two kinds may be identified: financial and social.[9] Financial crimes such as insider trading, restraint of trade, and fraudulent business practices victimize investors, consumers, business competitors, and government (the latter as investor and, in many cases, as loan guarantor of last resort). Social crimes, both environmental (air and water pollution), and health and safety crimes (unsafe workplaces, dangerous working conditions), victimize different, less powerful groups—workers, employees, and citizens as a whole. This basic fact of political economy means that rigorous enforcement benefits very different interests. Regulations requiring ventilators in factories, scrubbers in smokestacks and minimum pay (social corporate crime) threaten profit levels by increasing the cost of production. Financial regulations also add costs, but they create a level playing field and facilitate investor confidence, both factors essential to business prosperity. A state which monitors and sanctions those who loot company coffers or sell fraudulent stocks and trade on inside knowledge performs a vital function for capitalism by acting in the long term best interests of investors and corporations, of the capitalist system as a whole. Where cowboy capitalism runs wild, where regulatory and legal systems are known to be ineffective or absent, investors may flee. In today's wired world, this loss of confidence quickly escalates from local to global levels, possibly producing runs on the national currency and economic collapse.[10] If the *collective* financial interests of capital were the dominant forces behind strict enforcement, if maintaining "investor confidence" was the only goal of regulation, if pure reason dominated decision-making in complex organizations, installing and maintaining effective regulatory systems would be straightforward, though not easy. Like traditional policing aimed at deterring relatively powerless individuals, the primary constraints would be insufficient resources and technological limitations. That this has not happened signals that the relations of power at play are considerably more complex.

This paper examines the latest crackdown on insider trading and stock market fraud in Canada. First, it traces stock market regulation by state and non-state bodies from their origins to the present day; second, recent criminal (Bill C-13) and non-criminal measures to hold corporate actors accountable are outlined; third, it looks at factors which change the regulatory equation, particularly new technologies and social movements, versus those that reinforce existing relations of power. In theoretical terms, the paper uses Foucauldian arguments to show how meaning is constructed, negotiated, and defined, how resistance and power play into knowledge claims, and the discourses that construct the "good" corporate citizen and the "socially responsible corporation" today. In policy terms, the paper explores inequality. It seeks to understand the massive gulf in attitudes and policy between upper- and lower-world crime. The conclusion discusses the complexity of corporate crime and the difficulties of generalizing about its causes, remedies, and future.

History of Securities Regulation in Canada

The establishment of regulatory agencies to oversee stock exchanges in Canada originated in two "nation-building" priorities: first, the need to raise capital to promote the development of natural resources, particularly the mining industry; second, the need to control the industry's lamentable susceptibility to fraud. Mining has long been identified as central to the Canadian economy—resource development still accounts for more than 10 percent of Canada's GDP (Report on Business Magazine, June 2004, from Statistics Canada data). After the fur trade disappeared, and the easily exploitable timber resources were cut in Eastern Canada, before 1900, attention turned to wealth in the ground. Raising capital to allow private entrepreneurs to develop natural resources was an important duty of the Canadian capitalist class. It was also a major objective of the Canadian state. Stock exchanges were established in regional centres such as Toronto, Montreal, and Vancouver to give new mining companies a place to raise seed capital (as it was then called) to finance exploration and development. Given the nature of the terrain (wilderness), and of exploration (a low-tech, individualistic, labor-intensive process), finding, extracting, and processing wealth in the ground was a high-risk venture. Prospectors competed to survey and claim every likely looking chunk of muskeg and moose pasture. Rudimentary geology, rudimentary technologies, and basic (often nonexistent) systems of communication meant that, for much of the 20th century, anyone with an elementary knowledge of science could "salt" a likely section of land, (that is, plant valuable minerals on or in it), raise a fortune by selling dreams of riches to gullible investors, and disappear. In the first half of the 20th century, this happened frequently enough that key corporate and political actors became fearful. If too many scams became known, investment capital would disappear, and what would happen to the nation then? Worse, what would happen to their careers as stock promoters and bankers? At this juncture, provincial and territorial governments were forced to create regulatory bodies, designing each one to meet the capital-raising needs of resource industries in its particular region.

The history of regulation in Ontario, the economic engine of Canada and home of the largest and most influential stock exchange, illustrates the essential features of regulation as it developed. The granddaddy of Canada's regulatory agencies is the Ontario Securities Commission, established in 1945. This followed a recommendation of the 1944 Royal Commission on Mining aimed at repairing the Securities Act then in existence, which could only intervene once fraud was discovered. The OSC, in contrast, would be empowered to prevent as well as sanction fraud. Registration and disclosure were the vehicles through which public interest would be protected. Only companies meeting certain standards, standards which would ensure "the integrity of the applicant," would only be allowed to sell stocks in Ontario,[11] and applicants would have to file a prospectus disclosing "all material facts." The new rules would be backed with "more rigorous prosecution," and miscreants could face cancellation of registration in extreme cases.[12] However, because promoting the mining industry was the primary purpose of regulation, sanctions were not the regulatory strategy of choice. Facilitating the industry, seen as central to Canada's growth and prosperity, was where public interest lay. As regulatory goals, catching crooks and promoting ethical behavior hardly appeared in the debates. OSC listings illustrate the significance and centrality of resource industries at this time: in 1951, a total of 227 of 327 shares listed on the Toronto Stock Exchange were mining and oil stocks; in 1961 this fell slightly to 101 mining and oil stocks, 81 industrials, and 19 unclassified others.[13] Indeed, the Toronto Stock Exchange was the largest dealer in mining stocks in the world throughout the 1950s and 1960s.

The bulk of day-to-day regulation, however, was then and is today delegated to the industry itself, through the self-regulatory organization or SRO. The most important SRO was the Toronto Stock Exchange (TSE, now TSX). To government actors at the time, who were closely connected to key financial actors, it was "obvious" that members of the TSE were most knowledgeable and therefore best equipped to regulate and discipline members. The early OSC decision to allow mining companies registered on the TSE exemption from OSC disclosure requirements indicates both the centrality of the TSE and state reluctance to impede the mining industry's pursuit of capital in any way. That self-regulation necessarily involves serious conflicts of interest between the TSE as promoter and its obligations as policing agent, was not deemed problematic.

A second self-regulatory organization, the Broker-Dealers Association (now the Investment Dealers Association), was established in 1947. According to the OSC Chair at the time, the BDA was set up because the OSC felt that such an organization was necessary to limit OSC powers and territorial ambitions.[14] That a government regulatory agency would be so careful to limit its own powers explains the subsequent history of the OSC quite well. The BDA was also charged with promoting the industry. It would become the regulator of last resort, covering those who would otherwise escape regulation, such as prospectors and entrepreneurs who did not belong to professions. Membership in the BDA, originally not obligatory, became mandatory when the OSC refused to register non-BDA members. Since Ontario was Canada's richest province, being excluded from its stock exchange had serious financial consequences.[15]

In the 1960s, two highly visible public scandals occurred. In 1964 the Windfall mining company collapsed and its CEO was accused of selling worthless shares.[16] In 1965, the Atlantic Acceptance Finance Company went bankrupt due to illegal and unethical financial practices by senior executives. Following three Royal Commissions and a provincial inquiry, a new Securities Act was produced in 1966. It was shaped by struggles over the meaning of mandatory disclosure. The OSC argued that the goal of mandatory disclosure was greater investor protection, while the TSE and business in general argued that investors should be free to choose high-risk stocks if they wished. The TSE, labelled "a private gaming club" by one of the Royal Commissions, was not in a strong bargaining position until it repackaged its arguments. Business was represented as 100 percent in favor of investor protection, but the kind of mandatory disclosure sought by the OSC would prevent entrepreneurs from raising capital. Impeding resource exploitation was something both sides abhorred, and the OSC lost that battle.

In the 1970s, broker commission rates and merger mania took center stage. When the United States deregulated broker commission rates in 1975, many in the TSE were keen to copy, arguing that markets are the only guarantee of efficiency or of free and fair competition. The OSC argued the public had a right to rates that were "fair" and "reasonable." While the OSC won that battle in 1978, it reversed itself less than a decade later.[17] Merger issues revived struggles over mandatory disclosure. At what stage should investors be informed that a takeover bid or merger was under negotiation? How much were they entitled to know? OSC arguments for earlier, more comprehensive disclosure were unsuccessful. As Condon put it: "The attempt to require more detailed and contextual information to investors at the time of distribution of new securities largely failed".[18] However the struggles, compromises and negotiations which produced the revised Securities Act of 1978 altered the meaning of disclosure in a somewhat more investor-friendly way.

Developments Since 1980

In the 1980s and 1990s, monumental changes took place after the electoral victories of Ronald Reagan (USA) and Margaret Thatcher (UK). Neo-liberal doctrines celebrated capital as the engine of growth and guarantor of efficiency, and vilified government in general and regulation in particular. Regulation and government were no longer necessary evils, but impediments.[19] Two decades of privatization, deregulation, and decriminalization began. In the United States and Britain, regulatory agencies in all fields were attacked—often by appointing the business executive most critical of an agency as its new head (as with OSHA, the US Occupational Safety and Health Act.[20]

Although Canada was a late convert to neo-liberalism in many areas,[21] changes in competition policy began as early as 1986 with the replacement of the century old Combines Investigation Act (covering conspiracy, bid-rigging, predatory and discriminatory pricing, misleading advertising, and marketing practices such as pyramid sales), with the passage of the "flexible," business-oriented Competition Act.[22] Then on June 30, 1987, restrictions on banking, insurance, trust companies, and securities, laws meant to ensure that no single financial sector became too powerful, were removed. With restrictions gone, new players entered and competition to sell shares and financial advice increased. By the 1990s share-selling competition had gone global. Though wealth was not redistributed in a more egalitarian direction,[23] the number of share-owners in Canada increased dramatically.[24] While 23 percent of all Canadian adults owned publicly listed securities in 1990, this increased to 46 percent by 2003, accounting for 20 percent of total household assets per family.[25] This increased involvement, though mostly indirect, (in pension and mutual funds controlled by professional fund managers not individual "owners"), means greater public interest in and dependence on market integrity.

In the last decade, globalized capital and new communications technologies have destabilized regulation in all nation-states. With capital virtually unrestrained, money crosses borders and changes hands at log on speed. Businesses once dependent on local banks and exchanges now list on exchanges throughout the world. Multinational security firms trade on a 24/7 basis. Market volumes have increased: "between 1980 and 2000, private capital flows... increased more than six-fold to nearly US $4 trillion annually worldwide."[26] Stock exchanges have become more international—cross-border alliances are now common—but also more specialized. In Canada, the Toronto Stock Exchange handles senior equities, TSX Venture handles junior equities,[27] the *Bourse de Montreal* is the national derivatives exchange, while the Winnipeg Commodity Exchange specializes in commodity futures and option exchange.[28]

Capital markets have also become increasingly important suppliers of growth capital: in 2002, a total of 88 percent of long-term financing for Canadian firms came from markets, up from 73 percent in 1990. With the rise of the speculative economy and futures markets, investment requires no commitment to a particular nation-state, sector, or business. Buying and selling, getting in and out quickly, scoring maximum short-term profit, is all that counts. And while there are more ways to invest, waves of takeovers and mergers throughout the 1980s and 90s produced greater corporate concentration. In Canada today, 777 companies, worth more than $75M, account for 98 percent of all market capitalization; the largest 60 companies alone make up 51.6 percent of the total.

Numerous new disciplines and specialist roles have developed. As securities regulation became more complex, securities law became a new legal subfield. Securities lawyers now broker deals, negotiate takeovers, provide advice to business and to regulatory commissions, *and* compose a distinct new interest group. Within exchanges, more businesses and increased competition among them has weakened crucially important networks of informal social control. In a city such as Toronto, for example, key players were once geographically fixed, similar in class, ethnicity, religion, and gender.[29] The elites who ran the Toronto Stock Exchange typically attended the same set of private schools and summer camps, and belonged to the same social clubs, and economic and political organizations as adults. (Female elite members were wives, not competitors). Top regulators and politicians often shared similar backgrounds. Now this exclusive WASP gentleman's club is no longer the only game in town, and the common values and codes of behaviour these men promoted and enforced have been weakened. Whatever the flaws of old-boy networks (sexism, racism, ethnocentrism, classism, and more), a seldom understood consequence was that the rules of the game were understood and broadly respected by major players, if only because the consequences of deviation, both personal and professional, were so high.

Finally, three potentially important counter-hegemonic developments must be noted. First is the establishment and growing strength of oppositional stockholder rights groups. With the bursting of the technology-inspired market bubble of the 1990s, such groups have become increasingly aggressive, sometimes defying senior management by resisting takeovers, disputing key personnel changes, or questioning executive compensation and perks. Many have begun to lobby politically, demanding more disclosure, more information on profit levels and debt loads, and even (at times) questioning environmental practices and labour conditions.[30] Second, with 24-hour business news and increased public interest in investment and markets, investigative financial journalism has become more important. Canada's major national newspaper, the *Globe & Mail,* regularly issues reports on insider trading, or the gap between executive salaries (up) and profit levels (down). Third, new technologies offer unprecedented opportunities to monitor and discipline market players. Trades can be tracked as they happen, electronic "markers" differentiating insider trades can be purchased. Surveillance equipment is easy to acquire and install. And email has forever changed evidence-gathering, since it is impossible to render messages permanently irretrievable to those with sufficient time, resources, and computer savvy to retrieve them. Technological innovations allow regulators, in theory, to intervene as soon as "abnormal" trading patterns are discovered. They ease evidence-gathering and make convictions easier. But will they be used this way? The relative power of the parties involved may tell us more than the characteristics of the technologies.

Summing up: Canada today has a sophisticated and complex regulatory system of Self Regulatory Organizations (SROs) and government agencies. There are 13 official securities commissions, one in each province and territory, [31] originally established to facilitate resource extraction and capital raising in the mining industry. Securities commissions have long been viewed by government and by business as a necessary evil—sometimes more "evil" than "necessary," sometimes the reverse. However in 2004, oppositional groups and media are celebrating regulation as the saviour of free enterprise, [32] the quick fix to bring back investors and perpetuate prosperity. Section II examines measures which, it is hoped, will accomplish these goals.

The New Crackdown

On February 12, 2004, the federal government introduced a series of amendments to the *Criminal Code of Canada*. The Bill makes "improper insider trading" a criminal offense, increasing maximum penalties from 10 to 14 years.[33] Maximum penalties for "market manipulation" were doubled from 5 to 10 years. "Tipping," defined as "knowingly conveying inside information to another person with knowledge that it might be used to secure a trading advantage or illegal benefit," becomes a hybrid offense, where the Crown decides how to prosecute. If indictable, the maximum prison term is 5 years; if summary, fines are assessed.[34] The Minister of Justice emphasized in press releases that "stiff criminal penalties" would be reserved for "the most egregious cases."[35] To encourage judicial severity, sentencing guidelines—a list of "aggravating factors"—will be issued. Bill C-13 also provides whistleblower protection for employees who report illegal activities, and empowers courts to force third parties, such as banks, to provide all necessary documents.[36] Failure to comply can result in fines up to $250,000 and 6 months in jail. Changes in civil and administrative law are also under consideration, including measures strengthening corporate governance through the Canada Business Corporations Act (Canada, Department of Finance, 2003).

Bill C-13 is the Canadian government's most recent and visible response to wordwide corporate debacles such as Enron, Worldcom, and Parmalat, and its response to charges that Canada has been "too lenient" with corporate offenses in the past. Leniency is deemed problematic not because it imperils justice or threatens the rule of law, nor because it denies victims' compensation, but because it threatens investor confidence. Imposing new penalties on powerful financial elites is not something the federal government does often or easily. Attributing criminal liability to management for unsafe working conditions, for example, was under discussion for 50 years.[37] Constitutional issues add to the difficulties, because the provinces are legally responsible for stock exchanges and securities, while the federal government has jurisdiction over criminal law. Insider trading, then, was previously handled in administrative proceedings or by provincial courts on a quasi-criminal basis. Bill C-13 strengthens federal authority, giving the Attorney General of Canada concurrent jurisdiction with provincial Attorneys General in all cases that "threaten the national interest in the integrity of capital markets."[38]

Jurisdictional struggles are as old as Canada itself. The impetus for Bill C-13 was the necessity for Canada to respond to the *Sarbanes-Oxley Act* (2002). Since the passage of the North American Free Trade Agreement (NAFTA) in 1988, the Canadian economy has been ever more tightly tied to the United States. Canada is America's largest trading partner, and it has the largest number of non-American companies selling shares in the United States. Increasingly, American financial markets and stock exchanges, particularly the New York Stock Exchange, are the only ones that matter. Thus when the US government acts, Canada must respond. Indeed, precisely those terms were used to introduce and justify Bill C-13 in the House of Commons.[39]

The Canadian response was initially drafted at a private dinner meeting attended by a "select group of government officials, senior regulators and industry officials," including David Brown, head of the Ontario Securities Commission, David Dodge, governor of the Bank of Canada, and the deputy Minister of Finance. At this meeting, in March 2002, the implications of Enron, strategies to restore investor confidence, and policy options were discussed. Some of these recommendations have since been adopted by provincial regulatory commissions, albeit in piecemeal form. The Canadian Securities Administrators, a coordinating body which represents all 13 provincial regulators, urged its members to adopt a series of "Best Practices." These include mandatory halts in trading before major corporate announcements, real-time "markers" differentiating insider trades from others, measures to control "bucket shops" offshore, and the creation of international data bases. Ontario has taken the lead, decreeing that CEOs and CFOs must personally certify the accuracy of information in their financial statements. Audit committees must contain Directors who are independent of management and audits must be overseen by the Canadian Public Accountancy Board, (a new regulatory body created in July 2002). In addition, to obtain OSC permission to list on the TSX, publicly owned companies must have audits and financial statements done by a firm recognized by the CPAB. In September, 2003, Ontario and Quebec adopted a measure pioneered by Manitoba the preceding year, allowing Securities Commissions to order restitution to investors "where losses were incurred by illegal acts or improper advice."[40]

Self-regulatory organizations have also been active, particularly the chartered accounting profession. The Canadian Public Accountancy Board (CPAB), was created to set standards for auditors, although firms listed in Canada can bypass the CPAB by registering with the American body, (the Board of Public Companies' Accounting Oversight Board. Most recently, "independent" security analysts and mutual funds have come under scrutiny. Investment analysts, researchers who tell investors which stocks to buy and sell, are market investors themselves. They are also employees in stock-selling organizations. Potential conflicts of interest are endemic. In a 2001 report (*Setting Analyst Standards),* the Toronto Stock Exchange, the Broker Dealers Association, and the Canadian Venture Exchange recommended new conflict of interest rules, which were adopted in June, 2002.

Efforts have also been made to reform corporate governance.[41] A group of major institutional investors formed the Canadian Coalition for Good Governance in June 2002. This body issued a series of recommendations designed "to provide more power, oversight and independence to boards of directors and audit committees."[42] Although the TSX adopted new corporate governance guidelines in 1995, it is once again discussing the wisdom of requiring continuous disclosure. Even executive compensation is under scrutiny, as executive compensation levels soar while stock values and profit levels plummet.

Enforcement

Enforcement, portrayed in the 1990s as unnecessarily stringent, is now lamented as lax. "Canada suffers weak and inconsistent enforcement and investor protection. Wrongdoers too frequently go unpunished, and adjudication is unduly delayed." Enforcement, moreover, is "costly, duplicative and inefficient."[43] The lack of jail sentences is decried,[44] and now "global fraudsters" have identified Canada as the jurisdiction of choice. The Chair of the Canadian Securities Administrators (CSA) himself says that Canada has more inside trades prior to major announcements than the United States.

In September 2002 a provincial-federal task force with representatives from the government (Ontario, Quebec, BC, and Alberta Securities Commissions) and the private sector (the Investment Dealers Association, the *Bourse de Montreal*, and Market Regulation Services) was appointed. Its 32 recommendations called for more and better RCMP investigations, increased scrutiny of "offshore accounts" from regions with "inadequate regulatory regimes," and new directives for dealing with inside information for "senior managers, directors, lawyers and accountants."[45] To improve enforcement, multidisciplinary teams of accounting and economics professionals and municipal, provincial, and federal law enforcement personnel were recommended.

The federal government acted a year later, setting aside $120 million dollars. Dedicated interdisciplinary Integrated Market Enforcement Teams (IMET) will be set up in Toronto, Montreal, Vancouver, and Calgary. Two IMET teams now operating in Toronto contain staff from the RCMP, the OSC, the Investment Dealers Association (IDA), the Mutual Fund Dealers Association (MFDA), and Market Regulatory Services (MRS Inc., a TSX affiliate that monitors trading patterns. On June 14, 2004, IMET made its first arrest, charging Steve McRae of "no fixed address" with Theft over $5,000 and Laundering the Proceeds of Crime. McRae is accused of removing 17 securities certificates between July, 1998 and March, 2000 from unclaimed accounts at HSBC Canada, his employer at the time, and selling them for $370,000. IMET is presently working on a second case, described as a cross-border market manipulation and insider trading scheme.

Provincial agencies have also beefed up enforcement. Ontario increased penalties for illegal insider trading from two years to five, and maximum fines from $1 million to $5 million per count. Companies could be ordered to remit triple the profits made or losses avoided, whichever was greater. In a speech on May 27, 2004, OSC head David Brown boasted of progress since 2000: triple the number of inside trading cases prosecuted, more than 100 actions settled, judicial delay cut from 21 to 13 months, trial time from 15 to 11 months. Jail sentences were obtained when sought 80 percent of the time (unfortunately he does not say how often they were sought). Remaining enforcement delays, botched investigations and prosecutions are attributed to "lack of coordination" between three levels of police (federal, provincial, and city), three levels of government, and 13 Regulatory Commissions. His Director of Enforcement, Michael Watson, explained the problem this way: "A lot of people don't . . . think there is anything wrong with it [insider trading]"; moreover risks of detection are low, rewards high. He recommends better data tracking to deter "bad apples."

Despite all the rhetoric, many high profile cases remain in limbo. Bre-X Minerals imploded in the spring of 1997 when it was discovered that gold assays at their Indonesia mine ("the world's largest gold deposit") were "salted." Stocks became worthless overnight. Charges have only now been laid, eight counts of insider trading against a former executive who sold $84 million of Bre-X stock just before the fraud was discovered. Livent, a Toronto entertainment company, went bankrupt in 1998. Charges were laid by the SEC in the United States shortly thereafter, but the OSC waited three years before charging Livent's chief executives with manipulating financial records to hide losses of $100 million.

Similar examples of regulatory reluctance abound. Poonam Puri (2001)[46] examined enforcement under the Competition Act, the Income Tax Act and others; she found no significant change in historically lax enforcement patterns. Mary Condon[47] examined administrative sanctions assessed by securities regulators in 13 jurisdictions across Canada. Administrative sanctions are the most commonly used regulators prefer them to Criminal Code or penal statutes under securities law because regulators can act on their own, without going through courts or other external bodies. Thus they take the least time. Although Condon found significant inter-provincial differences in the severity, frequency, and rationale of administrative penalties, the total number of cases decided nationwide from 2000 to 2003 was 83.[48] The majority of cases, 213 in all, were "resolved" by settlement agreements—where no guilt is admitted and sanctions are moot. Such settlements were the regulatory instruments of choice in the most active provincial agencies (Alberta, British Columbia, and Ontario); used for a wide range of offenses, from failing to file insider-trading reports to distributing securities without registration.[49]

Self-regulatory agencies have similar enforcement records.[50] For example, the Investment Dealers Association, like most SROs, is both lobbyist and regulator for the brokerage industry. In 2003, the IDA received 1,506 complaints, mostly about "unsuitable" investments and unauthorized trading. Complaints were up 41 percent. Eleven members were hit with criminal charges, 629 with civil claims. Fifty-seven internal investigations were heard, 729 files opened, and fines totalling $265,189 (firms) and $3.2 million (individuals) were assessed.[51]

The mutual fund industry, which doubled in net worth from $131.5 billion in 1994 to $474 billion in 2004,[52] has been virtually ignored by regulators in the past. A task force established in 2002 by the Canadian Securities Administrators found significant conflicts of interest, lax enforcement, weak rules and standards. It recommended forcing companies to set up independent governance boards with the power to fire managers who put company interests before those of unit-holders. Similar proposals had been first endorsed back in 1969. However, CSA recommendations were once again blocked by powerful lobbies from the mutual funds industry. It argued that investor protection must be tied to market efficiency to avoid "burdening the industry with unnecessary and costly structures."[53] Another clever move was the hiring of the senior regulator who represented the OSC on the CSA task force. In her new capacity, she now argues, "The CSA was asking for the impossible and the unnecessary."[54] The Investment Funds Institute of Canada, a lobby group representing the 200 largest firms, asserted: "The interests of investors and the industry are the same." It characterized the industry's relations with regulators as "mature," a "give and take relationship."[55] Thus new regulations give oversight committees the power to "vet," not "veto," conflicts of interests; meaning committees will only see disputes that fund managers refer to them. Their strongest sanction is to "instruct" fund managers to "publicize the committee's displeasure."[56] Persuasion has replaced mandatory requirements. [57]

Thus, in the middle of the self-advertised greatest crackdown ever on financial crime, it is easy to find evidence that the power of business to resist, shape, and defeat regulatory initiatives remains.

Change, or Regulatory Status Quo?

The previous sections illustrates that there has been, thus far, more rhetoric and posturing from government and SROs than tough, zero-tolerance action. Neither the democratization of governance heralded by theorists[58] nor the crackdown trumpeted by media are apparent. Are these new laws and increased penalties purely symbolic? Will these initiatives outlast media interest and actually make such crimes unprofitable? Can they prevent the next Enron (or a scaled-down Canadian version)?

There *are* new developments with the potential to dramatically strengthen enforcement. Oppositional stockholder rights groups have become increasingly aggressive, lobbying for mandatory disclosure, bans on insider trading, and ceilings on executive compensation. Such groups supply pro-regulatory pressure to balance the constant, unremitting anti-regulatory pressure furnished by corporate lobbies, a countervailing force formerly in short supply. However investors are still a minority and a relatively privileged one at that, and investor lawsuits do little to protect the public. Lawsuits (even class actions) are basically individualistic, delivering the largest benefits to the biggest investors (and law firms!). They offer no public remedies, no symbolic redress, no "closure," nothing to compensate citizens for indirect losses when currencies decline and taxes increase to cover corporate malfeasance and theft. They typically deliver mere pennies, to the vast majority of unsecured creditors who see their life savings, pensions and nest-eggs destroyed. And there is no redress at all for employees facing job loss, pension loss, and unemployment.

Heightened public interest and the advent of investigative financial journalism also have counter-hegemonic potential. Publicity on the costs and ubiquity of corporate crime can direct public and political attention to the massive inequality in media outrage in regard to traditional offenders (bank robbers or "welfare cheats") in comparison to kid-glove, business-section coverage of corporate crime, which is typically a thousand times more costly.[59] Audiences can also be alerted to the massive discrepancy in sanctions. The multinational corporation steals millions and is fined the equivalent of its profits for a day; the penniless welfare cheat is imprisoned five years, and cut off welfare forever. Such exposes may strengthen oppositional groups seeking to stem corporate power, with possible long-term socio-cultural effects on popular beliefs about the beneficence of corporations.

But the most fervently promoted panacea is the technological fix. New technologies with the ability to "mark" inside trades, new surveillance capabilities, and the permanent nature of email communications make the democratization of control possible. If put into effect, these innovations increase trade visibility, make it harder for regulators and SROs to ignore suspicious trading patterns, and lay an evidence trail that makes conviction more certain. However, technologies interact with relations of power. Decisions about the design and deployment of new technologies within companies are made by CEOs and Boards of Directors. Decisions on surveillance equipment utilized by government agencies are made by politicians dependent on corporate goodwill ideologically, economically, and politically. Self-regulatory organizations typically play both regulatory and industry promotion roles. The primary targets of technological surveillance thus far, the recipients of the most intensive, intrusive monitoring, have been low-level employees—clerical staff, warehouse and call-center workers. [60]

There are other reasons for scepticism. Over the last three decades, maintaining nation-specific market regulation when capital is free to go anywhere is all but impossible. In Canada, and increasingly elsewhere, American stock exchanges and regulatory regimes are the only ones that count. This is why Sarbanes-Oxley impacted trading throughout the developed world. The United States has one of the most politicized regulatory systems in the world; under George Bush, Jr., business and free enterprise are worshipped, government and regulation reviled.[61] However, because the United States is a democratic country, major financial scandals routinely produce tough-sounding measures and relatively vigorous enforcement. But when stock markets bounce back, when media take up new scandals, when neo-liberal forces and business resume muscle-flexing, few indeed are the institutions and actors capable of mounting effective opposition. Budget cuts and regulatory rollbacks are therefore likely to return, repeating entrenched patterns of the past. As O'Brien notes, this "structural imbalance" is the Achilles heel of American regulatory systems.[62]

As nation-states' power has waned (with the dramatic exception of the world's only remaining superpower), the power of capital has increased.[63] Capital has a virtual monopoly on information about itself, a monopoly defended by the constitutional rights of corporations (which are extensive) and the barricades erected by an array of laws. Patents, definitions of privacy that privilege "trade secrets," and the commodification of everything from genes to breast cancer cures produce cultures where making money is accepted as the only legitimate goal of individuals and organizations.[64] Such messages are promoted through advertising, marketing, and public relations campaigns. Discourses lionizing the "free" individual and denigrating any kind of limit or regulation on profit-making and growth are inescapable: "U.S. business spent 60 percent more on marketing in 1992 than the U.S. as a nation spent on all private and public education."[65] The 100 largest transnational corporations in the world produce the bulk of these messages, shaping goals, belief systems, and "common-sense"expectations. Indeed, recent criticism of corporate behavior has spurred many transnational companies to seize the initiative. They have established and sponsored organizations to promote "social responsibility" and define "good corporate citizenship," thereby shaping what these terms should—and should not—mean.[66] No one should be surprised when such organizations produce codes which stress the importance of individual ethics and voluntary action over zero-tolerance regulation backed by criminal sanctions.[67]

The increased acceptance of profit-maximization as a legitimate life goal has significant impact on conscience and ethics, on patterns of socialization, on the all-important informal levels of social control. If doctrines of greed dominate socialization processes, value systems stressing honesty, social equality, and responsibility for others are weakened. Social control works most effectively when individuals shame themselves and significant others.[68] However, if family and peers accept values which tell executives that their only responsibility is to make the most money they can, for themselves and the company, and show increasing profits every quarter, no shaming is possible. There is no discrepancy between the way executives have been socialized to act and their present behaviour. The "star system," the cult of celebrity CEOs, the worship of cowboy capitalists sends similar criminogenic messages. Enron, for example, was lauded in 2001 for "dismantling the New Deal regulatory legacy;" shortly before it imploded, its CEO was named second-best in America, and it was voted the most innovative company by *Fortune* magazine six years in a row.[69] Such values promote codes of ethics that justify and promote law-breaking.

To understand the potential to secure rigorous enforcement, we must also look at the silences in the regulatory debates, the questions not asked, the issues not debated. For example, all the major players in regulatory debates—business, regulatory experts, and politicians—have assumed that the job of government was to promote the wealth of private investors and ensure the lasting prosperity of business. This is seen as fact, as simply "common sense." But such beliefs set real limits on regulatory agendas. If the main purpose of regulation is to make Canada safe for (corporate) investors, and stock markets safe for speculators, the regulatory debate will not address measures promoting equity and equality among citizens. *And once stock markets have recovered and investors are confident once more, the pressure on regulators to act will diminish.* As the major rationale for regulation, such an objective is perilously vulnerable. Moreover, the actors themselves, the voices attaching meanings to terms such as "regulatory crackdown," are primarily older white males from financially privileged backgrounds with similar educational credentials, lifestyles, and contacts. Actors from different backgrounds, with different "common sense" assumptions and value systems, are simply not in the room. The divergent ideas they might bring to the table are therefore not discussed, let alone debated. Such silences indicate how corporate-sponsored values set agendas at the most basic level, by shaping the ideas up for debate. When analysis is limited to debating the options these actors put on the regulatory table, the shape and overall slant of the table is neither seen nor problematized.

Conclusion

Globalization and the resilience of anti-regulatory arguments in neo-liberal states make it simplistic to take the latest state promises at face value. However, it is equally simplistic to assume that patterns of the past predict, circumscribe, or foretell the future. Cultures, human beings, financial forces and technological change are much too complex for deterministic formulae of the past. New voices, technologies, and laws are assuredly part of this new mix. At the most minimal level, they provide new and visible yardsticks against which regulatory efficiency and judicial zeal will be measured by oppositional groups. In this sense alone, today's crackdown on corporate crime is a significant event.

Acknowledgments

The author gratefully acknowledges the research support of the Social Science and Humanities Council of Canada, grant No. 410-2004-2230. I would also like to thank Mary Condon and Steve Bittle for their comments, and Justin O'Brien and participants in the International Conference on Governance, Belfast, September 21–22, 2004, where an early version of this paper was presented. This material will be published in an upcoming book of conference papers.

Endnotes

1. The legislation came into force June 4, 2004.
2. See Phelps, M., H. McKay, T. Allen, P. Brunet, W. Dobson, E. Harris, M. Tims, (2003) It's Time: Report of the Committee to Review the Structure of Securities Regulation in Canada. Canada: Department of Finance, December 17 (online at www.wise-averties.ca).
3. Archibald, T., K. Jull, and K. Roach (2004) "The Changed Face of Corporate Criminal Liability." *Criminal Law Quarterly* 48:367–96.
4. Carson, W. (1980) "The Institutionalization of Ambiguity: Early British Factory Acts." In G. Geis and E. Stotland, eds., *White-Collar Theory and Research.* Beverly Hills, Ca.: Sage, Carson, W. (1970) "White Collar Crime and the Enforcement of Factory Legislation." *British Journal of Criminology,* 10:383–98, and Snider, L. (1993) *Bad Business: Corporate Crime in Canada.* Scarborough, Ontario: Nelson.
5. Snider, L. (1978) "Corporate Crime in Canada: A Preliminary Report." *Canadian Journal of Criminology*, 20, 2:178–202; Stanbury, W. (1986-87) "The New Competition Act and Competition Tribunal Act: Not with a Bang but a Whimper?" *Canadian Business Law Journal* 12:2-42; Stanbury, W. (1977) *Business Interests and the Reform of Canadian Competition Policy 1971–75.* Toronto: Carswell/Methuen.
6. Which, ironically enough, required new regulations and new regulatory bodies! (Pearce and Tombs, 2003).

7. See Doern, B., and S. Wilks (1998) "Introduction," in B. Doern and S. Wilks, eds., *Changing Regulatory Institutions in Britain and North America.* Toronto: University of Toronto Press, 3–25, Doern B. and S. Wilks (1996) "Conclusions: International Convergence and National Contrasts." in B. Doern and S. Wilks, eds., *Comparative Competition Policy: National Institutions in a Global Market.* Oxford: Clarendon Press, 327–59; Fooks, G. (2003) "Auditors and the Permissive Society: Market Failure, Globalization and Financial Regulation in the United States." *Risk Management: An International Journal* 5(2):17–26; Tombs, S. (1996). "Injury, Death and the Deregulation Fetish: The Politics of Occupational Safety Regulation in United Kingdom Manufacturing Industries." *International Journal of Health Services*, 26(2):309–29.
8. See Snider, L. (1993) *Bad Business: Corporate Crime in Canada.* Scarborough, Ontario: Nelson, page 14; also Braithwaite, J. (1989) *Crime, Shame and Reintegration.* Cambridge: Cambridge University Press; Coleman, J. (1989) *The Criminal Elite.* New York: St. Martin's; Pearce, F., and S. Tombs (1998) *Toxic Capitalism: Corporate Crime and the Chemical Industry.* Aldershot: Ashgate/Dartmouth.
9. There are also splits within each designation: between industrial and financial capitalism (with many claiming that the needs of the latter have eclipsed the former), and between occupational health and safety movements (typically working class) and environmental movements (typically middle class).
10. The latest examples of this phenomenon occurred in Mexico and Argentina.
11. Condon, M. (1998) *Making Disclosure: Ideas and Interests in Ontario Securities Regulation.* Toronto: University of Toronto Press, Page 19.
12. Condon 1998, op. cit., 20.
13. Condon 1998, op. cit., 29.
14. Condon 1998, op. cit., 24–25.
15. The Prospectors and Developers Association predated the BDA, but it has never been a key player. Opposed to the establishment of the OSC in 1945, it was seen primarily as an interest group.
16. Sending Viola MacMillan to prison and cracking down on penny stock promoters in Toronto stimulated the growth of the Vancouver Stock Exchange. The VSE then became the favoured speculators' market, with lax or absent regulations and "a flaccid internal self-regulating body that would protect the name of any broker found chiselling..." (Macbeth, 1985:126).
17. This is a classic example of what Haines and Gurney (2003) call Regulatory Conflict, because the OSC argued that fixing rates would violate the Combines Investigation Act (now the Competition Act), federal legislation designed to promote competition.
18. Condon 1998, op. cit., 242.
19. Friedman, M. (1962) *Capitalism and Freedom.* Chicago: University of Chicago Press, Posner, R. (1976) *Antitrust Law.* Chicago: University of Chicago Press. Posner, R. (1977) *Economic Analysis of Law.* 2nd ed. New York: Little Brown.
20. Calavita, K. (1983) "The Demise of the Occupational Safety and Health Administration: A Case Study in Symbolic Action." *Social Problems* 30(4):437–48.
21. Clarkson, S. (2002) *Uncle Sam and Us: Globalization, Neoconservativisms and the Canadian State.* Toronto: University of Toronto Press; Snider, L. (2004) "Resisting Neo-Liberalism: The Poisoned Water Disaster in Walkerton, Ontario." *Social and Legal Studies* 13(2):265–90.
22. Stanbury, W. (1986–87) "The New Competition Act and Competition Tribunal Act: Not with a Bang but a Whimper?" *Canadian Business Law Journal* 12:2–42. Stanbury, W. (1977) Business Interests and the Reform of Canadian Competition Policy 1971–75. Toronto: Carswell/Methuen; Snider, L. (1993) *Bad Business: Corporate Crime in Canada.* Scarborough, Ontario: Nelson.
23. Barlow, M. and T. Clark (2002) *Global Showdown: How the New Activists are Fighting Corporate Rule.* Toronto: Stoddart, 2002; Fudge, J. and B. Cossman,

(2002) "Introduction: Privatization, Law and the Challenge to Feminism," in B. Cossman and J. Fudge, eds. *Privatization, Law and the Challenge:* 3–37; Sharp, A. (1998) "Income Distribution in Canada in the 1990s: The Offsetting Impact of Government on Growing Market Inequality." *Canada Watch* V6, June; Schrecker, E. (2001) "From the Welfare State to the No-Second-Chances State," in S. Boyd, D. Chunn, R. Menzies, editors, *[Ab]using Power: The Canadian Experience.* Halifax: Fernwood.

24. Control of companies is still concentrated within small corporate elites, and wealth distribution is wildly—and increasingly—unequal. In 1982 the average CEO in the US earned about 45 times as much as the average employee, by 2000 he (seldom she) earned 458 times as much (Cernetig, 2002).
25. Phelps, M., H. McKay, T. Allen, P. Brunet, W. Dobson, E. Harris, M. Tims, (2003) *It's Time: Report of the Committee to Review the Structure of Securities Regulation in Canada.* Canada: Department of Finance, December 17, page 6 (online at *www.wise-averties.ca*); also Report on Business Magazine, June 2004 (*Globe & Mail insert).*
26. Phelps et al 2003, page 2, op. cit.
27. The Toronto Stock Exchange now handles 95% of all equity trading in Canada, 30 million transactions a year, with 530 employees handling 1,340 senior equities (June 2004 *Report on Business Magazine).* These are essentially blue chip stocks from established, often trans-national corporations. The TSX Venture Exchange lists stocks from smaller, less established "emerging" companies, 2,275 in 2004. It was formed by combining the small capital components of the Toronto, Vancouver, Alberta and Winnipeg exchanges, to allow entrepreneurs to raise capital quickly. Allowing "a prospector to get a grubstake to go out and do his thing." is as important today—and probably as male-dominated—as it was when these words were written in 1945 (Advertising Supplement of the Toronto Stock Exchange, *Report on Business Magazine,* June 2004).
28. Phelps et al., 2003, Op. cit., p. 4.
29. Porter, J. (1965) *The Vertical Mosaic.* Toronto: University of Toronto Press; Clement, W. (1975) *The Canadian Corporate Elite.* Toronto: McClelland and Stewart.
30. Yaron, G. (2002) *Canadian Shareholder Activism in an Era of Global Deregulation.* Vancouver: Shareholder Association for Research and Education, at www.share.ca.
31. In the spring of 2003 the federal commission set up the "Wise Persons Committee." charged with investigating the practicality and efficiency of this arrangement (www.wise-averties.ca). A report issued in September, 2003 recommends that this system be abolished and replaced with one national regulatory body, controlled and administered by the federal government, with regional offices.
32. This includes self-regulatory bodies such as the Toronto Stock Exchange, which recently published a three-page advertisement in Canada's premier business journal touting its capacity to monitor every trade "in real time," and its power to reverse trades (Advertising Supplement, *Report on Business Magazine,* June, 2004).
33. Michael Watson, head of enforcement at the OSC, argued before the Senate Banking Committee that this wording would make successful prosecution impossible, forcing the Crown to prove suspects knew the information was not publicly disclosed, and sought to take advantage of this fact. He recommended "trading with knowledge of" inside information instead. However no wording changes were made.
34. Fines under the Criminal Code of Canada are in theory unlimited.
35. Mackay R. and M. Smith, (2004) "Bill C-13: An Act to Amend the Criminal Code (Capital markets Fraud and Evidence-Gathering). Ottawa: Parliamentary Research Branch, Legislative summary, LS-468E, page 4–5.
36. The Canadian Bankers Association argued such penalties would be "very unfair," and requested more time to comply. Their pleas were apparently not heard.
37. Bittle, S. (2004) "Constituting the Corporate Criminal: Corporate Criminal Liability in Post-Westray Canada," unpublished paper, Department of Sociology, Queen's

University; Glasbeek, H. (2002) *Wealth by Stealth. Corporate Crime, Corporate Law and the Perversion of Democracy.* Toronto: Between the Lines.

38. Mackay and Smith, 2004, op. cit., p. 2.
39. Department of Finance Canada (2003) "Fostering Confidence in Canada's Capital Markets," online at *www.fin.gc.ca/activty/pubs/fostering_e.html*; also Department of Justice Canada (2003) *Backgrounder: Federal Strategy to Deter.*
40. Department of Finance, op. cit..
41. The federal Ministry of Finance, however, insists corporate governance is "already strong." They argue that because Canada has more small public companies and closely held corporations than the US, it should place "greater reliance on principles and voluntary guidelines" than the Americans. One would assume this means they are against greater criminalization, a position quite different from that taken by the Ministry of Justice (Canada, Minister of Finance, *www.fin.gc.ca/toce/2003*, Sept. 10, 2003, accessed July 5, 2004).
42. As Ronen Shamir (2004) notes, multinational corporations are now attempting to shape the meaning of corporate social responsibility, in ways that minimize structural oversight and maximize voluntary, individualistic corporate-friendly initiatives.
43. Quotes from Phelps et al., op. cit., p. 25.
44. This is not new, concern that this might send the "wrong" signal to investors is. Canada has seldom imposed jail sentences in any kind of corporate crime, financial or social. Over the 100 year history of the Combines Investigation Act, passed in 1898, now the Competition Act, legislation that covers everything from price fixing to false advertising, no executives have ever served prison time. Orders of prohibition, which allow companies to escape liability by promising not to commit the offense again, have been the dominant disposition (Snider, 1978, 1993; Stanbury, 1977; also Puri, 2001).
45. *Toronto Star,* Nov. 13, 2003: C1; also Phelps, 2003, op. cit. at 26.
46. Puri, P. (2001) "Sentencing the Criminal Corporation." *Osgoode Hall Law Journal* Summer/Fall, 39(2/3):612–53.
47. Condon, M. (2003) "The Use of Public Interest Enforcement Orders by Securities Regulators in Canada." *Research Study Prepared for the Wise Persons' Committee,* October. Online at *www.wise-averties.ca.*
48. Condon, 2003, op. cit., at 419, footnote 4.
49. Condon, 2003 op. cit. at 439, footnote 22.
50. The most important Self-Regulatory Organizations (SROs) in Canada are the Investment Dealers Association of Canada, the Mutual Fund Dealers Association of Canada (MFDA), and the stock exchanges in Toronto and Montreal (the TSX, TSX Venture Exchange, and the *Bourse de Montreal* (ME). There are also specialized private services, notably Market Regulation Services Inc. (MRS), an independent body which does market surveillance, investigation and enforcement for the Toronto Exchanges, and the Canadian Investor Protection Fund (CIPF), an industry-funded body to prevent investment dealer insolvency (Phelps, 2003: 18).
51. An OSC report published in 2001 recommended that the lobbying and regulatory functions of the IDA be separated, due to extreme conflicts of interest. However the final version of the Report did not do this. As reported in the press, the investigators "were ultimately persuaded... .that such a move wasn't justified" (K. Howlett, *Globe & Mail,* Jan. 27, 2004: B5).
52. Damsell, K., (2004) "IFIC Lobbies for Grants, Critics Charge." *Globe & Mail,* June 22, 2004:B8.
53. Church, E. (2004) "Who's Standing Up for the Investor?" *Globe & Mail,* June 22: B9.
54. Church, E. (2004), op. cit.
55. Damsell (2004), op. cit.
56. E. Church (2004), op. cit..

57. The lobby group also tells us the industry has a new Code of Ethics which prevents members from "personal trading and receiving gifts" (Damsell, *Globe & Mail,* June 22, 2004: B8). Presumably the Code is silent on executive compensation, which rose steeply despite declining equity levels (11.3% in 2002, 2.8% in 2003) (Willis, *Globe & Mail,* June 23, 2004: B9).
58. See Rose, N., and P. Miller (1992) "Political Power beyond the State: Problematics of Government." *British Journal of Sociology* 43:173–205; Rose, N. (1999) *Powers of Political Freedom: Reframing Political Thought.* Cambridge: Cambridge University Press; Rose, N. (1990) *Governing the Soul: The Shaping of the Private Self.* London: Routledge; Gandy, O. (1993) *The Panoptic Sort: A Political Economy of Personal Information.* Boulder, Colo.: Westview Press; Ericson, R. and K. Haggerty (1997) *Policing the Risk Society.* Toronto: University of Toronto Press.
59. See Clarke, M. (2000) *Regulation: The Social Control of Business between Law and Politics.* London: Macmillan; Calavita, K., H. Pontell, and R. Tillman (1997) *Big Money Crime: Fraud and Politics in the Savings and Loan Crisis.* Berkeley: University of California Press; Rosoff, S., H. Pontell, and R. Tillman (2007) *Profit Without Honor: White-Collar Crime and the Looting of America.* Upper Saddle River, NJ: Prentice Hall.
60. Ehrenreich, B. ((2001) *Nickel and Dimed: On (Not) Getting By in America.* New York: Metropolitan Books; Snider, L. (2002) "Theft of Time: Disciplining through Science and Law." *Osgoode Hall Law Journal*, 40, 4, 1:89–113.
61. American business history is a case in point. A series of scandals, from the railway trusts of the 19th century, the price fixing scandals in the 1950s and 1960s, Penn Central in the 1970s, Mike Milken and the junk bond scandal in the 1980s and the 150 billion dollar savings and loan debacle (Calavita et al., 1997, Rosoff et al., 1998) all initially produced tough rhetoric and new measures, followed by deregulation, budget cuts and regulatory neglect.
62. O'Brien, J. (2003) *Wall Street on Trial.* Chicester, U.K.: Wiley, page 1.
63. See Mishra, R. (1999) *Globalization and the Welfare State*. Cheltenham: Edward Elgar; Monbiot, G. (2000) *The Captive State. The Corporate Takeover of Britain.* London: Macmillan; Pearce, F., and S. Tombs (1998) *Toxic Capitalism: Corporate Crime and the Chemical Industry.* Aldershot: Ashgate/Dartmouth.
64. Fooks, G. (2003) "Auditors and the Permissive Society: Market Failure, Globalization and Financial Regulation in the United States." *Risk Management: An International Journal* 5, 2:17–26; Tombs, S., and D. Whyte (2003) "Scrutinizing the Powerful" in S. Tombs and D. Whyte, eds., *Unmasking the Crimes of the Powerful.* New York: Peter Lang, pp. 3–48.
65. Glasbeek, H. (2002) *Wealth by Stealth. Corporate Crime, Corporate Law and the Perversion of Democracy.* Toronto: Between the Lines.
66. Shamir, R., (2004) "Between Self-Regulation and the Alien Tort Claims Act: On the Contested Concept of Corporate Social Responsibility." *Law & Society Review* 38(4):635–63.
67. International legal systems are in their infancy, and at this stage none of the world's most powerful countries is willing to cede any sovereignty to them.
68. Braithwaite, J. (1989) *Crime, Shame and Reintegration.* Cambridge: Cambridge University Press.
69. Fooks (2003), op. cit. at 17.

References

Archibald, T., K. Jull and K. Roach (2004) "The Changed Face of Corporate Criminal Liability." *Criminal Law Quarterly* 48:367–96.

Barlow, M., and T. Clark (2002) *Global Showdown: How the New Activists are Fighting Corporate Rule.* Toronto: Stoddart, 2002.

Bittle, S. (2004) "Constituting the Corporate Criminal: Corporate Criminal Liability in Post-Westray Canada," unpublished paper. Department of Sociology, Queen's University.
Braithwaite, J. (1989) *Crime, Shame and Reintegration.* Cambridge: Cambridge University Press.
Calavita, K., H. Pontell, and R. Tillman (1997) *Big Money Crime: Fraud and Politics in the Savings and Loan Crisis.* Berkeley: University of California Press.
Calavita, K. (1983) "The Demise of the Occupational Safety and Health Administration: A Case Study in Symbolic Action," *Social Problems* 30(4):437–48.
Carson, W. (1980) "The Institutionalization of Ambiguity: Early British Factory Acts." In *White-Collar Theory and Research,* Editors G. Geis and E. Stotland. Beverly Hills, CA: Sage.
Carson, W. (1970) "White-Collar Crime and the Enforcement of Factory Legislation," *British Journal of Criminology* 10:383–98.
Cernetig, M. (2002) "Witch Hunt on Wall Street?" *Globe & Mail,* June 1: F8.
Church, E., (2004) "Who's Standing Up for the Investor?" *Globe & Mail,* June 22:B9.
Clarke, M. (2000) *Regulation: The Social Control of Business between Law and Politics.* London: Macmillan.
Clarkson, S. (2002) *Uncle Sam and Us: Globalization, Neoconservativisms and the Canadian State.* Toronto: University of Toronto Press.
Clement, W. (1975) *The Canadian Corporate Elite.* Toronto: McClelland and Stewart.
Coleman, J. (1989) *The Criminal Elite.* New York: St. Martin's.
Condon, M. (2003) "The Use of Public Interest Enforcement Orders by Securities Regulators in Canada," *Research Study Prepared for the Wise Persons' Committee,* October. Online at *www.wise-averties.ca.*
Condon, M. (1998) *Making Disclosure: Ideas and Interests in Ontario Securities Regulation.* Toronto: University of Toronto Press.
Damsell, K., (2004) "IFIC Lobbies for Grants, Critics Charge," *Globe & Mail,* June 22, 2004:B.
Department of Finance Canada (2003) "Fostering Confidence in Canada's Capital Markets," online at www.fin.gc.ca/activty/pubs/fostering_e.html.
Department of Justice Canada (2003) *Backgrounder: Federal Strategy to Deter Serious Capital Market Fraud.* Online at www.canada.justice.gc.ca.
Doern, B., and S. Wilks (1998) "Introduction." Pp. 3–25 in *Changing Regulatory Institutions in Britain and North America,* Editors B. Doern and S. Wilks. Toronto: University of Toronto Press,.
Doern B., and S. Wilks (1996) "Conclusions: International Convergence and National Contrasts." Pp. 327–59 in *Comparative Competition Policy: National Institutions in a Global Market,* Editors B. Doern and S. Wilks. Oxford: Clarendon Press,.
Ehrenreich, B. (2001) *Nickel and Dimed: On (Not) Getting By in America.* New York: Metropolitan Books.
Ericson, R., and K. Haggerty (1997) *Policing the Risk Society.* Toronto: University of Toronto Press.
Fooks, G., (2003) "Auditors and the Permissive Society: Market Failure, Globalization and Financial Regulation in the United States." *Risk Management: An International Journal* 5(2):17–26.
Friedman, M. (1962) *Capitalism and Freedom.* Chicago: University of Chicago Press.
Fudge, J., and B. Cossman, (2002) "Introduction: Privatization, Law and the Challenge to Feminism," pp. 3–37 in *Privatization, Law and the Challenge*, Editors B. Cossman and J. Fudge. Toronto: University of Toronto Press.
Gandy, O. (1993) *The Panoptic Sort: A Political Economy of Personal Information.* Boulder, CO: Westview Press.
Glasbeek, H. (2002) *Wealth by Stealth. Corporate Crime, Corporate Law and the Perversion of Democracy.* Toronto: Between the Lines.

Haines, F., and D. Gurney, (2003) "The Shadows of the Law: Contemporary Approaches to Regulation and the Problem of Regulatory Conflict." *Law and Policy* 25 (4):353–79.

Howlett, K. (2004) "OSC Urges Securities Bill Change." *Globe & Mail*, March 11: B7.

Howlett, K., and J. McFarland, (2004) "OSC Says Enforcement a Priority." *Globe & Mail,* March 30, B10.

Leonhardt, D. (2002) "How Will Washington Read the Signs?" *The New York Times,* February 10, Money & Business, p. 1.

Macbeth, M. (1985) "Reining in the Cowboys," *Canadian Business,* May.

Mackay R., and M. Smith, (2004) "Bill C-13: An Act to Amend the Criminal Code (Capital markets Fraud and Evidence-Gathering). Ottawa: Parliamentary Research Branch, Legislative summary, LS-468E.

Mishra, R. (1999) *Globalization and the Welfare State.* Cheltenham: Edward Elgar.

Monbiot, G. (2000) *The Captive State. The Corporate Takeover of Britain.* London: Macmillan.

O'Brien, J. (2003) *Wall Street on Trial.* Chicester, U.K.: Wiley.

Pearce, F., and S. Tombs (2003) "'Dance Your Anger and Your Joys': Multinational Corporations, Power, 'Crime.'" In *Blackwell Companion to Criminology,* Editor C. Sumner. London: Blackwell.

Pearce, F., and S. Tombs (1998) *Toxic Capitalism: Corporate Crime and the Chemical Industry*. Aldershot, NH: Ashgate/Dartmouth.

Phelps, M., H. McKay, T. Allen, P. Brunet, W. Dobson, E. Harris, M. Tims, (2003) *It's Time: Report of the Committee to Review the Structure of Securities Regulation in Canada.* Canada: Department of Finance, December 17 (online at www.wise-averties.ca).

Porter, J. (1965) *The Vertical Mosaic.* Toronto: University of Toronto Press.

Posner, R. (1976) *Antitrust Law.* Chicago: University of Chicago Press.

Posner, R. (1977) *Economic Analysis of Law.* 2nd ed. New York: Little Brown.

Puri, P. (2001) "Sentencing the Criminal Corporation." *Osgoode Hall Law Journal* Summer/Fall 39(2/3):612–53.

Rose, N., and P. Miller (1992) "Political Power beyond the State: Problematics of Government." *British Journal of Sociology* 43:173–205.

Rose, N. (1999) *Powers of Political Freedom: Reframing Political Thought.* Cambridge: Cambridge University Press.

Rose, N. (1990) *Governing the Soul: The Shaping of the Private Self.* London: Routledge.

Rosoff, S., H. Pontell, and R. Tillman (2007) *Profit Without Honor. White-Collar Crime and the Looting of America.* Upper Saddle River, NJ: Prentice Hall.

Setting Analyst Standards: Recommendations for the Supervision and Practice of Canadian Securities Industry Analysts (2001, October). Toronto: Toronto Stock Exchange, Investment Dealers Association, Canadian Venture Exchange.

Schrecker, E. (2001) "From the Welfare State to the No-Second-Chances State." In *[Ab]using Power: The Canadian Experience,* Editors S. Boyd, D. Chunn, and R. Menzies. Halifax: Fernwood.

Shamir, R., (2004) "Between Self-Regulation and the Alien Tort Claims Act: On the Contested Concept of Corporate Social Responsibility." *Law & Society Review* 38(4):635–63.

Shapiro, S. (1990) "Collaring the Crime, not the Criminal: Reconsidering the Concept of White-Collar Crime." *American Sociological Review* 55:123–40.

Shapiro, S. (1984) *Wayward Capitalists: Target of the Securities and Exchange Commission.* New Haven: Yale University Press.

Sharp, A. (1998) "Income Distribution in Canada in the 1990s: The Offsetting Impact of Government on Growing Market Inequality." *Canada Watch* V6, June.

Slapper, G., and S. Tombs (1999) *Corporate Crime.* London: Longman.

Snider, L. (2004) "Resisting Neo-Liberalism: The Poisoned Water Disaster in Walkerton, Ontario." *Social and Legal Studies* 13(2):265–90.

Snider, L. (2002) "Theft of Time: Disciplining through Science and Law." *Osgoode Hall Law Journal* 40(4,1):89–113.

Snider, L. (2000), "The Sociology of Corporate Crime: An Obituary." *Theoretical Criminology* 4(2):169–205.

Snider, L. (1996) "Options for Public Accountability." In *Regulatory Efficiency and the Role of Risk Assessment,* Editor M. Mehta. Kingston, Ont.: School of Policy Studies, Queen's University.

Snider, L. (1993) *Bad Business: Corporate Crime in Canada.* Scarborough, Ontario: Nelson.

Snider, L. (1978) "Corporate Crime in Canada: A Preliminary Report." *Canadian Journal of Criminology* 20(2):178–202.

Stanbury, W. (1995) "Public Policy towards Individuals Involved in Competition-Law Offenses in Canada." Pp. 214–44 in *Corporate Crime: Contemporary Debates,* Editors F. Pearce and L. Snider.Toronto: University of Toronto Press:.

Stanbury, W. (1986–87) "The New Competition Act and Competition Tribunal Act: Not with a Bang but a Whimper?" *Canadian Business Law Journal* 12:2–42.

Stanbury, W. (1977) *Business Interests and the Reform of Canadian Competition Policy 1971–75.* Toronto: Carswell/Methuen.

Tombs, S. (1996). "Injury, Death and the Deregulation Fetish: The Politics of Occupational Safety Regulation in United Kingdom Manufacturing Industries." *International Journal of Health Services* 26(2):309–29.

Tombs, S. and D. Whyte (2003) "Scrutinizing the Powerful." Pp. 3–48 in *Unmasking the Crimes of the Powerful,* Editors S. Tombs and D. Whyte.New York: Peter Lang.

Willis, A. (2004) "Even in a Bear Market, Some Fund Managers Saw a Bonanza." *Globe & Mail,* June 23, B9.

Yaron, G. (2002) *Canadian Shareholder Activism in an Era of Global Deregulation.* Vancouver: Shareholder Association for Research and Education, at www.share.ca.

3

White-Collar Crime and Prosecution for "Industrial Manslaughter" as a Means To Reduce Workplace Deaths

Rick Sarre[1]

In 1949, Edwin Sutherland published his watershed *White-Collar Crime*. He proposed that criminologists ought to focus more of their attention upon the types of crimes committed by people of "respectability and high social status in the course of [their] occupation."[2] There has been much disagreement since that time on what constitutes or should constitute white-collar crime.[3] One can safely argue, however, that the phenomenon extends not only to what might be referred to as *occupational* crime (crime committed by persons in the course of their work), but also to *corporate* crime (crime committed by organizations using organizational resources). It is into this latter category that one can place crimes that involve violence or violations of rights, such as causing death in a workplace or making decisions in the workplace that have the effect of allowing a death to occur.[4] This category of crime (and recommended responses to it) provides the focus for the discussion below.

To understand the origins and current directions of the industrial manslaughter option, it is useful to begin with a review of the history and operation of the crime of manslaughter in the common law generally. That discussion is followed by an examination of the potential for specific occupational health and safety legislation to reduce the number of workplace deaths and injuries. For it is in the failures associated with manslaughter prosecutions and the inadequate deterrent effect of occupational health and safety legislation that one can gain perspective on the new industrial manslaughter laws.

The General Criminal Law: Corporate Manslaughter

Using the criminal law to prevent and punish corporate wrongdoing has traditionally been fraught with difficulty. The criminal law usually plays a very minor role in controlling corporate illegality.[5]

> Even when a formal criminal prosecution is undertaken, corporate defendants are well-positioned to defend themselves. Large companies are able to hire the best lawyers, secure "professional" expert witnesses, and engage in delaying tactics that will outlast the political pressure that prompted the government to initiate a prosecution in the first place ... The lesson seems to be that the criminal justice system, as presently constituted, is simply not a viable forum for tackling corporate wrongdoing.[6]

Corporate manslaughter prosecutions have rarely met with any degree of success. The first case of a prosecution alleging corporate manslaughter in Australia was probably *The Queen v. Denbo Pty Ltd.*[7] Denbo Pty Ltd was prosecuted when one of its drivers was killed when his truck's brakes failed. The company's vehicle service record was appalling. It pleaded guilty and was fined US $80,000. At the time of its conviction, however, Denbo Pty Ltd was in liquidation and owed creditors more than US $1.3 million. The company was wound up six months before sentencing and never paid the fine. Later it was reborn as under another name. The successor company did not pay the fine either.[8]

Assuming that a company which is the subject of a prosecution remains solvent, the success rate (measured by a guilty verdict) in manslaughter prosecutions against corporations and individual officers is very poor.[9] There are several reasons for this.[10] For a start, manslaughter was not created to deal with offenses committed by non-natural persons such as corporations. Hence, attributing the physical *(actus reus)* and fault *(mens rea)* elements of manslaughter to a corporation makes an uneasy "fit."

> [The] criminal law was not developed with companies in mind. Concepts such as *mens rea* and *actus reus*, which make perfectly good sense when applied to individuals, do not translate easily to an inanimate fictional entity such as a corporation. Trying to apply these concepts to companies is a bit like trying to squeeze a square peg into a round hole.[11]

In cases involving modern corporations, it is necessary to prosecute an individual person who is the "guiding mind" of the corporation in order to meet the requirements for criminal culpability.[12] Where many people participate in decision-making, it is extremely difficult to trace this culpability (usually criminal negligence) to a single individual. As Celia Wells puts it, "[c]orporations, whatever they are, are not individuals and do not act as unitary individuals."[13] A prosecution will fail even where it seems that the corporate employer *as a whole* was guilty of criminal negligence, because the "guiding mind" test focuses only on individuals.[14] For example, in *The Queen v. AC Hatrick Chemicals,*[15] a case involving the death of a welder following an explosion, manslaughter charges against a plant engineer and his manager were withdrawn before the trial. Hampel, J, directed a verdict of acquittal because the allegedly culpable individuals were clearly not the "guiding mind" of the corporation.

Occupational Health and Safety Laws

For the foregoing reasons, the main focus of lawmakers in the drive to protect workers has been on enacting specific occupational health, safety and welfare (OH&S) laws. These laws involve a mixture of *ex post facto* legal responses and prevention measures.[16] Their key focus is the imposition of penalties, principally fines. Again, legislators have placed a great deal of faith in the act of prosecuting as a means of eradicating harmful activities and changing public perceptions of workplace risks.[17]

Several Australian jurisdictions have recently strengthened their OH&S penalty regimes. For example, in Queensland in 2003, legislators increased terms of imprisonment for employers whose acts directly cause workplace death or serious injury.[18] The South Australian parliament, too, recently introduced penalties for aggravated breaches of its *Occupational Health, Safety and Welfare Act* 1986 which carry terms of imprisonment for a maximum of five years, in addition to fines. "Aggravated breaches" are defined as being those committed by an individual—

a. knowing that the contravention was likely to endanger seriously the health or safety of another; and
b. being recklessly indifferent as to whether the health or safety of another was so endangered.[19]

In New South Wales (NSW),[20] corporations can now be fined a maximum of US $400,000 for a first offense or US $600,000 subsequently for similar circumstances. Individuals face a maximum fine of US $40,000 for a first offense and, for repeat offenses, a maximum penalty of US $60,000 or two years imprisonment, or both. The failure of senior officers to ensure that their corporation complies with its OH&S obligations is itself an offense, but then the law goes a step further by imposing liability on individuals for the contraventions of their corporate "parent." Section 26(1) provides—

> If a corporation contravenes, whether by act or omission, any provision of this Act or the regulations, each director of the corporation, and each person concerned in the management of the corporation, is taken to have contravened the same provision unless the director or person satisfies the court that—
>
> a. he or she was not in a position to influence the conduct of the corporation in relation to its contravention of the provision, or
> b. he or she, being in such a position, used all due diligence to prevent the contravention by the corporation.

But there is little evidence that punishment, or the threat of punishment, is anything more than a fairly blunt instrument when it comes to workplace deterrence. While some corporate behavior can be identified as flowing from a rational cost-benefit analysis, reliance upon general deterrence is unrealistic. What is more likely is the existence of a corporate "personality" that may be impervious to such legal threats.

> This "corporate personality" or "corporate culture" is seen both formally, in the company's policies and procedures, but also informally. It is a dynamic process with the corporate culture affecting the actions of individuals, and the actions of individuals affecting the corporate personality. Corporate culture may exist independently of individual employees or officers and may continue to exist despite changes in personnel. ... For example, while a corporation may outwardly claim to be concerned with occupational health and safety, if the pressure on individual managers is to meet unrealistic financial or time pressures, then there may be a temptation for corners to be cut and worker safety compromised.[21]

One may suspect that increases in OH&S penalties motivate organizations to take a pragmatic approach to compliance by confining themselves to obvious changes, to limiting legal liability, and to leaving broader issues of safety and responsibility largely unaddressed.[22]

Experimenting with a New Offense: "Industrial Manslaughter"

Poor conviction rates for corporate manslaughter and the inability of even the most condign of punishments under OH&S legislation to curb workplace fatalities have spurred reformers to suggest other options for legislators. One such suggestion has been for lawmakers to create a new offense of "industrial manslaughter" designed to punish corporations by making their higher level employees criminally responsible for outcomes regardless of their direct complicity.

How does this happen? For a start, industrial manslaughter laws treat corporations as if they were natural persons. Moreover, industrial manslaughter laws allow for the joining of liability of any individuals who may have formed a "web of decisions" that led to the action that eventually caused the harm in question.[23] This is known as "aggregation."

> A theory of aggregation arguably better captures the nature of corporate fault than a theory which imputes to the company a crime of a particular individual. There are times when, as a result of employee negligence, victims are seriously injured. Negligence, however, is generally not deemed sufficient to warrant imposing criminal liability on an individual and therefore also insufficient . . . to hold a company liable for the agent's acts.[24]

The *naissance* of the Australian developments in this area can be found in the *Criminal Code Act 1995*, a Commonwealth of Australia Act.[25] The *Criminal Code Act* expands the notion of corporate criminal liability. It does this by providing for the attribution of recklessness and negligence to a corporation in new ways,[26] namely, that corporations may be found guilty of any offense, including those punishable by imprisonment, and that harm caused by employees acting within the scope of their employment is considered to be harm caused by the body corporate.[27] This allows for the *physical* element of manslaughter to be attributed to a body corporate where the actions involved were engaged in by more than one person, persons who may or may not have met the requirement of being the "guiding mind" of the corporation.

Regarding the attribution of a *mental* element to a body corporate, the Code provides several alternatives. A requisite mental element other than negligence can be attributed to a body corporate if it expressly, tacitly, or impliedly authorized or permitted the commission of the offense.[28] Two of the ways in which this authorization or permission may be established are through the state of mind of either the board of directors or "high managerial agents" within the body corporate,[29] or by virtue of the "corporate culture." "Corporate culture" is defined as including an "attitude, policy, rule, course of conduct, or practice existing within the body corporate generally. . . "[30] In other words, the body corporate could be deemed criminally liable for a workplace death, for example, if it has a corporate culture that actively or passively allows non-compliance with the law.[31] This change was designed to embrace situations where, despite the existence of documentation appearing to require compliance, the reality was that non-compliance was not unusual or was tacitly authorised by the company as a whole.[32]

The other possible mental element for manslaughter is negligence, and, again, it is difficult to attribute negligence to corporations at common law. However, the

Code allows the attribution of negligence to corporations through aggregation.[33] Negligence may exist on the part of the body corporate, says the legislation,[34] if the body corporate's conduct is negligent when *viewed as a whole* (that is, by adding together the conduct of any number of its employees, agents, or officers).

The Code thus introduces a new basis for liability and one that is markedly different from the common law. Both mental and physical elements can be attributed according to the behavior of the corporation *as an entity*, and its principals can be prosecuted and punished both individually and collectively by association with the corporation.

There is a major difficulty, however, for those wishing to use the Code to prosecute criminal conduct in Australia. The Code only applies to Commonwealth of Australia offenses, and manslaughter is not such an offense.[35] In order to give effect to these provisions, States and Territories would need to adopt similar provisions in their criminal codes or, in the case of common law jurisdictions, other criminal legislation. The Australian Capital Territory is the only jurisdiction to enact such laws. Other jurisdictions have considered them and rejected them. It is to these developments that we now turn.

The Australian Capital Territory Experiment

The Australian Capital Territory (ACT), in 2004, became the first jurisdiction in Australia to introduce the offense of industrial manslaughter it did so, via the Crimes (Industrial Manslaughter) Act 2003 (ACT). "Industrial manslaughter" is defined as causing the death of a worker while either being reckless in regard to causing serious harm to that worker or any other worker, or being negligent about causing the death of that or any other worker.[36] Chapter 2 of its Criminal Code incorporates the Commonwealth Criminal Code notions of "corporate culture."[37] Moreover, the Act provides for both employer and "senior officer" liability for industrial manslaughter, with maximum penalties of fines of up to US $750,000 million for large corporations, US $140,000 for individual senior officers, or 20 years imprisonment, or both.

The key to the legislation is section 51:

> (1) In deciding whether the fault element of intention, knowledge or recklessness exists for an offense in relation to a corporation, the fault element is taken to exist if the corporation expressly, tacitly or impliedly authorized or permits the commission of the offense.
>
> (2) The ways in which authorization or permission may be established include—
>
> (a) proving that the corporation's board of directors intentionally, knowingly or recklessly engaged in the conduct or expressly, tacitly or impliedly authorized or permitted the commission of the offense; or
>
> (b) proving that a high managerial agent of the corporation intentionally, knowingly or recklessly engaged in the conduct or expressly, tacitly or impliedly authorized or permitted the commission of the offense; or
>
> (c) proving that a corporate culture existed within the corporation that directed, encouraged, tolerated or led to noncompliance with the contravened law; or
>
> (d) proving that the corporation failed to create and maintain a corporate culture requiring compliance with the contravened law.
>
> (3) Subsection (2) (b) does not apply if the corporation proves that it exercized appropriate diligence to prevent the conduct, or the authorization or permission.

Significantly, negligence of a corporation can be attributed by aggregation,[38] and, similarly, the physical element of the offense (causing death either by an act or by omission) is not only attributable to the conduct of officers, but also to agents or employees of the corporation.[39]

One needs to acknowledge a limitation, however. The Australian Capital Territory is home to only 1.5% of the Australian population, and has no heavy industry. Most of its employers and employees are government departments and public servants, respectively. Indeed, the Australian government moved quickly in response to the Crimes (Industrial Manslaughter) Act 2003, and introduced (in 2004) a law that exempts Commonwealth of Australia employers and employees from its provisions (about 80% of employers and companies in the ACT). We await a test case to determine the effectiveness of these new provisions, but one can safely predict that the law is mostly symbolic.

Other Australian Developments

In late November 2001, the Victorian Liberal government introduced the *Crimes (Workplace Deaths & Serious Injuries) Bill* into the Victorian parliament. Like the Commonwealth of Australia *Criminal Code*, the bill was designed to allow a court to look at the conduct of the corporation as a whole in finding culpability and affixing a penalty. A corporation found guilty of industrial manslaughter, that is, where its conduct "materially contributed" to the outcome, would be liable for fines of up to US $3.75 million for a death and up to US $1.5 million for a serious injury. Where serious injury or death occurred, the bill allowed for periods of imprisonment of up to two years or five years, respectively, for senior officers found complicit in the offense.

The bill, however, was rejected in the Upper House in April 2002, following sustained pressure from the Australian Industry Group and the Victorian Employers Chamber of Commerce. Notwithstanding that it has had control of the Upper House since November 2002, the Labor Government has indicated it has no plans to reintroduce the bill. Instead, it will bolster existing OH&S legislation so that individual company officers, managers, and employees who ignore serious workplace safety problems will be liable for jail terms and fines of up to US $670,000. Victoria has thus abandoned any talk of industrial manslaughter.

The South Australian Labor government, in 2003, introduced the *Occupational Health, Safety and Welfare (SafeWork SA) Amendment Bill* 2003[40] to implement selected recommendations from the Stanley Report regarding OH&S reforms.[41] In keeping with the report, the bill does not propose an industrial manslaughter offense, although it includes other recommended non-pecuniary penalties, such as requiring employers (or responsible officers of a corporate employer) to undergo training programs and to publicize their breaches of the Act, for example, by notifying shareholders. The non-pecuniary penalties are designed to provide flexibility in sentencing and to ensure that the penalty fits the "circumstances of the offender."[42]

Unhappy with the above developments, an Upper House independent Nick Xenophon introduced in 2004 an amendment to the *Occupational Health, Safety and Welfare Act 1986* (SA) that provides for a specific offense of industrial manslaughter. His bill is modeled on the ACT provisions, and applies to a situation where an employer or a "senior officer" of the employer is either negligent about causing death or "recklessly indifferent about seriously endangering the health or safety of [an] employee or any other person at work." It also applies to omissions, deeming an omission to act an offense "if it is an omission to perform a duty to avoid or prevent danger to the life, safety or health of another." The danger may arise from either the act or undertaking of that person or, significantly, "anything in the person's possession or control." Penalties are similar in scope to those in the ACT, including fines of up to US $375,000 and the possibility of 20 years imprisonment. The bill will not succeed without the support of the Labor government and that support is highly unlikely.

In New South Wales, the *Crimes Amendment (Industrial Manslaughter) Bill 2004* was introduced into the Legislative Council by the Green Party's Lee Rhiannon, in part as a response to recommendations by the New South Wales General Purpose Standing Committee that offenses of industrial manslaughter and gross negligence causing serious injury be enacted into the *Crimes Act 1900* (NSW) "as a matter of urgency."[43] Any hope the Greens may have had in securing the cooperation of the NSW Labor Government,[44] however, was dashed when, on October 27, 2004, the government introduced an alternative bill to amend the *Occupational Health and Safety Act*.[45] The legislation, the Occupational Health and Safety Amendment (Workplace Deaths) Bill 2005, was given royal assent in June 2005. It introduces a new offense of "reckless conduct causing death at workplace by a person with OHS duties." The new offense imposes a maximum penalty of US $1.25 million for corporations and US $125,000 for individuals, with the possibility of five years' imprisonment. By virtue of this, move, the parliament has specifically rejected industrial manslaughter laws.

Western Australia steered clear of industrial manslaughter laws, too, in its recent review of its OH&S legislation. New provisions, which came into effect on January 1, 2005, substantially increased penalties, especially for corporations, including imprisonment in cases where gross negligence by an individual causes serious harm or death.[46]

United Kingdom

The UK Home Office, following sustained public pressure over the failure of the courts to secure convictions arising out of the *Herald of Free Enterprise* sinking,[47] the Southall rail crash in September 1997,[48] and a Law Commission Review in 1996, explored in 2000 the idea of a stand-alone offense of "corporate killing," an offense that would correspond to the (proposed) offense of "killing by gross carelessness."[49] "Corporate killing" could be alleged to have occurred when there is "management failure," that is, where the corporation's conduct in causing death fell far below what could reasonably have been expected. According to the Law Commission, such a failure should be regarded as *causative* of death even if the more immediate cause is the act or omission of an individual. In that case, both individual and corporate liability could flow from the same incident. In its consultation paper, the government, in accepting the thrust of the Law Commission's recommendations,[50] proposed that any individual who could be shown to have contributed to management failure that fell far below what could reasonably be expected should be subject to disqualification, and that any individual who substantially contributed to a death would be potentially liable for a term of imprisonment. But nothing happened in parliament.[51]

In May of 2003, the government again indicated its intention to introduce an offense of corporate killing.[52] The Trades Union Congress was in favor of provision for terms of imprisonment to be imposed on company directors if the circumstances require it, citing the need for deterrence.[53] But support was lukewarm, given the potential for companies, worried about more draconian penalties, moving operations offshore, with the attendant potential for job losses and economic downturn.[54] Hence, the government has indicated its intention not to include offenses aimed directly at corporate officers.

United States

The United States imposes corporate liability for negligence according to a variation of the principle of vicarious liability. This effectively circumvents the need to identify either one single "guiding mind" or to combine the actions and attitudes of several corporate officers or managers. It also applies to a wider range of individuals within the corporation. When applied to negligence liability, this test does not turn on subjective awareness. A corporate employer will be vicariously liable for the acts of officers, servants, or agents whose actions are within the scope of their employment. Moreover, the United States model indicates the possibilities of aggregation, best illustrated in the case of *United States v. Bank of New England*. In that case, the court held that what the bank "knew" about a violation consisted of the sum of what was known by its employees.[55] The vicarious liability model used by the United States has seen many corporations found guilty of manslaughter offenses. One such case is *Sea Horse Ranch v. Superior Court*[56] in which the corporation's president was successfully prosecuted for involuntary manslaughter.

Canada

Canadian occupational health and safety law operates at both provincial and at the national level with the same federal anomalies encountered in Australia. For example, in Ontario, corporate employers are vicariously liable for "any act or neglect on the part of any manager, agent, representative, officer, director or supervisor" who breaches any provision of the Act.[57] The *Canadian Criminal Code*, however, does not impose corporate *criminal* liability vicariously on employers. Canada continues to use the "identification" ("guiding mind") model used in the UK and in Australia. Corporations found guilty of indictable offenses under the Code are penalized by a fine set at the court's discretion in lieu of imprisonment.[58]

In 2002, the Canadian Standing Committee on Justice and Human Rights reported on the need for reform of Canada's laws regarding corporate criminal responsibility.[59] In considering the appropriate test of liability for negligence, the United States "vicarious liability" model and the Australian "corporate culture" model were examined. The "corporate culture" requirement was criticized as being too difficult to apply with necessary precision, and the vicarious model was seen to risk punishing a corporation which is not, in fact, blameworthy for the actions of its officers or managers. Although the Government decided that a separate offense of "corporate killing" was not needed, its response to the report concluded that reform should occur, because the use of the "guiding mind" principle as a basis of liability "does not reflect the reality of corporate decision-making and delegation of operational responsibility in complex organizations."[60]

The Arguments for and Against Industrial Manslaughter Laws

Given the persistence of deaths and injuries in workplaces around the world, there are many who now believe that general criminal law and OH&S prosecutions are inadequate protections against workplace harm, and that directors and managers of companies ought to be personally criminally liable in circumstances where a poor "corporate culture" pervades their organizations. It can be argued that aggregated negligence or vicarious liability *should* be appropriate tests of criminal liability if the harm is great, the risk obvious, and the precautionary work poor,[61] especially where conduct "conspicuously fail[s] to observe the standards laid down by law."[62] There are some who believe, in addition, that the penalties for culpable principals should include imprisonment. This possibility, it is said, sends a strong message of justice and deterrence to the community, namely that culpable conduct will not be tolerated even if it means scapegoating individuals.

On the other hand, since a corporation's "personality" is essentially a legal fiction, it may be unfair to make company principals criminally culpable by virtue of their status within the company. Without this association, the principals themselves could not have been prosecuted successfully. Imposing vicarious liability on corporations for regulatory breaches by its senior officers is one thing. Imposing vicarious personal liability on senior officers and jailing them as a result is quite another.

For example, if an otherwise defensible decision by management goes awry, with death occurring, it may be too harsh to expect one person to take the blame for a tragic consequence that came about because of a chain of errors. Moreover, how would the mooted imprisonment provisions apply to senior officers of non-corporations (such as partnerships and sole traders), transnational corporations, and government-owned enterprises? These bodies are never mentioned in industrial manslaughter provisions. Finally, there is evidence that the mere idea of industrial manslaughter raises the likelihood that collaboration between employers and employees will stall, an outcome that would be to the detriment of health and safety in the workplace generally.[63]

Others argue that there are more effective alternatives to the jailing of managers. In the case of *The Queen v. Leighton Contractors Pty Ltd*,[64] for example, a construction company (Leighton) had been convicted of serious breaches of the Victorian Occupational Health and Safety Act. Leighton had subcontracted with Sergi Services Pty Ltd to provide crane services for the construction of a bridge. On October 8, 2000, one of the concrete beams used in the construction collapsed, killing Sergi and injuring a number of his workers. Leighton was charged with failing to provide and maintain a plant that was safe and without risk to health. The company pleaded guilty.[65]

Judge Gebhardt found evidence of gross shoddiness and an indifference to a standard of engineering and construction precision which was required in that kind of work. He ordered that the company pay US $243,000 in fines, US

$52,000 to two charities, and a further US $67,000 into the trust funds for the deceased worker's children.

For the first time in legal history in Australia, an order was then made that the directors meet with Victorian WorkSafe representatives three times a year, and make note of these meetings in the company's annual reports.[66] The company was also ordered to assist in the implementation of a new industry standard for bridge beam construction by paying US $30,000 to the development of a training program for construction workers. Furthermore, the company agreed to approach two Melbourne universities for the purpose of improving OH&S training for engineers associated with the design of temporary structures for bridge construction.

Commentators have suggested that there is broad deterrent power in these and other options,[67] deterrent power that is arguably more potent that the risk of a short jail term for a scapegoated manager for whom many may have a great deal of sympathy. These other options include divestment of company equity, adverse publicity, corporate probation (with remedial and rehabilitative conditions), disqualifications from certain commercial activities, receiverships (or ordering someone else to run the company), the threat of the loss of limited liability,[68] and ultimately a company's winding-up. These options reinforce the value of a multi-faceted approach to sentencing corporations in the event of grossly culpable behavior. They endeavor, too, to find some alignment between the interests of the corporation and its employees and to focus on prevention of future occurrences.[69] One could also argue that they would rarely compromise the interests of victims' families.

Conclusion

The debate over the value of industrial manslaughter laws will continue to feature strongly in employment law and criminal law circles. Discussion to date has been hampered by the multi-layered complexities and political tensions involved in drafting laws designed to bring responsible persons to account while remaining faithful to basic precepts of criminal responsibility and punishment policy.

Legislators in Australia [70] clearly have indicated that they are decidedly nervous about moving toward a new offense of industrial manslaughter specifically or adopting the practice in the United States that endorses a "vicarious liability" approach more generally. In the absence of persuasive evidence that aggregating negligent minds and actions, locating corporate criminal liability in faulty organizational "culture," and allowing for the possibility of imprisonment in the most egregious of cases will significantly reduce death from the corporate workplace, changes to the *status quo* are unlikely. To appease critics who allege that too little is being done about workplace death rates, legislators are raising the penalties under existing occupational health and safety laws and are prescribing terms of imprisonment for individuals who have engaged in grossly culpable behavior (even in the absence of any evidence that these measures have a consequent deterrent effect).

Industrial manslaughter laws cannot by themselves lower workplace death rates because, arguably, corporate culture exists independently of corporate or individual employees' perceptions of risk. If that is the case, there needs to be embedded within corporate entities and their professional communities a variety of social control mechanisms.[71] For example, corporate entities should be paying greater attention to the organization of their businesses and their safety procedures and systems. The aim is to determine how best to encourage such attitudes and behaviors with or without the threat of legal sanction. Certainly, professional communities should be rewarding companies that display exemplary "corporate governance" behavior.[72] Whatever it takes, the development of good corporate culture, it is argued, is likely to be a far more effective regulatory regime than experimenting with a probably ineffective, possibly counterproductive, and largely unfair means of tackling corporate killing.

Endnotes

1. Felipe Estrada and Tove Pettersson of the Department of Criminology, Stockholm University is acknowledged with gratitude, along with the research assistance of Jenny Richards of Adelaide University Law School. Some of the material contained herein has been revised and updated from the previously published article: Sarre, R., and Richards, J.: "Responding to Culpable Corporate Behaviour: Current developments in the industrial manslaughter debate," Flinders Journal of Law Reform, 8(1), 93–111, 2005.
2. Sutherland, E. (1949/1983) White-Collar Crime: The Uncut Version, New Haven: Yale University Press, p 7. The term "white-collar crime" was first used in Sutherland's 1939 address to the American Sociological Society, published the following year in Vol 5, American Sociological Review as "White Collar Criminality" (1940) 1–12.
3. Discussed in Sutton, A. and Haines, F. (2003), "White Collar and Corporate Crime," in Goldsmith, A. Israel, M., and Daly, K (eds): Crime and Justice: An Australian Textbook in Criminology, 2*nd* ed, Pyrmont, NSW: Thomson Lawbook Co, 147–149.
4. Such as the improper disposal of toxic waste by a company that proves fatal. These considerations are found within the framework of a subset of critical criminology termed "environmental criminology," refer White, R and Haines, F (2004) Crime and Criminology: An Introduction (3rd ed), South Melbourne: OUP p 213–4.
5. Sarre, R. (2001) "Risk Management and Regulatory Weakness," in I. Ramsay (ed): Collapse Incorporated: Tales, Safeguards and Responsibilities of Corporate Australia, Sydney, CCH, 291–323.
6. Gobert, J and Punch, M, (2003) Rethinking Corporate Crime, London: LexisNexis Butterworths, 9.
7. (1994) 6 VIR 157.
8. Chesterton, S (1994) "The Corporate Veil, Crime and Punishment: The Queen v Denbo Pty Ltd and Timothy Ian Nadenbousch" 19 Melbourne University Law Review 1064.
9. For example, the failure of the prosecution in The Queen v AC Hatrick Chemicals Pty Ltd (Unreported, Supreme Court of Victoria, Hampel J, 29 November 1995), discussed below.
10. Refer to the discussion in Bronitt, S and McSherry, B (2000) Principles of Criminal Law 157–159, and also at 505–510 for a review of Australian law regarding negligence and manslaughter.
11. Gobert, J. and Punch, M. (2003) Rethinking Corporate Crime, 10
12. Tesco Supermarkets Ltd v Nattrass [1972] AC 153, followed in Meridian Global Funds Management Asia Ltd v Securities Commission [1995] 2 AC 500 and consistently in Australia, e.g. Hamilton v Whitehead (1988) 63 ALJR 80.
13. Wells, C (1993) Corporations and Criminal Responsibility 121.

14. See Wheelwright, K (2002), "Corporate Liability for Workplace Deaths and Injuries—Reflecting on Victoria's Laws in the Light of the Esso Longford Explosion" 7(2) Deakin Law Review 323. For a useful discussion on the imposition of corporate criminal liability generally, see Polk, K Haines, F and Perrone, S (1993), "Homicide, Negligence and Work Death: The Need for Legal Change," in M. Quinlan (ed): Work and Health: The Origins, Management and Regulation of Occupational Illness.
15. The Queen v AC Hatrick Chemicals Pty Ltd (Unreported, Supreme Court of Victoria, Hampel J, 29 November 1995).
16. Employers under the relevant legislation are obliged to ensure that conditions in their workplaces do not endanger the health or safety of their workers. The legislation is usually regulatory in its framework, invoking "strict" criminal liability for any person who fails to put in place required safety practices. For a discussion of the issues surrounding regulatory enforcement generally, see Fox, Richard (2002) "New Crimes or New Responses? Future Directions in Australian Criminal Law," 28(1) Monash University Law Review 103, 114–118.
17. Croall, H (2001) Understanding White Collar Crime, Buckingham: Open University Press, 151.
18. Workplace Health Safety and Other Acts Amendment Act 2003 (Qld).
19. Section 59(1) (a) and (b).
20. Under the Occupational Health and Safety Act 2000 (NSW) s 12.
21. Clough, Jonathan (2005) "Will the punishment fit the crime? Corporate manslaughter and the problem of sanctions," Flinders Journal of Law Reform, 8(1), 113–131 at 119.
22. Hall, Andy and Johnstone, Richard (2005) "Exploring the re-criminalising of OHS breaches in the context of industrial death," Flinders Journal of Law Reform, 8(1), 57–92 at 86.
23. Tomasic, R. (2005) "From White-Collar to Corporate Crime and Beyond," in Chappell, D, and Wilson, P (eds): Issues in Australian Crime and Criminal Justice, Chatswood NSW: LexisNexis Butterworths, p 264.
24. Gobert, J and Punch, M. Rethinking Corporate Crime 84
25. This Act applies to all Australians. Most Australian criminal law is the responsibility of the States or Territories and these laws are only applicable within the relevant jurisdiction.
26. Part 2.5, Division 12. For a useful discussion of this Part, see Woolf, T (1997) "The Criminal Code Act 1995 (Cth)—Towards a Realist Vision of Corporate Criminal Liability," 21(5) Criminal Law Journal 257.
27. Section 12.1 and 12.2.
28. Section 12.3(1).
29. Section 12.3(2) (a) and (b).
30. Section 12.3(6).
31. Sections 12.3(2) (c) and (d).
32. Section 12.3(2) (d).
33. Section 12.4(2).
34. Section 12.4.2(b).
35. In August of 2004, Greens Senator Kerry Nettle introduced into the Australian parliament the Criminal Code Amendment (Workplace Death and Serious Injury) Bill 2004, which was designed specifically to incorporate industrial manslaughter offenses into the Commonwealth Criminal Code. The Bill has stalled.
36. Crimes Act 1900 (ACT) ss 49C, 49D.
37. Crimes Act 1900 (ACT) s 7A.
38. Criminal Code 2002 (ACT) s 52.
39. Criminal Code 2002 (ACT) s 50.
40. The Bill was read a second time in the House of Assembly Wednesday 28 May 2003.

41. Stanley, B., Meredith, F. and Bishop, R. (2003) Review of the Occupational Health, Safety and Welfare System in South Australia, Vol 3.
42. Statement made by the Hon Michael J Wright, Minister for Industrial Affairs, during Question Time, SA House of Assembly Monday 28 April 2003.
43. General Purpose Standing Committee No 1, Parliament of New South Wales, Serious Injury and Death in the Workplace (2004), Recommendation 26. Refer also to the Advice in Relation to Workplace Death, Occupational Health and Safety Legislation and Other Matters ("The McCallum Report" to the WorkCover Authority of NSW June 2004) which also recommended against the introduction of a separate industrial manslaughter offense. *http://www.workcover.nsw.gov.au/publications* at 9 November 2004.
44. Rhiannon, L. (2004) "Greens to Workers: We'll Push for Industrial Manslaughter Laws" (Press Release, 11 August 2004).
45. McLean, T. (2004) "NSW: Govt to introduce tougher laws for negligent employers" (report from AAP, 27 October 2004).
46. Currently, Tasmania and the Northern Territory have no plans to legislate for industrial manslaughter laws.
47. See Sarre, R and Doig, M (2000) "Preventing Disaster by Building a Risk-Prevention Ethic into Corporate Governance," 15 Australian Journal of Emergency Management 54.
48. See Wells, C (2001) "Corporate Criminal Liability: Developments in Europe and Beyond," 39(7) Law Society Journal 62, 64. Refer also to Attorney-General's Reference No. 2/1999 [2000] 3 All ER 182, and P&O European Ferries (Dover) Ltd (1991) 93 Cr App R 72.
49. Home Office (2000) Reforming the Law in Involuntary Manslaughter: The Government's Proposals, Part 3: "Scope of the Proposals—A new offense of corporate killing." May 2000. See also the discussion of The Queen v Adomako [1995] 1 AC 171 in Gobert, J. and Punch, M. Rethinking Corporate Crime (2003), 92. The Queen v Adomako had the effect of replacing "recklessness" with "gross negligence" as the mens rea of manslaughter. The successful prosecution of a holiday company in Dorset arising out of the deaths of four teenagers in 1996 was based upon this standard (The Queen v Kite and OLL Ltd, discussed in Carver, A (2001) Hong Kong Business Law, (5th ed) Hong Kong: Longman, 69).
50. Home Office, Reforming the Law in Involuntary Manslaughter: The Government's Proposals, para 3.4.9.
51. Gobert, James. (2005) "The Politics of Corporate Manslaughter—the British Experience," Flinders Journal of Law Reform, 8(1), 1–38.
52. Home Office, "Government to Tighten Laws on Corporate Killing" (Press Release 21 May 2003).
53. Trades Union Congress, Corporate Accountability and Real Corporate Responsibility (2003) *http://www.tuc.org.uk/h_and_s/tuc-6546-f0.cfm* at 12 August 2003.
54. Gobert, James (2005) "The Politics of Corporate Manslaughter—the British Experience," Flinders Journal of Law Reform, 8(1), 1–38.
55. Reported in Gobert, J. and Punch, M. Rethinking Corporate Crime (2003), 83.
56. (1994) 24 Cal.App.4th 446.
57. Occupational Health and Safety Act R.S.O 1990 c. 0.1 s. 66(4).
58. Section 735(1) (a).
59. Glasbeek, Harry (2005) "More Criminalisation in Canada: More of the same?" Flinders Journal of Law Reform, 8(1), 39–55 at 43.
60. Department of Justice, Canada (2002) Government Response to the Fifteenth Report of the Standing Committee on Justice and Human Rights—Corporate Liability. *http://canada.justice.gc.ca/en/dept/pub/ccl_rpm/summary.html* at 12 August 2003.
61. Gobert, J. and Punch, M. Rethinking Corporate Crime (2003), 96, referring to A. Ashworth, Principles of Criminal Law, (3rd ed, 1999) 199.

62. Per Cummins J, DPP v Esso (Australia) Pty Ltd [2001] VSC 296 (Unreported, Supreme Court of Victoria, Justice Cummins, 30 May 2001) [4].
63. Per NSW Industrial Relations Minister John Della Bosca as cited by, and reported in "NSW: Govt to introduce tougher laws for negligent employers" (report from AAP, 27 October 2004).
64. Unreported, County Court of Victoria, per Judge Gebhardt, 27 May 2004.
65. The case is discussed in Catanzariti, J (2004) "Higher and novel penalties for serious safety breaches" Law Society Journal August 2004, 48.
66. Judgment at para 37.
67. Clough, Jonathan (2005) "Will the punishment fit the crime? Corporate manslaughter and the problem of sanctions," Flinders Journal of Law Reform, 8(1), 113–131 at 120–130 and Fisse, B (1990) "Sentencing Options Against Corporations," 1(2) Criminal Law Forum 211.
68. An idea explored in Sarre, R (2003) "Corporate governance in the wake of contemporary corporate collapses: some agenda items for evaluators," 3(1) Evaluation Journal of Australasia, (new series) (1), 48.
69. Clough, Jonathan (2005) "Will the punishment fit the crime? Corporate manslaughter and the problem of sanctions," Flinders Journal of Law Reform, 8(1), 113–131 at 120.
70. Outside of the Australian Capital Territory.
71. Tomasic, Roman (2005) "From White-Collar to Corporate Crime and Beyond," in Duncan Chappell and Paul Wilson (eds): Issues in Australian Crime and Criminal Justice, Chatswood NSW: LexisNexis Butterworths at 267.
72. See this connection made in Hill, J (2002) "Corporate Criminal Liability in Australia: An Evolving Corporate Governance Technique?" in Low Chee Keong (ed): Corporate Governance: An Asia-Pacific Critique, 519.

References

Bronitt, Simon, and Bernadette McSherry (2000) *Principles of Criminal Law*. Pyrmont, NSW: Thomson Lawbook Co.

Carver, Anne (2001) *Hong Kong Business Law* (5th ed). Hong Kong: Longman.

Catanzariti, Joe (2004) "Higher and Novel Penalties for Serious Safety Breaches." *Law Society J.* 48 (August).

Chesterton, Simon (1994) "The Corporate Veil, Crime and Punishment: The Queen v Denbo Pty Ltd and Timothy Ian Nadenbousch." *Melbourne University Law Rev.* 19:1064.

Clough, Jonathan (2005) "Will the Punishment Fit the Crime? Corporate Manslaughter and the Problem of Sanctions." *Flinders J. of Law Reform* 8(1):113–131.

Commonwealth of Australia (2003) Royal Commission into the Building and Construction Industry, Final Report, Canberra AGPS.

Croall, Hazel (2001) *Understanding White Collar Crime.* Buckingham: Open University Press.

Department of Justice, Canada (2002) Government Response to the Fifteenth Report of the Standing Committee on Justice and Human Rights—Corporate Liability *http://canada.justice.gc.ca/en/dept/pub/ccl_rpm/summary.html* (accessed 12 August 2003).

Fisse, Brent (1990) "Sentencing Options Against Corporations." *Criminal Law Forum* 1(2):211

Fox, Richard (2002) "New Crimes or New Responses? Future Directions in Australian Criminal Law." *Monash University Law Rev.* 28(1):103.

Glasbeek, Harry (2005) "More Criminalisation in Canada: More of the Same?" *Flinders J. of Law Reform* 8(1):39–55.

Gobert, James (2005) "The Politics of Corporate Manslaughter—the British Experience." *Flinders J. of Law Reform* 8(1):1–38.

Gobert, James, and Maurice Punch (2003) *Rethinking Corporate Crime.* London: LexisNexis.

Hall, Andy, and Richard Johnstone (2005) "Exploring the Re-Criminalising of OHS breaches in the Context of Industrial Death." *Flinders J. of Law Reform* 8(1):57–92.

Hill, Jennifer (2002) "Corporate Criminal Liability in Australia: An Evolving Corporate Governance Technique?" P. 519 in *Corporate Governance: An Asia-Pacific Critique*, Editor L.C. Keong. Hong Kong: Sweet & Maxwell Asia.

Home Office (2000) Reforming the Law in Involuntary Manslaughter: The Government's Proposals, Part 3: "Scope of the Proposals—A New Offence of Corporate Killing" (May).

McLean, Tamara (2004) "NSW: Govt To Introduce Tougher Laws for Negligent Employers" (report from AAP, 27 October 2004).

Polk, Ken, Fiona Haines , and Santina Perrone (1993) "Homicide, Negligence and Work Death: The Need for Legal Change." In *Work and Health: The Origins, Management and Regulation of Occupational Illness,* Editor M. Quinlan. Melbourne: Macmillan.

Rhiannon, Lee (2004) "Greens to Workers: We'll Push for Industrial Manslaughter Laws" (Press Release, 11 August 2004).

Sarre, Rick (2001) "Risk Management and Regulatory Weakness." Pp. 291–323 in *Collapse Incorporated: Tales, Safeguards and Responsibilities of Corporate Australia,* Editor I. Ramsay. Sydney: CCH.

Sarre, Rick (2003) "Corporate Governance in the Wake of Contemporary Corporate Collapses: Some Agenda Items for Evaluators." *Evaluation J. of Australasia* (new series) 3 (1):48–55.

Sarre, Rick, and Meredith Doig (2000) "Preventing Disaster by Building a Risk-Prevention Ethic into Corporate Governance." *Australian J. of Emergency Management* 15:54–57.

Sarre, Rick, and Jenny Richards (2005) "Responding to Culpable Corporate Behaviour: Current Developments in the Industrial Manslaughter Debate."*Flinders J. of Law Reform* 8(1):93–111.

Stanley, Brian, Frances Meredith, and Rod Bishop (2003) Review of the Occupational Health, Safety and Welfare System in South Australia, Vol 3, Adelaide: Government Printer.

Sutherland, Edwin H. (1949/1983) *White-Collar Crime: The Uncut Version.* New Haven: Yale University Press.

Sutton, Adam, and Fiona Haines (2003) "White Collar and Corporate Crime." In *Crime and Justice: An Australian Textbook in Criminology,* 2nd ed. Editors A. Goldsmith, M. Israel, and K. Daly. Pyrmont, NSW: Thomson Lawbook Co.

Tomasic, Roman (2005) "From White-Collar to Corporate Crime and Beyond." *In Issues in Australian Crime and Criminal Justice,* Editors Duncan Chappell and Paul Wilson. Chatswood NSW: LexisNexis Butterworths.

Wells, Celia (1993) *Corporations and Criminal Responsibility*. Oxford: OUP.

Wells, Celia (2001) "Corporate Criminal Liability: Developments in Europe and Beyond Law Society J." 39(7):62.

Wheelwright, Karen (2002) "Corporate Liability for Workplace Deaths and Injuries–Reflecting on Victoria's Laws in the Light of the Esso Longford Explosion." *Deakin Law Rev.* 7(2):323.

White, Rob, and Fiona Haines (2004) *Crime and Criminology: An Introduction* (3rd ed.). South Melbourne: OUP

Woolf, Tahnee (1997) "The Criminal Code Act 1995 (Cth)—Towards a Realist Vision of Corporate Criminal Liability." *Criminal Law J.* 21(5):257.

4

The Punishment of Corporate Crime in China

Ling Zhang and Lin Zhao

Corporate crime is usually studied as the economic product of a free market society. Certainly, corporate conglomerates when operated legally have helped a country's economy, and to a larger extent, have promoted a healthy global economy. Illegal operations, on the other hand, may not only harm the well-being of the country in which they occur but can and have harmed the well-being of not just one country but also globally. Therefore, more and more nations and global communities (e.g., The United Nations) now consider corporate crime more of a priority because of its tremendous global effects. The United States in particular is actively seeking new ways to prevent corporate crimes and is prosecuting white-collar criminals aggressively to offset the damage to its economic reputation done by the recent waves of corporate crimes. This international trend has acted as strong encouragement for study and research regarding white-collar crimes in China, especially concerning how to deal with its corporate crimes and how to effectively punish white-collar criminals. This analysis will discuss China's corporate crimes as well as issues regarding their punishment under Chinese law.

The Development of China's Modern Corporation

The definition of a corporation varies in different countries due to economic, legal, and historical differences. Moreover, researchers and scholars have defined corporations differently; there is no universal definition. In general, a corporation is an independent organization set forth and defined under specific legal terms with its primary goal being a profit for shareholders.

There are three key features of a corporation: (1) It exists in society as an economically independent organization that promotes the distribution of goods and services. (2) It has a specific goal of generating profits. This is the most important feature of a corporation as its survival depends on profit from economic activities and transactions. (3) Since it is a legally defined entity, it is expected to operate under these terms set forth in the law.

Unlike Western countries, China's socioeconomic infrastructure is based on the Marxian theory of a state-run socialist economy. Since the establishment of the New China in 1949, and before the period of Economic Reform, corporations in China were generally owned by the state or by the community. As a result, traditionally there were only two types of corporations in China: state-owned or collectively owned. However, given profit as a goal, these kinds of organizations provide ineffective models because they do not encourage motivation, creativity, or the general morale. Individual employees are not rewarded for making a profit for the company. In 1978, after the 11th Communist Party Conference, the policy of Economic Reform brought new life into state-owned corporations. Privatization is now possible, and the Chinese Constitution states that "under special legal terms, privately owned business (e.g., small companies) or individually owned establishments have now become an important part of the socialist economic market." Incorporating different types of privatized business inaugurated the Chinese-style socialist economic model and it also started an unprecedented economic reform. Only after this new beginning in China's economy did private and foreign investors start new business deals in China. During China's 14th Communist Party Conference in 1993, specific regulations regarding the economic infrastructure in a socialist society were passed which laid down the foundation for transitioning from state-owned and state-run businesses to private and individually owned business. Once again, state officials emphasized the importance of a privatized economy and its inextricable link to China's modernization and other economic reform efforts. The conference also pointed out that a modern business entity must be competitive in the marketplace, with clear goals of profit, differentiated levels of responsibilities, and modern scientific managerial methods. This model will essentially become the prototype of the "new corporation" in China. Multiple corporations must be able to coexist in the marketplace with limited state regulations and they must freely compete for the attention of consumers. In essence, this Conference adopted a laissez-faire attitude to encourage private business to enter China's market and to accelerate the Economic Reform movement.

Types of Corporations

A corporation is a living entity with many different facets. These differences directly affect how a corporation breaks the law because they involve the pragmatic venues or opportunities to accomplish illegal acts. Because corporate crimes are differentiated by their methods, there are also differentiated punishments for specific offenses. However, to study corporate crimes, one must first define the different types of corporations in terms of by their organization and responsibilities, such as whether they comprise a corporation business, co-oped business, or individual business.

Corporation Business

A corporation business is defined under corporate law as an organization with two or more investors, co-investing for profit. Corporate responsibilities of the investors are limited by the percentage of their investment or the value of their stock. However, the corporation is solely responsible and liable for all of its financial transactions and all other monetary dealings. Thus, the monetary assets of the individual investors and the corporation itself are separated. The corporation is in charge of its own finances or funds as an independent entity. The most common types of corporation businesses are companies with limited responsibilities and limited stock value. Under China's corporate law, besides these two types of corporations, there is also the state-invested corporation with limited responsibilities and operated by a government agency. There are no unlimited-responsibility corporations or other types of corporations with different formats from these.

The Co-op Corporation

A co-op business is an economic organization co-invested, co-operated, co-owned, and co-controlled by two or more people. These co-investors are solely responsible for their corporation's social, financial, and legal liabilities (or so-called unlimited responsibilities). In 1988, under China's business law, this type of corporation was recognized, and in 1999 during the 9th Conference of the People's Representatives, China's Co-Op Business Laws were passed, thereby formalizing the legality of these corporations.

Individual Business

An individual business (i.e., small business) is privately invested by one person and is an individually operated company. The private owner is completely in charge and solely responsible with unlimited responsibilities for all the company's social, financial, and legal obligations. In 1988, under China's business law, this organizational format was recognized and in 1999 during the 9th Conference of the People's Representatives, China's Individual Business Laws were passed, thereby recognizing the legality of this type of business.

Corporation Types as Defined by Ownership

Although there are certain commonalities regarding the definitions of corporations in different nations, the distribution of ownership and how it operates affects these legal definitions. For example, China has traditionally categorized a business by type of ownership. While China is developing its economy for a global market, it nonetheless maintains its communist-socialist origin, and the majority of the businesses are state-owned. Other types of businesses can also be distinguished by their ownership:

1. State-owned Business or Corporations: A state-owned[1] corporation is operated by the government. However, the categorization of corporations by state-ownership is only an organizing concept because there are many legal forms of state-owned organizations, including for-profit and non-profit businesses.
2. Collectively Owned Business or Corporation: The concept of a collectively owned business or corporation is that of a socialist organization owned and operated by the people. The wealth or profit is distributed to each individual according to their organizational responsibilities and contributions of labor. The profit gained by the corporation essentially belongs to the people or the collective unit. These collectively owned businesses are an essential part of China's economy.
3. Privately Owned Business or Corporation: A privately owned business is an enterprise owned and operated by a single citizen and all funds or profits belong to the individual. A privately owned corporation must have at least eight or more employees. Currently most of the privately owned businesses in China are individually owned, co-op, or Ltd. (corporations with limited responsibilities).
4. Foreign-Invested Corporations: Foreign-invested corporations are enterprises that are created and funded by foreign citizens or companies. These

corporations include solely foreign-invested firms, Chinese and foreign-invested firms, and Chinese and foreign co-op firms. In legal terms, all foreign-invested corporations have more independence under China's law because at least some, if not all, corporate assets belong to foreign interests.

5. Combination Corporations: A combination corporation involves multiple forms of economic organization that comprise a single for-profit enterprise. As Economic Reform efforts are implemented and China's economy gradually evolves into the larger global marketplace (i.e., it incorporates more features of a capitalist economy), many corporations are emerging as combination enterprises. For example, there are state-owned, collectively operated businesses, privately invested, collectively operated businesses, businesses co-invested by a single corporate legal representative (or *faren*) and all company employees, as well as other combination corporations with limited responsibilities or limited stockvalues.

China's Corporate Crimes

Definition

Corporate crime is a new type of crime which is not clearly defined in China's legal statutes. In Western countries, corporate crime is often synonymous with "white-collar" crime, company crime, and "CEO or CFO" crime. In the United States and United Kingdom, the research literature often refers to "corporate crime" as a type of organizational crime. Moreover, this type of organizational crime is defined differently from traditional organized crime, such as the Mafia, the mob, or other enterprises organized specifically for illegal activities. Currently, "corporate crime"[2] is still not clearly defined under China's criminal or civil laws. In fact, even scholars have not agreed upon a clear definition. Given these circumstances, we decided to define corporate crime to include crimes committed by a corporation's legal representative, or *faren*, defined as a person who is legally registered to head the corporation, and thus, at least theoretically, has responsibility for all the legal and financial liabilities of the corporation, and for crimes committed by those who are directly in charge of the operation of the organization and who may disregard the welfare of others and the law, in a way that has detrimental effects and thus deserves legal punishment.

Under China's current legal definition, "company crime"[3] generally describes and includes corporate crimes as the forms are similar in nature. Under China's Criminal Law Section 30, "When companies, corporations, firms, enterprises, or other forms of organizations commit harmful social behavior, under the law it is defined as company crime and therefore the organization must bear legal responsibilities and criminal liabilities." Although Criminal Law Section 30 specifies both company and corporate crimes as a type of organizational crime, it does not negate the legal responsibilities of the specific perpetrators of the crime, specifically regarding crimes committed by the *farens*. The reason the law defines it as an organizational crime is because the structure of an organization plays a heavy role in the perpetration of a corporate crime; it is not meant to undermine individual criminal liabilities. Currently, corporate crime in China is attracting increased attention as a consequential topic for research.

Trends in Chinese Corporate Crime

China's corporate crime can be divided into the following categories:

a. Start-Up Structural Corporate Crime: One type of corporate crime is the fake setup or start-up of a corporation and crimes committed for the purpose of this goal, and subsequently the illegal channeling of investor funds (similar to boiler rooms, phony investments, and ponzi schemes) Under the law, there must be appropriate measures taken or conditions met to set up a corporation, including enough initial monetary assets. There is also the expectation of good faith in doing business and in the exchange of goods and services on credit. Many of these start-up companies buy on credit, promising to pay after the purchase of certain goods and services, but then disappear, leaving creditors in ruins. Other start-up companies scam investors by lying about assets or issuing fake stocks and bonds, in some cases even setting up fake investment firms to scam unsuspecting victims. Once the victims invest, the company vanishes.
b. Production-Operational Corporate Crime: Prior to a corporation's legally producing goods and services, its operation must be evaluated and authorized by the state. Currently, however, many corporations produce and sell unsafe or contaminated products or provide inadequate services through misleading or false advertising. For example, corporations have produced and sold many unsafe medical products, cosmetics, contaminated foods, and unsafe agricultural products such as pesticides and fertilizers. In addition, some of these products have been exported, generating negative effects on the reputation of goods produced in China. Equally notable, there are companies that illegally produce, rent, sell, and export guns, bombs, and other weaponry. Other companies ignore official designations for retailers who have exclusive rights to sell certain goods (e.g., designated retailers protected by the state who sell certain goods such as tobacco and gasoline) and participate in the illegal sales of specialized goods and services. Such violations, when widespread, can have a crippling effect on China's controlled economy.
c. Unfair Competition in the Consumer Market: Corporations also commit crime by pirating well-known brand names in an attempt to gain a competitive edge in the consumer market. Pirating an established competitor's name brand, and stealing intellectual property, business secrets, and patents, has been done to generate profit. New technologies make this easier than ever before and lead to a diminished reputation of the victim company, as the pirated product is often of inferior quality. Thus, the victim is in fact victimized in two stages—through piracy and related sales loss, and by damage to its reputation, resulting in further sales losses. In other instances, corporations have used illegal and criminal means to denigrate their competitors by spreading rumors, false reports, and negative advertisements.
d. Fiduciary and Security Fraud: Fiduciary and security systems are increasingly important forces in China's economy as the country continues its Economic Reform efforts from a communist and socialist economy to a more capitalist economy. Because these institutions compose a relatively new sector in China's economy, their systems of management are not yet fully developed. This leaves structural imperfections that create opportunities for different kinds of white-collar and corporate crimes. For example, many corporations are set up as fake banking institutions or investment firms

that bilk both the public as well as private investors by selling phony stocks, bonds, checks, credit cards, money orders, promissory notes, among other financial services and instruments. These companies are assisted by legal institutions that often manipulate the public through false accounting, false advertising, and other data that provide the media with a fictitious picture of the company's financial health. Sometimes, several corporations help each other to increase the stock values through manipulation of the stock market. Controlling the sales or purchase of shares misleads the public regarding the true financial picture of the company. Other corporate crimes include various institutionalized frauds and insurance frauds involving staged "accidents."

e. Organized Illegal Smuggling of Goods and Tax Evasion: Since the 1980s, one of the biggest changes in the smuggling business is that it used to be a clandestine activity organized by a few individuals. Now, however, corporations increasingly participate in organized, illegal smuggling and the exportation/importation of illicit goods. The merchandise being smuggled both in and out of China's borders involves items that are strictly forbidden by Chinese law, including weapons, bombs, fake coins, pornography, rare antiques, precious metals, endangered species, and exotic flora. In addition, some companies smuggle non-forbidden items to avoid inspection and to evade taxes and tariffs. A large part of China's economy depends on income from corporate taxes. In fact, the majority of revenues collected by the Chinese government comes from corporate taxes or tariffs. Since 1994, after the establishment of China's new tax codes and laws, the effects of organized illegal smuggling and corporate tax evasion have been extremely damaging to China's economy and national treasury.

f. Corporate Fraud: The concept of business transactions being done on credit is still fairly new in China, and corporations have used this condition to their advantage in committing fraud. There are several general types of corporate fraud. First, there is contract fraud, which involves documents written in a way to legally defraud the signer of the document of funds, assets, and/or properties. This is the most common form of contract fraud. Second, corporations commit identity theft by using personal information obtained from their clients. The corporations open new accounts in their clients' names, producing financial and legal documents by forging the victim's signature. Third, corporations simply "take the money and run" by emptying client accounts and then disappearing afterwards. Persons fall for these scams because many of the companies appear very credible and dependable and offer deals that seem almost too good to be true.

Since the 1980s, there has been a dramatic increase in both the amount and seriousness of economic crime. In the span of 11 years between 1982 and 1993, official statistics show that China's regional superior courts received 618,915 economic crime cases, with an average yearly increase of 17.7%. About 30% of these were economic crimes. After 1993, as Economic Reform measures took place in China, corporate crimes in securities fraud, contract fraud, tax evasion, illegal smuggling, and unsafe consumer products have all increased exponentially. From 1994 to 1996, regional superior courts in China on average received more than 12,000 cases of economic crime per year; an increase of one-third from 1993.

In 1997,[4] there were a total of 8,680 cases of fiduciary/security frauds and tax evasion. There were also 9,876 cases of fraud involving unsafe consumer products or illegal smuggling. In 1998, there were 4,834 cases reviewed in all China's judiciary courts, four times the caseload of the previous year, of these, 1,468 were securities frauds (twice as much than the previous year), and 1,147 cases were tax frauds. Facing a dramatic rise in white-collar crime cases, the Chinese government issued an order[5] to all regional superior courts to review each case in an expeditious manner and to severely castigate perpetrators of these crimes in order to deter such offenses. To combat white-collar crimes, the government also imposed heavy fines, confiscated all corporate profits, and repossessed monetary assets and property of the perpetrators as a form of retribution. After these steps were implemented, the government was able to recover 95 billion yuan. In 2001,[6] there were a total of 14,953 cases of "severely destructive" economic crimes reviewed by the courts which saw 19,972 individuals criminally convicted and 22.3 billion yuan recovered. In 2003,[7] there were a total of 14,775 cases reviewed by courts involving unsafe products, smuggling, securities and fiduciary fraud against the free market, with 19,197 individuals criminally convicted and 15 billion yuan recovered. From these numbers,[8] we see that in the last 20 years or so, there has been a dramatic increase in economic crimes in China, especially in the number of corporate crimes.

Moreover, there has been a dramatic increase in corporate participation in subfields of economic crime, such as violating corporate regulations; illegally pirating the intellectual properties of others; producing imitations of patented or established name brands: producing, distributing, and selling illegal drugs; and smuggling illicit substances or forbidden goods in and out of the country. These organized corporate crimes are on the rise at an alarming rate. In fact, crimes that involve multiple individuals and financial investment have been committed by corporations and companies in an organized manner and have become one of the most important social problems in China.

Definition of a Criminal Perpetrator in Corporate Crime

China's Criminal Law, Section 30, specifically defines a company or a corporation as a perpetrator of a crime as long as it is an enterprise or organization, regardless of the type of ownership (state-owned, collectively owned, or privately owned) or how it is organized (state-invested, collectively invested, or privately invested). It is defined as a single perpetrator of a crime under this definition and therefore can be prosecuted under the criminal law and receive criminal punishment. Moreover, the statute also tacitly implies that those who receive criminal punishment must also be those who committed the crime. In China, both the individuals who are directly in charge of the corporation and the organization itself are charged as perpetrators of a corporate crime.

However, because of the inherent difficulties in pinpointing fault, not all corporate crimes are prosecuted under current legal and criminal definitions, and sometimes corporations may thus escape criminal punishment. Very often, there are organized crimes that are in fact corporate crimes; nonetheless, the intention of the criminal or how the crime was actually perpetrated will sometimes exclude these cases from being prosecuted as corporate crime. In these circumstances, only specific individual(s) will be punished and no other action is taken against the corporation as a whole. These offenses include the following categories of crime:

a. A corporation was created with criminal intent: There are individuals who form a company through illegal means and commit crimes under the company name or use the corporation as a front to cover criminal activities. To discourage such activities, on June 18, 1999, China's Supreme Court ruled in the document *Concerning the Prosecution of Corporate Crime and the Implementation of Penal Codes*, under Section 2, that "individuals who set up a corporation with criminal intent will not fall under the corporate penal code. Instead, the perpetrator will be individually punished with a harsher sentence than that allowed under corporate law."
b. Illegally using a corporation's name without consent and with the motive to commit crime: Under the same document, in Section 3, it defines that "those who profit by illegally obtaining the name of a (law-abiding) corporation without consent will be prosecuted as individuals.
c. Illegally setting up and operating a corporation against government regulations or without a legal representative (*faren*): In the same document, Section 1, it specifies that "Criminal Law, Section 30 stated that companies, corporations, organizations, and enterprises are defined as legal entities only when they follow government regulations and there is a legal registered *faren* or legal representative for the company." As a result, any corporation illegally formed and operated or without a *faren* is by definition an illegal entity, and therefore cannot be prosecuted under the corporate penal code because the legal status of a corporation was never granted by the state. These perpetrators are individually prosecuted and punished even if crime has been committed through the corporation.

The Principle and Basis for Punishment of Corporate Crime in China

The Principal of Punishment for Corporate Crimes

In general, corporate crime in China follows the guidelines of "company crime," and the creed for penal punishment has always been "to impose a two-tier punishment for most crime and rely on single-tier punishment as a secondary option." Under Criminal Law, Section 31, it states that "for corporate crime, the criminal punishment for the corporation is monetary fines and for those who are in charge of the organization, criminal punishment must be assigned." Therefore, the statue specifies that both the individual and the organization will be penalized criminally under the law, and all other details of the punishment must follow the principal of the two-tier punishment system. Generally, the current punishment model imposes monetary fines on the corporation and criminal sanctions on those who are either directly in charge or who have knowledge of the operations of the corporation. The two-tier punishment system attempts to censure both the perpetrators individually and the organization as a whole.

For example, under Criminal Law, Section 393 regarding corporate bribery, those who are in charge of the corporation who bribe or provide kickbacks to government officials during an otherwise legitimate business transaction, the two-tiered punishment will be applied. That is, the corporation will be fined and the individual will serve at least five years in prison.

The single-tier punishment model is applied only in circumstances where the individuals who are in charge of the corporation are prosecuted and penalized with a jail term; no further action is taken against the corporation. Under China's Criminal Law, Section 162, it states that when corporations fall under extreme economic hardship and commit economic crimes or fraud in an attempt to alleviate its financial burden, only those who are in charge of the corporation will be tried and penalized criminally but no further punishment will be assigned to the corporation. This is because imposing further monetary fines will only make the situation worse and will penalize investors. Crimes in these circumstances will fall under the single-tier punishment model, and the company will be exonerated from further criminal liability. Section 396 further states that if individuals in a corporation illegally distribute profit that belongs to the state, because the corporation did not gain any benefit from this crime, it is excluded from criminal prosecution and no monetary fines will be imposed. Instead, the individual perpetrators who benefited from the crime will be criminally punished.

The Basis of Punishment for Corporate Crime

Because corporate crime involves so many different facets of society and there can be many complex ties involved, differentiated punishments are necessary, depending on the specific nature of the offense. The punishment for a specific corporate crime depends on several legal evaluations. Aside from breaking specific criminal laws, a corporate crime also simultaneously breaks economic, administrative, and civil laws. Thus, multiple levels of punishment can be imposed upon perpetrators of corporate crime. Aside from criminal laws, a corporate crime also violates the following three types of legal codes and regulations:

1. Economic Laws and Regulations: Economic laws and regulations set legal boundaries regarding the nature of business activities and transactions allowed by the state. Any behavior outside these perimeters is by definition illegal, including corporate crime. Thus, the state often applies sanctions under economic laws for corporate crimes in addition to punishments which are applied under the criminal laws.
2. Administrative Laws and Regulations: Administrative laws and regulations also set rules regarding the operation of corporations. In general, there are two types of administrative regulations:
   a. Legal operational procedures and standards set by the judiciary branch of the state regarding business organizations (*The Standards and Legal Procedures for the Registration of a Faren* and *Tax Codes for Corporations*).
   b. Administrative and procedural legal codes that involve corporations such as accountings laws, patent laws, as well as other regulations. Corporate crime can also involve the violation of these administrative and procedural regulations.
3. Civil Laws: Under China's Civil Law, Section 2, civil laws mostly focus on the transfer of monetary assets or properties between two parties. Under these laws, corporate crime is essentially a business transition that goes awry and in which one party is wronged. Thus, a corporate crime usually violates both economic and civil laws, and the punishment of the perpetrator will also include an additional civil liability component.

Methods of Punishment for Corporate Crime

China's Criminal Law Section 31, specifies that "for corporate crime, monetary fines are imposed as a punishment against the corporation and all criminal punishment will be applied to those individuals who are directly in charge of the corporation or in the operation of the corporation for the crime." Therefore, under China's criminal law, any type of criminal punishment can be applied to those who were in charge of the company, which includes punishments that may impose limitations on the person's life, freedom, monetary assets, or intellectual or political rights. However, there is only one type of punishment for the organization or the corporation itself—monetary fines. Most corporate crimes are economic in nature with the goal of greater profit. Under such circumstances, the best punishment is the confiscation of all profit illegally earned in addition to a monetary fine, as it sends the message that "crime does not pay." English scholar Bensen states that "it is best to reward greed with monetary fines so long as it is within the means of the criminal. This form of economic retribution turns the crime around; the victims are rewarded and perpetrators are punished as a result of the crime."[9] As for the amount of monetary fines, under China's Criminal Law, Section 52, they depend on the specific crime.

There are three types of monetary fines under the criminal law: (1) preset amounts, (2) multiplied amount, and (3) unlimited amount. A preset fine is an amount established by the court, depending on the specific circumstances of the crime (generally the worse the crime, the heavier the fine). A multiple fine is also referred to as a ratioed fine, and also depends on the circumstance of the crime, but the court may set a baseline amount and then impose an extra amount—multiples of the baseline or an extra percentage of the baseline fees. There are specific guidelines in the criminal law for the first two kinds of monetary fines. The last type of fine is an "unlimited amount," meaning that there is no preset amount and no specific guidelines exist under the criminal code for this type of fine. Instead, the court may set any amount, depending on the seriousness of the crime and the harm it has done. Under China's criminal law, any type of these three monetary fines may be imposed upon an individual as a punishment. However, when punishing a corporation for a corporate crime as an organization, there is only one type of fine imposed—an undetermined amount. For example, under Criminal Law, Section 164, it states that, "Companies or corporations after gaining illegal profit, if the profit is distributed to the company employees and if it is a fair amount of monetary value, the corporation will be fined." There is no mention of how much the corporation should be fined under this statute. The amount depends on the situation and is unlimited. In some cases, even when an individual is fined in the multiplied or ratioed amount, the corporation can still be fined an undetermined amount. Also under Criminal Law, Section 180, it states "if an individual engages in unfair trade during a business transaction, the individual must serve 1 to 5 year(s) in jail and the corporation will be fined more than twice but less than five times the profit gained illegally. If the circumstances of the crimes are unusually heinous, the individual will serve more than 5 but less than 10 years in jail and the corporations will be fined more than twice but less than five times the amount of profit gained illegally through the crime." Therefore, no matter what kind of punishment the individual receives, the corporation will be liable for a variable amount of monetary fine as set by the court.

There are five ways of collecting monetary fines in China: (1) One-time full payment with a specific due date; (2) multiple-payment (e.g., monthly, yearly) with a specific due date; (3) forced payment; (4) anytime collection; and (5) reduced or forgiven payment.

1. One-time full payment with a specific due date. This method can be applied when the fine is not large or regardless of its size if the criminal has no financial difficulties in paying in full.
2. Multiple-payment with a specific (monthly or yearly) due date. This method applies when the fine is a large amount, the criminal has difficulties making a one-time payment in the full amount, and he or she needs to make several payments (in a specific length of time which is determined by the court).
3. Forced payment or collection. This applies when the criminal has the ability to pay monetary fines but does not meet the due date. The court will force the payment by seizing the criminal's monetary assets, including taking actions such as freezing bank accounts, revoking professional licenses, and the foreclosure or auction of monetary assets or properties.
4. Anytime collection. This applies when the criminal originally indicates that he/she is unable to pay the full amount due to financial difficulties, but the court subsequently discovers that the individual actually has sufficient monetary assets, in which case the court reserves the right for anytime collection of the payment.
5. Reduced or forgiven fines. This only applies when the criminal is unable to pay due to "unavoidable disasters."[10] If such an event occurs the criminal may apply for a reduced or forgiven payment, and if the circumstances are verified by the court, it may reduce the amount, or forgive the fine altogether.

Under China's criminal law, the payment of monetary fines as a punishment cannot be delayed, thus probation never applies to monetary fines. Under China's Criminal Law Section 72, convicted criminals who receive a sentence less than 3 years have the possibility for probation depending on repentance, cooperation, and good behavior. If the court can be assured that the individual will no longer be a threat to society, then probation or a delayed sentence may be applied. However, probation or the delay of punishment cannot be applied in the realm of dealing with one's personal freedom; therefore, monetary fines are not included in this provision. When monetary fines are imposed as a punishment, it must be a swift process and the criminal is expected to pay immediately.

Non-Criminal Punishment for Corporate Crime

Non-criminal punishment refers to other types of sanctions, excluding criminal processes, and specifically refers to administrative, economic, and civil sanctions. Non-criminal punishment applies to less serious corporate crimes. Since only monetary fines can be imposed as a sanction against a corporation. This makes it harder to prosecute certain corporate crimes. Thus, it is important that other types of sanctions be incorporated in addition to monetary fines. For less serious corporate crimes, which do not deserve criminal punishment, such crimes would be difficult to deter without non-criminal punishment. Therefore, besides criminal sanctions, other parts of the legal system should be used to coordinate a set of punishments that fit these crimes.

Guidelines for Different Types of Non-Criminal Punishment

Under China's criminal law, non-criminal punishment falls in the category of "other types of punishment." There are specific guidelines which are extremely important for helping to coordinate actions of different parts of the legal system in creating specific sanctions designed to protect victim's rights, and re-educate convicted criminals. There are several different types of non-criminal punishment under China's criminal law:

1. Court-Appointed and Court-Mandated Economic Compensation: Economic compensation refers to monetary fines in addition to the perpetrator's criminal conviction, where the criminal must pay for the "economic loss" of the victim as a result of the crime. The amount of the "economic loss" is determined by the court and depends on the specific circumstances and seriousness of the crime. Under Criminal Law, Section 36, "when the crime results in the economic loss to a victim, along with a criminal sentencing, the criminal must also compensate the victim for his/her economic loss."

   Corporate crime, especially crime that involves damages to the environment, production and sale of unsafe consumer products, and the making of unsafe and/or fake drugs, not only brings danger and harm to the society and the state, but also may cause bodily harm/injuries and economic loss to specific victims. Therefore, aside from determining the criminal responsibility of offending corporations, the welfare and the suffering of victims must also be factored into the punishment for these crimes, which includes both economic compensation and civil liabilities.

   When assigning "economic compensation" as a punishment against a corporation, there must be two preexisting conditions:

   a. The economic loss to the victim must be a direct result of the corporate crime.
   b. The corporation already has been convicted of a crime and has been sentenced.

   Moreover, if the corporation has been ordered to pay both monetary fines and economic compensation to victims, and does not have enough assets for both financial obligations at once, then the victim must come first. There is an established hierarchy of priorities to protect the individual, the community, and the state.

   If the nature of a corporate crime is less serious, charges may not be pursued by the courts, and therefore criminal liability may be reduced or "forgiven" altogether. However, even if the effect of the crime is minimal, as long as there is economic loss to individuals or the society as a result of the crime, the court may impose the sanction of "financial compensation for economic loss." Criminal Law, Sections 36 and 37, both deal with the nature of sentencing corporate financial compensation for a victim's economic loss, and explain the corporations' civil responsibilities.
2. Public Condemnation, Public Repentance, and Public Apology: All these forms of punishment apply only to non-serious corporate crimes with relatively minimal effects. The court may publicly condemn, denounce, or censure the individual perpetrator for the purpose of reeducation. Public repentance refers to the sanction whereby an individual criminal writes a letter or signs a contract for repentance including a guarantee to never commit the crime again. Finally, public apology may be ordered where a perpetrator

acknowledges the harm done to the victim in court, apologizing for the crime committed and for the suffering and inconvenience it caused.

These three forms of punishment (public condemnation, public repentance, and public apology) apply only to non-serious offenses. The court's goal is to reeducate the criminal and placate victims in order to promote social justice.

3. Recommendation of Departmental and Administrative Punishment or Demotion: For corporations that escape a criminal indictment and punishment, to better deter, educate, and forewarn these corporations for their criminal behavior, the court may recommend administrative punishment or demotion depending on the circumstances of the crime. This includes but is not limited to firing or demoting the officials in charge of corporations, reforming the administrative system of the corporation, selecting new leaders and staff, changing internal structural rules and regulations of the corporation, and improving the equipment and environment to reduce needs and/or motives for committing crime. These sanctions may be particularly effective in promoting compliance in state-run corporations.

Administrative Punishment

Administrative punishment applies when a citizen, *faren*, or an organization breaks administrative rules or regulations. When such an incident occurs, administrative punishment methods must follow the guidelines under the criminal codes. These forms of punishment are aimed at maintaining law and order socially and economically. For corporate crimes that commit violations of administrative regulations such as tax fraud, evasion of taxes or tariffs, practicing unfair competition in the free market, producing fake or unsafe consumer products, administrative punishment methods are most likely to be used. The following methods are the most common administrative punishments:

1. Warning: A warning is also referred to as reputation-affecting punishment and it is used to deter a corporation that committed non-serious offenses. The primary goal of the warning is public denunciation and degradation, which will in turn affect the reputation, brand name, or product(s) of the corporation. A warning is warranted generally if the corporate crime is relatively insignificant. If a corporation receives a warning, there would also be registration of the offense along with the dates and frequencies of the warnings received. The corporation is required to register their current system of operation and reform it quickly. Every time a corporation receives a warning it is counted in the registry. If a subsequent warning is received, there could be more serious punishment for the corporation.

   Generally, a warning is used for the first offense and before harsher forms of criminal punishment are imposed. The goal of this punishment is to warn the individual perpetrator or the organization to be "mentally alert"; if the criminal behavior does not end, there will be a more serious punishment that will affect the freedom and financial assets of the perpetrator or the organization.

   Warning as a formal criminal punishment must be behavioral, and it must also be stated in a formal letter from the legal institution giving the reprimand. An oral warning cannot be considered an administrative punishment. However, the effectiveness of an administrative warning depends on the size

of the corporation and its preexisting reputation, among other factors. As American scholar James Coleman explained, "any punishment that affects one's reputation is insignificant to anyone who had none to begin with."[11] On the other hand, it can be a severe punishment for a corporation with established brand names and a good reputation.
2. Confiscation of Illegal Gains and Illegal Goods: The confiscation of illegal gains refers to when a legal institution seizes all profits, including monetary assets and other illegal gains. The confiscation of illegal goods may entail such as items as pirated materials, pornography, unsafe food products, or any paraphernalia for illegal activities such tools for the production of guns and weapons and automobiles for the illegal transportation and smuggling of these goods.
3. Administrative Monetary Fines: Monetary fines are imposed by an administrative institution with a specific due date. The monetary fines must come out existing corporate assets or through legal sources. There is a baseline and a limit for the amount of the fine that is set by specific guidelines under the statute. However, a judge can decide whether to increase or decrease the "baseline" amount of the fine depending on the seriousness or the circumstances of the crime. Fiduciary and Securities Law, Section 199, explains that "if the investment company mishandles securities or stocks and illegally sells, buys, or exchanges securities, a formal reprimand should be issued to correct the behavior, and all illegal profit or gains should be confiscated and a fine should be imposed in the amount of at least twice the illegal profit but less than five times the same amount."
4. Forced Stopped Production: Forced stopped production refers to the shutdown of a corporation by the state for breaking laws and regulations. A temporary shutdown or forced stopped production is meant to make the corporation reform its administrative style and fulfill its legal responsibilities within a set time period. The company may resume the operation when these changes and obligations are met, and there is no need to reapply for a license or permit. A shutdown or forced stopped production is used mostly for two specific types of crime: (1) the production and sale of unsafe products; (2) the production or sale of products that threaten public safety (people's health) and the environment. Forced stopped production is a serious administrative punishment because many corporations rely on the production and sales of goods and services for their survival. The stopped production and halt of sales eliminate the means of current illegal activities and the venue for breaking laws and regulations. The judiciary must decide when to impose a shutdown and whether it should be a partial or complete.
5. Temporary Cancellation of Licenses and Revocation of Permits for Operation: A temporary revocation or cancellation of a specific license or permit for the operation of a business and the sales of certain goods may also be employed as an administrative punishment. The corporation must change its behavior and only after a certain period of time the hold or revocation may be cancelled and the license or permit restored.

Other Types of Non-Criminal Punishment

In China, aside from standard criminal and administrative sanctions, there are other punishments that are non-criminal and non-administrative. These methods of punishment can either be determined by the state judiciary or by the administrative committee of the corporation.

1. Barred or Forbidden Participation: Individual perpetrators of a corporate offense sometimes use their professional network to commit crime. In these cases individuals may be barred from their profession. Such a penalty not only punishes the individual, but the lack of access to the profession also potentially denies possibilities for future lawbreaking. China's Corporate Law, Section 219, states that "for those individuals who are in charge of the estimation or evaluation of monetary assets as public notaries, if these individuals provide false documentation for illegal profit, all illegal gains will be confiscated; the individual will be fined at least more than twice but less than five times the amount of the illegal profit, and the service institution will be shut down along with the permanent revocation of the individual's license."
2. Dissolving and Disbanding the Corporation: China's Corporate Law, Section 192, states, "any corporation that was shut down under administrative law as a result of a corporate crime may also be dissolved or disbanded as a business enterprise or organization." The courts order the dissolution of a business when very serious crimes are committed. A company may be dissolved due to extreme financial difficulties or monetary loss, and if the company is no longer able to survive under these circumstances, the investors may apply to dissolve the company. After evaluation, the court may grant a disbandment status to the company. However, this is very different than a court-ordered and forced disbandment as a criminal punishment. A court-ordered disbandment is warranted when a crime has been committed after the establishment of the corporation and during its production or operation. These crimes include, but are not limited to: covering up or falsifying information on the business registry of administrative institutions, falsifying and changing the accounting books, and participating in illegal sales of good and services.
3. Public Rendering of a Court Verdict: For corporations that escape indictment on criminal charges, the court may render a verdict publicly through the news media. In general, when the court renders a verdict, it is a closed case and the verdict is only sent to the defendant and those who are involved in the case. Therefore, for corporations that avoided a criminal indictment (and therefore a criminal sentence), public rendering of a court verdict is a public shaming mechanism that openly sets forth the facts of the crime and serves as a form of severe public condemnation. It is also functions to make the public feel that social justice has been restored. Large corporations are powerful establishments with enormous financial backing. Thus, when a corporation escapes criminal indictment or punishment, the public rendering of a verdict and public condemnation placate the popular demand for justice. In addition, such non-criminal punishment negatively affects the reputation of the corporation, which in turn will affect its economic activities.

Conclusion

This analysis explored China's methods of punishment against corporate crime, including criminal punishment and non-criminal punishment. The remaining and largely unexplored issue is how these potential sanctions are actually applied, and when they are, whether they are having the effects intended by state legislation. Conversely, if they are not being applied, research needs to examine why this is the case. Given the range of sanctions available in China for sanctioning white-collar and corporate crime, much more research is required regarding the willingness of authorities to bring such cases in the first place, and what cultural, political, legal, and resource obstacles remain in effectively preventing the growth of such offenses.

If the judiciary follows guidelines and implements punishment accordingly, they will play a major role in the prevention and deterrence of corporate crime. The principle behind the implementation of sanctions has always been to use both criminal and non-criminal punishment simultaneously with a main focus on the implementation of criminal punishment. The specific circumstances of each situation must be evaluated, and then one form or a combination of punishment methods carefully chosen as the most effective way to combat corporate crime.

Moreover, when punishing corporate crimes, there should be a limit on the severity of the criminal punishment—one should use the lightest or the most minimal criminal sentence to achieve maximum social justice for the public. Severe punishment should be imposed on the individual perpetrators of serious crimes. When the crime is relatively minor criminal punishment should be avoided, and instead non-criminal punishment methods should be imposed. Harsh criminal punishment cannot be viewed as a panacea for all offenses. In cases where criminal punishment is not used, perpetrators should be "reeducated" to become law-abiding citizens .

All the punishment methods can be seen as serving important roles in the prevention and deterrence of corporate crime in China. These methods can complement each other. China must also remain highly cognizant of international trends regarding corporate crime. As an emerging world power and major economy, the China must look to its government to study and evaluate research on the topic and exchange enforcement and legal experiences with other countries. It may then be better able to implement policies and punishment regimes that fit with China's unique social conditions effectively to control corporate offenses and to deter future illegalities.

Endnotes

* Translated by Helena Rene, American University.

1. State corporations refers to corporate enterprises that are both owned and operated by the state.
2. Chen Zhong Cheng (1992) *Legal Tales*. China: Chinese-Foreign Language Translation Press. p. 201.
3. In China, by law, a company is an economic organization with a certain amount of funds that functions under specific legal liabilities.
4. From China's *Supreme Court Report* as used in the 8th People's Representative's Conference, 2nd meeting in 1995.
5. From China's *Supreme Court Report* as used in the 9th People's Representative's Conference, 2nd meeting, in 1999
6. From China's *Supreme Court Report* as used in the 9th People's Representative's Conference, 2nd meeting in 1999.

7. From China's *Supreme Court Report* as used in the 9th People's Representative's Conference, 5th meeting in 2002.
8. From China's *Supreme Court Report* as used in the 10th People's Representative's Conference, 2nd meeting in 2004.
9. Bensen (1996) *The Foundations of Law–Theory of Criminal Law*. China: China's People's University of Public Security Press. p. 78.
10. "Unavoidable disasters" are defined in the document *The Supreme Court on the Provisions of Civil Properties* as monetary loss due to natural disasters, disabilities, the loss of bodily use due to serious injuries or illness, or if relatives of the criminal need large amount of money for the treatment of an illness.
11. James Coleman (1990) *Foundations of Social Theory*. Cambridge: Belknap Press. p. 315.

References

Bensen, Bill (1996) *The Foundations of Law–Theory of Criminal Law*. China: China's People's University of Public Security Press Beijing.
Chen, Zhong Cheng (1992) *Legal Tales*. China: Chinese-Foreign Language Translation Press Beijing.
Coleman, James (1990) *Foundations of Social Theory*. Cambridge: Belknap Press.
China's *Supreme Court Report* as used in the 8th People's Representative's Conference, 2nd meeting in 1995.
China's *Supreme Court Report* as used in the 9th People's Representative's Conference, 2nd meeting, in 1999.
China's *Supreme Court Report* as used in the 9th People's Representative's Conference, 2nd meeting in 1999.
China's *Supreme Court Report* as used in the 9th People's Representative's Conference, 5th meeting in 2002.

About the Authors

Michael L. Benson is Professor of Criminal Justice at the University of Cincinnati. Writing mainly in the areas of white-collar and corporate crime, he has been published in numerous journals, including *Criminology, Justice Quarterly, Journal of Research and Delinquency, American Sociological Review, American Journal of Sociology, and Social Problems*. He received the Outstanding Scholarship Award of the Society for the Study of Social Problems Division on Crime and Juvenile Delinquency for his co-authored book *Combating Corporate Crime: Local Prosecutors at Work*. His most recent book is *Crime and the Life Course: An Introduction*.

William K. Black is the Executive Director of the Institute for Fraud Prevention. He taught microeconomics, public financial management, financial regulation, and white-collar crime at the LBJ School of Public Affairs. He is the distinguished researcher in residence at Santa Clara University's law school and a scholar in SCU's Markkula Center for Applied Ethics. He is a World Bank consultant (anti-corruption initiatives). Black was a senior regulator during the savings and loan debacle. His book *The Best Way to Rob a Bank is to Own One* (University of Texas Press, 2005), uses the debacle as a case study of "control fraud." His undergraduate (economics) and law degrees are from the University of Michigan, his Ph.D. (criminology) is from the University of California (Irvine).

Chrisje Brants is Professor of Criminal Law at the Willem Pompe Institute of Criminal Law and Criminology, University of Utrecht, The Netherlands, of which she is also director. She studied criminology and law at the University of Amsterdam, where she also obtained a doctorate in social science in 1991 with "The Social Construction of Fraud." Her main fields of interest and research are international criminal law, comparative criminal law, crime and the media, comparative criminology, and the interrelationship between criminal law and the cultural and social construction of crime and criminal justice.

Bertrand Demonceau is an Assistant Lecturer at the University of Liège and a high-ranking civil servant in public finance. He holds degrees from both the School of Criminology and the School of Business Administration. He has held several positions in the banking industry, and is a member of the Belgian Royal Political Economy Society.

Michael Dantine is Senior Lecturer at the School of Criminology of the University of Liege, Belgium. He holds a Ph.D. in Criminology, and his dissertation focused on money laundering through securities and derivatives. He has been involved in research related to business crimes many years, has published several articles on white-collar crime and money laundering, and has taught "White Collar Crime and Business Crime" and "Crime and New Technologies" in the Master's Program in Criminology at the University of Liege.

Mary Dodge is an Associate Professor with the Graduate School of Public Affairs at the University of Colorado at Denver & Health Sciences Center. Her research has appeared in the *International Journal of Police Science & Management, Contemporary Issues in Criminology, International Journal of the Sociology of Law,* and the *Encyclopedia of White-Collar and Corporate Crime*. She is a co-editor with Gilbert Geis of *Lessons of Criminology* and co-author, with Gilbert Geis, of *Stealing Dreams: A Fertility Clinic Scandal.* She is an Associate Editor for Criminal Justice Research Reports in "Police, Law Enforcement, and Crime Prevention" and serves on the editorial advisory board for *The Prison Journal.*

Amitai Etzioni served as a Senior Advisor to the Carter White House; taught at Columbia University, Harvard Business School, University of California at Berkeley; and is the first University Professor at George Washington University, where he is the Director of the Institute for Communitarian Policy Studies. He served as the President of the American Sociological Association, and he founded the Communitarian Network (*www.communitariannetwork.org*).

A study by Richard Posner ranked him among the top 100 American intellectuals. He is the author of many op-eds and his voice is frequently heard in the media. He is the author of numerous books, including *The Active Society, Genetic Fix, The Moral Dimension, The New Golden Rule*, and *My Brother's Keeper*. His most recent books are *The Common Good, From Empire to Community: A New Approach to International Relations,* and *How Patriotic is the Patriot Act: Freedom Versus Security in the Age of Terrorism.* Dr. Etzioni is married and is the father of five sons.

Gabrio Forti is a Professor of Criminal Law and Criminology at the Catholic University of Milan. Editor of *White Collar Crime: The Uncut Version* by E.H. Sutherland (Giuffrè editore, Milano, 1987), he has published books on criminal negligence and corruption, as well as several essays on organized and economic crime and is the author of a criminology textbook (L'*Immane Concretezza*, Raffaello Cortina Editore, Milano, 2000). He has recently lead a vast study on television and crime, editing the book which encompasses, together with the main research results, the proceedings of an international conference thereon (*La Televisione del Crimine*, Vita e Pensiero, Milano, 2005).

David O. Friedrichs is Professor of Sociology/Criminal Justice at the University of Scranton. He is author of *Trusted Criminals: White Collar Crime in Contemporary Society* (Thomson/Wadsworth, 1996, 2004, 2007) and *Law in Our Lives: An Introduction* (Roxbury, 2001, 2006) and editor of *State Crime, Volumes I and II* (Ashgate/Dartmouth, 1998). He has also published some 100 journal articles, book chapters, encyclopedia entries, and essays. He served as President of the White Collar Crime Research Consortium (2002–2004), and received a Lifetime Achievement Award (Division on Critical Criminology) in 2005. In Spring, 2006, he was Visiting Professor of Law at Flinders University in Adelaide, Australia.

Jeannine A. Gailey is an Assistant Professor of Criminal Justice at Texas Christian University. Her scholarship focuses on organizational deviance, social psychology, violence against women, and masculinities. Her research has appeared in such journals as *Social Psychology Quarterly, Deviant Behavior*, and *The Journal of Applied Social Psychology*.

Gilbert Geis is Professor Emeritus, Department of Criminology, Law, and Society, University of California, Irvine. He is a former president of the American Society of Criminology and recipient of the Society's Edwin H. Sutherland Award for outstanding research. His most recent books are *Criminal Justice and Moral Issues*, with Robert Meier (Roxbury, 2006) and *White Collar and Corporate Crime* (Prentice Hall, 2007).

Harry Glasbeek B.A., LLB. (Hons.) University Of Melbourne, JD (Chicago), Professor Emeritus and Senior Scholar, Osgoode Hall Law School, York University, has taught at the universities of Melbourne and Monash in Australia and the University of Western Ontario in Canada. From 1974 to1996 he was a Professor at Osgoode Hall Law School. He has written books on Australian labor law and Australian evidence law, on Canadian labor law and evidence law, as well as more than 120 articles on tort law, labor law, Bills of Rights, legal education, corporate law, corporate social responsibility, corporate criminality, and occupational health and safety. His last book, the tenth, was *Wealth by Stealth: Corporate Crime, Corporate Law and the Perversion of Democracy,* Toronto: Between the Lines, 2003.

James Gobert received his undergraduate degree from Cornell University (B.A., with a major in psychology) in 1967 and his law degree from Duke University (J.D. with Distinction) in 1970. He has taught in both the United States (University of Tennessee, University of Michigan, Vanderbilt University) and in the United Kingdom at the University of Essex, where he was appointed to a chair in 1988. His primary teaching interests are in criminal law and criminology, jurisprudence, and law and mental health. His most recent books include *Rethinking Corporate Crime* (with M. Punch), and *Cases and Materials on Criminal Law* (with J. Dine).

Peter Grabosky is a Professor in the Research School of Social Sciences, Australian National University, and a Fellow of the Academy of the Social Sciences in Australia. His general interests are in computer crime, policing, and in harnessing non-governmental resources in furtherance of public policy. His publications include *Cyber Criminals on Trial* (with Russell Smith and Gregor Urbas, Cambridge University Press, 2004) which won the Distinguished Book Award of the American Society of Criminology's Division of International Criminology in 2005; *Electronic Theft* (with Russell Smith and Gillian Dempsey, Cambridge University Press, 2001); and *Crime in the Digital Age* (with Russell Smith, Federation Press/Transaction Publishers, 1998).

Stuart Green is the L.B. Porterie Professor of Law at Louisiana State University. A graduate of Yale Law School, he clerked on the U.S. Ninth Circuit Court of Appeals in Los Angeles and practiced law in Washington, D.C. before entering teaching. He has served as a Visiting Professor at the University of Michigan Law School (Fall 2005) and Fulbright Scholar in the United Kingdom (2002–03). The author of numerous works on moral and criminal law theory, including *Lying, Cheating, and Stealing: A Moral Theory of White Collar Crime* (Oxford University Press, 2006), he serves on the editorial board of *Criminal Law and Philosophy*.

Richard S. Gruner is a Professor of Law at the Whittier Law School in Costa Mesa, California, where he teaches courses in corporate law, white-collar crime, and intellectual property. He is a graduate of the California Institute of Technology (B.S. 1975), the USC Law School (J.D. 1978), and the Columbia Law School (LL.M. 1982). Professor Gruner is a former inside counsel to the IBM Corporation and consultant to the U.S. Sentencing Commission concerning corporate sentencing standards. He is the coauthor with Louis M. Brown and Anne Kandel of *The Legal Audit* (1990), published by West Group. His latest book, *Corporate Criminal Liability and Prevention*, was published by Law Journal Press in 2004.

Fiona Haines is Associate Professor in the Department of Criminology at the University of Melbourne. Fiona Haines' research spans broad areas concerned with corporate harm and its regulation. Previous work includes *Corporate Regulation: Beyond Punish or Persuade* (1997) and more recently *Globalization and Regulatory Character: Regulatory Reform after the Kader Toy Factory Fire* (2005), a study of globalization and occupational safety in Thailand. Her current research is an investigation (with Adam Sutton) into how critical sites deal with multiple regulatory demands emanating from the Longford explosion, the collapse of HIH, and the rise of terrorism.

Michael Indergaard is an Associate Professor of Sociology at St. John's University in New York City. He is the co-author of *Pump and Dump: The Rancid Rules of the New Economy* (Rutgers University Press, 2005). He is also wrote *Silicon Alley: The Rise and Fall of a New Media District* (Routledge, 2004). He has published in *Urban Studies, Urban Affairs Review, Social Problems, and Economic Development Quarterly*.

Paul Jesilow is an Associate Professor in the Department of Criminology, Law and Society at the University of California, Irvine. He is interdisciplinary by training and that is reflected in his use of several perspectives to approach his subject matter, as well as his use of qualitative and quantitative tools in his research, including interpretive historical methods, reviews of case files, interviews, and statistical techniques. He has used these methods to help understand the factors that affect sentencing by judges, the impact of California's "Three Strikes" law on the operation of the courts, police officers' behavior, the public's attitudes toward law enforcement, and fraud and abuse in health care.

David Johnson is Associate Professor of Sociology at the University of Hawaii and research associate at the Criminal Justice Research Program, University of California, Berkeley. He is author of *The Japanese Way of Justice* (Oxford, 2002).

Tomomi Kawasaki is an Associate Professor Of Criminal Law at Doshisha University in Kyoto, Japan. He received his Ph.D. from Doshisha University in 2005. He is author of *Corporate Criminal Liability* (published in Japanese). His current research focuses on several topics in white-collar crime, including corporate criminal liability, compliance programs, financial crime, securities fraud, and antitrust violations, both in the United States and Japan.

Georges Kellens is Professor Of Criminology and President of the School of Criminology, University of Liege, Belgium. He holds a doctorate in both law and criminology. He has published alone, or in collaboration, 20 books, including one on bankruptcy crimes. He is President-Elect of the International Penal and Penitentiary Foundation, Deputy Secretary General of the International Society of Criminology, and editor of the International Annals of Criminology.

Tokikazu Konishi is a research associate in the School of Law at Waseda University, Japan (since 2003), and is completing a doctorate in law at the Graduate School of Law at Waseda University. His areas of research include juvenile predelinquency and crimes by professionals. His most recent publications include a series of articles on "The Structure of the Concept of 'Pre-Delinquent Juvenile'" in *Waseda Law Review* (2004–2006, in Japanese).

Ronald C. Kramer is Professor of Sociology and Director of the Criminal Justice Program at Western Michigan University. His published works include *Crimes of the American Nuclear State*, *State-Corporate Crime: Wrongdoing at the Intersection of Business and Government*, and a number of articles on the crimes of the powerful.

Matthew T. Lee is an Assistant Professor of Sociology and Fellow at the Center for Conflict Management at the University of Akron. His scholarship focuses on immigration and violence, organizational deviance, and most recently, altruism. He is author of *Crime on the Border: Immigration and Homicide in Urban Communities* (LFB Scholarly, 2003). His research has appeared in such journals as *Criminology, Social Problems, Social Psychology Quarterly*, and*The Sociological Quarterly*.

Michael Levi has been Professor of Criminology at Cardiff University, Wales, United Kingdom since 1991, and has been researching organized and white-collar crime issues since 1972. He has degrees from Oxford, Cambridge, and Southampton universities. His books include *Drugs and Money* (with Petrus van Duyne), 2005; *Fraud: Organization, Motivation and Control I and II,* 1999; *Money-Laundering in the UK* (with Michael Gold), 1994; *The Investigation, Prosecution, and Trial of Serious Fraud*, 1993; *Regulating Fraud: White-Collar Crime and the Criminal Process*, 1987; and *The Phantom Capitalists: the Organisation and Control of Long-Firm Fraud*, 1981, to be republished by Ashgate in 2006 with a new introduction. He is currently completing *White-Collar Crime and its Victims* and *White-Collar Crime in the Media* for Clarendon Press, Oxford, and a variety of research studies on serious and organized crime.

Tamara D. Madensen is currently a doctoral candidate at the University of Cincinnati in the Division of Criminal Justice. Over the past several years, she served as the project manager for the Ohio Service for Crime Opportunity Reduction (OSCOR) project, which helps police and communities develop crime reduction strategies and conduct project evaluations. She also served as the managing editor for the *Security Journal*. Ms. Madensen recently accepted a faculty appointment at the University of Nevada, Las Vegas, in the Department of Criminal Justice.

Shin Matsuzawa is an Associate Professor in the School of Law at Waseda University, Japan (since 2004). Born in 1968, he received his Ph.D. in Law from St. Paul's University, Japan, in 1998. He was a researcher in the Institute of Legal Science at the University of Copenhagen, Denmark, from 1996 to 2002. His areas of research include the methodology of the study of criminal law, the comparative study of Japanese and Scandinavian (especially Danish) criminal law, and citizens' participation in criminal court. Major publications include *Theory on the Pragmatic Science of Criminal Law* (2001; in Japanese).

Raymond J. Michalowski is Arizona Regents Professor of Criminal Justice at Northern Arizona University. His published works include *Order, Law, and Crime*, *Radikale Kriminologie*, *Crime, Power and Identity*, *Run for the Wall: Remembering Vietnam on a Motorcycle Pilgrimage*, and *State-Corporate Crime: Wrongdoing at the Intersection of Business and Government.*

Derek Mitchell is a research associate at the Institute for Communitarian Policy Studies, George Washington University. He received his B.A. in Religion from Columbia University and studied Gandhian development theory as a Fulbright scholar in India. His research interests include the role of religion in international development, communitarian political and social theory, and South Asian religious traditions.

Frank Pearce is Professor of Sociology at Queen's University, Canada. He has taught elsewhere in Canada, The United States, and the United Kingdom. He has been researching corporate crime since 1973 and in 1976 his first book, *Crimes of the Powerful: Marxism, Crime and Deviance*, was published. Since then he has authored many articles, edited books, and journals and co-authored another book, with Steve Tombs, *Toxic Capitalism: Corporate Crime and the Chemical Industry (1998)*. He has also written widely on sociological theory—most recently, "Foucault and the Hydra-Headed Monster: The College de Sociologie" and the two Acéphales in A. Beaulieu and D. Gabbard (Eds) (2006) *Michel Foucault and Power Today. International Multidisciplinary Studies in the History of Our Present*, "The College de Sociologie and French Social Thought," special issue of *Economy and Society (200)* and the second edition of *The Radical Durkheim (2001)*. Currently he is exploring the relationship between capitalism and the sacrifice of human life.

Kenneth Polk is Professor of Criminology at the University of Melbourne in Australia. Before that he was for many years Professor of Sociology at the University of Oregon. His undergraduate degree was from San Diego State, and his Ph.D. from UCLA. Much of his research over the past decade has focused on violence and homicide, including the books *When Men Kill* (1994) and *Child Victims of Homicide* (2001, with Christine Alder). In addition, his most recent work has examined art crime, including the problem of the international traffic in plundered archeological material.

Henry N. Pontell is Professor of Criminology, Law, and Society and of Sociology at the University of California, Irvine. He has written on numerous topics in criminology, criminal justice, and law and society, and most recently on identity theft, cyber crime, and fraud in major financial debacles. His latest books include *Social Deviance* (5th ed. 2005), and *Profit Without Honor: White-Collar Crime and the Looting of America*, (4th ed. 2006) with Stephen Rosoff and Robert Tillman. He is a former Vice-President of the American Society of Criminology, and recipient of the Albert J. Reiss, Jr. Distinguished Scholarship Award from the American Sociological Association, and the Donald R. Cressey Award from the Association of Certified Fraud Examiners.

Maurice Punch studied and worked in the United Kingdom before moving to the Netherlands in 1975. He has researched corporate crime and police corruption (*Conduct Unbecoming*, Tavistock, 1985). He has published in English, Dutch, French, and American journals and has written several books, including *Dirty Business: Exploring Corporate Misconduct* (Sage: 1996) and, with Jim Gobert, *Rethinking Corporate Crime* (Butterworths, 2003). After almost 20 years teaching in Dutch universities he became an independent researcher and consultant in 1994 and in 1999 he became Visiting Professor at the Mannheim Centre for the Study of Criminology and Criminal Justice, London School of Economics.

Stephen M. Rosoff is Associate Professor of Sociology and Director of the Graduate Criminology Program at the University of Houston–Clearlake. He received his Ph.D. in social ecology from the University of California, Irvine. He has written extensively on white-collar crime and professional deviance. He is co-author of *Profit Without Honor* (4th ed., 2006), and *Looting America*. He is also co-author on two forthcoming books: *Who's Right? Whose Rights? Contemporary Legal Debates in America*, and *Deviance and Deviants*.

Rick Sarre is Professor of Law and Criminal Justice at the School of Commerce, University of South Australia, where he teaches criminal justice, media law, and commercial law. He continues to visit Hong Kong Baptist University, and has been a Visiting Professor at Graceland University, Iowa, on three occasions. He also enjoys an on-going association with the Law Department, Umeå University, Umeå, Sweden, where he was Visiting Research Professor in 2004. His latest book is *The Law of Private Security in Australia* (Sydney: Thomson Lawbook Co, 2005, with Tim Prenzler). He lives in Adelaide, South Australia, with his wife and two children.

David Shichor is Professor Emeritus of Criminal Justice, California State University San Bernardino. He received his B.A. in Sociology and History at the Hebrew University in Jerusalem and his Ph.D. in Sociology from the University of Southern California. He has written, edited, and co-edited nine books and has published over 80 articles in professional journals dealing mainly with penology, juvenile delinquency, victimology, and white-collar crime. During the last 15 years his major interests focused on the privatization of prisons and on white-collar crime victims and their victimization.

Neal Shover is Professor of Sociology at the University of Tennessee, Knoxville. His research has examined the criminal pursuits and careers of street offenders, dynamics of regulatory oversight, and victims of white-collar crime. He is the author of *Enforcement or Negotiation: Constructing a Regulatory Bureaucracy* (with Donald Clelland and John Lynxwiler); *Great Pretenders: Pursuits and Careers of Persistent Thieves*; *Crimes of Privilege* (with John Paul

Wright); and *Choosing White-Collar Crime* (with Andy Hochstetler). Professor Shover's current research examines the effects on unethical research practices by clinical researchers of conditions linked theoretically to deviance in organizational settings.

Laureen Snider is a Professor of Sociology at Queen's University, Kingston, Ontario, Canada, who has written extensively on corporate law, feminism, and punishment. Her most recent publications include "Resisting Neo-Liberalism: The Poisoned Water Disaster in Walkerton, Ontario," *Social and Legal Studies*, V5 (2):27–47, 2003; "Captured by Neo-Liberalism: Regulation and Risk in Walkerton Ontario," *Risk Management: An International Journal,* V5(2): March, 2003; and "Constituting the Punishable Woman: Atavistic Man Incarcerates Postmodern Woman," *British Journal of Criminology*, V43, No.2, 2003: 354–78.

Robert Tillman is Professor of Sociology at St. John's University in New York City. He received his Ph.D. from the University of California, Davis. He is the author and co-author of a number of books on white-collar crime, including, most recently, *Pump and Dump: The Rancid Rules of the New Economy* (Rutgers University Press, 2005). In addition he is co-author of *Big Money Crime: Fraud and Politics in the Savings and Loan Crisis* (University of California Press, 1997), which received the Albert J. Reiss Jr. Award for Distinguished Scholarship from the American Sociological Association in 2001.

Steve Tombs is a Professor of Sociology at Liverpool John Moores University and Chair of the human rights charity at the Centre for Corporate Accountability. He has a long-standing interest in the incidence, nature, and regulation of corporate crime, and in particular the regulation and management and health and safety at work. His other main current research interest is Politics of Knowledge. Recent publications include co-edited texts with Dave Gordon, Paddy Hillyard, and Christina Pantazis, entitled *Criminal Obsessions* (Crime and Society Foundation, 2005) and *Beyond Criminology? Taking Harm Seriously* (Pluto Press, 2004), as well as *Unmasking the Crimes of the Powerful: Scrutinising States and Corporations,* with Dave Whyte (Peter Lang, 2003). He is co-author of *Corporate Crime* (Longman, 1999), with Gary Slapper, and *Toxic Capitalism* (Ashgate, 1998, Canadian Scholars' Press, 1999), with Frank Pearce. He is currently preparing *Safety Crimes,* with Dave Whyte (Willan, 2006).

Diane Vaughan investigates "the dark side of organizations": mistake, misconduct, and disaster. Her work explores how institutional forces join with organizations' structure and culture to influence individual decision-making and action, producing harmful outcomes. In each of her books, *Controlling Unlawful Organizational Behavior*, *Uncoupling*, and *The Challenger Launch Decision*, the "normalization of deviance" contributed to the outcome. Currently she is working on*Theorizing: Analogy, Cases, and Comparative Social Organization* and *Dead Reckoning: Air Traffic Control in the Early 21st Century*. She has a Ph.D. in Sociology from Ohio State University, and she is Professor of Sociology and International and Public Affairs at Columbia University.

Arianna Visconti received her degree, summa cum laude, in the Faculty of Law at the Catholic University of Milan. A doctoral candidate in comparative criminal law at the University of Pavia, she is a researcher in criminal law and criminology at the Catholic University of Milan and has recently worked on a national research grant studying felonies against persons with a view toward criminal-code reform.

Sascha Walkley received her Ph.D. from The Australian National University. The focus of her research is the application of criminological theory to computer crime. She currently works as an analyst at the Australian Transaction Reports and Analysis Centre (AUSTRAC) in Sydney. Her current research involves the matter of trust in electronic commerce.

Dave Whyte is a Lecturer in Criminology at the University of Stirling, where he teaches and researches various aspects of criminal justice, with a specialist interest in the crimes of the powerful. His particular research interests include the politics of regulation, the criminalization of deaths and injuries at work and the regulation of the private military industry. He has recently completed a study on corporate corruption in occupied Iraq.

Peter Cleary Yeager is a Professor of Sociology at Boston University. He has co-authored two books on business compliance with the law, *Illegal Corporate Behavior* (U.S. Department of Justice, 1979) and *Corporate Crime* (The Free Press, 1980, 1983), the second of which was re-published in 2006 as a classic in criminology and law. His other works include *The Limits of Law: The Public Regulation of Private Pollution* (Cambridge University Press, 1991, 1993), on the environmental regulation of business in the United States, and articles in the research literatures of management policy, sociology, and law. He is writing a new book tentatively titled,*Markets, Morals and Mischief: Law and Order at Work.*

Minoru Yokoyama completed his B.A. in Law and M.A. in both Criminal Law and Sociology at Chuo University, Tokyo. He is a vice-president of Kokugakuin University, a professor and former Dean of the Faculty of Law, and president of the Information Center of Kokugakuin University in Tokyo. He is former 2nd Vice President of the Research Committee for the Sociology of Deviance and Social Control of the International Sociological Association. He is former president of the Japanese Association of Sociological Criminology, president of the Tokyo Study Group of Sociological Criminology, and a former member of the board of directors of the Japanese Association of Social Problems. He has presented numerous papers at national and international conferences and symposia, and has published numerous articles in professional journals.

Ling Zhang received Ph.D. degrees from both Jinlin University (China) and Waseda University (Japan), and is currently a professor in the School of Criminal Justice, and Director of the Asian Law Center at China University of Politics and Law. He is also Vice Chief Procurator of the Public Prosecutor Office, Chao Yang District, Beijing, and Director of the Chinese Criminology Society. His books include *The Comparative Research of Organizational Crime in Japan and China* (2004, Japanese), *Criminal Procedural Law in Japan* (2004, Chinese), and *Explanation and Comment on the Code of Criminal Law in China* (with Minoru Nomura, 2002, Japanese).

Lin Zhao is a postgraduate researcher in the School of Criminal Justice at China University of Politics and Law. She was born in Mudanjiang City, Heilongjiang Province, China. In 2005 she received the award for first-class scholarship from

China University of Politics and Law. She has published numerous academic papers on topics ranging from international perspectives on the death sentenceto contract deceit in the automotive finance industry.

Franklin E. Zimring is the William G. Simon Professor of Law and Chair of the Criminal Justice Research Program in the Institute for Legal Research at the University of California, Berkeley. His major fields of interest are criminal justice, juvenile justice, and family law, with special emphasis on the use of empirical research to inform legal policy. He has authored or co-authored books on deterrence, gun control, capital punishment, the scale of imprisonment, and drug control. His recent books include *The Contradictions of American Capital Punishment* (Oxford, 2003), and *American Juvenile Justice* (Oxford, 2005).

Index

Printed in the United States of America.